D1074933

This book was donated to
The King's Institute Library
from the library of
Sam F. Middlebrook
First Executive Director of
The King's Institute.

GESENIUS'
HEBREW GRAMMAR

AS EDITED AND ENLARGED BY THE LATE

E. KAUTZSCH

PROFESSOR OF THEOLOGY IN THE UNIVERSITY OF HALLE

SECOND ENGLISH EDITION

REVISED IN ACCORDANCE WITH THE TWENTY-EIGHTH GERMAN
EDITION (1909) BY

A. E. COWLEY

WITH A FACSIMILE OF THE SILOAM INSCRIPTION BY J. EUTING, AND
A TABLE OF ALPHABETS BY M. LIDZBARSKI

OXFORD
AT THE CLARENDON PRESS

PJ
4564
.G5
1910

Oxford University Press, Amen House, London E.C.4

GLASGOW NEW YORK TORONTO MELBOURNE WELLINGTON
BOMBAY CALCUTTA MADRAS KARACHI KUALA LUMPUR
CAPE TOWN IBADAN NAIROBI ACCRA

SECOND ENGLISH EDITION 1910

REPRINTED LITHOGRAPHICALLY IN GREAT BRITAIN
AT THE UNIVERSITY PRESS, OXFORD, 1946, 1949, 1952, 1956, 1960
FROM CORRECTED SHEETS OF THE SECOND EDITION

TRANSLATOR'S PREFACE

THE translation of the twenty-sixth German edition of this grammar, originally prepared by the Rev. G. W. Collins and revised by me, was published in 1898. Since that date a twenty-seventh German edition has appeared; and Prof. Kautzsch was already engaged on a twenty-eighth in 1908 when the English translation was becoming exhausted. He sent me the sheets as they were printed off, and I began revising the former translation in order to produce it as soon as possible after the completion of the German. The whole of the English has been carefully compared with the new edition, and, it is hoped, improved in many points, while Prof. Kautzsch's own corrections and additions have of course been incorporated. As before, the plan and arrangement of the original have been strictly followed, so that the references for sections and paragraphs correspond exactly in German and English. Dr. Driver has again most generously given up time, in the midst of other engagements, to reading the sheets, and has made numerous suggestions. To him also are chiefly due the enlargement of the index of subjects, some expansions in the new index of Hebrew words, and some additions to the index of passages, whereby we hope to have made the book more serviceable to students. I have also to thank my young friend, Mr. Godfrey R. Driver, of Winchester College, for some welcome help in correcting proofs of the Hebrew index and the index of passages. ‏בֵּן חָכָם יְשַׂמַּח אָב‎. Many corrections have been sent to me by scholars who have used the former English edition, especially the Rev. W. E. Blomfield, the Rev. S. Holmes, Mr. P. Wilson, Prof. Witton Davies, Mr. G. H. Skipwith, and an unknown correspondent at West Croydon. These, as well as suggestions in reviews, have all been considered, and where possible, utilized. I am also much indebted to the Press-readers for the great care which they have bestowed on the work.

Finally, I must pay an affectionate tribute to the memory of Prof. Kautzsch, who died in the spring of this year, shortly after finishing the last sheets of the twenty-eighth edition. For more than thirty years he was indefatigable in improving the successive editions of the Grammar. The German translation of the Old Testament first published by him in 1894, with the co-operation of other scholars, under the title *Die Heilige Schrift des A Ts*, and now (1910) in the third and much enlarged edition, is a valuable work which has been widely appreciated: the *Apocryphen und Pseudepigraphen des A Ts*, edited by him in 1900, is another important work: besides which he published his *Grammatik des Biblisch-Aramäischen* in 1884, two useful brochures *Bibelwissenschaft und Religionsunterricht* in 1900, and *Die bleibende Bedeutung des A Ts* in 1903, six popular lectures on *Die Poesie und die poetischen Bücher des A Ts* in 1902, his article 'Religion of Israel' in Hastings' *Dictionary of the Bible*, v. (1904), pp. 612–734, not to mention minor publications. His death is a serious loss to Biblical scholarship, while to me and to many others it is the loss of a most kindly friend, remarkable alike for his simple piety and his enthusiasm for learning.

A. C.

Magdalen College, Oxford,
Sept. 1910.

FROM THE GERMAN PREFACE

THE present (twenty-eighth) edition of this Grammar,[1] like the former ones, takes account as far as possible of all important new publications on the subject, especially J. Barth's *Sprachwissenschaftliche Untersuchungen zum Semitischen*, pt. i, Lpz. 1907 ; the important works of C. Brockelmann (for the titles see the heading of § 1 ; vol. i of the *Grundriss* was finished in 1908) ; P. Kahle's *Der masoretische Text des A Ts nach der Überlieferung der babylonischen Juden*, Lpz. 1902 (giving on p. 51 ff. an outline of Hebrew accidence from a Babylonian MS. at Berlin) ; R. Kittel's *Biblia Hebraica*, Lpz. 1905 f., 2 vols. (discriminating between certain, probable, and proposed emendations ; see § 3 *g*, end) ; Th. Nöldeke's *Beiträge zur semit. Sprachwissenschaft*, Strassburg, 1904 ; Ed. Sievers' *Metrische Studien* (for the titles of these striking works see § 2 *r*). The important work of J. W. Rothstein, *Grundzüge des hebr. Rhythmus*, &c. (see also § 2 *r*), unfortunately appeared too late to be used. The two large commentaries edited by Nowack and Marti have been recently completed ; and in P. Haupt's Polychrome Bible (*SBOT.*), part ix (Kings) by Stade and Schwally was published in 1904.

For full reviews of the twenty-seventh edition, which of course have been considered as carefully as possible, I have to thank Max Margolis (in *Hebraica*, 1902, p. 159 ff.), Mayer

---

[1] The first edition appeared at Halle in 1813 (202 pp. small 8vo) ; twelve more editions were published by W. Gesenius himself, the fourteenth to the twenty first (1845-1872) by E. Rödiger, the twenty-second to the twenty-eighth (1878-1910) by E. Kautzsch. The first abridged edition appeared in 1896, the second at the same time as the present (twenty-eighth) large edition. The first edition of the 'Übungsbuch' (Exercises) to Gesenius-Kautzsch's Hebrew Grammar appeared in 1881, the sixth in 1908.

Lambert (*REJ.* 1902, p. 307 ff.), and H. Oort (*Theol. Tijdschrift*, 1902, p. 373 ff.). For particular remarks and corrections I must thank Prof. J. Barth (Berlin), Dr. Gasser, pastor in Buchberg, Schaffhausen, B. Kirschner, of Charlottenburg, (contributions to the index of passages), Pastor Köhler, of Augst, Dr. Liebmann, of Kuczkow, Posen, Prof. Th. Nöldeke, of Strassburg, Pastor S. Preiswerk junior, of Bâle, Dr. Schwarz, of Leipzig, and Prof. B. Stade, of Giessen (died in 1906). Special mention must be made of the abundant help received from three old friends of this book, Prof. P. Haupt, of Baltimore, Prof. Knudtzon, of Kristiania, and Prof. H. Strack, of Berlin, and also, in connexion with the present edition, Prof. H. Hyvernat, of the University of Washington, who has rendered great service especially in the correction and enlargement of the indexes. I take this opportunity of thanking them all again sincerely. And I am no less grateful also to my dear colleague Prof. C. Steuernagel for the unwearying care with which he has helped me from beginning to end in correcting the proof-sheets.

Among material changes introduced into this edition may be mentioned the abolition of the term *S^ewâ medium* (§ 10 *d*). In this I have adopted, not without hesitation, the views of Sievers. I find it, however, quite impossible to follow him in rejecting all distinctions of quantity in the vowels. It is no doubt possible that such matters may in the *spoken* language have worn a very different appearance, and especially that in the period of nearly a thousand years, over which the Old Testament writings extend, very great variations may have taken place. Our duty, however, is to represent the language in the form in which it has been handed down to us by the Masoretes; and that this form involves a distinction between unchangeable, tone-long, and short vowels, admits in my opinion of no doubt. The discussion of any earlier stage of development belongs not to Hebrew grammar but to comparative Semitic philology.

The same answer may be made to Beer's desire (*ThLZ.* 1904,

col. 314 f.) for an 'historical Hebrew grammar describing the actual growth of the language on a basis of comparative philology, as it may still be traced within the narrow limits of the Old Testament'. Such material as is available for the purpose ought indeed to be honestly set forth in the new editions of Gesenius; but Beer seems to me to appraise such material much too highly when he refers to it as necessitating an 'historical grammar'. In my opinion these historical differences have for the most part been obliterated by the harmonizing activity of the Masoretes.

. . . .

E. KAUTZSCH.

HALLE,
July, 1909.

ADDITIONS AND CORRECTIONS

Page 42, line 13 from below, *for* note 1 *read* note 3.

Page 63, § 15 *p*. [See also Wickes, *Prose Accentuation*, 130 f., 87 *n*. (who, however, regards the superlinear, Babylonian system as the earlier); and Ginsburg, *Introduction to the Hebrew Bible*, 76, 78. In Ginsburg's *Hebrew Bible*, ed. 2 (1908), pp. 108 f., 267 f., the two systems of division are printed *in extenso*, in parallel columns—the 10 verses of the superlinear (Babylonian) system consisting (in Exodus) of v. [2.3-6.7.8-11.12.13.14.15.16.17] (as numbered in ordinary texts), and the 12 verses of the sublinear (Palestinian) system, consisting of v. [2-3.4.5.6.7.8.9.10.11.12.13-16.17].—S. R. D.]

Page 65, note 1, *for* אָֽנָּא *read* אָנָּא (as § 105 *a*).

[Editions often vary in individual passages, as regards the accentuation of the first syllable: but in the 7 occurrences of אנא, and the 6 of אנה, Baer, Ginsburg, and Kittel agree in having an accent on both syllables (as אָֽנָּא) in Gn 50¹⁷, Ex 32³¹, ψ 116¹⁶, and Metheg on the first syllable and an accent on the second syllable (as אָֽנָּה) in 2 K 20⁹=Is 38³, Jon 1¹⁴, 4², ψ 116⁴, 118²⁵·²⁵, Dn 9⁴, Ne 1⁵·¹¹, except that in ψ 116⁴ Ginsburg has אָנָּה.—S. R. D.]

Page 79, § 22 *s*, *before* הִרְדִּיפֻהוּ *insert* exceptions to *b* are. *After* Jer 39¹² *add* ψ 52⁵; *and for* Ez 9⁶ *read* Ezr 9⁶.

[So Baer (cf. his note on Jud 20⁴³; also on Jer 39¹², and several of the other passages in question): but Ginsburg only in 10 of the exceptions to *b*, and Jacob ben Ḥayyim and Kittel only in 5, viz. Jer 39¹², Pr 11²¹, 15¹, ψ 52⁵, Ezr 9⁶.—S. R. D.]

Page 111, line 12, *for* הַהוּה *read* הַהוּא.

Page 123, § 45 *e*, *add*: cf. also נֶהְפְּכָה followed by את, Is 13¹⁹, Am 4¹¹ (§ 115 *d*).

Page 175, § 67. *See* B. Halper, 'The Participial formations of the Geminate Verbs' in *ZAW*. 1910, pp. 42 ff., 99 ff., 201 ff. (also dealing with the regular verb).

Page 177, at the end of § 67 *g* the following paragraph has been accidentally omitted:

Rem. According to the prevailing view, this strengthening of the first radical is merely intended to give the bi-literal stem at least

a tri-literal appearance. (Possibly aided by the analogy of verbs פ״ן,
as P. Haupt has suggested to me in conversation.) But cf. Kautzsch,
'Die sog. aramaisierenden Formen der Verba ע״ע im Hebr.' in *Oriental.
Studien zum 70. Geburtstag Th. Nöldekes,* 1906, p. 771 ff. It is there
shown (1) that the sharpening of the 1st radical often serves to emphasize a particular meaning (cf. יִפֶּר, but יִגְרֹהוּ, יָחֵל and יָחַל, יִסֹּב and יָסֹב,
יִשֹּׁם and תֵּשַׁם), and elsewhere no doubt to dissimilate the vowels (as
יִדֵּל, יִפֶּר, never יֵדַל, יֵגַר, &c.) : (2) that the sharpening of the 1st
radical often appears to be occasioned by the nature of the first letter
of the stem, especially when it is a sibilant. Whether the masoretic
pronunciation is based on an early tradition, or the Masora has arbi-
trarily adopted aramaizing forms to attain the above objects, must be
left undecided.

Page 193, the second and third paragraphs should have the marginal
letters *d* and *e* respectively.

Page 200, § 72 *z*, line 2, *after* Est 2[18] *add* 4[14].

Page 232, § 84[a] *s, add* שְׁמֵמָה 2 S 13[20].

Page 236, § 85 *c, add* הַנְזְקָה Ezr 4[22].

Page 273, § 93 *qq* end, *add* מוֹסֵרוֹת Jer 5[5], רְבֵעִים, שְׁלֵשִׁים Ez 20[5],
שְׁמֵמוֹת Is 49[8], שְׁמֵמִים La 1[16] (cf. König, ii. 109).

LIST OF ABBREVIATIONS

The following abbreviations have occasionally been used for works and periodicals frequently quoted:—

AJSL. = American Journal of Semitic Languages.

CIS. = Corpus Inscriptionum Semiticarum.

Ed.Mant. = Biblia Hebraica ex recensione Sal. Norzi edidit Raphael Ḥayyim Basila, Mantuae 1742–4.

Jabl. = Biblia Hebraica ex recensione D. E. Jablonski, Berolini, 1699.

JQR. = Jewish Quarterly Review.

*KAT.*³ = Die Keilinschriften und das Alte Testament, 3rd ed. by H. Zimmern and H. Winckler, 2 vols., Berlin, 1902 f.

Lexicon = A Hebrew and English Lexicon of the Old Testament, based on the Thesaurus and Lexicon of Gesenius, by F. Brown, S. R. Driver, and C. A. Briggs, Oxford, 1906.

NB. = J. Barth, Die Nominalbildung in den semitischen Sprachen. Lpz. 1889–94.

NGGW. = Nachrichten der Göttinger Gesellschaft der Wissenschaften.

OLZ. = Orientalistische Literaturzeitung. Vienna, 1898 ff.

PRE. = Realencyclopädie für protestantische Theologie und Kirche, 3rd ed. by A. Hauck. Lpz. 1896 ff.

PSBA = Proceedings of the Society of Biblical Archæology. London, 1879 ff.

REJ. = Revue des Études Juives. Paris, 1880 ff.

Sam. = The (Hebrew) Pentateuch of the Samaritans.

SBOT. = Sacred Books of the Old Testament, ed. by P. Haupt. Lpz. and Baltimore, 1893 ff.

ThLZ. = Theologische Literaturzeitung, ed. by E. Schürer. Lpz. 1876 ff.

VB. = Vorderasiatische Bibliothek, ed. by A. Jeremias and H. Winckler. Lpz. 1907 ff.

ZA. = Zeitschrift für Assyriologie und verwandte Gebiete, ed. by C. Bezold. Lpz. 1886 ff.

ZAW. = Zeitschrift für die alttestamentliche Wissenschaft, ed. by B. Stade, Giessen, 1881 ff., and since 1907 by K. Marti.

ZDMG. = Zeitschrift der deutschen morgenländischen Gesellschaft, Lpz. 1846 ff., since 1903 ed. by A. Fischer.

ZDPV. = Zeitschrift des deutschen Palästinavereins, Lpz. 1878 ff., since 1903 ed. by C. Steuernagel.

CONTENTS

SECOND PART

ETYMOLOGY, OR THE PARTS OF SPEECH

CHAPTER I. THE PRONOUN

CHAPTER II. THE VERB

I. The Strong Verb.

A. *The Pure Stem, or Qal.*

Contents   xiii

PAGE

CHAPTER IV. THE PARTICLES

THIRD PART

SYNTAX

CHAPTER I. THE PARTS OF SPEECH

I. Syntax of the Verb.

A. *Use of the Tenses and Moods.*

Contents

B. *The Infinitive and Participle.*

C. *The Government of the Verb.*

II. Syntax of the Noun.

III. Syntax of the Pronoun.

Chapter II. The Sentence

I. The Sentence in General.

II. Special Kinds of Sentences.

HEBREW GRAMMAR

INTRODUCTION

§ 1. *The Semitic Languages in General.*

B. Stade, *Lehrb. der hebr. Gramm.*, Lpz. 1879, § 2 ff. ; E. König, *Hist.-krit. Lehrgeb. der hebr. Spr.*, i. Lpz. 1881, § 3 ; H. Strack, *Einl. in das A. T.*, 6th ed., Munich, 1906, p. 231 ff. (a good bibliography of all the Semitic dialects) ; Th. Nöldeke, article 'Semitic Languages', in the 9th ed. of the *Encycl. Brit.* (*Die semit. Sprachen*, 2nd ed., Lpz. 1899), and *Beitr. zur sem. Sprachwiss.*, Strassb., 1904 ; W. Wright, *Lectures on the Comparative Grammar of the Semitic Languages*, Cambr. 1890 ; H. Reckendorf, ' Zur Karakteristik der sem. Sprachen,' in the *Actes du Xᵐᵉ Congrès internat. des Orientalistes* (at Geneva in 1894), iii. 1 ff., Leiden, 1896 ; O. E. Lindberg, *Vergl. Gramm. der sem. Sprachen*, i A : *Konsonantismus*, Gothenburg, 1897 ; H. Zimmern, *Vergl. Gramm. der sem. Sprachen*, Berlin, 1898 ; E. König, *Hebräisch und Semitisch : Prolegomena und Grundlinien einer Gesch. der sem. Sprachen*, &c., Berlin, 1901 ; C. Brockelmann, *Semitische Sprachwissenschaft*, Lpz. 1906, *Grundriss der vergl. Gramm. der sem. Sprachen*, vol. i (Laut- und Formenlehre), parts 1–5, Berlin, 1907 f. and his *Kurzgef. vergleichende Gramm.* (Porta Ling. Or.) Berlin, 1908.—The material contained in inscriptions has been in process of collection since 1881 in the Paris *Corpus Inscriptionum Semiticarum.* To this the best introductions are M. Lidzbarski's *Handbuch der Nordsem. Epigraphik*, Weimar, 1898, in 2 parts (text and plates), and his *Ephemeris zur sem. Epigraphik* (5 parts published), Giessen, 1900 f. [G. A. Cooke, *Handbook of North-Semitic Inscriptions*, Oxford, 1903].

1. The Hebrew language is one branch of a great family of lan- *a* guages in Western Asia which was indigenous in Palestine, Phoenicia, Syria, Mesopotamia, Babylonia, Assyria, and Arabia, that is to say, in the countries extending from the Mediterranean to the other side of the Euphrates and Tigris, and from the mountains of Armenia to the southern coast of Arabia. In early times, however, it spread from Arabia over Abyssinia, and by means of Phoenician colonies over many islands and sea-boards of the Mediterranean, as for instance to the Carthaginian coast. No comprehensive designation is found in early times for the languages and nations of this family; the name *Semites* or *Semitic*[1] *languages* (based upon the fact that according to Gn 10²¹ ᶠᶠ· almost all nations speaking these languages are descended from Shem) is, however, now generally accepted, and has accordingly been retained here.[2]

---

[1] First used by Schlözer in Eichhorn's *Repertorium für bibl. u. morgenl. Literatur*, 1781, p. 161.

[2] From Shem are derived (Gn 10²¹ ᶠᶠ·) the Aramaean and Arab families as well as the Hebrews, but not the Canaanites (Phoenicians), who are traced back to Ham (vv. ⁶·¹⁵ ᶠᶠ·), although their language belongs decidedly to what is now called Semitic. The language of the Babylonians and Assyrians also was long ago shown to be Semitic, just as Aššur (Gn 10²²) is included among the sons of Shem.

B

b   2. The better known Semitic languages may be subdivided[1] as follows:—

I. The South Semitic or Arabic branch. To this belong, besides the classical literary language of the Arabs and the modern vulgar Arabic, the older southern Arabic preserved in the Sabaean inscriptions (less correctly called Himyaritic), and its offshoot, the Geʻez or Ethiopic, in Abyssinia.

II. The Middle Semitic or Canaanitish branch. To this belongs the Hebrew of the Old Testament with its descendants, the New Hebrew, as found especially in the Mishna (see below, § 3 *a*), and Rabbinic; also Phoenician, with Punic (in Carthage and its colonies), and the various remains of Canaanitish dialects preserved in names of places and persons, and in the inscription of Mêšaʻ, king of Moab.

c   III. The North Semitic or Aramaic branch. The subdivisions of this are—(1) The Eastern Aramaic or Syriac, the literary language of the Christian Syrians. The religious books of the Mandaeans (Nasoraeans, Sabians, also called the disciples of St. John) represent a very debased offshoot of this. A Jewish modification of Syriac is to be seen in the language of the Babylonian Talmud. (2) The Western or Palestinian Aramaic, incorrectly called also 'Chaldee'.[2] This latter dialect is represented in the Old Testament by two words in Gn 31[47], by the verse Jer 10[11], and the sections Dn 2[4] to 7[28]; Ezr 4[8] to 6[18], and 7[12-26], as well as by a number of non-Jewish inscriptions and Jewish papyri (see below, under *m*), but especially by a considerable section of Jewish literature (Targums, Palestinian Gemara, &c.). To the same branch belongs also the Samaritan, with its admixture of Hebrew forms, and, except for the rather Arabic colouring of the proper names, the idiom of the Nabataean inscriptions in the Sinaitic peninsula, in the East of Palestine, &c.

For further particulars about the remains of Western Aramaic (including those in the New Test., in the Palmyrene and Egyptian Aramaic inscriptions) see Kautzsch, *Gramm. des Biblisch-Aramäischen*, Lpz. 1884, p. 6 ff.

d   IV. The East Semitic branch, the language of the Assyrio-Babylonian cuneiform inscriptions, the third line of the Achaemenian inscriptions.

On the importance of Assyrian for Hebrew philology especially from a lexicographical point of view cf. Friedr. Delitzsch, *Prolegomena eines neuen*

---

[1] For conjectures as to the gradual divergence of the dialects (first the Babylonian, then Canaanite, including Hebrew, lastly Aramaic and Arabic) from primitive Semitic, see Zimmern, *KAT.*[3], ii. p. 644 ff.

[2] In a wider sense *all* Jewish Aramaic is sometimes called 'Chaldee'.

hebr.-aram. Wörterbuchs zum A. T., Lpz. 1886 ; P. Haupt, 'Assyrian Phonology, &c.,' in *Hebraica*, Chicago, Jan. 1885, vol. i. 3 ; Delitzsch, *Assyrische Grammatik*, 2nd ed., Berlin, 1906.

If the above division into four branches be reduced to two principal groups, No. I, as South Semitic, will be contrasted with the three North Semitic branches.[1]

All these languages stand to one another in much the same relation as those *e* of the Germanic family (Gothic, Old Norse, Danish, Swedish ; High and Low German in their earlier and later dialects), or as the Slavonic languages (Lithuanian, Lettish ; Old Slavonic, Serbian, Russian ; Polish, Bohemian). They are now either wholly extinct, as the Phoenician and Assyrian, or preserved only in a debased form, as Neo-Syriac among Syrian Christians and Jews in Mesopotamia and Kurdistan, Ethiopic (Ge'ez) in the later Abyssinian dialects (Tigrê, Tigriña, Amharic), and Hebrew among some modern Jews, except in so far as they attempt a purely literary reproduction of the language of the Old Testament. Arabic alone has not only occupied to this day its original abode in Arabia proper, but has also forced its way in all directions into the domain of other languages.

The Semitic family of languages is bounded on the East and North by another of still wider extent, which reaches from India to the western limits of Europe, and is called Indo-Germanic [2] since it comprises, in the most varied ramifications, the Indian (Sanskrit), Old and New Persian, Greek, Latin, Slavonic, as well as Gothic and the other Germanic languages. With the Old Egyptian language, of which Coptic is a descendant, as well as with the languages of north-western Africa, the Semitic had from the earliest times much in common, especially in grammatical structure ; but on the other hand there are fundamental differences between them, especially from a lexicographical point of view ; see Erman, ' Das Verhältnis des Aegyptischen zu den semitischen Sprachen,' in the *ZDMG.* xlvi, 1892, p. 93 ff., and Brockelmann, *Grundriss*, i. 3.

3. The *grammatical structure* of the Semitic family of languages, *f* as compared with that of other languages, especially the Indo-Germanic, exhibits numerous peculiarities which collectively constitute its distinctive character, although many of them are found singly in other languages. These are—(*a*) among the consonants, which in fact form the substance of these languages, occur peculiar gutturals of different grades ; the vowels are subject, within the same consonantal framework, to great changes in order to express various modifications of the same stem-meaning ; (*b*) the word-stems are almost invariably triliteral, i.e. composed of three consonants ; (*c*) the verb is restricted to two tense-forms, with a peculiarly regulated use ; (*d*) the noun has only two genders (masc. and fem.) ; and peculiar expedients are adopted for the purpose of indicating the case-relations ; (*e*) the

---

[1] Hommel, *Grundriss der Geogr. und Gesch. des alten Orients*, Munich, 1904, p. 75 ff., prefers to distinguish them as Eastern and Western Semitic branches. Their geographical position, however, is of less importance than the genealogical relation of the various groups of dialects, as rightly pointed out by A. Jeremias in *Th.LZ.* 1906, col. 291.

[2] First by Klaproth in *Asia Polyglotta*, Paris, 1823 ; cf. Leo Meyer in *Nachrichten d. Gött. Gesellschaft*, 1901, p. 454.

oblique cases of the personal pronoun, as well as all the possessive pronouns and the pronominal object of the verb, are denoted by forms appended directly to the governing word (suffixes); (*f*) the almost complete absence of compounds both in the noun (with the exception of many proper names) and in the verb; (*g*) great simplicity in the expression of syntactical relations, e. g. the small number of particles, and the prevalence of simple co-ordination of clauses without periodic structure. Classical Arabic and Syriac, however, form a not unimportant exception as regards the last-mentioned point.

g 4. From a lexicographical point of view also the vocabulary of the Semites differs essentially from that of the Indo-Germanic languages, although there is apparently more agreement here than in the grammar. A considerable number of Semitic roots and stems agree in sound with synonyms in the Indo-Germanic family. But apart from expressions actually borrowed (see below, under *i*), the real similarity may be reduced to imitative words (onomatopoetica), and to those in which one and the same idea is represented by similar sounds in consequence of a formative instinct common to the most varied families of language. Neither of these proves any *historic* or *generic* relation, for which an agreement in grammatical structure would also be necessary.

Comp. Friedr. Delitzsch, *Studien über indogermanisch-semitische Wurzelverwandtschaft*, Lpz. 1873; Nöldechen, *Semit. Glossen zu Fick und Curtius*, Magdeb. 1876 f.; McCurdy, *Aryo-Semitic Speech*, Andover, U. S. A., 1881. The phonetic relations have been thoroughly investigated by H. Möller in *Semitisch und Indogermanisch*, Teil i, *Konsonanten*, Copenhagen and Lpz. 1907, a work which has evoked considerable criticism.

h As onomatopoetic words, or as stem-sounds of a similar character, we may compare, e. g. לָקַק, לָחַךְ λείχω, lingo, Skt. *lih*, Eng. *to lick*, Fr. *lécher*, Germ. *lecken*; גָּלַל (cf. אָגַל, עָגַל) κυλίω, volvo, Germ. *quellen, wallen*, Eng. *to well*; גָּרַד, חָרַט, חָרַת χαράττω, Pers. *khâridan*, Ital. *grattare*, Fr. *gratter*, Eng. *to grate, to scratch*, Germ. *kratzen*; פָּרַק *frango*, Germ. *brechen*, &c. ; Reuss, *Gesch. der hl. Schriften A. T.'s*, Braunschw. 1881, p. 38, draws attention moreover to the Semitic equivalents for *earth, six, seven, horn, to sound, to measure, to mix, to smell, to place, clear, to kneel, raven, goat, ox*, &c. An example of a somewhat different kind is *am, ham* (*sam*), *gam, kam*, in the sense of the German *samt, zusammen, together*; in Hebrew אָמַם (whence אֻמָּה *people*, properly *assembly*), עַם (*with*) *samt*, בַּ also, moreover, Arab. בֹּמַע *to collect*; Pers. *ham, hamah* (*at the same time*); Skt. *samá* (*with*), Gk. ἅμα (ἄμφω), ὁμός, ὁμοῦ (ὅμιλος, ὅμαδος), and harder κοινός, Lat. *cum, cumulus, cunctus* ; with the corresponding sibilant Skt. *sam*, Gk. σύν, ξύν, ξυνός = κοινός, Goth. *sama*, Germ. *samt, sammeln* ; but many of these instances are doubtful.

i Essentially different from this internal connexion is the occurrence of the same words in different languages, where one language has borrowed directly from the other. Such *loan-words* are—

(*a*) In Hebrew: some names of objects which were originally indigenous in Babylonia and Assyria (see a comprehensive list of Assyrio-
Babylonian loan-words in the Hebrew and Aramaic of the Old Testament
in Zimmern and Winckler, *KAT.*³, ii. p. 648 ff.), in Egypt, Persia, or
India, e. g. יְאֹר (also in the plural) *river*, from Egyptian *yoor*, generally as the
name of the Nile (late Egypt. *yaro*, Assyr. *yaru'u*), although it is possible that
a pure Semitic יְאֹר has been confounded with the Egyptian name of the Nile
(so Zimmern); אָחוּ (Egyptian) Nile-reed (see Lieblein, ' Mots égyptiens dans
la Bible,' in *PSBA.* 1898, p. 202 f.); פַּרְדֵּס (in Zend *pairidaêza*, circumvalla-
tion = παράδεισος) *pleasure-garden, park*; אֲדַרְכֹּן *daric*, Persian gold coin; תֻּכִּיִּים
peacocks, perhaps from the Malabar *tôgai* or *tôghai*. Some of these words are
also found in Greek, as כַּרְפַּס (Pers. *karbâs*, Skt. *karpâsa*) cotton, κάρπασος,
carbasus. On the other hand it is doubtful if קוֹף corresponds to the Greek
κῆπος, κῆβος, Skt. *kapi*, ape.

(*b*) In Greek, &c. : some originally Semitic names of Asiatic products and
articles of commerce, e. g. בּוּץ βύσσος, *byssus* ; לְבֹנָה λίβανος, λιβανωτός, *incense* ;
קָנֶה κάνη, κάννα, *canna*, cane ; כַּמֹּן κύμινον, *cuminum*, cumin ; קְצִיעָה κασσία,
cassia ; גָּמָל κάμηλος, *camelus* ; עֵרָבוֹן ἀρραβών, *arrhabo, arrha*, pledge. Such
transitions have perhaps been brought about chiefly by Phoenician trade.
Cf. A. Müller, 'Semitische Lehnworte im älteren Griechisch,' in Bezzen-
berger's *Beiträge zur Kunde der Indo-germ. Sprachen*, Göttingen, 1877, vol. i.
p. 273 ff. ; E. Ries, *Quae res et vocabula a gentibus semiticis in Graeciam pervenerint*,
Breslau, 1890; Muss-Arnolt, 'Semitic words in Greek and Latin,' in the
Transactions of the American Philological Association, xxiii. p. 35 ff. ; H. Lewy, *Die
semitischen Fremdwörter im Griech.*, Berlin, 1895 ; J. H. Bondi, *Dem hebr.-phöniz.
Sprachzweige angehör. Lehnwörter in hieroglyph. u. hieratischen Texten*, Lpz. 1886.

5. No system of writing is ever so perfect as to be able to reproduce *k*
the sounds of a language in all their various shades, and the *writing
of the Semites* has one striking fundamental defect, viz. that only the
consonants (which indeed form the substance of the language) are
written as real letters,[1] whilst of the vowels only the longer are
indicated by certain representative consonants (see below, § 7).
It was only later that special small marks (points or strokes below
or above the consonants) were invented to represent to the eye all
the vowel-sounds (see § 8). These are, however, superfluous for
the practised reader, and are therefore often wholly omitted in
Semitic manuscripts and printed texts. Semitic writing, moreover,
almost invariably proceeds from right to left.[2]

---

[1] So also originally the Ethiopic writing, which afterwards represented
the vowels by small appendages to the consonants, or by some other change
in their form. On the Assyrio-Babylonian cuneiform writing, which likewise indicates the vowels, see the next note, ad fin.

[2] The Sabaean (Himyaritic) writing runs occasionally from left to right,
and even alternately in both directions (*boustrophedon*), but as a rule from
right to left. In Ethiopic writing the direction from left to right has become
the rule ; some few old inscriptions exhibit, however, the opposite direction.
The cuneiform writing also runs from left to right, but this is undoubtedly
borrowed from a non-Semitic people. Cf. § 5 *d*, note 3.

With the exception of the Assyrio-Babylonian (cuneiform), all varieties of Semitic writing, although differing widely in some respects, are derived from one and the same original alphabet, represented on extant monuments most faithfully by the characters used on the stele of Mêša', king of Moab (see below, § 2 *d*), and in the *old* Phoenician inscriptions, of which the bronze bowls from a temple of Baal (*CIS.* i. 22 ff. and Plate IV) are somewhat earlier than Mêša'. The old Hebrew writing, as it appears on the oldest monument, the Siloam inscription (see below, § 2 *d*), exhibits essentially the same character. The old Greek, and indirectly all European alphabets, are descended from the old Phoenician writing (see § 5 *i*).

l See the Table of Alphabets at the beginning of the Grammar, which shows the relations of the older varieties of Semitic writing to one another and especially the origin of the present Hebrew characters from their primitive forms. For a more complete view, see Gesenius' *Scripturae linguaeque Phoeniciae monumenta*, Lips. 1837, 4to, pt. i. p. 15 ff., and pt. iii. tab. 1-5. From numerous monuments since discovered, our knowledge of the Semitic characters, especially the Phoenician, has become considerably enlarged and more accurate. Cf. the all but exhaustive bibliography (from 1616 to 1896) in Lidzbarski's *Handbuch der Nordsemitischen Epigraphik*, i. p. 4 ff., and on the origin of the Semitic alphabet, ibid., p. 173 ff., and *Ephemeris* (see the heading of § 1 *a* above), i. pp. 109 ff., 142, 261 ff., and his 'Altsemitische Texte', pt. i, *Kanaanäische Inschriften* (Moabite, Old-Hebrew, Phoenician, Punic), Giessen, 1907.—On the origin and development of the *Hebrew* characters and the best tables of alphabets, see § 5 *a*, last note, and especially § 5 *e*.

m 6. As regards the relative *age* of the Semitic languages, the oldest literary remains of them are to be found in the Assyrio-Babylonian (cuneiform) inscriptions,[1] with which are to be classed the earliest Hebrew fragments occurring in the old Testament (see § 2).

The earliest non-Jewish *Aramaic* inscriptions known to us are that cf זכר king of Hamath (early eighth cent. B.C.), on which see Nöldeke, *ZA.* 1908, p. 376, and that found at Teima, in N. Arabia, in 1880, probably of the fifth cent. B.C., cf. E. Littmann in the *Monist*, xiv. 4 [and Cooke, *op. cit.*, p. 195]. The monuments of Kalammus of Sam'al, in the reign of Shalmanezer II, 859-829 B.C. (cf. A. Šanda, *Die Aramäer*, Lpz. 1902, p. 26), and those found in 1888-1891 at Zenjîrlî in N. Syria, including the Hadad inscription of thirty-four lines (early eighth cent. B.C.) and the Panammu inscription (740 B.C.), are not in pure Aramaic. The Jewish-Aramaic writings begin about the time of Cyrus (cf. Ezr 6³ ff.), specially important being the papyri from Assuan ed. by Sayce and Cowley, London, 1906 (and in a cheaper form by Staerk, Bonn, 1907), which are precisely dated from 471 to 411 B.C., and three others of 407 B.C. ed. by Sachau, Berlin, 1907.

---

[1] According to Hilprecht, *The Babylonian Expedition of the University of Pennsylvania*, i. p. 11 ff., the inscriptions found at Nippur embrace the period from about 4000 to 450 B.C.

Monuments of the *Arabic* branch first appear in the earliest centuries A. D. (Sabaean inscriptions, Ethiopic translation of the Bible in the fourth or fifth century, North-Arabic literature from the sixth century A. D.).

It is, however, another question which of these languages has adhered longest and most faithfully to the original character of the Semitic, and which consequently represents to us the earliest phase of its development. For the more or less rapid transformation of the sounds and forms of a language, as spoken by nations and races, is dependent on causes quite distinct from the growth of a literature, and the organic structure of a language is often considerably impaired even before it has developed a literature, especially by early contact with people of a different language. Thus in the Semitic group, the Aramaic dialects exhibit the earliest and greatest decay, next to them the Hebrew-Canaanitish, and in its own way the Assyrian. Arabic, owing to the seclusion of the desert tribes, was the longest to retain the original fullness and purity of the sounds and forms of words.[1] Even here, however, there appeared, through the revolutionary influence of Islam, an ever-increasing decay, until Arabic at length reached the stage at which we find Hebrew in the Old Testament.

Hence the phenomenon, that in its grammatical structure the ancient *n* Hebrew agrees more with the modern than with the ancient Arabic, and that the latter, although it only appears as a written language at a later period, has yet in many respects preserved a more complete structure and a more original vowel system than the other Semitic languages, cf. Nöldeke, ' Das klassische Arabisch und die arabischen Dialekte,' in *Beiträge zur semitischen Sprachwissenschaft*, p. 1 ff. It thus occupies amongst them a position similar to that which Sanskrit holds among the Indo-Germanic languages, or Gothic in the narrower circle of the Germanic. But even the toughest organism of a language often deteriorates, at least in single forms and derivatives, while on the contrary, in the midst of what is otherwise universal decay, there still remains here and there something original and archaic ; and this is the case with the Semitic languages.

Fuller proof of the above statements belongs to the comparative Grammar of the Semitic languages. It follows, however, from what has been said : (1) that the Hebrew language, as found in the sacred literature of the Jews, has, in respect

---

[1] Even now the language of some of the Bèdawî is much purer and more archaic than that of the town Arabs. It must, however, be admitted that the former exalted estimate of the primitiveness of Arabic has been moderated in many respects by the most recent school of Semitic philology. Much apparently original is to be regarded with Nöldeke (*Die semit. Spr.*, p. 5 [= *Encycl. Brit.*, ed. 9, art. SEMITIC LANGUAGES, p. 642]) only as a modification of the original. The assertion that the Arabs exhibit Semitic characteristics in their purest form, should, according to Nöldeke, be rather that 'the inhabitants of the desert lands of Arabia, under the influence of the extraordinarily monotonous scenery and of a life continually the same amid continual change, have developed most exclusively some of the principal traits of the Semitic race '.

to its organic structure, already suffered more considerable losses than the Arabic, which appears much later on the historical horizon ; (2) that, notwithstanding this fact, we cannot at once and in all points concede priority to the latter ; (3) that it is a mistake to consider with some that the Aramaic, on account of its simplicity (which is only due to the decay of its organic structure), is the oldest form of Semitic speech.

§ 2. *Sketch of the History of the Hebrew Language.*

See Gesenius, *Gesch. der hebr. Sprache u. Schrift,* Lpz. 1815, §§ 5–18 ; Th. Nöldeke's art., 'Sprache, hebräische,' in Schenkel's *Bibel-Lexikon,* Bd. v, Lpz. 1875 ; F. Buhl, 'Hebräische Sprache,' in Hauck's *Realencycl. für prot. Theol. und Kirche,* vii (1899), p. 506 ff.; A. Cowley, 'Hebrew Language and Literature,' in the forthcoming ed. of the *Encycl. Brit.* ; W. R. Smith in the *Encycl. Bibl.,* ii. London, 1901, p. 1984 ff. ; A. Lukyn Williams, 'Hebrew,' in Hastings' *Dict. of the Bible,* ii. p. 325 ff., Edinb. 1899.

a 1. The name *Hebrew Language* usually denotes the language of the sacred writings of the Israelites which form the canon of the *Old Testament.* It is also called *Ancient Hebrew* in contradistinction to the New Hebrew of Jewish writings of the post-biblical period (§ 3 *a*). The name Hebrew language (לְשׁוֹן עִבְרִית γλῶσσα τῶν Ἑβραίων, ἑβραϊστί) does not occur in the Old Testament itself. Instead of it we find in Is 19[18] the term *language of Canaan,*[1] and יְהוּדִית *in the Jews' language* 2 K 18[26.28] (cf. Is 36[11.13]) Neh 13[24]. In the last-cited passage it already agrees with the later (post-exilic) usage, which gradually extended the name *Jews, Jewish* to the whole nation, as in Haggai, Nehemiah, and the book of Esther.

b The distinction between the names *Hebrew* (עִבְרִים Ἑβραῖοι) and *Israelites* (בְּנֵי יִשְׂרָאֵל) is that the latter was rather a national name of honour, with also a religious significance, employed by the people themselves, while the former appears as the less significant name by which the nation was known amongst foreigners. Hence in the Old Testament *Hebrews* are only spoken of either when the name is employed by themselves as contrasted with foreigners (Gn 40[15], Ex 2[6 f.] 3[18] &c., Jon 1[9]) or when it is put in the mouth of those who are not Israelites (Gn 39[14.17] 41[12] &c.) or, finally, when it is used in opposition to other nations (Gn 14[13] 43[32], Ex 2[11.13] 21[2]). In 1 S 13[3-7] and 14[21] the text is clearly corrupt. In the Greek and Latin authors, as well as in Josephus, the name Ἑβραῖοι, Hebraei,[2] &c., alone occurs. Of the many explanations of the gentilic עִבְרִי, the derivation from עֵבֶר *a country on the other side* with the derivative suffix ־ִי (§ 86 *h*) appears to be the only one philologically possible. The name accordingly denoted the Israelites as being those who inhabited the *'eber,* i. e. the district on the other side of the Jordan (or according to others the Euphrates), and would therefore originally be only appropriate when used by the nations on this side of the Jordan or Euphrates. We must, then, suppose that after the crossing of the river in question it had been retained by the Abrahamidae as an old-established name, and within certain limits

---

[1] That Hebrew in its present form was actually developed in Canaan appears from such facts as the use of *yām* (sea) for the west, *nègeb* (properly *dryness,* afterwards as a proper name for the south of Palestine) for the south.

[2] The Graeco-Roman form of the name is not directly derived from the Hebrew עִבְרִי, but from the Palestinian Aramaic *'ebrāyā,* 'the Hebrew.'

(see above) had become naturalized among them. In referring this name to the patronymic Eber, the Hebrew genealogists have assigned to it a much more comprehensive signification. For since in Gn 10^{21} (Nu 24^{24} does not apply) Shem is called the *father of all the children of Eber*, and to the latter there also belonged according to Gn 11^{14} ff. and 10^{25} ff. Aramean and Arab races, the name, afterwards restricted in the form of the gentilic *'ibrî* exclusively to the Israelites, must have originally included a considerably larger group of countries and nations. The etymological significance of the name must in that case not be insisted upon.[1]

The term ἑβραϊστί is first used, to denote the old Hebrew, in the prologue C to Jesus the son of Sirach (about 130 B. c.), and in the New Testament, Rv 9^{11}. On the other hand it serves in Jn 5^{2}, $19^{13.17}$ perhaps also in 19^{20} and Rv 16^{16} to denote what was then the (Aramaic) vernacular of Palestine as opposed to the Greek. The meaning of the expression ἑβραῖς διάλεκτος in Acts 21^{40}, 22^{2}, and 26^{14} is doubtful (cf. Kautzsch, *Gramm. des Bibl.-Aram.*, p. 19 f.). Josephus also uses the term *Hebrew* both of the old Hebrew and of the Aramaic vernacular of his time.

The Hebrew language is first called the *sacred language* in the Jewish-Aramaic versions of the Old Testament, as being the language of the sacred books in opposition to the *lingua profana*, i. e. the Aramaic vulgar tongue.

2. With the exception of the Old Testament (and apart from the *d* Phoenician inscriptions; see below, *f–h*), only very few remains of old Hebrew or old Canaanitish literature have been preserved. Of the latter—(1) an inscription, unfortunately much injured, of thirty-four lines, which was found in the ancient territory of the tribe of Reuben, about twelve miles to the east of the Dead Sea, among the ruins of the city of Dîbôn (now Dîbân), inhabited in earlier times by the Gadites, afterwards by the Moabites. In it the Moabite king Mêša' (about 850 B.C.) recounts his battles with Israel (cf. 2 K 3^{4} ff.), his buildings, and other matters.[2] Of old Hebrew: (2) an inscription

---

[1] We may also leave out of account the linguistically possible identification of the 'Ibriyyîm with the Ḥabiri who appear in the Tell-el-Amarna letters (about 1400 B. c.) as freebooters and mercenaries in Palestine and its neighbourhood.

[2] This monument, unique of its kind, was first seen in August, 1868, on the spot, by the German missionary F. A. Klein. It was afterwards broken into pieces by the Arabs, so that only an incomplete copy of the inscription could be made. Most of the fragments are now in the Louvre in Paris. For the history of the discovery and for the earlier literature relating to the stone, see Lidzbarski, *Nordsemitische Epigraphik*, i. pp. 103 f., 415 f., and in the bibliography (under Me), p. 39 ff. The useful reproduction and translation of the inscription by Smend and Socin (Freiburg im Baden, 1886) was afterwards revised and improved by Nordlander, *Die Inschrift des Königs Mesa von Moab*, Lpz. 1896; by Socin and Holzinger, 'Zur Mesainschrift' (*Berichte der K. Sächsischen Gesell. d. Wiss.*, Dec. 1897); and by Lidzbarski, 'Eine Nachprüfung der Mesainschrift' (*Ephemeris*, i. 1, p. 1 ff.; text in his *Altsemitische Texte*, pt. 1, Giessen, 1907); J. Halévy, *Revue Sémitique*, 1900, pp. 236 ff., 289 ff., 1901, p. 297 ff.; M. J. Lagrange, *Revue biblique international*, 1901, p. 522 ff.; F. Prätorius in ZDMG. 1905, p. 33 ff., 1906, p. 402. Its genuineness was attacked by A. Löwy, *Die Echtheit der Moabit. Inschr. im Louvre* (Wien, 1903), and G. Jahn in *Das Buch Daniel*, Lpz. 1904, p. 122 ff. (also in ZDMG. 1905, p. 723 ff.), but without justification, as shown by E. König in ZDMG. 1905, pp. 233 ff. and 743 ff. [Cf. also Driver, *Notes on the Hebrew Text of the Books of Samuel*, Oxford, 1890, p. lxxxv ff.; Cooke, *op. cit.*, p. 1 ff.]

of six lines (probably of the eighth century B.C.[1]) discovered in June, 1880, in the tunnel between the Virgin's Spring and the Pool of Siloam at Jerusalem; (3) about forty engraved seal-stones, some of them pre-exilic but bearing little except proper names[2]; (4) coins of the Maccabaean prince Simon (from 'the 2nd year of deliverance', 140 and 139 B.C.) and his successors,[3] and the coinage of the revolts in the times of Vespasian and Hadrian.

e 3. In the whole series of the ancient Hebrew writings, as found in the Old Testament and also in non-biblical monuments (see above, *d*), the language (to judge from its consonantal formation) remains, as regards its general character, and apart from slight changes in form and differences of style (see *k* to *w*), at about the same stage of development. In this form, it may at an early time have been fixed as a literary language, and the fact that the books contained in the Old Testament were handed down as *sacred* writings, must have contributed to this constant uniformity.

f To this old Hebrew, the language of the Canaanitish or Phoenician[4] stocks came the nearest of all the Semitic languages, as is evident partly from the many Canaanitish names of persons and places with a Hebrew form and meaning which occur in the Old Testament (e.g. קִרְיַת סֵפֶר, מַלְכִּי־צֶדֶק, &c.;

---

[1] Of this inscription—unfortunately not dated, but linguistically and palaeographically very important—referring to the boring of the tunnel, a facsimile is given at the beginning of this grammar. See also Lidzbarski, *Nordsemitische Epigraphik*, i. 105, 163, 439 (bibliography, p. 56 ff.; facsimile, vol. ii, plate xxi, 1); on the new drawing of it by Socin (*ZDPV.* xxii. p. 61 ff. and separately published at Freiburg i. B. 1899), see Lidzbarski, *Ephemeris*, i. 53 ff. and 310 f. (text in *Altsemit. Texte*, p. 9 f.). Against the view of A. Fischer (*ZDMG.* 1902, p. 800 f.) that the six lines are the continuation of an inscription which was never executed, see Lidzbarski, *Ephemeris*, ii. 71. The inscription was removed in 1890, and broken into six or seven pieces in the process. It has since been well restored, and is now in the Imperial Museum at Constantinople. If, as can hardly be doubted, the name שִׁלֹחַ (i. e. *emissio*) Is 8[6] refers to the discharge of water from the Virgin's Spring, through the tunnel (so Stade, *Gesch. Isr.* i. 594), then the latter, and consequently the inscription, was already in existence about 736 B.C. [Cf. Cooke, *op. cit.*, p. 15 ff.]

[2] M. A. Levy, *Siegel u. Gemmen, &c.*, Bresl. 1869, p. 33 ff.; Stade, *ZAW.* 1897, p. 501 ff. (four old-Semitic seals published in 1896); Lidzbarski, *Handbuch*, i. 169 f.; *Ephemeris*, i. 10 ff.; W. Nowack, *Lehrb. d. hebr. Archäol.* (Freib. 1894), i. 262 f.; I. Benzinger, *Hebr. Archäol.*[2] (Tübingen, 1907), pp. 80, 225 ff., which includes the beautiful seal inscribed לשמע עבד ירבעם from the castle-hill of Megiddo, found in 1904; [Cooke, p. 362].

[3] De Saulcy, *Numismatique de la Terre Sainte*, Par. 1874; M. A. Levy, *Gesch. der jüd. Münzen*, Breslau, 1862; Madden, *The Coins of the Jews*, Lond. 1881; Reinach, *Les monnaies juives*, Paris, 1888.—Cf. the literature in Schürer's *Gesch. des jüd. Volkes im Zeitalter J. C.*[3], Lpz. 1901, i. p. 20 ff.; [Cooke, p. 352 ff.].

[4] כְּנַעֲנִי, כְּנַעַן is the native name, common both to the Canaanitish tribes in Palestine and to those which dwelt at the foot of the Lebanon and on the Syrian coast, whom we call Phoenicians, while they called themselves כנען on their coins. The people of Carthage also called themselves so.

on 'Canaanite glosses'[1] to Assyrian words in the cuneiform tablets of Tell-el-Amarna [about 1400 B.C.] cf. H. Winckler, 'Die Thontafeln von Tell-el-Amarna,' in *Keilinschr. Bibliothek*, vol. v, Berlin, 1896 f. [transcription and translation]; J. A. Knudtzon, *Die El-Amarna-Tafeln*, Lpz. 1907 f.; H. Zimmern, *ZA.* 1891, p. 154 ff. and *KAT.*[3], p. 651 ff.), and partly from the numerous remains of the Phoenician and Punic languages.

The latter we find in their peculiar writing (§ 1 *k, l*) in a great number of inscriptions and on coins, copies of which have been collected by Gesenius, Judas, Bourgade, Davis, de Vogüé, Levy, P. Schröder, v. Maltzan, Euting, but especially in Part I of the *Corpus Inscriptionum Semiticarum*, Paris, 1881 ff. Among the inscriptions but few public documents are found, e. g. two lists of fees for sacrifices; by far the most are epitaphs or votive tablets. Of special importance is the inscription on the sarcophagus of King Ešmûnazar of Sidon, found in 1855, now in the Louvre; see the bibliography in Lidzbarski, *Nordsem. Epigr.*, i. 23 ff.; on the inscription, i. 97 ff., 141 f., 417, ii. plate iv, 2; [Cooke, p. 30 ff.]. To these may be added isolated words in Greek and Latin authors, and the Punic texts in Plautus, *Poenulus* 5, 1-3 (best treated by Gildemeister in Ritschl's edition of Plautus, Lips. 1884, tom. ii, fasc. 5). From the monuments we learn the native orthography, from the Greek and Latin transcriptions the pronunciation and vocalization; the two together give a tolerably distinct idea of the language and its relation to Hebrew.

g Phoenician (Punic) words occurring in inscriptions are, e. g. אל *God*, אדם *man*, בן *son*, בת *daughter*, מלך *king*, עבד *servant*, כהן *priest*, זבח *sacrifice*, בעל *lord*, שמש *sun*, ארץ *land*, ים *sea*, אבן *stone*, כסף *silver*, ברזל *iron*, שמן *oil*, עת *time*, קבר *grave*, מצבת *monument*, מקם *place*, משכב *bed*, כל *all*, אחד *one*, שנים *two*, שלש *three*, ארבע *four*, חמש *five*, שש *six*, שבע *seven*, עשר *ten*, כן (=Hebr. היה) *to be*, שמע *to hear*, פתח *to open*, נדר *to vow*, ברך *to bless*, בקש *to seek*, &c. Proper names: צדן *Sidon*, צר *Tyre*, חנא *Hanno*, חנבעל *Hannibal*, &c. See the complete vocabulary in Lidzbarski, *Nordsem. Epigr.*, i. 204 ff.

h Variations from Hebrew in Phoenician orthography and inflection are, e. g. the almost invariable omission of the vowel letters (§ 7 *b*), as בת for בית *house*, קל for קול *voice*, צדן for צידן, כהנם for כֹּהֲנִים *priests*, אלנם (in Plaut. *alonim*) *gods*; the fem., even in the absolute state, ending in ת (*ath*) (§ 80 *b*) as well as א (*ô*), the relative אש (Hebr. אֲשֶׁר), &c. The differences in pronunciation are more remarkable, especially in Punic, where the וֹ was regularly pronounced as *û*, e. g. שפט *sûfeṭ* (judge), שלש *sālûs* (three), רש *rûs*=ראש *head*; *i* and *e* often as the obscure dull sound of *y*, e. g. הנגּוּ *ynnynnu* (ecce eum), את (אית) *yth*; the ע as *o*, e. g. מעקר *Mocar* (cf. מֶעְבָה LXX, Gn 22²⁴ Μωχά). See the collection of the grammatical peculiarities in Gesenius, *Monumenta Phoenicia*, p. 430 ff.; Paul Schröder, *Die phöniz. Sprache*, Halle, 1869; B. Stade, 'Erneute Prüfung des zwischen dem Phönic. und Hebr. bestehenden Verwandtschaftsgrades,' in the *Morgenländ. Forschungen*, Lpz. 1875, p. 169 ff.

i **4.** As the Hebrew writing on monuments and coins mentioned in *d* consists only of consonants, so also the writers of the Old

---

[1] Cf. inter alia: *aparu*, also *ḥaparu* (Assyr. *epru, ipru*)=עָפָר; *ḥullu*=על (with hard ע; cf. § 6 *c*, and Assyr. *ḥumri*=עָמְרִי, *ḥazzatu*=עַזָּה); *iazkur*=יִזְכֹּר, *zuruḥu*=זְרוֹעַ, *abadat*=אֲבְדָה, *šaḥri*=שַׁעַר, *gate*; *baṭnu*=בֶּטֶן, *belly*; *kilûbi*=כְּלוּב, *net*; *ṣaduk*=צָדֹק (צַדִּיק), &c. [Cf. Böhl, *Die Sprache d. Amarnabriefe*, Lpz. 1909.]

Testament books used merely the consonant-signs (§ 1 *k*), and even now the written scrolls of the Law used in the synagogues must not, according to ancient custom, contain anything more. The present pronunciation of this consonantal text, its vocalization and accentuation, rest on the tradition of the Jewish schools, as it was finally fixed by the system of punctuation (§ 7 *h*) introduced by Jewish scholars about the seventh century A.D.; cf. § 3 *b*.

k An earlier stage in the development of the Canaaniṭish-Hebrew language, i.e. a form of it anterior to the written documents now extant, when it must have stood nearer to the common language of the united Semitic family, can still be discerned in its principal features :—(1) from many archaisms preserved in the traditional texts, especially in the names of persons and places dating from earlier times, as well as in isolated forms chiefly occurring in poetic style; (2) in general by an *a posteriori* conclusion from traditional forms, so far as according to the laws and analogies of phonetic change they clearly point to an older phase of the language; and (3) by comparison with the kindred languages, especially Arabic, in which this earlier stage of the language has been frequently preserved even down to later times (§ 1 *m*, *n*). In numerous instances in examining linguistic phenomena, the same—and consequently so much the more certain—result is attained by each of these three methods.

Although the systematic investigation of the linguistic development indicated above belongs to comparative Semitic philology, it is nevertheless indispensable for the scientific treatment of Hebrew to refer to the ground-forms [1] so far as they can be ascertained and to compare the corresponding forms in Arabic. Even elementary grammar which treats of the forms of the language occurring in the Old Testament frequently requires, for their explanation, a reference to these ground-forms.

l 5. Even in the language of the Old Testament, notwithstanding its general uniformity, there is noticeable a certain progress from an earlier to a later stage. Two periods, though with some reservations, may be distinguished: the *first*, down to the end of the Babylonian exile; and the *second*, after the exile.

m To the former belongs, apart from isolated traces of a later revision, the larger half of the Old Testament books, viz. (*a*) of the prose and historical writings, a large part of the Pentateuch and of Joshua, Judges, Samuel, and Kings; (*b*) of the poetical, perhaps

---

[1] Whether these can be described simply as 'primitive Semitic' is a question which may be left undecided here.

a part of the Psalms and Proverbs; (*c*) the writings of the earlier prophets (apart from various later additions) in the following chronological order: Amos, Hosea, Isaiah I, Micah, Nahum, Zephaniah, Habakkuk, Obadiah (?), Jeremiah, Ezekiel, Isaiah II (ch. 40–55).

The beginning of this period, and consequently of Hebrew literature *n* generally, is undoubtedly to be placed as early as the time of Moses, although the Pentateuch in its present form, in which very different strata may be still clearly recognized, is to be regarded as a gradual production of the centuries after Moses. Certain linguistic peculiarities of the Pentateuch, which it was once customary to regard as archaisms, such as the epicene use of נַעַר *boy, youth,* for נַעֲרָה *girl,* and הוּא for הִיא, are merely to be attributed to a later redactor; cf. § 17 *c*.

The linguistic character of the various strata of the Pentateuch has been *o* examined by Ryssel, *De Elohistae Pentateuchici sermone,* Lpz. 1878; König, *De criticae sacrae argumento e linguae legibus repetito,* Lpz. 1879 (analysis of Gn 1–11); F. Giesebrecht, 'Der Sprachgebr. des hexateuchischen Elohisten,' in *ZAW.* 1881, p. 177 ff., partly modified by Driver in the *Journal of Philology,* vol. xi. p. 201 ff.; Kräutlein, *Die sprachl. Verschiedenheiten in den Hexateuchquellen,* Lpz. 1908.—Abundant matter is afforded also by Holzinger, *Einleitung in den Hexateuch,* Freib. 1893; Driver, *Introduction to the Literature of the Old Testament* [8], Edinburgh, 1908; Strack, *Einleitung ins A. T.* [6], Munich, 1906; König, *Einleitung in das A. T.,* Bonn, 1893.

6. Even in the writings of this first period, which embraces *p* about 600 years, we meet, as might be expected, with considerable differences in linguistic form and style, which are due partly to differences in the time and place of composition, and partly to the individuality and talent of the authors. Thus Isaiah, for example, writes quite differently from the later Jeremiah, but also differently from his contemporary Micah. Amongst the historical books of this period, the texts borrowed from earlier sources have a linguistic colouring perceptibly different from those derived from later sources, or passages which belong to the latest redactor himself. Yet the structure of the language, and, apart from isolated cases, even the vocabulary and phraseology, are on the whole the same, especially in the prose books.

But the *poetic language* is in many ways distinguished from *q* prose, not only by a *rhythm* due to more strictly balanced (parallel) members and definite metres (see *r*), but also by peculiar *words* and *meanings, inflexions* and *syntactical constructions* which it uses in addition to those usual in prose. This distinction, however, does not go far as, for example, in Greek. Many of these poetic peculiarities occur in the kindred languages, especially in Aramaic, as the ordinary modes of expression, and probably are to be regarded largely as archaisms which poetry retained. Some perhaps, also, are embellishments which the Hebrew poets who knew Aramaic adopted into their language.[1]

The prophets, at least the earlier, in language and rhythm are to be regarded almost entirely as poets, except that with them the sentences are often more extended, and the parallelism is less regular and balanced than is the case with the poets properly so called. The language of the later prophets, on the contrary, approaches nearer to prose.

r On the *rhythm* of Hebrew poetry, see besides the Commentaries on the poetical books and Introductions to the O. T., J. Ley, *Grundzüge des Rhythmus, &c.,* Halle, 1875 ; *Leitfaden der Metrik der hebr. Poesie,* Halle, 1887 ; ' Die metr. Beschaffenheit des B. Hiob,' in *Theol. Stud. u. Krit.,* 1895, iv, 1897, i ; Grimme, ' Abriss der bibl.-hebr. Metrik,' *ZDMG.* 1896, p. 529 ff., 1897, p. 683 ff. ; *Psalmenprobleme, &c.,* Freiburg (Switzerland), 1902 (on which see Beer in *ThLZ.* 1903, no. 11); ' Gedanken über hebr. Metrik,' in Altschüler's *Vierteljahrschrift,* i (1903), 1 ff. ; Döller, *Rhythmus, Metrik u. Strophik in d. bibl.-hebr. Poesie,* Paderborn, 1899 ; Schloegl, *De re metrica veterum Hebraeorum disputatio,* Vindobonae, 1899 (on the same lines as Grimme) ; but especially Ed. Sievers, *Metrische Studien* : i *Studien zur hebr. Metrik,* pt. 1 *Untersuchungen,* pt. 2 *Textproben,* Lpz. 1901 : ii *Die hebr. Genesis,* 1 *Texte,* 2 *Zur Quellenscheidung u. Textkritik,* Lpz. 1904 f. : iii *Samuel,* Lpz. 1907 ; *Amos metrisch bearbeitet* (with H. Guthe), Lpz. 1907 ; and his *Alttest. Miszellen* (1 Is 24–27, 2 Jona, 3 Deutero-Zechariah, 4 Malachi, 5 Hosea, 6 Joel, 7 Obadiah, 8 Zephaniah, 9 Haggai, 10 Micah), Lpz. 1904–7.—As a guide to Sievers' system (with some criticism of his principles) see Baumann, ' Die Metrik u. das A.T.,' in the *Theol. Rundschau,* viii (1905), 41 ff. ; W. H. Cobb, *A criticism of systems of Hebrew Metre,* Oxford, 1905 ; Cornill, *Einleitung ins A. T.*[3], Tübingen, 1905, p. 11 ff. ; Rothstein, *Zeitschr. für d. ev. Rel.-Unterricht,* 1907, p. 188 ff. and his *Grundzüge des hebr. Rhythmus,* Lpz. 1909 (also separately *Psalmentexte u. der Text des Hohen Liedes,* Lpz. 1909) ; W. R. Arnold, ' The rhythms of the ancient Heb.,' in *O. T. and Semitic Studies in memory of W. R. Harper,* i. 165 ff., Chicago, 1907, according to whom the number of syllables between the beats is only limited by the physiological possibilities of phonetics ; C. v. Orelli, ' Zur Metrik der alttest. Prophetenschriften,' in his *Kommentar zu den kl. Propheten*[3], p. 236 ff., Munich, 1908.— In full agreement with Sievers is Baethgen, *Psalmen*[3], p. xxvi ff., Göttingen, 1904. [Cf. Budde in *DB.* iv. 3 ff. ; Duhm in *EB.* iii. 3793 ff.]

Of all views of this matter, the only one generally accepted as sound was at first Ley's and Budde's discovery of the Qina- or Lamentation-Verse (*ZAW.* 1882, 5 ff. ; 1891, 234 ff. ; 1892, 31 ff.). On their predecessors, Lowth, de Wette, Ewald, see Löhr, *Klagelied*[2], p. 9. This verse, called by Duhm 'long verse', by Sievers simply ' five-syllabled ' (Fünfer), consists of two members, the second at least one beat shorter than the other. That a regular repetition of an equal number of syllables in *arsis* and *thesis* was observed by other poets, had been established by Ley, Duhm, Gunkel, Grimme, and others, especially Zimmern, who cites a Babylonian hymn in which the members are equally marked (*ZA.* x. 1 ff., xii. 382 ff. ; cf. also Delitzsch, *Das babyl. Weltschöpfungsepos,* Lpz. 1896, pp. 60 ff.). Recently, however, E. Sievers, the recognized authority on metre in other branches of literature, has indicated, in the works mentioned above, a number of fresh facts and views, which have frequently been confirmed by the conclusions of Ley and others. The most important are as follows :—

Hebrew poetry, as distinguished from the quantitative Classical and Arabic

---

[1] That already in Isaiah's time (second half of the eighth century B. C.) educated Hebrews, or at least officers of state, understood Aramaic, while the common people in Jerusalem did not, is evident from 2 K 18[26] (Is 36[11]).

and the syllabic Syriac verse, is *accentual*. The number of unstressed syllables between the beats (*ictus*) is, however, not arbitrary, but the scheme of the verse is based on an irregular anapaest which may undergo rhythmical modifications (e. g. resolving the ictus into two syllables, or lengthening the arsis so as to give a double accent) and contraction, e. g. of the first two syllables. The foot always concludes with the ictus, so that toneless endings, due to change of pronunciation or corruption of the text, are to be disregarded, although as a rule the ictus coincides with the Hebrew word-accent. The metrical scheme consists of combinations of feet in *series* (of 2, 3 or 4), and of these again in *periods*—double threes, very frequently, double fours in narrative, fives in Lamentations (see above) and very often elsewhere, and sevens. Sievers regards the last two metres as catalectic double threes and fours. Connected sections do not always maintain the same metre throughout, but often exhibit a mixture of metres.

It can no longer be doubted that in the analysis of purely poetical passages, this system often finds ready confirmation and leads to textual and literary results, such as the elimination of glosses. There are, however, various difficulties in carrying out the scheme consistently and extending it to the prophetical writings and still more to narrative : (1) not infrequently the required number of feet is only obtained by sacrificing the clearly marked parallelism, or the grammatical connexion (e. g. of the construct state with its genitive), and sometimes even by means of doubtful emendations ; (2) the whole system assumes a correct transmission of the text and its pronunciation, for neither of which is there the least guarantee. To sum up, our conclusion at present is that for poetry proper some assured and final results have been already obtained, and others may be expected, from the principles laid down by Sievers, although, considering the way in which the text has been transmitted, a *faultless* arrangement of metres cannot be expected. Convincing proof of the *consistent* use of the same metrical schemes in the prophets, and *a fortiori* in narrative, can hardly be brought forward.

The great work of D. H. Müller, *Die Propheten in ihrer ursprüngl. Form* (2 vols., Vienna, 1896 ; cf. his *Strophenbau u. Responsion*, ibid. 1898, and *Komposition u. Strophenbau*, ibid. 1907), is a study of the most important monuments of early Semitic poetry from the point of view of strophic structure and the use of the refrain, i. e. the repetition of the same or similar phrases or words in corresponding positions in different strophes.

The arrangement of certain poetical passages in verse-form required by early scribal rules (Ex 15$^{1-19}$; Dt 32$^{1-43}$; Ju 5 ; 1 S 2$^{1-10}$; 2 S 22, 23$^{1-7}$; ψ 18, 136 ; Pr. 31$^{10-31}$; 1 Ch 16$^{8-36}$: cf. also Jo 12$^{9-24}$; Ec 3$^{2-8}$; Est 9$^{7-10}$) has nothing to do with the question of metre in the above sense.

Words are used in poetry, for which others are customary in prose, e. g. ψ אָתָה ; רָאָה to see = חָזָה ; דָּבָר word = מִלָּה path = דֶּרֶךְ ; אֹרַח man = אָדָם ; אֱנוֹשׁ to come = בּוֹא.

To the poetic *meanings of words* belongs the use of certain poetic *epithets* as substantives ; thus, for example, אָבִיר (only in constr. st. אֲבִיר) *the strong one* for *God* ; אַבִּיר *the strong one* for *bull, horse* ; לְבָנָה *alba* for *luna* ; צָר *enemy* for אֹיֵב.

Of word-forms, we may note, e. g. the longer forms of prepositions of place (§ 103 n) עַד = עֲדֵי, אֶל = אֱלֵי, עַל = עֲלֵי ; the endings ־י ֫, וֹ in the noun (§ 90) ; the pronominal suffixes מוֹ, ־ֵמוֹ, ־ָמוֹ for ם, ־ָם, ־ֶם (§ 58) ; the plural ending ־ִין for ־ִים (§ 87 e). To the *syntax* belongs the far more sparing use of the article, of the relative pronoun, of the accusative particle אֵת ; the construct state even before prepositions ; the shortened imperfect with the same meaning as the ordinary form (§ 109 i) ; the wider governing power of prepositions ; and in general a forcible brevity of expression.

The King's Library

t 7. The *second* period of the Hebrew language and literature, after the return from the exile until the Maccabees (about 160 B.C.), is chiefly distinguished by a constantly closer approximation of the language to the kindred western Aramaic dialect. This is due to the influence of the Aramaeans, who lived in close contact with the recent and thinly-populated colony in Jerusalem, and whose dialect was already of importance as being the official language of the western half of the Persian empire. Nevertheless the supplanting of Hebrew by Aramaic proceeded only very gradually. Writings intended for popular use, such as the Hebrew original of Jesus the son of Sirach and the book of Daniel, not only show that Hebrew about 170 B.C. was still in use as a literary language, but also that it was still at least understood by the people.[1] When it had finally ceased to exist as a living language, it was still preserved as the *language of the Schools*—not to mention the numerous Hebraisms introduced into the Aramaic spoken by the Jews.

For particulars, see Kautzsch, *Gramm. des Bibl.-Aram.*, pp. 1-6. We may conveniently regard the relation of the languages which co-existed in this later period as similar to that of the High and Low German in North Germany, or to that of the High German and the common dialects in the south and in Switzerland. Even amongst the more educated, the common dialect prevails orally, whilst the High German serves essentially as the literary and cultured language, and is at least understood by all classes of the people. Wholly untenable is the notion, based on an erroneous interpretation of Neh 8⁸, that the Jews immediately after the exile had completely forgotten the Hebrew language, and therefore needed a translation of the Holy Scriptures.

u The Old Testament writings belonging to this second period, in all of which the Aramaic colouring appears in various degrees, are: certain parts of the Pentateuch and of Joshua, Ruth, the books of Ezra, Nehemiah, Chronicles, Esther; the prophetical books of Haggai, Zechariah, Isaiah III (56—66), Malachi, Joel, Jonah, Daniel; of the poetical books, a large part of Proverbs, Job, Song of Songs, Ecclesiastes, and most of the Psalms. As literary compositions, these books are sometimes far inferior to those of the first period, although work was still produced which in purity of language and aesthetic value falls little short of the writings of the golden age.

v *Later words* (Aramaisms) are, e.g. אַחֲוָה *declaration*, אָנַס *compel*, בַּר *son*, גִּיר *chalk*, זְמָן = עֵת *time*, זָקַף *raise up*, חסד Pi. *reproach*, טלל Pi. *roof over*,

---

[1] The extensive use of Hebrew in the popular religious literature which is partly preserved to us in the Midrašim, the Mišna, and the Liturgy, indicates, moreover, that Hebrew was widely understood much later than this. Cf. M. H. Segal, 'Mišnaic Hebrew and its relations to Biblical Hebrew and Aramaic,' in *J. Q. R.*, 1908, p. 647 ff. (also separately).

טָעָה *stray,* כֵּף *rock,* מלך *advise,* קֵץ = סוֹף *end,* לָקַח = קָבַל *take,* רָצַע = רָעַע *break,* שָׂנֵא *be many,* שָׁלַט = מָלַךְ *rule,* אָמֵץ = תָּקֵף *be strong.*—Later meanings are, e. g. אָמַר (to say) *to command* ; עָנָה (to answer) *to begin speaking.*—*Orthographical* and *grammatical* peculiarities are, the frequent *scriptio plena* of ‍ֹ and ‍ִ, e. g. דָּוִיד [1] (elsewhere דָּוִד), even קוֹדָשׁ for קֹדָשׁ, רוֹב for רֹב ; the interchange of ה‍ and א‍ final ; the more frequent use of substantives in וֹן, ‍ָן, וּת, &c. Cf. Dav. Strauss, *Sprachl. Studien zu d. hebr. Sirachfragmenten,* Zürich, 1900, p. 19 ff.; for the Psalms Cheyne, *Origin of the Psalter,* p. 461 ff., and especially Giesebrecht in *ZAW.* 1881, p. 276 ff. ; in general, Kautzsch, *Die Aramaismen im A. T.* (i, Lexikal. Teil), Halle, 1902.

But all the peculiarities of these later writers are not Aramaisms. Several do not occur in Aramaic and must have belonged at an earlier period to the Hebrew vernacular, especially it would seem in northern Palestine. There certain parts of Judges, amongst others, may have originated, as is indicated, e. g. by שֶׁ, a common form in Phoenician (as well as אֵשׁ), for אֲשֶׁר (§ 36), which afterwards recurs in Jonah, Lamentations, the Song of Songs, the later Psalms, and Ecclesiastes.

Rem. 1. Of dialectical varieties in the old Hebrew language, only one ‍ש express mention occurs in the O. T. (Ju 12⁶), according to which the Ephraimites in certain cases pronounced the שׁ as ס. (Cf. Marquart in *ZAW.* 1888, p. 151 ff.) Whether in Neh 13²⁴ by the *speech of Ashdod* a Hebrew, or a (wholly different) Philistine dialect is intended, cannot be determined. On the other hand, many peculiarities in the North Palestinian books (Judges and Hosea) are probably to be regarded as differences in dialect, and so also some anomalies in the Moabite inscription of Mêša‛ (see above, *d*). On later developments see L. Metman, *Die hebr. Sprache, ihre Geschichte u. lexikal. Entwickelung seit Abschluss des Kanons u. ihr Bau in d. Gegenwart,* Jerusalem, 1906.

2. It is evident that, in the extant remains of old Hebrew literature,[2] the entire store of the ancient language is not preserved. The canonical books of the Old Testament formed certainly only a fraction of the whole Hebrew national literature.

§ 3. *Grammatical Treatment of the Hebrew Language.*

Gesenius, *Gesch. der hebr. Sprache,* §§ 19–39 ; Oehler's article, 'Hebr. Sprache,' in Schmid's *Encykl. des ges. Erziehungs- u. Unterrichtswesens,* vol. iii. p. 346 ff. (in the 2nd ed. revised by Nestle, p. 314 ff.). Cf. also the literature cited above in the headings of §§ 1 and 2 ; also Böttcher, *Lehrb. der hebr. Spr.,* i. Lpz. 1866, p. 30 ff. ; L. Geiger, *Das Studium der Hebr. Spr. in Deutschl. vom Ende des XV. bis zur Mitte des XVI. Jahrh.,* Breslau, 1870 ; B. Pick, 'The Study of the Hebrew Language among Jews and Christians,' in *Bibliotheca Sacra,* 1884, p. 450 ff., and 1885, p. 470 ff. ; W. Bacher, article 'Grammar' in the *Jew. Encyclopaedia,* vol. vi, New York and London, 1904. Cf. also the note on *d*.

1. At the time when the old Hebrew language was gradually *a* becoming extinct, and the formation of the O. T. canon was

---

[1] דָּוִיד in the Minor Prophets throughout (Ho 3⁵, &c.) is due merely to a caprice of the Masoretes.

[2] According to the calculation of the Dutch scholar Leusden, the O. T. contains 5,642 different Hebrew and Aramaic words; according to rabbinical calculations, 79,856 altogether in the Pentateuch. Cf. also E. Nestle, *ZAW.* 1906, p. 2⁸3 ; H. Strack, *ZAW.* 1907, p. 69 ff. ; Blau, 'Neue masoret. Studien,' in *JQR.* xvi. 357 ff., treats of the number of letters and words, and the verse division in the O. T.

approaching completion, the Jews began to explain and critically revise their sacred text, and sometimes to translate it into the vernacular languages which in various countries had become current among them. The oldest *translation* is the Greek of the *Seventy* (more correctly *Seventy-two*) Interpreters (LXX), which was begun with the Pentateuch at Alexandria under Ptolemy Philadelphus, but only completed later. It was the work of various authors, some of whom had a living knowledge of the original, and was intended for the use of Greek-speaking Jews, especially in Alexandria. Somewhat later the Aramaic translations, or Targums (תַּרְגּוּמִים i.e. *interpretations*), were formed by successive recensions made in Palestine and Babylonia. The *explanations*, derived in part from alleged tradition, refer almost exclusively to civil and ritual law and dogmatic theology, and are no more scientific in character than much of the textual tradition of that period. Both kinds of tradition are preserved in the *Talmud*, the first part of which, the *Mišna*, was finally brought to its present form towards the end of the second century; of the remainder, the *Gemāra*, one recension (the *Jerusalem* or *Palestinian Gem.*) about the middle of the fourth century, the other (the *Babylonian Gem.*) about the middle of the sixth century A.D. The Mišna forms the beginning of the New-Hebrew literature; the language of the Gemaras is for the most part Aramaic.

b 2. To the interval between the completion of the Talmud and the earliest grammatical writers, belong mainly the vocalization and accentuation of the hitherto unpointed text of the O. T., according to the pronunciation traditional in the Synagogues and Schools (§ 7 *h*, *i*), as well as the greater part of the collection of critical notes which bears the name of Masōra (מָסוֹרָה *traditio* ?).[1] From this the text which has since been transmitted with rigid uniformity by the MSS.,

---

[1] On the name Masora (or Massora, as e. g. E. König, *Einleitung in das A. T.*, p. 38 ff.; *Lehrgeb. d. hebr. Sprache*, ii. 358 ff.), and the great difficulty of satisfactorily explaining it, cf. De Lagarde, *Mitteilungen*, i. 91 ff. W. Bacher's derivation of the expression (in *JQR.* 1891, p. 785 ff.; so also C. Levias in the *Hebrew Union College Annual*, Cincinnati, 1904, p. 147 ff.) from Ez 20³⁷ (מָסֹרֶת הַבְּרִית; מסרה, i. e. מוֹסֵרָה, being an equally legitimate form) is rightly rejected by König, l. c. The correctness of the form מָסְרָה (by the side of the equally well-attested form מַסֹּרֶת) does not seem to us to be invalidated by his arguments, nor by Blau's proposal to read מְסוֹרֶת (*JQR.* xii. 241). The remark of Levias (l.c.) deserves notice, that with the earlier Masoretes מסורת is equivalent to orthography, i. e. *plene-* and *defective* writing, and only later came to mean *traditio*.—G. Wildboer, in *ZAW.* 1909, p. 74, contends that as מסר *to hand on* is not found in the O. T., it must be a late denominative in this sense.

and is still the received text of the O.T., has obtained the name of the Masoretic Text.

E. F. K. Rosenmüller already (*Handbuch für d. Liter. der bibl. Kritik u. C Exegese*, 1797, i. 247; *Vorrede zur Stereotyp-Ausg. des A. T.*, Lpz. 1834) maintained that our O. T. text was derived from Codices belonging to a single recension. J. G. Sommer (cf. Cornill, *ZAW*. 1892, p. 309), Olshausen (since 1853), and especially De Lagarde (*Proverbien*, 1863, p. 1 ff.), have even made it probable that the original Masoretic text was derived from a single standard manuscript. Cf., however, E. König in *Ztschr. f. kirchl. Wiss.*, 1887, p. 279 f., and especially his *Einleitung ins A. T.*, p. 88 ff. Moreover a great many facts, which will be noticed in their proper places, indicate that the Masora itself is by no means uniform but shows clear traces of different schools and opinions ; cf. H. Strack in *Semitic Studies in memory of . . . Kohut*, Berlin, 1897, p. 563 ff. An excellent foundation for the history of the Masora and the settlement of the masoretic tradition was laid by Joh. Buxtorf in his *Tiberias seu Commentarius Masorethicus*, first published at Basel in 1620 as an appendix to the Rabbinical Bible of 1618 f. For more recent work see Geiger, *Jüdische Ztschr.*, iii. 78 ff., followed by Harris in *JQR*. i. 128 ff., 243 ff.; S. Frensdorff, *Ochla W'ochla*, Hanover, 1864; and his *Massor. Wörterb.*, part i, Hanover and Lpz. 1876; and Ch. D. Ginsburg, *The Massora compiled from Manuscripts, &c.*, 3 vols., Lond. 1880 ff., and *Introduction to the Massoretico-critical edition of the Hebr. Bible*, Lond. 1897 (his text, reprinted from that of Jacob b. Ḥayyîm [Venice, 1524–5] with variants from MSS. and the earliest editions, was published in 2 vols. at London in 1894, 2nd ed. 1906; a revised edition is in progress); H. Hyvernat, ʻLa langue et le langage de la Massoreʼ (as a mixture of New-Hebrew and Aramaic), in the *Revue biblique*, Oct. 1903, p. 529 ff. and B: ʻLexique massorétique,ʼ *ibid.*, Oct. 1904, p. 521 ff., 1905, p. 481 ff., and p. 515 ff. In the use of the Massora for the critical construction of the Text, useful work has been done especially by S. Baer, in the editions of the several books (only Exod.-Deut. have still to appear), edited from 1869 conjointly with Fr. Delitzsch, and since 1891 by Baer alone. Cf. also § 7 *h*.

The various readings of the Qᵉrê (see § 17) form one of the oldest and most important parts of the Masora. The punctuation of the Text, however, is not to be confounded with the compilation of the Masora. The former was settled at an earlier period, and is the result of a much more exhaustive labour than the Masora, which was not completed till a considerably later time.

3. It was not until about the beginning of the tenth century that *d* the Jews, following the example of the Arabs, began their grammatical compilations. Of the numerous grammatical and lexicographical works of R. Saʿadya,[1] beyond fragments in the commentary on the Sepher Yeṣira (ed. Mayer-Lambert, pp. 42, 47, 75, &c.), only the explanation in Arabic of the seventy (more correctly ninety) *hapax legomena* in the O. T. has been preserved. Written likewise in Arabic, but frequently translated into Hebrew, were the still extant works of the grammarians R. Yehuda Ḥayyûǵ (also called Abu Zakarya Yaḥya, about the year 1000) and R. Yôna (Abu ʼl-Walîd Merwân ibn Ǵanâḥ, about 1030). By the aid of these earlier labours, Abraham ben Ezra (commonly called Aben Ezra, ob. 1167) and R. David Qimḥi (ob. c. 1235) especially gained a classical reputation by their Hebrew grammatical writings.

---

[1] On his independent attitude towards the Masoretic punctuation, see Delitzsch, *Comm. zu den Psalmen*[4], p. 39.

From these earliest grammarians are derived many principles of arrangement and technical terms, some of which are still retained, e. g. the naming of the conjugations and weak verbs according to the paradigm of פָּעַל, certain *voces memoriales*, as בְּנֵדְכְּפַת and the like.[1]

e **4.** The father of Hebrew philology among Christians was John Reuchlin (ob. 1522),[2] to whom Greek literature also is so much indebted. Like the grammarians who succeeded him, till the time of John Buxtorf the elder (ob. 1629), he still adhered almost entirely to Jewish tradition. From the middle of the seventeenth century the field of investigation gradually widened, and the study of the kindred languages, chiefly through the leaders of the Dutch school, Albert Schultens (ob. 1750) and N. W. Schröder (ob. 1798), became of fruitful service to Hebrew grammar.

f **5.** In the nineteenth century[3] the advances in Hebrew philology are especially connected with the names of W. Gesenius (born at Nordhausen, Feb. 3, 1786; from the year 1810 Professor at Halle, where he died Oct. 23, 1842), who above all things aimed at the comprehensive observation and lucid presentation of the actually occurring linguistic phenomena; H. Ewald (ob. 1875, at Göttingen; *Krit. Gramm. der Hebr. Spr.*, Lpz. 1827; *Ausführl. Lehrb. d. hebr. Spr.*, 8th ed., Gött. 1870), who chiefly aimed at referring linguistic forms to general laws and rationally explaining the latter; J. Olshausen (ob. 1882, at Berlin; *Lehrb. der hebr. Sprache,* Brunswick, 1861) who attempted a consistent explanation of the existing condition of the language, from the presupposed primitive Semitic forms, preserved according to him notably in old Arabic. F. Böttcher (*Ausführl. Lehrb. d. hebr. Spr.* ed. by F. Mühlau, 2 vols., Lpz. 1866–8) endeavoured to present an exhaustive synopsis of the linguistic phenomena, as well as to give an explanation of them from the sphere of Hebrew

---

[1] On the oldest Hebrew grammarians, see Strack and Siegfried, *Lehrb. d. neuhebr. Spr. u. Liter.*, Carlsr. 1884, p. 107 ff., and the prefaces to the Hebrew Lexicons of Gesenius and Fürst; Berliner, *Beiträge zur hebr. Gramm. im Talmud u. Midrasch*, Berlin, 1879; Baer and Strack, *Die Dikduke ha-t^eamim des Ahron ben Moscheh ben Ascher u. andere alte grammatisch-massorethische Lehrstücke*, Lpz. 1879, and P. Kahle's criticisms in *ZDMG.* lv. 170, n. 2; Ewald and Dukes, *Beiträge z. Gesch. der ältesten Auslegung u. Spracherklärung des A. T.*, Stuttg. 1844, 3 vols.; Hupfeld, *De rei grammaticae apud Judaeos initiis antiquissimisque scriptoribus*, Hal. 1846; W. Bacher, ʻDie Anfänge der hebr. Gr.,ʼ in *ZDMG.* 1895, 1 ff. and 335 ff.; and *Die hebr. Sprachwissenschaft vom 10. bis zum 16. Jahrh.*, Trier, 1892.

[2] A strong impulse was naturally given to these studies by the introduction of printing—the Psalter in 1477, the Bologna Pentateuch in 1482, the Soncino O. T. complete in 1488: see the description of the twenty-four earliest editions (down to 1528) in Ginsburg's *Introduction*, p. 779 ff.

[3] Of the literature of the subject down to the year 1850, see a tolerably full account in Steinschneider's *Bibliogr. Handb. f. hebr. Sprachkunde*, Lpz. 1859.

alone. B. Stade, on the other hand (*Lehrb. der hebr. Gr.*, pt. i. Lpz.
1879), adopted a strictly scientific method in endeavouring to reduce
the systems of Ewald and Olshausen to a more fundamental unity.
E. König[1] in his very thorough researches into the phonology and
accidence starts generally from the position reached by the early
Jewish grammarians (in his second part ' with comparative reference
to the Semitic languages in general ') and instead of adopting the usual
dogmatic method, takes pains to re-open the discussion of disputed
grammatical questions. The syntax König has ' endeavoured to treat
in several respects in such a way as to show its affinity to the common
Semitic syntax '.—Among the works of Jewish scholars, special attention may be called to the grammar by S. D. Luzzatto written in
Italian (Padua, 1853–69).

The chief requirements for one who is treating the grammar of
an ancient language are—(1) that he should *observe* as fully and
accurately as possible the existing linguistic phenomena and *describe*
them, after showing their organic connexion (the empirical and
historico-critical element); (2) that he should try to *explain* these
facts, partly by comparing them with one another and by the analogy
of the sister languages, partly from the general laws of philology
(the logical element).

Such observation has more and more led to the belief that the *g*
original text of the O. T. has suffered to a much greater extent than
former scholars were inclined to admit, in spite of the number of
variants in parallel passages : Is $2^{2\,\text{ff.}}$=Mi $4^{1\,\text{ff.}}$, Is 36–39=2 K 18^{13}–
20^{19}, Jer 52 = 2 K 24^{18}–25^{30}, 2 S 22=ψ 18, ψ 14=ψ 53, ψ $40^{14\,\text{ff.}}$=
ψ 70, ψ 108=ψ $57^{8\,\text{ff.}}$ and $60^{7\,\text{ff.}}$. Cf. also the parallels between the
Chronicles and the older historical books, and F. Vodel, *Die konsonant.
Varianten in den doppelt überlief. poet. Stücken d. masoret. Textes*,
Lpz. 1905. As to the extent and causes of the corruption of the
Masoretic text, the newly discovered fragments of the Hebrew
Ecclesiasticus are very instructive; cf. Smend, *Gött. gel. Anz.*, 1906,
p. 763.

The causes of *unintentional* corruption in the great majority of
cases are :—Interchange of similar letters, which has sometimes taken
place in the early ' Phoenician ' writing; transposition or omission of

---

[1] *Historisch-krit. Lehrgeb. der hebr. Sprache mit steter Beziehung auf Qimchi und
die anderen Autoritäten* : I, 'Lehre von der Schrift, der Aussprache, dem Pron.
u. dem Verbum,' Lpz. 1881 ; II. 1, 'Abschluss der speziellen Formenlehre u.
generelle Formenl.,' 1895 ; ii. 2, 'Historisch-kompar. Syntax d. hebr. Spr.,'
1897.

single letters, words, or even whole sentences, which are then often
added in the margin and thence brought back into the text in the
wrong place; such omission is generally due to homoioteleuton (cf.
Ginsburg, *Introd.*, p. 171 ff.), i. e. the scribe's eye wanders from the
place to a subsequent word of the same or similar form. Other
causes are dittography, i. e. erroneous repetition of letters, words,
and even sentences; its opposite, haplography; and lastly wrong
division of words (cf. Ginsburg, *Introd.*, p. 158 ff.), since at a certain
period in the transmission of the text the words were not separated.[1]—
Intentional changes are due to corrections for the sake of decency or
of dogma, and to the insertion of glosses, some of them very early.

Advance in grammar is therefore closely dependent on progress
in *textual criticism*. The systematic pursuit of the latter has only
begun in recent years: cf. especially Doorninck on Ju 1–16, Leid.
1879; Wellhausen, *Text der Bb. Sam.*, Gött. 1871; Cornill, *Ezechiel*,
Lpz. 1886; Klostermann, *Bb. Sam. u. d. Kön.*, Nördl. 1887; Driver,
Notes on the Hebr. text of the Books of Sam., Oxf. 1890; Klostermann, *Deuterojesaja*, Munich, 1893; Oort, *Textus hebr. emendationes*,
Lugd. 1900; Burney on *Kings*, Oxf. 1903; the commentaries of Marti
and Nowack; the *Internat. Crit. Comm.*; Kautzsch, *Die heil.
Schriften des A.T.*[2], 1909–10. A critical edition of the O.T. with full
textual notes, and indicating the different documents by colours, is
being published in a handsome form by P. Haupt in *The Sacred Books
of the Old Test.*, Lpz. and Baltimore, 1893 ff. (sixteen parts have
appeared: Exod., Deut., Minor Prophets, and Megilloth are still to
come); Kittel, *Biblia hebraica*[2], 1909, Masoretic text from Jacob b.
Ḥayyim (see *c*), with a valuable selection of variants from the
versions, and emendations.

§ 4. *Division and Arrangement of the Grammar.*

The division and arrangement of Hebrew grammar follow the
three constituent parts of every language, viz. (1) articulate *sounds*
represented by *letters*, and united to form *syllables*, (2) *words*, and
(3) *sentences*.

The first part (the elements) comprises accordingly the treatment
of *sounds* and their representation in writing. It describes the nature
and relations of the sounds of the language, teaches the pronunciation

---

[1] This *scriptio continua* is also found in Phoenician inscriptions. The
inscription of Mêʿaʿ always divides the words by a point (and so the Siloam
inscription; see the facsimile at the beginning of this grammar), and frequently marks the close of a sentence by a stroke.

of the written signs (orthoepy), and the established mode of writing (orthography). It then treats of the sounds as combined in syllables and words, and specifies the laws and conditions under which this combination takes place.

The second part (etymology) treats of words in their character as parts of speech, and comprises: (1) the principles of the *formation of words,* or of the derivation of the different parts of speech from the roots or from one another; (2) the principles of *inflexion,* i. e. of the various forms which the words assume according to their relation to other words and to the sentence.

The third part (syntax, or the arrangement of words): (1) shows how the word-formations and inflexions occurring in the language are used to express different shades of ideas, and how other ideas, for which the language has not coined any forms, are expressed by periphrasis; (2) states the laws according to which the parts of speech are combined in sentences (the principles of the sentence, or syntax in the stricter sense of the term).

FIRST PART

ELEMENTARY PRINCIPLES OR THE SOUNDS AND CHARACTERS

CHAPTER I

THE INDIVIDUAL SOUNDS AND CHARACTERS

§ 5. *The Consonants: their Forms and Names.*

(Cf. the Table of Alphabets.)

Among the abundant literature on the subject, special attention is directed to : A. Berliner, *Beiträge zur hebr. Gramm.*, Berlin, 1879, p. 15 ff., on the names, forms, and pronunciation of the consonants in Talmud and Midrash; H. Strack, *Schreibkunst u. Schrift bei d. Hebräern*, PRE.[3], Lpz. 1906, p. 766 ff.; Benzinger, *Hebr. Archäologie*[2], Tübingen, 1907, p. 172 ff.; Nowack, *Lehrbuch d. hebr. Archäol.*, Freiburg, 1894, i. 279 ff.; Lidzbarski, *Handbuch d. nordsem. Epigraphik*, Weimar, 1898, i. 173 ff.; also his art. 'Hebrew Alphabet,' in the *Jewish Encyclopaedia*, i, 1901, p. 439 ff. (cf. his *Ephemeris*, i. 316 ff.); and 'Die Namen der Alphabet-buchstaben', in *Ephemeris*, ii. 125 ff.; Kenyon, art. 'Writing,' in the *Dictionary of the Bible*, iv. Edinb. 1902, p. 944 ff.; Nöldeke, 'Die semit. Buchstabennamen,' in *Beitr. zur semit. Sprachwiss.*, Strassb. 1904, p. 124 ff.; F. Praetorius, *Ueber den Ursprung des kanaan. Alphabets*, Berlin, 1906; H. Grimme, 'Zur Genesis des semit. Alphabets,' in *ZA.* xx. 1907, p. 49 ff.; R. Stübe, *Grundlinien zu einer Entwickelungsgesch. d. Schrift*, Munich, 1907; Jermain, *In the path of the Alphabet*, Fort Wayne, 1907.—L. Blau, *Studien zum althebr. Buchwesen, &c.*, Strassb. 1902; and his 'Ueber d. Einfluss d. althebr. Buchwesens auf d. Originale ', &c., in *Festschr. zu Ehren A. Berliners*, Frkf. 1903.

The best tables of alphabets are those of J. Euting in G. Bickell's *Outlines of Heb. Gram.* transl. by S. I. Curtiss, Lpz. 1877 ; in Pt. vii of the *Oriental Series* of the Palaeographical Soc., London, 1882 ; and, the fullest of all, in Chwolson's *Corpus inscr. Hebr.*, Petersburg, 1882; also Lidzbarski's in the *Jewish Encycl.*, see above.

a 1. The Hebrew letters now in use, in which both the manuscripts of the O. T. are written and our editions of the Bible are printed, commonly called the *square character* (כְּתָב מְרֻבָּע), also the *Assyrian character* (כְּ׳ אַשּׁוּרִי),[1] are not those originally employed.

Old Hebrew (or *Old Canaanitish*[2]) writing, as it was used on

---

[1] The name אַשּׁוּר (Assyria) is here used in the widest sense, to include the countries on the Mediterranean inhabited by Aramaeans; cf. Stade in *ZAW.* 1882, p. 292 f. On some other names for Old Hebrew writing. cf. G. Hoffmann, ibid. 1881, p. 334 ff.; Buhl, *Canon and Text of the O. T.* (transl. by J. Macpherson), Edinb. 1892, p. 200.

[2] It is tacitly assumed here that this was the mother of *all* Semitic alphabets. In *ZDMG.* 1909, p. 189 ff., however, Prätorius has shown good

public monuments in the beginning of the ninth and in the second
half of the eighth century B.C., is to be seen in the inscription of
Mêša', as well as in that of Siloam.   The characters on the Maccabaean coins of the second century B.C., and also on ancient gems,
still bear much resemblance to this (cf. § 2 d).   With the Old Hebrew
writing the Phoenician is nearly identical (see § 1 k, § 2 f, and the
Table of Alphabets).   From the analogy of the history of other kinds
of writing, it may be assumed that out of and along with this monu-
mental character, a less antique and in some ways more convenient,
rounded style was early developed, for use on softer materials, skins,
bark, papyrus, and the like.   This the Samaritans retained after their
separation from the Jews, while the Jews gradually [1] (between the
sixth and the fourth century) exchanged it for an Aramaic character.
From this gradually arose (from about the fourth to the middle of the
third century) what is called the *square character*, which consequently
bears great resemblance to the extant forms of Aramaic writing, such
as the Egyptian-Aramaic, the Nabatean and especially the Palmyrene.
Of Hebrew inscriptions in the older square character, that of 'Arâq
al-Emîr (15½ miles north-east of the mouth of the Jordan) probably
belongs to 183 B.C.[2]

The Jewish sarcophagus-inscriptions of the time of Christ, found in
Jerusalem in 1905, almost without exception exhibit a pure square character.
This altered little in the course of centuries, so that the age of a Hebrew MS.
cannot easily be determined from the style of the writing.   The oldest known
biblical fragment is the Nash papyrus (found in 1902), containing the ten
commandments and the beginning of Dt 6⁴ᶠ·, of the end of the first or
beginning of the second century A.D. ; cf. N. Peters, *Die älteste Abschr. der 10
Gebote*, Freibg. i. B. 1905.   Of actual MSS. of the Bible the oldest is probably
one of 820–850 A.D. described by Ginsburg, *Introd.*, p. 469 ff., at the head of
his sixty principal MSS. ; next in age is the codex of Moses ben Asher at
Cairo (897 A.D., cf. the art. 'Scribes' in the *Jew. Encycl.* xi and Gottheil in
JQR. 1905, p. 32).   The date (916 A.D.) of the Codex prophetarum Babylon.
Petropol. (see § 8 g, note) is quite certain.—In the synagogue-rolls a distinction is drawn between the Tam-character (said to be so called from Rabbi
Tam, grandson of R. Yišḥaqî, in the twelfth century) with its straight strokes,
square corners and 'tittles' (tāgîn), in German and Polish MSS., and the
foreign character with rounded letters and tittles in Spanish MSS.   See
further E. König, *Einl. in das A. T.*, Bonn, 1893, p. 16 ff.

---

grounds for believing that the South Semitic alphabet is derived not from
the Mêša' character, or from some kindred and hardly older script, but from
some unknown and *much* earlier form of writing.

[1] On the effect of the transitional mixture of earlier and later forms on the
constitution of the text, see R. Kittel, *Ueber d. Notwendigk. d. Herausg. einer
neuen hebr. Bibel*, Lpz. 1901, p. 20 ff.—L. Blau, 'Wie lange stand die althebr.
Schrift bei den Juden im Gebrauch?' in *Kaufmanngedenkbuch*, Breslau, 1900,
p. 44 ff.

[2] Not 176, as formerly held.   Driver and Lidzbarski now read עֲרָבִיה,
correctly, not טוּבִיה.

b　**2.** The Alphabet consists, like all Semitic alphabets, solely of consonants, twenty-two in number, some of which, however, have also a kind of vocalic power (§ 7 *b*). The following Table shows their form, names, pronunciation, and numerical value (see *k*):—

FORM.	NAME.	PRONUNCIATION.	NUMERICAL VALUE.
א	'*Ālĕph*	' *spiritus lenis*	1
ב	*Bêth*	*b* (*bh*, but see § 6 *n*)	2
ג	*Gimĕl* (*Giml*)	*g* (*gh*, „ „ „)	3
ד	*Dālĕth*	*d* (*dh*, „ „ „)	4
ה	*Hē*	*h*	5
ו	*Wāw* (*Wāu*)	*w* (*u*) [1]	6
ז	*Záyĭn*	*z*, as in English (soft *s*)	7
ח	*Ḥêth*	*ḥ*, a strong guttural	8
ט	*Ṭêth*	*ṭ*, emphatic *t*	9
י	*Yôd*	*y* (*i*) [1]	10
כ, final ך	*Kaph*	*k* (*kh*, but see § 6 *n*)	20
ל	*Lāmĕd*	*l*	30
מ, final ם	*Mêm*	*m*	40
נ, final ן	*Nûn*	*n*	50
ס	*Sāmĕkh*	*s*	60
ע	'*Áyĭn*	' a peculiar guttural (see below)	70
פ, final ף	*Pê*	*p* (*f*, see § 6 *n*)	80
צ, final ץ	*Ṣādê*	*ṣ*, emphatic *s*	90
ק	*Qôf*	*q*, a strong *k* [2] formed at the back of the palate	100
ר	*Rêš*	*r*	200
שׂ	*Śin*	*ś*	} 300
שׁ	*Šin* [3]	*š*, pronounced *sh*	
ת	*Tāw* (*Tāu*)	*t* (*th*, but see § 6 *n*)	400

[1] Philippi, 'Die Aussprache der semit. Consonanten ו und י,' in *ZDMG.* 1886, p. 639 ff., 1897, p. 66 ff., adduces reasons in detail for the opinion that 'the Semitic ו and י are certainly by usage consonants, although by nature they are vowels, viz. *u* and *i*, and consequently are consonantal vowels'; cf. § 8 *m*.

[2] As a representation of this sound the Latin *q* is very suitable, since it occupies in the alphabet the place of the Semitic ק (Greek κόππα).

[3] Nestle (*Actes du onzième Congrès . . . des Orientalistes*, 1897, iv. 113 ff.) has shown that the original order was שׂ, שׁ.

3. As the Table shows, five letters have a special form at the end *c* of the word. They are called final letters, and were combined by the Jewish grammarians in the mnemonic word כַּמְנֶפֵּץ *Kamnèphäṣ*, or better, with A. Müller and Stade, כַּמְנֻפֵּץ i. e. *as the breaker in pieces.*[1] Of these, ך, ן, ף, ץ are distinguished from the common form by the shaft being drawn straight down, while in the usual form it is bent round towards the left.[2] In the case of ם the letter is completely closed.

4. Hebrew is read and written from right to left.[3] Words must *d* not be divided at the end of the lines;[4] but, in order that no empty space may be left, in MSS. and printed texts, certain letters suitable for the purpose are dilated at the end or in the middle of the line. In our printed texts these *literae dilatabiles* are the five following: א ה ל ת ם (mnemonic word אֲהַלְתֶּם *ʾahaltèm*). In some MSS. other letters suitable for the purpose are also employed in this way, as ד, כ, ר; cf. Strack in the *Theol. Lehrb.*, 1882, No. 22; Nestle, *ZAW.* 1906, p. 170 f.

Rem. 1. The forms of the letters originally represent the rude outlines of *e* perceptible objects, the names of which, respectively, begin with the consonant represented (akrophony). Thus *Yôd*, in the earlier alphabets the rude picture of a hand, properly denotes *hand* (Heb. יָד), but as a letter simply the sound י (*y*), with which this word begins; *ʿAyin*, originally a circle, properly an *eye* (עַיִן), stands for the consonant ע. In the Phoenician alphabet, especially, the resemblance of the forms to the objects denoted by the name is still for the most part recognizable (see the Table). In some letters (ג, ו, ז, ט, שׁ) the similarity is still preserved in the square character.

It is another question whether the present names are all original. They may be merely due to a later, and not always accurate, interpretation of the forms. Moreover, it is possible that in the period from about 1500 to 1000 B.C. the original forms underwent considerable change.

The usual explanation of the present names of the letters[5] is: אֶלֶף *ox*, *f*

---

[1] In the Talmud, disregarding the alphabetical order, מִן־צֹפֵךְ *of thy watcher*, i. e. *prophet*. See the discussions of this mnemonic word by Nestle, *ZAW.* 1907, p. 119 ff., König, Bacher (who would read מִן־צֹפַיִךְ = proceeding *from thy prophets*, Is 52⁸), Krauss, Marmorstein, ibid. p. 278 ff. All the twenty-two letters, together with the five final forms, occur in Zp 3⁸.

[2] Chwolson, *Corpus Inscr. Hebr.*, col. 68, rightly observes that the more original forms of these letters are preserved in the *literae finales*. Instances of them go back to the time of Christ.

[3] The same was originally the practice in Greek, which only adopted the opposite direction exclusively about 400 B.C. On the *boustrophēdon* writing (alternately in each direction) in early Greek, early Sabaean, and in the Safa-inscriptions of the first three centuries A.D., cf. Lidzbarski, *Ephemeris*, i. 116 f.

[4] This does not apply to early inscriptions or seals. Cf. Mēšaʿ, ll. 1–5, 7, 8, &c., Siloam 2, 3, 5, where the division of words appears to be customary.

[5] We possess Greek transcriptions of the Hebrew names, dating from the fifth century B.C. The LXX give them (in almost the same form as Eusebius, *Praep. Evang.* 10. 5) in La 1–4, as do also many Codices of the Vulgate (e. g. the

בֵּית *house*, גְּמֶל *camel* (according to Lidzbarski, see below, perhaps originally גֻּרְוָן *axe* or *pick-axe*), דֶּלֶת *door* (properly *folding door*; according to Lidzbarski, perhaps דַּד *the female breast*), הֵא *air-hole* (?), *lattice-window* (?), וָו *hook, nail*, זַיִן *weapon* (according to Nestle, comparing the Greek ζῆτα, rather זַיִת *olive-tree*), חֵית *fence, barrier* (but perhaps only differentiated from ה by the left-hand stroke), טֵית *a winding* (?), according to others a *leather bottle* or a *snake* (but perhaps only differentiated from ת by a circle round it), יוֹד *hand*, כַּף *bent hand*, לָמֶד *ox-goad*, מַיִם *water*, נוּן *fish* (Lidzbarski, 'perhaps originally נָחָשׁ *snake*,' as in Ethiopic), סָמֶךְ *prop* (perhaps a modification of ז), עַיִן *eye*, פֵּא (also פֵּי) *mouth*, צָדֵי *fish-hook* (?), קוֹף *eye of a needle*, according to others *back of the head* (Lidzb., 'perhaps קֶשֶׁת *bow*'), רֵישׁ *head*, שִׁין *tooth*, תָּו *sign, cross*.

g   With regard to the origin of this alphabet, it may be taken as proved that it is not earlier (or very little earlier) than the fifteenth century B. C., since otherwise the el-Amarna tablets (§ 2 *f*) would not have been written exclusively in cuneiform.[1] It seems equally certain on various grounds, that it originated on Canaanitish soil. It is, however, still an open question whether the inventors of it borrowed

(*a*) From the Egyptian system—not, as was formerly supposed, by direct adoption of hieroglyphic signs (an explanation of twelve or thirteen characters was revived by J. Halévy in *Rev. Sémit.* 1901, p. 356 ff., 1902, p. 331 ff., and in the *Verhandlungen des xiii. . . . Orient.-Kongr. zu Hamb.*, Leiden, 1904, p. 199 ff.; but cf. Lidzbarski, *Ephemeris*, i. 261 ff.), or of hieratic characters derived from them (so E. de Rougé), but by the adoption of the *acrophonic* principle (see *e*) by which e. g. the hand, in Egyptian *tot*, represents the letter *t*, the lion = *laboi*, the letter *l*. This view still seems the most probable. It is now accepted by Lidzbarski ('Der Ursprung d. nord- u. südsemit. Schrift' in *Ephemeris*, i (1900), 109 ff., cf. pp. 134 and 261 ff.), though in his *Nordsem. Epigr.* (1898) p. 173 ff. he was still undecided.

(*b*) From the Babylonian (cuneiform) system. Wuttke's and W. Deecke's derivation of the old-Semitic alphabet from new-Assyrian cuneiform is impossible for chronological reasons. More recently Peters and Hommel have sought to derive it from the old-Babylonian, and Ball from the archaic Assyrian cuneiform. A vigorous discussion has been aroused by the theory of Frdr. Delitzsch (in *Die Entstehung des ält. Schriftsystems od. der Urspr. der Keilschriftzeichen dargel.*, Lpz. 1897; and with the same title 'Ein Nachwort', Lpz. 1898, preceded by a very clear outline of the theory) that the old-Semitic alphabet arose in Canaan under the influence both of the Egyptian system (whence the acrophonic principle) and of the old-Babylonian, whence the principle of the graphic representation of objects and ideas by means of simple, and mostly rectilinear, signs. He holds that the choice of the objects was probably (in about fifteen cases) influenced by the Babylonian system. The correspondence of names had all the more effect since, according to Zimmern (*ZDMG.* 1896, p. 667 ff.), out of twelve names which are certainly identical, eight appear in the same order in the Babylonian arrangement of signs. But it must first be shown that the present names of the

---

Cod. Amiatinus) in ψψ 111, 112, 119, but with many variations from the customary forms, which rest on the traditional *Jewish* pronunciation. The forms *Deleth* (and *delth*), *Zai, Sen* (LXX also χσεν, cf. Hebr. שֵׁן *tooth*) are to be noticed, amongst others, for *Daleth, Zain, Šin.* Cf. the tables in Nöldeke, *Beiträge zur sem. Sprachwiss.*, p. 126 f. In his opinion (and so Lidzbarski, *Ephemeris*, i. 134) the form and meaning of the names point to Phoenicia as the original home of the alphabet, since *alf, bêt, dalt, wâw, tâw, pei = pê, pi*, mouth, and the vowel of ρᾶ̂ = rôš, head, are all Hebraeo-Phoenician.

[1] In the excavations at Jericho in April, 1907, E. Sellin found a jar-handle with the Canaanite characters הי, which he dates (probably too early) about 1500 B. C.

'Phoenician' letters really denote the original picture. The identity of the objects may perhaps be due simply to the choice of the commonest things (animals, implements, limbs) in both systems.

The derivation of the Semitic alphabet from the signs of the Zodiac and their names, first attempted by Seyffarth in 1834, has been revived by Winckler, who refers twelve fundamental sounds to the Babylonian Zodiac. Hommel connects the original alphabet with the moon and its phases, and certain constellations; cf. Lidzbarski, *Ephemeris*, i. 269 ff., and in complete agreement with him, Benzinger, *Hebr. Archäologie²*, p. 173 ff. This theory is by no means convincing.

(c) From the hieroglyphic system of writing discovered in 1894 by A. J. Evans in inscriptions in Crete (esp. at Cnossus) and elsewhere. According to Kluge (1897) and others, this represents the 'Mycenaean script' used about 3000–1000 B.C., and according to Fries ('Die neuesten Forschungen über d. Urspr. des phöniz. Alph.' in *ZDPV*. xxii. 118 ff.) really supplies the original forms of the Phoenician alphabet as brought to Palestine by the Philistines about 1100 B.C., but 'the Phoenician-Canaanite-Hebrews gave to the Mycenaean signs names derived from the earlier cuneiform signs'. The hypothesis of Fries is thus connected with that of Delitzsch. But although the derivation of the Phoenician forms from 'Mycenaean' types appears in some cases very plausible, in others there are grave difficulties, and moreover the date, 1100 B.C., assigned for the introduction of the alphabet is clearly too late. [See Evans, *Scripta Minoa*, Oxf. 1909, p. 80 ff.]

(d) From a system, derived from Asia Minor, closely related to the Cypriote syllabary (Praetorius, *Der Urspr. des kanaan. Alphabets*, Berlin, 1906). On this theory the Canaanites transformed the syllabic into an apparently alphabetic writing. In reality, however, they merely retained a single sign for the various syllables, so that e.g. ק is not really *q*, but *qa*, *qe*, *qi*, &c. Of the five Cypriote vowels also they retained only the star (in Cypriote = *a*) simplified into an *'ālef* (see alphabetical table) to express the vowels at the beginning of syllables, and *i* and *u* as Yod and Waw. Praetorius claims to explain about half the twenty-two Canaanite letters in this way, but there are various objections to his ingenious hypothesis.

2. As to the *order* of the letters, we possess early evidence in the alphabetic[1] *h* poems: ψ 9 (ב–א, cf. ψ 10[1] ל, and vv[12-17] ת–ק; cf. Gray in the *Expositor*, 1906, p. 233 ff., and Rosenthal, *ZAW*. 1896, p. 40, who shows that ψ 9[3.15.17] נ, ל, כ, exactly fit in between ת, מ, י, and that ψ 10[1.3.5] therefore has the reverse order ל, כ, י); also ψψ 25 and 34 (both without a separate ו-verse and with פ repeated at the end[2]); 37, 111, 112, 119 (in which every eight verses begin with the same letter, each strophe, as discovered by D. H. Müller of Vienna, containing the eight leading words of ψ 19[8 ff.], *tôrā*, *'ēdûth*, &c.); La 1–4 (in 2–4 פ before ע[3], in chap. 3 every three verses with the same initial, see Löhr, *ZAW*. 1904, p. 1 ff., in chap. 5 at any rate as many verses as letters in the alphabet); Pr 24[1.3.5], 31[10-31] (in the LXX with פ before ע[3]); also in Na 1[2-10] Pastor Frohnmeyer of Württemberg (ob. 1880) detected traces of an alphabetic arrangement, but the attempt of Gunkel, Bickell, Arnold (*ZAW*. 1901,

---

[1] On the supposed connexion of this artificial arrangement with magical formulae ('the order of the letters was believed to have a sort of magic power') cf. Löhr, *ZAW*. 1905, p. 173 ff., and *Klagelieder²*, Gött. 1907, p. vii ff.

[2] On this superfluous פ cf. Grimme, *Euphemistic liturgical appendices*, Lpz. 1901, p. 8 ff., and Nestle, *ZAW*. 1903, p. 340 f., who considers it an appendage to the Greek alphabet.

[3] [Perhaps also originally in ψ 34.] פ before ע is probably due to a magic alphabet, see above, n. 1. According to Böhmer, *ZAW*. 1908, p. 53 ff., the combinations אב, גד, הו, &c., were used in magical texts; עם was excluded, but by a rearrangement we get סף and עץ.

p. 225 ff.), Happel (*Der Ps. Nah*, Würzb. 1900) to discover further traces, has not been successful. [Cf. Gray in *Expositor*, 1898, p. 207 ff.; Driver, in the Century Bible, *Nahum*, p.26.]—Bickell, *Ztschr f. Kath. Theol.*,1882, p. 319 ff., had already deduced from the versions the alphabetical character of Ecclus 51¹³⁻³⁰, with the omission of the ו-verse and with פ¹ at the end. His conjectures have been brilliantly confirmed by the discovery of the Hebrew original, although the order from נ to ל is partly disturbed or obscured. If ו before צ is deleted, ten letters are in their right positions, and seven can be restored to their places with certainty. Cf. N. Schlögl, *ZDMG*. 53, 669 ff.; C. Taylor in the appendix to Schechter and Taylor, *The Wisdom of Ben Sira*, Cambr. 1899, p. lxxvi ff., and in the *Journ. of Philol.*, xxx (1906), p. 95 ff.; *JQR*. 1905, p. 238 ff.; Löhr, *ZAW*. 1905, p. 183 ff.; I. Lévy, *REJ*. 1907, p. 62 ff.

The sequence of the three softest labial, palatal, and dental sounds ב, ג, ד, and of the three liquids ל, מ, נ, indicates an attempt at classification. At the same time other considerations also appear to have had influence. Thus it is certainly not accidental, that two letters, representing a hand (*Yôd*, *Kaph*), as also two (if *Qôph* = back of the head) which represent the head, and in general several forms denoting objects naturally connected (*Mêm* and *Nûn*, *'Ayin* and *Pê*), stand next to one another.

i   The order, names, and numerical values of the letters have passed over from the Phoenicians to the Greeks, in whose alphabet the letters A to Υ are borrowed from the Old Semitic. So also the Old Italic alphabets as well as the Roman, and consequently all alphabets derived either from this or from the Greek, are directly or indirectly dependent on the Phoenician.

k   3. *a*. In default of special arithmetical figures, the consonants were used also as numerical signs; cf. G. Gundermann, *Die Zahlzeichen*, Giessen, 1899, p. 6 f., and Lidzbarski, *Ephemeris*, i. 106 ff. The earliest traces of this usage are, however, first found on the Maccabean coins (see above, § 2 *d*, end). These numerical letters were afterwards commonly employed, e.g. for marking the numbers of chapters and verses in the editions of the Bible. The units are denoted by ט–א, the tens by צ–י, 100-400 by ת–ק, the numbers from 500-900 by ך (=400), with the addition of the remaining hundreds, e. g. תק 500. In compound numbers the greater precedes (on the right), thus יא 11, קכא 121. But 15 is expressed by טו 9+6, not יה (which is a form of the divine name, being the first two consonants of יהוה).² For a similar reason טז is also mostly written for 16, instead of יו, which in compound proper names, like יואל, also represents the name of God, יהוה.

The thousands are sometimes denoted by the units with two dots placed above, e. g. אׅׅ 1000.

l   *b*. The reckoning of the years in Jewish writings (generally ליצירה *after the creation*) follows either the *full chronology* (לפרט גדול or לפ׳ ג׳), with the addition of the thousands, or the *abridged chronology* (לפ׳ קטון), in which they are omitted. In the dates of the first thousand years after Christ, the Christian era is obtained by the addition of 240, in the second thousand years by the addition of 1240 (i. e. if the date falls between Jan. 1 and the Jewish new year; otherwise add 1239), the thousands of the Creation era being omitted.

m   4. Abbreviations of words are not found in the text of the O. T., but they occur on coins, and their use is extremely frequent amongst the later Jews.³

---

¹ See note 3 on p. 29.

² On the rise of this custom (יׅׅ having been originally used and afterwards יהׅׅ), cf. Nestle in *ZAW*. 1884, p. 250, where a trace of this method of writing occurring as early as Origen is noted.

³ Cf. Jo. Buxtorf, *De abbreviaturis Hebr.*, Basel, 1613, &c.; Pietro Perreau.

A point, or later an oblique stroke, serves as the sign of abridgement in old MSS. and editions, e. g. יִשְׂ׳ for יִשְׂרָאֵל, פְּ׳ for פְּלֹנִי *aliquis*, דָּ׳ for דָּבָר *aliquid*, וְגוֹ׳ for וְגוֹמֵר *et complens*, i. e. *and so on.* Also in the middle of what is apparently a word, such strokes indicate that it is an abbreviation or a *vox memorialis* (cf. e. g. § 15 *d* תא״ם). Two such strokes are employed, from § 41 *d* onward, to mark the different classes of weak verbs.—Note also יְ״ or יְ״ (also ה׳) for יְהוָֹה.

5. Peculiarities in the tradition of the O. T. text, which are already *n* mentioned in the Talmud, are—(1) The 15 *puncta extraordinaria*, about which the tradition (from Siphri on Nu 9[10] onwards) differs considerably, even as to their number; on particular consonants, Gn 16[5], 18[9], 19[33.35], Nu 9[10]; or on whole words, Gn 33[4], 37[12], Nu 3[39], 21[30], 29[15], Dt 29[28], 2 S 19[20], Is 44[9], Ez 41[20], 46[22], ψ 27[13],—all no doubt critical marks; cf. Strack, *Prolegomena Critica*, p. 88 ff.; L. Blau, *Masoretische Untersuchungen*, Strassburg, 1891, p. 6 ff., and *Einleitung in die hl. Schrift*, Budapest, 1894; Königsberger, *Jüd. Lit.-Blatt*, 1891, nos. 29–31, and *Aus Masorah u. Talmudkritik*, Berlin, 1892, p. 6 ff.; Mayer-Lambert, *REJ.* 30 (1895), no. 59; and especially Ginsburg, *Introd.*, p. 318 ff.; also on the ten points found in the Pentateuch, see Butin (Baltimore, 1906), who considers that they are as old as the Christian era and probably mark a letter, &c., to be deleted. (2) The *literae majusculae* (e. g. בּ Gn 1[1], ו Lv 11[42] as the middle consonant of the Pentateuch, ׳ Nu 14[17]), and *minusculae* (e. g. ה Gn 2[4]). (3) The *literae suspensae* (Ginsburg, *Introd.*, p. 334 ff.) נ Ju 18[30] (which points to the reading מֹשֶׁה for מְנַשֶּׁה), ע ψ 80[14] (the middle of the Psalms[1]) and Jb 38[13.15]. (4) The 'mutilated' *Wāw* in שלום Nu 25[12], and ק Ex 32[25] (בקמיהם), and Nu 7[2] (הפקודים). (5) *Mêm clausum* in למרבה Is 9[6], and *Mêm apertum* in הם פרוצים Neh 2[13]. (6) *Nûn inversum* before Nu 10[35], and after ver. 36, as also before ψ 107[23–28] and [40]; according to Ginsburg, *Introd.*, p. 341 ff., a sort of bracket to indicate that the verses are out of place; cf. Krauss, *ZAW.* 1902, p. 57 ff., who regards the inverted *Nûns* as an imitation of the Greek obelus.

§ 6. *Pronunciation and Division of Consonants.*

P. Haupt, 'Die Semit. Sprachlaute u. ihre Umschrift,' in *Beiträge zur Assyrio-logie u. vergleich. semit. Sprachwissenschaft*, by Delitzsch and Haupt, i, Lpz. 1889, 249 ff.; E. Sievers, *Metrische Studien*, i, Lpz. 1901, p. 14 ff.

1. An accurate knowledge of the original phonetic value of each *a* consonant is of the greatest importance, since very many grammatical peculiarities and changes (§ 18 ff.) only become intelligible from the nature and pronunciation of the sounds. This knowledge is obtained partly from the pronunciation of the kindred dialects, especially the still living Arabic, partly by observing the affinity and interchange

---

Oceano delle abbreviature e sigle[2], Parma, 1883 (appendix, 1884); Ph. Lederer, *Hebr. u. Chald. Abbreviaturen*, Frankf. 1893; Händler, *Lexicon d. Abbreviaturen* (annexed to G. Dalman's *Aram.-neuhebr. WB.*, Frankf. 1897); Levias, art. 'Abbreviations,' in the *Jew. Encycl.*, i. 39 ff.; F. Perles, 'Zur Gesch. der Abbrev. im Hebr.' (*Archiv f. Stenogr.*, 1902, p. 41 ff.). On abbreviations in biblical MSS. see Ginsburg, *Introd.*, 165 ff.

[1] According to Blau, *Studien zum althebr. Buchwesen*, Strassburg, 1902, p. 167, properly a large ע, called *t'lûyâ* because *suspended* between the two halves of the Psalter, and then incorrectly taken for a *littera suspensa*.

of sounds on Hebrew itself (§ 19), and partly from the tradition of the Jews.[1]

The pronunciation of Hebrew by the modern German Jews, which partly resembles the Syriac and is generally called ' Polish', differs considerably from that of the Spanish and Portuguese Jews, which approaches nearer to the Arabic. The pronunciation of Hebrew by Christians follows the latter (after the example of Reuchlin), in almost all cases.

b   The oldest tradition is presented in the transcription of Hebrew names in Assyrian cuneiform ; a later, but yet in its way very important system is seen in the manner in which the LXX transcribe Hebrew names with Greek letters.[2] As, however, corresponding signs for several sounds (ט, ע, צ, ק, שׁ) are wanting in the Greek alphabet, only an approximate representation was possible in these cases. The same applies to the Latin transcription of Hebrew words by Jerome, according to the Jewish pronunciation of his time.[3] On the pronunciation of the modern Jews in North Africa, see Bargès in the *Journ. Asiat.*, Nov. 1848 ; on that of the South Arabian Jews, J. Dérenbourg, *Manuel du lecteur*, &c. (from a Yemen MS. of the year 1390), Paris, 1871 (extrait 6 du *Journ. Asiat.* 1870).

c   2. With regard to the pronunciation of the several gutturals and sibilants, and of ט and ק, it may be remarked :—

1. Among the gutturals, the glottal stop א is the lightest, corresponding to the *spiritus lenis* of the Greeks. It may stand either at the beginning or end of a syllable, e. g. אָמַר *'āmár*, יֶאְשָׁם *yā'šám*. Even *before* a vowel א is almost lost to our ear, like the *h* in *hour* and in the French *habit, homme*. *After* a vowel א generally (and at the end of a word, always) coalesces with it, e. g. קָרָא *qārā* for an original *qāră'*, Arab. *qārắ* ; see further, § 23 *a*, 27 *g*.

d   ה before a vowel corresponds exactly to our *h* (spiritus asper) ; after a vowel it is *either* a guttural (so always at the end of a syllable which is not final, e. g. נֶהְפַּךְ *nähpakh* ; at the end of a word the consonantal ה has a point —Mappîq—in it, see § 14), *or* it stands inaudible at the end of a word, generally as a mere orthographic indication of a preceding vowel, e. g. גָּלָה *gālā* ; cf. §§ 7 *b* and 75 *a*.

e   ע is related to א, but is a much stronger guttural. Its strongest sound is a rattled, guttural *g*, cf. e. g. עַזָּה, LXX Γάζα, עֲמֹרָה Γόμορρα ; elsewhere, a weaker sound of the same kind, which the LXX reproduce by a *spiritus* (*lenis* or *asper*), e. g. עֵלִי 'Ηλί, עֲמָלֵק 'Αμαλέκ.[4] In the mouth of the Arabs one hears in the former case a sort of guttural *r*, in the latter a sound peculiar to themselves formed in the back of the throat.—It is as incorrect to omit the ע

---

[1] Cf. C. Meinhof, ' Die Aussprache des Hebr.,' in *Neue Jahrb. f. Philol. u. Pädag.*, 1885, Bd. 132, p. 146 ff. ; M. Schreiner, 'Zur Gesch. der Ausspr. des Hebr.,' in *ZAW.* 1886, p. 213 ff.

[2] Cf. Frankel, *Vorstudien zu der Septuag.*, Lpz. 1841, p. 90 ff. ; C. Könneke, ' Gymn.-Progr.,' Stargard, 1885. On the transcription of eleven Psalms in a palimpsest fragment of the Hexapla at Milan, see Mercati, *Atti della R. Accad.*, xxxi, Turin, 1896. [Cf. Burkitt, *Fragments of . . . Aquila*, Cambr. 1897, p. 13.]

[3] Numerous examples occur in *Hieronymi quaestiones hebraicae in libro geneseos*, edited by P. de Lagarde, Lpz. 1868 ; cf. the exhaustive and systematic discussion by Siegfried, ' Die Aussprache des Hebr. bei Hieronymus,' in *ZAW.* 1884, pp. 34–83.

[4] It is, however, doubtful if the LXX always consciously aimed at reproducing the actual differences of sound.

entirely, in reading and transcribing words (עֵלִי *Eli*, עֲמָלֵק *Amalek*), as to pronounce it exactly like *g* or like a nasal *ng*. The stronger sound might be approximately transcribed by *gh* or ^r*g*; but since in Hebrew the softer sound was the more common, it is sufficient to represent it by the sign ', as אַרְבַּע *'arba'*, עַד *'ad*.

ח is the strongest guttural sound, a deep guttural *ch*, as heard generally *f* in Swiss German, somewhat as in the German *Achat*, *Macht*, *Sache*, *Docht*, *Zucht* (not as in *Licht*, *Knecht*), and similar to the Spanish *j*. Like ע it was, however, pronounced in many words feebly, in others strongly.

As regards ר, its pronunciation as a palatal (with a vibrating uvula) seems *g* to have been the prevailing one. Hence in some respects it is also classed with the gutturals (§ 22 *q, r*). On the lingual ר, cf. *o*.

2. The Hebrew language is unusually rich in sibilants. These have, at any *h* rate in some cases, arisen from dentals which are retained as such in Aramaic and Arabic (see in the *Lexicon* the letters ז, צ and שׁ).

שׁ and שׂ were originally represented (as is still the case in the unpointed *i* texts) by only *one* form שׁ; but that the use of this one form to express two different sounds (at least in Hebrew) was due only to the poverty of the alphabet, is clear from the fact that they are differentiated in Arabic and Ethiopic (cf. Nöldeke in *Ztschr. f. wissensch. Theol.*, 1873, p. 121; Brockelmann, *Grundriss*, i. 133). In the Masoretic punctuation they were distinguished by means of the diacritical point as שׁ (*sh*) and שׂ (*s*).[1]

The original difference between the sounds שׂ and ס[2] sometimes marks *k* a distinction in meaning, e. g. סָכַר *to close*, שָׂכַר *to hire*, סָכַל *to be foolish*, שָׂכַל *to be prudent, to be wise*. Syriac always represents both sounds by ס, and in Hebrew also they are sometimes interchanged; as סָכַר for שָׂכַר *to hire*, Ezr 4⁵; שִׂכְלוּת for סִכְלוּת *folly*, Ec 1¹⁷.

ז (transcribed ζ by the LXX) is a soft whizzing *s*, the French and English *z*, *l* altogether different from the German *z* (*ts*).

3. ט, ק, and probably צ are pronounced with a strong articulation and *m* with a compression of the larynx. The first two are thus essentially different from ת and כ, which correspond to our *t* and *k* and also are often aspirated (see below, *n*). צ is distinguished from every other *s* by its peculiar articulation, and in no way corresponds to the German *z* or *ts*; we transcribe it by *ṣ*; cf. G. Hüsing, 'Zum Lautwerte des צ,' in *OLZ*. x. 467 ff.

3. Six consonants, the weak and middle hard Palatals, Dentals, *n* and Labials

(בְּגַדְכְּפַת) ב ג ד כ פ ת

have a twofold pronunciation, (1) a harder sound, as mutes, like

---

[1] The modern Samaritans, however, in reading their Hebrew Pentateuch pronounce שׁ invariably as שׂ.

[2] The original value of ס, and its relation to the original value of שׂ and שׁ, is still undetermined, despite the valuable investigations of P. Haupt, *ZDMG*. 1880, p. 762 f.; D. H. Müller, 'Zur Geschichte der semit. Zischlaute,' in the *Verhandlungen des Wiener Orient. Congresses*, Vienna, 1888, Semitic section, p. 229 ff.; De Lagarde, 'Samech,' in the *NGGW*. 1891, no. 5, esp. p. 173; Aug. Müller, *ZAW*. 1891, p. 267 ff.; Nöldeke, *ZDMG*. 1893, p. 100 f.; E. Glaser, *Zwei Wiener Publicationen über Habaschitisch-punische Dialekte in Südarabien*, Munich, 1902, pp. 19 ff.—On the phonetic value of צ see G. Hüsing, *OLZ*. 1907, p. 467 ff.

k, p, t, or initial *b, g* (hard), *d*; and (2) a softer sound as *spirantes.*[1] The harder sound is the original. It is retained at the beginning of syllables, when there is no vowel immediately preceding to influence the pronunciation, and is denoted by a point, *Dageš lene* (§ 13), placed in the consonants, viz. בּ *b,* גּ *g,* דּ *d,* כּ *k,* פּ *p,* תּ *t.* The weaker pronunciation appears as soon as a vowel sound immediately precedes. It is occasionally denoted, esp. in MSS., by *Rāphè* (§ 14 *e*), but in printed texts usually by the mere absence of the *Dageš.* In the case of ב, כ, פ, ת, the two sounds are clearly distinguishable even to our ear as *b* and *v, k* and German (weak) *ch, p* and *ph, t* and *th* (in *thin*). The Greeks too express this twofold pronunciation by special characters : כּ κ, כ χ; פּ π, פ φ; תּ τ, ת θ. In the same way גּ should be pronounced like the North German *g* in *Tage, Wagen,* and ד like *th* in *the,* as distinguished from גּ and דּ.

For more precise information on the cases in which the one or the other pronunciation takes place, see § 21. The modern Jews pronounce the aspirated ב as *v,* the aspirated ת as *s,* e.g. רַב *rav* (or even *raf*), בַּיִת *bais.* The customary transcription (used also in this Grammar) of the spirants ב, כ, ת by *bh, kh, th* is only an unsatisfactory makeshift, since it may lead (esp. in the case of *bh* and *kh*) to an erroneous conception of the sounds as real aspirates, *b–h, k–h.*

o   4. According to their special character the consonants are divided into—

    (*a*) Gutturals   א ה ע ח;

    (*b*) Palatals   ג כ ק;

    (*c*) Dentals   ד ט ת;

    (*d*) Labials   ב פ;

    (*e*) Sibilants   ז שׁ שׂ ס צ;

    (*f*) Sonants   נ מ, ר ל, ו י.

In the case of ר its hardest pronunciation as a *palatal* (see above, *g,* end) is to be distinguished from its more unusual sound as a lingual, pronounced in the front of the mouth.

On the twofold pronunciation of *r* in Tiberias, cf. Delitzsch, *Physiol. und Musik,* Lpz. 1868, p. 10 ff.; Baer and Strack, *Dikduke ha-ṭ^eamim,* Lpz. 1879, p. 5, note *a,* and § 7 of the Hebrew text, as well as p. 82.

p   In accordance with E. Sievers, *Metrische Studien,* i. 14, the following scheme of the Hebrew phonetic system is substituted for the table formerly given in this grammar :—

    i. Throat sounds (Gutturals): א ה ע ח.

---

[1] So at any rate at the time when the present punctuation arose.

ii. Mouth-sounds:		w.	m.	e.	w.	m.
1. Mutes and Spirants:	Palatal	ג	כ	ק	ג	כ
	Dental	ד	ת	ט	ד	ת
	Labial	ב	פ	—	ב	פ
2. Sibilants:		...	ז	שׁ שׂ ס	צ	
3. Sonants:		...	וי	ר ל	נ מ	

Rem. 1. The meaning of the letters at the top is, w. = weak, m. = middle *q* hard, e. = emphatic. Consonants which are produced by the same organ of speech are called *homorganic* (e.g. ג and כ as palatals), consonants whose sound is of the same nature *homogeneous* (e.g. ו and י as semi-vowels). On their homorganic character and homogeneity depends the possibility of interchange, whether within Hebrew itself or with the kindred dialects. In such cases the soft sound generally interchanges with the soft, the hard with the hard, &c. (e.g. ד = ז, ת = שׁ, ט = צ). Further transitions are not, however, excluded, as e.g. the interchange of ת and ק (ת = כ = ק). Here it is of importance to observe whether the change takes place in an initial, medial, or final letter; since e.g. the change in a letter when medial does not always prove the possibility of the change when initial. That in certain cases the character of the consonantal sound also influences the preceding or following vowel will be noticed in the accidence as the instances occur.

Rem. 2. Very probably in course of time certain nicer distinctions of *r* pronunciation became more and more neglected and finally were lost. Thus e.g. the stronger ע *ʿg*, which was known to the LXX (see above, *e*), became in many cases altogether lost to the later Jews; by the Samaritans and Galileans ע and ח were pronounced merely as א, and so in Ethiopic, ע like א, ח like *h*, שׁ like *s*.

Rem. 3. The consonants which it is usual to describe especially as *weak*, *§* are those which readily coalesce with a preceding vowel to form a long vowel, viz. א, ו, י (as to ה, cf. § 23 *k*), or those which are most frequently affected by the changes described in § 19 *b–l*, as again א, ו, י, and נ, and in certain cases ה and ל; finally the gutturals and ר for the reason given in § 22 *b* and *q*.

§ 7. *The Vowels in General, Vowel Letters and Vowel Signs.*

1. The original vowels in Hebrew, as in the other Semitic tongues, *a* are *a, i, u*. *E* and *o* always arise from an obscuring or contraction of these three pure sounds, viz. ĕ by modification from ĭ or ă; short ŏ from ŭ; ê by contraction from *ai* (properly *ay*); and ô sometimes by modification (obscuring) from â, sometimes by contraction from *au* (properly *aw*).[1]

In Arabic writing there are vowel signs only for *a, i, u*; the combined sounds *ay* and *aw* are therefore retained uncontracted and pronounced as diphthongs (*ai* and *au*), e.g. שׁוֹט Arab. *sauṭ*, and עֵינַיִם Arab. *ʿainain*. It was

[1] In proper names the LXX often use the diphthongs *ai* and *aú* where the Hebrew form has *ê* or *ô*. It is, however, very doubtful whether the *ai* and *aú* of the LXX really represent the true pronunciation of Hebrew of that time; see the instructive statistics given by Kittel in Haupt's *SBOT.*, on 1 Ch 1²·²⁰.

only in later Arabic that they became in pronunciation *ê* and *ô*, at least after weaker or softer consonants; cf. בֵּין Arab. *bain*, *bên*, יוֹם Arab. *yaum*, *yôm*. The same contraction appears also in other languages, e. g. in Greek and Latin (θαῦμα, Ionic θῶμα; *plaustrum = plostrum*), in the French pronunciation of *ai* and *au*, and likewise in the German popular dialects (*Oge* for *Auge*, &c.). Similarly, the obscuring of the vowels plays a part in various languages (cf. e. g. the *a* in modern Persian, Swedish, English, &c.).[1]

b 2. The partial expression of the vowels by certain consonants (ה, ו, י; א), which sufficed during the lifetime of the language, and for a still longer period afterwards (cf. § 1 *k*), must in the main have passed through the following stages [2]:—

(*a*) The need of a written indication of the vowel first made itself felt in cases where, after the rejection of a consonant, or of an entire syllable, a long vowel formed the final sound of the word. The first step in such a case was to retain the original final consonant, at least as a vowel letter, i. e. merely as an indication of a final vowel. In point of fact we find even in the Old Testament, as already in the Mêša‘ inscription, a ה employed in this way (see below) as an indication of a final *o*. From this it was only a step to the employment of the same consonant to indicate also other vowels when final (thus, e. g. in the inflection of the verbs ל״ה, the vowels *ā̆*,[3] *ē*, *è*). After the employment of ו as a vowel letter for *ô* and *û*, and of י for *ê* and *î*, had been established (see below, *e*) these consonants were also employed—although not consistently—for the same vowels at the end of a word.

c According to § 91 *b* and *d*, the suffix of the 3rd sing. masc. in the noun (as in the verb) was originally pronounced הֻ. But in the places where this הֻ with a preceding *a* is contracted into *ô* (after the rejection of the ה), we find the ה still frequently retained as a vowel letter, e. g. עִירֹה, סֻתֹה Gn 49[11], cf. § 91 *e*; so throughout the Mêša‘ inscription אַרְצֹה, בֵּיתֹה (also בֵּתֹה), הַלְתְּחֻמֹה, לֹה, בֹּה, בֹּנֹה; on the other hand already in the Siloam inscription רֵעֹו.[4] יָמֹה Mêša‘, l. 8 = יָמָיו *his days* is unusual, as also רֹשֹה l. 20 if it is for רֹאשׁיו *his chiefs*. The verbal forms with ה suffixed are to be read וַיַּחְלְפֶהָ (l. 6), וָאֶסְחָבֶהָ (l. 12 f.) and וַיִּגְרְשֵׁהָ (l. 19).

d As an example of the original consonant being retained, we might also include the י of the constr. state plur. masc. if its *ê* (according to § 89 *d*) is

---

[1] In Sanskrit, in the Old Persian cuneiform, and in Ethiopic, short *a* alone of all the vowels is not represented, but the consonant by itself is pronounced with short *a*.

[2] Cf. especially Stade, *Lehrb. der hebr. Gr.*, p. 34 ff.

[3] According to Stade, the employment of ה for *ā* probably took place first in the case of the locative accusatives which originally ended in ־ָה, as קָרִימָה, אַרְצָה.

[4] The form רֵעֹו contradicts the view of Oort, *Theol. Tijds.*, 1902, p. 374, that the above instances from the Mêša‘-inscription are to be read *benhu, bahu, lahu*, which were afterwards vocalized as *beno, bo, lo*.

contracted from an original *ay*. Against this, however, it may be urged that the Phoenician inscriptions do not usually express this *ê*, nor any other final vowel.[1]

(*b*) The employment of ו to denote *ô*, *û*, and of י to denote *ê*, *î*, may *e* have resulted from those cases in which a ו with a preceding *a* was contracted into *au* and further to *ô*, or with a preceding *u* coalesced into *û*, and where י with *a* has been contracted into *ai* and further to *ê*, or with a preceding *i* into *î* (cf. § 24). In this case the previously existing consonants were retained as vowel letters and were further applied at the end of the word to denote the respective long vowels. Finally א also will in the first instance have established itself as a vowel letter only where a consonantal א with a preceding *a* had coalesced into *â* or *ā*.

The orthography of the Siloam inscription corresponds almost exactly with *f* the above assumptions. Here (as in the Mêša' inscr.) we find all the long vowels, which have not arisen from original diphthongs, *without* vowel letters, thus צֻר, שָׁלֹשׁ, קֹל, אַמֹת ; (מִימָן or) מִימָן ; חֹצְבָם, אִשׁ. On the other hand מוֹצָא (from *mauṣa'*), עוֹד (from *'aud*) ; מִימָן also, if it is to be read מִימָן, is an instance of the retention of a י which has coalesced with *i* into *î*. Instances of the retention of an originally consonantal א as a vowel letter are מֵאתַיִם, מוֹצָא, and קָרָא, as also רֹאשׁ. Otherwise final *ā* is always represented by ה : נִקְבָה, זְדה, הָיָה, אַפֹּה. To this ם‎‏‎‎‎ alone would form an exception (cf. however the note on יֹם, § 96), instead of יוֹם (Arab. *yaum*) day, which one would expect. If the reading be correct, this is to be regarded as an argument that a consciousness of the origin of many long vowels was lost at an early period, so that (at least in the middle of the word) the vowel letters were omitted in places where they should stand, according to what has been stated above, and added where there was no case of contraction. This view is in a great measure confirmed by the orthography of the Mêša' inscription. There we find, as might be expected, דיבן (= *Daibōn*, as the Δαιβών of the LXX proves), חורֹנָן (*ô* from *au*), and בֵּיתֹה (*ê* from *ai*), but also even הָשָׁעֲנֵי [2] instead of הוֹשֵׁעֲנִי (from *hauš-*), בֵּת = וָאֹשִׁיב = וָאשֵׁב four times, בֵּתֹה once, for בֵּית and בֵּיתֹה (from *bait*) ; אֵין or אֵן = אֹן, לָיְלָה = ללה.

---

[1] Thus there occurs, e.g. in Melit. 1, l. 3 שנבן = שְׁנֵי בְּנֵי *the two sons*; elsewhere כ for כִּי (but כי in the Mêša' and Siloam inscrr.), ז for זֶה (the latter in the Siloam inscr.), בנת = בְּנֹתִי (so Mêša') or בְּנִיתִי, &c. Cf. on the other hand in Mêša', אנכ = אָנֹכִי (unless it was actually pronounced '*anôkh* by the Moabites!). As final *ā* is represented by ה and א and final *i* by י, so final *û* is almost everywhere expressed by ו in Mêša', and always in the Siloam inscription. It is indeed not impossible that Hebrew orthography also once passed through a period in which the final vowels were left always or sometimes undenoted, and that not a few strange forms in the present text of the Bible are to be explained from the fact that subsequently the vowel letters (especially ו and י) were not added in all cases. So Chwolson, 'Die Quiescentia הוי in der althebr. Orthogr.,' in *Travaux du Congrès . . . des Orientalistes*, Petersb. 1876 ; cf. numerous instances in Ginsburg, *Introd.*, p. 146 ff.

[2] השעני is the more strange since the name of king הושׁע is represented as *A-u si'* in cuneiform as late as 728 B.C.

g   (*c*) In the present state of Old Testament vocalization as it appears
in the Masoretic text, the striving after a certain uniformity cannot
be mistaken, in spite of the inconsistencies which have crept in.
Thus the final long vowel is, with very few exceptions (cf. § 9 *d*,
and the very doubtful cases in § 8 *k*), indicated by a vowel letter—
and almost always by the same letter in certain nominal and verbal
endings. In many cases the use of ו to mark an *ô* or *û*, arising from
contraction, and of י for *ê* or *î*, is by far the more common, while we
seldom find an originally consonantal א rejected, and the simple
phonetic principle taking the place of the historical orthography.
On the other hand the number of exceptions is very great. In many
cases (as e.g. in the plural endings ◌ים and וֹת) the vowel letters are
habitually employed to express long vowels which do not arise
through contraction, and we even find short vowels indicated. The
conclusion is, that if there ever was a period of Hebrew writing when
the application of fixed laws to all cases was intended, either these
laws were not consistently carried out in the further transmission of
the text, or errors and confusion afterwards crept into it. Moreover much remained uncertain even in texts which were plentifully
provided with vowel letters. For, although in most cases the context
was a guide to the correct reading, yet there were also cases where,
of the many possible ways of pronouncing a word, more than one
appeared admissible.[1]

h   3. When the language had died out, the ambiguity of such a writing
must have been found continually more troublesome ; and as there
was thus a danger that the correct pronunciation might be finally
lost, the vowel signs or vowel points were invented in order to fix it.
By means of these points everything hitherto left uncertain was most
accurately settled. It is true that there is no historical account
of the date of this vocalization of the O. T. text, yet we may at
least infer, from a comparison of other historical facts, that it was
gradually developed by Jewish grammarians in the sixth and seventh
centuries A.D. under the influence of different Schools, traces of which
have been preserved to the present time in various differences of
tradition.[2] They mainly followed, though with independent regard to

---

[1] Thus e.g. קטל can be read *qāṭal, qāṭāl, qāṭōl, qᵉṭōl, qōṭēl, qiṭṭēl, qaṭṭēl, quṭṭal,
qēṭel*, and several of these forms have also different senses.

[2] The most important of these differences are, (*a*) those between the
Orientals, i. e. the scholars of the Babylonian Schools, and the Occidentals,
i. e. the scholars of Palestine (Tiberias, &c.) ; cf. Ginsburg, *Introd.*, p. 197 ff. ;
(*b*) amongst the Occidentals, between Ben-Naphtali and Ben-Asher, who
flourished in the first half of the tenth century at Tiberias ; cf. Ginsburg,
Introd., p. 241 ff. Both sets of variants are given by Baer in the appendices

the peculiar nature of the Hebrew, the example and pattern of the older Syrian punctuation.[1]

See Gesenius, *Gesch. d. hebr. Spr.*, p. 182 ff. ; Hupfeld, in *Theol. Studien u. Kritiken*, 1830, pt. iii, who shows that neither Jerome nor the Talmud mentions vowel signs ; Berliner, *Beiträge zur hebr. Gramm. im Talm. u. Midrasch*, p. 26 ff. ; and B. Pick, in *Hebraica*, i. 3, p. 153 ff. ; Abr. Geiger, ʻ Zur Nakdanim-[Punctuators-]Literatur,ʼ in *Jüd. Ztschr. für Wissensch. u. Leben*, x. Breslau, 1872, p. 10 ff. ; H. Strack, *Prolegomena critica in Vet. Test. Hebr.*, Lips. 1873 ; ʻ Beitrag zur Gesch. des hebr. Bibeltextes,ʼ in *Theol. Stud. u. Krit.*, 1875, p. 736 ff., as also in the *Ztschr. f. die ges. luth. Theol. u. K.*, 1875, p. 619 ff. ; ʻ Massorah,ʼ in the *Protest. Real.-Enc.*[3], xii. 393 ff. (a good outline) ; A. Merx, in the *Verhandlungen des Orientalistenkongresses zu Berlin*, i. Berlin, 1881, p. 164 ff. and p. 188 ff. ; H. Graetz, ʻ Die Anfänge der Vokalzeichen im Hebr.,ʼ in *Monatsschr. f. Gesch. u. Wissensch. d. Judenth.*, 1881, pp. 348 ff. and 395 ff. ; Hersmann, *Zur Gesch. des Streites über die Entstehung der hebr. Punktation*, Ruhrort, 1885 ; Harris, ʻ The Rise . . . of the Massorah,ʼ *JQR*. i. 1889, p. 128 ff. and p. 223 ff. ; Mayer-Lambert, *REJ*. xxvi. 1893, p. 274 ff. ; J. Bachrach, *Das Alter d. bibl. Vocalisation u. Accentuation*, 2 pts. Warsaw, 1897, and esp. Ginsburg, *Introd.* (see § 3 *c*), p. 287 ff. ; Budde, ʻ Zur Gesch. d. Tiberiens. Vokalisation,ʼ in *Orient. Studien zu Ehren Th. Nöldekes*, i. 1906, 651 ff. ; Bacher, ʻ Diakrit. Zeichen in vormasoret. Zeit,ʼ in *ZAW*. 1907, p. 285 ; C. Levias, art. ʻ Vocalization,ʼ in the *Jewish Encycl.*—On the hypothesis of the origin of punctuation in the Jewish schools for children, cf. J. Dérenbourg in the *Rev. Crit.*, xiii. 1879, no. 25.

4. To complete the historical vocalization of the consonantal text *i* a phonetic system was devised, so exact as to show all vowel-changes occasioned by lengthening of words, by the tone, by gutturals, &c., which in other languages are seldom indicated in writing. The pronunciation followed is in the main that of the Palestinian Jews of about the sixth century A.D., as observed in the solemn reading of the sacred writings in synagogue and school, but based on a much older tradition. That the real pronunciation of early Hebrew is consistently preserved by this tradition, has recently been seriously questioned on good grounds, especially in view of the transcription of proper names in the LXX. Nevertheless in many cases, internal reasons, as well as the analogy of the kindred languages, testify in a high degree to the faithfulness of the tradition. At the same recension of the text, or soon after, the various other signs for reading (§§ 11–14, 16) were added, and the accents (§ 15).

§ 8. *The Vowel Signs in particular.*

P. Haupt, ʻThe names of the Hebrew vowels,ʼ *JAOS*. xxii, and in the *Johns Hopkins Semitic Papers*, Newhaven, 1901, p. 7 ff. ; C. Levias in the *Hebr. Union Coll. Annual*, Cincinnati, 1904, p. 138 ff.

---

to his critical editions. Our printed editions present uniformly the text of Ben-Asher, with the exception of a few isolated readings of Ben-Naphtali, and of numerous later corruptions.

[1] See Geiger, ʻ Massorah bei d. Syrern,ʼ in *ZDMG*. 1873, p. 148 ff. ; J. P. Martin, *Hist. de la ponctuation ou de la Massore chez les Syriens*, Par. 1875 ; E. Nestle, in *ZDMG*. 1876, p. 525 ff. ; Weingarten, *Die syr. Massora nach Bar Hebraeus*, Halle, 1887.

Preliminary Remark.

The next two sections (§§ 8 and 9) have been severely criticized (Philippi, *ThLZ.* 1897, no. 2) for assigning a definite quantity to each of the several vowels, whereas in reality ⟍, ⟍, ⟍ are merely signs for *ă, e, o*: 'whether these are long or short is not shown by the signs themselves but must be inferred from the rules for the pause which marks the breaks in continuous narrative, or from other circumstances.' But in the twenty-fourth and subsequent German editions of this Grammar, in the last note on § 8 *a* [English ed. p. 38, note 4], it was stated : 'it must be mentioned that the Masoretes are not concerned with any distinction between long and short vowels, or in general with any question of quantity. Their efforts are directed to fixing the received pronunciation as faithfully as possible, by means of writing. For a long time only שִׁבְעָה מְלָכִים *seven kings* were reckoned (*vox memor.* in Elias Levita (וַיֹּאמֶר אֵלָיהוּ), Šureq and Qibbuṣ being counted as one vowel. The division of the vowels in respect of quantity is a later attempt at a scientific conception of the phonetic system, which was not invented but only represented by the Masoretes (Qimchi, *Mikhlol*, ed. Rittenb. 136 *a*, distinguishes the five long as *mothers* from their five daughters).'

I have therefore long shared the opinion that 'the vowel-system represented by the ordinary punctuation (of Tiberias) was primarily intended to mark only differences of quality' (Sievers, *Metrische Studien,* i. 17). There is, however, of course a further question how far these 'later' grammarians were mistaken in assigning a particular quantity to the vowels represented by particular signs. In Philippi's opinion they were mistaken (excluding of course *î, ê, ô* when written *plene*) in a very great number of cases, since not only does ⟍ stand, according to circumstances, for *ā̆* or *ă̄*, and ⟍ for *ā̆* or *ă̆*, but also ⟍ for *ē* or *ĕ*, and ⟍ for *ō* or *ŏ*, e. g. כָּבֵד and קָטֹן, out of pause *kăbêd*, *qă̆ṭôn* (form קָטַל), but in pause *kā̆bêd, qā̆ṭôn.*

I readily admit, with regard to Qameṣ and *S*ᵉ*gol*, that the account formerly given in § 8 f. was open to misconstruction. With regard to Ṣere and Ḥolem, however, I can only follow Philippi so long as his view does not conflict with the (to me inviolable) law of a long vowel in an open syllable before the tone and (except Pathaḥ) in a final syllable with the tone. To me כָּבֵד = *kā̆bêd*, &c., is as impossible as e. g. עֵנָב = '*ênab* or בֹּרַךְ = *bŏrakh*, in spite of the analogy cited by Sievers (p. 18, note 1) that 'in old German e. g. original *ĭ* and *ŭ* often pass into *ĕ* and *ŏ* dialectically, while remaining in a closed syllable.

a   1. The full vowels (in contrast to the half-vowels or vowel trills, § 10 *a–f*), classified according to the three principal vowel sounds (§ 7 *a*), are as follows :—

First Class.   A-sound.

A {
  1. ⟍ [1] Qāmĕṣ denotes either *ā, â*, more strictly *ă̄* (the obscure Swedish *å*) and *ä̊*,[2] as יָד *yăd* (hand), רֵאשִׁים *rā'sîm* (heads), or *ă̆* (in future transcribed as *ŏ*), called Qāmeṣ *hă̆ṭûph*, i.e. hurried Qameṣ. The latter occurs almost exclusively as a modification of *ŭ*; cf. *c* and § 9 *u*.

  2. ⟍ Páthă̆ḥ, *ă*, בַּת *bă̆th* (daughter).

---

[1] In early MSS. the sign for Qameṣ is a stroke with a point underneath, i. e. according to Nestle's discovery (*ZDMG.* 1892, p. 411 f.), Pathaḥ with Ḥolem, the latter suggesting the obscure pronunciation of Qameṣ as *â*. Cf. also Ginsburg, *Introd.*, p. 609.

[2] Instead of the no doubt more accurate transcription *ā̆, ä̊* we have

Also 3. ◌ֶ *S^egôl*, an open *e*, *è* (*ā̈* or *ă̈*), as a modification of *ă*,[1] either in an untoned closed syllable, as in the first syllable of יֶדְכֶם *yädkhèm* (your hand) from *yădkhèm*—or in a tone-syllable as in פֶּסַח *pĕsaḥ*; cf. πάσχα, and on the really monosyllabic character of such formations, see § 28 *e*. But *S^egôl* in an open tone-syllable with a following י, as in גְּלֶ֫ינָה *g^elènā* (cf. § 75 *f*), יָדֶ֫יךָ *yādèkhā* (cf. § 91 *i*), is due to contraction from *ay*.

Second Class. I- and E-sounds.

I
1. ◌ִי *Ḥîrĕq* with *yod*, almost always *î*, as צַדִּיק *ṣaddîq* (righteous). *b*
2. ◌ִ either *î* (see below, *i*), as צַדִּקִים *ṣaddîqîm*, only orthographically different from צדיקים (צדיקם),—or *ĭ*, as צִדְקוֹ *ṣĭdqô* (his righteousness).

E
3. ◌ֵי *Ṣerî* or *Ṣērê* with *yod*=*ê*, e. g. בֵּיתוֹ *bêthô* (his house).
◌ֵ either *ê*, but rarely (see below, *i*), or *ē* as שֵׁם *šēm* (name). *Ṣere* can only be *ĕ*, in my opinion, in few cases, such as those mentioned in § 29 *f*.
4. ◌ֶ *S^egôl*, *ă̈*, a modification of *ĭ*, e.g. חֶפְצִי *ḥäfṣî* (ground-form *ḥĭfṣ*); שֶׁן־ *šän* (ground-form *šĭn*).

Third Class. U- and O-sounds.

U
1. וּ *Šûrĕq*, usually *û*, מוּת *mûth* (to die), rarely *ŭ*. *c*
2. ◌ֻ *Qibbûṣ*, either *ŭ*, e.g. סֻלָּם *sŭllām* (ladder), or *û*, e.g. קֻ֫מוּ *qūmū* (rise up), instead of the usual ק֫וּמוּ.

O
3. וֹ and ◌ֹ *Ḥōlĕm*, *ô* and *ō*, קוֹל *qôl* (voice), רֹב *rōbh* (multitude). Often also a defective ◌ֹ for *ô*; rarely וֹ for *ō*.
On the question whether ◌ֹ under some circumstances represents *ŏ*, see § 93 *r*.
4. ◌ָ On *Qāmĕṣ ḥāṭûph*=*ŏ*, generally modified from *ŭ*, as חָק־ *ḥŏq* (statute), see above, *a*.

---

retained *ā*, *â* in this grammar, as being typographically simpler and not liable to any misunderstanding. For *Qameṣ ḥaṭuph*, in the previous German edition expressed by *ă̊*, we have, after careful consideration, returned to *ŏ*. The use of the same sign ◌ָ for *ā̊* (*â̊*) and *ă̊*, shows that the Massoretes did not intend to draw a sharp distinction between them. We must not, however, regard the Jewish grammarians as making a merely idle distinction between *Qāmeṣ rāḥāb*, or broad Qameṣ, and *Qāmeṣ ḥaṭûph*, or light Qameṣ. It is quite impossible that in the living language an *ā* lengthened from *ă*, as in *dābār*, should have been indistinguishable from e.g. the last vowel in וַיָּשָׁב or the first in קָדָשִׁים.—The notation *â*, *ê*, *ô* expresses here the vowels essentially long, either naturally or by contraction; the notation *ā*, *ē*, *ō* those lengthened only by the tone, and therefore changeable; *ă*, *ĕ*, *ŏ* the short vowels. As regards the others, the distinction into *î* and *ĭ*, *û* and *ŭ* is sufficient; see § 9.—The mark ˂ stands in the following pages over the tone-syllable, whenever this is not the last, as is usual, but the penultimate syllable of the word, e. g. יָ֫שַׁב.

[1] These *S^egôls*, modified from *ă*, are very frequent in the language. The

d   The names of the vowels are mostly taken from the form and action of the mouth in producing the various sounds, as פֶּתַח *opening* ; צְרֵי *a wide parting* (of the mouth), also שֶׁבֶר (= *î*) *breaking, parting* (cf. the Arab. *kasr*) ; חִירֶק (also חֲרֶק) *narrow opening* ; חוֹלֶם *closing*, according to others *fullness*, i. e. of the mouth (also מְלֹא פוּם [1] *fullness of the mouth*). קָמֶץ [2] also denotes a slighter, as שׁוּרֶק and קִבּוּץ (also קבוץ פום) a firmer, compression or contraction of the mouth. S*e*gôl (סֶגוֹל *bunch of grapes*) takes its name from its form. So שְׁלֹשׁ נְקֻדּוֹת (*three points*) is another name for *Qibbúṣ*.

e   Moreover the names were mostly so formed (but only later), that the sound of each vowel is heard in the first syllable (קָמֶץ for קָמֶץ, פֶּתַח for פֶּתַח, צְרִי for צְרִי) ; in order to carry this out consistently some even write *Sägôl, Qomeṣ-ḥaṭúf, Qúbbúṣ.*

f   **2.** As the above examples show, the vowel sign stands regularly *under* the consonant, *after* which it is to be pronounced, רָ *rā*, רַ *rǎ*, רֵ *rē*, רֻ *rǔ*, &c. The *Pathaḥ* called *furtivum* (§ 22 *f*) alone forms an exception to this rule, being pronounced *before* the consonant, רוּחַ *rûᵃḥ* (wind, spirit). The *Ḥōlěm* (without *wāw*) stands on the left above the consonant; רֹ *rō* (but לֹ = *lō*). If א, as a vowel letter, follows a consonant which is to be pronounced with *ō*, the point is placed over its right arm, thus רֹאשׁ, בֹּא ; but e.g. בָּאם, since א here begins a syllable.

g   No dot is used for the Ḥolem when *ō* (of course without *wāw*) is pronounced after *sin* or before *šin*. Hence שֹׂנֵא *śōnē* (hating), נְשֹׂא *n*e*śō* (to bear), מֹשֶׁה *môše* (not מֹשֶׁה) ; but שֹׁמֵר *šōmēr* (a watchman). When *ō* precedes the *sin*, the dot is placed over its right arm, e.g. יִרְפֹּשׂ *yirpōś* (he treads with the feet), הַנֹּשְׂאִים *hannōś*e*'im* (those who carry).

In the sign וֹ, the ו may also be a consonant. The וֹ is then either to be read *ōw* (necessarily so when a consonant otherwise without a vowel precedes, e.g. לֹוֶה *lōwè*, lending) or *wō*, when a vowel already precedes the ו, e.g. עָוֹן *'āwôn* (iniquity) for עָוֹן. In more exact printing, a distinction is at least made between וֹ (*wo*) and וֹ (i. e. either *ō* or, when another vowel follows the *wāw, ōw* [3]).

Babylonian punctuation (see § 8 *g*, note 1) has only one sign for it and tone-bearing Pathah ; see also Gaster, 'Die Unterschiedslosigkeit zwischen Pathach u. Segol,' in *ZAW.* 1894, p. 60 ff.

[1] On the erroneous use of the term *melo pum*, only in Germany, for *šúreq* (hence also pronounced *melu pum* to indicate *û*), see E. Nestle, *ZDMG.* 1904, p. 597 ff. ; Bacher, ibid., p. 799 ff., Melopum ; Simonsen, ibid., p. 807 ff.

[2] The usual spelling קָמֶץ and פֶּתַח takes the words certainly rightly as Hebrew substantives; according to De Lagarde (*Gött. gel. Anz.* 1886, p. 873, and so previously Luzzatto), קָמֶץ and פֶּתַח are rather Aram. participles, like *Dageš*, &c., and consequently to be transliterated *Qámeṣ* and *Páthaḥ.*

[3] Since 1846 we have become acquainted with a system of vocalization different in many respects from the common method. The vowel signs, all except ו, are there placed *above* the consonants, and differ almost throughout in form,

3. The vowels of the first class are, with the exception of 'ַ in *h*
the middle and הָ, אָ, הָ at the end of the word (§ 9 *a–d, f*),
represented *only* by vowel signs, but the long vowels of the I- and
U-class largely by vowel letters. The vowel sound to which the letter

---

and some even as regards the sound which they denote: ◌ = *â, ā*, ◌ = tone-
bearing *ă* and *ĕ*, ◌ = *ê, ē*, ◌ = *î*, ◌ = *ô, ō*, ◌ or ◌ = *û*. In an unsharpened
syllable ◌ = toneless *ă* and *ĕ*, and also Ḥaṭeph Pathaḥ; ◌ = toneless *ĕ* and
Ḥaṭeph Seghôl; ◌ = *ĭ*, ◌ = *ŭ*, ◌ = *ŏ*, and Ḥaṭeph Qameṣ. Lastly in tone-
less syllables before Dageš, ◌ = *ă*, ◌ = *ĕ*, ◌ = *i*, ◌ = *ŭ*, ◌ = *ŏ̆*. Šewâ is ◌
The accents differ less and stand in some cases under the line of the consonants.
Besides this complicated system of the Codex Babylonicus (see below) and other
MSS., there is a simpler one, used in Targums. It is still uncertain whether the
latter is the foundation of the former (as Merx, *Chrest. Targ.* xi, and Bacher,
ZDMG. 1895, p. 15 ff.), or is a later development of it among the Jews of South
Arabia (as Praetorius, *ZDMG.* 1899, p. 181 ff.). For the older literature on
this *Babylonian punctuation* (נִקּוּד בַּבְלִי), as it is called, see A. Harkavy and
H. L. Strack, *Katalog der hebr. Bibelhandschr. der Kaiserl. öffentl. Bibliothek zu
St. Petersb.*, St. Petersb. and Lpz., 1875, parts i and ii, p. 223 ff. A more
thorough study of the system was made possible by H. Strack's facsimile
edition of the *Prophetarum posteriorum codex Babylonicus Petropolitanus* (St. Petersb.,
1876, la. fol.) of the year 916, which Firkowitsch discovered in 1839, in the
synagogue at Tschufutkale in the Crimea. The MS. has been shown by
Ginsburg (*Recueil des travaux rédigés en mémoire . . . de Chwolson*, Berlin, 1899,
p. 149, and *Introd.*, pp. 216 ff., 475 f.) to contain a recension of the Biblical text
partly Babylonian and partly Palestinian ; cf. also Barnstein, *The Targum of
Onkelos to Genesis*, London, 1896, p. 6 f. Strack edited a fragment of it in *Hosea
et Joel prophetae ad fidem cod. Babylon. Petrop.*, St. Petersb. 1875. Cf. also the
publication by A. Merx, quoted above, § 7 *h*, and his *Chrestomathia Targumica*,
Berlin, 1888; G. Margoliouth, in the *PSBA.* xv. 4, and M. Gaster, ibid.;
P. Kahle, *Der masoret. Text des A. T. nach d. Überlief. der babyl. Juden*, Lpz. 1902,
with the valuable review by Rahlfs in *GGA.* 1903, no. 5; Nestle, *ZDMG.* 1905,
p. 719 (Babylonian ◌ = ע. According to the opinion formerly prevailing,
this Babylonian punctuation exhibits the system which was developed in the
Eastern schools, corresponding to and contemporaneous with the Western or
Tiberian system, although a higher degree of originality, or approximation
to the original of both systems of punctuation, was generally conceded to the
latter. Recently, however, Wickes, *Accents of the Twenty-one Books*, Oxford,
1887, p. 142 ff, has endeavoured to show, from the accents, that the
'Babylonian' punctuation may certainly be *an* Oriental, but is by no means
the Oriental system. It is rather to be regarded, according to him, as a later
and not altogether successful attempt to modify, and thus to simplify, the
system common to all the Schools in the East and West. Strack, *Wiss.
Jahresb. der ZDMG.* 1879, p. 124, established the probability that the vowels
of the superlinear punctuation arose under *Arab* influence from the vowel
letters וֹאי (so previously Pinsker and Graetz), while the Tiberian system
shows *Syrian* influence.
A third, widely different system (Palestinian), probably the basis of the
other two, is described by A. Neubauer, *JQR.* vii. 1895, p. 361 ff., and
Friedländer, ibid., p. 564 ff., and *PSBA.* 1896, p. 86 ff. ; C. Levias, *Journ. of
Sem. Lang. and Lit.*, xv. p. 157 ff.; and esp. P. Kahle, *Beitr. zu der Gesch.
der hebr. Punktation*,' in *ZAW.* 1901, p. 273 ff. and in *Der masoret. Text des A. T.*
(see above), chiefly dealing with the Berlin MS. Or. qu. 680, which contains
a number of variants on the biblical text, and frequently agrees with the
transcriptions of the LXX and Jerome.

points is determined more precisely by the vowel sign standing before, above, or within it. Thus—

' may be combined with *Ḥîrĕq*, *Ṣērê*, *Sᵉgôl* ('⸗, '⸗, '⸗).

ו with *Šûrĕq* and *Ḥōlĕm* (וּ and וֹ).[1]

> In Arabic the long *a* also is regularly expressed by a vowel letter, viz. 'Alĕph (אָ), so that in that language three vowel letters correspond to the three vowel classes. In Hebrew א is rarely used as a vowel letter; see § 9 *b* and § 23 *g*.

i   **4.** The omission of the vowel letters when writing *î, û, ê, ô* is called *scriptio defectiva* in contrast to *scriptio plena*. קוֹל, קוּם are written *plene*, קֹלֹת, קֻם *defective*.

> Cf. Bardowitz, *Studien zur Gesch. der Orthogr. im Althebr.*, 1894; Lidzbarski, *Ephem.*, i. 182, 275; Marmorstein, 'Midrasch der vollen u. defekt. Schreibung,' in *ZAW.* 1907, p. 33 ff.

k   So far as the choice of the full or defective mode of writing is concerned, there are certainly some cases in which only the one or the other is admissible. Thus the full form is necessary at the end of the word, for *û, ô, ō, î, ê, ē*, as well as for *è* in חֹזֶה &c. (§ 9 *f*), also generally with *â, ā* (cf. however § 9 *d*), e.g. קָטְלוּ, קָטַלְתִּי, יָדִי, מַלְכֵי. (But the Masora requires in Jer 26⁶, 44⁸; Ezr 6²¹; 2 Ch 32¹³ גּוֹיִ instead of גּוֹיֵי; Zp 2⁹ גּוֹיִ [perhaps an error due to the following י] for גּוֹיֵי; Is 40³¹ וְקוֹיֵ [followed by י] for וְקוֹיֵי; Jer 38¹¹ בְּלוֹיֵ for בְּלוֹיֵי.) On the other hand the defective writing is common when the letter, which would have to be employed as a vowel letter, immediately precedes as a strong consonant, e.g. גֹּיִם (*nations*) for גּוֹיִים, מִצְוֺת (*commandments*) for מִצְווֹת.

l   That much is here arbitrary (see § 7 *g*), follows from the fact that sometimes the same word is written very differently, e.g. הֲקִימֹתִי Ez 16⁶⁰ : הֲקִמֹתִי and also הֲקִמוֹתִי Jer 23⁴; cf. § 25 *b*. Only it may be observed,

(*a*) That the scriptio plena in two successive syllables was generally avoided; cf. e.g. נָבִיא but נְבִאִים, צַדִּיק, but צַדִּקִים; קוֹל, קֹלֹת; יְהוֹשֻׁעַ; מְצָאֻהוּ.

(*b*) That in the later Books of the O. T. (and regularly in post-biblical Hebrew) the full form, in the earlier the defective, is more usual.

m   **5.** In the cognate dialects, when a vowel precèdes a vowel-letter which is not kindred (heterogeneous), e.g. וַ⸗, וֶ⸗, יַ⸗, יֶ⸗, יִ⸗, a diphthong (*au, ai*)[2] is formed if the heterogeneous vowel be *a*. This is also to be regarded as the Old Hebrew pronunciation, since it

---

[1] After the example of the Jewish grammarians the expression, 'the vowel letter rests (*quiesces*) in the vowel-sign,' has become customary. On the other hand, the vowel letters are also called by the grammarians, *matres lectionis* or *supports* (*fulcra*).

[2] Cf. T. C. Foote, *The diphthong ai in Hebrew* (Johns Hopkins Univ. Circulars, June, 1903, p. 70 ff.).

agrees with the vocalic character of ו and י (§ 5 b, note 2). Thus such words as וָו, חַי, גּוֹי, עָשׂוּי, גֵּו, בַּיִת are not to be pronounced according to the usual Jewish custom[1] as *vāv, ḥay, gôy, 'āsûy, gēv, bayith* (or even as *vaf*, &c.; cf. modern Greek *av af, ev ef* for αὐ, εὐ), but with the Italian Jews more like *wāu, ḥai*, &c. The sound of יְ‍ is the same as יִ‍, i.e. almost like *āu*, so that יִ‍ is often written defectively for יְ‍.

§ 9. *Character of the several Vowels.*

Numerous as are the vowel signs in Hebrew writing, they are yet *a* not fully adequate to express all the various modifications of the vowel sounds, especially with respect to length and shortness. To understand this better a short explanation of the character and value of the several vowels is required, especially in regard to their length and shortness as well as to their changeableness (§§ 25, 27).

I. *First Class. A-sound.*

1. *Qameṣ* (‍ָ‍), when it represents a long *a*, is, by nature and origin, of two kinds :—

(1) The essentially long *â* (in Arabic regularly written אָ‍), which is not readily shortened and never wholly dropped (§ 25 c), e.g. כְּתָב *kᵉthâbh* (writing); very seldom with a following א, as רֹאשׁ 2 S 12¹·⁴ (see the examples in § 72 p).[2]

The writing of קָאם Ho 10¹⁴ for קָם would only be justifiable, if the *â b* of this form were to be explained as a contraction of *ăă*; cf. however § 72 a; דָּאַג Neh 13¹⁶ for דָּג (*dāg*) is certainly incorrect.—The rarity of the *â* in Hebrew arises from the fact that it has for the most part become an obtuse *ô*; see below, *q*.

(2) *-ā*, lengthened only by position (i.e. tone-long or at all events *c* lengthened under the influence of the tone, according to the laws for the formation of syllables, § 27 *e–h*), either in the tone-syllable itself (or in the secondary tone-syllable indicated by *Mèthĕg*, see below), or just before or after it. This sound is invariably lengthened from an original *ă*,[3] and is found in open syllables, i.e. syllables ending in a vowel (§ 26 b), e.g. אָסִיר, יְקוּם, קָטַל, לְךָ (Arab. *lăkă, qătălă, yăqûmŭ, 'ăsîrŭ*), as well as in closed syllables, i.e. those ending in

---

[1] In MSS. ו and י, in such combinations as גֵּו, חַי, are even marked with Mappîq (§ 14 a).

[2] Of a different kind are the cases in which א has lost its consonantal sound by coalescing with a preceding a, § 23 a–d.

[3] In Arabic this *ă* is always retained in an open syllable.

a consonant, as יָד, כּוֹכָב (vulgar Arab. *yăd, kaukăb*). In a closed syllable, however, it can only stand when this has the tone, דָּבָר, עוֹלָם; whereas in an open syllable it is especially frequent *before* the tone, e.g. דְּבָר, לָכֶם, זָכֹן. Where the tone is moved forward or weakened (as happens most commonly in what is called the construct state of nouns, cf. § 89 a) the original short *ă* (*Pathaḥ*) is retained in a closed syllable, while in an open syllable it becomes *S̆ewâ* (§ 27 i): חָכָם, constr. state חֲכַם (*ḥᵃkhăm*); דָּבָר, דְּבַר (*dᵉbhăr*); קָטַל, קְטָלָם. For examples of the retention, in the secondary tone-syllable, of *ā* lengthened from *ă*, see § 93 xx.

d　In some terminations of the verb (תָ in the 2nd sing. masc. perf., ־ִי in the 2nd pl. fem. of the imperat., as well as in the 3rd and 2nd pl. fem. of the imperf.), in אַתָּ *thou* (masc.) and in the suffixes ךָ and הָ, the final *ā* can stand even without a vowel letter. A ה is, however, in these cases (except with הָ) frequently added as a vowel letter.

On ־ַ for *ŏ* see below, *f*.

e　**2. Pathaḥ,** or short *ă*, stands in Hebrew almost exclusively in a closed syllable with or without the tone (קָטַל, קְטַלְתֶּם). In places where it now appears to stand in an open syllable the syllable was originally closed, and a helping vowel (*ă*, *ĭ*) has been inserted after the second radical merely to make the pronunciation easier, e.g. נַחַל (ground-form *naḥl*), בַּיִת (Arab. *bait*), see § 28 d, and with regard to two cases of a different kind, § 26 g, h. Otherwise *ă* in an open syllable has almost without exception passed into *ā* (־ָ), see above, *c*.

On the very frequent attenuation of *ă* to *ĭ*, cf. below, *h*. On the rare, and only apparent union of Pathaḥ with א (א־ַ), see § 23 d, end. On *ă* as a helping-vowel, § 22 f (*Pathaḥ furtivum*), and § 28 e.

f　**3. Segôl** (*ĕ, ė* [*ā́*]) by origin belongs sometimes to the second, but most frequently to the first vowel class (§ 27 o, p, u). It belongs to the first class when it is a modification of *a* (as the Germ. *Bad*, pl. *Bäder*; Eng. *man*, pl. *men*), either in a toneless syllable, e.g. יֶדְכֶם (for *yadkhèm*), or with the tone, e.g. אֶרֶץ from *'arṣ*, קֶרֶן Arab. *qărn*, קֶמַח Arab. *qămḥ*. This *Segôl* is often retained even in the strongest tone-syllable, at the end of a sentence or of an important clause (in *pause*), as צֶדֶק, מֶלֶךְ (*mắlăkh, ṣắdăq*). As a rule, however, in such cases the *Pathaḥ* which underlies the *Segôl* is lengthened into *Qameṣ*, e.g. קָמַח, קָרֶן. A *Segôl* apparently lengthened from *S̆ewâ*, but in reality traceable to an original *ă*, stands in pausal forms, as פֶּרִי (ground-form *păry*), יֶהִי (*yăhy*), &c. On the cases where a י (originally consonantal) follows this Segôl, see § 75 f, and § 91 k.

II.   *Second Class. I- and E-sounds.*

4. The long *î* is frequently even in the consonantal writing indicated *g* by ' (a *fully* written *Ḥireq* 'ֵ֗—); but a naturally long *î* can be also written *defectively* (§ 8 *i*), e. g. צַדִּיק (*righteous*), plur. צַדִּיקִים *ṣaddîqîm*; יָרֵא (*he fears*), plur. יִרְאוּ. Whether a *defectively* written *Ḥireq* is long may be best known from the origin of the form; often also from the nature of the syllable (§ 26), or as in יִרְאוּ from the *Metheg* attached to it (§ 16 *f*).

5. The *short Ḥireq* (always[1] written *defectively*) is especially frequent *h* in sharpened syllables (אִמִּי, קִטֵּל) and in toneless closed syllables (מִזְמוֹר *psalm*); cf. however וַיִּשְׁבְּ in a closed tone-syllable, and even וַיִּפֶן, with a helping Seg̊ol, for *wayyíphn*. It has arisen very frequently by attenuation from *ă*, as in דִּבְרֵי from original *dăbărê*, צִדְק̣ (ground-form *ṣădq*),[2] or else it is the original *ĭ*, which in the tone-syllable had become *ē*, as in אֹיִבְךָ (*thy enemy*) from אֹיֵב (ground-form *'ăyĭb*).[3] It is sometimes a simple helping vowel, as in בַּיִת, § 28 *e*.

The earlier grammarians call every *Ḥireq* written *fully*, *Ḥireq magnum*; every one written *defectively*, *Ḥireq parvum*,—a misleading distinction, so far as quantity is concerned.

6. The longest *ê* 'ֵ֗— (more rarely defective —ֵ, e. g. עֵנִי for עֵינִי *i* Is 3[8]; at the end of a word also ה—ֶ) is as a rule contracted from '—ֶ *ay* (*ai*), § 7 *a*, e. g. הֵיכָל (*palace*), Arab. and Syriac *haikal*.

7. The *Ṣere* without Yôdh mostly represents the tone-long *ē*, which, *k* like the tone-long *ā* (see *c*), is very rarely retained except *in* and *before* the tone-syllable, and is always lengthened from an original *ĭ*. It stands in an open syllable with or before the tone, e. g. סֵפֶר (ground-form *sĭphr*) *book*, שֵׁנָה (Arab. *sĭnăt*) *sleep*, or with Metheg (see § 16 *d*, *f*) in the secondary tone-syllable, e. g. שְׁאֵלָתִי *my request*, נֵלְכָה *let us go*. On the other hand in a closed syllable it is almost always with the tone, as בֵּן *son*, אִלֵּם *dumb*.

Exceptions : (*a*) *ē* is sometimes retained in a toneless closed syllable, in *l* monosyllabic words before Maqqeph, e. g. עֵץ־ Nu 35[18], as well as in the examples of *nāsôg 'āḥôr* mentioned in § 29 *f* (on the quantity cf. § 8 *b* 3 end); (*b*) in a toneless open final syllable, Ṣere likewise occurs in examples of the *nāsôg 'āḥôr*, as יֵצֵא Ex 16[29]; cf. Ju 9[39].

8. The Seg̊ol of the I(E)-class is most frequently an *ĕ* modified from *m* original *ĭ*, either replacing a tone-long *ē* which has lost the tone, e. g.

---

[1] At least according to the Masoretic orthography; cf. Wellhausen, *Text der Bb. Sam.*, p. 18, Rem.

[2] Jerome (cf. Siegfried, *ZAW.* 1884, p. 77) in these cases often gives *ă* for *ĭ*.

[3] Cf. the remarks of I. Guidi, 'La pronuncia del ṣērē,' in the *Verhandl. des Hamburger Orient.-Kongr.* of 1902, Leiden, 1904, p. 208 ff., on Italian *e* for Latin *i*, as in *fede = fidem*, *pece = picem*.

תֶּן from תֵּן (*give*), יֹצְרֶךָ (*thy creator*) from יֹצֵר, or in the case discussed in § 93 *o*, עֶזְרִי, חֶלְקִי from the ground-forms *ḥilq*, *'izr*; cf. also § 64 *f*. *Segôl* appears as a simple helping-vowel in cases such as סֵפֶר for *siphr*, יֵגֶל for *yigl* (§ 28 *e*).

III.   Third Class.   U- and O-sounds.

n   **9.** For the U-sound there is—

(1) the *long û*, either (*a*) written fully, וּ *Šureq*, e.g. גְּבוּל (*boundary*), or (*b*) defectively written —֫ *Qibbûṣ*, גְּבֻלוֹ, יְמֻתוּן;

(2) the short *ŭ*, mostly represented by *Qibbûṣ*, in a toneless closed syllable and especially common in a sharpened syllable, in e.g. שֻׁלְחָן (*table*), סֻכָּה (*booth*).

O   Sometimes also *ŭ* in a sharpened syllable is written וּ, e. g. הוּכָּה ψ 102[5], יֻגְּלֶד Jb 5[7], כֻּלָּם Jer. 31[34], מְשׁוּבָתוֹ Is 5[5], עֲרוּמִּים Gn 2[25] for הֻכָּה, &c.

For this *u* the LXX write *o*, e.g. עֲדֻלָּם 'Οδολλάμ, from which, however, it only follows, that this *ŭ* was pronounced somewhat indistinctly. The LXX also express the sharp *Ḥireq* by ε, e. g. אִמֵּר = 'Εμμήρ. The pronunciation of the *Qibbûṣ* like the German *ü*, which was formerly common, is incorrect, although the occasional pronunciation of the U-sounds as *ü* in the time of the punctators is attested, at least as regards Palestine[1]; cf. the Turkish *bülbül* for the Persian *bulbul*, and the pronunciation of the Arabic *dunyā* in Syria as *dünyā*.

p   **10.** The O-sound bears the same relation to U as the E does to I in the second class. It has four varieties:—

(1) The *ô* which is contracted from *aw* (=*au*), § 7 *a*, and accordingly is mostly written fully; וֹ (*Holem plenum*), e.g. שׁוֹט (*a whip*), Arab. *sauṭ*, עוֹלָה (*iniquity*) from עַוְלָה. More rarely *defectively*, as שֹׁרְךָ (*thine ox*) from שׁוֹר Arab. *ṭaur*.

q   (2) The long *ô* which arose in Hebrew at an early period, by a general process of obscuring, out of an original *â*,[2] while the latter has been retained in Arabic and Aramaic. It is usually written *fully* in the tone-syllable, *defectively* in the toneless, e.g. קֹטֵל Arab. *qâṭil*. Aram. *qâṭēl*, אֱלוֹהַּ Arab. *'ilâh*, Aram. *'ᵉlâh*, plur. אֱלֹהִים; שׁוֹק (*leg*), Arab. *sâq*; גִּבּוֹר (*hero*), Arab. *gâbbâr*; חוֹתָם (*seal*), Arab. *ḥâtām*; רִמּוֹן (*pomegranate*), Arab. *rŭmmân*; שִׁלְטוֹן (*dominion*), Aram. שִׁלְטָן and שֻׁלְטָן Arab. *sŭlṭân*; שָׁלוֹם (*peace*), Aram. שְׁלָם, Arab. *sâlâm*. Sometimes the form in *â* also occurs side by side with that in *ô* as שִׁרְיָן and שִׁרְיוֹן (*coat of mail*; see however § 29 *u*). Cf. also § 68 *b*.

r   (3) The tone-long *ō* which is lengthened from an original *ŭ*, or from an *ŏ* arising from *ŭ*, by the tone, or in general according to the

---

[1] Cf. Delitzsch, *Physiologie u. Musik*, Lpz. 1868, p. 15 f.
[2] Cf. above, *b*, end. On Jerome's transliteration of *o* for *â*, see *ZAW.* 1884, p. 75.

laws for the formation of syllables. It occurs not only in the tone-syllable, but also in an open syllable before the tone, e.g. קֹדֶשׁ (ground-form *qŭdš*) *sanctuary*; בָּרַךְ for *burrakh*, יִלְקֹטוּ ψ 104²⁸, as well as (with *Metheg*) in the secondary tone-syllable; אָהֳלִים, בְּעֲלֵי. But the original *ŏ* (*ŭ*) is retained in a toneless closed syllable, whereas in a toneless open syllable it is weakened to *Šᵉwâ*. Cf. כֹּל *all*, but כָּל־ (*kŏl*), כֻּלָּם (*kŭllām*); יִקְטֹל, יִקְטָלְךָ and יִקְטְלוּ, where original *u* is weakened to *Šᵉwâ*: *yiqṭᵉlû*, Arab. *yaqtŭlû*. This tone-long *ō* is only as an exception written fully.

(4) ◌ָ *Qameṣ-ḥaṭuph* represents *ŏ* (properly *ằ*, cf. § 8 *a*, note 2) modified *s* from *ŭ* and is therefore classed here. It stands in the same relation to *Ḥolem* as the *Sᵉgôl* of the second class to *Sere*, כָּל־ *kŏl*, וַיָּקָם *wayyāqŏm*. On the distinction between this and *Qameṣ*, see below, *u*.

11. The following table gives a summary of the gradation of the *t* three vowel-classes according to the quantity of the vowels :—

First Class : A.	*Second Class* : I and E.	*Third Class* : U and O.
◌ָ original *â* (Arabic אַ◌ָ).	◌ֵי *ê*, from original *ay* (*ai*). ◌ִי or ◌ִ long *î*.	וֹ *ô*, from original *aw* (*au*). וֹ or ◌ֹ *ô* obscured from *â*. וּ or ◌ֻ *û*.
◌ָ tone-long *ā* (from original *ă*) chiefly in the tone-syllable but also just before it.	◌ֵ tone-long *ē* (from *ĭ*) generally in the tone-syllable but also just before it.	◌ֹ tone-long *ō* (from original *ŭ*) in the tone-syllable, otherwise in an open syllable.
◌ֶ (as a modification of *ă*) sometimes a tone-long *è*, sometimes *ĕ*. ◌ַ short *ă*. [◌ִ *ĭ* attenuated from *ă*; see *h*.] Utmost weakening to ◌ֲ *a*, ◌ֳ *ŏ*, ◌ְ *e*.	◌ֶ *ĕ*. ◌ִ short *ĭ*. Utmost weakening to ◌ֲ *a*, ◌ֳ *ŏ*, or ◌ְ *e*.	◌ָ *ŏ*, modified from *ŭ*. ◌ֻ short *ŭ*, especially in a sharpened syllable. Utmost weakening to ◌ֲ *a*, ◌ֳ *ŏ*, ◌ֳ *o*, or ◌ְ *e*.

Rem. *On the distinction between Qameṣ and Qameṣ-ḥaṭuph.*[1]   *u*

According to § 8 *a*, long *ā* or *ā̆* (*Qameṣ*) and short *ŏ* or *ă̆* (*Qameṣ-ḥaṭuph*) are in manuscripts and printed texts generally expressed by the same sign (◌ָ), e.g. קָם *qām*, כָּל־ *kŏl*. The beginner who does not yet know the grammatical

---

[1] These statements, in order to be fully understood, must be studied in connexion with the theory of syllables (§ 26) and *Metheg* (§ 16 *c–i*).

origin of the words in question (which is of course the surest guide), may depend meanwhile on the following principal rules :—

1. *The sign* —́[1] *is* ŏ *in a toneless closed syllable*, since such a syllable can have only a short vowel (§ 26 *o*). The above case occurs—

(a) When Šᵉwâ follows as a syllable-divider, as in חָכְמָה *ḥŏkh-mâ* (wisdom), אָכְלָה *'ŏkh-lấ* (food). With *Metheg* —́ is *â* (*ā̆*) and according to the usual view stands in an open. syllable with a following Šᵉwâ *mobile*, e.g. אָכְלָה *'ā-khᵉlấ* (she ate) ; but cf. § 16 *i*.

(b) When a closed syllable is formed by *Dageš forte*, e.g. חָנֵּנִי *ḥŏnnênî* (have mercy upon me); but בָּתִּים (with *Metheg*, § 16 *f* ζ) *bâttîm*.

(c) When the syllable in question loses the tone on account of a following *Maqqēph* (§ 16 *a*), e.g. כָּל־הָאָדָם *kŏl-hā-'ādám* (all men).

In ψ 35¹⁰ and Pr 19⁷ *Maqqēph* with כָּל is replaced by a conjunctive accent (*Merᵉkha*) ; so by *Darga*, Ju 19⁵ with סְעָד, and Ez 37⁸ with וַיִּקְרָם (so Baer after Qimḥi ; ed. Mant., Ginsburg, Kittel וַיִּקְרָם).

(d) In a closed final syllable without the tone, e.g. וַיָּקָם *wayyắqŏm* (and he stood up).—In the cases where *â* or *ā* in the final syllable has become toneless through *Maqqēph* (§ 16 *a*) and yet remains, e.g. כְּתָב־הַדָּת Est 4⁸, שְׁתָ־לִי Gn 4²⁵, it has a *Metheg* in correct manuscripts and printed texts.

In cases like הֲלָאָה, לָמָּה *lámmā*, the tone shows that —́ is to be read as *ā*.

v   2. The cases in which —́ appears to stand in an open syllable and yet is to be read as ŏ require special consideration. This is the case, (a) when *Ḥaṭeph-Qameṣ* follows, e.g. פָּעֳלוֹ *his work*, or simple vocal Šᵉwâ, e.g. דָּרְבָן *ox goad* ; בְּעָבְרוּ Jo 4⁷ ; שָׁמְרָה (so ed. Mant., Ginsb.) *preserve* ψ 86², cf. 16¹ and the cases mentioned in § 48 *i*, n., and § 61 *f*, n. ; other examples are Ob 11, Ju 14¹⁸); *Ḥaṭeph-Pathaḥ* follows in לְמָשְׁחֲךָ (so Ginsburg ; Baer לְמָשְׁחֶךָ) 1 S 15¹, לְהָרְגֶנָךְ 24¹¹, and יִפְנֶשְׁךָ (so Baer, Gn 32¹⁸, others יִפְנֶשְׁךָ) ; (b) before another *Qameṣ-ḥaṭuph*, e.g. פָּעֳלְךָ *thy work* ; on אָרֳח־לִי and קָבֳה־לִי Nu 23⁷, see § 67 *o* ; (c) in the two plural forms קָדָשִׁים *sanctuaries* and שָׁרָשִׁים *roots* (also written קָֽד־ and שָֽׁר־). In all these cases the Jewish grammarians regard the *Metheg* accompanying the —́ as indicating a Qāmeṣ raḥabh (broad Qameṣ) and therefore read the —́ as *ā* ; thus *pā-ŏlô, dā-rᵉbān, pā-ŏlᵉkhā, qā-dāšim*. But neither the origin of these forms, nor the analogous formations in Hebrew and in the cognate languages, nor the transcription of proper names in the

---

[1] In the Babylonian punctuation (§ 8 *g*, note) *ā* and ŏ are carefully distinguished. So also in many MSS. with the ordinary punctuation and in Baer's editions of the text since 1880, in which —̄: is used for ŏ as well as for ŏ. Cf. Baer-Delitzsch, *Liber Jobi*, p. 43. But the identity of the two signs is certainly original, and the use of —̄: for ŏ is misleading.

LXX, allows us to regard this view as correct. It is just possible that Qameṣ is here used loosely for *ắ*, as the equivalent of *ō*, on the analogy of בְּעָלוֹ &c., § 93 *q*. As a matter of fact, however, we ought no doubt to divide and read *pŏʿŏ-lô* (for *pŏʿ-lô*), *pŏʿŏ-lᵉkhā*, *qŏdā-šim*.—Quite as inconceivable is it for *Metheg* to be a sign of the lengthening into *ā* in בְּחָרִי־אָף (Ex 11⁸), although it is so in בָּאֳנִי *bā-ʾᵒnî* (in the navy), since here the *ā* of the article appears under the בּ.

§ 10. *The Half Vowels and the Syllable Divider* (Šᵉwâ).

1. Besides the full vowels, Hebrew has also a series of vowel *a* sounds which may be called *half vowels* (Sievers, *Murmelvokale*). The punctuation makes use of these to represent extremely slight sounds which are to be regarded as remains of fuller and more distinct vowels from an earlier period of the language. They generally take the place of vowels *originally short* standing in *open syllables*. Such short vowels, though preserved in the kindred languages, are not tolerated by the present system of pointing in Hebrew, but either undergo a lengthening or are weakened to Šᵉwâ. Under some circumstances, however, the original short vowel may reappear.

To these belongs first of all the sign ⸗, which indicates an ex- *b* tremely short, slight, and (as regards pronunciation) indeterminate vowel sound, something like an obscure half *ĕ* (*ͤ*). It is called *Šᵉwâ*,[1] which may be either *simple Šᵉwâ* (*Šᵉwâ simplex*) as distinguished from the compound (see *f*), or *vocal Šᵉwâ* (*Šᵉwâ mobile*) as distinguished from *Šᵉwâ quiescens*, which is silent and stands as a mere syllable divider (see *i*) under the consonant which closes the syllable.

The vocal *Šᵉwâ* stands under a consonant which is closely united, as *c* a kind of grace-note, with the following syllable, either (*a*) at the beginning of the word, as קְטֹל *qᵉṭōl* (to kill), מְמַלֵּא *mᵉmallē* (filling), or (*b*) in the middle of the word, as קוֹטְלָה *qŏ-ṭᵉlā*, יִקְטְלוּ *yiq-ṭᵉlû*.

In former editions of this Grammar *Šᵉwâ* was distinguished as *medium d* when it followed a short vowel and therefore stood in a supposed 'loosely closed' or 'wavering' syllable, as in בִּנְפֹל, מַלְכֵי. According to Sievers, *Metrische Studien*, i. 22, this distinction must now be abandoned. These syllables are really closed, and the original vowel is not merely shortened, but entirely elided. The fact that a following Bᵉgadkᵉphath letter (§ 6 *n*) remains spirant instead of taking *Dageš lene*, is explained by Sievers on the 'supposition that the change from hard to spirant is older than the elision

---

[1] On שְׁוָא, the older and certainly the only correct form (as in Ben Asher), see Bacher, *ZDMG*. 1895, p. 18, note 3, who compares Šewayya, the name of the Syriac accentual sign of similar form ⸗ (=Hebr. Zaqeph). The form שְׁבָא, customary in Spain since the time of Menaḥem b. Sarûq, is due to a supposed connexion with Aram. שְׁבַת *rest*, and hence would originally have denoted only *Šᵉwâ quiescens*, like the Arabic *sukūn* (rest). The derivation from שָׁוָה, שִׁיבָה (stem יָשַׁב, Levias, *American Journ. of Philol.*, xvi. 28 ff.) seems impossible.

of the vowel, and that the prehistoric *malakai* became *malakhai* before being shortened to *malkhe'*. In cases like בְּסָאוֹ (from כִּסֵּא), יָקְחוּ (from יִקַּח) the dropping of the *Dageš forte* shows that the original vowel is completely lost.

e   The sound ĕ has been adopted as the normal transcription of simple *Šᵉwâ mobile*, although it is certain that it often became assimilated in sound to other vowels. The LXX express it by ε, or even by η, כְּרוּבִים Χερουβίμ, הַלְלוּ־יָהּ ἀλληλούϊα, more frequently by α, שְׁמוּאֵל Σαμουήλ, but very frequently by assimilating its indeterminate sound to the following principal vowel, e.g. סְדֹם Σόδομα, שְׁלֹמֹה Σολομών (as well as Σαλωμών), צְבָאוֹת Σαβαώθ, נְתַנְאֵל Ναθαναήλ.[1] A similar account of the pronunciation of *Šᵉwâ* is given by Jewish grammarians of the middle ages.[2]

How the *Šᵉwâ* sound has arisen through the vanishing of a full vowel is seen, e.g. in בְּרָכָה from *bărăkă*, as the word is still pronounced in Arabic. In that language the full short vowel regularly corresponds to the Hebrew *Šᵉwâ mobile*.

f   2. Connected with the *simple Šᵉwâ mobile* is the *compound Šᵉwâ* or *Ḥâṭēph* (*correptum*), i.e. a *Šᵉwâ* the pronunciation of which is more accurately fixed by the addition of a short vowel. There are three *Šᵉwâ*-sounds determined in this way, corresponding to the three vowel classes (§ 7 *a*):—

(◌ֲ) *Ḥâṭēph-Páthăḥ*, e.g. חֲמוֹר *ḥᵃmôr*, ass.

(◌ֱ) *Ḥâṭēph-Sᵉgôl*, e.g. אֱמֹר *'ᵉmōr*, to say.

(◌ֳ) *Ḥâṭēph-Qámĕṣ*, e.g. חֳלִי *ḥᵒlî*, sickness.

These *Ḥâṭēphs*, or at least the first two, stand especially under the four guttural letters (§ 22 *l*), instead of a *simple Šᵉwâ mobile*, since these letters by their nature require a more definite vowel than the indeterminate *simple Šᵉwâ mobile*. Accordingly a guttural at the beginning of a syllable, where the *Šᵉwâ* is necessarily vocal, can never have a mere *Šᵉwâ simplex*.

On ◌ֲ the shorter Ḥatef as compared with ◌ֳ cf. § 27 *v*.

g   Rem. A. Only ◌ֲ and ◌ֳ occur under letters which are not gutturals. *Ḥaṭeph-Pathaḥ* is found instead of *simple Šᵉwâ* (especially *Šᵉwâ mobile*), chiefly (*a*) under strengthened consonants, since this strengthening (commonly called doubling) causes a more distinct pronunciation of the *Šᵉwâ mobile*, שֻׁבֲּלִי *branches*, Zc 4¹². According to the rule given by Ben-Asher (which, however, appears to be unknown to good early MSS. and is therefore rejected by Ginsburg, *Introd.*, p. 466; cf. Foote, *Johns Hopkins Univ. Circulars*, June 1903,

---

[1] The same occurs frequently also in the Greek and Latin transcriptions of Phoenician words, e.g. מַלְכָּא *Malaga*, גְּבֻלִים *gubulim* (Schröder, *Die phöniz. Spr.*, p. 139 ff.). Cf. the Latin augment in *momordi*, *pupugi*, with the Greek in τέτυφα, τετυμμένος, and the old form *memordi*.

[2] See especially *Yehuda Ḥayyûǵ*, pp. 4 f. and 130 f. in Nutt's edition (Lond. 1870), corresponding to p. 200 of the edition by Dukes (Stuttg. 1844); Ibn Ezra's *Ṣaḥoth*, p. 3; Gesenius, *Lehrgebäude der hebr. Sprache*, p. 68. The *Manuel du lecteur*, mentioned above, § 6 *b*, also contains express rules for the various ways of pronouncing *Šᵉwâ mobile*: so too the *Dikduke ha-tᵉamim*, ed. by Baer and Strack, Lpz. 1879, p. 12 ff. Cf. also Schreiner, *ZAW.* vi. 236 ff.

p. 71 f.), the *Ḥateph* is *necessary*[1] when, in a strengthened *medial* consonant with Š°wâ (consequently not in cases like וַיְהִי, &c.), preceded by a Pathaḥ, the sign of the strengthening (*Dageš forte*) has fallen away, e. g. הַלְלוּ (but ed. Mant. and Ginsb. הַלְלוּ) *praise ye!* וַתְּאָלְצֵהוּ Ju 16¹⁶; no less universally, where after a consonant with Š°wâ the same consonant follows (to separate them more sharply, and hence with a *Metheg* always preceding), e. g. סוֹרְרִים ψ 68⁷; קִלֲלַתְךָ (ed. Mant. and Ginsb. קִלְלַ) Gn 27¹³ (but not without exceptions, e. g. חִקְקֵי־ Ju 5¹⁵, Is 10¹; צֶלְלֵי Jer 6⁴, and so always הִנֲנִי *behold me*, הִנֲנוּ *behold us*; on בְ before the suffix ךָ, see § 20 *b*); also in certain forms under *Kaph* and *Rēš* after a long vowel and before the tone, e. g. תְּאָכֲלֶנָּה Gn 3¹⁷; בְּרֲכִי ψ 103¹; וְתִשֲׁרֲתֵהוּ 1 K 1⁴ (but וְיִתְבָּרֲכוּ ψ 72¹⁷, cf. Jer 4², 1 Ch 29²⁰, because the tone is thrown back on to the *ā*. After *ē* Š°wâ remains even before the tone, as בְּרֲכוּ, &c.; but before Maqqef אֶלֲכָה־נָּא Baer Ex 4¹⁸, 2 S 15⁷, Jer 40¹⁵, but ed. Mant., Jabl., Ginsb. אֵל־)[2]; (*b*) under initial sibilants after וּ copulative, e. g. וּזֲהַב Gn 2¹²; cf. Jer 48²⁰; וּסֲחַר Is 45¹⁴; וּשֲׂדֵה Lv 25³⁴; וּשֲׁקָה Gn 27²⁶; וּשֲׁמַע Nu 23¹⁸, Is 37¹⁷, Dn 9¹⁸, cf. Ju 5¹², 1 K 14²¹, 2 K 9¹⁷, Jb 14¹, Ec 9⁷—to emphasize the vocal character of the Š°wâ. For the same reason under the emphatic ט in הֻטֲלוּ Jer 22²⁸; cf. Jb 33²⁵; after *Qôph* in וְקָדֲרְתִּי (so Baer, but ed. Mant., Jabl., Ginsb. וְקָ) Ez 23⁴¹; וְקָרֲב־ ψ 55²²; cf. Jer. 32⁹; under *Rēš* in אָרֲדָה (ed. Mant. אָר־) Gn 18²¹; וְרָעֲם ψ 28⁹; even under ח Ezr 26²¹; under ב Est 2⁸; וּבֲרֶכְךָ so Jabl., Ginsb., but ed. Mant. וּבֵר־) Dt 24¹³; (*c*) under sonants, sibilants or *Qôph* after *i*, e. g. יִצֲחַק Gn 21⁶, cf. 30³⁸ and Ez 21²⁸ (under ק); אָמֲרוֹת ψ 12⁷; הִתֲמַלָּה Jer 22¹⁵; כִּנֲרוֹת Jos 11²; בְּכָבְ־ ψ 74⁵,—for the same reason as the cases under *b*[3]; according to Baer also in שְׂפֲמוֹת 1 S 30²⁸; יִפֲנֶשָׁ Gn 32¹⁸ after *ŏ* (cf. § 9 *v*), as well as after *a* in הַקֲשִׁיבָה Dn 9¹⁹; הַבֲרָכָה Gn 27³⁸; הַמֲצֹרָעִים 2 K 7⁸.

B. The *Ḥateph-Qameṣ* is less restricted to the gutturals than the first two, [*h*] and stands more frequently for a simple Š°wâ mobile when an original O-sound requires to be partly preserved, e. g. at the beginning, in רֳאִי (ground-form *rŏ'y*) *vision* (cf. § 93 *z*); בְּנֳנֵיהוּ 2 Ch 31¹², &c., *Q°rê* (*K°th.* כּוּן); עֳמָנִיּוֹת *Ammonitish women*, 1 K 11¹ (sing. עֳמֹנִית); יִרֳדֹּפֶךָ for the usual יִרְדֹּפֶךָ Ez 35⁶, from יָרַדֹּף; תְּקֳבֶנּוּ Nu 23²⁵, Jer 31³³, and elsewhere before suffixes, cf. § 60 *a*; קֳדְקֳדוֹ *his pate* (from קָדְקֹד) ψ 7¹⁷, &c.; אֶשְׁקֳטָה Is 18⁴ *Q°rê*. Further, like ‑, it stands under consonants, which ought to have *Dageš forte*, as in לֻקֳחָה (for לֻקְחָה) Gn 2²³. In this example, as in וּסֳעָדָה 1 K 13⁷; וּסֳאָה 2 K 7¹⁸; and וּצֳעָקִי Jer 22²⁰, the *Ḥateph-Qameṣ* is no doubt due to the influence of the

---

[1] See Delitzsch, 'Bemerkungen über masoretisch treue Darstellung des alttestam. Textes,' in the *Ztschr. f. luth. Theol. u. Kirche*, vol. xxiv. 1863, p. 409 ff.

[2] On the uncertainty of the MSS. in some cases which come under *a*, see *Minḥat shay* (the Masoretic comm. in ed. Mant.) on Gn 12³ and Ju 7⁶.

[3] Ben-Asher requires ‑ for ‑ (even for Š°wâ quiescens) generally before a guttural or ר; hence Baer reads in 2 S 15⁵ בְּקָרֲב־, ψ 187 אֶקֳרָא; 49¹⁵ לְשֳׁאוֹל; תֳּבֲחַר 65⁵; תֳּמֲחַץ 68²⁴; תֳּלֲעַג Pr 3c¹⁷; אָבֳחַר Jb 29²⁵; cf. Delitzsch, *Psalms*, 12⁷, note.

following guttural as well as of the preceding U-sound. (Elsewhere indeed after ו in similar cases *Ḥaṭeph-Pathaḥ* is preferred, see above, *b*; but with לָקְחָה cf. also סָבְלוֹ Is 9³, 10²⁷, 14²⁵, where the U-sound must necessarily be admitted to have an influence on the *Šᵉwâ* immediately following.) In וּטֳהָר־ (û-ṭᵒhŏr) Jb 17⁹ it is also influenced by the following O-sound. In קֳסָמִי 1 S 28⁸ *Qᵉré*, the original form is קְסָם, where again the *ō* represents an *ŏ*. It is only through the influence of a following guttural that we can explain the forms נִקְרָאָה Est 2¹⁴; נִבְהַל Pr 28²²; נֶסֶרְחָה Jer 49⁷; אֶפְשְׁעָה Is 27⁴; וָאֶשְׁמְעָה Dn 8¹³; שָׁמְעָה ψ 39¹³; בְּסַעְרָה 2 K 2¹ (Baer's ed. also in ver. 11); הַקְּהָתִים 2 Ch 34¹² (ed. Mant., Opitius, &c. הַקְּ). Finally in most of the examples which have been adduced, the influence of an emphatic sound (ק, ט, cf. also אֲלַקְטָה Ru 2²·⁷), or of a sibilant is also to be taken into account.

i 3. The sign of the *simple Šᵉwâ* ־ serves also as a mere syllable divider. In this case it is disregarded in pronunciation and is called *Šᵉwâ quiescens*. In the middle of a word it stands under every consonant which closes a syllable; at the end of words on the other hand it is omitted except in *final* ך (to distinguish it better from final ן), e.g. מֶלֶךְ *king*, and in the less frequent case, where a word ends with a mute after another vowelless consonant as in נֵרְדְּ *nard*, אַתְּ *thou* fem. (for *ʼant*), קָטַלְתְּ *thou* fem. *hast killed*, וַיַּשְׁקְ *and he watered*, וַיִּשְׁבְּ *and he took captive*, אַל־תֵּשְׁתְּ *drink thou not*; but וַיֵּרָא, חֲטָא.[1]

k However, in the examples where a mute closes the syllable, the final *Šᵉwâ* comes somewhat nearer to a vocal *Šᵉwâ*, especially as in almost all the cases a weakening of a final vowel has taken place, viz. אַתְּ *ʼattᵉ* from אַתִּי *ʼatti* (*ʼanti*), קָטַלְתְּ from קָטַלְתִּי (cf. in this form, the 2nd sing. fem. perf. Qal, even בָּאת, after a vowel, Gn 16⁸, Mi 4¹⁰, &c., according to the readings of Baer), יִשְׁבְּ *yišbᵉ* from יִשְׁבָה, &c. The Arabic actually has a short vowel in analogous forms. In נֵרְדְּ borrowed from the Indian, as also in קֹשְׁטְ (qōšṭ) Pr 22²¹; and in אַל־תּוֹסְףְּ *ne addas* (for which we should expect תּוֹסֵף) Pr 30⁶ the final mute of itself attracts a slight vowel sound.

l Rem. The proper distinction between *simple Šᵉwâ mobile* and *quiescens* depends on a correct understanding of the formation of syllables (§ 26). The beginner may observe for the present, that (1) *Šᵉwâ* is always *mobile* (*a*) at the beginning of a word (except in שְׁתַּיִם שְׁתֵּי § 97 *b*, note); (*b*) under a consonant with *Dageš forte*, e.g. גֻּדְּפוּ *gid-dᵉphû*; (*c*) after another *Šᵉwâ*, e.g. יִקְטְלוּ *yiqṭᵉlû* (except at the end of the word, see above, *i*). (2) *Šᵉwâ* is *quiescens* (*a*) at the end of a word, also in the ך; (*b*) before another *Šᵉwâ*.

§ 11. *Other Signs which affect the Reading.*

Very closely connected with the vowel points are the *reading-signs*, which were probably introduced at the same time. Besides the diacritical point over שׁ and שׂ, a point is placed *within* a consonant

---

[1] On יתְ־ as an ending of the 2nd sing. fem. perf. Qal of verbs ל״ה, see § 75 *m*.

to show that it has a stronger sound. On the other hand a horizontal stroke (*Rāphè*) over a consonant is a sign that it has *not* the stronger sound. According to the different purposes for which it is used the point is either (1) *Dageš forte*, a sign of strengthening (§ 12); or (2) *Dageš lene*, a sign of the harder pronunciation of certain consonants (§ 13); or (3) *Mappîq*, a sign to bring out the full consonantal value of letters which otherwise serve as vowel letters (§ 7 *b*), especially in the case of ה at the end of the word (§ 14 *a*). The *Rāphè*, which excludes the insertion of any of these points, has almost entirely gone out of use in our printed texts (§ 14 *e*).

§ 12. *Dageš in general,*[1] *and Dageš forte in particular.*

Cf. Graetz, ' Die mannigfache Anwendung u. Bedeut. des Dagesch,' in *Monatsschr. für Gesch. u. Wiss. d. Judent.*, 1887, pp. 425 ff. and 473 ff.

1. *Dageš*, a point standing in the middle of a consonant,[2] denotes, *a* according to § 11, (*a*) the *strengthening*[3] of a consonant (*Dageš forte*), e. g. קָטֵל *qiṭṭēl* (§ 20); or (*b*) the *harder* pronunciation of the letters בְּגַדְכְּפַת (*Dageš lene*). For a variety of the latter, now rarely used in our printed texts, see § 13 *c*.

The root רגש in Syriac means *to pierce through, to bore through* (with sharp *b* iron); hence the name *Dageš* is commonly explained, solely with reference to its form, by *puncture, point*. But the names of all similar signs are derived rather from their grammatical significance. Accordingly רגש may in the Masora have the sense : *acuere* (*literam*), i. e. to *sharpen* a letter, as well as to *harden* it, i. e. to pronounce it as hard and without aspiration. דָּגֵש *acuens* (*literam*) would then be a sign of sharpening and hardening (like *Mappiq* מַפִּיק *proferens*, as *signum prolationis*), for which purposes a *prick* of the *pen*, or *puncture*, was selected. The opposite of *Dageš* is רָפֶה *soft*, § 14 *e*, and § 22 *n*.

2. In grammar *Dageš forte*, the *sign of strengthening*, is the more *c* important. It may be compared to the *sicilicus* of the Latins (*Luculus* for *Lucullus*) or to the stroke over $\bar{m}$ and $\bar{n}$. In the unpointed text it is omitted, like the vowels and other reading signs.

For the different kinds of *Dageš forte*, see § 20.

---

[1] Oort, *Theol. Tijdschr.* 1902, p. 376, maintains that 'the Masoretes recognized no distinction between *Dageš lene* and *forte*. They used a *Dageš* where they considered that a letter had the sharp, not the soft or aspirated sound.' This may be true; but the old-established distinction between the two kinds of *Dageš* is essential for the right understanding of the grammatical forms.

[2] *Wāw* with *Dageš* (וּ) cannot in our printed texts be distinguished from a *wāw* pointed as *Šûrĕq* (וּ); in the latter case the point should stand higher up. The וּ *û* is, however, easily to be recognized since it cannot take a vowel before or under it.

[3] Stade, *Lehrb. der hebr. Gr.*, Lpz. 1879, pp. 44, 103, rightly insists on the expression *strengthened pronunciation* instead of the older term *doubling*, since the consonant in question is only written once. The common expression arises from the fact that in transcription a *strengthened* consonant can only be indicated by writing it as double.

§ 13. *Dageš lene.*

Ginsburg, *Introd.*, p. 114 ff. : Dagesh and Raphe.

a 1. *Dageš lene*, the sign of *hardening*, is in ordinary printed texts placed only within the בְּנַדְכְּפַת letters (§ 6 *n*) as a sign that they should be pronounced with their original hard sound (without aspiration), e. g. מֶלֶךְ *mèlĕkh*, but מַלְכּוֹ *maⁱ-kô* ; תָּפַר *tāphár*, but יִתְפֹּר *yith-pōr* ; שָׁתָה *šāthā*, but יִשְׁתֶּה *yiš-tè*.

b 2. The cases in which a *Dageš lene* is to be inserted are stated in § 21. It occurs almost exclusively at the beginning of words and syllables. In the middle of the word it can easily be distinguished from *Dageš forte*, since the latter always has a vowel before it, whereas *Dageš lene* never has; accordingly the *Dageš* in אַפִּי *'appî*, רַבִּים *rabbîm* must be *forte*, but in יִגְדַּל *yigdal* it is *lene*.

c A variety of the *Dageš lene* is used in many manuscripts, as well as in Baer's editions, though others (including Ginsburg in the first two cases, *Introd.*, pp. 121, 130, 603, 662) reject it together with the Ḥaṭefs discussed in § 10 *g*. It is inserted in consonants other than the *Bᵉgadkᵉphath* to call attention expressly to the beginning of a new syllable : (*a*) when the same consonant precedes in close connexion, e. g. בְּכָל־לִבִּי ψ 9², where, owing to the *Dageš*, the coalescing of the two *Lameds* is avoided ; (*b*) in cases like מַחְסִי ψ 62⁸ = *maḥ-si* (not *măḥᵃ-sî*) ; (*c*) according to some (including Baer ; not in ed. Mant.) in לֹא in the combination לֹא לִי Dt 32⁵, or לֹא לּוֹ Hb 1⁶, 2⁶ &c. (so always also in Ginsburg's text, except in Gn 38⁹) ; see also § 20 *e* and *g*.—Delitzsch appropriately gives the name of *Dageš orthophonicum* to this variety of *Dageš* (*Bibl. Kommentar*, 1874, on ψ 94¹²) ; cf. moreover Delitzsch, *Luth. Ztschr.*, 1863, p. 413 ; also his *Complutensische Varianten zu dem Alttest. Texte*, Lpz. 1878, p. 12.

d 3. When *Dageš forte* is placed in a *Bᵉgadkᵉphath*, the strengthening necessarily excludes its aspiration, e. g. אַפִּי *'appî*, from אַנְפִּי *'anpî*.

§ 14. *Mappîq and Rāphè.*

a 1. *Mappîq*, like *Dageš*, also a point *within* the consonant, serves in the letters א ה ו י as a sign that they are to be regarded as full consonants and not as vowel letters. In most editions of the text it is only used in the consonantal ה at the end of words (since ה can never be a vowel letter in the middle of a word), e. g. גָּבַהּ *gābháh* (to be high), אַרְצָהּ *'arṣāh* (her land) which has a consonantal ending (shortened from *-hā*), different from אַרְצָה *'árṣā* (to the earth) which has a vowel ending.

b Rem. 1. Without doubt such a *Hē* was distinctly aspirated like the Arabic *Hā* at the end of a syllable. There are, however, cases in which this ה has lost its consonantal character (the Mappîq of course disappearing too), so that it remains only as a vowel letter ; cf. § 91 *e* on the 3rd fem. sing.

c The name מַפִּיק means *proferens*, i. e. a sign which brings out the sound of the letter distinctly, as a consonant. The same sign was selected for this and for *Dageš*, since both are intended to indicate a hard, i. e. a strong, sound. Hence *Râphè* (see *e*) is the opposite of both.

2. In MSS. Mappîq is also found with א, ו, י, to mark them expressly as *d* consonants, e. g. גּוֹי (*gôy*), קָו (*qāw, qāu*), for which וּ is also used, as עָשׂוּ, &c. For the various statements of the Masora (where these points are treated as *Dageš*), see Ginsburg, *The Massorah, letter* א, § 5 (also *Introd.*, pp. 557, 609, 637, 770), and 'The Dageshed Alephs in the Karlsruhe MS.' (where these points are extremely frequent), in the *Verhandlungen des Berliner Orientalisten-Kongresses*, Berlin, i. 1881, p. 136 ff. The great differences in the statements found in the Masora point to different schools, one of which appears to have intended that every audible א should be pointed. In the printed editions the point occurs only four times with א (אַ or אָ), Gn 43²⁶, Lv 23¹⁷, Ezr 8¹⁸ and Jb 33²¹ (רָאוּ; where the point can be taken only as an orthophonetic sign, not with König as *Dageš forte*). Cf. Delitzsch, *Hiob*, 2nd ed., p. 439 ff.

2. *Râphè* (רָפֶה i. e. weak, soft), a horizontal stroke over the letter, *e* is the opposite of both kinds of *Dageš* and *Mappîq*, but especially of *Dageš lene*. In exact manuscripts every בגדכפת letter has either *Dageš lene* or *Râphè*, e. g. מֶלֶךְ *mèlĕkh*, תָּפַר, שָׁתָה. In modern editions (except Ginsburg's 1st ed.) *Râphè* is used only when the absence of a *Dageš* or *Mappîq* requires to be expressly pointed out.

§ 15. *The Accents*.

On the ordinary accents (see below, *e*), cf. W. Heidenheim, מִשְׁפְּטֵי הַטְּעָמִים *a* [*The Laws of the Accents*], Rödelheim, 1808 (a compilation from older Jewish writers on the accents, with a commentary); W. Wickes (see also below), טעמי כ״א ספרים [*The Accents of the Twenty-one Books*], Oxford, 1887, an exhaustive investigation in English; J. M. Japhet, *Die Accente der hl. Schrift* (exclusive of the books אמ״ת), ed. by Heinemann, Frankf. a. M. 1896; Prätorius, *Die Herkunft der hebr. Accente*, Berlin, 1901, and (in answer to Gregory's criticism in the *TLZ*. 1901, no. 22) *Die Uebernahme der früh-mittelgriech. Neumen durch die Juden*, Berlin, 1902; P. Kahle, 'Zur Gesch. der hebr. Accente,' *ZDMG*. 55 (1901), 167 ff. (1, on the earliest Jewish lists of accents; 2, on the mutual relation of the various systems of accentuation; on p. 179 ff. he deals with the accents of the 3rd system, see above, § 8 *g*, note); Margolis, art. 'Accents,' in the *Jewish Encycl.* i (1901), 149 ff.; J. Adams, *Sermons in Accents*, London, 1906.—On the accents of the Books תא״ם (see below, *h*), S. Baer, תורת אמת [*Accentual Laws of the Books* אמ״ת], Rödelheim, 1852, and his appendix to Delitzsch's *Psalmencommentar*, vol. ii, Lpz. 1860, and in the 5th ed., 1894 (an epitome is given in Baer-Delitzsch's *Liber Psalmorum hebr.*, Lpz. 1861, 1874, 1880); cf. also Delitzsch's most instructive 'Accentuologischer Commentar' on Psalms 1-3, in his *Psalmencommentar* of 1874, as well as the numerous contributions to the accentual criticism of the text, &c., in the editions of Baer and Delitzsch, and in the commentaries of the latter; W. Wickes, טעמי אמ״ת [*Accents of the Poet. Books*], Oxford, 1881; Mitchell, in the *Journal of Bibl. Lit.*, 1891, p. 144 ff.; Baer and Strack, *Dikduke ha-ṭᵉamim*, p. 17 ff.

1. As Prätorius (see above) has convincingly shown, the majority of *b* the Hebrew accents, especially, according to Kahle (see above), the 'Conjunctivi', were adopted by the Jews from the neums and punctuation-marks found in Greek gospel-books, and, like these, their primary purpose was to regulate minutely the public reading of the sacred

text. The complete transformation and amplification of the system (in three different forms, see § 8 *g*, note), which soon caused the Jews to forget its real origin, is clearly connected with the gradual change from the speaking voice in public reading to chanting or singing. The accents then served as a kind of musical notes.[1] Their value as such has, however, with the exception of a few traces, become lost in transmission. On the other hand, according to their original design they have also a twofold use which is still of the greatest importance for grammar (and syntax), viz. their value (*a*) as *marking the tone*, (*b*) as *marks of punctuation* to indicate the logical (syntactical) relation of single words to their immediate surroundings, and thus to the whole sentence.[2]

c 2. As a mark of the tone the accent stands almost invariably (but see below, *e*) with the syllable which has the principal tone in the word. This is usually the ultima, less frequently the penultima. Amongst the Jewish grammarians a word which has the tone on the ultima is called *Milra'* (Aram. מִלְּרַע i.e. accented below[3]), e.g. קָטַל *qāṭál*; a word which has the tone on the penultima is *Mil'êl* (Aram. מִלְּעֵיל, accented *above*), e.g. מֶלֶךְ *mèlĕkh*. Besides this, in many cases a *secondary tone* is indicated in the word by *Mèthĕg* (cf. § 16). Examples such as נַעֲמָדָה יַחַד Is 50[8] (cf. 40[18], Ex 15[8], Jb 12[15], La 2[16]) are regarded by the Jewish grammarians as even *proparoxytone*.[4]

d 3. As marks of interpunctuation the accents are subdivided into those which *separate* (*Distinctivi* or *Domini*) and those which *connect* (*Conjunctivi* or *Servi*). Further a twofold system of accentuation is to be noted : (*a*) the common system found in twenty-one of the Books (the כ״א i.e. twenty-one), and (*b*) that used in the first three Books of the *Hagiographa*, viz. Psalms, Proverbs, and Job, for which the *vox memor.* is אֱמֶת, from the initial consonants of the names, תְּהִלִּים Psalms, מִשְׁלֵי Proverbs, אִיּוֹב Job, or more correctly, according to their original sequence, תְּאֹם תא״ם (*twin*), so that טַעֲמֵי תא״ם means the accents (sing. טַעַם) of these three Books. The latter system is not only richer and more complicated in itself, but also musically more significant than the ordinary accentuation.

---

[1] On the attempts of Christian scholars of the sixteenth century to express the Hebrew accents by musical notes, cf. Ortenberg, *ZDMG.* 1889, p. 534.

[2] At the same time it must not be forgotten that the value of the accent as a mark of punctuation is always relative ; thus, e. g. *'Athnâḥ* as regards the logical structure of the sentence may at one time indicate a very important break (as in Gn 1[4]); at another, one which is almost imperceptible (as in Gn 1[1]).

[3] 'Above' in this sense means what comes before, 'below' is what comes after ; cf. Bacher, *ZAW.* 1907, p. 285 f.

[4] Cf. Delitzsch on Is 40[18].

I. *The Common Accents.*

Preliminary remark. The accents which are marked as *prepositive* stand to *e* the right over or under the initial consonant of the word ; those marked as *postpositive*, to the left over or under the last consonant. Consequently in both cases the tone-syllable must be ascertained independently of the accent (but cf. below, *l*).

A. Disjunctive Accents (*Distinctivi* or *Domini*).[1]   *f*

1. (–ֽ) סִלּוּק Sillûq (*end*) always with the tone-syllable of the last word before Sôph pāsûq (:), the verse-divider, e.g. הָאָֽרֶץ׃.

2. (–֑) אַתְנָח ’Athnâḥ or אַתְנַחְתָּא ’Athnaḥtā (*rest*), the principal divider within the verse.

3 a. (–֒) סְגוֹלְתָּא Seḡôltā, *postpositive*, marks the fourth or fifth subordinate division, counting backwards from ’Athnâḥ (e.g. Gn 1⁷·²⁸).

3 b. (׀–֓) שַׁלְשֶׁלֶת Šalšeleth (i. e. *chain*), as disjunctive, or Great Šalšeleth, distinguished by the following stroke[2] from the conjunctive in the poetic accentuation, is used for

---

[1] All the disjunctives occur in Is 39². — The earlier Jewish accentuologists already distinguish between מְלָכִים *Reges* and מְשָׁרְתִים *Servi*. The division of the disjunctive accents into Imperatores, Reges, Duces, Comites, which became common amongst Christian grammarians, originated in the *Scrutinium S. S. ex accentibus* of Sam. Bohlius, Rostock, 1636, and, as the source of manifold confusion, had better be given up. The order of the accents in respect to their disjunctive power is shown in general by the above classification, following Wickes. In respect to the height of tone (in chanting) 1, 2, 5, 4, 8, which were *low* and long sustained notes, are to be distinguished from the *high* notes (7, 3ᵃ, 6, 13, 9), and the highest (3ᵇ, 11, 12, 10); cf. Wickes, א״כ ט׳ p. 12 ff. — The name טְעָמִים (later = *accents* in general) was originally restricted to the disjunctives, see Kahle, l. c., p. 169.

[2] This stroke is commonly confused with *Paseq*, which has the same form. But Pāseq (= *restraining, dividing*, also incorrectly called Peṣiq) is neither an independent accent, nor a constituent part of other accents, but is used as a mark for various purposes ; see the Masoretic lists at the end of Baer's editions, and Wickes, *Accents of the Twenty-one Books*, p. 120 ff., where Pāseq is divided into *distinctivum, emphaticum, homonymicum*, and *euphonicum*. The conjecture of Olshausen (*Lehrb.*, p. 86 f.), that Pāseq served also to point out marginal glosses subsequently interpolated into the text, has been further developed by E. von Ortenberg, ' Die Bedeutung des Paseq für Quellenscheidung in den BB. d. A. T.,' in *Progr. des Domgymn. zu Verden*, 1887, and in the article, ' Paseq u. Legarmeh,' in *ZAW*. 1887, p. 301 ff. (but see Wickes, ibid. 1888, p. 149 ff. ; also E. König, in the *Ztschr. f. kirchl. Wiss. u. kirchl. Leben*, 1889, parts 5 and 6 ; Maas, in *Hebraica*, v. 121 ff., viii. 89 ff.). Prätorius, *ZDMG.* 1899, p 683 ff., pointed out that *Paseq* (which is pre-masoretic and quite distinct from Leḡarmēh) besides being a divider (used especially for the sake of greater clearness) also served as a sign of abbreviation. For further treatment of *Paseq* see H. Grimme, ' Pasekstudien,' in the *Bibl. Ztschr.*, i. 337 ff., ii. 28 ff., and *Psalmenprobleme*, &c., Freiburg (Switzerland), 1902, p. 173, where it is argued that *Paseq* indicates variants in a difficult sentence ; J. Kennedy, *The Note-line in the Heb. Scriptures*, Edinb. 1903, with an index of all the occurrences of *Paseq*, p. 117 ff. According to Kennedy the ' note-line ', of which he distinguishes sixteen different kinds, is intended to draw attention to some peculiarity in the text ; it existed long before the Masoretes, and was no longer understood by them. See, however, the reviews of E. König, *Theol.*

S^egôltā (seven times altogether) when this would stand
at the head of the sentence; cf. Gn 19[16], &c.

4 *a.* (ـֵ) גָּדוֹל זָקֵף Zâqēph gādôl, and

4 *b.* (ـֵ) קָטֹן זָקֵף Zâqēph qāṭôn. The names refer to their musical
character. As a disjunctive, Little Zâqēph is by nature
stronger than Great Zâqēph; but if they stand together,
the one which comes first is always the stronger.

5. (ـֵ) טִפְחָא Ṭiphḥā or טַרְחָא Ṭarḥā, a subordinate disjunctive
before Sillûq and 'Athnâḥ, but very often the principal
disjunctive of the whole verse instead of 'Athnâḥ; always
so when the verse consists of only two or three words
(e. g. Is 2[18]), but also in longer verses (Gn 3[21]).

6. (ـֵ) רְבִיעַ R^ebhîaʻ.

7. (ـֵ) זַרְקָא Zarqā, *postpositive.*

8 *a.* (ـֵ) פַּשְׁטָא Pašṭā, *postpositive,*[1] and

8 *b.* (ـֵ) יְתִיב Y^ethîbh, *prepositive,* and thus different from M^ehup-
pākh. Y^ethîbh is used in place of Pašṭā when the latter
would stand on a monosyllable or on a foretoned word,
not preceded by a conjunctive accent.

9. (ـֵ) תְּבִיר T^ebhîr.

10 *a.* (ـֵ) גֶּרֶשׁ Gèreš or טֶרֶס Ṭères, and

10 *b.* (ـֵ) גֵּרְשַׁיִם G^erāšayim[2] or Double Gèreš, used for Gèreš, when
the tone rests on the ultima, and 'Azlā does not precede.

11 *a.* (ـֵ) פָּזֵר Pâzēr, and

11 *b.* (ـֵ) גָּדוֹל פָּזֵר Pâzēr gādôl (Great Pâzēr) or פָרָה קַרְנֵי Qarnê phārā
(*cow-horns*), only used 16 times, for special emphasis.

12. (ـֵ) גְדוֹלָה תְּלִישָׁא T^elišā g^edôlā or Great T^elîšā, *prepositive.*

13. (|ـֵ) לְגַרְמֵהּ L^egarmēh, i. e. Mûnaḥ (see below) with a following
stroke.

Stud. u. Krit., 1904, p. 448 ff., G. Beer, *TLZ.* 1905, no. 3, and esp. A. Klostermann, *Theol. Lit.-blatt,* 1904, no. 13, with whom Ginsburg agrees (*Verhandlungen des Hamb. Or.-kongresses von 1902,* Leiden, 1904, p. 210 ff.) in showing
that the tradition with regard to the 479 or 480 uses of *Paseq* is by no means
uniform. The purpose of *Paseq* is clearly recognizable in the five old rules:
as a divider between identical letters at the end and beginning of two words;
between identical or very similar words; between words which are absolutely
contradictory (as *God* and *evil-doer*); between words which are liable to be
wrongly connected; and lastly, between heterogeneous terms, as 'Eleazar the
High Priest, and Joshua'. But the assumption of a far-reaching critical
importance in *Paseq* is at least doubtful.—Cf. also the important article by
H. Fuchs, 'Pesiq ein Glossenzeichen,' in the *Vierteljahrsschrift f. Bibelkunde,*
Aug. 1908, p. 1 ff. and p. 97 ff.

[1] If the word in question has the tone on the penultima, Pašṭā is placed
over it also, e. g תֹהוּ Gn 1[2]; cf. below, *l.*

[2] Wickes requires Geršáyim (גֵּרְשַׁיִם).

B. Conjunctive Accents (*Conjunctivi* or *Servi*).   g

14. (‐ֻ) מוּנַח Mûnaḥ.

15. (‐ֻ) מְהֻפָּךְ Meḥuppākh or מַהְפָּךְ Mahpākh.

16 *a*. (‐ֻ) מֵירְכָא or מֵאַרְכָא Mêrekhā, and

16 *b*. (‐ֻ) מ׳ כְּפוּלָה Mêrekhā khephûlā or Double Mêrekhā.

17. (‐ֻ) דַּרְגָּא Dargā.

18. (‐ֻ) אַזְלָא 'Azlā, when associated with Gèreš (see above) also
called Qadmā.

19. (‐ֻ) תְּלִישָׁא קְטַנָּה Telišā qeṭannā or Little Telišā, *postpositive.*

20. (‐ֻ) גַּלְגַּל Galgal or יֶרַח Yèraḥ.

[21. (‐ֻ) מְאַיְּלָא Me'ayyelā or מָאיְלָא Mâyelā, a variety of Ṭiphḥa,
serves to mark the secondary tone in words which have
Sillûq or 'Athnâḥ, or which are united by Maqqēph
with a word so accentuated, e.g. וַיֵּצֵא־נֹחַ Gn 8¹⁸.]

II.   *The Accents of the Books* תא״ם.

A. Distinctivi.   h

1. (‐ֻ) Sillûq (see above, I, 1).

2. (‐ֻ) עוֹלֶה וְיוֹרֵד 'Ôlè weyôrēd,[1] a stronger divider than

3. (‐ֻ) 'Athnâḥ (see above, I, 2). In shorter verses 'Athnâḥ
suffices as principal distinctive; in longer verses '*Ôlè
weyôrēd* serves as such, and is then mostly followed by
'Athnâḥ as the principal disjunctive of the second half
of the verse.

4. (‐ֻ) Rebhíaʿ gādôl (Great Rebhíaʿ).

5. (‐ֻ) Rebhíaʿ mugrāš, i.e. Rebhíaʿ with Gèreš on the same word.

6. (‐ֻ) Great Šalšèleth (see above, I. 3 *b*).

7. (‐ֻ) צִנּוֹר Ṣinnôr (Zarqā), as *postpositive*, is easily distinguished
from צִנּוֹרִית Ṣinnôrîth similarly placed, which is not an
independent accent, but stands only over an open syllable
before a consonant which has Mêrekhā or Mahpākh.

8. (‐ֻ) Rebhíaʿ qāṭôn (Little Rebhíaʿ) immediately before 'Ôlè
weyôrēd.

9. (‐ֻ) דְּחִי Deḥî or Ṭiphḥā, *prepositive*, to the right underneath
the initial consonant, e.g. הַגּוֹי (consequently it does not
mark the tone-syllable).

---

[1] Wrongly called also Mêrekhā meḥuppākh (*Mêrekha mahpakhatum*), although
the accent underneath is in no way connected with Mêrekhā; cf. Wickes, l. c.,
p. 14.

10. (–꜍) Pázēr (see above, I, 11 *a*).

11 *a*. (|–꜕) Mᵉhuppākh lᵉgarmēh, i.e. Mahpākh with a following
stroke.

11 *b*. (|–꜔) 'Azlā lᵉgarmēh, i.e. 'Azlā with a following stroke.

i   B. Conjunctivi.

12. (–꜓) Mêrᵉkhā (see above, I. 16 *a*).

13. (–꜓) Mûnaḥ (see above, I. 14).

14. (–꜌) עִלּוּי 'Illûy or Mûnaḥ superior.

15. (–꜖) טַרְחָא Ṭarḥā (under the tone-syllable, and thus easily
distinguished from No. 9).

16. (–꜐) Galgal or Yᵉraḥ (see above, I. 20).

17. (–꜕) Mᵉhuppākh or Mahpākh (see above, I. 15).

18. (–꜔) 'Azlā (see above, I. 18).

19. (–꜋) Šalšèleth qᵉṭannā (Little Šalšèleth).

The last three are distinguished from the disjunctives of
the same name by the absence of the stroke.

[20. (–꜏) Ṣinnôrîth, see above under No. 7.]

Remarks on the Accents.

I. *As Signs of the Tone.*

k   1. As in Greek and English (cf. εἰμί and εἶμι, cómpact and compáct) so also in
Hebrew, words which are written with the same consonants are occasionally
distinguished by the position of the tone, e.g. בָּנוּ *banú* (they built), בָּנוּ *bánu*
(in us) ; קָמָה *qama* (she stood up), קָמָה *qamá* (standing up, *fem.*).

l   2. As a rule the accent stands on the tone-syllable, and properly on its
initial consonant. In the case of prepositives and postpositives alone (see
above, *e*) the tone-syllable must be ascertained independently of the accent.
In many MSS. as well as in Baer's editions of the text, the postpositive sign
in foretoned words stands also over the tone-syllable after the analogy of
Paštā (see above, I. 8 *a*, note) ; e.g. יִשְׁכְּבוּ קָרֶם Gn 19⁴ ; so the prepositive
sign in cases like וַיְהִי Gn 8¹³.

II. *As Signs of Punctuation.*

m   3. In respect to this use of the accents, every verse is regarded as a period
which closes with Sillûq, or in the figurative language of the grammarians,
as a province (*ditio*) which is governed by the great distinctive at the end.
According as the verse is long or short, i. e. the province great or small, there
are several subordinate *Domini* of different grades, as governors of greater
and smaller divisions. When possible, the subdivisions themselves are also
split up into parts according to the law of dichotomy (see Wickes, *The Accents
of the Twenty-one Books*, p. 29 ff).—When two or more *equivalent* accents (Zâqēph,
Rᵉbhîaʻ) occur consecutively, the accent which precedes marks a greater
division than the one which follows ; cf. e. g. the Zâqēph, Gn 1²⁰ ᵃ.

n   4. In general a conjunctive (*Servus*) unites only such words as are closely
connected in sense, e. g. a noun with a following genitive or a noun with an

adjective. For the closest connexion between two or more words *Maqqēph* is added (§ 16 *a*).

5. The consecution of the several accents (especially the correspondence of O disjunctives with their proper conjunctives) conforms in the most minute details to strict rules, for a further investigation of which we must refer to the above-mentioned works. Here, to avoid misunderstanding, we shall only notice further the rule that in the accentuation of the books תא״ם, the *Rᵉbhiaʿ mugrāš* before *Sillùq*, and the *Dᵉḥi* before *'Athnāḥ*, must be changed into conjunctives, unless at least two toneless syllables precede the principal disjunctive. For this purpose Šᵉwâ *mobile* after Qameṣ, Ṣere, or Ḥolem (with Metheg) is to be regarded as forming a syllable. After 'Ôlè wᵉyōrēd the 'Athnāḥ does not necessarily act as pausal (cf. Delitzsch on ψ 45⁶). The condition of our ordinary texts is corrupt, and the system of accents can only be studied in correct editions [see Wickes' two treatises].

6. A double accentuation occurs in Gn 35²², from וישכב onward (where *p* the later accentuation, intended for public reading, aims at uniting vv. 22 and 23 into *one*, so as to pass rapidly over the unpleasant statement in v. 22); and in the Decalogue, Ex 20² ff.; Dt 5⁶ ff. Here also the later (mainly superlinear) accentuation which closes the first verse with עברים (instead of פני) is adopted simply for the purposes of public reading, in order to reduce the original twelve verses (with sublinear accentuation) to ten, the number of the Commandments. Thus עֲבָדִים at the end of v. 2 has Silluq (to close the verse) in the lower accentuation, but in the upper, which unites vv. 2–6 (the actual words of God) into a single period, only Rᵉbhiaʿ. Again פני, regarded as closing v. 3, is pointed פָּנַי (pausal Qameṣ with Silluq), but in the upper accentuation it is פָּנַי with Pathaḥ because not in pause. (Originally there may have been a third accentuation requiring עֲבָדִים and פָּנַי, and thus representing vv. 2 and 3 as the first commandment.) Further the upper accentuation unites vv. 8–11 into one period, while in vv. 12–15 the lower accentuation combines commandments 5–8 into one verse. Cf. Geiger, *Urschrift u. Übersetzungen der Bibel*, p. 373; Japhet, *op. cit.*, p. 158, and esp. K. J. Grimm, *Johns Hopkins Univ. Circ.* xix (May, 1900), no. 145.

§ 16. *Of Maqqēph and Mèthĕg.*

These are both closely connected with the accents.　　　　*a*

1. Maqqēph (מַקֵּף i.e. *binder*) is a small horizontal stroke between the upper part of two words which so connects them that in respect of tone and pointing they are regarded as one, and therefore have only one accent. Two, three, or even four words may be connected in this way, e.g. כָּל־אָדָם *every man*, אֶת־כָּל־עֵשֶׂב *every herb*, Gn 1²⁹, אֶת־כָּל־אֲשֶׁר־לוֹ *all that he had*, Gn 25⁵.

Certain monosyllabic prepositions and conjunctions, such as אֶל־ *to*, עַד־ *b until*, עַל־ *upon*, עִם־ *with*, אַל־ *ne*, אִם־ *if, whether*, מִן־ *from*, פֶּן־ *lest*, are almost always found with a following Maqqēph, provided they have not become independent forms by being combined with prefixes, e.g. מֵעַל, מֵעִם, in which case Maqqēph as a rule does not follow. Occasionally Maqqēph is replaced by a conjunctive accent (see above, § 9 *u*, 1 *c*), as, according to the Masora, in Dt 27⁹, 2 S 20²³, Jer 25³⁰, 29²⁵, Ec 9⁴ in the case of כָּל־אֶל; ψ 47⁵, 60², Pr 3¹² in the case of אֶת־, the objective particle. Longer words are, however, connected by Maqqēph with a following monosyllable, e.g. הִתְהַלֶּךְ־נֹחַ Gn 6⁹, וַיְהִי־כֵן Gn 1⁷; or two words of more than one syllable, e.g. שִׁבְעָה־עָשָׂר *seventeen*, Gn 7¹¹. Cf. the Greek proclitics ἐν, ἐκ, εἰς, εἰ, ὡς, οὐ, which are *atonic*, and lean on the following word.

c **2.** Mètheg (מֶתֶג i.e. *a bridle*), a small perpendicular stroke under the consonant to the left of the vowel, indicates most frequently the secondary stress or counter-tone, as opposed to the principal tone marked by the accents. It serves, however, in other cases to point out that the vowel should not be hastily passed over in pronunciation, but should be allowed its full sound. Hence other names of *Mètheg* are *Ma'aᵣîkh*, i.e. *lengthener*, and *Ga'yā*, i.e. *raising* of the voice, which is *Great Ga'yā* with long vowels, otherwise *Little Ga'yā*.[1]

d It is divided into: 1. The *light Mètheg*. This is subdivided again into (a) the ordinary Mètheg of the counter-tone, as a rule in the second (open) syllable before the tone, e.g. הָאָדָם (cf. also such cases as מֶלֶךְ־צֹר); but also in the third when the second is closed, e.g. הָאַרְבָּעִים (also in such cases as עֶבֶד־הַמֶּלֶךְ), and when the third is not suitable for it, even in the fourth (open) syllable before the tone. This Mètheg may be repeated in the fourth syllable before the tone, when it already stands in the second, e.g. שְׁבֻעֹתֵיכֶם. Finally it is always added to the vowel of an open ultima, which is joined by Maqqēph to a word beginning with a toneless syllable and so without Mètheg (e.g. בְּנֵי־יִשְׂרָאֵל, on the other hand לֹא־אֶהְיֶה, רִשְׁפֵי־קֶשֶׁת), or to a word beginning with *Šewâ* before the tone-syllable, e.g. שְׁלֹמֹה־בְנִי, מִי־לְךָ, &c.; the object being to prevent the *Šewâ* from becoming *quiescent*.

e The ordinary *light Mètheg* is omitted with a movable ו *copulative*, consequently we do not find וּבָנִים, &c. (nor even וּבְנֵי, &c., contrary to *b, a*; but וַחֲרֵב, &c., according to *b, δ*, cf. § 10 *g. b*).

f (b) The *firm* or *indispensable Mètheg*. (α) With all long vowels (except in certain cases, ו *copulative*, see above), which are followed by a *Šewâ mobile* preceding the tone-syllable; e.g. יִרְאוּ, יֵשְׁנוּ, &c. (β) To emphasize a long vowel in a closed syllable immediately before Maqqēph, e.g. שָׁת־לִי Gn 4²⁵ (not *šŏth-lî*); hence also with כָּל־ ψ 138², and אֶת־ Jb 41²⁶ (for כָּל־ and אֶת־; cf. also מֵאֵת־ Jo 15¹⁸, &c.). (γ) With Ṣere, which has become toneless through retraction of the tone, in order to prevent its being pronounced as Seghôl, e.g. אֹהֵב דַּעַת Pr 12¹ (not *'ôhĕbh*). (δ) With all vowels before composite *Šewâ*, e.g. יַעֲמֹד, צְעָקִים, &c. (except when the following consonant is strengthened, e.g. יְקֻבֶּנּוּ Is 62², because the strengthening by Dageš excludes the retarding of the vowel by Mètheg); so in the cases discussed in § 28 *c*, where a short vowel has taken the place of a Ḥateph, as יַעֲמֹדוּ, &c. (ε) In the preformative syllable of all forms of הָיָה *to be*, and חָיָה *to live*, when *Šewâ quiescens* stands under the ה or ח, e.g. תִּהְיֶה, יִהְיֶה (*yih-yĕ, tiḥ-yĕ*), &c., cf.

---

[1] Cf. as the source of this account of *Mètheg*, the exhaustive treatment by S. Baer, 'Mètheg-Setzung nach ihren überlieferten Gesetzen,' in A. Merx's *Archiv für die wissenschaftl. Erforschung des A. Test.*, Heft i, Halle, 1867, p. 56 ff., and Heft ii. 1868, p. 194 ff.; Baer and Strack, *Dikduke ha-ṭᵉamim*, p. 30 ff.

§ 63 q. (ζ) With the Qameṣ of the plural forms of בַּיִת *house* (thus בָּתִּים *báttim*, cf. § 96 under בַּיִת), and with אָנָּ֫א [1] *prithee!* to guard against the pronunciation *bŏttim*, *ŏnnā*.—Every kind of light Mèthĕg may in certain circumstances be changed into a conjunctive accent, e. g. בָּתִּים 2 Ch 34[11], &c.

2. The *grave Mèthĕg* (Ga‘yā in the more limited sense) is especially employed *g* in the following cases in order more distinctly to emphasize a short vowel or an initial Šewâ: (a) with the Pathaḥ of the article or of the prefixes בְּ, כְּ, לְ, בְּ, when followed by Šewâ under a consonant without Dageš, e. g. הַמְסִלָּה, לַמְסִלָּה, &c., but not before יְ (before which וַ also remains without Mèthĕg, with the exception of וַיְהִי and וַיְחִי, when they are followed by Maqqēph, or accented with Pašṭā), nor before the tone-syllable of a word, and neither *before* nor *after* the common Mèthĕg; likewise not in words which are connected by a conjunctive accent with the following word; (b) with the interrogative הֲ with Pathaḥ (except when it precedes יְ, Dageš forte or the tone-syllable of the word), e. g. הַאֵלֵךְ. When a Šewâ follows the הַ and after the Šewâ there is an untoned syllable, Baer places the Mèthĕg to the right of the Pathaḥ, e. g. הֲבְרָכָה Gn 27[38] (but ed. Mant. and Ginsb. 'הַב); (c) with the Pathaḥ or Segol of the article before a guttural (which cannot take Dageš), e. g. הֶהָרִים, הֶחַיִּים.—The Šewâ-Ga‘yā (ֽ) is especially important in the accentuation of the תא״ם, for purposes of musical recitation; it stands chiefly in words whose principal tone is marked by a disjunctive without a preceding conjunctive, e. g. וְהָיָה ψ 1[3].

3. The *euphonic Ga‘yā*, to ensure the distinct pronunciation of those con- *h* sonants which in consequence of the loss of the tone, or because they close a syllable, might easily be neglected, e. g. וַיִּשָּׁבַע לוֹ Gn 24[9]; פַּדֶּנָה אֲרָם (here to avoid a hiatus) 28[2], or in such cases as רוּחַ־אֵל Jb 33[4], &c.; תִּדְשָׁא Gn 1[11].

Mèthĕg (especially in the cases mentioned in 1, b, a) is a guide to correct *i* pronunciation, since it distinguishes ā from ŏ (except in the case noted in § 9 v, b) and î from ĭ; e. g. אָכְלָה '*ā-khelā* (she has eaten), but אָכְלָה '*ŏkhlā* (food), since the ָ stands here in a toneless closed syllable, and must therefore be a short vowel; thus also יִרְאוּ *yi-reʾû* (they fear), but יִרְאוּ *yirʾû* (they see), יִשְׁנוּ (they sleep), but יִשְׁנוּ (they repeat). The Jewish grammarians, however, do not consider the syllables lengthened by Mèthĕg as open. They regard the Šewâ as *quiescent* in cases like אָכְלָה, and belonging to the preceding vowel; cf. Baer, *Thorat ʾEmeth*, p. 9, and in Merx's *Archiv*, i. p. 60, Rem. 1, and especially *Dikduke ha-ṭeamim*, p. 13.

§ 17. *Of the Qerê and Kethîbh. Masora marginalis and finalis.*

On Qerê and Kethîbh see Ginsburg, *Intr.*, p. 183 ff.]

1. The margin of Biblical MSS. and editions exhibits variants *a* of an early date (§ 3 c), called קְרִי [2] *to be read*, since, according to

---

[1] The common form is אָנָּא, with an accent on both syllables, in which case, according to Qimḥi, the tone is always to be placed on the former. For the above mode of writing and position of the tone cf. Is 38[3], Jon 1[14], 4[2], ψ 116[4].

[2] On the necessity of the punctuation קְרִי as passive participle (= *legendum*)

the opinion of the Jewish critics, they are to be preferred to the כְּתִיב, i.e. what is *written* in the text, and are actually to be read instead of it.

On this account the vowels of the marginal reading (the *Qᵉrê*) are placed under the consonants of the text, and in order to understand both readings properly, the vowels in the text must be applied to the marginal reading, while for the reading of the text (the *Kᵉthîbh*) its own vowels are to be used. Thus in Jer 42⁶ אֲנַוּ occurs in the text, in the margin אנחנו קרי. Read אֲנוּ *we* (or according to Jewish tradition אָנוּ) in the text, in the margin אֲנַחְנוּ. A small circle or asterisk in the text always refers to the marginal reading.

b   2. Words or consonants which are to be passed over in reading, and are therefore left unpointed, are called כְּתִיב וְלֹא קְרֵי (*scriptum et non legendum*), e.g. את Jer 38¹⁶, אם 39¹², ידרך 51³. Conversely, words not contained in the text, but required by the Masora (as indicated by the insertion of their vowels), are called קְרֵי וְלֹא כְתִיב, e.g. 2 S 8³, Jer 31³⁸. See further Strack, *Prolegomena Critica*, p. 85; *Dikduke ha-ṭᵉamim*, §§ 62, 64; Blau, *Masoretische Untersuchungen*, p. 49 ff.

c   3. In the case of some very common words, which are *always* to be read otherwise than according to the *Kᵉthîbh*, it has not been considered necessary to place the *Qᵉrê* in the margin, but its vowels are simply attached to the word in the text. This *Qᵉrê perpetuum* occurs in the Pentateuch in הוא (Qᵉrê חִיא) wherever הוא stands for the feminine (§ 32 *l*), and in נַעֲרָ (Kᵉthîbh נער, Qᵉrê נַעֲרָה) always, except in Dt 22¹⁹ (but the Sam. text always has היא, נערה). The ordinary explanation of this supposed archaism, on the analogy of Greek ὁ παῖς and ἡ παῖς, our *child*, is inadequate, since there is no trace elsewhere of this epicene use; נער for נערה is rather a survival of a system of orthography in which a final vowel was written defectively, as in קָטַלְתָּ; cf. § 2 *n*.— Other instances are: יִשָּׂכָר (Q. יְשָׂכָר) Gn 30¹⁸ &c., see the *Lexicon*, and Baer and Delitzsch, *Genesis*, p. 84, and below, note to § 47 *b*; יְרוּשָׁלַיִם (Q. יְרוּשָׁלַיִם), properly יְרוּשָׁלֵם; יְהוָֹה (Q. אֲדֹנָי *the Lord*), or (after אֱלֹהִים) יֱהוִֹה (Q. אֲדֹנָי) properly יַהְוֶה *Yahwè* (cf. § 102 *m*, and § 135 *q*, note); on שְׁנַיִם, שְׁתַּיִם for שְׁנֵי, שְׁתֵּי, see § 97 *d*, end.

d   4. The masoretic apparatus accompanying the biblical text is divided into (*a*) *Masora marginalis*, consisting of (α) *Masora* (*marginalis*) *magna* on the upper and lower margins of MSS.; (β) *Masora* (*marginalis*) *parva* between and on the right and left of the columns;

---

instead of קְרִי *Qᵉri*, which was formerly common but is properly a past tense (= *lectum est*), see Kautzsch, *Gramm. des Bibl.-Aram.*, p. 81, note.

(b) *Masora finalis* at the end of the several books, counting Samuel, Kings, Minor Prophets, Ezra-Nehemiah, Chronicles, each as one book. On all three varieties see especially Ginsburg, *Introd.*, p. 423 ff., and the appendices containing (p. 983 ff.) the masoretic treatise from the St. Petersburg MS. of A.D. 1009, and (p. 1000 ff.) specimens of the *Masora parva* and *magna* on two chapters.

In nearly all printed editions only the *Masora finalis* is found, indicating the number of verses, the middle point of the book, &c., and a scanty selection from the *Masora parva*. The following alphabetical list of technical expressions (some of them Aramaic) and abbreviations, may suffice with the help of the lexicon to elucidate the subject. Further details will be found in the appendix to Teile's edition of the Hebrew O. T., p. 1222 ff.

אוֹת *letter.* אֶלָּא *nisi, except.* אֶמְצַע *middle.* אתנח סוף פסוק=אס״ף in the formula בְּלֹא אס״ף *without 'Athnaḥ or Soph-pasuq* i. e. *although no 'Athnaḥ or Soph-pasuq is written.*

בְּ *with,* before names of vowels or accents, as קָמֶץ בְּזָקֵף *Qameṣ with Zaqeph* used instead of Pathaḥ (§ 29 *i*).—בְּ as a numeral = *two,* as in טְעָמִים ב׳ *two accents.* במקצת, see מִקְצָת. בְּנֻסְחָא אַחֲרִינָא = בנ״א (Aramaic) *in another copy;* pl. בְּנֻסְחָן אַחֲרִינָן = בְּסְפָרִים אֲחֵרִים = בס״א. *in other books.* בָּתַר (Aram.) *after.*

דְּגוּשׁ fem. דְּגוּשָׁה *marked with Dageš (or Mappiq).* דַּף *leaf, page.*

זְעֵיר fem. זְעֵירָא (Aram.) *small.*

חֹל *profane, not sacred,* e. g. אֲדֹנָי Gn 19² because not referring to God. חוּץ *except.* חָסֵר *written defectively,* also *wanting* as ח׳ א׳ *'aleph is omitted.*

טַעַם *accent* (see ב); טָעַם in Hiphil *to chant an accent.* יָתִיר *superfluous.*

כָּאן *here.* כְּלָל (Aram.) *total,* as adv. *in general.*

לֵית=ל׳ (Aram., from לָא אִית) *non est*) = the form *is not found elsewhere.*

מְדוּיָּק *accurately corrected.* מָלֵא *full* i. e. *written plene.* מִלְמַטָּה *below* = מִלְרַע (§ 15 *c*). מִלְמַעְלָה=מִלְעֵיל (§ 15 *c*). מְנֻזָּרוֹת *separated,* the name of the strangely formed Nûns before ψ 107²³ ff. (§ 5 *n*). מִקְרָא *that which is read,* the name for all the O. T. scriptures. מִקְצָת *part.*

נָח fem. נָחָה *quiescent,* i. e. *not sounded.* נֶעְלָם *concealed,* i. e. *only retained orthographically.* נָקוּד *a point.* נָקוּד *pointed.*

ס״א see ב. סִימָן σημεῖον, *sign,* esp. *a mnemonic word* or, frequently, *sentence.* סכים=סך *total.* סוף פסוק=ס״ף (§ 15 *f*).

עַמּוּד *column of a page.*

פָּסוּק *a masoretic verse.* פִּסְקָא *a space,* esp. in the phrase פָּסוּק בָּאֶמְצַע *a space within a verse,* e. g. Gn 35²²; cf. H. Grätz, *Monatschrift für Gesch. u. Wiss. des Judentums,* 1878, p. 481 ff., and H. Strack, ibid. 1879, p. 26 ff.

קְרִי=ק׳, see above, *c.* קוֹדם *properly* קָדָם *before.* קָמוּץ fem. קְמוּצָה *pointed with Qameṣ.* קוֹרֵא *reader of the sacred text.*

רַבָּתִי, רַבָּתָה, רַבָּתָא (Aram., all fem. sing.) *large.*

תֵּיבָה *word* (consisting of more than one letter). תְּלוּיָה *suspensa* (§ 5 *n*, 3). תְּרֵי (Aram.) *two.*

CHAPTER II

PECULIARITIES AND CHANGES OF LETTERS: THE SYLLABLE AND THE TONE

§ 18.

THE changes which take place in the forms of the various parts of speech, depend partly on the peculiar nature of certain classes of letters and the manner in which they affect the formation of syllables, partly on certain laws of the language in regard to syllables and the tone.

§ 19. *Changes of Consonants.*

a   The changes which take place among consonants, owing to the formation of words, inflexion, euphony, or to influences connected with the progress of the language, are *commutation, assimilation, rejection, addition, transposition, softening.*

1. *Commutation*[1] may take place between consonants which are either *homorganic* or *homogeneous* (cf. § 6 *q*), e.g. עָלֵץ, עָלַם, עָלֵז, עָלַז *to exult*, לָהָה, לָאָה, Aram. לְעָא *to be weary*, לָחַץ and נָחַץ *to press*, סָגַר and סָכַר *to close*, מָלַט and פָּלַט *to escape*. In process of time, and partly under the influence of Aramaic, the harder and rougher sounds especially were changed into the softer, e.g. צָחַק into שָׂחַק *to laugh*, גָּעַל into גָּאַל *to reject*, and the sibilants into the corresponding mutes: ז into ד, שׁ into ת, צ into ט. In many cases these mutes may be regarded as a return to an earlier stage of the pronunciation.

The interchange of consonants, however, belongs rather to the lexicographical treatment of stems[2] than to grammatical inflexion. To the latter belong the interchange (*a*) of ת and ט in *Hithpaʿēl* (§ 54 *b*); (*b*) of ו and י in verbs *primae Yôd* (§ 69), יָלַד for וָלַד, &c.

b   **2.** *Assimilation* usually takes place when one consonant which closes a syllable passes over into another beginning the next syllable, and forms with it a strengthened letter, as *illustris* for *inlustris*, *affero* for *adfero*, συλλαμβάνω for συνλαμβάνω. In Hebrew this occurs,

---

[1] Cf. Barth, *Etymologische Forschungen*, Lpz. 1893, p. 15 ff. ('Lautverschiebungen').

[2] See in the *Lexicon*, the preliminary remarks on the several consonants.

(a) most frequently with נ, e.g. מִשָּׁם (for min-šām) *from there,* מִזֶּה c
(for min-zė) *from this,* יִתֵּן (for yinten) *he gives.* נ is *not* assimilated
after the prefix לְ, e.g. לִנְפֹּל, nor as a rule before gutturals (except
sometimes before ח), nor when it is the third consonant of the stem,
e.g. שָׁכַנְתְּ (cf. however נָתַתָּ for nāthántā) except when another *Nun*
follows, cf. § 44 o; nor in some isolated cases, as Dt 33⁹, Is 29¹, 58³,
all in the principal pause; on הַנְדֹּף and תִּנְדֹּף ψ 68³, see § 51 k, and
§ 66 f.

(b) Less frequently and only in special cases with ל, ת, ד, e.g. יִקַּח d
(for yilqaḥ) *he takes;* מִדַּבֵּר for mithdabbēr; יִטַּמָּא for yithṭammā; תִּכּוֹנֵן
for tithkônēn; תְּכַשָּׂא for tithkannaśā; אַחַת for 'aḥadt; but in 1 S 4¹⁹ for לַת
read probably לָלֶדֶת.

(c) In isolated cases with ה, ו, י, e.g. אָנָּא *prithee !* if from אָנָה נָא; c
ו and י mostly before sibilants in the verbal forms enumerated in § 71.

In all these cases, instead of the assimilated letter, a *Dageš forte* f
appears in the following consonant. *Dageš,* however, is omitted when
the strengthened consonant would stand at the end of a word, since
the strengthening would then be less audible (§ 20 l), e.g. אַף *nose*
(from 'anp), תֵּת *to give* (from tint).

The cases are less frequent where a weak letter is lost in pronunciation,[1]
and in place of it the preceding stronger sound is sharpened, i.e. takes *Dageš,*
e.g. קְטַלְתּוּ from קְטַלְתָּהוּ (§ 59 g). אָסָּלַק for אֶסָּלַק (§ 66 e) is an Aramaism.

3. Complete *rejection* takes place only in the case of weaker con- g
sonants, especially the sonants נ and ל, the gutturals א and ה, and the
two half vowels ו and י. Such rejection takes place,

(a) at the beginning of a word (*aphaeresis*), when these weak con- h
sonants (א, י, ל, נ) are not supported by a full vowel, but have only
Šewâ, e.g. נַחְנוּ *we,* also אֲנַחְנוּ; דַּע for וְדַע; קַח for לְקַח; גַּשׁ for נְגַשׁ,
הִי for נְהִי Ez 2¹⁰.

Aphaeresis of a weak consonant with a full vowel is supposed to occur in רַד i
Ju 19¹¹ for יֵרַד; in תַּתָּה 2 S 22⁴¹ for נָתַתָּה; in שׁוֹב for יָשׁוּב Je 42¹⁰; on קַח
Ez 17⁵ for לְקַח, and on קָחָם Ho 11³ for לְקָחָם, see § 66 g, end. In reality,
however, all these forms are to be regarded merely as old textual errors.

(b) In the middle of a word (*syncope*), when Šewâ precedes the k
weak consonant[2]; thus in the case of א (see further § 23 b–f, and

---

[1] Such a suppression of a letter is sometimes inaccurately called ' backward
assimilation '.
[2] Syncope of a strong consonant (ע) occurs in בִּי *prithee !* if this stands for
בְּעִי (see *Lexicon*), also in וּנְשָׁקָה Am 8⁸, *Kᵉthibh* for וְנִשְׁקְעָה (cf. וְשָׁקְעָה 9⁵), and

§ 68 *b–k*), e.g. in מוֹם for מְאוֹם. As a rule in such cases, however, the א is orthographically retained, e.g. לִקְרַאת for לִקְרַאת. Syncope occurs frequently in the case of ה, e.g. לַמֶּלֶךְ for לְהַמֶּלֶךְ (§ 23 *k* and § 35 *n*), יַקְטִיל for יְהַקְטִיל (§ 53 *a*).

Syncope of א with Šᵉwâ occurs in such cases as בַּאדֹנָי for בַּאדֹנָי (cf. § 102 *m*); וַאעֲשֵׂר Zc 11⁵.¹ On the cases in which א is wholly omitted after the article, see § 35 *d*.

Finally, the elision of ו and י in verbs ל״ה (§ 75 *h*) is an instance of syncope.—On the syncope of ה between two vowels, see § 23 *k*.

l (*c*) At the end of a word (*apocope*), e.g. גִּלֹה pr. name of a city (cf. גִּילֹנִי Gilonite); וַיַּרְא, where א though really rejected is orthographically retained, &c. On the apocope of ו and י in verbs ל״ה, see § 24 *g*, and § 75 *a*.

Bolder changes (especially by violent apocope), took place in earlier periods of the language, notably the weakening of the feminine ending ן__ *âth* to ן__ *â*, see § 44 *a*, and § 80 *f*.

m 4. To avoid harshness in pronunciation a helping sound, Aleph prosthetic² with its vowel, is prefixed to some words, e.g. אֶזְרוֹעַ and זְרוֹעַ *arm* (cf. χθές, ἐχθές; *spiritus*, French *esprit*).—A prosthetic ע occurs probably in עַקְרָב *scorpion*; cf. Arab. *ʿusfûr* bird (stem *safara*).

n 5. *Transposition*³ occurs only seldom in the grammar, e.g. הִשְׁתַּמֵּר for הִתְשַׁמֵּר (§ 54 *b*) for the sake of euphony; it is more frequent in the lexicon (כֶּבֶשׂ and כֶּשֶׂב *lamb*, שִׂמְלָה and שַׂלְמָה *garment*), but is mostly confined to sibilants and sonants.

o 6. *Softening* occurs e.g. in כּוֹכָב *star*, from *kaukabh=kawkabh* for *kabhkabh* (cf. Syriac *raurab = rabrab*); טוֹטָפוֹת *phylacteries* for *taphtâphôth*; according to the common opinion, also in אִישׁ *man* from *ʾinš*, cf. however § 96.

§ 20. *The Strengthening (Sharpening) of Consonants.*

a 1. The strengthening of a consonant, indicated by *Dageš forte*, is necessary and essential (*Dageš necessarium*)

(*a*) when the same consonant would be written twice in succession

---

in בָּלָה Jos 19³ for בַּעֲלָה (as in 15²⁹). Probably, however, ונשקה and בלה are only clerical errors, as is undoubtedly בָּאר Am 8⁸ for בְּיָאר (9⁵).

¹ Frensdorff, *Ochla W'ochla*, p. 97 f., gives a list of forty-eight words with quiescent א.

² This awkward term is at any rate as suitable as the name *Alef protheticum* proposed by Nestle, *Marginalien u. Materialien*, Tübingen, 1893, p. 67 ff.

³ Cf. Barth, *Etymologische Studien*, Lpz. 1893, p. 1 ff.; Königsberger, in *Zeitschrift f. wissenschaftliche Theologie*, 1894, p. 451 ff.

without an intermediate vowel or *Šᵉwâ mobile*; thus we have נָתַנּוּ for נָתַנְנוּ *nāthăn-nû* and שַׁתִּי for שַׁתְתִּי.

(*b*) in cases of assimilation (§ 19 *b–f*), e. g. יִתֵּן for *yintēn*.

In both these cases the *Dageš* is called *compensativum*.

(*c*) When it is characteristic of a grammatical form, e. g. לָמַד *he has learned*, לִמַּד *he has taught* (*Dageš characteristicum*). In a wider sense this includes the cases in which a consonant is sharpened by Dageš forte, to preserve a preceding short vowel (which in an open syllable would have to be lengthened by § 26 *e*), e. g. גְּמַלִּים *camels* for *gᵉmālîm*; cf. § 93 *ee* and *kk*, § 93 *pp*.

This coalescing of two consonants as indicated above does not take place *b* when the first has a vowel or *Šᵉwâ mobile*. In the latter case, according to the correct Masora, a *compound Šᵉwâ* should be used, preceded by *Méthĕg*, e. g. הַגֲלָלִים, קִלֲלַת, &c. (cf. §§ 10 *g*, 16 *f*). This pointing is not used before the suffix ךָ, e. g. תְּבָרֶכְךָ Gn 27⁴, but the first כ has a *vocal Šᵉwâ*, otherwise the second כ would have *Dageš lene*. Also when the former of the two consonants has been already strengthened by *Dageš forte*, it can only have a *vocal Šᵉwâ*, and any further contraction is therefore impossible. This applies also to cases where *Dageš forte* has been omitted (see below, *m*), e. g. הַלֲלוּ properly = הַלְלוּ *hal-lᵉlû*. The form חָנֵּנִי ψ 9¹⁴ (not חָנְנֵנִי) might be explained as imperat. Pi‘ēl = חַנְּנֵנִי; if it were imperat. *Qal* the non-contraction of the monosyllabic root would be as strange as it is in שָׁדְדוּ Jer 49²⁸, and in the imperf. יִשְׁדְּדֵם Jer 5⁶.

2. A consonant is sometimes strengthened merely for the sake of *c* euphony (*Dageš euphonicum*), and the strengthening is then not so essential. This occurs[1]—

(*a*) when two words are closely united in pronunciation by *Dageš forte conjunctivum*: (1) in the first letter of a monosyllable or of a word having the tone (or occasionally the counter-tone) on the first syllable,[2] when closely connected with the preceding word, if that word ends in a tone-bearing *Qameṣ* (ה‍ָ) with *Šᵉwâ mobile* preceding, or a tone-bearing ה‍ָ,—called דְּחִיק (i. e. *compressed*) by the Jewish grammarians.

The term monosyllable here and in *f* (by § 28 *e*) includes Segholates like בֶּסֶף, שַׁחַד, &c., as well as forms like פְּרִי, שְׁאָל, שְׁמוֹ, and even כְּנַעַן.

----

[1] Cf. Baer, ' De primarum vocabulorum literarum dagessatione,' in his *Liber Proverbiorum*, Lpz. 1880, pp. vii–xv ; F. Prätorius, ' Über den Ursprung des Dag. f. conjunctivum,' in *ZAW*. 1883, p. 17 ff. (ascribed to an original assimilation of ת or נ).

[2] לֶאֱמֹר alone, although having the tone on the ultima, invariably takes the *Dageš forte conj.* when מֹשֶׁה with a conjunctive accent precedes, Ex 6¹⁰·²⁹, 15²⁴, &c.

Some limit the use of the *Dᵉḥiq* to the closest connexion of a monosyllable with a following *Bᵉgadkᵉphath*. However, it also applies to cases like לְכָה־נָּא Nu 22⁶; לְקַחַת־זֹאת Gn 2²³; יַצֶּה־לָּךְ ψ 91¹¹; and even with *Rᵉḇâ*, מַעֲנֵה־רַךְ Pr 15¹; וּמִשְׁנֶה־כָּסֶף Gn 43¹⁵. In all these examples the tone, were it not for the Maqqēph, would be on the ultima of the first word.

d   Rem. 1. When זֶה *this* has *Maqqēph* after it, a *Dageš forte conj.* always follows, even if the next word is neither a monosyllable nor has the tone on the initial syllable; thus not only in וְזֶה־שְּׁמוֹ Jer 23⁶, but also in וְזֶה־פְּרִיָּהּ Nu 13²⁷, 1 Ch 22¹. In הִנֶּה־נָא Gn 19² (where Maqqēph is represented by a conjunctive accent, § 9 *u*, 1 *c*, and § 16 *b*), the Sᵉḡôl coincides with the secondary tone-syllable. On the origin of *Dag. f. conj.* after מַה־ (for מָה) *what?*, see § 37 *b, c.*

e   2. Such cases as גָּאֹה גָּאָה Ex 15¹·²¹, the 2nd כָּמֹכָה in ver. 11, גָּאַלְתָּ ver. 13, כָּאָבֶן ver. 16, ·do not belong here. In these the *Dageš* can only be intended for *Dag. lene*, see § 21 *d.*

f   (2) In the first letter of a monosyllable, or of a word with the tone on the first syllable after a closely connected *mil'êl* ending in ◌ָה— or ◌ֶה—. Such a mil'êl is called by the Jewish grammarians אָתֵי מֵרָחִיק (Aram. = Heb. אֹתֶה מֵרָחוֹק) *veniens e longinquo* (in respect of the tone). The attraction of the following tone-syllable by *Dageš forte conj.* is here also due to the exigencies of rhythm, e. g. שָׁבִיתָ שֶּׁבִי ψ 68¹⁹; הוֹשִׁיעָה נָּא ψ 118²⁵ (so ed. Mant., but Ginsburg and Kittel נָא); הִרְחִיבָה שְּׁאוֹל Is 5¹⁴; אַרְצָה כְּנַעַן Gn 11³¹. The Mil'êl may, however, also be due to a subsequent retraction of the tone (*nāsôg 'aḥôr*, § 29 *e*), as in עֹשֶׂה פֶּרִי Gn 1¹¹.—The prefixes בְ, כְ, לְ, and וְ alone do not take a Dageš in this case, except in לְךָ, always, and לְלַיְלָה ψ 19³. Such forms as הִשָּׁבְעָה לִּי Gn 21²³, מָלְאָה שָּׁחַד ψ 26¹⁰, רָחֲקָה מֶּנִּי Jb 21¹⁶, and even נֶעֶמְדָה יָּחַד Is 50⁸ (i. e. the cases where the tone is thrown back from the ultima on to the syllable which otherwise would have *Metheg*), are likewise regarded as *mil'êl*. On the other hand, e. g. חָרָה לָךְ Gn 4⁶, not לָּךְ since the first *ā* of חָרָה could not have *Metheg*. When words are closely united by *Maqqēph* the same rules apply as above, except that in the first word *Metheg*, in the secondary tone, takes the place of the accent, cf. עֹשֵׂה־פְּרִי Gn 1¹²; הַגִּידָה־נָּא Gn 32³⁰, &c. Finally, the *Dageš* is used when the attracted word does not begin with the principal tone, but with a syllable having *Metheg*, הֵּמָּה יִירְשׁוּ ψ 37⁹; אֵלֶּה יַּעֲקֹב Is 44²¹; עָשִׂיתָ קְּעֶרְתָיו Ex 25²⁹, provided that the second word does not begin with a *Bᵉgadkᵉphath* letter (hence e. g. אֵלֶּה תְוֹלְדוֹת Gn 2⁴).

g   Rem. Such cases as קָנֶּךָ Dt 32⁶, and כָּשִּׁיתָ 32¹⁵, and בָּעוֹת (so Baer, but not ed. Mant., &c.) 1 S 1¹³ are therefore anomalous; also, because beginning with a Beḡaḏkephaṯ, בָּאֵלָם Ex 15[11] (cf. however above, *e*); תֵּל־ Jos 8[28]; בְּזֹרֽוֹעַ ψ 77[16]; בֶּן־הִיא Jb 5[27].—It is doubtful whether we should include here those cases in which *Dageš forte* occurs after a word ending in a toneless *û*, such as קוּמוּ צְאוּ Gn 19[14], Ex 12[31]; Ex 12[15] (שְׂאָר), Dt 2[24]; also לֹא Gn 19[2], 1 S 8[19]; לוֹ Ju 18[19], Est 6[13] (where P. Haupt regards the *Dageš* as due to the enclitic character of the לוֹ); מְעַט Ho 8[10]; נֵדֽוּ Jer 49[30]; רְדֽוּ 1 S 15[6]. When we explained the *Dageš* in these examples not as conjunctive, but orthophonic (see above, § 13 *c*, and Delitzsch, *Psalmen*, 4th ed. on ψ 94[12 *a*]), we especially had in view those cases in which the consonant with *Dageš* has a *Šewâ*. The extension of the use of *Dageš* to consonants with a strong vowel, seems, however, to indicate that these are cases of the אָתֵי מֵרַחִיק, which was required by some Masoretes but not consistently inserted. On the other hand, the *Dageš forte* in י after a preceding *î* (ψ 118[5.18]), and even after *û* (ψ 94[12]), is due to an attempt to preserve its consonantal power; see König, *Lehrgeb.*, p. 54 *b*.

(*b*) When a consonant with *Šewâ* is strengthened by *Dageš forte* ʰ *dirĭmens* to make the *Šewâ* more audible. In almost all cases the strengthening or sharpening can be easily explained from the character of the particular consonant, which is almost always a sonant, sibilant, or the emphatic *Qôph*; cf. עִנְּבֵי Lv 25[5], Dt 32[32] (for עִנְבֵי); כַּנְּתְךָ Is 33[1] (where, however, כְּכַלּוֹתְךָ is to be read); cf. Na 3[17], Jb 9[18], 17[2], Jo 1[17] (with מ); Is 57[6] (with ל); Ju 20[43,][1] 1 S 1[6] (with ר); Gn 49[10.17] (and so always in עִקְּבֵי Ju 5[22], Ct 1[8] and עִקְּבוֹת ψ 77[20], 89[52]); Ex 15[17], Dt 23[11], Ju 20[32], 1 S 28[10] (ק)[2]; Ex 2[3], Is 58[3], Am 5[21], ψ 141[3], Pr 4[13] (צ); Pr 27[25] (שׂ); Is 5[28], ψ 37[15], Jer 51[56], Neh 4[7] (שׁ). Also, with כ Ho 3[2]; with ב Is 9[3], Jer 4[7]; with ת 1 S 10[11]. In many instances of this kind the influence of the following consonant is also observable.

(*c*) When a vowel is to be made specially emphatic, generally in *î* the principal *pause*, by a *Dageš forte affectuosum* in the following consonant. Thus in a following sonant, Ju 5[7] (חָדְֿלֽוּ), Jb 29[21] (וְיִחֵלּֽוּ), 22[12] (רְמֽוּ); Ez 27[19] (in נ); in ת Is 33[12], 41[17], Jer 51[58], perhaps also Jb 21[13] (יֵחַתּֽוּ).

(*d*) When the sonants ל, מ, נ are strengthened by *Dageš forte firma-* ᵏ *tivum* in the pronouns הֵמָּה, הֵנָּה, אֵלֶּה, and in לָמָּה *why?* cf. also בַּמֶּה, בַּמָּה *whereby?* בַּמָּה *how much?* (§ 102 *k, l*), to give greater firmness to the preceding tone-vowel.

3. Omission of the strengthening, or at least the loss of the *Dageš* ˡ *forte* occurs,

(*a*) *almost always* at the end of a word, since here a strengthened

---

[1] The ordinary reading הֻרְדִּיפֹהוּ, where ר is without *Dageš*, is only intelligible if the ר has *Dageš*.

[2] Also in ψ 45[10] read בִּיקְּרוֹתֶיךָ with Baer and Ginsburg, following Ben Asher, and in Pr 30[17] לִיקֲּהַת (Ben Naphthali בִּיקְּ and לִיקְּ).

consonant cannot easily be sounded.[1] In such cases the preceding vowel is frequently lengthened (§ 27 *d*), e. g. רֹב *multitude,* from רבב; עָם *people,* with a distinctive accent or after the article, עָם, from עמם; but e. g. גַּן *garden,* בַּת *daughter,* with the final consonant virtually sharpened. On the exceptions אַתְּ *thou* (fem.) and נָתַתְּ *thou* (fem.) *hast given* Ez 16³³, see § 10 *k*.

m   (*b*) Very frequently in certain consonants with *Šᵉwâ mobile,* since the absence of a strong vowel causes the strengthening to be less noticeable. This occurs principally in the case of ו and י (on יְ and יְ after the article, see § 35 *b*; on יְ after מַה־, § 37 *b*); and in the sonants מ,[2] נ and ל; also in the sibilants, especially when a guttural follows (but note Is 62⁹, מְאַסְפָיו, as ed. Mant. and Ginsb. correctly read, while Baer has מְאַסְּ' with compensatory lengthening, and others even מְאַסְּ'; מְשַׁמֵּי Gn 27²⁸·³⁹; מְשָׁלֵשׁ 38²⁴ for מְשֻׁ', מְשָׁ', הַשְּׁלָבִּים 1 K 7²⁸; מִשְׁתֵּים, אֶשְׁקָה־ 1 K 19²⁰ from נָשַׁק, הַשְּׂפַתַּיִם Ez 40⁴³ and לַשְּׁפַנִּים ψ 104¹⁸; הַצְפַרְדְּעִים Jon 4¹¹, Ex 8¹ &c.);—and finally in the emphatic ק.[3]

Of the *Bᵉgadkᵉphath* letters, ב occurs without *Dageš* in מִבְצִיר Ju 8²; נ in מִגְבֹּרֹתָם Ez 32³⁰; ד in נִדְחֵי Is 11¹² 56⁸, ψ 147² (*not* in Jer 49⁵⁶), supposing that it is the Participle Niph'al of נָדַח; lastly, ת in תִּרְצוּ Is 22¹⁰. Examples, עֹרִים, וַיְהִי (so always the preformative יְ in the *imperf.* of verbs), יִקְחוּ, יִשְׂאוּ, כְּסָאִי, מִלְאוּ, הֵלְלוּ, הִנְנִי, לַמְנַצֵּחַ, מִלְמַעְלָה, מְקָצֶה, מַקְלוֹת, &c. In correct MSS. the omission of the *Dageš* is indicated by the *Rāphè* stroke (§ 14) over the consonant. However, in these cases, we must assume at least a *virtual* strengthening of the consonant (*Dageš forte implicitum,* see § 22 *c*, end).

(*c*) In the Gutturals, see § 22 *b*.

n   Rem. 1. Contrary to rule the strengthening is omitted (especially in the later Books), owing to the lengthening of the preceding short vowel, generally *ḥireq* (cf. *mîle* for *mille*), e. g. יְחִתַּן *he makes them afraid,* for יְחַתֵּן Hb 2¹⁷ (where, however, it is perhaps more correct to suppose, with König, a formation on the analogy of verbs ע״וּ, and moreover to read יְחִיתָךְ with the LXX), זִיקוֹת Is 50¹¹ for זִקּוֹת.

o   2. Very doubtful are the instances in which compensation for the strengthening is supposed to be made by the insertion of a following נ. Thus for

---

[1] So in Latin *fel* (for *fell*), gen. *fellis; mel, mellis; os, ossis*. In Middle High German the doubling of consonants never takes place at the end of a word, but only in the middle (as in Old High German), e g. *val* (*Fall*), gen. *valles; swam* (*Schwamm*, &c., Grimm, *Deutsche Gramm.,* 2nd ed., i. 383.

[2] *Dageš forte* is almost always omitted in מ when it is the prefix of the participle Pi'el or Pu'al, hence ψ 104³ הַמְקָרֶה *who layeth the beams,* but הַמְּקָרֶה *the roof* Ec 10¹⁸ (cf. הַמְּלָאכָה *the work,* &c.).

[3] According to some also in ט in תִּמְטָעִי Is 17¹⁰; but see Baer on the passage.

מְעֻנֶּיהָ Is 23¹¹, read מְעֹנֶיהָ (or מְעֻנֶיהָ); and for חָֽמְנוּ La 3²², read תַּמּוּ. In Nu 23¹³ קָבְנוֹ is not an instance of compensation (see § 67 o, end).

§ 21. *The Aspiration of the Tenues.*[1]

The *harder* sound of the six *B⁰gadk⁰phath* letters, indicated by a *Dageš lene*, is to be regarded, according to the general analogy of languages, as their older and original pronunciation, from which the softer sound was weakened (§ 6 n and § 13). The original hard sound is maintained when the letter is initial, and after a consonant, but when it immediately follows a vowel or *Šⁱwā mobile* it is softened and aspirated by their influence, e. g. פָּרַץ *pāraṣ*, יִפְרֹץ *yiphrōṣ*, כֹּל *kōl*, לְכֹל *l⁰khōl*. Hence the *B⁰gadk⁰phath* take *Dageš lene*

(1) at the beginning of words : (a) without exception when the b preceding word ends with a vowelless consonant, e. g. עַל־כֵּן *'al-kēn* (*therefore*), עֵץ פְּרִי *'ēṣ p⁰rî* (*fruit-tree*); (b) at the beginning of a section, e. g. בְּרֵאשִׁית Gn 1¹, or at the beginning of a sentence, or even of a minor division of a sentence after a distinctive accent (§ 15 d), although the preceding word may end with a vowel. The distinctive accent in such a case prevents the vowel from influencing the following tenuis, e. g. וַיְהִי כַאֲשֶׁר *and it was so, that when*, Ju 11⁵ (but וַיְהִי כֵן Gn 1⁷).

Rem. 1. The vowel letters ה, י, ו, א, as such, naturally do not close a c syllable. In close connexion they are therefore followed by the aspirated *B⁰gadk⁰phath*, e. g. וּמָצָא בָהּ, &c. On the other hand, syllables are closed by the consonantal ו and י (except קַרֹֽתְהוּ Is 34¹¹; שָׁלַו בָּהּ Ez 23⁴²; ψ 68¹⁸), and by ה with *Mappiq* ; hence e. g. there is *Dageš lene* in עָלֶ פִּיהֶם and always after יְהֹוָה, since the *Q⁰rê perpetuum* of this word (§ 17) assumes the reading אֲדֹנָי.

2. In a number of cases *Dageš lene* is inserted, although a vowel precedes in d close connexion. This almost always occurs with the prefixes בְּ and כְּ in the combinations בְּ כְּ, כְּ כְ, בְּ כ (i. e. when a *B⁰gadk⁰phath* with Šⁱwā precedes the same or a kindred aspirate) and בְּמ (see Baer, *L. Psalmorum*, 1880, p. 92,[2] on ψ 23³); cf. e. g. 1 S 25¹, Is 10⁹, ψ 34², Jb 19²; כְּנ is uncertain ; כְּד ,בְּד, and בְכ according to David Qimḥi do not take Dageš, nor כְּנ ,כְּב, and כְּמ accord- ing to the *Dikduke ha-ṭ⁰amim*, p. 30. Sometimes the *B⁰gadk⁰phath* letters, even with a full vowel, take *Dageš* before a spirant (and even before ה in בַּחֲמִשָׁה 1 K 12³²) ; cf. the instances mentioned above, § 20 e (mostly *tenues* before א). In all these cases the object is to prevent too great an accumulation of aspirates. The LXX, on the other hand, almost always represent the כ and

---

[1] Cf. Delitzsch, *Ztschr. f. luth. Theol. u. Kirche*, 1878, p. 585 ff.
[2] Also *L. Proverbiorum*, 1880, Praef. p. ix ; and *Dikduke ha-ṭ⁰amim*, p. 30 (in German in König's *Lehrgeb.*, i. p. 62).

פ, even at the beginning of a syllable, by χ and φ ; Χερούβ, Χαλδαῖοι, Φαρφάρ, &c.—The forms בְּרְכֹּד (after וְשַׂמְתִּי) Is 54¹², and בַּלְכֵל (after וְנִלְאֵיתִי) Jer 20⁹ are doubly anomalous.

e   (2) In the middle of words after *Šᵉwâ quiescens*, i.e. at the beginning of a syllable immediately after a vowelless consonant,[1] e.g. יִרְפָּא *yirpā* (*he heals*), קְטַלְתֶּם *ye have killed* ; but after *Šᵉwâ mobile*, e. g. רְפָא *rᵉphā* (*heal thou*), בָּבְדָה *she was heavy*.

f   On וַיִּשְׁבְּ, קָטְלַתְ and similar forms, see § 10 *i*.

Whether *Šᵉwâ* be vocal and consequently causes the aspiration of a following *tenuis*, depends upon the origin of the particular form. It is almost always vocal

(*a*) When it has arisen from the weakening of a strong vowel, e.g. רְדְפוּ *pursue ye* (not רְדְפוּ) from רְדֹף ; מַלְכֵי (not מַלְכֵי), because originally *mǎlǎkhê*, but מַלְכִּי from the ground-form *malk*.

(*b*) With the כ of the pronominal suffixes of the 2nd pers. ךְ—, כֶם—, כֶן—, since Šᵉwâ mobile is characteristic of these forms (see § 58 *f* ; § 91 *b*).

Rem. Forms like שָׁלַחַתְּ *thou* (fem.) *hast sent*, in which we should expect an aspirated ת after the vowel, cf. וַתַּחַתְ Ex 18⁹, have arisen from יָחַדְ, שָׁלַחְתְּ, &c. ; Pathaḥ being here simply a helping vowel has no influence on the tenuis ; cf. § 28 *e*.

§ 22. *Peculiarities of the Gutturals.*

a   The four gutturals ח, ה, ע, א, in consequence of their peculiar pronunciation, have special characteristics, but א, as the weakest of these sounds, and sometimes also ע (which elsewhere as one of the harder gutturals is the opposite of א), differ in several respects from the stronger ה and ח.

b   1. They do not admit of *Dageš forte*, since, in consequence of a gradual weakening of the pronunciation (see below, note 2), the strengthening of the gutturals was hardly audible to the Masoretes. But a distinction must be drawn between (*a*) the complete omission of the strengthening, and (*b*) the mere *echo* of it, commonly called *half* doubling, but better, *virtual* strengthening.

c   In the former case, the short vowel before the guttural would stand in an open syllable, and must accordingly be lengthened or modified.[2]

---

[1] The exceptions יִקְתְאֵל Jos 15³⁸ (see *Minḥat shay*, on this passage), 2 K 14⁷, and יׇקְדְעָם Jos 15⁵⁶ may perhaps be due to the character of the ק.

[2] Cf. *terra* and the French *terre*, the German *Rolle* and the French *rôle* ; German *drollig* and French *drôle*. The omission of the strengthening shows a deterioration of the language. Arabic still admits of the strengthening of gutturals in all cases.

For a distinction must again be drawn between the full lengthening of
Pathaḥ into *Qameṣ*—mostly before א (*always* under the ה of the
article, see § 35), as a rule also before ע, less frequently before ה, and
least often before ח—and the modification of *Pathaḥ* to *Sᵉghôl*,
mostly before a guttural with *Qameṣ*. In the other case (*virtual*
strengthening) the *Dageš* is still omitted, but the strengthening is
nevertheless regarded as having taken place, and the preceding vowel
therefore remains short. This *virtual* strengthening occurs most
frequently with ח, usually with ה, less frequently with ע, and very
seldom with א. Examples of (*a*) מֵאֵן, הָאָדָם, הָעָם, הָהָר, הָחֵבָא (for
yiḥḥābhē') ; also אָחָד, הֶחָג, הֶהָרִים, הֶעָנִי (see more fully on the pointing
of the article before ע in § 35).—Of (*b*) הַחֹדֶשׁ, מָחוֹט (from *minḥûṭ*),
הַהוּא, בְּעֵר, נִאֵץ, &c.—In all these cases of virtual strengthening the
Dageš forte is to be regarded at least as implied (hence called *Dageš
forte implicitum*, *occultum*, or *delitescens*).

2. They prefer before them, and sometimes after them (cf. *h*), *d*
a short A-sound, because this vowel is organically the nearest akin
to the gutturals. Hence

(*a*) before a guttural, *Pathaḥ* readily (and always before ה, ח, ע
closing a syllable) takes the place of another short vowel or of
a rhythmically long *ē* or *ō*, e.g. זֶבַח *sacrifice*, not *zebĕḥ*; שֵׁמַע *report*,
not *šēmĕ'*. This is more especially so when *a* was the original vowel
of the form, or is otherwise admissible. Thus in the Imperat. and
Imperf. Qal of guttural verbs שְׁלַח *send thou*, יִשְׁלַח *he will send* (not
yišlōḥ) ; Perf. Pi'el שִׁלַּח (but in Pausa שִׁלֵּחַ) ; יַחְמֹד *he will desire* (not
yiḥmōd); וַיָּנַח *and he rested* (not *wayyānŏḥ*); נַעַר *a youth*. In שְׁלַח
and יַחְמֹד *ă* is the original vowel.

Rem. In such cases as דְּשֵׁא, מָנָא, פֶּלֶא, פֶּרֶא, the א has no consonantal *e*
value, and is only retained orthographically (see § 23 *a*).

(*b*) After a heterogeneous long vowel, i.e. after all except *Qameṣ*, *f*
the hard gutturals[1] (consequently not א), when standing at the end
of the word, require the insertion of a rapidly uttered *ă* (*Pathaḥ
furtivum*) between themselves and the vowel. This *Pathaḥ* is placed
under the guttural, but sounded *before* it. It is thus merely an
orthographic indication not to neglect the guttural sound in pronunciation, e.g. רוּחַ *rûᵃḥ*, נוֹעַ, רֵעַ, הִשְׁלִיחַ, גָּבֹהַּ (when consonantal ה is

---

[1] Prätorius, *Ueber den rückweich. Accent im Hebr.*, Halle, 1897, p. 17, &c.,
remarks that Pathaḥ furtivum has not arisen merely under the influence of
the guttural, but is due to a duplication of the accented syllable, so that e.g.
יָצוּד, יָשִׁיב would also be pronounced *yasi'bh*, *yaṣû"dh* although the short
intermediate vowel was not so noticeable as before a guttural.

final it necessarily takes Mappîq), but e. g. רוּחִי, &c., since here the rapidly uttered *ă* is no longer heard.

g　I*ᵃch* for *ich*, &c., in some Swiss dialects of German, is analogous ; a *furtive Pathah* is here involuntarily intruded before the deep guttural sound. In Arabic the same may be heard in such words as *mesîah*, although it is not expressed in writing. The LXX (and Jerome, cf. *ZAW.* iv. 79) write ε, sometimes α, instead of *furtive Pathah*, e. g. נֹחַ Νῶε, יַדּוּעַ 'Ιεδδούα (also 'Ιαδδού).

h　Rem. 1. The guttural may also have an influence upon the *following* vowel, especially in Segholate forms, e. g. נַעַר (not *na'ĕr*) *a youth*, פֹּעַל (not *po'ĕl*) *deed*. The only exceptions are אֹהֶל, בֹּהֶן, לֶחֶם, רֶחֶם.

i　2. Where in the present form of the language an *ĭ*, whether original or attenuated from *Pathah*, would stand before or after a guttural in the first syllable of a word, a *Sᵉghôl* as being between *ă* and *ĭ* is frequently used instead, e. g. עֶזְרִי, נֶאְדָּר, חֶבְלֵי, יֶהְגּוּ (יֶחְבַּשׁ), יֶחֱבַשׁ (also יֶחֱבַשׁ), &c.

k　On the other hand, the slighter and sharper *Hireq* is retained even under gutturals when the following consonant is sharpened by *Dageš forte*, e. g. חִטָּה, הִנֵּה, הִלֵּל ; but when this sharpening is removed, Sᵉghôl is again apt to appear, e.g. הַנִּיֹן constr. הֶנְיֹת, חִזָּיֹן constr. חֶזְיֹן.

l　3. Instead of *simple Šᵉwâ mobile*, the gutturals take without exception a *compound Šᵉwâ*, e. g. אֲנִי, אֱמֹר, אֲקַטֵּל, שְׁחָטוּ, &c.

m　4. When a guttural with quiescent *Šᵉwâ* happens to close a syllable in the middle of a word, the strongly closed syllable (with quiescent *Šᵉwâ*) may remain ; necessarily so with ח, ע, and ה at the end of the tone-syllable, e. g. שָׁלַחְתָּ, יָדַעְתָּ, but also *before* the tone (see examples under *i*), even with א.

But in the syllable before the tone and further back, the closed syllable is generally opened artificially by a *Hateph* (as being suited to the guttural) taking the place of the quiescent *Šᵉwâ*, and in particular that *Hateph* which repeats the sound of the preceding vowel, e. g. יַחֲשֹׁב (also יַחְשֹׁב) ; יֶחֱזַק (also יֶחְזַק) ; פָּעֳלוֹ *pŏʿŏlô* (for *pŏʿlô*). But when, owing to a flexional change, the strong vowel following the *Hateph* is weakened into *Šᵉwâ mobile*, then instead of the *Hateph* its full vowel is written, e. g. יַעַמְדוּ (from יַעֲמֹד), נֶעֶרְמוּ, פָּעֳלֶךָ (from פֹּעַל). The original forms, according to § 28 *c*, were *yaʿamᵉdhû, neʿĕrmû, pŏʿlᵉkhā*. Hence יַעַמְדוּ, &c., are really only different orthographic forms of יַעֲמְדוּ, &c., and would be better transcribed by *yaʿᵃmᵉdhû*, &c.

n　Rem. 1. On the use of simple or compound Šᵉwâ in guttural verbs, see further §§ 62–65.

o　2. Respecting the choice between the three *Hatephs*, it may be remarked : (*a*) ח, ה, ע at the beginning of a syllable prefer ﹷ, but א prefers ﹼ, e. g. חֲמוֹר ass, הֲרֹג *to kill*, אֱמֹר *to say* ; when farther from the tone syllable, however, the ﹷ even under א changes into the lighter ﹼ, e. g. אֱלַי (poetic for אֶל־) *to*, but אֲלֵיכֶם *to you*, אֱכֹל *to eat*, but אֲכָל־ (*ᵃkhŏl*, toneless on account

of Maqqêph). Cf. § 27 *w*. The 1st pers. sing. imperf. Pi'ēl regularly has ◌ֵ.
Likewise ◌ֱ is naturally found under א in cases where the *Ḥateph* arises
from a weakening of an original *ă* (e. g. אֲרִי *lion*, ground-form *'ary*), and ◌ֳ
if there be a weakening of an original *u* (e. g. אֳנִי *a fleet*, עֳנִי *affliction*, cf.
§ 93 *q*, *z*).

(*b*) In the middle of a word after a long vowel, a *Ḥateph-Pathaḥ* takes the *p*
place of a *simple Šᵉwâ mobile*, e. g. הֶעֱלָה מֵאֲנָה (see § 63 *p*) ; but if a short
vowel precedes, the choice of the *Ḥaṭeph* is generally regulated by it, e. g.
Perf. Hiph. הֶעֱמִיד (see above, *i*), *Infin.* הַעֲמִיד (regular form הַקְטִיל) ; *Perf.*
Hoph. הָעֳמַד (regular form הָקְטַל) ; but cf. שְׁחַדוּ Jb 6²² (§ 64 *a*).

5. The ר, which in sound approximates to the gutturals (§ 6 *g*), *q*
shares with the gutturals proper their first, and to a certain extent
their second, peculiarity, viz.

(*a*) The exclusion of the strengthening, instead of which the preceding vowel is almost always lengthened, e. g. בֵּרַךְ *he has blessed* for
birrakh, בָּרֵךְ *to bless* for *barrēkh*.

(*b*) The preference for *ă* as a preceding vowel, e. g. וַיַּרְא *and he saw* *r*
(from יִרְאֶה) ; וַיָּסַר both for וַיִּסָר *and he turned back*, and for וַיָּסַר *and*
he caused to turn back.

The exceptions to *a* are מָרַת *mŏrrăth*, Pr 14¹⁰ ; כָּרַת *khŏrrăth* and שֹׁרֶךְ *šŏrrēkh*, *S*
Ez 16⁴ (cf. Pr 3⁸) ; שֵׁרָאשִׁי Ct 5² ; הִרְעָמָהּ 1 S 1⁶ ; הִרְאִיתָם 1 S 10²⁴, 17²⁵,
2 K 6³² ; הִרְדִּיפֻהוּ Ju 20⁴³ (cf. § 20 *h*) ; מִרְדָּף 1 S 23²⁸, 2 S 18¹⁶ ; also on account
of דחיק (§ 20 *c*), Pr 15¹, 20²², 2 Ch 26¹⁰ ; and on account of אתי מרחיק
(§ 20 *f*) 1 S 15⁶, Jer 39¹², Hb 3¹³, Pr 11²¹, Jb 39⁹, Ez 9⁶. A kind of virtual
strengthening (after מ for מִן) is found in מֵרָחֹק Is 14³. In Samaritan and
Arabic this strengthening has been retained throughout, and the LXX write
e. g. Σάρρα for שָׂרָה.

§ 23. *The Feebleness of the Gutturals* א *and* ה.

1. The א, a light and scarcely audible guttural breathing, as a rule *a*
entirely loses its slight consonantal power whenever it stands without
a vowel at the end of a syllable. It then remains (like the German
h in *roh, geh, nahte*) merely as a sign of the preceding long vowel, e. g.
הוֹצִיא, מָלֵא, מָצָא (but when a syllable is added with an introductory
vowel, according to *b* below, we have, e. g. מְצָאֵנִי, הוֹצִיאֵנִי, since the א
then stands at the beginning of the syllable, not מְצָאֵנִי, הוֹצִיאֵנִי), מָצָא,
כָּלוּא (cf., however, § 74 *a*), מָצְאָת (for *māṣa'tā*), תִּמְצֶאןָה. Similarly
in cases like חָטָא, וַיֵּרְא, שָׁוְא, &c. (§ 19 *l*), and even in דֶּשֶׁא, פֶּלֶא (see
above, § 22 *e*), the א only retains an orthographic significance.

2. On the other hand, א is in general retained as a strong con- *b*
sonant whenever it begins a syllable, e. g. אָמַר ; מָאֲסוּ, or when it is
protected by a *Ḥateph* after a short syllable, e. g. לֶאֱכֹל, and finally,

when it stands in a closed syllable with quiescent *Šᵉwâ* after a preceding *Sᵉghôl* or *Pathaḥ*, e.g. נֶאְדָּר, וַיֶּאְסֹר, *nä'dār*, יַאְדִּימוּ *ya'dimû*. Even in such cases the consonantal power of א may be entirely lost, viz.

c   (*a*) when it would stand with a long vowel in the middle of a word after *Šᵉwâ mobile*. The long vowel is then occasionally thrown back into the place of the *Šᵉwâ*, and the א is only retained orthographically, as an indication of the etymology, e.g. רָאשִׁים *heads* (for *rᵉ'āšîm*), מָאתַיִם *two hundred* (for *mᵉ'ātháyim*), שָׁאטְךָ Ez 25⁶ for שְׁאטְךָ; פֹּארֶךָ for פֶּארֶךָ Is 10³³; בֹּורְאָם Neh 6⁸ for בְּורְאָם; מֹאוּם Jb 31⁷, Dn 1⁴ for מְאוּם; הֹטְאִים *ḥôṭîm*, 1 S 14³³ for הַטְאִים (cf. § 74 *h*, and § 75 *oo*); הָראוּבֵנִי Nu 34¹⁴, from רְאוּבֵן; so always חַטֹּאות or חַטֹּאת 1 K 14¹⁶, Mi 1⁵, &c., for חַטָּאות. Sometimes a still more violent suppression of the א occurs at the beginning of a syllable, which then causes a further change in the preceding syllable, e.g. מְלָאכָה *work* for מַלְאָכָה (as in the Babylonian punctuation), יִשְׁמָעֵאל for יִשְׁמָעֵאל; שְׂמֹאל or שְׂמֹאול *the left hand*, ground form *sim'âl*.

d   (*b*) When it originally closed a syllable. In these cases א is generally (by § 22 *m*) pronounced with a *Ḥaṭeph*, ⸗ or ⸗. The preceding short vowel is, however, sometimes lengthened and retains the following א only orthographically, e.g. וַיָּאצֶל Nu 11²⁵ for וַיַּאְצֶל (cf. Ju 9⁴¹), and פָּארוּר Jo 2⁶ for פַּארוּר; לֵאמֹר for לֶאְמֹר; לֵאלֹהִים for לֶאֱלֹהִים; but the contraction does not take place in לֶאֱלָלְיָה Is 10¹¹. The short vowel is retained, although the consonantal power of א is entirely lost, in וַארְדִּי, &c. (see § 102 *m*), וַיַּאת Is 41²⁵, וְאָבֶדְךָ Ez 28¹⁶ for וְאַאְבֶּדְךָ; cf. Dt 24¹⁰, 1 K 11³⁹, Is 10¹³.

e   Instead of this א which has lost its consonantal value, one of the vowel letters ו and י is often written according to the nature of the sound, the former with *ô* and the latter with *ê* and *î*, e.g. רֵים *buffalo* for רְאֵם. At the end of the word ה also is written for א, e.g. יִמְלֶה *he fills* for יִמְלָא Jb 8²¹ (see below, *l*).

f   3. When א is only preserved orthographically or as an indication of the etymology (quiescent), it is sometimes entirely dropped (cf. § 19 *k*), e.g. יָצָתִי Jb 1²¹ for יָצָאתִי; מָלֵתִי Jb 32¹⁸ for מָלֵאתִי; מָצָתִי Nu 11¹¹; וַתֵּהֶז 2 S 20⁹; וַיְרֻפּוּ Jer 8¹¹ for וַיְרַפְּאוּ; וַתֻּזְרֵנִי 2 S 22⁴⁰, but וַתְּאַזְּרֵנִי ψ 18⁴⁰; תּוּמָם Gn 25²⁴ for תְּאוּמָם; אַחַטֶּנָּה 31³⁹ for אֲחַטְּאֶנָּה; שְׁלַתֶךָ 1 S 1¹⁷ for שְׁאֵלָתֵךְ"; רֵמִים ψ 22²² for רְאֵמִים; גֻּוָה Jb 22²⁹ for גֵּאֲוָה; הַבֵּרְתִי 1 Ch 11³⁹ for "הַבְּאֵרִי, and so ב S 23³⁷; שֵׂרִית 1 Ch 12³⁸ for שְׁאֵרִית; לַהְשׁוֹת 2 K 19²⁵ *Keᵗhîbh* for לְהַשְׁאות (cf. Is 37²⁶); חֵמָה Jb 29⁶ for חֶמְאָה.¹ In מַבְּלָת

---

¹ In Jer 22²³, נֵחַנְתְּ is unquestionably a corruption of נאנחת for ננחת נֶאֱנַחַתְּ.

1 K 5²⁵ (for מֵאֵב״) the strengthening of the following consonant by Dageš compensates for the loss of the א; in מָֹסֶרֶת Ez 20³⁷, if for מֵאַס״ (but read מוּסָר, with Cornill), the preceding vowel is lengthened; cf. above, *c*. On אֹמַר for אֵאמַר, see § 68 *g*.

Rem. 1. In Aramaic the א is much weaker and more liable to change than *g* in Hebrew. In literary Arabic, on the other hand, it is almost always a firm consonant. According to Arabic orthography, א serves also to indicate a long *a*, whereas in Hebrew it very rarely occurs as a mere vowel letter after Qameṣ; as in קָאם Ho 10¹⁴ for קָם *he rose up*; רָאשׁ Pr 10⁴, 13²³ for רָשׁ *poor*; but in 2 S 11¹ the *Kᵉthîbh* הַמַּלְאָכִים *the messengers*, is the true reading; cf. § 7 *b*.

2. In some cases at the beginning of a word, the א, instead of a compound *h* Šᵉwâ, takes the corresponding full vowel, e.g. אֲזוֹר *girdle* for אֱזוֹר; cf. § 84 *a*, *q*, and the analogous cases in § 52 *n*, § 63 *p*, § 76 *d*, § 93 *r* (אֳהָלִים).

3. An א is sometimes added at the end of the word to a final *û*, *î*, or *ô*, e.g. *i* הָלְכוּא for הָלְכוּ Jos 10²⁴(before א!), אָבוֹא Is 28¹². These examples, however, are not so much instances of 'Arabic orthography', as early scribal errors, as in יִנְשֹׁוא Je 10⁵ for יִנָּשֵׂא; and in נָשֹׂוא ψ 139²⁰ for נָשְׂאוּ. Cf. also יְהוּא Ec 11³ (§ 75 *s*); נָקִיא for נָקִי *pure*; לוּא for לוּ *if*; אֵפוֹא for אֵפוֹ *then* (*enclitic*); רִבּוֹא for רִבּוֹ *myriad*, Neh 7⁶⁶·⁷¹. On הוּא and הִיא see § 32 *k*.

4. The ה is stronger and firmer than the א, and never loses its *k* consonantal sound (i.e. *quiesces*) in the middle of a word[1] except in the cases noted below, in which it is completely elided by syncope. On the other hand, at the end of a word it is always a mere vowel letter, unless expressly marked by *Mappîq* as a strong consonant (§ 14 *a*). Yet at times the consonantal sound of ה at the end of a word is lost, and its place is taken by a simple ה or more correctly ה֚, with *Râphè* as an indication of its non-consonantal character, e.g. לָה *to her* for לָהּ, Zc 5¹¹, &c. (cf. § 103 *g*, and §§ 58 *g*, 91 *e*); cf. also יָה for יָהּ (from יָהוּ) in proper names like יִרְמְיָה, &c.—Finally, in very many cases a complete elision of the consonantal ה takes place by *syncope*: (*a*) when its vowel is thrown back to the place of a preceding Šᵉwâ *mobile* (see above, *c*, with א), e.g. לַבֹּקֶר for לְהַבֹּקֶר (the ה of the article being syncopated as it almost always is); בַּיּוֹם for כְּהַיּוֹם [but see § 35 *n*], בַּשָּׁמַיִם for בְּהַשָּׁמַיִם; יֹנָתָן for יְהוֹנָתָן; perhaps also בְּנֵיהֶם for בְּנֵיהֶם Ez 27³². (*b*) By contraction of the vowels preceding and following the ה, e.g. סוּסוֹ (also written סוּסֹה) from *sûsahu* (*a* + *u* = *ô*).—A violent suppression of ה together with its vowel occurs in בָּם (from בָּהֶם), &c.

---

[1] Only apparent exceptions are such *proper names* as פְּדָהצוּר, עֲשָׂהאֵל, which are compounded of two words and hence are sometimes even divided. Cf. forms like חֲזָאֵל for חֲזָהאֵל. Another exception is יְפַהפִיָּה, the reading of many MSS. for the artificially divided form יְפֵה־פִיָּה in the printed texts, Je 46²⁰.

l Rem. In connexion with ŏ and ē, a ה which only marks the vowel ending is occasionally changed into ו or י (חַכֵּ=חַבֵּי, רָאֹה=רָאוֹ Ho 6⁹), and with any vowel into א in the later or Aramaic orthography, but especially with *ā*, e. g. שְׁנָא *sleep*, ψ 127² for שֵׁנָה; נָשָׁא Jer 23³⁹ for נָשָׁה, &c. Thus it is evident that final ה as a vowel letter has only an orthographical importance.

§ 24. *Changes of the Weak Letters* ו *and* י.

Philippi, *Die Aussprache der semit. Konsonanten* ו *und* י (mentioned above, § 5 *b*, note 1), a thorough investigation of their phonetic value as consonantal, i. e. non-syllabic, vowel-sounds, not palatal or labial fricatives; cf. also E. Sievers, *Metrische Studien*, i. 15.

a ו and י are, as consonants, so weak, and approach so nearly to the corresponding vowels *u* and *i*, that under certain conditions they very readily merge into them. This fact is especially important in the formation of those weak stems, in which a ו or י occurs as one of the three radical consonants (§ 69 ff., § 85, § 93).

1. The cases in which ו and י lose their consonantal power, i. e. merge into a vowel, belong almost exclusively to the middle and end of words; at the beginning they remain as consonants.¹

The instances may be classified under two heads:

b (*a*) When either ו or י with *quiescent Šᵉwâ* stands at the end of a syllable immediately after a *homogeneous* vowel (*u* or *i*). It then merges in the homogeneous vowel, or more accurately it assumes its vowel-character (ו as *u*, י as *i*), and is then contracted with the preceding vowel into *one* vowel, necessarily long, but is mostly retained orthographically as a (quiescent) vowel letter. Thus הוּשַׁב for *huwšab*; יִיקַץ. for *yiyqaṣ*; so also at the end of the word, e. g. עִבְרִי *a Hebrew*, properly *'ibriy*, fem. עִבְרִיָּה, pl. עִבְרִיִּים (and עִבְרִים); עָשׂוּ Jb 41²⁵ for עָשׂיו (cf. עָשׂוֹת 1 S 25¹³ *Kᵉthîbh*). On the other hand, if the preceding vowel be heterogeneous, ו and י are retained as full consonants (on the pronunciation see § 8 *m*), e. g. שָׁלֵו *quiet*, זִו *the month of May*, גוֹי *nation*, גָּלוּי *revealed*. But with a preceding *ă* the ו and י are mostly contracted into *ô* and *ê* (see below, *f*), and at the end of a word they are sometimes rejected (see below, *g*).

Complete syncope of ו before *î* occurs in אִי *island* for אֱוִי; עִי *ruins* for עֱוִי; רִי *watering* Jb 37¹¹ for רְוִי; [כִּי *burning* Is 3²⁴ for כְּוִי, cf. §§ 84ᵃ *c, e*, 93 *y*].

---

¹ Or as consonantal vowels (see above), and are then transcribed by P. Haupt, Philippi, and others, as *u̯*, *i̯*, following the practice of Indogermanic philologists. ו for וְ *and*, alone is a standing exception, see § 26. 1 and § 104 *e*. On י=*i* at the beginning of a word, cf. § 47 *b*, note. According to § 19 *a*, end, *initial* ו in Hebrew almost always becomes י; always in verbs originally פ״ו, § 69 *a*. Apart from a few proper names, initial ו occurs only in וָו *hook*, וָלָד *child* Gn 11³⁰, 2 S 6²³ *Kᵉthîbh* [elsewhere יֶלֶד], and the doubtful וָזָר Pr 21⁸.

Thus an initial יְ after the prefixes בְּ, וְ, כְּ, לְ, which would then be *c* pronounced with ĭ (see § 28 *a*), and also almost always after מִ (see § 102 *b*), coalesces with the ĭ to î, e.g. בִּיהוּדָה *in Judah* (for בְּיְ), וִיהוּדָה *and Judah*, כִּיאֹר *as the Nile*, לִיהוּדָה *for Judah*, מִידֵי *from the hands of*.

(*b*) When ו and י without a vowel would stand at the end of the *d* word after *quiescent Šᵉwâ*, they are either wholly rejected and only orthographically replaced by ה (e.g. בְּכֶה from *bikhy*, as well as the regularly formed בְּכִי *weeping*; cf. § 93 *x*) or become again vowel letters. In the latter case י becomes a homogeneous *Ḥireq*, and also attracts to itself the tone, whilst the preceding vowel becomes *Šᵉwâ* (e.g. פְּרִי from *piry*, properly *pary*); ו is changed sometimes into a toneless *u* (e.g. תֹּהוּ from *tuhw*).

Rem. In Syriac, where the weak letters more readily become vowel sounds, *e* a simple *i* may stand even at the beginning of words instead of יְ or יִ. The LXX also, in accordance with this, write Ἰουδά for יְהוּדָה, Ἰσαάκ for יִצְחָק. Hence may be explained the *Syriac usage* in Hebrew of drawing back the vowel *i* to the preceding consonant, which properly had a simple *vocal Šᵉwâ*, e.g. (according to the reading of Ben-Naphtali [1]) וַיִּלֶת Jer 25³⁶ for וַיְלֵת (so Baer), בִּיתְרוֹן Ec 2¹³ for בְּיִתְרוֹן, cf. also the examples in § 20 *h*, note 2 ; even וַיִּחְלוּ Jb 29²¹ (in some editions) for וְיִחְלוּ. According to Qimḥi (see § 47 *b*) יִקְטֹל was pronounced as *iqṭōl*, and therefore the 1st pers. was pointed אֶקְטֹל to avoid confusion. In fact the Babylonian punctuation always has ĭ for ă in the 1st pers.

2. With regard to the *choice* of the long vowel, in which ו and י *f* quiesce after such vocalization and contraction, the following rules may be laid down :

(*a*) With a short *homogeneous* vowel ו and י are contracted into the corresponding long vowel (û or î), see above, *b*.

(*b*) With short ă they form the diphthongs ô and ê according to § 7 *a*, e.g. מֵיטִיב from מַיְטִיב ; יוֹשִׁיב from יַוְשִׁיב, &c.[2]

Rem. The rejection of the half vowels ו and י (see above, *b*) occurs especially *g* at the end of words after a heterogeneous vowel (ă), if according to the nature of the form the contraction appears impossible. So especially in

---

[1] According to Abulwalid, Ben-Naphtali regarded the *Yodh* in *all* such cases as a vowel letter.

[2] Instances in which no contraction takes place after ă are, מַיְמִינִים 1 Ch 12² ; אִיסִירֵם הַיְשָׁר Ho 7¹² (but cf. § 70 *b*) ; ψ 5⁹ *Qᵉrê* ; the locatives בַּיְתָה, מִצְרַיְמָה, &c.—On the suffix יֵכִי for יֵךְ see § 91 *l*.—Sometimes both forms are found, as עַוְלָה and עוֹלָה ; cf. חַי *living*, constr. state חֵי. Analogous is the contraction of מָוֶת (ground-form *mawt*) *death*, constr. מוֹת ; עַיִן (ground-form *'ayn* ['ain]) *eye*, constr. עֵין.

verbs לְ״ה, e. g. originally גְּלְי = (גְּלַ(י) = גְּלָה, since *ă* after the rejection of the י
stands in an open syllable, and consequently must be lengthened to *ā*. The
ה is simply an orthographic sign of the long vowel. So also שָׁלָה for *šălaw*.[1]
On the origin of יִגְלֶה, see § 75 *e*; on קָם as perf. and part. of קוּם, see § 72 *b*
and *g*; on יֵלֵד, &c., from וְלַד, see § 69 *b*.—On the weakening of ו and י to א,
see § 93 *x*.

§ 25. *Unchangeable Vowels.*

a   What vowels in Hebrew are unchangeable, i. e. are not liable to
attenuation (to Š°wâ), modification, lengthening, or shortening, can
be known with certainty only from the nature of the grammatical
forms, and in some cases by comparison with Arabic (cf. § 1 *m*). This
holds good especially of the *essentially* long vowels, i. e. those long by
nature or *contraction*, as distinguished from those which are only
lengthened *rhythmically*, i. e. on account of the special laws which
in Hebrew regulate the tone and the formation of syllables. The
latter, when a change takes place in the position of the tone or in
the division of syllables, readily become short again, or are reduced to
a mere *vocal Š°wâ*.

b   1. The essentially long and consequently, as a rule (but cf. § 26 *p*,
§ 27 *n, o*), unchangeable vowels of the *second* and *third* class, *î, ê, û, ô*,
can often be recognized by means of the vowel letters which accom-
pany them ('ִ־, 'ֵ־, וּ, וֹ); e. g. יֵיטִיב *he does well*, הֵיכָל *palace*, גְּבוּל
boundary, קוֹל *voice*. The *defective* writing (§ 8 *i*) is indeed common
enough, e. g. יֵיטֵב and יֵטִיב for יֵיטִיב; גְּבֻל for גְּבוּל; קֹל for קוֹל, but this
is merely an orthographic licence and has no influence on the quantity
of the vowel; the *û* in גְּבֻל is just as necessarily long, as in גְּבוּל.

As an exception, a merely tone-long vowel of both these classes is sometimes
written *fully*, e. g. יְקְטוֹל for יִקְטֹל.

c   2. The essentially or naturally long *â* (*Qameṣ impure*),[2] unless it has
become *ô* (cf. § 9 *q*), has as a rule in Hebrew no representative among
the consonants, while in Arabic it is regularly indicated by א; on the
few instances of this kind in Hebrew, cf. § 9 *b*, § 23 *g*. The naturally
long *â* and the merely tone-long *ā* therefore can only be distinguished
by an accurate knowledge of the forms.

---

[1] The Arabic, in such cases, often writes etymologically גְּלִי, but pronounces
galā. So the LXX Σινᾶ סִינַי, Vulg. *Sina*; cf. Nestle, *ZAW.* 1905, p. 362 f.
But even in Arabic שלא is written for שָׁלַו and pronounced *salā*.

[2] By *vocales impurae* the older grammarians meant vowels properly followed
by a vowel letter. Thus כְּתָב *k°thâbh* was regarded as merely by a licence
for כְּתָאב, &c.

3. Short vowels in closed syllables (§ 26 *b*), which are not final, are *d*
as a rule unchangeable, e. g. מַלְבּוּשׁ *garment,* מִדְבָּר *wilderness,* כְּמַלְכָה
kingdom; similarly, short vowels in sharpened syllables, i. e. before
Dageš forte, e. g. גַּנָּב *thief.*

4. Finally, those long vowels are unchangeable which, owing to *e*
the omission of the strengthening in a guttural or ר, have arisen by
lengthening from the corresponding short vowels, and now stand in
an open syllable, e. g. מֵאֵן for *mi''ēn*; בֹּרַךְ for *burrakh.*

§ 26. *Syllable-formation*[1] *and its Influence on the Quantity of Vowels.*

Apart from the unchangeable vowels (§ 25), the use of short or long *a*
vowels, i. e. their lengthening, shortening, or change into vocal *Šewâ,*
depends on the *theory of syllable-formation.* The initial and final
syllables especially require consideration.

1. The *initial* syllable. A syllable regularly begins with a consonant,
or, in the case of initial ו and י (cf. note on § 5 *b*), a consonantal vowel.[2]
The copula is a standing exception to this rule. According to the
Tiberian pronunciation וְ *and* is resolved into the corresponding vowel
וּ before *Šewâ,* and the labials, e. g. וּדְבַר, וּמֶלֶךְ; the Babylonian punctuation in the latter cases writes וֹ, i. e. וְ before a full vowel.

2. The *final* syllable. A syllable may end— *b*

(*a*) With a vowel, and is then called an *open* or *simple* syllable,
e. g. in קָטְלָה where the first and last are open. See below, *e.*

(*b*) With *one* consonant, and is then called a *simple closed* or *com-* *c*
pound syllable, as the second in קָטַל, לְבַב. See below, *o, p.* Such are
also the syllables ending in a strengthened consonant, as the first in
קַטֵּל *qaṭ-ṭēl.* See below, *q.*

(*c*) With *two* consonants, a *doubly closed* syllable, as קֹשְׁטְ *qōšṭ,* קָטַלְתְּ. *d*
Cf. below, *r,* and § 10 *i–l.*

3. *Open* or *simple* syllables have a long vowel, whether they have *e*
the tone as in בְּךָ *in thee,* יֵלֵךְ *he goes,* or are toneless as in קָטַל, עֵנָב
a bunch of grapes.[3] A long vowel (Qameṣ, less frequently Ṣere) is

---

[1] Cf. C. H. Toy, 'The Syllable in Hebrew,' *Amer. Journal of Philol.,* 1884,
p. 494 ff.; H. Strack, 'The Syllables in the Hebrew Language,' *Hebraica,*
Oct. 1884, p. 73 ff.

[2] We are not taking account here of the few cases in which initial *Yodh* is
represented as simple *i,* by being written אִי or אִ, see § 24 *e,* and especially
§ 47 *b,* note; nor of certain other cases in which א with an initial vowel has
only a graphic purpose, though it is indispensable in an unpointed text.

[3] In opposition to this fundamental law in Hebrew (a *long* vowel in an *open*
syllable), the original short vowel is found always in Arabic, and sometimes

especially common in an open syllable before the tone (pretonic vowel),
e. g. לָהֶם, יָקוּם, קָטַל, לְבָב׳.

f *Short* vowels in *open* syllables occur :

(*a*) In apparently dissyllabic words formed by means of a helping vowel from monosyllables, as נַחַל *brook*, בַּיִת *house*, יֶרֶב *let him increase*, from *naḥl*, *bayt*, *yirb* ; cf. also יִם‑ the ending of the dual (§ 88). But see § 28 *e*.

g (*b*) In the verbal suffix of the 1st pers. sing. (נִי‑ *me*), e. g. קְטָלַנִי (Arab. *qătălănī*). The uncommon form נִּי‑, however (Gn 30⁶, cf. § 59*f*), proves that the tone-bearing *Pathaḥ* produces a sharpening of the following sonant, and thus virtually stands in a closed syllable, even when the *Nun* is not expressly written with *Dageš*. In cases like וָאֶרְדֹּנִי (§ 102 *m*) *Pathaḥ* is retained in the counter-tone after the א has become quiescent.

h (*c*) Sometimes before the toneless ה‑ *local* (§ 90 *c*), e. g. מִדְבָּרָה *towards the wilderness* ; only, however, in the constr. state (1 K 19¹⁵), since the toneless suffix ה‑ does not affect the character of the form (especially when rapidly pronounced in close connexion) ; otherwise it is מִדְבָּרָה.

In all these cases the short vowel is also supported by the tone, either the principal tone of the word, or (as in *h*) by the secondary tone in the constr. st., or by the counter-tone with *Metheg*, as in וָאֶרְדֹּנִי above, *g* ; cf. the effect of the *arsis* on the short vowel in classical prosody.

i (*d*) In the combinations ⸺, ⸺, ⸺, ⸺, e. g. נַעֲרוֹ *his boy*, יֶאְסֹר *he will bind*, פָּעֳלוֹ *his deed*. In all these cases the syllable was at first really closed, and it was only when the guttural took a *Ḥateph* that it became in consequence open (but cf. e. g. יֶאְסֹר and יֶאְסֹר). The same vowel sequence arises wherever a preposition בְּ, כְּ, לְ, or וְ copulative is prefixed to an initial syllable which has a *Ḥateph*, since the former then takes the vowel

in the other Semitic languages, except of course in the case of *naturally* long vowels. The above examples are pronounced in Arabic *bĭkă*, *qătălă*, *'ĭnăb*. Although it is certain therefore that in Hebrew also,·at an earlier period, *short* vowels were pronounced in open syllables, it may still be doubted whether the present pronunciation is due *merely* to an artificial practice followed in the solemn recitation of the O. T. text. On this hypothesis we should have still to explain, e. g. the undoubtedly very old lengthening of *ĭ* and *ŭ* in an open syllable into *ē* and *ō*.

¹ That these pretonic vowels are really *long* is shown by Brockelmann, *ZA*. xiv. 343 f., from the transcription of Hebrew proper names in the Nestorian (Syriac) punctuation, and e. g. from the Arabic 'Ibrâhîm = אַבְרָהָם. He regards their lengthening in the syllable before the tone as a means adopted by the Masoretes to preserve the pronunciation of the traditional vowels. This explanation of the pretonic vowels as due to a precaution against their disappearing, is certainly right ; as to whether the precaution can be ascribed to the Masoretes, see the previous note. For the pretonic vowel the Arabic regularly has a short vowel (*lăhŭm*, *yăqŭm*, &c.), the Aramaic simply a vocal *Šᵉwâ* (לְהוֹן, יְקוּם, קְטַל, לְבַב) ; and even in Hebrew, when the tone is thrown forward the pretonic vowel almost always becomes *Šᵉwâ*, see § 27. It would, however, be incorrect to assume from this that the pretonic vowel has taken the place of *Šᵉwâ* only on account of the following tone-syllable. It always arises from an original short vowel, since such a vowel is mostly lengthened in an open syllable before the tone, but when the tone is moved forward it becomes *Šᵉwâ*.

contained in the *Ḥaṭeph* (see § 102 *d* and § 104 *d*). To the same category belong also the cases where these prepositions with Hireq stand before a consonant with simple Šᵉwâ mobile, e. g. בְּדָבָר, בִּדְבַר, &c.

(*e*) In forms like יֶחֱזְקוּ *yāḥă-zᵉ-qû* (they are strong), פָּעֳלְךָ *pŏ'ŏ lᵉkhā* (thy *k* deed). These again are cases of the subsequent opening of closed syllables (hence, e. g. יֶחְזְקוּ also occurs) ; פָּעֳלְךָ is properly *pŏ'ŏlᵉkhā* ; cf. generally § 22 *m*, end, and § 28 *c*.

Such cases as הֶחָרֵשׁ, אָחִים (§ 96), הָחְתֹּת (§ 67 *w*) do not come under this *l* head, since they all have *ă* in a virtually sharpened syllable ; nor does the tone-bearing *Sᵉghôl* in suffixes (e.g. וּדְבָרֶךָ), nor *Sᵉghôl* for *ă* before a guttural with Qameṣ (§ 22 *c*). On שֶׁרָשִׁים and קָדָשִׁים, see § 9 *v*.

4. The independent syllables with a firm vowel which have been *m* described above, are frequently preceded by a single consonant with vocal Šᵉwâ, simple or compound. Such a consonant with vocal Šᵉwâ never has the value of an independent syllable, but rather attaches itself so closely to the following syllable that it forms practically one syllable with it, e. g. לְחִי (cheek) *lᵉḥî* ; חֳלִי (sickness) *ḥŏlî* ; יִלְמְדוּ *yil-* *mᵉdhû*. This concerns especially the prefixes וְ, בְּ, כְּ, לְ. See § 102.

The *Šᵉwâ mobile* is no doubt in all such cases weakened from an original *n* full vowel (e. g. יִקְטְלוּ Arab. *yaqtŭ'û*, בְּךָ Arab. *bĭkă*, &c.) ; from this, however, it cannot be inferred that the Masoretes regarded it as forming a kind of *open* syllable, for this would be even more directly opposed to their fundamental law (viz. that a long vowel should stand in an open syllable), than are the exceptions cited above, *f–k*. Even the use of Metheg with Šᵉwâ in special cases (see § 16 *f*) is no proof of such a view on the part of the Masoretes.

5. *Closed* syllables ending with one consonant, when without the *o* tone, necessarily have short vowels, whether at the beginning or at the end of words,[1] e. g. מַלְכָּה *queen*, חֶשְׁבּוֹן *understanding*, חָכְמָה *wisdom*, וַיָּסַר *and he turned back*, וַיָּקָם, וַיָּקֶם (*wayyāqŏm*).

A *tone-bearing* closed syllable may have either a long or short vowel, *p* but if the latter, it must as a rule be either Pathaḥ or Sᵉghôl.[2] The tone-bearing closed penultima admits, of the *long* vowels, only the tone-long *ā, ē, ō*, not the longest *î, ê, ô, û*; of the *short* vowels, only *ă, ĕ*, not *ĭ, ŭ, ŏ* (but on *ĭ* and *ŭ*, see § 29 *g*). Thus יַקְטִילוּ (3rd pl. masc. Imperf. Hiph.) but תַּקְטֵלְנָה 3rd pl. fem., and קֹטְמוּ (2nd pl. masc. Imperat. Qal) but קְטֹמְנָה fem.

---

[1] In exceptions such as שְׁתִי־לִי Gn 4²⁵ (where *šăt* is required by the character of the form, although the closed syllable has lost the tone owing to the following Maqqeph), Metheg is used to guard against a wrong pronunciation ; similarly *ē* is sometimes retained before Maqqeph, e.g. שֵׁם־ Gn 2¹³; עֵץ־ Gn 2¹⁶.

[2] See § 9 *e, f*. *ĭ* occurs thus only in the particles אִם, עִם, מִן ; but these usually (מִן always) are rendered toneless by a following Maqqeph. Cf. also such forms as וַיִּשָׁב § 26 *r* and § 75 *q*.

q 6. A special kind of closed syllables are the *sharpened*, i. e. those which end in the same (strengthened) consonant with which the following syllable begins, e. g. אִמִּי *'im-mî*, כֻּלּוֹ *kŭl-lô*. If without the tone, they have, like the rest, short vowels; but, if bearing the tone, either short vowels as כֻּלּוֹ, הִנֵּנוּ, or long, as שָׁמָּה, הֵמָּה.

On the omission of the strengthening of a consonant at the end of a word, see § 20 *l*.

r 7. Syllables ending with *two* consonants occur only at the end of words, and have most naturally short vowels, קָטַלְתְּ, וַיֵּשְׁבְּ; but sometimes *Ṣere*, as נֵרְדְּ, וַיֵּבְךְּ, or *Ḥolem*, תּוֹסְףְ קשְׁטְ. Cf., however, § 10 *i*. Usually the harshness of pronunciation is avoided by the use of a helping vowel (§ 28 *e*).

§ 27. *The Change of the Vowels, especially as regards Quantity.*

a The changes in sound through which the Hebrew language passed, before it assumed the form in which we know it from the Masoretic text of the O. T. (see § 2 *k*), have especially affected its vowel system. A precise knowledge of these vowel changes, which is indispensable for the understanding of most of the present forms of the language, is derived partly from the phenomena which the language itself presents in the laws of derivation and inflexion, partly from the comparison of the kindred dialects, principally the Arabic. By these two methods, we arrive at the following facts as regards Hebrew:

b 1. That in an open syllable the language has frequently retained only a half-vowel (*Šewâ mobile*), where there originally stood a full short vowel, e. g. עֲגָלָה (ground-form *'ăgălăt*) *a waggon*, צְדָקָה (ground-form *ṣădăqăt*) *righteousness*, קְטָלוֹ (Arab. *qătălû*), יְקַטְּלוּ (Arab. *jŭqattŭlû*).

c 2. That vowels originally short have in the tone-syllable, as also in the open syllable preceding it, been generally changed into the corresponding tone-long vowels, *ă* into *ā*, *ĭ* into *ē*, *ŭ* into *ō* (see § 9, *a–e*, *k*, *r*). If, however, the tone be shifted or weakened, these tone-long vowels mostly revert to their original shortness, or, occasionally, are still further shortened, or reduced to mere *Šewâ mobile*, or, finally, are entirely lost through a change in the division of syllables; e. g. מָטָר (Arab. *măṭăr*) *rain*, when in close dependence on a following genitive in the *construct state*), becomes מְטַר; עָקֵב (Arab. *'ăqĭb*) *heel*, dual עֲקֵבַיִם, dual *construct* (with attenuation of the original *ă* of the first syllable to *ĭ*) עִקְּבֵי [on the פ, see § 20 *h*]; יִקְטֹל (Arab. *yăqtŭl*), plur. יִקְטְלוּ (Arab. *yăqtŭlû*). For instances of complete loss, as in בְּכַסְפִּי, cf. § 93 *m*.

According to § 26, the following details of vowel-change must be observed :

1. The original, or a kindred short vowel reappears— *d*

(*a*) When a closed syllable loses the tone (§ 26 *o*). Thus, יָד *hand*, but יַד־יְהֹוָה *the hand of Yahwe*; בֵּן *son*, but בֶּן־הַמֶּלֶךְ *the son of the king*; כֹּל *the whole*, but כָּל־הָעָם *the whole of the people* ; so also when a tone-bearing closed syllable loses the tone on taking a suffix, e. g. אֹיֵב *enemy*, but אֹיִבְךָ *thy enemy*; finally, when the tone recedes, יָקֻם, but וַיָּקָם (*wayyāqŏm*) ; יֵלֵךְ, but וַיֵּלֶךְ.

(*b*) To the same category belong cases like סֵפֶר *book*, but סִפְרִי *my book*; קֹדֶשׁ *holiness*, but קָדְשִׁי *my holiness*. In spite of the helping vowel, סֵפֶר and קֹדֶשׁ are really closed syllables with a tone-long vowel; when the syllable loses the tone, the original *ĭ* or *ŏ* (properly *ŭ*) re-appears.

The same is true of syllables with a virtually sharpened final consonant: the lengthening of original *ĭ* to *ē* and *ŭ* to *ō* takes place only in a tone-bearing syllable; in a toneless syllable the *ĭ* or *ŏ* (or *ŭ*) remains, e. g. אֵם *mother*, but אִמִּי *my mother*; חֹק *law*, plur. חֻקִּים; but עֹז *strength*, עֻזִּי (and עֻזִּי) *my strength*.

2. The lengthening of the short vowel to the corresponding long, *e* takes place—

(*a*) When a closed syllable becomes open by its final consonant being transferred to a suffix beginning with a vowel, or in general to the following syllable, e. g. קְטָלוֹ, קָטַל *he has killed him*; קְטַלְתִּי primarily from קָטַלְתְּ. Similarly *ă* mostly becomes *ā* even before a suffix beginning with *Šᵉwâ mobile*; e. g. קְטָלְךָ from קָטַל, קְטַלְתְּךָ from קָטַלְתְּ.

(*b*) When a syllable has become open by complete loss of the *f* strengthening of its final consonant (a guttural or *Rêš*), e. g. בֵּרַךְ for *bĭrrakh*, see § 22 *c*. Cf. also § 20 *n*.

(*c*) When a weak consonant (א, ו, י) following the short vowel *g* quiesces in this vowel, according to § 23 *a, c, d*, § 24 *f*, e. g. מָצָא for מָצְא, where the א, losing its consonantal value, loses also the power of closing the syllable, and the open syllable requires a long vowel.

(*d*) Very frequently through the influence of the *pause*, i. e. the *h* principal tone in the last word of a sentence or clause (§ 29 *k*). Sometimes also through the influence of the article (§ 35 *o*).

3. When a word increases at the end and the tone is consequently *i* moved forward, or when, in the *construct state* (see § 89), or otherwise in close connexion with the following word, its tone is weakened, in such cases a full vowel (short or tone-long) may, by a change in the division of syllables, be weakened to *Sᵉwâ mobile*, or even be entirely lost, so that its place is taken by the mere syllable-divider (*Sᵉwâ quiescens*). Examples of the first case are, שֵׁם *name*, pl. שֵׁמוֹת, but שְׁמִי *my name*, שְׁמוֹתָם *their names*, דָּבָר *word*, constr. st. דְּבַר; צְדָקָה *righteousness*, constr. st. צִדְקַת; an example of the second case is, בְּרָכָה *blessing*, constr. st. בִּרְכַּת. Whether the vowel is retained or becomes *Sᵉwâ* (דָּם, דְּמִי, but שֵׁם, שְׁמִי), and which of the two disappears in two consecutive syllables, depends upon the character of the form in question. In general the rule is that only those vowels which stand in an open syllable can become *Sᵉwâ*.

Thus the change into *Sᵉwâ* takes place in—

k (a) The *ā* and *ē* of the first syllable, especially in the inflexion of nouns, e. g. דָּבָר *word*, plur. דְּבָרִים; גָּדוֹל *great*, fem. גְּדוֹלָה; לֵבָב *heart*, לְבָבִי *my heart*; but also in the verb, תָּשׁוּב *she will return*, plur. תְּשׁוּבֶינָה, and so always, when the originally short vowel of the prefixes of the Imperfect comes to stand in an open syllable which is not pretonic. On the other hand, an *ā* lengthened from *ă* before the tone is retained in the *Perfect consecutive* of Qal even in the secondary tone, e. g. וְקָטַלְתָּ; cf. § 49 *i*.

l (b) The short, or merely tone-long, vowels *a, e, o* of the ultima, especially in verbal forms, e. g. קָטַל, fem. קָטְלָה *qāṭᵉlā*; יִקְטְלוּ, יִקְטֹל *yiqṭᵉlû*; but note also תִּרְדְּקִין, יִלְקְטוּן, &c., according to § 47 *m* and *o*. The helping vowels are either entirely omitted, e. g. מֶלֶךְ *king* (ground-form *malk*), מַלְכִּי *my king*; or, under the influence of a guttural, are weakened to Ḥaṭeph, e. g. נַעַר *boy*, נַעֲרוֹ *his boy*. If the tone remains unmoved, the vowel also is retained, notwithstanding the lengthening of the word, e. g. יִקְטֹלוּ pausal-form for יִקְטְלוּ.

m Where the tone moves forward two places, the former of the two vowels of a dissyllabic word may be shortened, and the second changed into *Sᵉwâ*. Cf. דָּבָר *word*; in the plur. דְּבָרִים; with heavy suffix דִּבְרֵיהֶם (cf. § 28 *a*) *their words*. On the attenuation of the *ă* to *ĭ*, see further, *s*, *t*.

n Rem. 1. An *ô* arising from *aw = au*, or by an obscuring of *â* (see § 9 *b*), sometimes becomes *û*, when the tone is moved forward, e. g. נָקוֹם, נְקוּמוֹת (see Paradigm *Perf. Niph.* of קוּם); מָנוֹס *flight*, fem. מְנוּסָה, with suffix, מְנוּסִי. The not uncommon use of וּ in a sharpened syllable, as בְּחֻקֵּי Ez 20¹⁸ (for בְּחֻקֵּי, cf. also the examples in § 9 *o*), is to be regarded as an orthographic licence, although sometimes in such cases *û* may really have been intended by the *Kᵉthîbh*.

o Of the vowels of the *U*-class, *û* and tone-long *ō* stand in a tone-bearing closed final syllable, and *ŏ* in a toneless syllable, e.g. יָקוּם *he will arise*, יָקֹם jussive, *let him arise*, וַיָּקָם *and he arose*. The only instance of *ŭ* in an ultima which has lost the tone is וַיָּרָם Ex 16²⁰ (see § 67 *n*). Similarly, of vowels of the *I*-class, *ê*, *i*, and *ē* stand in a tone-bearing closed final syllable, and *ĕ* in a toneless syllable, e.g. יָקִים *he will raise*, יָקֵם *let him raise*, וַיָּקֶם *and he raised*. The only instance of *ĭ* in an ultima which has lost the tone is וַתֵּרֶץ Ju 9⁵³ (see § 67 *p*).

2. In the place of a *Pathaḥ* we not infrequently find (according to § 9 *f*) *p*
a *Sᵉghôl* (*ĕ*, *ē*) as a modification of *ă* :

(*a*) In a closed antepenultima, e.g. in the proper names אֶבְיָתָר and אֶבְיָסָף, where LXX 'Αβι-=אֲבִי, which is certainly the better reading, cf. Ulmer, *Die semit. Eigennamen*, 1901, p. 12 ; or in a closed penultima, e.g. יֶהְדֹּף, but also יֶדְכֶם *your hand*, for *yadᵉkhèm*. In all these cases the character of the surrounding consonants (see § 6 *q*) has no doubt had an influence.

(*b*) Regularly before a guttural with *Qameṣ* or *Ḥaṭeph Qameṣ*, *q*
where the strengthening has been dropped, provided that a lengthening of the *Pathaḥ* into *Qameṣ* be not necessary, e.g. אֶחָיו *his brothers*, for '*aḥāw* ; כֶּחָשׁ *false*, for *kaḥāš* ; פֶּחָה *governor*, constr. st. פַּחַת ; פֶּחָם *coal* ; הֶחָי *the living* (with the article, הֶ for הַ) ; יִתְנֶחָם Nu 23¹⁹, &c., and so always before חָ and חֶ, as הֶחֳדָשִׁים *the months*, see § 35 *k*.
Before הָ and עָ *Sᵉghôl* generally stands only in the second syllable before the tone, e.g. הֶהָרִים *the mountains* ; הֶעָוֹן *the guilt* ; immediately before the tone *Pathaḥ* is lengthened into a (pretonic) *Qameṣ*, e.g. הָעָם, הָהָר ; but cf. also הִפָּהֲרוּ Nu 8⁷. Before the weak consonants א and ר (cf. § 22 *c*, *q*), the lengthening of the *Pathaḥ* into *Qameṣ* almost always takes place, e.g. הָאָב *the father*, pl. הָאָבוֹת ; הָרֹאשׁ *the head*, pl. הָרָאשִׁים. Exceptions, הֶהָרָה *towards the mountain*, Gn 14¹⁰, in the tone-syllable, for *hárrā* ; יְבֶרֶכְיָהוּ (pr. name) for יְבָרֶכְיָהוּ. On הֶ as a form of the interrogative הַ (הֲ), see § 100 *n* ; on מֶה for מָה (מֶה), § 37 *e*, *f*. Finally, אָכֶלְךָ Ex 33³ also comes partly under this head, in consequence of the loss of the strengthening, for אֹכַלְךָ, and יְחֶזְקֵאל Ezekiel for יְחֶזְקֵאל=יְחַזְקֵאל *God strengthens*.

(*c*) As a modification of the original *Pathaḥ* in the first class of the segholate *r*
forms (§ 93 *g*), when a helping vowel (§ 28 *e*) is inserted after the second consonant. Thus the ground-form *kalb* (*dog*), after receiving a helping *Sᵉghôl*, is modified into כֶּלֶב (also in modern Arabic pronounced *kelb*),[1] *yarḥ* (*month*), with a helping *Pathaḥ*, יֶרַח. The same phenomenon appears also in the formation of verbs, in cases like יֶגֶל (jussive of the Hiph'îl of גָּלָה), with a helping *Sᵉghôl*, for *yagl*.

3. The attenuation of *ă* to *ĭ* is very common in a toneless closed syllable. *s*
(*a*) In a firmly closed syllable, מִדּוֹ *his measure*, for מַדּוֹ (in a sharpened syllable) ; יְלִדְתִּיךָ *I have begotten thee*, from יָלַדְתִּי with the suffix ךָ ; cf. Lv 11⁴⁴, Ez 38²³, and § 44 *d*. Especially is this the case in a large number of *segholates*

---

[1] So the LXX write Μελχισεδέκ for מַלְכִּי־צֶדֶק.

from the ground-form *qaṭl*, when combined with singular suffixes, e.g. צִדְקִי *my righteousness*, for *ṣadqi.*

t   (b) In a loosely-closed syllable, i. e. one followed by an aspirated *Begadkᵉphath*, as דִּמְכֶם *your blood*, for דַּמְכֶם, and so commonly in the *st. constr. plur.* of segholates from the ground-form *qaṭl*, e. g. בִּגְדֵי from בֶּגֶד (ground-form *bagd*) *a garment.* In most cases of this kind the attenuation is easily intelligible from the nature of the surrounding consonants. It is evident from a comparison of the dialects, that the attenuation was consistently carried out in a very large number of noun and verb-forms in Hebrew, as will be shown in the proper places.[1]

u   4. *Sᵉghōl* arises, in addition to the cases mentioned in *o* and *p*, also from the weakening of *ā* of the final syllable in the isolated cases (הָֽ‑ for הָ‑) in 1 S 28¹⁵ (? see § 48 *d*), ψ 20⁴ (?), Is 59⁵, Pr 24¹⁴ (see § 48 *l*); for examples of Locative forms in הָ‑ see § 90 *i* end.

v   5. Among the *Ḥaṭeph*-sounds ‑ is shorter and lighter than ‑, and consequently the vowel group ‑ ‑ is shorter than ‑ ‑; e. g. אֱדוֹם *Edom*, but אֲדֹמִי (*Edomite*), shortened at the beginning because the tone is thrown forward; אֱמֶת (*ᵉmèth*) *truth*, אֲמִתּוֹ *his truth*; נֶעְלָם *hidden*, pl. נֶעֱלָמִים; הֶעֱבַרְתִּי but וְהַעֲבַרְתִּי; but also conversely נַעֲשָׂה fem. נֶעֶשְׂתָה, cf. § 63 *f*, 3.

w   6. To the chapter on vowel changes belongs lastly the *dissimilation* of vowels, i. e. the change of one vowel into another entirely heterogeneous, in order to prevent two similar, or closely related vowels, from following one another in the same word.[2] Hence לוּלֵא for *lū lō* (unless). Cf. also חִיצוֹן from חוּץ; רִאשׁוֹן from רֹאשׁ; תִּיכוֹן from תּוֹךְ; נְכֹחוֹ from נָכַח; עֵירֹם from stem עוּר; most probably also יִלּוֹד *offspring*, קִפּוֹד *porcupine*, for יַל׳, קַפ׳, see § 68 *c*, note.— On the proper names יְהוֹא and יֵשׁוּעַ, which were formerly explained in the same way, see now Prätorius, *ZDMG.* 1905, p. 341 f.

§ 28. *The Rise of New Vowels and Syllables.*

a   1. According to § 26 *m* a half-syllable, i. e. a consonant with Šᵉwâ mobile (always weakened from a short vowel), can only occur in close dependence on a full syllable. If another half-syllable with simple Šᵉwâ follows, the first takes a full short vowel again.[3] This vowel is almost always *Ḥireq*. In most cases it is probably an attenuation of an original *ă*, and never a mere helping vowel. In some instances analogy may have led to the choice of the *ĭ*. Thus, according to § 102 *d*, the prefixes בְּ, כְּ, לְ before a consonant with Šᵉwâ mobile become בִּ, כִּ, לִ, e. g. לִפְרִי, כִּפְרִי, בִּפְרִי; before יְ they are pointed as in בִּיהוּדָה (from *bi-yᵉhûdā*, according to § 24 *c*); so too with *Wāw* copulative, e. g. וִיהוּדָה for וְי׳ attenuated from וַי׳. The first half-

---

[1] Analogous to this attenuation of *ă* to *ĭ* is the Lat. *tango, attingo; laxus, prolixus*; to the transition of *ă* to *ĕ* (see above, *a*), the Lat. *carpo, decerpo; spargo, conspergo.*

[2] Cf. Barth, *Die Nominalbildung in den semit. Spr.*, p. xxix; A. Müller, *Theol. Stud. u. Krit.*, 1892, p. 177 f., and Nestle, ibid., p. 573 f.

[3] Except וְ *and*, which generally becomes וּ before a simple Šᵉwâ, cf. § 104 *e*.

syllable, after the restoration of the short vowel, sometimes combines with the second to form a firmly closed syllable, e. g. לִנְפֹּל Nu 14³ for *linᵉphōl*, and so almost always in the infin. constr. after לְ (§ 45 g); in isolated cases also with כְּ, as כְּנֻפֹּר Jer 17².

2. If a guttural with *Ḥaṭeph* follows, the original *ă* of the prefixes *b* is retained before Ḥaṭeph Pathaḥ, but before Ḥaṭeph Seghol or Ḥaṭeph Qameṣ it is modified to the short vowel contained in the *Ḥaṭeph*. Thus arise the vowel groups ◌ֲ◌ַ, ◌ֱ◌ֶ, ◌ֳ◌ָ, e.g. וַאֲנִי *and I*, כַּאֲשֶׁר *as*, לַעֲבֹד *to serve*, לֶאֱכֹל *to eat*, לָחֳלִי *in sickness*. On the Metheg with every such short vowel, see § 16 *f*, δ. Sometimes here also a fully closed syllable is formed. In such a case, the prefix takes the short vowel, which would have belonged to the suppressed *Ḥaṭeph*, e. g. לַחְטֹב for לַחֲטֹב; לַחְמָם Is 47¹⁴ for לַחֲמָם (see § 67 *cc*); לֶאְסֹר but also לֶאֱסֹר; and even וַעְצֹר Jb 4², cf. Gn 32¹⁶. So always in the Infin. and Imperat. Qal of the verbs הָיָה *to be* and חָיָה *to live*, e. g. לִהְיוֹת *to be*, וִהְיִי *and be ye*; even with מִן, as מִהְיוֹת, on which cf. § 102 *b*; but וֶהְיֵה *and be*, וֶחְיֵה *and live*, have *ĕ* instead of *ĭ* under the prefix. For the Metheg, cf. § 16 *f*, ε.

3. When a *Ḥaṭeph* in the middle of a word, owing to flexional *c* changes, would stand before a vocal *Šᵉwâ*, it is changed into the short vowel, with which it is compounded. This applies especially to cases in which the *Ḥaṭeph* stands under a guttural instead of quiescent *Šᵉwâ*, as an echo of the preceding short vowel, e.g. יַעֲמֹד *he will stand* (for יַעְמֹד), but plur. יַעַמְדוּ for *ya'ᵃmᵉdhû*, and נֶהֶפְכוּ for *nĕhᵃphᵉkhû* (*they have turned themselves*), פָּעָלְךָ *thy work*, cf. § 26 *k*. The syllables are to be divided *yă'ă-mᵉdhû*, and the second *ă* is to be regarded exactly as the helping *Pathaḥ* in נַעַר, &c.[1]

4. At the end of words, syllables occur which close with two con- *d* sonants (§ 10 *i*, § 26 *r*), but only when the latter of the two is an emphatic consonant (ט, ק) or a tenuis (viz. ב, ד, ך, ת[2]), e.g. יֵשְׁטְ *let him turn aside*, וַיַּשְׁקְ *and he caused to drink*, אָמַרְתְּ *thou* (fem.) *hast said*, וַיֵּבְךְּ *and he wept*, וְיֵרְדְּ *and let him have dominion*, וַיִּשְׁבְּ *and he took captive*.

This harsh ending is elsewhere avoided by the Masora,[3] which *e* inserts between the two final consonants a helping vowel, usually

---

[1] In Ju 16¹³ read תְּאָרְגִי not (with Opitius, Hahn and others) תָּאַרְגִי.

[2] With a final ף, the only example is תּוֹסְף Pr 30⁶, where several MSS. and printed editions incorrectly have ף without Dageš. Instead of this masoretic caprice we should no doubt read תּוֹסֵף.

[3] An analogy to this practice of the Masora is found among the modern Beduin, who pronounce such a helping vowel before *h, ḥ, ḫ, ġ*; cf. Spitta, *Gramm. des arab. Vulgärdialektes von Aegypten*, Lpz. 1880, § 43 *d*.

Sᵉ*ghôl*, but with medial or final gutturals a *Pathaḥ*,[1] and after י
a *Ḥireq*, e. g. וַיִּגֶל and *he revealed*, for *wayyiḡl*; יֶרֶב *let it multiply*, for
yirb; קֹדֶשׁ *holiness*, ground-form *quds̆*; נַחַל *brook*, ground-form *naḥl*;
שָׁלַחַתְּ [2] for שָׁלַחְתְּ *thou hast sent*; בַּיִת *house*, ground-form *bayt*.   These
helping vowels are, however, to be regarded as exactly like *furtive*
Pathaḥ (§ 22 *f, g*); they do not alter the monosyllabic character of
the forms, and they disappear before formative suffixes, e. g. קָדְשִׁי *my*
holiness, בֵּיתָה *home-ward*.

f   5. On the rise of a full vowel in place of a simple Sᵉ*wâ*, under the
influence of the *pause*, see § 29 *m*; on initial א for אֱ, see § 23 *h*.

§ 29. *The Tone, its Changes and the Pause.*

a   1. The principal tone rests, according to the Masoretic accentuation
(cf. § 15 *c*), as a rule on the final syllable, e. g. קָטַל, דָּבָר, דְּבָרוֹ, דְּבָרִים,
קָדְרוֹן, קָטְלוּ, קְטַלְתֶּם—in the last five examples on the formative additions
to the stem.   Less frequently it rests on the penultima, as in לַיְלָה
night, קָטַלְתָּ, כֻּלּוֹ, קָמוּ; but a closed penultima can only have the tone
if the ultima is open (e. g. קֹמְנָה, לִכְנָה, קָטַלְתָּ), whilst a closed ultima
can as a rule only be without the tone if the penultima is open, e. g.
וַיָּקָם, וַיָּקֶם; see also below, *e*.

b   A kind of counter-tone or secondary stress, as opposed to the
principal tone, is marked by *Metheg* (§ 16 *c*).   Words which are closely
united by *Maqqeph* with the following word (§ 16 *a*) can at the most
have only a secondary tone.

c   2. The original tone of a word, however, frequently shifts its place
in consequence either of changes in the word itself, or of its close
connexion with other words.   If the word is increased at the end, the
tone is moved forward (*descendit*) one or two places according to the
length of the addition, e. g. דָּבָר *word*, plur. דְּבָרִים; דִּבְרֵיכֶם *your words*;
קֹדֶשׁ *holy thing*, plur. קָדָשִׁים; קָטַלְתָּ with suffix קְטַלְתָּהוּ, with *Wāw* con-
secutive וְקָטַלְתָּ.   On the consequent vowel-changes, see § 27 *d, i–m*.

d   3. On the other hand, the original tone is shifted from the ultima
to the penultima (*ascendit*):

---

[1] On the apparent exceptions דָּשֵׁא, &c., cf. § 22 *e*; other instances in which
א has entirely lost its consonantal value, and is only retained orthographically,
are חֵטְא *sin*, גֵּיא *valley* (also גַּי), שָׁוְא *vanity* (Jb 15³¹ *Kᵉthîbh* שֵׁו).

[2] In this form (§ 65 *g*) the *Dageš lene* remains in the final *Tāw*, although
a vowel precedes, in order to point out that the helping *Pathaḥ* is not to be
regarded as a really full vowel, but merely as an orthographic indication of
a very slight sound, to ensure the correct pronunciation.   An analogous case
is יֵחַד *yiḥad* from חָרָה (§ 75 *r*).

(a) In many forms of the Imperfect, under the influence of a pre-fixed *Wāw consecutive* (וַ see § 49 c–e), e. g. וַיֹּאמֶר *he will say*, וַיֹּאמֶר *and he said*; יֵלֵךְ *he will go*, וַיֵּלֶךְ *and he went*.   Cf. also § 51 n on the impf. Niphʿal, and § 65 g, end, on the impf. Piʿel; on these forms in Pause, when the ו consec. does not take effect, see below, p.

(b) For rhythmical reasons (as often in other languages), when *e* a monosyllable, or a word with the tone on the first syllable, follows a word with the tone on the ultima, in order to avoid the concurrence of two tone-syllables.[1]   This rhythmical retraction of the tone, however (נָסוֹג אָחוֹר *receding*, as it is called by the Jewish grammarians), is only admissible according to *a*, above, provided that the penultima, which now receives the tone, is an open syllable (with a long vowel; but see *g*), whilst the ultima, which loses the tone, must be either an open syllable with a long vowel, e. g. קָרָא לַיְלָה, Gn 1⁵, 4¹⁷, 27²⁵, Ex 16²⁹, ψ 5¹¹, 104¹⁴, Dn 11¹³, or a closed syllable with a short vowel, e. g. תֹּאכַל לֶחֶם Gn 3¹⁹, Jb 3³, 22²⁸.[2]   The *grave* suffixes ־כֶם, ־כֶן, ־הֶם, ־הֶן־ are exceptions, as they never lose the tone.   Moreover a fair number of instances occur in which the above conditions are fulfilled, but the tone is not retracted, e. g. esp. with הָיָה, and before א; cf. Qimḥi, *Mikhlol*, ed. Rittenberg (Lyck, 1862), p. 4ᵇ, line 13 ff.

Although *Ṣere* can remain in a closed ultima which has lost the tone, it *f* is perhaps not to be regarded in this case (see § 8 b) as a long vowel.   At any rate it then always has, in correct editions, a retarding *Metheg*, no doubt in order to prevent its being pronounced as *Seghôl*, e. g. לְבֵעֵר קֵין Nu 24²²; cf. Nu 17²³, Ju 20², Is 66³, Jer 23²⁹, Ez 22²⁵, ψ 37⁷, and even with a following *furtive Pathaḥ* Pr 1¹⁹, 11²⁶, &c., although there is no question here of two successive tone-syllables.   In other cases the shortening into *Seghôl* does take place, e. g. הֹלֶם פַּעַם *who smiteth the anvil*, Is 41⁷, for הֹלֶם פָּעַם; מֵאֵת שֵׁמֶר 1 K 16²⁴.—The retraction of the tone even occurs when a half-syllable with a Šewâ mobile precedes the original tone-syllable, e. g. וַיֹּאמְרוּ לוֹ Gn 19⁵, and frequently; יֹרְדֵי בוֹר ψ 28¹; שָׁמְנוּ לִי

---

[1] Even Hebrew *prose* proceeds, according to the accentuation, in a kind of iambic rhythm.   That this was intended by the marking of the tone, can be seen from the use of Metheg.—Jos. Wijnkoop in *Darche hannesigah sive leges de accentus Hebraicae linguae ascensione*, Ludg. Bat. 1881, endeavours to explain, on euphonic and syntactical grounds, the numerous cases in which the usual retraction of the tone does not occur, e. g. וּבוֹרֵא חֹשֶׁךְ Is 45⁷, where the object probably is to avoid a kind of hiatus; but cf. also Am 4¹³.   Prätorius, *Ueber den rückweich. Accent im Hebr.*, Halle, 1897, has fully discussed the *nasog 'aḥor*.

[2] The reading עֲרָיִם (so even Opitius and Hahn) Ez 16⁷ for עֶרְיָם is rightly described by Baer as 'error turpis'.—That an unchangeable vowel in a closed final syllable cannot lose the tone is shown by Prätorius from the duplication of the accent (see above, § 22 f).

ψ 31[5]; מְטֹעֲנֵי חָ֫רֶב Is 14[19]; as also when the tone-syllable of the second word is preceded by a half-syllable, e. g. עֹ֫שֶׂה פְּרִי Gn 1[11] (on the *Dag. f.*, cf. § 20 *f*); לָ֫תֶת לְךָ Gn 15[7] (cf. § 20 *c*).

g According to the above, it must be regarded as anomalous when the Masora throws back the tone of a closed ultima upon a *virtually* sharpened syllable with a short vowel, e.g. אַ֫חַר כֵּן 1 S 10[5], § 101 *a*; וְכִ֫חֶשׁ בּוֹ Jb 8[18], cf. Lv 5[22], Ho 9[2]; לְצַ֫חֶק בָּנוּ Gn 39[14.17]; whereas it elsewhere allows a closed penultima to bear the tone only when the ultima is open. Still more anomalous is the placing of the tone on a *really* sharpened syllable, when the ultima is closed, as in הֻקַּ֫ם עָל 2 S 23[1]; נִכַּר שׁוֹעַ Jb 34[19]; cf. also יֻקַּם־קָיִן Gn 4[24], with Metheg of the secondary tone. We should read either הֻקַּם, or, with Frensdorff, *Massora Magna*, p. 167, Ginsb., Kittel, after Bomb., הֻקַּם. Other abnormal forms are וַיַּ֫חֲזֶק בּוֹ Ex 4[4] (for similar instances see § 15 *c*, end) and וַיְהִ֫יוּ שָׁם Dt 10[5].

h (*c*) In *pause*, see *i–v*.

The meeting of two tone-syllables (see *e*, *f*) is avoided also by connecting the words with Maqqēph, in which case the first word entirely loses the tone, e. g. וַיִּכְתָּב־שָׁ֫ם *and he wrote there*, Jos 8[32].

i 4. Very important changes of the tone and of the vowels are effected by the *pause*. By this term is meant the strong stress laid on the tone-syllable in the last word of a sentence (verse) or clause. It is marked by a great *distinctive accent*, *Sillûq*, *'Athnâḥ*, and in the accentuation of the books תא"ם, *'Ôlè wᵉyôrēd* (§ 15 *h*). Apart from these principal pauses (*the great pause*), there are often pausal changes (*the lesser pause*) with the lesser distinctives, especially *Sᵉgolta*, *Zaqeph qaṭon*, *Rᵉbhîaᶜ*, and even with *Pašṭa*, *Tiphḥa*, *Gereš*, and (Pr 30[4]) *Pazer*.[1] The changes are as follows:

k (*a*) When the tone-syllable naturally has a short vowel, it as a rule becomes tone-long in *pause*, e. g. קָטַל, קָטָ֑ל; מַיִם, מָ֑יִם; קָטַלְתְּ, קָטָ֫לְתְּ. An *ă* which has been modified to *Sᵉghôl* usually becomes *ā* in *pause*, e. g. קֶ֫שֶׁר (ground-form *qašr*) in *pause* קָ֫שֶׁר 2 K 11[14]; אֶ֫רֶץ אָ֑רֶץ Jer 22[29];

---

[1] In most cases, probably on account of a following guttural or (at the end of a sentence) ו (cf. e.g. Ex 21[31], Jer 3[9] [but Ginsb. ותחנף], Ru 4[4], Ec 11[6] [but Ginsb. יכשר]; before ו Jer 17[11]) [see also § 29 *w*]. שָׁפָט אֶת־ 1 S 7[17], וָאָרֶץ Is 65[17], Pr 25[3], where *ā* has *munaḥ*, are very irregular, but the lengthening here is probably only to avoid the cacophony *šāphăṭ 'ĕt*. In the same way הַיִצְלָח Ez 17[15] (with Mahpakh before הֶ) and וַיִּקְרַם Ez 37[8] (with Darga before עָ) are to be explained. The four instances of אָ֫נִי for אֲנִי apparently require a different explanation; see § 32 *c*.—The theory of Olshausen and others that the phenomena of the *pause* are due *entirely* to liturgical considerations, i. e. that it is 'a convenient way of developing the musical value of the final accents by means of fuller forms' in liturgical reading (Sievers, *Metr. Studien*, i. 236, also explains pausal forms like יִקְטֹ֫לוּ, קָטָ֫לָה, as 'late formations of the grammarians'), is contradicted by the fact that similar phenomena are still to be observed in modern vulgar Arabic, where they can only be attributed to rhythmical reasons of a general character.

also in 2 K 4³¹ read קָשֵׁב with ed. Mant., &c. (Baer קָשֵׁב).—דִּבֶּר becomes in *pause* דִּבֵּר.

Sometimes, however, the distinct and sharper *ă* is intentionally retained *l* in *pause*, especially if the following consonant is strengthened, e. g. יִבַּחוּ Jb 4²⁰, or ought to be strengthened, e. g. כְּבַת 2 S 12³, בֵּן Is 8¹, &c.; but also in other cases as זָקַנְתִּי Gn 27², because from זָקֵן, cf. below, *q*; עַד Gn 49²⁷; וְהִקְדִּישָׁנוּ 2 Ch 29¹⁹ (so Baer, but Ginsb. 'הקד, ed. Mant. 'הקד); and regularly in the numeral אַרְבַּע *four*, Lv 11²⁰, &c. In the accentuation of the three poetical books (§ 15 *d*) the use of *Pathaḥ* with '*Athnaḥ* is due to the inferior pausal force of '*Athnaḥ*, especially after '*Ôlè weyôred* (§ 15 *o*); cf. ψ 100⁸, Pr 30⁹, and Qimḥi, *Mikhlol*, ed. Rittenberg, p. 5ᵇ, line 4 from below. Compare the list of instances of pausal *ă* and *è* in the appendices to Baer's editions.

(*b*) When a full vowel in a tone-bearing final syllable has lost the *m* tone before an afformative, and has become *vocal Šewâ*, it is restored in *pause* as tone-vowel, and, if short, is lengthened, e. g. קָטַל, *fem.* קָטְלָה (*qāṭelā*), in *pause* קָטָלָה; שִׁמְעוּ (*šimʻû*), in *pause* שְׁמָעוּ (from sing. שָׁמַע); יִקְטְלוּ ¹ (sing. יִקְטֹל). The fuller endings of the Imperfect וּ and וּן (§ 47 *m* and *o*) alone retain the tone even when the original vowel is restored. In segholate forms, like פְּרִי, לֶחִי (ground-form *laḥy*, *pary*), the original *ă* returns, though under the form of a tone-bearing *Seghôl*, thus לֶחִי, פֶּרִי; original *ĭ* becomes *ē*, e. g. חֲצִי, in *pause* חֵצִי; original *ŏ* (*ŭ*) becomes *ō*, חֳלִי (ground-form *huly*), in *pause* חֹלִי (§ 93 *x*, *y*, *z*).

On the analogy of such forms as לֶחִי, &c., the shortened Imperfects *n* יְהִי and יְחִי become in *pause* יֶחִי, יֶהִי, because in the full forms יִהְיֶה *he will be*, and יִחְיֶה *he will live*, the *ĭ* is attenuated from an original *ă*. Similarly שְׁכֶם *shoulder*, in *pause* שֶׁכֶם (ground-form *šakhm*), and the pron. אֲנִי *I*, in *pause* אָנִי; cf. also the restoration of the original *ă* as *è* before the suffix ךָ— *thy, thee*, e. g. דְּבָרְךָ *thy word*, in *pause* דְּבָרֶךָ; יִשְׁמָרְךָ *he guards thee*, in *pause* יִשְׁמָרֶךָ; but after the prepositions לְ, בְּ, (אֶת) the suffix ךָ— in *pause* becomes ךְ—, e. g. בָּךְ, לָךְ, אִתָּךְ.

(*c*) This tendency to draw back the tone in *pause* to the *penultima* *O* appears also in such cases as אָנֹכִי *I*, in *pause* אָנֹכִי; אַתָּה *thou*, in *pause* אָתָּה (but in the three poetically accented books also אַתָּה, since in those books '*Athnaḥ*, especially after '*Ôlè weyôred*, has only the force of a *Zaqeph*; hence also יִמְלָאוּ Pr 24⁴ instead of יִמְלְאוּ²; עַתָּה *now*, עָתָּה; and in other sporadic instances, like כָּלֹה ψ 37²⁰ for כָּלוּ; but in 1 S 12²⁵

---

¹ Such a pausal syllable is sometimes further emphasized by strengthening the following consonant, see § 20 *i*.

² יִפְּלוּ ψ 45⁶, cf. also יִבְּלְמוּ ψ 40¹⁵, is to be explained in the same way, but not הִמְלַטִי Zc 2¹¹, where, on the analogy of הִשָּׁמְרוּ Je 9³, we should expect הִמָּלַטִי.

תְּסַפּוּ with Baer and Ginsb., is to be preferred to the reading of ed. Mant., &c.

p   (*d*) Conversely all forms of imperfects consecutive, whose final syllable, when not in *pause*, loses the tone and is pronounced with a short vowel, take, when in *pause*, the tone on the ultima with a tone-long vowel, e. g. וַיָּ֫מָת *and he died*, in pause וַיָּמֹת.

q   Of other effects of the *pause* we have still to mention, (1) the transition of an *ĕ* (lengthened from *ĭ*) to the more distinct *ă* (see above, *l*), e.g. הֶחָן for הֶחֶן Is 18⁵ (cf. § 67 *v*; § 72 *dd*); קָמֵל Is 33⁹; אָצַל 1 Ch 8³⁸ (beside אָצֵל [, see *v*. 37. Cf. : טָבָאֵל Is 7⁶ (טָבְאֵל Ezr 4⁷); : שָׁשָׁר Jer 22¹⁴; סְפָרָד Ob 20; : וַיִּנָּפַשׁ Ex 31¹⁷; : וְאָנָשׁ 2 S 12¹⁵ (below, § 51 *m*)—S. R. D.]); הַפָּר Gn 17¹⁴; הַפָּצַר 1 S 15²³; תְּאָחַר ψ 40¹⁸; הַרְחַק Jb 13²¹, mostly before liquids or sibilants (but also הָשֵׁב Is 42²², and without the *pause* תֵּרַד La 3⁴⁸). So also וַיֵּ֫לֶךְ (shortened from יֵלֵךְ) becomes in pause וַיֵּלַךְ; cf. וַיֵּ֫לַךְ La 3²; תֵּלַךְ for תֵּלְךְ Ju 19²⁰. On Seghôl in pause instead of Ṣere, cf. § 52 *n*, 60 *d*, and especially § 75 *n*, on וְחָיָה Pr 4⁴ and 7².

r   (2) The transition from *ă* to *ē* in the ultima; so always in the formula לְעוֹלָם וָעֶד (for עַד) *for ever and ever*.

s   (3) The pausal Qameṣ (according to § 54 *k*, lengthened from original *ă*) in *Hithpa'ēl* (but not in *Pi'ēl*) for Ṣere, e.g. יִתְהַלָּ֫ךְ Jb 18⁸ for יִתְהַלֵּךְ. But pausal forms like שָׁ֫בֶט, סָ֫תֶר (in the *absol. st.* סֵ֫תֶר, שֵׁ֫בֶט) go back to a secondary form of the *abs. st.* שָׁ֫בֶט, סָ֫תֶר.

t   (4) The restoration of a final *Yodh* which has been dropped from the stem, together with the preceding vowel, e.g. אָתָ֫יוּ, בְּעָ֫יוּ Is 21¹², for אָתוּ, בְּעוּ, the latter also without the *pause* Is 56⁹·¹²; cf. Jb 12⁶, and the same occurrence even in the word *before* the *pause* Dt 32³⁷, Is 21¹².

u   (5) The transition from *ô* or *ō* to *ā* in *pause*: as שְׁאָלָה Is 7¹¹, if it be a locative of שְׁאֹל, and not rather imperat. Qal of שָׁאַל; שְׁבָלְתִּי Gn 43¹⁴ for שְׁכֹלְתִּי; עָז Gn 49³; יִטְרָף Gn 49²⁷; perhaps also שָׁרְיָן 1 K 22³⁴, Is 59¹⁷, and מְשָׁקֶ֫לֶת Is 28¹⁷, cf. 2 K 21¹³. On the other hand the regular pausal form יַחְפֹּץ (ordinary imperfect יַחְפֹּץ) corresponds to a perfect חָפֵץ (see § 47 *h*).

v   (6) When a *Pathaḥ* both precedes and follows a virtually strengthened guttural, the second becomes *ā* in *pause*, and the first *Seghôl*, according to § 22 *c* and § 27 *q*, e.g. אַחַי *my brothers*, in pause אֶחָי. Similarly in cases where an original *Pathaḥ* after a guttural has been attenuated to *i* out of *pause*, and then lengthened to *ē* with the tone (cf. § 54 *k*), e.g. יִתְנַחֵם, but in pause יִתְנֶחָם Dt 32³⁶; cf. Nu 8⁷, 23¹⁹, Ez 5¹³, ψ 135¹⁴.—On pausal Ṣere, for Seghôl, in infin., imperat., and imperf. of verbs ל"ה, see § 75 *hh*.

w   [Other instances of the full vowel in lesser pause, where the voice would naturally rest on the word, are Gn 15¹⁴ יַעֲבֹדוּ, Is 8¹⁵, 40²⁴, Ho 4¹², 8⁷, Dn 9¹⁵, and very often in such cases.]

SECOND PART

ETYMOLOGY, OR THE PARTS OF SPEECH

§ 30. Stems and Roots[1]: Biliteral, Triliteral, and Quadriliteral.

1. Stems in Hebrew, as in the other Semitic languages, have this *a* peculiarity, that by far the majority of them consist of three consonants. On these the meaning essentially depends, while the various modifications of the idea are expressed rather by changes in the vowels, e. g. עָמֵק (עָמֵק or עָמֹק; the 3rd pers. sing. perf. does not occur) *it was deep*, עָמֹק *deep*, עֹמֶק *depth*, עֵמֶק, *a valley, plain*. Such a stem may be either a verb or a noun, and the language commonly exhibits both together, e.g. זָרַע *he has sown*, זֶרַע *seed* ; חָכַם *he was wise*, חָכָם *a wise man*. For practical purposes, however, it has long been the custom to regard as the stem the *3rd pers. sing. Perf. Qal* (see § 43), since it is one of the simplest forms of the verb, without any formative additions. Not only are the other forms of the verb referred to this stem, but also the noun-forms, and the large number of particles derived from nouns ; e. g. קָדַשׁ *he was holy*, קֹדֶשׁ *holiness*, קָדוֹשׁ *holy*.

Sometimes the language, as we have it, exhibits only the verbal *b* stem without any corresponding noun-form, e. g. סָקַל *to stone*, נָהַק *to bray* ; and on the other hand, the noun sometimes exists without the corresponding verb, e. g. אֶבֶן *stone*, נֶגֶב *south*. Since, however, the nominal or verbal stems, which are not now found in Hebrew, generally occur in one or more of the other Semitic dialects, it may be assumed, as a rule, that Hebrew, when a living language, also possessed them. Thus, in Arabic, the verbal stem *'ăbĭnă* (*to become compact, hard*) corresponds to אֶבֶן, and the Aramaic verb *n*ᵉ*gab* (*to be dry*) to נֶגֶב.

Rem. 1. The Jewish grammarians call the stem (i.e. the 3rd pers. sing. *c* Perf. Qal) שֹׁרֶשׁ *root*. Hence it became customary among Christian grammarians to call the stem *radix*, and its three consonants *litterae radicales*, in contradistinction to the *litterae serviles* or *formative letters*. On the correct use of the term *root*, see *g*.

---

[1] On the questions discussed here compare the bibliography at the head of § 79.

d　2. Others regard the three stem-consonants as a *root*, in the sense that, considered as *vowelless* and unpronounceable, it represents the common foundation of the verbal and nominal stems developed from it, just as in the vegetable world, from which the figure is borrowed, stems grow from the hidden root, e.g.

Root : מָלַךְ, the indeterminate idea of *ruling*.

Verb-stem, מָלַךְ *he has reigned.*　　　Noun-stem, מֶלֶךְ *king.*

For the historical investigation of the language, however, this hypothesis of unpronounceable roots, with indeterminate meaning, is fruitless. Moreover, the term *root*, as it is generally understood by philologists, cannot be applied to the Semitic triliteral stem (see *f*).[1]

e　3. The 3rd sing. Perf. Qal, which, according to the above, is usually regarded, both lexicographically and grammatically, as the ground-form, is generally in Hebrew a dissyllable, e.g. קָטַל. The monosyllabic forms have only arisen by contraction (according to the traditional explanation) from stems which had a weak letter (ו or י) for their middle consonant, e.g. קָם from *qăwăm*; or from stems whose second and third consonants are identical, e.g. צַר and צָרַר (but see below, §§ 67, 72). The dissyllabic forms have themselves no doubt arisen, through a loss of the final vowel, from trisyllables, e.g. קָטַל from *qătălă*, as it is in literary Arabic.

f　2. The law of the triliteral stem is so strictly observed in the formation of verbs and nouns in Hebrew (and in the Semitic languages generally), that the language has sometimes adopted artificial methods to preserve at least an appearance of triliteralism in monosyllabic stems, e.g. שְׁבֶת for the inf. constr. of verbs פ״ו; cf. § 69 *b*. Conversely such nouns, as אָב *father*, אֵם *mother*, אָח *brother*, which were formerly all regarded as original monosyllabic forms (*nomina primitiva*), may, in some cases at least, have arisen from mutilation of a triliteral stem.

g　On the other hand, a large number of triliteral stems really point to a biliteral base, which may be properly called a *root* (*radix primaria, bilitteralis*), since it forms the starting-point for several triliteral modifications of the same fundamental idea. Though in themselves unpronounceable, these roots are usually pronounced with *ă* between the two consonants, and are represented in writing by the sign √, e.g. √כר as the root of אָכַר, כּוּר, כָּרָה, כָּרַר. The reduction of a stem to the underlying root may generally be accomplished with certainty when the stem exhibits one weak consonant with two strong ones, or when the second and third consonants are identical. Thus e.g. the stems דָּכָה, דָּכָא, דָּכַךְ, דּוּךְ, דָּכַךְ may all be traced to the idea of *striking, breaking,* and the root common to them all is evidently the two strong consonants דך (*dakh*). Very frequently, however, the development of the root into a stem is effected by the addition of

---

[1] Cf. Philippi, ' Der Grundstamm des starken Verbums,' in *Morgenländische Forschungen*, Leipz. 1875, pp. 69-106.

a strong consonant, especially, it seems, a sibilant, liquid or guttural.[1]
Finally, further modifications of the same root are produced when
either a consonant of the root, or the letter which has been added,
changes by phonetic laws into a kindred letter (see the examples
below). Usually such a change of sound is accompanied by a modification of meaning.

Examples: from the root קץ (no doubt *onomatopoetic*, i.e. imitating the
sound), which represents the fundamental idea of *carving off, cutting in pieces*,
are derived directly: קצץ and קצה *to cut, to cut off*; the latter also metaph. *to
decide, to judge* (whence קָצִין, Arab. *qâḍi, a judge*); also קָצַב *to cut off, to shear*,
קָצַף *to tear, to break*, קָצַע *to cut into*, קָצַר *to cut off, to reap*. With a dental instead
of the sibilant, קד, קט, whence קָטַב *to cut in pieces, to destroy*, קָטַל *to cut down,
to kill*, קָטַף *to tear off, to pluck off*. With the initial letter softened,
the root becomes כס, whence כָּסַח *to cut off*, and כָּסַם *to shave*; cf. also נכס
Syr. *to slay (sacrifice), to kill*. With the greatest softening to גו and גד; גָּזַז *to
cut off, to shear*; גָּזָה *to hew stone*; גּוּז, גּוּם, גָּוַע, גָּוַל, גָּזַר *to cut off, to tear off, eat up*;
similarly גָּדַד *to cut into*, גָּדַע *to cut off*; cf. also גָּדָה, גָּדַף, גָּדַר. Allied to this
root also is the series of stems which instead of a palatal begin with a
guttural (ח), e.g. חָדַר *to split, cut*; cf. also חדל, חדק, חדר, חדשׁ, and further
חצר, חצץ, חצה, חצב, חסף, חסם, חסל, חטף, חטם, חטב, חזו, חזה, חוץ, חוג, חום,
in the Lexicon.

The root הם expresses the sound of *humming*, which is made with the
mouth closed (μύω); hence הָמַם, הום, הָמָה, נָהַם (נָאַם), Arab. *hámhama, to buzz,
to hum, to snarl*, &c.

As developments from the root רע cf. the stems רָעַד, רָעַל, רָעַם, רָעַע, רָעַץ,
רָעַשׁ. Not less numerous are the developments of the root (פל, פר) בר and
many others.[2]

Closer investigation of the subject suggests the following observations:

(*a*) These roots are mere *abstractions* from stems in actual use, and are
themselves not used. They represent rather the hidden germs (*semina*) of the
stems which appear in the language. Yet these stems are sometimes so
short as to consist simply of the elements of the root itself, e.g. תַּם *to be
finished*, קַל *light*. The ascertaining of the root and its meaning, although in
many ways very difficult and hazardous, is of great lexicographical importance.
It is a wholly different and much contested question whether there ever was
a period in the development of the Semitic languages when purely *biliteral*
roots, either isolated and invariable or combined with inflexions, served for
the communication of thought. In such a case it would have to be admitted,
that the language at first expressed extremely few elementary ideas, which
were only gradually extended by additions to denote more delicate shades of
meaning. At all events this process of transformation would belong to
a period of the language which is entirely outside our range. At the most
only the gradual multiplication of *stems* by means of phonetic change (see
below) can be historically proved.

(*b*) Many of these monosyllabic words are clearly imitations of sounds, and

---

[1] That *all* triliteral stems are derived from biliterals (as König, *Lehrg.* ii. 1,
370; M. Lambert in *Studies in honour of A. Kohut*, Berl. 1897, p. 354 ff.) cannot
be definitely proved.

[2] Cf. the interesting examination of the Semitic roots QR, KR, XR, by
P. Haupt in the *Amer. Journ. of Sem. Lang.*, xxiii (1907), p. 241 ff.

sometimes coincide with roots of a similar meaning in the Indo-Germanic family of languages (§ 1 *h*). Of other roots there is definite evidence that Semitic linguistic consciousness regarded them as onomatopoetic, whilst the Indo-Germanic instinct fails to recognize in them any imitation of sound.

l　(c) Stems with the harder, stronger consonants are in general (§ 6 *r*) to be regarded as the older, from which a number of later stems probably arose through softening of the consonants ; cf. פזר and בזר, צחק and שחק, צעק and זעק, עלץ and עלז, עלם and עלן ; רקק and רכך, and the almost consistent change of initial ו to י. In other instances, however, the harder stems have only been adopted at a later period from Aramaic, e.g. טעה, Hebr. תעה. Finally in many cases the harder and softer stems may have been in use together from the first, thus often distinguishing, by a kind of sound-painting, the intensive action from the less intensive ; see above קצץ *to cut*, גזז *to shear*, &c.

m　(d) When two consonants are united to form a root they are usually either both emphatic or both middle-hard or both soft, e.g. קץ, קם, קט, כם, כס, גז, גד never קן, קץ, נס, גס, גט, גיז, כיץ. Within (triliteral) stems the first and second consonants are never identical. The apparent exceptions are either due to reduplication of the root, e.g. דדה (ψ 42⁵, Is 38¹⁵), Arabic דאדא, or result from other causes, cf. e.g. בבה in the Lexicon. The first and third consonants are very seldom identical except in what are called concave stems (with middle ו or י), e.g. נון, צוץ ; note, however, נגן, נתן, שמש, שרש, and on עלע Jb 39³⁰ see § 55 *f*. The second and third consonants on the other hand are very frequently identical, see § 67.[1]

n　(e) The softening mentioned under *l* is sometimes so great that strong consonants, especially in the middle of the stem, actually pass into vowels : cf. § 19 *o*, and עֲזָאזֵל Lv 16⁸ ᶠᶠ· if it is for עֲזַלְזֵל.

o　(f) Some of the cases in which triliteral stems cannot with certainty be traced back to a biliteral root, may be due to a combination of two roots—a simple method of forming expressions to correspond to more complex ideas.

p　3. Stems of *four*, or even (in the case of nouns) of *five* consonants[2] are secondary formations. They arise from an extension of the triliteral stem : (a) by addition of a fourth stem-consonant; (b) in some cases perhaps by composition and contraction of two triliteral stems, by which means even *quinquiliterals* are produced. Stems which have arisen from reduplication of the biliteral root, or from the mere repetition of one or two of the three original stem-consonants, e.g. כִּלְכֵּל from כּוּל or כִּיל, סְחַרְחַר from סחר, are usually not regarded as *quadriliterals* or *quinqueliterals*, but as *conjugational* forms (§ 55); so also the few words which are formed with the prefix שׁ, as שַׁלְהֶבֶת *flame* from לָהַב, correspond to the Aramaic conjugation *Šaph'ēl*, שַׁלְהֵב.

q　Rem. on (a). The letters *r* and *l*, especially, are inserted between the first and second radicals, e.g. כִּרְסֵם, כָּסַם *to eat up* ; שַׁרְבִיט = שֵׁבֶט *sceptre* (this insertion of an *r* is especially frequent in Aramaic) ; וְלַעֲפָה *hot wind* from זָעַף

---

[1] Consonants which are not found together in roots and stems are called *incompatible*. They are chiefly consonants belonging to the same class, e.g. גכ, קכ, גק, דט, טת, זד, בף, מף, ויץ, צם, אע, חע, הח, &c., or in the reverse order.

[2] In Hebrew they are comparatively rare, but more numerous in the other Semitic languages, especially in Ethiopic.

to be hot. Cf. Aram. עַרְגֵּל *to roll,* expanded from עַגֵּל (conjugation Pa'ēl, corresponding to the Hebrew Pi'ēl). In Latin there is a similar expansion of *fid, scid, tud, jug* into *findo, scindo, tundo, jungo.* At the end of words the commonest expansion is by means of ל and ן, e.g. גַּרְזֶן *axe,* כַּרְמֶל *garden-land* (from כֶּרֶם), גִּבְעֹל *corolla* (גְּבִיעַ *cup*) ; cf. § 85, xi.

Rem. on (*b*). Forms such as צְפַרְדֵּעַ *frog,* חֲבַצֶּלֶת *meadow-saffron,* צַלְמָוֶת *shadow* *r* *of death,*[1] were long regarded as compounds, though the explanation of them all was uncertain. Many words of this class, which earlier scholars attempted to explain from Hebrew sources, have since proved to be *loan-words* (§ 1 *i*), and consequently need no longer be taken into account.

4. A special class of formations, distinct from the fully developed *s* stems of three or four consonants, are (*a*) the *Interjections* (§ 105), which, as being direct imitations of natural sounds, are independent of the ordinary formative laws ; (*b*) the *Pronouns.* Whether these are to be regarded as the mutilated remains of early developed stems, or as relics of a period of language when the formation of stems followed different laws, must remain undecided. At all events, the many peculiarities of their formation[2] require special treatment (§ 32 ff.). On the other hand, most of the particles (adverbs, prepositions, conjunctions) seem to have arisen in Hebrew from fully developed stems, although in many instances, in consequence of extreme shortening, the underlying stem is no longer recognizable (see § 99 ff.).

§ 31. *Grammatical Structure.*

P. Dörwald, 'Die Formenbildungsgesetze des Hebr.' (*Hilfsbuch für Lehrer des Hebr.*), Berlin, 1897, is recommended for occasional reference.

1. The formation of the parts of speech from the stems (derivation), *a* and their inflexion, are effected in two ways : (*a*) internally by changes in the stem itself, particularly in its vowels: (*b*) externally by the addition of formative syllables before or after it. The expression of grammatical relations (e. g. the comparative degree and some case-relations in Hebrew) periphrastically by means of separate words belongs, not to etymology, but to syntax.

The external method (*b*) of formation, by affixing formative syllables, *b* which occurs e.g. in Egyptian, appears on the whole to be the more ancient. Yet other families of language, and particularly the Semitic, at a very early period had recourse also to the internal method, and during their youthful vigour widely developed their power of forming derivatives. But the continuous decay of this power in the later periods of language made syntactical circumlocution more and more necessary. The same process may be seen also e.g. in Greek (including modern Greek), and in Latin with its Romance offshoots.

---

[1] So expressly Nöldeke in *ZAW.* 1897, p. 183 ff. ; but most probably it is to be read צַלְמוּת *darkness* from the stem צלם [Arab. *zalima,* to be dark].

[2] Cf. Hupfeld, 'System der semitischen Demonstrativbildung,' in the *Ztschr. f. d. Kunde des Morgenl.,* vol. ii. pp. 124 ff., 427 ff.

c **2.** Both methods of formation exist together in Hebrew. The internal mode of formation by means of vowel changes is tolerably extensive (קָטַל, קָטֵל, קְטֹל; קֻטַּל, קֻטֵּל, &c.). This is accompanied in numerous cases by external formation also (נִקְטַל, הִקְטִיל, הִתְקַטֵּל, &c.), and even these formative additions again are subject to internal change, e.g. הָקְטַל, הָתְקַטַּל. The addition of formative syllables occurs, as in almost all languages, chiefly in the formation of the persons of the verb, where the meaning of the affixed syllables is for the most part still perfectly clear (see §§ 44, 47). It is also employed to distinguish gender and number in the verb and noun. Of case-endings, on the contrary, only scanty traces remain in Hebrew (see § 90).

CHAPTER I

THE PRONOUN

Brockelmann, *Semit. Sprachwiss.*, p. 98 ff.; *Grundriss*, i. 296 ff. L. Reinisch, 'Das persönl. Fürwort u. die Verbalflexion in den chamito-semit. Sprachen' (*Wiener Akad. der Wiss.*, 1909).

§ 32. *The Personal Pronoun. The Separate Pronoun.*

1. The personal pronoun (as well as the pronoun generally) belongs *a* to the oldest and simplest elements of the language (§ 30 *s*). It must be discussed *before* the verb, since it plays an important part in verbal inflexion (§§ 44, 47).

2. The independent principal forms of the personal pronoun serve *b* (like the Gk. ἐγώ, σύ, Lat. *ego, tu*, and their plurals) almost exclusively to emphasize the nominative-subject (see, however, § 135 *d*). They are as follows:

Singular.		Plural.	
1. *Com.* אָנֹכִי, in *pause* אָנֹכִי; אֲנִי, in *pause* אָנִי	} *I.*	1. *Com.* אֲנַחְנוּ, in *pause* אֲנָחְנוּ (אֲנוּ), נַחְנוּ, in *pause* נָחְנוּ	} *we.*
2. *m.* אַתָּה (אַתְּ), in *pause* אַתָּה or אָתָּה *f.* אַתְּ(אַתְּי) properly (אַתִּי), in *pause* אָתְּ	} *thou.*	2. *m.* אַתֶּם *f.* אַתֵּן (אַתֵּנָה); אַתֵּן אַתֵּן (אַתֵּנָה)	} *ye.*
3. *m.* הוּא *he (it).* *f.* הִיא *she (it).*		3. *m.* הֵם (הֵמָּה), הֵם (־הֵם) *f.* הֵנָּה after *prefixes* הֵן, הֵן	} *they.*

The forms enclosed in parentheses are the less common. A table of these pronouns with their shortened forms (*pronominal suffixes*) is given in Paradigm A at the end of this Grammar.

REMARKS.

I. *First Person.*

1. The form אָנֹכִי is less frequent than אֲנִי.[1] The former occurs in *c*

---

[1] On the prevalence of אָנֹכִי in the earlier Books compare the statistics collected by Giesebrecht in *ZAW*. 1881, p. 251 ff., partly contested by Driver in the *Journal of Philology*, 1882, vol. xi. p. 222 ff. (but cf. his *Introduction*, ed. 6, p. 135, line 1 f.), but thoroughly established by König in *Theol. Stud. u. Krit.*, 1893, pp. 464 ff. and 478, and in his *Einleitung in das A. T.*, p. 168, &c. In some of the latest books אנכי is not found at all, and hardly at all in the Talmud. [For details see the Lexicon, s. v. אֲנִי and אָנֹכִי.]

Phoenician, Moabite, and Assyrian, but in no other of the kindred dialects ;[1] from the latter the suffixes are derived (§ 33). The *ô* most probably results from an obscuring of an original *á* (cf. Aram. אֲנָא, Arab. *'ánâ*). The pausal form אָ֫נִי occurs not only with small disjunctive accents, but even with conjunctives; so always in חַי אָ֫נִי *as I live!* also Is 49[18] with Munaḥ, ψ 119[125] with Merkha (which, however, has been altered from Deḥî), and twice in Mal 1[6]. In all these cases there is manifestly a disagreement between the vocalization already established and the special laws regulating the system of accentuation.

d   2. The formation of the plural, in this and the other persons, exhibits a certain analogy with that of the noun, while at the same time (like the pronouns of other languages) it is characterized by many differences and peculiarities. The short form אֲנוּ (אָנוּ) from which the suffix is derived occurs only in Jer 42[6] *Kethîbh*. The form נַ֫חְנוּ (cf. § 19 *h*) only in Ex 16[7.8], Nu 32[32], La 3[42]; נָ֑חְנוּ in *pause*, Gn 42[11]; in Arabic *náḥnu* is the regular form. In the Mišna אָנוּ (אֲנוּ) has altogether supplanted the longer forms.

e   3. The pronoun of the 1st person only is, as a rule in languages, of the *common gender*, because the person who is present and speaking needs no further indication of gender, as does the 2nd person, who is addressed (in Greek, Latin, English, &c., this distinction is also lacking), and still more the 3rd person who is absent.

II. *Second Person.*

f   4. The forms of the 2nd person אַתָּה, אַתְּ, אַתֶּם, אַתֵּ֫נָה, &c., are contracted from *'antâ*, &c. The kindred languages have retained the *n* before the ת, e. g. Arab. *'antâ*, fem. *'ánti*, thou; pl. *'ántum*, fem. *'antúnna*, ye. In Syriac אַנְתְּ, fem. אַנְתִּי are written, but both are pronounced *'at*. In Western Aramaic אַנְתְּ is usual for both genders.

g   אַתְּ (without ה) occurs five times, e. g. ψ 6[4], always as *Kethîbh*, with אַתָּה as *Qerê*. In three places אַתְּ appears as a masculine, Nu 11[15], Dt 5[24], Ez 28[14].

h   The feminine form was originally אַתִּי as in Syriac, Arabic, and Ethiopic. This form is found seven times as *Kethîbh* (Ju 17[2], 1 K 14[2], 2 K 4[16.23], 8[1], Jer 4[30], Ez 36[13]) and appears also in the corresponding personal ending of verbs (see § 44 *f*), especially, and necessarily, before suffixes, as קְטַלְתִּ֫ינִי, § 59 *a* [*c*] ; cf. also *î* as the ending of the 2nd fem. sing. of the imperative and imperfect. The final *î* was, however, gradually dropped in pronunciation, just as in Syriac (see above, *f*) it was eventually only written, not pronounced. The י therefore finally disappeared (cf. § 10 *k*), and hence the Masoretes, even in these seven passages, have pointed the word in the text as אַתִּי to indicate the *Qerê* אַתְּ (see § 17). The same final י֫ appears in the rare (Aramaic) forms of the suffix ־יכִי, ־יכִי (§§ 58, 91).

i   5. The plurals אַתֶּם (with the second vowel assimilated to the fem. form) and אַתֵּן (אַתֵּ֫ן), with the tone on the ultima, only partially correspond to the assumed ground-forms *'antumû*, fem. *'antinnâ*, Arab. *'ántum* (Aram. אַתּוּן, אֲנַתּוּן) and *'antúnna* (Aram. אַתֵּין, אֲנַתֵּין). The form אַתֵּן is found only in Ez 34[31] (so Qimḥi expressly, others אַתֶּן); אַתֵּ֫נָה (for which some MSS. have

---

[1] In Phoenician and Moabite (inscription of Mêša', line 1) it is written אנך, without the final י֫. In Punic it was pronounced *anec* (Plaut. *Poen.* 5, 1, 8) or *anech* (5, 2, 35). Cf. Schröder, *Phöniz. Sprache*, p. 143. In Assyrian the corresponding form is *anaku*, in old Egyptian *anek*, Coptic *anok, nok*.

אַתֵּנָה) only four times, viz. Gn 31⁶, Ez 13¹¹·²⁰, 34¹⁷; in 13²⁰ אַתֵּם (before a מ) is even used as feminine.

III. *Third Person.*

6. (a) In הוּא and הִיא (*hû* and *hî*) the א (corresponding to the *'Elif of pro- k longation* in Arabic, cf. § 23 i) might be regarded only as an orthographic addition closing the final long vowel, as in לוּא, נְקִיא, &c. The א is, however, always written in the case of the separate pronouns,[1] and only as a toneless suffix (§ 33 a) does הוּא appear as הֻ, while הִיא becomes הָ. In Arabic (as in Syriac) they are written הו and הי but pronounced *húwă* and *hiyă*, and in Vulgar Arabic even *húwwa* and *hiyya*. This Arabic pronunciation alone would not indeed be decisive, since the vowel complement might have arisen from the more consonantal pronunciation of the ו and י; but the Ethiopic *we'etû* (=*hu'a-tû*) for הוּא, *ye'etî* (=*hi'a-tî*) for הִיא (cf. also the Assyrian *ya-u-a* for יֵהוּא) show that the א was original and indicated an original vocalic termination of the two words. According to Philippi (*ZDMG.* xxviii. 172 and xxix. 371 ff.) הוּא arose from a primitive Semitic *ha-ṛa*, הִיא from *ha-ya*.

(b) The form הוּא also stands in the consonantal text (*Kᵉthîbh*) of the l Pentateuch [2] (with the exception of eleven places) for the *fem.* הִיא. In all such cases the Masora, by the punctuation הִוא, has indicated the *Qᵉrê* הִיא (*Qᵉrê perpetuum*, see § 17). The old explanation regarded this phenomenon as an archaism which was incorrectly removed by the Masoretes. This assumption is, however, clearly untenable, if we consider (1) that no other Semitic language is without the quite indispensable distinction of gender in the separate pronoun of the 3rd pers.; (2) that this distinction does occur eleven times in the Pentateuch, and that in Gn 20⁵, 38²⁵, Nu 5¹³·¹⁴ הוּא and הִיא are found close to one another; (3) that outside the Pentateuch the distinc- tion is found in the oldest documents, so that the הִיא cannot be regarded as having been subsequently adopted from the Aramaic; (4) that those parts of the book of Joshua which certainly formed a constituent part of the original sources of the Pentateuch, know nothing of this epicene use of הוּא. Consequently there only remains the hypothesis, that the writing of הוּא for הִיא rests on an orthographical peculiarity which in some recension of the Pentateuch-text was almost consistently followed, but was afterwards very properly rejected by the Masoretes. The orthography was, however, peculiar to the Pentateuch-text alone, since it is unnecessary to follow the Masora in writing הִיא for הוּא in 1 K 17¹⁵, Is 30³³, Jb 31¹¹, or הוּא for הִיא in ψ 73¹⁶, Ec 5⁸, 1 Ch 29¹⁶. The Samaritan recension of the Pentateuch has the correct form in the *Kᵉthîbh* throughout. Levy's explanation of this strange practice of the Masoretes is evidently right, viz. that originally הא was written for both forms (see k, note), and was almost everywhere, irrespective of gender, expanded into הוא. On the whole question see Driver, *Leviticus* (in Haupt's Bible), p. 25 f. In the text Driver always reads הא.

7. The plural forms הֵם (הֵמָּה) and הֵנָּה (after *prefixes* הֶן, הֵן, הֵן) are of doubt- m ful origin, but הֵמָּה, הֵם have probably been assimilated to הֵנָּה which goes back to a form *hinnā*. In Western Aram. הִמּוֹן, הִמּוֹ (הִנּוּן, אַנּוּן), Syr. *henûn*

---

[1] In the inscription of King Mêša' (see § 2 d), lines 6 and 27, we find הא for הוא, and in the inscription of 'Ešmunʿazar, line 22, for הִיא, but in the Zenjirli inscriptions (see § 1 m) both הא and הו occur (Hadad i, l. 29).

[2] Also in twelve places in the Babylonian Codex (Prophets) of 916 A.D.; cf. Baer, *Ezechiel*, p. 108 f.; Buhl, *Canon and Text of the O. T.* (Edinb. 1892), p. 240.

('enûn), Arab. *húmú* (archaic form of *hum*), and Ethiop. *hômú*, an *ô* or *ú* is appended, which in Hebrew seems to reappear in the poetical suffixes מוֹ__, ‍ָ‍ַמוֹ‍, ‍ָ‍מוֹ‍ (§ 91 *l*, 3).

n   In some passages הֵמָּה stands for the feminine (Zc 5[10], Ct 6[8], Ru 1[22]; cf. the use of the suffix of the 3rd masc. for the 3rd fem., § 135 *o* and § 145 *t*). For the quite anomalous עַד־הֶם 2 K 9[18] read עֲדֵיהֶם (Jb 32[12]).

o   8. The pronouns of the 3rd person may refer to *things* as well as persons. On their meaning as *demonstratives* see § 136.

§ 33. *Pronominal Suffixes.*

Brockelmann, *Semit. Sprachwiss.*, p. 100 f.; *Grundriss*, i. 306 ff. J. Barth, 'Beiträge zur Suffixlehre des Nordsemit.,' in the *Amer. Journ. of Sem. Lang.*, 1901, p. 193 ff.

a   1. The independent principal forms of the personal pronoun (the *separate pronoun*), given in the preceding section, express only the nominative.[1]   The accusative and genitive are expressed by forms, usually shorter, joined to the end of verbs, nouns, and particles (*pronominal suffixes* or simply *suffixes*); e. g. הוּ (toneless) and וֹ (from *āhú*) *eum* and *eius*, קְטַלְתִּיהוּ *I have killed him* (also קְטַלְתִּיו, קְטַלְתָּהוּ or (with *āhú* contracted into *ô*) קְטַלְתּוֹ *thou hast killed him*; אוֹרוֹ (also אוֹרֵהוּ) *lux eius.*

The same method is employed in all the other Semitic languages, as well as in the Egyptian, Persian, Finnish, Tartar, and others; in Greek, Latin, and German we find only slight traces of the kind, e. g. German, *er gab's* for *er gab es*; Greek, πατήρ μου for πατήρ ἐμοῦ; Latin, *eccum, eccos*, &c., in Plautus and Terence for *ecce eum, ecce eos*.

b   2. The *case* which these suffixes represent is—

(*a*) When joined to verbs, the accusative (cf., however, § 117 *x*), e. g. קְטַלְתִּיהוּ I have killed *him*.

c   (*b*) When affixed to substantives, the genitive (like πατήρ μου, *pater eius*).   They then serve as *possessive pronouns*, e. g. אָבִי ('ābh-î) *my father*, סוּסוֹ *his horse*, which may be either *equus eius* or *equus suus*.

d   (*c*) When joined to particles, either the genitive or accusative, according as the particles originally expressed the idea of a noun or a verb, e. g. בֵּינִי, literally *interstitium mei, between me* (cf. *mea causa*); but הִנְנִי *behold me, ecce me*.

e   (*d*) Where, according to the Indo-Germanic case-system, the dative or ablative of the pronoun is required, the suffixes in Hebrew are joined to prepositions expressing those cases (לְ sign of the dative, בְּ *in*, מִן *from*, § 102), e. g. לוֹ *to him* (*ei*) and *to himself* (*sibi*), בּוֹ *in him*, מִנִּי (usually מִמֶּנִּי) *from me*.

---

[1] On apparent exceptions see § 135 *d*.

3. The suffixes of the 2nd person (‎ָךְ‎, &c.) are all formed with *f* a *k*-sound, not, like the *separate* pronouns of the 2nd person, with a *t*-sound.

So in all the Semitic languages, in Ethiopic even in the verbal form (*qatalka, thou hast killed* = Hebr. קְטַלְתָּ).

4. The *suffix of the verb* (the accusative) and the *suffix of the noun* (the *g* genitive) coincide in most forms, but some differ, e. g. ‏נִי‎— *me,* ‏־ִי‎ *my.*

Paradigm A at the end of the Grammar gives a table of all the forms of the *separate pronoun* and the *suffixes*; a fuller treatment of the *verbal suffix* and the mode of attaching it to the verb will be found in § 58 ff., of the *noun-suffix* in § 91, of the prepositions with suffixes in § 103, of adverbs with suffixes § 100 *o*.

§ 34. *The Demonstrative Pronoun.*

1. *Sing.* { *m.* זֶה ¹ *f.* זֹאת (זֹה, זוֹ)² } *this.* *Plur. com.* אֵלֶּה (rarely אֵל) *these. a*

Rem. 1. The feminine form זֹאת has undoubtedly arisen from זָאת, by *b* obscuring of an original *â* to *ô* (for זָאת = זֶה cf. the Arab. *hâ-ḏâ, this,* masc.; for ת as the feminine ending, § 80), and the forms זֹה, זוֹ, both of which are rare,³ are shortened from זֹאת. In ψ 132¹² זוֹ is used as a *relative,* cf. זוֹ below. In Jer 26⁶, Kᵉᵗʰîᵇʰ, הַזֹּאתָה (with the article and the demonstrative termination ה‏ָ‏) is found for זֹאת. The forms אֵלֶּה and אֵל are the plurals of זֶה and זֹאת by usage, though not etymologically. The form אֵל occurs only in the Pentateuch (but not in the Samaritan text), Gn 19⁸·²⁵, 26³·⁴, &c. (8 times), always with the article, הָאֵל [as well as הָאֵלֶּה, אֵלֶּה frequently], and in 1 Ch 20⁸ without the article [cf. Driver on Dt 4⁴²].⁴ Both the singular and the plural may refer to things as well as persons.

2. In combination with prepositions to denote the oblique case we find לָזֶה *c to this* (cf. for לְ, § 102 *g*), לָזֹאת, לְזֹאת *to this* (fem.), לָאֵלֶּה, לְאֵלֶּה *to these*; אֶת־זֶה *hunc,* אֶת־זֹאת *hanc,* אֶת־אֵלֶּה *hos,* also without אֶת־, even *before* the verb ψ 75⁸, &c. Note also מְחִיר זֶה *pretium huius* (1 K 21²), &c.

---

¹ In many languages the demonstratives begin with a *d*-sound (hence called the *demonstrative sound*) which, however, sometimes interchanges with a sibilant. Cf. Aram. דֵּן, דֵּךְ, דֵּךְ *masc.,* דָּא, דָּךְ, *fem.* (this); Sansk. *sa, sâ, tat*; Gothic *sa, sô, thata*; Germ. *da, der, die, das*; and Eng. *the, this, that,* &c. Cf. J. Barth, 'Zum semit. Demonstr. *d,*' in *ZDMG.* 59, 159 ff., and 633 ff.; *Sprachwiss. Untersuchungen zum Semit.,* Lpz. 1907, p. 30 ff. [See the Lexicon, s. v. זֶה, and Aram. דִּי, דָא.]

² That זֶה may stand for the feminine, cannot be proved either from Ju 16²⁸ or from the certainly corrupt passage in Jos 2¹⁷.

³ זוֹ 2 K 6¹⁹, and in seven other places; זוֹ only in Hos 7¹⁶, ψ 132¹².

⁴ According to Kuenen (cf. above, § 2 *n*) and Driver, on Lev 18²⁷ in Haupt's Bible, this אֵל is due to an error of the punctuators. It goes back to a time when the vowel of the second syllable was not yet indicated by a vowel letter, and later copyists wrongly omitted the addition of the ה. In Phoenician also it was written אל, but pronounced *ily* according to Plautus, *Poen,* v, 1, 9.

d   **2.** The secondary form זוּ occurs only in poetic style, and mostly for the relative, like our *that* for *who* [see Lexicon, s.v.]. Like אֲשֶׁר (§ 36), it serves for all numbers and genders.

e   Rem. 1. This pronoun takes the article (הָאֵל, הָאֵלֶּה, הַזֹּאת, הַזֶּה) according to the same rule as adjectives, see § 126 *u*; e.g. הָאִישׁ הַזֶּה *this man*, but זֶה הָאִישׁ *this is the man.*

f   2. Rarer secondary forms, with strengthened demonstrative force, are הַלָּזֶה Gn 24⁶⁵, 37¹⁹; הַלָּז *fem.* Ez 36³⁵; and shortened הַלָּז, sometimes *masc.*, as in Ju 6²⁰, 1 S 17⁷⁶, 2 K 23¹⁷, Zc 2⁸, Dn 8¹⁶, sometimes *fem.*, 2 K 4²⁵ : cf. 1 S 14¹ [and 20¹⁹ LXX; see Commentaries and Kittel].

g   3. The personal pronouns of the 3rd person also often have a demonstrative sense, see § 136.

§ 35. *The Article.*

J. Barth, 'Der heb. u. der aram. Artikel,' in *Sprachwiss. Untersuch. zum Semit.*, Lpz. 1907, p. 47 ff.

a   **1.** The article, which is by nature a kind of demonstrative pronoun, never appears in Hebrew as an independent word, but always in closest connexion with the word which is defined by it.   It usually takes the form הַ, with *ă* and a strengthening of the next consonant, e.g. הַשֶּׁמֶשׁ *the sun*, הַיְאֹר *the river*, הַלְוִיִּם *the Levites* (according to § 20 *m* for הַלְוִיִּם, הַיְאֹר).

b   Rem. With regard to the Dageš in יְ after the article, the rule is, that it is inserted when a ה or ע follows the יְ, e.g. הַיְּהוּדִים *the Jews*, הַיְּעֵפִים *the weary* (בַּיְעֵנִים La 4³ *Qᵉrê* is an exception), but הַיְאוֹר, הַיְסוֹד, הַיְלָדִים, &c.   *Dageš forte* also stands after the article in the prefix מְ in certain nouns and in the participles *Piʿēl* and *Puʿal* (see § 52 *c*) before ה, ע and ר, except when the guttural (or ר) has under it a short vowel in a sharpened syllable; thus הַמְּהוּמָה Ez 22⁵, הַמְּעָרָה *the cave*, בַּמְּרֵעִים ψ 37¹ (cf. Jb 38⁴⁰, 1 Ch 4⁴¹); but הַמְהַלֵּךְ ψ 104³ (Ec 4¹⁵, 2 Ch 23¹²; before ע ψ 103⁴); הַמְעֻשָּׁקָה Is 23¹², חֲמֻרָבְּלִים הַמְעֻלָּלִים Jos 6²². Before letters other than gutturals this מְ remains without Dageš, according to § 20 *m*.

c   **2.** When the article stands before a guttural, which (according to § 22 *b*) cannot properly be strengthened, the following cases arise, according to the character of the guttural (cf. § 27 *q*).

(1) In the case of the weakest guttural, א, and also with ר (§ 22 *c* and *q*), the strengthening is altogether omitted.   Consequently, the *Pathaḥ* of the article (since it stands in an open syllable) is always lengthened to *Qameṣ*; e.g. הָאָב *the father*, הָאַחֵר *the other*, הָאֵם *the mother*, הָאִישׁ *the man*, הָאוֹר *the light*, הָאֱלֹהִים ὁ θεός, הָרֶגֶל *the foot*, הָרֹאשׁ *the head*, הָרָשָׁע *the wicked.*

d   So also הַשְׁפוֹת Neh 3¹³, because syncopated from הָאַשְׁפוֹת (cf. verse 14 and Baer on the passage); הָאֻקִּים (as in Nu 11⁴, Ju 9⁴¹, 2 S 23³³, with the א

orthographically retained), for הָאֵז׳ Jer 40⁴ (cf. בָּאז׳ verse 1) ; הַסּוּרִים Ec 4¹⁴
for הָאֵס׳ ; הָרֵמִים 2 Ch 22⁵ for הָאֵר׳ (cf. 2 K 8²⁸).

(2) In the case of the other gutturals either the virtual strengthen- *e*
ing takes place (§ 22 *c*)—especially with the stronger sounds ח and
ה, less often with ע—or the strengthening is wholly omitted. In
the former case, the *Pathaḥ* of the article remains, because the syllable
is still regarded as closed; in the second case, the *Pathaḥ* is either
modified to *Seghôl* or fully lengthened to *Qameṣ*. That is to say :—

A. When the guttural has any other vowel than *ā* (–֫–) or *ŏ* (–֫֒–), *f*
then

(1) before the stronger sounds ח and ה the article regularly remains
הַ ; e. g. הַהוּא *that*, הַחֹרֶשׁ *the month*, הַחַיִל *the force*, הַחָכְמָה *the wisdom*.
Before ח, *ā* occurs only in הָחֵי Gn 6¹⁹ [not elsewhere], הֶחָרִיטִים Is 3²²,
הֶחָפְנִים Is 17⁸ [not elsewhere]; before ה, always in הָהֵם, הָהֵמָּה.

(2) before ע the *Pathaḥ* is generally ᵃlengthened to *Qameṣ*, e. g. הָעַיִן *g*
the eye, הָעִיר *the city*, הָעֶבֶד *the servant*, plur. הָעֲבָדִים; הָעֲלָמִים 1 K 12³²;
also in Gn 10¹⁷ הָעַרְקִי is the better reading. Exceptions are בְּעוֹבֶרֶת
Ex 15¹⁰, הַעִוְרִים 2 S 5⁶·⁸, Is 42¹⁸, בַּעֲבָד Is 24², הָעֹרְבִים Is 65¹¹, בָּעֶשֶׂק
Ez 22⁷, הַעֹּבְבִים Pr 2¹³ and הַעֹלֶבֶת Pr 2¹⁷, לָעֵינַיִם 1 S 16⁷, Ec 11⁷; but
לָעֵינ׳ Gn 3⁶, Pr 10²⁶. Cf. Baer on Is 42¹⁸.

B. When the guttural has *ā* (–֫–) then   *h*
(1) immediately before a tone-bearing הָ or עָ the article is always
הָ, otherwise it is הֶ; e. g. הָעָם *the people*, הָהָר *the mountain*, הָעָיִן (in
pause) *the eye*, הָהָרָה *towards the mountain*; but (according to § 22 *c*)
הֶהָרִים *the mountains*, הֶעָוֹן *the iniquity*.

(2) before חָ the article is invariably הֶ without regard to the tone ; *i*
e. g. הֶחָכָם *the wise man*, הֶחָג *the festival*.

C. When the guttural has –ֳ– the article is הֶ before חֳ; e. g. *k*
הֶחֳדָשִׁים *the months*; בֶּחֳרָבוֹת *in the waste places* (without the article בְּחׇ׳
bŏḥᵒrābhôth) Ez 33²⁷, הֶחֳרָבוֹת Ez 36³⁵·³⁸, cf. 2 Ch 27⁴; but הָ before עֳ, as
הָעֳמָרִים *the sheaves* Ru 2¹⁵.

The gender and number of the noun have no influence on the form
of the article.

Rem. 1. The original form of the Hebrew (and the Phoenician) article הַ *l*
is generally considered to have been הַל, the ל of which (owing to the proclitic
nature of the article) has been invariably assimilated to the following consonant, as in יִקַּח from *yilqaḥ*, § 19 *d*. This view was supported by the form
of the Arabic article אַל (pronounced *hal* by some modern Beduin), the ל of
which is also assimilated at least before all letters like *s* and *t* and before *l*, *n*,
and *r*, e. g. *'al-Qur'ân* but *'as-sănă* (Beduin *has-sana*) = Hebr. הַשָּׁנָה *the year*.

But Barth (*Amer. Journ. of Sem. Lang.*, 1896, p. 7 ff.), following Hupfeld and Stade, has shown that the Hebrew article is to be connected rather with the original Semitic demonstrative *hā*,[1] cf. Arab. *hāḏa*, Aram. *hāḏēn*, &c. The sharpening of the following consonant is to be explained exactly like the sharpening after וַ consecutive (§ 49 *f*; cf. also cases like בַּמֶּה, בַּמָּה, &c., § 102 *k*), from the close connexion of the *ha* with the following word, and the sharpening necessarily involved the shortening of the vowel.[2]

m The Arabic article is supposed to occur in the Old Testament in אַלְמֻגִּים 1 K 10[11.12] (also אַלְגּוּמִּים 2 Ch 2[7], 9[10.11]), *sandal-wood* (?), and in אֶלְגָּבִישׁ *hail, ice* = גָּבִישׁ (Arab. *ǧibs*) Ez 13[11.13], 38[22], but this explanation can hardly be correct. On the other hand, in the proper name אַלְמוֹדָד Gn 10[26] the first syllable is probably אֵל *God*, as suggested by D. H. Müller (see Lexicon, s. v.) and Nöldeke, *Sitzungsber. der Berl. Akad.*, 1882, p. 1186. אַלְקוּם Pr 30[31], commonly explained as = Arab. *al-qaum*, the militia, is also quite uncertain.

n 2. When the prefixes בְּ, לְ, כְּ (§ 102) come before the article, the ה is elided, and its vowel is thrown back to the prefix, in the place of the Š⁺wâ (§ 19 *k*, and § 23 *k*), e. g. בַּשָּׁמַיִם *in the heaven* for בְּהַשָּׁמַיִם (so ψ 36[6]); לָעָם for לְהָעָם *to the people*, בֶּהָרִים *on the mountains*, בֶּחֳדָשִׁים *in the months*; also in Is 41[2], read כֶּעָפָר instead of the impossible כֶּעָפָר. Exceptions to this rule occur almost exclusively in the later Books: Ez 40[25], 47[22], Ec 8[1], Dn 8[16], Neh 9[19], 12[3ⁱ], 2 Ch 10[7], 25[10], 29[27]; cf., however, 1 S 13[21], 2 S 21[20]. Elsewhere, e. g. 2 K 7[12], the Masora requires the elision in the *Q⁺rê*. A distinction in meaning is observed between כְּהַיּוֹם *about this time* (Gn 39[11], 1 S 9[13], &c.) and כַּיּוֹם *first of all* (Gn 25[31], &c.). After the copula וְ (*and*) elision of the ה does not take place, e. g. וְהָעָם.

o 3. The words אֶרֶץ *earth*, הַר *mountain*, חַג *feast*, עַם *people*, פַּר *bull*, always appear after the article with a long vowel (as in *pause*); הָעָם, הֶחָג, הָהָר, הָאָרֶץ, הַפָּר; cf. also אֲרוֹן *ark* (so in the absol. st. in 2 K 12[10], 2 Ch 24[8], but to be read אָרוֹן), with the article always הָאָרוֹן.

§ 36. *The Relative Pronoun.*

The relative pronoun (cf. § 138) is usually the indeclinable אֲשֶׁר (*who, which*, &c.), originally a demonstrative pronoun; see further §§ 138 and 155. In the later books, especially Eccles. and the late Psalms, also Lam. (4 times), Jon. (1[7]), Chron. (twice), Ezra (once),—and always in the Canticle (cf. also Ju 7[12], 8[26], 2 K 6[11]), שֶׁ is used instead; more rarely שַׁ Ju 5[7], Ct 1[7] (Jb 19[29]?); once שָׁ before א Ju 6[17] (elsewhere שֶׁ before a guttural), before ה even שֵׁ Ec 3[18], and according to some (e. g. Qimḥi) also in Ec 2[22].[3] [See Lexicon, s. v.]

---

[1] An original form *han*, proposed by Ungnad, 'Der hebr. Art.,' in *OLZ*. x (1907), col. 210 f., and *ZDMG*. 1908, p. 80 ff., is open to grave objections.
[2] In the Liḥyanitic inscriptions collected by Euting (ed. by D. H. Müller in *Epigraphische Denkmäler aus Arabien*, Wien, 1889) the article is ה, and also in a North Arabian dialect, according to E. Littmann, *Safa-inschriften*, p. 2, Rem., and p. 34.
[3] The full form אשר does not occur in Phoenician, but only שא (= אֲשֵׁ ?), pronounced *asse, esse* (also *as, es, is, ys, us*), or—especially in the later Punic

§ 37. *The Interrogative and Indefinite Pronouns.*

1. The interrogative pronoun is מִי *who?* (of persons, even before plurals, Gn 33[5], Is 60[8], 2 K 18[35], and sometimes also of things Gn 33[8], Ju 13[17], Mi 1[5] ; cf. also בַּת־מִי *whose daughter?* Gn 24[23] ; לְמִי *to whom?* אֶת־מִי *whom?*)—מָה, מַה (see *b*) *what?* (of things).—אֵי־זֶה *which? what?*

The form מַה, מָֽה, &c. (followed by *Dageš forte conjunct.*: even in וְ, Hb 2[1], &c., against § 20 *m*) may be explained (like the art. הַ־ § 35 *l*, and וְ in the *imperf. consec.*) from the rapid utterance of the interrogative in connexion with the following word. Most probably, however, the *Dageš forte* is rather due to the assimilation of an originally audible ה (מַה), as Olshausen), which goes back through the intermediate forms *math, mat* to an original *mant*: so W. Wright, *Comparative Grammar*, Cambridge, 1890, p. 124, partly following Böttcher, *Hebräische Grammatik*, § 261. A ground-form *mant* would most easily explain מָן (*what?*), used in Ex 16[15] in explanation of מָן *manna*, while מַן is the regular Aramaic for *who*. Socin calls attention to the Arabic *mah* (in pause with an audible *h*: *Mufaṣṣal*, 193, 8). Observe further that—

(*a*) In the closest connexion, by means of *Maqqeph*, מַה־ takes a following *Dageš* (§ 20 *d*), e.g. מַה־לָּךְ *what is it to thee?* and even in *one* word, as מַלָּכֶם *what is it to you?* Is 3[15] ; cf. Ex 4[2], Mal 1[13], and even before a guttural, מֵהֶם Ez 8[6] *Kethibh.*

(*b*) Before gutturals in close connexion, by means of *Maqqeph* or (e.g. Ju 14[18], 1 S 20[1]) a conjunctive accent, either מַה is used with a virtual strengthening of the guttural (§ 22 *c*), so especially before ה, and, in Gn 31[36], Jb 21[21], before ח —or the doubling is wholly omitted. In the latter case either (cf. § 35 *e-k*) *ă* is fully lengthened to *Qames* (so always before the ה of the article, except in Ec 2[12] ; also before הֵנָּה, הֵפַח, and so ה (Hb 2[18]), א (2 S 18[22], 2 K 8[14]), ע (Gn 31[22], 2 K 8[13]), or modified to *Seghôl*, especially before ע, חָ, and generally before הֶ. The omission of the strengthening also takes place as a rule with ה, ח, ע, when they have not *Qames*, and then the form is either מֶה or מָה, the latter especially before ח or ע, if *Maqqeph* follows.

The longer forms מָה and מֶה are also used (מֶה even before letters which are not gutturals) when not connected by *Maqqeph* but only by a *conjunctive accent*. As a rule מָה is then used, but sometimes מֶה when at a greater distance from the principal tone of the sentence, Is 1[5], ψ 4[3]. (On מֶה in the combinations בַּמֶּה, בַּמָּה, and even לָמֶה, 1 S 1[8], cf. § 102 *k* and *l*.)

(*c*) In the principal pause מָה is used without exception ; also as a rule with the smaller *disjunctives*, and almost always before gutturals (מֶה only in very few cases). On the other hand, מָה more often stands before letters which are not gutturals, when at a greater distance from the principal tone of the sentence, e.g. 1 S 4[6], 15[14], 2 K 1[7], Hag 1[9] (see Köhler on the passage), ψ 10[13], Jb 7[21] ; cf., however, Pr 31[2], and Delitzsch on the passage.

2. On מִי and מָה as indefinite pronouns in the sense of *quicunque, quodcunque*, and as relatives, *is qui, id quod*, &c., see § 137 *c*.

---

and in the *Poenulus* of Plautus—ש (*sa, si, sy, su*). Also in New Hebrew שְׁ has become the common form. Cf. Schröder, *Phön. Sprache*, p. 162 ff. and below, § 155 ; also Bergsträsser, 'Das hebr. Präfix שְׁ,' in *ZAW.* 1909, p. 40 ff.

CHAPTER II

THE VERB

§ 38. *General View.*

a Verbal stems are either original or derived. They are usually divided into—

(*a*) Verbal stems proper (*primitive verbs*), which exhibit the stem without any addition, e.g. מָלַךְ *he has reigned.*

b (*b*) *Verbal derivatives,* i.e. *secondary* verbal stems, derived from the pure stem (letter *a*), e.g. קִדֵּשׁ *to sanctify,* הִתְקַדֵּשׁ *to sanctify oneself,* from קָדַשׁ *to be holy.* These are usually called *conjugations* (§ 39).

c (*c*) *Denominatives,*[1] i.e. verbs derived from nouns (like the Latin *causari, praedari,* and Eng. *to skin, to stone*), or even from particles (see *d,* end) either in a primitive or derivative form, e.g. אָהַל, *Qal* and *Piʿēl, to pitch a tent,* from אֹהֶל *tent;* הִשְׁרִישׁ and שֵׁרֵשׁ *to take root,* and שֵׁרֵשׁ *to root out,* from שֹׁרֶשׁ *root* (§ 52 *h*).

d This does not exclude the possibility that, for nouns, from which denominative verbs are derived, the corresponding (original) verbal stem may still be found either in Hebrew or in the dialects. The meaning, however, is sufficient to show that the denominatives have come from the noun, not from the verbal stem, e.g. לְבֵנָה *a brick* (verbal stem לבן *to be white*), denomin. לָבַן *to make bricks;* דָּג *a fish* (verbal stem דָּנָה *to be prolific*), denomin. דּוּג *to fish;* חָרַף *to winter* (from חֹרֶף *autumn, winter,* stem חָרַף *to pluck*); קוּץ *to pass the summer* (from קַיִץ *summer,* stem קיץ *to be hot*).

On 'Semitic verbs derived from particles' see P. Haupt in the *Amer. Journ. of Sem. Lang.,* xxii (1906), 257 ff.

§ 39. *Ground-form and Derived Stems.*

Brockelmann, *Sem. Sprachwiss.,* p. 119 ff.; *Grundriss,* p. 504 ff.

a 1. The 3rd sing. masc. of the *Perfect* in the form of the pure stem (i.e. in *Qal,* see *e*) is generally regarded, lexicographically and grammatically, as the ground-form of the verb (§ 30 *a*), e.g. קָטַל *he has killed,* כָּבֵד *he was heavy,* קָטֹן *he was little.*[2] From this form the other

---

[1] Cf. W. J. Gerber, *Die hebr. Verba denom., insbes. im theol. Sprachgebr. des A. T.,* Lpz. 1896.

[2] For the sake of brevity, however, the meaning in Hebrew-English Lexicons is usually given in the Infinitive, e.g. לָמַד *to learn,* properly *he has learnt.*

persons of the *Perfect* are derived, and the *Participle* also is connected with it. קְטֹל or קָטַל, like the Imperative and Infinitive construct in sound, may also be regarded as an alternative ground-form, with which the Imperfect (see § 47) is connected.

In verbs ע״וּ (i.e. with וּ for their second radical) the stem-form, given both *b* in Lexicon and Grammar, is not the 3rd sing. masc. Perfect (consisting of two consonants), but the form with medial וּ, which appears in the Imperative and Infinitive; e. g. שׁוּב *to return* (3rd pers. perf. שָׁב): the same is the case in most stems with medial י, e. g. דִּין *to judge*.

2. From the pure stem, or *Qal*, the derivative stems are formed *c* according to an unvarying analogy, in which the idea of the stem assumes the most varied shades of meaning, according to the changes in its form (intensive, frequentative, privative, causative, reflexive, reciprocal; some of them with corresponding passive forms), e. g. לָמַד *to learn*, לִמַּד *to teach*; שָׁכַב *to lie*, הִשְׁכִּיב *to lay*; שָׁפַט *to judge*, נִשְׁפַּט *to contend*. In other languages such formations are regarded as new or *derivative* verbs, e. g. Germ. *fallen* (to fall), *fällen* (to fell); *trinken* (to drink), *tränken* (to drench); Lat. *lactere* (to suck, Germ. *saugen*), *lactare* (to suckle, Germ. *säugen*); *iacère* (to throw), *iacēre* (to lie down); γίνομαι, γεννάω. In Hebrew, however, these formations are incomparably more regular and systematic than (e. g.) in Greek, Latin, or English; and, since the time of Reuchlin, they have usually been called *conjugations* of the primitive form (among the Jewish grammarians בִּנְיָנִים, i. e. *formations*, or more correctly *species*), and are always treated together in the grammar and lexicon.[1]

3. The changes in the primitive form consist either in internal *d* modification by means of vowel-change and strengthening of the middle consonant (קָטֵל, קִטֵּל; קוֹטֵל, קוֹטֵל; cf. *to lie, to lay; to fall, to fell*), or in the repetition of one or two of the stem-consonants (קְטַלְטַל, קְטַלְל), or finally in the introduction of formative additions (נִקְטַל), which may also be accompanied by internal change (הִתְקַטֵּל, הִקְטִיל). Cf. § 31 *b*.

In Aramaic the formation of the conjugations is effected more by formative additions than by vowel-change. The vocalic distinctions have mostly become obsolete, so that, e. g. the reflexives with the prefix אֶת, אַת, הִת, הִת have entirely usurped the place of the passives. On the other hand, Arabic has preserved great wealth in both methods of formation, while Hebrew in this, as in other respects, holds the middle place (§ 1 *m*).

4. Grammarians differ as to the *number* and *arrangement* of these *e* conjugations. The common practice, however, of calling them by the

---

[1] The term *Conjugation* thus has an entirely different meaning in Hebrew and Greek or Latin grammar.

old grammatical terms, prevents any misunderstanding. The simple form is called *Qal* (קַל *light*, because it has no formative additions); the others (כְּבֵדִים *heavy*, being weighted, as it were, with the strengthening of consonants or with formative additions) take their names from the paradigm of פָּעַל *he has done*,[1] which was used in the earliest Jewish grammatical works. Several of these have passives which are distinguished from their actives by more obscure vowels. The common conjugations (including *Qal* and the passives) are the seven following, but very few verbs exhibit them all:

	Active.		Passive.	
f 1. Qal	קָטַל *to kill*.		(Cf. § 52 *e*.)	
2. Niph'al	נִקְטַל *to kill oneself* (rarely passive).			
3. Pi'ēl	קִטֵּל *to kill many, to massacre*.	4. Pu'al	קֻטַּל.	
5. Hiph'il	הִקְטִיל *to cause to kill*.	6. Hoph'al	הָקְטַל.	
7. Hithpa'ēl	הִתְקַטֵּל *to kill oneself*.	[Very rare, Hothpa'al	הָתְקַטַּל.]	

g   There are besides several less frequent conjugations, some of which, however, are more common in the kindred languages, and even in Hebrew (in the weak verb) regularly take the place of the usual conjugations (§ 55).

In Arabic there is a greater variety of conjugations, and their arrangement is more appropriate. According to the Arabic method, the Hebrew conjugations would stand thus: 1. *Qal*; 2. *Pi'ēl* and *Pu'al*; 3. *Pô'ēl* and *Pô'al* (see § 55 *b*); 4. *Hiph'il* and *Hoph'al*; 5. *Hithpa'ēl* and *Hothpa'al*; 6. *Hithpô'ēl* (see § 55 *b*); 7. *Niph'al*; 8. *Hithpa'ēl* (see § 54 *l*); 9. *Pi'lēl* (see § 55 *d*). A more satisfactory division would be into three classes: (1) The intensive *Pi'ēl* with the derived and analogous forms *Pu'al* and *Hithpa'ēl*. (2) The causative *Hiph'il* with its passive *Hoph'al*, and the analogous forms (*Šaph'ēl* and *Tiph'ēl*). (3) The reflexive or passive *Niph'al*.

---

[1] This paradigm was borrowed from the Arabic grammarians, and, according to Bacher, probably first adopted throughout by Abulwalîd. It was, however, unsuitable on account of the guttural, and was, therefore, usually exchanged in later times for פָּקַד, after the example of Moses Qimḥi. This verb has the advantage, that all its conjugations are actually found in the Old Testament. On the other hand, it has the disadvantage of indistinctness in the pronunciation of some of its forms, e. g. פְּקַדְתָּ, פְּקַדְתֶּם. The paradigm of קָטַל, commonly used since the time of Danz, avoids this defect, and is especially adapted for the comparative treatment of the Semitic dialects, inasmuch as it is found with slight change (Arab. and Ethiop. קתל) in all of them. It is true that in Hebrew it occurs only three times in *Qal*, and even then only in poetic style (ψ 139¹⁹, Jb 13¹⁵, 24¹⁴); yet it is worth retaining as a model which has been sanctioned by usage. More serious is the defect, that a number of forms of the paradigm of קָטַל leave the beginner in doubt as to whether or not there should be a *Dageš* in the Bᵉgadkᵉphath letters, and consequently as to the correct division of the syllables.

§ 40. *Tenses. Moods. Flexion.*

A. Ungnad, 'Die gegenseitigen Beziehungen der Verbalformen im Grundstamm des semit. Verbs,' in *ZDMG.* 59 (1905), 766 ff., and his 'Zum hebr.
Verbalsystem ', in *Beiträge zur Assyriologie* ed. by Fr. Delitzsch and P. Haupt,
1907, p. 55 ff.

1. While the Hebrew verb, owing to these derivative forms or *a*
conjugations, possesses a certain richness and copiousness, it is, on the
other hand, poor in the matter of *tenses* and *moods.* The verb has
only two *tense*-forms (*Perfect* and *Imperfect,* see the note on § 47 *a*),
besides an *Imperative* (but only in the active), two *Infinitives* and
a *Participle.* All relations of time, absolute and relative, are expressed
either by these forms (hence a certain diversity in their meaning,
§ 106 ff.) or by syntactical combinations. Of moods properly so
called (besides the *Imperfect Indicative* and *Imperative*), only the
Jussive and *Optative* are sometimes indicated by express modifications
of the Imperfect-form (§ 48).

2. The *inflexion* of the *Perfect, Imperfect,* and *Imperative* as to *b*
persons, differs from that of the Western languages in having, to a
great extent, distinct forms for the two genders, which correspond to
the different forms of the *personal pronoun. It is from the union
of the pronoun with the verbal stem that the personal inflexions of these
tenses arise.*

The following table will serve for the beginner as a provisional *c*
scheme of the formative syllables (*afformatives* and *preformatives*)
of the two *tenses.* The three stem-consonants of the strong verb are
denoted by dots. Cf. § 44 ff. and the Paradigms.

PERFECT.

	Singular.					Plural.			
3. *m.*		•	•	•	3. *c.*	וּ	•	•	•
3. *f.*	הָ	•	•	•					
2. *m.*	תָּ	•	•	•	2. *m.*	תֶּם	•	•	•
2. *f.*	תְּ	•	•	•	2. *f.*	תֶּן	•	•	•
1. *c.*	תִּי	•	•	•	1. *c.*	נוּ	•	•	•

IMPERFECT.

	Singular.					Plural.			
3. *m.*		•	•	•	י	3. *m.*	וּ	•	•	•	•	י
3. *f.*		•	•	•	תּ	3. *f.*	נָה	•	•	•	תּ
2. *m.*		•	•	•	תּ	2. *m.*	וּ	•	•	•	תּ
2. *f.*	יִ	•	•	•	תּ	2. *f.*	נָה	•	•	•	תּ
1. *c.*		•	•	•	א	1. *c.*		•	•	•	נ

§ 41. *Variations from the Ordinary Form of the Strong Verb.*

a　　The same laws which are normally exhibited in stems with strong (unchangeable) consonants, hold good for all other verbs. Deviations from the model of the strong verb are only modifications due to the special character or weakness of certain consonants, viz. : —

(*a*) When one of the stem-consonants (or *radicals*) is a guttural. In this case, however, the variations only occur in the vocalization (according to § 22), not in the consonants. The *guttural verbs* (§§ 62–65) are, therefore, only a variety of the *strong verb*.

b　　(*b*) When a stem-consonant (*radical*) disappears by assimilation (§ 19 *b-f*), or when the stem originally consisted of only two consonants (*verbs* פ״ן, ע״ע, and ע״ו, as נָשַׁ֥ל קַל, קוּם, §§ 66, 67, 72).

c　　(*c*) When one of the stem-consonants (*radicals*) is a weak letter. In this case, through aphaeresis, elision, &c., of the weak consonant, various important deviations from the regular form occur. Cf. § 68 ff. for these verbs, such as גָּלָה, מָצָא, יָשַׁב, דָּרַ.

d　　Taking the old paradigm פָּעַל as a model, it is usual, following the example of the Jewish grammarians, to call the first radical of any stem פ, the second ע, and the third ל. Hence the expressions, *verb* פ״א for a verb whose first radical is א (*primae radicalis* [*sc. literae*] א) ; ע״י for *mediae radicalis* י ; ע״ע for a verb whose second radical is repeated to form a third.

I. The Strong Verb.

§ 42.

As the formation of the strong verb is the model also for the weak verb, a statement of the general formative laws should precede the treatment of special cases.

Paradigm B, together with the Table of the personal preformatives and afformatives given in § 40 *c*, offers a complete survey of the normal forms. A full explanation of them is given in the following sections (§§ 43-55), where each point is elucidated on its first occurrence ; thus e. g. the inflexion of the Perfect, the Imperfect and its modifications, will be found under Qal, &c.

A. THE PURE STEM, OR QAL.

§ 43. *Its Form and Meaning.*

a　　The common form of the 3rd sing. masc. of the *Perfect Qal* is קָטַל, with *ă* (*Pathaḥ*) in the second syllable, especially in *transitive* verbs (but see § 44 *c*). There is also a form with *ē* (*Ṣere*, originally *ĭ*), and another with *ō* (*Ḥolem*, originally *ŭ*) in the second syllable, both of which, however, have almost always an *intransitive* [1] meaning,

---

[1] But cf. such instances as Jer 48[5]. In Arabic also, transitive verbs are found with middle *ĭ*, corresponding to Hebrew verbs with *ē* in the second

and serve to express states and qualities, e.g. כָּבֵד *to be heavy,* קָטֹן *to be small.*

In Paradigm B a verb *middle a,* a verb *middle ē,* and a verb *middle ō* are accordingly given side by side. The second example כָּבֵד is chosen as showing, at the same time, when the *Dageš lene* is to be inserted or omitted.

Rem. 1. The vowel of the second syllable is the principal vowel, and hence *b* on it depends the distinction between the transitive and intransitive meaning. The *Qameṣ* of the first syllable is lengthened from an original *ă* (cf. Arabic *qătălă*), but it can be retained in Hebrew only immediately before the tone, or at the most (with an open ultima) in the counter-tone with *Metheg*; otherwise, like all the pretonic vowels (*ā, ē*), it becomes *Šᵉwâ,* e. g. קְטַלְתֶּם 2nd *plur. masc.* In the Aramaic dialects the vowel of the first syllable is always reduced to Šᵉwâ, as קְטַל = Hebr. קָטַל. The intransitive forms in Arabic are *qătĭlă, qătŭlă;* in Hebrew (after the rejection of the final vowel) *ĭ* being in the tone-syllable has been regularly lengthened to *ē,* and *ŭ* to *ō.*

2. Examples of *denominatives* in Qal are : חָמַר *to cover with pitch,* from חֵמָר *c* *pitch;* מָלַח *to salt,* from מֶלַח *salt;* שָׁבַר (usually *Hiph.*) *to buy* or *sell corn,* from שֶׁבֶר *corn;* see above, § 38 *c.*

§ 44. *Flexion of the Perfect of Qal.*[1]

1. The formation of the persons of the Perfect is effected by the *a* addition of certain forms of the personal pronoun, and marks of the 3rd fem. sing. and 3rd pl. (as *afformatives*) to the *end* of the verbal-stem, which contains the idea of a predicate, and may be regarded, in meaning if not in form, as a *Participle* or *verbal adjective.* For the 3rd *pers. sing. masc. Perfect,* the pronominal or subject idea inherent in the finite verb is sufficient : thus, קָטַל *he has killed,* קָטַלְתָּ *thou hast killed* (as it were, *killing thou,* or *a killer thou*), *a killer wast thou* = קָטַל אַתָּה ; יָרֵא *he was fearing,* יְרֵאתֶם *ye were fearing* = יָרֵא אַתֶּם. The ending of the 1st pers. plur. (נוּ—) is also certainly connected with the termination of אֲנַחְנוּ, אנו *we* (§ 32 *b, d*). The afformative of the 1st pers. sing. (תִּי) is to be referred, by an interchange of כ and ת (cf. § 33 *f*), to that form of the pronoun which also underlies אָנֹכִי, I.[2] In the *third* person ה_ (originally ת_, cf. below, *f*) is the mark of the feminine, as in a great number of nouns (§ 80 *c*), and ו is the termination of the plural; cf., for the latter, the termination of the 3rd and 2nd pers. plur. Imperf. *ûna* in Arabic and *û* (often also וֹן)

syllable. Hence P. Haupt (*Proc. Amer. Or. Soc.,* 1894, p. ci f.) prefers to distinguish them as *verba voluntaria* (actions which depend on the will of the subject) and *involuntaria* (actions or states independent of the will of the subject).

[1] Cf. Nöldeke, 'Die Endungen des Perfects' (*Untersuchungen zur semit.* Gramm. ii.), in *ZDMG.* vol. 38, p. 407 ff., and more fully in *Beiträge zur sem. Sprachwiss.,* Strassb. 1904, p. 15 ff.

[2] According to Nöldeke, *l.c.,* p. 419, the original Semitic termination of the 1st sing. Perf. was most probably *kū* ; cf. the Ethiopic *qatalku,* Arabic *qataltu.*

in Hebrew, also *úna* (in the construct state *ú*) as the plural termination of masc. nouns in literary Arabic.

b 2. The characteristic *Pathaḥ* of the second syllable becomes *Šᵉwâ* before an afformative beginning with a vowel, where it would otherwise stand in an open syllable (as קָטְלוּ, קָטְלָה; but in *pause* קָטָלוּ, קָטָלָה). Before an afformative beginning with a consonant the *Pathaḥ* remains, whether in the tone-syllable (קְטַלְתָּ, קְטַלְתְּ, קְטַלְתִּי, קְטַלְנוּ; in *pause* קְטָלְתְּ &c.) or *before* it. In the latter case, however, the *Qames* of the first syllable, being no longer a pretonic vowel, becomes vocal *Šᵉwâ*; as קְטַלְתֶּם, קְטַלְתֶּן; cf. § 27 *i* and § 43 *b*. On the retention of *ā* with *Metheg* of the counter-tone in the *Perf. consecutive*, cf. § 49 *i*.

c Rem. I. Verbs middle *ē* in Hebrew (as in Ethiopic, but not in Arabic or Aramaic) generally change the *E*-sound in their inflexion into *Pathaḥ* (frequently so even in the 3rd sing. masc. Perf.). This tendency to assimilate to the more common verbs middle *a* may also be explained from the laws of vocalization of the tone-bearing closed penultima, which does not readily admit of *Sere*, and never of *Ḥireq*, of which the *Sere* is a lengthening (cf. § 26 *p*). On the other hand, *Sere* is retained in an open syllable; regularly so in the weak stems ל״א (§ 74 *g*), before suffixes (§ 59 *i*), and in the pausal forms of the strong stem in an open tone-syllable, e. g. דָּבֵקָה *it cleaveth*, Jb 29¹⁰ (not דָּבְקָה), cf. 2 S 1²³, Jb 41¹⁵; even (contrary to § 29 *q*) in a *closed* pausal syllable, e. g. שָׁכֵן, Dt 33¹² (out of pause שָׁכַן, Is 32¹⁶); but קָטֵל Is 33⁹, &c., according to § 29 *q*.

d 2. In some weak stems middle *a*, the *Pathaḥ* under the second radical sometimes, in a closed toneless syllable, becomes ֶ, and, in one example, ֵ. Thus from יָרֵשׁ: וִירִשְׁתָּהּ *and thou shalt possess it*, Dt 17¹⁴; וִירִשְׁתֶּם Dt 19¹; וִירִשְׁתֶּם Dt 4¹, and frequently; from יָלַד *to bring forth, to beget*; יְלִדְתִּיךָ ψ 2⁷ (cf. Nu 11¹², Jer 2²⁷, 15¹⁰); from פּוּשׁ; וּפִשְׁתֶּם Mal 3²⁰; from שָׁאַל; שְׁאִלְתִּיו *I have asked him*, I S 1²⁰ (Ju 13⁶), and three times שְׁאִלְתֶּם I S 12¹³, 25⁵, Jb 21²⁹. Qimḥi already suggests the explanation, that the *ĭ* (*ĕ*) of these forms of שָׁאַל and יָרֵשׁ is the original vowel, since along with שָׁאַל and יָרֵשׁ are also found שָׁאֵל and יָרֵשׁ (see the Lexicon). The possibility of this explanation cannot be denied (especially in the case of יָרֵשׁ, see § 69 *s*); the *ĭ* in these forms might, however, equally well have arisen from an attenuation of *ă* (§ 27 *s*), such as must in any case be assumed in the other instances. Moreover, it is worthy of notice that in all the above cases the *ĭ* is favoured by the character of the following consonant (a sibilant or dental), and in most of them also by the tendency towards assimilation of the vowels (cf. § 54 *k* and § 64 *f*).

e 3. In verbs middle *ō*, the *Ḥolem* is retained in the tone-syllable, e. g. יָכֹלְתָּ *thou didst tremble*; יָכֹלוּ in pause for יָכְלוּ *they were able*; but in a toneless closed syllable the original short vowel appears in the form of a *Qames ḥaṭuph*; יְכָלְתִּיו *I have prevailed against him*, ψ 13⁵; וְיָכָלְתָּ (see § 49 *h*) *then shalt thou be able*, Ex 18²³; in a toneless open syllable it becomes vocal *Šᵉwâ*, e. g. יָכְלָה, יָכְלוּ.

f 4. Rarer forms[1] are: Sing. 3rd *fem.* in ת ֵ (as in Arabic, Ethiopic, and

---

[1] Many of these forms, which are uncommon in Hebrew, are usual in the

Aramaic), e. g. אָזְלַת *it is gone*, Dt 32³⁶; וְנִשְׁבַּחַת Is 23¹⁵ (in the Aramaic form, for (וְנִשְׁבְּחָה); from a verb ע״ו, וְשָׁבַת, cf. § 72 *o*. This original feminine ending -*ath* is regularly retained before suffixes, see § 59 *a*; and similarly in stems ל״ה, either in the form *āth* (which is frequent also in stems ל״א § 74 *g*), or with the *Pathaḥ* weakened to *vocal Šᵉwâ* before the pleonastic ending ָה, e. g. גָּלְתָה § 75 *i*. In Ez 31⁵ the Aramaic form גָּבְהָא occurs instead of גָּבְהָה.

2nd *masc.* תָּה for תָּ (differing only orthographically), e. g. בָּגַרְתָּה *thou hast* *g* *dealt treacherously*, Mal 2¹⁴; cf. 1 S 15³, Gn 3¹² נָתַתָּה which is twice as common as נָתַתָּ, cf. § 66 *h*); Gn 21²³, 2 S 2²⁶, 2 K 9³, Is 2⁶, ψ 56⁹ (so also in *Hiph'il*; 2 K 9⁷, Is 37²³, ψ 60⁴).

2nd *fem.* has sometimes a Yodh at the end, as in הָלַכְתִּי *thou wentest*, Jer 31²¹; *h* cf. 2³³, 3⁴·⁵, 4¹⁹ (but read the ptcp. שֹׁמַעַת, with the LXX, instead of the 2nd fem.),46¹¹, and so commonly in Jeremiah, and Ez (16¹⁸, &c.); see also Mi 4¹³, Ru 3³·⁴. הָלַכְתִּי, &c., is really intended, for the vowel signs in the text belong to the marginal reading הָלַכְתְּ (without י)¹ as in the corresponding pronoun אַתִּי (אַתְּ) § 32 *h*. The ordinary form has rejected the final *i*, but it regularly reappears when pronominal suffixes are added (§ 59 *a*, *c*).

1st *pers. comm.* sometimes without Yodh, as יָדַעְתְּ ψ 140¹³, Jb 42², 1 K 8⁴⁸, *i* Ez 16⁵⁹ (all in Kᵉthîbh), ψ 16², without a Qᵉrê; in 2 K 18²⁰ also אָמַרְתְּ is really intended, as appears from Is 36⁵. The Qᵉrê requires the ordinary form, to which the vowels of the text properly belong, whilst the Kᵉthîbh is probably to be regarded as the remains of an earlier orthography, which omitted vowel-letters even at the end of the word.

תֶּן as the termination of the 2nd *plur. m.* for תֶּם Ez 33²⁶, might just possibly *k* be due to the following ת (cf., for an analogous case, Mi 3¹², § 87 *e*), but is probably a copyist's error. Plur. 2nd *fem.* in תֶּנָה- (according to others תֵּנָה-) Am 4³, but the reading is very doubtful; since ה follows, it is perhaps merely due to dittography; cf., however, אַתֵּנָה § 32 *i*.

3rd *plur. comm.* has three times the very strange termination וּן²; יְדָעוּן Dt *l* 8³·¹⁶ (both before א, and hence, no doubt, if the text is correct, to avoid a hiatus), and in the still more doubtful form עָקוּן Is 26¹⁶; on וּן in the Imperf. see § 47 *m*; on the affixed א in Jos 10²⁴, Is 28¹², see § 23 *i*.

It is very doubtful whether, as in most Semitic languages (see § 47 *c*, note), *m* the 3rd-*fem. plur.* in Hebrew was originally distinguished from the 3rd *masc.*

---

other Semitic dialects, and may, therefore, be called Aramaisms (Syriasms) or Arabisms. They must not, however, be regarded as cases of borrowing, but as a return to original forms.

¹ Where the Masora apparently regards the תִּי as the termination of the 2nd *sing. fem.*, e. g. in Jer 2²⁰ (twice), Mi 4¹³, it has rather taken the form as 1st *pers. sing.* (cf. Stade, *Gramm.*, p. 253); so in Ju 5⁷, where קַמְתִּי, on account of verse 12, must either have originally been intended as 2nd *sing. fem.*, or is due to an erroneous pronunciation of the form קמת as קַמְתִּי instead of 3rd *sing. fem.* קָמַת (as LXX).

² That these examples can hardly be referred to a primitive Semitic ending *ûn* in the 3rd plur. Perf., has been shown by Nöldeke in *ZDMG.* vol. 38, p. 409 ff.; cf. also *ZDMG.* vol. 32, p. 757 f., where G. Hoffmann proves that the terminations in *Nûn* of the 3rd plur. in Aramaic, formerly adduced by us, are secondary forms. [See also Driver, *Heb. Tenses*³, p. 6 *note*.]

plur. by the termination הָ֫__, as in Biblical Aramaic. Nöldeke (*ZDMG.* 38 [1884], p. 411) referred doubtfully to the textual readings in Dt 21⁷, Jos 15⁴, 18¹²·¹⁴·¹⁹, Jer 2¹⁵, 22⁶, where the Masora uniformly inserts the termination *û*, and to Gn 48¹⁰ in the Samaritan Pentateuch, Gn 49²², 1 S 4¹⁵, ψ 18³⁵, Neh 13¹⁰. In his *Beiträge zur sem. Sprachwiss.*, p. 19, however, he observes that the construction of a fem. plural with the 3rd sing. fem. is not unexampled, and also that ה is often found as a mistake for ו. On the other hand Mayer Lambert (*Une série de Qeré ketib*, Paris, 1891, p. 6 ff.) explains all these Kᵉthibh, as well as ψ 73², Jer 50⁶ (?), and (against Nöldeke) 1 K 22⁴⁹ (where ה is undoubtedly the article belonging to the next word), Jb 16¹⁶ (where the *masc.* פְּנֵי requires the marginal reading), also Jer 48⁴¹, 51⁵⁶, Ez 26², ψ 68¹⁴, as remains of the 3rd *fem. plur.* in הָ֫__. The form was abandoned as being indistinguishable from the (later) form of the 3rd *fem. sing.*, but tended to be retained in the perfect of verbs לְ"ה, as היה Kᵉthibh six times in the above examples.

n 5. The afformatives תָּ, (תְּ), תִּי, נוּ are generally toneless, and the forms with these inflexions are consequently *Mil'êl* (קָטַ֫לְתָּ, &c.); with all the other afformatives they are *Milra'* (§ 15 *c*). The place of the tone may, however, be shifted: (*a*) by the *pause* (§ 29 *i–v*), whenever a vowel which has become vocal Šᵉwâ under the second stem-consonant is restored by the *pause*; as קָטָ֫לָה for קָטְלָה (דָּבָ֫קָה for דָּבְקָה), and קָטָ֫לוּ for קָטְלוּ (מָלָ֫אוּ for מִלְאוּ); (*b*) in certain cases after *wāw consecutive* of the *Perfect* (see § 49 *h*).

o 6. Contraction of a final ת with the ת of the afformative occurs e. g. in כָּרַ֫תִּי Hag 2⁵, &c.; cf. Is 14²⁰, &c., in the *Perf. Po'el*; Dt 4²⁵ in the *Hiph'il* of שִׁחֵת; Is 21², &c., in the *Hiph'il* of שָׁבַת. Contraction of a final נ with the afformative נוּ occurs in נָתַ֫נּוּ Gn 34¹⁶; in *Niph.* Ezr 9⁷, cf. 2 Ch 14¹⁰; in *Hiph.* 2 Ch 29¹⁹; with the afformative נָה in the *Imperfect Qal* Ez 17²³; *Pi'êl* ψ 71²³, where with Baer and Ginsburg תְּרַנֶּ֫נָּה is to be read, according to others תְּרַנֶּ֫נָה (cf. in *Polel* תְּקוֹנֶ֫נָה Ez 32¹⁶), but certainly not תְּרַנֶּ֫נָה with the Mantua ed., Opitius and Hahn; with נָה in the *Imperat. Hiph.* Gn 4²³, Is 32⁹.

§ 45. *The Infinitive.*

F. Prätorius, 'Ueber den sog. Inf. absol. des Hebr.,' in *ZDMG.* 1902, p. 546 ff.

a 1. The Infinitive is represented in Hebrew by two forms, a shorter and a longer; both are, however, strictly speaking, independent *nouns* (*verbal substantives*). The shorter form, *the Infinitive construct* (in Qal קְטֹל,[1] sometimes incorrectly קְטוֹל), is used in very various ways, sometimes in connexion with pronominal suffixes, or governing a substantive in the genitive, or with an accusative of the object (§ 115), sometimes in connexion with prepositions (לִקְטֹל *to kill*, § 114 *f*), and sometimes in dependence upon substantives as genitive, or upon verbs as accusative of the object. On the other hand, the use of the longer form, the *Infinitive absolute* (in Qal קָטוֹל, sometimes also קָטֹל, obscured from original *qátâl*), is restricted to those cases in which it emphasizes

---

[1] Cf. the analogous forms of the noun, § 93 *t.*

the abstract verbal idea, without regard to the subject or object of the action. It stands most frequently as an adverbial accusative with a finite verb of the same stem (§ 113 *h-s*).[1]

The flexibility and versatility of the Infin. constr. and the rigidity *b* and inflexibility of the Infin. absol. are reflected in their vocalization. The latter has unchangeable vowels, while the *ō* of the Infin. constr. may be lost. For קְטֹל, according to § 84[a], *e*, goes back to the ground-form *qŭṭŭl*.

Other forms of the Infin. constr. Qal of the strong verb are— *c*

(*a*) קְטַל, e.g. שְׁכַב *to lie*, Gn 34[7]; שְׁפַל *to sink*, Ec 12[4]; especially with verbs which have *ă* in the second syllable of the Imperf.: hence sometimes also with those, whose second or third radical is a guttural (frequently besides the ordinary form). All the examples (except שְׁכַב, see above) occur in the closest connexion with the following word, or with suffixes (see § 61 *c*). In Ez 21[33] the Masora seems to treat לְטֶבַח (verse 20, in *pause* לְטָבַח) as an Infinitive = לִטְבֹּחַ; probably לְטֶבַח should be read.

(*b*) קִטְלָה and, attenuated from it, קִטְלָה; קָטְלָה and קִטְלָה (which are *d* feminine forms[2] of קְטַל and קְטֹל, mostly from intransitive verbs, and sometimes found along with forms having no feminine ending in use), e.g. לְאַשְׁמָה *to be guilty*, Lv 5[26], אַהֲבָה *to love*, שִׂנְאָה *to hate*; לְיִרְאָה, often in Dt., *to fear*; זִקְנָה *to be old*; קִרְאָה *to meet* (in לִקְרַאת § 19 *k*); לְרִבְעָה *to lie down*, Lv 20[16]; לְמָשְׁחָה *to anoint*, Ex 29[29]; לְרָחְצָה *to wash*, Ex 30[18], &c.; לְטֻמְאָה (also a subst. = *uncleanness*, like טֻמְאָה) *to be unclean*, Lv 15[32]; לְקָרְבָה *to approach*, Ex 36[2], &c.; cf. Lv 12[4,5], Dt 11[22], Is 30[19], Ez 21[16], Hag 1[6]; also רָחֳקָה *to be far off*, Ez 8[6]; חֶמְלָה *to pity*, Ez 16[5]; cf. Ho 7[4]. On the other hand in חֶמְלָה Gn 19[16], the original *ă* has been modified to *ĕ*; cf. חֶזְקָה Is 8[11], &c.

(*c*) In the Aramaic manner (מִקְטַל but cf. also Arab. *maqtal*) there occur as *e* *Infin. Qal*: מִשְׁלוֹחַ *to send*, Est 9[19]; מִקְרָא *to call* and מַסַּע *to depart*, Nu 10[2] (Dt 10[11]); מִקַּח *to take*, 2 Ch 19[7], &c.; מַשָּׂא *to carry*, Nu 4[24], &c. (cf. even לְמַשָּׂאוֹת Ez 17[9]); also with a feminine ending מַעֲלָה *to go up*, Ezr 7[9], &c.; cf. for these forms (almost all very late) Ryssel, *De Elohistae Pentateuchici sermone*, p. 50, and Strack on Nu 4[24].

(*d*) קְטֹלֶת in יַבֹּשֶׁת Gn 8[7]; יְבֹלֶת Nu 14[16]; probably also חֲרֹשֶׁת Ex 31[5], 35[33].

2. A kind of *Gerund* is formed by the *Infin. constr.* with the preposition *f* sition לְ; as לִקְטֹל *ad interficiendum*, לִנְפֹּל *ad cadendum* (see § 28 *a*).

---

[1] The terms *absolute* and *construct* are of course not to be understood as implying that the Infin. constr. קְטֹל forms the *construct state* (see § 89) of the Infin. absol. (קָטוֹל ground-form *qăṭāl*). In the Paradigms the *Inf. constr.*, as the principal form, is placed before the other, under the name of Infinitive simply.

[2] According to the remark of Elias Levita on Qimḥi's *Mikhlol*, ed. Rittenb., 14 *a*, these feminine forms occur almost exclusively in connexion with the preposition לְ.

g   The blending of the לְ with the *Infin. constr.* into a single grammatical form seems to be indicated by the firmly closed syllable, cf. לְשֶׁבֶת Gn 34⁷; לִנְפֹּל ψ 118¹³, with *Dageš lene* in the פ = *lin-pōl*; hence, also *liq-ṭōl*, &c.; but בִּנְפֹל *binephōl*, Jb 4¹³; כִּנְפֹל 2 S 3³⁴. Exceptions לִצְבָּא Nu 4²³, 8²⁴; לִנְתוֹשׁ וְלִנְתוֹץ Jer 1¹⁰, 18⁷, 31²⁸; לִשְׁדוֹד Jer 47⁴; לִטְבּוֹחַ Jer 11¹⁹, &c., ψ 37¹⁴; לִבְדֹּק 2 Ch 34¹⁰; according to some also לִסְבָב Nu 21⁴ and לִכְבָּשׁ 2 Ch 28¹⁰ (Baer לִכְבָּשׁ); on the other hand בִּשְׁכָּב Gn 35²²; בִּנְפֹּר Jer 17². For the meaningless לִדְרִיוֹשׁ Ezr 10¹⁶ read לִדְרֹשׁ.

§ 46. *The Imperative.*

a   1. The ground-forms of the Imperative, קְטֹל (properly *qeṭŭl*, which is for an original *quṭŭl*), and קְטַל (see below, *c*), the same in pronunciation as the forms of the Infin. constr. (§ 45), are also the basis for the formation of the Imperfect (§ 47).[1] They represent the *second* person, and have both fem. and plur. forms. The third person is supplied by the Imperfect in the Jussive (§ 109 *b*); and even the second person must always be expressed by the Jussive, if it be used with a negative, e. g. אַל-תִּקְטֹל *ne occidas* (not אַל-קְטֹל). The passives have no Imperative, but it occurs in the reflexives, as Niph'al and Hithpa'ēl.[2]

b   2. The Afformatives of the *2nd sing. fem.* and the *2nd plur. masc.* and *fem.* are identical in every case with those of the Imperfect (§ 47 *c*). In the same way, the Imperative of the *2nd sing. masc.*, in common with the Imperfect, admits of the lengthening by the ה⸗ *paragogicum* (§ 48 *i*), as, on the other hand, there are certain shortened forms of this person analogous to the Jussive (§ 48. 5).

c   Rem. 1. Instead of the form קְטֹל (sometimes also *plene*, e. g. שְׁמוֹר Ec 12¹³; before *Maqqeph* קְטָל־ with *Qameṣ ḥaṭuph*), those verbs which have an *a* in the final syllable of the *Imperf.* (i. e. especially verbs middle *ē*) make their Imperative of the form קְטַל, e. g. לְבַשׁ *dress!* (Perf. לָבַשׁ and לְבַשׁ); שְׁכַב *lie down!* in *pause* שְׁכָב 1 S 3⁵·⁶·⁹.

d   2. The first syllable of the sing. fem. and plur. masc. are usually to be pronounced with *Šewá mobile* (*qiṭelî, qiṭelû*, and so שִׁפְכִי, &c., without *Dageš lene*, and even מִשְׁכוּ with *Metheg*, Ex 12²¹; but cf. אִסְפִּי Jer 10¹⁷, and with the same phonetic combination חִשְׂפִּי Is 47²; see analogous cases in § 93 *m*); less frequently we find an *ŏ* instead of the *ĭ*, e. g. מָלְכִי *rule*, Ju 9¹⁰; מָשְׁכוּ *draw*, Ez 32²⁰; חָרְבוּ Jer 2¹² (cf. חָרְבִי Is 44²⁷); on קָסְמִי 1 S 28⁸ *Qerê*, צָעֳקִי Jer. 22²⁰ (cf. 1 K 13⁷), see § 10 *h*. This *ŏ* arises (see above, *a*) from a singular ground-form *quṭŭl*, not from a retraction of the original *ŭ* of the second syllable. We must abandon the view that the forms with *ĭ* in the first syllable (cf. also

---

[1] The *Infin. absol.*, like the Greek Infin., is also sometimes used for the Imperative (§ 113 *bb*). Cf. in general, Koch, *Der semitische Inf.* (Schaffhausen, 1874).

[2] In Hoph'al an Imperative is found only twice (Ez 32¹⁹, Jer. 49⁸), and closely approximating in meaning to the reflexive.

עֲבְרִי, חֲגְרִי, מִכְרִי, אִמְרִי) arise from a weakening of the characteristic vowel ŏ. They, or at least some of them, must rather be regarded with Barth (*ZDMG.* 1889, p. 182) as analogous to the original *ĭ*-imperfects. See further analogies in §§ 47 *i* and 48 *i* ; 61 *b,* 63 *n.*

The *pausal* form of the 2nd plur. masc. is גְּזֹרוּ 1 K 3²⁶; from שְׁמַע, שְׁמָעוּ, *e* &c. ; similarly the 2nd sing. fem. in *pause* is עֲבֹרִי Is 23¹² ; even without the *pause* מְלֹוכִי Ju 9¹⁰·¹², *Kᵉth.* ; קְסֹומִי 1 S 28⁸, *Kᵉth.* (cf. with this also מְלוֹכָה, &c., § 48 *i*); from שָׂמַח, שְׂמָחִי Jo 2²¹.

3. In the 2nd plur. fem. שְׁמַעַן occurs once, in Gn 4²³ (for שְׁמַעְנָה) with loss *f* of the ה֫— and insertion of a helping vowel, unless it is simply to be pointed שְׁמַעַן. Also instead of the abnormal קְרָאֶן Ex 2²⁰ (for קְרֶאנָה) we should perhaps read as in Ru 1²⁰ קְרָאן (cf. מְצָאֶן 1⁹ and לֶכֶן 1¹²).

On the examples of a 2nd plur. fem. in —֫, Is 32¹¹, see § 48 *i.*

§ 47. *The Imperfect and its Inflexion.*

1. The persons of the Imperfect,[1] in contradistinction to those of *a* the Perfect, are formed by placing abbreviated forms of the personal pronoun (preformatives) *before* the stem, or rather before the abstract form of the stem (קְטֹל). As, however, the tone is retained on the characteristic vowel of the Stem-form, or even (as in the *2nd sing. fem.* and the *3rd* and *2nd plur. masc.*) passes over to the afformatives, the preformatives of the Imperfect appear in a much more abbreviated form than the afformatives of the Perfect, only *one* consonant (נ, א, ת, י) remaining in each form. But as this preformative combined with the

---

[1] On the use of the Semitic Perfect and Imperfect cf. § 106 ff. and the literature cited in § 106. For our present purpose the following account will suffice :—The name *Imperfect* is here used in direct contrast to the Perfect, and is to be taken in a wider sense than in Latin and Greek grammar. The Hebrew (Semitic) *Perf.* denotes in general that which is *concluded, completed,* and *past,* that which has happened and has come into effect ; but at the same time, also that which is *represented* as accomplished, even though it be continued into present time or even be actually still future. The *Imperf.* denotes, on the other hand, the *beginning,* the *unfinished,* and the *continuing,* that which is just happening, which is conceived as in process of coming to pass, and hence, also, that which is yet future ; likewise also that which occurs repeatedly or in a continuous sequence in the past (Latin Imperf.). It follows from the above that the once common designation of the Imperf. as a *Future* emphasizes only *one* side of its meaning. In fact, the use of Indo-Germanic tense-names for the Semitic tenses, which was adopted by the Syrians under the influence of the Greek grammarians, and after their example by the Arabs, and finally by Jewish scholars, has involved many misconceptions. The Indo-Germanic scheme of three periods of time (past, present, and future) is entirely foreign to the Semitic tense-idea, which regards an occurrence only from the point of view of completed or incomplete action.—In the formation of the two tenses the chief distinction is that in the Perfect the verbal stem precedes and the indication of the person is added afterwards for precision, while in the Imperf. the subject, from which the action proceeds or about which a condition is predicated, is expressed by a prefixed pronoun.

stem-form was not always sufficient to express at the same time differences both of gender and number, the distinction had to be further indicated, in several cases, by special *afformatives*. Cf. the table, § 40 *c*.

b 2. The derivation and meaning, both of the preformatives and the afformatives, can still, in most cases, be recognized.

In the *first* pers. אֶקְטֹל, plur. נִקְטֹל, א is probably connected with אֲנִי, and נ with נַחְנוּ; here no indication of gender or number by a special ending was necessary. As regards the vocalization, the Arabic points to the ground-forms *'ăqtŭl* and *năqtŭl*: the *ĭ* of the 1st plur. is, therefore, as in the other preformatives, attenuated from *a*. The *Sᵉghôl* of the 1st sing. is probably to be explained by the preference of the א for this sound (cf. § 22 *o*, but also § 51 *p*); according to Qimḥi, it arises from an endeavour to avoid the similarity of sound between אֶקְטֹל (which is the Babylonian punctuation) and יִקְטֹל, which, according to this view, was likewise pronounced *iqtōl*.[1]

c The preformative ת of the *second* persons (תִּקְטֹל, ground-form *tăqtŭl*, &c.) is, without doubt, connected with the ת of אַתָּה, אַתֶּם. &c., and the *afformative* ־ִי of the 2nd fem. sing. תִּקְטְלִי with the *i* of the original feminine form אַתִּי (see § 32 *h*). The *afformative* ו of the 2nd masc. plur. תִּקְטְלוּ (in its more complete form, ן, see *m*) is the sign of the plural, as in the 3rd pers., and also in the Perfect (§ 44 *a*). In the Imperfect, however, it is restricted in both persons to the masculine,[2] while the afformative נָה (also ן,) of the 3rd and 2nd plur. fem. is probably connected with הֵנָּה *eae* and אַתֵּנָה *vos* (fem.).

d The preformatives of the *third* persons (י in the masc. יִקְטֹל, ground-form *yăqtŭl*, plur. יִקְטְלוּ, ground-form *yăqtŭlû*; ת in the fem. תִּקְטֹל, plur. תִּקְטֹלְנָה) have not yet met with any satisfactory explanation. With ת might most obviously be compared the original feminine

---

[1] Cf. § 24 *e*. In favour of the above view of Qimḥi may be urged the phonetic orthography אֵשׁ (in Pr 18²⁴ אִישׁ), 2 S 14¹⁹ (unless, with Perles, אָשֵׁב is to be read), Mi 6¹⁰, for יֵשׁ, and אִישֵׁי 1 Ch 2¹³ for יִשַׁי (as verse 12). Also הָאֻזְכֶּה Mi 6¹¹ is probably for הַאֶזְ'=הֲיִין, הֵין, אפקד Is 10¹² for יִפְקֹד; אנחמך Is 51¹⁹ for יְנַחֲמֵךְ; and conversely ישׁכר is for אשׁ'/אשׁשׁ=אִישׁ שָׂכָר. Similarly, ישׁוי 1 S 14⁴⁹ is probably for אִשְׁיוֹ or אִשְׁיָה; in 2 S 23⁸ ישׁב בשׁבת is, according to the LXX, an error for אֶשְׁבֹּשֶׁת=ישׁבשׁת. In Assyrian also the simple *i* corresponds to the Hebrew י as the preformative of the Impf. Qal.

[2] This is also the proper gender of the plural syllable *û*, *ûn*. In Hebrew, indeed, it is used in the 3rd plur. *Perfect* for both genders, but in the kindred languages even there only for the masculine, e.g. in Syriac *qᵉṭălû*, *qᵉṭălûn*, with the feminine form *qᵉṭălên*, in Western Aram. *qᵉṭălû*, fem. *qᵉṭălâ*; in Arab. *qătălû*, fem. *qătălnă*, Eth. *qătălû*, *qătălâ*.

ending ה◌ of nouns, and of the 3rd fem. sing. perfect. For the afformatives ִי (וֹן) and נָה, see *c*.

3. The characteristic vowel of the second syllable becomes Š⁰wâ *e* before tone-bearing afformatives which begin with a vowel, but is retained (as being in the tone-syllable) before the toneless afformative נָה.   Thus: תִּקְטְלוּ, יִקְטְלוּ, תִּקְטְלִי (but in *pause* תִּקְטֹלִי, &c.), תִּקְטֹלְנָה.

Rem. 1. The ō of the second syllable (as in the inf. constr. and imperat.), *f* being lengthened from an original *ŭ* in the tone-syllable, is only tone-long (§ 9 *r*). Hence it follows that: (*a*) it is incorrectly, although somewhat frequently, written *plene*; (*b*) before *Maqqeph* the short vowel appears as *Qameṣ ḥaṭuph*, e.g. וַיִּכְתָּב־שָׁם *and he wrote there*, Jos 8³² (but cf. also Ex 21³⁷, Jos 18²⁰); (*c*) it becomes Š⁰wâ before the tone-bearing afformatives ִי◌ and וּ (see above, *e*; but Jerome still heard e.g. *iezbuleni* for יִזְבְּלֵנִי; cf. *ZAW.* iv. 83).

Quite anomalous are the three examples which, instead of a shortening to *g* Š⁰wâ, exhibit a long *û*: יִשְׁפּוּטוּ הֶם Ex 18²⁶, immediately before the principal pause, but according to Qimḥi (ed. *Rittenb.* p.18ᵇ), ed. Mant., Ginsb., Kittel against the other editions, with the tone on the ultima; likewise לֹא־תַעֲבוּרִי מִזֶּה Ru 2⁸; תִּשְׁמוּרֵם (in principal pause) Pr 14³. In the first two cases perhaps יִשְׁפּוּטוּ and תַעֲבוּרִי (for יִשְׁפֹּטוּ, &c.) are intended, in virtue of a retrogressive effect of the pause; in Pr 14³ תִּשְׁמְרֻם is to be read, with August Müller.

2. The ō of the second syllable is to be found almost exclusively with transi- *h* tive verbs middle *a*, like קָטַל. Intransitives *middle a* and *ē* almost always take *ă* (*Pathaḥ*)[1] in the impf., e.g. יִרְבַּץ, רָבַץ *to couch*, יִשְׁכַּב, שָׁכַב *to lie down* (לָמַד, יִלְמַד *to learn* is also originally intransitive = *to accustom oneself*); יִגְדַּל, גָּדַל *to become great* (but cf. שָׁכֵן and שָׁכַן imperf. יִשְׁכֹּן *to dwell* and *to inhabit*, נָבֵל imperf. יִבֹּל *to wither*); also from verbs *middle ō*, as קָטֹן *to be small*, the imperf. has the form יִקְטַן.

Sometimes both forms occur together; those with ō having a transitive, *i* and those with *ă* an intransitive meaning, e.g. יִקְצֹר *he cuts off*, יִקְצַר *he is cut off*, i.e. *is short*; חָלַשׁ impf. ō, *to overcome*, Ex 17¹³; impf. *ă*, *to be overcome*, Jb 14¹⁰. More rarely both forms are used without any distinction, e.g. יִשֹׁךְ and יִשַּׁךְ *he bites*, יַחְפֹּץ and יַחְפַּץ *he is inclined* (but only the latter with a transitive meaning = *he bends*, in Jb 40¹⁷). On the *a* of the impf. of verbs middle and third guttural, cf. § 64 *b*; § 65 *b*. In some verbs first guttural (§ 63 *n*), ע״ע (§ 67 *p*), פ״י (§ 69 *b*), and פ״א (§ 68 *c*), and in יִתֵּן for *yintēn* from נָתַן *to give*, instead of *ă* or ō a movable *Ṣere* (originally *ĭ*) is found in the second syllable. A trace of these *i*-imperfects[2] in the ordinary strong verb is probably to be found in וַיִּטְמְנוּ 2 K 7⁸, since טמן otherwise only occurs in Qal. We call these three forms of the imperfect after their characteristic vowel impf. *o*, impf. *a*, impf. *e*.

3. For the 3rd sing. fem. תִּקְטֹל (= *tiq-ṭōl*), Baer requires in 1 S 25²⁰ תִּפְנֹשׁ *k* (but read with ed. Mant., &c. תִּפְגֹּשׁ). For the 2nd sing. fem. (תִּקְטְלִי) the form

---

[1] This *ă* is, however, by no means restricted to intransitive *strong* verbs; apart from verbs third guttural (§ 65 *b*), it is to be found in פ״ן and ע״ע, and in many verbs פ״א and פ״י (§§ 69–71).

[2] Cf. Barth, 'Das *i*-Imperfekt im Nordsemitischen,' *ZDMG.* 1889, p. 177 ff.

תִּקְטֹל is found in Is 57⁸, Jer 3⁵, Ez 22⁴, 23³², in every case after the regular form; but cf. also Ez 26¹⁴. In Is 17¹⁰, where the 2nd fem. precedes and follows, probably וּבְ תִּזְרָעִין is to be read with Marti for תִּזְרָעֶנּוּ.—For the 3rd plur. *fem.* תִּקְטֹלְנָה we find in Jer 49¹¹, in pause תִּבְטָחוּ (for תִּבְטַחְנָה), and thrice (as if to distinguish it from the 2nd pers.) the form יִקְטֹלְנָה with the preformative ' (as always in Western Aram., Arab., Eth., and Assyr.), in Gn 30³⁸, 1 S 6¹², Dn 8²². On the other hand, תִּקְטֹלְנָה appears in some cases to be incorrectly used even for the fem. of the 3rd pers. or for the masc. of the 2nd pers. *sing.* as תִּשְׁלַחְנָה Ju 5²⁶ (where, however, perhaps תִּשְׁלָחֶנָּה is to be read), and Ob¹³, for 2nd sing. masc., according to Olshausen a corruption of תִּשְׁלַח יָד; in Pr 1²⁰, 8³ for תָּרֹנָּה read תִּרְנֶה as in Jb 39²³; in Ex 1¹⁰ read תִּקְרָאֶנּוּ with the Samaritan.—In Is 27¹¹, 28⁸, as also in Jb 17¹⁶ (if we read טוֹבָתִי with LXX for the 2nd תִּקְוֹתִי), it is equally possible to explain the form as a plural. This small number of examples hardly justifies our finding in the above-mentioned passages the remains of an emphatic form of the Impf., analogous to the Arab. *Modus energicus I*, with the termination *ănnă*.

l   For נָה we frequently find, especially in the Pentateuch and mostly after *wāw consecutive*, simply ןָ *nă*, e. g. Gn 19³³·³⁶, 37⁷, Ex 1¹⁸·¹⁹, 15²⁰, Nu 25², Ez 3²⁰, 16⁵⁵; in Arab. always *nă*. According to Elias Levita תִּלְבַּשְׁןָ (2 S 13¹⁸) is the only example of this kind in the strong verb. The form וַתִּגְבְּהֶינָה (so also Qimḥi and ed. Mant.; but Baer, Ginsb. וַתִּגְבְּהֶנָה) for they were high, Ez 16⁵⁰, is irregular, with ' ֶ inserted after the manner of verbs ע״ע and ע״י, § 67 *d*; § 72 *i*; according to Olshausen it is an error caused by the following form.

m   4. Instead of the plural forms in ' there are, especially in the older books, over 300 forms¹ with the fuller ending וּן (with *Nûn paragogicum*), always bearing the tone; cf. § 29 *m* and § 44 *l*; on its retention before suffixes, see § 60 *e*; also defectively יְרִיבֻן Ex 21¹⁸, 22⁸, &c. This usually expresses marked emphasis, and consequently occurs most commonly at the end of sentences (in the principal pause), in which case also the (pausal) vowel of the second syllable is generally retained. Thus there arise full-sounding forms such as יִלְקְטוּן *they collect*, ψ 104²⁸; יִרְגָּזוּן *they tremble*, Ex 15¹⁴; תִּשְׁמָעוּן *ye shall hear*, Dt 1¹⁷; cf. Ex 34¹³, with Zaqeph qaṭon, Athnaḥ, and Silluq; Jos 24¹⁵, with Segolta; Is 13⁸ and 17¹³ with Zaqeph qaṭon, 17¹² with Athnaḥ and Silluq, 41⁵ after *wāw consec.* Without the pause, e. g. ψ 11², יִדְרְכוּן קֶשֶׁת, cf. 4³, Gn 18²⁸·²⁹·³⁰ ﬀ·, 44¹, Nu 32²³, Jos 4⁶ (וְיִשְׁאָלוּן); Is 8¹², 1 S 9¹³, Ru 2⁹ (יִקְצֹרוּן and יִשְׁאָבוּן); Ju 11¹⁸ after *wāw consec.*

Some of these examples may be partly due to euphonic reasons, e.g. certainly Ex 17², Nu 16²⁹, 32²⁰, 1 S 9¹³, 1 K 9⁶, and often, to avoid a hiatus before א or ע. It was, however, the pause especially which exerted an influence on the restoration of this older and fuller termination (cf. § 159 *c*, note), as is manifest from Is 26¹¹: בַּל־יֶחֱזָיוּן יֶחֱזוּ וְיֵבֹשׁוּ *they see not; may they see and become*

---

¹ [See details in F. Böttcher, *Lehrb.*, § 930; and cf. Driver on 1 S 2¹⁵.]

ashamed. All this applies also to the corresponding forms in the Imperfect of the derived conjugations.[1] In Aramaic and Arabic this earlier נ (old Arabic *ûnă*) is the regular termination; but in some dialects of vulgar Arabic it has also become *û*.

n — With an affixed א we find (in the imperf. Niph'al) יְּנָשׂוֹא Jer 10⁵, evidently an error for יִנָּשֵׂא, caused by the preceding נִשּׂא.—In יְשִׁשֻּׁם Is 35¹, since מ follows, the ם is no doubt only due to dittography.

o — 5. Corresponding to the use of ן for ו there occurs in the 2nd sing. fem., although much less frequently, the fuller ending ־ִין (as in Aram. and Arab.; old Arab. *înă*), also always with the tone, for ־ִי, generally again in the principal pause, and almost in all cases with retention of the vowel of the penultima; thus תִּדְבָּקִין Ru 2⁸·²¹, cf. 3⁴·¹⁸, 1 S 1¹⁴ (תִּשְׁתַּבָּרִין), Jer 31²², Is 45¹⁰.

p — 6. On the reappearance in pause of the *ō* which had become *Šᵉwâ* in the forms תִּקְטְלִי, &c., see above, *e*; similarly, the imperfects with *ă* restore this vowel in pause and at the same time lengthen it (as a tone-vowel) to *ā*, hence, e.g. יִגְדְּלוּ, תִּגְדְּלִי. This influence of the pause extends even to the forms without afformatives, e.g. וַיִּגְדַּל, in pause וַיִּגְדָּל. But the fuller forms in *ún* and *ín* have the tone always on the ultima, since the vowels *û* and *î* in a closed final syllable never allow of the retraction of the tone.

q — 7. On the numerous instances of passive forms in the imperfect, mostly treated as Hoph'al, see § 53 *u*.

§ 48. *Shortening and Lengthening of the Imperfect and Imperative. The Jussive and Cohortative.*

a — 1. Certain modifications which take place in the form of the imperfect, and express invariably, or nearly so, a distinct shade of meaning, serve to some extent as a compensation for the want of special forms for the *Tempora relativa* and for certain *moods* of the verb.

b — 2. Along with the usual form of the imperfect, there exists also a lengthened form of it (the *cohortative*), and a shortened form (the *jussive*).[2] The former occurs (with few exceptions) only in the 1st person, while the latter is mostly found in the 2nd and 3rd persons, and less frequently in the 1st person. The laws of the tone, however, and of the formation of syllables in Hebrew, not infrequently precluded the indication of the jussive by an actual shortening of the form; consequently it often—and, in the imperfect forms with afformatives, always—coincides with the ordinary imperfect (*indicative*) form.

In classical Arabic the difference is almost always evident. That language distinguishes, besides the indicative *yăqtŭlŭ*, (*a*) a subjunctive, *yăqtŭlă*; (*b*) a

---

[1] It is to be observed that the Chronicles often omit the *Nûn*, where it is found in the parallel passage in the Books of Kings; cf. 1 K 8³⁸·⁴³ with 2 Ch 6²⁹·³³; 1 K 12²⁴, 2 K 11⁵ with 2 Ch 11⁴, 23⁴.

[2] The perfect has only *one* form, since it cannot be used, like the imperfect, to express mood-relations (see § 106 *p*).

jussive, *yǎqtǔl*; (c) a double 'energetic' mood of the impf., *yǎqtǔlǎnnǎ* and *yǎqtǔlǎn*, in pause *yǎqtǔlǎ*, the last form thus corresponding to the Hebrew cohortative.

c 3. The characteristic of the cohortative form is an *ā* (הָ‍ָ) affixed to the 1st pers. sing. or plur., e. g. אֶקְטְלָה from אֶקְטֹל.[1] It occurs in almost all conjugations and classes of the strong and weak verb (except of course in the passives), and this final הָ‍ָ has the tone wherever the afformatives וֹ and יָ‍ָ would have it. As before these endings, so also before the הָ‍ָ cohortative, the movable vowel of the last syllable of the verbal form becomes *Šewâ*, e. g. in Qal אֶשְׁמְרָה *I will observe*, in Pi'el נְנַתְּקָה *let us break asunder*, ψ 2³; on אֶשְׁקְטָה Is 18⁴ *Qerê* (cf. also 27⁴, Ezr 8²⁵, &c.), see § 10 *h*; with the *Kethîbh* of these passages, compare the analogous cases יִשְׁפוֹטוּ, &c., § 47 *g*.—On the other hand, an unchangeable vowel in the final syllable is retained as tone-vowel before the הָ‍ָ, as (e. g.) in Hiph. אֲזַבִּירָה *I will praise*. In pause (as before *û* and *î*), the vowel which became *Šewâ* is restored as tone-vowel; thus for the cohortative אֶשְׁמְרָה the pausal form is אֶשְׁמֹרָה ψ 59¹⁰; cf. Gn 18²¹, Is 41²⁶.

d The change of הָ‍ָ into the obtuse הָ‍ָ seems to occur in 1 S 28¹⁵, unless, with Nestle, we are to assume a conflate reading, וָאֶקְרָא and וָאֶקְרָה; and with the 3rd pers. ψ 20⁴, in a syllable sharpened by a following *Dageš forte conjunct.*; cf. similar cases of the change of הָ‍ָ into the obtuse הָ‍ָ in *l* and in §§ 73 *d*, 80 *i*, 90 *i*. In ψ 20⁴, however, יְדַשְּׁנֶה—with suffix—is probably intended. An הָ‍ָ cohort. is also found with the 3rd pers. in Is 5¹⁹ (twice); Ez 23²⁰, and again in verse 16 according to the *Qerê*, but in both these cases without any effect on the meaning. Probably another instance occurs in Jb 11¹⁷, although there תָּעֻפָה might also, with Qimḥi, be regarded as 2nd masc. For the doubly irregular form תְּבוֹאָתָה Dt 33¹⁶ (explained by Olshausen and König as a scribal error, due to a confusion with תבואת in verse 14), read תְּבֹאֶנָה. For תְּבוֹאָתְךָ Jb 22²¹ the noun תְּבוּאָתְךָ *thine increase*, might be meant, but the Masora has evidently intended an imperfect with the ending *ath*, instead of הָ‍ָ, before the suffix, on the analogy of the 3rd sing. fem. perfect, see § 59 *a*; on ותבאתי 1 S 25³⁴, see § 76 *h*.

e The *cohortative* expresses the direction of the will to an action and thus denotes especially self-encouragement (in the 1st plur. an exhortation to others at the same time), a resolution or a wish, as an *optative*, &c., see § 108.

f 4. The general characteristic of the *jussive* form of the imperfect is rapidity of pronunciation, combined with a tendency to retract

---

[1] Probably this *ā* goes back to the syllable *an*, which in Arabic (see above, Rem. to *b*) is used for the formation of the 'energetic' mood, and in Hebrew (see the footnote to § 58 *i*) often stands before suffixes.

the tone from the final syllable, in order by that means to express the urgency of the command in the very first syllable. This tendency has, in certain forms, even caused a material shortening of the termination of the word, so that the expression of the command appears to be concentrated on a single syllable. In other cases, however, the jussive is simply marked by a shortening of the vowel of the second syllable, without its losing the tone, and very frequently (see above, *b*) the nature of the form does not admit of any alteration. It is not impossible, however, that even in such cases the jussive in the living language was distinguished from the indicative by a change in the place of the tone.

In the strong verb the jussive differs in *form* from the indicative *g* only in *Hiph'îl* (juss. יַקְטֵל, ind. יַקְטִיל), and similarly in the weak verb, wherever the imperfect indicative has *î* in the second syllable, e. g. from יָשַׁב impf. *Hiph.* יוֹשִׁיב, juss. יוֹשֵׁב; from מוּת יָמִית and יָמֵת; also in *Qal* of the verbs ע"י and ע"ו, as יָמֹת, ind. יָמוּת; יָגֶל, ind. יָגִיל; in all conjugations of verbs ל"ה, so that the rejection (*apocope*) of the ending הָ‎ in *Qal* and *Hiph.* gives rise to monosyllabic forms, with or without a helping vowel under the second radical, e. g. *Qal* ind. יִגְלֶה, juss. יִגֶל; *Hiph.* ind. יַגְלֶה, juss. יֶגֶל; and in the *Piʿēl* יְצַו from the indic. יְצַוֶּה (called apocopated imperfects). But almost all[1] the plural forms of the jussive coincide with those of the indicative, except that the jussive excludes the fuller ending וּן. Neither do the forms of the 2nd sing. fem., as תִּגְלִי, תָּמֹותִי, תַּקְטִילִי, &c., admit of any change in the jussive, nor any forms, whether singular or plural, to which suffixes are attached, e. g. תְּמִיתֵנִי as ind. Jer 38¹⁵, as jussive Jer 41⁸.

The meaning of the jussive is similar to that of the cohortative, *h* except that in the jussive the command or wish is limited almost exclusively to the 2nd or 3rd pers. On special uses of the jussive, e. g. in hypothetical sentences (even in the 1st pers.), see § 109 *h*.

5. The imperative, in accordance with its other points of connexion *i* with the imperfect in form and meaning, admits of a similar lengthening (by הָ‎, Arab. *imper. energicus*, with the ending *-ǎnnǎ* or *-ǎn*, in pause *-ā*) and shortening. Thus in *Qal* of the strong verb, the lengthened form of שְׁמֹר *guard* is שָׁמְרָה[2] (*šŏmᵉrâ*, cf. קְטָלִי *qǐṭᵉlî*, § 46 *d*); עָזְבָה, עֹזֶב, Jer 49¹¹; שִׁכְבָה, שְׁכַב *lie down*; שִׁמְעָה, שְׁמַע *hear*, in lesser pause שָׁמְעָה

---

[1] Only in 1st plur. do we find a few shortened forms, as נִשְׁאַר 1 S 14³⁶, parallel with cohortatives; and נֵרָא Is 41²³ *Kᵉth.*

[2] On the reading שָׁמְרָה (i. e. *šāmᵉra*, according to the Jewish grammarians), required by the Masora in ψ 86², 119¹⁶⁷ (cf. also Is 38¹⁴, and שָׁמְרֵנִי ψ 16¹), see § 9 *v*; on מְלוּכָה, Ju 9⁸ *Kᵉth.*, see § 46 *e*.

Dn 9¹⁹; in Niph'al הַשָּׁבְעָה Gn 21²³. Cf., however, also מִכְרָה *sell,*
Gn 25³¹, notwithstanding the impf. יִמְכֹּר; עָרְכָה Jb 33⁵ (cf. עֶרְכוּ Jer 46³),
but impf. יַעֲרֹךְ; אָסְפָה *collect,* Nu 11¹⁶ (for אֱסֹף cf. § 63 *l* and the plural
אִסְפוּ), but 2nd masc. אֱסֹף; נִצְרָה ψ 141³. Barth (see above, § 47 *i*
note) finds in these forms a trace of old imperfects in *i,* cf. § 63 *n.*
On the other hand, קָרְבָה ψ 69¹⁹ (also Imperat. קְרַב Lv 9⁷, &c.), but
impf. יִקְרַב. Without ה, we have the form לֵךְ *go,* Nu 23¹³, Ju 19¹³,
2 Ch 25¹⁷. The form קְטֹל in pause becomes קְטֹלָה, the form קְטַל
becomes קְטָלָה, e. g. יָרֵשָׁה Dt 33²³. But also without the pause we find
מְלוֹכָה Ju 9⁸ *Keth.* and צְרוּפָה ψ 26² *Keth.,* on which see § 46 *e.* On
the other hand חֲגֹרָה, עֹרָה, פְּשֹׁטָה, רְנֹּה Is 32¹¹ are to be explained as
aramaizing forms of the 2nd plur. fem.; also for חִרְדוּ v. 11 read חֲרָדָה,
and for סֹפְדִים v. 12 read סְפֹדָה.

k   The shortened imperative is found only in verbs ל״ה, e. g. in *Pi'ēl*
גַּל from גַּלֵּה. The shade of meaning conveyed by the imperatives
with ה‍ָ‍ is not always so perceptible as in the cohortative forms of the
imperfect, but the longer form is frequently emphatic, e. g. קוּם *rise up,*
קוּמָה *up!* תֵּן *give,* תְּנָה *give up!*

l   Rem. The form דְּעֶה for דְּעֶה, best attested in Pr 24¹⁴ (where it is taken
by the Masora as imperat., not as infin., דֵעָה) is evidently due to the influence
of the ה which follows it in close connexion (so Strack, on the analogy of
Jb 31²); for other examples of this change of *a* to Seghol, see above, under *d,*
§ 73 *d,* and § 80 *i.* On the other hand, it is doubtful whether רַבֶּה Ju 9²⁹ (from
רְבָה) is intended for רַבָּה, and not rather for the common form of the
imperative *Pi'ēl* רַבֵּה. In favour of the former explanation it may be urged
that the imperative צֵאָה (from יָצָא) follows immediately after; in favour of
the latter, that the ending ה‍ָ‍, with imperatives of verbs ל״ה, is not found
elsewhere, and also that here no guttural follows (as in Pr 24¹⁴).

§ 49. *The Perfect and Imperfect with Wāw Consecutive.*

a   1. The use of the two tense-forms, as is shown more fully in the
Syntax (§§ 106, 107, cf. above, § 47, note on *a*), is by no means
restricted to the expression of the past or future. One of the most
striking peculiarities in the Hebrew *consecution* of tenses [1] is the
phenomenon that, in representing a series of past events, only the first

---

[1] The other Semitic languages do not exhibit this peculiarity, excepting
the Phoenician, the most closely related to Hebrew, and of course the
Moabitish dialect of the *Mêša'* inscription, which is practically identical with
Old Hebrew. It also appears in the inscription of זכר of Hamâth (cf.
Nöldeke, *ZA.* 1908, p. 379) where we find וָאֶשָּׂא ידי *and I lifted up my hand,*
וַיַּעֲנֵנִי *and he answered me,* after a perfect of narration.

verb stands in the perfect, and the narration is continued in the imperfect. Conversely, the representation of a series of future events begins with the imperfect, and is continued in the perfect. Thus in 2 K 20¹, *In those days was Hezekiah sick unto death* (perf.), *and Isaiah . . . came* (imperf.) *to him, and said* (imperf.) *to him*, &c. On the other hand, Is 7¹⁷, *the Lord shall bring* (imperf.) *upon thee . . . days*, &c., 7¹⁸, *and it shall come to pass* (perf. וְהָיָה) *in that day . . .*

This progress in the sequence of time, is regularly indicated by *b* a pregnant *and* (called *wāw consecutive*[1]), which in itself is really only a variety of the ordinary *wāw copulative*, but which sometimes (in the imperf.) appears with a different vocalization. Further, the tenses connected by *wāw consecutive* sometimes undergo a change in the tone and consequently are liable also to other variations.

2. The *wāw consecutive* of the *imperfect* is (*a*) pronounced with *c* *Pathaḥ* and a *Dageš forte* in the next letter, as וַיִּקְטֹל *and he killed*; before א of the 1*st pers. sing.* (according to § 22 c) with *Qameṣ*, as וָאֶקְטֹל *and I killed*. Exceptions are, וָאֲכַפֶּךָ Ez 16¹⁰ according to the *Dikduke ha-ṭeamim*, § 71; also וַאֲמֹתְתֵהוּ 2 S 1¹⁰ according to Qimḥi; but in Ju 6⁹ וָאֲגָרֵשׁ should be read according to Baer, and וָאֵ in both places in Ju 20⁶. *Dageš forte* is always omitted in the preformative יְ, in accordance with § 20 *m*.

(*b*) When a shortening of the imperfect form is possible (cf. § 48 *g*), *d* it takes effect, as a rule (but cf. § 51 *n*), after *wāw consec.*, e.g. in Hiphil וַיַּקְטֵל (§ 53 *n*). The tendency to retract the tone from the final syllable is even stronger after *wāw consec.* than in the jussive. The throwing back of the tone on to the penultima (conditional upon its being an open syllable with a long vowel, § 29 *a*), further involves the greatest possible shortening of the vowel of the ultima, since the vowel then comes to stand in a toneless closed syllable, e.g. יָקֻם, juss.

---

[1] This name best expresses the prevailing syntactical relation, for by *wāw consecutive* an action is always represented as the direct, or at least temporal *consequence* of a preceding action. Moreover, it is clear from the above examples, that the *wāw consecutive* can only be thus used in immediate conjunction with the verb. As soon as *wāw*, owing to an insertion (e.g. a negative), is separated from the verb, the imperfect follows instead of the perfect *consecutive*, the perfect instead of the imperfect *consecutive*. The fact that whole Books (Lev., Num., Josh., Jud., Sam., 2 Kings, Ezek., Ruth, Esth., Neh., 2 Chron.) begin with the imperfect *consecutive*, and others (Exod., 1 Kings, Ezra) with *wāw copulative*, is taken as a sign of their close connexion with the historical Books now or originally preceding them. Cf., on the other hand, the independent beginning of Job and Daniel. It is a merely superficial description to call the wāw consecutive by the old-fashioned name *wāw conversive*, on the ground that it always converts the meaning of the respective tenses into its opposite, i.e. according to the old view, the future into the preterite, and vice versa.

יָקָם, with *wāw consec.* וַיָּקָם *and he arose* (§ 67 *n* and *x*, § 68 *d*, § 69 *p*, § 71, § 72 *t* and *aa*, § 73 *e*).[1]

e In the *first* pers. sing. alone the retraction of the tone and even the reducing of the long vowel in the final syllable (*û* to *ō*, *î* to *ē*, and then to *ŏ* and *ĕ*) are not usual,[2] at least according to the Masoretic punctuation, and the apocope in verbs ל״ה occurs more rarely ; e.g. always וָאָקוּם (or וָאָקֻם, a merely orthographic difference) *and I arose*; *Hiph.* וָאָקִים (but generally written וָאָקֶם, implying the pronunciation *wā'āqem*, as וָאָקֶם implies *wā'āqŏm*); וָאֶרְאֶה *and I saw*, more frequently than וָאֵרֶא, § 75 *t*. On the other hand, the form with final ה‑ is often used in the 1st pers. both sing. and plur., especially in the later books, e. g. וָאֶשְׁלְחָה *and I sent*, Gn 32⁶, 41¹¹, 43²¹, Nu 8¹⁹ (וָאֶתְּנָה, as in Ju 6⁹, 1 S 2²⁸, and often, probably a sort of compensation for the lost נ); Ju 6¹⁰, 12³, 2 S 22²⁴, ψ 3⁶, 7⁵, 90¹⁰, 119⁵⁵, Jb 1¹⁵ᶠᶠ·, 19²⁰, Ez 7²⁸, 8²⁵, 9³, Neh 2¹³, 5⁷·⁸·¹³, 6¹¹, 13⁷⁻¹¹·²¹ ᶠ·, &c.—Sometimes, as in ψ 3⁶, with a certain emphasis of expression, and probably often, as in Ju 10¹², וָאוֹשִׁיעָה before א, for euphonic reasons. In Is 8² וָאָעִידָה may have been originally intended ; in ψ 73¹⁶ וָאָח׳ and in Jb 30²⁶ וָאֲי׳. In Ez 3³ read וָאֹכְלָה or וָאֹכְלָה.

f This ‑וְ is in meaning a strengthened *wāw copulative*, and resembles in pronunciation the form which is retained in Arabic as the ordinary copula (*wă*).[3] The close connexion of this *wă* with the following consonant, caused the latter in Hebrew to take Dageš, especially as *ă* could not have been retained in an open syllable. Cf. לָמָּה, בַּמָּה, בַּמֶּה (for לְמָה), where the prepositions בְּ and לְ, and the particle כְּ, are closely connected with מָה in the same way (§ 102 *k*).

g The retraction of the tone also occurs in such combinations, as in לָמָּה (for לָמֶּה § 102 *l*).—The identity of many *consecutive* forms with jussives of the same conjugation must not mislead us into supposing an intimate relation between the moods. In the consecutive forms the shortening of the vowel (and the retraction of the tone) seems rather to be occasioned solely by the strengthening of the preformative syllable, while in the jussives the shortening (and retraction) belongs to the character of the form.

h 3. The counterpart of *wāw consecutive* of the *imperfect* is *wāw consecutive* of the *perfect*, by means of which perfects are placed as

---

[1] The plural forms in וּן also occur less frequently after *wāw consecutive* ; cf., however, וַיָּרִיבוּן Ju 8¹, 11¹⁸, Am 6³, Ez 44⁸, Dt 4¹¹, 5²⁰. The 2nd fem. sing. in יִן‑ never occurs after *wāw consecutive*.

[2] In the 1st plur. וַנַּעֲמִיד Neh 4³ is the only instance in which the vowel remains unreduced (cf. וַנָּשׁוּב, i. e. וַנָּשֻׁב, 4⁹ *Kᵉth.* ; *Qᵉrê* וַנָּשָׁב). On the treatment of the tone in the imperfect, imperative, and infinitive *Niph'al*, see § 51 *n*.

[3] In usage the Hebrew *wāw* does duty for the Arabic *fă* (*wāw apodosis*, see § 143 *d*) as well as *wă*.

the sequels in the future to preceding actions or events regarded as
incomplete at the time of speaking, and therefore in the imperfect,
imperative, or even participle. This *wāw* is in form an ordinary *wāw
copulative*, and therefore shares its various vocalization (וְ, וִ, וּ, as 2 K 7⁴,
and וַ); e. g. וְהָיָה, after an imperfect, &c., *and so it happens = and it
will happen*. It has, however, the effect, in certain verbal forms, of
shifting the tone from the penultima, generally on to the ultima, e.g.
הָלַכְתִּי *I went*, consecutive form וְהָלַכְתִּי *and I will go*, Ju 1³, where it is
co-ordinated with another *perfect consecutive*, which again is the consecutive to an *imperative*. See further on this usage in § 112.

As innumerable examples show, the *Qameṣ* of the first syllable is retained *i*
in the strong perf. consec. Qal, as formerly before the tone, so now in the
secondary tone, and therefore necessarily takes *Metheg*. On the other hand,
the *ō* of the second syllable in verbs *middle ō* upon losing the tone necessarily
becomes *ŏ*, e.g. וְיִכְלַת Ex 18²³.

The shifting forward of the tone after the *wāw consecutive* of the *perfect* is, *k*
however, not consistently carried out. It is omitted—(*a*) always in the
1st *pers. pl.*, e.g. וְיָשַׁבְנוּ Gn 34¹⁶; (*b*) regularly in Hiph'il before the afformatives
הָ and וּ, see § 53 *r*; and (*c*) in many cases in verbs לא״א and לה״ל, almost
always in the 1st sing. of לא״א (Jer 29¹⁴), and in לה״ל if the vowel of the
2nd syllable is *i*, Ex 17⁶, 26⁴·⁶·⁷·¹⁰ ᶠᶠ·, Ju 6²⁶, &c., except in Qal (only Lv 24⁵,
before א) and the 2nd sing. masc. of Hiph'il-forms before א, Nu 20⁸, Dt 20¹³,
1 S 15³, 2 K 13¹⁷; similarly in Pi'ēl before א, Ex 25²⁴, Jer 27⁴. On the other
hand the tone is generally moved forward if the second syllable has *ē* (in
לא״א Gn 27¹⁰ &c., in לה״ל Ex 40⁴, Jer 33⁶, Ez 32⁷); but cf. also וְיִרְאָת Lv 19¹⁴·³²
and frequently, always before the counter-tone, Jo 4²¹, ψ 19¹⁴.[1] With *ā* in
the penultima the form is וְנָשָׂאת Is 14⁴, and probably also וְקָרָאת Jer 2², 3¹²,
1 S 10² with little *Tᵉlîśā*, a postpositive accent.

But before a following א the ultima mostly bears the tone on phonetic *l*
grounds, e.g. וּבָאת אֶל־ Gn 6¹³, Ex 3¹⁸, Zc 6¹⁰ (by the side of וּבָאת), &c. (cf.,
however, וְקָרָאת, before א, Gn 17¹⁹, Jer 7²⁷, Ez 36²⁹); וְהִבֵּיתָ אֶת־ Ju 6¹⁶, cf.
Ex 25¹¹, Lv 24⁵ (but also וְצִוִּיתִי אֶת־ Lv 25²¹). Likewise, before ה, Am 8⁹, and ע,
e.g. Gn 26¹⁰, 27¹², Lv 26²⁵ (cf., however, וְקָרָאתִי עָלָיו, Ez 38²¹); on verbs ע״ע,
see § 67 *k* and *ee*.

(*d*) The tone always keeps its place when such a perfect stands in *pause*, *m*
e.g. וְשָׁבַעְתָּ Dt 6¹¹, 11¹⁵; וְאָמַרְתָּ Is 14⁴, Ju 4⁸; sometimes even in the lesser
pause, as Dt 2²⁸, Ez 3²⁶, 1 S 29⁸ (where see Driver), with *Zaqeph qaṭon*; and
frequently also immediately *before* a tone-syllable (according to § 29 *e*), as in
וְיָשַׁבְתָּה בָּהּ Dt 17¹⁴, Ez 14¹³, 17²², Am 1⁴·⁷·¹⁰·¹²—but also וְחָשַׁקְתָּ בָּהּ Dt 21¹¹, 23¹⁴·
24¹⁹, 1 K 8⁴⁶.

---

[1] The irregularity in the tone of these perfects manifestly results from
following conflicting theories, not that of Ben Asher alone.

§ 50. *The Participle.*

a　1. Qal has both an active participle, called *Pō'ēl* from its form (פֹּעֵל), and a passive, *Pā'ûl* (פָּעוּל).[1]

Pā'ûl is generally regarded as a survival of a passive of Qal, which still exists throughout in Arabic, but has been lost in Hebrew (see, however, § 52 *e*), just as in Aramaic the passives of *Pi'ēl* and *Hiph'îl* are lost, except in the participles. But instances of the form *quṭṭāl* are better regarded as remnants of the passive participle Qal (see § 52 *s*), so that פָּעוּל must be considered as an original verbal noun; cf. Barth, *Nominalbildung*, p. 173 ff.

b　2. In the intransitive verbs *mid. e* and *mid. o*, the form of the participle active of Qal coincides in form with the 3rd sing. of the perfect, e.g. יָשֵׁן *sleeping*, from יָשֵׁן; יָגוֹר (only orthographically different from the perf. יָגֹר) *fearing*; cf. the formation of the participle in *Niph'al*, § 51 *a*. On the other hand, the participle of verbs *mid. a* takes the form קֹטֵל (so even from the *transitive* שָׂנֵא *to hate*, part. שֹׂנֵא). The ô of these forms has arisen through an obscuring of the â, and is therefore unchangeable, cf. § 9 *q*. The form קָטֵל (with a changeable *Qameṣ* in both syllables), which would correspond to the forms יָשֵׁן and יָגֹר, is only in use as a noun, cf. § 84[a] *f*. The formation of the participle in *Pi'ēl*, *Hiph'îl*, and *Hithpa'ēl* follows a different method.

c　3. Participles form their feminine (קֹטְלָה or קֹטֶלֶת) and their plural like other nouns (§ 80 *e*, § 84[a] *r*, *s*, § 94).

d　Rem. 1. From the above it follows, that the *ā* of the form יָשֵׁן is lengthened from *ă*, and consequently changeable (e.g. *fem.* יְשֵׁנָה); and that the ô of קֹטֵל on the other hand is obscured from an unchangeable *â*.[1] In Arabic the verbal adjective of the form *qāṭil* corresponds to the form *qāṭēl*, and the part. *qāṭil* to *qōṭēl*. In both cases, therefore, the *ē* of the second syllable is lengthened from *ĭ*, and is consequently changeable (e.g. קֹטֵל, plur. קֹטְלִים; כָּבֵד, constr. pl. כִּבְדֵי).

e　תֹּמִיךְ ψ 16[5], instead of the form *qōṭēl*, is an anomaly; it is possible, however, that תֹּמֵיךְ (incorrectly written fully) is intended (cf. סֹבֵיב 2 K 8[21]), or even the *imperfect Hiph'il* of יָמַךְ. The form יֹסֵף in Is 29[14], 38[5] appears to stand for יֹסֵף, but most probably the Masora here (as certainly in יֹסִיף Ec 1[18]) intends the 3rd sing. imperf. Hiph., for which the better form would be יֹסֵף; אוֹבִיל 1 Ch 27[30], being a proper name and a foreign word, need not be considered.—אֹבֵד (constr. state of אֹבֵד), with *ă* in the second syllable, occurs in Dt 32[28] (cf. moreover, § 65 *d*). On הֹלֵם Is 41[7] (for הוֹלֵם), see § 29 *f*.

f　2. A form like the pass. ptcp. *Pā'ûl*, but not to be confused with it, is sometimes found from *intransitive verbs*, to denote an inherent quality, e.g. אָמוּן *faithful*; אָנוּשׁ *desperate*, Jer 15[18], &c.; בָּטוּחַ *trustful*, Is 26[3], ψ 112[7]; עָצוּם *strong*; שָׁכוּר *drunken*, Is 51[21]; and even from transitive verbs, אָחוּז *handling*, Ct 3[8]; זָכוּר *mindful*, ψ 103[14]; יָדוּעַ *knowing*, Is 53[3]; cf. § 84[a] *m*.

---

[1] The constr. st. נְאֻם in the formula נְאֻם יהוה, *the word* (properly the *whispering*) *of the Lord*, &c., is always written defectively.

[2] Cf. Vollers, 'Das Qâtil-partizipium,' in *ZA*. 1903, p. 312 ff.

B. Verba Derivativa, or Derived Conjugations.

§ 51. *Niph'al.*[1]

1. The essential characteristic of this conjugation consists in a *a* prefix[2] to the stem. This exists in two forms : (*a*) the (probably original) prepositive *nă*, as in the Hebrew perfect and participle, although in the strong verb the *ă* is always attenuated to *ĭ* : נִקְטַל for original *nă-qăṭăl*, participle נִקְטָל, infinitive absolute sometimes נִקְטוֹל; (*b*) the (later) proclitic *in* (as in all the forms of the corresponding Arabic conjugation VII. *'inqătăla*), found in the imperfect יִקָּטֵל for *yinqāṭēl*, in the imperative and infinitive construct, with a secondary ה added, הִקָּטֵל (for *hinqāṭēl*), and in the infinitive absolute הִקָּטֹל The inflexion of *Niph'al* is perfectly analogous to that of Qal.

The features of *Niph'al* are accordingly in the perfect and participle the *b* prefixed *Nûn*, in the imperative, infinitive, and imperfect, the *Dageš* in the first radical. These characteristics hold good also for the weak verb. In the case of an initial guttural, which, according to § 22 *b*, cannot take *Dageš forte*, the omission of the strengthening invariably causes the lengthening of the preceding vowel (see § 63 *h*).

2. As regards its meaning, *Niph'al* bears some resemblance to the *c* Greek *middle voice*, in being—(*a*) primarily *reflexive* of Qal, e.g. נִלְחַץ to thrust oneself (against), נִשְׁמַר to take heed to oneself, φυλάσσεσθαι, נִסְתַּר to hide oneself, נִגְאַל to redeem oneself; cf. also נַעֲנֶה to answer for oneself. Equally characteristic of *Niph'al* is its frequent use to express emotions which react upon the mind ; נִחַם to trouble oneself, נֶאֱנַח to sigh (to bemoan oneself, cf. ὀδύρεσθαι, *lamentari, contristari*); as well as to express actions which the subject allows to happen to himself, or to have an effect upon himself (*Niph'al tolerativum*), e. g. דָּרַשׁ to search, to inquire, Niph. *to allow oneself to be inquired of*, Is 65[1], Ez 14[3], &c.; so the Niph. of מָצָא to find, יָסַר to warn, to correct, Jer 6[8], 31[18], &c.

(*b*) It expresses *reciprocal* or mutual action. e.g. דִּבֶּר to speak, Niph. *d* to speak to one another; שָׁפַט to judge, Niph. *to go to law with one another*; יָעַץ to counsel, Niph. *to take counsel*, cf. the *middle* and *deponent* verbs βουλεύεσθαι (נוֹעַץ), μάχεσθαι (נִלְחַם), *altercari, luctari* (נִצָּה to strive with one another) *proeliari*.

(*c*) It has also, like *Hithpa'ēl* (§ 54 *f*) and the Greek *middle*, the *e* meaning of the active, with the addition of *to oneself* (*sibi*), *for one-*

---

[1] Cf. A. Rieder, *De linguae Hebr. verbis, quae vocantur derivata nifal et hitpael*, Gumbinnen (Progr. des Gymn.), 1884, a list of all the strong Niph'al forms (81) and Hithpa'ēl forms (36) in the Old Testament; and especially M. Lambert, 'L'emploi du Nifal en Hébreu,' *REJ.* 41, 196 ff.

[2] See Philippi in *ZDMG.* 1886, p. 650, and Barth, ibid. 1894, p. 8 f.

self, e. g. נִשְׁאַל *to ask* (something) *for oneself* (1 S 20⁶·²⁸, Neh 13⁶), cf. αἰτοῦμαί σε τοῦτο, ἐνδύσασθαι χιτῶνα, *to put on* (oneself) *a tunic*.

f   (*d*) In consequence of a looseness of thought at an early period of the language, *Niph'al* comes finally in many cases to represent the *passive*[1] of *Qal*, e. g. יָלַד *to bear*, Niph. *to be born*; קָבַר *to bury*, Niph. *to be buried*. In cases where *Qal* is intransitive in meaning, or is not used, *Niph'al* appears also as the passive of *Pi'ēl* and *Hiph'îl*, e.g. כָּבֵד *to be in honour*, Pi'ēl *to honour*, Niph. *to be honoured* (as well as Pu'al כֻּבַּד); פָּחַר Pi'ēl *to conceal*, Hiph. *to destroy*, Niph. passive of either. In such cases *Niph'al* may again coincide in meaning with Qal (חָלָה Qal and Niph. *to be ill*) and even take an accusative.

g   Examples of denominatives are, נִזְכַּר *to be born a male*, Ex 34¹⁹ (from זָכָר; but probably הַזָּכָר should here be read); נִלְבַּב *cordatum fieri*, Jb 11¹² (from לֵבָב *cor*); doubtless also נִבְנָה *to obtain children*, Gn 16², 30³.

h   The older grammarians were decidedly wrong in representing *Niph'al* simply as the *passive of Qal*; for *Niph'al* has (as the frequent use of its imperat. shows), in no respect the character of the other passives, and in Arabic a special conjugation ('*inqátălă*) corresponds to it with a passive of its own. Moreover, the forms mentioned in § 52 *e* point to a differently formed passive of *Qal*.— The form נִגְאָלוּ Is 59³, La 4¹⁴, is not to be regarded as a passive of Niph'al, but with König and Cheyne as a *forma mixta*, in the sense that the punctuators intended to combine two optional readings, נִגְאָלוּ, perf. Niph., and גֹּאֲלוּ, perf. Pu'al [cf. also Wright, *Compar. Gramm.*, p. 224]. Although the passive use of Niph'al was introduced at an early period, and became tolerably common, it is nevertheless quite secondary to the reflexive use.

i   Rem. 1. The *infin. absol.* נִקְטוֹל is connected in form with the perfect, to which it bears the same relation as קָטוֹל to קָטַל in Qal, the *ô* in the second syllable being obscured from an original *â*. Examples are, נִכְסֹף Gn 31³⁰; נִלְחֹם Ju 11²⁵; נִשְׁאֹל 1 S 20⁶·²⁸, all in connexion with the perfect.

k   Examples of the form הִקָּטֵל (in connexion with imperfects) are, הִנָּתֹן Jer 32⁴; הֵאָכֵל Lv 7¹⁸; once אִדָּרֵשׁ Ez 14³, where, perhaps, the subsequent אֶדְרֹשׁ has led to the substitution of א for ה.—Moreover, the form הִקָּטֵל is not infrequently used also for the infin. absol.,[2] e. g. Ex 22³, Nu 15³¹, Dt 4²⁶, 1 K 20³⁹. On the other hand, כְּהִנָּדֹף should simply be read for the wholly abnormal כְּהִנְדֹּף ψ 68³ (commonly explained as being intended to correspond in sound with the subsequent תִּנְדֹּף, but probably a 'forma mixta', combining the readings כְּנִדֹּף and כְּהִנָּדֵף).

---

[1] Cf. Halfmann, *Beiträge zur Syntax der hebräischen Sprache*, 1. Stück, Wittenb., 1888, 2. St. 1892 (Gymn.–Programm), statistics of the Niph'al (Pu'al, Hoph'al, and qātûl) forms at different periods of the language, for the purpose of ascertaining the meaning of Niph. and its relation to the passive; the selection of periods is, however, very questionable from the standpoint of literary criticism.

[2] But, like הַקְטֵל, *only* in connexion with imperfects, except Jer 7⁹. Barth is therefore right in describing (*Nominalbildung*, p. 74) both forms as later analogous formations (in addition to the original Semitic נִקְטוֹל), intended to assimilate the infinitive to the imperfect which it strengthens.

Elision of the ה after prepositions is required by the Masora in בְּכִשְׁלוֹ Pr *l*
24¹⁷ (for בְּהִכָּ'), בַּהֲרֹג Ez 26¹⁵ and בַּעֲטֹף La 2¹¹; also in verbs ל״ה Ex 10³
(לְעֲנֹת); 34²⁴, Dt 31¹¹, Is 1¹² (לִרְאוֹת); in verbs ע״ו Jb 33³⁰ (לְאוֹר). It is, however, extremely doubtful whether the *infin. Qal* of the *K⁽ᵉ⁾thîbh* is not rather
intended in all these examples; it certainly is so in La 2¹¹, cf. ψ 61³.

2. Instead of the *Ṣere* in the ultima of the imperfect, *Pathaḥ* often occurs *m*
in pause, e. g. וַיִּגְמָל Gn 21⁸; cf. Ex 31¹⁷, 2 S 12¹⁵ (with final שׁ); 17²³ (with
ק); Jon 1⁵ (with מ); see § 29 *q*. In the 2nd and 3rd plur. fem. *Pathaḥ* predominates, e. g. תִּזְכַּרְנָה Is 65¹⁷; *Ṣere* occurs only in תַּעֲנֶינָה Ru 1¹³, from עָנָה,
and hence, with loss of the doubling, for תֵּעָנֶינָה; cf. even תֵּאָמַנָה Is 60⁴.—
With *Nûn paragogicum* (see § 47 *m*) in the 2nd and 3rd plur. masc. are found,
תִּלָּחֲמוּן, יִבָּהֵלוּן, &c., in *pause* תִּשָּׁמֵדוּן, יִבָּחֲמוּ, &c.; but Jb 19²¹ (cf. 24²⁴)
יֶחֱצָבֻן.

3. When the imperfect, the infinitive (in *ē*), or the imperative is followed *n*
in close connexion by a monosyllable, or by a word with the tone on the first
syllable, the tone is, as a rule (but cf. וַיֵּאָבֵק אִישׁ Gn 32²⁵), shifted back from
the ultima to the penultima, while the ultima, which thus loses the tone,
takes *S⁽ᵉ⁾ghôl* instead of *Ṣere*; e. g. יִכָּשֶׁל בָּהּ Ez 33¹²; וַיֵּעָתֶר לוֹ Gn 25²¹; in the
imperative, 13⁹.—So always הִשָּׁמֶר לְךָ (since לְךָ counts as *one* syllable) Gn
24⁶, &c., cf. 1 S 19²; and even with *Pathaḥ* in the ultima, תֵּעֹב אָרֶץ Jb 18⁴
(but cf. וַיֵּעָתֵר אֱלֹהִים 2 S 21¹⁴). Although in isolated cases (e. g. Gn 32²⁵, Ezr
8²³) the tone is not thrown back, in spite of a tone-syllable following, the
retraction has become usual in certain forms, even when the next word
begins with a toneless syllable; especially after ו *consec.*, e. g. וַיִּשָּׁאֶר Gn 7²³;
וַיִּלָּחֶם Nu 21¹ and frequently, וַיִּצָּמֶד 25³; and always so in the imperative
הִשָּׁמֶר Ex 23²¹, Jb 36²¹, and (before Metheg of the counter-tone) Dt 24⁸, 2 K 6⁹.
On the avoidance of pausal-forms in the imperative (Am 2¹² with *Silluq*, Zc
2¹¹ with *Athnaḥ*), and imperfect (Pr 24⁴, &c.), see § 29 *o*, and note; on the
other hand, always יִמָּלֵט, הִמָּלֵט, &c.

In the *imperative*, נִקְבְּצוּ, for הִקָּבְצוּ, with the rejection of the initial ה, *o*
occurs in Is 43⁹, and in Joel 4¹¹ in *pause* נִקְבָּצוּ (cf. נֵלֵכוּ Jer 50⁵); but in these
examples either the reading or the explanation is doubtful. The 2nd sing.
imperat. of נִשְׁבַּע is always (with ה‿ *paragogicum*) הִשָּׁבְעָה לִּי *swear to me*,
Gn 21²³, &c. (also הִשָּׁבְעָה לִּי Gn 47³¹, 1 S 30¹⁵).

4. For the 1st sing. of the *imperfect*, the form אִקְטֵל is as frequent as אֶקְטֵל, *p*
e. g. אִדָּרֵשׁ *I shall be inquired of*, Ez 14³; אִשָּׁבֵעַ *I will swear*, Gn 21²⁴; cf. 16²,
Nu 23¹⁵, Ez 20³⁶, and so always in the cohortative, e. g. אִנָּקְמָה *I will avenge*
me, Is 1²⁴; cf. 1 S 12⁷, Ez 26², and in the impf. Niph. of פ״י (§ 69 *t*). The
Babylonian punctuation admits only *ĭ* under the preformative of the 1st
person.

§ 52. *Pi'ēl and Pu'al*.

1. The *characteristic* of this conjugation consists in the strengthening *a*
of the middle radical. From the simple stem *qaṭal* (cf. § 43 *b*) the
form קִטֵּל (cf. the Arabic conj. ii. *qăttălă*) would naturally follow as

the *perfect* of the active (*Pi̇ʿēl*). The *Pathaḥ* of the first syllable is, however, with one exception (see *m*), always attenuated to *ĭ* in the *perfect*. In the second syllable, *ă* has been retained in the majority of cases, so that the conjugation should more correctly be called *Piʿal*; but very frequently [1] this *ă* also is attenuated to *ĭ*, which is then regularly lengthened to *ē*, under the influence of the tone. Cf. in Aram. קַטֵּל; but in Biblical Aramaic almost always קַטֵּל. On the three cases in which *ă* before a final ר or ם has passed into *Sᵉghôl*, see below, *l*.— Hence, for the 3rd *sing. masc. perfect*, there arise forms like אִבֵּד, כִּבֵּד, גֵּרֵשׁ, קִדֵּשׁ, לִמֵּד, &c.—Before afformatives beginning with a consonant, however, *ă* is always retained, thus קִטַּלְתָּ, קְטַלְתֶּם, קִטַּלְנוּ, &c. In the *infinitives* (*absol.* קַטֹּל, obscured from *qaṭṭâl*; *constr.* קַטֵּל), *imperfect* (יְקַטֵּל), *imperative* (קַטֵּל), and *participle* (מְקַטֵּל) the original *ă* of the first syllable reappears throughout. The vocal *Šᵉwâ* of the preformatives is weakened from a short vowel; cf. the Arabic imperfect *yŭqáttĭl*, participle *mŭqáttĭl*.

b The *passive* (*Puʿal*) is distinguished by the obscure vowel *ŭ*, or very rarely *ŏ*, in the first syllable, and *ă* (in pause *ā*) always in the second. In Arabic, also, the passives are formed throughout with *ŭ* in the first syllable. The inflexion of both these conjugations is analogous to that of *Qal*.

c Rem. 1. The preformative מְ, which in the remaining conjugations also is the prefix of the participle, is probably connected with the interrogative or indefinite (cf. § 37) pronoun מִי *quis? quicunque* (fem. i. e. neuter, מָה); cf. § 85 *e*.

d 2. The Dageš *forte*, which according to the above is characteristic of the whole of *Piʿel* and *Puʿal*, is often omitted (independently of verbs *middle guttural*, § 64 *d*) when the middle radical has *Šᵉwâ* under it (cf. § 20 *m*), e. g. שִׁלְחָה for שִׁלְּחָה Ez 17¹⁷; בִּקְשׁוּ 2 Ch 15¹⁵ (but in the *imperative* always בַּקְּשׁוּ 1 S 28⁷, &c.), and so always in הַלְלוּ *praise*. The vocal character of the *Šᵉwâ* under the *litera dagessanda* is sometimes in such cases (according to § 10 *h*) expressly emphasized by its taking the form of a *Ḥaṭeph*, as in לְקָחָה Gn 2²³, with ـֳ owing to the influence of the preceding *u*, cf. פֻּעֲלוֹ for פֻּעֲלוֹ, &c.; Gn 9¹⁴, Ju 16¹⁶. In the *imperfect* and *participle* the *Šᵉwâ* under the preformatives (*Ḥaṭeph-Pathaḥ* under א in the 1st *sing. imperfect*) serves at the same time as a characteristic of both conjugations (Gn 26¹⁴ f.).

e 3. According to the convincing suggestion of Böttcher [2] (*Ausführliches Lehrbuch*, § 904 ff. and § 1022), many supposed perfects of *Puʿal* are in reality

---

[1] So in all verbs which end in *Nûn*, and in almost all which end in *Lamed* (Olsh. p. 538). Barth is probably right in supposing (*ZDMG.* 1894, p. 1 ff.) that the vowels of the strengthened perfects have been influenced by the *imperfect*.

[2] As Mayer Lambert observes, the same view was already expressed by Ibn Ġanâḥ (see above, § 3 *d*) in the *Kitâb el-luma'*, p. 161. Cf. especially Barth, 'Das passive Qal und seine Particípien,' in the *Festschrift zum Jubiläum Hildesheimer* (Berlin, 1890), p. 145 ff.

passives of Qal. He reckons as such all those *perfects*, of which the *Pi'ēl* (which ought to express the corresponding active) is either not found at all, or only (as in the case of יָלַד) with a different meaning, and which form their *imperfect* from another conjugation, generally Niph'al. Such *perfects* are the *quttal* form of the stems אָבַל, יָלַד, טֹרַף, חֻפַּשׁ (*imperfect* תְּאֻכְּלוּ Is 1²⁰), יֻצַּר, לֻקַּח, עֻבַּד, שֻׁגַּל, שֻׁטַּף, שֻׁפַּךְ. Barth (see below) adds to the list the apparent *Pu'al*-perfects of אֻסַּר, בֻּזַּז, זֹנָה, חֻצַּב, כֹּרַת, נֻפַּח, עֻזַּב, עֻשָּׂה, רֹאָה, and of verbs with middle ר (hence with *ŭ* of the first syllable lengthened to *ō*), הֹרַג, הֹרָה Jb 3³ [זֹרַה, see § 67 *m*], זֹרַע, זֹרַק, טֹרַף, מֹרַט, קֹרָא, שֹׁרַף; also the infinitives absolute הֹרֹו וְהֹגֹו Is 59¹³. In these cases there is no need to assume any error on the part of the punctuators; the sharpening of the second radical may have taken place in order to retain the characteristic *ŭ* of the first syllable (cf. Arab. *qŭtŭlă* as passive of *qătălă*), and the *a* of the second syllable is in accordance with the vocalization of all the other passives (see § 39 *f*). Cf. § 52 *s* and § 53 *u*.

2. The fundamental idea of *Pi'ēl*, to which all the various shades *f* of meaning in this conjugation may be referred, is *to busy oneself eagerly* with the action indicated by the stem. This intensifying of the idea of the stem, which is outwardly expressed by the strengthening of the second radical, appears in individual cases as—(*a*) a *strengthening* and *repetition* of the action (cf. the *intensive* and *iterative* nouns with the middle radical strengthened, § 84ᵇ),[1] e. g. צָחַק *to laugh*, Pi'ēl *to jest*, *to make sport* (to laugh repeatedly); שָׁאַל *to ask*, Pi'ēl *to beg*; hence when an action has reference to *many*, e. g. קָבַר *to bury* (a person) Gn 23⁴, Pi'ēl *to bury* (many) 1 K 11¹⁵, and often so in Syr. and Arab. Other varieties of the *intensive* and *iterative* meaning are, e. g. פָּתַח *to open*, Pi'ēl *to loose*; סָפַר *to count*, Pi'ēl *to recount*: [cf. הָלַךְ, חָשַׁב, כָּתַב, מָרַח, מְאֹהָב; תָּפַשׂ, חָפַשׂ, רָפָא].

The eager pursuit of an action may also consist in *urging* and *g* *causing* others to do the same. Hence *Pi'ēl* has also—(*b*) a *causative* sense (like *Hiph'il*), e. g. לָמַד *to learn*, Pi'ēl *to teach*. It may often be turned by such phrases as *to permit to, to declare* or *hold as* (*the declarative Pi'ēl*), *to help to*, e. g. חָיָה *to cause to live*, צָדֵק *to declare innocent*, יָלַד *to help in child-bearing*.

(*c*) *Denominatives* (see § 38 *b*) are frequently formed in this conju- *h* gation, and generally express a being occupied with the object expressed by the noun, either to form or to make use of it, e. g. קִנֵּן *to make a nest, to nest* (from קֵן), עִפֵּר *to throw dust, to dust* (from עָפָר),

---

[1] Analogous examples, in which the strengthening of a letter has likewise an *intensive* force, are such German words as *reichen, recken* (Eng. *to reach, to rack*); *streichen* (*stringo*), *strecken*: cf. *Strich* (a stroke), *Strecke* (a stretch); *wacker* from *wachen*; others, in which it has the *causative* sense, are *stechen, stecken*; *wachen* (*watch*), *wecken* (*wake*); τέλλω *to bring to an end* (cf. the stem τέλω *to end*, in τέλος, τελέω); γεννάω *to beget*, from the stem γένω *to come into being* (cf. γένος).

עֲנָן to gather the clouds together (from עָנָן), שִׁלֵּשׁ to divide in three parts, or to do a thing for the third time (from שָׁלֹשׁ); probably also דִּבֶּר to speak, from דָּבָר a word. Or again, the denominative may express taking away, injuring, &c., the object denoted by the noun (*privative Pi'ēl*, cf. our to skin, to behead, to bone), e. g. שֵׁרֵשׁ, from שֹׁרֶשׁ to root out, to extirpate, זִנֵּב prop. to injure the tail (זָנָב), hence to rout the rear of an army, to attack it; לִבֵּב to ravish the heart; דִּשֵּׁן to remove the ashes (דֶּשֶׁן), חִטֵּא to free from sin (חֵטְא), עִצֵּם to break any one's bones (עֶצֶם); cf., in the same sense, גֵּרֵם from גֶּרֶם); סְעֵף to lop the boughs, Is 10³³ (from סְעִיף a bough). Some words are clearly denominatives, although the noun from which they are derived is no longer found, e. g. סִקֵּל to stone, to pelt with stones (also used in this sense in *Qal*), and to remove stones (from a field), to clear away stones; cf. our to stone, used also in the sense of taking out the stones from fruit.

The meaning of the *passive* (*Pu'al*) follows naturally from the above, e. g. בִּקֵּשׁ Pi'ēl to seek, Pu'al to be sought.

i In *Pi'ēl* the literal, concrete meaning of the verb has sometimes been retained, when *Qal* has acquired a figurative sense, e.g. גִּלָּה, Pi'ēl to uncover, Qal to reveal, also to emigrate, i. e. to make the land bare.

k Also with an intransitive sense *Pi'ēl* occurs as an intensive form, but only in poetic language, e. g. חִתַּת in Pi'ēl to be broken in pieces, Jer 51⁵⁶; פִּחַד to tremble, Is 51¹³, Pr 28¹⁴; רִוָּה to be drunken, Is 34⁵·⁷; [מָעַט to be few, Ec 12³]; but in Is 48⁸, 60¹¹ instead of the Pi'ēl of פתח the Niph'al is certainly to be read, with Cheyne.

l Rem. 1. The (more frequent) form of the perfect with *Pathaḥ* in the second syllable appears especially before *Maqqeph* (Ec 9¹⁵, 12⁹) and in the middle of sentences in continuous discourse, but at the end of the sentence (in *pause*) the form with *Ṣere* is more common. Cf. גִּדַּל Is 49²¹ with גִּדֵּל Jos 4¹⁴, Est 3¹; מִלַּט Ez 33⁵ with מִלֵּט Ec 9¹⁵; קִצֵּץ 2 K 8¹⁶ with קִצֵּץ ψ 129⁴; but Qameṣ never appears in this pausal form. The *3rd sing. fem.* in pause is always of the form קִטְּלָה, except קִבְּצָה Mi 1⁷; the 3rd plur. always as קִטְּלוּ; the *2nd* and *1st sing.* and *1st plur.* of course as קִטַּלְתָּ, קִטַּלְתְּ, קִטַּלְתִּי (but always לִמַּדְתִּי and דִּבַּרְתִּי), קִטַּלְנוּ. In the *3rd sing. perf.* דִּבֶּר to speak, כִּפֶּר to pardon, and כִּבֶּס to wash clothes (also כִּבֶּס Gn 49¹¹) take *S'ghôl*, but become in pause דִּבֵּר, כִּבֵּס (2 S 19²⁵); the *pausal* form of כִּפֶּר does not occur.

m *Pathaḥ* in the first syllable (as in Aramaic and Arabic) occurs only once, Gn 41⁵¹, נַשַּׁנִי he made me forget, to emphasize more clearly the play on the name מְנַשֶּׁה.

n 2. In the *imperfect* (and *jussive* Ju 16²⁵), *infinitive*, and *imperative* *Pi'ēl* (as also in *Hithpa'ēl*) the *Ṣere* in the final syllable, when followed by *Maqqeph*, is usually shortened into *S'ghôl*, e. g. יְבַקֶּשׁ־לוֹ he seeks for himself, Is 40²⁰; קַדֶּשׁ־לִי sanctify unto me, Ex 13². Pausal-forms with *S'ghôl* instead of *Ṣere*, as יְרַחֶף Dt 32¹¹, אֲרַחֶם Ho 2⁶ (cf. Ex 32⁶ in the infinitive, and Gn 21⁹ in the participle), owe their origin to some particular school of Masoretes, and are wrongly accepted by Baer; cf. the analogous cases in § 75 *n* and *hh*. If the final syllable of the *imperfect Pi'ēl* has *Pathaḥ* (before a guttural or ר), it remains even in *pause*; cf. § 29 *s* and 65 *e*. In the 1st sing. imperfect the *e*-sound occurs in two words for *Ḥaṭeph-Pathaḥ*, under the preformative א; אֱזָרֶה Lv 26³³, Ez 5¹², 12¹⁴ and וָאֶסְעָרֵם Zc 7¹⁴ (in accordance with § 23 *h*).—Before the full plural ending וּן (see § 47 *m*) the Ṣere is retained in *pause*, e.g. תְּדַבְּרוּן ψ 58² (but Gn 32²⁰ תְּדַבְּרוּן), cf. 2 K 6¹⁹, Dt 12³; so before *Silluq* ψ 58³, Jb 21¹¹ and even before *Zaqeph qaṭon* Dt 7⁵. Instead of תְּקַפֵּלְנָה, forms like תְּקַפֵּלְנָה are also found, e.g. Is 3¹⁶, 13¹⁸, in both cases before a sibilant and in pause. Also פַּלֵּ ψ 55¹⁰ occurs as the 2nd sing. imperative (probably an intentional imitation of the sound of the preceding בַּלַּע) and קָרֵב (for *qarrabh*) Ez 37¹⁷.

3. The *infinite absolute* of Pi'ēl has sometimes the special form קַטֹּל given in the paradigm, e.g. יַסֹּר *castigando*, ψ 118¹⁸; cf. Ex 21¹⁹, 1 K 19¹⁰ (from a verb ל״א); ψ 40² (from a verb ל״ה); but much more frequently the form of the *infinitive construct* (קַטֵּל) is used instead. The latter has also, in exceptional cases, the form קִטֵּל (with *ă* attenuated to *ĭ* as in the *perfect*), e.g. in 1 Ch 8⁸ שִׁלְּחוֹ; perhaps also (if not a substantive) קִטֵּר Jer 44²¹; and for the sake of assonance even for *infinitive absolute* in 2 S 12¹⁴ (נִאֵץ נִאַצְתָּ). On the other hand, שַׁלֵּם Dt 32³⁵ and דִּבֶּר Jer 5¹³ are better regarded as substantives, while דְּבֶר Ex 6²⁸, Nu 3¹, Dt 4¹⁵ (in each case after בְּיוֹם), Ho 1² (after תְּחִלַּת), in all of which places it is considered by König (after Qimḥi) to be *infinitive construct*, is really perfect of Pi'ēl.

The infinitive construct Pi'ēl, with the *fem.* ending (cf. § 45 *d*), occurs in יַסְּרָה Lv 26¹⁸; זַמְּרָה ψ 147¹; with ת of the *fem.* before a suffix צַדְּקָתֵךְ Ez 16⁵². On the verbal nouns after the form of the Aram. inf. Pa'il (קַטָּלָה), see § 84ᵇ *e*.

Instead of the abnormal מְאַסְפָּיו (so Baer, Is 62⁹) as ptcp. Pi'el, read מְאַסְּ׳ with ed. Mant. and Ginsburg.

4. In Pu'al *ŏ* is sometimes found instead of *ŭ* in the initial syllable, e.g. מְאָדָּם *dyed red*, Ex 25⁵, &c., Na 2⁴, cf. 3⁷ שֹׁרָדָה; Ez 16⁴, ψ 72²⁰, 80¹¹. According to Baer's reading also in תֻּרְצְחוּ ψ 62⁴, and so also Ben Ašer, but Ben Naphtali תְּרָצְחוּ. It is merely an orthographic licence when *ŭ* is written fully, e.g. יֻלַּד Ju 18²⁹.

5. As *infinitive absolute* of Pu'al we find גֻּנֹּב Gn 40¹⁵.—No instance of the *inf. constr.* occurs in the strong verb in Pu'al; from ל״ה with suffix עֻנּוֹתוֹ ψ 132¹.

6. A few examples occur of the *participle* Pu'al without the preformative (מ), e.g. אֻכָּל Ex 3²; יֻלָּד (for מְיֻלָּד) Ju 13⁸; לֻקַּח 2 K 2¹⁰; סֹעֲרָה Is 54¹¹. These *participles* are distinguished from the *perfect* (as in Niph'al) by the *ā* of the final syllable. For other examples, see Is 30²⁴, Ec 9¹² (where יוּקָשִׁים, according to § 20 *n*, stands for יֻקָּ׳ = מְיֻקָּ׳); but, according to the Masora, *not* Ez 26¹⁷, since הֻהֲלָלָה as *Mil'ēl* can only be the *perfect*. The rejection of the מ may be favoured by an initial מ, as in Is 18²·⁷ (but also מְמֻשָּׁךְ); Pr 25¹⁹ (where, however, read מוּעָדֶת); so also in the participle Pi'ēl מְאָן Ex 7²⁷, 9² (always after אִם, but cf. also הַמְאָנִים Jer 13¹⁰, where, however, הַמְּאָנִים=הַמְּמָאֲנִים is to be read, with Brockelmann, *Grundriss*, p. 264 f.) and מַהֵר Zp 1¹⁴ (and Is 8¹·³ ?). Notice, however, Barth's suggestion (*Nominalbildung*, p. 273) that, as the active of forms like אֻכָל only occurs in *Qal*, they are perfect participles of former passives of Qal (see *e*), and in Jer 13¹⁰, 23³² perfect participles of Pi'ēl.—On מְרֻבָּע Ez 45², see § 65 *d*.

§ 53. *Hiph'îl and Hoph'al.*

a 1. The characteristic of the active (*Hiph'îl*) is a prefixed הַ (on its origin see § 55 *i*) in the perfect הִ (with the *ă* attenuated to *ĭ*, as in *Pi'ēl*), which forms a closed syllable with the first consonant of the stem. The second syllable of the perfect had also originally an *ă*; cf. the Arabic conj. IV. 'aqtălă, and in Hebrew the return of the *Pathaḥ* in the 2nd and 1st pers. הִקְטַלְתְּ, &c. After the attenuation of this *ă* to *ĭ*, it ought by rule to have been lengthened to *ē* in the tone-syllable, as in Aramaic אַקְטֵל, beside הַקְטֵל in Biblical Aramaic. Instead of this, however, it is always replaced in the strong verb by *î*,[1] ־ִי, but sometimes written defectively ־ִ; cf. § 9 *g*. Similarly in the infinitive construct הַקְטִיל, and in the imperfect and participle יַקְטִיל and מַקְטִיל, which are syncopated from יְהַקְטִיל and מְהַקְטִיל; § 23 *k*. The corresponding Arabic forms (*juqtĭl* and *muqtĭl*) point to an original *ĭ* in the second syllable of these forms. In Hebrew the regular lengthening of this *ĭ* to *ē* appears in the strong verb at least in the *jussive* and in the *imperfect consecutive* (see *n*), as also in the *imperative* of the 2nd sing. masc. (see *m*); on תַּקְטֵלְנָה, הַקְטֵלְנָה cf. § 26 *p*. On the return of the original *ă* in the second syllable of the *Imperat.*, *Jussive*, &c, under the influence of a guttural, cf. § 65 *f*.

b In the *passive* (*Hoph'al*) the preformative is pronounced with an obscure vowel, whilst the second syllable has *ă* (in pause *ā*), as its characteristic, thus :—*Perf.* הֻקְטַל or הָקְטַל, *Imperf.* יֻקְטַל (syncopated from יְהֻקְטַל) or יָקְטַל, *Part.* מֻקְטָל or מָקְטָל (from מְהֻקְטָל); but the *infinitive absolute* has the form הָקְטֵל.

Thus the characteristics of both conjugations are the ה preformative in the *perfect, imperative*, and *infinitive*; in the *imperfect* and *participle Hiph'il*, Pathaḥ under the preformatives, in the *Hoph'al* *ŏ* or *ŭ*.

c 2. The *meaning* of *Hiph'îl* is primarily, and even more frequently than in *Pi'ēl* (§ 52 *g*), *causative* of Qal, e. g. יָצָא *to go forth*, Hiph. *to bring forth, to lead forth, to draw forth*; קָדַשׁ *to be holy*, Hiph. *to sanctify*. Under the *causative* is also included (as in *Pi'ēl*) the *declarative* sense, e. g. הִצְדִּיק *to pronounce just*; הִרְשִׁיעַ *to make one an evil doer* (*to pronounce guilty*); cf. עָקֵשׁ, in *Hiph'îl*, Jb 9²⁰, *to represent as perverse*. If Qal has already a transitive meaning, *Hiph'îl* then takes two accusatives (see § 117 *cc*). In some verbs, *Pi'ēl* and *Hiph'îl* occur side by side in the same sense, e. g. אָבַד *periit*, Pi'ēl and Hiph'il, *perdidit*; as a rule,

---

[1] This *î* may have been transferred originally from the imperfects of verbs ע״וּ, as a convenient means of distinction between the indicative and jussive, to the *imperfect* of the strong verb and afterwards to the whole of *Hiph'îl*; so Stade, Philippi, Praetorius, *ZAW.* 1883, p. 52 f.

however, only one of these two conjugations is in use, or else they differ from one another in meaning, e.g. כָּבֵד *gravem esse*, Pi'ēl *to honour*, Hiph'il *to bring to honour*, also *to make heavy*. Verbs which are intransitive in *Qal* simply become transitive in *Hiph'il*, e.g. נָטָה *to bow oneself*, Hiph. *to bow, to bend*.

Among the ideas expressed by the *causative* and *transitive* are included, *d* moreover, according to the *Hebrew* point of view (and that of the Semitic languages in general, especially Arabic), a series of actions and ideas, which *we* have to express by periphrasis, in order to understand their being represented by the Hiph'il-form. To these *inwardly transitive* or *intensive* Hiph'ils belong: (*a*) Hiph'il stems which express the obtaining or receiving of a concrete or abstract quality. (In the following examples the *Qal* stems are given, for the sake of brevity, with the addition of the meaning which—often together with other meanings—belongs to the *Hiph'il*.) Thus יָפַע, זָהַר, אָהַל, צוּץ *to be bright, to shine* (to give forth brightness); opposed to חָשַׁךְ *to become dark*; חָזַק, נָבַר, אָמֵץ *to be strong* (to develop strength), עָטַף *to be weak*; אָרַךְ *to be long* (to acquire length); גָּבַהּ *to be high*; הוּם *to be in tumult*, זָעַק *to cry out*, רוּעַ, רָנַן *to make a noise, to exult*; חָלַף *to sprout* (to put forth shoots), cf. פָּרַח *to bloom*, עָדַף, שׁוּק *to overflow*; צָמַת, סָכַת, חָשָׁה, חָרַשׁ *to be silent* (silentium facere, Pliny); מָתַק *to be sweet*; צָלַח *to have success*; שָׁפֵל *to be low*; אָדַם *to become red*, לָבַן *to become white*.

(*b*) Stems which express in *Hiph'il* the entering into a certain condition and, *e* further, the being in the same: אָמַן *to become firm, to trust in*; בָּאַשׁ *to become stinking*; זוּד *to become boiling, to boil over*; חָלָה *to become ill*; הָסַר *to come to want*; חָרָה *to become hot*; יָבֵשׁ *to become dry, to become ashamed*; יָתַר *to attain superiority*; סָכַן *to become familiar*; קוּץ, עוּר *to become awake*; קָשָׁה *to become hard*; שָׁקַט, רָגַע *to become quiet* (to keep quiet); שָׁמֵם *to be astonished*. The Hiph'il forms of some verbs of motion constitute a variety of this class: נָגַשׁ *to draw near*; קָרַב *to come near*; רָחַק *to withdraw far off* (all these three are besides used as causatives); קָדַם *to come before*.

(*c*) Stems which express action in some particular direction: חָטָא *to err*; *f* חָלַק *to flatter* (to act smoothly); יָטַב *to act well, to do good*; סָכַל *to act foolishly*; שָׂכַל *to act wisely*; עָרַם *to act craftily*; צָנַע *to act submissively*; רָשַׁע, רָעַע *to act wickedly, godlessly*; תָּעַב, שָׁחַת *to act corruptly, abominably*; שָׁלֵם *to act peacefully, to be at peace, to be submissive*.

Further, there are in *Hiph'il* a considerable number of *denominatives* which *g* express the *bringing out*, the *producing* of a thing, and so are properly regarded as causatives,[1] e.g. אָצַר *to set over the treasury*, Neh 13:13 (unless וַאֲצַוֶּה is to be read, as in Neh 7:2); בָּכַר *to bring forth a firstborn*; גָּשַׁם *to cause to rain*; זָרַע *to produce seed*; יָמַן (*Hiph'il* הֵימִין) *to go to the right*, cf. הִשְׂמְאִיל *to go to the left*; פָּרַס *to get* or *to have hoofs*; קָרַן *to get* or *to have horns*; שָׁכַל *to produce abortion*; שָׁלַג *to become snow-white*; שָׁמַן *to grow fat*; שָׁרַשׁ *to put forth roots*, &c.: so also according to the ordinary acceptation הֶאֱזְנִיחוּ Is 19:6, *they have become stinking*, from אָזְנַח *stinking* or *stench*, with retention of the א prosthetic, § 19 m (but see below, *p*).

---

[1] The same ideas are also paraphrased by the verb עָשָׂה (*to make*), e.g. *to make fat*, for, *to produce fat upon his body*, Jb 15:27; *to make fruit, to make branches*, for, *to put forth, to yield*, Jb 14:9, Ho 8:7, cf. the Lat. *corpus, robur, sobolem, divitias facere*, and the Ital. *far corpo, far forze, far frutto*.

Of a different kind are the *denominatives* from: אָזַן (scarcely *to prick up the ears*, but) *to act with the ears, to hear*; cf. לָשַׁן *to move the tongue, to slander*, and the German *äugeln* (to make eyes), *füsseln, näseln, schwänzeln*; שָׁבַר *to sell corn*; שָׁכַם *to set out early* (to load the back [of the camel, &c.] ?) ; opposed to הֶעֱרִיב.

h   **3.** The meaning of *Hophʻal* is (*a*) primarily that of a *passive* of *Hiphʻîl*, e.g. הִשְׁלִיךְ *proiecit*, הָשְׁלַךְ or הֻשְׁלַךְ *proiectus est*; (*b*) sometimes equivalent to a passive of *Qal*, as נָקַם *to avenge*, Hoph. *to be avenged* (but see below, *u*).

i   Rem. 1. The *î* of the 3rd sing. masc. perf. *Hiphʻîl* remains, without exception, in the 3rd fem. (in the tone-syllable). That it was, however, only lengthened from a short vowel, and consequently is changeable, is proved by the forms of the *imperative* and *imperfect* where *ē* (or, under the influence of gutturals, *ă*) takes its place. In an open syllable the *î* is retained almost throughout; only in very isolated instances has it been weakened to *Šᵉwâ* (see *n* and *o*).

k   2. The *infinitive absolute* commonly has *Ṣere* without *Yodh*, e.g. הַקְדֵּשׁ Ju 17³; less frequently it takes יְ—ִ, e.g. הַשְׁמֵיד Am 9⁸; cf. Dt 15¹⁴, Is 59⁴, Jer 3¹⁵, 23³², 44²⁵, Jb 34³⁵, Ec 10¹⁰. With א instead of ה (probably a mere scribal error, not an Aramaism) we find אַשְׁכֵּים Jer 25³. Rare exceptions, where the form with *Ṣere* stands for the *infinitive construct*, are, e.g. Dt 32⁸ (Sam. בְּהַנְחִיל; read perhaps בְּהַנְחֵל), Jer 44¹⁹·²⁵, Pr 25², Jb 13³ (?); on the other hand, for לַעְשֵׂר Dt 26¹² (which looks like an infinitive Hiphʻîl with elision of the ה, for לְהַעְשִׂיר) the right reading is simply לְעַשֵּׂר, since elsewhere the Piʻēl alone occurs with the meaning *to tithe*; for בַּעְשֵׂר Neh 10³⁹ perhaps the inf. Qal (בַּעְשֹׂר) was intended, as in 1 S 8¹⁵·¹⁷ (=*to take the tithe*). At the same time it is doubtful whether the present punctuation does not arise from a conflation of two different readings, the Qal and the Piʻēl.

l   Instead of the ordinary form of the *infinitive construct* הַקְטִיל the form הַקְטִיל sometimes occurs, e.g. הַשְׁמִיד *to destroy*, Dt 7²⁴, 28⁴⁸; cf. Lv 14⁴⁶, Jos 11¹⁴, Jer 50³⁴, 51³³ and הַקְצֹת for הַקְצוֹת Lv 14⁴³ from קָצָה; scarcely, however, Lv 7³⁵ (see § 155 *l*), 2 S 22¹ (ψ 18¹), 1 K 11¹⁶ (after עַד), and in the passages so explained by König (i. 276) where הַשְׁאִיר appears after prepositions [1]; [cf. Driver on Dt 3³, 4¹⁵, 7²⁴, 28⁵⁵].

With *ă* in the second syllable there occurs הַזְבַּרְכֶם Ez 21²⁹ (cf. the substantival infin. הַפֵּצַר 1 S 15²³).—In the Aram. manner לְהַשְׁמָעוּת is found in Ez 24²⁶ (as a construct form) for the *infinitive Hiphʻîl* (cf. the *infinitive Hithpaʻel*, Dn 11²³). On the elision of the ה after prefixes, see *q*.

m   3. In the *imperative* the *î* is retained throughout in the open syllable, according to *i*, and consequently also before suffixes (see § 61 *g*) and ה—ָ *paragogic*, e.g. הַקְשִׁיבָה *attend to*, הוֹשִׁיעָה נָּא ψ 118²⁵, as in ed. Mant., Jabl., Baer, not הוֹשִׁיעָה נָא as Ginsb. and Kittel; with the tone at the end only הַצְלִיחָה ibid. v. 25ᵇ. On the other hand, in the 2nd sing. masc. the original *î* (cf. Arabic *ʼaqtil*) is lengthened to *ē*, e.g. הַשְׁמֵן *make fat*, and becomes *Sᵉghôl* before *Maqqeph*, e.g. הַסְכֶּן־נָא Jb 22²¹.—The form הַקְטֵל for הַקְטֵיל appears anomalously a few times: ψ 94¹, Is 43⁸, Jer 17¹⁸ (cf. § 69 *v* and § 72 *y*); elsewhere the Masora has preferred the punctuation הַקְטִיל, e.g. 2 K 8⁶; cf. ψ 142⁵.—In La 5¹ הַבִּיטָה is required by the *Qᵉrê* for הבט.

_____

[1] As to the doubtfulness, on general grounds, of this form of the Inf. Hiph., see Robertson Smith in the *Journ. of Philol.*, xvi. p. 72 f.

4. In the *imperfect Hiph'il* the *shorter* form with Ṣere prevails for the jussive *n*
in the 3rd *masc.* and *fem.* and 2nd *masc. sing.*, e. g. אַל־תַּגְדֵּל *make not great,*
Ob [12] ; יַכְרֵת *let Him cut off!* ψ 12[4] ; even incorrectly תַּגִּיד Ex 19[3] and יַגִּיד
Ec 10[20] ; cf. also יַבְעֶר Ex 22[4], where the jussive form is to be explained
according to § 109 *h*, and יַאֲבֵר Jb 39[26] before the principal pause. Similarly,
after ו consec., e. g. וַיַּבְדֵּל *and He divided*, Gn 1[4]. On the other hand, *i* is
almost always retained in the 1st sing., e. g. וְאַשְׁמִיד Am 2[9] (but generally
without י, as וָאַסְתִּר Ez 39[23] f., &c.) ; cf. § 49 *e* and § 74 *l*, but also § 72 *aa* ;
in 1st plur. only in Neh 4[3] ; in the 3rd sing. ψ 105[28]. With ă in the principal
pause וַתּוֹתַר Ru 2[14], and in the lesser pause, Gn 49[4] ; before a sibilant (see
§ 29 *q*) וַיַּפֵּשׁ Ju 6[19] ; in the lesser pause וַיָּקֶף La 3[5]. Before *Maqqeph* the Ṣere
becomes Sᵉghôl, e. g. וַיַּחֲזֶק־בּוֹ Ju 19[4]. In the plural again, and before suffixes,
i remains in the forms תַּקְטִילוּ, יַקְטִילוּ, even in the jussive and after ו consecutive, e. g. וַיַּרְבִּיקוּ Ju 18[22]. The only exceptions, where the *i* is weakened
to Šᵉwâ, are וַיַּדְרִכוּ Jer 9[2] ; וַיַּדְבִּקוּ 1 S 14[22], 31[2], 1 Ch 10[2] ; יַעַבְרוּ Jer 11[15] ;
וְאָוֹצְרָה Neh 13[13], if it is *Hiph'il* of אצר, but probably וַאֲצַוֶּה is to be read, as
in 7[2] ; perhaps also תְּהַכְּרוּ Jb 19[9] (according to others, *imperfect Qal*). The
same weakening occurs also in the imperfect in 3rd and 2nd masc. sing.
before suffixes, 1 S 17[25], 1 K 20[33], ψ 65[10], and in Jb 9[20], unless the form be
Pi'ēl=וְיַעַקְשֵׁנִי, since the *Hiph'il* is not found elsewhere. It is hardly likely
that in these isolated examples we have a trace of the ground-form, *yaqtîl*, or
an Aramaism. More probably they are due partly to a misunderstanding of
the defective writing, which is found, by a purely orthographic licence, in
numerous other cases (even in 3rd sing. יַשְׁלֵם Is 44[28]), and partly are intended,
as *formae mixtae*, to combine the forms of Qal and Hiph'il. Instead of the
firmly closed syllable, the Masora requires in Gn 1[11] תַּדְשֵׁא, with euphonic
Ga'ya (see § 16 *h*).

5. In the *participle*, מוֹצִא ψ 135[7] appears to be traceable to the ground-form, *O
maqtîl* ; yet the Ṣere may also possibly be explained by the retraction of the
tone. The Masora appears to require the weakening of the vowel to Šᵉwâ
(see above, *n*) in מַהֲלְכִים Zc 3[7] (probably, however, מַהְלְכִים should be read),
also in מַחְלְמִים Jer 29[8], מַעֲוְרִים 2 Ch 28[23] (but as ם precedes, and accordingly
dittography may well have taken place, the participle Qal is probably to be
read in both places ; the reading of the text is perhaps again intended to
combine Qal and Hiph'il, see above, *n*), and in the Qᵉrê מַחֲצְרִים 1 Ch 15[24] &c.
(where the Kᵉthîbh מַחְצְרִים is better).—The fem. is ordinarily pointed as
מֻזְכֶּרֶת Nu 5[15], מַשֵּׂנֶת Lv 14[21] ; in pause מַשְׁכֶּלֶת Pr 19[14].

6. In the *perfect* there occur occasionally such forms as הִכְלִמָּנוּ 1 S 25[7] ; *p*
cf. Gn 41[28], 2 K 17[11], Jer 29[1], Mi 6[3], Jb 16[7] ; with the original ă in the first
syllable וְהִרְאֵיתִי Na 3[5].—In אֶנְאַלְתִּי [1] *I have stained*, Is 63[3], א stands at the
beginning instead of ה, cf. above, *k*, on אַשְׁבֵּים. On the other hand, וְהַאֲזִינוּ

---

[1] Most probably, however, גֵּאַלְתִּי (*perfect Pi'ēl*) is to be read, and the א is
only an indication of the change of the *perfect* into the *imperfect*, as also
previously, by a change of punctuation, וְאָדְרְכֵם and וְיָן (instead of וָאֵדְרְ and
וַיָּן) are made future instead of past. Jewish exegesis applied these Edom-
oracles to the Roman (i. e. Christian) empire. So G. Moore in *Theol. Literaturzeitung*, 1887, col. 292.

Is 19⁶ (see above, g) is a mere error of the scribe, who had the Aramaic form in mind and corrected it by prefixing ה.

q 7. In the *imperfect* and *participle* the characteristic ה is regularly elided after the preformatives, thus מַקְטִיל, יַקְטִיל; but it is retained in the *infinitive* after prepositions, e.g. לְהַקְטִיל. The exceptions are in the imperfect, יְהוֹשִׁיעַ *He will save* for יוֹשִׁיעַ 1 S 17⁴⁷, ψ 116⁶ (in *pause*); יְהוֹדֶה *He will praise* for יוֹדֶה Neh 11¹⁷, ψ 28⁷, 45¹⁸ (cf. the proper name יְהוֹבָל Jer 37³, for which 38¹ יוּבַל [and יְהוֹסֵף ψ 81⁶]); (§ 70 d) יְהֵילִילוּ Is 52⁵, יְהָתֵלּוּ Jer 9⁴, תְּהְתָּלּוּ Jb 13⁹] and מְהִקְצָעוֹת Ez 46²²; in the *infinitive* (where, however, as in *Niph'al*, § 51 l, the *infinitive Qal* is generally to be read) לַסְתֵּר Is 29¹⁵ for לְהַסְתִּיר; לְנֹפֵּל and לַצְבּוֹת Nu 5²²; לַעֲבִיר 2 S 19¹⁹; לַהֲלֹק Jer 37¹²; לַחֲטִיא Ec 5⁵; לַכֵּן (doubly anomalous for וְלַשְׁבִּית (לְהַלְבִּין) Dn 11³⁵; לַשְׁמֵעַ ψ 26⁷; לַאֲדִיב 1 S 2³³; לַשְׁמֵד Is 23¹¹; Am 8⁴ (certainly corrupt); בָּעִיר for בְּהָעִיר ψ 73²⁰ (but *in the city* is probably meant); לָבִיא Jer 39⁷ (2 Ch 31¹⁰); לַמְרוֹת Is 3⁸, ψ 78¹⁷; לַנְחֹתָם Ex 13²¹; בַּגְּלוֹת (see, however, § 20 h) Is 33¹; לְרָאֹתְכֶם Dt 1³³: cf. further, from verbs ל״ה, Nu 5²², Jer 27²⁰; on Dt 26¹² and Neh 10³⁹, see above, k; for לַמְחוֹת Pr 31³ read לִמְחוֹת or לִמְמַחוֹת.

r 8. With regard to the tone it is to be observed that the afformatives וּ and הֶ__ in Hiph'il have *not* the tone, even in the *perfect* with *waw consecutive* (except in Ex 26³³ before ה, Lv 15²⁹ before א, to avoid a hiatus); but the plural ending וּן (see § 47 m) always has the tone, e.g. תַּקְרִבוּן Dt 1¹⁷.

s 9. The passive (Hoph'al) has *ŭ* instead of Qameṣ-ḥaṭuph in the first syllable (הָקְטַל), in the strong verb less frequently in the perfect and infinitive, but generally in the participle, through the influence of the initial מ (but cf. מָשְׁחָת Pr 25²⁶); e.g. הֻשְׁכַּב Ez 32³² (beside הֻשְׁכְּבָה 32¹⁹); יֻשְׁלַךְ *impf.* part. מֻשְׁלָךְ 2 S 20²¹ (beside הֻשְׁלַכְתָּ Is 14¹⁹) הֻמְלַחַת Ez 16⁴; in the partic. Hoph. without elision of the ה: מְהִקְצָעוֹת Ez 46²²; on the other hand, verbs פ״ן always have *ŭ* (in a sharpened syllable): יֻגַּד, הֻגַּד (cf. § 9 n).

t 10. The *infinitive absolute* has in Hoph'al (as in Hiph'il) Ṣere in the last syllable, e.g. הָמְלֵחַ and הָחְתֵּל Ez 16⁴; הֻגֵּד Jos 9²⁴. An *infinitive construct* does not occur in the strong verb.

11. With regard to the *imperative Hoph'al*, see above, § 46 a, note.

u 12. According to Böttcher (*Ausführliches Lehrbuch*, § 906) and Barth (see above, § 52 e) a number of supposed imperfects Hoph'al are, in fact, imperfects of the passive of Qal. As in the case of the perfects passive of Qal (see above, § 52 e) the question is again of verbs of which neither the corresponding causative (i. e. here the Hiph'il), nor the other tense of the same conjugation (i. e. here the perfect Hoph'al) is found; so with יֻקַּם (for יֻנְקַם, cf. *yuqtălŭ* as imperfect Qal in Arabic) and יֻתַּן, from נָתַן and נָתַן; יֻקַּח from לָקַח (cf. § 66 g); יוּאָר Nu 22⁶ from אָרַר; יֻחַן from חָנַן; יוּשַׁד Ho 10¹⁴ (cf. Is 33¹) from שָׁדַד; Barth adds the verbs פ״ן: תֻּתַּשׁ Ez 19¹² from נתשׁ; יֻתַּץ Lev 11³⁵ from נתץ; the verbs ע״ע: יֻחַק Jb 19²³ from חקק; יֻכַּת &c. from כתת; the verb ע״ו: יוּדַשׁ from דּוּשׁ; the verbs ע״י: יֻחָל, יוּשַׁר, יֻשַּׁת from חִיל, שִׁיר and שִׁית. On וַיֵּישֶׂם &c., § 73 f. In point of fact it would be very strange, especially in the case of יֻתַּן and יֻקַּח, that of these frequently used verbs, amongst all the forms of Hiph'îl and Hoph'al, only the *imperfect* Hoph'al should have been preserved. A passive of Qal is also indicated in the Tell-el-Amarna letters, according to Knudtzon, by a number of imperfect forms, which are undoubtedly due to Canaanite influence, cf. *Beitr. zur Assyriologie,* iv. 410.

§ 54. *Hithpaʿēl.*

1. The *Hithpaʿēl* [1] is connected with *Pi'ēl*, being formed by prefixing *a* to the *Pi'ēl*-stem (*qattēl, qattal*) the syllable הִתְ (Western Aramaic אִתְ, but in Biblical Aramaic הִתְ; Syr. *'et* [2]). Like the preformative נ (הִן) of *Niph'al*, הִתְ has also a reflexive force.

2. The ת of the prefix in this conjugation, as also in *Hothpaʿal* *b* (see *h*), *Hithpōʿēl, Hithpaʿlēl* and *Hithpalpel* (§ 55), under certain circumstances, suffers the following changes:

(*a*) When the stem begins with one of the harder sibilants ס, צ, or שׂ, the ת and the sibilant change places (cf. on this *metathesis,* § 19 *n*), and at the same time the ת after a צ becomes the corresponding emphatic ט: thus הִשְׁתַּמֵּר *to take heed to oneself,* for הִתְשַׁמֵּר; הִסְתַּבֵּל *to become burdensome,* for הִתְסַבֵּל; הִצְטַדֵּק *to justify oneself,* from צָדַק. The only exception is in Jer 49³, וְהִתְשׁוֹטַטְנָה, to avoid the cacophony of three successive *t*-sounds.

(*b*) When the stem begins with a *d*- or *t*-sound (ד, ט, ת), the ת of *c* the preformative is assimilated to it (§ 19 *d*), e.g. מִדַּבֵּר *speaking, conversing;* הִדַּכָּא *to be crushed,* הִטַּהֵר *to purify oneself,* הִטַּמֵּא *to defile oneself,* הִתַּמֵּם *to act uprightly.* (An exception occurs in Ju 19²².) The assimilation of the ת occurs also with נ and כ, e.g. הִנַּבֵּא *to prophesy,* as well as הִתְנַבֵּא (cf. Nu 24⁷, Ez 5¹³, Dn 11¹⁴); תִּכּוֹנֵן Nu 21²⁷ (cf. Is 54¹⁴, ψ 59⁵); תִּכַּפֶּה Pr 26²⁶; with שׂ Ec 7¹⁶; with ר Is 33¹⁰.

Rem. Metathesis would likewise be expected, as in the cases under *b*, *d* when ת and ז come together, as well as a change of ת to ד. Instead of this, in the only instance of the kind (הִזַּכּוּ Is 1¹⁶) the ת is assimilated to the ז, —unless indeed הִזָּכוּ, *imperative Niph'al* of זכך, is intended.

3. As in form, so also in meaning, *Hithpaʿēl* is primarily (*a*) *reflexive* of *Pi'ēl,* e.g. הִתְאַזֵּר *to gird oneself,* הִתְקַדֵּשׁ *to sanctify oneself.* Although in these examples the intensive meaning is not distinctly marked, it is so in other cases, e.g. הִתְנַקֵּם *to show oneself revengeful (Niph.* simply *to take revenge),* and in the numerous instances where the *Hithpaʿēl* expresses *to make oneself* that which is predicated by the stem, *to conduct oneself* as such, *to show oneself, to imagine oneself, to*

---

[1] A. Stein, *Der Stamm des Hithpael im Hebr.* pt. 1, Schwerin, 1893, gives alphabetical statistics of the 1151 forms.

[2] So also in Hebrew אֶתְחַבַּר 2 Ch 20³⁵; cf. ψ 76⁶ (אֶשְׁתּוֹלָלוּ).

affect to be of a certain character. E. g. הִתְגַּדֵּל *to make oneself great, to act proudly*; הִתְחַכֵּם *to show oneself wise, crafty*; הִתְחַלָּה *to pretend to be ill*; הִתְעַשֵּׁר *to make, i. e. to feign oneself rich*; הִשְׁתָּרֵר Nu 16¹³, *to make oneself a prince*; הִתְנַבֵּא 1 S 18¹⁰, *to act in an excited manner like a prophet, to rave*. The meaning of *Hithpaʿēl* sometimes coincides with that of *Qal*, both forms being in use together, e. g. אָבַל *to mourn*, in Qal only in poetic style, in *Hithpaʿēl* in prose. On the accusative after Hithpaʿel (regarded as a transitive verb), see § 117 *w*.

f   (*b*) It expresses *reciprocal* action, like *Niphʿal*, § 51 *d*, e. g. הִתְרָאָה *to look upon one another*, Gn 42¹; cf. ψ 41⁸;—but

    (*c*) It more often indicates an action less directly affecting the subject, and describes it as performed *with regard to* or *for* oneself, in one's own special interest (cf. *Niphʿal*, § 51 *e*). Hithpaʿel in such cases readily takes an accusative, e. g. הִתְפָּרֵק Ex 32³ and הִתְנַצֵּל Ex 33⁶ *to tear off from oneself*; הִתְפַּשֵּׁט *exuit sibi* (*vestem*), הִתְפַּתֵּחַ *solvit sibi* (*vincula*); הִצְטַיָּר Jos 9¹², *to take* (*something*) *as one's provision*; without an accusative, הִתְהַלֵּךְ *to walk about for oneself* (*ambulare*); הִתְפַּלֵּל *sibi intercedere* (see Delitzsch on Is 1¹⁵); הִתְחַקֶּה *to draw a line for oneself*, Job 13²⁷; on Is 14², see § 57, note.

g   (*d*) Only seldom is it *passive*, e. g. הִיא תִתְהַלָּל Pr 31³⁰ *she shall be praised*; הִשְׁתַּכַּח *to be forgotten*, Ec 8¹⁰, where the reflexive sense (*to bring oneself into oblivion*) has altogether disappeared. Cf. Niphʿal, § 51 *f*.

h   The passive form *Hothpaʿal* is found only in the few following examples: הֻטַּמָּא *to be defiled*, Dt 24⁴; *infinitive* הֻכַּבֵּס *to be washed*, Lv 13⁵⁵·⁵⁶; הֻדְּשְׁנָה (for הִתְדַּשְּׁנָה, the נָה being treated as if it were the afformative of the *fem. plur.*) *it is made fat*, Is 34⁶. On הִתְפָּקְדוּ, see *l*.

i   Denominatives with a reflexive meaning are הִתְיַהֵד *to embrace Judaism*, from (יְהוּדָה) יְהוּד *Judah*; הִצְטַיָּד *to provision oneself for a journey*, from צֵידָה *provision for a journey* (see § 72 *m*).

k   Rem. 1. As in *Piʿēl*, so in *Hithpaʿēl*, the perfect very frequently (in stems ending in ג, ק, מ, פ) has retained the original *Pathaḥ* in the final syllable (while in the ordinary form it is attenuated, as in *Piʿēl*, to *i* and then lengthened to *ē*), e. g. הִתְאַנַּף Dt 4²¹, &c.; cf. 2 Ch 13⁷, 15⁸; with ו *consecutive* Is 8²¹; so also in the imperfect and imperative, e. g. תִּתְחַכַּם Ec 7¹⁶; cf. Dt 9⁸·¹⁸, 1 S 3¹⁰, 2 S 10¹², 1 K 11⁹, Is 55², 58¹⁴, 64¹¹, ψ 55²; הִתְחַזַּק 1 K 20²², ψ 37⁴, Est 5¹⁰; וָאֶתְאַפַּק 1 S 13¹².—In Lv 11⁴⁴, 20⁷ and Ez 38²³, *i* takes the place of *ă* in the final syllable of the stem before שׁ (cf. § 44 *d*), and in the last passage before לְ. In the *perfect, imperfect* (with the exception of Ec 7¹⁶), and *imperative* of Hithpaʿēl (as well as of *Hithpōʿēl*, *Hithpaʿlēl*, *Hithpalpēl*, § 55) the original *ă* always returns in *pause* as Qameṣ, e. g. הִתְאַזָּר ψ 93¹; יִתְאַבָּל Ez 7²⁷; יִתְהַלָּךְ Jb 18⁸; הִתְקַדָּשׁוּ Jos 3⁵; cf. Jb 33⁵ and § 74 *b*.—The *ā* also appears before the fuller ending וּן in the plural of the imperfect (cf. § 47 *m*) in ψ 12⁹, Jb

9⁶, 16¹⁰.—Like the *Piʻēl* תְּקַפֵּלְנָה (§ 52 *n*), forms occur in *Hithpaʻēl* like תִּתְהַלֲּכְנָה Zc 6⁷; cf. Am 8¹³, and so in *Hithpoʻēl*, Jer 49³, Am 9¹³; with *e* only in La 4¹.— In the Aramaic manner an *infinitive Hithpaʻēl* הִתְחַבְּרוּת occurs in Dn 11²³ (cf. the *Hiphʻil* inf. הַשְׁמָעוּת in Ez 24²⁶).

2. As instances of the *reflexive* הִתְקַטֵּל (connected with *Piʻēl*) a few reflexive *l* forms of the verb פָּקַד (to examine) are also probably to be reckoned. Instead of a *Pathaḥ* in a sharpened syllable after the first radical, these take *Qameṣ* in an open syllable, e. g. הִתְפָּקְדוּ Ju 20¹⁵·¹⁷, *imperfect* יִתְפָּקֵד 20¹⁵, 21⁹. The corresponding passive form הָתְפָּקְדוּ also occurs four times, Nu 1⁴⁷, 2³³, 26⁶², 1 K 20²⁷. According to others, these forms are rather reflexives of *Qal*, in the sense of *to present oneself for review, to be reviewed*, like the Aramaic *'Ithpeʻēl* (Western Aramaic אִתְקְטֵל, Syr. אֶתְקְטֶל) and the Ethiopic *taqatēla*, Arab. *'iqtatala*, the last with the *t* always placed after the first radical (cf. above, *b*); but they are more correctly explained, with König, as *Hithpaʻēl* forms, the doubling of the פ being abnormally omitted.—Such a reflexive of *Qal*, with the ת transposed, occurs in הלתחם (on the analogy of O. T. Hebrew to be pronounced הִלָּתֵחֶם) in the inscription of the Moabite king *Mēšaʻ*, with the meaning of the O. T. *Niphʻal* נִלְחַם *to fight, to wage war*: see the inscription, lines 11, 15, 19, and 32; in the first two places in the *imperfect* with *wāw consecutive* וָאֶלְתַּחֵם; in line 19 in the *infinitive* with suffix, בְּהִלְתְּחֲמֹה בִי *in his fighting against me*.

§ 55. *Less Common Conjugations.*

Of the less common conjugations (§ 39 *g*) some may be classed with *a* *Piʻēl*, others with *Hiphʻil*. To the former belong those which arise from the lengthening of the vowel or the repetition of one or even two radicals, in fact, from an internal modification or development of the stem; to the latter belong those which are formed by prefixing a consonant, like the ה of Hiphʻil. Amongst the conjugations analogous to *Piʻēl* are included the *passive* forms distinguished by their vowels, as well as the reflexives with the prefix הִתְ, on the analogy of *Hithpaʻēl*.

The following conjugations are related to *Piʻēl*, as regards their *b* inflexion and partly in their meaning:

1. *Pōʻēl* קוֹטֵל, passive *Pōʻal* קוֹטַל, reflexive *Hithpōʻēl* הִתְקוֹטֵל, corresponding to the Arabic conj. III. *qātăla*, pass. *qûtĭlă*, and conj. VI. reflexive *tăqātălă*; *imperfect* יְקוֹטֵל, *participle* מְקוֹטֵל, *imperfect passive* יְקוֹטַל &c. Hence it appears that in Hebrew the *ô* of the first syllable is in all the forms obscured from *â*, while the passive form is distinguished simply by the *a*-sound in the second syllable. In the strong verb these conjugations are rather rare. Examples: *participle* מְשֹׁפְטִי *mine adversary, who would contend with me*, Jb 9¹⁵; (denominative from לָשׁוֹן *the tongue*) *slandering* (as if *intent on injuring with the tongue*) ψ 101⁵ Kᵉth. (The *Qᵉrē* requires מְלָשְׁנִי *mᵉlošni* as Na 1³ וּגְדוֹל־; זֹרְמוּ *they have poured out*, ψ 77¹⁸ (if not rather *Puʻal*); יוֹדַעְתִּי *I have appointed*, 1 S 21³ (unless הוֹדַעְתִּי should be read); יִסֹעֵר Ho 13³; שֹׁרֵשׁ *to take root*, passive

שׁוֹרֵשׁ, *denominative from* שֹׁרֶשׁ *root* (but שֵׁרֵשׁ *to root out*); in Hithpôʿēl הִתְגֹּעֲשׁוּ
they shall be moved, Jer 25¹⁶; imperf. 46⁸; from a verb ל״ה, שׁוֹשֵׁתִי Is 10¹³. The
participle מְנֹאָין Is 52⁵ is probably a *forma mixta* combining the readings מְנֹאָין
and מְחֹלָאִין.

c   Poʿel proper (as distinguished from the corresponding conjugations of verbs
ע״ע § 67 *l* and ע״וּ § 72 *m*, which take the place of the ordinary causative
Piʿēl) expresses an aim or endeavour to perform the action, especially with
hostile intent, and is hence called, by Ewald, the stem expressing *aim* (Ziel-
stamm), *endeavour* (Suche-stamm) or *attack* (Angriffs-stamm); cf. the examples
given above from Jb 9¹⁵, ψ 101⁵, and עוֹיֵן ı S 18⁹ Qᵉrē (probably for מְעוֹיֵן, cf.
§ 52 *s*; § 55 *f*: *seeking to cast an evil eye*).

With קוֹטֵל is connected the formation of quadriliterals by the insertion of
a consonant between the first and second radicals (§ 30 *p*, § 56).

d   2. Paʿlēl, generally with the *ă* attenuated to *ĭ*=Piʿlēl¹ (Piʿlal), קְטָלֵל and
קְטָלֵל; the *ē* in the final syllable also arises from *ĭ*, and this again from *ă*;
passive Puʿlal קְטָלֵל, reflexive Hithpaʿlēl הִתְקַטְלֵל, like the Arabic conjugations
IX. ʾiqtállä and XI. ʾiqtâllä, the former used of permanent, the latter of accidental
or changing conditions, e.g. of colours; cf. שַׁאֲנַן *to be at rest*, רַעֲנַן *to be green*,
passive אֻמְלֵל *to be withered*, all of them found only in the *perfect* and with
no corresponding *Qal* form. (For the barbarous form צִמְּתֻתֻנִי ψ 88¹⁷ read
צִמְּתֻתֻנִי; for נִפְלֵל Ez 28²³, which has manifestly arisen only from confusion
with the following חַלֵל, read נָפַל). These forms are more common in verbs
ע״וּ, where they take the place of Piʿēl and Hithpaʿēl (§ 72 *m*). Cf. also § 75 *kk*.

e   3. Peʿalʿal: קְטַלְטֵל with repetition of the last two radicals, used of move-
ments repeated in quick succession; e.g. סְחַרְחַר *to go about quickly, to palpitate*
(of the heart) ψ 38¹¹, from סָחַר *to go about*; passive חֲמַרְמַר *to be in a ferment,
to be heated, to be red*, Jb 16¹⁶, La 1²⁰, 2¹¹. Probably this is also the explanation
of חֲצֹצֵר (denom. from חֲצֹצְרָה *a trumpet*, but only in the *participle*, ı Ch 15²⁴
&c. Kᵉth.) for חֲצַרְצֵר, by absorption of the first ר, lengthening of *ă* in the
open syllable, and subsequent obscuring of *ā* to *ô*. On the other hand, for
the meaningless אֲהַבוּ הֵבוּ Ho 4¹⁸ (which could only be referred to this conjugation if it stood for אֲהַבְהֲבוּ) read אֲהַבוּ, and for the equally meaningless
יְפִיפִית ψ 45³ read יָפִיתָ. In both these cases a scribal error (*dittography*) has
been perpetuated by the punctuation, which did not venture to alter the
Kᵉthibh. On the employment of Peʿalʿal in the formation of nouns, cf. § 84ᵇ *n*.
Closely related to this form is—

f   4. Pilpēl (pass. Polpal), with a strengthening of the two essential radicals in
stems ע״ע, ע״וּ, and ע״ו, e.g. גִּלְגֵּל *to roll*, from גַּל=גָּלַל; *reflexive* הִתְגַּלְגֵּל *to
roll oneself down*; כִּלְכֵּל from כּוּל, passive כָּלְכַּל; cf. also טִאטֵא (so Baer and
Ginsb. after Qimḥi; others טֵאטֵא) Is 14²³, and with *ă* in both syllables
owing to the influence of ר, קַרְקַר from קוּר Nu 24¹⁷ (cf. however, in the
parallel passage, Jer 48⁴⁵, קָדְקֹד) and Is 22⁵, in the *participle*; שִׂכְשֵׂךְ Is 17¹¹ *to
hedge in*, acc. to others *make to grow*. Probably to this form also belongs
יְלַעְלְעוּ, the emended reading of Jb 39³⁰ instead of the impossible יְעַלְעוּ; also

---

¹ Cf. Wolfensohn, 'The Piʿlel in Hebrew,' *Amer. Journ. of Or. Studies*, XXVII
(1907), p. 303 ff.

סָאסְאָה Is 27⁶, if that form is to be referred to an *infinitive* סַאסֵּא ; perhaps also שֵׁישָׁא Ez 39² for שַׁאשָׁא. This form also commonly expresses rapidly repeated movement, which all languages incline to indicate by a repetition of the sound,[1] e.g. צִפְצֵף *to chirp*; cf. in the Lexicon the nouns derived from עוּף, גָּרַר, and צָלַל.

As *Hithpalpel* we find יִשְׁתַּקְשְׁקוּן Na 2⁵; וַתִּתְחַלְחַל Est 4⁴; וַיִּתְמַרְמַר Dn 8⁷, *g* 11¹¹. Of the same form is אֲדַדֶּה Is 38¹⁵, if contracted from אֶתְדַּוְדֶה or אתדידה from the root דו or דִי), and also הִתְמַהְמְהוּ *tarry ye*, Is 29⁹ (but read probably הִתַּמְּהוּ), וַיִּתְמַהְמָהּ (*in pause*) Gn 19¹⁶, &c., if it is to be derived from מָהַהּ, and not Hithpa‘el from מַהֲמַהּ.

Only examples more or less doubtful can be adduced of—　　　*h*

5. *Tiph‘ēl* (properly *Taph‘ēl* [2]): תִּקְטֵל, with ת prefixed, cf. תִּרְגַּלְתִּי *to teach to walk, to lead* (denominative from רֶגֶל *a foot?*) Ho 11³; from a stem ל״ה, the *imperfect* יַחֲרֶה *to contend with*, Jer 12⁵; *participle*, 22¹⁵ (from חָרָה *to be hot, eager*). Similarly in Aramaic, תַּרְגֵּם *to interpret*, whence also in Hebrew the *passive participle* מְתֻרְגָּם Ezr 4⁷.

6. *Šaph‘ēl*: שִׁקְטֵל, frequent in Syriac, e.g. שַׁלְהֵב from לְהַב *to flame*; whence *i* in Hebrew שַׁלְהֶבֶת *flame*. Perhaps of the same form is שַׁבְלוּל *a snail* (unless it be from the stem שׁבל), and שַׁעֲרוּרֹת *hollow strokes*, cf. § 85, No. 50. This conjugation is perhaps the original of *Hiph‘il*, in which case the ה, by a phonetic change which may be exemplified elsewhere, is weakened from a sibilant.

* * *

Forms of which only isolated examples occur are:—　　　*k*

7. קָטְלַט, *passive* קֻטְלַט; as מְחֻסְפָּס *peeled off, like scales*, Ex 16¹⁴, from חָסַף, חָשַׂף *to peel, to scale*.

8. קַטְקַל, in זַרְזִיף *a rain-storm*, from זָרַף.

9. נִתְקַטֵּל (regularly in Mishnic Hebrew [3]) a form compounded of *Niph‘al* and *Hithpa‘el*; as וְנִתוֹסְרוּ for וְנִתְוַסְּרוּ *that they may be taught*, Ez 23⁴⁸; נִכַּפֵּר probably an error for הִתְכַּפֵּר *to be forgiven*, Dt 21⁸. On נִשְׁתַּוָּה Pr 27¹⁵, see § 75 *x*.

§ 56. *Quadriliterals*.

On the origin of these altogether secondary formations cf. § 30 *p*. While quadriliteral *nouns* are tolerably numerous, only the following examples of the verb occur:

---

[1] Cf. Lat. *tinnio, tintinno*, our *tick-tack, ding-dong*, and the German *wirrwarr, klingklang*. The repetition of the radical in verbs ע״ע also produces this effect; as in לָקַק *to lick*, דָּקַק *to pound*, טָפַף *to trip along*. The same thing is expressed also by *diminutive* forms, as in Latin by the termination *-illo*, e.g. *cantillo*, in German by *-eln, -ern*, e.g. *flimmern, trillern, tröpfeln, to trickle*.

[2] The existence of a *Taph‘ēl* is contested on good grounds by Barth, *Nominalbildung*, p. 279.

[3] [See Segal, *Mišnaic Hebrew*, Oxf. 1909, p. 30 ff.]

(a) On the analogy of *Pi'ēl*: כִּרְסֵם, *imperfect* יְכַרְסְמֶנָּה *he doth ravage it*, ψ 80[14] from כָּסַם, cf. נָּם. *Passive* רֻטֲפַשׁ *to grow fresh again*, Jb 33[25]. *Participle* מְכֻרְבָּל *girt, clothed* (cf. Aramaic כְּבַל *to bind*), 1 Ch 15[27]. It is usual also to include among the quadriliterals פֵּרְשֵׁז Jb 26[9], as a *perfect* of Aramaic form with *Pathaḥ* not attenuated. It is more correctly, however, regarded, with Delitzsch, as the *infinitive absolute* of a *Pi'lel* formation, from פָּרַשׂ *to spread out*, with euphonic change of the first שׂ to שׁ, and the second to ז. Moreover, the reading פֵּרְשֵׁז also is very well attested, and is adopted by Baer in the text of Job; cf. the Rem. on p. 48 of his edition.

(b) On the analogy of *Hiph'îl*: הִשְׂמְאִיל, by syncope הִשְׂמָאִיל and הִשְׂמִיל *to turn to the left* (denom. from שְׂמֹאל) Gn 13[9], Is 30[21], &c. On הָאֳנִיחוּ cf. § 53 *p*.

C. STRONG VERB WITH PRONOMINAL SUFFIXES.[1]

§ 57.

The accusative of the personal pronoun, depending on an active verb,[2] may be expressed (1) by a separate word, אֵת the accusative sign (before a suffix אֹת, אֶת) with the pronominal suffix, e. g. קָטַל אֹתוֹ *he has killed him*; or (2) by a mere suffix, קְטָלֵהוּ or קְטָלוֹ *he has killed him*. The latter is the usual method (§ 33), and we are here concerned with it alone.[3] Neither of these methods, however, is employed when the accusative of the pronoun is *reflexive*. In that case a reflexive verb is used, viz. Niph'al or Hithpa'ēl (§§ 51 and 54), e. g. הִתְקַדֵּשׁ *he sanctified himself*, not קִדְּשׁוֹ, which could only mean *he sanctified him*.[4]

Two points must be specially considered here: the form of the suffix itself (§ 58), and the form which the verb takes when suffixes are added to it (§§ 59–61).

---

[1] This subject of the verbal suffixes is treated here in connexion with the strong verb, in order that both the forms of the suffixes and the general laws which regulate their union with verbal forms may be clearly seen. The rules which relate to the union of the suffixes with weak verbs will be given under the several classes of those verbs.

[2] An accusative suffix occurs with *Niph'al* in ψ 109[3] (since נִלְחַם is used in the sense of *to attack*), and according to some, in Is 44[21]; with *Hithpa'ēl* Is 14[2] (הִתְנַחֵל to appropriate somebody *to oneself as a possession*); cf. above, § 54 *f*, and § 117 *w*.

[3] On the cases where אֵת is necessary, see § 117 *e*.

[4] The exceptions in Jer 7[19], Ez 34[2.8.10] are only apparent. In all these instances the sharp antithesis between אֹתָם (*themselves*) and another object could only be expressed by retaining the same verb; also in Ex 5[19] אֹתָם after an active verb serves to emphasize the idea of *themselves*.

§ 58. *The Pronominal Suffixes of the Verb.*

Cf. the statistics collected by H. Petri, *Das Verbum mit Suffixen im Hebr.*,
part ii, in the נביאים ראשנים, Leipzig, 1890. W. Diehl, *Das Pronomen pers.
suff. . . . des Hebr.*, Giessen, 1895. J. Barth, 'Beiträge zur Suffixlehre des
Nordsem.,' *AJSL.* xvii (1901), p. 205 f. Brockelmann, *Semit. Sprachwiss.*, i.
159 f.; *Grundriss*, p. 638 ff.

1. The *pronominal suffixes* appended to the verb express the *a*
accusative of the *personal pronoun.* They are the following :—

	A.	B.	C.	
	To a form ending in a Vowel.	*To a form in the Perf. ending in a Consonant.*	*To a form in the Imperf. ending in a Consonant.*	
Sing. 1. com. נִי‸	נִי‸ַ (in *pause* נִי‸ָ)	נִי‸ַ	me.
2. m. ךָ‸	ךָ‸ַ (in *pause* ךָ‸ָ, also ךָ‸ָ) thee.		
f. ךְ—	ךְ‸ַ ךְ‸ַ, rarely ךְ‸ָ	ךְ‸..	
3. m. הוּ‸, וֹ	הוּ‸ַ, וֹ (הֹ)	הוּ‸ַ	him.
f. הָ‸	הָ‸ָ	הָ‸ַ	her.
Plur. 1. com. נוּ‸	נוּ‸ַ	נוּ‸ַ	us.
2. m. כֶם—		כֶם‸ָ	you (vos).
f. . . . .[1]			
3. m. הֶם,[1] ם	ם‸ָ (from הֶם‸ַ), ם‸ַ	ם— (from הֶם‸ַ) eos.	
poet. מוֹ‸	מוֹ‸ָ	מוֹ‸ַ	
f. ן—	ן‸ָ, ן‸ַ	. . . . .[1]	eas.

2. That these suffixes are connected with the corresponding *forms b
of the personal pronoun* (§ 32) is for the most part self-evident, and
only a few of them require elucidation.

The suffixes נִי, נוּ, הוּ, הָ (and ךָ, when a long vowel in an open *c*
syllable precedes) never have the tone, which always rests on the preceding syllable ; on the other hand, כֶם and הֶם always take the tone.

In the 3rd pers. masc. הוּ‸ָ, by contraction of *a* and *u* after the *d*
rejection of the weak ה, frequently gives rise to *ô* (§ 23 *k*), ordinarily
written וֹ, much less frequently הֹ (see § 7 *c*). In the *feminine*, the
suffix הָ should be pronounced with a preceding *a* (cf. below, *f*, note),
as הָ‸ַ or הָ‸ַ, on the analogy of *āhû*; instead of הָ‸ָ, however, it
was simply pronounced הָ‸ָ, with the rejection of the final vowel,

---

[1] According to Diehl (see above), p. 61, כֶם occurs only once with the
perfect (see § 59 *e*), 7 times with the imperfect, but never in pre-exilic
passages, whereas the accus. אֶתְכֶם occurs 40 times in Jer. and 36 times
in Ezek.—הֶם occurs only once as a *verbal* suffix (Dt 32²⁶, unless, with Kahan,
Infinitive u. Participien, p. 13, אֲפָאֵיהֶם from פָּאָה is to be read), while the forms
כֶן (2nd *f. pl.*) and ן‸ַ and הֶן (3rd *f. pl.*), added by Qimḥi, never occur.

and with *Mappiq*, since the ה is consonantal; but the weakening to
הָ is also found, see below, *g*.

e **3.** The *variety* of the suffix-forms is occasioned chiefly by the fact
that they are modified differently according to the form and tense of the
verb to which they are attached. For almost every suffix three forms
may be distinguished:

(*a*) One beginning with a consonant, as נִי֯, הוּ֯, וֹ (only after *î*),
נוּ֯, (הֶם) ם, &c. These are attached to verbal forms which end with
a vowel, e.g. יְקַטְלוּנִי; קְטַלְתִּיהוּ, for which by absorption of the ה we
also get קְטַלְתִּיו, pronounced *qᵉṭaltîu*; cf. § 8 *m*.

f (*b*) A second and third with what are called *connecting vowels*[1]
(נִי֯, נִי֯), used with verbal forms ending with a consonant (for
exceptions, see § 59 *g* and § 60 *e*). This *connecting vowel* is *a* with
the forms of the perfect, e.g. קְטָלַנִי, קְטָלָנוּ, קְטָלָם (on קְטָלֵךְ, the ordinary
form of the 3rd masc. perf. with the 2nd fem. suffix, cf. below, *g*); and
e (less frequently *a*) with the forms of the imperfect and imperative, e.g.
יִקְטְלֵהוּ, קָטְלֵם; also with the infinitive and participles, when these do
not take noun-suffixes (cf. § 61 *a* and *h*). The form וֹ also belongs to
the suffixes of the perfect, since it has arisen from הוּ֯ (cf., however,
§ 60 *d*). With ךָ, כֶם, the connecting sound is only a vocal *Šᵉwâ*,
which has arisen from an original short vowel, thus ךָ֯, כֶם֯, e.g.
קְטָלְךָ (*qᵉṭālᵉkhā*), or when the final consonant of the verb is a guttural,
ךָ֯, e.g. שְׁלָחֲךָ. In *pause*, the original short vowel (*ă*) reappears as
Sᵉghôl with the tone ךָ֯ (also ךָ֯, see *g*). On the appending of
suffixes to the final וּן of the imperfect (§ 47 *m*), see § 60 *e*.

g Rem. 1. As *rare* forms may be mentioned *sing.* 2nd pers. *masc.* כָה֯ Gn 27⁷,
1 K 18⁴⁴, &c., in *pause* also כָּה֯ (see below, *i*); *fem.* כִי, כִי֯ ψ 103⁴, 137⁶.
Instead of the form ךָ֯, which is usual even in the perfect (e.g. Ju 4²⁰,
Ez 27²⁶), ךָ֯ occurs as *fem.* Is 60⁹ (as *masc.* Dt 6¹⁷, 28⁴⁵, Is 30¹⁹, 55⁵ always in
pause); with *Munaḥ* Is 54⁶, Jer 23³⁷.—In the 3rd *masc.* ה Ex 32²⁵, Nu 23⁸;
in the 3rd *fem.* הָ without *Mappiq* (cf. § 91 *e*) Ex 2³, Jer 44¹⁹; Am 1¹¹, with

---

[1] We have kept the term *connecting* vowel, although it is rather a superficial
description, and moreover these vowels are of various origin. The connective
a is most probably the remains of the old verbal termination, like the *i* in
the 2nd pers. *fem.* sing. קְטַלְתִּיהוּ. Observe e.g. the Hebrew form *qᵉṭāl-ani* in
connexion with the Arabic *qatala-ni*, contrasted with Hebrew *qᵉṭālat-ni* and
Arabic *qatalat-ni*. König accordingly prefers the expression ' vocalic ending
of the stem', instead of 'connecting syllable'. The connective ē, ā, as
Prätorius (*ZDMG.* 55, 267 ff.) and Barth (ibid. p. 205 f.) show by reference to
the Syriac connective *ai* in the imperf. of the strong verb, is originally due
to the analogy of verbs ל״י מְחֵנִי=מַחֲנִי from *mᵉḥaini*), in which the final *ê*
was used as a connecting vowel first of the imperat., then of the impf.
(besides many forms with *a*, § 60 *d*), and of the infin. and participle.

retraction of the tone before a following tone-syllable, but read certainly
שָׁמַר לָנֶצַח.—The forms מוֹ ◌ֵּ, מוֹ ◌ָ, מוֹ ◌ֵ occur 23 times, all in poetry [1]
(except Ex 23³¹) [viz. with the perfect Ex 15¹⁰, 23³¹, ψ 73⁶; with the imperfect
Ex 15⁵ (מוֹ for מוֹ), 15⁷·⁹·⁹·¹²·¹⁵·¹⁷·¹⁷, ψ 2⁵, 21¹⁰·¹³, 22⁵, 45¹⁷, 80⁶, 140¹⁰; with the
imperative ψ 5¹¹, 59¹²·¹², 83¹²]. On the age of these forms, see § 91 *l* 3; on
◌ֵ and ◌ֶ as suffixes of the 3rd fem. plur. of the imperfect, § 60 *d*.—
In Gn 48⁹ קְחָם־נָא (cf. וַיִּכֵּם־שָׁם 1 Ch 14¹¹ according to Baer), ◌ָם has lost
the tone before *Maqqeph* and so is shortened to ◌ַם.—In Ez 44⁸ וַתְּשִׂימוּן is
probably only an error for וַתְּשִׂימוּם.

2. From a comparison of these verbal suffixes with the noun-suffixes (§ 91) *h*
we find that (*a*) there is a greater variety of forms amongst the verbal than
amongst the noun-suffixes, the forms and relations of the verb itself being
more various;—(*b*) the verbal suffix, where it differs from that of the noun,
is longer; cf. e.g. נִי ◌ֵ, נִי ◌ָ, נִי ◌ֶ (*me*) with י ◌ִ (*my*). The reason is that
the pronominal object is less closely connected with the verb than the
possessive pronoun (the genitive) is with the noun ; consequently the former
can also be expressed by a separate word (אֵת in אֹתִי, &c.).

4. A verbal form with a suffix gains additional strength, and some- *i*
times intentional emphasis, when, instead of the mere connecting vowel,
a special connecting-syllable [2] (*ăn*) [3] is inserted between the suffix and
the verbal stem. Since, however, this syllable always has the tone,
the *ă* is invariably (except in the 1st pers. sing.) modified to tone-
bearing *S°ghôl*. This is called the *Nûn energicum* [4] (less suitably
demonstrativum or *epentheticum*), and occurs principally (see, however,
Dt 32¹⁰ *bis*) in pausal forms of the imperfect, e. g. יְבָרֲכֶנְהוּ *he will bless
him* (ψ 72¹⁵, cf. Jer 5²²), אֲתַקֶּנְךָ Jer 22²⁴; יְכַבְּדָנְנִי *he will honour me*
(ψ 50²³) is unusual; rarely in the perfect, Dt 24¹³ בֵּרֲכֶךָ. On examples
like דָּנַנִּי Gn 30⁶, cf. § 26 *g*, § 59 *f*. In far the greatest number of
cases, however, this *Nûn* is assimilated to the following consonant
(נ, כ), or the latter is lost in pronunciation (so ה), and the *Nûn*
consequently sharpened. Hence we get the following series of suffix-
forms :—

---

[1] Thus in ψ 2 מוֹ ◌ָ occurs five times [four times attached to a noun or
preposition, §§ 91 *f*, 103 *c*], and ◌ָם only twice.

[2] It is, however, a question whether, instead of a connecting syllable, we
should not assume a special verbal form, analogous to the Arabic *energetic mood*
(see *l*, at the end) and probably also appearing in the Hebrew cohortative (see the footnote on § 48 *c*).—As M. Lambert has shown in *REJ*. 1903,
p. 178 ff. ('De l'emploi des suffixes pronominaux ...'), the suffixes of the 3rd
pers. with the impf. without *waw* in prose are נּוּ ◌ֶ and נָּה ◌ֶ, but with
waw consec. הוּ ◌ֵ and הָ ◌ֶ or הָ ◌ָ ; with the jussive in the 2nd and 3rd pers.
always הוּ ◌ֵ, הָ ◌ֶ, in the 1st pers. more often נּוּ ◌ֵ than הוּ ◌ֵ, and always
נָּה ◌ֶ.

[3] According to Barth 'n-haltige Suffixe' in *Sprachwiss. Untersuchungen*, Lpz.
1907, p. 1 ff., the connecting element, as in Aramaic, was originally *in*, which
in Hebrew became *en* in a closed tone-syllable.

[4] So König, *Lehrgeb.*, i. p. 226.

1st pers. יִ֫־ (even in pause, Jb 7¹⁴, &c.), ־ֶּ֫נִּי (for ־ֶ֫נְנִי, ־ַ֫נְנִי).

2nd pers. ךָ֫־ (Jer 22²⁴ in pause ־ֶ֫ךָּ) and, only orthographically different,

־ֶ֫כָּה (Is 10²⁴, Pr 2¹¹ in *pause*).

3rd pers. ־ֶ֫נּוּ (for ־ֶ֫נְהוּ),¹ *fem.* ־ֶ֫נָּה for ־ֶ֫נְהָ.

[*1st pers. plur.* ־ֶ֫נּוּ (for ־ֶ֫נְנוּ), see the Rem.]

In the other persons Nûn energetic does not occur.

k Rem. The uncontracted forms with *Nûn* are rare, and occur only in poetic or elevated style (Ex 15², Dt 32¹⁰ [*bis*], Jer 5²², 22²⁴); they are never found in the *3rd fem. sing.* and *1st plur.* On the other hand, the contracted forms are tolerably frequent, even in prose. An example of ־ֶ֫נּוּ as 1st plur. occurs perhaps in Jb 31¹⁵ [but read ־ֶ֫נוּ and cf. § 72 *cc*], hardly in Ho 12⁵; cf. הִנֶּ֫נּוּ *behold us*, Gn 44¹⁶, 50¹⁸, Nu 14⁴⁰ for הִנְנוּ (instead of הִנֶּ֫נוּ; see § 20 *m*).— In Ez 4¹² the Masora requires תְּעֻגֶ֫נָה, without Dageš in the Nûn.

l That the forms with *Nûn energicum* are intended to give greater emphasis to the verbal form is seen from their special frequency in *pause*. Apart from the verb, however, *Nûn energicum* occurs also in the union of suffixes with certain particles (§ 100 *o*).

This Nûn is frequent in Western Aramaic. In Arabic the corresponding forms are the two *energetic moods* (see § 48 *b*) ending in *an* and *anna*, which are used in connexion with suffixes (e.g. *yaqtulan-ka* or *yaqtulanna-ka*) as well as without them.

§ 59. *The Perfect with Pronominal Suffixes.*

a 1. The endings (*afformatives*) of the perfect occasionally vary somewhat from the ordinary form, when connected with pronominal suffixes; viz.:—

(*a*) In the *3rd sing. fem.* the original feminine ending תַ־ or תָ־ is used for ה־.

(*b*) In the *2nd sing. masc.* besides תָּ we find תְּ, to which the connecting vowel is directly attached, but the only clear instances of this are with ־ַ֫נִי.²

(*c*) In the *2nd sing. fem.* תִּי, the original form of תְּ, appears; cf. קְטַלְתִּי, אַתִּי, § 32 *f*; § 44 *g*. This form can be distinguished from the 1st pers. only by the context.

(*d*) *2nd plur. masc.* תוּ for תֶּם. The only examples are Nu 20⁵, 21⁵, Zc 7⁵. The *fem.* קְטַלְתֶּן never occurs with suffixes; probably it had the same form as the masculine.

b We exhibit first the forms of the perfect *Hiph'îl*, as used in connexion with suffixes, since here no further changes take place in the stem itself, except as regards the tone (see *c*).

---

¹ On נוּ=־ֶ֫נּוּ Nu 23¹³, see § 67 *o*.

² On the *ă* as an original element of the verbal form, see § 58 *f*, note.

Singular.		Plural.	
3. *m.*	הִקְטִיל	3. *c.*	הִקְטִילוּ
3. *f.*	הִקְטִילַת		
2. *m.*	הִקְטַלְתְּ, הִקְטַלְתָּ	2. *m.*	הִקְטַלְתּוּ
2. *f.*	הִקְטַלְתִּי, הִקְטַלְתְּ		
1. *c.*	הִקְטַלְתִּי	1. *c.*	הִקְטַלְנוּ

The beginner should first practise connecting the suffixes with these *Hiph'il* forms and then go on to unite them to the *Perfect Qal* (see *d*).

2. The addition of the suffix generally causes the tone to be thrown *c* forward towards the end of the word, since it would otherwise fall, in some cases, on the ante-penultima; with the *heavy* suffixes (see *e*) the tone is even transferred to the suffix itself. Considerations of tone, especially in the Perfect *Qal*, occasion certain vowel changes: (*a*) the *Qameṣ* of the first syllable, no longer standing *before* the tone, always becomes vocal *Šewâ*; (*b*) the original *Pathaḥ* of the second syllable, which in the 3rd *sing. fem.* and 3rd *plur.* had become *Šewâ*, reappears before the suffix, and, in an open syllable before the tone, is lengthened to *Qameṣ*; similarly original *ĭ* (as in the 3rd *sing. masc. without* a suffix) is lengthened to *ē*, e. g. אֲהֵבוּךָ 1 S 18²², Pr 19⁷.

The forms of the perfect of Qal consequently appear as follows:— *d*

Singular.		Plural.	
3. *m.*	קָטַל	3. *c.*	קְטָלוּ
3. *f.*	קְטָלַת (קָטְלָה, see *g*)		
2. *m.*	קְטָלְתָּ (קָטַלְתָּ, see *h*)	2. *m.*	קְטַלְתּוּ
2. *f.*	קְטָלְתִּי (קָטַלְתְּ, see *h*)		
1. *c.*	קָטַלְתִּי	1. *c.*	קְטַלְנוּ

The connexion of these forms with all the suffixes is shown in *Paradigm C*. It will be seen there also, how the *Ṣere* in the Perfect *Pi'ēl* changes sometimes into *Segôl*, and sometimes into *vocal Šewâ*.

Rem. 1. The suffixes of the 2nd and 3rd pers. plur. כֶם and הֶם, since they *e* end in a consonant and also always have the tone, are distinguished as *heavy* suffixes (*suffixa gravia*) from the rest, which are called *light* suffixes. Compare the connexion of these (and of the corresponding feminine forms כֶן and הֶן) with the *noun*, § 91. With a perfect כֶם alone occurs, ψ 118²⁶. The form קְטָל which is usually given as the connective form of the 3rd sing. masc. before כֶם and כֶן is only formed by analogy, and is without example in the O. T.

2. In the 3rd *sing. masc.* קְטָלָהוּ (especially in verbs ל״ה; in the strong verb *f* only in Jer 20¹⁵ in *Pi'ēl*) is mostly contracted to קְטָלוֹ, according to § 23 *k*; likewise in the 2nd sing. masc. קְטַלְתָּהוּ to קְטַלְתּוֹ.—As a suffix of the 1st sing. ־נִי occurs several times with the 3rd sing. masc. perf. Qal of verbs ל״ה, not only in *pause* (as עָנָנִי ψ 118⁵; קָנָנִי Pr 8²² with *Deḥi*), but even with a con-

junctive accent, as הֹרֵנִי Jb 30¹⁹; עֲנֵנִי 1 S 28¹⁵ (where, however, the reading עֲנֵנִי is also found). With a sharpened נ: דָּנַּנִי Gn 30⁶, יְסָרַּנִי ψ 118¹⁸.

g　3. The 3rd sing. fem. קָטְלַת (=קְטָלָה) has the twofold peculiarity that (*a*) the ending *ath* always takes the tone,[1] and consequently is joined to those suffixes which form a syllable of themselves (נוּ, הָ, הוּ, ךָ, נִי), without a connecting vowel, contrary to the general rule, § 58 *f*; (*b*) before the other suffixes the connecting vowel is indeed employed, but the tone is drawn back to the *penultima*, so that they are pronounced with shortened vowels, viz. ךְ——ַ, ם——ַ, e.g. אֲהֵבַתְךָ *she loves thee*, Ru 4¹⁵, cf. Is 47¹⁰; גְּנָבָתַם *she has stolen them*, Gn 31³²; שְׂרָפָתַם *it burns them*, Is 47¹⁴, Jos 2⁶, Ho 2¹⁴, ψ 48⁷. For ——ַתְךָ, ——ַתְנִי &c., in *pause* תְנִי—— is found, Jer 8²¹, ψ 69¹⁰, and תְךָ—— Ct 8⁵; and also without the *pause* for the sake of the assonance חִבְּלָתְךָ, *she was in travail with thee*, ibid. The form קְטָלַתּוּ (e.g. Ru 4¹⁵) has arisen, through the loss of the ה and the consequent sharpening of the ת (as in נּוּ—— and פָּה—— for נְהוּ—— and נְהָ——, cf. § 58 *i*), from the form קְטָלַתְהוּ, which is also found even in *pause* (אֲהֵבַתְהוּ 1 S 18²⁸; elsewhere it takes in *pause* the form סְמָכַתְהוּ Is 59¹⁶); so קְטָלַתָּה from קְטָלַתְהָ; cf. 1 S 1⁶, Is 34¹⁷, Jer 49²⁴, Ru 3⁶; in *pause* Ez 14¹⁵, always, on the authority of Qimḥi, without *Mappiq* in the ה, which is consequently always a mere vowel-letter.

h　4. In the 2nd sing. masc. the form קְטָלְךָ is mostly used, and the suffixes have, therefore, no connecting vowel, e.g. וְנִחַתְּנוּ פְרַצְתָּנוּ *thou hast cast us off, thou hast broken us down*, ψ 60³; but with the suff. of the 1st sing. the form קְטָלְתַּנִי is used, e.g. חֲקַרְתַּנִי ψ 139¹; in *pause*, however, with Qameṣ, e.g. עֲזַבְתָּנִי ψ 22²; Ju 1¹⁵ (with *Zaqeph qaton*); but cf. also צְרַפְתָּנִי ψ 17³ with *Merekha*.—In the 2nd sing. fem. תִּי—— is also written defectively, רְמִיתִנִי 1 S 19¹⁷, Ju 11³⁵, Jer 15¹⁰, Ct 4⁹. Occasionally the suffix is appended to the ordinary form תְּ——, viz. הִשְׁבַּעְתָּנוּ *thou (fem.) dost adjure us*, Ct 5⁹, Jos 2¹⁷·²⁰; cf. Jer 2²⁷, and, quite abnormally, with *Ṣere* הוֹרַדְתֵּנוּ *thou (fem.) didst let us down*, Jos 2¹⁸, where הוֹרַדְתִּנוּ would be expected. In Is 8¹¹ וְיִסְּרֵנִי is probably intended as an *imperfect*.

i　5. In verbs middle *ē*, the *ē* remains even before suffixes (see above, *c*), e.g. אֹהֶבְךָ Dt 15¹⁶, אֲהֵבַתְהוּ 1 S 18²⁸, cf. 18²²; יְרָאֻהוּ Jb 37²⁴. From a verb middle *ō* there occurs יְכָלְתִּיו *I have prevailed against him*, ψ 13⁵, from יָכֹל with *ŏ* instead of *ō* in a syllable which has lost the tone (§ 44 *e*).

§ 60. *Imperfect with Pronominal Suffixes.*

a　In those forms of the *imperfect* Qal, which have no afformatives, the vowel *ō* of the second syllable mostly becomes ——ְ (simple *Šewâ mobile*), sometimes ——ֳ; thus in the principal *pause*, Nu 35²⁰, Is 27³, 62², Jer 31³³, Ez 35⁶, Ho 10¹⁰; before the principal *pause*, ψ 119³³; before a secondary *pause*, Ez 17²³; even before a conjunctive accent, Jos 23⁵. Before ךָ——ְ,

---

[1] חִבְּלָתְךָ Ct 8⁵ is an exception. כֶם would probably even here have the tone (see *e*); but no example of the kind occurs in the O.T. In Is 51² the *imperfect* is used instead of the *perfect* with a suffix.

כֶם‎‑, however, it is shortened to *Qameṣ ḥaṭuph*, e. g. יִשְׁמָרְךָ (but in *pause* יִשְׁמְרֶךָ or יִשְׁמֹרֶךָ; with *Nûn energicum*, see § 58 i), יִשְׁמָרְכֶם, &c. Instead of תִּקְטֹלְנָה, the form תִּקְטְלִי [1] is used for the 2nd and 3rd *fem. plur.* before suffixes in three places: Jer 2¹⁹, Jb 19¹⁵, Ct 1⁶.

Rem. 1. יְחָבְרְךָ ψ 94²⁰ is an anomalous form for יַחְבָּרְךָ (cf. the analogous *b* יָחֶנְךָ § 67 n) and יִפְנְשְׁךָ (so Baer; others יִפְגָּשְׁךָ) Gn 32¹⁸ for יִפְגָּשְׁךָ. To the same category as יְחָבְרְךָ belong also, according to the usual explanation, תֵּעָבְדֵם (from תֵּעָבֹד), Ex 20⁵, 23²⁴, Dt 5⁹, and נַעֲבֹד Dt 13³. As a matter of fact, the explanation of these forms as imperfects of *Qal* appears to be required by the last of these passages; yet why has the retraction of the ŏ taken place only in these examples (beside numerous forms like וַיַּעַבְדֵנִי)? Could the Masora in the two Decalogues and in Ex 23²⁴ (on the analogy of which Dt 13³ was then wrongly pointed) have intended an imperfect *Hoph'al* with the suffix, meaning *thou shalt not allow thyself to be brought to worship them*?

Verbs which have *a* in the second syllable of the *imperfect*, and imperative, *c* *Qal* (to which class especially *verba tertiae* and *mediae gutturalis* belong, § 64 and § 65) do *not*, as a rule, change the *Pathaḥ* of the *imperfect* (nor of the imperative, see § 61 g) into Šewâ before suffixes; but the Pathaḥ, coming to stand in an open syllable before the tone, is lengthened to *Qameṣ*, e. g. וַלְבִּשֵׁנִי Jb 29¹⁴; יִנְאָלוּהוּ 3⁵; וַיִּשְׁלְחֵם Jos 8³; יִקְרָאֶהוּ ψ 145¹⁸; but יִקְרָאוֹ Jer 23⁶, is probably a *forma mixta* combining the readings יִקְרָאוֹ and יִקְרָאֵהוּ, cf. § 74 e.

2. Not infrequently suffixes with the connecting vowel *a* are also found *d* with the imperfect, e. g. תְּרְבְּקַנִי Gn 19¹⁹, cf. 29³², Ex 33²⁰, Nu 22³³, 1 K 2²⁴ *Qᵉrê*, Is 56³, Jb 9¹⁸; also ‑נִּ‑, Gn 27¹⁹.³¹, Jb 7¹⁴, 9³⁴, 13²¹ (in principal *pause*); וַיְּבִירֶהָ Gn 37³³, cf. 16⁷, 2 S 11²⁷, Is 26⁵, Jb 28²⁷, 1 Ch 20²; יַכִּירֵנוּ Is 63¹⁶ (manifestly owing to the influence of the preceding יְדָעָנוּ); יִלְבָּשָׁם Ex 29⁰, cf. 2¹⁷, Nu 21³⁰, Dt 7¹⁵, ψ 74⁸; even אֲמִילַם 118¹⁰⁻¹²; וַיּוֹשִׁיעֵן Ex 2¹⁷, and יַחְיֶתָן Hb 2¹⁷ (where, however, the ancient versions read יְחַתֶּךָ); even יִרְדְּפוּ (ô from *âhu*) Ho 8³; cf. Ex 22²⁹, Jos 2⁴ (but read וַתִּצְפְּנֵם); 1 S 18¹ *Kᵉth.*, 21¹⁴ (where, however, the text is corrupt); 2 S 14⁶ (where read with the old versions וַיָּךְ); Jer 23⁶ (see § 74 e), ψ 35⁸, Ec 4¹². — On pausal Sᵉghôl for Ṣere in וָאֲבָרֶכְם Gn 48⁹ and וַתְּאַלְּצֵהוּ (so Baer, but ed. Mant., Ginsb.) וַתְּאַלָּצֵהָ Ju 16¹⁶, see § 29 q.

3. Suffixes are also appended in twelve passages to the plural forms in וּן, *e* viz. תְּדַכְּאוּנַנִי *will ye break me in pieces?* Jb 19²; יְשָׁרְתוּנְךָ (here necessarily with a connecting vowel) Is 60⁷.¹⁰; Pr 5²² (וֹ but probably corrupt); elsewhere always without a connecting vowel; יִקְרָאֻנְנִי with two other examples Pr 1²⁸, 8¹⁷, Ho 5¹⁵; cf. ‑וּנְךָ‑ ψ 63⁴, 91¹²; ‑נְהוּ‑ Jer 5²²; ‑וּנְךָ‑ Jer 2²⁴, all in principal pause. [See Böttcher, *Lehrb.*, § 1047 f.]

4. In *Pi'ēl*, *Pō'ēl*, and *Po'lēl*, the *Ṣere* of the final syllable, like the ŏ in Qal, *f* becomes vocal Šewâ; but before the suffixes ךָ‑ and כֶם‑ it is shortened to Sᵉghôl, e. g. יְקַבְּצֶךָ Dt 30⁴, ψ 34¹², Is 51². With a final guttural, however, אֲשַׁלֵּחַךָ Gn 32²⁷; also in Pr 4⁸, where with Qimḥi תְּכַבְּדֵךָ is to be read. ē is

---

[1] This form is also found as feminine without a suffix, in Jer 49¹¹, Ez 37⁷. In the latter passage וַתִּקְרְבוּ is probably to be regarded, with König, as a clumsy correction of the original וַיִּק, intended to suggest the reading וַתִּקְרַבְנָה, to agree with the usual gender of עֲצָמוֹת.

retained in the tone-syllable; an analogous case in *Hiph'il* is וַיַּגֵּד Dt 32⁷. Less frequently Ṣere is sharpened to Ḥireq, e.g. אֲאַמִּצְכֶם Jb 16⁵, cf. Ex 31¹³, Is 1¹⁵, 52¹²; so in *Po'ēl*, Is 25¹, ψ 30², 37³⁴, 145¹, and probably also in *Qal* אֹסִפְךָ 1 S 15⁶; cf. § 68 *h*.

g　5. In *Hiph'il* the *i* remains, e.g. תַּלְבִּישֵׁנִי Jb 10¹¹ (after *wāw consecutive* it is often written defectively, e.g. וַיַּלְבֵּשׁ Gn 3²¹ and often); but cf. above, *f*, Dt 32⁷. Forms like תַּעְשְׁרֶ֫נָּה *thou enrichest it*, ψ 65¹⁰, 1 S 17²⁵, are rare. Cf. § 53 *n*.

h　6. Instead of the suffix of the 3rd plur. fem. (ן), the suffix of the 3rd plur. masc. (ם) is affixed to the afformative ו, to avoid a confusion with the personal ending וּן; cf. וַיִּמָּלְאוּם Gn 26¹⁵ (previously also with a perf. סְתֻמִ֑ים); Gn 26¹⁸, 33¹³, Ex 2¹⁷ (where וַיּ֫וֹשִׁעָן occurs immediately after); 39¹⁸·²⁰, 1 S 6¹⁰ (where also בְּנֵיהֶם is for בְּנֵיהֶן, a neglect of gender which can only be explained by § 135 *o*).—For יַהַרְגֶן Zc 11⁵ read perhaps יַהַרְגֵן with M. Lambert.

§ 61. *Infinitive, Imperative and Participle with Pronominal Suffixes.*

a　1. The *infinitive construct* of an *active verb* may be construed with an accusative, and therefore can also take a *verbal suffix*, i.e. the *accusative* of the personal pronoun. The only undoubted instances of the kind, however, in the O.T. are infinitives with the verbal suffix of the 1st pers. sing., e.g. לְדָרְשֵׁנִי *to inquire of me*, Jer 37⁷. As a rule the infinitive (as a *noun*) takes *noun*-suffixes (in the *genitive*, which may be either subjective or objective, cf. § 115 *c*), e.g. עָבְרִי *my passing by*; מָלְכוֹ *his reigning*, see § 115 *a* and *e*. The infinitive *Qal*, then, usually has the form *qŏṭl*, retaining the original short vowel under the first radical (on the probable ground-form *qŭṭŭl*, see § 46 *a*). The resulting syllable as a rule allows a following Begadkephath to be spirant, e.g. בְּכָתְבוֹ *in his writing*, Jer 45¹; cf., however, הָפְכִּי Gn 19²¹; נִגְפּוֹ (so ed. Mant.; others נָגְפוּ) Ex 12²⁷; עָצְבִּי 1 Ch 4¹⁰; before ךָ— and כֶם— also the syllable is completely closed, e.g. בְּאָסְפְּךָ Ex 23¹⁶, Lv 23³⁹ (but in pause לְהָרְגֶ֫ךָ Gn 27⁴²), unless the vowel be retained in the second syllable; see *d*. With the form קָטֹל generally, compare the closely allied nouns of the form קְטֹל (before a suffix קָטָל or קְטָל), § 84ᵃ *a*; § 93 *q*.

b　Rem. 1. The infin. of verbs which have ō in the last syllable of the *imperfect* of *Qal*, sometimes takes the form *qiṭl* before suffixes, e.g. מָכְרָם Ex 21⁸; בְּבִגְדוֹ Ex 21⁸; Am 2⁶ (but מָכְרָה Ex 21⁸), נִפְלוֹ 2 S 1¹⁰ (but נָפְלוֹ 1 S 29³), לְשָׁטְנוֹ Zc 3¹, שָׁבְרִי Lv 26²⁶, Ez 30¹⁸ &c. According to Barth (see above, § 47 *i* with the note) these forms with *i* in the first syllable point to former *i*-imperfects.

c　Infinitives of the form קְטֹל (§ 45 *c*) in verbs middle or third guttural (but cf. also שָׁכְבָה Gn 19³³·³⁵—elsewhere שָׁכְבְּךָ and שָׁכְבוֹ) before suffixes sometimes take the form *qaṭl*, as וַעֲטֹף Jon 1⁵ (and, with the syllable loosely closed,

פָּֽעֳמוֹ‎ Ju 13²⁵), מַחֲאֵךְ‎ and רָקְעֶךָ‎ Ez 25⁶; sometimes *qiṭl*, with the *a* attenuated to *i*, especially in verbs third guttural; as בְּטַחֲךָ‎, בְּלִעִי‎, בִּקְעָם‎, פִּגְעוֹ‎, פִּתְחִי‎, רִבְעָה‎.—Contrary to § 58 *f* נִי‎ (1 Ch 12¹⁷) and נוּ‎ (Ex 14¹¹) are sometimes found with the *infinitive* instead of נִי‎ and נוּ‎. On רָדוֹפִי‎ *my following* ψ 38²¹ (but *Qᵉrê* רָדְפִי‎), cf. the analogous examples in § 46 *e*.

2. With the suffixes ךָ‎ and כֶם‎, contrary to the analogy of the corre- *d* sponding nouns, forms occur like אֲכָלְךָ‎ *thy eating*, Gn 2¹⁷; אֲכָלְכֶם‎ Gn 3⁵; עָמְדָךְ‎ (others עָמְדְךָ‎) Ob ¹¹, i.e. with *ō* shortened in the same way as in the *imperfect*, see § 60. But the analogy of the nouns is followed in such forms as קָצְרְכֶם‎ *your harvesting*, Lv 19⁹, 23²² (with retention of the original *ŭ*), and מָאָסְכֶם‎ (read *mŏ'ŏskhèm*) *your despising*, Is 30¹²; cf. Dt 20²; on בְּמֹצַאֲכֶם‎ Gn 32²⁰ (for בְּמֹצָֽאֲ‎), see § 74 *h*.—Very unusual are the infinitive suffixes of the 2nd sing. masc. with נ *energicum* (on the analogy of suffixes with the imperfect, § 58 *i*), as יָפְרֶךָ‎ Dt 4³⁶, cf. 23⁵, Jb 33³², all in principal pause.

Examples of the *infinitive Niph'al* with suffixes are, הִשָּׁמֶרְךָ‎ הִבָּבְדִי‎ Ex 14¹⁸; *e* Dt 28²⁰ (in *pause*, הִשָּׁמְרֶךָ‎ verse 24); הִשָּׁפְטוֹ‎ ψ 37³³; הִזָּכְרְכֶם‎ Ez 21²⁹; הִשָּׁמְדָם‎ Dt 7²³. In the *infinitive* of *Pi'ēl* (as also in the *imperfect*, see § 60 *f*) the *ē* before the suff. ךָ‎, כֶם‎ becomes *Sᵉghôl*, e.g. דַּבֶּרְךָ‎ Ex 4¹⁰, and with a sharpening to *i* פָּרְשְׂכֶם‎ Is 1¹⁵ (see § 60 *f*). In the *infinitive Pō'ēl* בְּשַׂסְּכֶם‎ occurs (with *a* for *ĕ* or *ĭ*) Am 5¹¹, but probably בֻּסְּכֶם‎, with Wellhausen, is the right reading; the correction ם has crept into the text alongside of the *corrigendum* שׁ.

2. The leading form of the *imperative Qal* before *suffixes* (קָטְל‎) is *f* due probably (see § 46 *d*) to the retention of the original short vowel of the first syllable (ground-form *qŭṭŭl*). In the *imperative* also *ŏ* is not followed by *Dageš lene*, e.g. כָּתְבֵם‎ *kŏthbhēm* (not *kŏthbēm*), &c.[1] As in the *imperfect* (§ 60 *d*) and *infinitive* (see above, *c*), so also in the *imperative*, suffixes are found united to the stem by an *a*-sound; e.g. כָּתְבָה‎ Is 30⁸; cf. 2 S 12²⁸.—The forms קָטְלוּ‎, קָטְלִי‎, which are not exhibited in Paradigm C, undergo no change. Instead of קְטֹלְנָה‎, the masc. form (קִטְלוּ‎) is used, as in the *imperfect*.

In verbs which form the *imperative* with *a*, like שְׁלַח‎ (to which class *g* belong especially verbs *middle* and *third guttural*, §§ 64 and 65), this *a* retains its place when pronominal suffixes are added, but, since it then stands in an open syllable, is, as a matter of course, lengthened to *Qameṣ* (just as in *imperfects Qal* in *a*, § 60 *c*), e.g. שְׁלָחֵנִי‎ *send me*, Is 6⁸, בַּחֲנֵנִי‎ ψ 26², קְרָאֵנִי‎ ψ 50¹⁵, שְׁמָעֵנִי‎ Gn 23⁸. In Am 9¹ בְּצָעַם‎ (so ed. Mant., Baer, Ginsb., instead of the ordinary reading בְּצָֽעַם‎) is to be explained, with Margolis, *AJSL.* xix, p. 45 ff., from an original בְּצָעֵמוֹ‎, as וַהֲרַגְתֶּם‎ Am 9⁴ from original וַהֲרַגְתֵּמוֹ‎.—In the imperative *Hiph'îl*, the form used in conjunction with suffixes is not the 2nd *sing. masc.*

---

[1] שָׁמְרֵנִי‎ *šāmᵉrènî* required by the Masora in ψ 16¹ (also שָׁמְרָה‎ ψ 86², 119¹⁶⁷; cf. Is 38¹⁴ and עָמְדָךְ‎ Ob ¹¹), belongs to the disputed cases discussed in § 9 *v* and § 48 *i* note.

הַקְטֵל, but הַקְטִיל (with *i* on account of the open syllable, cf. § 60 *g*), e. g. הַקְרִיבֵ֫הוּ *present it*, Mal 1⁸.

h 3. Like the infinitives, the participles can also be united with either verbal or noun-suffixes; see § 116 *f*. In both cases the vowel of the participles is shortened or becomes *Šᵉwâ* before the suffix, as in the corresponding noun-forms, e. g. from the form קֹטֵל: רֹדְפִי, רֹדְפוֹ, &c.; but before *Šᵉwâ mobile* יֹצְרֵךְ, &c., or with the original *i*, אֹיִבְךָ Ex 23⁴, &c., אֹסְפְךָ 2 K 22²⁰ (coinciding in form with the 1st *sing. imperfect Qal*, 1 S 15⁶; cf. § 68 *h*); with a middle guttural (וְאֵלִי), נֹּאֵלְךָ; with a third guttural, בֹּרַאֲךָ Is 43¹, but שֹׁלְחֲךָ, מְשַׁלֵּחֲךָ Jer 28¹⁶, cf. § 65 *d*. The form מְקַטֵּל, with suffix מְקַטְּלִי; before *Šᵉwâ* sometimes like מְלַמֶּ֫דְךָ Is 48¹⁷, מְנַחֶמְכֶם 51¹², sometimes like מְאַסֶּפְכֶם 52¹². In Is 47¹⁰ רֹאָ֫נִי is irregular for רֹאָ֫נִי; instead of the meaningless בְּלֻה מְקַלְלֹ֫נִי Jer 15¹⁰ read בְּכֻלָּם קִלְלֹ֫נִי.

Also unusual (see above, *d*) with participles are the suffixes of the 2nd sing. masc. with נ *energicum*, as עֹשֶׂ֫ךָ Jb 5¹; cf. Dt 8⁵, 12¹⁴·²⁸.

§ 62. *Verbs with Gutturals.*

Brockelmann, *Grundriss*, p. 584 ff.

Verbs which have a guttural for one of the three radicals differ in their inflexion from the ordinary strong verb, according to the general rules in § 22. These differences do not affect the consonantal part of the stem, and it is, therefore, more correct to regard the guttural verbs as a subdivision of the strong verb. At the most, only the entire omission of the strengthening in some of the verbs *middle guttural* (as well as in the *imperfect Niphʿal* of verbs *first guttural*) can be regarded as a real weakness (§§ 63 *h*, 64 *e*). On the other hand, some original elements have been preserved in guttural stems, which have degenerated in the ordinary strong verb; e. g. the *ă* of the initial syllable in the *imperfect Qal*, as in יַחְמֹד, which elsewhere is attenuated to *i*, יִקְטֹל.—In guttural verbs א and ה are only taken into consideration when they are actual consonants, and not vowel-letters like the א in some verbs פ״א (§ 68), in a few ע״א (§ 73 *g*), and in most ל״א (§ 74). In all these cases, however, the א was at least originally a full consonant, while the ה in verbs ל״ה was never anything but a vowel letter, cf. § 75. The really consonantal ה at the end of the word is marked by *Mappîq*.—Verbs containing a ר also, according to § 22 *q*, *r*, share some of the peculiarities of the guttural verbs. For more convenient treatment, the cases will be distinguished, according as the guttural is the first, second, or third radical. (Cf. the Paradigms D, E, F, in which only those conjugations are omitted which are wholly regular.)

§ 63. *Verbs First Guttural*, e. g. עָמַד *to stand.*

In this class the deviations from the ordinary strong verb may be *a* referred to the following cases :—

1. Instead of a *simple Šᵉwâ mobile*, the initial guttural takes a *compound Šᵉwâ* (*Ḥaṭeph*, § 10 *f*, § 22 *l*). Thus the *infinitives* עֲמֹד, אֲכֹל *to eat*, and the *perfects*, *2nd plur. masc.* חֲפַצְתֶּם, עֲמַדְתֶּם from חָפֵץ *to be inclined*, correspond to the forms קְטֹל and קְטַלְתֶּם; also אֲכָלוֹ to קְטָלוֹ, and so always with initial ◌ֲ before a suffix for an original *ă*, according to § 22 *o*.

2. When a preformative is placed before an initial guttural, either *b* the two may form a closed syllable, or the vowel of the preformative is repeated as a *Ḥaṭeph* under the guttural. If the vowel of the preformative was originally *a*, two methods of formation may again be distinguished, according as this *a* remains or passes into Seghôl.

Examples: (*a*) of firmly closed syllables after the original vowel *c* of the preformative (always with *ō* in the second syllable, except וַתַּעְגַּב Ez 23⁵, תַּעְדֶּה &c. from עָדָה *to adorn oneself*, and יַעְטֶה; but cf. *e*): יַחְמֹד, יַחְמֹל, יַחְשֹׁב, יַחְשֹׁךְ, יַעְקֹב Jer 9³ (probably to distinguish it from the name יַעֲקֹב, just as in Jer 10¹⁹, &c., the participle fem. Niphʻal of נַחְלָה is חָלָה to distinguish it from נֶחֱלָה), &c., and so generally in the *imperfect Qal* of stems beginning with ח, although sometimes parallel forms exist, which repeat the *ă* as a *Ḥaṭeph*, e. g. יַחֲשֹׁב, &c. The same form appears also in the *imperfect Hiphʻîl* יַחְסִיר, &c. Very rarely the original *ă* is retained in a closed syllable under the preformative נ of the *perfect Niphʻal*: נֶחְבֵּאתָ Gn 31²⁷; cf. 1 S 19², Jos 2¹⁶; also the *infinitive absolute* נַחְתּוֹם Est 8⁸, נַעְתּוֹר 1 Ch 5²⁰, and the *participle fem.* נֶחְלָה (see above), *plur.* נַעְתָּרוֹת Pr 27⁶. In these forms the original *ă* is commonly kept under the preformative and is followed by *Ḥaṭeph-Pathaḥ*; thus in the *perfect* of some verbs ל״ה, e. g. נֶעֱשָׂה, &c.; in the *infinitive absolute*, נַהֲפוֹךְ Est 9¹; in the *participle* נֶעֱרָץ, ψ 89⁸, &c.

(*b*) Of the corresponding *Ḥaṭeph* after the original vowel: יַחֲבֹשׁ *d* (but יַחְבָּשׁ Jb 5¹⁸ in pause), יַחֲלֹם, יַעֲמֹד, יַהֲרֹס, and so almost always with ע and often with ה in the *imperfects* of *Qal* and *Hiphʻîl*; in *Hophʻal*, הָעֳמַד, יָעֳמַד; but cf. also הָחֳבְּאוּ Is 42²², הָחֵל Ez 16⁴.

The *ă* of the preformative before a guttural almost always (§ 22 *i*, *e* cf. § 27 *p*) becomes *Sᵉghôl* (cf., however, *q*). This *Sᵉghôl* again appears sometimes

(*c*) in a closed syllable, e. g. יֶאְשַׁם, יֶעְתַּר, יֶחְסַר, יֶחְבַּשׁ, always with *ă* in the second syllable, corresponding to the imperfects of verbs ע״ע,

with original *ĭ* in the first and *ă* in the second syllable, § 67 *n*, and also to the imperfects of verbs ו״ע, § 72 *h*; but cf. also יֶאְסֹר, יֶאְפֹּד and יֶהְדֹּף; in *Niph.*, e. g. נֶהְפַּךְ; נֶחְלָה Am 6⁶, &c.; in *Hiph.* הֶחְסִיר, הֶעְלִים, 2 K 4⁷, &c.: sometimes

(*d*) followed by *Ḥaṭeph-Seghôl*, e. g. יֶחֱרַב, יֶחֱשַׁף, יֶאֱסֹף, יֶחֱזַק in *imperfect Qal*; הֶעֱמִיד *Hiph'îl*; נֶעֱנַשׁ *Niph'al*.

f　Rem. With regard to the above examples the following points may also be noted: (1) The forms with a firmly closed syllable (called the hard combination) frequently occur in the same verb with forms containing a loosely closed syllable (the soft combination). (2) In the 1st *sing. imperfect Qal* the preformative א invariably takes *Seghôl*, whether in a firmly or loosely closed syllable, e. g. אֶחְבֹּשׁ (with the cohortative אֶחְבְּשָׁה), אֶחֱסָר (in *pause*), &c. In Jb 32¹⁷ אֶעֱנֶה must unquestionably be *Hiph'îl*, since elsewhere the pointing is always אַעֲ. Cohortatives like אַהֲרְנֶה Gn 27⁴¹ and אַחְדְּלָה Jb 16⁶, are explained by the next remark. (3) The shifting of the tone towards the end frequently causes the *Pathaḥ* of the preformative to change into *Seghôl*, and vice versa, e. g. נַעֲשָׂה, but נֶעֶשְׂתָה 3rd *sing. fem.*; יָאֹסֵף, but תֶּאֱסְפִי; הֶעֱמִיד, but with *wāw consecutive* וְהַעֲמַדְתָּ, &c.; so וַיֶּחֱסָר Gn 8³ the plur. of וַיֶּחְסַר, cf. Gn 11⁸; and thus generally a change of the stronger *Ḥaṭeph-Seghôl* group (　͜　) into the lighter *Ḥaṭeph-Pathaḥ* group takes place whenever the tone is moved one place toward the end (cf. § 27 *v*).

g　3. When in forms like יַעֲמֹד, נֶעֱמַד, the vowel of the final syllable becomes a *vocal Shewâ* in consequence of the addition of an afformative (וֹ, ◌ִי, הָ◌) or suffix, the *compound Shewâ* of the guttural is changed into the corresponding short vowel, e. g. יַעֲמֹד, *plur.* יַעַמְדוּ (*ya-'a-me-dhû* as an equivalent for *ya'-me-dhû*); נֶעֶזְבָה *she is forsaken*. But even in these forms the hard combination frequently occurs, e. g. יַחְבְּלוּ *they take as a pledge* (cf. in the *sing.* תֶּחְבֹּל, also יַחְבֹּל); יֶחֶזְקוּ (also יֶחֶזְקוּ) *they are strong*. Cf. *m* and, in general, § 22 *m*, § 28 *c*.

h　4. In the *infinitive, imperative,* and *imperfect Niph'al*, where the first radical should by rule be strengthened (הִקָּטֵל, יִקָּטֵל), the strengthening is always omitted, and the vowel of the preformative lengthened to *Sere*; יֵעָמֵד for *yi"āmēd*,[1] &c. Cf. § 22 *c*.—For תֵּעָשֶׂה Ex 25³¹ (according to Dillmann, to prevent the pronunciation תֵּעֲשֶׂה, which the LXX and Samaritan follow) read תֵּיעָשֶׂה.

REMARKS.

I. On Qal.

i　1. In verbs פ״א the *infinitive construct* and *imperative* take *Ḥaṭeph-Seghôl* in the first syllable (according to § 22 *o*), e. g. אֱזֹר *gird thou*, Jb 38³, אֱהַב *love thou*,

---

[1] אֶעֱנֶה Jb 19⁷ (so even the Mantua ed.) is altogether abnormal: read אֵעָנֶה, with Baer, Ginsb.

Ho 3¹, אֱחֹז *seize thou*, Ex 4⁴ (on אֵפוּ *bake ye*, Ex 16²³, see § 76 *d*); אֱכֹל *to eat*; infinitive with a prefix לֶאֱחֹז, בַּאֲכֹל, לֶאֱכֹל Is 5²⁴; לֶאֱחֹב Ec 3⁸. Sometimes, however, *Ḥaṭeph-Pathaḥ* is found as well, e. g. *infinitive* אֱחֹז 1 K 6⁶; בַּאֲכֹל הָעָם Nu 26¹⁰ (before a suffix אָמְרְךָ, אֲכָלְכֶם, אֲכָלְכֶם, אָמְרָם § 61 *d*); cf. Dt 7²⁰, 12²³, Ez 25⁸, ψ 102⁵, Pr 25⁷ (אֲמָר־לָךְ), Jb 34¹⁸, always in close connexion with the following word. With a firmly closed syllable after ל cf. לַחְסוֹת Is 30²; לַחְפֹּר Jos 22²ᶠ. (on Is 2²⁰, cf. § 84ᵇ *n*); לַחְתּוֹת Is 30¹⁴, Hag 2¹⁶; וַחֲשֹׁב Ex 31⁴, &c.; לַעְזֹר 2 S 18³ *Qᵉrê*, but also בַּעְזֹר 1 Ch 15²⁶.

הֶחֱדַלְתִּי Ju 9⁹·¹¹·¹³ is altogether anomalous, and only a few authorities give *k* הֶחְדַּלְתִּי (Hiph'il), adopted by Moore in Haupt's Bible. According to Qimḥi, Olshausen, and others, the Masora intended a *perfect Hoph'al* with syncope of the preformative after the ה interrogative = הֻהֳחֳדַלְתִּי, or (according to Olshausen) with the omission of the ה interrogative. But since the *Hiph'il* and *Hoph'al* of חָדַל nowhere occur, it is difficult to believe that such was the intention of the Masora. We should expect the *perfect Qal*, הֶחָדַלְתִּי. But the *Qameṣ* under the ה, falling between the tone and counter-tone, was naturally less emphasized than in חָדַלְתִּי, without the ה interrogative. Consequently it was weakened, not to simple *Šᵉwâ*, but to ◌ֱ, in order to represent the sound of the Qameṣ (likewise pronounced as *å*) at least in a shortened form. The *Sᵉghôl* of the ה interrogative is explained, in any case, from § 100 *n* (cf. the similar pointing of the article, e. g. in הֶחֳדָשִׁים, § 35 *k*). For the accusative after חָדַל, instead of the usual מִן, Jb 3¹⁷ affords sufficient evidence.

Also in the other forms of the *imperative* the guttural not infrequently *l* influences the vowel, causing a change of *ĭ* (on this *ĭ* cf. § 48 *i*) into *Sᵉghôl*, e. g. אֶסְפָה *gather thou*, Nu 11¹⁶; עֶרְכָה *set in order*, Jb 33⁵; חֶשְׂפִי *strip off*, Is 47² (on this irregular *Dageš* cf. § 46 *d*), especially when the second radical is also a guttural, e. g. אֶהֱבוּ Am 5¹⁵, ψ 31²⁴; cf. Zc 8¹⁹; אֶחֱזוּ Ct 2¹⁵; cf. also in verbs ל״ה, עֱנוּ *sing ye*, Nu 21¹⁷, ψ 147⁷ (compared with עֲנוּ *answer ye*, 1 S 12³) and אֱלַי Jo 1⁸.—*Pathaḥ* occurs in חַבְלֵהוּ *hold him in pledge*, Pr 20¹⁶, and probably also in ψ 9¹⁴ (חָנְנֵנִי).—As a pausal form for חָרְבִי (cf. the *plur.* Jer 2¹²) we find in Is 44²⁷ חֳרָבִי (cf. the *imperf.* יֶחֱרַב) with the *ŏ* repeated in the form of a *Ḥaṭeph-Qameṣ*. For other examples of this kind, see § 10 *h* and § 46 *e*.

2. The pronunciation (mentioned above, No. 2) of the imperfects in *ă* with *m* *Sᵉghôl* under the preformative in a firmly closed syllable (e. g. יֶחְכַּם, יֶחְדַּל) regularly gives way to the soft combination in verbs which are at the same time ל״ה, e. g. יֶחֱזֶה &c. (but cf. יֶהְגֶּה, יֶחְתֶּה Pr 6²⁷, אֶעֱשֶׂה ed. Mant., Ex 3²⁰). Even in the strong verb וַיֶּחֱזַק is found along with יֶחְזַק. Cf. also וַתַּעֲזֹב Ez 23⁵; וַיַּעֲקְבֵנִי Gn 27³⁶ (so Ben-Asher; but Ben-Naphtali וַיַּעְקְ); וַתַּחְלְקֵם Neh 9²², and so always in the *imperfect Qal* of עָזַר with suffixes, Gn 49²⁵, &c.—תֶּאֱהֲבוּ Pr 1²² is to be explained from the endeavour to avoid too great an accumulation of short sounds by the insertion of a long vowel, but it is a question whether we should not simply read תֶּאֱהֲבוּ with Haupt in his Bible, *Proverbs*, p. 34, l. 44 ff.; cf. the analogous instances under *p*, and

such nouns as בְּאֵר, זְאֵב, § 93 t.—On יַחְבְּרֶךָ ψ 94²⁰ for יְחָבְּרֶךָ (according to Qimḥi, and others, rather *Puʻal*) cf. § 60 b.

n   יַאְמֵם ψ 58⁵ and יָעְרֵם *to deal subtilly*, 1 S 23²², Pr 15⁵, 19²⁵, may be explained with Barth (*ZDMG.* 1889, p. 179) as *i*-imperfects (see above, § 47 *i*),—the latter for the purpose of distinction from the causative יַעְרִים ψ 83⁴.—Instead of the unintelligible form וַיְחַלְּקֵם (so ed. Mant.; Baer and Ginsb. as in 24³) 1 Ch 23⁶ and וַיְחַ' 24³ (partly analogous to תְּעָבְרֵם § 60 b) the Qal וַיַּחְלְקֵם is to be read. The form יְרַדְּף ψ 7⁶ which is, according to Qimḥi (in *Mikhlol*; but in his Lexicon he explains it as *Hithpaʻēl*), a composite form of Qal (יִרְדֹּף) and *Piʻēl* (יְרַדֵּף), can only be understood as a development of יִרְדֹּף (cf. § 64 *h* on יִצְחַק, and § 69 *x* on תְּהֲלַךְ Ex 9²³, ψ 73⁹). Pathaḥ has taken the place of Ḥaṭeph-Pathaḥ, but as a mere helping-vowel (as in שָׁמְעַתְּ § 28 *e*, note 2) and without preventing the closing of the syllable. It is much simpler, however, to take it as a *forma mixta*, combining the readings יִרְדֹּף (impf. Qal) and יְרַדֵּף (impf. Piʻel).

II. On Hiphʻil and Hophʻal.

o   3. The above-mentioned (*f,* 3) change of ⎯⎯ to ⎯⎯ occurs in the *perfect Hiphʻil*, especially when *wāw consecutive* precedes, and the tone is in consequence thrown forward upon the afformative, e. g. הֶעֱמַדְתָּ, but וְהַעֲמַדְתָּ Nu 3⁶, 8¹³, 27¹⁹; הֶעֱבַרְתִּי, but וְהַעֲבַרְתִּי Jer 15¹⁴, Ez 20³⁷; even in the 3rd *sing.* וְהָאָזִין ψ 77².—On the contrary ⎯⎯ occurs instead of ⎯⎯ in the *imperative Hiphʻil*, Jer 49⁸·³⁰; and in the *infinitive* Jer 31³². The preformative of עתר in *Hiphʻil* always takes *a* in a closed syllable: Ex 8⁴ הַעְתִּירוּ; verse 5 אַעְתִּיר; also verse 25 and Jb 22²⁷.

p   4. In the *perfect Hiphʻil* ⎯⎯ is sometimes changed into ⎯⎯, and in *Hophʻal* ⎯⎯ into ⎯⎯ (cf. § 23 *h*); הֶעֱבַרְתָּ Jos 7⁷, הֶעֱלָה Hb 1¹⁵, הֶעֱלָה Ju 6²⁸, 2 Ch 20³⁴, Na 2⁸, always before ע, and hence evidently with the intention of strengthening the countertone-syllable (הֶ or הָ) before the guttural. On a further case of this kind (זֶעֲמָה) see § 64 *c*. Something similar occurs in the formation of segholate nouns of the form *qŏṭl*; cf. § 93 *q*, and (on אֱמוּן &c. for אֲמוּן) § 84ᵃ *q*.—In the imperfect consecutive וַיֶּחֱזַק בּוֹ the tone is thrown back on to the first syllable. On the *Hophʻal* תָּעָבְרֵם Ex 20⁵, &c., see § 60 b.

III. הָיָה and חָיָה.

q   5. In the verbs הָיָה *to be*, and חָיָה *to live*, the guttural hardly ever affects the addition of preformatives; thus *imperfect Qal* יִהְיֶה and יִחְיֶה, *Niphʻal* נִהְיָה; but in the *perfect Hiphʻil* הֶחֱיָה (2nd *plur.* וִהְחֱיִתֶם Jos 2¹³, and even without *wāw consecutive*, Ju 8¹⁹). Initial ה always has *Ḥaṭeph-Seghól* instead of *vocal Šᵉwâ*; הֱיִיתֶם, הֱיוֹתָם, 1 S 25⁷, הֱיִיתָ (except הֱיִי *be thou! fem.* Gn 24⁶⁰). The 2nd *sing. fem. imperative* of חָיָה is חֲיִי *live thou*, Ez 16⁶; the infinitive, with suffix, חֲיוֹתָם Jos 5⁸. After the prefixes וְ, בְּ, כְּ, לְ, מִ (= מִן) both ה and ח retain the *simple Šᵉwâ* (§ 28 *b*) and the prefix takes *ĭ*, as elsewhere before strong consonants with *Šᵉwâ*; hence in the *perfect Qal* וִהְיִיתָ, *imperative* וִהְיִי, *infinitive* לִהְיוֹת, בִּהְיוֹת &c. (cf. § 16 *f, ε*). The only exception is the 2nd *sing. masc.* of the *imperative* after *wāw*; וֶהְיֵה Gn 12², &c., וֶחְיֵה Gn 20⁷.

§ 64.   *Verbs Middle Guttural*, e.g. שָׁחַט *to slaughter.*

The slight deviations from the ordinary inflexion are confined *a* chiefly to the following[1]:—

1. When the guttural would stand at the beginning of a syllable with simple *Šᵉwâ*, it necessarily takes a *Ḥaṭeph*, and almost always *Ḥaṭeph-Pathaḥ*, e.g. *perfect* שָׁחֲטוּ, *imperfect* יִשְׁחֲטוּ, *imperative Niph'al* הִשָּׁחֲטוּ. In the *imperative Qal*, before the afformatives *î* and *û*, the original *Pathaḥ* is retained in the first syllable, and is followed by *Ḥaṭeph-Pathaḥ*, thus, זַעֲקִי, זַעֲקוּ, &c.; in אֶהֱבוּ the preference of the א for *Sᵉghôl* (but cf. also וְיֶאֱחֹזְךָ Jer 13²¹) has caused the change from *ă* to *ĕ*; in שְׁחֲדוּ Jb 6²², even *ĭ* remains before a *hard* guttural.

So in the *infinitive Qal fem.*, e.g. אַהֲבָה *to love*, דַּאֲבָה *to pine*; and in the *infinitive* with a suffix לְסׇעֲדָה Is 9⁶; the doubtful form שַׁחֲטָה Ho 5², is better explained as *infinitive Pi'ēl* (= שַׁחֲתָה).

2. Since the preference of the gutturals for the *a*-sound has less *b* influence on the following than on the preceding vowel, not only is *Ḥolem* retained after the middle guttural in the *infinitive Qal* שָׁחֹט (with the fem. ending and retraction and shortening of the *o* רׇחְצָה and רׇחְקָה, cf. § 45 *b*), but generally also the *Ṣere* in the *imperfect Niph'al* and *Pi'ēl*, e.g. יִלָּחֵם *he fights*, יְנַחֵם *he comforts*, and even the more feeble *Sᵉghôl* after *wāw consecutive* in such forms as וַתִּפָּעֶם, וַיִּלָּחֶם Gn 41⁸ (cf., however, וַיִּפָּעַע 1 K 12⁶, &c.). But in the *imperative* and *imperfect Qal*, the final syllable, through the influence of the guttural, mostly takes *Pathaḥ*, even in transitive verbs, e.g. שָׁחַט, יִשְׁחַט; בָּחַר, יִבְחַר; זָעַק, זְעַק; with *suffixes* (according to § 60 *c*), *imperative* שְׁאָלוּנִי, בְּחָנֵנִי, *imperfect* יִנְאָלוֹהוּ.

With *ō* in the *imperative Qal*, the only instances are נְעֹל 2 S 13¹⁷; *c* אֱחֹז Ex 4⁴, 2 S 2²¹, *fem.* אֲחֳזִי Ru 3¹⁵ (with the unusual repetition of the lost *ō* as *Ḥaṭeph-Qameṣ*; 2nd *plur. masc.* in *pause* אֱחֹזוּ Neh 7³; without the *pause* אֲחֹזוּ Ct 2¹⁵); סְעָד Ju 19⁸.[2] Finally זֹעֲמָה for זׇעֲמָה, Nu 23⁷, is an example of the same kind, see § 63 *p*. Just as rare are the imperfects in *ō* of verbs *middle guttural*, as תִּמְעֹל Lv 5¹⁵, Nu 5²⁷, יֶאֱחֹז, יִנְהֹם (but וַיִּמְעַל 2 Ch 26¹⁶); cf. וַתִּשְׁחֳדִי Ez 16³³; תִּפְעֹל Jb 35⁶. Also in the *perfect Pi'ēl*, *Pathaḥ* occurs somewhat more frequently than in the strong verb, e.g. נִחַם *to comfort* (cf., however, שִׁחֵת, כִּחֵשׁ, כָּחַר, כָּהַן, בְּהֶן);

---

[1] *Hoph'al*, which is not exhibited in the paradigm, follows the analogy of *Qal*; *Hiph'il* is regular.

[2] Also Ju 19⁵ (where Qimḥi would read *sᵉ'ād*), read *sᵉ'ŏd*, and on the use of the conjunctive accent (here *Darga*) as a substitute for *Metheg*, cf. § 9 *u* (c) and § 16 *b*.

but א and ע always have *ē* in 3rd *sing*.—On the *infinitive* with suffixes, cf. § 61 *b*.

d   3. In *Pi'ēl*, *Pu'al*, and *Hithpa'ēl*, the *Dageš forte* being inadmissible in the middle radical, the preceding vowel, especially before ה, ח, and ע, nevertheless, generally remains short, and the guttural is consequently to be regarded as, at least, *virtually* strengthened, cf. § 22 *c*; e.g. *Pi'ēl* שָׂחֵק, נִחֲלוּ Jos 14¹, וּבְעַרְתִּי 1 K 14¹⁰, נִהַג Ex 10¹³ (cf., however, אֵחַר Gn 34¹⁹; נֶהֶלְתָּ Ex 15¹³, but in the *imperfect* and *participle* יְנַהֵל, &c.; in verbs ל"ה, e.g. רֵעָה), *infinitive* שַׂחֵק, *Pu'al* רֻחַץ (but cf. דֻּחֹה ψ 36¹³ from דָּחָה, also the unusual position of the tone in בֻּחַן¹ Ez 21¹⁸, and in the *perfect Hithpa'ēl* הִתְרָחַצְתִּי Jb 9³⁰); *Hithpa'ēl perfect* and *imperative* הִפָּהֲרוּ, &c.; in *pause* (see §§ 22 *c*, 27 *q*, 29 *v*, 54 *k*) הִפָּהֵרוּ Nu 8⁷, 2 Ch 30¹⁸; יִתְנֶחָם Nu 23¹⁹, &c.

e   The complete omission of the strengthening, and a consequent lengthening of the preceding vowel, occurs invariably only with ר (כָּרַת Ez 16⁴ is an exception; בֹּרָתָה also occurs, Ju 6²⁸), e.g. בֵּרַךְ (in pause בֵּרֵךְ), *imperfect* יְבָרֵךְ, *Pu'al* בֹּרַךְ. Before א it occurs regularly in the stems פֵּאֵר, מֵאֵן, גֵּאֵל, בֵּאֵר, and in the *Hithpa'ēl* of ראה, באש, and שאה; on the other hand, א is *virtually* strengthened in the *perfects*, נִאֵף (once in the imperfect, Jer 29²³) *to commit adultery*, נִאֵץ *to despise* (in the *participle*, Nu 14²³, Is 60¹⁴, Jer 23¹⁷; according to Baer, but not ed. Mant., or Ginsb., even in the *imperfect* יְנַאֵץ ψ 74¹⁰), נִאֵר *to abhor* La 2⁷ (also נֵאַרְתָּה ψ 89⁴⁰) and שָׁאֵל ψ 109¹⁰; moreover, in the *infinitive* יַאֵשׁ Ec 2²⁰, according to the best reading. On the *Mappîq* in the *Pu'al* רֻאָי Jb 33²¹, cf. § 14 *d*.

f   Rem. 1. In the verb שָׁאַל *to ask, to beg*, some forms of the *perfect Qal* appear to be based upon a secondary form *middle e*, which is *Ṣere* when the vowel of the א stands in an open syllable, cf. שָׁאֵלְךָ Gn 32¹⁸, Ju 4²⁰; שְׁאֵלוּנִי ψ 137³; but in a closed syllable, even without a suffix, שְׁאֶלְתֶּם 1 S 12¹³, 25⁵, Jb 21²⁹; שְׁאֶלְתִּיהוּ Ju 13⁶, 1 S 1²⁰. Cf., however, similar cases of attenuation of an original *ă*, § 69 *s*, and especially § 44 *d*. In the first three examples, if explained on that analogy, the *ĭ* attenuated from *ă* would have been lengthened to *ē* (before the tone); in the next three *ĭ* would have been modified to *ĕ*. Also in the *Hiph'il*-form הִשְׁאֶלְתִּיהוּ 1 S 1²⁸ the א is merely attenuated from אַ.

g   2. In *Pi'ēl* and *Hithpa'ēl* the lengthening of the vowel before the guttural causes the tone to be thrown back upon the penultima, and consequently the *Ṣere* of the ultima to be shortened to *Seghôl*. Thus (*a*) before monosyllables, according to § 29 *e*, e.g. לְשָׁרֶת שָׁם *to minister there*, Dt 17¹², even in the case of a guttural which is *virtually* strengthened, Gn 39¹⁴, Jb 8¹⁸ (see § 29 *g*). (*b*) after *wāw consecutive*, e.g. וַיְבָרֶךְ *and he blessed*, Gn 1²² and frequently, וַיְגָרֶשׁ *and he drove out*, Ex 10¹¹, וַתִּתְפָּעֶם Dn 2¹.

---

¹ בֻּחַן is explained by Abulwalîd as the 3rd pers. *perfect Pu'al*, but by Qimḥi as a noun.

3. The following are a few rarer anomalies; in the *imperfect Qal* יִצְחָק Gn 21⁶ *h* (elsewhere תִּצְחַק, &c., in *pause* יִצְחָק, cf. § 10 *g* (*c*) and § 63 *n*); וַיֶּאְחַר Gn 32⁵ (for וַיֶּאֱחַר); in the *perfect Pi'ēl* אֵחֲרוּ Ju 5²⁸ (perhaps primarily for אֶחֱרוּ; according to Gn 34¹⁹ אֵחֲרוּ would be expected), and similarly יְחַמְּתֵנִי ψ 51⁷ for יְחַמְּתֵנִי; in the *imperative Pi'ēl* קָרֶב Ez 37¹⁷ (cf. above, § 52 *n*); finally, in the *imperative Hiph'il* הַרְחֵק Jb 13²¹ and הַמְעֵד ψ 69²⁴, in both cases probably influenced by the closing consonant, and by the preference for *Pathaḥ* in *pause* (according to § 29 *q*); without the pause הַרְחֵק Pr 4²⁴, &c.; but also הַנְחֵת Jo 4¹¹.

4. As *infinitive Hithpa'ēl* with a suffix we find הִתְיַחְשָׂם Ezr 8¹, &c., with *i* a firmly closed syllable, also the *participle* מִתְיַחְשִׂים Neh 7⁶⁴; Baer, however, reads in all these cases, on good authority, הִתְיַחֲשָׂם &c.—The quite meaningless *K'thîbh* וּנְאִשְׁאַר Ez 9⁸ (for which the *Q're* requires the equally unintelligible וְנִשְׁאַר) evidently combines two different readings, viz. וְנִשְׁאַר (*part. Niph.*) and וָאֶשָּׁאֵר (*imperf. consec.*); cf. König, *Lehrgebäude*, i. p. 266 f.—In יְתָאֲרֵהוּ Is 44¹³ (also יִתְאָרֵהוּ in the same verse) an *imperfect Pō'ēl* appears to be intended by the Masora with an irregular shortening of the ō for תְֹ יִתְאֹר; cf. § 55 *b* מַלְשָׁנִי ψ 101⁵ *Q're*; on the other hand Qimḥi, with whom Delitzsch agrees, explains the form as *Pi'ēl*, with an irregular ֵ for ֵ, as in the reading אֲלַקְּטָה Ru 2²·⁷; cf. § 10 *h*.

5. A few examples in which א, as middle radical, entirely loses its consonantal value and quiesces in a vowel, will be found in § 73 *g*.

§ 65. *Verbs Third Guttural*, e.g. שָׁלַח *to send*.[1]

1. According to § 22 *d*, when the last syllable has a vowel incom- *a* patible with the guttural (i.e. *not* an *a*-sound), two possibilities present themselves, viz. either the regular vowel *remains*, and the guttural then takes *furtive Pathaḥ*, or *Pathaḥ* (in pause *Qameṣ*) takes its place. More particularly it is to be remarked that—

(*a*) The unchangeable vowels ־ִי, וֹ, וּ (§ 25 *b*) are always retained, even under such circumstances; hence *inf. abs. Qal* שָׁלוֹחַ, *part. pass.* שָׁלוּחַ, *Hiph.* הִשְׁלִיחַ, *imperf.* יַשְׁלִיחַ, *part.* מַשְׁלִיחַ. So also the less firm ō in the *inf. constr.* שְׁלֹחַ is almost always retained: cf., however, שְׁלַח, in close connexion with a substantive, Is 58⁹, and גְּעַ Nu 20³. Examples of the *infinitive* with suffixes are בְּבָרְחֲךָ Gn 35¹; בִּפְגְעוֹ Nu 35¹⁹; לְרִבְעָה Lv 18²³, &c.

(*b*) The *imperfect* and *imperative Qal* almost always have *ă* in the *b* second syllable, sometimes, no doubt, due simply to the influence of the guttural (for a tone-long ō, originally *ŭ*), but sometimes as being the original vowel, thus שְׁלַח, יִשְׁלַח, &c.; with suffixes שְׁלָחֵנִי, יִשְׁלָחֵנִי, see § 60 *c*.

---

[1] Verbs ל״ה in which the ה is *consonantal* obviously belong also to this class, e.g. גָּבַהּ *to be high*, תָּמַהּ *to be astonished*, מָהַהּ (only in *Hithpalpel*) *to delay*.

Exceptions, in the *imperfect* אסלוח Jer 5⁷, *Kᵉth.* (אֶסְלַח *Qᵉrê*); in the *imperative* טְבֹח Gn 43¹⁶. On such cases as אֶפְשְׁעָה Is 27⁴, cf. § 10 *h*.

c (*c*) Where *Ṣere* would be the regular vowel of the final syllable, both forms (with *ēᵃ* and *ă*) are sometimes in use; the choice of one or the other is decided by the special circumstances of the tone, i. e. :—

d Rem. 1. In the *absolute state* of the *participle* Qal, Pi'ēl and Hithpa'ēl, the forms שֹׁלֵחַ (with suff. שֹׁלְחִי, but שֹׁלֵחֲךָ), מְשַׁלֵּחַ (with suff. מְשַׁלֵּחֲךָ), and מִשְׁתַּנֶּה are used exclusively; except in verbs ל״ע where we find, in close connexion, also נֹטַע ψ 94⁹, רֹנַע Is 51¹⁵, Jer 31³⁵, רֹקַע Is 42⁵, 44²⁴, רוֹקַע ψ 136⁶, שֹׁגַע Lv 11⁷, all with the tone on the last syllable.—The part. Pu'al is מְרֻבַּע Ez 45² according to the best authorities (Kittel מְרֻבָּע).

e 2. Similarly, in the *imperf.* and *inf. Niph'al*, and in the *perf. inf.* and *imperf.* Pi'ēl the (probably more original) form with *ă* commonly occurs in the body of the sentence, and the fuller form with *ēᵃ* in *pause* (and even with the lesser distinctives, e.g. with *Dᵉhi* ψ 86⁴ in the imperative Pi'ēl; with *Ṭiphḥa* 1 K 12³² in the infinitive Pi'ēl; Jer 4³¹ imperfect Hithpa'ēl; Jer 16⁶ imperfect Niph'al), cf. e.g. יִזְרַע Nu 27⁴, with יִזְרָע 36³; וַיִּשְׁבַּע Dt 1³⁴, even with retraction of the tone in the *inf. abs. Niph'al* הִשָּׁבַע Nu 30³ (elsewhere הִשָּׁבֵעַ Jer 7⁹, 12¹⁶ twice, in each case without the pause); הִבָּקַע Hb 3⁹, with תִּבָּקַע Ez 13¹¹; בַּלַּע *to devour* Hb 1¹³, Nu 4²⁰ with בַּלַּע La 2⁸; for infinitive Hithpa'ēl, cf. Is 28²⁰. The *infinitive absolute* Pi'ēl has the form שַׁלֵּחַ Dt 22⁷, 1 K 11²²; the *infinitive construct*, on the other hand, when without the pause is always as שַׁלַּח except לְשַׁלֵּחַ Ex 10⁴.— זֹבֵחַ Hb 1¹⁶ has *ē*, though not in *pause*, and even וַיִּזְבַּח 2 K 16⁴, 2 Ch 28⁴; but *a* in *pause* in the *imperative Niph'al* הֵאָנַח Ez 21¹¹; *jussive Pi'ēl* תְּאַחַר ψ 40¹⁸; cf. § 52 *n*. An example of *ă* in the *imperative Pi'ēl* under the influence of a final ר is כַּתֵּר Jb 36², in the *imperfect Niph'al* וַתֵּעָצֵר Nu 17¹³, &c.—In יִפְרַח Jb 14⁹ (cf. ψ 92¹⁴, Pr 14¹¹), Barth (see above, § 63 *n*) finds an *i*-imperfect of Qal, since the intransitive meaning is only found in Qal.

f 3. In the 2nd *sing. masc.* of the *imperative*, and in the forms of the *jussive* and *imperfect consecutive* of *Hiph'il* which end in gutturals, *a* alone occurs, e.g. הַצְלַח *prosper thou*, יַבְטַח *let him make to trust*, וַיַּצְמַח *and he made to grow* (so in Hithpalpel יִתְמַהְמַהּ, &c., Hb 2³); even in *pause* וַיַּצְלַח 1 Ch 29²³, and, with the best authorities, וְיוֹכַח 1 Ch 12¹⁷; וְיֹשַׁע Is 35⁴ is perhaps to be emended into וְיֵשַׁע (=וְיוֹשִׁיעַ).—In the *infinitive absolute Ṣere* remains, e.g. הַגְבֵּהַּ *to make high*; as *infinitive construct* הוֹכֵחַ also occurs in close connexion (Jb 6²⁶); on הוֹשֵׁעַ as *infinitive construct* (1 S 25²⁶·³³), cf. § 53 *k*.

g 2. When the guttural with *quiescent Šᵉwâ* stands at the end of a syllable, the ordinary strong form remains when not connected with suffixes, e. g. שָׁלַחְתִּי, שָׁלַחְתָּ. But in the 2nd *sing. fem. perfect* a *helping-Pathaḥ* takes the place of the *Šᵉwâ*, שָׁבַחַתְּ Jer 13²⁵ (§ 28 *e*); also in 1 K 14³, לָקַחַתְּ is to be read, not לָקַחְתְּ.

h Rem. The soft combination with *compound Šᵉwâ* occurs only in the 1st *plur. perfect* with suffixes, since in these forms the tone is thrown one place farther forward, e.g. יְדַעֲנוּךָ *we know thee*, Ho 8² (cf. Gn 26²⁹, ψ 44¹⁸, 132⁶). Before the suffixes ךָ and כֶם, the guttural must have ◌ַ, e.g. אֲשַׁלֵּחֲךָ *I will send thee*, 1 S 16¹; וְאֶשְׁלָחֲךָ Gn 31²⁷; אַשְׁמִיעֲךָ Jer 18².

On the weak verbs ל״א, see especially § 74.

II. The Weak Verb.[1]

§ **66.** *Verbs Primae Radicalis Nûn* (פ״נ), e.g. נָגַשׁ *to approach*

Brockelmann, *Semit. Sprachwiss.*, p. 138 ff.; *Grundriss*, p. 595 ff.

The weakness of initial נ consists chiefly in its suffering *aphaeresis a* in the *infinitive construct* and *imperative* in some of these verbs (cf. § 19 *h*). On the other hand, the *assimilation* of the נ (see below) cannot properly be regarded as weakness, since the triliteral character of the stem is still preserved by the strengthening of the second consonant. The special points to be noticed are—

1. The *aphaeresis* of the Nûn (*a*) in the *infinitive construct*. This *b* occurs only (though not necessarily) in those verbs which have *a* in the second syllable of the *imperfect*. Thus from the stem נגשׁ, *imperfect* יִגַּשׁ, *infinitive* properly גַּשׁ, but always lengthened by the feminine termination ת to the segholate form גֶּשֶׁת [2]; with *suffix* גִּשְׁתּוֹ Gn 33[3]; with the concurrence of a guttural נָגַע *to touch*, imperfect יִגַּע, *infinitive* גַּעַת (also נְגֹעַ, see below); נָטַע *to plant*, *infinitive* טַעַת (also נְטֹעַ, see below); on the verb נָתַן *to give*, see especially *h* and *i*. On the other hand, *aphaeresis* does not take place in verbs which have *ō* in the *imperfect*, e. g. נָפַל *to fall*, imperfect יִפֹּל, *infinitive* נְפֹל, with *suffix* נָפְלוֹ, also נִפְלוֹ; לִנְדֹּר Nu 6[2], &c.; cf., moreover, לִנְגֹּעַ Gn 20[6], &c., וּנְגֹעַ Ex 19[12] (even לִנְגּוֹעַ Jb 6[7]; cf. Jer 1[10]); with *suffix* בְּנָגְעוֹ Lv 15[23]. Also לִנְטֹעַ Is 51[16] (but לָטַעַת Ec 3[2]); נְשֹׁא Is 1[14], 18[3]; with *suffix* בְּנָשְׂאִי ψ 28[2] (elsewhere שְׂאֵת, cf. § 74 *i* and § 76 *b*), לִנְשֹׁק 2 S 20[9].

(*b*) In the *imperative*. Here the *Nûn* is always dropped in verbs *c* with *a* in the *imperfect*, e. g. נגשׁ, *imperative* גַּשׁ (more frequently with *paragogic ā*, גְּשָׁה; before *Maqqeph* also גֶּשׁ־ Gn 19[9]), *plur.* גְּשׁוּ, &c. Parallel with these there are the curious forms with *ō*, גּוֹשִׁי Ru 2[14] (with *retarding* Metheg in the second syllable, and also *nasog 'aḥor*, according to § 29 *e*, before הֲלֹם) and גֹּשׁוּ Jos 3[9] (before הֵנָּה), 1 S 14[38] (before הֲלֹם) and 2 Ch 29[31]; in all these cases without the *pause*. With *Nûn* retained, as if in a strong verb, נְהַג *drive*, 2 K 4[24] (*imperfect* יִנְהַג, without assimilation of the *Nûn*), וְנִטְעוּ 2 K 19[29], Is 37[30], Jer 29[5.28]; cf. also the verbs ל״ה, which are at the same time פ״נ; נְחֵה Ez 32[18], נְחֵה Ex 32[34], נְטֵה Ex 8[1], &c.; the verb נָשָׂא ל״א, נְשָׂא ψ 10[12] (usually שָׂא); cf. § 76 *b*. But, as in the infinitive, the *aphaeresis* never takes place in verbs which have *ō* in the *imperfect*, e. g. נְצֹר, נְתֹץ, &c.

---

[1] Cf. the summary, § 41.
[2] The law allowing the addition of the feminine termination to the unlengthened form, instead of a lengthening of the vowel, is suitably called by Barth 'the law of compensation' (*Nominalbildung*, p. xiii).

d **2.** When, through the addition of a *preformative*, *Nûn* stands at the end of a syllable, it is readily assimilated to the second radical (§ 19 c); thus in the *imperfect Qal*,[1] e. g. יִפֹּל for yinpōl, *he will fall*; יִגַּשׁ for yingaš; יִתֵּן for yintēn, *he will give* (on this single example of an *imperfect* with original *i* in the second syllable, cf. *h*)[2]; also in the *perfect Niph'al* נִגַּשׁ for ningaš; throughout *Hiph'îl* (הִגִּישׁ, &c.) and *Hoph'al* (which in these verbs always has *Qibbuṣ*, in a sharpened syllable, cf. § 9 *n*) הֻגַּשׁ.

The other forms are all quite regular, e. g. the *perfect, infinitive absolute* and *participle Qal*, all *Piʿēl*, *Puʿal*, &c.

In Paradigm H, only those conjugations are given which differ from the regular form.

e The *characteristic* of these verbs in all forms with a preformative is *Dageš* following it in the second radical. Such forms, however, are also found in certain verbs פ״י (§ 71), and even in verbs ע״ע (§ 67). The *infinitive* גֶּשֶׁת and the *imperative* גַּשׁ, also גְּשָׁ־ (Gn 19⁹) and תֵּן, resemble the corresponding forms of verbs פ״י (§ 69).—On קַח, יִקַּח, and קַחַת, from לָקַח *to take*, see *g*.—In יָקוּם (*imperfect Niph'al* of קוּם), and in similar forms of verbs ע״ו (§ 72), the *full* writing of the *ô* indicates, as a rule, that they are not to be regarded as *imperfects Qal* of נָקַם, &c.—Also אֶפַּץ (ψ 139⁸) is not to be derived from נסק, but stands for אֶסְלַק (with a sharpening of the ס as compensation for the loss of the ל), from סָלַק *to ascend*, see § 19*f*, and Kautzsch, *Gramm. des Bibl.-Aram.*, § 44. Similarly the *Hiph'îl*-forms הִשִּׁיקוּ Ez 39⁹, יַשִּׁיק Is 44¹⁵, and the *Niph'al* נִשָּׁקָה ψ 78²¹ are most probably from a stem שׁלק, not נשׁק.

f Rem. 1. The instances are comparatively few in which the forms retain their *Nûn* before a firm consonant, e. g. נָטַר, imperfect יִנְטֹר Jer 3⁵ (elsewhere יִטֹּר); also from נָצַר the pausal form is *always* יִנְצֹרוּ (without the *pause* יִצְּרוּ Pr 20²⁸); similarly in Is 29¹, 58³, ψ 61⁸, 68³ (where, however, תִּנְרָךְ is intended), 140²·⁵, Pr 2¹¹, Jb 40²¹, the retention of the *Nûn* is always connected with the pause. In *Niph'al* this never occurs (except in the irregular *inf.* כְּהִנָּדֹף ψ 68³, cf. § 51 *k*), in *Hiph'îl* and *Hoph'al* very seldom ; e. g. לְהַנְתִּיךְ Ez 22²⁰, הִנְחֲקוּ Ju 20³¹ ; for לַנְפֵּל Nu 5²² read לְנִפֵּל, according to § 53 *q*. On the other hand, the *Nûn* is regularly retained in all verbs, of which the second radical is a guttural, e. g. יִנְחַל *he will possess*, although there are rare cases like יֵחַת (also יִנְחַת) *he will descend*, Jer 21¹³ (even תֵּחַת Pr 17¹⁰ ; without apparent reason accented as *Milʿēl*), plur. יֵחַתּוּ Jb 21¹³ (cf. § 20 *i*; the Masora, however, probably regards יֵחַת and יֵחַתּוּ as *imperfect Niph'al* from חָתַת (חָתַת); *Niph'al* נֶחַם for נָחַם *he has grieved*.

g **2.** The ל of לָקַח *to take* is treated like the *Nûn* of verbs פ״ן (§ 19 *d*). Hence *imperfect Qal* יִקַּח, cohortative (§ 20 *m*) אֶקְחָה, *imperative* קַח, in *pause* and

---

[1] Cf. Mayer Lambert, ' Le futur qal des verbes פ״י, פ״ן, פ״א,' in the *REJ.* xxvii. 136 ff.

[2] An imperfect in *a* (יִגַּשׁ) is given in the Paradigm, simply because it is the actual form in use in this verb.

before *suffixes* קַח (on קָחֶם־נָא Gn 48⁹, see § 61 *g*), *paragogic* form קָחָה; קְחִי, &c. (but cf. also לְקַח Ex 29¹, Ez 37¹⁶, Pr 20¹⁶, לְקָחִי 1 K 17¹¹, perhaps a mistake for לְךָ קְחִי, cf. LXX and Lucian); *infinitive construct* קַחַת (once קְחַת 2 K 12⁹, cf. § 93 *h*); with לְ, לָקַחַת; with *suffix* קַחְתִּי; *Hophʻal* (cf., however, § 53 *u*) *imperfect* יֻקַּח; *Niphʻal*, however, is always נִלְקַח.—The meaningless form קָח Ez 17⁵ is a mistake; for the equally meaningless קָחָם Ho 11³ read וָאֶקָּחֵם.

3. The verb נָתַן *to give*, mentioned above in *d*, is the only example of a *h* verb פ״נ with *imperfect* in ē (יִתֵּן) for *yinṭēn*; נִתֵּן¹ only in Ju 16⁵, elsewhere before *Maqqeph* ־יִתֶּן, &c.), and a corresponding *imperative* תֵּן or (very frequently) תְּנָה (but in ψ 8² the very strange reading תְּנָה is no doubt simply meant by the Masora to suggest נָתְנָה); before *Maqqeph* ־תֶּן, *fem.* תְּנִי, &c. Moreover, this very common verb has the peculiarity that its final *Nûn*, as a weak nasal, is also assimilated; נָתַתִּי for *nāthántī*, נָתַ or, very frequently, נָתַתָּה, with a kind of orthographic compensation for the assimilated *Nûn* (cf. § 44 *g*); *Niphʻal perfect* נִתַּם Lv 26²⁵, Ezr 9⁷.

In the *infinitive construct Qal* the ground-form *tint* is not lengthened to *tēneth i* (as גֶּשֶׁת from נָגַשׁ), but contracted to *titt*, which is then correctly lengthened to תֵּת, with the omission of *Dageš forte* in the final consonant, see § 20 *l*; but with suffixes תִּתִּי, תִּתּוֹ, &c.; before *Maqqeph* with the prefix לְ = לָתֶת־, e. g. Ex 5²¹, and even when closely connected by other means, e. g. Gn 15⁷. However, the strong formation of the *infinitive construct* also occurs in נְתֹן Nu 20²¹ and נָתָן־ Gn 38⁹; cf. § 69 *m*, note 2. On the other hand, for לָתֵתֶּן 1 K 6¹⁹ read either לְתִתּוֹ or simply לָתֵת, just as the *Qᵉrê*, 1 K 17¹⁴, requires תֵּת for תתן.

In other stems, the נ is retained as the third radical, e. g. שְׁכָנְתְּ, זָקַנְתִּי, cf. *k* § 19 *c* and § 44 *o*. On the entirely anomalous aphaeresis of the *Nûn* with a strong vowel in תַּתָּה (for נָתַתְּ) 2 S 22⁴¹, cf. § 19 *i*.—On the *passive imperfect* יֻתַּן, cf. § 53 *u*.

§ 67. *Verbs* ע״ע, e. g. סָבַב *to surround*.

Brockelmann, *Semit. Sprachwiss.*, p. 155 ff.; *Grundriss*, p. 632 ff.

1. A large number of Semitic stems have verbal forms with only *a* two radicals, as well as forms in which the stem has been made triliteral by a *repetition of the second radical*, hence called verbs ע״ע. Forms with two radicals were formerly explained as being due to contraction from original forms with three radicals. It is more correct

---

¹ P. Haupt on Ju 16⁵ in his Bible, compares the form of the Assyrian imperfect *iddan* or *ittan* (besides *inádin*, *inámdin*) from *nadánu* = נתן. But could this one passage be the only trace left in Hebrew of an imperf. in *a* from נתן?

to regard them as representing the original stem (with two radicals), and the forms with the second radical repeated as subsequently developed from the monosyllabic stem.[1] The appearance of a general contraction of triliteral stems is due to the fact that in biliteral forms the second radical regularly receives *Dageš forte* before afformatives, except in the cases noted in § 22 *b* and *q*. This points, however, not to an actual doubling, but merely to a strengthening of the consonant, giving more body to the monosyllabic stem, and making it approximate more to the character of triliteral forms.

The development of biliteral to triliteral stems (ע״ע) generally takes place in the 3rd *sing. masc.* and *fem.* and 3rd *plur.* perfect *Qal* of *transitive* verbs, or at any rate of verbs expressing an activity, e. g. חָנַן Gn 33[5] : סָבַב, סָבְבָה, סָבְבוּ (but with suffix חַנַּנִי, ver. 11); sometimes with an evident distinction between transitive and intransitive forms, as צָרַר *to make strait*, צַר *to be in a strait*; see further details, including the exceptions, in *aa*. The development of the stem takes place (*a*) necessarily whenever the strengthening of the 2nd radical is required by the character of the form (e. g. חָלַל, שָׁדַד), and (*b*) as a rule, whenever the 2nd radical is followed or preceded by an essentially long vowel, as, in Qal, סָבוֹב, סָבוּב, in Pô‘ēl and Pô‘al, סוֹבֵב, סוֹבַב.

b **2.** The biliteral stem always (except in *Hiph‘îl* and the *imperfect Niph‘al*, see below) takes the vowel which would have been required between the *second* and *third* radical of the ordinary strong form, or which stood in the ground-form, since that vowel is characteristic of the form (§ 43 *b*), e. g. תַּם answering to קָטַל, תַּמָּה to the ground-form *qăṭălăt*, תַּמּוּ to the ground-form *qăṭălû*; *infinitive*, סֹב to קְטֹל.

c **3.** The insertion of *Dageš forte* (mentioned under *a*), for the purpose of strengthening the second radical, never takes place (see § 20 *l*) in the final consonant of the word, e. g. סֹב, תַּם, not סֹבּ, תַּמּ; but it appears again on the addition of afformatives or suffixes, e. g. תַּמּוּ, סֹבּוּ, סַבּוּנִי, &c.

d **4.** When the afformative begins with a consonant (נ, ת), and hence the strongly pronounced second radical would properly come at the end of a closed syllable, a *separating vowel* is inserted between the stem-syllable and the afformative. In the *perfect* this vowel is וֹ, in the *imperative* and *imperfect* ◌ֶ, e. g. סַבּוֹת, סַבּוֹנוּ, *imperfect* תְּסֻבֶּינָה (for *sabb-tā, sabb-nû, tasōbb-nā*). The artificial opening of the syllable

---

[1] So (partly following Ewald and Böttcher) A. Müller, *ZDMG.* xxxiii. p. 698 ff. ; Stade, *Lehrbuch*, § 385 *b, c*; Nöldeke, and more recently Wellhausen, ‘ Ueber einige Arten schwacher Verba im Hebr.’ (*Skizzen u. Vorarb.* vi. 250 ff.). Against Böttcher see M. Lambert, *REJ.* xxxv. 330 ff., and Brockelmann, as above.

by this means is merely intended to make the strengthening of the
second radical audible.[1]

    The *perfect* תַּמֹּנוּ (for תַּמּוֹנוּ) Nu 17²⁸, ψ 64⁷ (Jer 44¹⁸ תַּמְנוּ with *Silluq*), owing *e*
to omission of the separating vowel, approximates, if the text is right, to the
form of verbs ע״וּ (cf. קָמְנוּ from קוּם).

    5. Since the preformatives of the *imperfect Qal*, of the *perfect* *f*
Niphʿal, and of *Hiphʿîl* and *Hophʿal* throughout, before a monosyllabic
stem form an open syllable, they take a *long* vowel before the tone
(according to § 27 *e*), e.g. *imperfect Hiphʿîl* יָסֵב for *yă-sēb*, *imperative*
הָסֵב for *hă-sēb*, &c. Where the preformatives in the strong verb have
ĭ, either the original ă (from which the ĭ was attenuated) is retained
and lengthened, e.g. יָסֹב in *imperfect Qal* for *yă-sōb*, or the ĭ itself is
lengthened to ē, e.g. הֵסֵב *perfect Hiphʿîl* for *hĭ-sēb* (see further under *h*).
The vowel thus lengthened can be maintained, however, only before
the tone (except the û of the *Hophʿal*, הוּסַב for *hŭ-săb*); when the
tone is thrown forward it becomes *Šᵉwâ*, according to § 27 *k* (under א
and ה *compound Šᵉwâ*), e.g. תָּסֹב, but תְּסֻבֶּינָה; *imperfect Hiphʿîl* תָּסֵב,
but תְּסִבֶּינָה; *perfect* הֲסִבֹּתִי, &c.

    Besides the ordinary form of the imperfects, there is another (common in *g*
Aramaic), in which the *imperfect Qal* is pronounced יִסֹּב or יִסַּב, the *first*
radical, not the second, being strengthened by *Dageš forte*, cf. יִשֹּׁם 1 K 9⁸,
וַיִּקֹּד Gn 24²⁶; with *a* in the second syllable, יִגַּר Lv 11⁷, יִדַּל Is 17⁴, וַיִּשַּׁח
Is 2⁹, &c., יִדַּם Am 5¹³ and frequently, וְאָכַּת Dt 9²¹, &c., יִסַּב (*turn* intrans.)
1 S 5⁸, &c., וַיִּקֹּב Lv 24¹¹, יִתֹּם Ez 47¹², &c., יֵחַם (with *Dageš forte implicitum*)
1 K 1¹; in the plural, יִתַּמּוּ Nu 14³⁵, &c. (in pause יִתָּמּוּ ψ 102²⁸); perhaps
also יִמַּל, יִמַּךְ, (unless these forms are rather to be referred to *Niphʿal*, like
יִדְּמוּ 1 S 2⁹; יָמֹלּוּ Jb 24²⁴); with suffix תִּקָּבֶנּוּ occurs (cf. § 10 *h*) in Nu 23²⁵;
Imperfect Hiphʿîl יָתַּם, *Hophʿal* יֻכַּת, &c. The vowel of the preformative (which
before *Dageš* is, of course, short) follows the analogy of the ordinary strong
form (cf. also *u* and *y*). The same method is then extended to forms with
afformatives or suffixes, so that even before these additions the second
radical is not strengthened, e.g. וַיִּקְדּוּ Gn 43²⁸, &c., for וַיִּקְּדוּ and *they bowed the*
head; וַיַּכֻּתוּ *and they beat down*, Dt 1⁴⁴ (from כָּתַת; וַיִּתְּמוּ Dt 32⁸; יִדְּמוּ Ex 15¹⁶,
Jb 29²¹ (cf., however, וַיֻּסַּבּוּ Ju 18²³, 1 S 5⁸, יֻכַּתּוּ Jer 46⁵, Jb 4²⁰). To the
same class of apparently strong formations belongs תִּצַּלְנָה (without the
separating vowel, for תִּצַּלֶּינָה, cf. 1 S 3¹¹ and below, *p*) *they shall tingle*,
2 K 21¹², Jer 19³.—On the various forms of the *Niphʿal*, see under *t*.

---

[1] Of all the explanations of these separating vowels the most satisfactory
is that of Rödiger, who, both for the *perfect* and *imperfect* (Ewald and Stade,
for the *imperfect* at least), points to the analogy of verbs ל״ה. We must,
however, regard סַבּוֹת as formed on the analogy not of גָּלִיתָ, but (with
P. Haupt) of a form גָּלוֹת (= *gālautā*, cf. Arab. *ǧazauta*), while תְּסִבֶּינָה follows
the analogy of תִּגְלֶינָה. [See also Wright, *Comp. Gr.*, 229 f.]

h   **6.** The original vowel is retained, see *f*, (*a*) in the preformative of the *imperfect Qal* יָסֹב for *yă-sōb* (cf. §§ 47 *b*, 63 *b*, and for verbs ע״וּ § 72); (*b*) in the *perfect Niph'al* נָסַב for *nă-săb* (§ 51 *a*); (*c*) in *Hoph'al* הוּסַב, with irregular lengthening (no doubt on the analogy of verbs פ״וּ) for *hōsăb* from *hŭ-sab*, imperfect יוּסַב from *yŭ-sab*, &c.

i   On the other hand, an already attenuated vowel (*i*) underlies the intransitive *imperfects Qal* with *ă* in the second syllable (probably for the sake of dissimilating the two vowels), e. g. יֵמַר for *yĭ-măr* (see *p*); and in the preformative of *Hiph'îl* הֵסֵב from *hĭ-sēb* (ground-form הַקְטֵל, § 53 *a*), as well as of the participle מֵסֵב (ground-form מַקְטֵל), on the analogy of the perfect. In the second syllable of the Perf. the underlying vowel is *ĭ*, attenuated from an original *ă*, which in the strong verb is abnormally lengthened to *î* (§ 53 *a*). The *ē* lengthened from *ĭ* is, of course, only tone-long, and hence when without the tone and before *Dageš forte* we have e. g. הֲסִבּוֹתָ. On the retention of the original *ă* in the second syllable, cf. *v*.

k   **7.** The *tone*, as a general rule, tends to keep to the stem-syllable, and does not (as in the strong verb) pass to the afformatives ◌ָה, וּ and ◌ִי (2nd *sing. fem. imperfect*); e. g. 3rd *sing. fem. perfect* חָתָּה, in pause חָתָה; with ר and gutturals מָרָה (for מַרָה), שָׁחָה ψ 44²⁶; on the other hand, with *wāw consecutive* וְרַבָּה Is 6¹² (but וְחָיָה Ex 1¹⁶). In the 3rd *plur. perfect* the tone-syllable varies; along with קַלּוּ, דַּלּוּ, we also find דַּלּוּ and קַלּוּ, רַבּוּ Is 59¹², שָׁחוּ Hb 3⁶, &c.; but in *pause* always תַּמּוּ, חָתּוּ, &c. The tone likewise remains on the stem-syllable in the *imperfect Qal* in תָּסֹבִּי, יָסֹב; *perfect Hiph'îl* הֵסַבָּה, הֵסַבּוּ; *imperfect* יָסֵבּוּ, תָּסֵבִּי, &c. In the forms with separating vowels, the tone is moved forward to these vowels (or to the final syllable, cf. *ee*), e. g. תִּסְבֶּינָה, סַבּוֹתָ, &c.; except before the endings חֶם and חֶן in the *perfect*, which always bear the tone. This shifting of the tone naturally causes the shortening of the merely tone-long vowels *ē* and *ō* to *ĭ* and *ŭ* (or *ŏ*, see *n*), hence הֲסִבּוֹתָ from הֵסַב, תְּסֻבֶּינָה from יָסֹב; on cases in which the vowel of the preformative becomes *Šⁱwâ*, see above, *f*.

l   **8.** In several verbs ע״ע, instead of *Pi'ēl*, *Pu'al* and *Hithpa'ēl*, the less frequent conjugation *Pô'ēl*, with its passive and reflexive, occurs (most probably on the analogy of the corresponding forms of verbs ע״וּ, cf. § 72 *m*), generally with the same meaning,[1] e. g. עוֹלֵל *to ill-treat*, passive עוֹלַל, reflexive הִתְעוֹלֵל (from עָלַל; cf. the *Hithpô'ēl* from רָעַע

---

[1] Sometimes both *Pi'ēl* and *Pô'ēl* are formed from the same stem, though with a difference of meaning, e. g. רִצֵּץ *to break in pieces*, רֹצֵץ *to oppress*; חִנֵּן *to make pleasing*, חוֹנֵן *to have pity*; סִבֵּב *to turn, to change*, סוֹבֵב *to go round, to encompass*.

and פָּרַר Is 24¹⁹ ꜰ·) ; in a few verbs also *Pilpēl* (§ 55 ꜰ) is found, e. g.
גִּלְגֵּל *to roll*, Hithpalpēl הִתְגַּלְגֵּל *to roll oneself* (from גָּלַל) ; imperative
with suffix סַלְסְלֶהָ *exalt her*, Pr 4⁸ ; שִׁעֲשַׁע *to comfort, to delight in*; passive
שֻׁעֲשַׁע *to be caressed* (from שָׁעַע). These forms cannot appear in a
biliteral form any more than *Piʿēl*, *Puʿal*, and *Hithpaʿēl*; cf. עֲוְעִים
(Is 19¹⁴) and קַוְקַו (Is 18²,⁷).—For תִּתְבָּר 2 S 22²⁷ read, according to
ψ 18²⁷, תִּתְבָּרָר.

REMARKS.

I. *On Qal*.

1. In the *perfect*, isolated examples are found with ō in the first syllable, *m*
which it is customary to refer to triliteral stems with middle ō (like יָכֹל,
§ 43 *a*) ; viz. רֹמּוּ *they are exalted*, Jb 24²⁴ to רָמַם ; רֹבּוּ *they shot*, Gn 49²³ to רָבַב;
זֹרוּ Is 1⁶ to זָרַר. But this explanation is very doubtful : זֹרוּ especially is
rather to be classed among the passives of Qal mentioned in § 52 *e*.

2. *Imperfects Qal* with ō in the second syllable keep the original *a* in the *n*
preformative, but lengthen it to *ā*, as being in an open syllable, hence יָחֹן,
יֵרַע, יָרֹן, יֵעֹז, יָמֹד (trans. *he breaks in pieces*, but יֵרַע *intrans.* = *he is evil*);
imperfects with *ă* have, in the preformative, an *ē*, lengthened from *ĭ*. See
the examples below, under *p*, § 63 *c* and *e*, § 72 *h*, and specially Barth in
ZDMG. 1894, p. 5 f.

The *Ḥōlem* of the *infinitive, imperative*, and *imperfect* (סֹב, יָסֹב) is only tone-
long, and therefore, as a rule, is written defectively (with a few exceptions,
chiefly in the later orthography, e. g. צוֹר *bind up*, Is 8¹⁶ ; גּוֹל ψ 37⁵; דּוֹם
ver. 7 ; לָבוֹז for לָבֹז *to plunder*, Est 3¹³, 8¹¹). When this ō loses the tone, it
becomes in the final syllable ŏ, in a sharpened syllable ŭ, or not infrequently
even ŏ (see above, *k*). Examples of ŏ are : (*a*) in a toneless final syllable, i. e.
before *Maqqeph* or in the *imperfect consecutive*, רָן־ (rŏn) *to rejoice*, Jb 38⁷ ; וַיָּסָב
Ju 11¹⁸ (once even with ŭ in a toneless final syllable, וַיָּרֶם Ex 16²⁰); on the
other hand, in the *plur.* וַיָּסֹבּוּ, *fem.* וַתְּסֻבֶּינָה ; (*b*) before a tone-bearing
afformative or *suffix*, e. g. *imperative 2nd sing. fem.* פֵּנִּי, רָנִּי (cf. ꜰ) ; חָנֵּנִי *pity me* ;
סֹלֻּוּה Jer 50²⁶ ; יֻשַּׁם Pr 11³ Qᵉrē ; תְּחֻנֵּהוּ Ex 12¹⁴ (for the defective writing,
cf. יִסֻּבֵּהוּ Jb 40²²). In יָחֻנְךָ Gn 43²⁹, Is 30¹⁹ (for יְחָנְךָ) this ŏ is thrown back
to the preformative.

On the 2nd *plur.* *fem.* *imperat.* עֹרָה *make yourselves naked* Is 32¹¹, cf. the *o*
analogous forms in § 48 *i*.—Quite abnormal is the *infinitive absolute* רֹעָה Is 24¹⁹
(as ה follows, probably only a case of dittography for רֹע, cf. קֹב Nu 23²⁵ and
שֹׁל Ru 2¹⁶); so also are the *imperatives* קָבְה־לִי Nu 22¹¹·¹⁷, and אָרָה־לִי 22⁶, 23⁷,.
with ה *paragogic*. We should expect קָבָּה, אָרָה. If these forms are to be
read *qŏballi, ʾŏralli*, they would be analogous to such cases as מְדֻבָּרָה (§ 90 *i*),
the addition of the *paragogic* ה causing no change in the form of the word
(רָן־ like קָב־ above). If, however, as Jewish tradition requires, they are to
be read *qābālli, ʾāralli*, then in both cases the Qameṣ must be explained, with

Stade, as the equivalent of ō (קָבְה־לִּי, &c.; cf. § 9 *v*). Still more surprising is קַבְנוּ *curse him*, Nu 23¹³, for קָבֵּנּוּ or קַב'.¹

p 3. Examples with *Pathaḥ* in the *infinitive*, *imperative*, and *imperfect* are בַּר (in לִבְרָם *to prove them*, Ec 3¹⁸); רַד Is 45¹; שַׁךְ Jer 5²⁶; בְּשַׁגָּם *in their error*, Gn 6³ (so ed. Mant., but there is also good authority for בְּשַׁגַּם, from שַׁ־ = שֶׁ־ = אֲשֶׁר and גַּם *also*; so Baer and Ginsburg). Also גַּל *take away*, ψ 119²²; and the imperfects יֵחַם *it is hot*, Dt 19⁶, &c. (on the ē of the preformative cf. *n*); יֵמַר *it is bitter*, Is 24⁹; יֵצַר *it is straitened*; יֵרַךְ *it is soft*, Is 7⁴; תֵּשַׁם *it is desolate*, Ez 12¹⁹ (in pause תֵּשָׁם Gn 47¹⁹); וַתֵּקַל *she was despised*, Gn 16⁴ (but elsewhere in the *impf. consec.* with the tone on the penultima, e. g. וַיֵּצֶר Gn 32⁸, &c.; וַיֵּרַע Gn 21¹¹, &c., cf. Ez 19⁷); in the 1st *sing. imperfect* אֵיתַם² ψ 19¹⁴, abnormally written fully for אֶתַּם, unless אֶתָּם is to be read, as in some MSS., on the analogy of the 3rd sing. יִתַּם.—In the *impf. Qal* of שָׁלַל the reading of Hb 2⁸ varies between יִשָׁלּוּךָ (Baer, Ginsb.) and יְשָׁלּוּךָ (ed. Mant., Jabl.).— The following forms are to be explained with Barth (*ZDMG*. xliii. p. 178) as imperfects Qal with original *ĭ* in the second syllable, there being no instances of their Hiph'il in the same sense: וַיִּגַּל Gn 29¹⁰; יִגַּן Is 31⁵, &c.; וַיִּסַךְ Ex 4c²¹, ψ 91⁴, &c.; perhaps also תִּצְלַיְנָה 1 S 3¹¹ and יָהֵל Jb31²⁶, &c.; in accordance with this last form, (בְּ)הִלּוֹ Jb 29³ would also be an *infinitive Qal*, not Hiph'il (for בְּהַהִלּוֹ), as formerly explained below, under *w*. Finally the very peculiar form וַתָּרֵץ Ju 9⁵³ may probably be added to the list.

q   Imperfects, with an original *u* in the second syllable, are also found with this *ŭ* lengthened to *û* (instead of *ō*), e. g. יָרוּן, if the text is correct, in Pr 29⁶; יָשׁוּד ψ 91⁶ (unless it be simply an imperfect from שׁוּד *to be powerful, to prevail*); יָרוּץ (if from רצץ) Is 42⁴, &c. (also defectively אָרֻץ ψ 18³⁰; but in Ec 12⁶, according to Baer, וְתָרֻץ); תָּחֹם Ez 24¹¹ (on the sharpening of the ת cf. *g* above).³

r   A similar analogy with verbs ע״וּ is seen in the infinitives לָבוּר (for בֹּר) Ec 9¹; בְּחֻקּוֹ Pr 8²⁷ (cf. בַּחוּקוֹ Pr 8²⁹) for בְּחֻקּוֹ, and in the *imperfect* אֲמֻשְׁךָ Gn 27²¹. (The forms חַנּוֹת in ψ 77¹⁰, שַׁמּוֹת Ez 36³, חַלּוֹתִי ψ 77¹¹, formerly treated here as infinitives from ע״וּ stems, are rather to be referred to ל״ה stems, with Barth, *Wurzeluntersuchungen*, Lpz. 1902, p. 21.) On other similar cases, see below, under *ee*. For examples of the *aramaïzing imperfect*, see above, *g*.

s   4. In the *participle*, the aramaïzing form שֹׁאֲסַיִךְ for שֹׁסְסַיִךְ occurs in Kᵉthibh, Jer 30¹⁶ (the *Qᵉrê* indicates a *participle* from שָׁסָה); רֹעָה Pr 25¹⁹ appears to be a contraction from רֹעֲעָה, *part. fem.* = *breaking in pieces*.

---

¹ For נוּ as suffix of the 3rd person a parallel might be found in יִשְׁנוּ, § 100 *o*, and probably also in the *Nún* of the Phoenician suffix נם: cf. Barth, *ZDMG*. xli. p. 643, and the note on § 100 *o*.

² Also in Ez 6⁶, instead of תִּישַׁמְנָה, which could only come from יָשֵׁם, תִּישַׁ' is intended, and יֶאְשְׁמוּ in the same verse is probably only an error for יֵשַׁמּוּ.

³ According to Stade, *Grammatik*, § 95, Rem., the pronunciation with *û*, since it also appears in Neo-Punic [and in Western Syriac, see Nöldeke, *Syr. Gramm.*, § 48], was that of everyday life.

II. On Niph'al.

5. Besides the ordinary form of the *perfect* נָסַב with *Pathaḥ* (in *pause t* נָסָב) and the *participle* נָסָב with *Qameṣ* in the second syllable, there is also another with *Ṣere*, and a third with *Ḥolem*, e.g. *perfect* נָמֵס *it melts*, Ez 21¹², 22¹⁵; נָסַבָּה (for נָסַבָּה) Ez 26²; *part.* נָמֵס *molten*, 1 S 15⁹, Na 2¹¹; נָקֵל *it is a light thing*, 2 K 20¹⁰, Is 49⁶ (*perf.* נָקֹל); with ō, e.g. נָגֹלּוּ *they are rolled together*, Is 34⁴; cf. 63¹⁹, 64², Am 3¹¹, Na 1¹², Ec 12⁶ᵇ. In the *imperfect* with ō in the second syllable, on the analogy of verbs ע״וּ (from which König would also explain the *perfects* with ō), we find תִּדֹּמִּי *thou shalt be brought to silence*, Jer 48² (unless this form should be referred to *Qal* with Qimḥi, Olshausen, König); יֵרוֹעַ *he suffers hurt*, Pr 11¹⁵, 13²⁰; תֵּרוֹץ (for *tirrōṣ*) Ez 29⁷; with ē in the second syllable תֵּחֵל *she profanes herself*, Lv 21⁹, but וְאֵחַל Ez 22²⁶, and יֵחַל Is 48¹¹, יֵחַת Is 7⁸, &c. For *infinitives*, cf. הִמֵּס *to melt*, ψ 68³ (as *inf. constr.*; 2 S 17¹⁰ as *inf. absol.*); again, with compensatory lengthening in the first syllable, הֵחַל Ez 20⁹, 14²², but with suffix הֵחַלּוֹ Lv 21⁴; also הִבּוֹז *to be plundered*, and הִבּוֹק *to be emptied*, Is 24³; in the *imperative*, only הִבָּרוּ *be ye clean*, Is 52¹¹. On הֵרֹמּוּ *get you up*, Nu 17¹⁰, and the corresponding *imperf.* יֵרֹמּוּ Ez 10¹⁷, &c., cf. 72 *dd*.

Examples of the *perfect Niph'al* with sharpening of the initial syllable are, *u* נִחַל *it is profaned*, Ez 22¹⁶, 25³ (from חָלַל); נָחַר (from חָרַר) ψ 69⁴, 102⁴ (also נָחַר Jer 6²⁹); נִחַת *fractus est* (from חָתַת) Mal 2⁵; cf. with this in the *participle*, נְחָמִים (for *niḥḥāmim*) Is 57⁵, and נֵאָרִים Mal 3⁹: in the *imperative* and *infinitive Niph'al* such a virtual strengthening of the guttural after preformatives never occurs.—The occurrence of *u* instead of ō as a separating vowel in the *perfect* נְשַׁדֻּנוּ Mic 2⁴ is abnormal.

III. On Hiph'il and Hoph'al.

6. The second syllable in *Hiph'il* sometimes has *Pathaḥ* instead of *Ṣere*, *v* especially under the influence of ר and the gutturals, e.g. *perfect* הֵמַר *he made bitter*, הֵשַׁח *he bowed*, הֵפַר *he hath broken*, Gn 17¹⁴, in *pause*, cf. § 29 *q*; otherwise הֵפֵר, *plur.* הֵפֵרוּ Is 24⁵. In הֵפִיר ψ 33¹⁰, Ez 17¹⁹, cf. ψ 89³⁴, and in הֵשִׁירוּ Ho 8⁴ (perhaps also in יָחִיתַן Hab 2¹⁷, but cf. § 20 *n*) there is an assimilation to the corresponding forms of verbs ע״וּ, see *z*. Also הֵצַר Dt 28⁵², הֵתַן (in *pause*) Is 18⁵; *inf.* לְהָבֵר *to cleanse*, Jer 4¹¹, in *pause*. But also with other consonants, e.g. הֵדַק 2 K 23¹⁵, הֵקַל Is 8²³; הֵרַךְ Jb 23¹⁶; *plur.* הֵסַבּוּ 1 S 5⁹·¹⁰ (and so usually in the 3rd *plur. perf.*, except before ר and gutturals, e.g. הֵרֵעוּ); *imper.* הֵשַׁע *besmear*, Is 6¹⁰; *plur.* הֵשַׁמּוּ *be astonished*, Jb 21⁵; *imperfect* תֵּרַע *Thou dost afflict*; *part.* מֵצַל (on ē in the first syllable, see under *i*) *shadowing*, Ez 31³ (but מֵסִיךְ Ju 3²⁴ is assimilated to the form of verbs ע״וּ, unless, with Moore, we simply read מֵסֵךְ, or, with incorrect spelling, מֵסִיךְ. So in the *imperative* הֲמִישֵׁנִי Ju 16²⁶ *Q°rê*, and in the *infinitive* הַתְמֵךְ Is 33¹').

The ē of the second syllable, when without the tone, may become *ĕ*, e.g. *w* הֵחֶל בִּי Gn 31⁷ (see also *x*). It is unusual (cf. § 53 *k*) to find the ē written fully as in the *infinitive* לְהָפִיר Zc 11¹⁰. Instead of *Ḥaṭeph-Pathaḥ* a *Ḥaṭeph-*

Sᵉghôl is found under the preformative in הֲקִלְּתַ֫נִי 2 S 19⁴⁴, and a *Pathaḥ* occurs before ה (with a virtual sharpening of the ה) in such forms as הַחְתַּ֫ת Is 9³; cf. Gn 11⁶, Dt 2³¹, 3²⁴, 1 S 22¹⁵, Est 6¹³—in all these cases before חַ.—On בְּהִלּוֹ Jb 29³, see above, *p* : on וְהַחֲתַתִּי Jer 49³⁷, see below, *dd*.

x 7. In the *imperfect consecutive* of verbs whose second radical is a guttural, *ă* is retained (§ 22 *d*) in the second syllable instead of *ĕ*, e.g. וַיִּרַע 1 K 16²⁵: so also with ר, as וַיֵּ֫צֶר 2 Ch 28²⁰, Dt 2⁹—but cf. also וַיֹּ֫פֶר Neh 4⁹.

y 8. Aramaïzing forms (but cf. Rem. to § 67 *g*) in *Hiph'il* and *Hoph'al* are, וַיֵּסַב Ex 13¹⁸, &c.; cf. Ju. 18²³; אַל־תֵּ֫מַר Ex 23²¹, but read אַל־תָּ֫מַר from מָרָה: וַיֵּבְתּוּ Dt 1⁴⁴ (cf. Nu 14⁴⁵), but וַיָּסֵ֫בּוּ Ju 18²³, 1 S 5⁸, 2 Ch 29⁶; אָחֵל *profanabo*, Ez 39⁷; תֵּ֫חַם Jb 22³; without elision of the ה (cf. § 53 *q*), וְיָהֵ֫תֶּל 1 K 18²⁷, but Jer 9⁴ יְהָתֵ֫לּוּ, Jb 13⁹ תְּהָתֵ֫לּוּ; with *î* in the second syllable יָשִׂ֫ים Jer 49²⁰, 50⁴⁵; cf. וַשִּׂ֫ים Nu 21³⁰; in the *perfect* הַזִּילוּהָ La 1⁸. In *Hoph'al*, הֻמְּכוּ *they are brought low*, Jb 24²¹; יֻכַּת *he is smitten*, Is 24¹² (*plur.* יֻכַּ֫תּוּ Jer 46⁵, Mi 1⁷); in *pause*, יֻכָּ֫קוּ Jb 19²³, but also יֻכַּ֫תּוּ Jb 4²⁰ (so Baer, Ginsb., but ed. Mant., Jabl. יֻכַּ֫תּוּ); with *ŏ* in the initial syllable, הָשַׁמָּה (*infinitive with suffix* = הָשַׁמָּה, cf. § 91 *e*) Lv 26³⁴ᶠ·, cf. 2 Ch 36²¹; בְּהִשַׁמָּה, with irregular syncope for בְּהַשַׁמָּה, Lv 26⁴³.

IV. *In General.*

z 9. Verbs ע״ע are most closely related as regards inflexion to verbs ע״וּ (§ 72). The form of verbs ע״ע is generally the shorter (cf. e.g. יָסֹב and הָסֵב, יָקוּם and הֵקִים); in a few cases, however, the two classes exactly coincide, e.g. in the *imperfect* Qal and *Hiph'il* with *wāw consecutive*, in *Hoph'al* and in the less common conjugations (see above, *l*).

aa 10. The developed forms (with three radicals), as mentioned in *a*, are especially frequent in the 3rd *sing. masc.* and *fem.*, and the 3rd *plur. perf. Qal* (i.e. in forms without an afformative or with an afformative beginning with a vowel) of transitive verbs, or verbs, at any rate, expressing action, e.g. סָבַב, סָבְבוּ (but before a suffix also סַבּ֫וּנִי, as well as סְבָב֫וּנִי, שְׁדָד֫וּנִי, &c.); אָפְפוּ, זֵמָה, זָמַם, &c. Sometimes the contracted, *as well as* the uncontracted form, is found, e.g. בַּז *to plunder*, *plur.* בַּזְזוּ; in other parts, only בֹּ֫זְזוּ Dt 2³⁵, as well as בַּזֹּ֫נוּ Dt 3⁷; זַמָּ֫תִי Zc 8¹⁴·¹⁵ and וָמֹ֫תִי Jer 4²⁸. Other examples of biliteral forms in 2nd *sing. masc.* are Dt 25¹², Pr 30³²; in 1st *sing.*, Jos 5⁹. Apart from Qal the only example of a developed form is וְהַחֲתַתִּי Jer 49³⁷.

bb On the other hand, the biliteral forms are the more common in the 3rd *sing.* and *plur.* of perfects which are *intransitive*, and express a state; cf. דַּק Dt 9²¹ (Ex 32²⁰ דָּק; elsewhere always a transitive verb); חַת, *fem.* חַתָּה; מַר, *fem.* מָ֫רָה (for *marrā*) צַר, *fem.* צָ֫רָה (cf. וְהָרָה Ez 24¹¹); שַׁח, רַךְ 1 S 3¹, *fem.* שָׁ֫חָה, תַּם, &c.; *plur.* חַ֫תּוּ, תַּ֫מּוּ, &c. (but on the tone, cf. *ee* below). Exception, עָשֹֹׁ֫שָׁה ψ 6⁸.

cc The intransitive but developed perfects נָדְדוּ, נֵדְדָה, חָלַל, חָלְלוּ (also דַּלּוּ), (in *pause* נָדֹ֫דוּ), סָרַר, עָשְׁשָׁה ψ 31¹¹), (*plur.* in *pause* עָשֵׁ֫שׁוּ (also שָׁ֫חֲחוּ, צָלְלוּ, שַׁ֫חוּ), almost all have, as Mayer Lambert observes, at least an active, not a stative meaning. Triliteral forms of the *infinitive* after לְ are לִסְבֹּב Nu 21⁴; לִשְׁדוֹד Jer 47⁴; לִנְזֹ֫ז Gn 31¹⁹ (also לָנֹ֫ז Gn 38¹³); cf. also לַחְמֹם Is 47¹⁴, in subordinate pause, for לַחְמֹם; with *suffix* לַחֲנַנְכֶם Is 30¹⁸, and, from the same form חַן, with retraction and modification of the vowel, לְחַנְנָה ψ 102¹⁴; also שָׁחוֹחַ Is 60¹⁴, בִּנְזוֹ 1 S 25², כְּמַסֵם Is 10¹⁸, בְּעָזוֹז Pr 8²⁸, כְּצָרוֹר Pr 26⁸.—*Imperative* שָׁדְדוּ Jer 49²⁸ (cf. § 20 *b*, and ibid. also on חָנְנֵנִי ψ 9¹⁴); in the *imperfect*, יָדוֹד Na 3⁷ (ψ 68¹³; cf. Gn 31⁴⁰) from נדד; the strong form here, after the assimilation of the *Nûn*, was unavoidable. On the other hand, יִשָּׁדְּדֵם Jer 5⁶ is anomalous for יָשָׁדֵּם (Pr 11³ *Qᵉrê*; the eastern school read the Poʿēl ישׁודדם in the *Kᵉthibh*); the strengthening of the second radical has been afterwards resolved by the insertion of a *vocal Šᵉwâ*. Cf. also יֶחֱמוּ Am 5¹⁵ (elsewhere יֵחַן). In *Niph'al*, the triliteral form יִלָּבֵב is found, Jb 11¹²; in *Hiph'il*, all the forms of רנן, thus *imperative* הַרְנִינוּ, *imperfect* תַּרְנִין; *infinitive* הַשַּׁמֵּם Mi 6¹³; *participle* מַשְׁמִים Ez 3¹⁵. That the developed (triliteral) forms possess a certain emphasis is seen from their frequent use in *pause*, as in ψ 118¹¹ after a biliteral form (סַבּוּנִי נַם־סְבָבוּנִי).

11. The above-mentioned (see *g*) neglect of the strengthening in aramaïzing *dd* forms, such as יָדֻמּוּ and the like, occurs elsewhere tolerably often; in the *perfect Qal* תַּמּוֹנוּ for תַּמּוֹנוּ Nu 17²⁸ (Jer 44¹⁸; cf. above, *e*); *imperfect* נָבוֹחַ 1 S 14³⁶ (ה ָ *parag.* without any influence on the form, cf. *o*); even with the firm vowel reduced to *vocal Šᵉwâ*, נְבְלָה Gn 11⁷ for נָבֹלָה (cohortative from בָּלַל); יְזֹמוּ for יָזֹמּוּ ibid. ver. 6, *they purpose*; following the analogy of verbs ע״וּ, אֲמֻשְׁךָ (see above, *r*); from *intransitive imperfects Qal*, תֵּצְרִי Is 49¹⁹ (*plur. masc.* Jb 18⁷); יֵרְעוּ Neh 2³; also תִּישְׁמְנָה Ez 6⁶ (for which read תֵּשַׁמְ/תֵּישׁ) might be explained in the same way.—*Perfect Niph'al* נָסֵבָּה for נָסַבָּה Ez 41⁷; נָזֹלּוּ Ju 5⁵ for נָזֹלּוּ, נְמַלְתֶּם for נִמַּלְתֶּם Gn 17¹¹ (as if from מָלַל not מוּל *to circumcise*), cf. Is 19³, Jer 8¹⁴; *imperfect* תִּפָּקֵנָה Zc 14¹²; *participle* נְחָמִים, cf. *u*. So also נָפֵץ 1 S 13¹¹, נִפְצָה Gn 9¹⁹ (cf. Is 33³), are perfects *Niph'al* from פצץ (= פּוּץ), not *Qal* from נָפַץ.—In *Hiph'il* הֵתַלְתָּ (for הֲתִלֹּת Ju 16¹⁰ (2 S 15³⁴); הֵעֵזָה for הֶעֱזָה Pr 7¹³ (cf. Ct 6¹¹, 7¹³).

No less irreguiar is the suppression of the vowel of the stem-syllable in לְהָפְרְכֶם Lv 26¹⁵.—On the perfect דַּלְיוּ Pr 26⁷, cf. § 75 *u*.

12. Cases in which the tone is thrown forward on the afformatives (see *cc* *k*) are (*a*) in the *perfect*, the 1st *sing*. regularly (but cf. וְהַצְרֹתִי Jer 10¹⁸ before לָהֶם) after ו *consec.*, Ex 33¹⁹·²², 2 K 19³⁴, &c., also Is 44¹⁶ (חַמּוֹתִי before ר); ψ 92¹¹ (but the text is certainly corrupt; see the Lexicon), 116⁶, perhaps also Jb 19¹⁷ וְחַנֹּתִי (though in this passage, and in ψ 17³, the form might be an *infinitive* in *ôth*; see Delitzsch on Jb 19¹⁷); in the 2nd *sing*. וְקַצֹּתָה (before א) Dt 25¹²; in the 3rd *plural*, רַבּוּ *multi sunt*, ψ 3², 104²⁴, Jer 5⁶, 1 S 25¹⁰; רַבּוּ *they are soft*, ψ 55²² קַלּוּ *they are swift*, Jer 4¹³, Hb 1⁸; זַכּוּ *they are pure*, Jb 15¹⁵, 25⁵, La 4⁷; שַׁחוּ *they did bow*, Hb 3⁶; חָרוּ *they are burned*, Is 24⁶. A by-form of שָׁתוּ (ע״וּ, cf. § 72 *dd*) is שַׁתּוּ ψ 49¹⁵, 73⁹.

(*b*) In the *imperative* (a command in an emphatic tone) רָנִּי *sing*, Is 54¹, *ff* Zp 3¹⁴, Zc 2¹⁴; רֹנִּי Is 44²³, 49¹³, Jer 31⁷ (but רֹבִּי *lament*, La 2¹⁹), חָגִּי *keep* (thy feasts), Na 2¹, Jer 7²⁹; עֻנֶּה (=עֲנֵה) before א, ψ 68²⁹. On the retention of the short vowels *ŭ* (*ŏ*) and *i* before *Dageš forte*, in place of the tone-long *ō* and *ē*, see above, *k*; on the change of the vowel of the preformative into *Šᵉwâ*, when it no longer stands before the tone, see *g*.

The Weakest Verbs (*Verba Quiescentia*).

§ 68. *Verbs* פ״א e.g. אָכַל *to eat.*

Brockelmann, *Semit. Sprachwiss.*, p. 140 ff. ; *Grundriss*, p. 589 ff.

a So far as א retains its full consonantal value as a guttural, these verbs share all the peculiarities of verbs *primae gutturalis*, mentioned in § 63. They are, however, to be treated as *weak* verbs, when the א loses its value as a consonant, and coalesces with the preceding vowel (originally short) to form one long syllable. This takes place only in the following very common verbs and forms, as if through phonetic decay :—

b 1. In the *imperfect Qal*, five verbs (viz. אָבַד *to perish*, אָבָה *to be willing*, אָכַל *to eat*, אָמַר *to say*, אָפָה *to bake*) regularly make the א quiesce in a long *ô*, e. g. יֹאכַל.[1] In a few others the ordinary (strong) form is also in use, as יֶאֱחֹז (18 times) and יַחֲזֹ (3 times) *he takes hold*; יֶאֱסֹף (see *h*), also יַאֲסֹף, *he collects*. This *ô* has primarily arisen from an obscuring of *â* (§ 9 *q*), and the *â* from אַ־, the weak consonant א coalescing with *ă* to *â*; cf. § 23 *a*.

c In the second syllable *ō* (for original *ŭ*) never appears, but either *ē*[2] or *ă*; and in *pause* almost always *ē*, even before the tone-bearing *heavy* afformative ֹון, e. g. יֹאכֵלוּן Dt 18¹, without the pause יֹאכְלוּן Dt 4²⁸. In the 3rd *sing. masc.* and 1st *sing.* of אָמַר, however, *ă* is always retained in pause, יֹאמַר and אֹמַר; but in the 2nd *masc.* תֹּאמֵר 1 K 5²⁰, in the 3rd *fem.* תֹּאמֵר Pr 1²¹; in the *plural* יֹאמְרוּ Jer 5², ψ 145⁶·¹¹, תֹּאמֵרוּ Jer 23³⁸, with *Sĕgolta*; cf. also תֹּאכֵל 1 S 1⁷, &c. But with conjunctive accents in the body of the sentence, *ă* (as being a lighter vowel) is used, e. g. תֹּאבַד לָעַד ψ 9¹⁹, but in *pause* תֹּאבַד ψ 1⁶; cf. a similar interchange of *ē* and *ă* in § 65 *c*. The 3rd *fem. plur. impf.* always has the form תֹּאבַלְנָה Zc 11⁹.

d When the tone moves back, the final syllable of the *imperfects* of אָבַד and אָכַל, with a conjunctive accent, also always takes *Pathaḥ*, e. g. יֹאבַד יוֹם Jb 3³, וַיֹּאכַל *and he did eat*; in אָמַר the loss of the tone from the final syllable only occurs in the form with *wāw consecutive*

---

[1] So in the modern vulgar Arabic of South Palestine, *ya'kul* (*he eats*) becomes *yôkul*.

[2] On this *ē* (originally *ĭ*) as a dissimilation from *ō* (originally *ŭ*), cf. § 27 *w*, and F. Philippi, in the *Zeitschrift für Völkerpsychologie und Sprachwissenschaft*, xiv. 178. The latter rightly observes that the existence of an original *u* in the *imperfect* of אָכַל is indicated by the form of the *imperative* אֱכֹל, the Arabic *ya'kul* and the Aramaic יֵאכַל, as well as by the fact that יֶאֱחֹז and יֶאֱסֹף are found along with יֹאחֶז and יֹאסֶף.

(but never in the 1st *sing.* וַיֹּאמֶר; cf. וַיֹּאכַל), and then the final syllable, if without the *pause*, always takes *Sᵉghôl*, וַיֹּאמֶר *and he said* (except וַתֹּאמַר לוֹ Pr 7¹³).

In *pause*, however, the *imperfect consecutive* (except the 1st pers. of אָכַל, see below) always has the form וַיֹּאכַל (but *plur.* always יֹאכֵלוּ, וַיֹּאמֵרוּ, (וַיֹּאכֵלוּ; except וַיֹּאמַר in the poetic portion of the book of Job, as 3², 4¹, &c., but not in 32⁶, in the middle of the verse. The weak *imperfect* of אָחַז is always יֹאחֵז and וַיֹּאחֶז, but in the 1st *sing.*, according to § 49 *e*, וָאֹחֵז Ju 20⁶; cf. וָאֹכַל Gn. 3¹².¹³ in pause.—אָבָה and אָפָה are, at the same time, verbs לה״ה, hence *imperfect* יֹאבֶה (§ 75 *c*).

f Before *light* suffixes the vowel of the second syllable becomes vocal Šᵉwâ, as תֹּאכְלֵם, יֹאכְלֵנוּ, but תֹּאכַלְכֶם.—In a few cases, instead of the ô in the first syllable an *ê* is found, which is due to contraction from the group (or) in place of; e.g. תֵּאתֶה *it shall come*, Mi 4⁸, from תֶּאֱתֶה (from אָתָה); אֵהַב (for אֶאֱהַב) *I love*, Pr 8¹⁷, also (four times) אֵהַב Mal 1², &c., with suffixes אֹהֲבֵהוּ Ho 11¹, 14⁵, &c. (but only in 1st *sing.*, otherwise יֶאֱהַב, &c., from אֶאֱהַב,אָהֵב); וָאֵשֵׁב *and I stayed*, Gn 32⁵. The *infinitive construct* of אָמַר with ל is always לֵאמֹר *dicendo*, for לֶאֱמֹר.—According to Barth (*ZDMG*. 1889, p. 179) וַיֵּאָצֶל Nu 11²⁵ is to be regarded as an *imᵖerfect Qal*, without the obscuring of אֶ to ô, not as *imperfect Hiph'il*, since אצל elsewhere occurs only in the *perfect Qal* and *Niph'al*; on the original *i* in the second syllable, see above, § 67 *p*. For תֵּאכְלֵהוּ Jb 20²⁶ we should simply emend תֹּאכְלֵ׳; the view that it is *imperfect Pô'ēl* (which nowhere else occurs) can, as regards the change of ô to ŏ, be supported only by the very doubtful analogies of ψ 62⁴ (see § 52 *q*) and ψ 101⁵ *Qᵉrê* (see § 55 *b*), while the view that it is *Pi'ēl* (תְּאָבֶ׳=תְּאָב׳=תְּאַבֶּ׳) rests on no analogy whatever. It would be more admissible to suppose that תְּאָכֶ׳ stands for תְּאַבֶּ׳, *Pu'al* (cf. אֻכְּלָךְ for אֲכֻלָךְ, § 27 *q*); but no reason has been discovered for this departure from the natural punctuation תֹּאכְ׳.

2. In the 1st *pers. sing. imperfect*, where two א's would ordinarily *g* come together, the second (which is radical) is regularly dropped (§ 23 *f*), as אֹמַר ¹ (for אֶאֱמַר), &c., and even *plene* וָאוֹמַר Neh 2⁷, &c., אוֹמְרָה ψ 42¹⁰. In the other cases, also, where the א is ordinarily regarded as *quiescing* in ô or ê, it is only retained orthographically, and on etymological grounds. Hence the possibility of its being dropped in the following cases:—

Always in the contracted forms of אָסַף, as תֹּסֵף for תֹּאסֵף ψ 104²⁹; וַיֹּסֶף *h* 2 S 6¹ (but for יֵאָסֵף Jb 27¹⁹ read יוֹסֵף=יֹאסֵף with the LXX); cf. also in

---

¹ The regularity of this orthography indicates that the contraction of אֶא to *â* in this 1st pers. occurred at a time when in the 3rd and 2nd persons the א was still audible as a consonant (which accordingly was almost always retained in writing). Nöldeke (*ZDMG*. xxxii. 593) infers this from the fact that also in Arabic the 3rd and 2nd persons are still written yăˈkŭlŭ, tăˈkŭlŭ, but the 1st pers. ˈăkŭlŭ, not ˈăˈkŭlŭ.

the 1st *pers.* Mi 4⁶ and אֹסְפֵךְ 1 S 15⁶, which is apparently (from the *Metheg* with the *i*), intended for an *imperfect Hiph'il*: instead of it, however, read, with the Mantua edition, אֶסְפֵּךְ (with *i*, according to § 60 *f*). But תֵּאָסְפוּן Ex 5⁷ (for 'תֹּם), וַיֹּאסֶף 1 S 18²⁹ (for 'וַיֹּסֶף), and יֹאסַ֫ף Jb 27¹⁹ (see above) are due to a mistake, since all three forms must be derived from the stem יָסַף. Furthermore, יְמָרוּךְ ψ 139²⁰ (where certainly 'יָמֵר is to be read) ; תֹּבֵא Pr 1¹⁰ (cf. § 75 *hh*) ; וַתֹּאפֵ֫הוּ 1 S 28²⁴ ; יֹאכְלוּ Ez 42⁵ ; תֹּמְרוּ 2 S 19¹⁴ ; וַתֹּ֫חֶז 2 S 20⁹ ; תֵּזְלִי *thou gaddest about* (from אָזַל), Jer 2³⁶ ; וַיֵּתֵא Dt 33²¹ (for יֶאֱתֶה), according to other readings (on the analogy of the cases mentioned in § 75 *p*) וַיֵּתָא, וַיֵּתָא or וַיֵּ֫תָא.

Paradigm I shows the weak forms of the *imperfect Qal*, and merely indicates the other conjugations, which are regular.

i Rem. 1. In the derived conjugations only isolated weak forms occur : *Perfect Niphal* נֶאֶחֲזוּ Nu 32³⁰, Jos 22⁹ ; *Hiph.* וַיֵּאָצֶל Nu 11²⁵ (but the statement in verse 17 is וְאָֽצַלְתִּי, therefore Qal) ; equally doubtful is the punctuation of וַיֶּ֫אֱרֹב (for 'וַיֶּאֱרַב ?) *and he laid wait*, 1 S 15⁵, and אַאֲזִין *I listen*, Jb 32¹¹ (on the analogy of verbs ע״י ; cf. also אוֹכִיל (*ô* from *â*) *I give to eat*, Hos 11⁴ ; אֹבִ֫ידָה (*ô* from *â*) *I will destroy*, Jer 46⁸ ; וַיֹּ֫אחֶז 2 S 20⁵ Q^e^rê (for 'וַיֵּאָחֵ) ; the K^e^thibh appears to require the *Pi'ēl* וַיְיַחֵר, from יחר as a secondary form of אחר ; but וַיְיַחֵר = וַיְאַחֵר for וַיְאַחֵר as *imperfect Qal* is not impossible. On וְאֹֽוצְרָה Neh 13¹³, cf. § 53 *n*.—*Infinitive* לְהָכִיל Ez 21³³ (=לְהַֽאֲבִ') unless it is rather *infin. Hiph.* from כּוּל) ; *Participle* מֵזִין *giveth ear*, Pr 17⁴ (clearly by false analogy of verbs ע״י, for מַֽאֲזִין) ; *Imperative* הֵתָ֫יוּ *bring* (from אָתָה) Jer 12⁹. (On the same form used for the *perfect* in Is 21¹⁴, cf. § 76 *d*.)

k 2. In the *Pi'ēl* the א is sometimes elided (like ה in יְהַקְטִיל, הַקְטִיל), thus מַלֵּף (as in Aramaic and Samaritan) *teaching*, for מְאַלֵּף Jb 35¹¹ ; יַהֵל (if not a mere scribal error) for יַאֲהֵל Is 13²⁰ ; וַתְּזָרֵ֫נִי *thou hast girded me*, 2 S 22⁴⁰, for וַתְּאַזְּרֵ֫נִי, as ψ 18⁴⁰ ; וַֽאֲבַדֵּךְ Ez 28¹⁶ ; cf. § 23 *c*.

§ 69. *Verbs* פ״י. *First Class, or Verbs originally* פ״ו, e. g. יָשַׁב *to dwell.*

Brockelmann, *Semit. Sprachwiss.*, p. 141 f. ; *Grundriss*, p. 596 ff.

a Verbs which at present begin with Yôdh when without preformatives are divided into two classes according to their origin and consequent inflexion : (*a*) Verbs which (as still in Arabic and Ethiopic) originally began with Wāw, e. g. יָלַד *to give birth to*, Arab. and Eth. *wălădă*. In consequence of a phonetic change which prevails also with few exceptions in the noun, this Wāw in Hebrew and Aramaic always becomes a Yôdh, at least when it is the initial consonant ; but after preformatives it either reappears, or is again changed into

Yôdh, or, lastly, is altogether elided; (*b*) Verbs which (as in Arabic) originally began with Yôdh (called *Verba cum Iod originario*, see § 70). A few verbs again (some with original Yôdh, and some with original Wâw) form a special class, which in certain forms assimilates the Wâw or Yôdh to the following consonant on the analogy of the Nûn in verbs פ״נ (see § 71).

With regard to verbs פ״ו (i. e. פ״י with original Wâw) it is to be *b* noticed that—

1. In the *imperfect, imperative* and *infinitive construct Qal* there is a twofold inflexion, according as the Wâw is wholly rejected or only changed into Yôdh. The complete rejection (or *elision*) takes place regularly in eight verbs (see *h*) in the following manner:

A. *Imperfect* יֵשֵׁב, יֵרַע with an unchangeable[1] Ṣere in the first syllable and original *ĭ* in the second, which in the tone-syllable (according to § 27 *c*) becomes *ē* (thus יֵלֵד; יֵרֵד, יֵצֵא, יֵלֵךְ, see *x*), or, under the influence of a guttural, with *ă* in the second (יֵדַע, יֵקַע, יֵחַר).

The tone-long *ē* of the second syllable is of course liable to be shortened or to become Šᵉwâ, e.g. וַיֵּשֶׁב, יֵשְׁבוּ, &c.; in the same way *ă* becomes Šᵉwâ in such cases as יֵדְעוּ, &c., but is lengthened to Qameṣ in *pause* (יֵדָעוּ) and before suffixes (יֵדָעֵם).

B. *Imperative* שֵׁב with *aphaeresis* of the Wâw and with tone-long *ē*, from *ĭ*, as in the *imperfect*.

C. *Infinitive* שֶׁבֶת from original *šibh*, by addition of the feminine ending (ת) lengthened to a *segholate* form; as in verbs פ״נ (cf. § 66 *b*) this lengthening affords a certain compensation for loss of the initial consonant.

Rem. Since the infinitives לֶדָה, דֵּעָה (see below, *m*) point to a ground- *c* form *di'at, lidat*, we must, with Philippi (*ZDMG.* xxxii. 42) and Barth (ibid. xli. 606), assign to שֶׁבֶת, &c., the ground-form *šibt* (which, therefore, reappears in שִׁבְתִּי, &c.); the apparent ground-form *šabt* rests upon the law that the *ĭ* of the stem-syllable is changed into *a* whenever the syllable becomes doubly closed by the addition of the vowelless feminine ending.

---

[1] The *e* of the first syllable is really *ê*, not tone-long *ē*, since it is retained not merely before the tone, and in the counter-tone (e.g. וְיֵרְעָם Ho 14¹⁰), but also in אֵרֵעֲךָ Ex 33¹³·¹⁷. It is no objection to this view that the *scriptio plena* of this *ê* occurs (with the exception of יֵיקַר ψ 72¹⁴, elsewhere pointed יֵקַר only in Mi 1⁸ and Ez 35⁹ *Kᵉth.*; in ψ 138⁶ the Masora prefers to point יֵדָע.—Of the various explanations of the *ê* the most satisfactory is that of Philippi (*ZDMG.* xl. p. 653) that an original *yălĭd*, for example (see above), became *yilĭd* by assimilation of the vowel of the first syllable to that of the second; this then became *yêlēd* instead of *yēlēd*, in an attempt to raise the word again in this way (by writing *ê* instead of *ē*) to a triliteral form.

d   In more than half the number of verbs פ״ו the original *Wāw* in the above-mentioned forms gives place to *Yôdh*, which, unless it suffers aphaeresis (see *f*), appears:—

in the *imperatives* יְרַשׁ, יְצֵק and *infinitives* יְסֹד, יְרֹא, as a strong consonant, but

in the *imperfect* יִירַשׁ, properly *yiyraš*, merges with the preceding *i* into *î*.

In the second syllable *imperfects* of this form regularly have *ă*.

e   (*a*) That the latter forms are derived from verbs with an original *Wāw* (not *Yôdh*) is shown partly by the inflexion of these verbs in *Niphʿal*, *Hiphʿil*, and *Hophʿal* (where the original *Wāw* reappears throughout), and partly by the Arabic, in which verbs פ״ו likewise exhibit a twofold formation; cf. *wălădă*, imperf. *yălidu*, with elision of the *Wāw*, and *wăǧïlă*, *yauǧalu*, with retention of the *Wāw*.

f   (*b*) Sometimes both forms, the weaker and the stronger, occur in the same verb; cf. צֶק 2 K 4⁴¹ and יְצֹק *pour*, Ez 24³ (cf. יִצֹק 1 K 18³⁴ and the *infin.* צֶקֶת Ex 38²⁷) ; רֵשׁ *take possession*, Dt 1²¹, 1 K 21¹⁵ (but cf. *s*), רָשׁ (in pause for רֵשׁ) Dt 2²⁴·³¹ ; *plur.* רְשׁוּ Dt 1⁸, 9²³, but also, with הֵ *paragogic*, יְרָשָׁה Dt 33²³. In the *imperfect* יִיקַד Dt 32²² and יֵקַד Is 10¹⁶ *it shall be kindled*; וַיִּיקַר *it was precious*, 1 S 18³⁰ and יֵקַר ψ 49⁹ (cf. וַיֵּיקַר ψ 72¹⁴).—The form וַיֶּחֱמוּ Gn 30³⁹, for וַיֵּחַמּוּ, beside וַיֵּחַמְנָה verse 38, is remarkable ; cf. § 47 *k*.

g   (*c*) On רַד Ju 19¹¹ for יְרָד and שׁוֹב Jer 42¹⁰ for the *infinitive absolute* יָשׁוֹב, cf. § 19 *i*.—But יֵרְד Ju 5¹³ (twice) is not intended by the Masora either as *perfect* (for יָרַד, which really should be restored) or as *imperative* of יָרַד, but as an apocopated *imperfect* Piʿēl from רָדָה (=יְרַדֶּה) *to have dominion*.

h   (*d*) The eight verbs,[1] of which the initial consonant in the above-mentioned forms always suffers elision or aphaeresis, are יָלַד *to bring forth*, יָצָא *to go forth*, יָשַׁב *to sit, to dwell*, יָרַד *to descend*, also הָלַךְ *to go* (cf. below, *x*) ; and with *ă* in the second syllable of the *imperfect*, יָדַע *to know*, יָחַד *to be united*, יָקַע *to be dislocated*. Examples of the other formation (יִירַשׁ, &c.) are יָעֵף *to be wearied*, יָעַץ *to counsel*, יָשֵׁן *to sleep*, יָרֵא (*imperfect* יִירָא, *imperative* יְרָא) *to fear*.

i   2. The original *Wāw* is retained as a firm consonant: (*a*) in the *infinitive, imperative*, and *imperfect Niphʿal*, being protected by the strengthening, e. g. הִוָּשֵׁב, יִוָּשֵׁב, which are consequently strong forms like הִקָּטֵל, יִקָּטֵל; (*b*) in the *Hithpaʿel* of some verbs, e. g. הִתְוַדַּע from יָדַע, הִתְוַכַּח, יָכַח, הִתְוַדָּה from יָדָה; otherwise a radical *Wāw* at the beginning of a word is now found only in a few nouns, e. g. וָלָד *offspring* from יָלַד *to bear*. At the end of a syllable *Wāw* with the homogeneous

---

[1] A ninth יָסַף *to add*, is also to be included. In the Mêšaʿ-inscription, l. 21, the *infinitive* is written לספת (cf. יספתי, l. 29); hence read in Is 30¹ (Nu 32¹⁴, Dt 29¹⁸) סְפֵת for סְפוֹת. The 2nd *plur. masc. imperative* סְפוּ Is 29¹, Jer 7²¹ corresponds to שְׁבוּ; thus in proof of a supposed סָפָה *addere*, there remains only אַסְפָה Dt 32²³, for which, according to 2 S 12⁸, read אֹסִפָה.

vowel *ŭ* coalesces into *û*; so throughout *Hoph'al*, e. g. הוּשַׁב for
hŭwšabh; but with a preceding *a* the *Wāw* is contracted into *ô* (וֹ);
so in the *perfect* and *participle Niph'al* and throughout *Hiph'îl*, e. g.
נוֹשַׁב from an original *nāwšābh*, הוֹשִׁיב from an original *hāwšîbh*.

The first radical always appears as *Yôdh* in the *perfect* and *participle k*
Qal, יָשַׁב, &c., יָשׁוּב, יָשֵׁב, even when וְ precedes, e. g. וְיָשַׁב (but וִישַׁבְתֶּם,
according to § 24 *b*), also throughout *Pi'ēl* and *Pu'al*, e. g. יִחַל *to wait*,
יֻלַּד *to be born*, and in the *imperfect* and *participle* מְיֻדָּע, יְיַחֵל *known*
(from יָדַע), and, as a rule, also in *Hithpa'el*, e. g. הִתְיַחֵשׂ, הִתְיַצֵּב, הִתְיַלֵּד
(as against הִתְוַדַּע, &c., with *Wāw*).

The beginner may recognize verbs פ"י in the *imperfect Qal* partly by the *l*
Ṣere under the preformatives; in *Niph'al* and *Hiph'îl* by the *Wāw* (וֹ, וֹ) before
the second radical. (The defective writing, as in הֵלִיד, is rare.) Verbs
פ"ו have forms like שֵׁב (דַּע), שֶׁבֶת, in common with verbs פ"ן. Similarly
Hoph'al has the same form as in verbs ע"ע and ע"ו.

Rem. 1. The *infinitive Qal* of the weaker form (שֶׁבֶת, ground-form *šibt*, *m*
רֶשֶׁת; cf. above, *c*) with suffixes is pointed as שִׁבְתִּי,[1] רִשְׁתּוֹ (the strong form
only in לְיָרְשֶׁנּוּ Ju 14¹⁵). The masculine form is very rare, e. g. דֵּעַ *to know*,
Jb 32⁶·¹⁰, as also the feminine ending ה—, e. g. דֵּעָה[2] Ex 2⁴, לֵדָה Is 37³
(2 K 19³); Jer 13²¹, Ho 9¹¹; מֻרְדָה[2] *to descend*, Gn 46³, where the change of
the *ē* into vocal *Šewā* is to be explained, with König, from its position
between the principal and secondary tone. From יָדַע, under the influence
of the guttural, דֵּעַת is formed, with *suff.* דַּעְתִּי, &c.; but from יָצָא, צֵאת.
From יָרַד there occurs in ψ 30⁴ in *Qᵉrê* מִיָּרְדִי (the *Kᵉth.* requires מִיּוֹרְדִי) a very
remarkable case of the strong form (for מֵרִדְתִּי). For לַת 1 S 4¹⁹ (generally
explained as a case of assimilation of ד to ת in the supposed ground-form
ladt; according to Mayer Lambert pausal of לַת = *lidt*, see above, *c*) read
simply לֶדֶת.

Examples of the strong form of the *infinitive* are יְרֹא *to fear*, Jos 22²⁵, with *n*
preposition לִיסֹד Is 51¹⁶ (but 2 Ch 31⁷ according to Ben Naphtali לִיסֹד, where
the י is only retained orthographically, but is really assimilated to the ס;
the reading of Ben Asher, לִיסוֹד, accepted by Baer, is meaningless); לִישׁוֹן
Ec 5¹¹; לְרֹא 1 S 18²⁹ is irregular, but probably לִרֹא (for לִירֹא) is intended. With *suff.* בְּיִסְדָּה Jb 38⁴, cf. Ju 14¹⁵, Ezr 3¹²; with ת *fem.* יְכֹלֶת
to be able, Nu 14¹⁶. On יַבֶּשֶׁת, which is likewise usually referred to this class,
cf. the note on § 70 *a*.

---

[1] וְשַׁבְתִּי ψ 23⁶ can hardly be intended for an *infin.* with suffix from יָשַׁב,
but rather for a *perf. consec.* from שׁוּב; but read וְיָשַׁבְתִּי.

[2] The infinitives דֵּעָה and רְדָה belong to the source marked E (Dillmann's B)
in the modern criticism of the Pentateuch. The same document also has
נָתֹן *to give*, for תֵּת; הָלֹךְ *to go*, for לֶכֶת; and עָשֹׂה *to make*, for עֲשׂוֹת. See
Dillmann, *Die BB. Num., Deut., Jos.*, p. 618.

O 2. The *imperative Qal* frequently has the lengthening by הָ‎, e.g. שְׁבָה
sit thou, רְדָה descend thou. From יָהַב *to give*, Arab. *wăhăbă*, only the *imperative*
is used in Hebrew; it has the form הַב *give*, lengthened הָבָה generally with
the meaning *age, go to*, hence in Gn 11³·⁴ even addressed to several persons
(Gn 29²¹ הָבָה before א to avoid the hiatus); *fem.* הָבִי Ru 3¹⁵, *Milra'* on the
analogy of the plural הָבוּ (once in Jb 6²² הְבוּ before the tone-syllable; but cf.
Dt 32³), whilst, on the analogy of other *imperatives Qal* of verbs פ״י, הָבִי, הַבוּ
would be expected.—On דְּעֶה Pr 24¹⁴, cf. § 48 *l*.

p 3. The *imperfect* with ו elided takes ă in the second syllable, besides the
cases mentioned above (under *f*), also in תֵּרֶד Jer 13¹⁷ (cf. La 3⁴⁸) and in
the pausal form יֵלַךְ Jb 27²¹, &c. (from הָלַךְ, see *x*); on יֵקַד Is 10¹⁶ see above, *f*.
The ă in the second syllable, when followed by the affirmative תֵּרַדְנָה (נָה
&c.), is in accordance with the law mentioned above (under *c*), by which
ă takes the place of ĭ in a doubly closed syllable. Forms with ē in the
second syllable shorten the ē to *Sᵉghôl*, when the tone is drawn back (before
a tone-syllable or after *wāw consecutive*), e.g. וַיֵּשֶׁב, וַיֵּרֶד; יֵשֶׁב־נָא Gn 44³³;
but ē is retained in an open syllable, even with Mil'el-tone, in יֵצֵא Ex 16²⁹,
Ju 9³⁹, in both cases with *nasog 'aḥor*, § 29 *e*. The *pausal* is either of the
form וַיֵּשֵׁב Ru 4¹ or וַיֵּרַד ψ 18¹⁰; the 1st pers. sing., whether in or out of
pause, is וָאֵלֵךְ, וָאֵרֵד, &c., except וְאֵלַךְ Jb 19¹⁰, see *x*.—For יֵדַע ψ 138⁶ (cf. the
note above, on *b* and the analogous cases in § 70 *d*) יֵדֵע is intended.

q The *imperfect* of the form יִירָא is frequently (especially before afformatives)
written defectively, in which case the *i* can always be recognized as a long
vowel by the *Metheg* (see § 16 *f*), e.g. יָעֵפוּ Is 40³⁰, יִגְעוּ Is 65²³; and so always
יִרְאוּ *they fear*, as distinguished from יִרְאוּ *they see* (*imperf. Qal* of רָאָה).—On
וַיִּישֶׁם Gn 50²⁶, 24³³ *Kᵉth*, and יֵסַךְ Ex 30³², see § 73 *f*.

r From יָכֹל *to prevail, to be able*, the *imperfect Qal* is יוּכַל, which can only have
arisen through a depression of the vowel from יוֹכַל (ground-form *yaukhal =
yawkhal*), to distinguish it, according to Qimḥi, from אֹכַל, just as, according
to § 47 *b*, אֶקְטֹל is differentiated from יִקְטֹל. Cf. the Arabic *yauru'u* (*yôru'u*)
from *waru'a*, *yauǵalu* (*yôǵalu*) from *waǵila*, as also the vulgar Arabic (among
towns-people) *yûṣal*, &c., from *waṣala*. Others regard יוּכַל as an *imperfect Hoph'al*
(*he is enabled = he can*), always used instead of the *imperfect Qal*; cf., however,
§ 53 *u*.—וַתּוּכְל occurs in Jer 3⁵ as 2nd *sing. fem.* for וַתּוּכְלִי, according to
König because the 2nd *fem.* had been sufficiently indicated previously.—
Further יוֹרֶה or יֹרֶה is to be regarded with M. Lambert (*REJ*. xxxvii, no. 73)
as *impf. Qal* (not *Hiph'il*) of יָרָה *to throw, shoot* (the supposed *impf. Qal* וַיִּירָם
Nu 21³⁰ is critically very doubtful). This is shown especially by the passages in which the *impf*. יוֹרֶה is immediately preceded by the *imperat. Qal*
(2 K 13¹⁷) or *infin. Qal* (ψ 64⁶), or is followed by the *participle Qal* (2 Ch 35²³;
but in 2 S 11²⁴ by the *participle Hiph'il*).

s 4. The attenuation of ă to ĭ in the *perfect* (in a toneless, closed syllable)
which is discussed in § 44 *d* (cf. § 64 *f*) occurs in verbs פ״י in a few forms
of יָלַד Nu 11¹², Jer 2²⁷, ψ 2⁷, &c. (always after י), as well as of יָרֵשׁ, e.g.
וַיִּרְשְׁתֶּם, &c., Dt 4¹, 8¹, 17¹⁴, 19¹, 26¹, 31³ (always after וְ for וַ). In both
cases the attenuation might be explained from the tendency to assimilate
the vowels, especially if the initial י was pronounced, as in Syriac, like *i*
(§ 47 *b*). In the case of יָרֵשׁ, however, a secondary form יָרַשׁ (cf. § 44 *d*) is
probably to be assumed, since in Arabic also the verb was *wăriṯă*. The forms

וַיִּרֻשֹּׁוּךְ Ez 36¹² and וַיִּרְשׁוּהָ ψ 69³⁶, &c., are most simply explained from the return of this *i*.

5. As an exception, the *imperfect Niph'al* sometimes has a י instead of the *t* ו, e.g. וַיִּחַל *and he stayed*, Gn 8¹² (unless the Pi'ēl or וַיְחַל, as in ver. 10, is to be read), cf. Ex 19¹³; 1 S 13⁸ *Kethibh.*—The first person always has the form אִוָּשֵׁב, not אִוָּשֵׁב, cf. § 51 *p*.—In the *participle* the plural נוֹגֵי (from יָנָה, with depression of *ô* to *û*, cf. § 27 *n*) is found in Zp 3¹⁸; cf. La 1⁴. While in these cases some doubt may be felt as to the correctness of the Masoretic pointing, much more is this so in the perfect נוֹלְדוּ *nulledhû*, 1 Ch 3⁵, 20⁸, for נוֹלְדוּ which appears to be required by the *wāw* in the initial syllable.

6. In the *imperfect Pi'ēl* elision of the first radical (י) sometimes takes place *u* after *wāw consec.* (as in the case of א, § 68 *k*), e.g. וַיַּגֶּה for וַיִּיגֶּה *and he has grieved*, La 3³³, and וַיַּדּוּ for וַיִּידּוּ *and they have cast*, verse 53, from יָרָה, which may also be a true verb פ״י (on the other hand, in יַדּוּ גוֹרָל *they have cast lots*, Jo 4³, Ob¹¹, Na 3¹⁰, a *perfect Qal* of יָדַד is required by the context; but as this, being a *transitive* perfect, ought to have the form יָדְדוּ according to § 67 *a*, perhaps we should read יַדּוּ). So from a verb פ״י, of the second class, וַיְבַּשֵּׁהוּ for וַיְיַבְּשֵׁהוּ *and he made it dry*, Na 1⁴; cf. וַיַּשְׁרֶם 2 Ch 32³⁰ *Qerê* (the *Keth.* points either to Pi'ēl וַיְיַשְּׁרֶם or Hiph'il וַיַּישִׁרֶם).

7. The *imperative Hiph'il*, instead of the usual form הוֹשֵׁב, sometimes has *i* in *v* the second syllable; הוֹצִיא Is 43⁸; הוֹפִיעַ ψ 94¹ (before ה, hence probably a mere mistake for הוֹפִיעָה). On the uncertainty of the tone in הוֹשִׁיעָה־נָּא see § 53 *m*. When closed by a guttural the second syllable generally has *ă*, as הוֹדַע הוֹשַׁע, cf. also הֹקַר Pr 25¹⁷ (as in the *infin. constr.* הוֹכַח Jb 6²⁶; see § 65 *f*). On the other hand, *i* always appears when the syllable is open, thus הוֹשִׁיבִי הוֹשִׁיבָה, and so also before suffixes (§ 61 *g*). הַיְצֵא Gn 8¹⁷ *Qerê* (*Keth.* הוֹצֵא, see § 70 *b*) is irregular.—The *jussive* and the *imperfect consecutive Hiph'il* when the tone is drawn back take *Seghôl* in the second syllable, as in Qal, e.g. יוֹסֵף *that he may increase*, Pr 1⁵, before לֶקַח; cf. Ex 10²⁸ and Dt 3²⁶ after אַל־; וַיֹּסֶף (תּוֹסֵף Pr 30⁶ is anomalous); in *pause*, however, also תֹּסַף as *jussive*, Jb 40³² (usual *jussive* in *pause* יוֹשֵׁב, &c., which occurs even without the pause after *wāw consecutive*, Gn 47¹¹, Jos 24³, 2 S 8⁴, &c.). With a final guttural יֹדַע and יוֹכַח (*jussive*) and וַיּוֹכַח, &c.; with a final ר in *pause* וַתֹּתַר Ru 2¹⁴: on וַיְשַׁעְכֶם Is 35⁴, cf. § 65 *f*).—On forms like יְהוֹשִׁיעַ, see § 53 *q*.

In *Hoph'al ô* stands instead of ו, in הוֹרַע (for הוּרַע) Lv 4²³·²⁸, הֹנַח 2 S 20¹³, *w* and perhaps in יוֹרָא (for יוּרָה) Pr 11²⁵; but cf. Delitzsch on the passage.— Ptcp. מוּרַעַת Is 12⁵ *Qere* (מוֹדַעַת *Keth*).—An *infinitive Hoph'al* with feminine ending occurs in הֻלֶּדֶת Gn 40²⁰, for הֻלָּדֶת = הֻגַּל/; cf. above, *t*, on נוֹלְדוּ, and § 71 at the end.

8. The verb הָלַךְ *to go*, also belongs in some respects to the פ״י class, since it *x* forms (as if from וָלַךְ) *imperfect* יֵלֵךְ, with *wāw consecutive* וַיֵּלֶךְ (in *pause* וַיֵּלַךְ Gn 24⁶¹, &c.), 1st sing. וָאֵלֵךְ (but in Jb 19¹⁰ וָאֵלַךְ); *infinitive construct* לֶכֶת with suff. לֶכְתִּי (*Seghôl* under the influence of the following palatal, as in נֶכְדִּי, cf. also נֶגְדִּי); *imperative* לֵךְ, לֶךְ־ לָךְ, in the lengthened form לְכָה (as an interjection referring even to a *feminine*, Gn 19³², or a *plural*, Gn 31⁴⁴) and לָךְ (Nu 23¹³, Ju 19¹³, 2 Ch 25¹⁷); *Hiph.* הוֹלִיךְ (also in Ex 2⁹ הוֹלִיכִי 2nd *fem.* *imperative* is to be read for הֵילִיכִי, which probably arose merely through

confusion with the following וְהִנִּקֻהוּ) ; *imperfect* יוֹלִיךְ, but in the 1st sing. of the *imperfect consecutive* always וָאֹלֵךְ Lv 26¹³, Am 2¹⁰, &c. Rarely, and almost exclusively late or in poetry, the regular inflexions of הָלַךְ are also found : *imperf.* יֶהֱלַךְ (ψ 58⁹, &c. ; but תְּהֲלַךְ Ex 9²³, ψ 73⁹ ; cf. § 64 *a* and *h*) ; אֶהֱלֹךְ Jb 16²², also Mêša' inscription, line 14, אהלך ; *infin.* הֲלֹךְ (Ex 3¹⁹, Nu 22¹³ f.¹⁶, 1 Ec 6⁸·⁹) ; *imperative plur.* הִלְכוּ Jer 51⁵⁰. On the other hand, the *perfect Qal* is always הָלַךְ, *participle* הֹלֵךְ, *infinitive absolute* הָלוֹךְ, *Niph'al* נֶהֱלַךְ, *Pi'êl* הִלֵּךְ, *Hithpa'êl* הִתְהַלֵּךְ, so that a י never appears unmistakably as the first radical. The usual explanation of the above forms is nevertheless based on a supposed obsolete יָלַךְ. It is, however, more correct to regard the apparent פ"ו forms of הלך with Praetorius (*ZAW.* ii. 310 ff.) as originating with the Hiph'il, of which the ground-form *hahlikh* became *hâlikh*, and this again, on the analogy of the *imperfect Qal* of verbs פ"א, *hôlîkh.* This *hôlîkh* being referred to a supposed *haulikh* (properly *hawlikh*) gave rise to new formations after the manner of verbs פ"ו.

§ 70. Verbs פ"י. Second Class, or Verbs properly פ"י, e. g. יָטַב to be good. Paradigm L.

Brockelmann, *Semit. Sprachwiss.*, p. 143 ff. ; *Grundriss*, p. 603 ff.

Verbs properly פ"י differ from verbs פ"ו in the following points :

a　1. In *Qal* the initial Yôdh never suffers aphaeresis or elision ; hence the *infinitive* has the form יְבֹשׁ,² the *imperfect* יִיטַב, יִיקַץ, יִינַק (in *pause* יִיקָץ), also written יֵטַב, &c. ; and so always with a tone-bearing *ă* in the second syllable, even after *wāw consec.*, e. g. וַיִּיטֶב, except וַיִּיקֶץ Gn 9²⁴, and וַיִּיצֶר Gn 2⁷·¹⁹, unless יָצַר is to be included among verbs פ"ו (cf. נוֹצַר Is 43¹⁰).

b　2. In *Hiph'îl* the original form הַיְטִיב is regularly contracted to הֵיטִיב (rarely written הֵיטֵב, הֵימֵב, &c.) ; *imperfect* יֵיטִיב, וַיֵּיטֶב. Instances of the uncontracted form are יְיַשְּׁרוּ Pr 4²⁵, according to Barth (see above, § 67 *p*), an example of an *i-imperfect* of *Qal*, since the *Hiph'îl* is otherwise always *causative* ; הַיְשֵׁר (*imperative*) ψ 5⁹ *Qerê* (the *Keth.* requires הוֹשֵׁר according to the form of verbs פ"ו ; cf. Is 45², אוֹשִׁר *Keth.*, אֲיַשֵּׁר *Qerê*), cf. Gn 8¹⁷ *Qerê* ; מֵימִינִים 1 Ch 12², to be explained as a denominative from יָמִין ; אֵיסִירֶם Ho 7¹² (§ 24 *f*, note), but perhaps the punctuation here is only intended to suggest another reading אֲיַסְּרֵם.

---

¹ Cf. above, *m*, note 2.

² This may be inferred from בִּיבֹשׁ (= בְּיִ) Is 27¹¹, which with its fem. יְבֹשֶׁת Gn 8⁷, is the only example of an infinitive *construct Qal* of these verbs. No example of the *imperative Qal* is found : consequently the forms יְטַב, &c. (in Paradigm L of the earlier editions of this Grammar), are only inferred from the *imperfect*.

Rem. 1. The only verbs of this kind are : יָטַב *to be good* (only in the C *imperfect Qal* and in *Hiph'il* ; in the *perfect Qal* טוֹב, a verb ע״ו, is used instead), יָנַק *to suck*, יָקץ *to awake*, יָצַר *to form* (but see above, *a*), יָלַל only in *Hiph'il* הֵילִיל *to bewail*, יָשַׁר *to be straight, right*, also יָבֵשׁ (Arabic *yábïsä*) *to be dry* (but *Hiph'il* הוֹבִישׁ 2 S 19⁶, on the analogy of verbs פ״ו ; on Is 30⁵, cf. § 72 *x*), and the *Hiph'il* הֵימִין (denominative from יָמִין), infin. לְהֵימִן 2 S 14¹³ *to go to the right*.

2. In some examples of the *imperfect Hiph'il* the preformative has been subsequently added to the contracted form : יֵיטִיב Jb 24²¹ ; יְיֵלִיל Is 15²·³, 16⁷ ; אֲיֵלִיל Jer 48³¹ ; plur. יְיֵלִילוּ Ho 7¹⁴, cf. Is 65¹⁴. Qimḥi and others explain the above forms from a phonetic interchange of *Yôdh* and *He*, arising from the unsyncopated forms יְהֵילִיל, &c. (cf. Is 52⁵). It is, perhaps, more correct to suppose that the regular forms (יֵילִיל יֵיטִיב) were originally intended, but that in the later pronunciation the syllable was broken up in order to restore artificially the preformative which had become merged in the first radical.

Isolated anomalies are : *perfect Hiph'il* וְהֵיטַבְתִּי Ez 36¹¹ with separating vowel (for הֵיטַבְתִּי) on the analogy of verbs ע״ו ; *imperfect* יֵיטִיב for יֵיטִב 1 K 14⁷ ; תֵּיטְבִי (*imperfect Qal* for תִּיטְבִי) Na 3⁸ ; וַתִּינְקֵהוּ *imperfect Hiph'il* Ex 2⁹, either an error for וַתֵּינִק, or an irregular shortening of the first syllable, caused by the forward movement of the tone. Similarly, the *Hiph'il* הֵקִיץ (from קִיץ) is always used instead of הֵיקִיץ from יָקֵץ ; hence also הֲקִיצֹתִי, הֲקִיצֹות, *imperat.* הָקִיצָה, *infin.* הָקִיץ.—On וַיַּבְשֵׁהוּ Na 1⁴, see § 69 *u*).

§ 71. Verbs פ״י. *Third Class, or Verbs with Yôdh assimilated.*

In some verbs פ״י, the *Yôdh* (or the original *Wāw*) does not quiesce in the preceding vowel, but is regarded as a full consonant, and, like *Nûn*,[1] is assimilated to the following consonant. These forms, therefore, belong properly to the class of strong verbs. Assimilation invariably takes place in יָצַע (prop. וצע) *to spread under* ; *Hiph'il* הִצִּיעַ, *Hoph'al* הֻצַּע ; יָצַת *to burn*, imperfect יִצַּת, *Niph'al* נִצַּת, *Hiph'il* הִצִּית (in Is 27⁴ also אַצִּיתֶנָּה is to be read with König ; in 2 S 14³⁰ the Masora has rightly emended the *Kethîbh* והוצתיה, which could only be the 1st sing. perf. of a verb פ״ו, to the imperative וְהַצִּיתוּהָ in agreement with the context and all the early versions) ; יָצַג, *Hiph'il* הִצִּיג *to place*, *Hoph'al* הֻצַּג ; and probably also in the forms ordinarily derived from נָצַב, viz. נִצַּב (*Niph'al*), הִצִּיב, יַצִּיב, הַצֵּב ; at any rate a stem יָצַב is implied by the *Hithpa'ēl* הִתְיַצֵּב ; instead of the anomalous וַתְּתַצַּב Ex 2⁴ read with the Samaritan ותתיצב, i.e. וַתִּתְיַצֵּב. Besides the common form we find once אֶצָּק in Is 44³ (from יָצַק *to pour*) with a *transitive* meaning, beside וַיִּצֶק *intransitive*, 1 K 22³⁵. Elsewhere the *imperfect*

---

[1] These verbs, like verbs ע״ע (cf. above, note on § 67 *g*), may perhaps have been influenced by the analogy of verbs פ״ן.

consecutive has the form וַיִּצֶק Gn 28¹⁸, 35¹⁴, &c., cf. § 69*f*, where also other forms of יָצַק are given; וַיִּיצֶר and יָצֹר (Is 44¹², 49⁸, Jer 1⁵ *Qᵉrê*), from יָצַר *to form*, are, however, used in the same sense. Cf. also אֶפְרֵם Ho 10¹⁰; וַיִּשְׁרֵנָה (for וַתְּ according to § 47 *k*) 1 S 6¹²; לִיסֹד 2 Ch 31⁷ (cf. § 69 *n*) and מוּפָד Is 28¹⁶. This assimilation is found always with sibilants (most frequently with צ) except in the case of וַיִּקַּץ 1 K 3¹⁵ (εo ed. Mant., Ginsb., Kittel; but Jabl., Baer וַיָּקַץ) and in הֻלֶּדֶת Gn 40²⁰, Ez 16⁵ (cf. הֻלֶּדֶת verse 4), *infinitive Hophʿal* of יָלַד (cf. נוּלְדוּ § 69 *t*).

§ 72. Verbs ע״וּ (*vulgo* ע״ו), e. g. קוּם *to rise up. Paradigm M.*

Brockelmann, *Semit. Sprachwiss.*, p. 144 ff. ; *Grundriss*, p. 605 ff.

a 1. According to § 67 *a* a large number of monosyllabic stems were brought into agreement with the triliteral form by a strengthening, or repetition, of the second radical, i. e. of the *consonantal* element in the stem. In another large class of stems the same object has been attained by strengthening the *vocalic* element. The ground-form used for these verbs is not, as in other cases (§ 39 *a*), the 3rd *sing. masc. perfect*, but always the *infinitive construct* form (§ 39 *b*), the *û* of which is characteristic also of the *imperative* and of the *imperfect indicative Qal*. These stems are consequently termed verbs ע״ו or more correctly (see below) ע״וּ.[1]

---

[1] The term ע״ו was consequent on the view that the *Wāw* (or ' in the case of verbs ע״י) in these stems was originally consonantal. This view seemed especially to be supported by the return of the *Wāw* in *Piʿēl* (עֵוֵר, the ו usually passing into ' as in קִים, cf. Arabic *qáwwămă*), and by certain forms of the *absolute state* of the nouns of such stems, e. g. מָוֶת *death*, compared with מוּת *to die*. Hence in explaining the verbal forms a supposed stem *qawam* (in verbs ע״י e. g. *šayat*) was always assumed, and יָקוּם was referred to an original *yaqwăm*, the *infinitive absolute* קוֹם to original *qawôm*, the *participle passive* קוּם to original *qawûm*. It must, however, be admitted : (1) that forms like עֵוֵר, קִים (see *m*) are only to be found in the latest books, and are hence evidently secondary as compared with the pure Hebrew forms קוֹמֵם, &c. ; (2) that to refer the verbal forms invariably to the stem קַום, leads in many cases to phonetic combinations which are essentially improbable, whereas the assumption of original *middle-vowel* stems renders a simple and natural explanation almost always possible. These ע״וּ stems are therefore to be rigidly distinguished from the real ע״ו stems of the strong forms, such as גָּוַע, רָוַח, &c. (see below, *gg*).—As early as the eleventh century the right view with regard to ע״וּ stems was taken by Samuel Hannagîd (cf. Bacher, *Leben und Werke des Abulwalʿid*, p. 16) ; recently by Böttcher (*Lehrbuch*, § 1112), and (also as to ע״י stems) especially by Müller, Stade, and Wellhausen (see above, § 67 *a*, note). On the other hand, the old view of ו and ' as consonants has been recently revived by Philippi, Barth, M. Lambert, and especially Brockelmann (op. cit.).

2. As in the case of verbs ע״ע, the monosyllabic stem of verbs ע״י *b* generally takes the vowel which would have been required in the *second* syllable of the ordinary strong form, or which belonged to the ground-form, since this is essentially characteristic of the verbal form (§ 43 *b*; § 67 *b*). However, it is to be remarked: (*a*) that the vowel, short in itself, becomes of necessity long in an open syllable as well as in a tone-bearing closed *ultima* (except in *Hoph'al*, see *d*), e. g. 3rd *sing. masc. perf.* קָם, *fem.* קָמָה, *plur.* קָמוּ, but in a closed *penultima* קַמְתְּ, &c.[1]; (*b*) that in the forms as we now have them the lengthening of the original short vowel sometimes takes place irregularly. Cf. *f*.

Intransitive verbs *middle e* in the *perfect Qal* have the form מֵת *he* *c* *is dead*; verbs *middle o* have the form אוֹר *he shone*, בֹּשׁ *he was ashamed*, טוֹב *he was good*.[2] Cf. *n–r*.

3. In the *imperfect Qal, perfect Niph'al*, and throughout *Hiph'il* and *d* *Hoph'al* the short vowel of the preformatives in an open syllable before the tone is changed into the corresponding tone-long vowel. In *Qal* and *Niph'al* the original *ă* is the basis of the form and not the *ĭ* attenuated from *ă* (§ 67 *h*; but cf. also *h* below, on יֵבֹשׁ), hence יָקוּם, for *yăqûm*; נָקוֹם for *năqôm*; on the other hand, in the *perfect Hiph'il* הֵקִים for *hĭqîm*; *participle* מֵקִים (on the Ṣere cf. *z*); *perfect Hoph'al* הוּקַם for *hŭqam*.

A vowel thus lengthened before the tone is naturally changeable and *e* becomes *vocal Šĕwâ* when the tone is moved forward, e.g. יְמִיתֶנּוּ *he will kill him*; so also in the 3rd *plur. imperfect Qal* with *Nûn paragogic*; יְמוּתוּן (without *Nûn* יְמוּתוּ). The wholly abnormal *scriptio plena* of *ē* in הַהֵימִיר Jer 2[11] (beside הֵמִיר in the same verse) should, with König, be emended to הֲיָמִיר; the incorrect repetition of the interrogative necessarily led to the pointing of the form as *perfect* instead of *imperfect*.—But in *Hoph'al* the *û* is retained throughout as an unchangeable vowel, when it has been introduced by an abnormal lengthening for the tone-long *ō* (as in the *Hoph'al* of verbs ע״ע).

---

[1] In Aramaic, however, always קָמַת; also in Hebrew grammars before Qimḥi קָמְתָּ, קָמְתִּי, &c., are found, but in our editions of the Bible this occurs only in *pause*, e. g. קַמְתִּי Mi 7[8], מַתְנוּ 2 K 7[3,4].

[2] According to Stade (*Grammatik*, § 385 *e* and *f*) the *e* in מֵת is of the nature of a diphthong (from *ai*, which arose from the union of the vowel *ĭ*, the sign of the intransitive, with the *ă* of the root), and likewise the *o* in אוֹר, &c. (from *au*). But *ô* (from *au*) could not, by § 26 *p*, remain in a closed penultima (בֹּשְׁתְּ, &c.); consequently the *o* of these forms can only be tone-long, i. e. due to lengthening of an original *ŭ*, and similarly the *ē* of מֵת to lengthening of an original *ĭ*. This is confirmed by the fact that the *ō* in בֹּשְׁתְּ בֹּשְׁתִּי, בֹּשְׁנוּ is always, and in בֹּשׁוּ, 3rd *plur. perfect*, nearly always (the instances are 11 to 2), written defectively. Forms like בּוֹשָׁה בּוֹשׁוּ, אוֹרוּ, &c., are therefore due to orthographic licence.

f   4. The cases of unusual vowel lengthening mentioned in *b* are: imperfect Qal יָקוּם (also in Arabic *yăqûmu*), but *jussive* with normal lengthening (§ 48 *g*), יָקֹם, with retraction of the tone יָ֫קֹם (*yāqŏm*), וַיָּ֫קֹם (in *pause* יָקֹ֑ם); *imperative* קוּם, with normal lengthening of the *ŭ* in the 2nd *plur. fem.* קֹ֫מְנָה, since, according to § 26 *p*, the *û* cannot be retained in a closed penultima; *infinitive construct* קוּם. In *Hiph'il* the original *ĭ* is naturally lengthened to *î* (הֵקִים, imperfect יָקִים, jussive יָקֵם, with retraction of the tone יָ֫קֵם, וַיָּ֫קֵם); on the transference of this *î* to the *Hiph'îl* of the strong verb, cf. § 53 *a*.

g   The following forms require special consideration: the *participle Qal* קָם is to be traced to the ground-form with *â* unobscured, Arab. *qâtil*, § 9 *q*, and § 50 *b*. On this analogy the form would be *qâim*,[1] which after absorption of the *ĭ* became קָם, owing to the predominating character of the *â*. The unchangeableness of the *â* (*plur.* קָמִים, constr. קָמֵי, &c.) favours this explanation.

h   In the *imperfect Qal*, besides the forms with original *ŭ* (now *û*) there are also forms with original *ă*. This *ă* was lengthened to *ā*, and then further obscured to *ô*; hence especially יָבוֹא (יָבֹא), וַיָּבֹא, &c., from the perfect בָּא *he has come*. In the *imperfects* יָאוֹר (but cf. וַתָּאֹ֫רְנָה 1 S 14²⁷) and יֵבוֹשׁ from the *intransitive perfects* אוֹר, בֹּשׁ (see above, *c*), most probably also in יֵאֹ֫תוּ 2 K 12⁹, נֵאוֹת Gn 34¹⁵ from an unused אוֹת *to consent*, and perhaps in וַתֵּהֹם 1 S 4⁵, &c., as in the cases noticed in § 63 *e* and especially § 67 *n*, the *ē* of the preformative is lengthened from *ĭ* (which is attenuated from original *ă*) and thus *yĭ-băš* became *yĭ-bāš*, and finally *yē-bôš*. Finally the *Niph.* נָקוֹם (*nă-qām*), *imperfect* יִקּוֹם from *yiqqām*, originally (§ 51 *m*) *yinqăm*, arises in the same way from the obscuring of *ā* lengthened from *ă*.

i   5. In the *perfect Niph'al* and *Hiph'îl* a ו is inserted before the afformatives beginning with a consonant in the 1st and 2nd persons, and ־ֶי regularly (but see Rem.) in the *imperfect Qal*, sometimes also in the *imperfect Hiph'îl* (as in תְּבִיאֶ֫ינָה Lv 7³⁰, cf. תְּהִימֶ֫נָה Mi 2¹²), before the termination of נָה. As in verbs ע״ע (§ 67 *d* and note) these *separating vowels* serve as an artificial opening of the preceding syllable, in order to preserve the long vowel; in the *perfect Hiph'îl*, however, before the ו, instead of the *î* an *ē* is somewhat often found[2] (as a normal lengthening of the original *ĭ*), especially after *wāw con-*

---

[1] So in Arabic, prop. *qâ'im*, since the two vowels are kept apart by the insertion of an א, cf. Aram. קָאֵם; but also contracted, as *šâk*, *hâr*, for *šā'ik*, &c. (cf. Wright's *Gramm. of the Arabic Language*, 2nd ed. vol. i. p. 164).

[2] וַהֲשִׁיבֹתֶם 1 S 6⁷ (cf. 2 Ch 6²⁵) could only be an orthographic licence for וַהֲשִׁבֹ׳; perhaps, however, וַהֲשִׁיב׳ was originally intended.

secutive, Dt 4³⁹, 30¹, as well as before the afformatives תֶּם and תֶּן or before suffixes, Dt 22², 1 S 6⁸, 1 K 8³⁴, Ez 34⁴. For in all these cases the tone is removed from the ־ֵ to the following syllable, and this forward movement of the tone produces at the same time a weakening of the *i* to *ē*; thus הֲקִימֹ֫וֹת, הֲקֵים (or הֲקֵ֑ם; on הַעֲרֹ֫תָה Ex 19²³, cf. x), but וַהֲקֵמֹתָ, &c., Ex 26³⁰, &c.; Dt 4³⁹, Nu 18²⁶ (cf., however, וַהֲקֵמֹנוּ Mi 5⁴). In the same way in the 1st *pers. sing.* of the *perfect Niph'al*, the *ô* before the separating vowel is always modified to *û* (נְקוּמֹ֫ותִי); cf. *v*. In the *imperfect Qal* and *Hiph'îl* the separating vowel ־ֶ֫י always bears the tone (תְּקוּמֶ֫ינָה).

Without the separating vowel and consequently with the tone-long *ō* and *k ē* instead of *û* and *i* we find in *imperfect Qal* תָּבֹ֫אנָה (see § 76 *g*); תֵּשֹׁ֫בְןָ Ez 16⁵⁵ (also תְּשׁוּבֶ֫ינָה in the same verse); וַתָּשֹׁ֫בְנָה 1 S 7¹⁴ (cf. Ez 35⁹ Q°rê; on the K°thibh תֵּשַֹׁ֫בְנָה cf. above, note on § 69 *b*); וַתָּאֹ֫רְנָה 1 S 14²⁷ from אוֹר (K°thibh וַתִּרְאֶ֫נָה *and they saw*, see § 75 *w*); in *Hiph'îl*, e.g. הֲנִבַּ֫פַת Ex 20²⁵, also הֲנִיפֹ֫ותִי Jb 31²¹; וַהֲטִלְתִּי Jer 22²⁶; תֵּשַֹׁ֫בְנָה Jb 20¹⁰; with a separating vowel, e.g. תְּבִיאֶ֫ינָה Lv. 7³⁰ from בּוֹא. S°ghôl without ־י occurs in the *imperfect Qal* in תְּמוּתֶ֫נָה Ez 13¹⁹, Zc 1¹⁷; and in *Hiph'îl* Mi 2¹²: the Dageš in the *Nûn* is, with Baer, to be rejected in all three cases according to the best authorities. Wholly abnormal is תָּקֵ֫ימְנָה Jer 44²⁵, probably an erroneous transposition of ימ (for תְּקֵימֶ֫נָה), unless it originates from an incorrect spelling תָּקֵימְנָה or תְּקִימֶ֫נָה.

6. The tone, as in verbs ע"ע (cf. § 67 *k*), is also generally retained *l* on the stem-syllable in verbs ע"י before the afformatives ־ָה, ־ו, ־ִי; thus קָ֫מָה (but also בָּזָ֫ה לְךָ 2 K 19²¹, probably for the sake of rhythmical uniformity with the following לַעֲנָה לָךְ; after *wāw consecutive* וְשָׁ֫בָה Is 23¹⁷); קָ֫מוּ (but also קָ֫מוּ, cf. Is 28⁷, 29⁹, Na 3¹⁸, ψ 76⁶, Pr 5⁶, La 4¹⁸; וְרָ֫צוּ 1 S 8¹¹; so especially before a following א, cf. § 49 *l*, Nu 13³²; וְנָ֫עוּ Is 19¹; before ע, ψ 131¹, Pr 30¹³, La 4¹⁴); יָק֫וּמוּ, תָּק֫וּמִי, but before a *suffix* or with *Nûn paragogic* וִיסֻבּ֫וּם 2 Ch 28¹⁵; יְקוּמ֫וּן Dt 33¹¹, &c.

7. The formation of the conjugations *Pi'ēl, Pu'al,* and *Hithpa'ēl* is, *m* strictly speaking, excluded by the nature of verbs ע"י. It is only in the latest books that we begin to find a few secondary formations, probably borrowed from Aramaic, on the analogy of verbs ע"י (with consonantal ו, see below, *gg*); e.g. the *Pi'ēl* עֻוֵּד *to surround,* only in עֹֽוְדֵ֫נִי ψ 119⁶¹; and with change of ו to י, קַיֵּם Est 9³¹, קִיְּמוּ Est 9²⁷, impf. וָאֲקַיְּמָה ψ 119¹⁰⁶, infin. קַיֵּם Ez 13⁶, Ru 4⁷ &c., Est 9²¹ &c., imperat. קַיְּמִי ψ 119²⁸; וְחַיַּבְתֶּם Dn 1¹⁰ from חוּב *to be guilty.* The *Hithpa'ēl* הִצְטַיָּד Jos 9¹², which belongs to the older language, is probably a denominative from צֵיד. On the other hand the otherwise less common conjugation *Pôlēl* (see § 55 *c*), with its passive and reflexive, is usually

employed in the sense of *Piʿēl* and as a substitute for it, e. g. קוֹמֵם *to set up* from קוּם; מוֹתֵת *to slaughter*, 1 S 14¹³, 17⁵¹, 2 S 1⁹, from מות; רוֹמֵם *to exalt*, passive רוֹמַם, from רום; reflexive הִתְעוֹרֵר *to stir up oneself* (cf. יִתְעֹרָר Jb 17⁸ in *pause*) from עוּר; reciprocal הִתְבּשֵׁשׁ *to be ashamed before one another*, Gn 2²⁵. The conjugation *Pilpēl* (§ 55 *f*), on the analogy of verbs ע″ע, is less common, e. g, טִלְטֵל *to hurl away* from טול; כִּלְכֵּל *to contain* from כול; קַרְקַר *to destroy* from קור.

R E M A R K S.

I. *On Qal.*

n   1. Of verbs *middle e* and *o*, in which, as in the strong verb, the *perfect* and *participle* have the same form (§ 50. 2), the following are the only examples: מֵת *he is dead*, *fem.* מֵתָה, 2nd *masc.* מַתָּה (cf. § 44 *g*; § 66 *h*); 1st *sing.* מַתִּי, וָמַתִּי (even in *pause*, Gn 19¹⁹); *plur.* מֵתוּ, 1st *pers.* מַתְנוּ, in *pause* מָתְנוּ; בּשׁ *he was ashamed*, בִּשְׁתָּ, בִּשְׁתִּי, בּשְׁנוּ; בּשׁ; אוֹר *it has shone*, *plur.* אוֹרוּ; טוֹב *to be good*, טֹבוּ. *Participles* מֵת *a dead man* (*plur.* מֵתִים); מֵתֵי) בּשִׁים *ashamed*, Ez 32³⁰. For גֵּר Is 27¹¹ read נֵד, or, with LXX, עַד.

o   Isolated anomalies in the *perfect* are: וְשָׁבַת (with the original ending of the *fem.* for וְשָׁבָה) Ez 46¹⁷ (see § 44 *f*); צָקוּן Is 26¹⁶ (see § 44 *l*).—In בָּנוּ 1 S 25⁸ (for בָּאנוּ from בּוֹא) the א has been dropped contrary to custom. In יָבֹאוּ Jer 27¹⁸ (instead of בָּאוּ) the Masora seems to point to the *imperfect* which is what would be expected; as *Yôdh* precedes, it is perhaps simply a scribal error.

p   The form קָם occurs (cf. § 9 *b*) with א in the *perfect*, קָאם Ho 10¹⁴, also in the *participles* לָאט *softly*, Ju 4²¹, רָאשׁ *poor*, 2 S 12¹·⁴, Pr 10⁴, *plur.* 13²³; שָׁאטִים *doing despite unto* (unless שָׁאֲטִים is to be read, from a stem שׁאט whence שָׁאט Ez 25¹⁵, 36⁵), Ez 28²⁴·²⁶; *fem.* 16⁵⁷; also in Zc 14¹⁰ רָאֲמָה is to be read with Ben-Naphtali for רָאֲמָה. On the analogy of participles of verbs *middle ō* (like בּשִׁים, see above) קוֹמִים occurs for קָמִים 2 K 16⁷ and even with a transitive meaning לוֹט *occultans*, Is 25⁷; בּוֹסִים Zc 10⁵.—*Participle passive*, מוּל *circumcised*; but סוּג *a backslider*, Pr 14¹⁴, and סוּרָה *put aside*, Is 49²¹ (cf. Jer 17¹³ Q⁰rê), are verbal adjectives of the form *qāṭūl* (§ 50 *f*), not passive participles. For חֻשִׁים *hastening*, Nu 32¹⁷, read חֲמֻשִׁים as in Ex 13¹⁸; for שׁבִי Mi 2⁸ read שֵׁבִי.

q   2. Imperfects in *û* almost always have the corresponding *imperative* and *infinitive construct* in *û*, as יָקוּם, *imperative* and *infinitive* קוּם (also defectively written קֻם, יָקֻם); but יָדֹשׁ *he threshes* (*infin.* דּוֹשׁ), has *imperative* דּוֹשִׁי (*fem.*), Mi 4¹³; יָמוֹט *it slippeth*, *infinitive* מוֹט (ψ 38¹⁷, 46³); cf. נוֹחַ (also נֻחַ) Nu 11²⁵ and נוֹעַ Is 7² (elsewhere נוּעַ) with the *imperfects* יָנוּחַ and יָנוּעַ; לָעוּז Is 30²; שׁוּב Jos 2¹⁶; רוּם Ez 10¹⁷ (verse 16 רֻם).

r   Where the *imperfect* (always intransitive in meaning) has *ô* the *imperative* and *infinitive* also have it; thus *imperfect* יָבוֹא (יָבֹא), *infin.* and *imper.* בּוֹא or בֹּא¹; וַיָּאר 2 S 2³², אוֹרוּ, אֹרוּ; בּוֹשׁ, יָבוֹשׁ, &c.—יָקוֹם Jb 8¹⁴ (if it be a verb at all and not rather a substantive) is formed on the analogy of verbs ע″ע,

---

¹ In 1 K 14¹² בְּבֹאָה before a genitive), the text is evidently corrupt: read with Klostermann after the LXX בְּבֹאֵךְ.

since the *imperfect* of קוּט appears as אָקוּט in ψ 95¹⁰. On the other hand יִקְשׁוּן (as if from קוֹשׁ, on the analogy of יָבוֹא, &c.) occurs as *imperfect* of יָקֹשׁ (פ״י). The *imperfect* יָדוֹן, with ô, Gn 6³, probably in the sense of *to rule*, has no corresponding *perfect*, and is perhaps intentionally differentiated from the common verb יָדִין *to judge* (from דִּין, ע״י). Or can יָדוֹן be a *jussive* after לֹא (cf. § 109 *d*)? Similarly לֹא תָחוֹם עֵינִי (עֵינְךָ) might be taken as a case of a *jussive* after לֹא, with irregular *scriptio plena* (as in Ju 16³⁰), in Dt 7¹⁶, 13⁹, 19¹³·²¹, 25¹², Ez 5¹¹, 7⁴·⁹, 8¹⁸, 9¹⁰. But perhaps in all these cases לֹא תָחוֹם was originally intended, as in Is 13¹⁸, Jer 21⁷, while cases like יָחֹם ψ 72¹³ are to be explained as in § 109 *k*.—The *infinitive absolute* always has ô, e.g. קוֹם יָקוּמוּ Jer 44²⁹.

3. In the *imperative* with afformatives (קֻמוּ, קֹמִי) the tone is on the stem *s* syllable (cf., however, עוּרִי Ju 5¹² intentionally varied from עֹרִי; also עוּרִי Zc 13⁷ and Is 51⁹ beside עֹרִי, עוּרִי כִּימֵי; גִּילִי Zc 9⁹; צוּרִי Is 21², שׁוּבִי ψ 116⁷, likewise for rhythmical reasons). So also the lengthened form, as שׁוּבָה Jer 3¹², ψ 7⁸, and עוּרָה verse 7. But if an א follows in close connexion, the lengthened *imperative* usually has the form קוּמָה, &c.,¹ in order to avoid a hiatus, e.g. Ju 4¹⁸, ψ 82⁸; hence also before יְהֹוָה, *Qerê perpetuum* אֲדֹנָי (§ 17 *c*), e.g. ψ 3⁸, 7⁷ קוּמָה (cf., however, in the same verse עוּרָה and in Jer 40⁵, שֵׁבָה before א), and so even before ר ψ 43¹, 74²², &c. (רִיבָה).

4. In the *jussive*, besides the form יָקֹם (see above, *f*), יָקוֹם also occurs *t* (as subjunctive, Ec 12⁴; נָסֹג ψ 80¹⁹ may also, with Delitzsch, be regarded as a voluntative), incorrectly written *plene*, and יָקֻם (Gn 27³¹; cf. Ju 6¹⁸, Pr 9⁴·¹⁶), which, however, is only orthographically different from יָקֹם (cf. Jer 46⁶). In the *imperfect consecutive* (וַיָּקָם, in *pause* וַיָּקֹם, see above, *f*) if there be a guttural or ר in the last syllable, ă often takes the place of ŏ, e.g. וַיָּנַח *and he rested*; וַיָּנַע *and it was moved*; וַיָּסַר *and he turned aside*, Ju 4¹⁸, Ru 4¹ (distinguished only by the sense from *Hiph'îl* וַיָּסַר *and he removed*, Gn 8¹³); וַיָּצַר Ex 21⁴, 2 K 5²³, 17⁵ (but also וַיָּגָר from both גּוּר *to sojourn*, and גּוּר *to fear*); וַיָּעַף (to be distinguished from וַיָּעָף *and he flew*, Is 6⁶) *and he was weary*, Ju 4²¹, 1 S 14²⁸·³¹, 2 S 21¹⁵, but probably in all these cases וַיָּעַף for וַיִּיעַף from יָעַף is intended. For ותלש 2 S 13⁸ *Keth.*, the *Qerê* rightly requires וַתָּלָשׁ. On the other hand, in an open syllable always וַיָּקוּמוּ, וַיָּסֹרוּ, &c. On וָאָקוּם (וָאָקֻם), see § 49 *e*.

Examples of the full plural ending וּן with the tone (see above, *l*) are *u* תְּמֻתוּן Gn 3³·⁴; יְנוּסוּן ψ 104⁷; יְרֻצֹּן Jo 2⁴·⁷·⁹.

II. On Niph'al.

5. The form of the 1st *sing. perf.* נְקוּמֹּתִי, which frequently occurs (נָסֻגֹּתִי, *v* נְפֻגֹּתִי, cf. also the *ptcp. plur.* נְבֹכִים Ex 14³), serves as a model for the 2nd *sing.* נְקוּמֹּתָ, נְקוּמֹות, and the 1st *plur.* נְקוּמֹּנוּ given in the paradigm, although no instances of these forms are found; but of the 2nd *plur.* the

---

¹ Cf. Delitzsch's commentary on ψ 3⁸.

only examples found have ô (not û), viz. נְפוֹצֹתֶם *ye have been scattered*, Ez 11¹⁷, 20³⁴·⁴¹, and וּנְקֹטֹתֶם *and ye shall loathe yourselves*, Ez 20⁴³, 36³¹.—To the ĭ (instead of ă) of the preformative may be traced the *perfect* נֵעוֹר Zc 2¹⁷ (analogous to the *perfect* and *participle* נָמוֹל, see below, *ee*), *imperfect* יֵעוֹר for *yiʿʿōr*.—The *infinitive construct* הִדּוֹשׁ occurs in Is 25¹⁰; in לָאוֹר Jb 33³⁰, the Masora assumes the elision of the ה (for לְהָאוֹר); but probably לָאוֹר (*Qal*) is intended (see § 51 *l*).—נָמוֹג Is 14³¹, נָסוֹג Is 59¹³ are to be regarded as *infinitives absolute*.

III. On Hiph'il, Hoph'al, and Pi'lel.

w 6. Examples of the *perfect* without a separating vowel (see above, *k*) are: הֵבֵאתָ, &c. (see further, § 76 *g*); הֵמֵתָּה (from מוּת) for *hēmáth-tā* (cf. § 20 *a*); הֲבִנֹּנּוּ 1st *plur. perfect Hiph'il* from בּוּן 2 Ch 29¹⁹, even הֲמִתֶּם (§ 27 *s*) Nu 17⁶, &c.; cf. 1 S 17³⁵, 2 S 13²⁸, also וַהֲמִתֶּיהָ Ex 1¹⁶, and וַהֲמִתִּיהָ Ho 2⁵; but elsewhere, with *wāw consecutive* וַהֲמַתִּי Is 14³⁰; cf. וְהִטַלְתִּי Jer 16¹³, and וְהֵנֵפְתָּ Ex 29²⁴, &c.—In these cases the ē of the first syllable is retained in the secondary tone; elsewhere in the second syllable before the tone it becomes ◌ֵ (1 Ch 15¹², &c.) or more frequently ◌ֲ, and in the syllable before the antepenultima it is necessarily ◌ֲ (e. g. וַהֲקֵמֹתִי Gn 6¹⁸). Before a suffix in the 3rd *sing. masc.* (except Gn 40¹³) and *fem.*, and in the 3rd *plur.*, the vowel of the initial syllable is *Ḥaṭeph-Seghôl*, in the other persons always *Ḥaṭeph-Pathaḥ* (König); on הֲקֵמֹתוֹ 2 K 9², ψ 89⁴⁴, cf. Ex 19²³, Nu 31²⁸, Dt 4³⁹, 22², 27², 30¹, Ez 34⁴, and above, *i*. The 3rd *fem. perf. Hiph.* הֵסַתָּה 1 K 21²⁵ is quite abnormal for הֱסִיתָה from סוּת or סִית.

x As in verbs ע″ע with ח for their first radical (§ 67 *w*), all the forms of עוּד Ex 19²³ (where against the rule given under *i* we find הַעֵרֹתָה with ē instead of *i*), Dt 8¹⁹, Neh 9³⁴, Jer 42¹⁹, and עוּר Is 41²⁵, 45¹³, take Pathaḥ in these conjugations instead of ◌ֲ. The irregular וְהֹשַׁבּוֹתִים Zc 10⁶ has evidently arisen from a combination of two different readings, viz. וְהוֹשַׁבְתִּים (from יָשַׁב) and וַהֲשִׁבוֹתִים (from שׁוּב): the latter is to be preferred.—On הֵבִישׁ and הוֹבִישׁ as a (metaplastic) *perfect Hiph'il* of בּוֹשׁ, cf. § 78 *b*.

y 7. In the *imperative*, besides the short form הָקֵם (on הָשֵׁב Is 42²² with Silluq, cf. § 29 *q*; but in Ez 21³⁵ for הָשֵׁב read the *infinitive* הָשֵׁב) the lengthened form הָקִימָה is also found. With *suffix* הֲקִימֵנִי, &c. The *imperative* הָבִיא Jer 17¹⁸ is irregular (for הָבֵא Gn 43¹⁶); perhaps הָבֵא (as in 1 S 20⁴⁰; cf. 2 K 8⁶) is intended, or it was originally הָבִיאָה.

z In the *infinitive*, elision of the ה occurs in לָבִיא Jer 39⁷, 2 Ch 31¹⁰ (for לְהָבִיא); ה◌ָ *fem.* is added in לְהָנֵפָה Is 30²⁸; cf. Est 2¹⁸ and the analogous *infinitive Haph'el* in biblical Aramaic, Dn 5²⁰.—As *infinitive absolute* הָכֵין occurs in Ez 7¹⁴ (perh. also Jos 4³, Jer 10²³).—The *participles* have ē, on the analogy of the *perfect*, as the vowel of the preformative, like verbs ע″ע (§ 67 *i*). On מֵבִי 2 S 5², &c. (in Kᵉ*thibh*), see § 74 *k*.

aa On the shortened forms of the *imperfect* (יָקֶם, וַיָּקֶם, but always וַיָּבֵא; in the *jussive* also with retraction of the tone אַל־תֵּשֵׁב 1 K 2²⁰) see above, *f*. With a guttural or ר the last syllable generally has *Pathaḥ* (as in *Qal*), e. g. וַיָּעַד *and he testified*, 2 K 17¹³; יָרַח *let him smell*, 1 S 26¹⁹; וַיָּרַח Gn 8²¹; וַיָּסַר

and he took away, Gn 8¹³. The 1st *sing.* of the *imperfect consecutive* commonly
has the form וָאָשִׁיב Neh 2²⁰, or, more often, defectively וָאָעַד 1 K 2⁴², less
frequently the form וָאָשֶׁב Jos 14⁷.—For אָסַף Zp 1² (after אָסֹף) and in
verse 3, read אֹסֵף from אָסַף, on the analogy of אֹמֵר § 68 *g*: similarly in
Jer 8¹³ אֲסִיפֵם instead of אֲסִפֵם.

In the *imperfect Pôlēl* the tone is moved backwards before a following tone- *bb*
syllable, but without a shortening of the vowel of the final syllable ; e.g.
וַתִּתְבֹּנֶן גּוֹ תְּרוֹמֵם Pr 14³⁴; תְּחוֹלֵל לוֹ Jb 35¹⁴; cf. Pr 25²³, and acc. to Baer בִּי
Jb 30²⁰ (ed. Mant., Ginsb. בִּי וַתִּתְבֹּנֵן), always in principal pause; on the
Metheg with *Ṣere*, cf. § 16 *f. γ*.—As *Pôlal* cf. יְרֹעַע Is 16¹⁰.

As *participle Hoph'al* הַמּוּשָׁב occurs in close connexion, Gn 43¹²; cf. § 65 *d*.

Peculiar contracted forms of *Pôlēl* (unless they are transitives in *Qal*) are *cc*
וַיְכֻנְנֵנּוּ Jb 31¹⁵, יְעֹרְרֶנּוּ 41², וַתְּמֹגְנֵנוּ Is 64⁶ for וַיְכוֹנְנֵנוּ, &c. [but read יְכֻנְנֵנוּ
(§ 58 *k*), יְעוֹרְרֶנּוּ or יְעִירֶנּוּ, and וַתְּמֻגְּנֵנוּ];—also תְּרֹמֵם Jb 17⁴, for תְּרֹמֵם.—In
Is 15⁵ יְעֹעֵרוּ appears to have arisen from the *Pilpel* יְעַרְעֵרוּ, the *ă* after the loss
of the ר having been lengthened to *ā*, which has then been obscured to *ô*.—
For the strange form בְּתִקּוֹמְמֶיךָ ψ 139²¹, which cannot (according to § 52 *s*)
be explained as a *participle* with the מ omitted, read בְּמִתְקוֹ.

IV. *In General.*

8. The verbs ע״וּ are primarily related to the verbs ע״ע (§ 67), which were *dd*
also originally biliteral, so that it is especially necessary in analysing them
to pay attention to the differences between the inflexion of the two classes.
Several forms are exactly the same in both, e.g. *imperfect Qal* and *Hiph'il* with
wāw consecutive, the whole of *Hoph'al*, the *Pi'lēl* of verbs ע״וּ, and the *Pô'ēl* of
verbs ע״ע; see § 67 *z*. Owing to this close relation, verbs ע״וּ sometimes
have forms which follow the analogy of verbs ע״ע, e.g. *perfect Qal* בַּז *he has
despised* (from בּוּז, as if from בָּזַז) Zc 4¹⁰; *perfect Niph'al* נָמַר Jer 48¹¹ (for נָמוֹר
from מוּר, as if from מָרַר). The same explanation equally applies to נָקֹטָה
Jb 10¹ for נָקְטָה (cf. § 67 *dd*)=נָקוֹטָה from קוּט, and נָסֹבּוּ Ez 6⁹ (for נָסוֹבּוּ);
יָרֹמּוּ Ez 10¹⁷ and וַיָּרֹמּוּ verse 15; הָרֹמּוּ (*imperative*) Nu 17¹⁰; יָסַב Mi 2⁶;
Hiph'il perfect הֲתֵן Is 18⁵ for הֲתֵן (cf. § 29 *q*), which is for הָתִין from תּוּן. On
the other hand the *imperfects* יָמֶר Ez 48¹⁴ (unless it be intended for יָמֹר,
cf. ψ 15⁴) and יָפַח Hb 2³, are to be regarded according to § 109 *i*, simply as
rhythmically shortened forms of יָמִיר and יָפִיחַ.

9. In common with verbs ע״ע (§ 67 *g*) verbs ע״וּ sometimes have in *Niph'al* *ee*
and *Hiph'il* the quasi-Aramaic formation, by which, instead of the long
vowel under the preformative, they take a short vowel with *Dageš forte* in the
following consonant; this variety is frequently found even along with
the ordinary form, e.g. הֵסִית *to incite*, imperfect יָסִית (also הֵסִית, יָסִית;
הֵסִיג, imperfect יָסִיג *to remove* (from סוּג), also *Hoph'al* הֻסַּג Is 59¹⁴ (on הֻקַּם
cf. § 29 *g*); sometimes with a difference of meaning, as הֵנִיחַ *to cause to rest*,¹
but הִנִּיחַ (*imperfect* יַנִּיחַ, *consecutive* וַתַּנַּח Gn 39¹⁶; *imperative* הַנַּח, plur. הַנִּיחוּ) *to
set down*; for וְהֻנִּיחָה (Baer, Ginsburg וְהֻנְחָה) Zc 5¹¹ (which at any rate could
only be explained as an isolated passive of *Hiph'il* on the analogy of the
biblical Aramaic הֻקִּמַת Dn 7⁴) we should probably read וְהִנִּיחָהּ with

---

¹ As the passive of this *Hiph'il* we should expect the *Hoph'al* הוּנַח, which
is, no doubt, to be read for הוּגַּן in La 5⁵.

Klostermann after the LXX. In Dn 8¹¹ the *K^ethîbh* הרים is intended for a *perfect Hiph'îl.* There is also a distinction in meaning between ילן *to spend the night, to remain,* and ילין Ex 16⁷ *Q^erê* (*K^ethîbh* תלונו ; conversely, verse 2 *K^ethîbh* ילינו, *Q^erê* ילונו), *participle* מלין Ex 16⁸, Nu 14²⁷, 17²⁰, *to be stubborn, obstinate*: in the latter sense from the form ילין only וילן is found, Ex 17³. Other examples are *Niph'al* נמול *he was circumcised,* Gn 17²⁶ ᶠ·; *participle* 34²² (from מול, not נמל ; נעור *he is waked up,* Zc 2¹⁷ (see above, *v*) ; *Hiph'îl* הדילגה La 1⁸ ; יליזו Pr 4²¹.

ff Perhaps the same explanation applies to some forms of verbs *first guttural* with *Dageš forte implicitum,* which others derive differently or would emend, e. g. ותחש for ותחוש *and she hastened* (from חוש) Jb 31⁵ ; ויעט (another reading is ויעט,) 1 S 15¹⁹, 25¹⁴ (14³² *Q^erê*) from עוט or עיט *to fly at anything.* Both, as far as the form is concerned, would be correct *apocopated imperfects* from חשה and עטה (ל״ה), but these stems only occur with a wholly different meaning.

gg 10. Verbs with a consonantal *Wāw* for their second radical, are inflected throughout like the strong form, provided the first or third radical is not a weak letter, e. g. חור, *imperfect* יחור *to be white* ; גוע, *imperfect* יגוע *to expire* ; רוח *to be wide* ; צוה *to cry* ; *Pi'ēl* עול, *imperfect* יעול *to act wickedly* ; עוה *to bend,* *Hithpa'ēl* התעות *to bend oneself* ; and this is especially the case with verbs which are at the same time ל״ה, e. g. צוה, *Pi'ēl* צוה *to command,* קוה *to wait,* רוה *to drink,* *Pi'el* רוה (on ארוך Is 16⁹, see § 75 *dd*) and *Hiph'îl* הרוה *to give to drink,* &c.

§ 73. *Verbs middle i (vulgo* ע״י), *e. g.* בין *to discern.* ## Paradigm N.

a 1. These verbs agree, as regards their structure, exactly with verbs ע״ו, and in contrast to them may be termed ע״י, or more correctly, '*ayin-î* verbs, from the characteristic vowel of the *impf., imper.,* and *infin. constr.* This distinction is justified in so far as it refers to a difference in the pronunciation of the *imperfect* and its kindred forms, the *imperative* and *infin. constr.*—the ע״ו verbs having *û* lengthened from original *ŭ* and ע״י having *î* lengthened from original *ĭ.* In other respects verbs ע״ו simply belong to the class of really monosyllabic stems, which, by a strengthening of their *vocalic* element, have been assimilated to the triliteral form ¹ (§ 67 *a*). In the *perfect Qal* the monosyllabic stem, as in ע״ו, has *ā* lengthened from *ă*, thus : שת *he has set* ; *infinitive* שית, *infinitive absolute* שות, *imperative* שית, *imperfect* ישית, *jussive* ישת (§ 48 *g*), *imperfect consecutive* וישת.—The *perfect Qal* of some verbs

¹ That verbs ע״ו and ע״י are developed from biliteral roots at a period before the differentiation of the Semitic languages is admitted even by Nöldeke (*Beiträge zur sem. Sprachwiss.,* Strassburg, 1904, p. 34 ff.), although he contests the view that ביֵנֹתַי and ריבֹות are to be referred to *Hiph'îl* with the preformative dropped.

used to be treated as having a double set of forms, a regular series, and others like *Hiph'il* without the preformative, e. g. בִּינֹ֫תִי Dn 10¹; בִּין Dn 10¹; Dn 9², also בַּ֫נְתָּ ψ 139²; רִיבֹ֫ותָ *thou strivest*, Jb 33¹³, also רַ֫בְתָּ La 3⁵⁸. The above *perfects* (רִיב, בִּין, &c.) might no doubt be taken as forms *middle ē* (properly *ĭ*), the *ĭ* of which has been lengthened to *î* (like the *ŭ* lengthened to *û* in the *imperfect Qal* of קוּם). It is more probable, however, that they are really shortened forms of *Hiph'il*. This is supported by the fact that, especially in the case of בִּין, the shortened forms are few and probably all late, while the corresponding unshortened forms with the same meaning are very numerous, e. g. *perfect* הֵבִין (but בִּין only in Dn 10¹), הֲבִינֹתָ֫ם, *infinitive* הָבִין (but *infin. abs.* בִּין only in Pr 23¹), *imperative* הָבֵן (only in Dn 9²³ וּבִין immediately before וְהָבֵן, also בִּ֫ינוּ three times, and בִּ֫ינָה ψ 5²), *participle* מֵבִין.¹ Elsewhere *Hiph'il*-forms are in use along with actual *Qal*-forms with the same meaning, thus : מֵרִיב (also רָב), מֵשִׂים *placing* (but only in Jb 4²⁰, which, with the critically untenable הַשִׂ֫ימִי Ez 21²¹, is the only instance of שׂוּם in *Hiph'il*), מֵנִיץ *breaking forth* Ju 20³³, with *infin. Qal* הֵחִ֫ישׁוּ ; נִ֫יחֹו ; *they rushed forth* Ju 20³⁷, with חָשׁ ; חָשַׁ֫תִּי מֵצִיץ *glancing*, also in *perfect* צָץ ; הֵקִיא *he spat out*, with *imperat. Qal* קִיא. As *passives* we find a few apparent *imperfects Hoph'al*, which are really (according to § 53 *u*) *imperfects passive of Qal*, e. g. יוּחַל Is 66⁸ from חִיל *to turn round*, יוּשַׁר from שִׁיר *to sing*, יוּשַׁת from שִׁית *to set*.

b 2. The above-mentioned *Hiph'il*-forms might equally well be derived from verbs ע״ו ; and the influence of the analogy of verbs ע״ו is distinctly seen in the *Niph'al* נָבֹון (ground-form *nabān*), *Pôlēl* בֹּונֵן, and *Hithpôlēl* הִתְבֹּונֵן. The very close relation existing between verbs ע״ו and ע״י is evident also from the fact that from some stems both forms occur side by side in *Qal*, thus from חִיל *to turn round, imperative* also ח֫וּלִי Mi 4¹⁰; שִׂים *to place, infinitive construct* commonly שׂוּם (2 S 14⁷ שִׂים *Qᵉre*), *imperfect* יָשִׂים, but Ex 4¹¹ יָשׂוּם. In other verbs one form is, at any rate, the more common, e. g. גִּיל *to exult* (גּוּל only in Pr 23²⁴ *Kᵉthîbh*); from לִין (perhaps denominative from לַ֫יִל) *to spend the night,* לָלִין occurs six times as *infinitive construct,* לָלוּן only in Gn 24²³ ; but the *imperative* is always לִין, &c.—Of verbs ע״י the most common are שִׁית *to set,* רִיב *to strive,* דִּין *to judge,* שִׂישׂ *to rejoice* ; cf. also *perfect* בָּל (*middle*

---

¹ Since בנת ψ 139² might be intended for בָּנַ֫תְ, there remains really no form of בין which must *necessarily* be explained as a Qal, except the *ptcp. plur.* בָּנִים Jer 49⁷. Nevertheless it is highly probable that all the above instances of Hiph'il-forms, parallel with Qal-forms of the same meaning, are merely due to a secondary formation from the *imperfects Qal* יָשִׂים, יָבִין, &c., which were wrongly regarded as *imperfects Hiph'il*: so Barth, *ZDMG.* xliii. p. 190 f., and *Nominalbildung*, p. 119 f.

Yôdh in Arabic) *to comprehend, to measure,* Is 40¹²; עִיט (as in Arabic and Syriac) *to rush upon,* and the denominative *perfect* קָץ (from קַיִץ) *to pass the summer,* Is 18⁶. On the other hand, וְדִיגוּם *and they shall fish them,* Jer 16¹⁶, generally explained as *perfect Qal,* denominative from דָּג *fish,* probably represents a denominative *Pi'ēl,* וְדִיגוּם.

c Corresponding to verbs properly ע״ו, mentioned in § 72 *gg,* there are certain verbs ע״י with consonantal *Yôdh,* as אָיַב *to hate,* עָיֵף *to faint,* הָיָה *to become, to be,* חָיָה *to live.*

d Rem. 1. In the *perfect Qal* 3rd *fem. sing.* וָלֶנָה occurs once, Zc 5⁴, for וָלָנָה, with the weakening of the toneless *ā* to *ĕ* (as in the *fem. participle* זוֹרָה Is 59⁵); cf. the analogous examples in § 48 *l* and § 80 *i.*—2nd *sing. masc.* שַׁתָּה ψ 90⁸, *Qᵉrê* (before ע; cf. § 72 *s*); 1st *sing.* once שַׁתִּי ψ 73²⁸, *milra',* without any apparent reason; 1st *plur.* וָלָנוּ Ju 19¹³ for *lán-nú.* The lengthened *imperative* has the tone on the ultima before gutturals, רִיבָה יהוה ψ 35¹; see further, § 72 *s.*—Examples of the *infinitive absolute* are: רֹב *litigando,* Ju 11²⁵, Jb 40²; שׂוֹם Jer 42¹⁵, שֵׁת *ponendo,* Is 22⁷. On the other hand, רִיב יָרִיב (for רֹב) Jer 50³⁴, בִּין תָּבִין Pr 23¹, חוּל תָּחִיל Ez 30¹⁶ *Keth.,* are irregular and perhaps due to incorrect *scriptio plena;* for the last the *Qᵉrê* requires חוּל תָּחוּל, but read חוֹל; cf. § 113 *x.*

e 2. The *shortened imperfect* usually has the form יָשֵׁשׁ, יָשֵׁת, יָבֶן; more rarely, with the tone moved back, e.g. יָרֶב לוֹ Ju 6³¹, cf. Ex 23¹, אַל-תֵּשֶׁת 1 S 9²⁰. So with *wāw consecutive* וַיָּשֶׂם *and he placed,* וַיָּבֶן *and he perceived;* with a middle guttural וַיָּעַט בָּהֶם 1 S 25¹⁴ (see § 72 *ee*); with ר as 3rd radical, וַתָּשַׁר Ju 5¹. As jussive of לִין, תָּלֶן is found in Ju 19²⁰ (in *pause*) and Jb 17², for תָּלֶן.—For אַל-תָּרוֹב Pr 3³⁰ *Keth.* (*Qᵉrê* תָּרִיב) read תָּרֵב.

f 3. As *participle active Qal* לָן *spending the night,* occurs once, Neh 13²¹; *participle passive* שִׂים Nu 24²¹, 1 S 9²⁴, Ob⁴; *feminine* שׂוּמָה 2 S 13³², in the *Qᵉrê,* even according to the reading of the Oriental schools (see p. 38, note 2): the *Kᵉthibh* has שָׂמָה. A *passive* of *Qal* (cf. above, § 52 *e* and *s,* and § 53 *u*) from שִׂים may perhaps be seen in וַיִּשֶׁם Gn 50²⁶ (also Gn 24³³ *Kᵉthibh* ויישם, *Qᵉrê* וַיִּישֶׂם; the Samaritan in both places has ויושם), and also in יֻסַּךְ Ex 30³², Samaritan יוסך. Against the explanation of יֻסַּךְ as a *Hoph'al*-form from סוּךְ, Barth (*Jubelschrift . . . Hildesheimer,* Berlin, 1890, p. 151) rightly urges that the only example of a *Hiph'îl* of סוּךְ is the doubtful וַיָּסֶךְ, which is probably an *ĭ-imperfect* of *Qal.*—The explanation of יִשַּׂם, &c., as a *passive* of *Qal* arising from *yiysam,* &c. = *yuysam* (so Barth, ibid., note 1), is certainly also unconvincing, so that the correctness of the traditional reading is open to question.

* * * * * *

g 4. In verbs ע״א the א always retains its consonantal value; these stems are, therefore, to be regarded as verbs *middle Guttural* (§ 64). An exception is יְנָאץ Ec 12⁵ if it be *imperfect Hiph'il* of נאץ (for יַנְאִיץ); but if the form has really been correctly transmitted, it should rather be referred to נָצַץ, and regarded as incorrectly written for יָנֵץ. On נָאוּ (from נָאֲוָה), which was formerly treated here as ע״א, see now § 75 *x.*

§ **74.** *Verbs* לא״ל, e. g. מָצָא *to find.* *Paradigm* O.

The א in these verbs, as in verbs פ״א, is treated in some cases as *a*
a consonant, i. e. as a guttural, in others as having no consonantal
value (as a quiescent or vowel letter), viz.:

1. In those forms which terminate with the א, the final syllable
always has the regular vowels, if long, e. g. מֹצֵא, מָצָא, מָצוּא, הִמְצִיא, i. e.
the א simply quiesces in the long vowel, without the latter suffering
any change whatever. It is just possible that after the altogether
heterogeneous vowel *û* the א may originally have preserved a certain
consonantal value. On the other hand, if the final א quiesces in
a preceding *ă* (as in the *perfect, imperfect,* and *imperative Qal,* in the
perfect Niph'al, and in *Pu'al* and *Hoph'al*) this *ă* is necessarily
lengthened to *ā*, by § 27 *g*, as standing in an open syllable; e. g. מָצָא,
יִמְצָא, &c.

The *imperfect* and *imperative Qal* invariably have *ā* in the final syllable, on *b*
the analogy of verbs *tertiae gutturalis*; cf., however, § 76 *e.*—In the *imperfect*
Hithpa'ēl ā occurs in the final syllable not only (according to § 54 *k*) in the
principal pause (Nu 31²³), or immediately before it (Jb 10¹⁶), or with
the lesser disjunctives (Lv 21¹·⁴, Nu 19¹³·²⁰), but even out of pause with
Merᵉkha, Nu 6⁷, and even before *Maqqeph* in Nu 19¹².

2. When א stands at the end of a syllable before an afformative *c*
beginning with a consonant (ת, נ), it likewise quiesces with the
preceding vowel; thus in the *perfect Qal* (and *Hoph'al,* see below)
quiescing with *ă* it regularly becomes *Qameṣ* (מָצָאתָ for מָצָאתְ, &c.);
but in the *perfect* of all the other active and reflexive conjugations,
so far as they occur, it is preceded by *Ṣere* (נִמְצֵאת, &c.), and in the
imperative and *imperfect* by *Sᵉghôl,* תִּמְצֶאנָה, מְצֶאנָה.

(*a*) The *Sᵉghôl* of these forms of the imperfect and imperative might be *d*
considered as a modification, and at the same time a lengthening of an
original *ă* (see § 8 *a*). In the same way the *ē* of the *perfect* forms in *Pi'ēl,*
Hithpa'ēl, and *Hiph'îl* might be traced to an original *î* (as in other cases the
ē and *î* in the final syllable of the 3rd *sing. masc. perfect* of these conjugations), although this *î* may have only been attenuated from an original *ă*.
According to another, and probably the correct explanation, however, both
the *Ṣere* and the *Sᵉghôl* are due to the analogy of verbs לה״ה (§ 75 *f*) in
consequence of the close relation between the two classes, cf. § 75 *nn.*—No
form of this kind occurs in *Pu'al*; in the *perfect Hoph'al* only the 2nd *masc.*
sing. הֻבָאתָ Ez 40⁴, lengthened according to rule.

(*b*) Before suffixes attached by a connecting vowel (e. g. יִקְרָאֵנִי) the א *c*
retains its consonantal value; so before ךָ and כֶם, e. g. אֶמְצָאֲךָ Ct 8¹;
הַבְּרַאֲךָ Ez 28¹³ (cf. § 65 *h*), not אֶמְצָאֲךָ, &c., since these suffixes, by § 58 *f*,
are likewise attached to the verb-form by a connecting vowel in the form of
Sᵉwâ mobile.—As *infinitive Qal* with suffix notice מְחָאֲךָ Ez 25⁶; *participle* with
suffix בֹּרַאֲךָ Is 43¹; *infinitive Pi'ēl* בְּטַמְּאֲכֶם.—The doubly anomalous form
יִקְרָאוּ Jer 23⁶ (for יִקְרָאֵהוּ or יִקְרָאֻנּוּ) is perhaps a *forma mixta* combining the
readings יִקְרָאוּ and יִקְרָאֻ.

f 3. When א begins a syllable (consequently before afformatives which consist of or begin with a vowel, as well as before suffixes) it is necessarily a firm consonant, and the form then follows the analogy of the strong verb, e.g. מָצְאָה *māṣᵉʾā*, מָצְאוּ, &c. (in *pause* מָצָאוּ, מָצָאָה).

REMARKS.

g 1. Verbs *middle e*, like מָלֵא *to be full*, retain the Ṣere also in the other persons of the *perfect*, e.g. מָלֵאתִי (מָלֵאוּ) Est 7⁵ has ‗ owing to its transitive use; for יְרֵאתֶם Jos 4²⁴ read with Ewald יְרָאתֶם). Instead of מָצְאָה the form קָרָאת *she names*, on the analogy of the ל״ה-forms noticed in § 75 *m*, occurs in Is 7¹⁴ (from קָרָאת, cf. § 44 *f*), and with a different meaning (*it befalls*) in Dt 31²⁹, Jer 44²³, in both places before א, and hence, probably, to avoid a hiatus (on the other hand, וְחָטָאת Ex 5¹⁶, could only be the 2nd *sing. masc.*; the text which is evidently corrupt should probably be emended to וְחָטָאת לְעַמֶּךָ with the LXX); in *Niph'al* נִפְלָאת ψ 118²³; in *Hoph'al* הֻבָאת Gn 33¹¹.—The 2nd *fem. sing.* is written קָרָאתְ by Baer, Gen 16¹¹, &c., according to early MSS.

h 2. The *infin. Qal* occurs sometimes on the analogy of verbs ל״ה (גְּלוֹת, &c., see § 75 *nn*) in the feminine form; so always מְלֹאת *to fill* (as distinguished from מְלֹא *fullness*), Lv 8³³, 12⁴·⁶, 25³⁰, Jer 29¹⁰, Ez 5², also written מְלֹאות Jer 25¹², Jb 20²², &c., and מְלֹאת Est 1⁵. Cf. further, קָרֹאת Ju 8¹; שְׂנֹאת Pr 8¹³; before suffixes, Ez 33¹²; and likewise in *Niph.* Zc 13⁴; also in *Pi'ēl* לְמַלֹּאת Ex 31⁵, 35³³, or לְמַלֹּאות Dn 9², &c. *Kᵉthîbh*; with suffix 2 S 21².—On the (aramaïzing) *infinitives* מַשָּׂא and מַשָּׂאות, see § 45 *e*; on לִקְרַאת *obviam*, § 19 *k*.—בְּמֹצַאֲכֶם *when ye find*, Gn 32²⁰, stands, according to § 93 *q*, for מָצְאֲכֶם. The tone of the lengthened *imperative* רְפָאָה Ps 41⁵ as *Milʻraʻ* (before נַפְשִׁי) is to be explained on rhythmical grounds; cf. the analogous cases in § 72 *s*.—The 2nd *fem. plur. imperative* in Ru 1⁹ has, according to Qimḥi, the form מְצֶאןָ and in verse 20 קְרֶאןָ; on the other hand, the Mantua edition and Ginsburg, on good authority, read קְרֶאןָ, מְצֶאןָ.

i 3. The *participle fem.* is commonly contracted, e.g. מֹצֵאת (for מֹצֶאֶת) 2 S 18²², cf. Est 2¹⁵; so *Niph'al* נִפְלֵאת Dt 30¹¹, Zc 5⁷ (but נִשָּׂאָה Is 30²⁵), and *Hoph'al*, Gn 38²⁵; less frequent forms are מוֹצֵאת Ct 8¹⁰ (cf. § 76 *b*, נִשֵּׂאת 1 K 10²² (cf. § 76 *b*, שֵׂאת beside לָשֵׂאת as *infinitive construct* from נָשָׂא) and without א (see *k*) יֹצֵת (from יָצָא) Dt 28⁵⁷. In the forms חֹטָאים *sinning*, 1 S 14³³, cf. ψ 99⁶; בֹּרְאָם *feigning them*, Neh 6⁸, the א is elided, and is only retained orthographically (§ 23 *c*) after the retraction of its vowel; see the analogous cases in § 75 *oo*.—On the *plur. masc. ptcp. Niph.* cf. § 93 *oo*.

k 4. Frequently an א which is quiescent is omitted in writing (§ 23 *f*): (*a*) in the middle of the word, e.g. בֵּנוּ 1 S 25⁸; מָצָתִי Nu 11¹¹, cf. Jb 1²¹; צָמֵתִי Ju 4¹⁹, cf. Jb 32¹⁸. In the *imperfect* תִּשֶּׂנָה Jer 9¹⁷, Zc 5⁹, Ru 1¹⁴ (but the same form occurs with *Yôdh* pleonastic after the manner of verbs ל״ה in Ez 23⁴⁹, according to the common reading; cf. § 76 *b* and Jer 50²⁰); in *Pi'ēl* אַחַטֶּנָּה (after elision of the א, cf. § 75 *oo*) Gn 31³⁹; and also in *Niph'al* נִטַּמְתֶם Lv 11⁴³; cf. Jos 2¹⁶. (*b*) at the end of the word; וַיָּבֹו 1 K 12¹² *Kᵉthîbh*; *Hiph'îl* הֶחֱטִי 2 K 13⁶, cf. Is 53¹⁰ (הֶחֱלִי for הֶחֱלִיא) *perfect Hiph'îl* of חָלָה formed after the manner of verbs ל״א); in the *imperfect Hiph'il* יֶשִׁי ψ 55¹⁶ *K*ᵉ*thîbh* ; יְנִי ψ 141⁵; אָבִי ı K 21¹⁹, Mi ı¹⁵; in the *infinitive*, Jᴄr 32³⁵; in the *participle*, 2 S 5², ı K 21²¹, Jer 19¹⁵, 39˙⁶, all in *K*ᵉ*thîbh* (מֵבִי, always before א, hence perhaps only a scribal error).

5. In the *jussive, imperfect consecutive*, and *imperative Hiph'il* a number of cases *l* occur with *î* in the final syllable; cf. יַשָּׁא Is 36¹⁴ (in the parallel passages 2 K 18²⁹, 2 Ch 32¹⁵ (וַיַּשִּׁיא); וַיָּבִיא Neh 8² (before ע); וַיֶּחְטָא 2 K 21¹¹ (cf. ı K 16², 21²²); וַתַּחְתְּבָא 2 K 6²⁹; וַיּוֹצֵא Dt 4²⁰, 2 K 11¹², ψ 78¹⁶, 105⁴³; *imperative* הָבִיא Jer 17¹⁸; הוֹצִיא Is 43⁸ (in both cases before ע). If the tradition be correct (which at least in the defectively written forms appears very doubtful) the retention of the *î* is to be attributed to the open syllable; while in the closed syllable of the 3rd *sing. masc.* and *fem.*, and the 2nd *sing. masc.* after ו *consecutive*, the *î* is always reduced to *ē*. In the examples before ע considerations of euphony may also have had some influence (cf. § 75 *hh*).—In Ez 40³, Baer reads with the Western school וַיָּבִיא, while the Orientals read in the *K*ᵉ*thîbh* וִיבוא, and in the *Q*ᵉ*rē* וַיָּבֵא.

On the transition of verbs ל״א to forms of ל״ה see § 75 *nn*.

§ 75. *Verbs* ל״ה, e.g. גָּלָה *to reveal.* *Paradigm P.*

Brockelmann, *Semit. Sprachwiss.*, p. 149 ff.; *Grundriss*, p. 618 ff.—G. R. Berry, 'Original Waw in ל״ה verbs' in *AJSL.* xx. 256 f.

These verbs, like the verbs פ״י (§§ 69, 70), belong to two different *a* classes, viz. those originally ל״ו and those originally ל״י,¹ which in Arabic, and even more in Ethiopic, are still clearly distinguished. In Hebrew, instead of the original ו or י at the end of the word, a ה always appears (except in the *ptcp. pass. Qal*) as a purely orthographic indication of a final vowel (§ 23 *k*); hence both classes are called ל״ה, e.g. גָּלָה for גָּלִי *he has revealed* ; שָׁלָה for שָׁלִו *he has rested.* By far the greater number of these verbs are, however, treated as originally ל״י; only isolated forms occur of verbs ל״ו.

שָׁלָה *to be at rest* may be recognized as originally ל״ו, in the forms in which *b* the *Wāw* appears as a strong consonant, cf. 1st *sing. perfect Qal* שָׁלַוְתִּי Jb 3²⁶, the *participle* שְׁלֵו and the derivative שַׁלְוָה *rest*; on the other hand the *imperfect* is יִשְׁלָיוּ (with *Yôdh*). In עָנָה (Arab. עני) *to answer*, and עָנָה (Arab. ענו) ² *to be afflicted*, are to be seen two verbs originally distinct, which have been assimilated in Hebrew (see the Lexicon, s. v. עָנָה).

---

¹ According to Wellhausen, 'Ueber einige Arten schwacher Verba' in his *Skizzen*, vi. p. 255 ff., the ל״ה verbs, apart from some true ל״ו and some probable ל״י, are to be regarded as originally biliteral. To compensate for their arrested development they lengthened the vowel after the 2nd radical, as the ע״ו verbs did after the 1st radical. But although there is much to be said for this view, it fails to explain pausal forms like חָסָיָה (see *u*). It seems impossible that these should all be *late* formations.

² In the Mêša' inscription, line 5, ויענו *and he oppressed* occurs as 3rd *sing. masc. imperfect Pi'ēl*, and in line 6, אענו *I will oppress* as 1st *sing.*

Of quite a different class are those verbs of which the third radical is a *consonantal* ה (distinguished by *Mappiq*). These are inflected throughout like verbs *tertiae gutturalis*. Cf. § 65 note on the heading.

c　　The grammatical structure of verbs ל״ה (see Paradigm *P*) is based on the following laws :—

1. In all forms in which the original *Yôdh* or *Wāw* would stand at the end of the word, it is dropped (cf. § 24 *g*) and ה takes its place as an orthographic indication of the preceding long vowel. Such an indication would have been indispensable, on practical grounds, in the still unvocalized consonantal text. But even after the addition of the vowel signs, the orthographic rule remained, with insignificant exceptions (see § 8 *k*, and *ā* in קָטַ֫לְתָּ, &c.), that a final vowel must be indicated by a vowel letter. In verbs ל״ה the ה which is here employed as a vowel letter is preceded by the same vowel in the same part of the verb throughout all the conjugations. Thus the endings are—

ה ָ in all perfects, גָּלָה, נִגְלָה, גֻּלָּה, &c.

ה ֶ in all imperfects and participles, גֹּלֶה, יִגְלֶה, &c.

ה ֵ in all imperatives, גְּלֵה, גַּלֵּה, &c.

ה ֹ in the infinitive absolute (גָּלֹה, &c.), except in *Hiph'il, Hoph'al,* and generally also *Piēl*, see *aa* and *ff*.

The *participle passive Qal* alone forms an exception, the original י (or ו, see *v*) reappearing at the end, גָּלוּי ; and so also some derived nouns (§ 84[a], *c*, ε, &c.).

The *infinitive construct* always has the ending וֹת (with ת *feminine*); *Qal* גְּלוֹת, *Pi'ēl* גַּלּוֹת, &c.; for exceptions, see *n* and *y*.

d　　These forms may be explained as follows :—in the *perfect Qal* גָּלָה stands, according to the above, for גָּלַי(ו), and, similarly, in *Niph'al, Pu'al,* and *Hoph'al.* The *Pi'ēl* and *Hithpa'ēl* may be based on the forms קִטֵּל, הִתְקַטֵּל (§ 52 *l*; and § 54 *k*), and *Hiph'il* on the form הִקְטֵל, on the analogy of the *ă* in the second syllable of the Arabic *'aqtălă* (§ 53 *a*). Perhaps, however, the final *ā* of these conjugations simply follows the analogy of the other conjugations.

e　　The explanation of the final tone-bearing ה ֶ of the *imperfect* is still a matter of dispute. As to the various treatments of it, see Barth, *Nominalbildung*, i. p. xxx ff., with § 136, Rem., and *ZDMG*. xliv. 695 f., against Philippi's objections in the *Zeitschrift für Völkerpsychologie*, 1890, p. 356 f. ; also *ZDMG*. lvi. 244, where Barth appeals to the rule that, in the period before the differentiation of the North Semitic dialects, final *iy* becomes ֶ (constr. ה ֶ), not *i* ; M. Lambert, *Journ. Asiat.* 1893, p. 285 ; Prätorius, *ZDMG*. lv. 365. The most probable explanation now seems to be, first, that the uniform pronunciation of *all* imperfects and participles with *S*[e]*ghôl* in the last syllable merely follows the analogy of the *impf. Qal*, and secondly, that the *S*[e]*ghôl* of the *impf. Qal* does perhaps ultimately represent a contraction of the original termination י ֶ (= *ai*), although elsewhere (e.g. in the *imperative* of ל״ה) *ai* is usually contracted to *ê*.

2. When the original *Yôdh* stands at the end of the syllable before *f* an afformative beginning with a consonant (ת, נ) there arises (*a*) in the *perfects*, primarily the diphthong *ai* ('ַ֖י). In the middle of the word this ought always to be contracted to *ê* ('ֵ֫י), but this *ê* is only found consistently in the passive conjugations, whilst regularly in *Qal*, and frequently in the other active and reflexive conjugations (especially in *Pi'ēl*), it appears as *î* (cf. *x*, *z*, *ee*). This *î*, however, in the *perf. Qal* is not to be explained as a weakening of an original *ê*, but as the original vowel of the *intransitive* form. It then became usual also in the *transitive* forms of *Qal* (and in some other conjugations on this analogy), whereas e. g. in Syriac the two kinds of forms are still carefully distinguished.—(*b*) In the *imperfects* and *imperatives*, 'ֶ֫ינָ with the tone always appears before the afformative נָה. On the most probable explanation of this 'ֶ֫ינָ, see above, *e*.

Summary. Accordingly before afformatives beginning with a con- *g* sonant the principal vowel is—

In the perfect *Qal* *î*, e. g. גָּלִ֫יתָ ;

In the perfects of the other active and reflexive conjugations, sometimes *ê*, sometimes *î*, גִּלִּ֫יתָ and גִּלֵּ֫יתָ ; נִגְלֵ֫יתָ and נִגְלִ֫יתָ ;

In the perfects passive always *ê*, e. g. גֻּלֵּ֫יתָ ;

In the imperfects and imperatives always 'ֶ֫ינָ, e. g. תִּגְלֶ֫ינָה, גְּלֶ֫ינָה.

The diphthongal forms have been systematically retained in Arabic and Ethiopic; only as an exception and in the popular language is the diphthong contracted. In Aramaic the contracted forms predominate, yet the Syriac, for example, has in *Qal* 2nd *pers. sing.* *g^elait* (but 1st *pers. sing.* גְּלִית), and so too the Western Aramaic גְּלֵ֫ית, but also גְּלִ֫ית.

3. Before the vocalic afformatives (וּ, 'ֵ֫י, הָ֫) the *Yôdh* is usually *h* dropped altogether, e. g. גָּלוּ (ground-form *gălăyû*), תִּגְלִי, *participle fem.* גֹּלָה, *plur. masc.* גֹּלִים; yet the old full forms also not infrequently occur, especially in *pause*, see *u*. The elision of the *Yôdh* takes place regularly before *suffixes*, e. g. גָּלְךָ (see *ll*).

4. In the 3rd *sing. fem. perfect*, the original feminine ending ־ַת *i* was appended to the stem; hence, after elision of the *Yôdh*, arose properly forms like גָּלָת, with *ā* in the final syllable with the tone. This form, however, has been but rarely preserved (see below, *m*). The analogy of the other forms had so much influence, that the common ending הָ֫ was added pleonastically to the ending ־ָת. Before the הָ֫ the vowel of the ending ־ָת, which thus loses the tone, becomes *Š^ewâ*, and thus there arise such forms as נִגְלְתָה, גָּלְתָה, &c. (but in *pause* גָּלָ֫תָה, &c.).

For similar cases see § 70 *d*; § 91 *m*.

k 5. Finally, a strongly-marked peculiarity of verbs ל״ה is the rejection of the ending הָ‑ in forming the *jussive* and the *imperfect consecutive*. This shortening c curs in all the conjugations, and sometimes also involves further changes in the vocalization (see *o, y, bb, gg*). Similarly, in some conjugations a *shortened imperative* (cf. § 48 *k*) is formed by *apocope* of the final הָ‑ (see *cc, gg*).

l 6. The ordinary form of the *imperfect* with the ending הָ‑ serves in verbs ל״ה to express the cohortative also (§ 48 *c*); cf. Gn 1²⁶, 2¹⁸, 2 Ch 25¹⁷, &c. With a final הָ‑ there occur only: in *Qal*, אֶשָּׁעָה ψ 119¹¹⁷, אֶהְמָיָה (with the י retained, see below, *u*) ψ 77⁴; and in *Hithpa'ēl* וְנִשְׁתָּעָה Is 41²³ (with *Ṭiphḥa*, therefore in lesser pause).

REMARKS.

I. *On Qal.*

m 1. The older form of the *fem.* of the 3rd *sing. perf.* גָּלַת, mentioned above, under *i* (cf. § 74 *g*), is preserved in עָשָׂת (before א) Lv 25²¹ (cf. 2 K 9³⁷ *Kethibh*)[1]; likewise in *Hiph'il* הִרְצָת (before א) Lv 26³⁴, הֶחֱלָאת Ez 24¹²; and in *Hoph'al* הָגְלָת (before יְ) Jer 13¹⁹.—The 2nd *sing. fem.* is also written יתְ‑‑; thus in the textus receptus וְהָיִית 2 S 14², and always in Baer's editions (since 1872), as in most other verbs; חָזִית and פָּלִית Is 57⁸; עָשִׂית Jer 2²³, Ez 16⁴⁸, &c. (so וְהוֹצֵאת 1 K 17¹³ from יָצָא). In the 3rd *pers. plur.* the tone, instead of keeping its usual place (גָּלוּ, &c.), is retracted in ψ 37²⁰, כָּלוּ, both on account of the *pause* and also in rhythmical antithesis to the preceding כָּלוּ; also in Is 16⁸ תָּעוּ (according to Delitzsch for the sake of the assonance with נָגְעוּ); and in Jb 24¹ חָזוּ.—On the tone of the *perfect consecutive* see § 49 *k*.

n 2. The *infin. absol.* frequently has וֹ (probably a survival of the older orthography) for הֹ‑‑, e. g. הָיוֹ Gn 18¹⁸; עָשׂוֹ Jer 4¹⁸, &c., Ez 31¹¹; קָנֹו 2 S 24²⁴; רָאוֹ Gn 26²⁸, Is 6⁹ (cf. 1 S 6¹²), &c., beside רָאֹה. The form שָׁתוֹת Is 22¹³ (beside שָׁתֹו in the same verse) appears to have been chosen on account of its similarity in sound to שָׁתֹם; so in Is 42²⁰ *Qerê* and Ho 10⁴, אָלוֹת (unless it is a substantive, *oaths*) and כָּרֹת; cf. also עָרוֹת Hb 3¹³.—Conversely, instead of the *infinitive construct* גְּלוֹת such forms are occasionally found as גְּלֹה or גָּלֹו, cf. רְאֹה Gn 48¹¹; קְנֹה Pr 16¹⁶; עֲשֹׂה Gn 50²⁰, ψ 101³, also עֲשֹׂו Gn 31²⁸ (cf. Pr 31⁴), and even with the *suffix* הוּ the very remarkable form עֲשֹׂהוּ Ex 18¹⁸.[2]—The feminine form רְאָוָה (for רְאֹות) Ez 28¹⁷, analogous to nouns like גַּאֲוָה (cf. § 45 *d*), is strange, but הָיָה as *infin.* Ez 21¹⁵ is quite inexplicable.—The forms הֹגֹו and הֹרֹו Is 59¹³ are perhaps to be regarded with Barth, *Nominalbildung*, § 51 *a*, as *infinitives absolute* of the *passive* of *Qal* (see above, § 53 *u*), not of *Pô'ēl*.—The 2nd *sing. masc. imperative* וַחֲיֵה occurs in the principal pause in Pr 4⁴ and 7²; but

---

[1] In the Siloam inscription also (see above, § 2 *d*), line 3, הית may be read הָיָת quite as well as [הָיְתָ‑ה].

[2] All these infinitives construct in *ô*, in the Pentateuch, belong to the document called E; cf. § 69 *m*, second note.

probably these forms are simply to be attributed to ≈ Masoretic school, which in general marked the difference between certain forms by the use of *è* for *ē*, and conversely *ē* for *è*; cf. the analogous examples in § 52 *n*, and especially § 75 *hh*, also Kautzsch, *Grammatik des Bibl.-Aram.*, § 17, 2, Rem. 1.—On the reading וּרְאֵינָה Ct 3¹¹ (for וּרְאֶינָה, on the analogy of the reading מְצֶאנָה, &c., § 74 *h*), see Baer's note on the passage.

3. The *shortening* of the *imperfect* (see above, *k*, and the note on *hh*) occasions **O** in *Qal* the following changes:

(*a*) As a rule the first radical takes a helping *S⁰ghôl*, or, if the second radical is a guttural, a helping *Pathaḥ* (according to § 28 *e*). Thus וַיִּגֶל for יִגֶל; וַיִּבֶן *and he despised*, Gn 25³⁴, וַיִּבֶן *and he built*; יֵשַׁע *he looks*; וַיִּמַח *and he destroyed*, Gn 7²³.

(*b*) The *ĭ* of the preformative is then sometimes lengthened to *ē*, e. g. יֵרֶא **P** *he sees.* This, however, mostly happens only after the preformative ת, whilst after י the homogeneous *ĭ* remains, e. g. וַתֵּרֶב (but וְיִכֶל), וַיֶּפֶן (but וַיִּפֶן), (but וַיִּרֶב); with middle guttural תֵּחַם וַתֵּכַּה Jb 17⁷ (from כָּבָה). The unusual position of the tone in תֵּרֶא Zc 9⁵, וְתֵרֶא Mi 7¹⁰ (so Baer and Ginsb.; ed. Mant. וַיֵּרֶא, יֵרֶא) is best explained (except in יֵרֶא Gn 41³³, before פ) on the analogy of קוּמָה, &c., § 72 *s*, as due to the following א. But cf. also *hh.*

(*c*) The helping vowel is elsewhere not used under the circumstances men- **Q** tioned in § 28 *d*; וַיֵּשְׁבְּ Nu 21¹, Jer 41¹⁰, cf. וַיְּפְתּ Jb 31²⁷; on the other hand, with *ĭ* lengthened into *ē* (see *p*), יֵשְׁתְּ ,וַיֵּבְךְ, וַיֵּרְדְּ. The form יֵרֶא *he sees*, occurs parallel with וַיַּרְא *and he saw* (but 3rd *fem.* always וַתֵּרֶא), the latter with the original *Pathaḥ* on account of the following ר, and identical with the 3rd *sing. masc.* of the *imperf. consec. Hiph'il*, 2 K 11⁴.

(*d*) Examples of verbs *primae gutturalis* (§ 63), and at the same time ל״ה, **r** are וַיַּעַשׂ, in *pause* וַיָּעַשׂ *and he made*, from עָשָׂה; וַיַּעַן *and he answered*, from עָנָה (always identical with the corresponding forms in *Hiph'il*), וַיַּחַץ *and he divided*, from חצה. On some similar forms of פ״א see § 76 *d*.—In the following cases the initial (hard) guttural does not affect the form: וַיִּחַר *and he was wroth*, וַיִּחַן *and he encamped* (3rd plur. וַיֶּחֱנוּ), יַחְדְּ (with *Dageš lene* and *Š⁰wâ*) *let it rejoice*, Jb 3⁶; cf. Ex 18⁹.—On וַיִּן ,וַיֵּן (ל״ה as well as פ״ן), &c., see § 76 *b, c, f.*

(*e*) The verbs הָיָה *to be*, and חָיָה *to live*, of which the shortened imperfects **S** ought to be *yihy* and *yiḥy*, change these forms to יְהִי and יְחִי, the second *Yôdh* being resolved into *î* at the end of the word; but in *pause* (§ 29 *n*) יֶחִי ,יֶהִי, with the original *ă* modified to *S⁰ghôl* with the tone (cf. also *nouns* like בְּכִי for *bakhy.* in *pause* בֶּכִי; עֶנִי for *'ŏny*, &c., § 84ᵃ *c*, and § 93 *x*). For תְּשִׁי, however, in Dt 32¹⁸, since no verb שָׁיָה exists, we must read either תֵּשׁ, or better תִּשֶּׁה (Samaritan תשׁא), as *imperfect Qal* of נָשָׁה *to forget*.—Analogous to יְהִי from הָיָה, there occurs once, from הָוָה *to be*, the form יְהוּא for יְהוּ *he will be*, Ec 11³, but no doubt הוּא is the right reading.

The *full* forms (without apocope of the הָ—, cf. § 49 *c*) not infrequently **t** occur after *wāw consecutive*, especially in the 1st pers. and in the later books, e. g. וָאֶרְאֶה *and I saw*, twenty times, and Jos 7²¹ in *K⁰thîbh*, but never in the Pentateuch (וָאֵרָא fifteen times, of which three are in the Pent.); also in the

3rd pers. וַיִּרְאֶה Ez 18²⁸, Jb 42¹⁶ Qᵉrê; וַיַּעְשֶׂה *and he made*, four times (but וַיַּעַשׂ over 200 times); cf. also Ju 19² (וַתְּזְנֶה); ı K 10²⁹ (וַתַּעֲלֶה); Dt ı¹⁶ (וָאֲצַוֶּה), and Gn 24⁴⁸. So also occasionally for the *jussive*, cf. Gn ı⁹, 41³⁴, Jer 28⁶.—For the well attested, but meaningless תִּרְאוּ Jb 6²¹ (doubtless caused by the following וַתִּירְאוּ), read תִּרְאוּ *ye see*, with Ginsburg.

u 4. The original י sometimes appears even before afformatives beginning with a vowel (cf. above, *h* and *l*), especially in and before the *pause*, and before the full plural ending וּן_, or where for any reason an emphasis rests on the word. *Perfect* חָסָיָה ψ 57², חָסָיוּ Dt 32³⁷, cf. ψ 73² Qᵉrê; *imperative* בְּעָיוּ Is 21¹². *Imperfect* יֶאֱתָיוּ Jb 16²², 30¹⁴ (without the pause, ψ 68³²); יִשְׁלָיוּ ψ 122⁶, Jb 12⁶, cf. ψ 77⁴; יִרְבָּיֻן Dt 8¹³; ψ 36⁹: more frequently like יִשְׁתָּיוּן ψ 78⁴⁴; Is 17¹², 21¹², 26¹¹, 31³, 33⁷, 41⁵, ψ 36⁸, 39⁷, 83³; before a suffix, Jb 3²⁵. Also in Pr 26⁷ דָּלְיוּ, as *perf. Qal* from דָּלָה, was perhaps originally intended, but hardly דָּלְיוּ, since these full forms, though they may stand out of pause, do not begin sentences; דַּלְיוּ probably points to דַּלּוּ from דָּלַל as the right reading, since the sense requires an intransitive verb. Cf. further, *v*, *x*, *dd*, *gg*.

v 5. The *participle active* (cf. Vollers, 'Das Qâtil-Partizipium,' *ZA.* 1903, p. 312 ff., and on the participles of ל״ה, *ibid.*, p. 316 ff.), besides feminine forms like עֹלָה Ju 20³¹, &c., רֹאֶה Pr 20¹², has also a *feminine* which retains the 3rd radical י, viz. בּוֹכִיָּה (=בֹּכָה) *weeping*, La 1¹⁶; הֹמִיָּה *tumultuous*, Is 22² (*plur.* Pr 1²¹); צוֹפִיָּה *spying*, Pr 31²⁷, פֹּרִיָּה *fruitful*, ψ 128³, plur. אֹתִיּוֹת *the things that are to come*, Is 41²³. With the ordinary strong inflexion י appears in עֹטְיָה Ct 1⁷, but perhaps there also עֹטִיָּה was intended, unless it should be טֹעִיָּה *a wanderer*. For רֹאֶנִי Is 47¹⁰, רֹאֵנִי is to be read.—On עֹשֶׂה ı K 20⁴⁰ for עֹשֶׂה, cf. § 116 *g*, note. —In the *participle passive* the 3rd radical still sometimes appears as ו (§ 24 *b*), cf. עָשׂוּ *made*, Jb 41²⁵, צָפוּ Jb 15²², contracted from עָשׂווּ, צָפווּ; and before a formative ending, it even has its consonantal sound, הָעֲשׂווּם (read הָעֲשׂוּוּם) 2 K 23⁴; עֲשׂווֹת (read *ʿᵃsûwôth*) ı S 25¹⁸ Kᵉthîbh, נטווֹת (read *nᵉṭûwôth*) Is 3¹⁶ Kᵉthîbh. The shortening of the *û* in רְאִיּוֹת Est 2⁹ is irregular.

w 6. The defective writing is rare in such forms as וְהָיִתִ 2 S 15³³; בָּנִתִ ı K 8⁴⁴, cf. ı K 9³; וַתִּרְדְּלָה Ex 2¹⁶ (cf. Jer 18²¹, 48⁶, ı Ch 7¹⁵, Jb 17⁵, &c.), and the pronunciation תִּרְאֶינָה Mi 7¹⁰, cf. תַּעֲנֶנָה Ju 5²⁹ (unless they are *sing.* with *suff.* of the 3rd *sing. fem.*). Both cases are probably to be explained according to § 20 *i*.

II. *On Niphʿal.*

x 7. Here the forms with יִ_ in the ıst and 2nd *pers. sing.* of the *perfect* predominate (ı_ only in נִקֵּתִ Gn 24⁸); on the other hand in the ıst *plur.* always יִ_, as נִגְלֵינוּ ı S 14⁸. No examples of the 2nd *plur.* occur.—With י retained in *pause* נָפָּיוּ Nu 24⁶; once with an initial guttural נֶחֱרוּ Ct 1⁶ for נֶחְרוּ, probably arising from the ordinary strong form *niḥru*, but the harshness of ח immediately followed by ר is avoided by pronouncing the ח with *Ḥaṭeph-Pathaḥ*.—In the 3rd *sing. fem.* נִשְׁתַּוָה Pr 27¹⁵ (in *pause* for נִשְׁתָּוָה) ו and ת may be transposed for euphonic reasons; but probably we should simply read נִשְׁוָתָה.—Among Niphʿal forms of ל״ה must be classed, with Buxtorf and others (cf. Nöldeke, *ZDMG.* xxx. 185), נָאוָה from אָוָה, not Pi'lel of נאה=נאו; hence, according to § 23 *d*, נָאווּ *they are beautiful* (for נָאֲוּ) Is 52⁷, Ct 1¹⁰; but in ψ 93⁵, where Baer requires נָאֲוָה, read נָאוָה with ed. Mant., Ginsb.

8. The *apocope* of the *imperfect* causes no further changes beyond the rejection **y** of the הֶ—, e.g. יִגֶל from יִגְלֶה; in one verb *middle guttural*, however, a form occurs with the Qameṣ shortened to *Pathaḥ*, viz. יְמַח (for יִמְחֶה) ψ 109¹³, as in verbs ע״ע; but in *pause* תִּמָּח verse 14. Cf. *bb*.—The *infinitive absolute* נִגְלוֹת emphasizing an *infinitive construct*, 2 S 6²⁰, is very extraordinary; probably it is a subsequent correction of an erroneous repetition of הַגְלוֹת.—The *infin. constr.* לְחַרְאָה occurs in Ju 13²¹, 1 S 3²¹ for לְהֵרָאֹת; cf. above, *n.*—On the infinitive Niph'al with the ה elided, see § 51 *l.*—The irregular תֵּעָלוּ Ez 36³ has probably arisen from a combination of the readings תֵּעָלוּ (Qal) and תֵּעָלוּ (Niph'al). Similarly the solecism מְמַבְזֶה 1 S 15⁹ might be due to a combination of the *participle fem.* Niph'al (נִבְזָה, cf. נַחְלָה, נֶחְפָּה, נֶעְשָׂה) with the Hoph'al (מֻבְזֶה); but it is more correct, with Wellhausen, to explain the מ from a confusion with נמס and to read, in fact, נִבְזָה וְנִמְאָסֶת.

III. *On Pi'ēl, Pô'ēl, Pu'al, and Hithpa'ēl.*

9. In the 1st and 2nd persons of the *perfect* Pi'ēl the second syllable in **z** most of the instances has ִי— on the analogy of Qal (see *f*), as קוּיתִי, דִּמִּיתִי; always so in the first *plur.*, and before *suffixes*, e.g. כִּסִּינוּ Gn 37²⁶, דִּכִּיתָנוּ ψ 44²⁰. The form with ֵי— is found only in the 1st *sing.* (e.g. Jo 4²¹; Is 5⁴, 8¹⁷ along with the form with î). On the tone of the *perf. consec.* Pi'el of ל״ה, see § 49 *k.*—Hithpa'ēl has (besides ִי— Jer 17¹⁶) as a rule ֵי— (Pr 24¹⁰, 1 K 2²⁶, Jer 50²⁴). On the other hand, Pu'al always has ֵי—, e.g. עֻשֵּׂיתִי ψ 139¹⁵.—A 1st *sing. perfect* Pô'ēl שׁוֹשֵׂתִי (=שׁוֹשֵׂיתִי) occurs in Is 10¹³.

10. The *infinitive absolute* Pi'ēl takes the form כַּלֵּה, קַוֵּה (like קַטֵּל, the more **aa** frequent form even in the strong verb, see § 52 *o*); with ô only in ψ 40² קַוֹּה; with ôth Hb 3¹³ עָרוֹת (cf. above, *n*). On הֹגוֹ and הֹרוֹ, *infinitives absolute* of the passive of Qal, not of Pô'ēl, see above, *n.*—As *infinitive construct* חַכֵּי occurs in Pi'ēl, Ho 6⁹ (only orthographically different from חַכֵּה, if the text is correct); לְכַלֵּא Dn 9²⁴ (on the א see *rr*); עַד־לְכַלֵּה 2 Ch 24¹⁰, 31¹, for which in 2 K 13¹⁷·¹⁹, Ezr 9¹⁴ עַד־כַּלֵּה with *infin. abs.*; in *Pu'al* עֻנּוֹת ψ 132¹.

11. The *apocopated imperfect* must (according to § 20 *l*) lose the *Dageš forte* **bb** of the second radical, hence וַיְצַו *and he commanded*, תְּעַר (for תְּעָרֶה = *te'arrè*) ψ 141⁸; cf. Gn 24²⁰; even in the principal pause אַל־תְּגַל Pr 25⁹; Hithpa'ēl וַיִּתְגַּל *and he uncovered himself*, Gn 9²¹; תִּתְרַע Pr 22²⁴; cf. ψ 37¹·⁷·⁸. With the lengthening of *Pathaḥ* to Qameṣ, וַיְתָו *and he made marks*, 1 S 21¹⁴ (but read with Thenius וַיְתָף, and instead of the meaningless וַיִּשַׁנּוֹ *ibid.* read וַיְשַׁן). In Hithpa'ēl אַל־תִּתְגָּר, in close connexion, Dt 2⁹·¹⁹; תִּשְׁתָּע Is 41¹⁰; according to Qimḥi also תִּתְאָו, יִתְאָו ψ 45¹², Pr 23³·⁶, 24¹, 1 Ch 11¹⁷, whilst Baer and Ginsburg read with the best authorities תִּתְאָו, יִתְאָו (but cf. König, *Lehrgebäude*, i. 597).[1]—On אֲחַוְךָ Jb 15¹⁷ (for אֲחַוְּךָ) cf. § 20 *m*; on אֹכֶלְךָ Ex 33³, see § 27 *q*;

---

[1] In Nu 34⁷·ᶠ·, according to verse 10, תִּתְאָו (=תִּתְאַוּ) is intended to be read for תִּתְאָו (*imperfect* Pi'ēl from תָּאָה).

on יָרַד Ju 5[13], see § 69 *g*. Finally, on דְּלִיָּ, which is referred to *Piʿēl* by some, as a supposed *imperative*, see above, *u*.

cc 12. Examples of apocopated *imperatives* in *Piʿēl* and *Hithpaʿēl* are : צַו, also צַוֵּה *command thou*, גַּל *open thou*, ψ 119[18.22] ; כֵּן *prepare thou*, ψ 61[8] ; נַס for נַסֵּה *prove thou*, Dn 1[12] ; הִתְחַל *feign thyself sick*, 2 S 13[5] ; cf. Dt 2[24].—On רְבֶה Ju 9[29], cf. § 48 *l*.—In ψ 137[7] עָרוּ *rase it*, is found twice instead of עֹרוּ (for ʿ*arrû*) for rhythmical reasons (cf., however, וַיְעָרוּ in the *imperfect*, 2 Ch 24[11]).

dd 13. Examples of forms in which the *Yôdh* is retained are the *imperfects* תִּרְמְיוּן Is 40[18], cf. verse 25 and 46[5] ; יְכַסְיֻמוּ *they cover them*, Ex 15[5] ; *participle Puʿal* מְחֻיִּם Is 25[6] ; for אַרְיֻוְךָ Is 16[9] (from רָוָה) read with Margolis, אַרְוֵךְ.

IV. On Hiphʿil and Hophʿal.

ee 14. The 3rd *sing. perfect Hiphʿil* sometimes has *Sᵉghôl* in the first syllable instead of *i* (§ 53 *p*), especially in הֶגְלָה (but *perfect consecutive* וְהִגְלָה 2 K 24[14]), הֶרְאָה, הֶלְאָה ; also with *suffixes*, e. g. הֶגְלָם 1 Ch 8[7], הֶלְאָנִי Jb 16[7], וְהֶפְדָּה Ex 21[8]. The *Sᵉghôl* also occurs in the 1st *sing.*, e. g. הֶלְאֵתִיךָ Mi 6[3]. On וְהִרְאֵיתִי Na 3[5], cf. § 53 *p*. The forms with *ê* in the second syllable (also written defectively, as וְהִכֵּתִי Jer 21[6]) are found throughout in the 1st *sing.* (except Pr 5[13]), rarely in the 2nd *sing. masc.*, and never in the 1st *plur*. In the other persons they are about equally common with *i*, except in the 2nd *plur.*, where *i* predominates. Before *suffixes* the forms with *i* predominate throughout ; cf., however, *ê* in Ex 4[12], Mi 6[3], Pr 4[11]. On the tone of the *perf. consec. Hiph.* of ל״ה, see § 49 *k*. In *Hophʿal* only יֹ‿ occurs in the 2nd syllable.

ff 15. In the *infinitive Hiphʿil* of רָבָה *to be abundant*, besides the *construct* הַרְבּוֹת we find the *absolute* הַרְבָּה taking the place of the common form הַרְבֵּה, which had come to be used invariably (but König calls attention to its use as *infinitive construct* in Ez 21[20]) as an adverb, in the sense of *much* ; in 2 S 14[11] the *Qᵉrê* requires הַרְבַּת for the *Kᵉthîbh* הַרְבִּית, an evident scribal error for הַרְבּוֹת. Cf. Gn 41[49], 22[17], Dt 28[63] ; the pointing הַרְבֵּה Jer 42[2] probably arises from regarding this form as a noun.—On הַמְרוֹת Jb 17[2] (with *Dageš f. dirimens*) see § 20 *h*.—In 2 K 3[24] הַכּוֹת (before א) is probably *infinitive absolute*, used in order to avoid the hiatus, cf. § 113 *x*, and on a similar case in *Qal*, see above, *n*.—On the *infinitives* with elision of the ה, cf. § 53 *q*.

gg 16. The *shortened imperfect Hiphʿil* either takes no helping vowel, as יַפְתְּ *let him enlarge*, Gn 9[27] ; יַרְדְּ *he shall subdue*, Is 41[2] ; וַיַּשְׁקְ *and he watered*, Gn 29[10], &c. ; וַיַּרְא *and he showed*, 2 K 11[4] (see § 28 *d*) : or else has a helping vowel, as יֶגֶל (for יַגְל, see § 27 *r*), e. g. 2 K 18[11] ; וַיֹּפֶר ψ 105[24] ; וַתֵּחַע Ez 5[6] ; וַיֵּתַע 2 Ch 33[9] ; וָאֶרֶב i. e. probably וָאֶרְבֶּ Jos 24[3] *Kᵉthîbh* (וָאַרְבֶּה *Qᵉrê*).—Examples of verbs *first guttural* : וַיַּעַל Nu 23[2], וָאָעַל, &c., which can be distinguished as *Hiphʿil* from the similar forms in *Qal* only by the sense.—The apocopated *imperative Hiphʿil* always (except in verbs פ״ן, e. g. הַךְ, הַט, § 76 *c*) has a helping vowel, *Sᵉghôl* or *Pathaḥ*, e. g. הֶרֶב *increase thou* (for *harb*, הַרְבֵּה) ψ 51[4] *Qᵉrê*, also Ju 20[38] ; where, however, it cannot be explained the text stands ; הֶרֶף *let alone* (for הַרְף, הַרְפֵּה Dt 9[14], &c. ; הַעַל (for הַעֲלֵה) Ex 8[1], 33[12] ; but for הַשַׁע ψ 39[14], which could only be *imperative Hiphʿil* of שָׁעַע (= *smear over*, as in Is 6[10]), read with Baethgen שְׁעֵה *look away*.—The *imperfect Hiphʿil* with *Yôdh* retained occurs only in תּוֹנִיּֽוּן Jb 19[2], from יָנָה. Cf. *u*.

V. *In General.*

17. In Aramaic the *imperfect* and *participle* of all the conjugations terminate *hh*
in אָ‍ or יִ‍. The Hebrew *infinitives*, *imperatives*, and *imperfects* in ה‍, less
frequently אָ‍ or יִ‍, may be due to imitation of these forms. On the
infinitive construct Pi'ēl חַפֵּא, see above, *aa*; *imperative* Qal הֱוֵא Jb 37⁶ (in the sense
of *fall*); *imperfect* יֵרֵא *let him look out*, Gn 41³³ (but see above, *p*); יֵעֶשֶׂה *he will
do*, Is 64³; אַל־תִּהְיֶה Jer 17¹⁷; אַל־תֹּבֵא *consent thou not*, Pr 1¹⁰; אַל־תַּעֲשֶׂה *do
thou not*, 2 S 13¹² (the same form in Gn 26²⁹, Jos 7⁹, Jer 40¹⁶ Q°rē); אֶהְיֶה (so
Baer and Ginsburg, after cod. Hillel, &c.) *I will be*, Jer 31¹; וַנַּעֲשֶׂה Jos 9²⁴;
תֵּרָאֶה Dn 1¹³. Cf. also in *Niph'al* יִמָּצֵא Lv 5⁹; תִּבָּנֶה (according to Qimḥi)
Nu 21²⁷; in *Pi'ēl* תְּכַלֶּה Lv 18⁷·⁸·¹²⁻¹⁷, 20¹⁹, in each case לֹא תְכַלֶּה, beside תְּכַלֶּה
with a minor distinctive; יֵנָקֵה (Baer יְנַקֶּה) Na 1³; אֱזָרֶה Ez 5¹² (with *Zaqeph*;
Baer אֱזָרֶה). The fact, however, that a great number of these forms occur in
pause and represent at the same time a *jussive* or *voluntative* (Jos 7⁹), suggests
the view that the *Ṣere* is used merely to increase the emphasis of the
pausal form, and at the same time to make a distinction in sound between
the *jussive* or *voluntative* and the ordinary *imperfect*.[1] Elsewhere (Gn 26²⁹,
Lv 5⁹, Jer 40¹⁶, Dn 1¹³; according to Baer also Mi 7¹⁰, Zc 9⁵) the pronunciation
with *ê* is probably intended to soften the hiatus caused by a following א or
ע; cf. the analogous cases above, § 74 *l*.

The ending יִ‍ appears to stand for ה‍ in the *imperfect* Qal in וַתִּזְנִי־שָׁם *ii*
and there hath she played the harlot, Jer 3⁶; perhaps, however, the 2nd *sing. fem.*
is intended, or it may have been introduced into the text of Jeremiah from
Ez 16¹⁵, &c. Still more strange is it in the *imperfect* Hiph'il אַל־תָּמְחִי Jer 18²³;
but the *Mil'ēl*-tone probably points to תֶּמַח as the correct reading (cf. Neh 13¹⁴).
The יִ‍ stands for ה‍ in the *perfect* Hiph'il הֶחֱלִי *he made sick*, Is 53¹⁰, which
is probably for החלִיא from חלָא, a secondary form of חלה; see *rr*. The *plur.*
הִמְסִיו (Baer הִמְסִין) *they made to melt*, Jos 14⁸, is a purely Aramaic form.

18. In two verbs the rare conjugation Pa'lēl or its reflexive (§ 55 *d*) occurs: *kk*
מְטַחֲוֵי *archers*, Gn 21¹⁶ (from טָחָה); but most frequently in שָׁחָה *to bend*, Pa'lēl
שַׁחֲוָה not in use, whence reflexive הִשְׁתַּחֲוָה *to bow oneself, to prostrate oneself*,
2nd *pers.* in יְתָ‍ and 1st *pers.* in יְתִי‍, *imperfect* יִשְׁתַּחֲוֶה, *consecutive* 3rd *sing.
masc.* וַיִּשְׁתַּחוּ for *wayyištaḥw* (analogous to the noun-forms, like שָׂחוּ for *saḥw*);
3rd *plur.* יִשְׁתַּחֲווּ.—Instead of the aramaizing *infinitive* with *suffix* בְּהִשְׁתַּחֲוִיתוֹ
2 K 5¹⁸ read with König בְּהִשְׁתַּחֲווֹתִי; in Ez 8¹⁶ מִשְׁתַּחֲוִיתֶם is still more certainly
a scribal error for מִשְׁתַּחֲוִים.

19. Before *suffixes* in all forms ending in ה, a connecting vowel is employed *ll*
instead of the ה and the connecting vowel which precedes it (§ 58 *f*), e.g.
נָחֵנִי Gn 24²⁷; in *pause* עָנָנִי 1 K 2³⁰, &c., even with lesser disjunctives, ψ 118⁵,
Pr 8²², or with a conjunctive accent, 1 S 28¹⁵ (but Baer עָנָנִי), Jb 30¹⁹; cf.
§ 59 *h*; עִנְּךָ, in *pause* עִנָּךְ, Is 30¹⁹ (and even when not in *pause* Jer 23³⁷) or
like קָנֶךָ Dt 32⁶; וְיִפְרְךָ, וְיַרְבְּךָ Gn 28³; cf. also עָנָהוּ, עָנָם, *imperfect* יַעֲנֵהוּ,
הִבָּהוּ, הֶעֱלָךְ, Hiph'il הַבֵּנִי, יַעֲנֶךָ.

Only very seldom does the *imperat.* or *impf.* end in יִ‍ before suffixes, e.g. *mm*

---

[1] Possibly these examples (like the cases of S°ghôl in *pause*, see *n*) represent
the view of a particular Masoretic school, which was intended to be consistently carried out.

אַפְאֵיהֶם Dt 32²⁶ ; יְכַסְּיֻמוֹ ψ 140¹⁰ Qᵉrê ; הַבֵּינִי *smite me*, 1 K 20³⁵·³⁷ ; cf. Hb 3², Is 38¹⁶. Even in these examples a return to the original ending *ay* might be assumed ; but perhaps they are merely due to a less correct *plene* writing. In the 3rd *sing. perf. fem.* the older form גָּלַת (see *i*) is always used before a suffix, e. g. כְּלָתוּ (for כְּלָתְהוּ) Zc 5⁴ ; *in pause* עֲשָׂתְנִי Jb 33⁴ ; רָאָתְךָ 42⁵.

VI. *The Relation between Verbs* ל״ה *and* ל״א.

nn 20. The close relation existing between verbs ל״א and ל״ה is shown in Hebrew by the fact that the verbs of one class often borrow forms from the other, especially in the later writers and the poets.

oo 21. Thus there are forms of verbs ל״א—

(*a*) Which have adopted the vowels of verbs ל״ה, e. g. *perfect Qal* כָּלָאתִי *I have refrained*, ψ 119¹⁰¹ ; *participle* חוֹטֵא (חֹטֵא) *sinning*, Ec 2²⁶, 8¹², 9²·¹⁸ ; cf. Is 65²⁰ ; מוֹצֵא Ec 7²⁶ ; נֹשֵׁא *lending*, 1 S 22² ; *Pi'ēl perfect* מִלֵּא *he has filled*, Jer 51³⁴ ; cf. 1 K 9¹¹, Am 4² (where, however, the *perfect Niph.* is perhaps intended), ψ 89¹¹, 143³ ; רִפֵּאתִי *I heal*, 2 K 2²¹ ; cf. Jer 51⁹ ; *imperfect* יַנְמֵא Jb 39²⁴ ; *Niph'al perfect* נִפְלְאָתָה (like נִגְלְתָה) *it was wonderful*, 2 S 1²⁶ ; *Hiph'il perfect* הִפְלֵא Dt 28⁵⁹ ; הֶחְבֵּאתָה (not אָתָ—, cf. above, 2 S 1²⁶) *she hid*, Jos 6¹⁷. On the other hand, forms like חֹטְאִים 1 S 14³³, קֹרְאִים ψ 99⁶, נִרְפְּאוּ Ez 47⁸, תְּרַכְּאוּנַנִי, according to the correct reading, Jb 19² (cf. Gn 31³⁹ אֶחֱטֶנָּה), and יִרְאוּ *imperative plur. masc.* from יָרֵא Jos 24¹⁴, 1 S 12²⁴, ψ 34¹⁰, are due to the elision of the א, see § 74 *i*. On יִשָּׂוֹא Jer 10⁵ and נָשׂוֹא ψ 139²⁰, see § 23 *i*.

pp (*b*) Forms in ה, but keeping their ל״א vowels, e. g. *imperfect Qal* אֶרְפֶּה Jer 3²² ; *imperative* רְפֵה *heal thou*, ψ 60⁴ ; *Niph'al* נֶחְבָּה Jer 49¹⁰ (which must evidently be a *perfect* ; read with Ewald the *infinitive absolute* נַחְבֹּה as in verse 23), and הֵחָבֵה *to hide oneself*, 1 K 22²⁵, cf. Jer 19¹¹ ; *Pi'ēl imperfect* יְמַלֶּה *he will fill*, Jb 8²¹.

qq (*c*) Forms entirely of a ל״ה character, e. g. *perfect Qal* וְצָמִת *and when thou art athirst*, Ru 2⁹, cf. 2 S 3⁸ ; כָּלוּ *they shut up*, 1 S 6¹⁰ ; cf. 25³³ ; מָלוּ *they are full*, Ez 28¹⁶, cf. 39²⁶ ; *infinitive* חֲטוֹ (see above, *n*) *to sin*, Gn 20⁶ (on מְלֹאת see above, § 74 *h*) ; *imperative sing. fem.* חֲבִי Is 26²⁰ ; *imperfect* יִכְלֶה (for יִכְלָא) *he will keep back*, Gn 23⁶ ; תִּרְפֶּינָה *they heal*, Jb 5¹⁸ ; *participle* בוֹטֶה Pr 12¹⁸ ; *fem.* יֹצֵא Ec 10⁵ ; *plur.* צֹבֶיהָ Is 29⁷ ; *participle passive* נָשׂוּי ψ 32¹ ; *Niph'al* נִרְפֶּתָה Jer 51⁹ ; *thou hast prophesied*, Jer 26⁹ (cf. ψ 139¹⁴, Jb 18³) ; *imperfect* וַיִּרְפוּ 2 K 2²² (*infinitive* Jer 19¹¹) ; *Pi'ēl imperfect* וַיְרַפּוּ Jer 8¹¹, cf. Gn 31³⁹ ; *Hiph'il participle* מַקְנֶה Ez 8³ ; *Hithpa'el* הִתְחַבֵּית 1 S 10⁶ ; *infinitive* הִתְנַבּוֹת 1 S 10¹³. For the Kᵉthîbh לַהֲשׂות 2 K 19²⁵, Jablonski and others require as Qᵉrê the form לְהַשְׁאוֹת (so Is 37²⁶) ; the Kᵉthîbh would have to be read לְהַשּׂות, with elision of the א and retraction of the vowel.

rr 22. On the other hand, there are forms of verbs ל״ה, which wholly or in part follow the analogy of verbs ל״א, e. g. in their consonants אָתָא *he comes*, Is 21¹² ; בָּרָא 2 S 12¹⁷ (*textus receptus*) בָּרָה ; וְרָאָתִי Ez 43²⁷ ; יִשְׁנָא Jb 8¹¹ ; יִשְׁנָא La 4¹ ; וַיַּחְלָא 2 Ch 16¹² ; תִּקְרֶאנָה Ex 1¹⁰, Lv 10¹⁹ ; תְּלָאִים Dt 28⁶⁶ (cf. Ho 11⁷) ; נִקְרָא (*infin. absol. Niph'al* beside נִקְרֵיתִי) 2 S 1⁶ ; שָׂנֵא 2 K 25²⁹ ; מְרֻפָּא

Jer 38⁴; יֵשְׁנָא Ec 8¹: in their vowels, אָתָנוּ Jer 3²² ; יִקְרַח Dn 10¹⁴ ; תִּכְלֶה לִירוּא 1 K 17¹⁴: in both, יִקְרָא Gn 49¹ ; cf. 42⁴, Is 51¹⁹; תִּלְאִים 2 S 21¹² Qᵉré; 2 Ch 26¹⁵ (cf. וַיִּרְאוּ הַמּוֹרִאים 2 S 11²⁴ Kᵉthibh) ; מֹרָאָה (*participle fem. Qal*) Zp 3¹ ; יַפְרִיא Ho 13¹⁵; מְסֻלָּאִים La 4².—For פֹּרֹאות (so Baer, Ez 17⁶, cf. 31⁸), which can only be intended for פֹּרֹאות *participle fem. plur.* from פָּרָה = פָּרָא, read פֹּארֹות *branches*, according to Ez 31⁵, &c.

§ 76. *Verbs Doubly Weak.*

a **1.** In a tolerably large number of verbs two radicals are weak letters, and are consequently affected by one or other of the anomalies already described. In cases where two anomalies might occur, usage must teach whether one, or both, or neither of them, takes effect.

Thus e.g. from נָדַד *to flee*, the *imperfect* is יִדּוֹד in Na 3⁷ and יִדַּד in Gn 31⁴⁰ (on the analogy of verbs פ״ן); *Hiph'il* הֵנַד (like a verb ע״ע), but the *imperfect Hoph'al* again יֻדַּד (as פ״ן).

b **2.** The following are examples of difficult forms, which are derived from doubly weak verbs:

(*a*) Verbs פ״ן and ל״א (cf. § 66 and § 74), e.g. נָשָׂא *to bear*, imperative שָׂא (ψ 10¹² נְשָׂא, of which נְסָה ψ 4⁷ is probably only an orthographical variation); *infinitive construct* שְׂאֵת (for שְׂאֶת ; see the analogous noun-formations in § 93 *t*), also נְשׂא Is 1¹⁴, 18³; Gn 4¹³ נְשׂוֹא ; ψ 89¹⁰ שׂוֹא (perhaps only a scribal error) ; after the *prefix* ל always לָשֵׂאת (otherwise the contracted form only occurs in מִשֵּׂתוֹ Jb 41¹⁷, with rejection of the א); *imperfect* תִּשֶּׂנָה for תִּשְׂאֶנָה Ru 1¹⁴; wholly irregular are תִּשָּׂאֶינָה Ez 23⁴⁹ (so Baer after Qimḥi; *textus receptus*, and also the Mantua ed., and Ginsburg, תִּשֶּׂאֶינָה) and נָשֵׂאת 2 S 19⁴³ as *infinitive absolute Niph'al* (on the analogy of the *infinitive construct Qal?*); but most probably נְשׂא is to be read, with Driver.

c (*b*) Verbs פ״ן and ל״ה (cf. § 66 and § 75), as נָטָה *to bow, to incline*, נָכָה *to smite*. Hence *imperfect Qal* יִטֶּה, *apocopated* וַיֵּט (Gn 26²⁵) *and he bowed*; וַיַּז (so, probably, also Is 63³ for וַיַּזֵּן) 2 K 9³³ *and he sprinkled* (from נָזָה); *perfect Hiph'il* הִכָּה *he smote*, imperfect יַכֶּה, *apocopated* וַיַּךְ (even with *Athnaḥ* 2 K 15¹⁶; but also ten times וַיַּכֶּה), וַנַּךְ Dt 2³³; so also וַיַּ Lv 8¹¹·³⁰; אַל־תַּם ψ 141⁴ (cf. Jb 23¹¹); *imperative* הַכֵּה, *apocopated* הַךְ *smite thou* (like הַט *incline*, with הַטֵּה), *infinitive* הַכּוֹת, *participle* מַכֶּה; *Hoph'al* הֻכָּה, *participle* מֻכֶּה.

d (*c*) Verbs פ״א and ל״ה (cf. § 68 and § 75), as אָבָה *to be willing*, אָפָה *to bake*, אָתָה *to come*. E.g. *imperfect Qal* יֹאפֶה, יֹאבֶה, *plur.* יֹאפוּ; וַיֵּתֶא (cf. § 68 *h*) Dt 33²¹ for וַיֶּאְתָה (= וַיֶּאֱתָה); *imperfect apocopated* וַיֵּאת Is 41²⁵ for וַיֶּאְתְּ; *imperative* אֱתָיוּ Is 21¹², 56⁹·¹² (cf. אֱפוּ *bake ye*, Ex 16²³) for אֱתָיוּ אֵתֶיוּ (§ 23 *h*; § 75 *u*); *Hiph'il perfect* הֵתָיוּ for הֶאֱתָיוּ (הַאֱתָיוּ) Is 21¹⁴; *imperfect apocopated* וַיֹּאֶל *and he adjured*, 1 S 14²⁴, properly יַאֲלֶה (יַאֲלֶה) from אָלָה, whence יָאַלֶה, and, with the obscuring to ô, יֹאלֶה; instead of the simple apocope (וַיֹּאל) the א which had already become quiescent, is made audible again by the helping *Seghôl* (unless perhaps there is a confusion with the *imperfect consecutive Hiph'il* of יאל).

e   (*d*) Verbs פ״י and ל״א (cf. § 69, § 70, and § 74), as יָצָא *to go forth, imperative* צֵא *go forth*, with ה‎_ *paragogic* צֵאָה Ju 9²⁹ in principal pause for צְאָה; 2nd *fem. plur.* צֶאנָה Ct 3¹¹; *infinitive* צֵאת; *Hiph'il* הוֹצִיא *to bring forth.*—יָרֵא *to fear, imperfect* יִירָא and יִירָא (or וַיִּרָא), *imperative* יְרָא; *imperfect Niph'al* יִוָּרֵא ψ 130⁴, *participle* נוֹרָא.

f   (*e*) Verbs פ״י and ל״ה (cf. § 69, § 70, and § 75), e.g. יָדָה *to throw*, Hiph'il *to confess, to praise*, and יָרָה *to throw* (both properly verbs פ״ו), and יָפָה *to be beautiful. Infinitive* יָרֹה, יְרוֹת; *imperative* יְרֵה; *imperfect consecutive* וַיִּיף Ez 31⁷ (cf. also וַתִּיפִי 16¹³); *with suffixes* וַנִּירָם *we have shot at them* (from יָרָה) Nu 21³⁰; perhaps, however, it should be read with the LXX וְנִינָם *and their race* (also in the very corrupt passage ψ 74⁸ נִינָם is probably a *substantive*, and not the *imperfect Qal* with *suffix* from יָנָה); *Piʻēl* וַיַּדּוּ for וְיִידּוּ (§ 69 *u*). *Hiph'il* הוֹרָה, הוֹרָה; *infinitive* הוֹרֹת (as *infinitive absolute* 2 Ch 7³); *imperfect* יוֹרֶה, cf. אַל־תֹּאֵנוּ Jer 22³; *apocopated* וַיּוֹר 2 K 13¹⁷.

g   (*f*) Verbs ע״י and ל״א, particularly בּוֹא *to come. Perfect* בָּא, בָּאת, or בָּאת (Gn 16⁸, 2 S 14³, Mi 4¹⁰; cf. § 75 *m*), once בָּנוּ for בָּאנוּ 1 S 25⁸; for בֹּאוּ Jer 27¹⁸, which is apparently the *perfect*, read יָבֹאוּ. In the *imperfect Qal* the separating vowel occurs (תְּבֹאֶינָה instead of the more common תְּבֹאנָה, cf. also תֵּבֹאןָ Gn 30³⁸) only in Jer 9¹⁶, ψ 45¹⁶, and 1 S 10⁷ *Kethibh*.

h   For וְתָבֵאת 1 S 25³⁴ *Qerê* (the *Kethibh* ותבאתי evidently combines the two readings וּבָאת and וְתָבֹאי; cf. Nestle, *ZAW.* xiv. 319), read וְתָבֹאי; on the impossible forms Dt 33¹⁶ and Jb 22²¹ cf. § 48 *d*.—In the *perfect Hiph'il* הֵבִיא, הֵבֵאת and (only before a suffix) הֲבִיאֹת; the latter form is also certainly intended in Nu 14³¹, where the Masora requires וְהֵבֵיאתִי, cf. 2 K 9², 19²⁵, Is 43²³, Jer 25¹³, Ct 3⁴. Before suffixes the *ē* of the first syllable in the 3rd *sing.* always becomes *Hateph-Seghôl*, e.g. הֱבִיאֲךָ, הֱבִיאַנִי; elsewhere invariably *Hateph-Pathah*, e.g. הֲבִיאֹתָנוּ or הֲבִיאָתָנוּ. On the other hand, *ē* is retained in the secondary tone in the *perfect consecutive* when without suffixes, e.g. וְהֵבֵאתָ. Cf. moreover, וַהֲקֵאתוֹ (וַהֲקֵאתוֹ in Opitius and Hahn is altogether incorrect), Pr 25¹⁶, from קִיא; but קִיא *spue ye*, Jer 25²⁷ (perhaps only a mistake for קִיאוּ), is not to be referred to קִיא but to a secondary stem קָיָה. In the *imperfect* וַתָּקֵא is found once, Lv 18²⁵, besides וַיָּקֵא (analogous to וַיָּבֵא).—On אָבִי (for אָבִיא), יָנֵי, מֵבִי, see § 74 *k*.

i   (*g*) The form חָיַי *to live*, in the *perfect Qal*, besides the ordinary development to חָיָה (*fem.* חִיְתָה), is also treated as a verb ע״ע, and then becomes חַי in the 3rd *pers. perfect*, in pause חָי, and with *wāw consecutive* וָחַי Gn 3²², and frequently. In Lv 25³⁶ the contracted form וְחֵי is perhaps *st. constr.* of חַי *life*, but in any case read וָחַי *perfect consecutive* as in verse 35. The form וְחָיָה occurs in Ex 1¹⁶ in *pause* for וְחָיְתָה (3rd *fem.*) with *Dageš* omitted in the י on account of the pausal lengthening of *ă* to *ā*.

§ 77.   *Relation of the Weak Verbs to one another.*

The close relation which exists between some classes of the weak *a* verbs (e. g. between פ״ו and פ״י, ל״א and ל״ה, ל״ע and ע״ע, ע״ע and ל״ה) appears not only in their similarity or identity of inflexion, or their mutual interchange of certain forms, but especially from the fact that frequently the same root (*radix bilittera*, see § 30 *g*) recurs in various weak stems of similar meaning. The meaning accordingly is inherent in the two constant root-consonants, while the third consonant, which is weak (and the particular class of weak verbs with it), does not establish any difference in the meaning. Thus from the root דך there occur with the same meaning דָּכָא, דּוּךְ, דָּכַךְ *to strike, to crush*; and from the root נד there are נוּד, נָדַד, נָדָה *to flee*.

In this manner the following classes are related in form and *b* meaning:

1. Verbs ע״וּ and ע״ע in which the first and third consonants are the same in both, as being essential to the meaning; e. g. מוּךְ and מָכַךְ *to become poor*; מוּשׁ and מָשַׁשׁ *to feel*; נוּד and נָדַד *to flee.*

2. Verbs פ״י and פ״ן; e. g. יָצַב and נָצַב *to place,* נָקַשׁ and יָקֹשׁ (yāqōš) *to lay C snares.* Moreover, stems belonging to the classes mentioned in 1 (especially ע״וּ) are frequently related also to verbs פ״ו and פ״י, e. g. גּוּר and יָגֹר *to fear*; טוֹב and יָטַב *to be good*; נָפַח and פּוּחַ *to blow*; נָפֵץ and פּוּץ *to dash to pieces.* Verbs פ״א are less frequently connected with these classes, e. g. אָרַשׁ and דּוּשׁ *to thresh,* &c.

3. Verbs ל״א and ל״ה (in which the first two consonants form the real *d* body of the stem) are sometimes related to each other, and sometimes to the above classes. To each other, in דָּכָא and דָּכָה *to crush,* קָרָא and קָרָה *to meet* (cf. § 75 *nn*); to verbs of the other classes, in מָצָה and מָצַץ *to suck,* דָּחָה and דּוּחַ *to thrust,* &c.

4. Verbs ע״ע and ל״ה, on which cf. Grimm, *Journal of Bibl. Lit.*, 1903, p. 196; *e* e. g. אָנָה and אָנַן *to sigh,* דָּמָה and דָּמַם *to be quiet,* חָנָה and חָנַן *to incline,* כָּלָה and בָּלַל *to end,* קָלָה and קָלַל *to despise,* שָׁנָה and שָׁנַן *to err,* שָׁחָה and שָׁחַח *to bend down,* שָׁסָה and שָׁסַם *to plunder.*

5. Verbs ע״וּ and ע״ה; e. g. מוּל and מָהַל (New Hebrew; in O. T. only *f* מָהוּל Is 1²²) *to circumcise,* מוּר and מָהַר *to exchange,* נוּר (in מְנוֹרָה *a light*) and נָהַר *to shine;* cf. also לְהָטִים *secret arts,* Ex 7¹¹ with לָט *secret,* from לוּט.

§ 78.   *Verba Defectiva.*

It often happens, when two kindred weak verbs are in use with *a* the same meaning, that both are *defective,* i. e. do not occur in all the forms. Since, however, those tenses and forms which are not in use in the one verb are generally supplied by the other, they mutually complete one another, and thus form together, as it were, an entire verb, as in Greek ἔρχομαι, aor. ἦλθον, fut. ἐλεύσομαι, and in Latin *fero, tuli, latum, ferre,* &c., but with this difference, that in Hebrew the roots of these verbs are almost always closely related.

b The most common verbs of this kind are—

בּשׁ *to be ashamed. Hiph'il* הֵבִישׁ (inferred from הֲבִישׁוֹת), but also הֹבִישׁ, הוֹבִישׁ, as if from יבשׁ, on the analogy of verbs פ״ו; also in Is 30⁵ the *Q'rê* requires הֵבִישׁ, where the *K'thibh* has הִבְאִישׁ from בָּאַשׁ.

טוֹב *to be good. Perfect* טוֹב; but *imperfect* יִיטַב and *Hiph'il* הֵיטִיב from יָטַב (but cf. הֵטִיבֹתָ 2 K 10³⁰).

יָנֹר *to be afraid. Imperfect* יָנֹר (from נגר).

יָקֵץ *to awake,* only in the *imperf.* יִיקַץ; for the *perfect,* the *Hiph'il* הֵקִיץ is used (from קוּץ).

נָפַץ *to break in pieces. Imperfect* יָפוּץ (from פוּץ). *Imperative* פּוּץ. *Niph'al* נָפֹּיץ. *Pi'ël* נִפֵּץ (from נָפַץ). *Pôlēl* פּוֹצֵץ (from פוּץ). *Reflexive* הִתְפּוֹצֵץ. *Hiph'il* הֵפִיץ. Also פִּצְפֵּץ Jb 16¹².

נָצַב (*Qal* in post-biblical Hebrew, in Aramaic and Arabic) *to place,* whence (possibly) *Niph'al* נִצַּב and *Hiph'il* הִצִּיב (see above, § 71); but *Hithpa'ēl* הִתְיַצֵּב.

שָׁתָה *to drink,* used in *Qal*; but in *Hiph.* הִשְׁקָה *to give to drink,* from a *Qal* שָׁקָה which is not used in Hebrew.

On (יָלַךְ) הָלַךְ *to go,* see above, § 69 x.

c Rem. 1. To the same category belong also, to a certain extent, those cases where the *tenses* or *moods* not in use in one conjugation, are supplied by forms having the same meaning in other conjugations of the same verb. Thus:

יָסַף *to add.* The *infinitive* (but cf. § 69 h, note) and *imperfect,* unused in *Qal,* are supplied by the *Hiph'il* הוֹסִיף, יוֹסִיף (on יֹסֵף as *imperfect indicative,* see § 109 d, cf. also § 109 i).

כָּשַׁל *to stumble. Perfect* from *Qal, imperfect* from *Niph'al.*

נָגַשׁ *to approach,* unused in *perf. Qal,* instead of which *Niph'al* נִגַּשׁ is used; but *imperfect* יִגַּשׁ, *imperative* גַּשׁ, and *infinitive* גֶּשֶׁת from *Qal* only are in use.

נָחָה *to lead. Perfect* usually נָחָה in *Qal,* so *imperative* נְחֵה, but *imperfect* and *infinitive* always in *Hiph'il.*

נתך *to be poured out. Perfect Niph'al* נִתַּךְ with *imperfect Qal* יִתַּךְ, but the *perfect Qal* and *imperfect Niph'al* are not in use.

2. The early grammarians often speak of *mixed forms* (*formae mixtae*), i. e. forms which unite the supposed character and meaning of two different tenses, genders, or conjugations. Most of the examples adduced are at once set aside by accurate grammatical analysis; some others appear to have arisen from misapprehension and inaccuracy, especially from erroneous views of unusual *plene* forms. Others, again, are either merely wrong readings or represent an intentional conflation of two different readings.

CHAPTER III

THE NOUN

§ 79. *General View.*

For the literature, see De Lagarde, *Uebersicht über die im Aram., Arab. und Hebr. übliche Bildung der Nomina*, Göttingen, 1889; Index and Additions, 1891; J. Barth, *Die Nominalbildung in den semitischen Sprachen*, first half, *Simple nouns*, Leipzig, 1889; second half, *Nouns with external additions*, 1891; second edition, with indices of words and subjects, 1894; E. König, *Historisch-kritische Lehrgebäude*, &c., ii. 1, Leipzig, 1895, see above, § 3 *f.*—Of these three important works the first two especially have given rise to various articles. In support of De Lagarde : Hommel in *ZDMG*. xliv, p. 535 ff. (against De Lagarde and Hommel : Barth, *ibid.*, p. 679 ff.), and dealing with the Index, *ZDMG*. xlv, p. 340 ff.—Against Barth (though with many points of agreement) : Philippi in the *Zeitschrift für Völkerpsychologie*, 1890, p. 344 ff. (answered by Barth in *ZDMG*. xliv, p. 692 ff.), and *ZDMG*. xlvi, p. 149 ff. (answered again by Barth, *ibid.*, xlviii, p. 10 ff.), also in the *Beiträge zur Assyriologie*, ii (1892), p. 359 ff. 'Die semitische Verbal- und Nominalbildung,' and lastly, in *ZDMG*. xlix, p. 187 ff.—Cf. also A. Müller, 'Semitische Nomina. Bemerkungen zu de Lagarde und Barth,' *ZDMG*. xlv, p. 221 ff.—The main points at issue in the works of De Lagarde and Barth are indicated below, § 83 *d.*—Brockelmann, *Semit. Sprachwiss.*, p. 104 ff.; *Grundriss*, p. 329 ff.

1. Since, according to § 30 *a*, most word-stems are developed into *a* verbal stems as well as into noun-stems, it has become customary (especially in the Lexicon) to refer the noun to the most simple ground-form of the verbal formation, viz. the 3rd *pers. sing. perfect Qal*, and, as it were, to derive it from that form. This is usual, not only in those noun-stems which can be directly connected with a corresponding verbal stem (*Nomina verbalia* or *derivativa*, § 83 ff.), but also with *Nomina primitiva*, i. e. those of which no verbal stem is now found in Hebrew (see § 82), as well as finally with *Nomina denominativa*, which have evidently been derived from other nouns (§ 86).

The adjective agrees in form entirely with the substantive. On the formation of adjectival ideas by giving to abstracts a concrete sense, see § 83 *c*.

2. A special inflexion of the noun to express the various cases does *b* not exist in Hebrew; only a few ancient and almost extinct traces of case-endings have survived (§ 90). The syntactical relation of a noun can therefore in general only be inferred from its position in the sentence, or from its being joined to prepositions. In either case, the form of the noun undergoes no change (except for the *construct*

state, § 89), and the representation of case-relations belongs therefore almost exclusively to the syntax (§ 117 ff.). The comparative and superlative of adjectives also can be expressed only by a syntactical combination (§ 133). On the other hand, several changes in the forms of nouns are occasioned by the additions of the plural, dual, and feminine terminations, as well as of the pronominal suffixes, and also by the close connexion of two nouns, by means of the *construct state*.[1]

§ 80. *The Indication of Gender in Nouns.*

Brockelmann, *Grundriss*, p. 404 ff.; 'Ueber die Femininendung *at, ah, ā*' in *Semit. Sprachwiss.*, p. 106 f.; *Grundriss*, pp. 105, 405 ff.; 'Die Femininendung *T* im Semit.' (*Sitzung d. orient.-sprachwiss. Sektion d. schlesischen Gesellschaft*, Feb. 26, 1903); against him J. Barth, *ZDMG.* 1903, p. 628 ff.; Brockelmann's reply, *ibid.*, p. 795 ff.; and Barth again, *ibid.*, p. 798 ff.

a   **1.** The Hebrew, like all Semitic languages, recognizes only two genders in the noun, a *masculine* and a *feminine*. Inanimate objects and abstract ideas, which other languages sometimes indicate by the *neuter*, are regarded in Hebrew either as masculine or feminine, more often the latter (see the Syntax, § 122 *q*).

b   **2.** The *masculine*, as being the more common and important gender, has no special indication.

Feminine nouns are also without an indication of gender when the meaning of the word naturally denotes a feminine, as אֵם *mother*, אָתוֹן *a she-ass*, עֵז *a she-goat*, רָחֵל *an ewe* (cf. § 122 *b*). As a rule, however, the *feminine* had originally the ending ת—ָ, as in the 3rd *sing. perfect* of verbs (§ 44 *a*). This ת—ָ, however, is regularly retained in Hebrew only in close connexion with a following genitive or suffix (cf. § 89 *e* and § 91 *o*), except where the form has arisen through the addition of a simple ת[2] (see below, *d*). Otherwise, the feminine ending of the independent form (the *absolute state*, § 89 *a*) is—

c   (*a*) Most commonly a tone-bearing ה—ָ, e.g. סוּס *equus*, סוּסָה *equa*. Of nouns ending in —ִ, like עִבְרִי, the feminine (by § 24 *b*) is עִבְרִיָּה, cf. § 86 *h*. As in the 3rd *sing. fem. perfect* (קָטְלָה, &c.), this ה—ָ seems to have arisen by the rejection of the final ת, and the lengthening of the *ǎ* in the open syllable, whereupon the ה was added as an orthographic indication of the final long vowel: cf. the exactly similar origin of such forms as גָּלָה for גָּלָי, § 75 *c*. It must, however, be

---

[1] To speak of these changes as a declension of the Hebrew noun, as is usually done, is accordingly incorrect.

[2] In Mal 1¹⁴ מָשְׁחָת (so e.g. ed. Mant.) would stand for מָשְׁחָתֶת, the ptcp. fem. Hoph'al; but מָשְׁחָת (so Baer and Ginsb.) is also supported by good authority.

noticed that in Arabic (see *m* and note) the pausal form of *at* is *ah*, of
which a trace may be preserved in the Hebrew הָ‍.

d   (*b*) Simple ת with nouns ending in a vowel, e. g. יְהוּדִי *Jew*, יְהוּדִית
Jewess. The same ending ת is very frequently added to stems ending
in a consonant, but only (except before suffixes) by means of a helping
vowel, which, as a rule, is *Sᵉghôl*, but after gutturals *Pathaḥ*, e. g. קֹטֶל,
fem. קֹטֶלֶת, *killing* ; before suffixes, e. g. קְטַלְתִּי, according to the rule
given in § 69 *c*, cf. also § 84ᵃ *s*; מוֹדָע *an acquaintance, fem.* מוֹדַעַת.
The forms which arise in this way follow in every respect the analogy
of the *segholate* forms (§ 94 *f*). The forms which have been developed
by means of a helping vowel are retained even in the connective form
(*construct state*) ; except וַיֹּלֶדְתְּ (for יֹלֶדֶת, which is used elsewhere)
Gn 16¹¹, Ju 13⁵·⁷ ; cf. Jer 22²³ and 51¹³ *Qᵉrê*, also מְשָׁרַת 1 K 1¹⁵, *participle fem. Piēl*, properly *mᵉšāratt* = מְשָׁרֶתֶת; also מְבַעְתֶּךָ (*participle
fem. Piēl* with suffix) arises from the form מְבַעַתְּ which was developed
into מְבַעֲתֶת.

e   Rem. 1. The fem. form in ‍ת‍ֶ is in general less frequent, and occurs
almost exclusively when the form in הָ‍ is also in use. It is only in the
participles and infinitives that it is the commoner, e. g. קֹטֶלֶת more common
than קְטָלָה, לֶדֶת than לֵדָה.

f   2. *Rarer* feminine endings áre—(*a*) ‍ת‍ַ with the tone, e. g. בָּרֶקֶת *emerald*,
Ez 28¹³ (also בָּרְקַת Ex 28¹⁷) ; שִׁפְעַת *a company*, 2 K 9¹⁷, unless the reading is
wrong ; more frequently in proper names, especially of places among the
Canaanites or Phoenicians (in whose language ‍ת‍ַ was the usual fem. ending,
§ 2 *d*) and other neighbouring tribes,[1] e. g. צָרְפַת *Zarephath*, גִּבְעַת *Gibeath*, קִרְיַת
Kiriath, אֵילַת Greek *Ailana* in Idumea ; אֲחֻזַּת Gn 26²⁶ : on the reading גָּלְיַת
cf. *g*. Cf., moreover, נְגִינַת ψ 61¹ (prob. originally נְגִינֹת); חַיַּת (LXX חַיּוֹת) 74¹⁹ᵃ;
פּוּנַּת La 2¹⁸ ; [רַבַּת *much*, in ψ 65¹⁰, 120⁶, 123⁴, 129¹·², is a form borrowed from
the Aramaic (Syriac *rabbath*) in which the original *t* of the *fem.* is often retained
to form *adverbs*, see Wright, *Comparative Grammar*, p. 135.]

g   (*b*) ‍ת‍ָ, which likewise occurs in some names of places, e. g. חֶלְקַת, בַּעֲלַת,
as well as in the *masc.* proper name גָּלְיָת 1 S 17⁴, &c. (in 17²³, and 21¹⁰, ed. Mant.
has גָּלְיַת), and in the *fem.* proper name שִׁמְעָת ; otherwise, almost only in poetry,
viz. זָמְרָת Ex 15², Is 12², ψ 118¹⁴ (really for זִמְרָתִי *my song* ; the absorption of the *î*,
however, can scarcely have 'taken place in the Aramaic manner', as suggested
by Duhm on Is 12², nor is it due merely to the following *Yôdh*, but is intended
'to facilitate the absorption of יָה' ; so Geiger, *Urschrift*, p. 277 f.) ; נַחֲלָת
heritage, ψ 16⁶ (either again for נַחֲלָתִי *my heritage*, or for נַחֲלָתָה, cf. § 90 *g*, as
probably also עֶזְרָת *help*, ψ 60¹³, 108¹³ for עֶזְרָתָה). These forms are possibly

---

[1] In the list of Palestinian towns taken by Pharaoh Shoshenq, the feminine
town-names all end in *t*. Cf. also the Mēša' inscription, line 3, הבמת זאת
this high place ; line 26, המסלת *the highway* [see also Driver, *Tenses*, § 181, *note*].

survivals from a period when even final vowels were not supported by a
vowel-letter. Cf. also פָּרָת *fecunda* (*a fruitful tree*) Gn 49²²; יִתְרַת *abundance*,
Jer 48³⁶ (before ע; but in Is 15⁷ יִתְרָה); שְׁנַת *sleep* (for שֵׁנָה ψ 132⁴; and
(unless the ת is radical) in prose קָאַת *pelican* (which reading is also preferable,
in Is 34¹¹, to the form קָאָה), also מָחֳרָת *the morrow*, but in *construct state* always
מִמָּחֳרָת.—¹ תְּהִלָּת־ Jer 45²⁵ Qᵉrê is no doubt intended to indicate the reading
תְּהִלָּתִי, parallel to מְשׁוֹשִׂי; cf. above, on זִמְרָת, &c.

h   (c) אָ__, the Aramaic orthography for הָ__, chiefly in the later writers;
זָרָא *loathing*, Nu 11²⁰; חָתָּא *a terror*, Is 19¹⁷; שֵׁנָא *sleep*, ψ 127²; לְבִיָא *a lioness*,
Ez 19² (unless לְבִיָא is intended); מַטָּרָא *a mark*, La 3¹²; cf. also דָּשָׁא *threshing*
(*participle Qal* from דּוּשׁ) Jer 50¹¹; מָרָא *bitter*, Ru 1²⁰. On the other hand,
according to the western Masora, קָרְחָה *baldness* is to be read in Ez 27³¹; see
Baer on the passage.

i   (d) הָ__, an obtuse form of הֶ__ (§ 27 *u*), only in הַאֹזְרָה for הָאֹזְרָה Is 59⁵
(unless it is again a *forma mixta* combining the *active ptcp. masc.* הָאֹזֵר and the
passive ptcp. fem. (הָאֲזוּרָה; cf. לָנָה for לָנָה Zc 5⁴; אָנָה 1 K 2³⁶·⁴² (§ 90 *i*, and
§ 48 *d*).

k   (e) הָ__◡ without the tone, e.g. תַּנּוּר בֹּעֵרָה Dt 14¹⁷ [Lv 11¹⁸ רְחָם; רַחֲמָה
an oven heated, Ho 7⁴; cf. Ez. 40¹⁹, 2 K 15²⁹, 16¹⁸. In all these examples the
usual tone-bearing הָ__ is perhaps intended, but the Punctuators, who considered the feminine ending inappropriate, produced a kind of *locative* form
(see § 90 *c*) by the retraction of the tone. [In 2 K 16¹⁸, Is 24¹⁹, Ez 21³¹ (note
in each case the following ה), and in Jb 42¹³, Ho 7⁴, the text is probably in
error.]

l   (f) י__, as an old feminine termination, preserved also in Syriac (*ai*; see
examples in Nöldeke's *Syrische Gram*, § 83), in Arabic and (contracted to *ê*) in
Ethiopic, very probably occurs in the proper name שָׂרַי *Sarai*, cf. Nöldeke,
ZDMG. xl. 183, and xlii. 484; also עֲשָׂרָה *ten* (*fem.*) undoubtedly arises
from an original 'esray; so Wright, *Comparative Grammar*, p. 138; König, *Lehrgebäude*, ii. 427.

m   3. It is wholly incorrect to regard the *vowel*-ending הָ__² as the original
termination of the feminine, and the *consonantal* ending ת__ as derived from
it. The Ethiopic still has the ת throughout, so too the Assyrian (*at, it*); in
Phoenician also the feminines end for the most part in ת, which is pronounced
at in the words found in Greek and Latin authors; less frequently in א (see
Gesenius, *Monumm. Phoen.*, pp. 439, 440; Schröder, *Phön. Sprache*, p. 169 ff.).
The ancient Arabic has the obtuse ending (*ah*) almost exclusively in *pause*;
in modern Arabic the relation between the two endings is very much as in
Hebrew.

---

¹ In 1 S 2c²⁷ also, where the Masora (see Baer on Jos 5¹¹) for some unknown
reason requires מִמָּחֳרָת, read with ed. Mant., Jablonski, Opitius, and Ginsburg,
מִמָּחֳרָת.

² In this ending the ה *h* can only be considered consonantal in the sense
that the ת was originally aspirated, and afterwards 'the mute ת was dropped
before *h*, just as the old Persian *mithra* became in modern Persian *mihr* '; so
Socin, who also points to the Arabic pausal form in *ah*, and observes that
among some of the modern Beduin an *h* is still heard as a fem. ending, cf.
Socin, *Diwan aus Centralarabien*, iii. 98, ed. by H. Stumme, Lpz. 1901. In
Hebrew this consonantal termination was entirely abandoned, at any rate in
later times.

§ 81. *Derivation of Nouns.*

Brockelmann, *Grundriss*, p. 329 ff.

Nouns are by their derivation either *primitive*, i. e. cannot be *a* referred to any verbal stem at present extant (see § 82), such as אָב *father*, אֵם *mother* (but see both words in the Lexicon; according to Stade and others בַּא, אֵם, &c., are children's words and terms of endearment, and so really primitive nouns), or *derivative*, i. e. either *Derivativa verbalia* (§§ 83–5), e. g. רָם *high*, רָמָה *high place*, מָרוֹם *height*, from רוּם *to be high*, or less frequently *Derivativa denominativa* (§ 86), e. g. מַרְגְּלוֹת *the place at the feet*, from רֶגֶל *foot*.

Rem. 1. The earlier grammarians consider the verb alone as stem, and *b* therefore *all* nouns as verbals, dividing them into (*a*) *Formae nudae*, i. e. such as have only the *three* (or *two*) radicals, and (*b*) *Formae auctae*, such as have formative letters or syllables added at the beginning or end, e. g. מַמְלָכָה, מַלְכוּת. The formative letters used for this purpose are ה א מ נ ת י ו (הָאֵמַנְתִּיו),[1] and the treatment of nouns formerly followed this order.

According to the view of *roots* and *stems* presented in § 30 *d*, nouns (other *c* than *denominatives*) are derived not from the verbal stem, but either from the (abstract) root or from the still undefined stem. In the following pages, however, the arrangement according to the verbal stem is retained as being simpler for the beginner. Cf. § 79 *a*.

2. *Compound* nouns as *appellatives* are very rare in Hebrew, e. g. בְּלִיַּעַל *d* *worthlessness*, *baseness*. On the other hand, they very frequently occur as proper names, e. g. גַּבְרִיאֵל (*man of God*), יְהוֹיָקִים (*Yahwe raises up*), יְהוֹנָתָן (*Yahwe gave*), &c.[2]

§ 82. *Primitive Nouns.*

The number of *primitive* nouns in the sense used in § 81 is small, since nouns, which in other languages are represented as independent noun-stems, can easily be traced back in Hebrew to the verbal idea, e. g. names of animals and natural objects, as שָׂעִיר *he-goat* (prop. *shaggy*, from שָׂעַר), שְׂעֹרָה *barley* (prop. *prickly*, also from שָׂעַר), חֲסִידָה *stork* (prop. *pia*, sc. *avis*), זָהָב *gold* (from זָהַב=צָהַב *to shine*, *to be yellow*). Thus there remain only a few nouns, e. g. several names of members of the body in men or beasts, to which a corresponding verbal stem cannot be assigned at all, or at any rate only indirectly (from other Semitic dialects), as קֶרֶן *horn*, עַיִן *eye*.

---

[1] From this *vox memorialis* the *nomina aucta* are also called by the older grammarians *nomina heemantica*.

[2] G. Rammelt (*Über die zusammengesetzten Nomina im Hebr.*, Halle, 1883, and Leipzig, 1884) recognizes as appellatives only צַפַּרְדֵּעַ (cf. below, § 85 *w*) and צַלְמָוֶת (the latter certainly incorrectly [see, however, Nöldeke, *ZATW.* 1897, p. 183 ff.]). In p. 8 ff. the author gives a list of 'logical compounds', i. e. new terms formed by composition with the negatives לֹא, בְּלִי, מִבְּלִי.

§ 83. *Verbal Nouns in General.*

a   **1.** In Hebrew, as in Greek and Latin, the *verbal nouns* are connected in form and meaning primarily with certain forms of the verb, especially the participles and infinitives, which are themselves, even in their ordinary form, frequently used precisely like nouns, e. g. אֹיֵב *enemy,* דַּעַת *to know, knowledge.* Still oftener, however, certain forms of the infinitive and participle, which are seldom or never found as such in the strong verb, though in use in the weak verb and in the kindred dialects, came to be commonly used for the verbal noun ; e. g. the participial form קָמֵל, the infinitives of the (Aramaic) form מִקְמַל (as a *noun* also מִקְטָל), further קְטֹלֶת, קְטֹלָה, קַטְלָה, קְטֻלָּה (§ 45 *d*), &c.   Others (as the Arabic shows) are properly intensive forms of the participle.

b   **2.** As regards their meaning, it follows from the nature of the case that nouns which have the form of the infinitive regularly denote the *action* or *state*, with other closely related ideas, and are therefore mostly *abstract* ; while the participial nouns, on the contrary, denote for the most part the *subject* of the action or state, and are therefore *concrete*.   Moreover, it is to be noticed, that a particular meaning is attached to many of the special forms of derivative nouns, although it does not appear equally in them all.

c   Rem. It need not appear strange, when we consider the analogy of other languages, that a noun which in form is properly *abstract* afterwards acquired a *concrete* sense, and vice versa.   So in English, we say *his acquaintance,* for the *persons* with whom he is *acquainted* ; the *Godhead* for *God* himself ; in Hebrew מוֹדָע *acquaintance* and *an acquaintance.*

d   The inner connexion in thought between Semitic noun-forms and the corresponding verbal forms is investigated in the works of De Lagarde and Barth (see the titles at the head of § 79) on very different lines, but with many points of agreement.   De Lagarde starts from the fact that language consists of sentences.   A sentence which consists of only *one* word is called a verb, and anything which serves as a complement to it is a noun.   The oldest form of the sentence is the imperative.   Closely related to it are three kinds of sentences of the nature of verbal forms, differing according as the property of the particular object of sense is to be represented as invariable (form *qatula*), or as liable to change (form *qatila*), or, finally, as a circumstance which takes place before our eyes (form *qatala*).   Like the imperative, these three forms of sentences have also been transformed into nouns, by means of certain phonetic changes,—especially by the omission of the final vowels and the addition of different terminations to the last consonant of the stem. But just as the forms of the verbal sentence undergo numerous modifications (in the tenses, moods, and conjugations), so also do the nouns, sometimes by assimilation of the unessential to the characteristic vowel (*qutul, qitil*), sometimes by the lengthening of the characteristic vowel (*qatûl, qatil, qatâl*), or else through the displacement of the accent and the consequent reduction of the noun to a monosyllabic form (*qatl, qutl, qitl*), or, finally, by their being formed from the derived stems (or conjugations), e. g. *qattal, qattâl ; qittil, qittâl,* &c.   Further modifications arise from the use of the various imperfect and infinitive forms, and also from the employment of the prefix *m*. Lastly, *denominalia* are formed from *deverbalia* by appending certain suffixes.

De Lagarde does not, however, claim to be able to show in the case of each particular noun the sense it conveyed in primitive times ; the origin of a number of nouns can now no longer be detected. In those, however, which are clearly derived from verbs, the original meaning is chiefly determined by the characteristic vowel.

Barth's system is based on the thesis that ' all Semitic nouns, adjectives, and participles are derived from either the perfect or the imperfect stem '. Thus, e. g. קְטֹל is the infinitive of the perfect stem, קְטֹל the infinitive of the imperfect stem, שְׁכַב infinitive of יִשְׁכַּב, &c. In dissyllabic noun-forms the second vowel is always alone characteristic and essential, the first vowel unessential, and therefore variable. Further modifications of the simple form are effected by strengthening (sharpening) the second or third consonant, by lengthening the characteristic vowel (instead of which, however, the feminine termination may also be used), or by ' metaplasm ', i. e. by the use of noun-forms derived from one of the two intransitive stems for the other, e. g. *qutl* for *qitl*, and vice versa.

In nouns of the perfect stem, the vowels *i* and *u* indicate intransitive formations, the vowel *a* a transitive sense. In nouns of the imperfect stem on the contrary, *u* and *i*, being characteristic vowels, indicate a transitive and *a* an intransitive sense : for *yaqtŭlŭ* is imperfect of the transitive perfect *qatala*, and *yaqtălŭ* imperfect of the intransitive perfects *qatila* and *qatula*, &c. This explains how nouns, apparently identical in form, may yet in sense belong to different classes : a *qutl*-form from a *u*-imperfect has a transitive meaning, but the same form from a *u*-perfect has an intransitive meaning. This double system of perfect and imperfect forms runs through the whole scheme of noun-formation, not only the forms connected with the conjugations, but also the forms with prefixes and suffixes.

Against the whole theory it has been urged that it postulates for the development of the language a much too abstract mechanism, and further, that the meanings of words as we find them may in many cases be due to a modification of the original sense. But though many of the details (e. g. the alleged unessential character of the vowel of the first syllable) remain doubtful, yet the agreement between the characteristic vowel of certain noun formations and that of the perfect or imperfect stem, is supported by such a number of incontestable instances, that there can be no doubt as to a systematic, intimate connexion between the two. At the same time it must be admitted that De Lagarde has put forward many important and suggestive points, and both scholars agree in laying stress on *one* characteristic vowel as indicative of the meaning.

§ 84ᵃ. *Nouns derived from the Simple Stem.*

Preliminary remark.—From the statement made above, § 83 *d*, it follows that *a* an external similarity between forms is no proof of their similar origin, and, vice versa, external difference does not exclude the possibility of their being closely related both in origin and meaning.

I. *Nouns with One Vowel, originally Short.*

R. Rŭzička, ' Beiträge zur Erklärung der nomina segolata,' in *Sitz.-ber. d. böhmischen Ges. d. Wiss.*, Prag, 1904.

1. Nouns with one of the three short vowels after the first radical : *present* ground-form *qătl, qĭtl, qŭtl*.

The supposition of *monosyllabic* ground-forms appeared to be required by the character of forms now existing in Hebrew, as well as in Arabic, &c. But there are strong reasons for believing that at least a large proportion of these forms go back to original dissyllabic bases with a short vowel in each syllable. When formative additions were made, the vowel of the 2nd syllable was dropped, i.e. before case-endings in Assyrian and early Arabic, and before pronominal suffixes in Hebrew. From the forms thus produced, the bases *qaṭl*, *qiṭl*, *quṭl* have been assumed, although they never appear in Hebrew except in the singular and then in connexion with suffixes.

In support of this view of a large number of original dissyllabic bases, we must not, however, appeal to the Sᵉghôl or Pathaḥ under the 2nd consonant of the existing developed forms, סֵ֫פֶר, זֶ֫רַע, &c. These are in no sense survivals or modifications of an original full vowel in the 2nd syllable, but are mere helping-vowels (§ 28 *e*) to make the monosyllabic forms pronounceable,[1] and consequently disappear when no longer needed. Under certain circumstances even (e.g. in קֹ֫שְׁטְ) they are not used at all. Actual proofs of such original toneless full vowels in the 2nd syllable of existing Segholates are—

1. Forms like Arab. *málik*, for which rarely *malk*, corresponding to the Hebrew ground-form; cf. De Lagarde, *Uebersicht*, p. 72 ff.

2. In Hebrew כָּתֵף, כָּבֵד, יָרֵךְ, גָּדֵר, the connective forms of יְרֵךְ, גְּדֵר, &c., which latter can only come from ground-forms *gădĭr*, *yărĭk*, *kăbĭd*, *kătĭp*.

3. The forms treated under *e*, which are in many ways related to the Segholates proper, in so far as they are to be referred to original dissyllabic bases.

4. The plurals of Hebrew Segholates, since, with very rare exceptions, they take *Qameṣ* under the 2nd radical before the termination ־ִים, fem. ־וֹת, of the *absolute state*, as סְפָרִים, מְלָכוֹת, מְלָכִים, &c. This *Qameṣ* (see note 1 on § 26 *e*) can only be due to a lengthening of an original short vowel in the 2nd syllable, and hence it would seem as though the vowel were always *ă*. This is impossible from what has been said, especially under 1 and 2. Hence the explanation of the consistent occurrence of *Qameṣ* in the plurals of *all* Segholates can only be that the regularly formed plurals (i.e. from singulars with original *ă* in the 2nd syllable) became the models for all the others, and ultimately even for some really monosyllabic forms.[2]

(*a*) From the strong stem the above three ground-forms are further developed to קֶ֫טֶל, קֵ֫טֶל, קֹ֫טֶל,[3] (cf. § 27 *r* and in § 93 the explanations of Paradigm I, *a–c*); without a helping vowel (§ 28 *d*) קֹשְׁטְ *truth*. If the second

---

[1] According to Delitzsch (*Assyr. Gram.*, p. 157 f.) the same is true in Assyrian of the corresponding *qaṭl*-forms. Without case-endings they are *kalab*, *šamaš*, *aban* (= כְּלָב, שֶׁ֫מֶשׁ, אֶ֫בֶן), with case-endings *kalbu*, *šamsu*, *abnu*. On the other hand, acc. to Sievers, *Metrik*, i. 261, Hebrew ground-forms probably have a twofold origin: they are shortened according to Hebrew rules partly from old absolute forms like *kálbu*, *sífru*, *qúdšu*, and partly from old construct-forms like the Assyrian types *kalab*, *sifir*, *quduš*.

[2] On the other hand, Ungnad, *ZA.* 1903, p. 333 ff., rejecting all previous explanations, maintains that the *a* in *mᵉlākhîm*, *mᵉlākhôth* is inserted merely to facilitate the pronunciation. From *qaṭlim* arose *qaṭᵃlim*, then *qaṭalim* and finally *qᵉṭālim*. See, however, Nöldeke, 'Zur semit. Pluralendung,' *ZA.* 1904, p. 68 ff., who points out that the Semitic nouns *faʿl*, *fiʿl*, *fuʿl* with their corresponding feminines *faʿla*, &c., on assuming the plural termination commonly take an *a* before the 3rd radical, but that no satisfactory account can be given for it. M. Margolis, 'The plural of Segolates' (*Proc. of the Philol. Assoc. of the Pacific Coast*, San Francisco, 1903, p. 4 ff.), and S. Brooks, *Vestiges of the broken plural in Hebrew*, Dublin, 1883, explain *mᵉlākhîm* as a *pluralis fractus*.

[3] It is worthy of notice that St. Jerome also (cf. Siegfried, *ZAW.* iv. 76) frequently represents the vowel of the first syllable by *a*, e.g. *gader*, *aben*, *ader*, *areb*, for גְּדֵר, אֶ֫בֶן, אֶ֫דֶר, חֶ֫רֶב, but *cedem*, *secel*, *deber*, &c., for קֶ֫דֶם, שֵׁ֫קֶל, דֶּ֫בֶר, &c.

or third radical be a guttural, a helping *Pathaḥ* takes the place of the helping *Sᵉghôl*, according to § 22 *d*, e. g. זֶרַע *seed*, נֶצַח *eternity*, פֹּעַל *work* ; but with middle ה or ח, note לֶחֶם *bread*, רֶחֶם (as well as רַחַם) *womb*, אֹהֶל *tent*, בֹּהֶן *thumb* ; so with final א, פֶּרֶא *a wild ass*, &c. ; with a middle guttural also the modification of the principal vowel *ă* to *ĕ* does not occur, e. g. לַחַץ, נַעַר, רַהַב (exceptions, again, רֶחֶם, לֶחֶם). On the inflexion, cf. § 93, Paradigm I, *a–f*, and the explanations. In חֵטְא *sin*, the א has wholly lost its consonantal value.

Examples of feminines : מַלְכָּה (directly from the ground-form *malk*, *king*), *b* סִתְרָה *a covering* (also סֵתֶר), אָכְלָה *food* (also אֹכֶל) ; with a middle guttural נַעֲרָה *girl*, טָהֳרָה *purity* (also טֹהַר). Cf. § 94, Paradigm I.

(*b*) From weak stems : (*a*) from stems ע״ן, e. g. אַף *nose* (from *'ănp*, hence *c* with formative additions, e. g. אַפִּי for *'anpi*, *my nose*) ; עֵז *a she-goat* (ground-form *'inz*) ; fem. חִטָּה *wheat* ; (*β*) from stems ע״ע (§ 93, Paradigm I, *l–n*) ; פַּת *a morsel*, עַם *people* (so, when in close connexion with the next word ; unconnected עָם ; with the article הָעָם, לָעָם, &c.) ; רַב in the sense of *much*, but רָב *great*, *numerous* (in close connexion also רַב) ; רָע *evil*, with the article in close connexion הָרַע, unconnected הָרָע ; with the *ă* always lengthened to *ā*, יָם *sea* ; fem. חַיָּה *life*, and with attenuation of the *ă* to *ĭ*, מִדָּה *measure* ; from the ground-form *qŭṭl*, אֵם *mother* ; fem. גִּזָּה *a shearing* ; from the ground-form *qŭṭl*, חֹק *statute*, fem. חֻקָּה. (*γ*) from stems ע״ו (Paradigm I, *g* and *i*) ; מָוֶת *death* (from *mă-ut*, the u passing into the corresponding consonant, as in תָּוֶךְ *middle*) or contracted יוֹם *day*, שׁוֹט *whip*, שׁוֹר *a bull* ; fem. עַוְלָה *perverseness* (also contracted עוֹלָה) ; from the ground-form *qŭṭl*, צוּר *a rock* ; fem. סוּפָה *a storm*.

(*δ*) from stems ע״י (Paradigm I, *h*) ; זַיִת *an olive-tree* (with a helping *Ḥireq* instead of a helping *Sᵉghôl*) from *ză-it*, the i passing into the corresponding consonant ; or contracted חֵיק *bosom*, חַיִל 2 K 18¹⁷ (elsewhere חֵיל) *host* ; fem. שֵׂיבָה *grey hair* ; from the ground-form *qŭṭl*, דִּין *judgement* ; fem. בִּינָה *understanding*. (*ε*) from stems ל״ה (Paradigm I, *k*) ; partly forms such as בֶּכֶה *weeping*, הֶגֶה *murmuring*, נֶדֶה *a present*, קֶצֶה *the end*, partly such as בְּכִי, אֲרִי *a lion* (ground-form *băky*, *'ăry*) ; cf. also the forms from stems originally ל״ו, שָׂחוּ *swimming* (ground-form *săḥw*) ; fem. שַׁלְוָה *rest*, גַּאֲוָה *exaltation* ; from stems ל״י, אַלְיָה *a fat tail*, and with attenuation of *ă* to *ĭ*, שִׁבְיָה *captivity*, also שְׁבִית, formed no doubt directly from the masc. שְׁבִי with the fem. termination ת ; from the ground-form *qŭṭl*, חֲצִי (from *ḥĭṣy*) ; fem. חֶדְוָה *joy*, עֶרְיָה and עֶרְוָה *nakedness* ; from the ground-form *qŭṭl*, בֹּהוּ (from *bŏhw*) *waste*, תֹּהוּ *emptiness* ; דְּלִי, for דַּלְי, *bucket* ; fem. אֳנִיָּה *a ship* (directly from אֳנִי *a fleet*).

The masculines as well as the feminines of these *segholate* forms may have *d* either an *abstract* or a *concrete* meaning. In the form קֹטֶל the *passive* or at any rate the *abstract* meaning is by far the more common (e. g. נֹעַר *youthfulness*, abstract of נַעַר *boy* ; אֹכֶל *food*, &c.).[1]

---

[1] M. Lambert also (*REJ*. 1896, p. 18 ff.), from statistics of the Segholates, arrives at the conclusion that the *qaṭl*-form is especially used for concretes (in nouns without gutturals he reckons twenty concretes as against two abstracts), and the *qiṭl*-form, and less strictly the *quṭl*, for abstracts.

e 2. Nouns with one of the three short vowels under the second radical (present ground-form qᵉṭăl, qᵉṭĭl, qᵉṭŭl), e. g. דְּבַשׁ *honey*, דְּוַי *sickness*, חֲתַת *terror*; and so always with middle א, בְּאֵר *a well*, זְאֵב *a wolf*, בְּאֹשׁ *stench*. In reality these forms, like the segholates mentioned in No. I (see above, *a*), are, probably, for the most part to be referred to original *dissyllabic* forms, but the tone has been shifted from its original place (the penultima) on to the ultima. Thus *dibăš* (originally *dibăš*) as ground-form of דְּבַשׁ is supported both by the Hebrew דִּבְשִׁי (with suffix of the first person), and by the Arabic *dibs*, the principal form; *bi'ir* (according to Philippi with assimilation of the vowel of the second syllable to that of the first) as ground-form of בְּאֵר is attested by the Arabic *bi'r*; for בְּאֹשׁ (Arabic *bu's*) similarly a ground-form *bu'uš* may be inferred, just as a ground-form *qŭṭŭl* underlies the infinitives of the form קְטֹל.[1]

II. *Nouns with an original Short Vowel in both Syllables.*

f 3. The ground-form qăṭăl, fem. qăṭălăt, developed in Hebrew to קָטָל (§ 93, Paradigm II, *a*, *b*) and קְטָלָה (§§ 94, 95, Paradigm II, *a*, *b*), mostly forms intransitive adjectives, as חָכָם *wise*, חָדָשׁ *new*, יָשָׁר *upright*; but also substantives, as דָּבָר *a word*, and even abstracts, as אָשָׁם *guilt*, רָעָב *hunger*, שָׂבָע *satiety*; in the fem. frequently abstract, as צְדָקָה[2] *righteousness*; with an initial guttural אֲדָמָה *earth*.—Of the same formation from verbs ע״ע are בָּדָד *alone*, עָנָן *cloud*; passive חָלָל *pierced*.—In verbs ל״ה a final Yôdh is almost always rejected, and the ă of the second syllable lengthened to ė. Thus שָׂדַי *field*, after rejection of the י and addition of ה as a vowel-letter, becomes שָׂדֶה (cf. § 93, Paradigm II, *f*); fem. e. g. שָׁנָה *year*; cf. § 95, Paradigm II, *c*. From a verb ל״י the strong form עָנָו *afflicted* occurs.

g 4. The ground-form qăṭĭl, fem. qăṭĭlăt, developed to קָטֵל (§ 93, Paradigm II, *c–e*) and קְטֵלָה, is frequently used as participle of verbs middle *e* (§ 50 *b*), and hence mostly with an intransitive meaning; cf. זָקֵן *old, an old man*; כָּבֵד *heavy*; fem. בְּהֵמָה *cattle*, אֲפֵלָה and חֲשֵׁכָה *darkness*.—From verbs פ״י: irregularly, דָּלִיּוֹתָיו *the branches of it*, Jer 11¹⁶, &c., generally referred to a *sing.* דָּלִית (stem דָּלָה), and הָרִיֹּתָיו Ho 14¹ *their women with child* (from הָרָה, *st. constr.* הֲרַת, *plur. st. absol.* and *constr.* הָרוֹת).—From a verb ל״ו with consonantal Wāw: שָׁלֵו *at ease*, incorrectly written *plene* שָׁלֵיו Jb 21²³.

h 5. The ground-form qăṭŭl, developed to קָטֹל (also written קָטוֹל), generally forms adjectives, e. g. אָיֹם *terrible*, בָּרֹד *piebald*, מָתוֹק *sweet*, נָקֹד *speckled*, עָבֹת *interwoven*, עָגֹל *round*, עָמֹק *deep*, עָקֹב *hilly*, צָהֹב *golden*; קָטֹן *small*, only in sing. masc., with a parallel form קָטָן of the class treated under *f*, fem. קְטַנָּה, plur. קְטַנִּים. These forms are not to be confounded with those in No. III, from

---

[1] On this theory cf. Stade, *Hebräische Grammatik*, § 199 *b*; De Lagarde, *Übersicht*, p. 57 f.; A. Müller, *ZDMG.* xlv, p. 226, and especially Philippi, *ZDMG.* xlix, p. 208.

[2] In St. Jerome's time these forms were still pronounced *ṣadaca* (צְדָקָה), *ṣaaca* (צְעָקָה), *nabala* (נְבָלָה), &c., see Siegfried, *ZAW.* iv. 79. Moreover, the numerous abstracts of this form (e. g. even קְצָפָה *a splintering*, צְוָחָה *a crying*, &c.) are undoubtedly to be regarded (with Barth, *Nominalbildung*, p. 87) as feminines of infinitives of the form qăṭăl, the lengthening of the second syllable being balanced, as in other cases, by the addition of the feminine termination.

the ground-form *qáṭál*.—Fem. אֵימָה, כְּבוּדָּה (*glorious*), עֲבֻתָּה, עֲנֻגָּה (*delicate*),
עֲמֻקָּה, עֲנֻלָּה, with sharpening of the third radical, in order to keep the original
ŭ short, and similarly in the plurals אֲסֻפִּים, עֲנֻלִים, נְקֻדִּים, בְּרֻדִּים *stores*, &c.

6. The ground-form *qíṭál* develops to קְטָל (cf. § 93, Paradigm II, Rem. 1), *i*
e. g. לְבָב *heart*, עֵנָב *a bunch of grapes*, שֵׁכָר *strong drink*; from a verb לְ״ה, probably
of this class is רֵעָה, generally contracted to רֵע *friend*, ground-form *ri'ay*: the
full form is preserved in רֵעֵהוּ *his friend*, for רֵעִיהוּ.

III. *Nouns with an original Short Vowel in the First and a Long Vowel*
in the Second Syllable.

7. The ground-form *qáṭál* in Hebrew always develops to the form קָטוֹל, the *k*
á becoming an obscure *ô*. The fact that this form is also written קָטֹל must
not lead to the confusion of these forms with those mentioned in No. 5, from
the ground-form *qáṭŭl*.[1] Moreover the *qaṭôl*-class includes forms of various
origin, and therefore of various meaning, as (*a*) intransitive adjectives like
גָּדוֹל *great*, קָדוֹשׁ *holy*, fem. גְּדוֹלָה, the short vowel becoming Šᵉwâ, whereas in
גְּדוֹל, &c., *before the tone* it is lengthened to *â*; (*b*) the *infinitives absolute* of the
form קָטוֹל (§ 45 *a*) as representing the abstract idea of the verb, and abstract
substantives like כָּבוֹד *honour*, שָׁלוֹם *peace* (Arab. *sâlâm*); (*c*) substantives and
adjectives in an active sense, as בָּחוֹן *assayer* (of metals), עָשׁוֹק *an oppressor*,
חָמוֹץ *oppressing*; in the feminine בָּגוֹדָה *treacherous* Jer 3⁷·¹⁰, the irregular
retention of the *â* in the third syllable from the end is no doubt to be
explained, with Brockelmann, from Aramaic influence, the punctuator having
in mind the Aramaic nomen agentis *qâṭôl*.

8. The ground-form *qáṭíl* develops to קָטִיל (cf. § 93, Paradigm IV, *a* and *b*). *l*
Here also forms of various origin and meaning are to be distinguished: (*a*)
adjectives used substantivally with a passive meaning to denote duration
in a state, as אָסִיר *a prisoner*, מָשִׁיחַ *an anointed one*. These proper *qáṭíl*-forms
are parallel to the purely passive *qaṭŭl*-forms (see *m*), but others are due to
a strengthening of original *qaṭíl*-forms. These are either (*b*) intransitive in
meaning, as צָעִיר *small*, and, from לְ״י stems, נָקִי *pure*, עָנִי *poor* (see § 93 *vv*), or (*c*)
active, as נָבִיא *a speaker* (prophet), פָּקִיד *an overseer*.—Of a different kind again
(according to De Lagarde, infinitives) are (*d*) forms like אָסִיף *the ingathering*,
בָּצִיר *vintage*, חָרִישׁ *ploughing time*, קָצִיר *harvest*. On *qáṭṭíl*-forms with a kindred
meaning, cf. § 84ᵇ *f*.

9. The ground-form *qáṭŭl* develops to קָטוּל. As in the *qaṭál* and *qaṭíl*-forms *m*
(see *k* and *l*), so here forms of various kinds are to be distinguished: (*a*)
qaṭŭl-forms proper, with passive meaning, especially all the passive participles
of Qal; fem. e. g. בְּתוּלָה *virgin* (properly *secluded*). On the other hand, by
strengthening an original *qaṭŭl*-form we get (*b*) certain stative adjectives
(§ 50 *f*), as אָנוּשׁ *incurable*, עָצוּם *strong*, עָרוּם *subtil*, or even transitive, as אָחוּז
holding; (*c*) active substantives, as יָקוּשׁ *a fowler*. Further, some of the forms
mentioned in § 84ᵇ *g* belong to this class; see above, the remark on *l*.

10. The ground-form *qíṭál* or *qŭṭál*[2] in Hebrew changes the *ĭ* to vocal Šᵉwâ, *n*

---

[1] In Na 1³ only the *Qᵉrê* requires גְּדָל־ (in the constr. state) for the Kᵉthîbh
גְּדוֹל.

[2] On the *fu'âl*-forms (regarded by Wellhausen as original diminutives) see
Nöldeke, *Beiträge* (Strassb. 1904), p. 30 ff. He includes among them נֹעֶרֶת *tow*,
and טְחֹרִים *hemorrhoids*.

and develops to קְטָל (cf. § 93, Paradigm IV, c) or קְטוֹל, with *â* obscured to *ô* (as above, *k*). Cf. שְׁאָר *remnant*, יְקָר *honour*, כְּתָב *book* (Arab. *kĭtâb*), קְרָב *war* (the last three probably loan-words from the Aramaic); of the other form, חֲלוֹם *a dream*, חֲמוֹר *an ass* (Arab. *ḥimâr*), אֱלוֹהַּ *God* (Arab. *'ilâh*); with א *prosthetic* (§ 19 *m*), אֶזְרוֹעַ *arm* (twice: usually זְרוֹעַ); fem. בְּשׂוֹרָה *good news* (Arab. *bĭšârăt*); עֲבוֹדָה *service*, כְּתֹבֶת (Arab. *kĭtâbăt*) *tattooing*.

o   11. The ground-form *qĭṭŭl* seems to occur e. g. in Hebrew אֱוִיל *foolish*, אֱלִיל *vanity*, בְּדִיל *lead*, כְּסִיל *a fool*, חֲזִיר *a swine* (the prop. name חֲזִיר points to the ground-form *qĭṭĭl*, cf. Arab. *ḥinzîr*).

p   12. The ground-form *qĭṭûl* or *qŭṭûl*, Hebr. קְטוּל, e. g. גְּבוּל *a boundary*, לְבוּשׁ *a garment*; fem. גְּבוּרָה *strength*, אֱמוּנָה *faithfulness*.

q   Rem. When the forms *qᵉṭûl* and *qᵉṭôl* begin with א, they almost invariably take in the singular a Ṣere under the א instead of the ordinary Ḥaṭeph-Sᵉghôl; cf. אֵבוּס *a crib*, אֵטוּן *thread*, אֵמוּן *faithful*, אֵזוֹב *hyssop*, אֵזוֹר, אֵסוּר *a waist-band*, *a bond*, אֵפוֹד *an 'ephod'*; cf. § 23 *h*, and the analogous cases of Ṣere for Ḥaṭeph-Sᵉghôl in verbal forms § 52 *n*, § 63 *p*, § 76 *d*.

IV. *Nouns with a Long Vocal in the First Syllable and originally a Short Vowel in the Second Syllable.*

r   13. The ground-form *qâṭăl*, in Hebrew, always changes the *â* into an obscure *ô*, קוֹטֶל (קוֹטָל), e. g. עוֹלָם (§ 93, Paradigm III, *a*), Arab. *'âlăm*, *eternity*; חוֹתָם (Arab. *ḥâtăm*) *a seal* (according to Barth a loan-word of Egyptian origin), fem. חֹתֶמֶת (from *ḥôtămt*); תּוֹלָע *worm* (unless from a stem ולע, like תּוֹשָׁב from ושׁב; see the analogous cases in § 85 *b*). On the participles Qal of verbs ל״ה (§ 93, Paradigm III, *c*), cf. § 75 *e*; on the feminines of the participles Qal, which are formed with the termination ת, see below, *s*.

Rem. Of a different kind (probably from a ground-form *qauṭal*) are such forms as אוֹפָן (or אוֹפַן Ez 10⁹ in the same verse) *a wheel*; גּוֹזָל *a young bird*, דּוֹנַג *wax*, &c.

s   14. The ground-form *qâṭĭl* also becomes in Hebrew almost invariably קוֹטֵל (קֹטֵל). Besides *participles active masc. Qal* this class includes also feminines of the form קֹטֶלֶת, if their ground-form *qôṭelt* (§ 69 *c*) goes back to an original *qâṭĭlt*. The substantives of this form, such as כֹּהֵן *priest* (Arab. *kâhin*), were also originally participles Qal. The fem. of the substantives has *ē* (lengthened from *ĭ*) retained before the tone, e. g. יֹלֵדָה *a woman in travail* (cf. also בֹּגֵדָה *the treacherous woman*, Jer 3⁸; הַצֹּלֵעָה *her that halteth*, Mi 4⁶ ⁷·, Zp 3¹⁹; סֹחֵרָה *a buckler*, ψ 91⁴); the participles as a rule have the form יֹלֶדָה, &c., the original *ĭ* having become Šᵉwâ; however, the form with Ṣere occurs also in the latter, Is 29⁶·⁸, 34⁹, ψ 68²⁶, 118¹⁶ (all in principal *pause*; in subordinate *pause* 2 S 13²⁰, Is 33¹⁴; with a conjunctive accent, Ct 1⁶).

t   15. The ground-form *qâṭŭl*, Hebrew קוֹטֶל (as יוּבַל *river*, Jer 17⁸) or קוֹטֶל e. g. עוּגָב *a pipe*, commonly עֻגָב, and to be so read, with Baer, also in ψ 150⁴, not עֹגָב.

V. *Nouns with a Long Vowel in each Syllable.*

u   16. קִיטוֹל, e. g. קִיטוֹר *smoke*. The few forms of this kind are probably derived from the ground-form *qîṭâl* (*qĭṭṭâl*?), i. e. the original *â* has become an obscure *ô*.

§ 84^b. *Formation of Nouns from the Intensive Stem.*

This includes all forms which have arisen, either through the *a* doubling of the middle radical, or the repetition of one or of two consonants of the simple stem.

VI. *Nouns with the Middle Consonant sharpened.*

As in the corresponding verbal stems (cf. § 52 *f*), so also in some noun-formations of this class, the Dageš in the second radical expresses an intensification of the idea of the stem, either emphasizing the energy of the action or relation, or else indicating a longer continuance of the relation or state. Other nouns of this character are evidently only by-forms of the nouns derived from the simple stem, which were treated in the last section : cf. the instances adduced under *f* and *g*, and Barth, *Nominalbildung*, Introd., p. x.

17. The ground-form *qăṭṭăl* is mostly lengthened in Hebrew to קַטָּל ; cf. *b* אַיִל *a stag*, fem. אַיָּלָה, *constr. st.* אַיֶּלֶת (from *'ăyyălt*) ; cf. also the fem. (originating from Qal) לֶהָבָה *a flame* (according to § 27 *q* for *lăhhābhā*), חָרָבָה *dry land* (for *ḥarrābhā*), דַּלֶּקֶת and קַדַּחַת *a burning fever*, יַבֶּשֶׁת and יַבָּשָׁה *dry land*, טַבַּעַת *a seal-ring*, שַׁחֶפֶת *consumption*. Adjectives of this class ('intensified participles of the active verb', Barth, *ibid.*, § 33) are חַטָּא *sinful*, נַגָּח *wont to gore*, קַנָּא *jealous*, כָּחָשׁ (for *kaḥḥāš*, by § 22 *c*) *lying*. Nomina opificum also, curiously enough, are so treated in Hebrew (at least in the *constr. state* of the sing.), although the corresponding Arabic form *qăṭṭāl* points to an original (unchangeable) *ā* in the second syllable ; cf. גַּנָּב *a thief*, דַּיָּן *a judge* (constr. st. דַּיַּן ψ 68⁶), טַבָּח *a cook*, חָרָשׁ (for *ḥarrāš*) *artificer* (constr. st. חָרַשׁ, but *plur. constr.* חָרָשֵׁי ; פָּרָשׁ *horseman* (for *parrāš*), *const. st.* פָּרַשׁ Ez 26¹⁰.

18. The ground-form *qĭṭṭăl* appears in צָחֶה *dry*, גֵּאֶה *haughty* (the *i* being *c* lengthened to *ē* according to § 22 *c*), if these forms go back to original *ṣiḥḥăy*, *gĭ'*ăy. On the analogy, however, of the adjectives denoting defects (see *d* below), we should rather expect a ground-form *qĭṭṭŭl*; moreover, *'iwwalt*, ground-form of the fem. אִוֶּלֶת *foolishness*, goes back to an original *iwwilt*, see § 69 *c*.

19. The ground-form *qŭṭṭăl* and *qŭṭṭŭl* ; cf. the fem. כֻּסֶּמֶת *spelt*, כֻּתֹּנֶת *coat*.

20. The ground-form *qăṭṭŭl* ; from the intensive stem, the infinitives Pi'ēl of *d* the form קַטֵּל.

21. The ground-form *qĭṭṭŭl*, in Hebrew lengthened to קִטֵּל. Of this form are a considerable number of adjectives which denote a bodily or mental fault or defect. Cf. אִטֵּר *disabled*, אִלֵּם *dumb*, גִּבֵּן *hump-backed*, עִוֵּר *blind*, חֵרֵשׁ *deaf* (for *ḥirrēš*), פִּסֵּחַ *lame*, קֵרֵחַ *bald*, עִקֵּשׁ *perverse* ; פִּקֵּחַ *open-eyed* follows the same analogy.

22. The ground-form *qăṭṭāl*, cf. the remarks in *b* above, on the *nomina e opificum* ; moreover, to this class belong infinitives Pi'ēl of the Aramaic form בַּקָּרָה *a searching out* ; בַּקָּשָׁה *a request* ; with middle guttural (see § 22 *c*) נָאָצָה *contumely* ; but cf. also נָאָצֹתֶיךָ Ez 35¹², with full lengthening of the original *ă* before א ; נֶחָמָה *comfort*. From the attenuation of the *ă* of this form to *ĭ*, arises undoubtedly :

23. The ground-form *qĭṭṭāl*, e. g. אִכָּר *husbandman* (Arab. *'ăkkār*).

24. The ground-form *qĭṭṭōl*, most probably only a variety of the form *qăṭṭāl* with the *ă* attenuated to *ĭ* (as in No. 23), and the *ā* obscured to *ō* (as in *n* and

r); cf. גִּבּוֹר *hero* (Arab. *găbbár*), יְסוֹר *caviller*, צִפּוֹר (*piper* or *chirper*) *a bird*, שִׁכּוֹר *drunkard*. On the other hand, יִלּוֹד *born* probably arises from *yullôd*, an old participle passive of *Qal*, the *ŭ* being dissimilated in the sharpened syllable before *ô*: so Barth, *ibid.*, p. 41 f.

f 25. The ground-form *qăṭṭîl*, קָטִיל, almost exclusively of persons, who possess some quality in an intensive manner, e. g. אַבִּיר *strong*, צַדִּיק *righteous*, בָּרִיחַ *fugitive* (for *barrîᵃḥ*), עָרִיץ *violent* (for *'ărrîṣ*).

That some of these are only by-forms of the *qăṭîl*-class (see above, remark on *a*), appears from the *constr. st.* פָּרִיץ *ravenous*, Is 35⁹ (but פָּרִיצִים, פְּרִיצֵי always), and according to Barth (*ibid.*, 35 *a*) also from the *constr. st.* אַבִּיר (but also אֲבִיר 1 S 21⁸) of אַבִּיר. However, the form אֲבִיר, as a name of God, may be intentionally differentiated from אַבִּיר, a poetic term for the bull.

In the same way אַסִּיר *prisoner*, סָרִים *eunuch* (*constr. st.* always סָרִיס, plur. סָרִיסִים, *constr. st.* סָרִיסֵי Gn 40⁷, but in the book of Esther always סָרִיסֵי, with *suffix* סָרִיסָיו, &c.), and עָתִיק *weaned*, may be regarded as by-forms of the *qăṭîl*-class wⁱᵗʰ passive meaning, see § 84ᵃ *l*.

g 26. The ground-form *qăṭṭûl*, קָטוּל, e. g. חַנּוּן *gracious*, רַחוּם *compassionate* (with virtual strengthening of the ח), חָרוּץ *diligent* (for *ḥarrûṣ*), probably, again, to a large extent by-forms of the *qăṭûl*-class, § 84ᵃ *m*. The same applies to substantives like אַשֻּׁר *a step* (in אַשֻּׁרִי, as well as אֲשֻׁרוֹ, &c.), עַמּוּד *pillar*; fem. חַבּוּרָה *a stripe* (also חֲבֻרָתוֹ, חַבֻּרוֹת), בַּטֻּחוֹת *security*: cf. Barth, *ibid.*, § 84.

h 27. The ground-form *qăṭṭôl*; besides the infinitives absolute *Piʿēl* of the form קַטֹּל, also קַנּוֹא *jealous* (as well as קַנָּא, an obscured form of *qăṭṭâl*, see *e*).

i 28. The ground-form *qĭṭṭûl*, קִטּוּל, e. g. צִפּוּי *a coating of metal*, שִׁלּוּם *requital*, שִׁקּוּי *drink*, שִׁקּוּץ *detestable thing*; with concrete meaning לִמּוּד *a disciple*, עִזּוּז *strong*; frequently in the plural in an abstract sense, as גִּדּוּפִים *reproach*, מִלֻּאִים *filling* (the induction of a priest), נִחֻמִים *consolations, compassion*, שִׁכֻּלִים *bereavement*, שִׁלּוּחִים *dismissal*, שִׁמֻּרִים *observance*.

VII. *Nouns with the Third Consonant repeated.*

k 29. The ground-form *qăṭlăl*, e. g. שַׁאֲנָן *quiet*, fem. שַׁאֲנַנָּה (with sharpening of the second *Nûn*, in order to keep the preceding vowel short); רַעֲנָן *green*, plur. רַעֲנַנִּים.

l 30. The ground-form *qăṭlĭl*, in Hebrew קְטַלְל; of this form are e. g. the infinitives *Piʿlēl* (prop. *Paʿlēl*), cf. § 55 *d*.

m 31. The ground-form *qăṭlŭl*; so the plur. גַּבְנֻנִּים *ridges* (with sharpening of the *Nûn*, as in No. 29).

32. The ground-form *qĭṭlăl*, in פִּרְחָח *a brood*.

33. The ground-form *qŭṭlăl*, in אֻמְלָל *faint*.

34. The ground-form *qăṭlîl*, e. g. עַבְטִיט *plunder*, סַגְרִיר *rain-storm*, שַׁפְרִיר *glittering tapestry*, Jer 43¹⁰ *Qᵉrê*; with attenuation of the *ă* to *i* in כְּמָרִירִים *all that maketh black*, Jb 3⁵ (but the better reading is כַּמְרִירֵי).

35. The ground-form *qăṭlûl*, e. g. שַׁפְרוּר Jer 43¹⁰ *Kᵉth.*; נַאֲפוּפִים *adulteries*.

VIII. *Nouns with the Second and Third Consonants repeated.*

n 36–39. *Qᵉṭălṭăl*, *qᵉ;ălṭŭl*, *qᵉṭălṭŭl*; *qᵉṭălṭôl*, *qᵉṭălṭôl* (in *fem.* and *plur.* often with the last consonant sharpened for the reason given in *a* above); cf. הֲפַכְפַּךְ

crooked, חֲלַקְלַקּוֹת *slippery places*, עֲקַלְקַלּוֹת *crooked (ways)* ; פְּתַלְתֹּל *tortuous* ; also words denoting colours, אֲדַמְדָּם (Lv 13⁴²·⁴⁹ in pause) *reddish*, fem. אֲדַמְדֶּמֶת, plur. אֲדַמְדַּמֹּת ; יְרַקְרַק *greenish*, plur. fem. יְרַקְרֹקֶת ; יְפֵיפִיָּה *very fair* (to be read in Jer 46²⁰ for יְפֵהפִיָּה) ; qᵉṭalṭûl, שְׁחַרְחֹרֶת (fem.) *blackish* ; אֲסַפְסֻף *a rabble* (augmented from אָסוּף *collected*). From a verb פ״ו with aphaeresis of the initial syllable צֶאֱצָאִים *offspring*. Moreover, of the same form, probably, is חֲצֹצְרָה *a trumpet* (for חֲצַרְצְרָה, cf. § 55 e). Also in Is 2²⁰ לַחְפַּרְפֵּרוֹת is to be read instead of לַחְפֹּר פֵּרוֹת (from the *sing.* חֲפַרְפֵּרָה a *digging* or *burrowing* animal, perhaps the *mole*). But פְּקַחְקוֹחַ *opening*, Is 61¹ (ed. Mant., Baer, Ginsb. פְּקַח־קוֹחַ), is an evident mistake due to dittography ; read פְּקֹחַ as in 42⁷.

IX. *Nouns in which the Whole (Biliteral) Stem is repeated.*

Naturally this class includes only isolated forms of the stems ע״ו and ע״ע *o* (on פִּיפִיּוֹת see § 96 under פֶּה). Thus :—

40. גַּלְגַּל *a wheel*, and, with attenuation of the first ă to ĭ, גִּלְגָּל (from גלל) ; fem. חַלְחָלָה *anguish* (from חוּל or חִיל) ; כִּכָּר (for kirkar) *a talent* ; cf. also כּוֹכָב *a star* (from kăwkăb, Arabic kaukăb, for כַּבְכַּב), טוֹטָפֹת *bands*, for טַפְטָפֹת ; צְלָצַל probably *a whirring locust*.

41. כִּלְכֵּל infin. *Pilpēl* (prop. *Palpīl*) from כּוּל ; fem. טַלְטֵלָה *a hurling* (from *p* טוּל).

42. כַּרְפֹּד perhaps a *ruby* (for kădkŭd), from כדד.

43. קָדְקֹד *the crown of the head* (for qŭdqŭd), from קדד ; fem. גֻּלְגֹּלֶת *a skull* (for gŭlgŭlt), from גלל.

44. זַרְזִיר *girded*, from זרר ; בַּקְבּוּק *a bottle*, from בקק ; בַּרְבֻּרִים *fattened birds* (?).

§ 85. *Nouns with Preformatives and Afformatives.*

These include nouns which are directly derived from verbal forms *a* having preformatives (*Hiphʿîl, Hophʿal, Hithpaʿēl, Niphʿal, &c.*), as well as those which are formed with other preformatives (א, י, מ, נ, ת), and finally those which are formed with afformatives. The quadri-literals and quinqueliterals also are taken in connexion with these formations, inasmuch as they arise almost always by the addition or insertion of one or two consonants to the triliteral stem.

X. *Nouns with Preformatives.*

45. Nouns with א prefixed. Cf. the substantives with א *prosthetic* (§ 19 m), *b* such as אֶזְרוֹעַ *arm* (Jer 32²¹, Jb 31²²; elsewhere always זְרוֹעַ) ; אֶצְבַּע *a finger*; אַרְבֶּה *a locust*, אֶגְרוֹף *fist* (others *mattock*, or *clod*), אַשְׁמוּרָה or אַשְׁמֹרֶת *a watch*. In these examples the א is a 'euphonic' prefix (Barth, *ibid.*, § 150 b) ; in other cases it is 'essential' ; cf. especially the adjectives, אַכְזָב *deceitful*, אַכְזָר *cruel*, אֵיתָן *perennial* (for *'aitan*) [=the Arab. 'elative', used for expressing the compar. and superl. degrees]. The fem. אַזְכָּרָה *fragrant part*¹ (of the meal-

---

¹ Or perhaps more correctly with Jacob, *ZAW.* 1897, p. 79, 'declaration,' i.e. the part of the meal-offering which 'announces the sacrifice and its object'.

offering) is a *nomen verbale* of *Hiph'il*, answering to the Aramaic infinitive of the causal stem (*'Aph'êl*), hence with suff. אַזְכָּרָתָהּ Lv 2², &c.

c 46. Nouns with ה prefixed. Besides the ordinary infinitives of *Hiph'il* הַקְטֵל and הַקְטִיל, of *Niph'al* הִקָּטֵל, הִקָּטֹל (for *hinq.*), and of the conjugations formed with the prefix הִתְ, this class also includes some rare *nomina verbalia* derived from *Hiph'il* (cf. § 72 *z*), viz. הַכָּרָה *appearance* (from נָכַר), Is 3⁹; הֲנָפָה a swinging (from נוּף), [Is 30²⁸; הֲנָחָה a *rest-giving*, Est 2¹⁸]; הַצָּלָה *deliverance* (from נָצַל), [Est 4¹⁴ an Aram. form : cf. הֶזְדָּה Dn 5²⁰]; perhaps also הֵיכָל *palace*, from *haikâl*, unless it is borrowed from the Assyrian ; see the Lexicon.

d 47. Nouns with י prefixed, as יִצְהָר *oil*, יַלְקוּט *wallet*, יַנְשׁוּף *owl*(?) ; from verbs ע״וּ, e. g. יְקוּם a *living thing*, יָתוּר a *range* ; from a verb ע״י, יָרִיב an *adversary*. Of a different character are the many proper names which have simply adopted the imperfect form, as יִצְחָק, יַעֲקֹב, &c.

e 48. Nouns with מ prefixed. This *preformative Mêm*, which is no doubt connected with מִי *who*, and מָה *what* (see § 37 and § 52 *c*), appears in a very large number of nouns, and serves to express the most varied modifications of the idea of the stem : (1) מ *subjective*, when preformative of the participles *Pi'êl*, *Hiph'il*, *Hithpa'êl*, and other active conjugations. (2) מ *objective*, when preformative of the participles *Pu'al*, *Hoph'al*, and other passive conjugations, as well as of numerous nouns. (3) מ *instrumental*, as in מַפְתֵּחַ a *key*, &c. (4) מ *local*, as in מִדְבָּר a *drive for cattle*, &c.

f As regards the formation of these nouns, it is to be remarked that the preformative מ was originally in most cases followed by a short *ă*. This *ă*, however, in a closed syllable is frequently attenuated to *ĭ* ; in an open syllable before the tone it is lengthened to *ā* (so also the *ĭ*, attenuated from *ă*, is lengthened to *ê*), and in מָגֵן *shield* (with suff. מָגִנִּי) it even becomes unchangeable *â*. But in an open syllable which does *not* stand before the tone, the *a* necessarily becomes *Sᵉwâ*.

g The following forms are especially to be noticed : (*a*) ground-form *măqtăl*, in Hebrew מַקְטֵל,¹ e. g. מַאֲכָל *food* ; fem. מַמְלָכָה *kingdom*, מַאֲכֶלֶת a *knife*, (for מַלְאָכָה by § 23 *c*) *business* ; from a verb פ״ן, מַתָּן a *gift* ; from verbs פ״י, מוֹצָא a *going forth*, מוֹשָׁב a *seat* ; from verbs פ״ו, מֵיטָב the *best* (from *maiṭăb*) ; with י (or ו) assimilated, מַצָּע a *bed* ; from verbs ע״ע, מָסָךְ a *screen*, and with the shortening of the *ă* under the preformative, מְמֶר *bitterness* (from מְמַר developed to a segholate), fem. מְשַׁמָּה *desolation* ; from a verb ע״ו, probably of this class is מָקוֹם *place*, the *ă* lengthened to *ā* and obscured to *ô* (Arabic *măqâm*) ; from verbs ל״ה, מַרְאֶה *appearance*, מַעַן (for מַעֲנֶה) prop. *intention*, only in לְמַעַן *on account of*, *in order that*.

h (*b*) Ground-form *miqtăl* (the usual form of the infin. *Qal* in Aramaic), Hebr. מִקְטָל, e. g. מִדְבָּר (in Jer 2³¹ also, where Baer requires הַמִּדְבָּר, read with ed. Mant., Ginsburg, &c. הַמִּדְבָּר) a *cattle-drive*, fem. מִלְחָמָה *war*, מֶרְכָּבָה a *chariot* (with *Sᵉghôl* instead of *ĭ*, but in constr. st. מִרְכֶּבֶת Gn 41⁴³ ; cf. מֶרְחָק *distance*), מִשְׁמֶרֶת a *watch* ; from verbs ע״ע, e. g. מֵסַב *surroundings* (from *mĭ-săb* ; *ĭ* in the open syllable being lengthened to *ê* ; but cf. also מַשָּׁק Is 33⁴ as constr. state from שׁקק with sharpening of the first radical ; cf. § 67 *g*) ; from verbs ל״ה, מִקְנֶה a *possession*, fem. מִקְנָה.

---

¹ In כְּמִתְקִים Ct 5¹⁶, Neh 8¹⁰, the first syllable is artificially opened to avoid the cacophony ; on the *ă* of the second syllable cf. § 93 *ee*.

(*c*) Ground-form *măqṭŭl*, Hebr. מַקְטֵל, e.g. מַשְׁעֵן *a support* (fem. מַשְׁעֵנָה), *i*
מַסְגֵּר *a smith*, מַעֲשֵׂר *a tithe*; fem. מַכְשֵׁלָה *a ruin*; from a verb פ״נ, מַגֵּפָה *an*
overthrow, מַצֵּבָה *a pillar*; from verbs ע״ע, מָגֵן *a shield*; fem. מְגִלָּה *a roll* (from
גָּלַל), מְאֵרָה *a curse* (for *me'irrā* from אָרַר); from a verb פ״ו, מוֹקֵשׁ *a snare*
(from *măwqiš*).

(*d*) Ground-form *miqṭŭl*, Hebr. מִקְטֵל, e.g. מִסְפֵּד *mourning*, מִזְבֵּחַ *an altar* *k*
(*place of sacrifice*); from a verb ע״ע, e.g. מֵסַב (מִסַּב?) *consessus*; (*e*) ground-
form *măqṭŭl*, Hebr. מַקְטֹל; fem. מַאֲכֹלֶת *food*, מַשְׂכֹּרֶת *wages*; from a verb ע״ע,
fem. מְסִבָּה *a covering* (from סָכַךְ). Also from ע״ע, according to the Masora,
מָעֹז *a refuge*, with suffixes מָעֻזִּי and מָעוּזִּי, plur. מָעֻזִּים, but, very probably,
most if not all of these forms are to be referred to the stem עוז *to flee for safety*,
and therefore should be written מָעוֹזִי, &c. The form מָעֹז, if derived from
the stem עזז, would mean *stronghold*.—Cf. also מֹרֶךְ *faintness*, developed to a
segholate, probably from מֹרֶךְ, for *mărōkh* from רָכַךְ, like מְתֹם *soundness of*
body, from תָּמַם.

With a long vowel in the second syllable: (*f*) ground-form *maqṭāl*, with *á* *l*
always obscured to *ô*, e.g. מַחְסוֹר *want*, מַלְקוֹחַ *booty*; from verbs ע״ע, e.g. מָגוֹר
fear, fem. מְגוֹרָה and מְגוּרָה (with the *ô* depressed to *ú* in a toneless syllable;
cf. § 27 *n*), מְהוּמָה, &c., Is 22⁵. (*g*) Ground-form *miqṭāl*, in Hebr. again מִקְטוֹל,
e.g. מִסְתּוֹר *a covert*, מִכְשׁוֹל *a stumbling-block* (cf. above under *i*, *măkh*ᵉ*šēlā*); fem.
מִכְמֹרֶת *a fishing-net*; (*h*) the ground-forms *maqṭil*, *miqṭil* (cf. מֵקִים) are found
only in participles Hiph'il; the fem. מַבְלִיגִית, *cheerfulness*, is a denominative
formed from a participle Hiph'il; (*i*) ground-form *măqṭūl*, as מַלְבּוּשׁ *a garment*.

Rem. On מ as preformative of the participles of all the conjugations except *m*
Qal and Niph'al, cf. § 52 *c*. Many of these participles have become substantives,
as מַזְמֵרָת *snuffers*, מַשְׁחִית *destroyer, destruction*.

49. Nouns with נ prefixed. Besides the participles Niph'al (ground-form *n*
năqṭăl, still retained e.g. in נוֹלָד for *năwlād*, but commonly attenuated to *niqṭăl*,
Hebr. נִקְטָל) and the infinitive Niph'al of the form נִקְטֹל, the prefix נ is found
in נַפְתּוּלִים *wrestlings*, Gn 30⁸, which is also to be referred to Niph'al, and נָזִיד
boiled pottage (stem זיד).

50. With שׁ prefixed, e.g. שַׁלְהֶבֶת *a flame*. On this *Šaph'ēl* formation, cf. § 55 *i*. *o*

51. Nouns with ת prefixed. Examples of this formation are numerous, *p*
especially from weak stems, for the purpose of strengthening them phoneti-
cally (see Barth, *ibid.*, p. 283), and notably from verbs פ״ו and ע״ע. They
may be classified as follows:—(*a*) the ground-form *tăqṭăl* in תַּחְמָס *ostrich* (?);
from verbs פ״ו, תּוֹשָׁב *a settler*; fem. תּוֹחֶלֶת *expectation*, תּוֹכַחַת (from the Hiph'il
הוֹכִיחַ) *correction*; from a verb פ״י, תֵּימָן *the south*; from verbs פ״ו and ל״ה,
תּוֹדָה *thanksgiving*, and תּוֹרָה *law*, both from Hiph'il; from a verb פ״ו and ל״א,
תּוֹצָאוֹת *issues*; probably belonging to this class, from verbs ע״ע, תֶּבֶל *confusion*,
and תֶּמֶס *a melting away* (developed from תֵּבֵל and תֵּמֵס, from בָּלַל and מָסַס).

(*b*) *Tiqṭăl*, e.g. fem. תִּפְאָרָה and תִּפְאֶרֶת *glory*; from a verb ל״ה, e.g. תִּקְוָה *q*
hope; (*c*) *tăqṭŭl*, e.g. תַּשְׁבֵּץ *chequer work*; fem. תַּרְדֵּמָה *deep sleep* (probably from
the Niph'al נִרְדַּם); from a verb פ״נ, תּוֹכֵחָה *correction* (from the Hiph'il-stem,
like the *constr. st. plur.* תּוֹלְדוֹת *generations*); from verbs ע״ע, תְּהִלָּה *praise*, תְּפִלָּה
prayer (from the Pi'ēl of the stems הָלַל and פָּלַל).

r　With a long vowel in the second syllable : (*d*) *tiqṭâl*, as תְּהוֹם *the ocean, the deep* (for *tihâm* ; in Assyrian the fem. *tiâmtu*, constr. st. *tiâmat*, is the usual word for *sea*), unless it is to be derived with Delitzsch, *Prolegomena*, p. 113, from the stem תהם ; (*e*) *tåqṭîl* (in Arabic the usual form of the infinitive of conjugation II. which corresponds to the Hebrew *Piʿēl*), e. g. from a verb ל״ה, fem. תַּכְלִית *completeness* ; תַּרְבִּית *increase, usury*, with a parallel form מַרְבִּית ; in a passive sense, תַּלְמִיד *a disciple* ; (*f*) תַּקְטוּל, e. g. תַּפּוּחַ *an apple* (for *tånpûaḥ*) ; very frequently used to form abstracts, e. g. תַּגְמוּל *a benefit* (also גְּמוּל) ; from verbs ע״וּ תְּבוּסָה *a treading down*, תְּנוּפָה *a waving* (like תְּרוּמָה *a lifting up*, from the *Hiphʿîl* stem), תְּשׁוּקָה *a longing*, &c. ; very frequently also as an abstract plural, e. g. תַּהְפֻּכוֹת *perverseness*, תַּחְבֻּלוֹת *guidance*, תַּמְרוּרִים *bitterness*, תַּנְחוּמִים and תַּנְחֻמוֹת *consolation* ; from a verb ע״וּ תְּאָנִים *toil*.

XI. Nouns with Afformatives.

s　52. **Nouns with ל affixed.** Perhaps חַשְׁמַל *amber* (?), and probably בַּרְזֶל *iron*, כַּרְמֶל *garden-land* (Sᵉghôl in both cases is probably a modification of the original *ă* in the tone-syllable), גִּבְעֹל *bloom*, cf. § 30 *q*.—According to Prätorius, *ZDMG.* 1903, p. 530 ff., *al* is an affix of endearment in the proper names מִיכָל, חֲמוּטַל (*little lizard* ?) אֲבִינַל (also אֲבִינָיֵל).

t　53. **Nouns with ם affixed.** With an original *ăm* as afformative, אוּלָם *vestibule* (although the *â* in the *sing.* remains unchangeable), plur. אֻלַמִּים ; but in כְּנָם *a swarm of gnats*, the ם is radical. With original afformative *ûm*, עֵירֹם (also עֵרֹם) *naked* (from עוּר), plur. עֵירֻמִּים Gn 3⁷, parallel form עָרוֹם, plur. עֲרוּמִּים Gn 2²⁵.—To this class also belong the adverbs in *âm* and *ôm*, mentioned in § 100 *g*, and many proper names, as גֵּרְשֹׁם, also גֵּרְשׁוֹם, and גֵּרְשֹׁן (patronymic גֵּרְשֻׁנִּי), מַלְכָּם, עַמְרָם, &c. ; but for פִּדְיֹם *ransom* (?), Nu 3⁴⁹, probably פִּדְיוּם is to be read.

u　54. **Nouns with ן affixed.** The ן is added by means of a simple helping vowel in כְּנַעַן *Canaan*, and צִפֹּרֶן *a finger nail* ; more frequently the addition is made by means of a tone-bearing *ă*, which in Hebrew is modified to Sᵉghôl (as גַּרְזֶן *axe*) or lengthened to *â* (but cf. also אָחֳרַנִּית and קָדְרַנִּית) ; e. g. קִנְיָן *a possession*, שֻׁלְחָן *a table*, קָרְבָּן *an offering*. From an original *â* being changed into an obscure *ô* we may probably explain such forms as דִּאָבוֹן *a pining away* ; דְּרָבוֹן (also דָּרְבָן) *a goad* ; רְעָבוֹן *hunger* ; from verbs ל״ה, גָּאוֹן *pride*, הָמוֹן *noise*, חָזוֹן *a vision* ; שִׁרְיוֹן *a coat of mail* ; from a verb פ״ן מַשָּׁאוֹן *guile* (the only instance with both מ preformative and *ôn* afformative) [1] ; very frequently from the simple stem with an unorganic sharpening of the second radical, e. g זִכָּרוֹן *memorial*, כִּלָּיוֹן *destruction* (constr. st. זִכְרוֹן and כִּלְיוֹן), &c. ; cf. also הֵרָיוֹן *pregnancy* (for הֶרְ׳) and § 93 *uu* ; קִיקָלוֹן *shame*, for קַלְקָלוֹן. Proper names occur with the termination *ûn*, as יְשֻׁרוּן, § 86 *g*, and others.

---

[1] The plurals נִצָּנִים *flowers*, Ct 2¹², and קִמְּשֹׂנִים *thorns* appear to be formed directly from the singulars נֵץ (cf. נִצָּה) and קִמּוֹשׂ with the insertion of *ân* (which in קִמְּ׳ is obscured to *ôn*). See Nöldeke, *Mand. Gr.*, p. 169, Rem. 3 ; similarly, according to Hoffmann, 'Einige phöniz. Inschriften,' p. 15 (*Abh. der Gött. Ges. der Wiss.*, xxxvi), עֻבּוֹנִים *wares*, Ez 27¹⁴·¹⁶ from עֶצֶב=עָצָב.

Rem. A large number of proper names now ending in הָ‎ֶ or וֹ‎ָ used to *v*
be classed as nouns originally formed with the affix וֹן‎ָ. The subsequent
rejection of the final *Nûn* seemed to be confirmed by the form מִגְדּוֹן‎, once
used (Zc 12¹¹) for מִגְדּוֹ‎ (and conversely in Pr 27²⁰ *K*ᵉ*thibh* אֲבַדֹּה‎, *Q*ᵉ*rê* אֲבַדּוֹ‎ for
אֲבַדּוֹן‎ *destruction*), also by the fact that for שְׁלֹמֹה‎ the LXX give the form
Σολωμών or Σαλωμών, and especially that in patronymics and tribal names
(§ 86 *h*) a *Nûn* appears before the termination *î*, as גִּילֹנִי‎ *Gilonite* from גִּלֹה‎ and
שִׁילֹנִי‎ from שִׁילֹה‎ (modern name *Sailûn*). Wetzstein, however (in Delitzsch's
Commentary on Job, 1st ed., p. 599), explained the *Nûn* in מִגְדּוֹן‎ as a secondary
addition to the common old-Palestinian termination *ô* (רִמּוֹנוֹ‎, עַכּוֹ‎, יְרִיחוֹ‎,
&c.), and Barth (*Nominalbildung*, § 224 *b*) has since shown the unsoundness of
the prevailing view on other grounds: the rejection of the *Nûn* would be
much more likely to occur in the numerous appellatives in *ôn* than in proper
names, and גִּילֹנִי‎ and שִׁילֹנִי‎ are due to the necessity of avoiding, for euphonic
reasons, such forms as *gilô-î*, *šilô-î*, &c.; cf. also שְׁלָנִי‎ from שֵׁלָה‎.

On the afformatives יָ‎ִ, יֶ‎ָ, וּת‎, ית‎ָ, see below, § 86 *h–l*.

XII. *Quadriliterals and Quinqueliterals.*

55. גַּלְמוּד‎ *barren,* חַלָּמִישׁ‎ *a flint,* and the fem זַלְעָפָה‎ *heat,* &c., have probably *w*
arisen from the insertion of a ל‎; חַרְגֹּל‎ *a locust,* קַרְדֹּם‎ *an axe,* סַרְעַפָּה‎ *a branch,*
Ez 31⁵ (verses 6, 8 סְעַפָּה‎), שַׂרְעַפִּים‎ (also שְׂעִפִּים‎) *anxious thoughts,* שַׁרְבִיט‎ *sceptre,*
from insertion of a ר‎, which is common in Aramaic. Cf., moreover, חֶרְמֵשׁ‎
a sickle, סְמָדַר‎ *vine-blossom;* with an initial ע‎, עֲטַלֵּף‎ *a bat,* עַכָּבִישׁ‎ *a spider,* עַכְבָּר‎
a mouse, עַקְרָב‎ *a scorpion,*[1] &c.—Quinqueliteral, צְפַרְדֵּעַ‎ *a frog.*

§ 86. *Denominative Nouns.*

1. Such are all nouns formed *immediately* from another noun, *a*
whether the latter be primitive or derived from a verb, e. g. קַדְמוֹן‎
eastern, immediately from קֶדֶם‎ *the east* (verbal stem קָדַם‎ *to be in front*).

2. Most of the forms which nouns of this class assume have already *b*
been given in §§ 84 and 85, since the denominatives, as secondary
(although in some cases very old) forms, invariably follow the analogy
of the verbal derivatives. As, for instance, the verbals with a prefixed
מ‎ (§ 85 *e* to *m*) express the place, &c., of an action, so the denominatives with מ‎ *local* represent the place where a thing is found or its
neighbourhood (see *e*).

The most common forms of denominatives are—   *c*

1. Those like the *participle Qal* (§ 84ᵃ *s*), e. g. שֹׁעֵר‎ *a porter,* from שַׁעַר‎ *a gate;*
בֹּקֵר‎ *a herdsman,* from בָּקָר‎ *a herd;* כֹּרֵם‎ *a vinedresser,* from כֶּרֶם‎ *a vineyard.*
2. Those like the form *qáṭṭāl* (§ 84ᵇ *b*), e. g. קַשָּׁת‎ *an archer,* from קֶשֶׁת‎ *a bow. d*

---

[1] Derenbourg (*REJ.*, 1883, p. 165) infers from the above examples and a
comparison of the Arabic *'uṣfûr*, *sparrow* (from *ṣafara, to chirp*), that ע‎ was
especially employed to form quadriliteral names of animals.

Both these forms (*c* and *d*) indicate customary occupations, inhering in the subject, like Greek nouns in τηϛ, τεύϛ, e. g. πολίτηϛ, γραμματεύϛ.

e　3. Nouns with מ prefixed, denoting the place where a thing is (cf. § 85 *e*), or its neighbourhood, e. g. מַעְיָן *a place of fountains*, from עַיִן; מַרְגְּלוֹת *the place about the feet*, מְרַאֲשׁוֹת *the place about the head*, from רֶגֶל, ראֹשׁ; מִקְשָׁה (for מִקְשָׁאָה) *a cucumber field*, from קִשֻּׁא *cucumber*. Cf. ἀμπελών from ἄμπελοϛ.

f　4. Nouns with the termination ָ‍ן or וֹן expressing adjectival ideas : קַדְמוֹן *eastern*, from קֶדֶם; אַחֲרוֹן *posterior*, from אַחַר; חִיצוֹן *exterior*, from חוּץ; probably also לִוְיָתָן *coiled*, hence *coiled animal*, *serpent*, from לִוְיָה *a winding*; נְחֻשְׁתָּן *brazen*, from נְחֹשֶׁת *brass*. Also abstracts, e. g. עִוָּרוֹן *blindness*, from עִוֵּר. Cf. § 85 *u*.— With a double termination (*ôn* or *ân* with *î*) אַדְמֹנִי *reddish*, יִדְעֹנִי *a knowing* (spirit); צִפְעֹנִי *basilisk*; רַחֲמָנִיּוֹת *merciful* [fem. plur.].

g　וֹן appears to be used as a diminutive ending (cf. the Syriac וּן) in אִישׁוֹן *little man* (in the eye), *apple of the eye*, from אִישׁ[1]; on the other hand שְׁפִיפֹן *adder*, which was formerly regarded as a diminutive, is properly an adjectival form from שָׁפַף *to rub* (hence, as it were, a *rubbing creature*); in the same way יְשֻׁרוּן is a *denominative* from יָשֻׁר (=יָשָׁר), properly *upright* (*righteous people*), and not a *diminutive* (*pious little people*, and the like); finally, שַׁהֲרֹן is not *lunula*, but *an artificial moon* (used as an ornament), and צַוְּרֹנִים not *little neck*, but *necklace* (from צַוָּאר *neck*). Cf. Delitzsch on Ct 4[9].

h　5. Peculiar to denominatives is the termination ִ‍י, which converts a substantive into an adjective, and is added especially to numerals and names of persons and countries, in order to form *ordinals*, *patronymics*, and *tribal names*; e. g. רַגְלִי *footman*, plur. רַגְלִים, from רֶגֶל *foot*; נָכְרִי *cruel*, אַכְזָרִי *strange*, from נֵכָר *strangeness*, תַּחְתִּי *lower*, from תַּחַת *below*, fem. תַּחְתִּית and תַּחְתֹּנָה, plur. תַּחְתִּיּוֹת תַּחְתִּים; שִׁשִּׁי *the sixth*, from שֵׁשׁ *six*; מוֹאָבִי *Moabite*, from מוֹאָב, plur. מוֹאָבִים, fem. מוֹאֲבִיָּה and מוֹאָבִית, plur. מוֹאֲבִיּוֹת; עִבְרִי *Hebrew*, plur. עִבְרִים and עִבְרִיִּם, fem. עִבְרִיָּה, plur. עִבְרִיּוֹת; יִשְׂרְאֵלִי *Israelite*, from יִשְׂרָאֵל. When the original substantive is a *compound*, it is resolved again into two words, e. g. בֶּן־יְמִינִי *Benjamite*, from בִּנְיָמִין (cf. on the use of the article in such cases, § 127 *d*).

i　Instead of ִ‍י we find in a few cases (*a*) the ending ַ‍י (as in Aram.), e. g. פִּילַי (*crafty*, or, according to others, *churlish*) if it stands for נְכִילַי and is not rather from a stem כְּלָא or כלה; חוֹרַי *white cloth*, Is 19[9] in pause; perhaps also גּוֹבַי *a swarm of locusts*, Am 7[1] (גּוֹבָי Na 3[17]); hardly נְגִינוֹתַי Is 38[20], Hb 3[19]; but certainly in proper names as בַּרְזִלַּי (*ferreus*) *Barzillai*;[2] and (*b*) ה ָ‍,

---

[1] Cf. Barth, § 212; König, ii. 1, 413. Diminutives in Semitic languages are, however, most commonly formed by inserting a *y* after the second radical, e. g. Aram. עוּלֵּימָא, Syr. ܟܠܝܼܠܵܐ, Arab. غُلَيِّم *a very young man*, *kulaib*, *a little dog*, &c. Since Olshausen (§ 180), עָיִר *a little* (Is 28[10.13], Jb 36[2]) has commonly been regarded as an example of the same form, to which others have added שְׁבִיסִים Is 3[18] (as though a foreign dialectical form for *šumais*, *little sun*), and אֲמִינוֹן 2 S 13[20], as a contemptuous diminutive form of אַמְנוֹן; cf. Ewald, § 167, W. Wright, *Arab. Gramm.*[2] i. § 269, De Lagarde, *Nominalbildung*, pp. 85–87, König. ii. 1, p. 143 f. The existence of the form in Hebrew is disputed by Barth, § 192 *d*.]

[1] On ָ‍י as an old fem. ending, see above, § 80 *l*.

arising from *ǎy*, in אִשֶּׁה *belonging to fire* (אֵשׁ), i. e. *a sacrifice offered by fire*; לִבְנֶה (prop. *milky*) *the storax-shrub*, Arabic *lubnay*.

6. *Abstract* nouns formed from *concretes* by the addition of וּת ,ת‐[‐‐ְ‐ִ] *k* (§ 95 *t*), cf. our terminations *-dom, -hood, -ness*, e.g. יַלְדוּת *youth*, מַלְכוּת *kingdom* (the omission of the *Dageš* in כ shows that the *Šewâ* is weakened from a full vowel; on *malik* as underlying the present form מֶלֶךְ cf. § 84*ª a*); אַלְמָנוּת *widowhood*, from אַלְמָן *widower*, אַלְמָנָה *widow*. In Aram. this fem. ending וּת (or וּ with rejection of the ת) is a common termination of the infinitive in the derived conjugations (cf., as substantival infinitives of this kind, הַשְׁמָעוּת *the announcing*, Ez 24²⁶, and הִתְחַבְּרוּת *the making of a league*, Dn 11²³); in Hebr. וּת as a termination to express abstract ideas (including some which appear to be directly derived from the verbal stem, as סִכְלוּת *folly*, רְפֻאוּת *a healing*[1]) becomes more common only in the later books. It is affixed to adjectives ending in *î* (see above, *h*) in אַכְזְרִיּוּת *cruelty*, and קוֹמְמִיּוּת *upright position* (Lv 26¹³, used adverbially).

The ending ‐ִית is found earlier, e.g. in שְׁאֵרִית *remainder*, רֵאשִׁית *prin-* *l* *cipium*, from רֵאשׁ=רֹאשׁ (*head*) *princeps*. The termination *ôth* seems to occur in חָכְמוֹת *wisdom* (in Pr 1²⁰, 9¹, joined to a *singular*; so also חַכְמוֹת Pr 14¹, where, probably, חָכְמוֹת should likewise be read) and in הוֹלֵלוֹת Ec 1¹⁷, &c., with the parallel form הוֹלֵלוּת Ec 10¹³.

§ 87. *Of the Plural.*

Brockelmann, *Grundriss*, i. 426 ff., and on the feminines, p. 441 ff.; M. Lambert, 'Remarques sur la formation du pluriel hébreu,' *REJ.* xxiv. 99 ff., and 'Les anomalies du pluriel des noms en Hébreu,' *REJ.* xliii. 206 ff.; P. Lajčiak, *Die Plural- u. Dualendungen im semit. Nomen*, Lpz. 1903; J. Barth, 'Beiträge zur Pluralbildung des Semit.,' *ZDMG.* 1904, p. 431 ff., i. 'the *ai* of the constr. st.'

1. The regular *plural* termination for the *masculine gender* is ‐ִים, *a* always with the tone, e.g. סוּס *horse*, plur. סוּסִים *horses*; but also very often written defectively ‐ִם, especially when in the same word one of the vowel letters, ו or י, precedes, e.g. Gn 1²¹ תַּנִּינִם. Nouns in ‐ִי make their plural in ‐ִיִּים, e.g. עִבְרִי *a Hebrew*, plur. עִבְרִים (Ex 3¹⁸); but usually contraction takes place, e.g. עִבְרִים; שָׁנִים *crimson garments*, from שָׁנִי.

Nouns in ‐ֶה lose this termination when they take the plural *b* ending, e.g. חֹזֶה *seer*, plur. חֹזִים (cf. § 75 *h*).—In regard to the loss of the tone from the ‐ִם in the two old plurals מַיִם *water* and שָׁמַיִם *heaven*, cf. § 88 *d* and § 96.

The termination ‐ִים is sometimes assumed also by feminines (cf. *c* נָשִׁים *women*, § 96 under אִשָּׁה; שָׁנִים *years*, from שָׁנָה; רְחֵלִים *ewes*, from רָחֵל), so that an indication of gender is not necessarily implied in it (cf. also below, *m–p*).—On the use of this termination ‐ִים to express abstract, extensive, and intensive ideas, cf. § 124.

---

[1] [See a complete list of instances in König, *Lehrgebäude*, ii. 1, p. 205 f.]

d The ending *îm* is also common in Phoenician, e. g. צדנם *Sidonii* ; Assyrian has *âni* (acc. to P. Haupt originally *âmi*, cf. § 88 *d*) ; Aramaic has *în* ; Arabic *ûna* (nominative) and *ína* (in the oblique cases, but in vulgar Arabic *în* is also used for the nominative) ; Ethiopic *ân*. Cf. also the verbal ending וּן in the 3rd plur. perf. (§ 44 *l*) and in the 3rd and 2nd plur. impf. (§ 47 *m*).[1]

e Less frequent, or only apparent terminations of the plur. masc. are—

(*a*) יִן__ , as in Aramaic,[2] found almost exclusively in the later books of the O. T. (apart from the poetical use in some of the older and even the oldest portions), viz. מְלָכִין *kings*, Pr 31³, צֹדְנִין 1 K 11³³, רָצִין *the guard*, 2 K 11¹³, חִטִּין *wheat*, Ez 4⁹ ; defectively אִיִּן *islands*, Ez 26¹⁸ ; יָמִין *days*, Dn 12¹³. Cf. also מִדִּין *carpets*, Ju 5¹⁰, in the North-Palestinian song of Deborah, which also has other linguistic peculiarities ; עָיִין *heaps*, Mi 3¹² (before ת ; cf. § 44 *k*) ; מִלִּין *words* (from the really Aram. מִלָּה), Jb 4², and twelve other places in Job (beside מִלִּים, ten times in Job) ; further, חַיִּין Jb 24²², אַחֲרִין 31¹⁰, and שׁוֹמֵמִין La 1⁴, תַּנִּין 4³.—The following forms are doubtful :

f (*b*) יִ__ (with the ם rejected, as, according to some, in the *dual* יָדַי for יָדַיִם Ez 13¹⁸, cf. § 88 *c*), e. g. מִנִּי *stringed instruments*, ψ 45⁹ for מִנִּים (unless it is to be so written)[3] ; עַמִּי *peoples*, ψ 144², and, probably, also La 3¹⁴ (in 2 S 22⁴⁴ it may be taken as עַמִּי *my people* ; cf. in the parallel passage ψ 18⁴⁴ עָם ; also in Ct 8² the *î* of רִמֹּנִי is better regarded as a *suffix*) ; see also 2 S 23⁸ as compared with 1 Ch 11¹¹, and on the whole question Gesenius, *Lehrgebäude*, p. 524 ff. More doubtful still is—

g (*c*) יֵ__ (like the constr. state in Syriac), which is supposed to appear in e. g. שָׂרֵי *princes*, Ju 5¹⁵ (perhaps *my princes* is intended : read either the constr. st. שָׂרֵי, which also has good authority, or with LXX שָׂרִים) ; for וְסֹ' חַלּוֹנֵי Jer 22¹⁴ (according to others *dual*, see § 88 *c*, or a loan word, cf. *ZA*. iii. 93) read חַלּוֹנָיו סָפוּן. On גּוֹבֵי and חוֹרֵי, which have also been so explained, see above, § 86 *i*.—חֲשׂוּפַי Is 20⁴ (where the right reading is certainly חֲשׂוּפֵי) must be intended by the Masora either as a singular with the formative syllable יַ__ *=bareness*, or more probably, as a constr. st. with the original termination *ay* (cf. § 89 *d*) to avoid the harsh combination *ḥᵃśûfê šēt*[4]; in אֲדֹנָי *the Lord* (prop. *my lord*, from the plur. *majestatis*, אֲדֹנִים *lord*), the *ay* was originally a *suffix*, § 135 *q*.

h (*d*) ם__ a supposed *plural* ending in כִּנִּם=כִּנָּם *gnats* (or *lice*), and סֻלָּם *ladder* (supposed by some to be a plur. like our *stairs*) ; but cf. on the former, § 85 *t*.

i 2. The plural termination of the *feminine gender* is generally indicated by the termination וֹת (often written defectively ת__, e. g. תְּהִלָּה *song of praise, psalm*, plur. תְּהִלּוֹת (only in post-biblical Hebrew

---

[1] On the connexion between all these endings see Dietrich's *Abhandl. zur hebr. Gramm.*, Leipzig, 1846, p. 51 ff. ; Halévy, *REJ*. 1888, p. 138 ff. [cf. also Driver, *Tenses*, § 6, *Obs*. 2].

[2] So also always in the Mêša‘ inscription, e. g. line 2 שלשן *thirty* ; line 4 מלכן *kings* ; line 5 ימן רבן *many days*, &c.

[3] According to some this *î* is simply due to a neglect of the point (§ 5 *m*), which in MSS. and elsewhere is marked the abbreviation of the plur. ending.

[4] Prätorius, *ZDMG*. 1903, p. 525, regards חֲשׂוּפַי as an instance of the affix of endearment (cf. כְּלוּבַי, אֲחוּמַי) transferred to an appellative, but such an explanation is rendered unlikely by the meaning of this isolated instance.

סֵפֶר תְּהִלּוֹת ,תְּהִלִּים, as in the headings of the printed editions, as well as
the *Book of Psalms*); אִגֶּרֶת *a letter*, plur. אִגְּרוֹת; בְּאֵר *a well*, plur.
בְּאֵרוֹת. Feminines in ‑ית form their plural in ‑יּוֹת, e.g. מִצְרִית
an Egyptian woman, plur. מִצְרִיּוֹת; and those in וּת either make ‑יּוֹת,
as מַלְכוּת *kingdom*, plur. מַלְכִיּוֹת, Dn 8²² (cf. חֲנִיּוֹת *cells*, Jer 37¹⁶), or are
inflected like עֵדְוֹת *testimonies* (pronounced *ʿēdhᵉwôth* for *ʿēdhŭwôth*).

It is only from a mistake or disregard of these feminine endings וּת‑ and *k*
‑ית that some words ending with them form their plural by the addition
of ‑ים or ‑וֹת, e.g. חֲנִית *spear*, plur. חֲנִיתִים and חֲנִיתוֹת; זְנוּת *whoredom*,
plur. זְנוּתִים (by the side of אַלְמְנוּתִים ;(זְנוּנִים *widowhood*; שְׁחִיתוֹת *pits*, כְּסָתוֹת
amulets (if connected with Assyr. *kâsu, to bind*), &c.

The termination -*ôth* stands primarily for -*âth* (which is the form it has in *l*
Arab., Eth., in the *constr. st.* of Western Aramaic, in Eastern Syriac, and also
in Assyrian; on the change of *â* into an obscure *ô*, see § 9 *q*). On the other
hand, it is doubtful whether this *âth* is to be regarded as a lengthened and
stronger form of the singular fem. ending *ăth* (cf. § 80 *b*).

How the changeable vowels of a noun are shortened or become
Šᵉwâ in consequence of the addition of the plural endings is explained
in §§ 92–5.

3. Words which in the singular are used both as masculine and *m*
feminine (§ 122 *d*), often have in the plural parallel forms with the
masculine and feminine terminations, e.g. עָב *cloud*, plur. עָבִים and
עָבוֹת; and each form may be treated either as masculine or feminine,
according to the usage of the particular word.—But even those words,
of which the gender is invariable, sometimes have both plural forms,
e.g. דּוֹר masc. *a generation*, plur. דּוֹרִים and דּוֹרוֹת; שָׁנָה fem. *a year*,
plur. שָׁנִים and שָׁנוֹת (see the Rem.). In these words the gender of
both plural forms remains the same as in the singular, e.g. אֲרִי masc.
a lion, plur. אֲרָיוֹת masc., Zp 3³, דּוֹרוֹת masc., Jb 42¹⁶.

Sometimes usage makes a distinction between the two plural forms of the *n*
same word. Thus, יָמִים *days*, שָׁנִים *years* are the usual, but יָמוֹת (only twice,
in the *constr. st.* Dt 32⁷, ψ 90¹⁵) and שָׁנוֹת (also only in the *constr. st.* and before
suffixes) are rarer poetic forms.

A difference of meaning appears in several names of members of the body, *o*
the dual (see § 88) denoting the living members themselves, while the plur.
in וֹת expresses something like them, but without life (§ 122 *u*), e.g. יָדַיִם
hands, יָדוֹת *artificial hands*, also e.g. the *arms* of a throne; כַּפַּיִם *hands*, כַּפּוֹת
handles (Lat. *manubria*); פַּעַם *foot*, פְּעָמוֹת *artificial feet* (of the ark), קַרְנַיִם *horns*,
קְרָנוֹת *horns* (of the altar); עֵינַיִם *eyes*, עֲינוֹת *fountains*; cf. also אֲרָיִים *lions*, אֲרָיוֹת
the *figures of lions* on Solomon's throne, תָּמָר *palm*, תִּמֹרָה *a palm-like column*,
plur. תִּמֹרִים and תִּמֹרוֹת.

4. A considerable number of masculines form their plural in וֹת, *p*
while many feminines have a plural in ‑ים. The gender of the
singular, however, is as a rule retained in the plural.

Undoubted instances of masculines with (masculine) plural in וֹת‍ are :
אָב *father,* אוֹצָר *treasure,* בְּאֵר and בּוֹר *cistern,* זָנָב *tail,* חֲלוֹם *dream,* כִּסֵּא *throne,*
לֵב and לְבַב *heart,* לוּחַ *tablet,* לֵיל and לַיְלָה *night,* מִזְבֵּחַ *altar,* מָקוֹם *place,* נֹאד
skin-bottle, נֵר *lamp,* עוֹר *skin,* קוֹל *voice,* שֻׁלְחָן *table,* שֵׁם *name,* שׁוֹפָר *trumpet.*

q   Feminines ending in ה‍ which take in the plural the termination ים‍
are אֵלָה *terebinth,* אֵימָה *terror* (but also אֵימוֹת), דְּבֵלָה *a cake of figs,* חִטָּה *wheat,*
לְבֵנָה *a brick,* מִלָּה (only in poetry) *a word,* סְאָה *seā, a dry measure,* שְׂעוֹרָה *barley,*
and the following names of animals דְּבוֹרָה *a bee* and יוֹנָה *a dove* ; also, for
בֵּיצִים *fem. eggs,* a singular בֵּיצָה is to be assumed. אֲלֻמָּה *sheaf* and שָׁנָה *year*
(see above, *n*) take both ים‍ and וֹת ; cf. finally שִׁבֹּלֶת *an ear of corn,* plur.
שִׁבֳּלִים, and without the fem. termination in the singular פִּילֶגֶשׁ *concubine,*
plur. פִּילַגְשִׁים.

r   **5.** A strict distinction in gender between the two plural endings
is found, in fact, only in adjectives and participles, e. g. טוֹבִים *boni,*
טוֹבוֹת *bonae,* קְטֻלִים masc., קְטֻלוֹת fem. So also in substantives of the
same stem, where there is an express distinction of sex, as בָּנִים *filii,*
בָּנוֹת *filiae;* מְלָכִים *reges,* מְלָכוֹת *reginae.*

s   Rem. 1. In some few words there is added to the plural ending וֹת a
second (masculine) plural termination (in the form of the constr. st. ‍ֵי‍ , cf.
§ 89 *c*), or a dual ending יִם‍ , e. g. בָּמָה *a high place,* plur. בָּמוֹת, constr. st.
בָּמֳתֵי (also בָּמֳתֵי bāmŏthê, Is 14[14], Jb 9[8], &c., sometimes as Qᵉrê to the Kᵉthîbh
במותי ; see § 95 *o*) ; מֵרַאֲשֹׁתֵי שָׁאוּל *from Saul's head,* 1 S 26[12] ; חוֹמָה *wall,* plur.
חוֹמוֹת *moenia,* whence dual חוֹמֹתַיִם *double walls.* This double indication of
the plural appears also in the connexion of suffixes with the plural ending
וֹת (§ 91 *m*).

t   2. Some nouns are only used in the singular (e. g. אָדָם *man,* and collectively
men) ; a number of other nouns only in the plural, e. g. מְתִים *men* (the old
sing. מְתוּ is only preserved in proper names, see § 90 *o* ; in Eth. the *sing.* is
mĕt, man) ; some of these have, moreover, a singular meaning (§ 124 *a*), as
פָּנִים *face.* In such cases, however, the same form can also express plurality,
e. g. פָּנִים means also *faces,* Gn 40[7], Ez 1[6] ; cf. אֱלֹהִים *God,* and also *gods* (the
sing. אֱלֹהַּ, a later formation from it, occurs only ten times, except in Job
forty-one and in Daniel four times).

§ 88. *Of the Dual.*

Cf. the literature on the Semitic dual in Grünert, *Die Begriffs-Präponderanz
und die Duale a potiori im Altarab.* (Wien, 1886), p. 21 ; Brockelmann, *Grundriss,*
p. 455 ff.

a   **1.** The *dual* is a further indication of number, which originated
in early times. In Hebrew, however, it is almost exclusively used
to denote those objects which naturally occur in pairs (see *e*). The
dual termination is never found in adjectives, verbs, or pronouns.
In the noun it is indicated in both genders by the termination יִם‍

appended to the ground-form,[1] e. g. יָדַיִם *both hands*, יוֹמַיִם *two days*.
In the feminine the dual termination is always added to the old ending
ath (instead of ה‏ָ‏—), but necessarily with *ā* (since it is in an open syllable
before the tone), thus ‏ַ‏תַיִם‏, e. g. שָׂפָה *lip*, שְׂפָתַיִם *both lips*. From
a feminine with the ending ‏ת‏ֶ‏—, e. g. נְחֹשֶׁת (from *nᵉḥušt*) the dual
is formed like נְחֻשְׁתַּיִם *double fetters*.

With nouns which in the singular have not a feminine ending, the *b*
dual termination is likewise really added to the ground-form; but
the latter generally undergoes certain changes in consequence of the
shifting of the tone, e. g. כָּנָף *wing* (ground-form *kănăph*), dual כְּנָפַיִם,
the first *ă* becoming *Šᵉwâ*, since it no longer stands before the tone,
and the second *ă* being lengthened before the new tone-syllable.
In 1 K 16²⁴, 2 K 5²³ᵇ the form כִּכְּרַיִם (which should be כִּכָּרַיִם) evidently
merely points to the *constr. st.* כִּכְּרֵי, which would be expected before
כֶּסֶף; cf. כִּכְּרַיִם in 2 K 5²³ᵃ, and on the syntax see § 131 *d*. In the
segholate forms (§ 84ᵃ *a*) the dual ending is mostly added to the
ground-form, e. g. רֶגֶל *foot* (ground-form *răgl*), dual רַגְלַיִם; cf., however,
קַרְנַיִם (only in the book of Daniel), as well as קַרְנַיִם from קֶרֶן *horn*, and
לְחָיַיִם from לְחִי *cheek* (as if from the plurals לְחָיִם, קְרָנוֹת).—A feminine
dual of an adjective used substantivally occurs in עֲצַלְתַּיִם *a sluggish
pair* (of hands) Ec 10¹⁸ from the sing. עָצֵל.

Rem. 1. Certain place-names were formerly reckoned as dual-forms (so in *c*
earlier editions of this Grammar, and still in König's *Lehrgebäude*, ii. 437), viz.—
(*a*) those in ‏יִן‏ַ‏—‏ and ‏‏ן‏ַ‏—‏, e. g. דֹּתָיִן Gn 37¹⁷ᵃ (locative דֹּתַיְנָה, but in 17ᵇ דֹּתָן),
and דֹּתָן 2 K 6¹³; קַרְתָּן Jos 21³², identical with קִרְיָתַיִם in 1 Ch 6⁶¹ (cf. also the
Moabite names of towns in the Mêša‛ inscription, line 10 קריתן = Hebrew
קִרְיָתַיִם; line 30 בֵּית דִּבְלָתַיִם=בת דבלתן Jer 48²²; lines 31, 32 חורנן=חֹרוֹנָיִם
Is 15⁵, &c.); (*b*) in ‏ם‏ַ‏—‏, Jos 15³⁴ הָעֵינָם (=עֵינָיִם Gn 38²¹). The view that
‏ן‏ַ‏—‏ and ‏ם‏ַ‏—‏ arise from a contraction of the dual terminations ‏יִן‏ַ‏—‏ (as in
Western Aramaic, cf. also nom. *âni*, accus. *aini*, of the dual in Arabic) and
‏יִם‏ַ‏—‏ seemed to be supported by the Mêša‛ inscription, where we find
(line 20) מאתן *two hundred*=מָאתַיִן, Hebrew מָאתַיִם. But in many of these
supposed duals either a dual sense cannot be detected at all, or it does not
agree at any rate with the nature of the Semitic dual, as found elsewhere.
Hence it can hardly be doubted that ‏יִן‏ַ‏—‏ and ‏יִם‏ַ‏—‏ in these place-names
only arise from a subsequent expansion of the terminations ‏ן‏ַ‏—‏ and ‏ם‏ַ‏—‏: so
Wellhausen, *Jahrbücher für Deutsche Theologie*, xxi. 433; Philippi, *ZDMG*. xxxii.
65 f.; Barth, *Nominalbildung*, p. 319, note 5; Strack, *Kommentar zur Genesis*,
p. 135. The strongest argument in favour of this opinion is that we have
a clear case of such an expansion in the *Qᵉrê perpetuum* (§ 17 *c*) יְרוּשָׁלַיִם for
יְרוּשָׁלֵם (so, according to Strack, even in old MSS. of the Mišna; cf. *Urusalim*
in the Tel-el-Amarna tablets, and the Aramaic form יְרוּשְׁלֵם): similarly in

---

[1] On dual endings appended to the plural see § 87 *s* and § 95 *o* at the
beginning.

the Aramaic שָׁמְרִין = שָׁמְרַיִן for the Hebrew שֹׁמְרוֹן *Samaria*.—We may add to this list נַהֲרַיִם, אֲפִרַיִם the river country (in the Tel-el-Amarna letters *nârima*, *na'rima*), מִצְרַיִם *Egypt*, Phoenician מצרם ; also the words denoting time, צָהֳרַיִם *midday* (Mêša' inscription, line 15 צהרם), and perhaps עַרְבַּיִם *in the evening*, if the regular expression בֵּין־הָעַרְבַּיִם Ex 12⁶, 16¹², &c., is only due to mistaking עַרְבַּיִם for a dual : LXX πρὸς ἑσπέραν, τὸ δειλινόν, ὀψέ, and only in Lv 23⁵ ἀνὰ μέσον τῶν ἑσπερινῶν. The Arabs also say *el 'išâ'ân*, *the two evenings*, cf. Kuhn's *Literaturblatt*, iii. 48.

Instead of the supposed dual יְדֵי Ez 13¹⁸ read יָדַיִם. On חַלּוֹנֵי (generally taken to be *a double window*) Jer 22¹⁴, see above, § 87 *g*.

d   2. Only apparently dual-forms (but really plural) are the words מַיִם *water* and שָׁמַיִם *heaven*. According to P. Haupt in *SBOT*. (critical notes on Isaiah, p. 157, line 18 ff.), they are to be derived from the old plural forms (found in Assyrian) *mâmi*, *šamâmi*, whence the Hebr. מים, שמים arose by inversion of the *i*, *mâmi*, *mâimi*, *maim*. It is simpler, however, to suppose that the primitive singulars *may* and *šamay*, when they took the plural of extension (§ 124 *b*), kept the tone on the *ay*, thus causing the *im* (which otherwise always has the tone, § 87 *a*) to be shortened to *im*. Cf. the analogous formations, Arab. *tarḍaina*, 2nd fem. sing. imperf. of a verb ל״י, for *tarḍay* + *ina*, corresponding to *taqtulina* in the strong verb ; also bibl.-Aram. בָּנַיִן the abs. st. plur. of the ptcp. *Qal* of בְּנָה (ל״י), which otherwise always ends in *in* with the tone, e.g. in the ptcp. *Qal* of the strong verb, דָבְחִין *sacrificing*.

e   2. The use of the dual in Hebrew is confined, except in the numerals 2, 12, 200, &c. (see § 97), practically to those objects which are by nature or art always found in *pairs*, especially to the double members of the body (but not necessarily so, cf. זְרֹעִים and זְרֹעוֹת *arms*, never in the dual), e. g. יָדַיִם *both hands*, אָזְנַיִם *both ears*, שִׁנַּיִם *teeth* (of both rows), also נַעֲלַיִם *a pair of sandals*, מֹאזְנַיִם *a pair of scales*, Lat. *bilanx*, &c.; or things which are at least thought of as forming a pair, e. g. יוֹמַיִם *two* (successive) *days*, Lat. *biduum* ; שְׁבֻעַיִם *two weeks* ; שְׁנָתַיִם *two years* (in succession), Lat. *biennium* ; אַמָּתַיִם *two cubits*.[1]

f   In the former case the dual may be used for a plural, either indefinite or defined by a numeral, where it is thought of in a double arrangement, e. g. אַרְבַּע רַגְלַיִם *four feet*, Lv 11²³ ; שֵׁשׁ כְּנָפַיִם *six wings* (i. e. three pairs), Is 6², Ez 1⁶; even שִׁבְעָה עֵינַיִם *seven eyes*, Zc 3⁹, כָּל־בִּרְכַּיִם *all knees*, Ez 7¹⁷ ; כָּל־יָדַיִם *all hands*, Ez 21¹² ; מְצִלְתַּיִם *cymbals*, Ezr 3¹⁰ ; שְׁפַתָּיִם *double-hooks*, Ez 40⁴³.—To express a certain emphasis the numeral *two* is used with the dual, as in Ju 16²⁸, Am 3¹².—See some other remarks on the use of the dual in § 87 *o* and *s*.

g   It is not impossible that Hebrew at an earlier period made a more extensive and freer use of the dual, and that the restrictions and limitations of its use, mentioned above, belong to a relatively later phase of development. The

---

[1] But for דְּרָכַיִם Pr 28⁶·¹⁸ (which the Masora takes as two roads leading from the cross-ways) דְּרָכִים is to be read.

Arabic literary language forms the dual in the noun, pronoun, and verb, almost as extensively as the Sanskrit or Greek; but in modern Arabic it has almost entirely disappeared in the verb, pronoun, and adjective. The Syriac has preserved it only in a few stereotyped forms, with which such duals as the Latin *duo, ambo, octo* may be compared. In the same way, the dual of the Sanskrit is lost in the modern Indian languages, and its full use in Old Slavonic has been restricted later, e.g. in Bohemian, just as in Hebrew, to *pairs*, such as hands, feet, eyes, ears. On the Germanic dual, see Grimm's *Gramm.*, 2nd ed., i. p. 814.

§ 89. *The Genitive and the Construct State.*

Philippi, *Wesen und Ursprung des Stat. Constr. im Hebr.* . . . , Weimar, 1871, p. 98 ff: on which cf. Nöldeke in the *Gött. Gel. Anzeigen*, 1871, p. 23.— Brockelmann, *Grundriss*, p. 459 ff.

1. The Hebrew language no longer makes a living use of *case-* *a* *endings*,[1] but either has no external indication of case (this is so for the *nominative*, generally also for the *accusative*) or expresses the relation by means of prepositions (§ 119), while the *genitive* is mostly indicated by a close connexion (or interdependence) of the *Nomen regens* and the *Nomen rectum*. That is to say, the noun which as genitive serves to define more particularly an immediately preceding *Nomen regens*, remains entirely unchanged in its form. The close combination, however, of the governing with the governed noun causes the tone first of all to be forced on to the latter,[2] and the consequently weakened tone of the former word then usually involves further changes in it. These changes to some extent affect the consonants, but more especially the vocalization, since vowels which had been lengthened by their position *in* or *before* the tone-syllable necessarily become shortened, or are reduced to *Šĕwâ* (cf. § 9 *a, c, k*; § 27 *e–m*); e. g. דָּבָר *word*, דְּבַר אֱלֹהִים *word of God* (a sort of compound, as with us in inverted order, *God's-word, housetop, landlord*); יָד *hand*, יַד הַמֶּלֶךְ *the hand of the king*; דְּבָרִים *words*, דִּבְרֵי הָעָם *the words of the people*. Thus in Hebrew only the noun which stands *before a genitive* suffers a change, and in grammatical language is said to be dependent, or in the *construct state*, while a noun which has not a genitive after it is said to be in the *absolute state*. It is sufficiently evident from the above that the *construct state* is not strictly to be regarded as a *syntactical* and *logical* phenomenon, but rather as simply *phonetic* and *rhythmical*, depending on the circumstances of the tone.

---

[1] On some remains of obsolete case-endings see § 90.
[2] The same phenomenon of the tone may also be easily seen in other languages, when two words are closely connected in a similar way. Observe, for example, in German the natural stress on the last word in '*der Thron des Königs*'; though here the other order of the words (inadmissible in Hebrew) '*des Königs Thron*' exhibits the same peculiarity.

b   Very frequently such interdependent words are also united by *Maqqeph*
(§ 16 *a*); this, however, is not necessary, but depends on the accentuation in
the particular case. On the wider uses of the *constr. st.* see the Syntax, § 130.

c   2. The *vowel* changes which are occasioned in many nouns by the
construct state are more fully described in §§ 92–5. But besides these,
the *terminations* of the noun in the construct state sometimes assume
a special form. Thus:

(*a*) In the *construct state*, plural and dual, the termination is ◌ֵי,
e. g. סוּסִים *horses*, סוּסֵי פַרְעֹה *the horses of Pharaoh*; עֵינַיִם *eyes.* עֵינֵי
הַמֶּלֶךְ *the eyes of the king.*

d   Rem. The ◌ֵי of the dual has evidently arisen from ◌ַי (cf. יָדַיִם), but the
origin of the termination ◌ֵי in the *constr. st.* plur. is disputed. The Syriac
constr. st. in *ay* and the form of the plural noun before suffixes (סוּסֶיךָ, סוּסֵי,
&c., § 91 *h*) would point to a contraction of an original ◌ַי, as in the dual.
But whether this *ay* was only transferred from the dual to the plural (so
Olshausen, and Nöldeke, *Beitr. zur sem. Sprachwiss.*, Strassb. 1904, p. 48 ff.),
or is to be regarded as the *abstract, collective* termination, as in אִשָּׁה (see *f*) and
חֹרִי (so Philippi, *ThLZ*. 1890, col. 419 ; Barth, *ZDMG*. 1904, p. 431 ff.), must be
left undecided.

e   (*b*) The original תֿ◌ is regularly retained as the feminine termination in the *construct state* sing. of those nouns which in the *absolute*
state end in ה◌, e. g. מַלְכָּה *queen*, מַלְכַּת שְׁבָא *the queen of Sheba*. But
the feminine endings ת◌, ת◌, and also the plural וֹת, remain
unchanged in the *construct state*.

f   (*c*) Nouns in ה◌ (cf. § 75 *e*) from verbs ל״ה (§ 93, Paradigm III *c*)
form their *constr. st.* in ה◌, e. g. רֹאֶה *seer*, constr. רֹאֵה. If this ה◌
is due to contraction of the original ◌ַי, with ה added as a vowel
letter, we may compare דַּי, constr. דֵּי *sufficiency* ; חַי, constr. חֵי *life* ;
גַּיְא (גַּי), constr. גֵּיא (גֵּי) *valley*.

On the terminations וֹ and ◌ֵי in the *constr. st.* see § 90.

§ 90. *Real and Supposed Remains of Early Case-endings.*
ה◌ *local,* וֹ *in compound proper names,* ◌ֵי *and* וֹ *in the Construct State.*

K. U. Nylander, *Om Kasusändelserna i Hebräiskan*, Upsala, 1882 ; J. Barth,
'Die Casusreste im Hebr.,' *ZDMG*. liii. 593 ff.

a   1. As the Assyrian and old Arabic distinguish three cases by special
endings, so also in the Hebrew noun there are three endings which,
in the main, correspond to those of the Arabic. It is, however, a
question whether they are all to be regarded as real remnants of
former case-endings, or are in some instances to be explained other-

wise. It can hardly be doubted (but cf. *h*, Rem.) that the (locative) termination הָ־ is a survival of the old accusative termination *a*, and that י in certain compound proper names is the old sign of the nominative. The explanation of the *î* as an old genitive sign, which, as being no longer understood in Hebrew, was used for quite different purposes, and the view that ו is a form of the nominative termination י, are open to grave doubts.

In Assyrian the rule is that *u* marks the nominative, *i* the genitive, and *a* the accusative,[1] 'in spite of the many and various exceptions to this rule which occur' (Delitzsch, *Assyrische Gramm.*, § 66). Similarly, the Arabic case-endings in the fully declined nouns (*Triptotes*) are : -*u* for the nominative, -*i* for the genitive, and -*a* for the accusative ; in the *Diptotes* the ending -*a* represents the genitive also. In modern Arabic these endings have almost entirely disappeared, and if they are now and then used, as among the Beduin, it is done without regularity, and one is interchanged with another (Wallin, in *ZDMG*. v, p. 9, xii, p. 874; Wetzstein, *ibid.*, xxii, p. 113 f., and especially Spitta, *Gramm. des arab. Vulgärdialekts von Ägypten*, Lpz. 1880, p. 147 ff.). Even as early as the Sinaitic inscriptions, their regular use is not maintained (Beer, *Studia Asiatica*, iii. 1840, p. xviii ; Tuch, *ZDMG*. iii. 139 f.). Ethiopic has preserved only the -*a* (in proper names -*hâ*), which is, however, still used for the whole range of the accusative, and also (the distinction of case being lost) as a termination of the *constr. st.* to connect it with a following genitive.

2. As remarked above, under *a*, the *accusative* form is preserved in Hebrew most certainly and clearly in the (usually toneless) ending הָ־, originally *ă*, as in the old Arabic accusative. This is appended to the substantive :

(*a*) Most commonly to express *direction towards* an object, or *motion to a place*,[2] e. g. יָמָּה *seaward, westward,* קֵדְמָה *eastward,* צָפוֹנָה *northward,* אַשּׁוּרָה *to Assyria,* בָּבֶלָה *to Babylon,* הָרָה (from הַר) *to the mountain,* Gn 14[10], אַרְצָה *to the earth,* בַּיְתָה *to the house,* תִּרְצָתָה *to Tirzah* (תִּרְצָה) 1 K 14[17], &c., עַזָּתָה *to Gaza* (עַזָּה) Ju 16[1]; with the article הָהָרָה *to the mountain,* הַבַּיְתָה *into the house,* הַחַדְרָה *into the chamber,* 1 K 1[15]; הָאֹהֱלָה[3] *into the tent,* Gn 18[6], &c.; similarly with adverbs, as שָׁמָּה *thither,* אָנָה *whither?* ; even with the *constr. st.* before a genitive בֵּיתָה יוֹסֵף *into Joseph's house,* Gn 43[17.24]; אַרְצָה הַנֶּגֶב *toward the land of the south,* Gn 20[1]; אַרְצָה מִצְרַיִם *to the land of Egypt,* Ex 4[20]; מִדְבַּרָה דַמֶּשֶׂק *to the wilderness of Damascus,* 1 K 19[15]; מִזְרָחָה שֶׁמֶשׁ *toward the sun-rising,* Dt 4[41]; and even with the plural כַּשְׂדִּימָה *into Chaldea,* Ez 11[24]; הַשָּׁמַיְמָה *towards the heavens.*

---

[1] This rule is almost always observed in the Tell-el-Amarna letters (see § 2 *f*) ; cf. the instances cited by Barth, l. c., p. 595, from Winckler's edition.

[2] On this meaning of the accusative see the Syntax, § 118 *d*, and cf. the Latin accusative of motion to a place, as in *Romam profectus est, domum reverti, rus ire.*

[3] הָאֹהֵלָה in Baer's text, Gn 18[6], is an error, according to his preface to Isaiah, p. v.

Rem. The above examples are mostly rendered definite by the article, or by a following genitive of definition, or are proper names. But cases like בֵּיתָה‎, הָרָה‎, יָמָּה show that the locative form *of itself* possessed a defining power.

d (*b*) In a somewhat weakened sense, indicating the place *where* something is or happens (cf. § 118 *d*), e.g. מַחֲנַיְמָה in Mahanaim, 1 K 4¹⁴; שָׁמָּה *there* (usually *thither*, see *c*), Jer 18², cf. 2 K 23⁸, and the expression *to offer a sacrifice* הַמִּזְבֵּחָה, properly *towards the altar* for *on the altar*. On the other hand, בָּבֶלָה Jer 29¹⁵, and וְבָלָה Hb 3¹¹, are to be regarded as ordinary accusatives of direction, *to Babylon, into the habitation*; also expressions like פְּאַת צָפוֹנָה *the quarter towards the north*, Jos 15⁵ (at the beginning of the verse, גְּבוּל קֵדְמָה *the border toward the east*), cf. 18¹⁵·²⁰, Ex 26¹⁸, Jer 23⁸.

e (*c*) The original force of the ending ה‎ָ is also disregarded when it is added to a substantive with a preposition prefixed (cf. also עַד־אָנָה *how long?*), and this not only after לְ‎, אֶל־ or עַד־ (which are easily explained), e.g. לְמַעְלָה *upwards*, לְמַטָּה *downwards*, לִשְׁאוֹלָה *to Sheol*, ψ 9¹⁸; עַד־אֲפֵקָה *unto Aphek*, Jos 13⁴, אֶל־הַצָּפוֹנָה *toward the north*, Ez 8¹⁴, cf. Ju 20¹⁶; but also after בְּ‎, and even after מִן‎, e.g. בַּנֶּגְבָּה *in the south*, Jos 15²¹, cf. Ju 14², 1 S 23¹⁵·¹⁹, 31¹³, 2 S 20¹⁵, Jer 52¹⁰; מִבָּבֶלָה *from Babylon*, Jer 27¹⁶; cf. 1¹³, Jos 10³⁶, 15¹⁰, Ju 21¹⁹, Is 45⁶.

f Rem. Old locative forms (or original accusatives) are, according to the Masora, still to be found in

(*a*) לַיְלָה‎, in *pause* לָיְלָה‎, the usual word in prose for *night*, which is always construed as masculine. The nominative of this supposed old accusative [1] appeared to be preserved in the form לֵיל‎, only used in poetry, Is 16³, constr. st. לֵיל (even used for the *absol. st.* in pause Is 21¹¹). Most probably, however, לַיְלָה is to be referred, with Nöldeke and others, to a reduplicated form לֵילִי‎; cf. especially the western Aramaic לֵילְיָא‎, Syr. *lilya*, &c.—Another instance is מְאוּמָה *something*, probably from מאוּם‎, מוּם *spot, point*, generally with a negative = *nothing*. Similarly אַרְצָה Is 8²³ and (in pause) Jb 34¹³, סוּפָתָה Ho 8⁷, and the place-name יַהְצָה 1 Ch 6⁶³, might be explained as accusatives. Elsewhere, however, the toneless ה‎ָ can be regarded only as a meaningless appendage, or at the most as expressing poetic emphasis; thus אַרְצָה (in *pause*) Jb 37¹²; הַמָּוְתָה *death*, ψ 116¹⁵; נֶגְדָּה־נָּא ψ 116¹⁴·¹⁸; נַחְלָה *stream*, ψ 124⁴; הַחַשְׁמַלָה *amber*, Ez 8² [in 1⁴ הַחַשְׁמַל‎, cf. § 80 *k*], &c. In Jos 15¹² הַיָּמָּה is probably only a scribal error (dittography). In Ju 14¹⁸ instead of the quite unsuitable poetic word הַחַרְסָה (towards the sun??) read as in 15¹ הַחַדְרָה *to the bride-chamber*.

---

[1] Brockelmann, *Sem. Sprachwiss.*, p. 113, also takes it as such, *láylā* being properly *at night*, then *night* simply. Barth, however (*Sprachwiss. Abhandlungen*, p. 16, note 1), refers it to an original לֵילָה‎, like אָנָה from אָן‎.

(b) In the termination תָ֫ה ֵ֫ ‐ often used in poetry with feminines, viz. *g* אֵימָ֫תָה terror (= אֵימָה), Ex 15¹⁶ ; עֶזְרָ֫תָה help (= עֶזְרָה), ψ 44²⁷, 63⁸, 94¹⁷ ; יְשׁוּעָ֫תָה salvation (= יְשׁוּעָה), ψ 3³, 80³, Jon 2¹⁰ ; עַוְלָ֫תָה unrighteousness (= עַוְלָה), Ez 28¹⁵, Ho 10¹³, ψ 125³ ; עֹלָ֫תָה ψ 92¹⁶ *K*ᵉ*th.* Jb 5¹⁶ ; צָרָ֫תָה ψ 120¹ ; עֵיפָ֫תָה darkness, Jb 10²² ; הַמֻּזְפָּ֫תָה Jer 11¹⁵ is corrupt, see the LXX and Commentaries. These cases are not to be taken as double feminine endings, since the loss of the tone on the final syllable could then hardly be explained, but they are further instances of an old accusative of direction or intention. In examples like עֶזְרָ֫תָה *for help* (ψ 44²⁷) this is still quite apparent, but elsewhere it has become meaningless and is used merely for the sake of poetical emphasis.[1]

This termination הָ ‐ usually has reference to *place* (hence called *h* הָ ‐ *locale*[2]) ; sometimes, however, its use is extended to time, as in מִיָּמִים יָמִ֫ימָה *from year to year*. Its use in הֲלִ֫ילָה, properly *ad profanum ! = absit !* is peculiar.

As the termination הָ ‐ is almost always toneless (except in מִזְרָ֫חָה *constr. st.* *i* Dt 4⁴¹ ; גֻּ֫תָּה and עַ֫תָּה Jos 19¹³) it generally, as the above examples show, exercises no influence whatever upon the vowels of the word ; in the *constr. st.* מִדְבָּ֫רָה Jos 18¹², 1 K 19¹⁵, and in the proper names גִּ֫בְעָתָה 1 K 2⁴⁰, דָּ֫נָה 2 S 24⁶ (so Baer ; ed. Mant. and Ginsb. דָּ֫נָה), צָרְפַ֫תָה 2 Ch 14⁹, צָרְפַ֫תָה 1 K 17⁹, צָרְתָ֫נָה 1 K 4¹², an *ă* is retained even in an open tone-syllable (cf., however, הָרָ֫ה Gn 14¹⁰, פַּדֶּ֫נָה Gn 28² from פַּדָּן, with modification of the *a* to *è* ; also כַּרְמֶ֫לָה 1 S 25⁵ from כַּרְמֶל). In segholate forms, as a general rule, the הָ ‐ *local* is joined to the already developed form of the *absol. st.*, except that the helping-vowel before הָ ‐ naturally becomes *S*ᵉ*wâ*, e.g. הָאֹ֫הֱלָה בֵּ֫יתָה Gn 18⁶, &c. ; הַיַּ֫עְרָה Jos 17¹⁵, הַשַּׁ֫עְרָה[3] Ju 20¹⁶, &c., but also נַ֫חֲלָה Nu 34⁵ (*constr. st.* ; likewise to be read in the *absolute* in Ez 47¹⁹, 48²⁸) and שַׁ֫עְרָה Is 28⁶ (with *Silluq*) ; cf. גֶּ֫נְבָּה Ez 47¹⁹ and גֹּ֫רְנָה (Baer, incorrectly, גֹּרְנָ֫ה) Mi 4¹² (both in *pause*).—In the case of feminines ending in הָ ‐ the הָ ‐ *local* is added to the original feminine ending תְ ‐ (§ 80 *b*), the *ă* of which (since it then stands in an open tone-syllable) is lengthened to *ā*, e.g. תִּרְצָ֫תָה.—Moreover the termination הָ ‐ is even weakened to הֶ ‐ in נֹ֫בֶה *to Nob*, 1 S 21², 22⁹ ; אָ֫נֶה *whither*, 1 K 2³⁶·⁴² and דְּדָ֫נֶה *to Dedan*, Ez 25¹³.

3. Of the three other terminations וֹ may still be regarded as a *k* survival of the old nominative ending. It occurs only in the middle

---

[1] The form clings also to a few place-names, as גֻּדְגֹּ֫דָה Dt 10⁷ ; שִׁלֹ֫שָׁה 1 S 9⁴, 2 K 4⁴² ; קְהֵלָ֫תָה Nu 33²² ᶠ· ; יָטְבָ֫תָה *verse* 33 f. ; תִּמְנָ֫תָה Jos 19⁴³, &c. ; אֶפְרָ֫תָה Mi 5¹, &c.]

[2] Cf. Sarauw, 'Der hebr. Lokativ,' *ZA.* 1907, p. 183 ff. He derives the הָ ‐ from the adverbs אָ֫נָה, שָׁ֫מָּה and holds that it has nothing whatever to do with the old accusative.

[3] So Qimḥi, and the Mant. ed. (Baer הַשַּׁ֫עֲרָה), i.e. locative from שַׁ֫עַר (Is 7²⁰). The reading הַשַּׁעֲרָ֫ה (Opit., Ginsb.) implies a feminine in הָ ‐ .

of a few (often undoubtedly very old) proper names,[1] viz. אֲחוּמַי (if compounded of אָחוּ and מִי), חֲמוּטַל (for which in Jer 52[1] *K*[e]*th*. חֲמִיטַל), מְתוּשָׁאֵל and מְתוּשֶׁלַח (otherwise in Hebrew only in the plur. מְתִים *men*; to מְתוּ corresponds most probably בְּתוּ in בְּתוּאֵל), פְּנוּאֵל Gn 32[31] (but in ver. 32 פְּנִיאֵל) *face of God* (otherwise only in the plur. פָּנִים *constr. st.* פְּנֵי).[2]—גַּשְׁמוּ Neh 6[6] (elsewhere גֶּשֶׁם), is the name of an Arab, cf. 6[1]. On the other hand the terminations ִ֑י and וֹ are most probably to be regarded (with Barth, l. c., p. 597) as having originated on Hebrew soil in order to emphasize the *constr. st.*, on the analogy of the *constr. st.* of terms expressing relationship.

In view of the analogies in other languages (see *b*) there is nothing impossible in the view formerly taken here that the *litterae compaginis* ִ֑י and וֹ are obsolete (and hence no longer understood) case-endings, *i* being the old genitive and *ô* for the nominative sign *u*. Barth objects that the *i* and *ô* almost invariably have the tone, whereas the accusative ָה is toneless, and that they are long, where the Arab. *i* and *ŭ* are short. Both these objections, however, lose their force if we consider the special laws of the tone and syllable in Hebrew. The language does not admit a final *ĭ* or *ŭ*, and the necessarily lengthened vowel might easily attract the tone to itself. On the other hand a strong argument for Barth's theory is the fact that these *litterae compaginis* are almost exclusively used to emphasize the close connexion of one noun with another, hence especially in the *constr. st.* Consequently it seems in the highest degree probable that all these uses are based upon forms in which the *constr. st.* is expressly emphasized by a special termination, i. e. the *constr. st.* of terms of relationship, חָמִי, אָחִי, אֲחִי, אֲבִי from אָב *father*, אָח *brother*, חָם *father-in-law* (cf. § 96). The instances given under *l* and *m* followed this analogy.

Like *i*, וֹ is also used only to emphasize the *constr. st.* (see *o*), and must therefore have a similar origin, but its exact explanation is difficult. According to Barth, this וֹ corresponds to a primitive Semitic *â* (cf. § 9 *q*) and is traceable to *'abâ, 'aḫâ*, the accusatives of terms of relationship in the *constr. st.*, which have *â* only before a genitive. Against this explanation it may be objected that there is no trace of the supposed Hebrew accusatives אֲבוֹ, אֲחוֹ, חָמוֹ, and only of the analogous בְּנוֹ. It is also remarkable that so archaic a form should have been preserved (except in בְּנוֹ) only in two words and those in quite late passages. However we have no better explanation to offer in place of Barth's.

Finally we cannot deny the possibility, in some cases, of Barth's explanation of the וֹ in compound proper names like בְּתוּאֵל, &c. (see above), as due to the analogy of terms of relationship with nominative in וֹ. But this in no way militates against the view expressed above, that in some very old names, like בְּתוּאֵל, פְּנוּאֵל, &c., the original common nominative sign has simply been preserved.

---

[1] Cf. the list in L. Kaila, *Zur Syntax des in verbaler Abhängigkeit stehenden Nomens im alttest. Hebr.*, Helsingfors, 1906, p. 54.

[2] The name שְׁמוּאֵל formerly regarded as a compound of שְׁמוּ = שֵׁם *name* and אֵל, is better explained with Prätorius, *ZDMG*. 1903, p. 777, as a name of affection, for יִשְׁמָעֵאל = שְׁמוּעַ אֵל [but see Driver on 1 S 1[20]]; similarly, according to Prätorius, פְּתוּאֵל = פָּתוּחַ אֵל and many others.

The instances found are:

(*a*) Of the ending יֵ֫—: בְּנִי אֲתֹנוֹ *his ass's colt*, Gn 49[11]; עֹזְבִי הַצֹּאן *l* *that leaveth the flock*, Zc 11[17] (cf. the preceding רֹעִי הָאֱלִיל); שֹׁכְנִי סְנֶה *the dweller in the bush*, Dt 33[16] (on שֹׁכְנִי cf. below Jer 49[16a], Ob[3]); appended to the feminine גְּנֻֽבְתִי יוֹם וּגְנֻֽבְתִי לָ֑יְלָה *whether stolen by day or stolen by night*, Gn 31[39] (in prose, but in very emphatic speech); מְלֵאֲתִי מִשְׁפָּט *plena iustitiae*, Is 1[21]; רַבָּ֫תִי עָם *full of people*, La 1[1] (on the retraction of the tone before a following tone-syllable, cf. § 29 *e*; in the same verse the second רבתי and שָׂרָ֫תִי, see below, follow the example of רַבָּ֫תִי, although no tone-syllable follows; cf. also Ho 10[11] below); עַל־דִּבְרָתִי מַלְכִּי־צֶ֫דֶק *after the order of Melchizedek*, ψ 110[4]; cf. also ψ 113[9], Jer 49[16b]. To the same category belong the rather numerous cases, in which a preposition is inserted between the *construct state* and its genitive (cf. § 130 *a*), without actually abolishing the dependent relation, e. g. רַבָּ֫תִי בַגּוֹיִם *she that was great among the nations*, שָׂרָ֫תִי בַּמְּדִינוֹת *princess among the provinces*, La 1[1]; אֹהַ֫בְתִּי לָדוּשׁ *that loveth to tread*, Ho 10[11]; cf. also Jer 49[16a], Ob[3].—In Ex 15[6] נֶאְדָּרִי can only be so explained if it is a vocative referring to יהוה, but perhaps we should read נֶאְדָּרָה as predicate to יְמִינְךָ.

Further, the *Ḥireq compaginis* is found with certain particles which are really also nouns in the *constr. st.*, as זוּלָתִי (=זוּלָת) *except*, מִנִּי (poetical for מִן) *from*, בִּלְתִּי *not*, אַפְסִי *not* (thrice in the formula אֲנִי וְאַפְסִי עוֹד *I am, and there is none else beside me*; but many take the יֵ֫— as a suffix here), Is 47[8.10], Zp 2[15]. [The above are all the cases in which this יֵ֫— is attached to independent words in the O.T.; it occurs, however, besides] in compound proper names (again attached to the *constr. st.*), as מַלְכִּי־צֶ֫דֶק (*king of righteousness*), גַּבְרִיאֵל (*man of God*), חַנִּיאֵל (*favour of God*), and others (cf. also the Punic name *Hannibal*, i. e. חַנִּבַ֫עַל *favour of Ba'al*).

Otherwise than in the *constr. st.* the *Ḥireq compaginis* is only found *m* in participial forms, evidently with the object of giving them more dignity, just as in the case of the construct forms in *î*. We must distinguish, however, between passages in which the participle nevertheless does stand in close connexion, as Gn 49[11], Is 22[16] (הֹצְבִי and חֹקְקִי, also in impassioned speech), Mi 7[14] (probably influenced by Dt 33[16]), ψ 101[5], 113[7]; and passages in which the *î* added to the participle with the article merely serves as an ornamental device of poetic style, e. g. in the late Psalms, 113[5.6.7.9] (on verse 8 see *n*), 114[8], 123[1].

In *Kethîbh* the termination *i* also occurs four times in יושבתי, i. e. יֹשַׁבְתִּי, *n* Jer 10[17], 22[23] (before בְּ), Ez 27[3] (before עַל־), La 4[21] (before בְּ). The *Qᵉre* always requires for it יוֹשֶׁבֶת (or יֵשׁ), except in Jer 22²³ יֹשַׁבְתְּ ; cf. ibid. מִקְנַנְתִּי *K^eth.*, מִקְנַנְתְּ *Q^ere*, and finally Jer 51¹³ שָׁבַנְתִּי *K^eth.*, שָׁבַנְתְּ *Q^ere*. Perhaps יָשַׁבְתִּי and שָׁבַנְתִּי are *formae mixtae*, combining the readings יֹשַׁבְתְּ, &c. and יָשַׁבְתְּ (2*nd fem. perf.*), &c., but מִקְנַנְתִּי may be merely assimilated to יְשַׁבְתִּי which immediately precedes it.

The following are simply textual errors : 2 K 4²³ הֹלַכְתְּ *K^eth.*, due to the preceding אֹתִי, and to be read הַהֹלֶכֶת as in the *Q^ere*; ψ 30⁸ (read הַרְרִי), 113⁸ (read לְהוֹשִׁיבוֹ), 116¹ (read קוֹל תַּחֲ, as in five other places). On בְּרִיתִי, thrice, in Lv 26⁴² cf. § 128 *d*.

o (*b*) Of the ending וֹ[1] (always with the tone): in prose only in the Pentateuch, but in elevated style, Gn 1²⁴ חַיְתוֹ־אֶרֶץ *the beast of the earth* (= חַיַּת הָאָרֶץ ver. 25); similarly in ψ 50¹⁰, 79², 104¹¹·²⁰, Is 56⁹ (twice), Zp 2¹⁴; otherwise only in בְּנוֹ צִפֹּר *son of Zippor*, Nu 23¹⁸; בְּנוֹ בְעֹר *son of Beor*, Nu 24³·¹⁵; and מַעְיְנוֹ מָיִם *a fountain of waters*, ψ 114⁸.

§ 91. *The Noun with Pronominal Suffixes.*

W. Diehl, *Das Pronomen pers. suffixum* 2 *u.* 3 *pers. plur. des Hebr.*, Giessen, 1895 ; A. Ungnad, 'Das Nomen mit Suffixen im Semit.,' *Vienna Oriental Journal*, xx, p. 167 ff.

a With regard to the connexion of the noun with pronominal suffixes, which then stand in a genitive relation (§ 33 *c*) and are, therefore, necessarily appended to the *construct state* of the noun, we shall first consider, as in the verb (§ 57 ff.), the forms of the suffixes themselves, and then the various changes in the form of the noun to which they are attached. The nouns are also tabulated in the Paradigms of the flexion of the noun in § 92 ff. Cf. also Paradigm A in the Appendix. We are here primarily concerned with the different forms of the suffixes when added to the singular, plural, and dual.

b 1. The Suffixes of the singular are—

With nouns ending in a—

	Vowel.		Consonant.	
Sing. 1.	*c.* ִי		ִי֔	*my.*
2.	*m.* ךָ		ךָ֔ (pause ךָ֔)	*thy.*
	f. ךְ		ךְ	
3.	*m.* וֹ, הוּ		וֹ (ה׳), הוּ	*his.*
	f. הָ		הָ, הָ֔	*her.*

---

[1] Cf. Kaila, l.c., p. 59 ff.

	Vowel.		Consonant.	
Plur. 1. c.	נוּ		־ַנוּ	our.
2. { m.	כֶם		כֶם ־ַ }	your.
f.	כֶן		כֶן ־ַ }	
3. { m.	הֶם		־ָם	} eorum.
	מוֹ		(poet. מוֹ ־ָ)	
f.	הֶן (הֵן)		־ָן	earum.

Rem. 1. There is less variety of forms in these than in the verbal suffixes; *c*
the particular forms are used as follows:—

(*a*) Those without a connecting vowel (on the derivation of these 'connecting vowels' from original stem-vowels, see note on § 58 *f*) are generally
joined to nouns of a peculiar form (see § 96), the *constr. st.* of which ends in
a vowel, as אָבִיךָ, אָבִיהוּ and אָבִיו, אָבִיהָ, אָבִיהֶם, אֲבִיכֶם, אֲבִיכֶן, אֲבִיהֶם, אֲבִיהֶן,
sometimes also to segholate forms ending in *i* from ל״ה stems (see § 93 *x, y*),
e. g. פִּרְיָם *the fruit of them*, Am 9[14] (also פִּרְיָם Is 37[30], &c.), פִּרְיְהֶן Jer 29[28] (also
פִּרְיָן verse 5); cf., moreover, חֶלְבְּהֶן Lv 8[16.25] and similar examples with הֶן
(Is 3[17] הֵן) Gn 21[28], Ez 13[17], 16[53]. [1] Also in Gn 1[21], 4[4], Ez 10[12], Nah 2[8], &c., the
K^eth. perhaps intends the singular, לְמִינָהֶם, &c., but the Masora requires the
plural with defective *ê*.

(*b*) The forms with connecting vowels (§ 58 *f*) are joined to nouns ending *d*
in a consonant. The connecting vowel is regularly *a* in the 3rd sing. fem. הָ־
(for *aha*) and 3rd plur. ־ָם, ־ָמוֹ, ־ָן, also in the 3rd sing. masc. וֹ (הֹ), since
the *ô* is contracted from *a[h]û*, and in the pausal form of the 2nd masc. ־ָךְ
(a modification of original ־ְךָ).

The forms with *ē* in the above-mentioned persons are common only with
nouns in הַ־ (from stems ל״ה), constr. st. הֶ־ (cf. § 89 *f*), e. g. שָׂדֵהוּ (from
sadaihû) *his field*, עָלֵהוּ *its leaf*, Is 1[30]; מַרְאֵה *the appearance thereof*, Lv 13[4] (from
mar'aihā; on the S^eghôl see *k*); but שָׂדֶהָ *her field*. The orthographic retention
of the ׳, e. g. מַעֲשָׂיו, מַעֲשֵׂי, gives to many forms the appearance of plurals;
see the instances in § 93 *ss*.

Apart from these ל״ה forms the connecting vowel *ē* in the 3rd pers. occurs
only in isolated cases; אוֹרֵהוּ *his light*, Jb 25[3]; לְמִינֵהוּ *after its kind*, Gn 1[12.25]
[+ 12 times]; Na 1[13]; in Ju 19[24] read פִּילַנְשׁוֹ as in vv. 2, 25. On the other
hand ־ֶךָ in the 2nd sing. fem. and ־ֵנוּ in the 1st plur. are by far the more
common forms, while ־ָךְ, ־ֵנוּ are of rare occurrence; see *e*.—Instead of
־ְךָ ־ֶכָה in Gn 10[19], Ex 13[16], Jer 29[25], &c., cf. לְכָה, בְּכָה § 103 *g*), ־ֶכֶם, ־ֶכֶן
(with S^ewâ mobile), if the last consonant of the noun is a guttural, the forms
are ־ֲךָ, ־ֲכֶם, ־ֲכֶן, e. g. רוּחֲךָ *thy spirit*, בֹּרַאֲךָ *thy creator*, Is 43[1], רֵעֲכֶם *your
friend*, Jb 6[27] (on such cases as בְּחוּבְכֶם Hag 2[5], see § 10 *g*).—With *Nun
energicum* (cf. § 58 *i*, and on עֹנֶךָ Jb 5[1], &c., cf. § 61 *h*) הֶיךָ occurs in Pr 25[16],
in principal pause.

2. Rare or incorrect forms are—

Sing. 1st pers. ־ִי in בִּשׁוּבֵנִי Ez 47[7] (certainly only a scribal error, caused *e*
by וַיְשִׁבֵנִי in verse 6).

---

[1] Also in Jer 15[10] read (according to § 61 *h*, end) כֻּלְּהֶם קִלְלוּנִי; in Ho 7[6]
probably אַפֵּהֶם for אֹפֵהֶם.

2nd pers. *m.* in pause כָה‎ ֶ֫‎ ‑, e.g. כַּפֶּ֫כָה (*thy hand*), ψ 139⁵, cf. Pr 24¹⁰; once הֹנֶךָ ψ 53⁶ (cf. the analogous cases in the verbal suffix § 7 *ll*); *fem.* ־יךְ‎ Ez 5¹² (in 16⁵³ also for שְׁבִיתַיִךְ probably שְׁבִיתֵךְ is intended), כִי‎ ‑ֵ‑ Jer 11¹⁵, ψ 103³, 116¹⁹, 135⁹ (corresponding to the Aramaic suffix of the *2nd fem. sing.*; on the wholly abnormal כֶה‎ ‑ֵ‑ Na 2¹⁴, cf. *l*), לֵכִי *Keth.* 2 K 4², Ct 2¹³. Also ־ךְ‎ ‑ֵ‑ Is 22¹, Ez 23²⁸, 25⁴.

3rd pers. ה‎ ‑ֹ‑ (cf. § 7 *c*), e.g. אָהֳלֹה Gn 9²¹, 12⁸, 13³, 35²¹ (always with *Qerê* אָהֳלוֹ); נָחֹה Nu 10³⁶; לֵחֹה Dt 34⁷; בַּלֹּה Jer 20⁷, Na 2¹ *Qerê*; קָצֹה 2 K 19²³ *Keth.*, for which קָצוֹ is read in Is 37²⁴; עִירֹה and סֻתֹה Gn 49¹¹, cf. Ex 22²⁶ (*Qerê* סוּתוֹ, עִירוֹ); סֻכֹּה ψ 10⁹, 27⁵ *Keth.*; הֲמוֹנֹה Ez 31¹⁸, &c., *Keth.*; תְּבוּאָתֹה Ez 48·⁸ [altogether fourteen times in the Pentateuch, and some forty times in other books: see Driver, *Samuel*, p. xxxv, and on 2 S 2⁹, 21¹].

3rd *fem.* ה‎ ‑ָ‑ for ה‎ ‑ָ‑ (with the softening of the *Mappiq*, cf. § 23 *k*, and the analogous cases in § 58 *g*) occurs repeatedly before *Beghadhkephath* and other soft consonants, Ex 9¹⁸ (before וְ, if the text is right), Lv 13⁴ (before לְ), Nu 15²⁸·³¹, 1 S 1⁹ (unless אָכְלָה, the infin. with fem. termination, is intended; שָׁתָה follows), Ez 16⁴⁴, 24⁶ (before בְ), 1 S 20²⁰, 2 K 8⁶, Pr 12²⁸ (before אֶ), Na 3⁹ (before וְ), ψ 48¹⁴ (before פְ), Ez 47¹⁰, Jb 31²² twice (before תְ), Is 21², Jer 20¹⁷ (before הֹ), Nu 32⁴², Am 1¹¹ (before נְ), Lv 6² (before עֲ); even in *pause*, Lv 12⁴ᵃ and ⁵ᵇ; Is 23¹⁷, Pr 21²², also with Zaqeph, Is 45⁶, Jer 6⁶ (probably), 44¹⁹; on הַשָּׁמָּה Lv 26³⁴, &c., see § 67 *y*. Cf. also אַ‎ ‑ֶ‑ Ez 36⁵.—Sometimes the Masora appears (but this is very doubtful) to regard the ה‎ ‑ָ‑ with feminines as a shortening of תָה‎ ‑ָ‑, e.g. נָצָה Gn 40¹⁰ for נָצְתָה, פֶּנָּה Pr 7⁸ for פִּנְּתָה; also ם‎ ‑ָ‑ for תָם‎ ‑ָ‑ in כְּתוּבָנָם Ho 13², and עֲרֻמָם Jb 5¹³. The examples, however, are for the most part uncertain, e.g. in Is 28⁴ the reading is simply to be emended to בְּכּוּרָה, and in Zc 4² to גֻּלָּה, Jb 11⁹ to מִדָּה, Neh 5¹⁴ to פֶּחָה. [See also, after prepositions, § 103 *g*.]

f Plur. 1st pers. נוּ‎ ‑ֵ‑, in *pause* קִימֹ֫נוּ Jb 22²⁰ (where, however, קָמֹ֫נוּ is certainly to be read); cf. Ru 3² [Is 47¹⁰, cf. § 61 *c*, *h*], and so always כֻּלָּ֫נוּ *all of us*, Gn 42¹¹, &c [cf. עֲמֵ֫נוּ, אִתָּ֫נוּ, לָ֫נוּ, בָּ֫נוּ.].

2nd pers. *fem.* בֶנָה Ez 23⁴⁸·⁴⁹.

3rd pers. *masc.* מוֹ‎ ψ 17¹⁰ (on מוֹ in פִּ֫ימוֹ in the same verse, and in ψ 58⁷ see *l*); הֶם‎ ‑ַ‑ 2 S 23⁶, according to Sievers probably to call attention to the reading בַּלֹּהֶם. *Fem.* הֶנָה‎ ‑ֵ‑ 1 K 7³⁷, Ez 16⁵³ (in *pause*); נָה‎ ‑ֶ‑ Gn 41²¹; פֶּה‎ ‑ֵ‑ Gn 30⁴¹; נָה‎ ‑ֶ‑ Ru 1¹⁹; elsewhere generally in *pause* (Gn 21²⁹, 42³⁶, Jer 8⁷, Pr 31²⁹, Jb 39²); finally הֶן as suffix to a noun, only in Is 3¹⁷.

For examples of singulars with plural suffixes see *l*.

g **2.** In the *plural masc.* and in the *dual* the suffixes are to be regarded primarily as affixed to the original ending of the *construct state* (‑ַי‎ ‑ֵ‑, cf. § 89 *d*). This ending, however, has been preserved unchanged only in the *2nd fem.* In most cases it is contracted to ‑ַי‎ ‑ֵ‑, as in the *constr. st.* without suffixes (so throughout the plur. and in the poetical suffix ‑ֵיהוּ of the *3rd sing. masc.*); in the *2nd masc.* and *3rd fem. sing.* it is ‑ַי‎ ‑ֵ‑ (cf. *k*). On the *1st pers.* and *3rd masc. sing.* see *i*.—Thus there arise the following

Suffixes of Plural Nouns.

h

Singular.	Plural.
1. c. ‏יַ־‎, pause ‏יָ־‎ *my.*	1. c. ‏ֵינוּ‎ *our.*
2. { *m.* ‏ֶיךָ‎ *f.* ‏ַיִךְ‎, pause ‏ָיִךְ‎ } *thy.*	2. { *m.* ‏ֵיכֶם‎ *f.* ‏ֵיכֶן‎ } *your.*
3. { *m.* ‏יו‎, poet. ‏ֵיהוּ‎ *his.* *f.* ‏ֶיהָ‎ *her.* }	3. { *m.* ‏ֵיהֶם‎, poet. ‏ֵימוֹ‎ *f.* ‏ֵיהֶן‎ } *their.*

Thus the original ‏יַ־‎ is (*a*) contracted in the 3rd sing. masc. *i* ‏ֵיהוּ‎ and throughout the *plural*, as ‏סוּסֵיהוּ‎ ‏סוּסֵינוּ‎, &c.; (*b*) retained unchanged in the 1*st* sing. ‏סוּסַי‎, the real suffix-ending ‏י‎ (see *b*) being united with the final Yôdh of the ending ‏יַ־‎; and in the 2*nd fem.* sing. ‏סוּסַיִךְ‎, with a *helping-Ḥireq* after the Yôdh. On the other hand (*c*) the Yôdh of ‏יַ־‎ is lost in pronunciation and the *ă* lengthened to *ā* in the 3rd masc. sing. ‏סוּסָיו‎, i. e. *sûsāw* (pronounced *susā-u*).[1] The 2*nd masc.* sing. ‏סוּסֶיךָ‎ and the 3rd *fem.* sing. ‏סוּסֶיהָ‎ were formerly also explained here as having really lost the ‏י‎, and modified the *a* of *sûsakā, sûsahā* to *Sᵉghôl*; but cf. the view now given in *g* and *k*.

Rem. 1. As ‏סוּסֵינוּ‎ represents *sûsai-nû*, so ‏סוּסֶיךָ‎ and ‏סוּסֶיהָ‎ represent *sûsai-kā*, *k* *sûsai-hā*, and the use of *Sᵉghôl* instead of the more regular *Ṣere* is to be explained from the character of the following syllable,—so P. Haupt who points to ‏יִקְטְלָהּ‎ as compared with ‏יִקְטְלֵהוּ‎. In support of the view formerly adopted by us that the ‏י‎ is only orthographically retained, too much stress must not be laid on the fact that it is sometimes omitted,[2] thereby causing confusion in an unpointed text with the singular noun. A number of the examples which follow may be due to an erroneous assumption that the noun is a plural, where in reality it is a singular, and others may be incorrect readings. Cf. ‏דְּרָכֶךָ‎ *thy ways* (probably ‏דַּרְכְּךָ‎ is intended), Ex 33¹³, Jos 1⁸, ψ 119³⁷; for other examples, see Jos 21¹¹ ff. (‏מִגְרְשֶׁהָ‎; but in 1 Ch 6⁴⁰ ff. always ‏ֶיהָ‎), Ju 19⁹, 1 K 8²⁹, Is 58¹³, ψ 119⁴¹·⁴³·⁹⁸ (probably, however, in all these cases the *sing.* is intended); ‏אֲסָרֶהָ‎ Nu 30⁸ (cf. v. 5); ‏מַכֹּתָהּ‎ Jer 19⁸, 49¹⁷; ‏מְבִיאָהּ‎ Dn 11⁶. For the orthographic omission of ‏י‎ before suffixes cf. ‏רֵעֹהוּ‎ for ‏רֵעֵיהוּ‎ *his friends* 1 S 30²⁶, Pr 29¹⁸; Jb 42¹⁰ (but it is possible to explain it here as a *collective singular*); ‏עֲוֹנֵנוּ‎ *our iniquities*, Is 64⁵·⁶, Jer 14⁷; Ex 10⁹, Neh 10¹ (‏לִוְֵנוּ‎ from ‏לֵוִים‎ which is always written defectively); ‏נְסִכֵּכֶם‎ Nu 29³³; ‏רָעֹתֵכֶם‎ Jer 44⁹; ‏יְדֵכֶם‎ ψ 134²; ‏לְמִינֵהֶם‎ *after their kinds*, Gn 1²¹ (but see *c*), cf. 4⁴ and Na 2⁸. The

---

[1] In the papyrus of the decalogue from the Fayyûm, line 16, ‏ויקרשׁין‎ occurs for ‏ויקרשׁהו‎ Ex 20¹¹. Gall, *ZAW.* 1903, p. 349, takes this as an indication that the traditional forms of the noun-suffix ‏יו‎ or ‏ו‎ represent *aiŭ* or *eŭ*. P. Haupt aptly compares the Greek use of the *iota subscript* (ᾳ).

[2] So in the Mêša‘ inscription, l. 22 ‏מגדלתה‎ *its towers* (along with ‏שׁעריה‎ *its gates*). Can it have been the rule to omit ‏י‎ after the termination *ôth*? Cf. below, *n*.

defective writing is especially frequent in the 3rd masc. sing. יֵ֫ו, which in *Qᵉrê* is almost always changed to יו, e. g. חִצֵּו *his arrows*, ψ 58⁸, *Qᵉrê* חִצָּיו. On יַחְדֵּו, only three times יַחְדִּיו, cf. § 135 *r*.

l   2. Unusual forms (but for the most part probably only scribal errors) are— Sing. 2nd pers. *fem* יֵ֫ךְ (after אַשְׁרֵי *happy!* Ec 10¹⁷, which has become stereotyped as an interjection, and is therefore unchangeable; cf. Delitzsch on the passage); יְכִי (cf. Syr. כִי) 2 K 4³, and ⁷ in *Kᵉth.*, ψ 103³⁻⁵, 116⁷ (יְכִי in *pause*).—In Ez 16³¹ יֵ֫ךְ (so יֵכֶם in 6⁸) occurs with an *infin.* ending in וֹת, the וֹת being therefore treated as a plural ending; similarly, the plural suffix is sometimes found with the feminine ending וּת (Nu 14³³, Is 54⁴, Jer 3⁸, Ez 16¹⁵, 23⁷, as well as in 16²⁰ *Qᵉrê*, and Zp 3²⁰), with the ending *ith* (Lv 5²⁴, reading חֲמִשָׁתוֹ), and even with the ordinary feminine ending *ath*; Is 47¹³, Ez 35¹¹, ψ 9¹⁵, Ezr 9¹⁵.—Wholly abnormal is מַלְאָכֶ֫כָה *thy messengers*, Na 2¹⁴, evidently a case of dittography of the following ה : read מַלְאָכֶ֫יךָ.

3rd masc. יֵ֫הוּ Hb 3¹⁰, Jb 24²³; יֵ֫הוּ 1 S 30²⁶, Ez 43¹⁷, Na 2⁴; וְהִי (a purely Aramaic form) ψ 116¹².—3rd fem. יֵ֫הָא Ez 41¹⁵.

Plur. The strange 2nd pers. masc. תְּפוֹצוֹתִיכֶם (with *i*, so Qimḥi; cf. Norzi) Jer 25³⁴, is probably a mixed form combining תָּפ֫וֹצוּ and הֲפִיצוֹתִיכֶם; *fem.* יְכֵ֫נָה Ez 13²⁰.

3rd masc. יְהֵ֫מָה Ez 40¹⁶; fem. יְהֵ֫נָה Ez 1¹¹.

3. The termination מוֹ (also with the *dual*, e. g. ψ 58⁷, 59¹³), like מוֹ and מוֹ, occurs with the noun (as with the verb, § 58 *g*) almost exclusively in the later poets [viz. with a substantive in the singular, ψ 21¹¹, 17¹⁰·¹⁰, 58⁷, 59¹³, 89¹⁸; with a dual or plural, Dt 32²⁷·³²·³⁷·³⁸, 33²⁹, ψ 2⁸·³, 11⁷, 35¹⁶, 49¹², 58⁷, 59¹⁴, 73⁵·⁷, 83¹²·¹², 140⁴·¹⁰, Jb 27²³; after prepositions, see § 103 *f, o*, notes], and cannot, therefore, by itself be taken as an indication of archaic language. On the other hand there can be no doubt that these are revivals of really old forms. That they are consciously and artificially used is shown by the evidently intentional accumulation of them, e. g. in Ex 15⁵·⁷·⁹, ψ 2³·⁵, and 140⁴·¹⁰, and also by the fact observed by Diehl (see the heading of this section) that in Ex 15 they occur *only* as verbal suffixes, in Dt 32 *only* as noun suffixes.

m   3. It is clear and beyond doubt that the *Yôdh* in these suffixes with the plural noun belongs, in reality, to the ending of the *construct state* of the masculine plural. Yet the consciousness of this fact became so completely lost as to admit of the striking peculiarity (or rather inaccuracy) of appending those *suffix*-forms which include the plural ending יֵ֫, even to the feminine plural in וֹת (סוּסוֹתֵ֫ינוּ, סוּסוֹתֶ֫יךָ, &c.), so that in reality the result is a double indication of the plural.[1]

n   Such is the rule: the singular suffix, however (see *b*), also occurs with the ending וֹת (probably through the influence of Aramaic), e. g. עֵדְוֹתַי ψ 132¹² (unless it be *sing.* for עֵדוּתִי, as, according to Qimḥi in his Lexicon, תְּחָתַי 2 K 6⁸ is for תַּחְתֻּנִתִי); מַכֹּתְךָ Dt 28⁵⁹ (treated on the analogy of an *infin.* ל״ה);

---

[1] See an analogous case in § 87 *s*. Cf. also the double feminine ending in the 3rd sing. perf. of verbs ל״ה, § 75 *i*.

אֲחִיוֹתֵךְ Ez 16⁵². On the other hand מִצְוֹתָךְ (so Baer, Ginsb.; but Opit. יִ֖ךָ‎)
ψ 119⁹⁸, Dn 9⁵ is merely written defectively, like נֶּרְרֹתֶךָ according to Baer
(not Ginsb.) in Pr 1⁹, &c. In the 3rd plur. the use of the singular suffix is
even the rule in the earlier Books (see the instances in Diehl, l. c., p. 8),
e. g. אֲבוֹתָם (*their fathers*) oftener than אֲבֹתֵיהֶם (this only in 1 K 14¹⁵, and in
Jer, Ezr, Neh, and Ch [in 1 K, Jer, Ezr, however, אֲבוֹתָם is more common]);
so always שְׁמוֹתָן, שְׁמוֹתָם *their names*, דּוֹרֹתָם *their generations*. From parallel
passages like 2 S 22⁴⁶ compared with ψ 18⁴⁶, Is 2⁴ with Mi 4³, it appears that
in many cases the longer form in יהֶם‎ can only subsequently have taken
the place of ם‎ָ.

4. The following Paradigm of a masculine and feminine noun
with suffixes is based upon a monosyllabic noun with one unchangeable
vowel. With regard to the ending ת‎ַ in the *constr. st.* of the fem.
it should be further remarked that the short *ă* of this ending is only
retained before the *grave* suffixes כֶם and כֶן; before all the others
(the *light* suffixes) it is lengthened to *ā*.

Singular.

	Masculine.		Feminine.	
	סוּס	*a horse.*	סוּסָה	*a mare.*
Sing. 1. com.	סוּסִי	*my horse.*	סוּסָתִי	*my mare.*
2. m.	סוּסְךָ	*thy horse.*	סוּסָתְךָ	*thy mare.*
2. f.	סוּסֵךְ	*thy horse.*	סוּסָתֵךְ	*thy mare.*
3. m.	סוּסוֹ	*equus eius (suus).*	סוּסָתוֹ	*equa eius (sua).*
3. f.	סוּסָהּ	*equus eius (suus).*	סוּסָתָהּ	*equa eius (sua).*
Plur. 1. com.	סוּסֵנוּ	*our horse.*	סוּסָתֵנוּ	*our mare.*
2. m.	סוּסְכֶם	*your horse.*	סוּסַתְכֶם	*your mare.*
2. f.	סוּסְכֶן	*your horse.*	סוּסַתְכֶן	*your mare.*
3. m.	סוּסָם	*equus eorum (suus).*	סוּסָתָם	*equa eorum (sua).*
3. f.	סוּסָן	*equus earum (suus).*	סוּסָתָן	*equa earum (sua).*

Plural.

	Masculine.		Feminine.	
	סוּסִים	*horses.*	סוּסוֹת	*mares.*
Sing. 1. com.	סוּסַי	*my horses.*	סוּסוֹתַי	*my mares.*
2. m.	סוּסֶיךָ	*thy horses.*	סוּסוֹתֶיךָ	*thy mares.*
2. f.	סוּסַיִךְ	*thy horses.*	סוּסוֹתַיִךְ	*thy mares.*
3. m.	סוּסָיו	*equi eius (sui).*	סוּסוֹתָיו	*equae eius (suae).*
3. f.	סוּסֶיהָ	*equi eius (sui).*	סוּסוֹתֶיהָ	*equae eius (suae).*
Plur. 1. com.	סוּסֵינוּ	*our horses.*	סוּסוֹתֵינוּ	*our mares.*
2. m.	סוּסֵיכֶם	*your horses.*	סוּסוֹתֵיכֶם	*your mares.*
2. f.	סוּסֵיכֶן	*your horses.*	סוּסוֹתֵיכֶן	*your mares.*
3. m.	סוּסֵיהֶם	*equi eorum (sui).*	סוּסוֹתֵיהֶם	*equae eorum (suae).*
3. f.	סוּסֵיהֶן	*equi earum (sui).*	סוּסוֹתֵיהֶן	*equae earum (suae).*

§ 92. *Vowel Changes in the Noun.*

a 1. Vowel changes in the noun may be caused (*a*) by dependence on a following genitive; (*b*) by connexion with pronominal suffixes, (*c*) by the plural and dual terminations, whether in the form of the absolute state or of the construct (before a following genitive of a noun or suffix).

b 2. In all these cases, the tone of the noun is moved forward either one or two syllables, while the tone of the *construct state* may even be thrown upon the following word. In this way the following changes may arise :—

(*a*) *When the tone is moved forward only one place*, as is the case when the plural and dual endings ‏ים‎ָ, ‏ות‎ and ‏ַ֫יִם‎ are affixed, as well as with all monosyllabic or paroxytone suffixes, then in dissyllabic nouns the originally short vowel of the first syllable (which was lengthened as being in an open syllable before the tone) becomes *Šewâ*, since it no longer stands before the tone. On the other hand, the originally short, but tone-lengthened vowel, of the second syllable is retained as being now the pretonic vowel ; e. g. ‏דָּבָר‎ *word* (ground-form *dâbăr*), plur. ‏דְּבָרִים‎; with a light suffix beginning with a vowel, ‏דְּבָרֵנוּ‎; plur. ‏דְּבָרַי‎, ‏דְּבָרֶיךָ‎, &c.; ‏כָּנָף‎ *wing*, dual ‏כְּנָפַ֫יִם‎. With an unchangeable vowel in the second syllable : ‏פָּקִיד‎ *overseer*, plur. ‏פְּקִידִים‎; with the *suffix* of the sing. ‏פְּקִידֵ֫נוּ‎, ‏פְּקִידִי‎, &c.; with the *suff.* of the plur. ‏פְּקִידֶ֫יךָ‎, ‏פְּקִידַי‎, &c. With an unchangeable vowel in the first syllable : ‏עוֹלָם‎ *eternity*, plur. ‏עוֹלָמִים‎, with *suff.* ‏עוֹלָמִי‎, &c.[1]

c But in participles of the form ‏קֹטֵל‎, with tone-lengthened *ē* (originally *ĭ*) in the second syllable, the *ē* regularly becomes *Šewâ mobile* before a tone-bearing affix, e. g. ‏אֹיֵב‎ *enemy*, plur. ‏אֹיְבִים‎, with *suff.* ‏אֹיְבִי‎, &c. Likewise in words of the form ‏קַטֵּל‎, ‏קִטֵּל‎, &c. (with *ē* in the second syllable ; § 84*b d, l, p* ; § 85 *i* and *k*), e. g. ‏אִלֵּם‎ *dumb*, plur. ‏אִלְּמִים‎.

d (*b*) When the tone of the *construct state*, plural or dual, is carried over to the following word, or, in consequence of the addition of the grave suffixes to the *constr. st.* plur. or dual, *is moved forward two places* within the word itself, in such cases the originally short vowel of the second syllable becomes *Šewâ*, while the vowel of the first syllable reverts to its original shortness, e. g. ‏דִּבְרֵי הָעָם‎ *the words of the people*, ‏דִּבְרֵיכֶם‎ *your words*, ‏דִּבְרֵיהֶם‎ *their words* (in all which instances the *ĭ* of the first syllable is attenuated from an original *ă*).

---

[1] The participles *Niph'al* ‏נִדְּחֶךָ‎ Dt 30⁴, ‏נִדְּחוֹ‎ 2 S 14¹³, and some plurals of the participle Niph. of verbs ‏ל״א‎ form an exception ; cf. § 93 *oo*.

In the segholate forms in the singular and mostly in the dual the suffix is *e*
appended to the ground-form (מַלְכִּי *my king*, מַלְכֵּנוּ, &c.) ; on the other hand,
before the endings ‎ִים, וֹת (sometimes also before ‎ַיִם) a *Qames* regularly
occurs,[1] before which the vowel of the first syllable then becomes vocal *Šewâ*
(מְלָכוֹת, מְלָכִים). This *Qames* (on which cf. § 84ᵃ *a*) remains even before the
light suffixes, when attached to the plur. masc. (מְלָכַי, מְלָכֶיךָ, &c.). On
the other hand, the *constr. st.* plur. and dual, regularly, according to *d*, has
the form מַלְכֵי, with grave suffix מַלְכֵיכֶם,&c., דַּלְתֵי from דְּלָתַיִם *folding-doors*.

(*c*) Before the *Šewâ mobile* which precedes the suffix ךָ when *f*
following a consonant, the *a*-sound, as a rule, is the only tone-
lengthened vowel which remains in the final syllable (being now
in an open syllable *before* the tone), e. g. דְּבָרְךָ, דָּמְךָ, &c. (on the
forms with *ē* in the second syllable, see § 93 *qq*) ; but before the grave
suffixes ‎ְכֶם and ‎ְכֶן in the same position it reverts to its original
shortness, as דְּבַרְכֶם (*debharkhèm*), &c. In the same way the tone-
lengthened *ā* or *ē* of the second syllable in the *constr. st.* sing. also
becomes short again, since the *constr. st.* resigns the principal tone to
the following word, e. g. חֲצַר הַבַּיִת (from חָצֵר) ; דְּבַר אֱלֹהִים.

Rem. The Masora (cf. *Diqduqe ha-ṭeamim*, p. 37) reckons thirteen words *g*
which retain *Qames* in the *constr. st.*, some of which had originally *á* and
therefore need not be considered. On the other hand, אֶלָם or אוּלָם ı K 7⁶,
Ez 40⁴⁸, &c. (in spite of the *constr. st.* plur. אֻלַמֵּי) ; מִבְטָח ψ 65⁶, Pr 25¹⁹ ; מַצָּב
ı S 13²³ (so Baer, but ed. Mant., Ginsburg, &c. מַצַּב) ; מִשְׁקָל Ezr 8³⁰ and מַתָּן
Pr 18¹⁶ are very peculiar.

3. The vowel changes in the inflexion of *feminine nouns* (§ 95) are *h*
not so considerable, since generally in the formation of the feminine
either the original vowels have been retained, or they have already
become *Šewâ*.

Besides the vowel changes discussed above in *a–g*, which take place according *i*
to the general formative laws (§§ 25–28), certain further phenomena must also
be considered in the inflexion of nouns, an accurate knowledge of which
requires in each case an investigation of the original form of the words in
question (see §§ 84–86). Such are, e. g., the rejection of the ה of לַ״ה stems
before all formative additions (cf. § 91 *d*), the sharpening of the final consonant
of עַ״ע stems in such cases as חֹק, חֻקִּי, &c.

A striking difference between the vowel changes in the verb and noun is *k*
that in a verb when terminations are added it is mostly the second of two
changeable vowels which becomes *Šewâ* (קָטַל, קָטְלָה, קָטְלוּ), but in a noun,
the first (דָּבָר, דְּבָרִי, דְּבָרִים), cf. § 27. 3.

---

[1] For the rare exceptions see § 93 *l* and § 97 *f*, note 2.

§ 93. *Paradigms of Masculine Nouns.*[1]

a Masculine nouns from the simple stem may, as regards their form and the vowel changes connected with it, be divided into *four* classes. A synopsis of them is given on pp. 264, 265, and they are further explained below. Two general remarks may be premised :

(*a*) That all feminines without a distinctive termination (§ 122 *h*) are treated like these masculine nouns, e. g. חֶרֶב *f. sword*, like מֶלֶךְ *m. king*, except that in the *plural* they usually take the termination וֹת_; thus חֲרָבוֹת, *constr.* חַרְבוֹת (and so always before *suffixes*, see § 95).

b (*b*) That in the plural of the first three classes a changeable vowel is always retained even before the light suffixes as a lengthened pretonic vowel, whenever it also stands before the plural ending ים_. All suffixes, except כֶם, כֶן, כֶן, הֶם, הֶן (יכֶם_, _יכֶן_, _יהֶם_, _יהֶן_), are called *light*. Cf. § 92 *e*.

Explanations of the Paradigms (see pp. 264, 265).

c 1. Paradigm I comprises the large class of *segholate* nouns (§ 84[a] *a–e*). In the first three examples, from a strong stem, the ground-forms, *mălk, siphr, qŭdš* have been developed by the adoption of a helping *Seghôl* to מֶלֶךְ (with *ă* modified to *è*), סֵפֶר (*ĭ* lengthened to *ē*), קֹדֶשׁ (*ŭ* lengthened to *ō*).[2] The next three examples, instead of the helping *Seghôl*, have a helping *Pathaḥ*, on account of the middle (*d, f*) or final guttural (*e*). In all these cases the *constr. st. sing.* coincides exactly with the *absolute*. The singular suffixes are added to the ground-form ; but in *c* and *f* an *ŏ* takes the place of the original *ŭ*, and in *d* and *f* the guttural requires a repetition of the *ă* and *ŏ* in the form of a *Ḥateph* (נַעֲרִי, פָּעֳלִי) ; before a following *Šewâ* this *Ḥateph* passes into a simple helping vowel (*ă, ŏ*), according to § 28 *c*; hence נַעַרְךָ, &c.

d In the plural an *a*-sound almost always appears before the tone-bearing affix ים_ (on the analogy of forms with original *a* in the

---

[1] A sort of detailed commentary on the following scheme of Hebrew declensions is supplied by E. König in his *Hist.-krit. Lehrgeb. der hebr. Spr.*, ii. 1, p. 1 ff.

[2] According to P. Haupt 'The book of Nahum' in the *Journ. of bibl. Lit.*, 1907, p. 29, the *e* in סֵפֶר and the *o* in קֹדֶשׁ are not long but accented, and hence to be pronounced σέφρ, όζν (אֹזֶן), a theory unknown at any rate to the Jewish grammarians.

second syllable; cf. § 84^a *a*), in the form of a pretonic *Qameṣ*, whilst the short vowel of the first syllable becomes vocal *Š^ewâ*. The original *a* of the 2nd syllable is elided in the *construct state*, so that the short vowel under the first radical then stands in a closed syllable. The omission of *Dageš* in a following *Begadkephath* (מַלְכֵי, not מַלְבִּי, &c.) is due to the loss of a vowel between ל and כ. On the other hand, the pretonic *Qameṣ* of the *absolute state* is retained before the light plural suffixes, whilst the grave suffixes are added to the form of the *construct state.*—The ending of the *absolute state* of the dual is added, as a rule, to the ground-form (so in *a–d* and *h*, but cf. *k*). The *construct state* of the dual is generally the same as that of the plural, except, of course, in cases like *m*.

Paradigms *g* and *h* exhibit forms with middle *u* and *i* (§ 84^a *c*, γ *e* and δ); the ground forms *maut* and *zait* are always contracted to *môth*, *zêth*, except in the *absol. sing.*, where *u* and *i* are changed into the corresponding consonants ו and י.

Paradigm *i* exhibits one of the numerous forms in which the contraction of a middle *u* or *i* has already taken place in the *absol. sing.* (ground-form *šauṭ*).

Paradigm *k* is a formation from a stem ל״ה (§ 84^a *c*, ε).

Paradigms *l*, *m*, *n* are forms from stems ע״ע, and hence (see § 67 *a*) *f* originally biliteral, *yam*, *'im*, *ḥuq*, with the regular lengthening to יָם, אֵם, חֹק. Before formative additions a sharpening, as in the inflexion of verbs ע״ע, takes place in the second radical, e.g. אִמִּי, יַמִּים, &c. (see § 84^a *c*, β).

REMARKS.

1. A. On I. *a* and *d* (ground-form *qaṭl*). In *pause* the full lengthening to *ā* *g* generally takes place, thus כֶּ֫רֶם *vineyard*, זָ֫רַע *seed* (from זֶ֫רַע), and so always (except ψ 48^{11}), in אֶ֫רֶץ *earth* with the article, הָאָ֫רֶץ, according to § 35 *o* (cf. also in the LXX the forms Ἀβέλ, Ἰαφέθ for הֶ֫בֶל, יֶ֫פֶת). However, the form with *è* is also sometimes found in pause, along with that in *ā*, e.g. חֶ֫סֶד together with חָ֫סֶד; and very frequently only the form with S^eghôl, e.g. מֶ֫לֶךְ, דֶּ֫שֶׁא *grass*, נֶ֫צַח *perpetuity*, פֶּ֫לֶא *a wonder*, צֶ֫דֶק *righteousness*, קֶ֫דֶם *the East*, יֶ֫שַׁע *help*, &c.—With two S^eghôls, although with a middle guttural, we find לֶ֫חֶם *bread* (in pause לֶ֫חֶם) and רֶ֫חֶם *womb* (in pause רָ֫חֶם), besides רַ֫חַם Ju 5^{30} (in pause רָ֫חַם). A helping S^eghôl always stands before a final א, as דֶּ֫שֶׁא, טֶ֫נֶא (with suff. טַנְאֲךָ), פֶּ֫לֶא, פֶּ֫רֶא (also written פֶּ֫רֶה), except in גֵּיא, see *v*.

B. The *constr. st.* is almost always the same as the *absolute*. Sometimes, *h* however, under the influence of a final guttural or ר, Pathaḥ appears in the second syllable as the principal vowel (see below, *s*), e.g. גֶּ֫בֶר ψ 18^{26}; זֶ֫רַע

Paradigms of

I.

	a.	b.	c.	d.	e.	f.
Sing. absolute	מֶ֫לֶךְ	סֵ֫פֶר	קֹ֫דֶשׁ	נַ֫עַר	נֵ֫צַח	פֹּ֫עַל
	(king)	(book)	(sanctuary)	(a youth)	(perpetuity)	(work)
,, construct	מֶ֫לֶךְ	סֵ֫פֶר	קֹ֫דֶשׁ	נַ֫עַר	נֵ֫צַח	פֹּ֫עַל
,, with light suff.	מַלְכִּי	סִפְרִי	קָדְשִׁי	נַעֲרִי	נִצְחִי	פָּעֳלִי
	מַלְכְּךָ	סִפְרְךָ	קָדְשְׁךָ	נַעַרְךָ	נִצְחֲךָ	פָּעָלְךָ
,, with grave suff.	מַלְכְּכֶם	סִפְרְכֶם	קָדְשְׁכֶם	נַעַרְכֶם	נִצְחֲכֶם	פָּעָלְכֶם
Plur. absolute	מְלָכִים	סְפָרִים	[קָדָשִׁים]	נְעָרִים	נְצָחִים	פְּעָלִים
,, construct	מַלְכֵי	סִפְרֵי	קָדְשֵׁי	נַעֲרֵי	נִצְחֵי	פָּעֳלֵי
,, with light suff.	מְלָכַי	סְפָרַי	[קָדָשַׁי]	נְעָרַי	נְצָחַי	פְּעָלַי
,, with grave suff.	מַלְכֵיכֶם	סִפְרֵיכֶם	קָדְשֵׁיכֶם	נַעֲרֵיכֶם	נִצְחֵיכֶם	פָּעֳלֵיכֶם
Dual absolute	רַגְלַ֫יִם	קֻבְצַ֫יִם	מָתְנַ֫יִם	נַעֲלַ֫יִם		
	(feet)	(two heaps)	(loins)	(sandals)		
		[proper name.]				
,, construct	רַגְלֵי	מָתְנֵי	נַעֲלֵי			

II.

	a.	b.	c.	d.	e.	f.
Sing. absolute	דָּבָר	חָכָם	זָקֵן	כָּתֵף	חָצֵר	שָׂדֶה
	(word)	(wise)	(an old man)	(shoulder)	(court)	(field)
,, construct	דְּבַר	חֲכַם	זְקַן	כֶּ֫תֶף	חֲצַר	שְׂדֵה
,, with light suff.	דְּבָרִי	חֲכָמִי	זְקֵנִי	כְּתֵפִי	חֲצֵרִי	שָׂדִי
	דְּבָרְךָ	חֲכָמְךָ				שָׂדְךָ
,, with grave suff.	דְּבַרְכֶם	חֲכַמְכֶם				
Plur. absolute	דְּבָרִים	חֲכָמִים	זְקֵנִים		חֲצֵרִים	פָּנִים
,, construct	דִּבְרֵי	חַכְמֵי	זִקְנֵי		חַצְרֵי	פְּנֵי
,, with light suff.	דְּבָרַי	חֲכָמַי	זְקֵנַי		חֲצֵרַי	פָּנַי
,, with grave suff.	דִּבְרֵיכֶם	חַכְמֵיכֶם	זִקְנֵיכֶם		חַצְרֵיכֶם	פְּנֵיכֶם
Dual absolute	כְּנָפַ֫יִם	חֲלָצַ֫יִם	יְרֵכַ֫יִם			
	(wings)	(loins)	(thighs)			(face)
,, construct	כְּנָפֵי					

Masculine Nouns.

I.

g.	h.	i.	k.	l.	m.	n.
מָוֶת	זַיִת	שׁוֹט	פְּרִי	יָם	אֵם	חֹק
(death)	(olive)	(whip)	(fruit)	(sea)	(mother)	(statute)
מוֹת	זֵית	שׁוֹט	פְּרִי	יַם ,יָם	אֵם	חָק־
מוֹתִי	זֵיתִי	שׁוֹטִי	פִּרְיִי	יַמִּי	אִמִּי	חֻקִּי
מוֹתְךָ	זֵיתְךָ	שׁוֹטְךָ	פֶּרְיְךָ	יַמְּךָ	אִמְּךָ	חָקְךָ
מוֹתְכֶם	זֵיתְכֶם	שׁוֹטְכֶם	פֶּרְיְכֶם	יַמְּכֶם	אִמְּכֶם	חָקְכֶם
[מוֹתִים]	זֵיתִים	שׁוֹטִים	גְּדָיִים	יַמִּים	אִמּוֹת	חֻקִּים
מוֹתַי	זֵיתַי	שׁוֹטַי	גְּדָיַי	יַמַּי	אִמּוֹת	חֻקִּי
	זֵיתַי	שׁוֹטַי	(kids)	יַמַּי	אִמּוֹתַי	חֻקִּי
	זֵיתֵיכֶם	שׁוֹטֵיכֶם	לְחָיַיִם	יַמֵּיכֶם	אִמּוֹתֵיכֶם	חֻקֵּיכֶם
	עֵינַיִם	יוֹמַיִם	(cheeks)	כַּפַּיִם	שִׁנַּיִם	
	(eyes)	(two days, biduum)		(hands)	(teeth)	
	עֵינַי	יוֹמַי	לְחָיַי	כַּפַּי	שִׁנַּי	

III.

a.	b.	c.
עוֹלָם	אֹיֵב	חֹזֶה
(eternity)	(enemy)	(seer)
עוֹלָם	אֹיֵב	חֹזֶה
עוֹלָמִי	אֹיְבִי	חֹזִי
עוֹלָמְךָ	אֹיִבְךָ	חֹזְךָ
עוֹלָמְכֶם	אֹיִבְכֶם	חֹזְכֶם
עוֹלָמִים	אֹיְבִים	חֹזִים
עוֹלָמֵי	אֹיְבַי	חֹזַי
עוֹלָמֵי	אֹיְבַי	חֹזַי
עוֹלָמֵיכֶם	אֹיְבֵיכֶם	חֹזֵיכֶם
מֶלְקָחַיִם	מֹאזְנַיִם	
(pair of tongs)	(balance)	
	מֹאזְנַי	

IV.

a.	b.	c.
פָּקִיד	עָנִי	כְּתָב
(overseer)	(poor)	(writing)
פָּקִיד	עָנִי	כְּתָב
פְּקִידִי		כְּתָבִי
פְּקִידְךָ		כְּתָבְךָ
פְּקִידְכֶם		כְּתָבְכֶם
פְּקִידִים	עֲנִיִּים	[כְּתָבִים]
פְּקִידִי	עֲנִיַּי	[כְּתָבִי]
פְּקִידִי		[כְּתָבִי]
פְּקִידֵיכֶם	עֲנִיֵּיכֶם	[כְּתָבֵיכֶם]
שְׁבֻעַיִם		
(two weeks)		

(only in Nu 11⁷, before Maqqeph), חֲדַר Ju 3²⁴ (but Ct 3⁴ וְחֶדֶר), נָטַע, סָחַר as well as זֶרַע, &c. ; cf., moreover, קַחַת 2 K 12⁹ (for קַחַת, *infin. constr.* from לָקַח).

i　C. The ה‍ָ *locale* is, according to § 90 *i*, regularly added to the already developed form, e. g. נֶגְדָּה ψ 116¹⁴·¹⁸ : הַפֶּתְחָה Gn 19⁶, *to the door* ; but also with a firmly closed syllable גָּנְבָּה Ex 40²⁴ ; under the influence of a guttural or ר, אַרְצָה, חַדְרָה, in *pause* אָרְצָה (cf. גֹּרֶן 1 Ch 14¹⁶, from גֹּרֶן).

k　D. The suffixes of the singular are likewise added to the ground-form, but forms with middle guttural take *Ḥaṭeph-Pathaḥ* instead of the *Šᵉwâ quiescens* ; נַעֲרִי, &c. (but also לַחְמִי, וַעֲמָ, &c.). In a rather large number of *qaṭl*-forms, however, before. suffixes in the sing., as well as in the *constr. st.* plur. and dual, the *ă* of the first syllable is attenuated to *ĭ*,[1] thus בִּטְנִי *my womb*, יִתְרוֹ ; so in שִׁמְשָׁ, רִשְׁעָ, קִרְבָּ, קִבְרָ, צִדְקָ, פֶּתְחָ, פִּשְׁעָ, טֶבַח, זֶבַח, מֶלַח, בֶּצַע, גֶּזַע, בֶּגֶד, and many others. In some cases of this kind besides the form with *ă* there most probably existed another with original *ĭ* in the first syllable ; thus certainly with יֵשַׁע beside יֵשַׁע, נֵצַח beside נֵצַח, &c. (According to the *Diqduqe ha-ṭᵉamim*, § 36, the *absolute st.* in such cases takes *ĕ*, the *constr. ē* ; cf. נֵדֶר Nu 30⁴ (*absol.*) and נֶדֶר 30¹⁰ (*constr.*) ; שֵׁכֶר Lv 24²⁰ (*absol.*) and שֵׁכֶר Am 6⁶ (*constr.*). According to this theory[2] פֶּלֶא (so the best authorities) Is 9⁵ would be the *constr. st.*, although the accentuation requires an *absol. st.*)—A weakening of the firmly closed syllable occurs in בִּנְדִי, &c. from בֶּגֶד and יָקֹבְךָ Dt 15¹⁴, 16¹³, in both cases evidently owing to the influence of the palatal in the middle of the stem. With *Sᵉghôl* for *ĭ* : נֶגְדִּי, יִשְׁעֶךָ, הֶבְלִי, &c.

l　E. In the plural the termination וֹת is found as well as יִם‍ֵ‍, e. g. נְפָשׁוֹת, עֲצָמוֹת together with נְפָשִׁים (Ez 13²⁰ [but read חַפָּשִׁים ; see comm.]), &c., *constr. st.* נַפְשׁוֹת. Other nouns have only the ending וֹת, e. g. אֲרָצוֹת, *constr.* אַרְצוֹת from אֶרֶץ. Without *Qameṣ* before the ending יִם‍ֵ‍ we find רַחֲמִים (*bowels*) *mercy*. On the numerals עֶשְׂרִים *twenty*, &c., cf. § 97 *f*, note 2. Moreover *a* is not inserted before plural suffixes with the tone on the penultima in אַשְׁרֶיךָ, &c., properly *thy happiness!* (a word which is only used in the *constr. st. pl.* and at an early period became stereotyped as a kind of interjection).

m　F. In the *constr. st. plural* a firmly closed syllable is sometimes found, contrary to the rule, e. g. כַּסְפֵּיהֶם Gn 42²⁵·³⁵ ; רִשְׁפֵי Ct 8⁶ (רִשְׁפֵי ψ 76⁴) ; טַרְפֵּי Ez 17⁹ ; צָמְדֵי Is 5¹⁰, and so always in נִסְפֵּיכֶם Nu 29³⁹, נִסְפֵּיהֶם ψ 16⁴, &c. (on the other hand, according to the best authorities *not* in חַסְדֵי Is 55³, &c., though in ψ 107⁴³ Ginsburg reads חֲסְדֵי) ; cf. § 46 *d*. Even with a middle guttural בַּעֲלֵיהֶן Est 1¹⁷·²⁰.—The attenuation of *ă* to *ĭ* also occurs sometimes in this form (see above, *k*), e. g. זִבְחֵי, &c., even יִלְדֵי Is 57⁴ beside יַלְדֵי Ho 1², &c.

n　G. In the *dual absol.* beside forms like רַגְלַיִם *feet*, with suff. רַגְלֶיךָ, רַגְלָיו, &c. אַלְפַּיִם *two thousand*, נְעָלַיִם *sandals*, בִּרְכַּיִם *knees* (*ă* attenuated to *ĭ*, *constr. st.* בִּרְכֵּי with a firmly closed syllable), with suffixes בִּרְכֵּי, &c. (cf., however, בִּרְכֵּיהֶם Ju 7⁶), forms with pretonic *Qameṣ* are also found (in consequence of the

---

[1] According to M. Lambert, *REJ.* 1896, p. 21, *a* tends to remain with labials ; so in 14 cases out of 22 masculines, and in 3 out of 6 feminines.

[2] Probably only a theory of one particular school and not generally accepted, or at any rate not consistently carried out ; cf. König, *Lehrgeb.*, ii. 22.

tendency to assimilate the dual to the plural in form: so König, *Lehrgeb.*,
ii. 17), as קַרְנַיִם *horns*, with suff. קַרְנָיו (Dn 8³ ᶠᶠ·; elsewhere always קַרְנַיִם,
קַרְנָיו, &c.), and so always דְּלָתַיִם, constr. st. דַּלְתֵי *folding-doors*, דְּרָכַיִם (?) *double
way*.

2. On Paradigms *b* and *e*. With a final א rejected (but retained ortho- *O*
graphically) we find חֵטְא *sin*. An initial guttural before suffixes generally
receives Sᵉghôl instead of the original *ĭ*, e.g. עֶזְרִי, חֶלְקִי, &c., so in the constr. st.
plur. עֶגְלֵי, &c.; חֵטְא forms חֲטָאֵי 2 K 10²⁹, &c., retaining the *Qameṣ* of חֲטָאִים
before the weak א.—The pausal forms סָתֶר and שָׁבֶט (out of pause always
שֶׁבֶט, סֶתֶר) go back to by-forms סֶתֶר, שֶׁבֶט.—On עֲשָׂבוֹת (constr. st. plur. of עֵשֶׂב)
Pr 27²⁵, cf. § 20 *h*; שִׁקְמִים *sycamores*, without *Qameṣ* before the termination
יִם‑‑ (see above, *l*), is probably from the sing. שִׁקְמָה found in the Mišna.

3. On Paradigms *c* and *f*. קֶשְׁט occurs in Pr 22²¹ without a helping vowel; *p*
with a middle guttural פֹּעַל, &c., but with ה also בֹּהֶן, אֹהֶל; with a final
guttural רֹבַע גֹּבַהּ, &c., but with א, גֻּמָּא; with a firmly closed syllable אֹסְפֵי
Mi 7¹.

Before suffixes the original *ŭ* sometimes reappears in the sing., e.g. גָּדְלוֹ *q*
(ψ 150²) beside גֻּדְלוֹ, from גֹּדֶל *greatness*; סֻבֳּלוֹ (with *Dageš forte dirimens*, and
the *ŭ* repeated in the form of a Ḥaṭeph-Qameṣ, cf. § 10 *h*) Is 9³, &c.; גִּשְׁמָה
Ez 22²⁴.—Corresponding to the form פָּעֳלְכֶם *poʿŏlkhèm* we find קָטְבֵךְ Ho 13¹⁴,
even without a middle guttural; similarly קְטָנִי (so Jablonski and Opitius)
1 K 12¹⁰, 2 Ch 10¹⁰, from קֹטֶן *little finger*; but the better reading is, no doubt,
קְטָנִּי (so ed. Mant., 'the ק proleptically assuming the vowel of the following
syllable'; König, *Lehrgeb.*, ii. 69), and the form is to be derived, with König,
from קֹטֶן, not *qŏṭŭn*, as Brockelmann quotes him, in *Grundriss*, p. 103. The
reading קְטָנִי (Baer and Ginsburg) is probably not due to a confusion of the
above two readings, but ‑‑ is merely intended to mark the vowel expressly
as *ŏ*. In the forms בְּעֳלוֹ Is 1³¹ (for פֹּעֲלוֹ) and תָּאֳרוֹ Is 52¹⁴ (for תָּאֳרוֹ 1 S 28¹⁴),
the lengthening of the original *ŭ* to *ō* has been retained even before the suffix;
cf. § 63 *p* and § 74 *h* (בְּמֹצַאֲכֶם Gn 32²⁰).—In the same way *ō* remains before
ה‑‑ *locale*, e.g. הָאֹהֱלָה, רֹנָּה Gn 18⁶, 24⁶⁷, &c. Dissimilation of the vowel (or
a by-form נֵכַח?) seems to occur in נִכְחוֹ Ex 14², Ez 46⁹, for נָכְחוֹ.

In the absol. st. plur. the original *ŭ* generally becomes Šᵉwâ before the *Qameṣ*, *r*
e.g. בְּקָרִים from בֹּקֶר *morning*, פְּעָלִים *works*, רְמָחִים *lances*, שְׁעָלִים *handfuls* (constr.
st. שַׁעֲלֵי Ez 13¹⁹); on the other hand, with an initial guttural the *ŭ*-sound reappears as Ḥaṭeph Qameṣ, e.g. חֳדָשִׁים *months*, עֳפָרִים *gazelles*, אֳרָחוֹת *ways*; and
so even without an initial guttural, הַגֳּרָנוֹת *the threshing-floors*, 1 S 23¹, Jo 2²⁴;
קֳדָשִׁים *sanctuaries*, and שֳׁרָשִׁים *roots* (*qŏdhāšim*, &c., with *ŏ* for ‑֯‑); also קָדָשַׁי
[but קֳדָשָׁיו, קֳדָשֶׁיךָ, once 'קָ], where, however, the reading frequently fluctuates
between 'קָ and 'קֳ; with the article 'הַקָ, 'בַּקֳ, 'לַקֳ, according to Baer and
Ginsburg. On these forms cf. especially § 9 *v*. From אֹהֶל *tent*, both
בָּאֳהָלִים and אֹהָלִים (cf. § 23 *h* and 'פֹּעֲ above) are found; with light suffixes
אָהֳלִי, &c.; so from אֹרַח *way*, אָרְחֹתָיו (also אֳרְחֹתַי)—hence only with initial א,
'on account of its weak articulation' (König, *Lehrgeb.*, ii. 45). It seems that
by these different ways of writing a distinction was intended between the

plural of אֹרְחָה *caravan*, and of אֹרַח *way*; however, אֲרָחוֹת is also found in the former sense (in *constr. st.* Jb 6¹⁹) and אֳרָחוֹת in the latter (e.g. Jb 13²⁷ according to the reading of Ben Naphtali and Qimḥi); cf. also אֹנִיּוֹת 2 Ch 8¹⁸ *K*ᵉ*th.* (אֳנִי *Q*ᵉ*rê*).—The *constr. st.* plural of בֹּהֶן *thumb* is בְּהֹנוֹת Ju 16ᶠ·, as if from a sing. בֹּהַן: of נֹגַהּ *brightness*, Is 59⁹ נְגֹהוֹת (on these *q*ᵉ*ṭōl*-forms, cf. *t*).—If אָפְנָיו Pr 25¹¹ is not dual but plural (see the Lexicon) it is then analogous to the examples, given in *l* and *o*, of plurals without a pretonic Qameṣ; cf. בָּטְנִים *pistachio nuts*, probably from a sing. בָּטְנָה. According to Barth, *ZDMG.* xlii, 345 f. אָפְנָיו is a sing. (אֹפֶן, the ground-form of אָפְנֶה, with suffix).

In the *constr. st. plur.* the only example with original *ŭ* is רִכְסֵי ψ 31²¹; otherwise like אָהֳלֵי, קָדְשֵׁי, &c.

s 4. Besides the forms treated hitherto we have to consider also a series of formations, which have their characteristic vowel under the *second* radical, as is ordinarily the case in Aramaic (on the origin of these forms see further, § 84ᵃ *e*). Thus (*a*) of the form קְטַל: דְּבַשׁ *honey*, מְעַט *little*; in pause, דְּבָשׁ; מְעָט; גְּבַר *man* (as *constr. st.*, see above, *h*), ψ 18²⁶ (elsewhere always גֶּבֶר), and infinitives like שְׁכַב (§ 45 *c*; on קְחַת, see above, *h*); שְׁכֶם *shoulder*, *ă* being modified to *è* (but in *pause* שְׁכֶם); locative שְׁכֶמָה, also שְׁכֶמָה Ho 6⁹. With suffixes in the usual manner שִׁכְמִי, שִׁכְבָהּ Gn 19³³·³⁵ (an infin. with suffix, therefore not שָׁכְבָהּ). On the other hand, the *ă* is retained in the *plur. absol.* by sharpening the final consonant: הֲדַסִּים *myrtles*, אֲגַמִּים (*constr.* אַגְמֵי) *marshes*, מְעַטִּים *few*.

t (*b*) Of the form קְטֵל: בְּאֵר *a well*, זְאֵב *wolf*, &c.¹; locative בְּאֵרָה, with *suff.* בְּאֵרִי, *plur.* זְאֵבִים, זְאֵבֵי; but בְּאֵרוֹת, *constr.* בְּאֵרֹת; on the *infin. constr.* שְׂאֵת, cf. § 76 *b*.

(*c*) of the form קְטֹל: בְּאֹשׁ *stench* (with *suff.* בָּאְשׁוֹ, just as סָבְכוֹ occurs in Jer 4⁷ along with the *constr. st.* סְבָךְ ψ 74⁵; cf. for the Dageš, § 20 *h*), perhaps also לְאֹם *nation*, pl. לְאֻמִּים.

u 5. Paradigms *g-i* comprise the segholate forms with middle ו or י: (*a*) of the form *qăṭl* with *Wāw* as a strong consonant, in which cases the original *ă* is almost always lengthened to *ā* (Paradigm *g*), thus מָוֶת, אָוֶן *vanity*, עָוֶל *iniquity*, תָּוֶךְ *midst*; with final א, שָׁוְא *falsehood*; cf. however, also רֶוַח *space*. In the *constr. st.* contraction always occurs, מוֹת, &c. (from original *maut*), and likewise before suffixes מוֹתוֹ, &c. Exception, עָוֶל as *constr. st.* Ez 28¹⁸ (according to Qimḥi) and with *suff.* עַוְלוֹ. The contraction remains also in all cases in the plural (but see below, *w*).

v (*b*) Of the form *qăṭl* with consonantal *Yôdh* (Paradigm *h*). With final א, גֶּיְא (also גֵּי), in Is 40⁴ גַּיְא, in the *constr. st.* (also *absol.* Zc 14⁴) גֵּיא (also גֵּי); plur. 2 K 2¹⁶ and Ez 6³ *K*ᵉ*th.* according to Baer גֵּאוֹת, i.e. doubtless גֵּאָיוֹת (cf. גֵּיאוֹתֶיךָ Ez 35⁸; according to another reading [and so Ginsburg] גֵּאָיוֹת,

---

¹ The proposal of Haupt (*SBOT.* 'Proverbs', p. 34, l. 44 ff.) to read זְאָב, בְּאָר, &c., does not seem to be warranted. The case here is quite different from that in Pr 1²² where the Masora requires תְּאֵהֲבוּ, no doubt on the analogy of בְּאָר, &c., for תְּאֵהֲבוּ, which was probably intended, see § 63 *m*.

i. e. doubtless גְּיָאוֹת), but in *Qᵉrê*, and all other passages, גֵּאָיוֹת. The uncontracted form (in the *absol. st.* with helping *Ḥireq*) remains also before ה‑ *locale*, e. g. בֵּיתָה (but in the *constr. st.* e. g. בֵּיתָה יוֹסֵף).—עִירָה (from עִיר) Gn 49¹¹ is peculiar, so also שִׁיתוֹ Is 10¹⁷ (from שַׁיִת).—In the *plural absol.* uncontracted forms occur, like חֲיָלִים *hosts*, עֲיָנוֹת *springs*, עֲיָרִים *young asses*, תְּיָשִׁים *he-goats*, &c.; as *constr. st.* Pr 8²⁸ עֵינוֹת for עֲיָנוֹת.

(c) With the contraction of the ו and י even in the *absol. st.* sing. (Paradigm *i*). In this way there arise formations which are unchangeable throughout; thus from the ground-form *qáṭl* : יוֹם (cf., however, § 96), סוֹף, שׁוֹר, &c.; with middle *Yôdh*, חֵיל 1 Ch 9¹³ (elsewhere חַיִל), לֵיל Is 21¹¹ (elsewhere לַיִל, in prose לַיְלָה, see above, § 90 *f*); from the ground-form *qíṭl*, דִּין, עִיר שִׁיר (see, however, § 96); from the ground-form *qúṭl*, גּוּר רוּחַ, &c. The plurals דְּוָדִים *pots*, שְׁוָקִים *streets*, שְׁוָרִים *oxen*, have a strong formation (but for חֲוָחִים 1 S 13⁶ read חֹרִים as in 14¹¹). Finally, forms with a quiescent middle א also belong to this class, such as רֹאשׁ *head* (obscured from רָאשׁ = *ra'š*, see § 96) and צֹאן *sheep*.

6. On Paradigm *k* : segholate forms from ל״ה stems. Besides the formations mentioned in § 84ᵃ *c*, *ε*, like בֶּכֶה, &c., and שָׁחוּ Ez 47⁵, with the original ו resolved, according to § 24 *d* (cf. the *constr. plur.* חַגְוֵי *clefts*, Ob ³, &c., and קַצְוֵי *ends*, ψ 48¹¹, &c., where the ו becomes again a strong consonant,[1] from חֵמוּ and קֵצוּ or חָמוּ and קָצוּ), there occur also (*a*) commonly, of the ground-form *qaṭl*, forms like צְבִי, לָחִי, בֶּכִי, פְּרִי, &c.; in *pause* פֶּרִי, בֶּכִי, לֶחִי, אֲרִי (cf. § 29 *m*), but אֲרִי Ju 14¹⁸; with suffixes פִּרְיוֹ (attenuated from *páryô*), בִּכְיִי ψ 6⁹, but also לְחָיִו, פֶּרְיִךְ, &c.; before a grave suffix פֶּרְיָתֶם, but also פֶּרְיְכֶם. Plur. גְּדָיִים (*constr.* גְּדָיֵי, see above, *o*), חֲטָאֵי), אֲרָיִים and אֲרָיוֹת; with softening of the י to א (as elsewhere in בְּלוֹאֵי Jer 38¹² for which there is בְּלוֹי in verse 11, according to § 8 *k*; עֲרָבִיאִים 2 Ch 17¹¹, cf. 26⁷ *Kᵉth.*; probably in לְאוֹת, דּוּדָאִים from דּוּדַי and לוּלַי; also חֲלְכָּאִים ψ 10¹⁰ *Kᵉth.*, divided into two words by the Masora, is to be referred to a sing. חֵלְכַּי *hapless*): חֲלָאִים *jewels*, Ct 7² (from חֲלִי, טְלָאִים *lambs*, Is 40¹¹ (from טְלִי); but instead of פְּתָאִים and צְבָאִים (from פֶּתִי and צְבִי) the Masora requires פְּתָאִים and צְבָאִים; dual: לְחָיַיִם, *constr. st.* לְחָיֵי, with *suff.* לְחָיַי, &c. On דַּל *door*, cf. § 95 *f*, and on such formations generally, see Barth on biliteral nouns in *ZDMG*. 1887, p. 603 ff., and *Nominalbildung* (isolated nouns), p. 1 ff.

(*b*) From the ground-form *qiṭl*, חֲצִי *half*, in *pause* חֶצְיִ, with suff. חֶצְיוֹ, &c.— From stems with middle *Wāw* arise such forms as אִי (from *'iwy*), עִי, צִי *ship*, plur. אִיִּים, צִיִּים, &c.; instead of the extraordinary plur. צִים Nu 24²⁴ read with the Samaritan יוֹצְאִים, and for בַּצִּים Ez 30⁹ read probably with Cornill אֳצִים.

(*c*) From the ground-form *qúṭl* sometimes forms like בֹּהוּ תֹּהוּ (from *tühw*, *bühw*), sometimes like חֳלִי, עֳנִי, and even without an initial guttural דְּמִי יְדִי, פִּי,

---

[1] Nöldeke, *Beiträge*, p. 58 : the direct or indirect retention of this ו is hardly a feature of early Hebrew. The true Hebrew forms from קָצֶה would be קְצֵה, קְצוֹת קָצוֹת, the aramaizing forms קָצֶה, קְצָת, קְצָוֹת, קְצָוֹת.

צְרִי (also צְרִי, יָפִי, דְּמִי), רָאִי, &c ; in *pause* חֹלִי,&c., with suff. חֶלְיוֹ, plur. חֲלָיִים.
From עֳפִי *branch*, there occurs in ψ 104¹² the plur. עֳפָאִים (analogous to פְּתָאִים,
&c., see above, *x*) ; the K*eth.* evidently intends עֳפָאִים (so Opitius and others).
Dual, with *suff.* דְּלָיָו Nu 24⁷, *bucket* (from דְּלִי, for דְּלָיְ), more correctly, with the
Masora, דָּלְיָו with Munaḥ for Metheg. This unusual Metheg is to be treated
as following the analogy of the cases mentioned in § 9 *v*.

aa   7. On Paradigms *l–n* : segholate forms from stems ע״ע (see § 84ª *c, β*).

(*a*) In the *qaṭl*-form the *ă* of the contracted formation is sometimes lengthened
in the *absol. st.*, sing. as in יָם (so also in the *constr. st.*, except in the combination יַם־סוּף *the Red sea*; and even before *Maqqeph*, יָם־הַמֶּלַח *the salt sea*),
sometimes it remains short, e. g. פַּת *morsel*, עַם *people*, but even these formations generally have *Qameṣ* in pause, as well as after the article (e. g. הָעָם).
Adjectives under the influence of a guttural either have forms like לַחִים,
צַחִים or, with *compensatory lengthening*, רָעִי, רָעִים. In the *constr. st.* חַי *living*
(in the plural חַיִּים also a substantive, *life*), and דַּי *sufficiency*, are contracted to
חֵי¹ and דֵּי. As a locative form notice הָהָרָה *to the mountain*, Gn 14¹⁰ (see § 27 *q*)
beside הַהֶרָה. The stem is expanded to a triliteral form in הָרָרִי (unless it is
simply derived from a by-form הָרָר on the analogy of *qáṭál*-forms) Jer 17³
(but in ψ 30⁸ for הָרָרִי read הֶרָרִי) and הָרָרַם Gn 14⁶ ; plur. *constr.* הָרָרֵי Nu 23⁷,
&c. (but only in poetical passages), with suffix, הָרָרֶיךָ Dt 8⁹ ; עֲמָמִים Ju 5¹⁴
(where, however, read probably בְּעַמֶּךָ), Neh 9²² ; עֲמָמֵי Neh 9²⁴ : elsewhere
עַמְּמִים, עַמֵּי.—Before *suffixes* and in the plur. *ă* is sometimes attenuated to *ĭ*,
e. g. פִּתִּי, פִּתִּים, from פַּת ; סִפִּים and סִפּוֹת (also סַפּוֹת 2 S 17²⁸) from סַף.
Before ח *ă* is retained in a virtually sharpened syllable, e. g. פַּחִים *traps*.

bb   (*b*) *Qiṭl*-forms : אֵם אֶם, אֵשׁ *fire* (with suff. אִשִּׁי, but cf. also אֶשְׁכֶם Is 50¹¹),
חֵן *favour*, &c. ; of a triliteral form, the plur. חֲצָצֶיךָ ψ 77¹⁸.

(*c*) *Quṭl*-forms : חֹק, כֹּל, חֹק *totality*, before *Maqqeph* חָק־, כָּל־, with suff. חֻקִּי, &c.,
with omission of *Dageš forte* (according to § 20 *m*) always חֻקְּכֶם, חֻקְּכֶם, but from
עֹז, עֻזְּ, עֻזֶּךָ, עֻזְּכֶם, for which עֻזִּי and עֻזְּךָ are also found. חֻקְקֵי, expanded to
a triliteral form, Ju 5¹⁵ and Is 10¹, generally explained as a secondary form
of חֻקֵּי with abnormal weakening of the *ŭ* to *ĭ*, is more probably to be referred
to a *qiṭl*-form = Arabic *ḥiqq*.

cc   The forms with assimilated middle *Nûn* likewise follow the analogy of
Paradigms *l–n*, e. g. אַף *nose, anger* (אַפַּי, dual אַפַּיִם, also *face*) for *'anp* ; חֵךְ *palate*
for *ḥink*, זִקִּים *fetters*, עֵז *goat*, plur. עִזִּים, for *'inz*, probably also אֵב *green herb*,
for *'inb*.

dd   2. Paradigm II comprises all formations with original short vowels,
whether in the first or second syllable ; cf. § 84ª *f–i*, and the general
laws of formation, § 92 *b–g*.

---

¹ חֵי only in Dn 12⁷ as *constr. st.*, since in the asseverative formulae (cf.
§ 149) חֵי נַפְשְׁךָ, חֵי פַרְעֹה (otherwise only in 2 S 15²¹, after חַי יהוה, and
Amos 8¹⁴), חֵי is a contracted form of the *absol. st.* (prop. *living is Pharaoh !* &c.).
It is evidently only a rabbinical refinement which makes the pronunciation חֵי
distinctive of an oath by God (or of God by himself), as in the regular
formulae חַי יְהוָה Dt 32⁴⁰) and חַי אָנֹכִי חַי אָנִי (= חַי אֲדֹנָי).

Rem. 1. On Paradigms *a* and *b*: ground-form *qăṭăl*. The lengthening of the second *ă* to *ā* is maintained in the *constr. st. sing.* only in ל״א-forms, e.g. צְבָא *army*, צְבָא. For the construct forms חֲלֵב *milk*, לְבֶן־ *white*, Gn 49¹², instead of the ordinary *absolutes* חָלָב, לָבָן, a secondary form לְבֶן, חֲלֵב must be assumed; from עָשָׁן *smoke*, the *constr. st.* עֲשַׁן occurs once, Ex 19¹⁸, beside עֲשַׁן, from הָדָר *ornament* the *constr. st.* הֲדַר Dn 11²⁰, beside the common form הֲדַר.—The plur. פְּרָשִׁים *horses*, Is 21⁷ (instead of פְּרָשִׁים, ground-form *părăš*) is no doubt due to a confusion with the *qaṭṭâl*-form פָּרָשׁ *horseman*.

A. Sometimes a sharpening of the third radical takes place, in order to *ee* keep the preceding vowel short, e.g. גְּמַלִּים *camels*, קְטַנִּים *small ones*, פְּלַגּוֹת *brooks* (see § 20 *a*).—The attenuation of the *ă* of the first syllable to *ĭ* does not take place in the *constr. st. plur.* as a rule after an initial guttural, as חַכְמֵי, עַנְוֵי, but חִזְקֵי, and never before a middle guttural, e.g. נַהֲרֵי; nor (according to König, owing to the influence of the nasal) in the non-guttural forms זַנְבוֹת *tails*, כַּנְפוֹת, and (in the dual) כַּנְפֵי *wings*, from זָנָב, כָּנָף.—The dual נַהֲרַיִם from נָהָר *river*, shows an abnormal omission of the lengthening of the *ă* before a tone-bearing termination, but cf. § 88 *c*.

B. From ע״ע stems, forms like חָלָל, עָנָן, &c., belong to this class. *ff*

C. The few nouns of the ground-form *qiṭăl* follow the same analogy, such as *gg* לֵבָב *heart*, שֵׁכָר *strong drink*, עֵנָב *grape*, &c. From שֵׂעָר *hair*, in the *constr. st.* besides שֵׂעַר the form שַׂעַר is also found (perhaps a survival of a secondary form like those in Paradigm I, *d*); so from צֵלָע *rib*, צֶלַע and even צְלַע 2 S 16¹³ (so ed. Mant., Ginsb.; but Baer צֵלַע), both, probably, old secondary forms (also used for the *absol. st.*) of צֵלָע; cf. also צַלְעִי and צַלְעוֹ, as well as the *constr. st. plur.* צַלְעוֹת; also from נֵכָר *strangeness*, the *constr. st.* נֵכַר־ is found, Dt 31¹⁶.

2. On Paradigms *c–e*: ground-form *qăṭĭl*, developed to *qāṭēl*; with a final *hh* guttural, e.g. שָׂבֵעַ *satisfied*. In the *constr. st.* the original *ĭ* of the second syllable, probably on the analogy of the forms discussed in § 69 *c*, becomes *ă*, e.g. זְקַן, חֲסַר, חֲדַל, &c., but not before suffixes, כְּתֵפִי, &c., nor in forms from ל״א stems, e.g. מָלֵא *full*, מְלָא; cf., moreover, עָקֵב Gn 25²⁶ from עָקֵב *heel*, and אֲבֶל־ ψ 35¹⁴, *mourning*. Paradigm *d* represents forms which in the *constr. st.* instead of the ordinary כְּתֵף, &c., have a segholate form, as עָרֵל, גֹּדֶל, יֶרֶךְ, אֶרֶךְ (Ez 44⁹), *constr. st.* of אָרֵךְ *long*, גֶּדֶר *wall*, יֶרֶךְ *thigh*, גֵּזֶל *robbery*, עָרֵל *uncircumcised*. In Is 11¹⁴ בְּכָתֵף would be altogether without precedent as a *constr. st.* (for בְּכֶתֶף); most probably the *absol. st.* is intended by the Masora (according to Nöldeke, *Gött. Gel. Anzeigen*, 1871, No. 23 [p. 896] for בכ׳ אֶחָד *with one shoulder*, i.e. *shoulder to shoulder*); [cf. Driver, *Tenses*, § 190, *Obs.*].

In the *plur. constr.* the *ē* lengthened from *ĭ* is frequently retained in verbal *ii* adjectives of this formation, e.g. חֲפֵצֵי, יְשֵׁנֵי, אֲבֵלֵי, שְׂמֵחֵי, שְׂבֵחֵי; cf. also יְתֵדְתָיו (with *ē* under the protection of the secondary tone) from יָתֵד *tent-peg*. On the other hand from יָרֵא *fearing*, always יִרְאֵי; cf. also רַגְעֵי ψ 35²⁰ from רָגֵעַ.—With *ă* retained in the initial syllable cf. אַחֵר *alius* (with a virtual sharpening of the ח).—From ע״י stems come forms like מֵת *dead person*, גֵּר *resident stranger*, עֵד *witness*, with unchangeable Ṣērê; hence מֵתִים, מֵתֵי, &c.

Kindred in character are the formations from the ground-form *qăṭŭl*. This *kk* ground-form is regularly lengthened to *qāṭōl*, e.g. עָגֹל *round*, עָמֹק *deep*, אָדֹם *red* ; but before formative additions the short *ŭ* returns, protected by the sharpening of the following consonant (see *ee* above), as עֲגֻלִּים, &c. (but in stems with a third guttural or ר, גְּבֹהָה‎, שְׁחֹרִים). The form עָגוֹל, 1 K 10¹⁹, is abnormal ; likewise עֲמֻוקָה Pr 23²⁷, Jablonski (ed. Mant. עֲמֻקָה, Baer and Ginsburg עֲמֻקָה).

ll 3. On Paradigm *f*: ground-form *qāṭāl* from ל״ה stems. As in verbs ל״ה § 75 *h*, the general rule is that before the terminations of the plur. and dual and before suffixes beginning with a vowel, the third radical is usually elided altogether. But besides שָׂדֶה the form שָׂדַי, with the final *Yôdh* retained, is also found in poetry (cf. also the singulars with suffixes, like מַשְׁתֵּיהֶם, in *ss*) ; in the same way final ו is retained in עֲנָוִים *the poor*, constr. עֲנָוֵי. The plur. of שָׂדֶה is שָׂדוֹת, constr. שְׂדוֹת (also שְׂדֵי, unless this is a *sing.*, contracted from שְׂדָי ; so Barth, *ZDMG*. xlii, p. 351). The *qiṭāl*-form (see § 84ᵃ *i*) רָעֶה 2 S 15³⁷, 16¹⁶, 1 K 4⁵ is remarkable as a *constr. st.* (the reading רֵעֶה of Opitius and others is opposed to the express statement of the Masora). To the category of these forms also belongs without doubt פָּנִים *face* (only in *plur.*), פְּנֵי, פְּנֵי, פְּנֵיכֶם, &c.

mm In a few formations of this kind the vowel of the second syllable appears to have been already lost in the *absol. st. sing.*; so according to the ordinary view, in יָד *hand*, constr. יַד, with *suff.* יָדוֹ, but יֶדְכֶם ; plur. יָדוֹת, constr. יְדוֹת, dual יָדַיִם, יְדֵי, with *suff.* יָדַי, יְדֵיכֶם, &c., and in דָּם *blood*, constr. דַּם, with *suff.* דָּמִי, but דִּמְכֶם (*ă* attenuated to *ĭ*), plur. דָּמִים, דְּמֵי. But perhaps both these nouns are to be regarded as primitive (§ 81), and as original monosyllabic formations.

nn 3. Paradigm III comprises forms with an unchangeable vowel in the first syllable, whilst the vowel of the second syllable has been lengthened from an original short vowel, and is therefore changeable. The special cases are to be distinguished in which the original short vowel is lengthened both *in* and *before* the tone, but in an open syllable becomes *Šₑwâ* (Paradigm *a*, but cf. also examples like אוֹפַנִּים *wheels*, for אוֹפָנִים, and אֻלַמִּים *porches*), secondly, the cases in which the vowel becomes *Šₑwâ* even *before* the tone (Paradigm *b*), and finally, those in which the termination of ל״ה formations is entirely lost (Paradigm *c*).

oo Rem. 1. On the model of עוֹלָם (which, moreover, is obscured from *'âlăm*), the following forms also are inflected : מִקְטָל (§ 85 *h*), in some cases with virtual sharpening of the third radical (see § 20 *a*), as מִבְטַחוֹ Jer 17⁷, ψ 40⁵, Jb 8¹⁴, &c. ; ל״א nouns of this form maintain the *Qames* in the constr. st. plur., e.g. מִקְרָאֵי from מִקְרָא¹; on the other hand, in the plur. of the *participles Niph.* (§ 85 *n*) of verbs ל״א (which likewise belong to this class), are found not only regular forms like נִקְרָאִים but also נֶחְבָּאִים Jos 10¹⁷, נְטְמָאִים Ez 20³⁰ᶠ·,

---

¹ מִקְרָשֵׁיהֶם Ez 7²⁴ for מִקְרְשֵׁ (from מִקְרָשׁ) is wholly irregular; perhaps, however, the *part. Pi'ēl* is intended, without *Dageš* in the ר (according to § 20 *m*).

and so always נְבִיאִים (except Ez 13² הַנִּבְּאִים) and נִמְצָאִים ₁ S 13¹³, ₂ K 14¹⁴, &c. (except Ezr 8²⁵ הַנִּמְצָאִים in pause).[1]

Moreover, the other participles in *ā* also follow the analogy of עוֹלָם as *pp* regards the final syllable (מָקְטָל, מָקְטָל; cf., however, הַפּוּשָׁב Gn 43¹² in close connexion; see the analogous cases in § 65 *d*); also שֻׁלְחָן *table* (§ 85 *u*; plur. שֻׁלְחָנוֹת, constr. שֻׁלְחָנוֹת), קָרְבָּן, constr. קָרְבַּן, hence in plur. constr. with suff. קָרְבְּנֵיהֶם Lv 7³⁸; עָקְרָב (§ 85 *w*), plur. עָקְרַבִּים (with sharpening of the final consonant for עָקְרָבִים, cf. also עֵירָם *naked*, plur. עֵירֻמִּים Gn 3⁷ [but in 2²⁵ עֲרוּמִּים, according to § 90 an orthographic licence for עֲרֻמִּים from עָרֹם] *nakedness*, 2 Ch 28¹⁵; קַרְדֻּמּוֹ, קַרְדֹּם; מֵעֲמַקֵּי Is 51¹⁰; נִכְבַּדֵּי Is 23⁸ ᶠ·; מִשְׁנַבִּי ψ 18³; even with attenuation of the *ă* to *ĭ*, מוֹרִגִּים *threshing instruments*, 2 S 24²², ₁ Ch 21²³, from (מוֹרַג), מַתָּן (§ 85 *g*), מָגֵן (§ 85 *i*), מָעֹז (§ 85 *k*), inasmuch as they retain the *ā* of the first syllable, contrary to rule, even when not pretonic, e.g. מָעֵנִי, מָעֵנּי; מוֹשָׁב (§ 85 *g*); תּוֹשָׁב (§ 85 *p*), constr. st. plur. תֹּשְׁבֵי ₁ K 17¹; also isolated forms according to § 84ᵃ *t*, and § 84ᵇ *b*, *c*, *k*, *m*, *n*, *o*. Cf. finally, צַוָּאר *neck* (from *ṣaw'ăr*), constr. st. צַוַּאר Jer 28¹⁰ ᶠᶠ·, constr. st. plur. צַוְּארֵי Gn 45¹⁴, &c.

2. (Paradigm *b*; cf. § 84ᵃ *s*.) Instead of the original *ĭ* in such forms as *qq* אֹיִבְכֶם (cf. 2 K 22²⁹), the second syllable more frequently has *ĕ*, e.g. יֹצֶרְךָ *thy creator*; with a closing guttural (according to § 91 *d*; but cf. also אָבַד Dt 32²⁸) forms are found sometimes like שֻׁלְחָךְ, sometimes like בֹּרַאֲךָ; constr. st. without suff. נֹטַע ψ 94⁹ (according to § 65 *d*); with a middle guttural וְאֵלֵךְ Is 48¹⁷; cf. 43¹⁴.—The same analogy also is followed in the flexion of the other participles which have *ē* in the final syllable (מְקַטֵּל, מִתְקַטֵּל, &c.), see further, in § 84ᵇ *d*, גִּבֵּן, &c. (but with exceptions, as שֻׁלֵּשִׁים, רַבְעִים), and ibid. *l*, *p*; § 85 *i*, *k* (מִזְבֵּחַ *altar*, constr. st. מִזְבַּח, plur. מִזְבְּחוֹת), and ibid. *q*, but here also there are exceptions like מַקְהֵלִים ψ 26¹².

3. (Paradigm *c*: part. Qal of verbs ל״ה, differing from Paradigm II, *f* in the *rr* unchangeableness of the vowel of the first syllable.) In Ez 17¹⁵ *ē* in the absol. st. is abnormal, and *Sᵉghôl* in the constr. st. in 2 S 24¹¹ (so Opitius, Ginsburg; but Baer חֹזֶה, Ec 2¹⁵ (according to Baer, but not the Mantua ed.; מִקְרֶה Ec 3¹⁹ is in the absol. st.). To this class belong, as regards their formation, the ל״ה-forms mentioned in § 84ᵃ *r*, § 85 *g* (with suff., e.g. הַמַּעַלְךָ Dt 20¹, *which brought thee up*), and *h*.

In a few instances, before a suffix beginning with a consonant, the original *ss* *ăy* of the termination has been contracted to *ê*, and thus there arise forms which have apparently *plural suffixes*; as מַרְאֵיהֶם Is 5¹², Dn 1¹⁰.¹⁶; *their appearance*, Dn 1¹⁵, Gn 41²¹, cf. Na 2⁵; נוֹטֵיהֶם *who stretched them forth*, Is 42⁵; *defectively* אֹפֵהֶם Ho 7⁵ (cf. נֹחֶם Ez 34¹⁴); on the other hand, the examples in Is 14¹¹, Gn 47¹⁷, which were formerly classed with the above, are really plurals. But מַחֲנֶיךָ *thy camp*, Dt 23¹⁵ (מַחֲנֶךָ occurs just before),

---

[1] Brockelmann, *Grundriss*, p. 659, observes that except in 2 Ch 5¹¹, 35¹⁷ הַנִּמְצָאִים is always followed by a preposition governing a word, so that the punctuators perhaps intended to indicate a sort of *constr. st.*

מִקְנֶיךָ *thy cattle*, Is 30²³ (probably also שָׁדֶיךָ 1 K 2²⁶), מַרְאַיִךְ Ct 2¹⁴, and מַרְאָיו *the sight of him*, Jb 41¹ (with the יְ here retained orthographically), מֵעָלָיו Ez 40³¹, &c., are still to be explained as singulars.—On a few other examples which may perhaps be thus explained, see § 124 *k*. Before the plural ending the original termination *ay* reappears in מְמֻחָיִם Is 25⁶ (*part. Pu.* from מָחָה).

tt 4. Paradigm IV comprises the forms with a changeable vowel (*a, b*), or a vowel which has already become Šᵉwâ (*c*), in the first syllable, and an unchangeable vowel in the second. With Paradigm *c* (which, however, for the most part consists merely of forms based on analogy, without biblical parallels) are also connected all the forms which have unchangeable vowels in both syllables, and therefore (like כְּתָב) cannot undergo any vowel changes.

uu Rem. 1. Analogous to פָּקִיד (ground-form *pāqîd*) are § 84ᵃ *k*, גְּדוֹל, &c. (with *ô*, not changeable ō for *ŭ*); in substantives like שָׁלוֹם, this *ô* is demonstrably obscured from *á* (Arab. *sálám*); ibid. *l, m*, אָסִיר,אָסוּר, &c. ; § 85 *u*, זָכְרוֹן, *constr.* זִכְרוֹן ; חִזָּיוֹן, *constr.* חֶזְיוֹן ; בִּלָּיוֹן, *constr.* בִּלְיוֹן (cf., however, the forms in the *constr. st.* עֶצְבּוֹן, קִנְמוֹן, and with the plural suffix עִזְּבוֹנַיִךְ Ez 27¹² ff.) ; § 85 *w*, חַלָּמִישׁ, *constr.* חַלְמִישׁ ; § 85 *l*, מָקוֹם, &c.

vv 2. עָנִי (ground-form *'ăniy*, stem עָנָה) represents forms in which a final Yôdh has been resolved into *î*; before formative additions the original Yôdh under the protection of a Dageš forte again becomes audible as a firm consonant, whilst the (originally short) vowel of the first syllable becomes Šᵉwâ; cf. § 84ᵃ *l*, נָקִי, plur. נְקִיִּים, and § 87 *a*.

ww 3. כְּתָב with unchangeable *á* in the second syllable, whilst the Šᵉwâ is weakened from a short vowel (Arab. *kitáb*); *constr. st.* כְּתָב־ Est 4⁸ (readings like כְּתָב 2 Ch 35⁴ are incorrect, although יְקָר Est 1⁴ and כְּתָב־ 4⁸ are supported by fairly good authority; however, these *qᵉṭâl*-forms in Hebrew are probably all loan-words from the Aramaic). The only plural form found in the O. T. is עֲבָדֵיהֶם *their deeds*, Ec 9¹. In a narrower sense the forms enumerated in § 84ᵃ *n–p* belong to this class; in a wider sense all those which have unchangeable vowels throughout, thus § 84ᵃ *u*, § 84ᵇ *e* קַטָּל, cf., however, the anomalous forms mentioned there), ibid. *f–i, m* (No. 34 f.), *n* (No. 39), *p* (No. 44), also partly § 85 *b–w* (especially *l* and *r*).

xx In opposition to the anomalous shortening of the form קַטָּל (see above), cases are also found where pretonic vowels are retained even in the antepenultima (with the secondary tone); cf. above, *ii* and *pp*, also of the form קָטִיל (properly *qăṭîl*) the examples שְׁלִישִׁים, פְּרִיצִים, סָרִיסִים, whilst the *constr. st. sing.* according to the rule, changes the *á* into Šᵉwâ (פְּרִיץ, סָרִים). (These are not to be confounded with forms like עָרִיץ *tyrant*, which is for עָרִיר, and consequently has an unchangeable Qameṣ.) Of the form קָטוּל (*qăṭûl*) in this class are שָׁבוּעַ *week*, plur. שְׁבֻעִים and שָׁבֻעוֹת, *constr.* שְׁבֻעוֹת, but with Metheg of the secondary tone in the fifth syllable from the end, שְׁבֻעֹתֵיכֶם.—On מָעוֹז, מְעֻזִּי, &c., cf. § 85 *k*.

§ 94. *Formation of Feminine Nouns.*

1. The feminine ending הָ֫-, when appended to the masculine *a* forms treated in § 93, effects in almost all cases the same changes as are produced in the masculine forms by the addition of a light suffix, since in both cases the tone is moved one place farther forward (see § 92 *b*). The following scheme is based on the same division into four classes, with their subdivisions, as in § 93; a few special forms will be treated in § 95 in connexion with the paradigms of feminine nouns.

Paradigm I: segholate forms, with the feminine ending always *b* added to the ground-form, (*a*) מַלְכָּה *queen*, כַּבְשָׂה, and with attenuation of *ă* to *ĭ* כִּבְשָׂה *lamb*, רִצְפָּה *hot stone*, Is 6⁶ (from another root רְצָפָה; see Baer on Ez 40¹⁷), חָזְקָה *strength* (unless belonging to Paradigm *b*); (*b*) סִתְרָה *covering* (masc. סֵתֶר); עֶדְנָה *pleasure* (עֵדֶן), not to be confounded with the unchangeable forms with a prefixed מ, derived from ל״ה stems, as מִצְוָה *command*, plur. מִצְוֹת; (*c*) חֶלְדָּה, proper name (חֹלֶד *mole*), אָכְלָה *food* (אֹכֶל); (*d*) נַעֲרָה *girl* (נַעַר); (*f*) בָּאְשָׁה *weed*, טָהֳרָה *purity* (טֹהַר); (*g*) עַוְלָה *wrong* (also עוֹלָה, Paradigm *i*); (*i*) צֵידָה *victuals* (masc. צַיִד, cf. Paradigm *h*); from *qiṭl* and *quṭl*-forms, בִּינָה *understanding*, סוּפָה *tempest*; (*k*) אַלְיָה *fat tail* (as if from אֲלִי), שִׁבְיָה (*ă* attenuated to *ĭ*) *captivity* (שְׁבִי), לִוְיָה *wreath* (probably an original *qiṭl*-form); (*l*) חַיָּה *life*, מִדָּה *measure* (attenuated from מַדָּה). Adjectives derived from ע״ע stems also belong in flexion to this class, as רַבָּה *multa*, with middle guttural רָעָה *mala*; (*m*) זִמָּה *plan*; (*n*) חֻקָּה *statute* (חֹק).

Paradigm II: ground-form *qăṭălăt*, &c., (*a*) נְקָמָה *vengeance* (נָקָם); *c* (*b*) אֲדָמָה *earth*; (*c*) נְבֵלָה *corpse*; (*d*) עֲיֵפָה *languida*; (*f*) יָפָה *beautiful*, קָצָה *end* (from קָצֶה, יָפֶה). From stems ע״וּ arise such forms as עֵרָה (masc. עֵר, properly *part.* Qal from עוּר) *female witness*. From the ground-form *qăṭŭl*, עֲמֻקָּה *profunda* (masc. עָמֹק), עֲבֻדָּה *servitude*, &c.

Paradigm III: unchangeable vowel in the first, changeable in the *d* second syllable, (*a*) יֹלֵדָה *a woman with child* (cf. the examples in § 84ᵃ *s*, and the retention of the *ē* in the *part.* Pi̇ʿēl, Ex 22¹⁷, 23²⁶; in the Hithpaʿēl 1 K 14⁵ᶠ·), but also with the change of the *ē* (originally *ĭ*) into *Sᵉwâ*, יֹשְׁבָה *dwelling*, Na 3⁸. However, in these participial forms the feminine is mostly indicated by ת--- (see below, *h*); (*c*) גּוֹלָה *those of the captivity* (masc. גּוֹלֶה), but also with a return of the final Yôdh, הֹמִיָּה *clamorous*, Pr 7¹¹, and the examples in § 75 *v*. On the *â* of the participles of verbs ע״וּ, which also belong to this class, such as זָרָה *peregrina*, cf. § 72 *g*.

e Paradigm IV: originally changeable vowel in the first syllable, unchangeable in the second, (*a*) גְּדֻלָה *magna*, חֲסִידָה *stork*, properly *pia*; בְּתוּלָה *virgin*, properly *seiuncta*; (*b*) עֲנִיָּה *misera*.

f 2. A simple ת is added as feminine ending in forms like בְּכִית *weeping* (masc. בְּכִי, § 93 *x, a*), בְּרִית *covenant*; but *feminine participles* of verbs ל״א, as יֹצֵאת, מֹצֵאת, may be due to contraction from *yôṣè'et*, &c. (hardly to lengthening of the ĭ in the ground-form *môṣi*), whilst forms like נִשְׂאֵת, מוֹצֵאת (see § 74 *i*) are to be explained on the analogy of the forms treated in § 93 *t*. Apart from the ל״ה formations, we find the simple ת in the participle מְשָׁרַת 1 K 1¹⁵, contracted from מְשָׁרַתְּ. But וַיֹּלֶדְתְּ Gn 16¹¹, Ju 13⁵·⁷ is the ground-form of the ptcp. וְיֹלֶדֶת (as in the same connexion in Gn 17¹⁹, Is 7¹⁴), cf. § 80 *d* and the *Qᵉre* שֹׁבַתְּ, &c., discussed in § 90 *n*.

g The forms which arise by appending the ת feminine to masculine nouns with a changeable vowel in a closed final syllable are, as a rule, developed exactly in the same way as masculine segholate forms. Thus there arise in Paradigm I (*a*) from גְּבִרְתְּ (for original *gᵉbirt*; § 69 *c*), the form גְּבֶרֶת *mistress* (but only in *construct st.*; in Is 47⁷ also גְּבֶרֶת עַד are to be taken together; the *absolute st.* is גְּבִירָה); from מַלְכַּת, מַלְכָּת *queen* (in Paradigm II, *a*); פַּחַת=פֶּחֶת (פַּחַת *pit*) Lv 13⁵⁵; (*c*) גֶּדֶר *wall*, גְּדֵרֶת (from גְּדִרְתְּ=*gᵉdirt*; cf. זֵק as construct st. of זָק); on the other hand, חֲמֵשֶׁת is construct st. of חֲמִשָּׁה *five*, with lengthening of the original ĭ of חֲמִשְׁתְּ.

h Formations with a changeable ō in the second syllable belonging to this class are נְחֹשֶׁת *bronze* (from נְחֻשְׁתְּ), כֻּתֹּנֶת the *constr. st.* of כֻּתֹּנֶת *coat*, perhaps also כְּתֹבֶת *writing* (unless it be obscured from כְּתָב, § 93, Paradigm IV, *c*).—Paradigm III, (*a*) חֹתֶמֶת (from חֹתַמְתְּ), masc. חוֹתָם *seal*; (*b*) יוֹנֶקֶת (properly *sucking*) *sprout* (in *pause*, e. g. הַבְּרֹכֶת Ex 26⁴, &c.), and so most feminines of participles קֹטֵל. On this transition of the ground-form *qôṭilt* to קֹטֶלֶת (regularly before suffixes in יוֹנַקְתּוֹ, יֹלַדְתּוֹ, &c.), cf. § 69 *c*; *qôṭalt* serves as the ground-form under the influence of a guttural as well as before suffixes, e. g. יֹדַעַת, feminine of יֹדֵעַ *knowing*; in a wider sense, גֻּלְגֹּלֶת *skull* may also be included here, see § 95, Paradigm IV, *c*.

On the endings וּת and י־ת, see § 86 *k, l*, § 95 at the end.

§ 95. *Paradigms of Feminine Nouns.*

a In accordance with the general formative laws, stated in § 92 *b–k*, the following cases have chiefly to be considered in the flexion of feminines also: (1) a tone-lengthened vowel on the removal of the tone reverts to its original shortness (thus the *ā* of the termination הָ becomes again *ă* in the *construct st.* תַ). On the other hand, even an originally short vowel is retained as (a long) pretonic vowel *before* the endings הָ and וֹת in the *abs. st.*, e.g. צְדָקָה; (2) without the tone or foretone an originally short vowel almost always becomes *Šᵉwâ*; on the other hand, *before* a vowel which had thus become *Šᵉwâ* the *ă* in the first syllable which had hitherto also been reduced to *Šᵉwâ* returns, although usually attenuated to *ĭ*, e.g. צִדְקַת from *ṣădhăqăth*; (3) in the plural of the feminines of segholate forms before the termination of וֹת or יִם, and in formations of the latter kind also before the light suffixes, a *pretonic Qameṣ* reappears, while the short vowel of the first syllable becomes *Šᵉwâ*. This short vowel, however, returns in the *construct st. plur.*, whether ending in וֹת or יִ; in formations of the latter kind also before the grave suffixes.

The following Paradigms (with the exception of I, *d*) deal only with such of the forms treated in § 94 as incur some vowel changes or other. All forms with unchangeable vowels follow the analogy of Paradigm I, *d*.

	I.					*b*
	a.	*b.*		*c.*	*d.*	*e.*
Sing. absolute	מַלְכָּה (queen)	[כִּלְיָה] (kidney)	חֶרְפָּה (reproach)	חָרְבָּה (waste)	חֻקָּה (statute)	[גְּבִירָה] (mistress)
„ *construct*	מַלְכַּת		חֶרְפַּת	חָרְבַּת	חֻקַּת	גְּבֶרֶת
„ *with light suff.*	מַלְכָּתִי		חֶרְפָּתִי	חָרְבָּתִי	חֻקָּתִי	גְּבִרְתִּי
„ *with grave suff.*	מַלְכַּתְכֶם		חֶרְפַּתְכֶם	חָרְבַּתְכֶם	חֻקַּתְכֶם	גְּבִרְתְּכֶם
Plur. absolute	מְלָכוֹת	כְּלָיוֹת	חֲרָפוֹת	חֲרָבוֹת	חֻקּוֹת	
„ *construct*	מַלְכוֹת	כִּלְיוֹת ¹	חֶרְפוֹת	חָרְבוֹת	חֻקּוֹת	
„ *with suff.*	מַלְכוֹתַי	כִּלְיוֹתַי		חָרְבוֹתַי	חֻקּוֹתַי	
Dual absolute		רִקְמָתַיִם (a double piece of embroidery)				מְצִלְתַּיִם (cymbals)

---

¹ Only in ψ 69¹⁰, contrary to rule, with a firmly closed syllable, cf. § 93 *m.*

c

	II.			III.	
	a.	*b.*	*c.*	*a.*	*b.*
Sing. absolute	צְדָקָה	זְעָקָה	שָׁנָה	יוֹנֶקֶת	גֻּלְגֹּלֶת
	(righteousness)	(outcry)	(year)	(sprout)	(skull)
„ construct	צִדְקַת	זַעֲקַת	שְׁנַת	יוֹנֶקֶת	גֻּלְגֹּלֶת
„ with light suff.	צִדְקָתִי	זַעֲקָתִי	שְׁנָתִי	יוֹנַקְתִּי	גֻּלְגָּלְתִּי
„ with grave suff.	צִדְקַתְכֶם	זַעֲקַתְכֶם	שְׁנַתְכֶם	יוֹנַקְתְּכֶם	גֻּלְגָּלְתְּכֶם
Plur. absolute	צְדָקוֹת		שָׁנוֹת [1]	[יוֹנְקוֹת]	
„ construct	צִדְקוֹת		שְׁנוֹת	יוֹנְקוֹת	גֻּלְגְּלוֹת
„ with suff.	צִדְקוֹתַי		שְׁנוֹתַי	יוֹנְקוֹתַי	גֻּלְגְּלוֹתַי
Dual absolute	[נְחֻשְׁתַּיִם]		שְׂפָתַיִם		
	(fetters of brass)		(lips)		
„ construct			שִׂפְתֵי		

Remarks.

d   1. **Paradigm I: feminines of segholate forms.** (a) The locative of this class has the form גִּבְעָתָה *towards Gibeah* (masc. גִּבְעַ). In some cases, especially with an initial guttural, there is no means of deciding whether the form in question is to be referred to a *qăṭl* or a *qĭṭl* base, e.g. חָזְקָה *strength* (cf. חָרְפָּה under *b*). A *dual* of this form occurs in שִׁבְעָתַיִם *seven times* (cf. שֶׁבַע *seven*, fem.). Analogous to masculine forms like דְּבַשׁ (§ 93 *s*) is הֲדַסָּה *myrtle*.—From masculines of the form פְּרִי ל״ה, cf. § 93 I, *k*) arise feminines sometimes like אַלְיָה, שַׁלְוָה, גַּאֲוָה (see above, § 94 *b*), sometimes like בְּכִית (§ 94 *f*); occasionally the final ת is retained before the plural ending, as if it belonged to the stem (cf. § 87 *k*), e.g. חֲנִיתוֹת *spears*. Forms like גְּדִיָּה (cf. אֳנִיָּה, a *qŭṭl* form) are derived directly from the masculine forms גְּדִי *kid*, אֳנִי *a fleet*.—(b) From a stem ע״ן חִטָּה *wheat* (for חִנְטָה), plur. חִטִּים.—(c) From עָרְלָה *foreskin*, the plur. absol. is עֲרָלוֹת (cf. פְּעָלִים, § 93, Paradigm I, *f*), constr. עָרְלוֹת.—(d) Example of a feminine segholate form from a stem ע״ע (ground-form *qŭṭl*, like חַיָּה of the form *qăṭl*, זִמָּה of the form *qĭṭl*), with ŏ for ŭ, חַגָּא *terror*, Is 19[17] (Aramaic orthography for חָגָּה).

e   (e) To the list of segholate forms with ת fem. belong also the infinitives of verbs פ״ן and פ״י, which have rejected the weak consonant at the beginning, as שֶׁבֶת (from יָשַׁב), דַּעַת (from יָדַע), גֶּשֶׁת (from נָגַשׁ), as well as קַחַת (from לָקַח); cf. § 69 *m* and § 66 *b* and *g*. The infinitives of verbs פ״ו are, however, also found in the form דֵּעָה, לֵדָה, צֵאָה, and of the same origin also are עֵדָה *congregation* (from יָעַד), עֵצָה *counsel* (from יָעַץ), שֵׁנָה *sleep* (from יָשֵׁן), constr. שְׁנַת, עֲדַת, while in the constr. forms זֵעַת *sweat*, Gn 3[19] (from יָזַע *to flow*), and צֵאַת *excrement*, Ez 4[12], the Ṣere has remained firm.

f   From a stem ע״ו (cf. בּוֹשׁ *to be ashamed*) is בֹּשֶׁת *shame*, with suffix בָּשְׁתִּי.

---

[1] On שָׁנוֹת as a less frequent (poetic) form for שָׁנִים see § 87 *n*.

From a stem ל״ה (דָּלָה, cf., however, Barth, *ZDMG.* 1887, p. 607, who assumes a stem (ידל the masculine דַּל appears to have been formed after the rejection of the final *Yôdh*, and afterwards the feminine דֶּלֶת *door*; but in the *plural* דְּלָתוֹת, *constr.* דַּלְתוֹת, the ת of the termination is retained (see above, *d*, חֲנִיתוֹת). In a similar way רְפָתִים *stalls*, Hb 3¹⁷, has arisen, if it is from the stem רפה, and שֹׁקֶת *trough* (from שָׁקָה), of which the masc. must have been שֹׁק = שְׁקִי; on the other hand, the *plur. constr.* שִׁקֲתוֹת Gn 30³⁸ (again retaining the feminine ת as an apparent radical) can only be an abnormal formation from the *singular* שֹׁקֶת, not from a kindred form שֶׁקֶת or שָׁקֶת.

2. Paradigm II: ground-form *qăṭălăt*, &c., cf. § 94 *c*, Paradigm II, *a* and *b*. **g** Analogous to the masculine forms like קָטָן, plur. קְטַנִּים, we find קְטַנָּה *parva*, &c.—The *constr.* forms, like צִדְקַת (*ṣidhᵉqăth*), are distinguished by the vocal *Šᵉwâ* (§ 10 *d*) from the segholate forms, like כִּבְשַׂת (*kibh-săth*). Consequently the *constr. st.* בִּרְכַּת Gn 28⁴, &c. (from בְּרָכָה *blessing*), and חֶרְדַּת 1 S 14¹⁵, &c. (from חֲרָדָה *a trembling*), are abnormal.—Under the influence of a guttural (see Paradigm *b*) the original *ă* is retained in the first syllable in the *constr. st.* (cf. also אֲדָמָה *earth*, אַדְמַת); in other cases it is modified to *Sᵉghôl*, e. g. עֲגָלָה *wagon*, עֶגְלָתוֹ. Frequently from an *absol. st.* in ◌ָה the *constr.* is formed with the termination ת, e. g. עֲטָרָה *crown*, constr. עֲטֶרֶת (from עֲטַרְתְּ); along with עֲצָרָה *assembly*, עֲצֶרֶת is found usually, even in the *absol. st.*; יְבֶמֶת (from יָבָם *levir*) before suffixes is pointed as in יְבִמְתִּי, and thus entirely agrees with גְּבֶרֶת (Paradigm I *e*). From a stem ל״י (אָמַן) is formed אֱמֶת *truth* (from *'ămant*, and this no doubt for an original *'ămint*, § 69 *c*) before suffixes אֲמִתִּי, &c.

From the masc. form קָטֵל (*qăṭil*) are formed, according to rule, גְּדֵרָה *wall*, **h** נְבֵלָה *corpse*, constr. נִבְלַת; בְּהֵמָה *cattle*, constr. בֶּהֱמַת (for בְּהֶמַת), with suffix בֶּהֶמְתְּךָ Lv 19¹⁹. More frequently, however, the *ē* of the second syllable is retained before the termination *ath* of the *constr. st.*; thus from נְבֵלָה once נְבֵלַת Is 26¹⁹, and always בְּרֵכַת *pool*, גְּזֵלַת *prey*, טְמֵאַת *unclean*, מְלֵאָתִי *full*, Is 1²¹ (with *Ḥireq compaginis*, see § 90 *l*), מְרִירְתִי Jb 16¹³; שְׁאֵלָתִי 1 S 1²⁷, &c. (with elision of the א, שְׁלָתֵךְ 1 S 1¹⁷), also שְׁאֵלָתִי Jb 6⁸. Cf. the analogous forms of the *constr. st.* מַגֵּפַת *plague*, תִּרְדֵּמַת *deep sleep*, from מַגֵּפָה, תַּרְדֵּמָה.

As dual we find יַרְכָתַיִם *sides* (cf. יַרְכְתוֹ Gn 49¹³, from the obsolete יָרְכָה, **i** feminine of יָרֵךְ; the *constr. st.* יַרְכְּתֵי is perhaps to be referred to a segholate form (יַרְכָּה, cf. יֶרֶךְ as *constr. st.* of יָרֵךְ), unless the closed syllable be due to the analogy of בִּרְכַּת and חֶרְדַּת (see *g*).

In the forms with simple ת feminine the ground-form *qăṭilt* is developed **k** (§ 69 *c*) to *qᵉṭalt*, and this again regularly to קְטֶלֶת. Thus the feminine of חָבֵר *companion* is חֲבֶרֶת (with suffix חֲבֶרְתָּהּ Mal 2¹⁴, cf. שְׁכֶנְתָּהּ Ex 3²²), of גֵּר fem. גְּרֶרֶת besides גְּרָרָה.—Of ע״ע stems the segholate forms נַחַת *rest* and שַׁחַת *pit* (from נוּחַ, שׁוּחַ) belong to this class; Böttcher (*Gram.* i. 411) rightly distinguished the latter from שַׁחַת *corruption* (stem שָׁחַת); in the same way also נַחַת *rest* is distinct from נַחַת *a lighting down* (stem נָחַת).

The feminines of the form *qăṭil* from stems ע״וּ, as מֵתָה *mortua*, עֵרָה fem. **l** *witness* (from עוּד, מוּת), have likewise an unchangeable vowel in the first syllable. Cf., on the other hand, the forms from פ״י stems mentioned above, under *e*, such as שֵׁנָה *sleep*, constr. st. שְׁנַת ; moreover, חֵמָה *anger*, constr. st. חֲמַת (but חֵמֶת *a leathern bottle*, in *pause* חֵמָת [so Baer, Ginsb., but Kittel 'חַ] Gn 21¹⁵, constr. *st.* חֵמַת מַיִם Gn 21¹⁴, perhaps from a stem חמת).

m   The feminines of the form *qăṭŭl*, like עֲמֻקָּה (masc. עָמֹק), maintain the original *ŭ* by sharpening the following consonant (cf. § 93 *kk*); on the other hand, by appending the fem. ת, segholate forms arise like נְחֹשֶׁת, before suff. נְחֻשְׁתָּם, &c.   Dual נְחֻשְׁתַּיִם (see Paradigm II, *a*) ; but cf. נְחֻשְׁתִּי La 3⁷.

n   A few (aramaising) feminines from ל״ה stems (Paradigm II, *c*) are found with the ending *âth*, due to the rejection of the final *Wāw* or *Yôdh* and contraction of the preceding *ă* with the *ă* of the termination *ăth* ; thus מְנָת *portion* (for *mănăyăth* or *mănăwăth*), קֵץ *end* (also קָצֶה and קְצֵה), plur. מְנָיוֹת (constr. *st.* Neh 12⁴⁷, 13¹⁰) and מְנָאוֹת (Neh 12⁴⁴) ; קְצָוֹת Ex 38⁵ ; cf. 37⁸ and 39⁴ *K*ᵉ*th.* ; on גֵּאָיֹת *valleys*, see § 93 *v.*—אוֹת *sign* (stem אוה) is obscured from אָת, and this is contracted from '*ăyăth* = '*ăwăyăth* ; plur. אֹתוֹת, with the double feminine ending ; cf. above, *f*, and § 87 *k*.—The retention of the *ā* in the first syllable in אֱלָתִי, &c., Gn 24⁴¹, &c., is abnormal.

o   3. Paradigm III, cf. the various forms in § 94 *d* and *f-h*. The *dual* חוֹמָתַיִם *two walls*, Is 22¹¹, &c., taken directly from the plur. חוֹמוֹת, for חוֹמָתַיִם, is abnormal (cf. § 87 *s*, and the proper name גְּדֵרֹתַיִם Jos 15³⁶).—Among the forms resembling participles Qal of verbs ע״ו, such as זָרָה (masc. זָר from *zâir*, hence with unchangeable *â*), must be reckoned also בָּמָה *high place* (from בּוּם), which has for its *constr. st. plur.* the pleonastic form בָּמֹתֵי, or written defectively בָּמֹתֵי (see § 87 *s*) ; for this the Masora everywhere requires בָּמֳתֵי, which is to be read *bāmᵒthê* (not *bŏmᵒthê*), with an anomalous shortening of the *ô* to ◌ֳ ; but with suffixes בָּמוֹתֵי, &c.

p   In a wider sense the feminines of the form קַטָּל (§ 84ᵇ *e*) belong to this class, in so far as they shorten the *â* of the second syllable before the termination ת, e. g. דַּלֶּקֶת *inflammation* (from *dallăqt*), with suff. צַדִּקָתֶךָ Ez 16⁵² ; טַבַּעַת *signet* ; also fem. of the forms קְטָל and קְטֹל (§ 84ᵇ *c* and *d*), as אִוֶּלֶת *folly* (for '*iwwălt*), and of all the forms which have a changeable vowel in the second syllable, and are formed with the prefix מ (§ 85 *g-k*), e. g. מַמְלָכָה *kingdom*, constr. always מַמְלֶכֶת ; מַזְמֵרָה (not used in the sing.) *pruning-hook*, plur. מַזְמֵרוֹת ; מַשְׂכֹּרֶת *reward*, with suff. מַשְׂכֻּרְתִּי ; cf. also the examples given in § 85 *g* and *p*, like מוֹלֶדֶת *birth* (but from ל״א, מוֹצָאָה *outgoing*), תּוֹלֶדֶת *generation*, תּוֹעֵבָה *abomination*, constr. תּוֹעֲבַת, &c.

q   Sometimes the plural of these forms is to be traced to a secondary form, e. g. אִגֶּרֶת *a letter*, plur. אִגְּרוֹת (as if from אִגְּרָה) ; also יוֹנְקוֹת, which is merely formed on the analogy of the other plur. fem. of participles Qal, is to be referred to a sing. יוֹנֶקֶת. Cf., moreover, מַחֲרֶשֶׁת *ploughshare*, plur. מַחֲרֵשׁוֹת (as if from מַחֲרֵשָׁה¹ ; on the other hand, כֹּתָרֹת *capitals* (of columns), and תּוֹכָחֹת *reproofs*, are the regular plurals of כֹּתֶרֶת and תּוֹכַחַת.

---

¹ עַשְׁתֹּרֶת *Astarte* (plur. עַשְׁתָּרוֹת), which was formerly included among these examples, is most probably due to an intentional alteration of the

In כֻּתֹּנֶת *coat* the original *ŭ* of the first syllable is maintained by the *r* sharpening of the following consonant (cf. Arab. *qŭṭŭn*), with suff. כֻּתָּנְתִּי, the *constr. st.*, however, is כְּתֹנֶת (as also in the *absol. st.* in Ex 28³⁹); plur. כֻּתֳּנוֹת, constr. כָּתְנוֹת.—The form גֻּלְגֹּלֶת given in Paradigm III, *b* is a *Pŭlpŭl*-form of the stem גָּלַל, cf. קָדְקֹד, § 84ᵇ *p*.

4. To the fourth class, for which no Paradigm is required, belong all the *s* numerous forms which in classical Hebrew have unchangeable vowels throughout, the originally short vowel of the first syllable having become *Šᵉwâ*, owing to the tone being thrown forward. Of the forms mentioned in §§ 84 and 85 those from ע״ע stems especially belong to this class, as מְגִלָּה *scroll*, תְּהִלָּה *praise*, תְּפִלָּה *prayer* (§ 85 *i* and *q*), as well as the feminine of the participle *Hiph'il* of verbs ע״וּ, e.g. מְאִירָה *enlightening* (from מֵאִיר), and generally the feminines of ע״וּ stems which are compounded with the *preformative* מ, as מְנוּחָה *rest* (from מָנוֹחַ), see § 85 *l*; from ל״ה stems perhaps also תְּעָלָה *conduit* (*constr. st.* תְּעָלַת Is 7³, &c.) and תְּלָאָה *travail*. Thus all these forms coincide externally with those which already, in the masculine form, have unchangeable vowels throughout (see the list of them in § 93 *ww*).

5. The feminine ending ־ית (apart from ל״ה-forms like בְּכִית, § 94*f*) arises *t* from the addition of the feminine ת to the ending ־י, which is employed to form adjectives, &c., see § 86 *d*, *h*, and *k*. The ending וּת, mentioned there, is attached, in segholate forms, sometimes to the ground-form, as עַשְׁתּוּת Jb 12⁵ (v.l. עֶשְׁתּוֹת), sometimes to forms with a loosely-closed syllable, as מַלְכוּת *kingdom*; from ל״ה stems we find forms sometimes like שְׁבוּת *captivity* (according to others from the stem שׁוּב, like לְזוּת *perverseness* from לוּז), sometimes like בְּכוּת *weeping*, גָּלוּת *exile*, חָזוּת *vision*; the latter retain the *ā* of the first syllable even in the *constr. st.* and before *suffixes*. From a *qāṭŭl*-form is formed כְּבֵדוּת *heaviness*; from a *qāṭŭl*-form פְּקֻדוּת, &c.

In the plural of these forms different methods of treatment may be distin- *u* guished. In some cases the whole ending וּת is retained, as if belonging to the stem (cf. above, *f*), e.g. אַלְמְנוֹתַיִךְ from אַלְמָנוּת, in others this ending is resolved, as in מַלְכֻיּוֹת Dn 8²² (no doubt for *mǎlᵉkhuwwôth*), and עֵדְוֺת *'ēdhᵉwôth*, from עֵדוּת *testimony*, but only with suffixes, עֵדְוֺתֶיךָ ψ 119¹⁴, &c.; עֵדְוֺתָיו 1 K 2³, &c.

§ 96. *Nouns of Peculiar Formation.*

In the following Paradigms,¹ pp. 282 to 284, a number of frequently used nouns are arranged, whose flexion presents more or less striking peculiarities. These peculiarities, however, are almost always subordinate to the usual phonetic laws, and the usual designation of the nouns as *irregular* is, therefore, not justified, when once the ground-forms are properly recognized on which the present forms are based.

---

original עַשְׁתֶּרֶת, like מֹלֶךְ Lv 18²¹, &c. (for מֶלֶךְ), with the vowels of בֹּשֶׁת *shame*, the latter word being substituted in reading for the name of the goddess.

¹ The only omissions from these Paradigms are אָחָד, חָם, and חָמוֹת (on which see the remarks), and all forms which are not found in the O. T.

		אָב (father)	אָח (brother)	אָחוֹת (sister)	אִישׁ (man)	אִשָּׁה (woman)
Sing. absolute		אָב	אָח	אָחוֹת	אִישׁ	אִשָּׁה
„	construct	אֲבִי	אֲחִי	אֲחוֹת	אִישׁ	אֵשֶׁת
„	with suff. of 1 sing.	אָבִי	אָחִי	אֲחוֹתִי	אִישִׁי	אִשְׁתִּי
„	2 masc.	אָבִיךָ	אָחִיךָ	אֲחוֹתְךָ		אִשְׁתְּךָ
„	2 fem.	אָבִיךְ	אָחִיךְ	אֲחוֹתֵךְ	אִישֵׁךְ	
„	3 masc.	אָבִיו (אֲבִיהוּ)	אָחִיו (אֲחִיהוּ)	אֲחֹתוֹ	אִישׁוֹ	אִשְׁתּוֹ
„	3 fem.	אָבִיהָ	אָחִיהָ	אֲחֹתָהּ	אִישָׁהּ	
„	1 Pl.	אָבִינוּ	אָחִינוּ	אֲחֹתֵנוּ		
„	2 masc.	אֲבִיכֶם	אֲחִיכֶם	[אֲחוֹתְכֶם]		
„	2 fem.	אֲבִיכֶן				
„	3 masc.	אֲבִיהֶם	אֲחִיהֶם	אֲחֹתָם		
„	3 fem.	אֲבִיהֶן				
Plur. absolute		אָבוֹת	אַחִים		אֲנָשִׁים	נָשִׁים
„	construct	אֲבוֹת	אֲחֵי		אַנְשֵׁי	נְשֵׁי
„	with suff. of 1 sing.	אֲבֹתַי, אַחַי (אָחָי, pause)	אֶחָי	אֲחִיוֹתַי	אֲנָשַׁי	נָשַׁי
„	2 masc.	אֲבֹתֶיךָ	אַחֶיךָ	אֲחוֹתֶיךָ	אֲנָשֶׁיךָ	נָשֶׁיךָ
„	2 fem.		אַחַיִךְ	אֲחוֹתַיִךְ		
„	3 masc.	אֲבֹתָיו	אֶחָיו	אֲחִיֹתָיו	אֲנָשָׁיו	נָשָׁיו
„	3 fem.		אַחֶיהָ	אֲחֶיהָ	אֲנָשֶׁיהָ	
„	1 Pl.	אֲבֹתֵינוּ	אַחֵינוּ		אֲנָשֵׁינוּ	נָשֵׁינוּ
„	2 masc.	אֲבֹתֵיכֶם	אֲחֵיכֶם	אֲחוֹתֵיכֶם		נְשֵׁיכֶם
„	3 masc.	אֲבֹתָם (אֲבֹתֵיהֶם)	אֲחֵיהֶם	אֲחִיֹתֵיהֶם	אַנְשֵׁיהֶם	נְשֵׁיהֶם
„	3 fem.				אַנְשֵׁיהֶן	

REMARKS.

אָב *father*; the *constr.* אֲבִי, like אֲחִי and בְּנִי (which occurs once), belongs to the connective forms discussed in § 90 k, which serve as the model for the Ḥireq compaginis. However, אַב also occurs in compound proper names, e.g. אֲבִשָׁלוֹם, beside אֲבִישָׁלוֹם, &c.; also Gn 17⁴ ᶠ· אַב־הֲמוֹן for the purpose of explaining the name אַב[רָ]הָם. On the plur. אָבוֹת see § 87 p.

אָח *brother.* The plur. *absol.* אַחִים has *Dageš forte implicitum* (§ 22 c); אֶחָי stands for אַחָי according to the phonetic law stated in § 27 q, and so also אֶחָי in *pause* for אַחָי. The sharpening of the ח merely serves to keep the preceding *Pathaḥ* short, as in גְּמַלִּים, &c. (§ 93 ee).

אֶחָד *one* (for אַחָד, likewise with *Dageš forte implicitum*, § 22 c, cf. § 27 q), *constr.* and otherwise in close connexion, אַחַד, Gn 48²², 2 S 17²², Is 27¹²,

אָמָה (handmaid)	בַּיִת (house)	בֵּן (son)	בַּת (daughter)	יוֹם (day)	כְּלִי (vessel)
	בֵּית	בֶּן־	בַּת	יוֹם	כְּלִי
אֲמָתִי	בֵּיתִי	בְּנִי	בִּתִּי		
אֲמָתְךָ	בֵּיתְךָ, בֵּיתֵךְ	בִּנְךָ, pause בְּנֶךָ	בִּתְּךָ, pause בִּתֶּךָ		כְּלְיֶךָ
	בֵּיתֵךְ	בְּנֵךְ			
אֲמָתוֹ	בֵּיתוֹ	בְּנוֹ	בִּתּוֹ	יוֹמוֹ	
אֲמָתָהּ	בֵּיתָהּ	בְּנָהּ	בִּתָּהּ		
		בְּנֵנוּ			
	בֵּיתְכֶם		בִּתְּכֶם		
	בֵּיתָם			יוֹמָם	
אֲמָהוֹת	בָּתִּים	בָּנִים	בָּנוֹת	יָמִים	כֵּלִים
אַמְהוֹת	בָּתֵּי	בְּנֵי	בְּנוֹת	יְמֵי	כְּלֵי
אַמְהֹתַי	בָּתַּי	בָּנַי	בְּנֹתַי	יְמַי	כְּלַי
	בָּתֶּיךָ	בָּנֶיךָ	בְּנֹתֶיךָ	יָמֶיךָ	כֵּלֶיךָ
	בָּתַּיִךְ	בָּנַיִךְ	בְּנֹתַיִךְ	יָמַיִךְ	
אַמְהֹתָיו		בָּנָיו	בְּנֹתָיו	יָמָיו	כֵּלָיו
אַמְהֹתֶיהָ		בָּנֶיהָ	בְּנֹתֶיהָ	יָמֶיהָ	כֵּלֶיהָ
	בָּתֵּינוּ	בָּנֵינוּ	בְּנֹתֵינוּ	יָמֵינוּ	כֵּלֵינוּ
אַמְהֹתֵיכֶם	בָּתֵּיכֶם	בְּנֵיכֶם	בְּנֹתֵיכֶם	יְמֵיכֶם	כְּלֵכֶם
	בָּתֵּיהֶם	בְּנֵיהֶם	בְּנֹתֵיהֶם	יְמֵיהֶם	כְּלֵיהֶם
אַמְהֹתֵיהֶן	בָּתֵּיהֶן	בְּנֵיהֶן			

Zc 11[7]; and especially before מִן (מֶ) Gn 3[22], Ex 30[14], Nu 16[15], Ju 17[5], 1 S 9[3], Ez 18[10]; fem. אַחַת *una* (for אַחֲדְתְּ, according to § 19 *d*), in *pause* אָחָת. Once חַד masc. (by aphaeresis, § 19 *h*), Ez 33[30], as in Aramaic; plur. אֲחָדִים *some*, but also *iidem*.

אָחוֹת *sister*, from *'ăḥăwăt* or *'ăḥăyăt*, with elision of the ו or י, and with the *â*, which has arisen from *ăă*, obscured to *ô*.[1] In Nu 6[7] אֲחֹתוֹ stands for אֲחֹתוֹ (with virtual sharpening of the ח). The plur. *absol.* (אֲחָיוֹת) does not happen

---

[1] This explanation of אָחוֹת (and חָמוֹת q. v.) still seems to us more probable than the assumption that the fem. ending *ăth* is lengthened to compensate for the loss of the 3rd radical (so Wellhausen, *Skizzen*, vi. 258), or that the form is derived from *'ahâ*, the old-semitic *constr. st.* of the accusative, with ת feminine (so Barth, ZDMG. 1899, p. 598).

	[מַי] (water)	עִיר (city)	פֶּה (mouth)	רֹאשׁ (head)	שֵׁם (name)	[שָׁמַי] (heaven)
Sing. absolute						
,, construct		עִיר	פִּי	רֹאשׁ	שֶׁם־, שֵׁם	
,, with suff. of 1 sing.		עִירִי	פִּי	רֹאשִׁי	שְׁמִי	
,, 2 masc.		עִירְךָ	פִּיךָ	רֹאשְׁךָ, שִׁמְךָ, *pause* שְׁמֶךָ		
,, 2 fem.				רֹאשֵׁךְ	שְׁמֵךְ	
,, 3 masc.		עִירוֹ	פִּיו, פִּיהוּ	רֹאשׁוֹ	שְׁמוֹ	
,, 3 fem.		עִירָהּ	פִּיהָ	רֹאשָׁהּ	שְׁמָהּ	
,, 1 Pl.			פִּינוּ	רֹאשֵׁנוּ	שְׁמֵנוּ	
,, 2 masc.			פִּיכֶם	רֹאשְׁכֶם	שִׁמְכֶם	
,, 3 masc.		עִירָם	פִּיהֶם	רֹאשָׁם	שְׁמָם	
,, 3 fem.			פִּיהֶן	רֹאשָׁן		
Plur. absolute	מַיִם	עָרִים	פִּיוֹת	רָאשִׁים	שֵׁמוֹת	שָׁמַיִם
,, construct	מֵי, מֵימֵי	עָרֵי		רָאשֵׁי	שְׁמוֹת	שְׁמֵי
,, with suff. of 1 sing.	מֵימַי	עָבַי				שְׁמֵי
,, 2 masc.	מֵימֶיךָ	עָרֶיךָ				שְׁמֶיךָ
,, 2 fem.		עָרַיִךְ				
,, 3 masc.	מֵימָיו	עָרָיו		רָאשָׁיו		שְׁמָיו
,, 3 fem.	מֵימֶיהָ	עָרֶיהָ		רָאשֶׁיהָ		
,, 1 Pl.	מֵימֵינוּ	עָרֵינוּ		רָאשֵׁינוּ		
,, 2 masc.		עָרֵיכֶם		רָאשֵׁיכֶם		שְׁמֵיכֶם
,, 3 masc.	מֵימֵיהֶם	עָרֵיהֶם		רָאשֵׁיהֶם	שְׁמוֹתָם	
,, 3 fem.				רָאשֵׁיהֶן	שְׁמוֹתָן	

to occur. In Ez 16⁵² אֲחָיוֹתֵךְ occurs (for אֲחִיתֵךְ). In the forms אֲחוֹתִי
Jos 2¹³ *Keth.*, אֲחוֹתָיִךְ Ez 16⁵¹·⁵⁵·⁶¹ (to be read also in verse 45 for אֲחוֹתֵךְ, which
has been erroneously assimilated to the singular occurring in vv. 48, 49, 56),
and אֲחוֹתֵיכֶם Ho 2³ (for which, however, read אֲחוֹתְכֶם), the third radical has
been entirely lost.

אִישׁ *man*, according to the common opinion either incorrectly lengthened
for אֵשׁ (from '*iš*, with assimilation of the *Nûn* of the ground-form '*inš*, which
again has been attenuated from '*anš* from the stem אָנַשׁ), or softened directly
from '*inš*. It is, however, probable that a separate stem (אִישׁ *to be strong*?) is
to be assumed for the singular[1]; consequently the stem אָנַשׁ *to be sociable*,

---

[1] So already Gesenius in his *Thes. linguae Hebr.*, i. 83 f., and recently again
Friedr. Delitzsch, *Prolegg.*, p. 160 ff., Praetorius in Kuhn's *Orient. L.-B.*, 1884,
p. 196; König, *Lehrgeb.*, ii. 38; while Nöldeke (*ZDMG.* 1886, p. 739 f.), against
Delitzsch, would connect both אִישׁ and נָשִׁים with the stem אָנַשׁ.

would be connected only with the plur. אֲנָשִׁים (אִישִׁים is found only in Is 53³, ψ 141⁴, Pr 8⁴).

אָמָה *slave, handmaid*; with the plur. אֲמָהוֹת, with consonantal ה, cf. in Aram. אֲבָהָן *fathers*, and similarly in Phoen. דלהת from דלת, also Arab. *'abahât* (fathers), *'ummahât* (mothers), with an artificial expansion into a triliteral stem.

אִשָּׁה *woman*, probably for אִנְשָׁה; from אָנַשׁ i.e. not (as Aram. אִתְּתָא shows) אָנַשׁ *to be sociable* (see above, on אִישׁ) but אָנַשׁ *to be weak* (Arab. *'ănŭṣă*). So De Lagarde, *Uebersicht*, p. 68; König, *Lehrgeb.*, ii. 159 f. The form אֵשֶׁת (for *'išt*, with ת fem., from *'išš*, after rejection of the doubling and lengthening of the ĭ to ē) occurs in Dt 21¹¹, 1 S 28⁷, ψ 58⁹, even in *absol. st.* [cf., however, below, § 130. 4, 5].—In ψ 128³ אֶשְׁתְּךָ is found for אִשְׁתְּךָ. Instead of the plur. נָשִׁים, we find in Ez 23⁴⁴ אִשֹּׁת.[1]

בַּיִת *house*, locative הַבַּיְתָה, בַּיְתָה, in *pause* הַבָּיְתָה, בָּיְתָה, constr. בֵּית, plur. בָּתִּים (but in Dt 6¹¹, 1 Ch 28¹¹ בָּתִּים without *Metheg*), pronounced *bâttim*. The explanation of the Dageš in the ת is still a matter of dispute. The Syriac *bâttin*, however, shows that the *Dageš* is original, and belongs to the character of the form.[2] According to Wright, *Comparative Grammar*, p. 88, בָּתִּים is simply contracted from *bai-tim* (as אָן from אַיִן, עֵינָם from עֵינַיִם, &c.), and the Dageš, therefore, is *lene*; König, *Lehrgeb.*, ii. 56, proposes the name *Dageš forte orthoconsonanticum*; on the other hand Rahlfs, *ThLZ*. 1896, col. 587, suggests that the י is assimilated to the ת, while Philippi, *ZDMG.* xlix, p. 206, assumes for the plural a stem distinct from that of the singular. A definite solution is at present impossible. The incorrectness of the formerly common pronunciation *bottim* is sufficiently shown by the Babylonian punctuation (see § 8 *g*, note 3), which leaves no doubt as to the *â*.

בֵּן *son* (Gn 30¹⁹ בֶּן־שִׁשִּׁי) constr. usually בֶּן־ (also with a conjunctive accent as an equivalent for *Maqqeph*, Gn 17¹⁷, Is 8², &c., 1 Ch 9²¹; even with smaller disjunctives, especially in the combination מִבֶּן־, Ex 30¹⁴, Lv 27³, &c. [מִבֶּן־ only after וְאִם and before חֹדֶשׁ, also in Is 51¹²; see Strack on Ex 30¹⁴]), rarely בִּן־ (Dt 25², Jon 4¹⁰ twice, Pr 30¹, and so always in the combination בִּן־נוּן, and in the proper names בִּנְיָמִין [but בֶּן־יְמִינִי *Benjamite*] and בִּן־יָקֶה Pr 30¹), once בְּנִי (cf. § 90 *l*) Gn 49¹¹, and בְּנוֹ (§ 90 *o*) Nu 23¹⁸, 24³·¹⁵.—In Gn 49²² בֵּן, for which בֶּן־ ought to be read, is intended by the Masora for the *absol. st.*, not the *constr.*

---

[1] Friedr. Delitzsch (in his Babylonian glosses to Baer's text of Ezekiel, p. xi) on Ez 23⁴⁴ remarks that in Assyro-Babylonian the plur. of *aššatu* (woman) is *aššâti*, corresponding, therefore, to אִשֹּׁות, not to the ordinary plur. נָשִׁים. The *a* of נָשִׁים (instead of *i* as in Arab. or *e* as in Syr.) is to be explained with Barth (*Orient. Studien zu Ehren Th. Nöldekes*, Giessen, 1906, p. 792) from the natural connexion of the ideas 'men' and 'women', נָשִׁים and אֲנָשִׁים.

[2] This disposes of the traditional view that the *Dageš* (after a firm Metheg, see § 16 *f* ζ) only serves to distinguish it from בָּתִים *passing the night*, ptcp. Qal of בּוּת, a stem which never occurs in the O. T. According to P. Haupt the stem is בא *to go in*, ת therefore being the feminine termination, as in *bint daughter*, and the original form *ba'tu*, *bâtu* (*entrance*) is preserved in the plural *bâttim* where the *tt* is to be explained as due to the analogy of trisyllabic stems. In the singular *bât* passed into *bēt* (?), and this was resolved into *bait*, as *Yerūšālēm* into *Yerūšālayim*.

בַּת *daughter* (from *bant*, and this again, according to the law stated in § 69 *c*, for *bint*, fem. of בֵּן), with suff. בִּתִּי for בִּנְתִּי. Plur. בָּנוֹת, from the sing. בָּנָה, comp. בָּנִים *sons*.

חָם *husband's father*, only with suff. חָמִיךָ, חָמִיהָ ; and חָמוֹת *husband's mother*, only with suff. חֲמוֹתֵךְ, חֲמוֹתָהּ. Cf. אָב, אָח, and especially אָחוֹת.

יוֹם *day* (Arab. *yaum*),[1] dual יוֹמַיִם ; the plur. יָמִים is probably from a different sing. (יָם *yām*), constr. יְמֵי and (poetically) יְמוֹת, Dt 32[7], ψ 90[15].

כְּלִי *vessel*, in pause כֶּלִי (with suff. כֶּלְיֶךָ Dt 23[25]) from כָּלָה *to contain*, plur. כֵּלִים (as if from כֵּל, כֶּלֶה ; according to König, ii. 63, shortened from *kilyim*).

מַיִם *water* ; on the plur. cf. § 88 *d*.

עִיר *city*. The plur. עָרִים is scarcely syncopated from עֲיָרִים, as it is pointed in Ju 10[4] (no doubt erroneously, in imitation of the preceding עֲיָרִים *ass colts*), but from a kindred sing. עָר, which still occurs in proper names.

פֶּה *mouth*, constr. st. פִּי (for original פִּי = פֶּה ?). Its origin is still disputed. According to Gesenius and König (ii. 103), פֶּה stands for פָּאֶה (ground-form *pi'ay*) from פָּאָה *to breathe, to blow* ; according to Olshausen, for פִּי, from a stem פֶּוָה or פָּוָה. But parallel with the Hebrew פֶּה are Assyr. *pû*, Arab. *fû, fam, famm, fumm*, bibl. Aram. פֻּם, פֻּמָּא, Syr. *pûm, pûmā*, so that Barth, *ZDMG.* xli, p. 634, assumes two forms of development from the same stem (פמו), viz. *fm* and *fw*. פִּי *my mouth*, from *pi-y* ; for פִּיהֶם we find in ψ 17[10], 58[7], 59[13] פִּימוֹ. The supposed plur. פִּים 1 S 13[21] is generally explained as a contraction from פִּפִים, but the text is altogether corrupt. The plur. פִּיּוֹת, for the *edges* of a sword, occurs in Pr 5[4] ; reduplicated פִּיפִיּוֹת Is 41[15], ψ 149[6].

רֹאשׁ *head* (obscured from רָאשׁ = *rā'š*) ; plur. רָאשִׁים (for רְאָשִׁים, § 23 *c*) ; רָאשָׁיו only in Is 15[2].

שֶׂה *a head of small cattle* (*sheep* or *goat*), constr. st. שֵׂה, with suff. שֵׂיהוּ 1 S 14[34] and שְׂיוֹ Dt 22[1], according to König, ii. 131, from a ground-form *si'ay*, but according to De Lagarde, *Uebersicht*, 81 f., from a stem ושׂי (שֶׂה = *say* = *wísay*).

שֵׁם *name*, constr. generally שֶׁם (only six times שֶׁם־) ; cf. בֵּן.

שָׁמַיִם *heaven* (§ 88 *d*).

§ 97. *Numerals.* (*a*) *Cardinal Numbers.*

Brockelmann, *Sem. Sprachwiss.*, p. 116 ff. ; *Grundriss*, i. 484 ff.

a 1. The formation of the cardinal numbers from 3 to 10 (on 1 and 2 see below) has this peculiarity, that numerals connected with a mascu-

---

[1] Cf. Nöldeke, *Beiträge*, p. 58, *yaum*, probably an extension of a biliteral word which has survived in יְמֵי, יָמִים. Barth, however, *Orient. Studien*, p. 791 (see above on אִשָּׁה), sees in יְמֵי, יָמִים, יְמוֹת new formations in Hebrew, caused by the naturally close connexion and association of these plurals with שָׁנִים, שְׁנֵי, שְׁנוֹת *years*, to which they became assimilated in form. The view that יוֹם is merely an incorrect obscuring of יָם, and therefore distinct from the Arab. *yaum*, is contradicted by the invariable spelling יוֹם, &c., notwithstanding the spelling ובים (= וּבְיֹם ?) in the Siloam inscription, line 3 (cf. § 7 *f*), and מִימֵיהֶם Ho 6[2]. Cf. also the note on § 100 *g*.

line substantive take the feminine form, and those with a feminine
substantive take the masculine form. The common explanation of this
strange phenomenon used to be that the primary form of the numeral
was an abstract noun in the feminine (cf. § 122 *p*). This was originally
attached in the *constr. st.* to the word qualified, then came to be also
used in apposition to it, and finally was placed after it like an adjective.
The consequence of the appositional, and finally adjectival, construction
was, that for numerals connected with feminine nouns a special shorter
form came to be used, whilst the original forms, with the abstract
feminine ending, were used in connexion with masculine nouns, after
as well as before them.

On this view the historical process would have been that originally the
abstract numerals (like Latin *trias, decas*, Greek πεντάς, δεκάς, &c.) were placed
in the *constr. st.* before masculines and feminines alike, e. g. שְׁלֹשֶׁת בָּנִים *trias
filiorum*, עֲשֶׂרֶת נָשִׁים *decas mulierum*. A trace of this earlier usage was seen in
the examples mentioned under *c*, like שְׁלֹשֶׁת נָשִׁים.—Further, it was possible to
say שְׁלֹשָׁה בָנִים *trias*, sc. *filii*, as well as בָּנִים שְׁלֹשָׁה *filii, trias*. From this
second appositional construction it was only a step to the treatment of
the abstract numeral as an adjective, *filii tres*. Similarly the subsequently
shortened forms of the abstract numeral, which were used in connexion with
feminines, might stand either in the *constr. st.* before, or in apposition before
or after the word numbered, thus שְׁלֹשׁ בָּנוֹת *trias filiarum*, or בָּנוֹת שְׁלֹשׁ *trias*,
sc. *filiae*, or בָּנוֹת שְׁלֹשׁ *filiae, trias*, or adjectivally *filiae tres*.

A different and much more intelligible explanation of the striking
disagreement between the gender of the numeral and that of the word
numbered has recently been given by Reckendorf, *Die syntaktischen
Verhältnisse des Arabischen*, pt. ii, Leiden, 1898, p. 265 ff. He also
considers that the earliest forms were abstract numerals which were
placed in the *constr. st.* before the noun numbered, the latter depending
on them in the genitive. The original form, however, of the abstract
numerals from 3 to 9 is not the feminine, but the masculine, used for
both genders, as it still is in the tens, 20, 30, &c. The feminine
abstract numeral was first distinguished by a special form in the
numbers from 13 to 19 (see further, below) when connected with
masculines, and this distinction was afterwards extended to the numbers
from 3 to 10. This explanation does not affect the view stated above
that the appositional and adjectival use of the abstract numerals was
only adopted later in addition to their use in the genitive construction.

The differentiation of the numerals (originally of common gender) into
masculine and feminine forms in the second decade, was occasioned, according to Reckendorf, by the use of the abstract feminine עֲשָׂרָה in compounds.

So long as it was felt that שָׁלֹשׁ עֶשְׂרֵה simply meant *the three of the decade*, the gender of the noun numbered made no difference. When, however, the consciousness of this meaning became weakened and the combination of units and tens came to be felt as a copulative rather than a genitive relation, it seemed suitable to connect only feminine nouns with the feminine form עֶשְׂרֵה. New forms were therefore invented, both of the units and the tens, for use with masculine nouns. The former, however, no longer had the form of the *constr.* but of the absolute state, clearly showing that the consciousness of the original syntactical relation in שָׁלֹשׁ עֶשְׂרֵה, &c., was lost. On the other hand, after the extension of these new formations to the first decade, the new feminine forms readily came to be used also in the genitive construction (and therefore in the *constr. st.*) on the analogy of the earlier masculine forms.

Of the first two numerals, אֶחָד *one*, with its fem. אַחַת (see § 96), may be recognized, from its form and use, as an adjective, although even so it admits of such combinations as אַחַד הֶהָרִים *unus e montibus*. The numeral two, as would be expected, appears as an abstract in the *dual*, but, like the other numerals, can also stand in apposition to the noun numbered. In form it always agrees with the gender of its noun. Accordingly, the numerals from 1 to 10 are as follows:

b

	With the Masculine.		With the Feminine.	
	Absol.	Constr.	Absol.	Constr.
1.	אֶחָד	אַחַד	אַחַת	אַחַת
2.	שְׁנַיִם	שְׁנֵי	שְׁתַּיִם [1]	שְׁתֵּי
3.	שְׁלֹשָׁה	שְׁלֹשֶׁת	שָׁלֹשׁ	שְׁלֹשׁ
4.	אַרְבָּעָה	אַרְבַּעַת	אַרְבַּע	אַרְבַּע
5.	חֲמִשָּׁה [2]	חֲמֵשֶׁת	חָמֵשׁ	חֲמֵשׁ
6	שִׁשָּׁה	שֵׁשֶׁת	שֵׁשׁ	שֵׁשׁ
7.	שִׁבְעָה	שִׁבְעַת	שֶׁבַע	[שְׁבַע] [3]
8.	שְׁמֹנָה	שְׁמֹנַת	שְׁמֹנֶה	שְׁמֹנֶה
9.	תִּשְׁעָה	תִּשְׁעַת	תֵּשַׁע	[תְּשַׁע] [3]
10.	עֲשָׂרָה	עֲשֶׂרֶת	עֶשֶׂר	עֶשֶׂר

---

[1] Shortened from שְׁנָתַּיִם, which would be the regular feminine form of שְׁנַיִם. Nevertheless, the *Dageš* in שְׁתַּיִם, &c. (even after מִן; מִשְׁתֵּים Jon 4¹¹; cf., however, מִשְׁתֵּי Ju 16²⁸), can by no means be regarded as a *Dageš forte* arising from assimilation of the *Nûn*, for in that case the word could only be שְׁתַּיִם (cf. Arab. *ṯintāni*). This form does occur in the Codex Babylonicus of A.D. 916, but it is only a later correction for שְׁתַּיִם, while in the Berlin MS. or. qu. 680 described by Kahle (Lpz. 1902) there is no trace of the *Dageš*. It is rather to be read *štáyim*, *štē* (with *Dageš lene*), cf. אֶשְׁתַּיִם, representing the later Palestinian pronunciation (Philippi, *ZDMG*. xlix, p. 206), and Arab. *'iṯnātāni* (with a kind of prosthetic א; cf. § 19 *m*), as a further feminine form of

On the connective forms שֶׁבַע, תֵּשַׁע, cf. the analogous forms in § 93 *h*.

The other Semitic languages also exhibit the same peculiarity in the C external differentiation of the numerals from 3 to 10 as regards gender. The fem. form of the numeral abstracts is only rarely found in connexion with feminine nouns,[4] e. g. שְׁלֹשֶׁת נָשִׁים Gn 7¹³, 1 S 10³, Jb 1⁴, Ez 7² *K*ᵉ*th.*; probably also Jos 17¹¹, where we should read with Dillmann שׁ׳ הַנְּפוֹת. In apposition, Zc 3⁹, 4², cf. Jer 36²³. From what was said above, under *a*, it follows that these cases are not a return to original usage, but only an intrusion of the form used before masculines into the sphere of the feminine. Conversely in Gn 38²⁴ שְׁלֹשׁ חֳדָשִׁים (but in the Samaritan שְׁלֹשֶׁת).—For שִׁבְעָה *seven*, there occurs in Jb 42¹³ the strange form שִׁבְעָנָה, according to Ewald [*Ausführl. Lehrb.*[8], § 269 *b*] an old feminine substantive (German *ein Siebend, a set of seven*), but more probably a scribal error.

2. The numerals from 11 to 19 are formed by placing the units, *d* without the *copula*, before the number ten (in the form עָשָׂר masc., עֶשְׂרֵה fem.), but without the two words being joined into one. As was said above, under *a*, and as is proved by the use of אַחַת, אַחַד in the numeral 11, the feminine numerals from 13 to 19 are to be regarded as *construct* forms in a genitive connexion. The connective forms of the masculine abstracts, like שְׁלֹשֶׁת, &c., are not admitted in combination with עָשָׂר, since they are merely in apposition, and not in a genitive relation (see the rare exceptions at the end of *e*). On the other hand שְׁנֵי and שְׁתֵּי in the numeral 12 are undoubtedly true *constructs*, like אַחַד and the fem. numerals 13–19. But instead of שְׁנֵי (Ex 28²¹, Jos 3¹² and four other places) and שְׁתֵּי (Jos 4⁸ and three times in Ezek.), we generally find שְׁנַיִם and שְׁתַּיִם. Two explanations have been given of these forms: (1) that the *K*ᵉ*thîbh* really intends שְׁנַיִם, שְׁתַּיִם, in the *absol. st.*, which was first introduced in the case of שְׁנַיִם, on the analogy of עֶשְׂרֵה, &c., and then extended to שְׁתַּיִם; the Maṣora, however, required שְׁתֵּי, שְׁנֵי (but see below), and therefore pointed שְׁתַּיִם, שְׁנַיִם as a *Q*ᵉ*rê perpetuum* (see § 17).—(2) that the *absolute* forms שְׁתַּיִם, שְׁנַיִם (introduced on the analogy of שְׁלֹשָׁה, &c.) were contracted to שְׁתֵּי, שְׁנֵי to facilitate the pronunciation of the duals when closely

---

'*iṯnāni, duo.* According to Barth (*Orient. Studien ... Th. Nöldeke*, ii. 792 f.) the irregularity of שְׁתַּיִם (he takes the Dageš as *Dageš forte*) is due to the complete assimilation of its vowels to those of the masc. שְׁנַיִם where the *Š*ᵉ*wâ mobile* is normal.

[2] With Dageš probably on the analogy of שִׁשָּׁה, as שֵׁשֶׁת on the analogy of חֲמֵשֶׁת. Cf. also J. K. Blake on חֲמִשָּׁה, חֲמִשִׁים in *JAOS.* 1905, p. 117 ff.

[3] שֶׁבַע and תֵּשַׁע appear only as connective forms before עֶשְׂרֵה and מֵאוֹת.

[4] In the vulgar dialects of Arabic, and in Ethiopic, the feminine form of the numeral is by far the more common. This form appears also in Hebrew, when the number is regarded in the abstract, as in the multiplicatives (see § 97 *h*).

connected with עֶשֶׂר עָשָׂר and עֶשְׂרָה, and that the contraction is founded on an early and correct tradition. The second explanation is supported by the large number of examples of שָׁנִים (66) and שָׁתִים (34). It would be strange if the Masora required the alteration of the far commoner forms on account of isolated instances of שְׁנֵי and שְׁתֵּי. As a matter of fact even in regard to the latter forms the tradition often varies between שְׁנֵי and שְׁנַיִם, &c., cf. e. g. Ginsburg on Jos 3¹². We cannot therefore assume a *Qᵉrê perpetuum*.

e Accordingly the numbers from 11 upwards are—

Masculine.	Feminine.
אַחַד עָשָׂר	אַחַת עֶשְׂרֵה
11. ⎰ עַשְׁתֵּי¹ עָשָׂר	עַשְׁתֵּי עֶשְׂרֵה
12. ⎰ שְׁנֵים עָשָׂר	שְׁתֵּים עֶשְׂרֵה
⎱ שְׁנֵי עָשָׂר	שְׁתֵּי עֶשְׂרֵה
13. שְׁלֹשָׁה עָשָׂר	שְׁלֹשׁ עֶשְׂרֵה

&c., on the analogy of the last. These numerals regularly have only the above form. In regard to their syntax, cf. § 134 *f*.

Very rarely the units appear in the *masc.* in the *constr. st.*, as חֲמֵשֶׁת עָשָׂר *fifteen*, Ju 8¹⁰, 2 S 19¹⁸ ; שְׁמֹנַת עָשָׂר *eighteen*, Ju 20²⁵.—Connected by וְ we find עֶשְׂרֵה וַחֲמִשָּׁה in Ex 45¹².

f 3. The tens from 30 to 90 are expressed by the plural forms of the units (so that the plural here always stands for *ten times* the unit), thus, שְׁלֹשִׁים 30, אַרְבָּעִים 40, חֲמִשִּׁים 50, שִׁשִּׁים 60, שִׁבְעִים 70, שְׁמֹנִים 80, תִּשְׁעִים 90. But *twenty* is expressed by עֶשְׂרִים, plur. of עֶשֶׂר *ten*.² These numerals are all of common gender, and do not admit of the *construct state*.—In compound numerals, like 22, 23, 44, &c., the units

---

¹ עַשְׁתֵּי, which remained for a long time unexplained, was recognized (first by J. Oppert) in the Assyro-Babylonian inscriptions in the form *ištin* or *ištên* ; cf. Friedr. Delitzsch, *Assyrische Grammatik*, p. 203, and P. Haupt, in the *American Journal of Philology*, viii. 279. Accordingly, עַשְׁתֵּי עָשָׂר is a compound, like the Sansk. *ékádaçan*, ἕνδεκα, *undecim* (analogous to the combination of units and tens in the numerals from 12 to 19), and is used at the same time in the composition of the feminine numeral eleven. On the gradual substitution of עַשְׁתֵּי עֲ׳ for אַחַד עֲ׳ and אַחַת עֲ׳ see Giesebrecht in *ZAW*. 1881, p. 226 ; עַשְׁתֵּי עֲ׳ occurs only in Jer., Ez., in the prologue to Deuteronomy (1³), in the Priestly Code, and in passages undoubtedly post-exilic, so that it may very well be a loan-word from the Babylonian.

² For עֶשְׂרִים, שְׁבְעִים, תִּשְׁעִים (from the *segholates* עֶשֶׂר, שֶׁבַע, תֵּשַׁע), we should expect *ᵃsārîm, šᵉbhāʿîm, tᵉšāʿîm*. Is this very unusual deviation from the common formation (see above, § 93 *l, o, r*) connected with the special meaning of these plurals, or are these survivals of an older form of the plural of segholates?

may precede (*two and twenty*, as in Arabic and English), e. g. Nu 3³⁹, 26¹⁴. Very frequently, however, the reverse order is found (*twenty and two*, as in Syriac, cf. French and English *twenty-two*), e. g. 1 Ch 12²⁸, 18⁵.[1] In all cases the units and tens are connected by the *copula*, ordinarily וְ, but וַ before numerals with the tone on the penultima, וָ before ﬞ, וּ before *Šᵉwâ*; see § 104 *d, e, g*.

The remaining numerals are the substantives—

g

100 מֵאָה fem., *constr.* מְאַת.

200 מָאתַֽיִם dual (contracted from מְאָתַֽיִם; cf. § 23 *c*).

300 שְׁלֹשׁ מֵאוֹת plur. (but in 2 K 11⁴·⁹·¹⁰·¹⁵, *Kᵉth.* הַמֵּאיּוֹת).

1000 אֶ֫לֶף masc.

2000 אַלְפַּֽיִם dual.

3000 שְׁלֹ֫שֶׁת אֲלָפִים plur., and so on (except עֲשָׂרָה אֲלָפִים in 2 S 18³, 2 K 24¹⁴ *Kᵉth.*; elsewhere always עֲשֶׂ֫רֶת אֲלָפִים).

10000 רְבָבָה, in the later books the aramaising[2] forms רִבּוֹ, רִבּוֹא, רִבּוֹת (properly *multitude*, cf. μυριάς).

20000 רִבֹּתַ֫יִם dual (see below, *h*); but שְׁתֵּי רִבּוֹת Neh 7⁷⁰ (also שְׁתֵּי רִבּוֹא Neh 7⁷¹).

40000 אַרְבַּע רִבּוֹא Neh 7⁶⁶.

60000 שֵׁשׁ־רִבּאוֹת Ezr 2⁶⁹ (Baer and Ginsburg רִבּאוֹת, as in Dn 11¹²).

אַלְפֵי רְבָבָה *thousands of myriads*, Gn 24⁶⁰.

Rem. 1. The dual form which occurs in some of the units has the meaning *h* of our ending *-fold*, e. g. אַרְבַּעְתַּ֫יִם *fourfold*, 2 S 12⁶; שִׁבְעָתַ֫יִם *sevenfold*, Gn 4¹⁵·²⁴, Is 30²⁶, ψ 12⁷, 79¹² (cf. § 134 *r*). The dual רִבֹּתַ֫יִם ψ 68¹⁸ (explained by אַלְפֵי שִׁנְאָן *thousands of duplication*) is not meant to be taken in the sense of *two myriads* or *twice the number of myriads*, but in a multiplicative sense.[3]—Besides the plural which denotes the tens, there are also the plurals אֲחָדִים *some*, also *iidem*, and עֲשָׂרוֹת *decades* (not *decem*) Ex 18²¹·²⁵.

2. The *suffixes* to numerals are, as with other nouns, properly genitives, *i* although they are translated in English as nominatives, e. g. שְׁלָֽשְׁתְּכֶם *your triad*, i. e. *you three*, Nu 12⁴; חֲמִשָּׁיו *his fifty* (i. e. the 50 belonging to him) 2 K 1⁹⁻¹³, and חֲמִשֶּׁ֫יךָ 2 K 1¹⁰·¹².

---

[1] According to the conclusions of König (*De Criticae Sacrae Argumento*, p. 61, and *Lehrgeb.*, ii. p. 215 ff.), the smaller number more commonly precedes in Ezek. and the Priestly Code, but the larger always elsewhere. S. Herner (*Syntax der Zahlwörter im A. T.*, Lund, 1893, p. 71 ff.) arrives at the same conclusion by a full examination of the statistics; cf. also his remarks on König in *ZAW*. 1896, p. 123, and König's reply, *ibid.*, p. 328 f.

[2] Cf. Kautzsch, *Die Aramaismen im A.T.* (Halle, 1902), p. 79 f.

[3] Cf. D. H. Müller, 'Die numeralia multiplicativa in den Amarnatafeln u. im Hebr.,' *Semitica*, i, Wien, 1906, p. 13 ff.

§ 98. *Numerals.* (*b*) *Ordinal Numbers.*

a   The ordinal numbers from 2 to 10 are formed from the corresponding cardinals by adding the termination יִ֫־ (§ 86 *h*), before which
another יִ־ also is generally inserted between the second and
third radicals.   They are as follows: שֵׁנִי *second*, שְׁלִישִׁי, רְבִיעִי (like
רֶ֫בַע, רֹ֫בַע, רִבְּעִים, without the prosthetic א, which appears in אַרְבַּע,
&c.), חֲמִישִׁי or חֲמִשִׁי (which, according to Strack, is always to be read
for חֲמִשִׁי), שִׁשִּׁי, שְׁבִיעִי, שְׁמִינִי, תְּשִׁיעִי, עֲשִׂירִי.   The ordinal *first* is expressed by רִאשׁוֹן (cf. § 27 *w*), from רֹאשׁ *head, beginning*, with the
termination וֹן (§ 86 *f*).   On the use of אֶחָד as an ordinal in numbering
the days of the month, cf. § 134 *p*; in such cases as Gn 1[5], 2[11], the
meaning of *first* is derived solely from the context.

b   The feminine forms have the termination ־ִית, more rarely (and
only in the case of 3 and 10) ־ִיָּה.   They are employed also to express
fractions, e. g. חֲמִשִׁית *fifth* or *fifth part*, עֲשִׂירִית and עֲשִׂירִיָּה *tenth part*.
Side by side with these, in the same sense, there are also forms like
רֹ֫בַע and רֶ֫בַע *a quarter*, חֹ֫מֶשׁ *a fifth part*, and with the afformative וֹן,
עִשָּׂרוֹן (plur. עֶשְׂרֹנִים) *a tenth part*; these are to be regarded as abstracts,
and are denominatives from the cardinal numbers.   Cf. finally שָׁבוּעַ
ἑβδομάς, *a week*; עָשׂוֹר *a decade* (of days), and also the *tenth day*.

On the expression of the other relations of number, for which the Hebrew
has no special forms, see the Syntax, § 134 *q* and *r*.

CHAPTER IV

THE PARTICLES

§ 99. General View.

Brockelmann, *Grundriss*, i. 492 f.

1. The particles, which in general express the secondary modi- *a* fications of thought in speech, the closer relation of words to one another, and the mutual connexion of sentences, are for the most part either borrowed or derived from noun-forms, sometimes also from pronouns and verbs (§ 30 *s*). *Primitive* particles (apart from a few demonstrative forms, see § 100 *i*) can only be so called in the sense defined in § 81 f.

2. So far as the origin of the particles can be discovered with *b* certainty, they are either (1) *borrowed* from other parts of speech; i. e. certain forms of the noun, pronoun, or verb, with more or less loss of their original meaning, have come to be employed as particles; cf. in the Indo-Germanic languages, e. g. the Latin *certo, falso, partim, verum, causa,* the German *statt, anstatt, wegen, weg,* and the English *instead, away;* or (2) *derived* from other parts of speech, either (*a*) by the *addition* of formative syllables, as יוֹמָם *by day,* from יוֹם (cf., however, § 100 *g*); or most commonly (*b*) by *abbreviations* effected in various ways, the extent of their mutilation being in proportion to the frequency of their use, so that in some cases (see below) the original stem has become wholly unrecognizable.

Cf. in German *gen,* from *gegen, Gegend;* *seit,* from *Seite;* *weil* (originally a particle of time, like our *while*), from *Weile.*
Still more violent abbreviations occur in Greek, Latin, and the Romance languages, e. g. ἀπό, *ab, a;* ἐξ, *ex, e; ad,* Fr. *à; aut,* Fr. *ou,* Ital. *o; super,* Ital. *su.*[1]

The greatest shortening occurs in those particles which have *c* entirely lost the character of an independent word, by being reduced to a single consonant with its vowel (generally short) or *Šᵉwâ.* According to the laws of syllable formation in Hebrew (§ 26 *m*),

---

[1] Even short phrases are contracted into one word: Lat. *forsitan,* from *fors sit an,* δηλονότι, δηλαδή, Fr. *peut-être,* Eng. *prithee* from *I pray thee.* — In Chinese most of the particles are verbs or nouns; e. g. *iù* (to give), also the sign of the dative; *ì* (to make use of), *to, for;* *něi* (the interior), *in.*

such particles cannot stand by themselves, but are united, as prefixes, with the following word (§ 102), very much like the preformatives of the imperfect (§ 47 *a–d*).

d The view that this shortening of whole words to single letters has actually taken place in the gradual course of linguistic development is rendered highly probable by the fact that similar abbreviations in later Hebrew and in Aramaic, i.e. as the development of the original Semitic speech progresses, become more and more striking and frequent. Thus the Biblical Aramaic דִּי becomes at a later period דְּ; in modern Arabic, e.g. *hallaq* (now) is from *halwaqt*; *lêš* (why?) from *li-ayyi-šaïn,* &c. Cf. also the analogous cases mentioned above from the Western languages. Nevertheless, the use of the simplest particles is found already in the earliest periods of the Hebrew language, or, at any rate, in the earliest documents which have come down to us.

e 3. Less frequently particles are formed by *composition*; as מַדּוּעַ *wherefore ?* for מַה־יָּדוּעַ *quid edoctus ?* (τί μαθών ;) or *quid cognitum ?* ; בִּלְעֲדֵי (from בַּל and עֲדֵי) *besides* ; מִלְמַעְלָה (from מִן, לְ, מַעְלָה) *from above, above.*

More frequent is the combination of two words into one without contraction, e.g. כִּי־עַל־כֵּן, אַף־כִּי, כִּי־אִם, אַחֲרֵי־כֶן; cf. also the compounds of אֵי with demonstrative pronouns, as אֵי־מִזֶּה *from what?* ; אֵי לָזֹאת *wherefore ?* [R.V. *how*]. See the lexicon under אֵי.

§ 100. *Adverbs.*

On demonstrative adverbs cf. Brockelmann, *Grundriss,* i. 323 ; on interrogative adverbs, *ibid.,* i. 328 ; on adverbs in general, i. 492 ff.

a 1. The negative לֹא *not,* and a few particles of place and time, as שָׁם *there,* are of obscure origin.

b 2. Forms of other parts of speech, which are used adverbially without further change, are—

(*a*) Substantives with prepositions, e.g. בִּמְאֹד (with might) *very* ; לְבַד *alone* (prop. *in separation,* Fr. *à part*), with suffix לְבַדִּי *I alone* ; מִבַּיִת *from within, within* ; cf. also כְּאֶחָד (as one) *together,* לְעֻמַּת and מִלְּעֻמַּת (originally *in connexion with*) *near to, corresponding to, like,* &c., cf. § 161 *b.*

c (*b*) Substantives in the accusative (the adverbial case of the Semites, § 118 *m*), cf. τὴν ἀρχήν, δωρεάν, e.g. מְאֹד (might) *very,* אֶפֶס (cessation) *no more,* הַיּוֹם (the day) *to-day* (cf. § 126 *b*), מָחָר [1] *to-morrow,* יַחַד (union) *together.* Several of these continued to be used, though rarely, as substantives, e.g. סָבִיב, plur. סְבִיבִים and סְבִיבוֹת, *circuit,* as adverb

---

[1] Generally derived from the ptcp. Puʿal מְאֻחָר *meʾŏḥār* (= *meʾoḥḥār*) and hence to be read *mŏḥār* (cf. מְחֻרַת *morning*) ; but according to P. Haupt (notes to Esther, p. 159) from יוֹם אַחַר.

circum, around; others have quite ceased to be so used, e.g. כְּבָר (length)
long ago [Aram.: only in Ec.]; עוֹד (repetition, duration) *again* or *further*.

(c) Adjectives, especially in the feminine (corresponding to the *d*
Indo-Germanic neuter), e.g. רִאשׁוֹנָה *primum, formerly* (more frequently
בָּרִאשׁוֹנָה, also לָרִאשׁוֹנָה); רַבָּה and רַבַּת [both rare] *multum, much, enough*;
נִפְלָאוֹת *wonderfully* (properly *mirabilibus*, sc. *modis*), יְהוּדִית *Jewish*,
i. e. in the Jewish language.

(d) Verbs in the infinitive absolute, especially in *Hiph'îl*, which *e*
are likewise to be regarded as accusatives (§ 113 *h*), e.g. הַרְבֵּה (prop.
a multiplying) *much* [frequent], לְהַרְבֵּה [rare and late] *in multitude*;
הַשְׁכֵּם (*mane faciendo*) *early*; הַעֲרֵב (*vespere faciendo*) *in the evening*.

(e) Pronouns and numerals, e.g. זֶה (prop. *there=at this place*) *here*, *f*
הֵנָּה *here, hither* (also of time, עַד־הֵנָּה *till now*, cf. the late and rare עֶדֶן
and עֶדֶנָּה=עַד־הֵן); אַחַת, שְׁתַּיִם, שֶׁבַע, מֵאָה *once, twice, seven times, a
hundred times*; שֵׁנִית *for the second time*.

3. Some adverbs are formed by the addition of formative syllables *g*
(most frequently ◌ָם) to substantives or adjectives, e.g. אָמְנָם and
אֻמְנָם *truly* (from אֹמֶן *truth*); חִנָּם (by favour) *gratis* (from חֵן *gratia*);
רֵיקָם *in vain, frustra*, but also *empty* (from רֵיק *empty, emptiness,
vanum*), Ru 1²¹, parallel with the *fem.* מְלֵאָה *full*; יוֹמָם *by day* (from יוֹם)¹;
with *ô* in the last syllable, פִּתְאֹם, for פִּתְעֹם, *in a twinkling, suddenly*
(from פֶּתַע *a twinkling*, the *ô* being probably obscured from an original
â).² — Moreover, cf. אֲחֹרַנִּית *backward*, and קְדֹרַנִּית *darkly attired*, Mal 3¹⁴.
In both these cases, the formative syllable *an* has been first attached
to the stem, and then the feminine ending *îth*, which is elsewhere
used to form adverbs, has been added to it.

The termination ◌ָם occurs also in the formation of substantives, e.g. *h*
אוּלָם *porch*, and hence the above adverbs may equally well be regarded as
nouns used adverbially, so that ◌ָם, ◌ִם, would correspond to ◌ָ‍‍י, ◌ֹ‍ן (§ 85,
Nos. 53, 54), cf. בְּפִתְאֹם (with prep.) *suddenly*, 2 Ch 29³⁶. According to others,
this *am* is an obsolete accusative ending, to be compared with the indeterminate accusative sing. in *ăn* in Arabic.

---

¹ Is this ◌ָם an instance of the locative or temporal termination (cf.
especially צָהֳרַיִם) mentioned in § 88 *c*? Nöldeke, *ZDMG.* xl. p. 721, considers
יוֹמָם a secondary substantival form (used adverbially like לַיְלָה *noctu*), corresponding to the Phoenician and Aramaic יִמָּם, Syr. *'imāmā*; cf. on the other
hand, König, ii. 255, who follows Olshausen in maintaining that the *ăm* is an
adverbial termination.

² דּוּמָם *silent* (an adjective in Is 47⁵, La 3²⁶; a substantive in Hb 2¹⁹), which
was formerly included under this head, is better taken, with Barth (*Nominalbildung*, p. 352, Rem. 2), as a participle formed like עוֹלֵל, שׁוֹבָב, so that דּוּמָם
(perhaps assimilated to דּוּמָה) stands for original דֻּוְמָם.

i 4. A number of forms standing in very close relation to the demonstrative pronoun may be regarded as primitive adverbs, since they arise directly from a combination of demonstrative sounds. Some of these have subsequently suffered great mutilation, the extent of which, however, can now very rarely be ascertained with certainty. Such are e. g. אָז *then*, הֵנָּה *here* (according to Barth, *Sprachwiss. Abhandlungen*, p. 16, formed from the two demonstrative elements *hin* and *na*), כֵּן, כֹּה *thus* (cf. אֵיכָה, אֵיכָכָה *how ?*), אַךְ *only*, אָכֵן *truly* (on all these adverbs, see the Lexicon), and especially the interrogative הֲ (*Hē interrogativum*), e. g. הֲלֹא (Dt 3¹¹ הֲלֹה) *nonne ?*, הֲגַם *num etiam ?* This *Hē interrogativum* is perhaps shortened from הַל, which is still used in Arabic, and, according to the view of a certain school of Masoretes, occurs also in Hebrew in Dt 32⁶.[1]

k The ה interrogative takes—(1) *Ḥaṭeph-Paṭhaḥ* generally before non-gutturals (even before ר), with a firm vowel, e. g. הֲשַׂמְתָּ *hast thou set?* see the interrogative clause, § 150 *c* (הַיֵּיטַב Lv 10¹⁹ is an exception).

l (2) Before a consonant with *Šᵉwâ*, usually *Paṭhaḥ* without a following *Dageš forte*, e. g. הַבְרָכָה Gn 27³⁸, cf. 18¹⁷, 29⁵, 30¹⁵, 34³¹; less frequently (in about ten passages), *Paṭhaḥ* with a following *Dageš forte*, e. g. הַבְּדֶרֶךְ *num in via*, Ez 20³⁰, הַלְּבֶן Gn 17¹⁷, 18²¹, 37³², Nu 13¹⁹, Jb 23⁶; even in ר, 1 S 10²⁴, 17²⁵, 2 K 6³².

m (3) Before gutturals, not pointed with either *Qameṣ* or *Ḥaṭeph-Qameṣ*, it takes *Paṭhaḥ*, e. g. הַאֵלֵךְ *shall I go ?*, הַאַתָּה *num tu ?*, הַאִם *num si* ; הַאֶרְצֶה Mal 1¹³ ; also in Ju 6³¹ read הַאַתֶּם (not הַא׳), likewise ה in Ju 12⁵, Jer 8¹⁹, Neh 6¹¹.— In הַאִישׁ Nu 16²², the Masora intends the article ; read הָאִישׁ, and cf. Dt 20¹⁹; in Ec 3²¹ read הַעֹלָה and הַיֹּרֶדֶת ; the article is a correction due to doctrinal considerations.

n (4) The ה takes *Sᵉghôl* before gutturals pointed with *Qameṣ* or (as in Ju 9⁹ff.) *Ḥaṭeph-Qameṣ*, e. g. הֶאָמוֹר Mi 2⁷ ; הֶאָנֹכִי Jb 21⁴ ; הֶחָיְתָה Jo 1² ; הֶהָשֵׁב Gn 24⁵ (cf. the analogous instances in § 22 *c*, § 35 *k*, § 63 *k*). The place of this interrogative particle is always at the beginning of the clause [but see Jb 34³¹, Neh 13²⁷, Jer 22¹⁵, where one or more words are prefixed for emphasis].

o 5. Some adverbs occur also in connexion with suffixes, thus יֶשְׁךָ *thou art there*, 3rd sing. masc. יֶשְׁנוֹ[2] (but see note below), 2nd plur. masc. יֶשְׁכֶם ; אֵינֶנִּי *I am not*, 2nd sing. אֵינְךָ, fem. אֵינֵךְ, 3rd sing. אֵינֶנּוּ, fem. אֵינֶנָּה, 2nd plur. אֵינְכֶם, 3rd plur. masc. אֵינָם.—Also עוֹדֶנִּי *I am yet* (La 4¹⁷ *Qᵉrê* ; עוֹדֵינָה only in בְּעוֹדִי and (מֵעוֹדִי), עוֹדְךָ, עוֹדָךְ, עוֹדֵינוּ (עוֹדִי)

---

[1] The separation of the ה at the beginning of Dt 32⁶, expressly noticed by Qimḥi (ed. Rittenb., p. 40 b) as an unique instance, is perhaps a protest against admitting a particle הַל.

[2] This form, which occurs in Dt 29¹⁴, 1 S 14³⁹, 23²³, Est 3⁸, is textually very doubtful, and cannot be supported by the equally doubtful קָבְנוּ (for קַבֵּנּוּ) Nu 23¹³. Most probably, with Stade, *Gramm.*, § 370 b, and P. Haupt, *SBOT* Numbers, p. 57, line 37, we should read יֶשְׁנֻוּ.

*K*eth.; the oriental school [see above, p. 38, note 2] recognize only
the reading עוֹרְ֫ינוּ), עוֹרָם.—אַיֵּ֫כָה *where art thou ?*, אַיּוֹ *where is he ?*, אַיָּם
where are they ? The same applies to הֵן) הֵ֫ן־) and הִנֵּה *behold !* (prop.
here, here is; see § 105 *b*), only in Gn 19² הִנֵּה־נָא; with suffixes, הִנְנִי,
once הִנֶּ֫נִּי (Gn 22⁷ with *Munaḥ*), in pause הִנֵּ֫נִי *behold me* (*here am I*),
הִנְּךָ (*pause* הִנֶּ֫ךָּ ψ 139⁸), הִנּוֹ, הִנָּ֫ה, and הִנֵּהוּ [both very rare], הִנְנוּ (*behold
us*). and הִנֶּ֫נּוּ (in *pause* הִנֵּ֫נוּ), הִנָּם, הִנְּכֶם; [see more fully in the Lexicon,
p. 243].

The usual explanation of these suffixes (especially of the forms with *Nún* *p*
energicum) as verbal suffixes, which ascribes some power of verbal government
even to forms originally substantival (e.g. יֶשְׁנוֹ *there is, he is*), is at least
inadmissible for forms (like אַיּוֹ, בְּעוֹרִי) which are evidently connected with
noun-suffixes; even for the other forms it is questionable. Brockelmann
suggests that the נ in connexion with these particles is a survival from הנה
corresponding to the Arab. *'ánna* which introduces dependent clauses.

101. *Prepositions.*

Brockelmann, *Grundriss*, i. 494 ff.

1. All words, which by usage serve as prepositions, were originally *a*
substantives, viz.:

(*a*) Substantives in the accusative and in the construct state, so that
the noun governed by them is to be considered as in the genitive,
and in Arabic actually has the genitive ending, cf. in German *statt
dessen, kraft dessen*, in Greek τούτου χάριν, in Latin *huius rei causa*,
or *gratia, montis instar*.[1] Cf. אַחַר (hinder part *) *behind, after* (*Mil'êl*
in אַחַר כֵּן Lv 14³⁶, Dt 21¹³, 1 S 10⁵; אַחַר זֶה 2 Ch 32⁹); אֵ֫צֶל (side)
close by; בֵּין (intermediate space *) *between*; בַּ֫עַד (distance²)
behind, around; זוּלַת, or with *Ḥireq compaginis* זוּלָתִי (removal, want)
except; יַ֫עַן (purpose) *on account of*; מוּל) מוֹל only in Dt 1¹) *before, over
against*; מִן־ (separation; cf. § 119 *v*) *from, out of*; נֶ֫גֶד (coming in
front, that which is over against) *before, over against*; עַד־ (progress,
duration *) *during, until*; עַל־ (height, upper part *) *upon, over*; עִם־
(connexion ?) *with*; it is doubtful whether this is to be derived from
the same stem as עֻמַּת, לְעֻמַּת *near, beside, like*; תַּ֫חַת (under part *)
under, instead of.

(*b*) Substantives in the construct state, but to be regarded as in the *b*
genitive, since they depend on prepositions (especially the inseparable),
e. g. לִפְנֵי (in the face of *) *before*; לְפִי, כְּפִי (according to the mouth,

---

[1] In the examples which follow, the meaning of the noun is added in
parentheses, and, when it is actually in use [though it is mostly in such cases
very rare], is marked with an asterisk.—On a similar use in other languages,
see W. von Humboldt, *Über die Kawisprache*, iii, p. 621.

[2] So also J. Hoch de Long, *Die hebr. Präpos.* בְּעַד, Lpz. 1905.

i. e. the command of *) *according to*; בִּגְלַל (in the concern of) *on account of*; לְמַעַן (for the purpose of) *on account of*.

c   2. Substantives used adverbially very frequently become prepositions in this way, e.g. בְּאֶפֶס, בְּאֵין, בִּלְתִּי, מִבְּלִי, בִּבְלִי, בְּלִי (with cessation) *without*, בְּעוֹד (in the duration of) *during*; כְּדִי, כְּדֵי (according to the requirement of) *for, according to*.

§ 102. *Prefixed Prepositions.*

a   1. Of the words mentioned in § 101, מִן *from, out of*, frequently occurs as a prefix (§ 99 c), with its *Nûn* assimilated to the following consonant (by means of *Dageš forte*), e. g. מִיַּעַר *out of a forest*.

b   Rem. The separate מִן־ (always with a following *Maqqeph*) is usual (but not necessary, cf. Ju 20¹⁴ with verse 15, Ez 43⁶, &c.) only before the article, e. g. מִן־הָאָרֶץ, and sometimes occurs before the softer consonants, e. g. מִן־אָז Jer 44¹⁸, מִן־בְּנֵי Jo 1¹², 1 Ch 5¹⁸; cf. Ex 18¹⁴, Lv 1¹⁴, 14³⁰, Ju 7²³, 10¹¹, 19¹⁶, ψ 104⁷ (2 K 23³⁶ before ר; also before ק in ψ 18⁴⁹), and elsewhere in the later books (as in Aramaic)¹; there is besides a poetic by-form מִנִּי (cf. § 90 m) and מִנֵּי Is 30¹¹. Its form is most commonly מִ־ *with a following Dageš*, which may, however, be omitted in letters which have *Šewâ* (cf. § 20 m). With a following י the מִ is, as a rule, contracted to מִי, e. g. מִידִי = מִידֵי or מִידֵי (but cf. מִישְׁנֵי Dn 12²; מִירֶשְׁתֶךָ 2 Ch 20¹¹); before gutturals it becomes מֵ (according to § 22 c), e. g. מֵעָם, מֵאָדָם; before ח the מ occurs with the guttural virtually sharpened in מָחוּץ *on the outside*, and in מֵחוּטם Gn 14²³; before ה in מִהְיוֹת (cf. § 28 b and § 63 q. The closed syllable here is inconsistent with the required virtual sharpening of the ה; probably מִהְיוֹת is merely due to the analogy of לִהְיוֹת); similarly Is 14³ before ר; but in 1 S 23²⁸, 2 S 18¹⁶ מֵהִרְדֹּף is to be read, according to § 22 s.

c   2. There are also three other particles, the most commonly used prepositions and the particle of comparison, which have been reduced by abbreviation (§ 99 c) to a single prefixed consonant with *Šewâ* (but see below, and § 103 e), viz.:

בְּ [poet. בְּמוֹ] *in, at, with*.

לְ [poet. לְמוֹ] *towards*, (belonging) *to, for*, Lat. *ad*.

כְּ [poet. כְּמוֹ] *like, as, according to* (no doubt the remnant of a substantive with the meaning of *matter, kind, instar*).

d   With regard to the pointing it is to be observed that—

(a) The *Šewâ mobile*, with which the above prefixes are usually pronounced, has resulted from the weakening of a short vowel (an original *ă*, according to f)²; the short vowel is regularly retained before *Šewâ*: before *Šewâ simplex*

---

¹ König, *Einleitung ins A. T.*, p. 393 (cf. also the almost exhaustive statistics in his *Lehrgebäude*, ii. 292 ff.), enumerates eight instances of מִן before a word without the article in 2 Samuel and Kings, and forty-five in Chronicles.

² Jerome (see Siegfried, *ZAW.* iv. 79) almost always represents בְּ by *ba*.

in the form of an *ĭ*, attenuated from *ă*: before a *Ḥaṭeph* the prefix takes the vowel of the *Ḥaṭeph*, e.g. לִפְרִי *for fruit*, כַּאֲרִי *as a lion*, בְּעָנְיִ *bŏ'ŏnî, in affliction* (sometimes with the syllable subsequently closed, cf. § 28 *b*, and the infinitives with לְ § 63 *i*): before weak consonants it follows the rule given in § 24 *c*, e.g. לִיהוּדָה for לִי׳.   When the prefixes לְ, כְּ, וְ, בְּ precede אֱלֹהִים *God*, the *Šᵉwâ* and *Ḥaṭeph Sᵉghôl* regularly coalesce in *Ṣērê*, e.g. בֵּאלֹהִים, &c., for בֶּאֱל׳; so with suffixes וֵאלֹהָיו, &c. (once also in the sing. לֵאלֹהוֹ Hb 1¹¹); also regularly לֵאמֹר *to say*, for לֶאֱמֹר, see § 23 *d*.

(*b*) When the prefixes precede the article, the ה is almost always dropped, *e* and they take its vowel.   See further in § 35 *n*.

(*c*) Immediately before the tone-syllable, i.e. before monosyllables and dis- *f* syllables with the tone on the penultima (in the fore-tone), they take *Qameṣ* (undoubtedly a lengthening of an original *ă*, cf. § 26 *e*, § 28 *a*), but only in the following cases:

(*aa*) לְ before infinitives of the above-mentioned forms, as לָתֵת *to give*, לָדִין *to judge*, לָבֹז *to plunder*, לָגֹז *to shear*, לָחֹג *to keep a festival*, לָלֶדֶת *to bring forth*, לָלֶכֶת *to go*, לָקַחַת *to take*, except when the infinitive (as a *nomen regens*) is closely connected with another word (especially its subject, § 115 *e*), and consequently, as being in a sort of *constr. state*, loses the principal tone, e.g. לְצֵאת Ex 19¹, לְשֶׁבֶת Gn 16³, and so always לְבֹא חֲמָת Nu 13²¹, &c. (in such cases as לְתֵת־חֶרֶב Ex 5²¹ the *ā* is protected by the secondary tone; before infinitives of verbs ע״וּ, the לְ is retained even in close connexion; cf. Ez 21²⁰·²⁵, 22³);

(*bb*) before many pronominal forms, e.g. בָּזֶה (so also in 1 S 21¹⁰; not בַּזֶּה), *g* לָזֹאת, בָּזֶה, לָזֶה (in close connexion, however, לְזֹאת Gn 2²³; כָּזֹאת Gn 45²³); כָּאֵלֶּה *as these*; and especially (בָּהֶם) and בָּהֶם, לָהֶם, בָּכֶם, לָכֶם, בָּכֶם (כָּכֶם), see § 103 *e*;

(*cc*) לְ before monosyllables or fore-toned nouns in such combinations as *h* פֶּה לָפֶה *mouth to mouth*, 2 K 10²¹, בֵּין מַיִם לָמָיִם *between waters and waters*, Gn 1⁶; לָטֹרַח *for a trouble*, Is 1¹⁴, but always before the principal pause.   The instructive example in Dt 17⁸ also shows that the punctuation לָ is only possible with at least the lesser pause after it; in Is 28¹⁰·¹³ the לָ is twice repeated, even before the small and smallest disjunctives;

(*dd*) in certain standing expressions, which have become stereotyped almost *i* as adverbs, e.g. לָעַד *to eternity*, לָרֹב *in multitude*, לָבֶטַח *in security*, לָנֶצַח *to eternity*, but לָנֶצַח נְצָחִים *to all eternity*, Is 34¹⁰.   Cf. also לָנֶפֶשׁ *for the dead*, Lv 19²⁸, Nu 5², 9¹⁰.

(*d*) With the interrogative מָה they are pointed as in בַּמֶּה; in *pause* and *k* before א as in בַּמֶּה *by what?* (before a following relative clause, as in Ec 3²², בַּמֶּה; cf. Delitzsch, *Jesaia*, 4th ed., on Is 2²²); כַּמֶּה *how much?* but also כַּמָּה 1 K 22¹⁶, in close connexion, and at a greater distance from the *pause*.   The *Sᵉghôl* in these forms arises from a modification of the original *ă*, while the מ is sharpened in order to maintain the original *ă* of the prefixes.

When לְ (prop. *la*) is united to מָה, it takes, according to § 49 *f*, *g*, the form *l* לָמָּה (Jb 7²⁰), לָמָה 1 S 1⁸, לָמֶה, all *Mil'êl*, and hence the *ă* in the tone is lengthened to *ā*) *for what? why?*   Before the gutturals א, ה, ע, לָמָה is used for euphonic reasons (exceptions 1 S 28¹⁵, 2 S 14³¹, Jer 15¹⁸, before ה; 2 S 2²², ψ 49⁶, before א) ; לָמָּה, however, remains before ה. Before letters which are not gutturals, לָמֶה is found in ψ 42¹⁰, 43² (immediately after a tone-syllable).

m Rem. The divine name יְהוָֹה, which has not its original vowels (יֱהֹוִה) but those of אֲדֹנָי (see § 17 c), except that the י has simple not compound Šᵉwâ, takes the prefixes also, after the manner of אֲדֹנָי, thus בֵּיהוָֹה, לַיהוָֹה, וַיהוָֹה, מֵיהוָֹה (since they are to be read מֵאֲדֹנָי, בַּאדֹנָי, לַאדֹנָי, וַאדֹנָי); for the א of אֲדֹנָי, as of אֲדֹנִים, אֲדֹנָי, &c. (see below), *quiesces* after the prefixes בּ, כּ, לְ, וּ, but is *audible* after מֶ (for מִן), שֶׁ (no instance in the O. T.), and הָ (in הָאֲדֹנִים Dt 10¹⁷, ψ 136³, the article, not הֲ interrog., is intended ; the only example with הֲ interrog.,· Jer 8¹⁹, is to be pointed הַיהוָֹה, i.e. הַאֲדֹנָי, not הֲיהוָֹה). Hence the rule, מֹשֶׁה מוֹצִיא *Moses brought out* (i. e. מ, שׁ, ה make the א audible), וְכָלֵב מַכְנִים *and Caleb brought in* (i. e. ו, כ, ל, בּ allow it to quiesce).[1]—As regards the other plural forms of אָדוֹן, elision of the א always takes place after בּ, וּ, כּ, לְ, except in the form אֲדֹנָי, thus לַאדֹנָיו, לַאדֹנֶיךָ, &c. ; but לַאֲדֹנָי, &c., לַאֲדֹנֵינוּ, &c., לַאֲדֹנֵיהֶם, &c.

§ 103. *Prepositions with Pronominal Suffixes and in the Plural Form.*

a 1. As all prepositions were originally nouns (§ 101) in the accusative, they may be united with the noun-suffixes (§ 91 *b-l*), e. g. אֶצְלִי (prop. at my side) *by me*, אִתִּי (in my proximity) *with me*, תַּחְתָּם (in their place) *instead of them*, like the Latin *mea causa, for my sake.*

b Rem. 1. The preposition אֵת (usually אֶת־) *near, with*, is distinguished from אֵת (see below, and § 117 a, note 4), the sign of the definite accusative (§ 117 a), in its connexion with suffixes, by a difference of pointing, the former making אִתִּי, אִתְּךָ, in *pause* אִתָּךְ, 2nd fem. אִתָּךְ (Is 54¹⁰), (אִתֵּךְ), אִתּוֹ, אִתָּהּ, אִתָּנוּ, אִתְּכֶם, אִתָּם (also in the later books, especially in Kings, and always in Jer. and Ezek., incorrectly אוֹתִי *with me* ; מֵאוֹתָךְ *from thee*, 1 K 20²⁵ ; מֵאוֹתוֹ *from him*, 1 K 22⁷ ; אוֹתָם *with them*), while the latter retains its ô (obscured from â) before the light suffixes, but before grave suffixes is pointed with Sᵉghôl. This Sᵉghôl is to be explained, with Praetorius, *ZDMG.* lv. 369 f., as the modification of an *ă* which again was shortened from original *â* (in 'áthî, 'áthô, &c.) in a closed syllable ('ăth-hem, &c.). The same shortening and modification of the original *â* takes place before words in close connexion, hence אֶת־כֹּל, &c. When not in close connexion, the toneless אֶת becomes tone-long אֵת, e. g. אֵת הַשָּׁמַיִם Gn 1¹. Hence the following forms arise :—

	Sing.			Plur.	
1.		אֹתִי *me.*		אֹתָנוּ *us.*	
2.	m.	אֹתְךָ, *pause* (אֹתָךְ)		אֶתְכֶם *you.*	} *thee.*
	f.	אֹתָךְ	} *thee.*	. . . . .	
3.	m.	אֹתוֹ *him.*		אֶתְהֶם, rarely אֹתָם	} *them.*
	f.	אֹתָהּ *her.*		אֶתְהֶן, rarely אֹתָן	

---

[1] Another *vox memor.* is כָּל־בּוֹ נֶעְלָם *all is hidden in him.*

Less common are the *plene* forms אוֹתִי‎, אוֹתְךָ‎, אֹתְכָה‎ (Nu 22³³ before ה‎), אוֹתָךְ‎ (Ex 29³⁵), (אֹתְכָה)‎, אוֹתָהּ‎, אוֹתָנִי‎, אוֹתוֹ‎, אוֹתָם‎. Moreover, for אֶתְכֶם‎ we find אוֹתְכֶם‎ Jos 23¹⁵; for אֶתָם‎, five times אֶתְהֶם‎ (Gn 32¹, Ex 18²⁰, &c.), and in Ez 23⁴⁵ אוֹתְהֶם‎; for אֶתְהֶן‎ (Gn 19⁸, &c. [13 times]), אֹתָן‎ (only found in Ez 16⁵⁴; Ex 35²⁶ אֹתָנָה‎; Ez 34²¹ (אוֹתָנָה)‎, and אוֹתְהֶן‎ Ez 23⁴⁷.—No instance of the 2nd fem. plur. אֶתְכֶן‎ occurs in the O.T.; in Cant 2⁷, &c., אֶתְכֶם‎ is used instead.

2. The preposition עִם־‎ *with* (with suffixes on the model of stems ע״ע‎, עִמִּי‎, *c* עִמְּךָ‎ [1 S 1²⁶ (עִמָּכָה)‎], in *pause* עִמָּךְ‎; 2nd fem. עִמָּךְ‎; עִמּוֹ‎, עִמָּהּ‎ (עִמָּה)‎ is united with the suffixes נוּ‎, כֶם‎, and הֶם‎ by a (pretonic) *Qameṣ*, which causes the sharpening of the *Mêm* to be distinctly audible: עִמָּנוּ‎, עִמָּכֶם‎, עִמָּהֶם‎ (so in Nu 22¹², Dt 29¹⁶, both in principal pause, and often in very late passages, otherwise עִמָּם‎ is generally used). In the first person, besides עִמִּי‎, we also find עִמָּדִי‎ (probably from original עִנְדִי‎; cf. Arab. *'inda*, beside, with).

3. It is but seldom that prepositions occur with verbal suffixes, as תַּחְתֵּנִי‎ *d* 2 S 22³⁷·⁴⁰·⁴⁸ (for which ψ 18³⁷·⁴⁰·⁴⁸ תַּחְתָּי‎), תַּחְתֶּנָּה‎ Gn 2²¹ and בַּעֲדֵנִי‎ ψ 139¹¹ (here probably for the sake of the rhyme with יְשׁוּפֵנִי‎).[1]

2. When pronominal suffixes are added to the prefixes (§ 102), there *e* appears occasionally, especially in the case of the shorter suffixes, an endeavour to lengthen the preposition, so as to give it more strength and body. Hence to כְּ‎ is appended the syllable מוֹ‎ (see below, *k*), and בְּ‎ and לְ‎ take at least a full vowel, בָּ‎ and לָ‎ (§ 102 *d, f*).—The following deviations from the analogy of the noun with suffixes are to be noticed (*a*) in the pausal forms בָּךְ‎, לָךְ‎, אֹתָךְ‎, אִתָּךְ‎, עִמָּךְ‎ (not *bĕkhā*, &c.); (*b*) in the similar forms with the suffix of the 2nd sing. fem. (not *bēkh*, &c.) and in עָמָּנוּ‎, לָנוּ‎, בָּנוּ‎, &c. (not *bēnû*, &c.).

(*a*) לְ‎ *with Pronominal Suffixes.*   *f*

	Sing.		Plur.	
1.	לִי‎ *to me.*		לָנוּ‎ *to us.*	
2.	*m.* לְךָ‎ (לְכָה)‎, in *pause* לָךְ‎ } *to thee.*		לָכֶם‎ [לָכֶן]²‎ *to you.*	
	f. לָךְ‎ . . . . }			
3.	*m.* לוֹ‎ *to him.*		לָהֶמָּה‎, לָהֶם‎, *poet.* לָמוֹ‎ [53 times]³	} *to them.*
	f. לָהּ‎ *to her.*		לָהֵנָּה‎⁴, לָהֶן‎	

---

[1] *Fini* and *bini* (in me), in vulgar Arabic for *fiyya* and *bi*, are compared by Socin. Brockelmann, *ZA.* xiv. 347, note 1, suggests that תחתני‎, תחתנה‎, בעדני‎ are later formations on the model of מִמֶּנִּי‎ when its origin from the reduplication of the preposition had become obscured, but see below, *m*.

[2] לָכֶן‎ does not occur in the O.T., by a mere accident, no doubt; Ez 13¹⁸ לָכֵנָה‎.

[For notes 3 and 4 see next page.]

g   בְּ takes suffixes in the same manner : בִּי, בְּךָ (Ex 7²⁹, 2 S 22³⁰, ψ 141⁸ בְּכָה, as in Gn 27³⁷, 2 S 18²², Is 3⁶ לְכָה [for 2nd fem. לָךְ the *Kᵉthîbh* לכי occurs in 2 K 4², Ct 2¹³, cf. § 91 *e*]), בֹּו, &c.; except that for the 3rd plur., besides בָּהֶם (especially in the later books) and בָּהֵמָּה (only in Ex 30⁴, 36¹, Hb 1¹⁶; לָהֵמָּה only in Jer 14¹⁶), the form בָּם is also used; and for the feminine, besides בָּהֵנָּה (three times), בָּהֵן is found fifteen times, and בָּהֶן only in 1 S 31⁷, Is 38¹⁶, Ez 42¹⁴.—According to the Masora, לֹא is found fifteen times for לֹו (as conversely in 1 S 2¹⁶, 20² לֹו for לֹא), e. g. Ex 21⁸, 1 S 2³, Is 9², ψ 100³ (and, as has been con-jectured, also Jb 41⁴); cf. Delitzsch on ψ 100³.—In Nu 32⁴², Zc 5¹¹, Ru 2¹⁴, the Masora requires לָהּ instead of לָהּ (in all three places before a following tone-syllable; cf. § 23 *k*, and the analogous cases of the loss of *Mappîq* in § 58 *g*, § 91 *e*).

h   (*b*) כְּ *with Pronominal Suffixes.*

Sing.		Plur.	
1.	כָּמֹונִי⁵ *as I.*	כָּמֹונוּ *as we.*	
2. { *m.* כָּמֹוךָ⁵	} *as thou.*	כָּמֹוכֶם, כָּכֶם, rarely כְּמֹוכֶם	} *as ye.*
{ *f.* ...		....	
3. { *m.* כָּמֹוהוּ	*as he.*	כְּמֹוהֶם, [כָּהֵמָּה], כָּהֶם, כָּהֵם	} *as they.*
{ *f.* כָּמֹוהָ	*as she.*	כָּהֵנָּה, [כָּהֵן]	

---

³ The question whether לָמֹו can also stand for the sing. לֹו, which Rödiger and recently W. Diehl (*Das Pronomen pers. suff. . . . des Hebr.*, p. 20 f.) and P. Haupt (*SBOT.* on Pr 23²⁰, a contraction of *la-humû*) have altogether denied, must be answered in the affirmative unless we conclude with Diehl and Haupt that *all* the instances concerned are due to corruptions of the text. It is true that in such places as Gn 9²⁶·²⁷, Dt 33², Is 30⁵, ψ 73¹⁰ (all *in* or immediately before the principal pause; in Dt 33² with *Zaqeph qaṭon* at least) לָמֹו can be better explained as plural (in reference to collective nouns); and in Is 53⁸ for נֶגַע לָמֹו we should read with the LXX נֻגַּע לָמֶּוֶת. On the other hand, in Is 44¹⁵ its explanation as plural would be extremely forced. Even then there would remain—presuming the traditional text to be correct— פָּנֵימֹו ψ 11⁷ and כַּפֵּימֹו Jb 27²³, as well as עָלֵימֹו, three times, Jb 20²³, 27²³ (beside עָלָיו), and especially Jb 22². In all these places the most extreme exegetical artifices can only be avoided by simply admitting a singular suffix (=עָלָיו, כַּפָּיו, פָּנָיו).—On the question of the antiquity of the suffixes in מֹו see § 91 *l*.

⁴ The form לָהֵן in Ru 1¹³ is Aramaic (=*therefore*).

⁵ The use of נִי here for ִי__ (cf. above, *d*) might be due to euphonic reasons.—כָּמֹנִי (defectively) only in the Pentateuch, כָּמֹךָ Ex 15¹¹.

(c) מִן־ *with Pronominal Suffixes.*

	Sing.	Plur.
1.	מִמֶּנִּי, poet. מִנִּי [4 times], in *pause* also מֶנִּי [6 times] *from me.*	מִמֶּנּוּ *from us.*
2.	{ m. מִמְּךָ, in *pause* (וּמִמֶּךָּ) f. מִמֵּךְ } *from thee.*	מִכֶּם מִכֶּן } *from you.*
3.	{ m. מִמֶּנּוּ, Jb 4¹² in *pause* מֶנְהוּ, [מִנֶּהוּ מִמֶּהוּ or מִנְהוּ: see below] *from him.* f. מִמֶּנָּה *from her.*	מֵהֶם, מֵהֵמָּה [twice], מֵהֶם Jb 11²⁰ מֵהֶן, מֵהֵנָּה [7 times] } *from them.*

The syllable מוֹ (in Arabic *mâ*= מָא =Heb. מָה *what*) in כָּמוֹנִי (probably from כְּמָה אֲנִי, prop. *according to what I, for as I*) is, in poetry, appended to the three simple prefixes בְּ, כְּ, לְ, even without suffixes, so that לְמוֹ, כְּמוֹ, בְּמוֹ appear as independent words, equivalent in meaning to בְּ, כְּ, לְ. Poetry is here distinguished from prose by the use of longer forms; in the case of מִן, on the other hand, it prefers the shorter, which resemble the Syriac and Arabic.

The form כָּהֶם, enclosed in brackets above, occurs only in 2 K 17¹⁵ (in *pause*), כָּהֵמָּה only in Jer 36³² (in *pause*); כָּהֵן (Baer following Qimḥi כָּהֶן) only in Ez 18¹⁴. Cf. Frensdorff, *Massora Magna*, p. 234 ff.—For כָּכֶם *as ye*, Qimḥi requires כְּכֶם (invariably or only in Jb 16⁴?); in Jos 1¹⁵, Ju 8², Ezr 4² Baer gives כָּכֶם.

With regard to מִן with suffixes, מִמֶּנִּי *from me* is usually explained as arising, by a reduplication of מִן, from an original מִנְמִנִי, just as מִמֶּנּוּ *from him*, from מִנְמִנ־הו, identical in form with מִמֶּנּוּ [1] *from us*, from מִנְמִנ־נו, while מִמֶּנָּה *from her*, goes back to מִנְמִנה. Far simpler, however, is Mayer Lambert's explanation (*REJ.* xxiii. 302 ff.), that מִמֶּנִּי, &c., have arisen from מִנֶּנִּי, &c., and that the forms of the suffixes are to be explained on the analogy of תַּחְתֶּנָּה, אֵינֶנִּי, עוֹדֶנּוּ, § 100 *o*.—The bracketed form מִנֶּהוּ, for which Baer, following Qimḥi and others, writes מִנְהוּ, occurs only in ψ 68²⁴, and is there regarded by Delitzsch, Hupfeld, and others (following Simonis) as a substantive (מֵן= *portion*). The expression מִן־הוּא (for מִמֶּנּוּ?) Is 18²·⁷ is very strange.—מֵהֵמָּה occurs only in Jer 10², Ec 12¹² (Jb 11²⁰ מֵהֶם); מֵהֶן (so Baer and Ginsburg, following the best authorities, instead of the ordinary reading מֵהֵן) only in Ez 16⁴⁷·⁵².

---

[1] The Babylonian Masora writes מִמֶּנּוּ (to distinguish it from the 3rd sing.), which is justly blamed by Ibn Ezra.

n **3.** Several prepositions, especially those which express relations of space and time, are (like the German *wegen*) properly plural nouns (for the reason, see § 124 *a*), and are, therefore, joined with the pronominal suffixes in the form of the plural *construct state*, just like other plural nouns (§ 91 *g*). On the other hand, the apparent connexion of עַל, עַד־, אֶל־ with plural suffixes is explained from the ground-forms of those prepositions (from stems ל״ה) עֲלֵי (וַאֲלֵי), אֲלֵי, עֲדֵי, עֲלֵי (contracted to אֱלֵי, אֲלֵי, &c.).[1]

o Without suffixes these prepositions are—

אַחַר, more frequently אַחֲרֵי (prop. *hinder parts*) *behind, after.*

אֶל־,[2] poet. [4 times in Job] also אֱלֵי (*region, direction*), *towards, to, according to.*

בֵּין (*interval*) *between*; the suffixes indicating the singular are added to the singular בֵּין, thus בֵּינְךָ, בֵּינִי, &c. (Gn 16⁵ בֵּינֶיךָ, the second *Yôdh* is, however, marked with a point as critically doubtful; בֵּינֵיו, which occurs three times, is only the Masoretic *Qᵉrê* for בֵּינוֹ, which is found e. g. in Gn 30³⁶). On the other hand, the suffixes indicating a plural are attached to the plural forms בֵּינֵי or בֵּינוֹת.

סָבִיב (*circuit*) *around*, as a preposition, always has the plural form, sometimes masc. סְבִיבָיִךְ, &c. [10 times], but much more frequently in the fem. סְבִיבוֹת (*surroundings*). In Ez 43¹⁷ סָבִיב אוֹתָהּ is a corruption of סְבִיבֹתֶיהָ; [in 1 K 6⁵ סָבִיב אֶת also is so contrary to usage, that it must be due to some textual error].

עַד־ (*continuation, duration*, from עָדָה) *as far as, unto*, poet. עֲדֵי [12 times]. In Jb 32¹² עֲדֵיכֶם, with the *ā* retained in the secondary tone, is abnormal. Also in 2 K 9¹⁸ for עַד־הֶם read עֲדֵיהֶם.

עַל־ *upon, over* (cf. the rare subst. עַל *height* [see Lexicon], from עָלָה *to ascend*), poet. עֲלֵי [40 times, and 2 *Qᵉrê*].

תַּחַת *under* (prop. *what is beneath*). On תַּחְתֵּנִי, &c.; cf. above, *d*.

---

[1] The reference of these forms to original plurals has been again expressly supported by De Lagarde, *Symmicta*, ii. 101 ff.; *Nachrichten der G. g. G.*, 1881, p. 376, cf. *Mittheilungen*, 1884, p. 63; also *GGA*. 1884, p. 280 f. According to Barth, *ZDMG*. xlii. p. 348 ff., and *Nominalbildung*, p. 375 ff., תַּחְתֶּיךָ, &c., was only formed on the analogy of עָלֶיךָ, &c., and אַחֲרֶיךָ, &c., only on the analogy of לְפָנַי, &c., since the real plural forms ought to be אֲחָרֶיךָ, תְּחָתֶיךָ, &c.; cf., however, König, *Lehrgebäude*, ii. 305 f.

[2] On the use of this particle see § 119 *g*.

With Suffixes.

	after me	between me	around me	beneath me	to me	unto me	on me (p)
1 *Sing.*	אַחֲרַי	בֵּינִי	סְבִיבוֹתַי	תַּחְתַּי	אֵלַי	עָדַי	עָלַי
	(after me)	(between me)	(around me)	(beneath me)	(to me)	(unto me)	(on me)
2 *S. m.*	אַחֲרֶיךָ	בֵּינְךָ	סְבִיבוֹתֶיךָ & סְבִיבֶיךָ	תַּחְתֶּיךָ	אֵלֶיךָ	עָדֶיךָ	עָלֶיךָ
2 *S. f.*	אַחֲרַיִךְ		סְבִיבוֹתַיִךְ & סְבִיבַיִךְ		אֵלַיִךְ		עָלַיִךְ
3 *S. m.*	אַחֲרָיו	בֵּינוֹ	סְבִיבוֹתָיו & סְבִיבָיו	תַּחְתָּיו	אֵלָיו	עָדָיו	עָלָיו
3 *S. f.*	אַחֲרֶיהָ		סְבִיבוֹתֶיהָ & סְבִיבֶיהָ	תַּחְתֶּיהָ	אֵלֶיהָ	עָדֶיהָ	עָלֶיהָ
1 *Plur.*	אַחֲרֵינוּ &	בֵּינֵינוּ & בֵּינוֹתֵינוּ¹	סְבִיבוֹתֵינוּ	תַּחְתֵּינוּ	אֵלֵינוּ		עָלֵינוּ
2 *Pl. m.*	אַחֲרֵיכֶם	בֵּינֵיכֶם	סְבִיבוֹתֵיכֶם	תַּחְתֵּיכֶם	אֲלֵיכֶם	עֲדֵיכֶם	עֲלֵיכֶם
3 *Pl. m.*	אַחֲרֵיהֶם	בֵּינֵיהֶם & בֵּינוֹתָם &	סְבִיבוֹתֵיהֶם & סְבִיבוֹתָם &	תַּחְתֵּיהֶם usually תַּחְתָּם &	אֲלֵיהֶם & אֲלֵהֶם & [אֱלֵימוֹ²]	[עֲדֵיהֶם]	עֲלֵיהֶם . [עֲלֵימוֹ²]
3 *Pl. f.*	אַחֲרֵיהֶן			תַּחְתֵּיהֶן	אֲלֵיהֶן & אֲלֵהֶן		עֲלֵיהֶן

§ 104. *Conjunctions.*

1. The conjunctions serve to connect sentences, and to express their relations one to another. They may be either—

(*a*) Original pronouns, e. g. the demonstrative כִּי *that, because, for.*

(*b*) Original substantives, which afterwards were reduced to the rank of pronouns, adverbs, or conjunctions; so perhaps אֲשֶׁר (see § 36), which is sometimes used to express the general idea of relation, sometimes as a relative pronoun (properly a demonstrative), but in many cases stands simply for כִּי; also אַל־ (*nothing*), *that not*; פֶּן *that not* (the Greek μή of *prohibition*), &c. To these may be added the adverbial combination of substantives with prepositions, e. g. בְּטֶרֶם

---

¹ As Mayer Lambert observes, usage (cf. esp. Gn 26[28]) distinguishes between the two forms: בינותינו means *between us and you*, whereas בינינו (Jos 22[25,27,28] before וביניכם) means *between us on the one side.*

² The poetical form אֱלֵימוֹ only in ψ 2[5]; עֲלֵימוֹ, on which see note 3 on *f,* 12 times [viz. Dt 32[23], ψ 5[12], 55[16], 64[9], Jb 6[16], 20[23], 21[17,22], 27[23], 29[22], 30[2,5]].

(*in the not yet*) *earlier, before*, for which מִטֶּרֶם is also used. On the combination of two particles to express complex ideas (e. g. אַף־כִּי *added to this, that=much more*), see the Syntax, § 163 f.

b　(c) Prepositions, which with the addition of the conjunction אֲשֶׁר or כִּי together form one single conjunction, e. g. יַעַן אֲשֶׁר *because*, prop. *on account of the fact that*; אַחַר אֲשֶׁר, and more frequently אַחֲרֵי אֲשֶׁר, *after that*; כַּאֲשֶׁר *according as* (with כְּ); עֵקֶב אֲשֶׁר and עֵקֶב כִּי *in consequence of the fact that, for the reason that, because*. Sometimes, however, the conjunction in such cases is omitted, and the preposition itself used as a conjunction, e. g. עַל־ (for עַל־אֲשֶׁר) *although*, Jb 16¹⁷.

So, at any rate, according to our linguistic principles. It would, however, be more correct to say, that instead of the intermediary אֲשֶׁר the whole of the succeeding sentence is regarded as *one* substantival idea, under the immediate government of the preposition. In the same way, all prepositions governing the gerund in English may be paraphrased by conjunctions with the finite verb, see §§ 114 and 115, *passim*.

c　2. Besides those already mentioned, there are certain other small words now used as conjunctions, of which the derivation or original meaning is altogether obscure, thus אוֹ *or*, אִם *if* (also *or* before the second member of a double question), אַף *also*, וְ *and*, and others.

d　Rem. The pointing of the וְ (originally וַ, as still before *Ḥaṭeph Pathaḥ* and—with a following *Dageš forte*—in *wāw consecutive* of the imperfect; cf. § 49 *f*) is in many respects analogous to that of the prefixes בְּ, כְּ, לְ (§ 102 *d-i*), but as being a weak consonant, the *wāw copulative* has some further peculiarities :

(a) Usually it takes simple *Šᵉwâ* (וְ).

(b) Before words which begin with a guttural having a *compound Šᵉwâ*, it takes the vowel with which the *Šᵉwâ* is compounded (according to § 28 *b*), e. g. וַחֲכַם *and be thou wise*, וַעֲבָדִים *and servants*, וֶעֱזוּז *and strength*, וֶאֱכֹל *and eat thou*, וֳחֳלִי *and sickness*. On וֵאלֹהַי, וֵאלֹהִים, &c., see § 102 *d* ; on וַאדֹנָי, &c., see § 102 *m* ; on such cases as וַעְצַר Jb 4², cf. § 28 *b*.

e　(c) Before words with simple *Šᵉwâ* under the first consonant (except in the cases under *f*), the *Wāw* becomes the vowel *û* (cf. § 26 *a*), e. g. וּלְכֹל *and to all*, so also (except in the case under *g*) before the cognate labials ב, מ, פ, hence וּמֶלֶךְ. On the cases in which *simple Šᵉwâ* has become a *Ḥaṭeph* after וּ *copulative* (e. g. וְזָהָב Gn 2¹²), cf. § 10 *g*.

f　(d) With a following יְ the וְ coalesces to form וִי according to § 24 *b*, as וִיהִי *and let him be*. On the peculiar punctuation of the *wāw copulative* before forms with initial *Šᵉwâ* from הָיָה *to be* and חָיָה *to live* (e. g. וִהְיִיתֶם Jos 8⁴, וְחָיָה Gn 20⁷), cf. § 63 *q*.

g　(e) Immediately before the tone-syllable it frequently takes *Qameṣ*, like בָּ, כָּ, לָ (see § 102 *f*), but in most cases only at the end of a sentence or clause (but cf. also וָבֹא 2 K 22³⁰), e. g. וָמֵת Ex 21¹² (on the other hand, in verse 20

וּמֵת is in closer logical connexion with what follows) ; 2 K 7⁴ שָׁם וָמֵתְנוּ, וָמֵתָה
and וָמֵתְנוּ ; Ru 3³ וְסַכְתְּ ; ψ 10¹⁵ וָרָע ; 1 S 9⁴ וָאַ֫יִן ; 2 S 13²⁶ וָלֹא ; Ez 47⁹ וָחָי ; cf.
also (with *Ṭiphḥa*) Gn 33¹³, 2 S 15¹². The very frequent connexion of nouns
expressing kindred ideas, by means of וְ, is due simply to considerations of
rhythm, for even in such cases the *Wāw* must immediately precede the tone-
syllable, which must be marked by a disjunctive accent, e. g. תֹּהוּ וָבֹהוּ Gn 1²,
יוֹם וָלַ֫יְלָה Gn 8²² (see also the previous examples) ; Gn 13¹⁴ (thrice) ; Ex 25³
נֹח וְשֵׁם־וְחָם וָיֶ֫פֶת ; Gn 7¹³ ; וְרֶ֫כֶב וָסוּס ψ 76⁷ ; כָּבוֹד וָעֹז ψ 96⁷ ; זָהָב וָכֶ֫סֶף 1 K 21¹⁰
כֹּה וָכֹה ; אֱלֹהִים וָמֶ֫לֶךְ *thus and thus* ; Est 1⁸ אִישׁ־וָאִישׁ at the end of the verse,
but in ψ 87⁵ אִישׁ וְאִישׁ in spite of the *D*ᵉ*ḥi* with the second אִישׁ, because it is
closely connected with the following predicate. Also with three words
פַּ֫חַד וָפַ֫חַת וָפָח Is 24¹⁷. On the other hand, the rapid pronunciation וְ occurs
before a conjunctive accent (and, when farther removed from the principal
pause, even with the smaller disjunctives, in spite of a following tone-syllable),
e. g. צֵא וַעֲבֹד Gn 32⁶ ; cf. Gn 31⁴⁰, Lv 7²³, Dt 2²¹, and among the examples
given above, Gn 7¹³ and ψ 76⁷. (Exceptions : וְקִדְּמָה Gn 13¹⁴, where evidently
the וְ is intended to ensure the slow and solemn recitation of the promise,
but also וָחַי Jos 15⁵⁵, וָעֶתֶר 19⁷, וָבֶ֫טֶן 19²⁵, all immediately before the pause.)
For the same rhythmical reason וָ (not וְ) is used regularly with certain
monosyllables which, by their nature, lean more closely upon the following
word, thus וָזֶה, וָאֵת, וָגַם, וָלֹא (to be distinguished from וְלֹא *if not*, with *Zaqeph
gadol*, 2 K 5¹⁷), and others.

§ 105. *Interjections.*

1. Among the interjections some (as in all languages) are simply *a*
natural sounds, or, as it were, vocal gestures, called forth involuntarily
by certain impressions or sensations, e. g. אָח (Ez 30² הָהּ), אֲהָהּ *ah !*
aha ! (cf. this אָח also in אַחֲלֵי and אַחֲלַי *utinam !*), אָנָּא Ex 32³¹, &c.
(Gn 50¹⁷ אָנָּא) *ah !* (from אָהּ and נָא), otherwise written אָנָּה 2 K 20³,
Jn 1¹⁴, ψ 116⁴ ; also הַס (in pause הָס, even in the plural הַ֫סּוּ *hold your
peace !* Neh 8¹¹) *hush !* הוֹי (Am 5¹⁶ הוֹ־הוֹ) *ha ! woe !* אוֹיָה, אוֹי (ψ 120⁵),
אִי (in Ec 4¹⁰ אִי־לָךְ ; אִילוֹ 10¹⁶) *woe !*

2. Others, however, originally expressed independent ideas, and *b*
become interjections only by rapid pronunciation and by usage, e. g.
הֵן (הֵא) or הִנֵּה *behold !* (prop. *here*) ; רְאֵה *behold !* (prop. imperative) ;
הָבָה, plur. הָבוּ (prop. *give*, imperative of יָהַב ; as to the tone, cf. § 69*o*),
come, the Latin *age, agite !* לְכָה (also לֵךְ), לְכוּ (prop. *go*, imperative
of הָלַךְ) with the same meaning¹ ; חָלִ֫ילָה *far be it !* (prop. *ad profanum !*)

---

¹ רְאֵה (Dt 1⁸), הָבָה and לְכָה are also used in connexion with the feminine
and the plural, which proves that they have become quite stereotyped as
interjections.

בְּ (see the Lexicon) *I beseech, hear me!* נָא *pray!* [1] used to emphasize a demand, warning, or entreaty, and always placed after the expression to which it belongs.[2]

---

[1] נָא serves to express the most various shades of expression, which are discussed in the various parts of the syntax. It is used especially (*a*) after the *imperative*, either in commands or entreaty, see § 110 *d*; (*b*) with the *imperfect*, either in the cohortative (§ 108 *b*) or jussive (§ 109 *b*); (*c*) once with *perfect*, Gn 40[14]; (*d*) after various particles: הִנֵּה־נָא *behold now*; particularly after the conjunctions אַל and אִם: אַל־נָא *ne quaeso* and אִם־נָא *if now*, εἴπερ, εἴποτε, *if*, in a deprecatory sense, expressive of politeness or modesty. In Nu 12[13] נָא stands after a noun; but we ought certainly to read אַל־נָא.— In polite language this particle is used constantly in all these ways, Gn 18[3.4], 19[7.8.19], and 50[17].

[2] Against the usual view which regards נָא as a hortatory particle (= *up! come!* analogous to the original imperatives הָבָה and לְכָה and the Ethiopic *nǎʿâ*, properly *hither*, also *come!*), P. Haupt, in the *Johns Hopkins University Circulars*, xiii, no. 114, p. 109, justly observes that we should then expect the particle to be *prefixed* to the imperative, &c. He proposes to describe נָא as an emphatic particle. Haupt's suggested identification of this נָא with the Assyrian, Arabic, and Ethiopic particle *mā* (which is also an enclitic of emphasis), and ultimately with the interrogative *mā*, we shall not discuss here.

THIRD PART

SYNTAX[1]

CHAPTER I

THE PARTS OF SPEECH

I. Syntax of the Verb.

A. USE OF THE TENSES AND MOODS.[2]

§ 106. *Use of the Perfect.*

The perfect serves to express actions, events, or states, which the *a* speaker wishes to represent from the point of view of completion, whether they belong to a determinate past time, or extend into the present, or, while still future, are pictured as in their completed state.

The definition formerly given here ('the perfect serves to express *completed* actions') applies, strictly speaking, only to some of the varieties of the perfect discussed under *b–p*: hence the above modification based on the arguments of Knudtzon (for the title see note 2, and cf. further § 107 *a*).

More particularly the uses of the perfect may be distinguished as follows :—

1. To represent actions, events, or states, which, after a shorter *b*

---

[1] Recent works on Hebrew syntax are: A. B. Davidson, *Introductory Heb. Gram.*, vol. ii, *Heb. Syntax*, Edinburgh, 1894; Ed. König. *Hist.-compar. Syntax der hebr. Sprache*, Lpz. 1897 (see above, § 3 *f*). Important contributions to Hebrew syntax are also contained in H. Reckendorf's work *Die syntakt. Verhältnisse des Arab.*, 2 pts., Leiden, 1895, 1898, of which we have already made use in § 97 *a*. Cf. also the same author's very instructive discussions *Ueber syntakt. Forschung*, Munich, 1899.

[2] Cf. the sketch of the tenses and moods used in Hebrew in § 40; and on the general characteristics of the perfect and imperfect see the note on § 47 *a*; also Driver, *A Treatise on the Use of the Tenses in Hebrew* (Oxford, 1874; 3rd ed. 1892); Bennett, 'Notes on the Use of the Hebrew Tenses' (*Hebraica*, 1886, vols. ii, iii). A partial modification of the accepted definition of the Semitic perfect and imperfect was proposed by J. A. Knudtzon, *Om det saakaldte Perfektum og Imperfektum i Hebraisk*, Kristiania, 1890; of which a summary entitled 'Vom sogenannten Perf. und Imperf. im Hebr.' appeared in the *Transactions of the Oriental Congress at Stockholm*, section sémitique *b*, p. 73 ff. (Leiden, 1893). Cf. also Knudtzon's articles, 'Zur assyrischen und allgemein semitischen Grammatik' in the *Zeitschrift für Assyriologie*, especially vi. 422 ff. and vii. 33 ff.

or longer duration, were terminated in the past, and hence are finally concluded, viz.:

(*a*) Corresponding to the perfect proper in Latin and the English perfect definite, in assertions, negations, confirmations, interrogations, &c., e.g. Gn 18¹⁵ *then Sarah denied, saying, I laughed not* (לֹא צָחַקְתִּי)......; *and he said, Nay, but thou didst laugh* (צָחָקְתְּ); Gn 3¹¹ מִי הִגִּיד לָךְ *who told thee* . . . . ? Cf. 3¹³·¹⁴·¹⁷·²². Also pointing to some undefined time in the past, e.g. Is 66⁸ מִי־שָׁמַע כָּזֹאת *who hath* (*ever yet*) *heard such a thing* ?

c Rem. In opposition to this express use of the perfect to emphasize the completion of an event, the imperfect is not infrequently used to emphasize that which is still future, e.g. Jos 1⁵ *as I was* (הָיִיתִי) *with Moses, so will I be* (אֶהְיֶה) *with thee;* Jos 1¹⁷, Ex 10¹⁴, Dt 32²¹, 1 K 2³⁸, Is 46⁴·¹¹, Jo 2², Ec 1⁹.

d (*b*) As a simple *tempus historicum* (corresponding to the Greek aorist) in narrating past events, e.g. Gn 4⁴ *and Abel, he also brought* (הֵבִיא), &c.; Gn 7¹⁹ *the waters did prevail* (גָּבְרוּ), &c.; Jb 1¹ *there was a man* (אִישׁ הָיָה) *in the land of Uz*, &c.; even in relating repeated actions, 1 S 18³⁰.

e Rem. As the above examples indicate, the perfect of *narration* occurs especially at the head of an entire narrative (Jb 1¹; cf. Dn 2¹) or an independent sentence (e.g. Gn 7¹¹·¹³), but in co-ordinate sentences, as a rule, only when the verb is separated from the copulative ו by one or more words (cf. above Gn 4⁴ and 7¹⁹). In other cases, the narrative is continued in the imperfect consecutive, according to § 111 *a*. The direct connexion of the narrative perfect with ו copulative (not to be confounded with the perfect consecutive proper, § 112) agrees rather with Aramaic syntax (cf. Kautzsch, *Gramm. des Biblisch-Aram.*, § 71, 1 *b*). On the examples (which are in many respects doubtful) in the earlier texts, see § 112 *pp–uu*.

f (*c*) To represent actions, &c., which were already completed in the past, at the time when other actions or conditions took place (pluperfect),[1] e.g. 1 S 28³ *now Samuel was* (*long since*) *dead*[2] ... *and Saul had put away* (הֵסִיר) *those that had familiar spirits* ... *out of the land.* Both these statements, being as it were in parentheses, merely assign a reason for the narrative beginning at verse 6. Cf. 1 S 9¹⁵, 25²¹, 2 S 18¹⁸.—Gn 20¹⁸ (*for the Lord had fast closed up*, &c.); 27³⁰, 31¹⁹·³⁴, Dt 2¹⁰; and in a negative statement, Gn 2⁵ *for the Lord God had not* (up to that time) *caused it to rain*, &c. This is especially frequent, from the nature of the case, in relative, causal, and temporal clauses, when the main clause contains a tense referring to the past, e.g. Gn 2² *and he rested* ... *from all his work which he had made* (עָשָׂה); Gn 7⁹,

---

[1] Cf. P. Haupt in the *Notes on Esther*, 9².

[2] Incorrectly, e.g. in the Vulgate, *Samuel autem mortuus est* ... *et Saul abstulit magos*, &c.

19²⁷, &c.; 29¹⁰ *now when Jacob had seen Rachel* (כַּאֲשֶׁר רָאָה) . . . , *Jacob went near*, &c.; so also in clauses which express the completion or incompleteness of one action, &c., on the occurrence of another, as in Gn 24¹⁵, 27³⁰, &c.; cf. § 164 *b*, with the note, and *c*.

2. To represent actions, events, or states, which, although completed *g* in the past, nevertheless extend their influence into the present (in English generally rendered by the present):

(*a*) Expressing facts which were accomplished long before, or conditions and attributes which were acquired long before, but of which the effects still remain in the present (present perfect), e. g. ψ 10¹¹ הִסְתִּיר פָּנָיו *he hath hidden his face* (*and still keeps it hidden*); ψ 143⁶ פֵּרַשְׂתִּי *I have spread forth my hands* (*and still keep them spread forth*). This applies particularly to a large number of perfects (almost exclusively of intransitive¹ verbs, denoting affections or states of the mind) which in English can be rendered only by the present, or, in the case mentioned above under *f*, by the imperfect.² Thus, יָדַעְתִּי *I know* (prop. *I have perceived, have experienced*) Jb 9², 10¹³, לֹא יָדַעְתִּי *I know not* Gn 4⁹, &c.; on the other hand, e. g. in Gn 28¹⁶, Nu 22³⁴, the context requires *I knew not*; זָכַרְנוּ *we remember* Nu 11⁵; מֵאֲנָה *she refuseth* Jb 6⁷; עָלַץ *it exulteth*; שָׂמַחְתִּי *I rejoice* 1 S 2¹; בִּקֵּשׁ *he requireth* Is 1¹²; קִוִּיתִי *I wait* Gn 49¹⁸, ψ 130⁵ (parallel with הוֹחָלְתִּי); חָפַצְתִּי *I delight* ψ 40⁹ (mostly negative, Is 1¹¹, &c.); אָהַבְתִּי *I love* Gn 27⁴; שָׂנֵאתִי *I hate* ψ 31⁷; מָאַסְתִּי *I despise* Am 5²¹; תְּעֵבוּנִי *they abhor me* Jb 30¹⁰; בָּטַחְתִּי *I trust* ψ 25²; חָסִיתִי *I put my trust* ψ 31²; צָדַקְתִּי *I am righteous* Jb 34⁵; פָּקַדְתִּי *I have decided to requite* 1 S 15².—We may further include a number of verbs which express bodily characteristics or states, such as גָּדַלְתָּ *thou art great* ψ 104¹; קָטֹנְתִּי *I am little* Gn 32¹¹; גָּבְהוּ *they are high* Is 55⁹; רָחֵקוּ *they stand aloof* Jb 30¹⁰; טֹבוּ *they are goodly* Nu 24⁵; נָאווּ *they are beautiful* Is 52⁷; זָקַנְתִּי *I am old* Gn 18¹³; יָגַעְתִּי *I am weary* ψ 6⁷; שָׂבַעְתִּי *I am full* Is 1¹¹, &c.

Rem. To the same category probably belong also the perfects after עַד־מָתַי *h* Ex 10³ *how long hast thou* already *been refusing* (and refusest still . . . ? which really amounts to *how long wilt thou refuse ?*), ψ 80⁵, Pr 1²² (co-ordinate with the imperf.), and after עַד־אָנָה Ex 16²⁸, Hb 1².

(*b*) In direct narration to express actions which, although really *i* only in process of accomplishment, are nevertheless meant to be repre-

---

¹ With regard to the great but very natural preponderance of intransitive verbs (expressing an existing state), cf. the lists in Knudtzon (see above, p. 309, note 2), pp. 117 and 122 in the Danish text.

² Cf. *novi, odi, memini;* οἶδα, μέμνημαι, ἔοικα, δέδορκα, κέκραγα; in the New Testament, ἤλπικα, ἠγάπηκα.

sented as already accomplished in the conception of the speaker, e. g.
הֲרִמֹ֫תִי *I lift up* (my hand in ratifying an oath) Gn 14²² ; נִשְׁבַּ֫עְתִּי *I swear*
Jer 22⁵ ; הַעִרֹ֫תִי *I testify* Dt 8¹⁹ ; יָעַ֫צְתִּי *I counsel* 2 S 17¹¹ (but in a
different context in ver. 15, *I have counselled*) ; אָמַ֫רְתִּי (prop. *I say*)
I decide (*I consider as hereby settled*) 2 S 19³⁰ ; *I declare* Jb 9²², 32¹⁰.

k   (*c*) To express facts which have formerly taken place, and are still
of constant recurrence, and hence are matters of common experience
(the Greek *gnomic aorist*), e. g. ψ 9¹¹ *for thou, Lord, hast not forsaken*
(לֹא־עָזַ֫בְתָּ) *them that seek thee.* Cf. ver. 13, also ψ 10³, 119⁴⁰ and Gn 49¹¹
(כִּבֵּס).

l   Rem. In almost all the cases discussed in No. 2 (included under the English
present) the imperfect can be used instead of the perfect, wherever the action
or state in question is regarded, not as already completed, but as still continuing or just taking place (see § 107 *a*). Thus, לֹא יָכֹ֫לְתִּי *I am not able* ψ 40¹³
and לֹא אוּכַל Gn 31³⁵ have practically the same meaning. Hence also it very
frequently happens that the imperfect corresponds to such perfects in poetic
or prophetic parallelism, e. g. Is 5¹², ψ 2¹ᶠ·, Pr 1²², Jb 3¹⁷.

m   3. To express *future* actions, when the speaker intends by an
express assurance to represent them as finished, or as equivalent to
accomplished facts :

   (*a*) In contracts or other express stipulations (again corresponding
to the English present, and therefore closely related to the instances
noted under *i*), e. g. Gn 23¹¹ *the field I give* (נָתַ֫תִּי) *thee* ; cf. ver. 13 and
48²², 2 S 14²¹, 24²³, Jer 40⁴ ; in a threat, 1 S 2¹⁶, 2 S 5⁶ (unless, with
Wellhausen, יְסִירְךָ is to be read).—Especially in promises made by God,
Gn 1²⁹, 15¹⁸, 17²⁰, Ju 1².

n   (*b*) To express facts which are undoubtedly imminent, and, therefore,
in the imagination of the speaker, already accomplished (*perfectum
confidentiae*), e. g. Nu 17²⁷ הֵן גָּוַ֫עְנוּ אָבַ֫דְנוּ כֻּלָּ֫נוּ אָבָ֫דְנוּ *behold, we perish, we
are undone, we are all undone.* Gn 30¹³, Is 6⁵ (נִדְמֵ֫יתִי *I am undone* [1]),
Pr 4². Even in interrogative sentences, Gn 18¹², Nu 17²⁸, 23¹⁰, Ju 9⁹·¹¹,
Zc 4¹⁰ (?), Pr 22²⁰. [2] This use of the perfect occurs most frequently in
prophetic language (*perfectum propheticum*). The prophet so trans-

---

[1] Cf. the similar use of ὄλωλα (διέφθορας, *Il.* 15. 128) and *perii!* On the
kindred use of the perfect in conditional sentences, cf. below, *p*.

[2] In Gn 40¹⁴ a *perf. confidentiae* (after כִּי אִם ; but cf. § 163 *d*) appears to be
used in the expression of an earnest desire that something may happen (*but
have me in thy remembrance,* &c.). Neither this passage, however, nor the use of
the perfect in Arabic to express a wish or imprecation, justifies us in assuming
the existence of a *precative* perfect in Hebrew. In Jb 21¹⁶, 22¹⁸, also, translate
the counsel of the wicked is far from me. Cf. Driver, *Tenses*³, p. 25 f. In Is 43⁹
either נִקְבְּצוּ is *imperative* (see § 51 *o*) or we must read יִקָּבְצוּ, corresponding to
יֵאָסְפוּ which follows.

ports himself in imagination into the future that he describes the future event as if it had been already seen or heard by him, e.g. Is 5¹³ *there-fore my people are gone into captivity* (גָּלָה); 9¹ᶠᶠ·, 10²⁸, 11⁹ (after כִּי, as frequently elsewhere); 19⁷, Jb 5²⁰, 2 Ch 20³⁷. Not infrequently the imperfect interchanges with such perfects either in the parallel member or further on in the narrative.

(*c*) To express actions or facts, which are meant to be indicated as *o* existing in the future in a completed state (*futurum exactum*), e.g. Is 4⁴ אִם רָחַץ *when he has washed away*=*when he shall have washed away* (an *imperfect* follows in the co-ordinate sentence; cf. the con-ditional sentences in § 107 *x*); Is 6¹¹ (after עַד אֲשֶׁר אִם, as in Gn 28¹⁵, Nu 32¹⁷; also 2 S 17¹³ after עַד אֲשֶׁר, Gn 24¹⁹ after עַד אִם and elsewhere frequently after temporal conjunctions); Mi 5² (יֵלֵדָה); Gn 43¹⁴ וַאֲנִי כַּאֲשֶׁר שָׁכֹלְתִּי שָׁכָלְתִּי *and I—if I am bereaved* (*orbus fuero*), *I am bereaved,* an expression of despairing resignation. Cf. Pr 23¹⁵, Est 4¹⁶.

4. To express actions and facts, whose accomplishment in the past *p* is to be represented, not as actual, but only as possible (generally corresponding to the Latin imperfect or pluperfect subjunctive), e.g. Gn 31⁴² *except the God of my father . . . had been with me, surely now hadst thou sent me away empty* (שִׁלַּחְתָּנִי); Gn 43¹⁰, Ex 9¹⁵ שָׁלַחְתִּי *I had almost put forth,* &c.); Nu 22³³, Ju 13²³, 14¹⁸, 1 S 13¹³ (הֵכִין); 2 K 13¹⁹; so frequently after כִּמְעַט *easily, almost,* Gn 26¹⁰, Is 1⁹ (where כִּמְעַט is probably to be connected with the word after it), ψ 73², 94¹⁷, 119⁸⁷, Pr 5¹⁴. Cf. also Jb 3¹³, 23¹⁰ (בְּחָנַנִי), Ru 1¹² (*if I should think,* &c.; cf. 2 K 7⁴); in the apodosis of a conditional sentence, 1 S 25³⁴.—So also to express an unfulfilled desire, Nu 14² לוּ מַתְנוּ *would that we had died . . . !* (לוּ with the imperfect would mean *would that we might die!* 1 S 14³⁰). Finally, also in a question indicating astonishment, Gn 21⁷ מִי מִלֵּל *who would have said . . . ?   quis dixerit ?* ψ 73¹¹.

§ 107. *Use of the Imperfect.*[1]

The imperfect, as opposed to the perfect, represents actions, events, *a* or states which are regarded by the speaker at any moment as still continuing, or in process of accomplishment, or even as just taking place. In the last case, its occurrence may be represented as certainly imminent, or merely as conceived in the mind of the speaker, or simply as desired, and therefore only contingent (the modal use of the imperfect).

---

[1] Cf. the literature cited above, p. 309, note 2.

Knudtzon (see above, Rem. on § 106 *a*), comparing the Ass.-Bab. usage, would prefer the term *present* rather than imperfect, on the ground that the tense expresses what is either actually or mentally present. In any case, the essential difference between the perfect and imperfect consists, he argues, in this, that the perfect simply indicates what is actually complete, while the imperfect places the action, &c., in a more direct relation to the judgement or feeling of the speaker.

More precisely the imperfect serves—

1. In the sphere of *past time*:

b   (*a*) To express actions, &c., which *continued* throughout a longer or shorter period,[1] e. g. Gn 2⁶ *a mist went up* continually (יַעֲלֶה), 2²⁵, 3⁷, 48¹⁰, Ex 1¹², 8²⁰, 13²², 15⁶.¹².¹⁴.¹⁵, Nu 9¹⁵ ᶠ. ²⁰ ᶠ., 23⁷, Ju 2¹, 5⁸, 1 S 3², 13¹⁷ ᶠ., 2 S 2²⁸, 23¹⁰, 1 K 3⁴, 7⁸, 21⁶, Is 1²¹, 6⁴ (יֻפְלָא), 17¹⁰ ᶠ., 51² ², Jer 13⁷, 36¹⁸, ψ 18⁷.¹⁴.¹⁷ ᶠᶠ.³⁸ ᶠᶠ., 24², 32⁴.⁵ (אוֹדִיעֲךָ), 47⁵, 68¹⁰.¹², 104⁶ ᶠᶠ., 106¹⁹, 107¹⁸.²⁹, 139¹³, Jb 3¹¹, 4¹².¹⁵ ᶠ., 10¹⁰ ᶠ., 15⁷ ᶠ.—very frequently alternating with a perfect (especially with a frequentative perfect; cf. Nu 9¹⁵⁻²³ and § 112 *e*), or when the narration is continued by means of an imperfect consecutive.[2]

c   Rem. 1. The imperfect is frequently used in this way after the particles אָז *then*, טֶרֶם *not yet*, בְּטֶרֶם *before*, עַד־ *until*, e. g. Ex 15¹ אָז יָשִׁיר־מֹשֶׁה *then sang Moses*, &c.; Nu 21¹⁷, Dt 4⁴¹, Jos 10¹², 1 K 3¹⁶, 8¹, ψ 126², Jb 38²¹. (The *perfect* is used after אָז when stress is to be laid on the fact that the action has really taken place, and not upon its gradual accomplishment or duration in the past, e. g. Gn 4²⁶ אָז הוּחַל *then began*, &c.; Gn 49⁴, Ex 15¹⁵, Jos 22³¹, Ju 5¹¹, ψ 89²⁰.)[3] After טֶרֶם e. g. Gn 19⁴ טֶרֶם יִשְׁכָּבוּ *before they lay down*; Gn 2⁵, 24⁴⁵, 1 S 3³.⁷, always in the sense of our *pluperfect*. (In Gn 24¹⁵ instead of the perf. כִּלָּה, the imperf. should be read, as in verse 45; so also in 1 S 3⁷ [וּגְלָה] an imperf. is co-ordinated with יָדַע). After בְּטֶרֶם (sometimes also simply טֶרֶם Ex 12³⁴, Jos 3¹), e.g. Jer 1⁵ בְּטֶרֶם תֵּצֵא *before thou camest forth*; Gn 27³³, 37¹⁸, 41⁵⁰, Ru 3¹⁴ (perhaps also in ψ 90² an imperf. was intended instead of יֻלָּדוּ; cf. Wellhausen on 2 S 3²; but note also Pr 8²⁵, in a similar context, *before the mountains were settled*, הָטְבָּעוּ, the predicate being separated from בְּטֶרֶם by הָרִים, as in ψ 90²). After עַד־ Jos 10¹³, ψ 73¹⁷ (*until I went*), 2 Ch 29³⁴; on the other

---

[1] Cf. the Meša' inscription, l. 5, כי יאנף כמש בארצה *for Chemosh was angry with his land*. As Driver, *Tenses*, 3rd ed., § 27, 1 *a*, remarks, this vivid realization of the accomplishment of the action is especially frequent in poetic and prophetic style.

[2] According to the Masora such imperfects occur in Is 10¹³ ᵇⁱˢ (where, however, וְאָסִיר might also mean *I am wont to remove*, &c.), Is 45³, 57¹⁷, ψ 18³⁸ᵃ, also (according to § 49 *c*) in 2 S 1¹⁰ and Ez 16¹⁰. In some other cases וְ is no doubt a dogmatic emendation for וְ (*imperf. consec.*) in order to represent historical statements as promises; cf. Is 42⁶, 43²⁸ [contrasted with 42²⁵], 51² ᵇⁱˢ, 63³ ᶠᶠ. and the note on § 53 *p*.

[3] After אָז *then* (to announce future events) the imperf. is naturally used in the sense of a future, Gn 24⁴¹, Ex 12⁴⁸, Mi 3⁴, Zp 3⁹, ψ 51²¹.

hand, with the perf., e.g. Jos 2²². As after אָז, so also after בְּטֶרֶם, טֶרֶם, and עַד־ the imperf. may be used, according to the context, in the sense of our *future*, e.g. 2 K 2⁹, Is 65²⁴, Jb 10²¹; after עַד־ e.g. Is 22¹⁴. The imperf. is used in the sense of our *present* after טֶרֶם in Ex 9³⁰, 10⁷.

2. Driver (*Tenses*³, p. 35 f.) rightly lays stress upon the inherent distinction *d* between the *participle* as expressing *mere* duration, and the *imperfect* as expressing *progressive* duration (in the present, past, or future). Thus the words וְנָהָר יֹצֵא Gn 2¹⁰ represent the river of Paradise as going out of Eden in a continuous, uninterrupted stream, but יִפָּרֵד, which immediately follows, describes how the parting of its waters is always taking place afresh. In the same way יַעֲלֶה Gn 2⁶ represents new mists as constantly arising, and יִמָּלֵא Is 6⁴ new clouds of smoke. Also those actions, &c., which might be regarded in themselves as single or even momentary, are, as it were, broken up by the imperfect into their component parts, and so pictured as gradually completing themselves. Hence תְּבַלְעֵמוֹ Ex 15¹² (after a *perf.* as in verse 14) represents the Egyptians, in a vivid, poetic description, as being swallowed up one after another, and יַנְחֵנִי Nu 23⁷ the leading on by stages, &c.

(*b*) To express actions, &c., which were *repeated* in the past, either *e* at fixed intervals or occasionally (the *modus rei repetitae*), e.g. Jb 1⁵ *thus did* (יַעֲשֶׂה) *Job continually* (after each occasion of his sons' festivities); 4³ᶠ·, 22⁶ᶠ·, 23¹¹, 29⁷·⁹·¹²ᶠ·, Gn 6⁴, 29², 30·⁸, 42³¹·³⁹ (*I used to bear* the loss of it), Ex 1¹², 19¹⁹, 33⁷ᶠᶠ· (יִקַּח *used to take* every time), 40³⁶ᶠᶠ·, Nu 9¹⁷ᶠ·²⁰ᶠᶠ·, 11⁵·⁹, Ju 6⁴, 14¹⁰, 21²⁵, 1 S 1⁷, 2²², 9⁹, 13¹⁹, 18⁵, 27⁹, 2 S 1²², 12³, 13¹⁸, 1 K 5²⁵ (of tribute repeated year by year), 10⁵, 13³³, 14²⁸, 2 K 4⁸, 8²⁹, 13²⁰, 25¹⁴, Jer 36²³, ψ 42⁵, 44³, 78¹⁵·⁴⁰, 103⁷, Est 2¹⁴; even in a negative dependent clause, 1 K 18¹⁰.

2. In the sphere of *present time*, again   *f*

(*a*) To express actions, events, or states, which are *continued* for a shorter or longer time,¹ e.g. Gn 37¹⁵ מַה־תְּבַקֵּשׁ *what seekest thou?* 19¹⁹ לֹא־אוּכַל *I cannot*; 24⁵⁰, 31³⁵, Is 1¹³. Other examples are Gn 2¹⁰, 24³¹, 1 S 1⁸, 11⁵, 1 K 3⁷, ψ 2², and in the prophetic formula יֹאמַר יְהֹוָה *saith the Lord*, Is 1¹¹·¹⁸, &c., cf. 40¹. So especially to express facts known by experience, which occur at all times, and consequently hold good at any moment, e.g. Pr 15²⁰ *a wise son maketh a glad father*; hence especially frequent in Job and Proverbs. In an interrogative sentence, e.g. Jb 4¹⁷ *is mortal man just before God?* In a negative sentence, Jb 4¹⁸, &c.

(*b*) To express actions, &c., which may be *repeated* at any time, *g* including therefore the present, or are *customarily* repeated on a given occasion (cf. above, *e*), e.g. Dt 1⁴⁴ *as bees do* (are accustomed to

---

¹ It is not always possible to carry out with certainty the distinction between *continued* and *repeated* actions. Some of the examples given under *f* might equally be referred to *g*.

do); Gn 6²¹, 32³³, 43³², Ju 11⁴⁰, 1 S 2⁸, 5⁵, 20², 2 S 15³², Is 1²³, 3¹⁶, ψ 1³. So again (see *f*) especially to express facts known by experience which may at any time come into effect again, e. g. Ex 23⁸ *a gift blindeth* (יְעַוֵּר), &c.; Gn 2²⁴, 22¹⁴, Is 32⁶, Am 3⁷, Mal 1⁶, Jb 2⁴, &c. Of the same kind also is the imperfect in such relative clauses (see § 155), as Gn 49²⁷ *Benjamin is* זְאֵב יִטְרָף *a wolf that ravineth* (properly, is accustomed to ravin). Finally, compare also the formulae יֵאָמֵר *it is* (wont to be) *said* (to introduce proverbial expressions) Gn 10⁹, 22¹⁴, &c.; לֹא־יֵעָשֶׂה כֵן *it is not* (wont to be) *so done* (and hence *may not, shall not be*, see *u*), Gn 29²⁶, 20⁹, 34⁷, 2 S 13¹².

h (*c*) To express actions, &c., which although, strictly speaking, they are already finished, are regarded as still lasting on into the present time, or continuing to operate in it, e. g. Gn 32³⁰ *wherefore is it that thou dost ask* (תִּשְׁאַל) *after my name?* 24³¹, 44⁷, Ex 5¹⁵, 2 S 16⁹. In such cases, naturally, the perfect is also admissible, and is sometimes found in the same formula as the imperfect, e. g. Jb 1⁷ (2²) מֵאַיִן תָּבֹא *whence comest thou* (just now)? but Gn 16⁸ (cf. 42⁷) אֵי־מִזֶּה בָאת *whence camest thou?* The imperfect represents the coming as still in its last stage, whereas the perfect represents it as an accomplished fact.

i 3. In the sphere of *future time*. To express actions, &c., which are to be represented as about to take place, and as continuing a shorter or longer time in the future, or as being repeated; thus:

(*a*) From the standpoint of the speaker's present time, e. g. Ex 4¹ *they will not believe* (יַאֲמִינוּ) *me, nor hearken* (יִשְׁמְעוּ) *unto my voice: for they will say* (יֹאמְרוּ), &c., 6¹, 9⁵, &c.

k (*b*) In dependent clauses to represent actions, &c., which from some point of time in the past are to be represented as future, e. g. Gn 43⁷ could we in any wise know *that he would say* (יֹאמַר)? 2¹⁹, 43²⁵, Ex 2⁴, 2 K 3²⁷ אֲשֶׁר־יִמְלֹךְ *qui regnaturus erat*; 13¹⁴, Jon 4⁵, Jb 3³, Ec 2³, ψ 78⁶ *that the generation to come might know*, בָּנִים יִוָּלֵדוּ *the children which should be born* (*qui nascituri essent*); the imperfect here with the collateral idea of the occurrence being repeated in the future).

l (*c*) To represent a *futurum exactum*; cf. Is 4⁴, 6¹¹ (co-ordinated with a perfect used in the same sense, see § 106 *o*); so also sometimes after the temporal particles עַד, ψ 132⁵, and עַד אֲשֶׁר *until*, Gn 29⁸, Nu 20¹⁷, &c.

m 4. Finally to the sphere of future time belong also those cases in which the (modal) imperfect serves to express actions, events, or states, the occurrence of which is to be represented as willed (or not willed), or as in some way conditional, and consequently only contingent. More particularly such imperfects serve—

(a) As an expression of will, whether it be a definite intention and *n* arrangement, or a simple desire, viz.:

(1) Sometimes in positive sentences in place of the cohortative (cf. e. g. ψ 59¹⁷ with verse 18; 2 S 22⁵⁰ with ψ 18⁵⁰; Ju 19¹¹, &c.), of the imperative (Is 18³), or of the jussive (which, however, in most cases, does not differ from the ordinary form of the imperfect), e. g. תֵּרָאֶה *let it appear* Gn 1⁹, 41³⁴, Lv 19²·³, 2 S 10¹² (and so frequently in verbs ל"ה; cf. § 109 *a*, note 2); Zc 9⁵ (תָּחִיל); ψ 61⁷ (תּוֹסִיף); Pr 22¹⁷ (תָּשִׁית); 23¹, Jb 6²³ (co-ordinated with the imperative), 10²⁰ *Keth.*; so probably also יָדִין *let him judge!* ψ 72².—So also in the 1st pers., to express a wish which is asserted subsequently with reference to a fixed point of time in the past, e. g. Jb 10¹⁸ אֶגְוַע *I ought to* [not *should* as A.V., R.V.] *have*, (then,·immediately after being born) *given up the ghost*; cf. verse 19 אֶהְיֶה and אוּבַל Lv 10¹⁸, Nu 35²⁸. Even to express an obligation or necessity according to the judgement of another person, e. g. Jb 9²⁹ אֶרְשָׁע *I am to be guilty*, 12⁴. Cp. Jb 9¹⁵, 19¹⁶; in a question, ψ 42¹⁰, 43².

(2) To express the definite expectation that something will not *o* happen. The imperfect with לֹא represents a more emphatic form of prohibition than the jussive [1] with אַל־ (cf. § 109 *c*), and corresponds to our *thou shalt not do it!* with the strongest expectation of obedience, while אַל־ with the jussive is rather a simple warning, *do not that!* Thus לֹא with the imperfect is especially used in enforcing the divine commands, e. g. לֹא תִגְנֹב *thou shalt not steal* Ex 20¹⁵; cf. verses 3, 4, 5, 7, 10 ff. So לֹא with the 3rd pers. perhaps in Pr 16¹⁰.

Rem. The *jussive*, which is to be expected after אַל־, does not, as a rule *p* (according to *n*, and § 109 *a*, note 2), differ in form from the simple imperfect. That many supposed jussives are intended as simple imperfects is possible from the occurrence after אַל־ of what are undoubtedly imperfect forms, not only from verbs ל"ה (cf. § 109 *a*, note 2), but also from verbs ע"ו, to express a prohibition or negative wish, אַל־נָא יָשִׂים 1 S 25²⁵, אַל־תָּסֻר Jos 1⁷, אַל־תָּבִיט Gn 19¹⁷, 1 S 25²⁵. Even with the 1st pers. plur. (after an imperative) וְאַל־נָמוּת *that we die not*, 1 S 12¹⁹. Also to express the conviction that something cannot happen, אַל־יָנוּם *he will not slumber*,[2] ψ 121³; cf. Jer 46⁶, 2 Ch 14¹⁰.

---

[1] As stated in § 46 *a*, a prohibition cannot be expressed by אַל־ and the imperative.

[2] To regard this as an optative (so Hupfeld) is from the context impossible. It is more probably a strong pregnant construction, or fusion of two sentences (such as, *do not think he will slumber!*). Verse 4 contains the objective confirmation, by means of לֹא with the imperf., of that which was previously only a subjective conviction.

q   (3) In dependent clauses after final conjunctions (§ 165 *b*), as אֲשֶׁר, Gn 11⁷ (אֲשֶׁר לֹא יִשְׁמְעוּ *that they may not understand*); בַּעֲבוּר Gn 21³⁰, 27⁴·¹⁹, Ex 9¹⁴, &c.; לְמַעַן אֲשֶׁר Nu 17⁵; לְמַעַן Dt 4¹, ψ 51⁶, 78⁶, and יַעַן אֲשֶׁר ¹ Ez 12¹², *in order that* ²; לְבִלְתִּי *that . . . not*, Ex 20²⁰, 2 S 14¹⁴; also after פֶּן *that not, lest*, Gn 3²², 11⁴, 19¹⁵, &c.³; cf. also the instances introduced by וְלֹא in § 109 *g*.—In Lv 9⁶ such an imperfect (or jussive? see the examples in § 109 *f*) is added to the expression of the command by an asyndeton, and in La 1¹⁹ to the principal clause simply by וְ: *while they sought them food* וְיָשִׁיבוּ אֶת־נַפְשָׁם *to refresh their souls* (cf. also La 3²⁶, *it is good and let him hope*, i. e. *that he should hope*); so after an interrogative clause, Ex 2⁷. Finally also in a relative clause, ψ 32⁸ בְּדֶרֶךְ־זוּ תֵלֵךְ *in the way which thou shouldst go.*

r   (*b*) To express actions, &c., which are to be represented as possibly taking place or not taking place (sometimes corresponding to the *potential* of the classical languages, as also to our periphrases with *can, may, should* ⁴). More particularly such imperfects are used—

s   (1) In a permissive sense, e. g. Gn 2¹⁶ *of every tree of the garden* (אָכֹל תֹּאכֵל) *thou mayest freely eat* (the opposite in verse 17); 3², 42³⁷, Lv 21³·²², Jb 21³. In the 1st pers. ψ 5⁸, 22¹⁸ (*I may, or can, tell*); in a negative sentence, e. g. ψ 5⁵.

t   (2) In interrogative sentences, e. g. Pr 20⁹ מִי־יֹאמַר *quis dixerit?* Cf. Gn 17¹⁷, 18¹⁴, 31⁴³, 1 S 11¹², 2 K 5¹² הֲלֹא־אֶרְחַץ בָּהֶם *may I not wash in them?* Is 33¹⁴, ψ 15¹, 24³, Ec 5⁵. So especially in a question expressing surprise after אֵיךְ, e. g. Gn 39⁹ *how then can I . . . ?* 44³⁴, Is 19¹¹, ψ 137⁴, and even with regard to some point of time in the past, looking forward from which an event might have been expected to take place, e. g. Gn 43⁷ הֲיָדוֹעַ נֵדַע *could we in any wise know . . . ?* Cf. 2 S 3³³ (יָמוּת) *was Abner to die as a fool*, i. e. *was he destined to die . . . ?*), and so probably also Gn 34³¹ (*should he deal . . . ?*). Very closely connected with this is the use of the imperfect—

u   (3) In a consecutive clause depending on an interrogative clause, e. g. Ex 3¹¹, *who am I* (כִּי אֵלֵךְ) *that I should* (*ought, could*) *go?* 16⁷, Nu 11¹², Ju 9²³, 1 S 18¹⁸, 2 K 8¹³, Is 29¹⁶, Jb 6¹¹, 21¹⁵, similarly after אֲשֶׁר Gn 38¹⁸, Ex 5².

---

¹ But יַעַן אֲשֶׁר in a causal sense (*because, since*), e. g. Ju 2²⁰ (as אֲשֶׁר Gn 34²⁷) is followed by the perfect. On Jos 4²⁴ see above, § 74 *g*.

[² R.V. *because he shall not see.*]

³ In 2 K 2¹⁶ פֶּן occurs with the perf. in a vivid presentment of the time when the fear is realized and the remedy comes too late. (In 2 S 2c⁶, since a *perfect consec.* follows, read with Driver יִמְצָא.)

⁴ By this, of course, is not meant that these finer distinctions were consciously present to the Hebrew mind. They are rather mere expedients for making intelligible to ourselves the full significance of the Semitic imperfect.

Rem. In passages like 1 S 11⁵, ψ 8⁵, 114⁵, the context shows that the imperfect corresponds rather to our present. In such sentences the perfect also is naturally used in referring to completed actions, e. g. Gn 20¹⁰, Ju 18²³, 2 S 7¹⁸, Is 22¹.

(4) In *negative sentences* to express actions, &c., which cannot or should not happen, e. g. Gn 32¹³ אֲשֶׁר לֹא־יִסָּפֵר מֵרֹב *which cannot be numbered for multitude*; 20⁹ *deeds* (אֲשֶׁר לֹא־יֵעָשׂוּ) *that ought not to be done* (cf. above, *g*); ψ 5⁵.

(5) In *conditional clauses* (the *modus conditionalis* corresponding to the Latin present or imperfect conjunctive) both in the protasis and apodosis, or only in the latter, ψ 23⁴ לֹא־אִירָא רָע . . . גַּם כִּי־אֵלֵךְ *yea, though I walk* (or *had to walk*) . . . *I fear* (or *I would fear*) *no evil*; Jb 9²⁰ *though I be righteous, mine own mouth shall condemn me*. After a perfect in the protasis, e. g. Jb 23¹⁰. Very frequently also in an apodosis, the protasis to which must be supplied from the context, e. g. Jb 5⁸ *but as for me, I would seek unto God* (were I in thy place); 3¹³·¹⁶, 14¹⁴ᶠ, ψ 55¹³, Ru 1¹². However, some of the imperfects in these examples are probably intended as jussive forms. Cf. § 109 *h*.

§ 108. *Use of the Cohortative.*

The cohortative, i. e. according to § 48 *c*, the 1st pers.[1] sing. or plur. of the imperfect lengthened by the ending הָ‐,[2] represents in general an endeavour directed expressly towards a definite object. While the corresponding forms of the indicative rather express the mere announcement that an action will be undertaken, the cohortative lays stress on the determination underlying the action, and the personal interest in it.

Its uses may be divided into—

1. The cohortative standing alone, or co-ordinated with another cohortative, and frequently strengthened by the addition of the particle נָא:

(*a*) To express self-encouragement, e. g. Ex 3³ אָסֻרָה־נָּא וג' *I will turn aside now, and see . . .!* So especially as the result of inward deliberation (in soliloquies), e. g. Gn 18²¹, 32²¹ (rarely so used after אֶל־, Gn 21¹⁶ *let me not look . . .!* Jer 18¹⁸), and also as a more or less emphatic statement of a fixed determination, e. g. Is 5¹ *I will sing*[3] . . .! 5⁶, 31⁸. Cf. also Gn 46³⁰ *now let me die (I am willing to die)*,

---

[1] For the few examples of cohortatives in the 3rd sing., see § 48 *d*.

[2] But verbs ל״ה, according to § 75 *l*, even in the cohortative, almost always have the ending הֶ‐ ; cf. e. g. in Dt 32²⁰ אֶרְאֶה after אַסְתִּירָה.

[3 R.V. *let me sing*.]

since I have seen thy face; and ψ 31⁸. In the 1st pers. plur. the cohortative includes a summons to others to help in doing something, e. g. ψ 2³ נְנַתְּקָה *come! let us break asunder!* &c., and Gn 11³.

c (b) To express a wish, or a request for permission, that one should be allowed to do something, e. g. Dt 2²⁷ אֶעְבְּרָה *may I be allowed to pass through* (*let me pass through*)! Nu 20¹⁷ נַעְבְּרָה־נָּא *may we be allowed to pass through!* Jer 40¹⁵ *let me go, I pray thee!* &c.; 2 S 16⁹; so after לֹא 2 S 18¹⁴; after אַל־ 2 S 24¹⁴, Jer 17¹⁸, ψ 25² (אַל־אֵבוֹשָׁה *let me not be ashamed*; cf. ψ 31²,¹⁸, 71¹); 69¹⁵. After אַל־נָא Jon 1¹⁴.

d 2. The cohortative in dependence on other moods, as well as in conditional sentences: (a) In dependence (with *wāw copulative*; ψ 9¹⁵ after לְמַעַן) on an imperative or jussive to express an intention or intended consequence, e. g. Gn 27⁴ *bring it to me*, וְאֹכֵלָה *that I may eat*, prop. *then will I eat*; Gn 19⁵, 23⁴, 24⁵⁶, 27²⁵, 29²¹, 30²⁵ᶠ·, 42³⁴, 49¹, Dt 32¹, Ho 6¹, ψ 2⁸, 39¹⁴, Jb 10²⁰ Qᵉrê; Is 5¹⁹ *and let the counsel of the Holy One of Israel draw nigh and come*, וְנֵדְעָה *that we may know* (*it*)! Gn 26²⁸, 1 S 27⁵. Also after negative sentences, Gn 18³⁰·³², Ju 6³⁹, and after interrogative sentences, 1 K 22⁷, Is 40²⁵, 41²⁶, Am 8⁵.

e (b) In conditional sentences (with or without אִם) to express a contingent intention, e. g. Jb 16⁶ אִם־אֲדַבְּרָה *should I determine to speak, my grief is not assuaged*, וְאַחְדְּלָה *and should I forbear, what am I eased?* without אִם Jb 19¹⁸, 30²⁶ (where, however, וְאִיחַלָה is probably intended); ψ 73¹⁶ (unless וָאֵח' should be read), 139⁸ᶠ·. After the 3rd person, Jb 11¹⁷ *though it be dark*, &c. So perhaps also 2 S 22³⁸ אֶרְדְּפָה *if I determined to pursue, then . . .*, but cf. ψ 18³⁸.

f (c) Likewise in the apodosis of conditional sentences, e. g. Jb 31¹ᶠ· *if my step hath turned out of the way . . .*, אֶזְרָעָה *then let me sow*; cf. 16⁴ᶠ· *I also could speak as ye do, if . . . . !* So even when the condition must be supplied from the context, e. g. ψ 40⁶ *else would I declare and speak of them*; 51¹⁸ *else would I* (*gladly*) *give it*, i. e. if thou didst require it (cf. the precisely similar וְאֶשָּׂא ψ 55¹³); Jb 6¹⁰. In the 1st plur. Jer 20¹⁰. To the same category belong the cohortatives after the formula expressing a wish מִי־יִתְּנֵנִי, מִי־יִתֵּן, e. g. Jer 9¹ *oh, that I had . . .*, וְאֶעֶזְבָה *then* (i. e. if I had) *should I* (or *would I*) *leave my people*, &c.; Ju 9²⁹; without *Wāw* Is 27⁴, ψ 55⁷, Jb 23⁴ (cf. also verse 7).

g Rem. 1. The question, whether a resolution formed under compulsion (a *necessity*) is also expressed by the cohortative (so, according to the prevailing opinion, in Is 38¹⁰ אֵלֵכָה; Jer 3²⁵, 4¹⁹·²¹, 6¹⁰, ψ 55³·¹⁸ (?); 57⁵, where, however, with Hupfeld, שָׁכְבָה should be read; 77⁷, 88¹⁶, and in the 1st plur. Is 59¹⁰), is to be answered in the sense that in these examples the cohortative *form* is used after its meaning has become entirely lost, merely for the sake of its fuller sound, instead of the ordinary imperfect. This view is strongly supported by the rather numerous examples of cohortative forms after *wāw consec.* of the imperfect (cf. § 49 *e*, as also ψ 66⁶ שָׁם נִשְׂמְחָה *there did we rejoice* ¹; ψ 119¹⁶³ וָאֶתְעֵבָה; Pr 7⁷), which can likewise only be explained as forms chosen merely for euphony, and therefore due to considerations of rhythm.

2. The cohortative is strange after עַד־ ψ 73¹⁷ *until I went* . . . אָבִינָה *I con-* *h* *sidered their latter end*; possibly a pregnant construction for 'until I made up my mind, saying, I will consider', &c. (but אָבִינָה Pr 7⁷ is still dependent on the preceding וְ); עַד־אֲרֻגִּיעָה Pr 12¹⁹ is at any rate to be explained in the same way (in Jer 49¹⁹, 50⁴⁴ we have כִּי־א׳ with a similar meaning), *as long as I* (intentionally) *wink with the eyelashes* (shall wink). On the other hand, in Ex 32³⁰ אֲכַפֵּר is to be read, with the Samaritan, instead of אֲכַפְּרָה after אוּלַי.

§ 109. *Use of the Jussive.*

As the *cohortative* is used in the 1st pers., so the *jussive* is especially *a* found in the 2nd and 3rd pers. sing. and plur. to express a more or less definite desire that something should or should not happen (cf. for its form, which frequently coincides with that of the ordinary *imperfect*,² § 48 *f*, *g*). More particularly its uses may be distinguished as follows:

1. The *jussive* standing alone, or co-ordinated with another jussive:

(*a*) In affirmative sentences to express a command, a wish (or a *b* blessing), advice, or a request; in the last case (the optative or precative) it is frequently strengthened by the addition of נָא. Examples: Gn 1³ יְהִי אוֹר *let there be light!* Gn 1⁶·⁹·¹¹, &c. (the creative commands); Nu 6²⁶ *the Lord lift up his countenance upon thee, and give thee peace!* cf. verse 25. After particles expressing a wish, Gn 30³⁴ לוּ יְהִי *I would it might be;* ψ 81⁹ אִם־תִּשְׁמַע־לִי *if thou wouldest hearken unto me!* As a humble request, Gn 44³³ . . . יֵשֶׁב־נָא עַבְדְּךָ . . . וְהַנַּעַר יַעַל *let thy servant, I pray thee, abide,* &c., *and let the lad go up,* &c., Gn 47⁴.

(*b*) In negative sentences to express prohibition or dissuasion, *c* warning, a negative wish (or imprecation), and a request. The prohibitive particle used before the jussive (according to § 107 *o*) is almost always אַל־ (in negative desires and requests frequently

---

¹ Analogous to this cohortative (as equivalent to the imperfect) after שָׁם is the use of the historic imperf. after אָז, § 107 *c*.

² With regard to verbs ל״ה, it is true that the full form of the imperfect is frequently used with the meaning of the jussive (as also for the cohortative, see § 108 *a*, note 2), e.g. אַל־יִרְאֶה Jb 3⁹ (but previously יְקַו *let it look for!*): especially *in* (Neh 2³) and immediately *before* the principal pause, Gn 1⁹ תֵּרָאֶה; Ju 6³⁹ יִהְיֶה, but previously יְהִי־נָא; Is 47³ תֵּרָאֶה, previously תִּגָּל; ψ 109⁷. On the attempt to distinguish such jussives from the imperfect by means of a special meaning הָ—, see § 75 *hh*.

אַל־נָא); e.g. Ex 34³ אִישׁ אַל־יֵרָא *neither let any man be seen!* Pr 3⁷ *be not* (אַל־תְּהִי) *wise in thine own eyes!* Jb 15³¹ אַל־יַאֲמֵן *ne confidat.* In the form of a request (prayer), Dt 9²⁶ אַל־תַּשְׁחֵת *destroy not!* 1 K 2²⁰, ψ 27⁹, 69¹⁸.

d　Rem. I. The few examples of לֹא with the jussive could at most have arisen from the attempt to moderate subsequently by means of the jussive (voluntative) form what was at first intended to be a strict command (לֹא with imperf. indic.); probably, however, they are either cases in which the defective writing has been misunderstood (as in 1 K 2⁶, Ez 48¹⁴), or (as in Gn 24⁸) instances of the purely rhythmical jussive form treated below, under *k*. Moreover, cf. לֹא יוֹסֵף Jo 2² and from the same verb Gn 4¹² (unless it is to be referred to *h*) and Dt 13¹. The same form, however, appears also to stand three times for the cohortative (see below), and in Nu 22¹⁹ for the ordinary imperfect (but see below, *i*). Thus it is doubtful whether an imaginary by-form of the ordinary imperf. is not intended by the Masora in all these cases, and whether consequently יוֹסֵף, &c., should not be restored.—On לְאֹ־תָחוּם עֵינֶךָ, &c., Dt 7¹⁶, 13⁹, &c., Ez 5¹¹, &c., cf. § 72 *r*, according to which תָחֹם should probably be read in every case.—The jussive appears in the place of the cohortative after לֹא 1 S 14³⁶ (וְלֹא־נַשְׁאַר co-ordinated with two cohortatives), 2 S 17¹²; cf. Is 41²³ *Keth.* (וְנֵרֶא, i.e. וְנֵרָא, after another cohortative); also (see above) לֹא אֹסֵף Dt 18¹⁶, Ho 9¹⁵, and even without לֹא Ez 5¹⁶.

e　2. אַל־ with the jussive (or imperf., cf. § 107 *p*) is used sometimes to express the conviction that something cannot or should not happen; cf. Is 2⁹ (where, however, the text is very doubtful) וְאַל־תִּשָּׂא לָהֶם *and thou canst not possibly forgive them* [R.V. *therefore forgive them not*]; ψ 34⁶, 41³, 50³, 121³ (אַל־יִתֵּן); Pr 3²⁵, Jb 5²² אַל־תִּירָא *neither needest thou be afraid;* 20¹⁷, 40³².

f　2. The jussive depending on other moods, or in conditional sentences: (*a*) Depending¹ (with *Wāw*) on an imperative or cohortative to express an intention or an assurance of a contingent occurrence, e.g. Gn 24⁵¹ *take her and go, and let her be* (וּתְהִי) prop. *and she will be*)...; 30³, 31³⁷, 38²⁴, Ex 8⁴, 9¹³, 10¹⁷, 14², Jos 4¹⁶, Ju 6³⁰, 1 S 5¹¹, 7³, 1 K 21¹⁰, ψ 144⁵, Pr 20²², Jb14⁶. Also after interrogative sentences, which include a demand, Est 7² (say) *what is thy desire...,* וְתֵעָשׂ *and it shall* (i.e. in order that it may) *be granted!* 1 K 22²⁰, Is 19¹², Jb 38³⁴ᶠ. Depending on a cohortative, e.g. Gn 19²⁰ אִמָּלְטָה נָּא שָׁמָּה *oh, let me escape thither...* וּתְחִי נַפְשִׁי *that my soul may live;* even after a simple imperf. (cf. below, *g*), 1 K 13³³ *whosoever would, he consecrated him...* וִיהִי *that he might be a priest* (read כֹּהֵן) *of the high places,* but probably the LXX reading וַיְהִי is to be preferred.

──────────

¹ This does not include the cases in which the jussive is not logically dependent on a preceding imperat., but is merely co-ordinated, e.g. Gn 20⁷, ψ 27¹⁴, &c.

Rem. In 2 Ch 35²¹ a negative final clause with וְאַל־ is dependent on an g
imperative, *forbear from* (meddling with) *God . . . that he destroy thee not.*
As a rule, however, negative final clauses are attached to the principal
sentence by means of וְלֹא and a following imperfect; so after an imperative,
Gn 42², 1 K 14², 18⁴⁴; after a jussive, Ex 30²⁰, Neh 6⁹; after a perfect consec.,
Ex 28³⁵·⁴³, 30¹², Nu 18⁵; after לֹא with an imperfect, Lv 10⁶, Nu 18³, Dt 17¹⁷
neither shall he multiply wives unto himself (וְלֹא יַסוּר לְבָבוֹ) *that his heart turn not
away*; 1 S 20¹⁴, 2 S 21¹⁷, Jer 11²¹; after אַל־ with jussive, Lv 10⁹, 11⁴³, 16²,
2 S 13²⁵, Jer 25⁶, 37²⁰, 38²⁴ ᶠ·; after the asseverative אִם with the impft., Gn 14²³;
even after a simple imperfect, Jer 10⁴ *with nails . . . they fasten it* (וְלֹא יָפִיק) *that
it move not*; after a participle, Jb 9⁷.

(*b*) Frequently in conditional sentences (as in Arabic), either in the h
protasis or in the apodosis, cf. ψ 45¹² יִתְאָו *should he desire . . . then . . .*;
104²⁰ וִיהִי . . . . תָּשֶׁת *if thou makest darkness, then it is night*; so also in
the protasis, Ex 22⁴, Lv 15²⁴, Is 41²⁸, Ez 14⁷ (וְיָעַל), Jb 34²⁹; in the
apodosis, Ex 7⁹ *then will it* (not, *then shall it*) *become a serpent*; Pr 9⁹
after an imperat. in the protasis; Jb 10¹⁶, 13⁵, 22²⁸. In a negative
apodosis, Gn 4¹² לֹא־תֹסֵף, but see above, *d*). In 2 K 6²⁷ אַל־יוֹשִׁעֵךְ (*if
the Lord do not help thee*, &c.) is to be explained as a jussive in
a negative protasis.

Rem. Undoubtedly this use of the jussive (in conditional sentences) is based i
on its original *voluntative* meaning; let something be so and so, then this or
that must happen as a consequence. Certain other examples of the *jussive*,
however, show that in the consciousness of the language the *voluntative* has
in such cases become weakened almost to a *potential* mood, and hence the
jussive serves to express facts which may happen *contingently*, or may be
expected, e. g. Nu 22¹⁹ (מַה־יֹּסֵף, but cf. above, *d*); Jb 9³³ *there is no daysman
betwixt us, that might lay* (יָשֵׁת, hence plainly a *subjunctive = qui ponat*; also in
Nu 23¹⁹ וִיכַזֵּב *that he should lie* is probably intended as a jussive); Ec 5¹⁴; so
after interrogative sentences, Jer 9¹¹ *who is the wise man*, וְיָבֵן *qui intelligat hoc?*;
Ho 14¹⁰.
Moreover, in not a few cases, the jussive is used, without any collateral k
sense, for the ordinary imperfect form, and this occurs not alone in forms,
which may arise from a misunderstanding of the defective writing, as Dt 28²¹·³⁶,
32⁸, 1 K 8¹, Is 12¹, Mi 3⁴, 5⁸, ψ 11⁶, 18¹², 21² *Qᵉré* מַה־יָגֶל, *Kᵉth.* (יָגִיל), 25⁹, 47⁴, 90³,
91⁴, 107²⁹, Pr 15²⁵, Jb 13²⁷, 15³³, 18⁹, 20²· יֹתֵר 22, 33¹¹, 36¹⁴, 38²⁴, Ec 12⁶ (verse 7 יֹשֵׁב
but immediately afterwards תָּשׁוּב), Dn 8¹²,—but also in shortened forms,
such as יְהִי Gu 49¹⁷ (Sam. וִיהִי), Dt 28⁸, 1 S 10⁵, 2 S 5²⁴, Ho 6¹, 11⁴, Am 5¹⁴, Mi 1²,
Zp 2¹³, Zc 9⁵, ψ 72¹⁶ᶠ· (after other jussives), 104³¹, Jb 18¹², 20²³·²⁶·²⁸, 27⁸, 33²¹, 34³⁷,
Ru 3⁴. This use of the jussive can hardly be due merely to poetic licence, but
is rather to be explained on rhythmical grounds. In all the above-cited
examples, in fact, the jussive stands at the beginning of the sentence (and
hence removed as far as possible from the principal tone), in others it is
immediately before the principal pause (Is 42⁶, 50², ψ 68¹⁵, Pr 23²⁵, Jb 24¹⁴, 29³,
40¹⁹), or actually *in* pause (Dt 32¹⁸, Jb 23⁹·¹¹, La 3⁵⁰), and is then a simply
rhythmical shortening due to the strong influence of the tone. Moreover,
since the jussive in numerous cases is not distinguished in form from the
imperfect (§ 48 g), it is frequently doubtful which of the two the writer
intended. This especially applies to those cases, in which a *subjunctive* is to be
expressed by one or other of the forms (cf. § 107 k and m–x).

§ 110. *The Imperative.*

Mayer Lambert, 'Sur la syntaxe de l'impératif en hébreu,' in
REJ. 1897, p. 106 ff.

a 1. The imperative,[1] which, according to § 46, is restricted to the
2nd pers. sing. and plur., and to *positive* commands, &c., may stand
either alone, or in simple co-ordination (as in 1 K 18⁴⁴, Is 56¹, 65¹⁸)
with other imperatives :

(*a*) To express real commands, e. g. Gn 12¹ *get thee out of thy
country*; or (like the jussive) mere admonitions (Ho 10¹²) and requests,
2 K 5²², Is 5³; on the addition of נָא see below, Rem. 1. The imperative
is used in the sense of an ironical challenge (often including a threat)
in 1 K 2²² *ask for him the kingdom also*; 22¹⁵, Ju 10¹⁴, Is 47¹² (with
נָא), Jer 7²¹, Ez 20³⁹, Am 4⁴, Jb 38³ᶠ·, 40¹⁰ᶠᶠ·, La 4²¹. The imperative
has a concessive sense in Na 3¹⁵ (though thou *make thyself many*, &c.),
and in the cases discussed under *f*, e. g. Is 8⁹ᶠ·, 29⁹.

b (*b*) To express permission, e. g. 2 S 18²³ after previous dissuasion,
(then) *run* (as far as I am concerned)! Is 21¹², 45¹¹.

c (*c*) To express a distinct assurance (like our expression, *thou shalt
have it*) [2] or promise, e. g. Is 65¹⁸ *but be ye glad*, &c. (i. e. ye will have
continually occasion to be glad); and Is 37³⁰, ψ 110²; in a threat,
Jer 2¹⁹. So especially in commands, the fulfilment of which is
altogether out of the power of the person addressed, e. g. Is 54¹⁴ *be far
from anxiety* (meaning, thou needst not fear any more); Gn 1²⁸, &c. (for
other examples, such as 1 K 22¹², 2 K 5¹³, see below, *f*). Most clearly
in the case of the *imperative Niph'al* with a passive meaning, e. g.
Gn 42¹⁶ וְאֵֽסָרוּ הָאָסְרוּ *and ye shall be bound*; Dt 32⁵⁰, Is 49⁹ (Is 45²², see
below, *f*).

d Rem. 1. The particle נָא *age!* (§ 105) is frequently added to the imperative,
as to the jussive, sometimes to soften down a command, or to make a request
in a more courteous form (see above, *a*), Gn 12¹³, 24², sometimes to strengthen
an exhortation uttered as a rebuke or threat (Nu 16²⁶, 20¹⁰) or in ridicule
(Is 47¹²).

e 2. The imperative after the desiderative particle לוּ Gn 23¹³ (at the end of
verses 5 and 14 also read לִי for לוּ and join it to the following imperative) is
due to an anacoluthon. Instead of the imperfect which would be expected
here after לוּ, the more forcible imperative is used in a new sentence.

f 2. The imperative in logical dependence upon a preceding imperative, jussive (or cohortative), or an interrogative sentence, serves to

---

[1] On the close relation between the imperative and jussive (both in meaning and form), cf. § 46 and § 48 *i*.

[2] Like the threatening formulae in the Latin comic writers, e. g. *vapula*,
Ter. Phorm. v. 6, 10 = *vapulare te iubeo*, Plaut. Curc. vi. 4, 12.

express the distinct assurance or promise that an action or state will
ensue as the certain consequence of a previous action. So especially:

(*a*) The imperative when depending (with *wāw copulative*) upon
another imperative. In this case the first imperative contains, as a
rule, a condition, while the second declares the consequence which the
fulfilment of the condition will involve. The imperative is used for
this declaration, since the consequence is, as a matter of fact, intended
or desired by the speaker (cf. *divide et impera*), e. g. Gn 42[18] זֹאת עֲשׂוּ
וִחְיוּ *this do, and live*, i. e. thus shall ye continue to live. Gn 17[1],
1 K 22[12], 2 K 5[13], Is 36[16], 45[22] (וְהִוָּשְׁעוּ), Jer 6[16], Am 5[4.6], ψ 37[27], Pr 3[3f.],
4[4], 7[2], 13[20] *K*[eth]., Jb 2[9], 2 Ch 20[20]; in Jer 25[5], Jb 22[21] נָא is added to
the first imperative. In other cases, the first imperative contains a
mocking concession, the second an irrevocable denunciation, e. g. Is 8[9]
רֹעוּ עַמִּים וָחֹתּוּ (continue to) *make an uproar, O ye peoples, and ye shall
be broken in pieces*; cf. verse 9 *b*.

Rem. 1. If a promise or threat dependent on an imperative be expressed in
the 3rd pers. then the jussive is naturally used instead of the 2nd imperative *g*
Is 8[10], 55[2].
2. In Pr 20[13] the second imperative (containing a promise) is attached by *h*
asyndeton; elsewhere two imperatives occur side by side without the copula,
where the second might be expected to be subordinated to the first, e. g.
Dt 2[24] הָחֵל רָשׁ (where רָשׁ is virtually, as it were, an object to הָחֵל) *begin, take
in possession* for *to take in possession* (cf., however, Ju 19[6] הוֹאֶל־נָא וְלִין *be content,
I pray thee, and tarry all night*, and on this kind of co-ordination in general,
cf. § 120 *d*). But such imperatives as (קוּמוּ) קוּם (לְכוּ) לֶךְ, when immediately
preceding a second imperative, are for the most part only equivalent to interjections, *come! up!*

(*b*) The imperative, when depending (with *wāw copulative*) upon *i*
a jussive (cohortative), or an interrogative sentence, frequently expresses also a consequence which is to be expected with certainty,
and often a consequence which is intended, or in fact an intention;
cf. Gn 20[7] *and he shall pray for thee*, וֶחְיֵה *and thou shalt live*; cf.
Ex 14[16], 2 K 5[10], Jb 11[6], ψ 128[5] *the Lord bless thee . . . so that* (or *in
order that*) *thou seest*, &c.; Ru 1[9], 4[11]; after a cohortative, Gn 12[2],
45[18], Ex 3[10] וְהוֹצֵא *that thou mayest bring forth*; Ex 18[22], 1 S 12[17],
1 K 1[12]; Jer 35[15] (after imperative and jussive); after an interrogative
sentence, 2 S 21[3] *wherewith shall I make atonement*, וּבָרְכוּ *that ye may
bless*, &c.—In Nu 5[19] the imperative without וְ (in 32[23] with וְ) is used
after a conditional clause in the sense of a definite promise.

Rem. The 2nd *sing. masc.* occurs in addressing feminine persons in Ju 4[20] *k*
(עֲמֹד, according to Qimḥi an infinitive, in which case, however, the infinitive
absolute עָמוֹד should be read; but probably we should simply read עִמְרִי with
Moore), Mi 1[13] and Zc 13[7] (after עוּרִי); and in Is 23[1], the 2nd *plur. masc.* (On

the four forms of the *2nd fem. plur. imperative* in Is 32¹¹, erroneously explained here in former editions, see now § 48 *i*). In Na 3¹⁵ the interchange of masc. and fem. serves to express totality (the nation in all its aspects). Cf., moreover, § 145 *p* on other noticeable attempts to substitute the corresponding masculine forms for the feminine.

§ 111. *The Imperfect with Wāw Consecutive.*

a　　1. The *imperfect* with *wāw consecutive* (§ 49 *a–g*) serves to express actions, events, or states, which are to be regarded as the temporal or logical sequel of actions, events, or states mentioned immediately[1] before. The *imperfect consecutive* is used in this way most frequently as the *narrative tense*, corresponding to the Greek *aorist* or the Latin *historic perfect*. As a rule the narrative is introduced by a perfect, and then continued by means of imperfects with *wāw consecutive* (on this interchange of tenses cf. § 49 *a*, and especially § 112 *a*), e. g. Gn 3¹ *now the serpent was* (הָיָה) *more subtil . . . and he said* (וַיֹּאמֶר) *unto the woman*; 4¹, 6⁹ᶠᶠ·, 10⁹ᶠ·, 15¹⁹, 11¹²ᶠᶠ· ²⁷ᶠᶠ·, 14⁵ᶠ·, 15¹ᶠ·, 16¹ᶠ·, 21¹ᶠᶠ·, 24¹ᶠ·, 25¹⁹ᶠᶠ·, 36²ᶠᶠ·, 37².

b　　Rem. 1. To this class belong some of the numerous *imperfects consec.* after various expressions of time, whenever such expressions are equivalent in meaning to a perfect[2] (viz. הָיָה *it came to pass*), e. g. Is 6¹ *in the year that king Uzziah died, I saw* (וָאֶרְאֶה), &c.; Gn 22⁴, 27³⁴, Ju 11¹⁶, 1 S 4¹⁹, 17⁵⁷, 21⁶, Ho 11¹: on the use of וַיְהִי to connect expressions of time, see below, *g*.—It is only in late books or passages that we find the simple *perfect* in a clause following an expression of time, as 1 S 17⁵⁵ (cf. Driver on the passage), 2 Ch 12⁷, 15⁸, &c., Dn 10¹¹, 15¹⁹; the *Perfect* after וְ and the subject, 2 Ch 7¹.

c　　2. The continuation of the narrative by means of the imperfect consec. may result in a series of any number of such imperfects, e. g. there are forty-nine in Gn. 1. As soon, however, as the connecting *Wāw* becomes separated from the verb to which it belongs, by the insertion of any word, the perfect necessarily takes the place of the imperfect, e. g. Gn 1⁵ *and God called* (וַיִּקְרָא) *the light Day, and the darkness he called* (וְלַחֹשֶׁךְ קָרָא) *Night*; verse 10, 2²⁰, 11³ and frequently.

d　　3. Of two co-ordinate *imperfects consecutive* the former (as equivalent to a temporal clause) is most frequently subordinate in sense to the latter, e. g. Gn 28⁸ ᶠ· . . . וַיֵּלֶךְ . . . וַיַּרְא עֵשָׂו *when Esau saw that . . .*, *he went*, &c.; so also, frequently וַיִּשְׁמַע, &c., Gn 37²¹, &c. On the other hand, a second *imperfect consecutive* is seldom used in an explanatory sense, e. g. Ex 2¹⁰ (וַתֹּאמֶר *for she said*); cf. 1 S 7¹². Other examples of the imperfect consecutive, which apparently represent a progress in the narrative, in reality only refer to the same time, or explain what precedes, see Gn 2²⁵ (וַיִּהְיוּ *they were*; but Jos 4⁹, 1 K 8⁸ *they are*); Gn 36¹⁴ (וַתֵּלֶד), 36³² (וַיִּמְלֹךְ), 1 K 1⁴⁴.

---

[1] On an apparent exception (the *imperf. consec.* at the beginning of whole books) see § 49 *b* note.

[2] Cf. Is 45⁴, where the *imperf. consec.* is joined to an abrupt statement of the cause, and Jb 36⁷, where it is joined to an abrupt statement of the place.

4. The imperfect consecutive sometimes has such a merely *external* con- *e* nexion with an immediately preceding perfect, that in reality it represents an antithesis to it, e. g. Gn 32³¹ *and (yet) my life is preserved*; 2 S 3⁸ *and yet thou chargest me*; Jb 10⁸, 32³; similarly in dependence on noun-clauses, Pr 30²⁵ ᶠᶠ.

2. The introduction of independent narratives, or of a new section *f* of the narrative, by means of an *imperfect consecutive*, likewise aims at a connexion, though again loose and external, with that which has been narrated previously. Such a connexion is especially often established by means of וַיְהִי (καὶ ἐγένετο) *and it came to pass*, after which there then follows either (most commonly) an *imperfect con- secutive* (Gn 4³·⁸, 8⁶, 11², Ex 12²⁹, 13¹⁷, &c.), or *Wāw* with the perfect (separated from it), Gn 7¹⁰, 15¹², 22¹, 27³⁰, or even a perfect without *Wāw* (Gn 8¹³, 14¹ᶠ·, 40¹, Ex 12⁴¹, 16²², Nu 10¹¹, Dt 1³, 1 S 18³⁰, 2 K 8²¹, &c.), or finally a noun-clause introduced by *Wāw*, Gn 41¹.

Rem. 1. This loose connexion by means of וַיְהִי¹ is especially common, *g* when the narrative or a new section of it begins with any expression of time, see above, *b*; cf., in addition to the above-mentioned examples (e.g. Gn 22¹ *and it came to pass after these things, that God did prove Abraham*), the similar cases in Gn 19³⁴, 21²², 1 S 11¹¹, Ru 1¹. Elsewhere the statement of time is expressed by בְּ or כְּ with an infinitive (Gn 12¹⁴, 19¹⁷·²⁹ 39¹³, 15¹⁸ᶠ·, Ju 16²⁵) or by an independent sentence with the perfect (equivalent to a pluperfect, cf. § 106*f*), e. g. Gn 15¹⁷, 24¹⁵, 27³⁰, or by a temporal clause introduced by כִּי *when*, Gn 26⁸, 27¹¹, Ju 16¹⁶, כַּאֲשֶׁר *when*, Gn 12¹¹, 20¹³, מֵאָז *from the time that*, Gn 39⁵; or, finally, by a noun-clause (cf. § 116 *u*), e.g. 2 K 13²¹ וַיְהִי הֵם קֹבְרִים אִישׁ *and it came to pass, as they were* (just) *burying a man* (prop. they bury), *that . . .*; Gn 42³⁵, 2 K 2¹¹ (the apodosis in both these cases being introduced by וְהִנֵּה); 1 S 7¹⁰, 2 S 13³⁰, 2 K 6⁵·²⁶, 19³⁷ (= Is 37³⁸).—In 1 S 10¹¹, 11¹¹, 2 S 2²³, 15² a noun standing absolutely follows וַיְהִי (as the equivalent of a complete sentence; see below, *h*), and then an *imperfect consecutive* follows.

2. Closely related to the cases noticed in *g* are those in which the *imperfect* *h* *consecutive*, even without a preceding וַיְהִי, introduces the apodosis either— (*a*) to whole sentences, or (*b*) to what are equivalent to whole sentences, especially to nouns standing absolutely. As in certain cases of the *perfect consecutive* (see § 112 *x*), so the *imperfect consecutive* has here acquired a sort of independent force. Cf. for (*a*) 1 S 15²³ *because thou hast rejected the word of the Lord*, וַיִּמְאָסְךָ *he hath rejected thee* (cf. Nu 14¹⁶, Is 48⁴, where the causal clause precedes in the form of an infinitive with preposition), Ex 9²¹; for (*b*) Gn 22²⁴ וּפִילַגְשׁוֹ *and* (as to) *his concubine . . .*, וַתֵּלֶד *she bare*, &c.; Ex 38²⁴, Nu 14³⁶ᶠ·, 1 S 14¹⁹, 17²⁴, 2 S 4¹⁰, 19⁴¹ *Keth.*, 21¹⁶, 1 K 9²⁰ᶠ·, 12¹⁷, 2 K 25²², Jer 6¹⁹, 28⁸, 33²⁴, 44²⁵.²—In 1 K 15¹³, 2 K 16¹⁴ the preceding noun, used absolutely, is even regarded as the object of the following imperfect consecutive, and is therefore introduced by אֶת־.

---

¹ Exhaustive statistics of the use of וַיְהִי in its many and various connexions are given by König in *ZAW.* 1899, p. 260 ff.

² Cf. the Mēša‘ inscription, l. 5 (*Omri*) *the king of Israel*, וַיְעַנּוּ *he oppressed Moab*, &c.—The peculiar imperfect consecutive in Gn 30²⁷ᵇ (in the earlier editions explained as equivalent to an object-clause) arises rather from a preg- nant brevity of expression: *I have observed and* have come to the conclusion, *the Lord hath blessed me*, &c.—In Gn 27³⁴ read, with LXX, וַיְהִי before כִּשְׁמֹעַ.

i 3. The *imperfect consecutive* serves, in the cases treated under *a–h*, to represent either expressly, or at least to a great extent, a *chronological* succession of actions or events; elsewhere it expresses those actions, &c., which represent the logical consequence of what preceded, or a result arising from it by an inherent necessity. Thus the *imperfect consecutive* is used—

k (*a*) As a final summing up of the preceding narrative, e. g. Gn 2¹, 23²⁰ וַיָּקָם הַשָּׂדֶה וג׳ *so* (in this way) *the field became* (legally) *the property of Abraham*, &c.; 1 S 17⁵⁰, 31⁶.

l (*b*) To express a logical or necessary consequence of that which immediately precedes, e. g. Gn 39², Jb 2³ *and he still holdeth fast his integrity,* וַתְּסִיתֵנִי וג׳ *so that thou thus* (as it now appears) *groundlessly movedst me against him;* ψ 65⁹ *so that they are afraid . . .;* even a consequence which happens conditionally, Jer 20¹⁷ וַתְּהִי *so that my mother should have been . . .* Another instance of the kind perhaps (if the text be correct) is Jer 38⁹ וָיָּמָת *so that he dies* (must die).

m Rem. Such consecutive clauses frequently occur after interrogative sentences, e. g. Is 51¹² *who art thou* (i. e. art thou *so helpless*), וַתִּירָא *that thou art* (*must needs be*) *afraid?* ψ 144³ (cf. ψ 8⁵, where in a very similar context כִּי *that* is used with the imperfect); Gn 12¹⁹ (וָאֶקַּח); 31²⁷ וָאֲשַׁלֵּחֲךָ *so that I might have sent thee away.*

4. As regards the range of time it is to be carefully noticed—

n (*a*) That the *imperfect consecutive* may represent all varieties in the relations of tense and mood, which, according to § 107 *a*, follow from the idea of the imperfect;

o (*b*) That the more precise determination of the range of time to which an *imperfect consecutive* relates must be inferred in each case from the character of the preceding tense (or tense-equivalent), to which it is attached, in a more or less close relation, as temporal or logical sequence. Thus the *imperfect consecutive* serves—

p (1) To represent actions, events, or states, which are *past* (or were repeated in past time), when it is united with tenses, or their equivalents, which refer to an actual past.

q Cf. the examples given above, under *a* and *f*, of the imperfect consecutive as an historic tense. The imperfect consecutive also frequently occurs as the continuation of a perfect (*preterite*) in a subordinate clause; e. g. Gn 27¹, Nu 11²⁰, Dt 4³⁷, 1 S 8⁸, 1 K 2⁵, 11³³, 18¹³, &c.; also in Is 49⁷ וַיִּבְחָרֶךָ is the continuation of a preterite, contained, according to the sense, in the preceding אֲשֶׁר נֶאֱמָן.—In Jb 31²⁶·³⁴ the imperfect consecutive is joined to an imperfect denoting the past in a conditional sentence. An imperfect consecutive occurs in dependence on a perfect which has the sense of a pluperfect (§ 106 *f*), e. g. in Gn 26¹⁸, 28⁶ ᶠ·, 31¹⁹·³⁴ (*now Rachel had taken the teraphim,* וַתְּשִׂמֵם *and had put them*, &c.) ; Nu 14³⁶, 1 S 28³, 2 S 2²³, Is 39¹. Finally there are the cases in which an infinitival or participial construction representing past time, according to § 113 *r*, § 116 *x*, is taken up and continued by an imperfect consecutive.

(2) To represent *present* actions, &c., in connexion with tenses, or *r* their equivalents, which describe actions and states as being either present or lasting on into the present (continuing in their effect) ; so especially,

(*a*) In connexion with the present perfects, described in § 106 *g*, e. g. ψ 16⁹ *therefore my heart is glad* (שָׂמַח) *and my glory rejoiceth* (וַיָּ֫גֶל); Is 3¹⁶ (parallel with a simple imperfect). Cf. also such examples as ψ 29¹⁰ וַיֵּ֫שֶׁב (prop. he sat down, *and has been enthroned ever since*), ψ 41¹³.

(β) In connexion with those perfects which represent experiences *s* frequently confirmed (see § 106 *k*), e. g. Jb 14² *he cometh up* (יָצָא) *like a flower, and is cut down* (וַיִּמָּל) ; *he fleeth* (וַיִּבְרַח) *also as a shadow*, וְלֹא יַעֲמוֹד *and continueth not* ; Jb 20¹⁵, 24²·¹¹, Is 40²⁴, Pr 11².

(γ) In connexion with imperfects which, in one of the ways *t* described in § 107. 2, are used in the sense of the present ; e. g. Jb 14¹⁰ *but man dieth* (יָמוּת) *and becometh powerless* (וַיֶּחֱלָשׁ), &c., i. e. remains powerless ; Jb 4⁵, Ho 8¹³, Hb 1⁹ᶠ·, ψ 55¹⁸, 90³, Jb 5¹⁵, 7¹⁸, 11³ (*when thou mockest*), 12²⁵, 34²⁴, 37⁸ (parallel with a simple imperfect) ; 39¹⁵. In the apodosis of a conditional sentence, ψ 59¹⁶, so also after an interrogative imperfect, 1 S 2²⁹, ψ 42⁶ וַתֶּהֱמִי for which in verse 12 and in 43⁵ we have וּמַה־תֶּהֱמִי *and why art thou disquieted ?*).

(δ) In dependence on participles, which represent what at present *u* continues or is being repeated, e. g. Nu 22¹¹, 1 S 2⁶, 2 S 19² *behold the king weepeth* (בֹּכֶה) *and mourneth* (וַיִּתְאַבֵּל) *for Absalom* ; Am 5⁸, 9⁵ᶠ·. Na 1⁴, ψ 34⁸, Pr 20²⁶, Jb 12²²ᶠᶠ·, but cf. e. g. Jb 12⁴ קֹרֵא לֶאֱלוֹהַּ *who called upon God*, וַיַּעֲנֵ֫הוּ *and he answered him*.

(ε) In dependence on other equivalents of the present, as in Is 51¹², *v* ψ 144³ (see above, *m*); Jb 10²². So especially as the continuation of an infinitive, which is governed by a preposition (cf. § 114 *r*), Is 30¹², Jer 10¹³, ψ 92⁸, &c.

(3) To represent *future* actions, &c., in dependence on—(*a*) an *w* imperfect which refers to the future, ψ 49¹⁵, 94²²ᶠ· ;—(β) a perfect consecutive, or those perfects which, according to § 106 *n*, are intended to represent future events as undoubtedly certain, and therefore as though already accomplished (*perf. propheticum*); cf. Is 5¹⁵ (parallel with a simple imperfect separated from וֹ) ; 5¹⁶ (cf. 2¹¹·¹⁷, where the same threat is expressed by the perfect consecutive) ; 5²⁵, 9⁵·¹⁰ᶠ·,

13¹⁵·¹⁷ᶠᶠ·, 22⁷ᶠᶠ·, Jo 2²³, Mi 2¹³, Ez 33⁴·⁶, ψ 7¹³, 64⁸ᶠᶠ·;—(γ) a future participle, Jer 4¹⁶. ¹

x   Rem. An imperfect consecutive in dependence on a perfect or imperfect, which represents an action occurring only conditionally, is likewise used only in a hypothetical sense, e. g. Jb 9¹⁶ אִם־קָרָאתִי וַיַּעֲנֵנִי *if I had called, and he had answered me, yet* . . .; ψ 139¹¹ וָאֹמַר *if I should say* (previously, in verse 8 f., hypothetical imperfects are used).—In Is 48¹⁸ ᶠ· an imperfect consecutive occurs in dependence on a sentence expressing a wish introduced by לוּא *utinam* (וַיְהִי *and it*, or *so that it were*, equivalent to *then should it be*). Cf. also the examples mentioned above, under *l* (Jer 20¹⁷) and *m* (Gn 31²⁷), where the imperfect consecutive expresses facts occurring *contingently*.

§ 112. *The Perfect with Wāw Consecutive.*

G. R. Berry, 'Waw consecutive with the perfect in Hebrew,' in *Bibl. Lit.*, xxii. (1903), pp. 60–69.

a   1. The perfect, like the imperfect (§ 111), is used with *wāw consecutive* (cf. § 49 *a*; on the external differentiation of the perfect consecutive by a change in the position of the tone, see § 49 *h*) to express actions, events, or states, which are to be attached to what precedes, in a more or less close relation, as its *temporal* or *logical* consequence. And as, according to § 111 *a*, the narrative which begins with a perfect, or its equivalent, is continued in the imperfect consecutive, so, vice versa, the perfect consecutive forms the regular continuation to a preceding imperfect, or its equivalent.

b   Rem. 1. This alternation of perfect and imperfect or their equivalents is a striking peculiarity of the *consecutio temporum* in Hebrew. It not only affords a certain compensation for the lack of forms for tenses and moods, but also gives to Hebrew style the charm of an expressive variety, an action conceived as being still in progress (*imperfect*, &c.), reaching afterwards in the *perfect* a calm and settled conclusion, in order to be again exhibited in movement in the imperfect, and vice versa.² The strict regularity of this

---

¹ Also in Jer 51²⁹ the imperfects consecutive are attached to the threat virtually contained in the preceding imperatives. On the other hand וְיָחֵלּוּ Ho 8¹⁰ would be very remarkable as expressing a future; the text is, however, certainly corrupt, and hence the Cod. Babyl. and the Erfurt MS. 3 endeavour to remedy it by וַיְחַל׳, and Ewald reads וַיָּחֵלּוּ.—In Ez 28¹⁶ (cf. Jer 15⁶ᶠ·) וָאֲחַלֶּלְךָ appears to announce an action irrevocably determined upon, and therefore represented as already accomplished; cf. the prophetic perfects in verse 17 ff.

² It is difficult to give a proper explanation of this phenomenon (according to § 49 *a*, note, to be found only in the Canaanitish group of languages), when we have given up the theory of a special *wāw conversivum* in the unscientific sense mentioned in § 49 *b*, note, at the end, and if we accept the fact that the *perfect* and *imperfect consecutive* cannot possibly be used in a way which contradicts their fundamental character as described in §§ 106 and 107. In other words, even the *perfect consecutive* originally represents a finally completed action, &c., just as the *imperfect consecutive* represents an action which

alternation belongs indeed rather to the higher style, and even then it depends upon the view and intention of the speaker, whether he wishes the action, &c., to be regarded as the logical consequence of what has preceded, or as simply co-ordinate with it, and so in the same tense.

2. A succession of any number of other *perfects consecutive* may be co-or- **c** dinated with a *perfect consecutive* (cf. e. g. Ez 14[18], Am 5[19], Ru 3[3], four perfects in each case, Is 8[7] five, Ex 6[6f.] eight). It is true, however, of the perfect (as conversely of the *imperfect*, § 111 c), that as soon as the *Wāw* is separated by any intervening word from the verb to which it belongs, an *imperfect* necessarily takes the place of the *perfect*, e. g. Gn 12[12] *when the Egyptians shall see thee, they shall say* (וְאָמְרוּ), *This is his wife: and they will kill me* (וְהָרְגוּ אֹתִי) *but thee they will save alive* (וְאֹתָךְ יְחַיּוּ).

2. The perfect consecutive, like the imperfect consecutive, always **d** belongs to the period of time expressed by the preceding tense, or its equivalent, with which it is connected as the temporal or logical consequence. The particular cases may be classed under three heads : (*a*) the perfect consecutive in *immediate* dependence (see *e*), (*b*) in loose connexion (see *x*) with the preceding, and (*c*) the perfect consecutive at the beginning of the apodosis to other sentences, or their equivalents (see *ff*).

3. The perfect consecutive in immediate dependence on the pre- **e** ceding tense, or its equivalent, serves

(*a*) As a frequentative tense to express *past* actions, &c., i. e. actions repeatedly brought to a conclusion in the past, and follows tenses, or their equivalents, representing actions which have *continued* or been *repeated in the past*:

(*a*) After a simple imperfect, e. g. Gn 2[6] אֵד יַעֲלֶה *there went up a mist* (again and again) *from the earth,* וְהִשְׁקָה *and watered* (as it were, *and ever watered afresh*), &c. This frequentative use of the perfect consecutive is equally evident after frequentative imperfects, Gn 2[10] (וְהָיָה *and it became* again every time; וַיְהִי *would mean, and it became so once for all*); 29[2f.] (four perfects consecutive referring to actions repeated daily); Ex 33[7–11] יִקַּח *he used to take* at each new encampment *the tent,* וְנָטָה *and to pitch it* again every time *without the camp*; notice, amongst the numerous frequent. perff. consec., the imperf. in vv. 7, 8, 9, 11, always in a frequentative sense ; 34[34f.], Nu 9[19.21] (among several simple imperfects), 10[17], Ju 2[19], 1 S 2[19] תַּעֲשֶׂה

---

is only beginning, becoming or still continuing, and hence in any case incomplete. The simplest view is to suppose, that the use of the *perfect consecutive* originated from those cases, in which it had to express the conclusion (or final consequence) of an action which was continued (or repeated) *in past time* (see the examples above), and that this use was afterwards extended to other cases, in which it had to represent the temporal or logical consequence of actions, &c., still in progress, and thus in the end a regular interchange of the two tenses became recognized.

she used to make . . . וְהַעֲלָתָה *and brought it to him from year to year*;
27⁹ (וְלָקַח), 1 K 14²⁸, 2 K 3²⁵, 12¹⁵ (in verses 16ᶠ· imperfects occur
again). So also in dependent sentences, Gn 6⁴ (וְיָלְדוּ) as a continuation
of יָבֹאוּ), Jb 31²⁹.[1]

f (β) After an imperfect consecutive, e. g. Ex 39³ (Samaritan וקצצו),
1 S 5⁷ (? see § 112 *rr*), 7¹⁶, 2 S 15²·⁵, 16¹³ *and he threw stones at him*,
וְעִפַּר *and cast dust continually*; 12¹⁶·³¹, 2 K 6¹⁰, 12¹¹ ff· ¹⁵, Jer 37¹⁵, Jb 1⁵.

g Rem. The frequentative perfect consecutive is sometimes joined even with
imperfects consecutive which simply express one *single* action or occurrence
in the past; thus Ex 18²⁶, 4ᶜ³¹ᶠ·, 1 S 1⁴, 2 S 15¹ᶠ·, 1 K 14²⁷ (cf. verse 28); 1 K 18⁴,
2 K 12¹⁰. For other examples of a loosely connected frequentative perfect
consecutive, see below, *dd*.

h (γ) After a perfect, Gn 37³ (וְעָשָׂה לוֹ), i. e. as often as he needed
a new garment)[2]; Gn 31⁷, Nu 11⁸, 1 S 16¹⁴, 2 K 3⁴, ψ 22⁶;[3] in
interrogative sentences, 1 S 26⁹ *who has ever*, &c.; ψ 80¹³, Jb 1·⁴, Ru 4⁷.

i (δ) After an infinitive, Am 1¹¹ עַל־רָדְפוֹ *because he did pursue his
brother*, וְשִׁחֵת *and* (on each occasion) *did cast off all pity* (then an
imperfect consecutive); after an infinitive absolute, Jos 6¹³, 2 S 13¹⁹,
Jer 23¹⁴.

k (ε) After a participle, Is 6³ (וְקָרָא), &c., frequentative, as a continuation of עֹמְדִים, verse 2); 1 S 2²², 2 S 17¹⁷.[4]

l (ζ) After other equivalents of tenses, e. g. Gn 47²² *the priests had
a portion from Pharaoh*, וְאָכְלוּ *and did eat* (year by year), &c.; 1 K 4⁷.

m (*b*) To express *present* actions, &c., as the temporal or logical consequence of actions or events which continue or are repeated in the
present, especially such as have, according to experience, been at all
times frequently repeated, and may be repeated at any time:

(α) After a simple imperfect, e. g. Gn 2²⁴ *therefore a man leaves*
(יַעֲזֹב *is accustomed to leave*) . . . וְדָבַק *and cleaves*, &c., here, as
frequently elsewhere, clearly with the secondary idea of purpose, i. e.
in order to cleave; Is 5¹¹ (if וְהָיָה is to be taken as a continuation

---

[1] Also in Ez 44¹² (where Stade, *ZAW*. v. 293, would read שֵׁרְתוּ and וְהָיוּ)
the unusual tenses may have been intentionally chosen: *because they continually
ministered and so always became afresh* . . .

[2] Driver, on this passage, rightly refers to 1 S 2¹⁹.

[3] Am 4⁷ would also come under this head, if וְהִמְטַרְתִּי is really intended,
and the statement refers to the past; מָנַעְתִּי might, however, also be a perfect
expressing positive assurance (§ 106 *m*), and the passage would then come
under *s*.

[4] That וְהָלְכָה, &c., are frequentatives (*the maidservant used to go repeatedly and
tell them*) may be seen from יֵלְכוּ (necessarily an imperfect, since it is separated
from וְ by הֵם) and יוֹכְלוּ; on the other hand in verse 18 וַיָּרָא and וַיֵּלְכוּ of
actions which happened only once.

of (יַדְלִיקֶם); Is 28²⁸, Jer 12³, Ho 4³, 7⁷, ψ 90⁶, Jb 14⁹; also in dependent clauses, Lv 20¹⁸, Is 29⁸·¹¹ᶠ·, Am 5¹⁹.

(β) After a participle, as the equivalent of a sentence representing *n* a contingent action, &c., e. g. Ex 21¹² מַכֵּה אִישׁ וָמֵת (instead of מַכֵּה there is in verse 20, &c. (וְכִי יָכֶּה אִישׁ) *if one smite a man and* (so that) *he die*, &c., Ex 21¹⁶, Is 29¹⁵, Am 6¹, Hb 2¹².

(γ) After an infinitive absolute, Jer 7⁹ᶠ· *will ye steal, murder, and* *o* *commit adultery* (simple infinitives absolute; cf. § 113 *ee*), וּבָאתֶם *and* *then come and stand before me . . . and say*, &c.; cf. below, *u.*

(*c*) To express *future* actions, &c., as the temporal or logical con- *p* sequence of tenses, or their equivalents, which announce or require such future actions or events.   Thus—

(*a*) After imperfects in the sense of a simple future, e. g. Am 9³ᶠ· מִשָּׁם אֲחַפֵּשׂ וּלְקַחְתִּים *I will search and take them out thence*, &c.; Gn 4¹⁴, 40¹³, Ex 7³, 1 S 17³², 2 K 5¹¹, Jb 8⁶ᶠ· (also with a change of subject, Gn 27¹², Ju 6¹⁶, &c.); and in interrogative sentences, Gn 39⁹, Ex 2⁷, 2 S 12¹⁸, 2 K 14¹⁰, Am 8⁸, ψ 41⁶; cf. also Ru 1¹¹; in sentences expressing a wish, 2 S 15⁴; as well as in almost all kinds of dependent clauses.   Also in conditional clauses after אִם־ Gn 32⁹, Ex 19⁵, 1 S 1¹¹, or כִּי Gn 37²⁶, or הֵן Jer 3¹; in final clauses after לְמַעַן Gn 12¹³, Nu 15⁴⁰, Is 28¹³; after אֲשֶׁר Dt 2²⁵, or פֶּן Gn 3²², 19¹⁹, 32¹², Is 6¹⁰, Am 5⁶; in temporal clauses, Is 32¹⁵, Jer 13¹⁶; and in relative clauses, Gn 24¹⁴, Ju 1¹², 1 S 17²⁶.

(β) After the jussive (or an imperfect in the sense of a jussive or *q* optative) or cohortative, with the same or a different subject, e. g. Gn 1¹⁴ᶠ· וְהָיוּ , . . . יְהִי מְאֹרֹת *let there be lights . . . and let them be*, &c.; Gn 24⁴, 28³, 31⁴⁴, 1 K 1², 22¹³, Ru 2⁷, 1 Ch 22¹¹; after a jussive expressing an imprecation, ψ 109¹⁰.

(γ) After an imperative, also with the same or a different subject, *r* e. g. 2 S 7⁵ וְאָמַרְתָּ לְךָ *go and tell* (that thou mayst tell), &c., and often, *perf. consec.* after לֵךְ (as also the *perf. consec.* of אָמַר and דִּבֶּר very frequently follows other imperatives);. Gn 6¹⁴, 8¹⁷, 27⁴³ᶠ·, 1 S 15³·¹⁸, 1 K 2³⁶, Jer 48²⁶.

(δ) After perfects which express a definite expectation or assurance *s* (cf. § 106 *m* and *n*), e. g. Gn 17²⁰ הִנֵּה בֵּרַכְתִּי אֹתוֹ וְהִפְרֵיתִי אֹתוֹ *behold*, *I have blessed him, and will make him fruitful*, &c.; Is 2¹¹, 5¹⁴; on Am 4⁷ see above, note 3 on *h*; in an interrogative sentence, Ju 9⁹, 11¹³.

(ε) After a participle, e. g. Gn 7⁴ *for yet seven days*, אָנֹכִי מַמְטִיר *t* *and I will cause it to rain . . .* וּמָחִיתִי *and I will* (i. e. in order to) *destroy*, &c.; Jer 21⁹; also with a different subject, Gn 24⁴³ᶠ· *the maiden which cometh forth* (הַיֹּצֵאת) . . . , וְאָמַרְתִּי אֵלֶיהָ *to whom I shall say* . . . , וְאָמְרָה *and she* (then) *shall say*, &c. This use of the perfect consecutive is especially frequent after a participle introduced by הִנֵּה, e. g. Gn 6¹⁷ᶠ·; with a different subject 1 K 20³⁶, Am 6¹⁴; after a complete noun-clause introduced by הִנֵּה (cf. § 140), Ex 3¹³ *behold, I come* (i.e. if I shall come) . . . וְאָמַרְתִּי לָהֶם *and shall say unto them* . . . , וְאָמְרוּ *and they* (then) *shall say*, &c.; 1 S 14⁸ᶠᶠ·, Is 7¹⁴, 8⁷ᶠ·, 39⁶.

u   (ζ) After an infinitive absolute, whether the infinitive absolute serves to strengthen the finite verb (see § 113 *t*), e. g. Is 31⁵, or is used as an emphatic substitute for a cohortative or imperfect (§ 113 *dd* and *ee*), e. g. Lv 2⁶, Dt 1¹⁶, Is 5⁵, Ez 23⁴⁶ᶠ·.

v   (η) After an infinitive construct governed by a preposition (for this change from the infinitive construction to the finite verb, cf. § 114 *r*), e. g. 1 S 10⁸ עַד־בֹּאִי אֵלֶיךָ וְהוֹדַעְתִּי לְךָ *till I come unto thee* (prop. *until my coming*) *and show thee*, &c.; Gn 18²⁵, 27⁴⁵, Ju 6¹⁸, Ez 39²⁷; cf. 1 K 2³⁷·⁴².

w   Rem. To the same class belong 1 S 14²⁴, where the idea of time precedes, *until it be evening and* until *I be avenged*, &c., and Is 5⁸, where the idea of place precedes, in both cases governed by עַד־.

x   4. The very frequent use of the perfect consecutive in direct dependence upon other tenses (see above, *d–v*) explains how it finally obtained a kind of independent force—especially for the purpose of announcing future events—and might depend loosely on sentences to which it stood only in a wider sense in the relation of a temporal or logical consequence. Thus the perfect consecutive is used—

(a) To announce *future* events, &c., in loose connexion with a further announcement, e. g. Gn 41³⁰ וְקָמוּ and two co-ordinate perfects consecutive, equivalent to *but then shall arise*, &c.; frequently so after הִנֵּה with a following substantive (1 S 9⁸), or a participial clause (cf. the analogous instances above, under *t*), e. g. 1 S 2³¹ *behold, the days come,* וְגָדַעְתִּי *that I will cut off*, &c.; Is 39⁶, Am 4², 8¹¹, 9¹³, and very often in Jeremiah; after an expression of time, Ex 17⁴, Is 10²⁵, 29¹⁷, Jer 51³³, Ho 1⁴. Further, when joined to a statement concerning present or past facts, especially when these contain the reason for the action, &c., expressed in the perfect consecutive; cf. Is 6⁷ *lo, this hath touched thy lips,* וְסָר *therefore thine iniquity shall be taken away*, &c. (not copulative *and it is taken away*, since it is parallel with a simple imperfect), Gn 20¹¹, 26²², Ju 13³ (here in an adversative sense); Ho 8¹⁴. In loose connexion with a noun-clause, a long succession of perfects consecutive occurs in Ex 6⁶ᶠᶠ·. Also in Amos 5²⁶ וּנְשָׂאתֶם may be an announcement *yea, ye shall take up*; but cf. below, *rr*.

Rem. 1. Very frequently the announcement of a future event is attached *y*
by means of וְהָיָה[1] *and it shall come to pass* (cf. the analogous continuation in
the past by means of וַיְהִי, § 111, 2), after which the event announced (sometimes after a long parenthesis) follows in one or more (co-ordinate) perfects
consecutive, Gn 9¹⁴, 12¹² וְהָיָה כִי=*if*, as in 46³³, Ex 1¹⁰, 22²⁶ and frequently),
1 K 18¹², Is 14³ ꜰ·, Am 8⁹; or in the imperfect, Gn 4¹⁴, Is 2², 3²⁴, 4³, 7¹⁸·²¹ ꜰꜰ·
(cf. 29⁸); or in the jussive, Lv 14⁹. It very rarely happens that the verb
which is thus loosely added, agrees in gender and number with the following
subject, as in Nu 5²⁷, Jer 42¹⁶ וְהָיְתָה (before הַחֶרֶב), and in Jer 42¹⁷ וְיִהְיֶה (before
כָּל־הָאֲנָשִׁים).

2. The jussive form וִיהִי occurs (in the sense described in *y*) instead of וְהָיָה *z*
in 1 S 10⁵, 2 S 5²⁴ (1 Ch 14¹⁵), 1 K 14⁵, Ru 3⁴, although in the first three places
a jussive is wholly inadmissible in the context, and even in Ru 3⁴ (where an
admonition follows) וְהָיָה would be expected (see below, *bb*). In 1 K 14⁵ the
form is a textual error, and the pointing should simply be וַיְהִי. In the other
passages וִיהִי (always before an infinitive with a preposition) stands at the
beginning of the sentence at an unusually long distance from the principal
tone, and hence is certainly to be explained according to § 109 *k*, except that
in 1 S 10⁵, &c., the simply rhythmical jussive form takes the place, not of the
full imperfect form, but (exceptionally) of the perfect consecutive.

(*b*) To introduce a command or wish: Dt 10¹⁹ *love ye therefore the* *aa*
stranger; 1 S 6⁵, 24¹⁶, 1 K 2⁶ (in Gn 40¹⁴ the precative perfect consecutive, as elsewhere the cohortative, jussive, and imperative, is
strengthened by means of נָא). So, also, in loose connexion with
participial and other noun-clauses (see above, *x*), Gn 45¹²ꜰ·, 1 K 2²ꜰ·,
Ru 3³ꜰ·, 3⁹.—In Gn 17¹¹ the perfect consecutive (וּנְמַלְתֶּם *and ye shall
be circumcised*, &c.) is used to explain a preceding command.

Rem. As in the cases mentioned above under *y*, the connexion may be *bb*
made by means of וְהָיָה. Thus with a following perfect consecutive, e. g.
Gn 46³³, 47²⁴, Ju 4²⁰. Cf. also Gn 24¹⁴, where the real wish, at least as regards
the sense, is contained in the next sentence.

(*c*) To introduce a question, whether in loose connexion with *cc*
another interrogative sentence (see above, *p*), e. g. Gn 29¹⁵ *art thou my
brother* (equivalent to, *Surely thou art*), וַעֲבַדְתַּנִי *and shouldest thou then
serve me for naught ?* or with a positive statement, e. g. Ex 5⁵ וְהִשְׁבַּתֶּם
will ye then make them rest ?); Nu 16¹⁰, 1 S 25¹¹, and (if it is *Milʿra*')
ψ 50²¹ (וְהֶחֱרַשְׁתִּי).

(*d*) To introduce actions frequently repeated (hence analogous to *dd*
the numerous examples of a frequentative perfect consecutive, above,
under *e*), e. g. 1 S 1³ (וְעָלָה) of annual festival journeys); 13²¹ (where,
however, the text appears radically corrupt); 27⁹ (וְהִכָּה, i. e. every
time, therefore continued by means of וְלֹא יְחַיֶּה); 1 K 5⁷ (וְכִלְכְּלוּ,

---

[1] On the various combinations with וְהָיָה see König's statistics in *ZAW*.
xix. 272 ff.

parallel with a simple imperfect); 9²⁵, Jer 25⁴, Ho 12¹¹, Dn 8⁴.—In Jb 1⁴ᶠ· a series of frequentative perfects consecutive is interrupted by an imperfect consecutive, while a simple imperfect (as the *modus rei repetitae*) forms the conclusion. In Jer 6¹⁷ a similar perfect is expressly marked, by placing the tone on the final syllable (according to § 49 *h*), as parallel with the real perfects consecutive.

ee Rem. The loose connexion of *tempora frequentativa* by וְהָיָה (cf. the Rem. on *y* and *bb*) is also very common in this sense; thus with a following perfect consecutive, Gn 30⁴¹ᶠ· (but in verse 42ᵃ, where the verb is separated from the *Wāw* by an insertion, we find לֹא יָשִׂים *he used not to put them in*, according to § 107 *e*); Gn 38⁹, Ex 17¹¹, 33⁷ ᶠᶠ· (see above, *e*), Nu 21⁹, Ju 6³, 19³⁰, 1 S 16²³ (followed by five perfects consecutive); 2 S 15⁵; with a following imperfect (as the *modus rei repetitae*), Ju 2¹⁹, 2 S 14²⁶.—In Ju 12⁵ᶠ· וְהָיָה, contrary to what would be expected, is continued by means of the imperfect consecutive, and in 1 S 13²² by וְלֹא with the perfect (instead of the imperfect).

ff **5.** Further, the perfect consecutive is very frequently employed with a certain emphasis to introduce the apodosis after sentences (or their equivalents) which contain a condition, a reason, or a statement of time. Such an apodosis, as in the cases already treated, may represent either future events, or commands and wishes, or even events which have been often repeated in the past. Thus—

(*a*) The perfect consecutive occurs in the apodosis to conditional sentences [1] (§ 159 *g, o, s*):

(α) After אִם with the imperfect, e. g. 2 K 7⁴ᵇ אִם־יְמִיתֻנוּ וָמָתְנוּ *if they kill us, (well then) we shall but die*; here the perfect consecutive is used obviously with greater emphasis than the imperfect (נִחְיֶה) which immediately precedes; Gn 18²⁶, 24⁸·⁴¹, 32⁹, Nu 30¹⁵, Ju 4²⁰, 1 S 1¹¹, 20⁶, 1 K 3¹⁴, Na 3¹², Ec 4¹¹.

gg (β) After אִם with the perfect (in the sense of a *futurum exactum*), Nu 5²⁷, 2 K 5²⁰, 7⁴ᵃ, Is 4¹ᶠ·; as precative apodosis after אִם־נָא with the *perf. preteritum*, Gn 33¹⁰; as a frequentative perfect consecutive, to represent past events in the apodosis after אִם with a perfect, Gn 38⁹, Nu 21⁹, Ju 6³, Jb 7⁴; after אִם with imperfect, Gn 31⁸.

hh (γ) After כִּי (*in case, suppose that*) with the imperfect, Gn 12¹², Ex 18¹⁶, Ju 13¹⁷, Is 58⁷, Ez 14¹³. [2] Frequentative with reference to the past, after כִּי with frequentative perfect, Ju 2¹⁸, Jb 7¹³ᶠ·.

---

[1] In a number of the examples of this kind the protasis is already loosely connected by means of וְהָיָה, and hence some of them had to be already mentioned above, under *y*, *bb*, *ee*.

[2] In 1 S 24¹⁹ a question appears to be expressed by the perfect consecutive, *for if a man find his enemy, will he let him go well away?* Probably, however, with Klostermann, וּמִי should be read for וְכִי.

(δ) After אֲשֶׁר with the imperfect, Gn 44⁹ וָמֵת ... אִתּוֹ יִמָּצֵא אֲשֶׁר *ii* *with whomsoever ... it be found, let him die*; with the perfect, Ex 21¹³ *and if a man lie not in wait, &c.*; Ju 1¹².

(ε) Very frequently after a perfect consecutive (one or more) con- *kk* taining the condition, e. g. Gn 44²⁹ וְהוֹרַדְתֶּם ... זֶה־אֶת גַּם וּלְקַחְתֶּם *and if ye take* (or *shall have taken*) *this one also ... ye shall bring down*, &c.; cf. Gn 33¹³, 42³⁸, 44⁴·²², 47³⁰, Nu 30¹², Ru 2⁹, and probably also Ez 39²⁸.— Also frequentative in reference to the past, e. g. 1 S 17³⁴ᶠ· ... הָאֲרִי וּבָא וְיָצָאתִי *and when there came* (as sometimes happened) *a lion ... I went out*, &c.; Ex 33¹⁰, Nu 10¹⁷ ᶠᶠ·, 1 K 18¹⁰, Jer 20⁹ (the perfects consecutive being regularly continued in the apodosis by וְלֹא with an imperfect[1]).

Rem. The perfect consecutive may be used also in the protasis to express *ll* a condition when the employment of the perfect consecutive in the apodosis has become impossible, owing to an emphatic word having to stand before it; thus in Ez 14¹⁴ on account of הֵמָּה; 33⁴ on account of דָּמוֹ.—In 1 S 14⁵² the imperfect consecutive, contrary to what might be expected, stands in the apodosis, *and when Saul saw any ... valiant man, he took him unto him*, where וַיַּאַסְפֵהוּ suggests the special case, rather than a repeated occurrence; cf. 2 S 15². Conversely, in 1 S 2¹⁶ (וַיֹּאמֶר) perhaps a mere mistake for וְאָמַר), 17³⁵ ᵇ an imperfect consecutive stands in the protasis.

(ζ) After various equivalents of sentences, which contain a condition; *mm* thus, after a substantive standing absolutely, or a participle (a *casus pendens*), Gn 17¹⁴ וְנִכְרְתָה וג׳ ... זָכָר וְעָרֵל *and the uncircumcised male* (in case such an one be found), *he shall be cut off*, &c.; cf. Gn 30³², Ex 12¹⁵, 2 S 14¹⁰, Is 6¹³, and (after an infinitive with a preposition) 2 S 7¹⁴; in a wider sense also Ex 4²¹, 9¹⁹, 12⁴⁴, Is 9⁴, 56⁵.

(*b*) The perfect consecutive serves as the apodosis to causal clauses; *nn* thus e. g. after כִּי יַעַן with the perfect, Is 3¹⁶ᶠ·; after אֲשֶׁר יַעַן with perfect, 1 K 20²⁸; after עֵקֶב with perfect, Nu 14²⁴; also after what are equivalent to causal clauses, e. g. ψ 25¹¹ (וְסָלַחְתָּ ... שִׁמְךָ לְמַעַן *for thy name's sake ... pardon ...*); Is 37²⁹ after יַעַן with an infinitive.

(*c*) The perfect consecutive occurs as the apodosis to temporal *oo* clauses or their equivalents, e. g. 1 S 2¹⁵ וּבָא ... הַחֵלֶב־אֶת יַקְטִרוּן בְּטֶרֶם הַכֹּהֵן נַעַר *before they burnt the fat, the priest's servant came* (used to come), &c., hence a frequentative perfect consecutive relating to the past, as in Ex 1¹⁹; also after participial clauses (§ 116 *w*), e. g. 1 S 2¹³ᶠ· וּבָא ... זֶבַח זֹבֵחַ אִישׁ־כָּל *when(ever) any man offered sacrifice, then came,*

---

[1] In all these examples (not only in the frequentative perfects consecutive) the original idea of the perfect, which also underlies the perfect consecutive, comes out very distinctly. Gn 44²⁹ (see above) implies in the mind of the speaker, If it ever shall have come to this, that ye *have taken* this one also, then *ye have* thereby brought me down to Sheol.

&c. (so Ju 19³⁰, 2 S 20¹²), with a frequentative perfect consecutive. The perfect consecutive is very frequently used to announce future actions or events after simple expressions of time of any kind; thus Gn 3⁵, Ex 32³⁴ (after בְּיוֹם with the infinitive), cf. also such examples as Gn 44³¹, Ju 16², Jos 6¹⁰, 1 S 1²², 16²³ (numerous frequentative perfects consecutive after the infinitive with a preposition; so 2 S 15⁵, see above, *ee*); 1 S 20¹⁸, 2 S 14²⁶, 15¹⁰, Is 18⁵; moreover, Ex 17⁴, Is 10²⁵, 29¹⁷, 37²⁶; even after single disconnected words, e. g. Ex 16⁶ עֶרֶב וִידַעְתֶּם *at even* (when it becomes evening) *then ye shall know*; cf. verse 7, Lv 7¹⁶, 1 K 13³¹, Pr 24²⁷.

pp   6. Finally there still remains a number of passages which cannot be classed with any of those hitherto mentioned. Of these, some are due to the influence of Aramaic modes of expression, while in others the text is evidently corrupt.[1] In a few instances we can do no more than merely call attention to the incorrectness of the expression. (We are not of course concerned here with the cases—usually occurring in dependent clauses—in which a 2nd pers. *perf.* with Wāw copulative is simply co-ordinate with what precedes, as in Gn 28⁶, and probably Nu 21¹⁵, Dt 33².)

(*a*) The influence of the Aramaic construction of the perfect with וֹ as the narrative tense, instead of the Hebrew imperfect consecutive (cf. Kautzsch, *Gramm. des Bibl.-Aram.*, § 71 *b*), is certainly to be traced in *Qoheleth*, and sporadically in other very late books,[2] perhaps also in a few passages in the books of Kings, which are open to the suspicion of being due to later interpolation; so probably 1 K 12³² וְהֶעֱמִיד; 2 K 11¹ *Keth.* וראתה; 14¹⁴ וְלָקַח (in the parallel passage, 2 Ch 25²⁴, the word is wanting); 2 K 23⁴ וְנָשָׂא, &c.; verse 10 וְטִמֵּא, &c.; verse 12 וְהִשְׁלִיךְ, &c.; verse 15 וְשָׂרַף, &c.[3] Cf. also Ez 37².⁷.¹⁰.

qq   (*b*) The text is certainly corrupt in Is 40⁶ (read with the LXX and Vulgate

---

[1] Mayer Lambert, *REJ.* xxvi. 55, is probably right in pointing some of these forms as *infin. abs.* instead of *perfects*.

[2] In the whole of *Qoheleth* the imperfect consecutive occurs only in 1¹⁷ and 4¹.⁷. Several of the perfects with וֹ can no doubt be explained as frequentatives, e. g. 1¹³, 2⁵.⁹.¹¹.¹³.¹⁵, 5¹⁸, compared with 6²; but this is impossible in such passages as 9¹⁴ ff. In Ezra, Driver reckons only six examples of the historical perfect with וֹ, in Nehemiah only six, and in Esther six or seven.

[3] Stade in *ZAW.* v. 291 ff. and in *Ausgewählte akad. Reden*, Giessen, 1899, p. 194 ff. and appendix p. 199, discusses, in connexion with 2 K 12¹², a number of critically questionable perfects with וֹ. He considers that the whole section, 2 K 23⁴ from וְנָשָׂא to verse 5 inclusive, is to be regarded as a gloss, since the continuation of an imperfect consecutive by means of a perfect with וֹ never occurs in pre-exilic documents, except in places where it is due to corruption of the original text. The theory of frequentative perfects consecutive (even immediately after imperfects consecutive), which has been supported above, under *f* and *g*, by a large number of examples, is quite inconsistent with the character of the action in 2 K 23⁵ וְהִשְׁבִּית, verse 8 וְנָתַץ, and verse 14 וְשִׁבַּר.

וַיֹּאמֶר) ; Jer 38²⁸, where the narrative breaks off in the middle of the sentence ;
40³ (וְהָיָה), &c., wanting in the LXX) ; also in Ju 7¹³ וְנָפַל הָאֹהֶל is altogether
redundant ; in 1 S 3¹³ read, with Klostermann, the 2*nd sing. masc.* instead of
וְהִגַּדְתִּי ; in 1 K 21¹² וְהוֹשִׁיבוּ is, no doubt, incorrectly repeated from verse 9,
where it is an imperative.

Of other questionable instances, (*a*) the following, at any rate, may also be *rr*
explained as frequentatives, Gn 21²⁵, 49²³, Ex 36³⁸, 38²⁸, 39³, 1 S 5⁷, 17²⁰, 24¹¹ (but
even so וְאָמְרוּ would be expected) ; 2 K 23¹², Is 28²⁶ (parallel with an imperfect) ; Am 5²⁶ (unless it is rather, *yea, ye shall take up* ; see above, *x*) ; ψ 26³,
Ez 8³⁶.

(β) A longer or constant continuance in a past state is perhaps represented *ss*
by the perfect with וְ (as a variety of the frequentative perfect with וְ), in
Gn 15⁶, 34⁵, Nu 21²⁰, Jos 9¹², 223 *b*, Is 22¹⁴, Jer 3⁹. But the unusual *perfects consec.*
in Jos 1:³⁻¹¹, 16²⁻⁸ (ultimately parallel with an imperf. as in 17⁹, 18²⁰), 18¹²⁻²¹,
19¹¹⁻¹⁴·²²·²⁶⁻²⁹·³⁴, are without doubt rightly explained by Bennett (*SBOT.*, Joshua,
p. 23) as originally containing the directions either of God to Joshua or of
Joshua to the people ; cf. the evident trace of this in 15⁴ *b*. A redactor
transformed the directions into a description but left the *perfects consec.*, which
are to be explained as in *aa*. In the same way וְהָיוּ Ex 36²⁹ is most simply
explained as repeated from 26²⁵.

(γ) The following are due to errors in the text, or to incorrect modes of *tt*
expression : Ex 36²⁹ *f.*, Ju 3²³, ¹ 16¹⁸ (read וַיַּעֲלוּ), 1 S 4¹⁹, 17³⁸, 2 S 16⁵, 19¹⁸ *f.* (read
צָלֵחוּ and וַיַּעַבְרוּ), 1 K 3¹¹ (where וְשָׁאַלְתָּ is, no doubt intentionally, assimilated to the four other perfects) ; 13³, 20²¹ ; 2 K 14⁷ (where, with Stade,
וְאֶת־הַסֶּלַע תָּפַשׂ should be read) ; 14¹⁴, 18⁴ (where, at any rate, וְשִׁבַּר might
be taken as a frequentative, but not וְכָרַת, &c. ; evidently the perfects are
co-ordinated only in form with הוּא הֵסִיר) ; 18³⁶, 21¹⁵, 24¹⁴, Jer 37¹⁵ (where
וְהִכּוּ, but not וּנְתָנֻנוּ, might be frequentative) ; Ez 9⁷ (omit וְיָצְאוּ with Stade,
and read וְהִכּוּ) ; 20²² וַהֲשִׁבֹתִי *Mil'ēl* before an imperfect consecutive) ; Am 7⁴
(וְאָכְלָה after an imperfect consecutive) ; Jb 16¹².

Finally, in 1 S 1¹², 10⁹, 17⁴⁸, 25²⁰, 2 S 6¹⁶, 2 K 3¹⁵, Jer 37¹¹, Am 7² וְהָיִי is to be *uu*
read throughout instead of וְהָיָה, but in Gn 38⁵ וְהָיָא with the LXX.

B. The Infinitive and Participle.

§ 113. *The Infinitive Absolute.*

Cf. the dissertation of J. Kahan, and, especially, the thorough investigation
by E. Sellin, both entitled, *Ueber die verbal-nominale Doppelnatur der hebräischen
Participien und Infinitive*, &c., Lpz. 1889 ; F. Prätorius, 'Ueber die sogen. Infin.
absol. des Hebr.' in *ZDMG.* 1902, pp. 546 ff.

1. The infinitive absolute is employed according to § 45 to emphasize *a*
the idea of the verb *in the abstract,* i. e. it speaks of an action (or
state) without any regard to the agent or to the circumstances
of time and mood under which it takes place. As the *name* of an
action the infinitive absolute, like other nouns in the stricter sense,

---

¹ Or does וְנָעַל, as a frequentative, imply fastening with several bolts ? It is,
at all events, to be noticed, that in 2 S 13¹⁸ also וְנָעַל follows an imperfect
consecutive.

may form part of certain combinations (as a subject, predicate, or object, or even as a genitive,[1] see below); but such a use of the infinitive absolute (instead of the infinitive construct with or without a preposition) is, on the whole, rare, and, moreover, open to question on critical grounds. On the other hand, the infinitive absolute frequently exhibits its character as an expression of the *verbal idea* by taking an object, either in the accusative or even with a preposition.

b　　Examples of the use of the infinitive absolute :—

(*a*) As subject, Pr 25²⁷ אָכֹל דְּבַשׁ הַרְבּוֹת לֹא טוֹב *it is not good to eat much honey* ; Jer 10⁵, Jb 6²⁵, Ec 4¹⁷ ; epexegetically, after a demonstrative pronoun, Is 58⁵ ᶠ·, Zc 14¹².

c　　(*b*) As predicate, Is 32¹⁷ *and the effect of righteousness* (is) הַשְׁקֵט וָבֶטַח *quietness* (prop. *to find rest*) *and confidence.*

d　　(*c*) As object, Is 1¹⁷ לִמְדוּ הֵיטֵב *learn to do well* ; Is 7¹⁵, Pr 15¹², Jb 9¹⁸ ; according to the sense also Jer 9²³ 23¹⁴, as well as Is 5⁵ הָסֵר and פָּרֹץ virtually depend on the idea of the wish contained in עָשָׂה) ; Is 22¹³, where a long series of infinitives absolute is governed by הִנֵּה, and 59¹³ (six infinitives governed by יְדַעֲנוּם in verse 12) ; Dt 28⁵⁶ is strange since the object precedes the infinitive absolute which governs it,[2] also Is 42²¹, where the statement of place precedes the infinitive absolute.—In Jer 9⁴, Jb 13³ the infinitive absolute as the object of the verb is placed before it for the sake of emphasis (with the verb negatived by לֹא in Is 57²⁰, Jer 49²³), so also in La 3⁴⁵ where it is the remoter object and co-ordinated with a substantive.

e　　(*d*) As genitive, Is 14²³ בְּמַטְאֲטֵא הַשְׁמֵד *with the besom of destruction* ; so perhaps also 4⁴ בְּרוּחַ בָּעֵר ; cf. further, Pr 1³, 21¹⁶. The infinitive absolute is never used in immediate connexion with prepositions[3] (which as being originally substantives govern the genitive), but always the infinitive construct ; but if a second infinitive is co-ordinated by וְ with such an infinitive construct, it has the form of the infinitive absolute (since it is released from the immediate government of the preposition), e. g. 1 S 22¹³ . . . בְּתִתְּךָ לוֹ לֶחֶם וְשָׁאוֹל לוֹ בֵּאלֹהִים *in that thou hast given him bread . . . and hast enquired of God for him* ; Ez 36³ ; 1 S 25²⁶·³³ (after מִן) ; after לְ Ex 32⁶, Jer 7¹⁸, 44¹⁷.

f　　(*e*) Governing an accusative of the object, e. g. Is 22¹³ הָרֹג בָּקָר וְשָׁחֹט צֹאן *slaying oxen and killing sheep* ; cf. Ex 20⁸, 23³⁰, Dt 5¹², Is 37¹⁹, Ez 23³⁰, and of the examples in *a–d*, Dt 28⁵⁶, Is 5⁵, 58⁶ ᶠ·, Pr 25²⁷, &c. ; followed by a preposition, e. g. Is 7¹⁵ מָאוֹס בָּרָע וּבָחוֹר בַּטּוֹב *to refuse the evil and choose the good* ; Pr 15¹² (הוֹכֵחַ לוֹ).

g　　If the object be a personal pronoun, then, since the infinitive absolute can never be united with a suffix (see the note on *a*), it is affixed by means of the accusative-sign אֵת (אֹת), e. g. Jer 9²³ וְיָדֹעַ אֹתִי *and knoweth me* ; Ez 36³.

---

[1] The infinitive absolute can never be joined with a genitive or a pronominal suffix.

[2] Perhaps הָגֵן according to § 53 *k* should be explained as an infinitive construct, or should be written הַגֵּן.

[3] וְאַחֲרֵי שָׁתֹה 1 S 1⁹ is impossible Hebrew, and as the LXX shows, a late addition.

2. Analogous to the use of the infinitive absolute as the accusative *h* of the object, mentioned in *d*, is its employment as a *casus adverbialis* [1] in connexion with some form of the finite verb, to describe more particularly the manner or attendant circumstances (especially those of time and place) under which an action or state has taken place, or is taking place, or will take place; e. g. Jer 22¹⁹ *he shall be buried with the burial of an ass,* סָחוֹב וְהַשְׁלֵךְ *a drawing and casting forth,* i. e. being drawn and cast forth, &c.; Gn 21¹⁶ (הַרְחֵק *a removing,* i. e. distant; cf. Ex 33⁷, Jos 3¹⁶); Gn 30³², Ex 30³⁶, Nu 6⁵·²³, 15³⁵ (where a subject is added subsequently; see below, *gg*); Jos 3¹⁷, 1 S 3¹² (הָחֵל וְכַלֵּה *a beginning and ending,* i. e. from beginning to end); 2 S 8², Is 7¹¹ (הַעֲמֵק and הַגְבֵּהַּ, prop. *a making deep . . .,* and *a making high,* i. e. whether thy request extend to the world below or to the height above); 57¹⁷ (הַסְתֵּר *in hiding,* sc. my face); Jer 3¹⁵ דֵּעָה וְהַשְׂכֵּיל *with knowledge and understanding*); Hb 3¹³ (עָרוֹת, for the form cf. § 75 *aa*); Zc 7³, ψ 35¹⁶ (חָלֹק, to define more precisely קָרְעוּ verse 15); Jb 15³. [2]

Rem. 1. To an adverbial infinitive absolute of this kind, there may further *i* be added a *casus adverbialis* (the accusative of state or circumstance), or even a circumstantial clause, to define more exactly the manner in which the action is performed, e. g. Is 20² *and he did so* הָלֹךְ עָרוֹם וְיָחֵף *walking naked and barefoot,* prop. in the condition of one naked, &c.; Is 30¹⁴ *a breaking in pieces* (acc. to the reading כָּתוֹת; the Masora requires כָּתוּת) *without sparing.*

2. A few infinitives of this kind, all of which are in Hiphʿil, have, through *k* frequent use, come to be treated by the language as simple adverbs; so especially הַרְבֵּה (cf. § 75 *ff*) *multum faciendo,* i. e. *multum,* very frequently strengthened by מְאֹד *very* and even used without connexion with a finite verb (see the Lexicon); also הֵיטֵב *bene faciendo,* i. e. *bene,* used especially to express the careful and thorough performance of an action (e. g. Dt 13¹⁵); in Dt 9²¹, 27⁸ it is added epexegetically to another adverbial infinitive absolute, in Jon 4⁹ it twice precedes the verb for the sake of emphasis. Finally, הַשְׁכֵּם *mane faciendo,* i. e. *early in the morning,* then in general *early* with the additional idea of earnestness; in 1 S 17¹⁶ joined with the infinitive absolute וְהַעֲרֵב a denominative from עֶרֶב *evening* (*morning and evening,* i. e. *early and late*), elsewhere (with the exception of Pr 27¹⁴) always joined with the infinitive absolute of the governing verb, e. g. Jer 11⁷ *for I earnestly protested* (הַעִידֹתִי) *unto your fathers . . .* הַשְׁכֵּם וְהָעֵד *rising early and protesting,* i. e. with earnest protestation; Jer 25³, 26⁵ (where ן should be omitted before 'ה); Jer 29¹⁹, 32³³, 2 Ch 16¹⁵.

---

[1] That this *casus adverbialis* also was originally regarded as an accusative, may be seen from classical Arabic, where an infinitive of this kind expressly retains the accusative ending. In Latin the ablative of the gerund corresponds in many ways to this use of the infinitive absolute.

[2] Also in 2 K 21¹³ for מָחָה וְהָפַךְ read with Stade and Klostermann מָחֹה וְהָפֹךְ; similarly, with Stade, וְקָשֹׁה in Ju 4²⁴; וְחָזוֹק in Jer 23¹⁴, and on Is 31⁵ cf. *t*.

l 3. The infinitive absolute occurs most frequently in immediate connexion with the finite verb of the same stem, in order in various ways *to define more accurately* or *to strengthen the idea of the verb*.[1]

m   These infinitives absolute joined immediately to the finite verb belong in a sense to the *schema etymologicum* treated in § 117 *p*, i.e. they are objects of the finite verb in question, except that the infinitive absolute (as a *nomen abstractum*) lays stress rather on the actual occurrence or the energy of the action (see the examples below), while the noun proper emphasizes the result or extent of the action; cf. e.g. Ex 22²² אִם־צָעֹק יִצְעַק אֵלַי *if* it actually happens that *he cries to me*, with Gn 27³⁴ (as it were, *he cried*, so that *a great cry was heard*).

We must further distinguish—

n   (a) The infinitive absolute used *before* the verb to *strengthen* the verbal idea, i.e. to emphasize in this way either the certainty (especially in the case of threats) or the forcibleness and completeness of an occurrence. In English, such an infinitive is mostly expressed by a corresponding adverb, but sometimes merely by putting greater stress on the verb; e.g. Gn 2¹⁷ מוֹת תָּמוּת *thou shalt surely die*, cf. 18¹⁰,¹⁸, 22¹⁷, 28²², 1 S 9⁶ (*cometh surely to pass*); 24²¹, Am 5⁵, 7¹⁷, Hb 2³, Zc 11¹⁷; with the infinitive strengthened by אַךְ Gn 44²⁸ (but 27³⁰ *and Jacob was yet scarce gone out*, &c.); Gn 43³ הָעֵד הֵעִד בָּנוּ *he did solemnly protest unto us*; 1 S 20⁶ נִשְׁאֹל נִשְׁאַל *David earnestly asked leave of me*; Jos 17¹³, Ju 1²⁸ וְהוֹרֵשׁ לֹא הוֹרִישׁוֹ *and did not utterly drive them out*; especially typical instances are Am 9⁸ *I will destroy it from off the face of the earth* אֶפֶס כִּי לֹא הַשְׁמֵיד אַשְׁמִיד וג' *saving that I will not utterly destroy*, &c.; Jer 30¹¹ *and will in no wise leave thee unpunished*; cf. further Gn 20¹⁸, 1 K 3²⁶, Jo 1⁷, Jb 13⁵.

o   The infinitive absolute is used before the verb with less emphasis:

(1) Frequently at the beginning of the statement; cf. Driver on 1 S 20⁶. However, in these cases a special emphasis on the following verb is sometimes intended; cf. above, *n*, on Gn 43³, 1 S 20⁶; also Gn 3¹⁶, 26²⁸, 32¹⁷, 1 S 14²⁸, 20³. Elsewhere the infinitive absolute is evidently used only as possessing a certain fullness of sound (hence for rhythmical reasons, like some uses of the separate pronoun, § 135 *a*), as in Gn 15¹³, 43⁷·²⁰, Ju 9⁸, 1 S 10¹⁶, 23¹⁰, 2 S 1⁶, 20¹⁸.

(2) Very frequently in conditional sentences after אִם, &c. The infinitive absolute in this case emphasizes the importance of the con-

---

[1] Cf. A. Rieder, *Die Verbindung des Inf. abs. mit dem Verb. fin* . . . *im Hebr.*, Lpz., 1872; also his *Quae ad syntaxin Hebraicam* . . . *planiorem faciendam ex lingua Graeca et Latina afferantur*, Gumbinnen (Programm des Gymnasiums), 1884. G. R. Hauschild, *Die Verbindung finiter und infiniter Verbalformen desselben Stammes in einigen Bibelsprachen*, Frankfurt a. M., 1893, discussing especially the rendering of such constructions in the Greek and Latin versions.

dition on which some consequence depends, e. g. Ex 15²⁶ *if thou wilt diligently hearken*, &c., Ex 19⁵, 21⁵, 22³·¹¹ᶠ· ¹⁶·²² (see above, *m*); 23²², Nu 21², Ju 16¹¹, 1 S 1¹¹, 12²⁵; after לֹא 1 S 14³⁰.

The infinitive absolute is used to give emphasis to an antithesis, e. g. *p* 2 S 24²⁴ *nay; but I will verily buy* (קָנוֹ אֶקְנֶה) *it of thee*, &c. (not receive it as a gift); Ju 15¹³ *no; but we will bind thee fast . . . but surely we will not kill thee*; cf. further Gn 31³⁰ (thou art indeed gone=) *though thou wouldst needs be gone* (Vulg. *esto*), *because thou sore longedst*, &c.; ψ 118¹³·¹⁸, 126⁶ (the second infinitive absolute as a supplement to the first—see below, *r*—comes *after* the verb).—Hence also, as permissive, Gn 2¹⁶ᶠ· אָכֹל תֹּאכֵל *thou mayest freely eat, but*, &c. (so that verse 16 is in antithesis to verse 17); or concessive, 1 S 2³⁰ *I said indeed . . .*, 14⁴³.

The infinitive absolute is used to strengthen a question, and *q* especially in impassioned or indignant questions, e. g. Gn 37⁸ הֲמָלֹךְ תִּמְלֹךְ עָלֵינוּ *shalt thou indeed reign over us?* Gn 37¹⁰, 43⁷, Ju 11²⁵, 1 S 2²⁷, 2 S 19⁴³, Jer 3¹, 13¹², Ez 28⁹, Am 3⁵, Zc 7⁵; but cf. also Gn 24⁵ *must I needs bring again?*

(*b*) The infinitive absolute *after the verb*, sometimes (as in *n*) to *r* intensify[1] the idea of the verb (especially after imperatives and participles, since the infinitive absolute can never precede either, e. g. Nu 11¹⁵, Jb 13¹⁷, 21², 37² שִׁמְעוּ שָׁמוֹעַ *hearken ye attentively*; Jer 22¹⁰; after participles, e. g. Is 22¹⁷, also elsewhere, e. g. Nu 23¹¹, 24¹⁰ *thou hast altogether blessed them*; Jos 24¹⁰, 2 K 5¹¹, Dn 11¹⁰, and with the infinitive absolute strengthened by means of גַּם Gn 31¹⁵, 46⁴, Nu 16¹³); sometimes to express the long *continuance* of an action; here again after an imperative, Is 6⁹ שִׁמְעוּ שָׁמוֹעַ *hear ye continually*; after a perfect, Jer 6²⁹; after a participle, Jer 23¹⁷; after an imperfect consecutive, Gn 19⁹, Nu 11³².

To this class belong especially those cases in which a second infini- *s* tive absolute is co-ordinated with the first; the latter then expresses either an accompanying or antithetical action or the aim to which the principal action is directed; e. g. 1 S 6¹² הָלְכוּ הָלֹךְ וְגָעוֹ *lowing as they went* (lowing continually; so after a participle, Jos 6¹³ᵇ *Qerê*); Gn 8⁷ *it went forth to and fro*[2]; Is 19²² *smiting and* (i. e. but also) *healing again*; Jo 2²⁶ (see above, *m*).

Rem. 1. Instead of a second infinitive absolute (see above) there is some- *t* times found a perfect consecutive (Jos. 6¹³ᵃ and 2 S 13¹⁹ [but Stade's וְזָעוֹק is

---

[1] In Arabic also, the intensifying infinitive regularly stands *after* the verb, but in Syriac *before* the verb.

[2] Also in Ez 1¹⁴ for the distorted form רָצוֹא reads simply יָצֹא יֵצֵא.

is preferable], in both places as perfect frequentative ; Is 31⁵ referring to the future, unless with Stade, *ZAW.* vi. 189, we read וְהַצִּיל and וְהַמְלִיט), or an imperfect consecutive (1 S 19²³, 2 S 16¹³) or participle (2 S 16⁵) ; cf. also *u.*

u 2. The idea of long *continuance* is very frequently expressed by the verb הָלַךְ *to go,* along with its infinitive absolute, or even by the latter alone, and this occurs not only when it can be taken in its literal sense (*to go, to walk,* as in the examples given above, Jos 6⁹·¹³, 1 S 6¹², 2 S 3¹⁶, 13¹⁹ ; cf. also, Is 3¹⁶, where both infinitives stand *before* the verb, and ψ 126⁶, where הָלוֹךְ precedes), but also in cases where הָלַךְ in the sense of *to go on, to continue,* merely performs the function of an adverb. The action itself is added in a second infinitive absolute, or sometimes (see above, *t*) in a participle or verbal adjective. Examples, Gn 8³ הָלוֹךְ וָשׁוֹב ... וַיָּשֻׁבוּ הַמַּיִם *and the waters returned ... continually* ; Gn 8⁵, 12⁹, Ju 14⁹, 2 K 2¹¹ ; with a participle following, Jer 41⁶ (unless we read וּבְכֹה, as in 2 S 3¹⁶) ; with an adjective following, Gen 26¹³, Ju 4²⁴, 1 S 14¹⁹, 2 S 5¹⁰ (1 Ch 11⁹), 2 S 18²⁵. [1]

On the other hand, in 1 S 17⁴¹ the participle הֹלֵךְ is used instead of the infinitive absolute. Of a different kind are the instances in which the participle הֹלֵךְ is used as predicate along with the co-ordinate adjective (Ex 19¹⁹, 1 S 2²⁶, 2 S 3¹, 15¹², Est 9⁴, 2 Ch 17¹²) or participle (1 S 17¹⁵, Jon 1¹¹, Pr 4¹⁸, Ec 1⁶).

v 3. The regular place of the negative is between the intensifying infinitive absolute and the finite verb,[2] e.g. Ex 5²³ וְהַצֵּל לֹא־הִצַּלְתָּ *neither hast thou delivered at all,* Ju 15¹³, Jer 13¹², 30¹¹ ; cf. Mi 1¹⁰ (אַל). Exceptions are Gn 3⁴ (where the negation of the threat pronounced in 2¹⁷ is expressed in the same form of words) ; Am 9⁸, ψ 49⁸.

w 4. With a finite verb of one of the derived conjugations, not only the infinitive absolute of the *same* conjugation may be connected (Gn 28²² Pi‘ēl ; 17¹³, Ex 22³, Ez 14³ Niph‘al ; Gn 40¹⁵ Pu‘al ; Ho 4¹⁸ Hiph‘îl ; Ez 16⁴ Hoph‘al), but also (especially with Niph‘al, rarely with Pi‘ēl or Hiph‘îl ; see Driver on 2 S 20¹⁸) that of *Qal* as the simplest and most general representative of the verbal idea, 2 S 20¹⁸ (with Pi‘ēl ; but in Gn 37³³, 44²⁸ טָרֹף is a passive of Qal, § 52 *e*) ; 46⁴ (with Hiph‘îl) ; Ex 19¹³, 21²⁰, 2 S 23⁷, Is 40³⁰, Jer 10⁵, Jb 6² (with Niph‘al) ; Is 24¹⁹ (with Hithpo‘ēl) רֹעָה in the same verse must also, according to the Masora, certainly be the infinitive absolute Qal ; see § 67 *o*), and so always מוֹת יוּמַת *he shall surely be put to death.* Elsewhere the infinitive absolute of a conjugation with kindred meaning is found, Lv 19²⁰, 2 K 3²³ Hoph‘al for Niph‘al (but most probably we should read, with Driver, the *infin. Niph.* in both places, הָפְדֵה and הֶחֱרֵב) ; 1 S 2¹⁶ (Pi‘ēl for Hiph‘îl, unless יִקְטֹרוּן is to be read) ; Ez 16⁴ (Hoph‘al for Pu‘al).[3] Finally, the infinitive absolute may

---

[1] Cf. in French, *Le mal va toujours croissant, la maladie va toujours en augmentant et en empirant,* ‘ *continually increases and becomes worse and worse.*’

[2] Cf. Rieder, *Quo loco ponantur negationes* לֹא *et* אַל ... (*Zeitschrift für Gymn.-Wesen,* 1879, p. 395 ff.).

[3] In three passages even the infinitive absolute of another stem of like sound occurs ; but in Is 28²⁸ אָדוֹשׁ is no doubt a mere textual error for דּוֹשׁ, and in Jer 8¹³, according to § 72 *aa,* we should read אָסְפֵם, and in Zp 1² אָסֵף. Barth, *Nom.-bildung,* § 49 *b,* sees in אָדוֹשׁ and אָסוֹף infinitives *Hiph‘îl,* exactly corresponding in form to *'aqâm[â]* the Aram. infin. 'Aph‘ēl of קוּם ; but there is no more evidence for a *Hiph.* of דּוּשׁ in Hebrew than for a stem אָדַשׁ.

equally well be represented by a *substantive* of kindred stem.[1] In Is 29[14] the substantive intensifying the verb is found *along with* the infinitive absolute.

5. Instead of the infinitive absolute immediately connected with the finite *x* verb, an infinitive construct form appears (cf. § 73 *d*), in Nu 23[25] קֹב גַּם ; cf. Ru 2[16] (שָׁל גַּם) ; Jer 50[34] (יָרִיב רִיב) ; Pr 23[1] (תָּבִין בִּין). In the last instances the infinitive is probably assimilated to the imperfect, like the infinitive Niph'al in the forms noticed in § 51 *k* and note.—Cf. also 2 K 3[24] בֹא וַיָּבֹאוּ וְהַכּוֹת (read so with the LXX) before א, hence, no doubt due to the dislike of a hiatus ; so in ψ 50[21], Neh 1[7] (חֲבֹל), all in rapid style ; *after* the verb, Jos 7[7], unless הַעֲבִיר is intended.

4. Finally the infinitive absolute sometimes appears as *a substitute* *y* *for the finite verb*, either when it is sufficient simply to mention the verbal idea (see *z*), or when the hurried or otherwise excited style intentionally contents itself with this infinitive, in order to bring out the verbal idea in a clearer and more expressive manner (see *aa*).

(*a*) The infinitive absolute as the continuation of a preceding finite *z* verb. In the later books especially it often happens that in a succession of several acts only the first (or sometimes more) of the verbs is inflected, while the second (or third, &c.) is added simply in the infinitive absolute. Thus after several perfects, Dn 9[5] (cf. verse 11) *we have sinned . . . and have transgressed thy law*, וְסוֹר *and have turned aside* (prop. *a turning aside* took place); so after a *perfect* Ex 36[7] (?), 1 S 2[28], Is 37[19], Jer 14[5], 19[13], Hag 1[6] (four infinitives), Zc 3[4] (but read with Wellhausen, after the LXX, אֹתוֹ וַהַלְבִּשׁוּ), 7[5], Ec 8[9], 9[11], Est 3[13], 9[6.16.18], 12[6ff.], Neh 9[8.13], 1 Ch 5[20], 2 Ch 28[19]; [2] after the *perfect consecutive*, Zc 12[10]; after the *perfect frequentative* 1 K 9[25] (unless וְהִקְטִיר be intended); after the simple *imperfect*, Lv 25[14], Nu 30[3], Jer 32[44] (three infinitives), 36[23], 1 Ch 21[24]; after a *cohortative*, Jos 9[20]; after the *imperfect consecutive*, Gn 41[43] (as a continuation of וַיַּרְכֵּב); Ex 8[11], Ju 7[19], Jer 37[21], Neh 8[8], 1 Ch 16[36], 2 Ch 7[3]; with אוֹ *or* after the *jussive*, Dt 14[21], Est 2[3], 6[9]; after the *imperative*, Is 37[30b], Am 4[f.]; after the *participle*, Hb 2[15] (strengthened by אַף, and regarded, like the participle itself, as an adverbial accusative); Est 8[8].

(*b*) At the beginning of the narrative, or at least of a new section *aa* of it. The special form of the finite verb which the infinitive absolute represents must be determined from the context. The infinitive

---

[1] On these substantives (and on the use of the infinitive absolute generally as absolute object, see above, *m*), cf. the *schema etymologicum* treated in connexion with the government of the verb in § 117 *p, q.*

[2] In Ez 7[14] a perfect appears to be continued by means of an infinitive construct; but the text is quite corrupt; Cornill reads הַכֵּן הֲבִינוּ תָּקוֹעַ תִּקְעוּ.

absolute is most frequently used in this way, corresponding to the infinitive of command in Greek, &c.[1] :—

bb (*a*) For an emphatic imperative,[2] e. g. שָׁמוֹר (thou shalt, ye shall), *observe* Dt 5¹²; זָכוֹר (thou shalt) *remember*, Ex 13³, 20⁸ (the full form occurs in Dt 6¹⁷ שָׁמוֹר תִּשְׁמְרוּן; 7¹⁸ זָכֹר תִּזְכֹּר); Lv 2⁶, Nu 4², 25¹⁷, Dt 1¹⁶, 2 K 5¹⁰, Is 38⁵, Jer 2², followed by a *perfect consecutive*; Jos 1¹³, 2 K 3¹⁶, Is 7⁴, 14³¹ (parallel with an *imperative*; in Na 2² three imperatives follow). But הַבֵּים ψ 142⁵ may be only an incorrect spelling of הַבֵּט imperative.[3]

cc (*β*) For the jussive, Lv 6⁷, Nu 6⁵, 2 K 11¹⁵, Ez 23⁴⁶; cf. also Pr 17¹² (*let it* rather *meet*).

dd (*γ*) For the cohortative, Is 22¹³ᵇ אָכוֹל וְשָׁתוֹ (the exclamation of the mocker); Ez 21³¹, 23³⁰·⁴⁶; perhaps also Jer 31² (הָלוֹךְ).[4]

ee (*δ*) For the imperfect in emphatic promises, e. g. 2 K 4⁴³ ye shall *eat and leave thereof*; 19²⁹ (Is 37³⁰), 2 Ch 31¹⁰; also in indignant questions, Jb 40² *shall he that cavilleth contend with the Almighty ?*[5] (on the addition of the subject cf. the Rem. below); Jer 3¹ *and thinkest thou to return again to me ?* Jer 7⁹ ff. (six infinitives, continued by means of the *perfect consecutive*; cf. § 112 *o*).

ff (*ε*) For any historical tense (like the Latin *historic* infinitive) in lively narration (or enumeration) and description, even of what is still taking place in present time, e. g. Hos 4² *swearing and breaking faith, and killing, and stealing, and committing adultery* (in these they are busied); 10⁴ (after a *perfect*); Is 21⁵, 59⁴, Jer 8¹⁵, 14¹⁹, Jb 15³⁵; cf. further Jer 32³³, Ec 4².—In Ez 23³⁰, Pr 12⁷, 15²², and 25⁴, the infinitive absolute is best rendered by the passive.

---

[1] Cf. also such infinitives in French as *voir* (page so and so, &c.), *s'adresser . . . , se méfier des voleurs !*

[2] Prätorius, *op. cit.*, p. 547 : the extraordinarily common use of the infinitive form *qātŏl* in the sense of an imperative, jussive, or cohortative has long since caused it to be compared with the Arab. *fa'āli*. It thus appears that the infin. *qātŏl* in Hebrew could be used from early times as a kind of fixed, invariable word of command.

[3] In Ez 21³¹, for the infinitives construct הָסִיר, הָרִים, הַשְׁפִּיל, הַשְׁפֵּל (beside הַגְבֵּהַ) read with Cornill the infinitives absolute הָסֵר, &c. The Kᵉthîbh probably intends הָסִיר, &c.

[4] In 2 S 3¹⁸ the infinitive construct appears to be used instead of the cohortative, but אוֹשִׁיעַ should certainly be read for הוֹשִׁיעַ. Also in 1 K 22³⁰ (2 Ch 18²⁹), which was formerly included under this head (I will *disguise myself and go into the battle*), read אֶתְחַפֵּשׂ וָאָבֹא.

[5] In Jb 34¹⁸ in a similar question instead of the infinitive constr. we should rather expect the infinitive absolute (הֶאָמֹר), unless with the LXX and Vulg. the participle with the article (הָאֹמֵר) is to be read.

Rem. The subject is sometimes added to the infinitive absolute when it *gg*
takes the place of the finite verb, e.g. Lv 6⁷, Nu 15³⁵, Dt 15², ψ 17⁵, Pr 17¹²,
Jb 40², Ec 4², Est 9¹. So, probably, also in Gn 17¹⁰, Ex 12⁴⁸, although here
כָּל־יָכֹר according to § 121 *a* might also be taken as *an object* with a passive
verb; cf. Est 3¹³. In 1 S 25²⁶·³³ the subject follows an infinitive absolute
which is co-ordinated with an infinitive construct, see above, *e*.

§ 114. *The Infinitive Construct.*

1. The infinitive construct, like the infinitive absolute, may also *a*
represent a *nomen verbale* (§ 45 *a*), but of a much more flexible
character than the infinitive absolute (cf. § 113 *a*). Its close relation
with nouns properly so called is especially seen in the readiness with
which the infinitive construct may be used for any case whatever;
thus,

(*a*) As the nominative of the subject, e.g. Gn 2¹⁸ לֹא־טוֹב הֱיוֹת
הָאָדָם לְבַדּוֹ, literally, *not good is the being of man in his separation*;
Gn 30¹⁵, 1 S 23²⁰, Is 7¹³, Pr 17²⁶, 25⁷·²⁴ (but cf. 21⁹ טוֹב לְשֶׁבֶת in the
same statement); ψ 32⁹ prop. *there is not a coming near unto thee*,
but the text is probably corrupt. With a *feminine* predicate, 1 S 18²³,
Jer 2¹⁷.

(*b*) As genitive, e.g. Ec 3⁴ עֵת סְפוֹד וְעֵת רְקוֹד *a time of mourning b
and a time of dancing*; Gn 2¹⁷, 29⁷, Neh 12⁴⁶, 2 Ch 24¹⁴. This
equally includes, according to § 101 *a*, all those cases in which the
infinitive construct depends on a preposition (see below, *d*) [and
Driver, *Tenses*, § 206].

(*c*) As accusative of the object, e.g. 1 K 3⁷ לֹא אֵדַע צֵאת וָבֹא *I know c
not the going out or the coming in* (*I know not* how *to go out and come
in*); Gn 21⁶, 31²⁸, Nu 20²¹, Is 1¹⁴, 37²⁸ (even with אֵת), Jer 6¹⁵, Jb 15²²
(cf. for the use of the infinitive absolute as object, § 113 *f*); as
accusative with a verb expressing fullness, Is 11⁹.

2. The construction of the infinitive with prepositions (as in Greek, *d*
ἐν τῷ εἶναι, διὰ τὸ εἶναι, &c.) may usually be resolved in English into
the finite verb with a conjunction, e.g. Nu 35¹⁹ בְּפִגְעוֹ־בוֹ *in his meeting
him*, i.e. if (as soon as) he meets him; Gn 27⁴⁵ (עַד־שׁוּב); Is 30¹²
יַעַן כָּאׇסְכֶם *because ye despise*; Jer 2³⁵ עַל־אָמְרֵךְ *because thou sayest*;
Gn 27¹ *and his eyes were dim* מֵרְאֹת *from seeing*, i.e. so that he could
not see.

This use of the infinitive construct is especially frequent in con- *e*
nexion with בְּ or כְּ to express time-determinations (in English resolved
into a temporal clause, as above the combination of the infinitive with
יַעַן or עַל־ is resolved into a causal clause), especially after וַיְהִי (see the

examples, § 111 *g*), e.g. 1 S 2²⁷ בִּהְיוֹתָם בְּמִצְרָ֑יִם *when they were in Egypt*; Gn 24³⁰ ... וּכְשָׁמְעוֹ וג׳ וַיְהִי כִרְאֹת אֶת־הַנֶּ֫זֶם *and it came to pass, when he saw* (prop. in the seeing) *the ring* ..., *and when he heard* (prop. in his hearing), &c.

f But by far the most frequent is the connexion of the infinitive construct with לְ.¹ Starting from the fundamental meaning of לְ, i.e. *direction towards something*, infinitives with לְ serve to express the most varied ideas of purpose or aim, and very commonly also (with a weakening or a complete disregard of the original meaning of the לְ) to introduce the object of an action, or finally even (like the infinitive absolute used adverbially, § 113 *h*, and the Latin gerund in -*ndo*) to state motives or attendant circumstances. See the instances in the Remarks.

g Rem. 1. The original meaning of the לְ is most plainly seen in those infinitives with לְ which expressly state a purpose (hence as the equivalent of a final clause), e.g. Gn 11⁵ *and the Lord came down*, לִרְאֹת אֶת־הָעִיר *to see the city*; also with a change of subject, e.g. 2 S 12¹⁰ *and thou hast taken the wife of Uriah the Hittite* לִהְיוֹת לְךָ לְאִשָּׁה *to be* (i.e. that she may be) *thy wife*; cf. Gn 28⁴, Jer 38²⁶ (לָמוּת).—If there is a special emphasis on the infinitive with לְ, it is placed, with its complement, before the governing verb, e.g. Gn 42⁹, 47⁴, Nu 22²⁰, Jos 2³, 1 S 16² with בּוֹא; Ju 15¹⁰, 1 S 17²⁵ with עָלָה.

h 2. Just as clearly the idea of aiming at a definite purpose or turning towards an object may be seen in the combination of the verb הָיָה *to be*, with לְ and an infinitive. In fact הָיָה לַעֲשׂוֹת may mean, either (*a*) *he was in the act of, he was about to* (as it were, he set himself), *he was ready, to do* something, or (*b*) *he or it was appointed* or *compelled*, &c., to do the action in question. In the latter case הָיָה לַעֲשׂוֹת corresponds to the Latin *faciendum erat*, cf. also the English *I am to go*. In both cases הָיָה (as elsewhere when copula) is often omitted.

i Examples of (*a*) Gn 15¹² וַיְהִי הַשֶּׁ֫מֶשׁ לָבוֹא *and when the sun was going down* (just about to set); 2 Ch 26⁵ וַיְהִי לִדְרֹשׁ אֱלֹהִים *and he set himself to seek God* (here with the secondary idea of a continuous action); with the omission of הָיָה Is 38²⁰, יְהֹוָה לְהוֹשִׁיעֵ֑נִי *the Lord is ready to save me*; 1 S 14²¹ (?), Jer 51⁴⁹, ψ 25¹⁴ (*et foedus suum manifestaturus est eis*); Pr 18²⁴ (?), 19⁸ (לִמְצֹא *consecuturus*

---

¹ Cf. § 45 *g*, according to which the close union of the לְ with the first consonant of the infinitive (לִכְתֹּב with a firmly closed syllable, as opposed to בְּכָתֹב, כִּכְתֹב, &c.) seems to point to the formation of a special new verbal form. Quite distinct are the few examples where the infinitive with לְ serves to express time, as Gn 24⁶³ לִפְנוֹת עָ֑רֶב *at the eventide* (prop. at the time of the return of evening); cf. Dt 23¹², Ex 14²⁷, Ju 19²⁶; 2 S 18²⁹ *when Joab sent the king's servant*.

est, unless we simply read יִמְצָא with the LXX)[1] ; 20²⁵, Ec 3¹⁵ אֲשֶׁר לִהְיוֹת *quod futurum est* ; 2 Ch 11²², 12¹² (in a negative statement) ; in a question, Est 7⁸ (*will he even . . . ?*). Cf. also 1 S 4¹⁹.

Of (*b*) Jos 2⁵ וַיְהִי הַשַּׁעַר לִסְגּוֹר *and the gate was to be shut* (had to be shut) ; *k* Is 37²⁶, ψ 109¹³.[2]   Mostly with the omission of הָיָה, e.g. 2 K 4¹³ מֶה לַעֲשׂוֹת לָךְ וג׳ *what is to be done for thee?* (הֲיֵשׁ לְדַבֶּר־לָךְ) *wouldest thou be* (lit. is it to be) *spoken for to the king*, &c. ? 2 K 13¹⁹ לְהַכּוֹת *it was to smite* equivalent to *thou shouldest have smitten* ; Is 5⁴, ψ 32⁹, 68¹⁹ (?), Jb 30⁶ (*habitandum est iis*), 1 Ch 9²⁵, 10¹³, 22⁵, 2 Ch 8¹³ (?), 11²², 19², 36¹⁹ (?), Ho 9¹³, Hb 1¹⁷.   In a question 2 Ch 19² ; after לֹא 1 Ch 5¹, 15² ; after אֵין 1 Ch 23²⁶, 2 Ch 5¹¹ and frequently.

Of the same kind also are the cases, in which the infinitive with לְ depends *l* on the idea of an obligation or permission (or prohibition) ; especially in such forms of expression as 2 S 18¹¹ עָלַי לָתֶת לְךָ וג׳ *it was upon me*, i. e. it would have been *my duty to give thee*, &c.[3] ; cf. Mi 3¹ (2 Ch 13⁵) *it is not for you to* (i. e. are ye not bound to) ?[4] with a negative, 2 Ch 26¹⁸ לֹא לְךָ וג׳ *it pertaineth not unto thee, Uzziah, to burn incense unto the Lord, but only to the priests* ; also אֵין לְ with an infinitive expresses *it is not permitted* (*nefas est*), *may not*, e.g. Est 4² כִּי אֵין לָבוֹא *for none might enter* ; 8⁸, 1 Ch 15²;[5] לֹא with an infinitive is used in a somewhat different sense, equivalent to *it is not feasible, not possible*, e.g. in ψ 40⁶, Ec 3¹⁴, 2 Ch 5¹¹.[6]—With either meaning לֹא can be used instead of אֵין, e.g. Am 6¹⁰ לֹא לְהַזְכִּיר *nefas est, to make mention* of the name of the Lord : but Ju 1¹⁹ *for it was not possible to drive out*, &c., perhaps, however, the text originally stood as in Jos 17¹² לֹא יָכְלוּ לְהֹ׳ ; 1 Ch 15².

---

[1] P. Haupt (*SBOT.*, Proverbs, p. 52, lines 10 ff. ; *Critical Notes on Esther*, p. 170, on 7⁸) considers it possible that here and in Pr 2⁸, 6²⁴, 7⁵, 16³⁰, 30¹⁴, as well as in 14³⁵, 17²¹ before a noun, the לְ is a survival of the emphatic לְ with an *imperf.*, which is especially common in Arabic. In that case לִמְצָא must be read לְמְצָא, i. e. ־ר יִמְצָא. But all the above instances can be taken as infinitives with לְ without difficulty.

[2] Somewhat different are the cases where הָיָה לְ with the infinitive (which is then used exactly as a substantive) implies *to become something*, i. e. to meet with a particular fate, as Nu 24²² (cf. Is 5⁵, 6¹³) לְבָעֵר *for wasting*, for which elsewhere frequently לְשַׁמָּה and the like ; probably also לְבַלּוֹת ψ 49¹⁵ is to be explained in this way, the הָיָה being omitted.

[3] 2 S 4¹⁰ (*cui dandum erat mihi*) appears to be similar ; it may, however, be better, with Wellhausen, to omit the אֲשֶׁר.

[4] But in 1 S 23²⁰ after וְלָנוּ *and our part shall be* the infinitive without לְ stands as the subject of the sentence.

[5] Quite different of course are such cases as Is 37³ וְכֹחַ אַיִן לְלֵדָה *and there is not strength to bring forth* ; cf. Nu 20⁵, Ru 4⁴.

[6] In 2 S 14¹⁹ אִשׁ (=יֵשׁ *it is, there is*) is used in a similar sense after אִם, the negative particle of asseveration, *of a truth it is not possible to turn to the right hand or to the left*.

m 3. A further class comprises the very numerous cases, in which the infinitive with לְ is used as the object[1] of a governing verb, hence, again, for *the direction* which an action takes. The verbs (or conjugations) which occur most frequently in this combination with לְ and an infinitive are: הֵחֵל (with an infinitive without לְ, e. g. Dt 2²⁵·³¹, Jos 3⁷), הוֹאִיל *to begin*, יָסַף, הוֹסִיף (prop. *to add*) *to continue*, very frequently, even in prose, with an infinitive without לְ, as Gn 4¹², 8¹⁰·¹², 37⁵, 1 S 3⁸, Jb 27¹, &c.; חָדַל *to cease from, to desist*; כִּלָּה *to complete, to make an end of*; תָּמַם *to be finished*; הִקְרִיב *to come near to*, Gn 12¹¹; מִהַר *to hasten* (with an infinitive without לְ Ex 2¹⁸); אָבָה *to be willing* (with an infinitive without לְ Is 28¹², 30⁹, Jb 39⁹); חָפֵץ *to will, to desire*; מֵאֵן *to refuse (to be unwilling)*; בִּקֵּשׁ *to seek*; יָכֹל *to be able* (with an infinitive without לְ, e. g. Gn 24⁵⁰, 37⁴, Ex 2³, 18²³, Nu 22³⁸, Jb 4²); נָתַן with an accusative of the person in the sense of *to give up to some one, to cause*, or *permit* him *to do something*, e. g. Gn 20⁶, ψ 16¹¹ (with an infinitive abs. Jb 9¹⁸, see § 113 *d*); יָדַע *to understand* how to do something (in Jb 3⁸ הָעֲתִידִם עֹרֵר is analogous); לָמַד *to learn*; קִוָּה *to wait, expect* (with a change of subject, e. g. Is 5² *and he waited for it to bring forth grapes*).

n We must further mention here a number of verbs in Hiph'il (partly denominatives), which express an action in some definite direction (cf. § 53 *f*), as הִגְדִּיל *to do greatly*, הִשְׁפִּיל *to make* (it) *low*, הִגְבִּיהַּ *to make* (it) *high*, הֶעֱמִיק *to make* (it) *deep*, הִרְחִיק *to make* (it) *far, distant*, הֵיטִיב *to make* (it) *good* (with an infinitive without לְ ψ 33³, but 1 S 16¹⁷, in the same combination, with לְ); הִשְׁכִּים *to do* anything *early* (ψ 127², along with its opposite אֵחַר *to do* something *late*, with an infinitive without לְ); הִרְבָּה *to make* (it) *much*, הִפְלָא *to make* (it) *wonderful* (even with a passive infinitive 2 Ch 26¹⁵),[2] &c.

---

[1] This view is based upon the fact, that in numerous expressions of this kind (see the examples above) the לְ may be omitted, and the infinitive consequently stand as an actual accusative of the object (see above, *c*). However, the connexion of the verb with the object is in the latter case closer and more emphatic (hence especially adapted to poetic or prophetic diction), than the looser addition of the infinitive with לְ; thus לֹא אָבוּ שְׁמוֹעַ Is 28¹² is equivalent to *they desired not obeying* (לֹא אָבוּ also with the infin. abs. in Is 42²⁴; cf. § 113 *d*); but לֹא אָבוּ לִשְׁמֹעַ Ez 20⁸ rather expresses *they could not make up their mind as to hearkening*. When connected with לְ, the governing verb has a more independent sense than when it directly governs the accusative of the object.

[2] In almost all these examples the principal idea is properly contained in the infinitive, whilst the governing verb strictly speaking contains only a subordinate adverbial statement, and is therefore best rendered in English by an adverb; e. g. Gn 27²⁰ *how is it that thou hast found it so quickly?* (prop. how thou hast hastened to find!), Gn 31²⁷ *wherefore didst thou flee secretly?* So frequently with הִרְבָּה (= *often, abundantly*), Ex 36⁵, 1 S 1¹², 2 K 21⁶, Is 55⁷, Am 4⁴, ψ 78³⁸, &c.; with שׁוּב (= *again*), Dt 30⁹, 1 K 13¹⁷, Ho 11⁹, Ezr 9¹⁴; cf. also 2 S 19⁴, Jer 1¹², Jn 4², and the analogous instances in § 120 *g*; also 2 K 2¹ *thou hast asked a hard thing.*

4. Finally, the infinitive with לְ is very frequently used in a much looser *O* connexion to state motives, attendant circumstances, or otherwise to define more exactly. In English, such infinitive constructions (like the Latin gerund in *-do*; cf. *f*) must frequently be turned by *that* or a gerund; e.g. 1 S 12¹⁷ לִשְׁאָל לָכֶם מֶלֶךְ *in asking you a king*; 14³³, 19⁵, 20³⁶, Gn 3²², 18¹⁹, 34⁷·¹⁵, Ex 23², Lv 5⁴·²²·²⁶, 8¹⁵, Nu 14³⁶, 2 S 3¹⁰, 1 K 2³ᶠ·, 14⁸, Jer 44⁷ᶠ·, ψ 63³, 78¹⁸, 101⁸, 103²⁰, 104¹⁴ᶠ·, 111⁶, Pr 2⁸, 8³⁴, 18⁵, Neh 13¹⁸. Sometimes the infinitive with לְ is used in this way simply by itself, e.g. 1 Ch 12⁸ *as the roes upon the mountains* לְמַהֵר (as regards hasting) *in swiftness*; Gn 2³, 2 S 14²⁵ (לְהַלֵּל); Is 21¹ (לַחֲלוֹף); Jo 2²⁶, Pr 2², 26² and so very frequently the infinitive לֵאמֹר *dicendo* which has become stereotyped as an adverb to introduce direct narration (in the sense of *thus, as follows*).[1]

5. In a number of instances—especially in the later books—the infin. *P* constr. with לְ appears to be attached by *Wāw* (like the infinitive absolute, § 113 *z*), as the continuation of a previous finite verb. In most examples of this kind it is, however, evident that the infinitive with לְ virtually depends on an idea of intention, effort, or being in the act of, which, according to the sense, is contained in what has preceded, whilst the copula, as sometimes also elsewhere, is used in an emphatic sense (*and that too*); thus e.g. Ex 32²⁹ (if the text be right) *fill your hand to-day* (sc. with an offering) *for the Lord . . . and that to bring a blessing upon you*, i. e. that ye may be blessed; cf. 1 S 25³¹ (otherwise in verses 26 and 33 where the infinitive absolute is used, see § 113 *e*); ψ 104²¹,[2] Jb 34⁸, Ec 9¹, Neh 8¹³, 2 Ch 7¹⁷.—In Lv 10¹⁰ ᶠ· וּלֲהַבְדִּיל might be regarded as an explanatory addition to the command contained in verse 9 *b* (= this prohibition of wine before the service shall ye observe, and that in order to put a difference, &c.); but probably the text has been disturbed by a redactor.—In 2 Ch 30⁹ וְלָשׁוּב depends on the idea of receiving a favour which lies in לְרַחֲמִים. On the other hand, in 1 S 8¹² it is sufficient to explain *and in order to appoint them unto him for captains of thousands* (sc. he will take them). In Is 44²⁸ translate *and he* (Cyrus) *shall perform all my pleasure, and that in saying of Jerusalem*, &c.

3. The period of time to which an action or occurrence represented *q* by the infinitive construct belongs, must sometimes be inferred from the context, or from the character of the principal tenses; cf. e.g. Gn 2⁴ *these are the generations of the heaven and of the earth,* בְּהִבָּרְאָם *when they were created* (prop. in their being created); Ju 6¹⁸ עַד־בֹּאִי וג׳ *until*

---

[1] לֵאמֹר is very often so used after וַיְדַבֵּר in the Priestly document (Gn 8¹⁵, 17³, &c., and numberless times in the legal parts of Exod., Lev., and Num.)—a pleonasm which is not surprising considering the admittedly prolix and formal style of the document.

[2] When Delitzsch on ψ 104²¹, referring to Hb 1¹⁷, explains the infinitive with לְ as an elliptical mode of expressing the *coniugatio periphrastica* (equivalent to *flagitaturi sunt a deo cibum suum*), this is, in point of fact, certainly applicable to this and a few other places mentioned above; but all these passages, in which the infinitive with וְ follows, are to be distinguished from the cases treated above under *h*, where the infinitive with לְ *without Wāw* corresponds to a Latin gerundive, or is actually used to express the *coniugatio periphrastica*.

I come unto thee, and bring forth, &c. Cf. 1 S 18¹⁹ (=*when she should have been given*); 2 K 2¹, Ho 7¹.

r　Rem. 1. The constructions of the infinitive with a preposition, described above under *d*, are almost always continued in the further course of the narrative by means of the *finite verb*, i. e. by an independent sentence, not by a co-ordinate infinitive. Such a finite verb *we* regard as governed by a conjunction, which corresponds to the preposition standing before the infinitive. Thus the infinitival construction (frequently even with a change of subject) is continued by a perfect (with לֹא), Jer 9¹² *because they have forsaken* (עַל־עָזְבָם) *my law* . . . וְלֹא שָׁמְעוּ *and have not obeyed my voice*; Gn 39¹⁰, 1 S 24¹², Am 1⁹; without לֹא Jb 28²⁵ (perf. after לְ and infin.) ; by a perfect with וְ (cf. § 112 *i* and *v*) Am 1¹¹ עַל־רָדְפוֹ וג׳ *because he did pursue his brother with the sword,* וְשִׁחֵת *and did cast off* continually *all pity* (a frequentative perfect ; for examples of the perfect consecutive proper see Gn 27⁴⁵, Ju 6¹⁸, 1 S 10⁸, 2 K 18³² [Is 36¹⁷], always after עַד־בֹּאִי *until I come*) ; by a simple imperfect, e. g. Pr 1²⁷ (after בְּ) ; Is 30²⁶ (after בְּיוֹם *in the day,* a temporal phrase which has here become equivalent to a preposition) ; Is 5²⁴ (after בְּ), 10², 13⁹, 14²⁵, 45¹, 49⁵, 1 S 2⁸, Pr 2⁸, 5², 8²¹ (always after לְ) ¹ ; by an imperfect consecutive, e. g. Gn 39¹⁸ *and it came to pass,* בַּהֲרִימִי קוֹלִי וָאֶקְרָא *as I lifted up my voice and cried, that* . . . ; 1 K 10⁹, Jb 38¹³ (after לְ) ; 1 K 18¹⁸, Is 38⁹, Jb 38⁷·⁹ ff. (after בְּ) ; Is 30¹², Jer 7¹³, Ez 34⁸ (after יַעַן).

s　2. The negation of an infinitive construct, on account of the predominance of the noun-element in its character, is effected not by the verbal negative לֹא (except in the compound בְּלֹא, which has come to be used as a preposition, *without,* Nu 35²³, Pr 19²), but by בִּלְתִּי, originally a substantive (see the Lexicon), with לְ prefixed (but also Nu 14¹⁶ מִבִּלְתִּי), e. g. Gn 3¹¹ לְבִלְתִּי אֲכָל־מִמֶּנּוּ *not to eat of it* ; in a final sense, 4¹⁵ *lest any finding him should smite him* ; only in 2 K 23¹⁰ is לְ repeated before the infinitive. In ψ 32⁹ (if the text be right) בַּל negatives, not the infinitive, but the predicate which is understood.

§ 115. *Construction of the Infinitive Construct with Subject and Object.*

a　1. Like the infinitive absolute (see § 113 *a*), the character of the infinitive construct as a *verbal* noun is shown by its power of taking the case proper to its verb, and hence in transitive verbs² *the accusative of the object,* e. g. Nu 9¹⁵ בְּיוֹם הָקִים אֶת־הַמִּשְׁכָּן *on the day the*

---

¹ The great frequency of examples of this kind, especially in the poetical books, is due to a striving after what is called *chiasmus* in the arrangement of the parallel members in the two halves of the verse, i. e. in the instances given, the finite verb *at the end* of the second (co-ordinate) clause is parallel with the infinitive *at the beginning* of the first. In this way the verbal form necessarily became separated from the וְ, and consequently the imperfect had to be used instead of the perfect consecutive. Such a parallelism of the *external* and *internal* members of a verse is frequent also in other cases, and was evidently felt to be an elegance of elevated—poetic or prophetic—style.

² For examples of the accus. of the object with a pass. infin., see § 121 *c*.

tabernacle was reared up; 1 S 19¹ לְהָמִית אֶת־דָּוִד that they should slay David; Gn 14¹⁷, 19²⁹, Ex 38²⁷, 1 K 12¹⁵, 15⁴; with a negative, e. g. Lv 26¹⁵ לְבִלְתִּי עֲשׂוֹת אֶת־כָּל־מִצְוֹתַי so that ye will not do all my command-ments; with the accusative of the personal pronoun, e. g. Dt 29¹² לְמַעַן הָקִים־אֹתְךָ that he may establish thee; Gn 25²⁶, Jer 24⁷; with a verbal suffix, e. g. Ex 2¹⁴ לְהָרְגֵנִי to kill me; Jer 38²⁶ לְבִלְתִּי הֲשִׁיבֵנִי that he would not cause me to return (on the suffix, cf. c). In Is 49⁶ the object even precedes the infinitive with לְ; on this order cf. the note on § 114 r.—If the verb governs a double accusative, the infinitive may also take the same, e. g. Gn 41³⁹ אַחֲרֵי הוֹדִיעַ אֱלֹהִים אוֹתְךָ אֶת־כָּל־זֹאת forasmuch as God hath showed thee all this; Dt 21¹⁶.

Rem. 1. The object after the infinitive construct must also always be *b* regarded as in the accusative, even when it is not expressly introduced (as in all the above examples) by the *nota accusativi* אֶת־, and when therefore the substantive in question might easily be taken as the *genitive of the object* governed by the infinitive (the usual construction in Arabic), e. g. Pr 21¹⁵ עֲשׂוֹת מִשְׁפָּט *to do judgement*. Against regarding it as a genitive, which is in itself possible (*the doing, the executing of judgement*), is the fact (*a*) that elsewhere the *nota accusativi* is so frequently added; (*b*) that in such a case the secondary forms of the infinitive, such as רְאֹה for רְאֹת (פָּנֶיךָ) Gn 48¹¹ (cf. ψ 101³, Pr 16¹⁶), would be unintelligible; (*c*) that certain infinitive forms, if they were to be regarded as in the construct state, could hardly retain the pretonic Qames without exception, whereas, when connected with suffixes (i. e. with real genitives; cf. § 33 c), this Qames necessarily becomes Šewâ; e. g. Gn 18²⁵ לְהָמִית צַדִּיק *to slay the righteous* (never as לְהָמִית; cf., on the other hand, above, וְהֲשִׁיבֵנִי); 2 K 21⁸, Ez 44³⁰. Similarly in such cases as Is 3¹³ (ψ 50⁴) instead of לָדִין עַמִּים we should rather expect לְדִין, if the infinitive were regarded as in the construct state, and עַמִּים as the genitive. Hence also in cases like Is 58⁹ (שְׁלַח for שְׁלֹחַ) we must assume, with Sellin, op. cit., p. 78, a merely 'external phonetic connexion' and not the genitive construction.

2. The verbal suffixes added to the infinitive are (with the exception of *c* לְהוֹצִיאֵהוּ Jer 39¹⁴) only the suffix of the 1st pers. sing. (besides the above examples cf. also 1 S 5¹⁰, 27¹, 28⁹, Ru 2¹⁰, 1 Ch 12¹⁷, &c.) and plural; e. g. לְהַשְׁמִידֵנוּ *to destroy us*, Dt 1²⁷ (immediately after לָתֶת אֹתָנוּ, so that נוּ ֵ‑ is doubtless a *verbal* not a *noun*-suffix, although in form it might be either); לַהֲמִיתֵנוּ Nu 16¹³, Ju 13²³ (after חָפֵץ). Elsewhere the pronominal object is appended either by means of the accusative sign (e. g. Gn 25²⁶ בְּלֶדֶת אֹתָם prop. *in the bearing them*; לָדַעַת אֹתִי *to know me*, Jer 24⁷) or in the form of a noun-suffix (as genitive of the object). The latter occurs almost always, whenever the context excludes the possibility of a misunderstanding; e. g. 1 S 20³³ לְהַכֹּתוֹ (prop. for his smiting) *to smite him*, not, as the form might also mean, *in order that he might smite*; cf. 1 K 20³⁵; with the suffix of the 3rd sing. fem. Nu 22²⁵; of the 3rd plur. Jos 10²⁰, 2 S 21², &c. Hence also the suffixes of the 2nd sing. with the infinitive, as לְהַכֹּתְךָ Jer 40¹⁴, cf. Mi 6¹³, and even גַּדֶּלְךָ *to magnify thee*, Jos 3⁷, must certainly be regarded as *nominal* not *verbal* suffixes. The connexion of the noun-suffix, as genitive of the object, with the infinitive,

was so fully established, that it could be used not only in such strange cases, as Gn 37⁴ לֹא יָכְלוּ דַּבְּרוֹ לְשָׁלֹם *they could not speak to him peaceably*, cf. Zc 3¹ לְשִׂטְנוֹ *to be an adversary to him*, but ultimately even in the 1st sing., as in Nu 22¹³ לְתִתִּי *to give me leave* [Dt 25⁷ לֹא אָבָה יַבְּמִי *he will not perform the duty of a husband's brother unto me*; 1 Ch 4¹⁰ לְבִלְתִּי עָצְבִּי *that it may not grieve me !*]

d   3. The power of governing like a verb is also retained in those verbal nouns which, although originally secondary forms of the infinitive, have fully acquired the value of nouns, e. g. Is 11⁹ דֵּעָה אֶת־יְהוָה (prop. *to know the Lord*) *the knowledge of the Lord*; לְיִרְאָה אֹתִי *to fear me*, Dt 4¹⁰, 5²⁶, 10¹²; an accusative follows לְאַהֲבָה Dt 10¹²·¹⁵, Is 56⁶ (cf. also 1 K 10⁹, Ho 3¹); לַהֲנָפָה Is 30²⁸; בְּשִׂנְאַת יְהוָה אֹתָנוּ Dt 1²⁷; after verbal nouns formed with the prefix מ (cf. § 45 *e*), Nu 10², Is 13¹⁹, Am 4¹¹, Ez 17⁹. The accusative of the object likewise remains after infinitives (or their secondary forms) which have the article, e. g. Gn 2⁹, Jer 22¹⁶, or a suffix, e. g. Gn 5⁴, &c., 28⁴·⁶, 29¹⁹ ᶠ·, 30¹⁵, 38⁵, 2 S 3¹¹, Is 29¹³.

e   **2.** The subject of the action represented by the infinitive is mostly placed immediately[1] after it, either in the *genitive* or *nominative*. The subject is in the genitive (§ 33 *c*) whenever it has the form of a noun-suffix, and also when the infinitive has the termination of the constr. st. fem. sing. (see *f*); probably also in many other cases, where the infinitive in form and meaning is used more like a substantive, and accordingly governs like a noun. On the other hand, the subject of the infinitive is certainly to be regarded as a nominative, when it is separated from the infinitive by any insertion, and according to certain indications (see *g*) very probably in many other instances.

f   Rem. 1. Examples of genitives of the subject after infinitives in the connective form are Dt 1²⁷ בְּשִׂנְאַת יְהוָה אֹתָנוּ prop. *in the Lord's hating us*; cf. 7⁸, Gn 19¹⁶, 1 K 10⁹, Is 13¹⁹, 47⁹, Ho 3¹, Am 4¹¹. The subject of the infinitive is probably also to be regarded as genitive in such cases as Ex 17¹ *and there was no water* לִשְׁתֹּת הָעָם *for the people to drink* (prop. *for the drinking of the people*), and in cases like Gn 16¹⁶ (בְּלֶדֶת הָגָר); Gn 16³, Ex 19¹, Nu 20³·⁴, 33³⁸, 1 K 6¹, ψ 133¹, 2 Ch 7³, &c.

g   2. Examples in which the subject is separated from the infinitive by an insertion, and hence must certainly be regarded as a nominative, are Jb 34²² לְהִסָּתֶר שָׁם פֹּעֲלֵי אָוֶן *that the workers of iniquity may hide themselves there* (prop. for the hiding themselves there the workers of iniquity); cf. Gn 34¹⁵, Nu 35⁶, Dt 19³, Ju 9², 2 S 24¹³, ψ 76¹⁰, and below, *i*. The subject is likewise to be regarded as a *nominative*, whenever the *Lamedh* is prefixed to the infinitive by means of a pretonic Qames (cf. *b* above), e. g. 2 S 19²⁰ לָשׂוּם הַמֶּלֶךְ אֶל־לִבּוֹ,

---

[1] In Gn 24³⁰ the subject of כִּרְאֹת is wanting (but כִּשְׁמֹעַ follows); the original reading was undoubtedly כְּרֹאתוֹ, and the text is now in a state of confusion; verse 30*a* should come before verse 29*b*. In Gn 19²⁹, 25²⁶, Ex 9¹⁶, 13²¹, 1 S 18¹⁹, Jer 41⁶, ψ 42⁴ the subject, although not indicated, is easily supplied from the context. The infinitive in such cases is best rendered in English by a passive.

since, if the infinitive were used as a *nomen regens*, we should rather expect לְשׂוּם according to § 102 *f*. That the subject of the infinitive is regarded elsewhere also as nominative is again (see above, *b*) probable, since in such forms as הֲנִיחַ Dt 25¹⁹, Is 14³, הָמִיר ψ 46³, &c., the pretonic Qameṣ is retained without exception, whereas on the analogy of הֲנִיחִי Ez 24¹³, הֲקִימוֹ Jer 23²⁰, &c., we should expect הֲמִיר, הֲנִיחַ, &c., if the infinitive were regarded as a *nomen regens*. Or was the retention of the Qameṣ (assuming the thorough correctness of the Masoretic punctuation) rendered possible even before a following genitive, because that vowel was characteristic of the form? It is at all events certain that owing to the lack of case-endings,[1] a distinction between the genitival and nominatival constructions could not have been consciously made in the case of most infinitives, e. g. in unchangeable forms like קְטֹל, קוּם, &c.

3. When both a *subject* and an *object* are connected with the *h* infinitive, the rule is, that the subject should immediately follow the infinitive, and then the object. The latter, in such a case, is necessarily in the accusative, but the subject (as in *e*) may be either in the genitive or in the nominative. The noun-suffixes again are, of course, to be regarded as genitives, e. g. Gn 39¹⁸ כַּהֲרִימִי קוֹלִי *as I lifted up my voice* (cf. 1 K 13²¹, and the examples, Gn 5⁴, &c., enumerated above, under *d*), and so also substantives which follow a connective form, Dt 1²⁷, &c.; see above, *d* and *f*.

On the other hand, the subject appears necessarily to be in the *i* nominative in such cases as Is 10¹⁵ כְּהָנִיף שֵׁבֶט אֶת־מְרִימָיו *as if a rod should shake them that lift it up* (for the plur. מרימיו cf. § 124 *k*), not כְּהָנִיף, as would be expected (see *g* above), if שֵׁבֶט were in the genitive; cf. 2 S 14¹³, Jb 33¹⁷. And so probably also in other cases, as Gn 5¹, 13¹⁰, Jos 14⁷, 1 K 13⁴, 2 K 23¹⁰, Is 32⁷. The subject is separated from the infinitive by an insertion (and consequently must necessarily be in the nominative; see *g* above), e. g. in Jer 21¹.

Rem. Less frequently the object is placed immediately after the infinitive, *k* and then the nominative of the subject, as a subsequent complement, e. g. Is 20¹ בִּשְׁלֹחַ אֹתוֹ סַרְגוֹן *when Sargon sent him*; Gn 4¹⁵, Jos 14¹¹, 2 S 18²⁹, Is 5²⁴, ψ 56¹, Pr 25⁸. In Nu 24²³ the subject follows an infinitive which has a noun-suffix in place of the object.

§ 116. *The Participles.*

Cf. Sellin (see above at the head of § 113), p. 6 ff., and Kahan, p. 11 ff.

1. Like the two infinitives, the participles also occupy a middle *a* place between the noun and the verb. In form they are simple nouns,

---

[1] In Arabic, where the case-endings leave no doubt as to the construction, it is equally possible to say either *qatlu Zaidin* (gen. of subj.) *'Amran* (acc.), literally *Zaid's killing 'Amr*, or *qatlu 'Amrin* (gen. of obj.) *Zaidun* (nom. of subj.), or even *el-qatlu* (with article) *Zaidun* (nom. of subj.) *'Amran* (acc. of obj.).

and most nearly related to the adjective; consequently they cannot in themselves be employed to represent definite relations of tense or mood. On the other hand, their verbal character is shown by their not representing, like the adjectives, a fixed and permanent quality (or state), but one which is in some way connected with an *action* or *activity*. The *participle active* indicates a person or thing conceived as being in the continual uninterrupted *exercise* of an activity. The *participle passive*, on the other hand, indicates the person or thing in a state which has been brought about by external *actions*.

b　Rem. That the language was fully conscious of the difference between a state implying action (or effected by external action) and mere passivity, is seen from the fact, that participles proper cannot be formed from the purely stative Qal, but only verbal adjectives of the form *qāṭēl* (כָּבֵד, מָלֵא, &c.) or *qāṭōl* (גְּבֹהַּ, &c.), whereas the *transitive* Qal שָׂנֵא *to hate*, although it coincides in form with the intransitive Qal (as a verb middle *e*), nevertheless forms a participle active שֹׂנֵא, and participle passive שָׂנוּא (cf. the feminine שְׂנוּאָה).— In cases where the participle proper and the verbal adjective both occur, they are by no means synonymous. When the Assyrians are called in Is 28[11] לְעֵגֵי שָׂפָה *men of stammering lips*, a character is ascribed to them which is inseparably connected with their personality. On the other hand כָּלֵּה לֹעֵג לִי Jer 20[7], describes those about the prophet as continually engaged in casting ridicule upon him. Cf. also ψ 9[18] (שְׁכֵחַי) with 50[22] (שֹׁכְחֵי).

c　On the difference between the participle as expressing *simple* duration and the imperfect as expressing *progressive* duration, cf. what has been stated above in § 107 *d*. Nevertheless the participle is sometimes used—especially in the later books, cf. e.g. Neh 6[17], 2 Ch 17[11]—where we should expect the action to be divided up into its several parts, and consequently should expect the finite verb. But the substitution of the participle for the *tempus historicum*, which becomes customary in Aramaic (cf. Kautzsch, *Gramm. des Bibl.-Aram.*, § 76. 2, *d* and *e*), is nevertheless quite foreign to Hebrew.

d　2. The period of time indicated by (*a*) a participle active, either as an attribute or predicate, must be inferred from the particular context. Thus מֵת may mean either *moriens* (Zc 11[9]), or *mortuus* (so commonly; with the article הַמֵּת regularly=*the dead man*), or *moriturus* (Dt 4[22]); בָּא *coming, come* Gn 18[11], &c., *venturus* 1 S 2[31], &c.; נֹפֵל *falling*, but also *fallen*, Ju 3[25], 1 S 5[3], and *ready to fall* (threatening ruin, Is 30[13], Am 9[11]). For other examples of perfect participles see Gn 27[33], 43[18] (הַשָּׁב *that was returned*; cf. Ezr 6[21], &c., הַשָּׁבִים *which were come again* from the captivity); Gn 35[3], Ex 11[5], Zc 12[1], ψ 137[7], Pr 8[9], Jb 12[4] (קֹרֵא), and see *m* below. For future participles see Gn 41[25], 1 K 18[9], Is 5[5], Jon 1[3], &c., probably also לֹקֵחַ Gn 19[14]. On the *futurum instans* (esp. after הִנֵּה) see *p* below.

e　(*b*) Of the passive participles, that of *Qal* (e.g. כָּתוּב *scriptus*) always corresponds to a Latin or Greek perfect participle passive, those of the other conjugations, especially *Niph'al*, sometimes to a Latin gerundive (or to an adjective in *-bilis*), e. g. נוֹרָא *metuendus*, to be feared, ψ 76⁸, &c.; נֶחְמָד *desiderandus* (*desiderabilis*) Gn 3⁶, ψ 19¹¹, &c.; נִבְרָא *creandus* ψ 102¹⁹; נוֹלָד, usually *natus*, but also (like הַיִּלֵּד Ju 13⁸) *procreandus, nasciturus* 1 K 13², ψ 22³²; נֶעְרָץ *terribilis* ψ 89⁸; נִתְעָב *abominable* Jb 15¹⁶; נֶחְשָׁב *aestimandus* Is 2²²; הַנֶּאֱכֶלֶת that may be eaten (an animal) Lv 11⁴⁷. In *Puʿal* מְהֻלָּל *laudandus*, worthy to be praised ψ 18⁴. In *Hophʿal*, 2 S 20²¹ מֻשְׁלָךְ; 2 K 11² מוּדַעַת; Is 12⁵ *Qerê*.¹

3. The participles active, in virtue of their partly verbal character, *f* possess the power of governing like verbs, and consequently, when used in the absolute state, may take after them an object either in the accusative, or with the preposition with which the verb in question is elsewhere usually construed, e. g. 1 S 18²⁹ אֹיֵב אֶת־דָּוִד *hating David*; Gn 42²⁹; with the suffix of the accusative, e. g. עֹשֵׂנִי *that made me* Jb 31¹⁵; מִי רֹאֵנוּ *who seeth us?* Is 29¹⁵ (in Is 47¹⁰ רֹאָנִי is abnormal); רֹדֵם *ruling them* ψ 68²⁸, sometimes also with the article, e. g. ψ 18³³ הַמְאַזְּרֵנִי *that girdeth me* (LXX ὁ κραταιῶν με); Dt 8¹⁴⁻¹⁶, 13⁶·¹¹, 20¹, 2 S 1²⁴, Is 9¹² (where, however, Cheyne omits the article), 63¹¹, ψ 81¹¹, 103⁴, Dn 11⁶; followed by a preposition, e. g. 1 K 9²³ הָרֹדִים בָּעָם *which bare rule over the people*; 2 K 20⁵ הִנְנִי רֹפֵא לָךְ *behold, I will heal thee*.²

By an exhaustive examination of the statistics, Sellin (see the title at the head of § 113), p. 40 ff., shows that the participle when construed as a *verb* expresses a single and comparatively transitory act, or relates to particular cases, historical facts, and the like, while the participle construed as a *noun* (see *g*) indicates repeated, enduring, or commonly occurring acts, occupations, and thoughts.

So also the verbal adjectives of the form *qāṭēl* may take an accusative of the person or thing, if the finite verb from which they are derived governs an accusative, e. g. Dt 34⁹ מָלֵא רוּחַ חָכְמָה *full of the spirit of wisdom*; ψ 5⁵ חָפֵץ רֶשַׁע *that hath pleasure in wickedness*.

As a sort of noun the participle may, however, also exercise the *g* same government as a noun, being in the construct state, and followed by the object of the action in the genitive (see § 89 *a*; and cf. § 128 *x*), e. g. ψ 5¹² אֹהֲבֵי שְׁמֶךָ *that love thy name*; cf. ψ 19⁸ᶠ·; also when a verbal adjective, e. g. Gn 22¹² and often יְרֵא אֱלֹהִים *one fearing*

---

¹ Such examples as נוֹרָא, נֶחְמָד, מְהֻלָּל show plainly the origin of this gerundive use of the participle passive. A person or thing *feared, desired*, or *praised* at all times is shown thereby to be *terrible, desirable*, or *praiseworthy*, and therefore also *to be feared*, &c.

² On the other hand, in Is. 11⁹ *as the waters* לַיָּם מְכַסִּים *covering the sea*, the לְ serves only to introduce the object preceding the participle [cf. the Arabic parallels cited by Driver, *Tenses*, § 135, 7 *Obs*.]. Cf. Hab. 2¹⁴.

God; Hb 2¹⁵; with an infinitive, ψ 127²; with a noun-suffix (which, according to § 33 c, also represents a genitive), e. g. Gn 4¹⁴ כָּל־מֹצְאִי *whosoever findeth me* (prop. *my finder*; cf. עֹשִׂי *my maker*); 12³ מְבָרֲכֶיךָ *that bless thee*, מְקַלֶּלְךָ *that curseth thee* (but read either מְבָרֲכֶיךָ, or מְקַלְלֶיךָ in the preceding clause); 27²⁹, 1 S 2³⁰, Is 63¹³, ψ 18⁴⁹. In Jer 33²² read מְשָׁרְתִים אֹתִי.¹

h Rem. To the class of objective genitives belong also specifications of place after the participles בָּא *iniens* and יֹצֵא *egrediens*, since the verbs בּוֹא and יָצָא, in the sense of *ingredi, egredi*, can be directly connected with an accusative; e. g. Gn 23¹⁰·¹⁸ בָּאֵי שַׁעַר עִירוֹ *that went in at the gate of his city*; La 1⁴; after יֹצֵא Gn 9¹⁰, 34²⁴, 46²⁶, &c.—In poetic language the participle in the construct state may be connected not only with a genitive of the object, but also with any other specifications (especially of space) which otherwise can only be made to depend on the verb in question by means of a preposition; cf. Is 38¹⁸, and frequently, יֹרְדֵי־בוֹר *they that go down into the pit* (the grave); ψ 88⁶ שֹׁכְבֵי קֶבֶר *that lie in the grave*; Dt 32²⁴ (Mi 7¹⁷); 1 K 2⁷, 2 K 11⁵·⁷·⁹ *those that came in* (or *went out*) *on the sabbath*, Pr 2⁷, 1 Ch 5¹⁸, &c.; instead of the construction with מִן, e. g. Is 59²⁰ (*those who turn from transgression*), Mi 2⁸ (cf. § 72 *p*).

i These genitives of nearer definition appear also in the form of a noun-suffix, e. g. ψ 18⁴⁰·⁴⁹ קָמָי (for קָמִים עָלַי) *that rise up against me*; cf. Ex 15⁷, Dt 33¹¹, ψ 44⁶, Ex 32²⁵, Is 1²⁷ שָׁבֶיהָ *her converts*; ψ 53⁶ (חֹנָךְ); Pr 2¹⁹ כָּל־בָּאֶיהָ *all that go unto her*; the construction is especially bold in Is 29⁷ כָּל־צֹבֶיהָ וּמְצֹדָתָהּ *all that fight against her and her stronghold* (for כָּל־הַצֹּבְאִים עָלֶיהָ וְעַל־מְ'); ψ 102⁹ even with a participle Poʻal, מְהוֹלָלַי *they that are mad against me* (?), but read perhaps with Olshausen מְחוֹלְלַי *who pierce me*.—In Is 1³⁰ *as a terebinth* נֹבֶלֶת עָלֶהָ *fading as regards its leaf*, it remains doubtful whether נֹבֶלֶת is in the absolute state, and consequently עָלֶהָ in the accusative, or whether it is to be regarded as construct state, and עָלֶהָ as the genitive. In the latter case it would be analogous to Pr 14² (see *k*).

k 4. The passive participles also may either be in the absolute state, and take the determining word in the accusative,² or may be connected

---

¹ When, as in Jb 40¹⁹, the participle with the noun-suffix הָעֹשׂוֹ *he that made him*, also has the article (cf. § 127 *i*), the anomaly is difficult to understand, since a word determined by a genitive does not admit of being determined by the article.—No less remarkable is the use of the constr. st. of the participle before the accusative in Jer 33²² מְשָׁרְתֵי אֹתִי *that minister unto me* (for which there is מְשָׁרְתַי in verse 21). In Am 4¹³ an accusative of the product follows the genitive of the object, עֹשֵׂה שַׁחַר עֵיפָה *maker of the morning into darkness*. In Jer 2¹⁷ בְּעֵת מֹלִכֵךְ is supposed to mean *at the time when he led thee*; perhaps the perfect (הֹלִיךְ) should be read as in 6¹⁵. In Ez 27³⁴, the ancient versions read עַתָּ(ה) נִשְׁבַּרְתְּ *now thou art broken*, instead of the difficult עֵת נִשְׁבֶּרֶת. In 1 K 20⁴⁰ read עֹשֶׂה before הִנֵּה וָהֵנָּה.

² On the proper force of this accusative when retained in the passive con-

with it in the construct state, e. g. Ju 18[11], 1 S 2[18], Ez 9[2] לָבֻשׁ בַּדִּים *clothed in linen*, cf. verse 3 הַלָּבֵשׁ הַבַּדִּים; (even with a suffix קָרֻעַ כֻּתָּנְתּוֹ *rent as regards his coat* 2 S 15[32]; with the participle following Ju 1[7]); but Ez 9[11] לְבֻשׁ הַבַּדִּים *the one clothed with linen*; 2 S 13[31] קְרֻעֵי בְגָדִים *rent in respect of clothes*, equivalent to *with their clothes rent* (cf. Jer 41[5]); Nu 24[4], Dt 25[10], Is 3[3], 33[24], Jo 1[8], ψ 32[1] (נְשׂוּי־פֶּשַׁע) *forgiven in respect of transgression*, כְּסוּי חֲטָאָה *covered in respect of sin*); with a suffix to the noun, Pr 14[2] נְלוֹז דְּרָכָיו *he that is perverse in his ways*.

Rem. The passive participle occurs in the construct state before a genitive *l* of the *cause*, e. g. in Is 1[7] שְׂרֻפוֹת אֵשׁ *burnt with fire*; cf. Gn 41[6], Ex 28[11], Dt 32[24]; before a genitive denoting the *author*, e. g. Gn 24[31] בְּרוּךְ יְהֹוָה *blessed of the Lord* (but ψ 115[15] בְּרוּכִים לַיהֹוָה, see § 121 *f*); cf. Is 53[4], ψ 22[7], Jb 14[1] (15[14], 25[4]); hence also with noun-suffixes (which are accordingly genitive) Pr 9[18] קְרֻאֶיהָ *her invited ones*, i. e. those invited by her; cf. 7[26], ψ 37[22].

5. The use of the participle as predicate is very frequent in noun- *m* clauses (which, according to § 140 *e*, describe established facts and states), in which the period of time intended by the description must again (see above, *d*) be inferred from the context. Thus:

(*a*) As *present*, in speaking of truths which hold good at all times, e. g. Ec 1[4] *n* דּוֹר הֹלֵךְ וְדוֹר בָּא *one generation goeth, and another generation cometh; and the earth abideth* (עֹמָדֶת) *for ever*; cf. verse 7; also to represent incidental (continuous) occurrences which are just happening, Gn 3[5], 16[8] (*I am fleeing*); 32[12], Ex 9[17], 1 S 16[15], 23[1], 2 K 7[9], Is 1[7]; when the subject is introduced by the emphatic demonstrative הִנֵּה *behold!* (§ 100 *o* and § 105 *b*), e. g. Gn 16[11] הִנָּךְ הָרָה *behold, thou art with child*, &c.; 27[42]; frequently also in circumstantial clauses (connected by *Wāw*), cf. § 141 *e*, e. g. Gn 15[2], &c.

(*b*) To represent *past* actions or states, sometimes in independent noun- *o* clauses, e. g. Ex 20[18] וְכָל־הָעָם רֹאִים אֶת־הַקּוֹלֹת *and all the people saw the thunderings*, &c.; 1 K 1[5]; in negative statements, e. g. Gn 39[23 *a*]; sometimes in relative clauses, e. g. Gn 39[23 *b*], Dt 3[2] (cf. also the frequent combination of the participle with the article as the equivalent of a relative clause, e. g. Gn 32[10] הָאֹמֵר *which saidst*; 12[7], 16[13], 35[1.3], 36[35], 48[16], 2 S 15[31], &c.); sometimes again (see *n*) in *circumstantial* clauses, especially those representing actions or states which occurred simultaneously with other past actions, &c., e. g. Gn 19[1] *and the two angels came to Sodom* וְלוֹט יֹשֵׁב *and* (i. e. *while*) *Lot sat*, &c.; 18[1.8.16.22], 25[26], Ju 13[9], 2 Ch 22[9]; also with the subject introduced by הִנֵּה 37[7], 41[17]. (On הֹלֵךְ with a following adjective or participle to express an action constantly or occasionally recurring, cf. § 113 *u*.)

(*c*) To announce *future* actions or events, e. g. 1 K 2[2], 2 K 4[16] *at this season p when the time cometh round,* אַתְּ חֹבֶקֶת בֵּן *thou shalt embrace a son*; so after a specification of time, Gn 7[4], 15[14], 17[19], 19[13], Hag 2[6] (but in Is 23[15], where, after וְהָיָה we should rather expect a perfect consecutive, it is better to explain

struction cf. below, § 117 *cc*, &c., and § 121 *c, d*. So also Neh 4[12] is to be understood, *and the builders were* אִישׁ חֲרָבוֹ אֲסוּרִים עַל־מָתְנָיו *girded every one with his sword on his side, and building.*

וְנִשְׁבַּ֫חַת, with Qimḥi, as the 3rd sing. fem. of the perfect; on the form, cf. § 44 *f*); or in relative clauses, Gn 41²⁵, Is 5⁵ *what I am doing,* i.e. am in the act of doing; in a deliberative question, Gn 37³⁰; but especially often when the subject is introduced by הִנֵּה (especially also if the subject be attached as a suffix to הִנֵּה as הִנְנִי, הִנָּךְ, &c.), if it is intended to announce the event as imminent, or at least near at hand (and sure to happen), when it is called *futurum instans,* e.g. Gn 6¹⁷, 15³, 20³, 24¹³ ᶠ·, 48²¹, 50⁵, Ex 3¹³, 8²⁵, 9³, 34¹⁰, Jos 2¹⁸, Ju 7¹⁷, 9³³, 1 S 3¹¹, 2 K 7², Is 3¹, 7¹⁴, 17¹, Jer 30¹⁰, Zc 2¹³, 3⁸; with a participle passive, 2 S 20²¹: cf. also § 112 *t.*

q Rem. 1. As the above examples show, a noun-clause with a participle as predicate may have for its subject either a substantive or a personal pronoun; in both cases the participle, especially if there be a certain emphasis upon it, may precede the subject. Also in noun-clauses introduced by הִנֵּה the subject may be either a substantive, or (e.g. Gn 37⁷) a separate personal pronoun, or a suffix attached to הִנֵּה. In the same way, the subject may also be introduced by יֵשׁ (*est,* see the Lexicon) with a suffix, and in negative sentences by אַיִן (*non est*) with a suffix, e.g. Ju 6³⁶ אִם־יֶשְׁךָ מוֹשִׁיעַ *if thou wilt save;* Gn 43⁵ אִם־אֵינְךָ מְשַׁלֵּחַ *if thou wilt not send;* 1 S 19¹¹.—In such cases as Is 14²⁷ יָד֣וֹ הַנְּטוּיָה *the stretched out hand is his,* הַנְּטוּיָה is not, like נְטוּיָה in 9¹¹·¹⁶, &c., the predicate (in which case the participle could not take the article), but the subject; cf. Gn 2¹¹, 45¹², Is 66⁹, Ez 20²⁹, Zc 7⁶ (cf. § 126 *k*), where the participle with the article likewise refers to the present, also Nu 7², Dt 3²¹, 4³, &c., 1 S 4¹⁶, where it refers to the past. In 1 K 12⁸ and 21¹¹ even in relative clauses after אֲשֶׁר.

r 2. To give express emphasis to an action continuing in the *past,* the perfect הָיָה in the corresponding person is sometimes added to the participle, and similarly the imperfect יִהְיֶה (or the jussive יְהִי, or the imperfect consecutive) is used to emphasize an action continuing in the *future,* e.g. Jb 1¹⁴ הַבָּקָר הָי֣וּ חֹרְשׁוֹת *the oxen* (cows) *were plowing;* Gn 37², 39²², Ex 3¹, Dt 9²⁴, Ju 1⁷, 1 S 2¹¹, 2 S 3⁶; the same occurs with a passive participle, e.g. Jos 5⁵, Zc 3³; יִהְיֶה with a participle is found e.g. in Is 2²; the jussive in Gn 1⁶, ψ 109¹²;[1] and וִיהִי with a participle in Ju 16²¹, Neh 1⁴.

s 3. The *personal pronoun* which would be expected as the subject of a participial clause is frequently omitted, or at least (as elsewhere in noun-clauses, cf. Is 26³, ψ 16⁸, Jb 9³²) the pronoun of the 3rd pers. הוּא, e.g. Gn 24³⁰, 37¹⁵, 38²⁴, 41¹, 1 S 10¹¹, 15¹², Is 29⁸ (the participle always after הִנֵּה); cf., moreover, Gn 32⁷, Dt 33³, 1 S 17²⁵, 20¹, Is 33⁵, 40¹⁹, ψ 22²⁹, 33⁵, 55²⁰, Jb 12¹⁷·¹⁹ ᶠᶠ·, 25², 26³.— הִיא is omitted in Lv 18²⁸; הֵ֫מָּה in Is 32¹², Ez 8¹², Neh 9³; in a relative clause, Gn 39²², Is 24².—The personal pronoun of the 2nd pers. masc. (אַתָּה) is omitted in Hb 2¹⁰; the 2nd fem. (אַתְּ) in Gn 20¹⁶ (where, however, for the participle וְנִכְבַּ֫חַת the 2nd fem. perf. וְנִכְבַּ֫חַתְּ is to be read); the pronoun of the 1st sing. in Hb 1⁵ (?), Zc 9¹², Mal 2¹⁶; the 2nd plur. (אַתֶּם) 1 S 2²⁴ (if the text be right), 6³, Ez 13⁷ (?). But these passages are all more or less doubtful.

t Of a different kind are the cases in which some undefined subject is to be supplied with the participle; e.g. Is 21¹¹ אֵלַי קֹרֵא *there is one calling unto me* (= one calleth; § 144 *d*); cf. Is 30²⁴, 33⁴.—So with participles in the plur., e.g. Ex 5¹⁶ אֹמְרִים sc. the taskmasters); Jer 38²³ (in 33⁵ the text is corrupt), Ez 13⁷ (?), 36¹³, 37¹¹ (equivalent to *sunt qui dicant*).

---

[1] A jussive is practically to be supplied also in the formulae of blessing and cursing, בָּרוּךְ *blessed be* ... Gn 9²⁶, &c.; אָרוּר *cursed art thou* ... 3¹⁴, &c.

4. We must mention as a special class those noun-clauses which occur at *u* the beginning of a period, and are intended to lay stress upon the fact that the first action still continues on the occurrence of the second (always introduced by וְ) ; e. g. Jb 1¹⁶ f. עוֹד זֶה מְדַבֵּר וְזֶה בָא *he was yet speaking, and* (=*when*) *another came*, &c.[1] ; cf. Gn 29⁹, 1 S 9¹¹·²⁷, 20³⁶, 1 K 14¹⁷ *she was entering the threshold of the house, when the child died* ; 2 K 2²³, 4⁵, Dn 9²⁰ f· ; also in Ju 19²², 1 S 9¹⁴, 17²³, 1 K 1⁴², Jb 1¹⁸ f·, in all which passages the apodosis is introduced by וְהִנֵּה.— On the other hand, in 1 K 1¹⁴ the noun-clause itself is introduced by הִנֵּה (as in verse 22 by וְהִנֵּה), and denotes an action only just impending.[2] Finally, when the whole sentence is introduced by means of וַיְהִי (cf. § 111 *g*), and the apodosis by וְהִנֵּה, Gn 42³⁵, 2 K 2¹¹, 13²¹ ; without הִנֵּה in the apodosis, 1 S 7¹⁰, 2 K 19³⁷ (Is 37³⁸).

Participles active, which are used in the sense of the perfect participle, and *v* also *participles passive*, in accordance with their meaning, express in such noun-clauses a state still continuing on the occurrence of the principal action, e. g. Gn 38²⁵ הוּא מוּצֵאת וְהִיא שָׁלְחָה *she was being brought forth, when she sent*, &c. ; cf. Gn 50²⁴. [See further in Driver, *Tenses*, §§ 166–169.]

5. Different from the examples treated in *u* and *v* are the instances in *w* which a participle (either alone or as the attribute of a noun) stands at the beginning of the sentence as a *casus pendens* (or as the subject of a *compound noun-clause*, see § 143 *c*) to indicate a condition, the contingent occurrence of which involves a further consequence ; e. g. Gn 9⁶ שֹׁפֵךְ דַּם הָאָדָם בָּאָדָם דָּמוֹ יִשָּׁפֵךְ *shedding man's blood*, i. e. if any one sheddeth man's blood, *by man shall his blood be shed* ; Ex 21¹², ψ 75⁴, Pr 17¹⁴, Jb 41¹⁸ ; so especially if כָּל־ *every* precedes the participle, Gn 4¹⁵, 1 S 3¹¹ (2 K 21¹²), 2 S 5⁸ (*whosoever smiteth*), 1 Ch 11⁶. The apodosis is very often introduced by וְ (*wāw apodosis*), e. g. Ex 12¹⁵ (with a following perfect consecutive), Nu 35³⁰ ; 1 S 2¹³ זֹבֵחַ זֶבַח וּבָא נַעַר הַכֹּהֵן *when any man offered sacrifice, the priest's servant came*, &c. ; 2 S 14¹⁰ (participle with article) ; 22⁴¹ (where, however, the text is to be emended in accordance with ψ 18⁴¹) ; 2 S 23³ f·, Pr 23²⁴ *Keth.* ; 29⁹.—As in the instances discussed under *u*, such sentences are sometimes preceded by וַיְהִי, cf. 1 S 10¹¹, 11¹¹, 2 S 2²³ וַיְהִי כָל־הַבָּא *and it came to pass, that as many as came*, &c. [or by וְהָיָה, frequentative, Ju 19³⁰].—On the other hand, וְהַנִּשְׁבֶּרֶת Dn 8²² is a mere catchword (equivalent to *and as for that which was broken*) to call to mind the contents of verse 8.

6. On the use of the participle after the infinitive absolute הָלוֹךְ cf. § 113 *u*.

7. Almost as a rule the participial construction beginning a sentence (like *x* the infinitival constructions according to § 114 *r*) is continued by means of a finite verb with or without וְ, before which the English construction requires us to supply the relative pronoun implied in the participle ; thus,

---

[1] The independent noun-clause here lays stress upon the simultaneous occurrence (and consequently the overlapping) of the events far more forcibly than could be done by a subordinate expression of time (as e. g. וַיְהִי בְדַבְּרוֹ). In English it may be represented by *scarcely had he finished speaking when*. . . . As the above examples show, the apodosis also frequently consists of a noun-clause.

[2] At the same time the preceding עוֹד *still* shows that what is announced is not merely a future event, but a future event *contemporaneous* with something else ; the case thus entirely differs from the examples given in § 112 *t*, where הִנֵּה refers to the following participle, while here it belongs properly to the apodosis, before which it is therefore generally placed ; see the examples.

continued by means of a perfect, Is 14[17] שָׂם תֵּבֵל כַּמִּדְבָּר וְעָרָיו הָרָס *that made the world as a wilderness, and overthrew the cities thereof* [1]; 43[7], Ez 22[3], ψ 136[13 ff.], Pr 2[17]; by a perfect without *Wāw*, Gn 49[11]; by a simple imperfect (as the *modus rei repetitae* in the present), Is 5[23], 46[6], Pr 7[8], Jb 12[17.19 ff.], 24[21]; by an imperfect without *Wāw*, e. g. 1 S 2[8], Is 5[8], Pr 2[14], 19[26]; by an imperfect consecutive, Gn 27[33], 35[3], 1 S 2[6], Jer 13[10] (after several participles), ψ 18[33], 136[10t.]

C. The Government of the Verb.

§ 117. *The Direct Subordination of the Noun to the Verb as Accusative of the Object. The Double Accusative.*

L. Kaila, *Zur Syntax des in verbaler Abhängigkeit stehenden Nomens im alttest. Hebr.*, Helsingfors, 1906.

a   1. The simplest way in which a noun is subordinated to a verbal form is by the addition of an accusative of the object to a transitive verb.[2] In the absence of case-endings,[3] this accusative can now be recognized only from the context, or by the particle אֵת־ (אֶת, before suffixes also אֹת, אוֹת)[4] prefixed to it. The use of this *nota accusativi*

---

[1] On the parallelism between the *external* and *internal* members, which appears here and in many other examples of this kind, see the note on § 114 *r*.

[2] The verb in question may either have been originally transitive, or only have become transitive by a modification of its original meaning. Thus the vocalization shows that חָפֵץ (*to have pleasure*, usually with בְּ) *to desire*, מָלֵא (*to be full* of something, also transitive) *to fill*, were originally intransitive. Cf. also such cases as בָּכָה *to weep* (generally with עַל־, אֶל־ or לְ), but also *to bewail* with an accusative; יָשַׁב *to dwell* (usually with בְּ), but also *to inhabit* with an accusative (cf. further, under *u*).—The examples are different in which verbs of motion such as בּוֹא *intrare*, also *aggredi*, יָצָא *egredi* (cf. § 116 *h* above), שׁוּב *redire*, Is 52[8], take an accusative of the aim of the motion, while בּוֹא according to the Old Semitic usage, even takes an accusative of the person (at least in poetry, equivalent to בּוֹא אֶל־ in prose).

[3] On traces of these endings, especially the remains of a former accusative ending in *a*, cf. § 90 *c*.

[4] אֵת־ (toneless owing to the following Maqqeph), and אֵת (with a tone-long *ē*, אֵת־ only in Jb 41[26]), אֹת or אוֹת before the light suffixes (on all these forms cf. § 103 *b*: the underlying form *āth* was obscured in Hebrew to *ôth*, shortened to *ăth* before suffixes beginning with a consonant and then modified to אֶת־, whence finally the secondary form אֵת with the tone), Phoenician אית i. e. probably *iyyāth* (for the Phoenician form, cf. G. Hoffmann, *Einige phönik. Inschriften*, Göttingen, 1889, p. 39 f.), Punic *yth* or (according to Euting) pronounced even as a mere prefixed *t*, Arabic, before suffixes, *'iyyâ*, Aram. יָת, יַת. It was no doubt originally a substantive, meaning *essence, substance, self* (like the Syriac *yāth*; on the other hand, any connexion with the Hebrew אוֹת, Syriac *'ātā*, Arabic *'āyat, a sign*, must, with Nöldeke, *ZDMG.* xl. 738, be rejected), but now united in the construct state with a following noun or suffix stands for the pronoun *ipse*, αὐτός. In common use, however (cf. Wilson, 'The particle את in Hebrew,' *Hebraica*, vi. 2, 3, and the precise statistics of the use

is, however, somewhat rare in poetry, and even in prose it is not
invariably necessary but is restricted to those cases in which the
accusative of the object is more closely determined by being a proper
name, or by having the article, or by a following determinate genitive
(hence also by the suffixes), or in some other way (see below, *c*), e. g.
Gn 4¹ *and she bare* אֶת־קַיִן *Cain* ; 6¹⁰, 1¹ *God created* אֵת הַשָּׁמַיִם וְאֵת הָאָרֶץ
the heaven and the earth (but 2⁴ אֶרֶץ וְשָׁמַיִם) ; 1²⁵ *and God made* אֶת־חַיַּת
הָאָרֶץ *the beast of the earth*; 2²⁴.

Rem. 1. The rare occurrence of the *nota accusativi* in poetic style (e. g. it *b*
never occurs in Ex 15²⁻¹⁸, Dt 32, Ju 5, 1 S 2, &c., though it is frequent in the
late Psalms) may be explained from the fact that in this as in other respects
(cf. § 2 *q*) poetry represents a somewhat more archaic stage of the language
than prose. The need of some external means of indicating the accusative
could only have been felt after the case-endings had become wholly extinct.
Even then the אֵת would probably have been used at first to indicate only
an object placed *before* the verb (when it followed, it was already sufficiently
characterized by its position as depending on the verb), or proper names.[1]
Finally, however, the *nota accusativi* became so customary everywhere in prose,
that even the pronominal object was expressed rather by אֵת with suffixes
than by verbal suffixes, even when none of the reasons mentioned under *e*
can be assigned for it; cf. Giesebrecht in *ZAW.* 1881, p. 258 ff., and the
statistics of H. Petri, cited above at the head of § 58.   Such examples as
כְּכֹל אֲשֶׁר־צִוָּהוּ כֵּן עָשָׂה Gn 6²² in the *Priestly Code*, beside כְּכֹל אֲשֶׁר צִוָּה אֹתוֹ אֱלֹהִים
7⁵ in the *Jahvist*, are especially instructive.

2. As accusatives determined in other ways, we have in the first place to *c*
consider the collectives introduced by כֹּל *entirety*, without a following article
or determinate genitive, inasmuch as the meaning of כֹּל includes a deter-
minative sense, cf. e. g. Gn 1²¹·³⁰, 8²¹, Dt 2³⁴, 2 K 25⁹. אֶת־כֹּל is used absolutely
in Gn 9³, cf. 39²³; similarly, מִי is determinate of itself, since it always denotes
a person, hence אֶת־מִי *quem?* e. g. Is 6⁸, 37²³, &c., but never אֶת־מָה *quid?* So
also the relative אֲשֶׁר in the sense of *eum qui* or *quem*, &c., e. g. 1 S 16³, or *id
quod*, Gn 9²⁴, &c.   Cf. also such examples as Jos 2¹⁰, 1 S 24¹⁹, where אֵת אֲשֶׁר
is equivalent to *the circumstance, that*, &c.—Elsewhere אֵת stands before nouns
which are determinate in sense, although the article is omitted, which
according to § 126 *h* is very frequently the case in poetic or otherwise elevated
style ; thus Lv 26⁵, Jos 24¹⁴·¹⁵, Is 41⁷ (to distinguish the object from the subject) ;
50⁴ (with the first of two accusatives, also for the sake of clearness) ; Ez 13²⁰,
43¹⁰, Pr 13²¹ (where the צַדִּיקִים are to be regarded as a distinct class) ; Jb 13²⁵

___

of אֵת on p. 140 ff.), it has so little force (like the oblique cases αὐτοῦ, αὐτῷ,
αὐτόν, sometimes also *ipsius, ipsum,* and the Germ. *desselben,* &c.) that it merely
serves to introduce a determinate object ; אֵת הַשָּׁמַיִם prop. αὐτὸν τὸν οὐρανόν
(cf. αὐτὴν Χρυσηΐδα, Iliad i. 143) is no stronger than the simple הַשָּׁמַיִם τὸν
οὐρανόν. Cf., further, P. Haupt on Pr 18²⁴ in his Rainbow Bible, and also in
the *Notes on Esther,* p. 191.

[1] Thus, in Dt 33, אֵת occurs only in verse 9 (twice, with an object preceding
the verb), in Gn 49 in the blessing of Jacob only in verse 15 with a co-ordinate
second object (consequently farther removed from the verb). Of the thirteen
instances of אֵת in the Mêša' inscription, seven stand directly and four
indirectly before proper names.

(unless, with Beer and others, we read אִם וְ for (וְאֶת־); also Ec 7⁷ may be
a quotation of an ancient maxim.

d　　On the other hand אֶת occurs very seldom in prose before a noun actually
or apparently undetermined. In 1 S 24⁶ כָּנָף is more closely defined by
means of the following relative clause; in 2 S 4¹¹ אִישׁ צַדִּיק refers to Ishbo-
sheth (as if it were *him, who was an innocent man*); in 1 K 6¹⁶ עֶשְׂרִים אַמָּה
refers to the particular twenty cubits. In Ex 21²⁸ (otherwise in verse 29)
perhaps the אֶת־ is used in order to avoid the combination שׁוֹר אִישׁ (as in
Nu 21⁹ to avoid the cacophony נָשַׁךְ הַנָּחָשׁ אִישׁ ?); in Lv 7⁸ and 20¹⁰ the accusatives are at any rate defined by the context.—In Nu 16¹⁵ אֶת־אַחַד מֵהֶם
probably means *even a single one* (and then *ipso facto* a definite one) *of them*, as also
in 1 S 9³ מֵהַנְּעָרִים אֶת־אַחַד may refer to some definite one of the men-servants.
In Gn 21³⁰ we should read אֶת־שֶׁבַע הַכְּבָשֹׂת with the Samaritan, since the
seven lambs have been already mentioned; in Ex 2¹ translate with Meyer,
Die Israeliten, p. 79, אֶת־בַּת־לֵוִי *the daughter of Levi*; in Ex 28⁹ read הַשֹּׁהַם with
the Samaritan; in Lv 20¹⁴ אֶת־אִשָּׁה is probably a scribal error due to
וְאֶת־אִמָּה; in 1 S 26²⁰ read נַפְשִׁי with the LXX for פַּרְעֹשׁ אֶחָד; in 2 S 5²⁴ read
הַצְּעָדָה as in 1 Ch 14¹⁵; in 2 S 15¹⁶ the אֶת־ is incorrectly inserted from 20³,
where it refers to the women already mentioned; in 2 S 18¹⁸ read הַמַּצֶּבֶת,
or omit both אֶת־ and אֲשֶׁר with the LXX and Lucian; in 1 K 12³¹ omit אֶת־;
in 2 K 23²⁰ probably אֶת־עַצְמוֹתָם is to be read; in 2 K 25⁹ the text is corrupt.
In Ez 16³² אֶת־זָרִים might refer to *the strangers in question*; but see Smend on
the passage.

e　　3. The pronominal object *must* be represented by אֵת with a suffix (instead
of a verbal suffix), when (*a*) it precedes the verb, e.g. Nu 22³³ אֹתְכָה הָרַגְתִּי
וְאוֹתָהּ הֶחֱיֵיתִי *I had slain thee and saved her alive*; Gn 7¹, Lv 22²⁸, 1 S 8⁷, Is 43²²,
57¹¹, Jer 4¹⁷·²², 7¹⁹; (*b*) when a suffix is already attached to the verb, and as
a rule when a second accusative with וְ follows, e.g. 2 S 15²⁵ וְהִרְאַנִי אֹתוֹ *and
he will show me it*; Ex 17³ לְהָמִית אֹתִי וְאֶת־בָּנַי *to kill us and our children*; Nu 16³²,
1 S 5¹¹, 2 S 14¹⁶ (but cf. also Dt 11⁶, 15¹⁶, &c., and Driver on 1 S 5¹⁰); (*c*) after
an infinitive absolute, see above § 113 *a* note; (*d*) after an infinitive construct, when it is immediately followed by the subject, e.g. Gn 41³⁹, or when
the combination of a suffix with the infinitive might lead to a misunderstanding, e.g. Gn 4¹⁵ לְבִלְתִּי הַכּוֹת־אֹתוֹ *lest one should smite him*, &c., where
לְבִלְתִּי הַכֹּתוֹ might also mean *lest he should smite*.

f　　4. The pronominal object is very frequently omitted, when it can be easily
supplied from the context; so especially the neuter accusative referring to
something previously mentioned (the English *it*) after *verba sentiendi* (שָׁמַע) and
dicendi, e.g. Gn 9²², &c., וַיַּגֵּד *and he told* (it); also after נָתַן *to give*, Gn 18⁷, 24⁴¹,
&c., לָקַח *to take*, הֵבִיא *to bring*, שִׂים *to lay*, Gn 9²³, &c., מָצָא *to find*, Gn 31³³, &c.
A personal object is omitted, e.g. in Gn 12¹⁹, 24⁵¹ (after לָקַח.—The omission
of the plural object is remarkable, because it leaves an opportunity for
a misunderstanding, in Gn 37¹⁷ שָׁמַעְתִּי אֹמְרִים ¹ *I heard* them *saying*; perhaps,
however, we should read שְׁמַעְתִּים with the Samaritan.

g　　5. In common formulae the substantival object is also sometimes omitted

---

¹ According to the ordinary rules of syntax (cf. § 116 *t*) we should translate,
I heard men who said, &c.

(an elliptical expression); thus e.g. כָּרַת 1 S 20¹⁶, &c. (see the Lexicon) stands for כָּרַת בְּרִית like the English *to close* (sc. a bargain) *with any one*; נָטַר *to keep* (sc. אַף *anger*) equivalent to *to be resentful*, ψ 103⁹, &c.; so also שָׁמַר Jer 3⁵ (beside נָטַר); נָשָׂא for נָשָׂא קוֹל *to lift up the voice*, Is 3⁷; נָשָׂא לְ for נָשָׂא עָוֹן לְ *to take away any one's sin* (to forgive), Gn 18²⁴,²⁶, Is 2⁹; שָׁלַח *to put forth* (sc. יָד *the hand*) equivalent to *to reach after something*, 2 S 6⁶, ψ 18¹⁷.

6. *Verba sentiendi* may take a second object, generally in the form of a parti- *h* ciple or adjective and necessarily indeterminate, to define more exactly the action or state in which the object is perceived, e.g. Nu 11¹⁰ וַיִּשְׁמַע מֹשֶׁה אֶת־הָעָם בֹּכֶה *and Moses heard the people weeping*; Gn 7¹ אֹתְךָ רָאִיתִי צַדִּיק *thee have I seen righteous*. Frequently, however, the second object is expressed by a separate clause. This is especially frequent with רָאָה *to see*, e.g. Gn 1⁴ *and God saw the light, that it was good*; Gn 6², 12¹⁴, 13¹⁰, 49¹⁵, Ex 2², ψ 25¹⁹, Pr 23³¹, Jb 22¹², Ec 2²⁴, 8¹⁷; so with יָדַע *to know*, Ex 32²², 2 S 3²⁵, 17⁸ (with two objects); 1 K 5¹⁷.

7. In certain instances אֵת serves apparently to introduce or to emphasize *i* a nominative. This cannot be regarded as a reappearance of the original substantival meaning of the אֵת, since all unquestionable examples of the kind belong to the later Books of the Old Testament. They are rather (apart from textual errors or other explanations) cases of virtual dependence on an implied *verbum regens* understood. The constant use of אֵת to indicate a clause governed by the verb, necessarily led at length to the use of אֵת generally as a defining particle irrespective of a governing verb. So in the Hebrew of the Mishna[1] (see above, § 3 *a*) אוֹתוֹ and אוֹתָהּ are prefixed even to a nominative without any special emphasis.

Naturally the above does not apply to any of the places in which אֵת is not *k* the *nota accusativi*, but a preposition (on אֵת *with*, cf. § 103 *b*), e.g. Is 57¹⁵, 1 S 17³⁴ (וְאֶת־הַדּוֹב *and that, with a bear*; אֶת־ here, however, has probably been interpolated from verse 36, where it is wanting); nor the places in which the accusative is subordinate to a passive (according to § 121 *c*) or to a verb of wanting as in Jos 22¹⁷ and Neh 9³², see below, *z*. In Ez 43¹⁷ סָבִיב *about* governs like a verb, being followed by אוֹתָהּ.

Other cases are clearly due to attraction to a following relative pronoun in *l* the accusative (Ez 14²², Zc 8¹⁷; but Hag 2⁵ᵃ, to מִמִּצְרַיִם, must be omitted, with the LXX, as a later addition), or the accusative depends on a verbal idea, virtually contained in what has gone before, and consequently present to the speaker's mind as governing the accusative. Thus Nu 3²⁶ the verbal idea contained in וּמֵישָׁרֶת verse 25 is *they had to take charge of*); in Jos 17¹¹ וַיְהִי לְ implies *it was given up* or *they gave him*; 1 S 26¹⁶ *see where* is equivalent to *search now for*; in 2 S 11²⁵ אַל־יֵרַע בְּעֵינֶיךָ is used in the sense of *noli aegre ferre*[2]; Jer 36³³ *and he had the brazier before him*; in Ec 4³ a verb like *I esteem* is mentally supplied before אֵת אֲשֶׁר. On Jos 22¹⁷, Neh 9³², see below, *aa*.— Aposiopesis occurs in Dt 11² *for not your children* (do I mean); still more boldly in Zc 7⁷, where either שְׁמַעְתֶּם or (תַּעֲשׂוּ) תִּשְׁמְעוּ is to be supplied.

Setting aside a few undoubtedly corrupt passages[3] there still remain the *m*

---

[1] Cf. Weiss, משפט לשון המשנה (Vienna, 1867), p. 112.

[2] So also in 1 S 20¹³ the Qal (יִיטַב) is, with Wellhausen, to be read instead of the Hiphʻil.

[3] Thus 1 S 26¹⁶, where וְאַי is to be read for וְאֵת; 1 K 11²⁵, where at present the predicate of the relative clause is wanting; in 2 K 6⁵ the אֵת is probably

following examples, in which אֶת־ in the later Hebrew manner (almost in the sense of the Latin *quod attinet ad*) introduces a noun with more or less emphasis, Nu 3⁴⁶, 5¹⁰, 35⁶, Ju 20⁴⁴·⁴⁶, Ez 17²¹, 20¹⁶, 35¹⁰, 44³, Neh 9¹⁹·³⁴, Dn 9¹³, 2 Ch 31¹⁷.—In Ez 47¹⁷⁻¹⁹ (cf. also 43⁷) it is simplest to emend זֹאת for אֶת־, according to verse 20. However, even the LXX, who have ταῦτα only in verse 18, càn hardly have known any other reading than את; consequently in all these passages את must be regarded as virtually dependent on some governing word, such as *ecce* (LXX 43⁷ ἑώρακας), and 47¹⁷ᶠᶠ. as equivalent to *thou shalt have* as a border, &c.

n 8. Another solecism of the later period is finally the introduction of the object by the preposition לְ (prop. *in relation to, in the direction of*), as sometimes in Ethiopic[1] and very commonly in Aramaic.[2] Less remarkable is this looser connexion of the object with a participle, as with אֹכַל La 4⁵, אֹסֵף Nu 10²⁵, זָקֵף ψ 145¹⁴ (but cf. 146⁸), צֹרֵר Nu 25¹⁸, הַשֹּׂנִא and שֹׁמַח Jb 12²³; *before* the participle Is 11⁹.—To introduce an object *preceding* the finite verb לְ is employed in Jb 5² (cf. also Dn 11³³); also *after* אָהַב Lv 19¹⁸·³⁴; הֶאֱרִיךְ ψ 129³; הִבְדִּיל Ezr 8²⁴, 2 Ch 25¹⁰; הֵבִין Jb 9¹¹; בֵּרֵךְ 1 Ch 29²⁰ (immediately before with an accusative); הִגְלָה 1 Ch 5²⁶; דָּרַשׁ Ezr 6²¹, 1 Ch 22¹⁹, 2 Ch 17¹³; הֶחֱיָה Gn 45⁷, where, however, read פְּלֵיטָה with the LXX for לפליטה and take לָכֶם as a *dativus commodi*; הִלֵּל 1 Ch 16³⁶, 2 Ch 5¹³; הָרַג 2 S 3³⁰, ψ 135¹¹ (verse 10 with accusative), 136¹⁹ᶠ·; חָבַשׁ (*to bind up*) Is 61¹ (Ez 34⁴ *before* the verb); יָדַע ψ 69⁶; כִּבֵּד ψ 86⁹; לָקַח Jer 40², 2 Ch 23¹; הִמְלִיךְ and מָשַׁח 1 Ch 29²²; נִהֵל 2 Ch 28¹⁵; סָמַךְ ψ 145¹⁴; עָזַב 1 Ch 16³⁷; הֶעֱלָה Ez 26³; פִּתַּח ψ 116¹⁶; רָדַף Jb 19²⁸; הַצַּדִּיק Is 53¹¹; שָׂכַר 2 Ch 24¹² (previously accusatives); שִׂים 1 S 22⁷ (but probably וְכִלְּכֶם is to be read); הֵשִׁיב (in the connexion, הֵשִׁיב דָּבָר לְ) 2 Ch 10⁶ (but verse 9 and 1 K 12⁹ with an accusative); שִׁחֵת Nu 32¹⁵, 1 S 23¹⁰; שִׁית 73¹⁸; שָׁלַח Ezr 8¹⁶, 2 Ch 2¹², 17⁷; שָׁמַר 1 Ch 29¹⁸, 2 Ch 5¹¹.

o 9. Sometimes the verb, on which an accusative of the object really depends, is contained only in sense in the verb which apparently governs, e.g. Is 14¹⁷ אֲסִירָיו לֹא־פָתַח בַּיְתָה *his prisoners he let not loose* nor sent them back *to their home*. On this *constructio praegnans* in general, see § 119 *ff*.

p 2. With the proper accusatives of the object may also be classed what is called the *internal* or *absolute object* (also named *schema etymologicum* or *figura etymologica*), i.e. the addition of an object in the form

derived from a text which read the Hiph'il instead of נָפַל. In Jer 23³³ instead of the artificial explanation *what a burden* (is, do ye ask?) we should read with the LXX and Vulg. אַתֶּם הַמַּשָּׂא *ye are the burden*. In Ez 10²² מַרְאֵיהֶם וְאוֹתָם is unintelligible; in 37¹⁹ read with Hitzig אֶל־ for את; in Hag 2¹⁷ for אתכם read with the LXX שְׁבַכֶם [or אֶינְכֶם; for the אֶל cf. 2 K 6¹¹, Jer 15¹, Ez 36⁹].

[1] Dillmann, *Grammatik der äthiopischen Sprache*, p. 349.
[2] With regard to Biblical Aramaic, see Kautzsch's *Grammatik des Bibl.-Aram.*, p. 151 f. In other ways, also, a tendency may be observed in later Hebrew to make use of the looser connexion by means of prepositions instead of the closer subordination of the noun in the accusative.

of a noun derived from the same stem,[1] e.g. ψ 14⁵ פָּחַד פָּחֲדוּ *they feared
a fear* (i.e. they were in great fear), Pr 15²⁷; also with the object
preceding, e.g. La 1⁸ חֵטְא חָטְאָה יְרוּשָׁלַ͏ִם *Jerusalem hath sinned a sin*;
with a double accusative (see below, *cc*), e.g. 1 K 1¹² אִיעָצֵךְ נָא עֵצָה *let
me, I pray thee, give thee counsel*; 1 K 1¹².[2]

Rem. (*a*) Strictly speaking the only cases of this kind are those in which *q*
the verbal idea is supplemented by means of an *indeterminate* substantive (see
the examples above). Such a substantive, except in the case of the addition
of the internal object to denominative verbs (see below), is, like the infinitive
absolute, never altogether without force, but rather serves like it to strengthen
the verbal idea. This strengthening is implied in the indeterminateness of
the internal object, analogous to such exclamations as, *this was a man!*[3]
Hence it is intelligible that some intensifying attribute is very frequently (as
in Greek usually) added to the internal object, e.g. Gn 27³⁴ וַיִּצְעַק צְעָקָה גְּדֹלָה
וּמָרָה עַד־מְאֹד *he cried* (with) *an exceeding great and bitter cry*; cf. the Greek
νοσεῖν νόσον κακήν, ἐχάρησαν χαρὰν μεγάλην (Matt. 2¹⁰); *magnam pugnare pugnam,
tutiorem vitam vivere*, &c.

Examples of an internal object *after* the verb, and without further addition,
are Ex 22⁵, 2 S 12¹⁶, Is 24²², 35², 42¹⁷, Ez 25¹⁵, 26¹⁵, 27³⁵, Mic 4⁹, Zc 1², Pr 21²⁶;
with an intensifying attribute, Gn 27³³, Ex 32³¹, Ju 15⁸, 2 S 13³⁶, 1 K 1⁴⁰ (cf.
Jon 4⁶, 1 Ch 29⁹); Is 21⁷, 45¹⁷, Jon 1¹⁰, Zc 1¹⁴, 8²ᵃ, Dn 11³; along with an object
proper the internal object occurs with an attribute in Gn 12¹⁷, 2 S 13¹⁵; cf.
also Is 14⁶, Jon 4¹.—An internal object without an attribute *before* the verb:
Is 24¹⁶, Jer 46⁵, Hb 3⁹, Jb 27¹²; with an attribute *before* the verb: Jer 14¹⁷, Zc 1¹⁵
(cf. also Gn 30⁸, Jer 22¹⁹, 30¹⁴, ψ 139²²). Instead of the substantive which
would naturally be expected, another of kindred meaning is used in Zc 8².

(*b*) Only in a wider sense can the *schema etymologicum* be made to include *r*
cases in which the denominative verb is used in connexion with the noun
from which it is derived, e.g. Gn 1¹¹, 9¹⁴, 11³, 37⁷, Ez 18², ψ 144⁶, probably also
Mi 2⁴, or where this substantive, made determinate in some way, follows
its verb, e.g. Gn 30³⁷, Nu 25¹¹, 2 K 4¹³, 13¹⁴, Is 45¹⁷, La 3⁵⁸, ⁴ and, determinate
at least in sense, Jer 22¹⁶; or precedes it, as in 2 K 2¹⁶, Is 8¹², 62⁵, Zc 3⁷; cf.
also Ex 3⁹. In both cases the substantive is used, without any special
emphasis, merely for clearness or as a more convenient way of connecting
the verb with other members of the sentence.

3. Verbs which denote *speaking* (*crying out, weeping*), or any *s*
external act, frequently take a direct accusative of the organ or means
by which the action is performed. In this case, however, the accusative must be more closely determined by an attributive adjective or
a noun in the genitive. This fact shows the close relation between
these accusatives and the *internal objects* treated under *p*, which also,

---

[1] On a kindred use of the infinitive absolute as an *internal object*, see above,
§ 113 *w*.

[2] Cf. βουλὰς βουλεύειν, Iliad x. 147.

[3] The Arab grammarians assign to the indeterminate cases generally an
intensive sense in many instances; hence the commentators on the Qorân
usually explain such cases by adding *and what . . . !* see § 125 *b*.

[4] Also in ψ 13⁴ *lest I sleep the* sleep of *death*, הַמָּוֶת is only used pregnantly
for שְׁנַת הַמָּוֶת (cf. Jer 51³⁹), as צְדָקוֹת Is 33¹⁵ for דֶּרֶךְ צְדָקוֹת. On the similar
use of הֹלֵךְ תָּמִים in ψ 15², see § 118 *n*.

according to *q*, mostly take an intensifying attribute. On the other hand, they must not be regarded as adverbial (instrumental) accusatives, nor are they to be classed with the second (neuter) subjects treated below in § 144 *l*.

t Examples of the accusative following the verb are וָאֶזְעַק קוֹל־גָּדוֹל *and I cried a loud voice*, i. e. with a loud voice, Ez 11[13], 2 S 15[23] (after the proper object, Dt 5[19], 1 K 8[55]) ; ψ 109[2] *they have spoken unto me* לְשׁוֹן שֶׁקֶר *a tongue of deceit*, i. e. with a lying tongue ; Pr 10[4] *he becometh poor* עֹשֶׂה כַף־רְמִיָּה *dealing a slack hand*, i. e. who dealeth with a slack hand ; cf. the German *eine schöne Stimme singen*, to sing a fine voice, *eine tüchtige Klinge schlagen*, to smite a trusty sword, *Schlittschuhe laufen*, to run skates (i. e. to skate), and our *to write a good hand, to play ball*, &c.—Examples of the accusative preceding are שְׂפָתֵי רְנָנוֹת יְהַלֶּל־פִּי *my mouth shall praise with joyful lips*, ψ 63[6] ; cf. ψ 12[3], where a *casus instrumenti* with בְּ follows the accusative.

u 4. Many verbs originally intransitive (sometimes even in form; see *a*, note 2) may be used also as transitives, in consequence of a certain modification of their original meaning, which has gradually become established by usage; cf. e. g. רִיב *to strive*, but also with an accusative *causam alicuius agere* (so even in Is 1[17], &c.; elsewhere with לְ of the person for whom one strives) ; יָכֹל *absolutely to be able*, with an accusative *to prevail over* any one ; חָפֵץ *to be inclined* and רָצָה *to have pleasure* (usually with בְּ), with an accusative *to wish for some one* or *something* ; שָׁכַב *cubare*, then in the sense of *concumbere*, originally joined with עִם־ *cum*, but quite early also with the accusative, equivalent to *comprimere* (*feminam*), &c. So in 2 S 13[14], &c., unless in all or some of the passages the preposition אֵת is intended, e. g. אֹתָהּ for אֹתָהּ ; in the earlier passages עִם־ is the more usual.

v Rem. 1. It is certainly difficult to decide whether some verbs, which were afterwards used absolutely or joined with prepositions, were not nevertheless originally *transitive*, and consequently it is only the supposed original meaning, usually assigned to them in English, which causes them to appear *intransitive*.[1] In that case there is of course no syntactical peculiarity to be considered, and a list of such verbs would at the most be requisite only for practical purposes. Moreover, it is also possible that certain verbs were originally in use at the same time both as transitive and intransitive, e. g. perhaps לָבֵשׁ *to be clothed* along with לָבֵשׁ *to put on* (a garment). Finally the analogy of certain transitives in constant use may have led to intransitives of kindred meaning being also united directly with the accusative, so that, in other words, whole classes of verbs came to be regarded in a particular aspect as transitives. See below, *y*.

---

[1] Thus e. g. עָנָה *to reply to* (ἀμείβεσθαί τινα), *to answer any one* ; צִוָּה *to command* (*iubere aliquem*) ; זָכַר *to remember* ; קִוָּה (also with לְ) *to wait for ary one* (to expect any one) ; בִּשַּׂר *to bring glad tidings to any one* (see the Lexicon) ; נָאַף and נָאַף *to commit adultery* (*adulterare matronam*) ; עָבַד *to serve* (*colere*) ; עָרַב *to become surety for* . . ., and many others.

2. The modification of the original meaning becomes especially evident **w** when even reflexive conjugations (*Niph'al, Hithpa'ēl*, &c.) take an accusative (cf. § 57, note 2); e.g. נִבָּא *to prophesy*, Jer 25¹³; נָסַב (prop. *to put oneself round*) *to surround*, Ju 19²²; נִלְחַם *to fight*, ψ 109³ (where, however, the *Qal* וַיְלַחֲמוּנִי should be read; cf. ψ 35¹); also הִתְגַּלַּח *to shave* (something) *for oneself*, Num 6¹⁹; הִתְנַחֵל *to take* some one *for oneself as a possession*, Is 14²; הִתְנַכֵּל *to make* some one *an object of craft*, Gn 37¹⁸; הִתְנַצֵּל *to strip* a thing *off oneself*, Ex 33⁶; הִתְעַבֵּר *to bring on oneself the anger* of any one, *to anger him*; הִתְבּוֹנֵן *to consider* something, Jb 37¹⁴; הִתְפָּרֵק *to break* something *off from oneself*, Ex 32³. In Gn 34⁹ after הִתְחַתְּנוּ *make ye marriages*, read אֹתָנוּ instead of אֹתָנוּ. Cf. § 54 f.

3. So also it is only owing to a modification of the original meaning of **x** a verb (except where the expression is incorrect, and perhaps derived from the popular language), when sometimes the remoter object (otherwise introduced by לְ) is directly subordinated in the form of an accusative suffix, e.g. Zc 7⁵ הֲצוֹם צַמְתֻּנִי אָנִי *did ye fast at all unto me, even to me?* as though to say, have ye *be-fasted* me? have ye reached me with your fasting? Still more strange is Jb 31¹⁸ גְּדֵלַנִי כְאָב *he* (the orphan) *grew up to me as to a father*; cf. Is 27⁴, 65⁵, Jer 31³, and in Aramaic Dn 5⁶; but אֶרֶץ הַנֶּגֶב נְתַתָּנִי Jos 15¹⁹ is to be regarded as a double accusative after a verb of *giving*, see ff. In 1 S 2²⁵ read וּפִלְלוֹ for וּפִלְלוּ; in Is 44²¹, instead of the Niph'al, read תִּנָּשֵׁנִי; in Ez 29³ either עֲשִׂיתִיו is to be read with Olshausen or עֲשִׂיתִים (and previously יְאֹרִי) with Smend; in ψ 42⁵ אֶדַּדֵּה or אֲדַדֵּם; in ψ 55²³ (where König takes יְהָבְךָ as *he has given it to thee*) we must certainly assume a substantive יְהָב (= *fate*?).

4. Whole classes of verbs, which, according to *v* above, are regarded as **y** transitive, either on account of their original meaning or (for the sake of analogy) by a modification of that meaning, are—

(*a*) Verba *induendi* and *exuendi*, as לָבַשׁ *to put on*, פָּשַׁט *to put off* a garment, עָדָה *to put on* ornaments, *to adorn oneself with* (cf. also מֻשְׁבָּצִים זָהָב *enclosed in gold*, Ex 28²⁰). Also in poetic expressions such as ψ 65¹⁴ לָבְשׁוּ כָרִים הַצֹּאן *the pastures are clothed with flocks*, cf. ψ 109²⁹; 104² (עָטָה); 65¹⁴ᵇ (עָטַף), &c.[1]

(*b*) Verba *copiae* and *inopiae* (also called verba *abundandi* and *deficiendi*), as **z** מָלֵא, *to be full* of something, Ex 8¹⁷; here, and also frequently elsewhere, construed with אֶת־, and hence evidently with an accusative; Gn 6¹³; with a personal object, Ex 15⁹ *my lust shall be satisfied upon them*; with an accusative *preceding* the verb for the sake of emphasis, e.g. Is 1¹⁵ *your hands* דְּמִים מָלֵאוּ *are full of blood*, cf. Is 22²; so also the *Niph.* נִמְלָא *to fill oneself with* something, e.g. Gn 6¹¹, Ex 1⁷ (where the object is connected by אֶת); Is 2⁷ᶠ, 6⁴, Pr 3¹⁰; וָזְרַע *to be fructified with*, Nu 5²⁸; שָׁרַץ *to swarm with*, Gn 1²⁰·²¹ Ex 7²⁸; שָׂבַע (שָׂבֵעַ) *to be full of*, Is 1¹¹, Jo 2¹⁹, Pr 12¹¹; גָּבַר *to become strong, to wax mighty in* something, Jb 21⁷; פָּרַץ *to overflow with* something, Pr 3¹⁰ (with the object preceding); יָרַד prop. *to descend*, poetically also *to pour down, to overflow with* something (cf. in Greek προρέειν ὕδωρ, δάκρυα στάζειν), e.g. La 3⁴⁸ פַּלְגֵי מַיִם תֵּרַד עֵינִי *mine eye runneth*

---

[1] From the idea of *covering oneself with* something, we might also, if necessary, explain Ex 30²⁰ יִרְחֲצוּ מַיִם *they shall wash themselves with water*; but the reading is simply to be emended to the ordinary בַּמָּיִם.

down (*with*) *rivers of water*; 1¹⁶, Jer 9¹⁷, 13¹⁷, ψ 119¹³⁶; so also הָלַךְ *to run over with, to flow with*, Jo 4¹⁸; נָזַל *to gush out with*, Jer 9¹⁷; נָטַף *to drop, to overflow with*, Ju 5⁴, Jo 4¹⁸ᵃ; פָּרַח *to break forth*, Ex 9⁹; שָׁטַף *to overflow*, but also (transitively) *to overflow with*, probably in Is 10²²; נוּב *to bud with*, Pr 10³¹; so perhaps also עָבַר *to pass over, to overflow with*, Jer 5²⁸; יָצָא *to go forth* with, Am 5³.—Especially bold, but still on the analogy of the above examples, is Is 5⁶, where it is said of a vineyard וְעָלָה שָׁמִיר וָשָׁיִת *but it shall come up* (it shall be overgrown) *with briers and thorns*; cf. Pr 24³¹, and still more boldly, Is 34¹³.

aa   With the opposite idea, חָסֵר *to be in want of, to lack*, Gn 18²⁸; שָׁכַל *to be bereaved of* (as though it were *to lose*), Gn 27⁴⁵.—In Jos 22¹⁷ even הַמְעַט־לָנוּ (prop. *was there too little for us of . . . ?*) as being equivalent to a *verbum inopiae* (= *had we too little of . . . ?*) is construed with an accusative; cf. Neh 9³².

bb   (*c*) Several verbs of *dwelling*; the accusative in this case expresses either the place or the thing at which or *with* which any one tarries; thus Gn 4²⁰, ψ 22⁴ after יָשַׁב, cf. § 118 *g*; Ju 5¹⁷, Is 33¹⁴ after גּוּר; ψ 57⁵ after שָׁכַב; ψ 68⁷, Pr 8¹², Is 33¹⁶ with שָׁכַן; or even the person (the people) with whom any one dwells or is a guest, as ψ 5⁵, 120⁵ after גּוּר, Gn 30²⁰ after זָבַל, ψ 68¹⁹ with שָׁכַן.

cc   **5.** *Two accusatives* (usually one of the person and one of the thing) are governed by—

(*a*) The causative conjugations (*Piʿēl, Hiphʿîl*, sometimes also *Pilpel*, e.g. כִּלְכֵּל Gn 47¹², &c.) of verbs which are simply transitive in *Qal*, and hence also of *verba induendi* and *exuendi*, &c. (cf. above *a* and *u*, and also *y, z*), e.g. Ex 33¹⁸ הַרְאֵנִי נָא אֶת־כְּבֹדֶךָ *show me, I pray thee, thy glory*. Thus very frequently הוֹדִיעַ *to cause some one to know* something; לִמֵּד *docere aliquem aliquid*, &c.; cf. further, Gn 41⁴² וַיַּלְבֵּשׁ אֹתוֹ בִגְדֵי־שֵׁשׁ *and he caused him to put on vestures of fine linen* (*he arrayed him in vestures*, &c.); cf. in the opposite sense, Gn 37²³ (both accusatives after הִפְשִׁיט introduced by אֵת); so with מִלֵּא *to fill, to fill up* with something, Gn 21¹⁹, 26¹⁵, Ex 28³; אָזַר *to gird* some one with something, ψ 18³³; עִטֵּר *to crown*, ψ 8⁶, &c.; חִסֵּר *to cause* some one *to lack* something, ψ 8⁶; הֶאֱכִיל *to feed* some one with something, Ex 16³²; הִשְׁקָה *to make* some one *drink* something, Gn 19³²ᶠᶠ.

dd   (*b*) Many verbs (even in *Qal*) which express an influence upon the object through some external means. The latter, in this case, is attached as a second object. They are especially—

ee   (*a*) Verbs which express *covering, clothing, overlaying*, חָמַר Ex 29⁹, צָפָּה Ex 26²⁹, &c., טוּחַ Ez 13¹⁰ᶠᶠ·, עָטַר ψ 5¹³; cf. also רָגַם אֶבֶן Jos 7²⁵, &c.; hence also verbs which express *sowing* (זָרַע Jud 9⁴⁵, Is 17¹⁰, 30²³), *planting* (Is 5²), *anointing* (ψ 45⁸) *with* anything.

ff   (*β*) Expressions of *giving*, thus נָתַן Jos 15¹⁹ where the accusative of the thing precedes; *endowing*, זָבַר Gn 30²⁰; and its opposite *taking away*, as קָבַע Pr 22²³; *to bless some one with something*, בֵּרַךְ Gn 49²⁵, Dt 15¹⁴; *to give graciously*, חָנַן Gn 33⁵; *to sustain* (i.e. to support, to maintain, to furnish) *with* anything, e.g. Gn 27³⁷, ψ 51¹⁴ (סָמַךְ‎); Ju 19⁵ (סָעַד‎); *to do something to one*, גָּמַל‎ Gn 50¹⁵·¹⁷, 1 S 24¹⁸; cf. also קִדֵּם‎ *to come to meet any one with* something, ψ 21⁴, שִׁלֵּם‎ *to repay some one with* something (with two accusatives, ψ 35¹², Pr 13²¹), and for the accusative of the person cf. εὖ, κακῶς πράττειν τινά. In a wider sense we may also include such phrases as *they hunt every man his brother with a net*, Mi 7²; *to shoot at one with arrows*, ψ 64⁸ (though this is against the accents); Pr 13²⁴ *seeks him early* (with) *discipline*, i.e. *chastises him betimes*, &c.

(γ) Expressions of *asking* some one *for* something, *desiring* something *from* gg some one (שָׁאַל‎ Dt 14²⁶, ψ 137³); *answering* any one anything (עָנָה‎ Mi 6⁵, &c.; cf. in the other conjugations הֵשִׁיב דָּבָר‎ prop. *verbum reddere*, with an accusative of the person, 1 K 12⁶, &c., also in the sense of *announcing*; sometimes also הִגִּיד‎ *to declare* something *to* some one, Jb 26⁴, &c., for הִגִּיד לְ‎); צִוָּה‎ *to enjoin a person* something, Ex 34³², Dt 1¹⁸, 32⁴⁶, Jer 7²³.

(δ) Expressions which mean *to make, to form, to build* something *out of* some- hh thing; in such cases, besides the accusative of the object proper, another accusative is used for the material of which the thing is made, e.g. Gn 2⁷ וַיִּיצֶר יְהֹוָה אֱלֹהִים אֶת־הָאָדָם עָפָר מִן־הָאֲדָמָה‎ *and the Lord formed man of the dust of the ground*; so with יָצַר‎ also in 1 K 7¹⁵; further Ex 38³ כָּל־כֵּלָיו עָשָׂה נְחֹשֶׁת‎ *all the vessels thereof made he of brass* (for another explanation of the accusative נְחֹשֶׁת‎ [*into brass*], linguistically possible but excluded by the context, see below, *ii* with *kk*); cf. Ex 25¹⁸·²⁸, 26¹·¹⁴ᶠ·²⁹, 27¹, 36⁸, 1 K 7²⁷; with a preceding accusative of the material, Ex 25²⁹, 29², Dt 27⁶ אֲבָנִים שְׁלֵמוֹת תִּבְנֶה אֶת־מִזְבַּח יְהֹוָה‎ *of unhewn stones shalt thou build the altar of the Lord*.

(c) Verbs which express *making, preparing, forming into* anything, *ii* along with the object proper, take a second accusative of the product, e.g. Gn 27⁹ אֶעֱשֶׂה אֹתָם מַטְעַמִּים‎ *I will make them* (the kids) *into savoury meat*; cf. Gn 6¹⁴·¹⁶, Ex 26¹ᵇ, 30²⁵, 32⁴, Is 44¹⁵, Ho 8⁴, 1 K 18³² וַיִּבְנֶה אֶת־הָאֲבָנִים מִזְבֵּחַ‎ *and he built the stones* (into) *an altar*; cf. 10¹². So also אָפָה‎, with two accusatives, *to bake* something *into* something, Ex 12³⁹, Lv 24⁵; שִׂים‎ (prop. *to set up for* something, cf. Gn 27³⁷, 28¹⁸, ψ 39⁹, and similarly הֵרִים‎ Gn 31⁴⁵) *to change into* something, Jos 8²⁸, Is 50², 51¹⁰, Mi 1⁷, 4¹³; with two accusatives of the person (*to appoint, promote* any one to the position of a . . .), Is 3⁷; נָתַן‎ is also used in the same sense with two accusatives, Gn 17⁵, and שִׁית‎ 1 K 11³⁴; as a rule, however, the description of the office, and also frequently of the product, is introduced by לְ‎ *to*, § 119 *t*; also שִׁית‎ *to make a thing so and so* (Is 5⁶, 26¹; with a personal object, ψ 21⁷,¹ 91⁹); הֶחְשִׁיךְ‎ *to make dark*, Am 5⁸. Of the same class also are instances like Jb 28² אֶבֶן יָצוּק נְחוּשָׁה‎ *a stone they smelt into brass*; 1 K 11³⁰ וַיִּקְרָעֶהָ שְׁנַיִם עָשָׂר קְרָעִים‎ *and rent it* (the garment) *into twelve pieces*; cf. Is 37²⁶, accusative of the product before the object proper, after לְהַשְׁאוֹת‎ *to lay waste*.

---

¹ Cf. a very pregnant expression of this kind in ψ 21¹³ כִּי תְשִׁיתֵמוֹ שֶׁכֶם‎ *for thou shalt make them* (as) *a neck*, i.e. *thou shalt cause them to turn their necks* (backs) *to me*; similarly ψ 18⁴¹ (2 S 22⁴¹, Ex 23²⁷); אֹיְבַי נָתַתָּה לִּי עֹרֶף‎ *thou hast given mine enemies unto me as a back*; cf. Jer 18¹⁷.

On a second object with *verba sentiendi* (as יָדַע *to know* something *to be* something, Ec 7²⁵; רָאָה *to see, find to be,* Gn 7¹; חָשַׁב *to esteem* one *to be* something, Is 53⁴, elsewhere always construed with לְ or כְּ), cf. *h.*

kk Rem. At first sight some of the examples given above appear to be identical in character with those treated under *hh*; thus it is possible, e. g. in 1 K 18³², by a translation which equally suits the sense, *he built from the stones an altar,* to explain מִזְבֵּחַ as the nearer object and אֶת־הָאֲבָנִים as an accusative of the material, and the construction would then be exactly the same as in Dt 27⁶. In reality, however, the fundamental idea is by no means the same. Not that in the living language an accusative of the material in the one case, and in the other an accusative of the product were consciously distinguished. As Driver (*Tenses,* § 195) rightly observes, the remoter accusative in both cases is, strictly speaking, in apposition to the nearer. This is especially evident in such examples as Ex 20²⁵ *thou shalt not build them* (the stones of the altar) גָּזִית as *hewn stones,* cf. also Gn 1²⁷. The main point is, which of the two accusatives, as being primarily affected (or aimed at) by the action, is to be made the more prominent; and on this point neither the position of the words (the nearer object, mostly determinate, as a rule follows immediately after the verb), nor even the context admits of much doubt. Thus in 1 K 18³² the treatment of the stones is the primary object in view, the erection of the altar for which they were intended is the secondary; in Dt 27⁶ the case is reversed.

ll (*d*) Finally, the second accusative sometimes more closely determines the nearer object by indicating the part or member specially affected by the action,[1] e. g. ψ 3⁸ *for thou hast smitten all mine enemies* לֶחִי (as to) *the cheek bone,* equivalent to *upon the cheek bone;* cf. Gn 37²¹ *let us not smite him* נֶפֶשׁ in *the life,* i. e. let us not kill him; Dt 22²⁶, 2 S 3²⁷; also with שׁוּף Gn 3¹⁵; with רָעָה Jer 2¹⁶; in poetry the object specially concerned is, by a bold construction, even placed first, Dt 33¹¹ (with מָחַץ).

§ 118. *The Looser Subordination of the Accusative to the Verb.*

a 1. The various forms of the looser subordination of a noun to the verb are distinguished from the different kinds of the accusative of the object (§ 117) by their specifying not the persons or things directly affected by the action, but some *more immediate circumstance* under which an action or an event takes place. Of such circumstances the most common are those of *place, time, measure, cause,* and finally the *manner* of performing the action. These nearer definitions are, as a rule, placed *after* the verb; they may, however, also precede it.

b Rem. That the cases thus loosely subordinated to the verb are to be regarded as *accusatives* is seen first from the fact that in certain instances the *nota accusativi* (אֵת) is prefixed; secondly from the fact that in one form of

---

[1] Analogous to this is the σχῆμα καθ' ὅλον καὶ κατὰ μέρος in Greek epic poetry, e. g. ποῖόν σε ἔπος φύγε ἕρκος ὀδόντων.

the *casus loci* a termination (הָ‏‗) is employed, in which (according to § 90 *c*) the old accusatival ending is preserved ; and finally from the consistency with which classical Arabic puts these nearer definitions in the accusative (which may be recognized by its form) even under circumstances in which one would be rather inclined to expect a nominative in apposition.

The relation subsisting between the circumstantial accusative and the *C* accusative of the object is especially apparent when the former (as e. g. in a statement of the goal after a verb of motion) is immediately connected with its verb. But even the more loosely connected circumstantial definitions are certainly to be regarded as originally objects of a governing word habitually omitted, only that the consciousness of this closer government was at length lost, and the accusative more and more acquired an independent value as a *casus adverbialis*.

2. The accusative serves to define more precisely the *place* (*accus. d loci*), either (*a*) in answer to the question *whither ?* after verbs of motion,[1] or (*b*) in answer to the question *where ?* after verbs of *being, dwelling, resting*, &c. (but also after transitive verbs, see the examples), or finally (*c*) to define more precisely the *extent* in space, in answer to the question *how far ? how high ? how much ?*, &c.

Instead of the simple accusative, the locative (see above, § 90 *c*)[2] is fre- *e* quently found in the cases mentioned under *f* (sometimes also in those under *g*) or the preposition אֶל־,[3] especially before persons as the aim of the movement, or בְּ, usually, to express being *at* a place.

Examples of (*a*) : נֵצֵא הַשָּׂדֶה *let us go out into the field*, 1 S 20¹¹ ; cf. Gn 27³, 31⁴, *f* Jb 29⁷ ; לָלֶכֶת תַּרְשִׁישׁ *to go to Tarshish*, 2 Ch 20³⁶ ; cf. Gn 10¹¹, 13⁹, 24²⁷, 26²³, 31²¹, Ex 4⁹, 17¹⁰, Ju 1²⁶, 2 K 11¹⁹, Na 1⁸ (?), ψ 134² ; with לָקַח Nu 23¹⁴ ; with נָתַן Jos 6²⁴ ; with the *accus. loci* emphatically preceding (cf. Driver on 1 S 5⁸), 1 K 2²⁶, Is 23¹², Jer 2¹⁰, 20⁶, 32⁵ ; with בּוֹא (in the sense of *aggredi*, equivalent to בּוֹא עַל־, cf. § 117 *a*, note 2) the *personal* aim also is poetically added in the accusative, Ez 32¹¹, 38¹¹, Pr 10²⁴, 28²², Jb 15²¹, 20²² ; but in the last passage it is better taken as an accusative of the object (cf. the German *einen ankommen, überkommen*). See also Nu 10³⁶ (where שׁוּב can hardly be transitive) ; Ju 11²⁹, 1 S 13²⁰ (where, however, אֶל־ has probably fallen out after יִשְׂרָאֵל ; so Strack).—Finally, cf. also the use of אֲשֶׁר for שָׁמָּה . . . אֲשֶׁר *whither*, Nu 13²⁷.—The *accus. loci* occurs after a passive, e. g. Gn 12¹⁵.

Examples of (*b*) : Gn 38¹¹ *remain a widow* בֵּית אָבִיךְ *in thy father's house* ; cf. *g* Gn 24²³, 1 S 17¹⁵, 2 S 2³², Is 3⁶, Hos 12⁵, Mi 6¹⁰, 2 Ch 33²⁰ ; פֶּתַח הָאֹהֶל *in the tent door*, Gn 18¹.¹⁰, 19¹¹, and frequently. As observed by Driver on 1 S 2²⁹, accusatives of this kind are almost without exception (but cf. 1 K 8³², Is 16², 28⁷, 2 Ch 33²⁰) connected with a noun in the genitive. In all the above examples, however, the accusative may have been preferred to the natural construction with בְּ (which is not rare even with בֵּית and פֶּתַח) for euphonic reasons, in order to avoid the combination of such sounds as בְּבֵּ and בְּפֶ ; cf., moreover, Gn 2¹⁴, 4¹⁶, Ex 18⁵, Lv 6⁸ (הַמִּזְבֵּחָה) instead of the usual הַמִּזְבֵּחָ

---

[1] So commonly in Sanskrit ; in Greek only poetically, e. g. Iliad i. 317 κνίση δ' οὐρανὸν ἷκεν : in Latin, e. g. *rus ire, Romam proficisci.*

[2] Hence e. g. in 1 S 9²⁶ the Masora requires הַגָּגָה instead of the *Kᵉth.* הַגָּג.

[3] So in Ju 19¹⁸ for י׳ אֶת־בֵּית the better reading is אֶל־בּ׳.

Ex 29¹³, &c.); Dt 1².¹⁹, ¹ 2 S 17²⁶, 1 K 7⁸, Pr 8³, 9¹⁴. On Is 1³⁰ see § 116 *i*; on יָשַׁב, with the *accus. loci*, see § 117 *bb*. On the other hand, in Dt 6³, according to the LXX, a verb of *giving* has dropped out before אֶרֶץ.

h Examples of (*c*): Gn 7²⁰ *fifteen cubits upward did the waters prevail*; Gn 31²³, 41⁴⁰ רַק הַכִּסֵּא אֶגְדַּל מִמֶּךָ *only in the throne will I be greater than thou*; Dt 1¹⁹ *we went* (through) *all that great and terrible wilderness*; cf. Jb 29³. Of the same kind also are such cases as Ex 16¹⁶ (*according to the number of your persons*, for which elsewhere לְמִסְפַּר־ is used); 1 S 6⁴ (with the accus. preceding); 6¹⁸, 2 S 21²⁰, Jb 1⁵.—A statement of weight is put in the accusative in 2 S 14²⁶.

i 3. The accusative is employed to determine more precisely the *time* (*accus. temporis*), (*a*) in answer to the question *when?* e. g. הַיּוֹם *the day*, i. e. *on the day* (in question), *at that time*, but also *on this day*, i. e. *to-day*, or finally *by day*, equivalent to יוֹמָם, like עֶרֶב *at evening*, לַיְלָה *noctu*, בֹּקֶר *in the morning, early*, ψ 5⁴, &c., צָהֳרַיִם *at noonday*, ψ 91⁶; יוֹם אֶחָד *on one and the same day*, Gn 27⁴⁵; שֵׁנָא *in sleep*, ψ 127²; תְּחִלַּת קְצִיר שְׂעֹרִים (*Qᵉrê* בִּתְ) *at the beginning of barley harvest*, 2 S 21⁹; in stating a date, Gn 11¹⁰, 14⁴ *in the thirteenth year*.

k (*b*) In answer to the question *how long?* e. g. Gn 3¹⁴, &c., כָּל־יְמֵי חַיֶּיךָ *all the days of thy life*; 7⁴ *forty days and forty nights*; 7²⁴, 14⁴, 15¹³, 21³⁴, 29¹⁸, Ex 20⁹ (*for six days*); 23¹⁵, 31¹⁷; עוֹלָמִים *for ever*, 1 K 8¹³; also with the accusative made determinate, Ex 13⁷ אֵת שִׁבְעַת הַיָּמִים *throughout the seven days* in question, mentioned immediately before; cf. Ju 14¹⁷, Dt 9²⁵.

l 4. The accusative is sometimes used of abstract ideas to state the reason (*accus. causae*), e. g. Is 7²⁵ *thou shalt not come thither* יִרְאַת שָׁמִיר *for fear of briers*.

m 5. Finally the accusative is used very variously (as an *accus. adverbialis* in the narrower sense), in order to describe more precisely the *manner* in which an action or state takes place. In English such accusatives are mostly rendered by *in, with, as, in the form* or *manner of* . . ., *according to, in relation to, with regard to*. For more convenient classification we may distinguish them as—

n (*a*) Adjectives expressing *state*, placed *after* the verb to describe more accurately some bodily or other external condition, e. g. Is 20² *walking* עָרוֹם וְיָחֵף *naked and barefoot*; cf. verse 3, 8²¹, Gn 15², 33¹⁸ (שָׁלֵם), Ju 8⁴, Mi 1⁸, ψ 107⁵ (but in 15² תָּמִים is rather a substantive directly dependent on הֹלֵךְ = *he that walketh in uprightness*; cf. § 117 *r*, note); Jb 30²⁸. After an accusative, e. g. Dt 15¹⁸; to specify some mental state, e. g. Gn 37³⁵ (אָבֵל).—*Before* the verb (and then with a certain emphasis), Am 2¹⁶, Jb 1²¹, Ec 5¹⁴; Lv 20²⁰, Jb 19²⁵, 27¹⁹, 31²⁶

---

¹ In ψ 2¹² דֶּרֶךְ is not to be taken as an *accus. loci* (*on the way*), but as an *accus. of respect* (*with regard to the way*); see below, *m*.

(unless יָקָר be a substantive); Ru 1²¹ (מְלֵאָה) parallel with the adverb רֵיקָם).
In Mi 2⁷ the text is clearly corrupt.

Those examples are especially instructive in which the adjective expressing *o*
a state, although referring to several, is nevertheless used in the singular,
e.g. Jb 24¹⁰ עָרוֹם הִלְּכוּ *naked*, i.e. in the condition of one naked, *they go about*;
cf. verse 7 and 12¹⁷. In Is 20⁴ the singular occurs *after* a plural object, and
in Is 47⁵ the *masc.* after the 2nd sing. *fem.* imperative, which clearly proves
that the term expressing the state is not conceived as being in apposition,
but as an indeclinable adverb.

(*b*) Participles, again either *after* the verb, Nu 16²⁷, Jer 2²⁷, 43², ψ 7³, Jb 24⁵, *p*
Ct 2⁸, or *before* it, Gn 49¹¹, Is 57¹⁹, Ez 36³⁵, ψ 56², 92¹⁴, Pr 20¹⁴; cf. also the
substantival use of the participles Niph'al נוֹרָאוֹת *in a fearful manner* (ψ 139¹⁴)
and נִפְלָאוֹת *in a wonderful manner*, Jb 37⁵, Dn 8²⁴.—Also participles in connexion with genitives, as מִתְהַלֵּךְ Gn 3⁸ (cf. also בָּאָה 1 K 14⁶), are to be
regarded as expressing a state and not as being in apposition, since in the
latter case they would have to take the article.—In 2 S 13²⁰, 1 K 7⁷ and Hb 2¹⁰
the *explicative Wāw* (equivalent to *and that too*) is also prefixed to the
participle. In ψ 69⁴ for מִיַּחֵל read מְיַחֵל.—On 1 K 11⁸, 2 K 10⁶, 19², Hag 1⁴,
cf. the note on § 131 *h*.

(*c*) Substantives[1] in the most varied relations: thus, as describing an *q*
external state, e.g. Mi 2³ וְלֹא תֵלְכוּ רוֹמָה *neither shall ye walk haughtily* (as
opposed to שָׁחוֹחַ Is 60¹⁴); Lv 6⁹ (accus. before the verb = as *unleavened cakes*),
Dt 2⁹, 4¹¹, Ju 5²¹, Is 57², Pr 7¹⁰, Jb 31²⁶, La 1⁹; as stating the position of a
disease, 1 K 15²³ *he was diseased* אֶת־רַגְלָיו in *his feet* (2 Ch 16¹² בְּרַגְלָיו), analogous
to the cases discussed in § 117 *ll* and § 121 *d* (*d*); as describing a spiritual,
mental, or moral state, e.g. Nu 32¹⁴, Jos 9² פֶּה אֶחָד *with one accord*, 1 K 22¹³;
cf. Ex 24³, Zp 3⁹), 1 S 15³², 2 S 23³, Is 41³ (unless שָׁלוֹם is adjectival, and the
passage is to be explained as in *n*); Jer 31⁷, Ho 12¹⁵, 14⁵, ψ 56³, 58², 75³, Pr 31⁹,
Jb 16⁹, La 1⁹; Lv 19¹⁶, &c., in the expression הֹלֵךְ רָכִיל *to go up and down* as
a tale-bearer; also בֶּטַח *unawares*, Gn 34²⁵, Ez 30⁹; מֵישָׁרִים *uprightly*, ψ 58², 75³
(in both places *before* the verb); as stating the age, e.g. 1 S 2³³ (if the text be
right) יָמוּתוּ אֲנָשִׁים *they shall die* as *men*, i.e. *in the prime of life*; cf. 1 S 2¹⁸
(נַעַר), Is 65²⁰, and Gn 15¹⁶; as specifying a number more accurately, Dt 4²⁷,
1 S 13¹⁷, 2 K 5², Jer 31⁸ [in Jer 13¹⁰ שְׁלוֹמִים *wholly* (?) is corrupt; read גֹּלוֹת שְׁלֵמָה
with LXX for שֵׁ הָגְלַת]; as stating the consequence of the action, Lv 15¹⁸, &c.

The description of the external or internal state may follow, in poetry, in *r*
the form of a comparison with some well-known class, e.g. Is 21⁸ וַיִּקְרָא אַרְיֵה
and he cried as a lion; cf. ψ 22¹⁴, Is 22¹⁸ (כַּדּוּר) *like a ball*); Is 24²², Zc 2⁸, ψ 11¹
(unless צִפּוֹר be vocative); 58⁹ᵇ (unless the force of the preceding כְּ is carried
on, as in ψ 90⁴); ψ 144¹², Jb 24⁵ (פְּרָאִים, before the verb); 41⁷ *shut up together*
as with *a close seal*.[2]

6. To the expressions describing a state belong finally those nouns *s*
which are introduced by the comparative particle כְּ,[3] since the כְּ is to

---

[1] Cf. above, § 100 *c*, on certain substantives which have completely become
adverbs; and § 113 *h* and *k* on the adverbial use of the infinitive absolute.

[2] It is, as a matter of fact, permissible to speak of the above examples as
comparatio decurtata, but it must not be assumed that the comparative particle
כְּ, which is otherwise regularly prefixed (see *s*), has actually dropped out.

[3] On the use of כְּ as a prefix, cf. § 102 *c*.

be regarded as originally a substantive [1] in the sense of *amount, kind* (*instar*), standing in the accusative (so that כְּ is equivalent to *as a kind of, after the manner of, according to*), while the following noun represents a genitive governed by the כְּ. From this, which is the proper meaning of the כְּ, may be explained its power of representing a great many pregnant relations, which in English can only be rendered by the help of prepositions.[2] Thus the comparison may refer to—

t　(a) The *place*, e.g. Is. 5[17] כְּדָבְרָם *after the manner of*, i.e. *as in their pasture*; 23[15] as (it is said) *in the song of the harlot*; 28[21], 29[7] כַּחֲלוֹם *as in a dream*.

u　(b) The *time*, especially in the combination כַּיּוֹם *after the manner of the day*, equivalent to *as in the day*, Is 9[3], Ho 2[5]; כִּימֵי *as in the days of* . . ., Is 51[9], Ho 2[17], 9[9], 12[10], Am 9[11]; cf. moreover, Lv 22[13], Ju 20[39], Is 17[6], Jb 5[14], 29[2], and the expressions כְּיוֹם בְּיוֹם *as day by day*=*as in the former days*, 1 S 18[10]; כְּפַעַם בְּפַעַם *as at other times*, 1 S 3[10], &c.; כְּשָׁנָה בְשָׁנָה *as in former years*, 2 K 17[4]; cf. § 123 *c*. Of a different character is the use of כְּ as a simple particle of time, e.g. Gn 18[10] כָּעֵת חַיָּה *at this time* (not *about the time*), when it lives again, i.e. at the end of a year; כָּעֵת מָחָר *to-morrow at this time*; cf. Is 23[5], and the frequent connexion of כְּ with the infinitive construct to express a definite time (in the sense of a pluperfect), Gn 12[14], 27[34], Ex 9[29], &c.

v　(c) The *person*, e.g. Gn 34[31] should he deal with our sister *as* with *a harlot*?

w　(d) The *thing*, e.g. Is 10[14], ψ 33[7], Jb 28[5] כְּמוֹ־אֵשׁ *as a fire*, i.e. *as it were by fire* (cf. Is 1[25] כַּבֹּר *as with lye*); Jb 29[23] כַּמָּטָר *as for the rain* (they waited for me); Jb 38[14] (*as in a garment*); 38[30] כָּאֶבֶן *as to stone* (the waters are solidified in freezing).

x　Rem. According to the earlier grammarians, כְּ is sometimes used pleonastically, i.e. not to indicate a similarity (as in Lv 14[35] *as it were*, i.e. *something like*), but simply to introduce the predicate (*Kaph veritatis*), e.g. Neh 7[2] *for he was* כְּאִישׁ אֱמֶת *a faithful man*; cf. 1 S 20[3] כְּפֶשַׂע, La 1[20] כַּפָּוֹת. Such a pleonasm is of course out of the question. At the most a *Kaph veritatis* can only be admitted in the sense that the comparison is sometimes introduced by כְּ with a certain emphasis (equivalent to *in every respect like*); thus כְּאִישׁ אֱמֶת in Neh 7[2] means simply *of the nature of a faithful man*, i.e. *as only a faithful man can be*; cf. Nu 11[1], Is 1[7], 13[6], Ho 4[4], 5[10], Ob 11, Jb 24[14], 27[7], La 1[20], 2[4]; also כִּמְעַט in such passages as ψ 105[12] *yea, very few*; but e.g. in Is 1[9] *only just, a very small* . . .

---

[1] Schwabe (כְּ *nach seinem Wesen und Gebrauch im alttestam. Kanon gewürdigt*, Halle, 1883) contests this explanation (which is defended especially by Fleischer and is certainly indisputable). He, with Gesenius and Ewald, places כְּ as a preposition on the same footing as בְּ and לְ, and believes it to be probably connected with the stem כּוּן as well as with כִּי and כֵּן. The above view of כְּ as a substantive of course does not imply that the language as we have it is still in every case conscious of the substantival meaning.—On כְּ in numerical statements, in the sense of *about, nearly*, see the Lexicon.

[2] It would be altogether unsuitable here also (see above, note 2 on *r*) to assume a loss of the preposition. Such examples as Is 1[26] (כְּבָרִאשֹׁנָה and כְּבַתְּחִלָּה), Lv 26[37] (כְּמִפְּנֵי) are to be explained from the fact that here the

§ 119. *The Subordination of Nouns to the Verb by means of Prepositions.*

1. In general. As is the case with regard to the looser subordina- *a* tion of nouns to the verbal idea (§ 118), so also their subordination by means of prepositions is used to represent the more immediate circumstances (of place, time, cause, purpose, measure, association, or separation) under which an action or event is accomplished. In the case of most prepositions some idea of a relation of *space* underlies the construction, which then, in a wider sense, is extended to the ideas of time, motive, or other relations conceived by the mind.

On the origin of the prepositions and the original case-relation in which they stand to the nouns governed by them, cf. § 101, where a list of the prepositions is given with their original meanings. Cf. also § 102 on the prefixes, and § 103 on the union of prepositions with suffixes.

2. A not unimportant part is played in Hebrew by the *compounding* *b* of prepositions to represent more accurately the relations of place, which either precede or follow the action. In the former case מִן, and in the latter (which is not so frequent) אֶל־ occurs before other prepositions of place; cf. e. g. Am 7¹⁵ *the Lord took me* מֵאַחֲרֵי הַצֹּאן *from behind the flock*; 2 K 9¹⁸ *turn thee* אֶל־אַחֲרָי *to behind me*, i. e. *turn thee behind me*; מֵאֵת, מֵעִם *from being with* . . . , as in French *de chez, d'après quelqu'un.*[1] For further examples, see *c*.

Rem. 1. We must *not* regard as combined prepositions in the above sense *c* either those *substantives* which have become prepositions only by their union with prefixes, as לִפְנֵי *before*, מִפְּנֵי, לְמַעַן *on account of* (but e. g. מִלִּפְנֵי *from before*, Gn 4¹⁶, &c., is such a compound); nor *adverbs*, which are also formed by combining words which were originally substantives (also used as preposi- tions) with prepositions, as מָחוּץ *without*, מִתַּחַת *in the sense of below*,[2] מֵעַל

preposition and substantive had already become simply *one* word before the בְּ was prefixed. We find also בְּעַל Is 59¹⁸, 63⁷, ψ 119¹⁴, and 2 Ch 32¹⁹; cf. Driver on 1 S 14¹⁴ (כְּבִנְחָצִי), where the text is wholly corrupt.

[1] In other cases French, as well as English and German, can only emphasize *one* of the two combined ideas; thus, such expressions as *il prend le chapeau sur la table*, German and English *er nimmt den Hut vom Tisch, he takes his hat from the table*, all regard the action from one point of view only; the Hebrew here brings out both aspects of it by means of מֵעַל־ *from upon*, cf. e. g. Is 6⁶.

[2] Hence not to be confounded with מִתַּחַת *from under*, in such examples as Pr 22²⁷, which is a real compound preposition. In the above-mentioned adverbs also the מִן was *originally* by no means pleonastic; מִתַּחַת denotes properly the locality, regarded primarily as a place *from beneath* which some- thing proceeds, and so on. This original sense of the מִן, however, has become so much obscured by its regular combination with words of place to form independent adverbs, that it is even prefixed (evidently only on the analogy of such common adverbs as מִתַּחַת, מֵעַל־) in cases where it is really inadmissible, owing to the meaning of the adverb, e. g. in מִבַּלְעֲדֵי, מִלְּבַד

above (so also in Gn 27³⁹, 49²⁵, not *from above*). These adverbs of place, however, may become prepositions by the addition of לְ, e.g. מִחוּץ לְ *outside as regards* ..., i.e. *outside of something*, in 1 K 21¹³ even after a transitive verb of motion ; מִתַּחַת לְ *below as regards* ..., i.e. *under something* (cf. עַד־מִתַּחַת לְ *until they came under* ..., 1 S 7¹¹), מֵעַל לְ *over something*, &c.; לְבַד prop. *in separation* ; לְבַד מִן־ *in separation from*, i.e. *apart from*, *besides*. Only rarely in such a case is the לְ omitted for the sake of brevity, e.g. Jb 26⁵ מִתַּחַת מַיִם *beneath the waters* ; Neh 3²⁸ (מֵעַל).

d   2. Real combinations of prepositions (each retaining its full force) occur—

(a) With מִן־, in מֵאַחֲרֵי, מֵאַחַר (see above) *from behind something* ; מֵאֵת and מֵעִם *from with* (see above) ; מִבֵּין or מִבֵּינוֹת *from between something* (with motion in either direction, see e.g. Gn 49¹⁰) ; מִלִּפְנֵי *from before* (see above) ; sometimes also מִמּוּל Lv 5⁸, &c.; מֵעַל *from upon*, i.e. *off from* ; מִתַּחַת *away from under* (see footnote 2 on p. 377).

e   (b) With אֶל־, אֱלֵי, in אֶל־אַחֲרֵי *to behind*; אֶל־בֵּינוֹת *to between* ; אֶל־מִבֵּית לְ *forth between* 2 K 11¹⁵; אֶל־מִחוּץ לְ *forth without*, i.e. *out in front of*, Nu 5³; אֶל־תַּחַת *down under*.[1]—In Jb 5⁵ the two prepositions of motion are combined in a peculiarly pregnant construction, אֶל־מִצִּנִּים (he goes thither and takes it) *out of the thorns*, i.e. he taketh it *even out of the thorns*, but the text is hardly correct.

f   3. A general view of the union of certain verbs, or whole classes of verbs, with particular prepositions, especially in explanation of certain idioms and pregnant expressions.[2]

g   (a) אֶל־ (אֱלֵי)[3] *towards*, properly an expression of *motion* or at least *direction towards something* (either in the sense of *up to* = עַד, or *into* = אֶל־תּוֹךְ), is used after verbs not only in answer to the question *whither?* but by a specially pregnant construction, in answer to the question *where?* e.g. Jer 41¹² they

without, cf. also such examples as מִבְּלִי, מִמּוּל, מִנֶּגֶד, מִשָּׁם (*there*), &c. Since a מִן־ is not usually repeated after מִלְּבַד, it appears as if מִלְּבַד by a transposition of the מִן־ stood for the usual לְבַד מִן־. In reality, however, the preposition which forms the adverb into a preposition is omitted here, as in מֵעַל, מִתַּחַת, without a following לְ (see above). Properly מִלְּבַד has a purely adverbial meaning = *taken by itself*, like מִלְמַעְלָה מִפָּעַל (Syriac *men leʿēl*) *above* (adv.), as distinguished from מֵעַל־לְ or מִפָּעַל לְ (Syriac *leʿēl men*), *over, upon something*.—Also לְמִן־ *from ... onward* is not for מִן־לְ, but the לְ serves merely (just like the Latin *usque* in *usque a, usque ad, usque ex*) to indicate expressly the starting-point, as an exact *terminus a quo* (of place or time).

[1] Also in 1 S 21⁵ אֶל־תַּחַת by a pregnant construction is virtually dependent on the idea of *coming into*, contained in the preceding אֵין־.

[2] A summary of *all* the relations and senses in which a preposition may be used, belongs not to the Grammar but to the Lexicon.

[3] Cf. Mitchell, 'The preposition *el*,' in the *Journal of the Society of Biblical Literature and Exegesis*, 1888, p. 143 ff., and especially A. Noordtzij, *Het hebreeuwsche voorzetsel* אל, Leiden, 1896, a thorough examination of its uses, and especially of the relation between אֶל־ and עַל־.

found him אֶל־מַיִם רַבִּים *by the great waters*; cf. Dt 16⁶, 1 K 13²⁰, and a still more remarkable instance in 8³⁰ אֶל־מְקוֹם שִׁבְתְּךָ אֶל־הַשָּׁמַיִם. This combination of *two* different ideas, of motion *to* a place and being or acting *in* the place (very plainly seen in Dt 16⁶ *but to the place which the Lord thy God shall choose . . . shalt thou bring thine offering and there shalt thou sacrifice, &c.*), is the same as the Greek use of εἰς, ἐς for ἐν, the Latin *in potestatem, in amicitiam ditionemque esse, manere* (Cic. Verr. 5, 38 ; Div. 2, 14, &c.) ; cf. also the common German expressions *zu* Hause, *zu* Leipzig sein, *zu* Bette liegen, &c.

(b) בְּ.¹ Underlying the very various uses of this preposition is either the *h* idea of being or moving within some definite region, or some sphere of space or time (with the infinitive, a simultaneous action, &c.), or else the idea of *fastening on* something, *close connexion with* something (also in a metaphorical sense, following some kind of pattern, e.g. the advice or command of some one בְּעֵצַת פ׳, בִּדְבַר פ׳, or in a comparison, as in Gn 1²⁶ בְּצַלְמֵנוּ כִּדְמוּתֵנוּ *in our image, after our likeness*; cf. 1²⁷, 5¹·³·), or finally the idea of *relying* or *depending* upon . . ., or even of merely *striking* or *touching* something.

Thus the use of בְּ is explained—

(1) In the sense of *among* (in the domain of), e.g. Mi 7² יָשָׁר בָּאָדָם אַיִן *there is none upright among men*; in the sense of *consisting of*, in specifying the constituents of a collective idea, e.g. Gn 7²¹ *and all flesh died . . . in* (= consisting of) *fowl, &c.* 8¹⁷, 9¹⁰, Ho 4³. Also after ideas of *appearing, manifesting oneself, representing, being*, in the sense of *as, in the capacity of* (prop. in the sphere, after the manner of, see above), *consisting of . . ., tanquam*, the בְּ *essentiae* of the earlier grammarians, corresponding to the Greek ἐν, the Latin *in*,² and the French *en*, e.g. Ex 6³ *I appeared unto Abraham . . .* בְּאֵל שַׁדַּי *as El Shaddai*; Jb 23¹³ וְהוּא בְאֶחָד *but he is* (manifests himself as) *one*, i.e. he remains always the same; Dt 26⁵, 28⁶² בִּמְתֵי מְעָט *in the condition of being few*, cf. 10²² *to the number of seventy*; Is 40¹⁰, ψ 39⁷.—Cf. also such examples as Ex 18⁴ (ψ 35², 146⁵) בְּעֶזְרִי *as my help*; Dt 26¹⁴ *being unclean*; Is 28¹⁶ *in Sion* (i.e. *I make Sion a foundation*); Ez 20⁴¹ *as a sweet savour*; Pr 3²⁶, perhaps also Ex 3² *in* (i.e. *as*) *a flame of fire*; Is 66¹⁵ *with* (i.e. *like*) *fire*; ψ 31²², 37²⁰ (102⁴). For the origin of all these forms of expression ψ 54⁶ is especially instructive, since אֲדֹנָי בְּסֹמְכֵי נַפְשִׁי is not meant to refer to the Lord as *belonging to* the סֹמְכִים, but only to ascribe to him a similar character, i.e. *the Lord is one who upholds my soul*; so also ψ 99⁶, 118⁷, Ju 11³⁵ [the plur. as in § 124 *g–i*].³—Cf. Gesenius, *Thes. Linguae Hebr.*, i. 174 f., and Delitzsch on ψ 35².

(2) To introduce the object after transitive verbs, which denote *touching, striking, reaching to* (thus to some extent a fastening on, see above) something, in English sometimes rendered by *at, on*, &c., and in German generally by compounds with *an*, e.g. *anfassen* = אָחַז בְּ, *anrühren* = נָגַע בְּ, &c. To the same category belongs also the construction of verbs denoting *authority* (מָשַׁל, מָלַךְ, רָדָה, נָגַשׂ, the last prop. *to tread on* . . .) with בְּ, inasmuch as the exercise of the authority is regarded as a laying hold of the person ruled; so also, the introduction of the object by בְּ after certain *verba dicendi*, or when the mental action is to be represented as extending *to* some one or something: e.g.

---

¹ Cf. Wandel, *De particulae Hebr.* בְּ *indole, vi, usu*, Jena, 1875.

² e.g. *res in praeda captae*, i.e. things taken as spoil; see Nägelsbach, *Lat. Stilistik*, § 123⁴. On the Hebrew בְּ *essentiae*, see Hauschild in the *Festschrift zur Einweihung des Goethegymn.* Frankf. a. M. 1897, p. 163.

³ Other instances formerly cited here (Is 26⁴, ψ 55¹⁹, where בְּ is used before the subject) as well as ψ 68⁵ בְּיָהּ שְׁמוֹ *Jah is his name*, are textually very uncertain. Cf. Cheyne, *SBOT.* Isaiah, p. 173, on Is 26⁴.

קָרָא בְ to call *on* some one, נִשְׁבַּע בְ *iurare per aliquem*, שָׁאַל בְ to enquire *of* some one. Again; רָאָה בְ *to look upon*, שָׁמַע בְ *to hearken to* (but cf. also *m*), generally with the secondary idea of participation, or of the pleasure with which one sees or hears anything, especially pleasure at the misfortunes of others, hence רָאָה בְ *to see his desire on any one* or *anything*; cf. however, Gn 21¹⁶ *let me not look upon the death of the child*; 1 S 6¹⁹ *because they had looked [irreverently] at the ark of the Lord*.

Closely related to this is the use of בְ:

l (3) To introduce the person or thing, which is the object of a *mental* act, e.g. הֶאֱמִין בְ *to trust in* (to cleave trustingly *to*) somebody or something; בָּטַח בְ *to have confidence in* . . .; שָׂמַח בְ *to rejoice in* or *at* something, &c.; דִּבֶּר בְ *to speak of* (*about*) some one or something, Dt 6⁷, 1 S 19³ ᶠ·, &c.

m (4) The idea of an action as extending *to* something, with at the same time the secondary idea of participation *in* something, underlies finally the *partitive* use of בְ, e.g. אָכַל בְ *to share in eating* something, Ex 12⁴³ ᶠᶠ·, Lv 22¹¹; also simply *to eat, to taste of* something, Ju 13¹⁶, Jb 21²⁵; so also בְ לָחַם *to eat of*, and שָׁתָה בְ¹ *to drink of* something, Pr 9⁵; שָׁמַע בְ *to hear* a whisper *of something*, Jb 26¹⁴; מָצָא בְ *they found* remaining *of her only*. . ., 2 K 9³⁵; נָשָׂא בְ *to bear a share of* something, Nu 11¹⁷, Ez 18²⁰, Jb 7¹³. Cf. also חָלַק בְ *to give a share of* something, Jb 39¹⁷; בָּנָה בְ *to do building to*, Neh 4⁴.

n (5) With the idea of *touching, striking against anything* is naturally connected that of *proximity* and *vicinity near*, and further that of *association with* something; cf. Gn 9⁴ בְּנַפְשׁוֹ *with the life thereof*; 15¹⁴, 32¹¹ בְּמַקְלִי *with my staff*. Sometimes בְ combined with a verb of motion (*to come with* something), expresses the idea of *bringing*, e.g. Ju 15¹ *Samson visited his wife with a kid*, i.e. he brought her a kid; Dt 23⁵, ψ 66¹³, 1 Ch 15¹⁹ ᶠᶠ·, 16⁶.

o (6) From the idea of connexion with something, being accompanied by something (see *n*), is developed, finally, the *instrumental* use of בְ, which represents the means or instrument (or even the personal agent), as something *with which* one has associated himself in order to perform an action; cf. Mi 4¹⁴ בַּשֵּׁבֶט *they smite with the rod*; Is 10²⁴; ψ 18³⁰ בְּךָ *by thee* (so also 44⁶, parallel with בְּשִׁמְךָ); Is 10³⁴, Ho 1⁷, 12¹⁴; cf. also עָבַד בְ *to labour by means of* some one, i.e. to cause him to labour at it, Ex 1¹⁴, &c. On בְ with the passive to introduce the means or the author, see § 121 *f*.

p A variety of the בְ *instrumenti* is בְ *pretii* (the price being considered as the means of acquiring a thing), cf. Gn 23⁹, 29¹⁸ (בְּרָחֵל); 30¹⁶, 33¹⁹, 34¹⁵ (בְּזֹאת) *on this* condition); 37²⁸; also, in a wider sense, Gn 18²⁸ בַּ *for the sake of*; 1 S 3¹³.

q Rem. The use of בְ *instrumenti* to introduce the object is peculiar in such expressions as ψ 44²⁰ *and thou coveredst over us* בְּצַלְמָוֶת *with the shadow of death*; Jb 16¹⁰ פָּעֲרוּ עָלַי בְּפִיהֶם *they have opened wide their mouth against me* (prop. *have made an opening with their mouth*); cp. ψ 22⁸, Ex 7²⁰ *he lifted up* בַּמַּטֶּה *the rod*; Lv 16⁴ חָגַר and צָנַף followed by בְ; Jos 8¹⁸, La 1¹⁷. Analogous to some English expressions we find both *to gnash the teeth*, ψ 35¹⁶, and *to gnash with the teeth*, Jb 16⁹; *to wink the eye*, Pr 10¹⁰, and *to wink with the eye*, Pr 6¹³; *shake the head*, ψ 22⁸, and *to shake with the head*, Jer 18¹⁶, Jb 16⁴.—In all these instances

---

¹ To be distinguished from שָׁתָה בְ = *to drink from* (a cup, &c., Gn 44⁵, Am 6⁶), as in Arabic and Aramaic (Dn 5²). Cf. also ἐν ποτηρίοις (Xen. Anab. vi. 1, 4), ἐν χρυσώμασι πίνειν (3 Ezr 3⁶), *venenum in auro bibitur*, Seneca, Thyestes 453, and the French *boire dans une tasse*.

the verb (intransitive) construed with בְּ has a greater independence, and consequently more emphasis than the verb construed with a direct accusative; the latter conveys a sort of necessary specification of the action, while the noun introduced by בְּ is used rather as a merely adverbial complement. An instructive example of this is נָתַן קוֹל *vocem emittere, to utter a voice,* also *to thunder,* while in נָתַן בְּקוֹלוֹ ψ 46⁷ (68³⁴, Jer 12⁸), נָתַן has an independent sense = *he thundered with his voice* (i.e. mightily).

(*c*) לְ¹ *to,* a very general expression of *direction towards* anything, is used to *r* represent the most varied *relations* of an action or state with regard to a person or thing. On the use of לְ as a periphrasis for the *genetivus possessoris* or *auctoris* (the idea of belonging to), see § 129; on לְ with the passive, to introduce the author or the cause, see § 121 *f*; on לְ in a purely local sense (e.g. לִימִינֶךָ *at thy right hand,* prop. *towards thy right hand*), or temporal (e.g. לָעֶרֶב *at evening,* &c.) or distributive, see the Lexicon.

The following uses of לְ properly belong to the government of the verb:

(1) As a *nota dativi*² to introduce the remoter object; also   *s*

(2) To introduce the *dativus commodi.* This *dativus commodi* (or *incommodi,* e.g. Ez 37¹¹) is used—especially in colloquial language and in later style— in the form of a pronoun with לְ, as an apparently pleonastic *dativus ethicus,* with many verbs, in order to give emphasis to the significance of the occurrence in question *for a particular subject.* In this construction the person of the pronoun must always agree with that of the verbal form.³ By far the most frequent use of this לְ is with the pronoun of the 2nd person after imperatives, e.g. לֶךְ־לְךָ *go, get thee away,* Gn 12¹, 22², Dt 2¹³ (also in the feminine, Ct 2¹⁰·¹³); וּנְטֵה לְךָ *turn thee aside,* 2 S 2²¹; סְעוּ לָכֶם *take your journey,* Dt 1⁷; עִבְרוּ לָכֶם *pass ye over;* בְּרַח־לְךָ *flee* (to save thyself), Gn 27⁴³; עֲלִי־לָךְ *get thee up,* Is 40⁹; פְּנוּ לָכֶם *turn you,* Dt 1⁴⁰; שֻׁבוּ לָכֶם *return ye,* Dt 5²⁷; קוּמִי לָךְ *rise up,* Ct 2¹⁰; שְׁבוּ לָכֶם *abide ye,* Gn 22⁵; חֲדַל לְךָ *forbear thee,* 2 Ch 35²¹ (in the plural, Is 2²²); הָבוּ לָכֶם *take you,* Dt 1¹³, Jos 18⁴, Ju 20⁷, 2 S 16²⁰, and so almost regularly הִשָּׁמֶר לְךָ (see above, § 51 *n*) *cave tibi!* and הִשָּׁמְרוּ לָכֶם *take heed to yourselves,* דְּמֵה לְךָ *be thou like,* Ct 2¹⁷ (cf. verse 9), 8¹⁴, is remarkable; after a perfect consecutive, 1 K 1⁷³, 1 S 22⁵; after an imperfect consecutive, e.g. Is 36⁹ וַתִּבְטַח לָךְ *and puttest thy trust.*—In the 3rd person, e.g. וַתֵּשֶׁב לָהּ *and sat her down,* Gn 21¹⁶, cf. 22⁵, Ex 18²⁷, ψ 120⁶, 123⁴, Jb 6¹⁹; even after a participle, Ho 8⁹.—In the 1st person plural, Ez 37¹¹.

(3) To introduce the result after verbs of making, forming, changing, *t* appointing *to* something, esteeming *as* something; in short, in all those cases in which, according to § 117 *ii,* a second accusative may also be used.

(4) In loose connexion with some verbal idea in the sense of *in reference to, u with regard to* ... (§ 143 *e*); so after a *verbum dicendi,* Gn 20¹³; 1 K 10²³, cf.

---

¹ Cf. Giesebrecht, *Die hebr. Präpos. Lamed,* Halle, 1876.

² Just as in the Romance languages the Latin preposition *ad* (Italian *a,* before vowels *ad,* French *à,* Spanish *á*) and in English *to* are used as a periphrasis for the dative.—On the introduction of the nearer object by לְ, cf. § 117 *n*.

³ Such expressions as the analogous English *he plucked me ope his doublet, but me no buts,* and the like, are accordingly inadmissible in Hebrew.

Is 36[9]; even before the verb, Jer 9[2].—To the same class belongs also the *Lamedh inscriptionis* (untranslatable in English, and hardly more than a mere quotation-mark) which introduces the exact wording of an inscription or title; thus Is 8[1] *write upon it* ... (the words) מַהֵר שָׁלָל וגו׳ (cf. verse 3, where the לְ naturally is not used); Ez 37[16].

v (*d*) מִן, originally (according to § 101 *a*) *separation*,[1] represents both the idea of *distance, separation* or *remoteness from* something, and that of *motion away from* something, hence also *descent, origin from* a place, Am 1[1].

w (1) From the idea of *separation* is naturally derived on the one hand the sense of (*taken*) *from among* ..., *e numero*, e. g. Gn 3[1] *subtil as none other of the beasts*, &c.; cf. 3[14], Dt 33[24], 1 S 15[33], Ju 5[24] (so especially after the idea of choosing *out of*[2] a larger class, 1 S 2[28]; cf. Ex 19[5], &c.), and on the other hand, the sense of *without* (separated, free from ...), e. g. Is 22[3] מִקֶּשֶׁת אֻסָּרוּ *without the bow* (i. e. without one needing to bend a bow against them) *they were made prisoners*; cf. Jer 48[45] מִכֹּחַ *without strength*; Ho 6[6], as the first half-verse shows, not *more than burnt offerings* (as R. V.), but *and not burnt offerings*; Mi 3[6], ψ 52[5], Jb 11[15], 19[26], 21[9], also such examples as Nu 15[24] *far from the eyes*, i. e. unobserved by the congregation; Pr 20[3].

x Here also belongs the use of מִן after the ideas of *restraining, withholding from, refusing to* any one, frequently in pregnant expressions, which we can render only by complete final or consecutive clauses, e. g. 1 S 15[23] *he hath rejected thee* מִמֶּלֶךְ *away from* (being) *king*, instead of מִהְיוֹת מ׳ (as in verse 26), *that thou be no longer king*; cf. 1 K 15[13], Is 17[1] מֵעִיר *so that it is no longer a city*; Jer 17[16], Jb 28[1]° *he bindeth the streams* מִבְּכִי *that they trickle not*; Gn 16[2], 23[6] מִקְּבֹר *that thou shouldst not bury thy dead*; Is 24[10].

y The מִן has a still more pregnant force in those examples in which the idea of *precluding from* anything is only indirectly contained in the preceding verb, e. g. Gn 27[1] *his eyes were dim* מֵרְאֹת *away from seeing*, i. e. *so that he could not see*; Is 7[8] *Ephraim shall be broken in pieces* מֵעָם *that it be not a people* (just as in Is 23[1], Jer 48[2.42], ψ 83[5]); Lv 26[13], Is 5[6], 49[15], 54[9], Ezr 2[62] (for other pregnant constructions with מִן see below, *ff*)[3]; on מִבְּלִי and מֵאֵין *without*, cf. § 152 *y*.

---

[1] Cf. O. Molin, *Om prepositionen min i Bibelhebreisken*, Upsala, 1893, and especially N. Zerweck, *Die hebr. Praep.* min, Leipzig, 1893, who, instead of the partitive meaning (formerly accepted by us also), more correctly takes 'separation' as the starting-point of its various uses.

[2] All the *partitive* uses of מִן also come most naturally under this idea of separation *out of* a larger class. Thus מִן is used in the sense of *some, something*, and even *one*, in such expressions as *and he slew* ... *also* מִשָּׂרֵי יִשְׂרָאֵל (*divers*) *of the princes of Israel*, 2 Ch 21[4]; מִכָּל־ Lv 4[2]; 1 K 18[5]; מִדַּם הַפָּר *some of the blood of the bullock*, Ex 29[12], &c.; Jb 27[6] *my heart doth not reproach me* מִיָּמָי *for any*, i. e. for one, *of my days*; 38[12] מִיָּמֶיךָ *one of thy days*, i. e. *ever in thy life* (this explanation is confirmed by 1 K 1[6]; cf. also 1 S 14[45], 25[28]). In this way also, the frequently misunderstood Hebrew (and Arabic) idiom is to be explained, by which מִן before אַחַת אֶחָד is equivalent to *ullus*; e. g. Lv 4[2] *and shall do* מֵאַחַת מֵהֵנָּה *any one of these things*; 5[13], Dt 15[7], Ez 18[10]; so before a *nomen unitatis* (see § 122 *t*), 1 S 14[45] (2 S 14[11], 1 K 1[52]) מִשַּׂעֲרַת רֹאשׁוֹ *not one hair of his head*.—מִן is used in the sense of the Arabic *min el-beyān* or explicative *min* (often to be simply translated by *namely*), e. g. in Gn 7[22] *of all that was*, i. e. *so far as it was*, probably also Gn 6[2] (= *whomsoever they chose*).

[3] On the use of מִן to express the comparative, which likewise depends on the idea of *distance from* ..., cf. below, § 133 *a*; on מִן as expressing the

(2) On the sense of *motion away from* anything depends the use of מִן after ≥ such ideas as *to take away from, to beware, to be afraid of, to flee, to escape, to hide oneself from* (cf. καλύπτω ἀπό, *custodire ab*), sometimes again in pregnant expressions, e. g. Is 33[15]. On the idea of *starting from* anything depends finally the very frequent *causative* use of מִן *on account of, in consequence of* (cf. our *that comes from . . .*), *prae*, e. g. מֵרֹב *for multitude*, 1 K 8[5].

(e) עַל.[1] The two original local meanings of this preposition are *upon aa* (ἐπί)[2] and *over* (ὑπέρ, *super*).

(1) From the original meaning *upon* is explained the use of עַל־ after ideas of *commanding, commissioning* (פָּקַד עַל־), &c., inasmuch as the command, obligation, &c., is *laid upon* the object. The construction is self-evident in the case of *to lie, rest, lean, rely, press upon* something; cf. also, for the last, such examples as Is 1[14], Jb 7[20], 23[2], and especially 2 S 18[11] וְעָלַי prop. *upon me* would it have been, it would have been incumbent *upon me*, &c.

(2) From the original meaning *over* is explained the use of עַל־ after ideas *bb* of *covering, protecting, guarding* עַל־ בָּכָה, עַל־ גָּנֵן ; also the combinations עַל־ רִחַם *to have compassion upon . . .*, עַל־ חוּס, עַל־ חָמַל *to spare* some one, arise from the idea of a compassionate or protective *bending over* something. Cf. also עַל־ נִלְחַם Ju 9[17] = *to fight for* some one, i. e. in his defence.

(3) Moreover עַל־ is used after verbs of *standing* and *going*, to express *cc* a towering *over* some one or something, sometimes in phrases, in which the original local idea has altogether fallen into the background, and which are therefore to be rendered in English by means of other prepositions (*by, with, before, near*), e. g. Gn 41[1], &c., *Pharaoh . . . stood* עַל־הַיְאֹר *by the Nile* (above the water level ; cf. ψ 1[3]), and so especially עַל־ עָמַד in the pregnant sense *to stand serving before* some one (prop. *over* one who sits or reclines at table) Zc 4[14] (cf. Is 6[2], where לְ מִמַּעַל is used for עַל־) ; עַל־ הִתְיַצֵּב *to present oneself* by command *before* some one, Jb 1[6], &c. Cf. also עַל־יַד, עַל־יְדֵי (Jb 1[14]) *near, at* (*on*) *the side* of some one or something.

(4) From the original meaning *above* (not, as formerly explained, *on to dd* something, *at* something, there arise finally all the various constructions with עַל־ in the sense of *towards, against*. The original idea (which in many of these constructions has become wholly unrecognizable) starts from the view that the assailant endeavours to take up his position *over* the person attacked, so as to reach him from above, or to *overpower* him ; cf. especially עַל־ קוּם *to rise up over*, i. e. *against* some one, then with a transference of

---

distance of time from a fixed limit, in the sense of *after*, e. g. ψ 73[20] מֵהָקִיץ *after awaking* (cf. ἐξ ἀρίστου, *ab itinere*), or *after the lapse of . . .*, e. g. Gn 38[24], Ho 6[2], and very frequently מִקֵּץ *from the end of*, i. e. *after the lapse of . . .*, see the Lexicon ; also for the use of מִן to represent *resting beside* anything, like the Latin *prope abesse ab . . .*

[1] Cf. Budie, *Die hebr. Präpos. 'Al* (עַל), Halle, 1882.

[2] Since the placing *upon* anything is an addition to it, עַל־ also implies *in addition to* something, cf. Gn 28[9] (31[50]) ; 30[40], 32[12] (probably a proverbial saying = *mother and children*) ; Dt 22[6]. Also עַל *notwithstanding* is no doubt properly *in addition to*, e. g. Jb 10[7] *although thou knowest*, prop. *in addition to thy knowing*.—From the original meaning *upon* is also derived that of *on account of* (prop. *upon the ground of*) and *in agreement with, according to*, since the pattern is regarded as the foundation *upon* which a thing stands or rests.

thought applied to any kind of hostile approach, נִלְחַם עַל־ *to fight against* . . . , חָנָה עַל־ *to encamp against* . . . , נֶאֱסַף עַל־ *to be gathered together, to assemble against* (Mi 4¹¹; cf. ψ 2²), &c.; even after verbs which express a mental action, e. g. חָשַׁב רָעָה עַל־ *to imagine evil against* any one, &c.

ee **4.** Sometimes a preposition appears to be under the immediate government of a verb, which, by its meaning, excludes such a union. In reality the preposition is dependent on a verb (generally a verb of motion), which, for the sake of brevity, is not expressed, but in sense is contained in what is apparently the governing verb.

ff Various examples of this *constructio praegnans* have been already noticed above in *x* and *y* under מִן־; for מִן־ cf. also ψ 22²² וּמִקַּרְנֵי רֵמִים עֲנִיתָנִי *and thou hast answered* and saved *me from the horns of the wild oxen* (in Is 38¹⁷, which Delitzsch translates by *thou hast loved* and delivered *my soul from the pit*, read חָשַׁכְתָּ with the LXX); Gn 25²³, 2 S 18¹⁹, Jb 28¹²; cf. also זָנָה מִן־ ψ 73²⁷ *to 'go a whoring from* any one i. e. *to be unfaithful to him*; רָשַׁע מִן־ ψ 18²² = *to depart wickedly from God*; חָרַשׁ מִן־ ψ 28¹ *to be silent from* one (*to turn away in silence*); cf. Jb 13¹³ [; so with מֵעַל Jb 30¹⁷·³⁰].

gg Pregnant constructions with אַחֲרֵי: Nu 14²⁴ equivalent to וַיְמַלֵּא לָלֶכֶת אַחֲרֵי *and he made full to walk* i. e. *walked fully after me*; in 1 S 13⁷ read with the LXX חָרְדוּ מֵאַחֲרָיו *they trembled*, i. e. *went trembling away from him*; with דָּרַשׁ אֶל־, Gn 43³³ תָּמְהוּ אֶל־ *to turn in astonishment to* some one (cf. Is 13⁸); Is 11¹⁰, &c., *to turn inquiringly to* some one; הֶחֱרִישׁ אֶל־ Is 41¹ *to turn in silence to* some one; חָרַד אֶל־ Gn 42²⁸ *to turn trembling to* some one (cf. חָרַד לִקְרַאת *to come trembling to meet*, 1 S 21² [also with שָׁאַג, הֵרִיץ, שָׂמַח and other verbs, Ju 14⁵, 15¹⁴, 19⁸; see Lexicon]); cf. further Jer 41⁷, ψ 7⁷, 2 Ch 32¹; with בְּ ψ 55¹⁹ *he hath redeemed* and hath put *my soul in peace*, exactly like ψ 118⁵; with לְ ψ 74⁷ *they have profaned* and cast . . . *even to the ground*; cf. 89⁴⁰.

hh **5.** In poetic parallelism the governing power of a preposition is sometimes extended to the corresponding substantive of the second member;[1] e. g. בְּ Is 40¹⁹, 48¹⁴ *he shall perform his pleasure* בְּבָבֶל *on Babylon, and his arm shall be* כַּשְׂדִּים (for בַּכַּשְׂדִּים) *on the Chaldaeans*; Jb 15³; לְ Is 28⁶, 42²² (but probably לְ has fallen out after another לְ), Ez 39⁴, Jb 34¹⁰ (perhaps also Gn 45³; מָשַׁל may, however, be taken here as a second accusative according to § 117 *ii*); לְמַעַן Is 48⁹; מִן־ Is 58¹³, ψ 141⁹ (unless וּמִמְקֹשׁוֹת is to be read); עַד־ Is 15³; תַּחַת Is 61⁷.

ii **6.** Adverbs which have acquired a substantival value are sometimes governed by prepositions, e. g. אֶל־חִנָּם *in vain*, Ez 6¹⁰; אַחֲרֵי־כֵן *after this*; בְּכֵן (Ec 8¹⁰, Est 4¹⁶) *then, on this condition*; לָכֵן *and* עַל־כֵּן *therefore*; עַד־כֵּן *hitherto*.

---

[1] Similarly the force of a negative is sometimes extended to the parallel member; see § 152 *z*.

§ 120. Verbal Ideas under the Government of a Verb. Co-ordination of Complementary Verbal Ideas.

1. When a *relative* verb (incomplete in itself) receives its necessary *a* complement in the form of a verbal idea, the latter is, as a rule, subordinated in the infinitive construct (with or without לְ), less frequently in the infinitive absolute, in a few instances in the form of a participle (or verbal adjective), or finally in the imperfect without the copula. In these combinations the principal idea is very frequently represented by the subordinate member of the sentence, whilst the governing verb rather contains a mere definition of the manner of the action; cf. *d* and *g* below, and § 114 *n*, note 2.

(*a*) On the subordination of an infinitive construct as an accusative of the *b* object, and as the complement of relative verbal ideas, see above, § 114 *c*, and the numerous examples given in § 114 *m*; on the infinitive absolute as object, see § 113 *d*.—The complement in the form of a participle (as in Greek, and also frequently in Syriac) occurs in Is 33¹ שׁוֹדֵד כַּהֲתִמְךָ (cf. for the form, § 67 *v*) *when thou hast ceased as a spoiler*, i. e. to spoil ; Jer 22³⁰ יֹשֵׁב ... לֹא יִצְלַח *he shall never prosper, sitting*, i. e. so as to sit, &c. ; Jon 1⁶ *what meanest thou, sleeping?* i. e. that thou sleepest ;[1] by a verbal adjective, 1 S 3² *now his eyes* הֵחֵלּוּ כֵהוֹת *had begun being dim*, i. e. to wax dim (unless we read לִכְהוֹת=כֵּהוֹת, cf. § 114 *m*); by a substantive, Gn 9²⁰ *and Noah began to be an husbandman* (omitting the article before אֲדָמָה).

(*b*) Examples of the subordination of the complementary verbal idea in the *c* imperfect[2] (in English usually rendered by *to, in order to* or *that*) are—(1) with both verbs in the same person : after the perfect, Is 42²¹ יַגְדִּיל ... יְהוָה חָפֵץ *it pleased the Lord ... to magnify*, &c. ; Jb 30²⁸, 32²² לֹא יָדַעְתִּי אֲכַנֶּה *I know not to give flattering titles* ; after a perfect consecutive, 1 S 20¹⁹ (where for תֵּרֵד we should read with the LXX תִּפָּקֵד) ; after an imperfect, ψ 88¹¹, 102¹⁴, Jb 19³, 24¹⁴; after an imperf. consec., Jb 16⁸; after a participle, Is 5¹¹ᵃ.—(2) with a difference in the persons : after a perfect, Lv 9⁶ *this is the thing* אֲשֶׁר־צִוָּה יְהוָה תַּעֲשׂוּ *which the Lord commanded* (that) *ye should do* ; a negative imperfect follows צִוָּה in La 1¹⁰; after the imperfect, Is 47¹ (⁵) כִּי לֹא תוֹסִיפִי עוֹד יִקְרְאוּ־לָךְ *for thou shalt no more continue* (that) *they call thee*, i. e. thou shalt no longer be called, &c. ; Ho 1⁶ לֹא אוֹסִיף עוֹד אֲרַחֵם *I will no longer continue* (and) *have mercy*, i. e. *I will no more have mercy* ; Is 52¹, Pr 23³⁵.—Nu 22⁶ *peradventure I shall prevail* (that) *we may smite them, and* (that) *I may drive them out of the land* (אוּכַל may, however, be a scribal error for נוּכַל, due to the preceding אוּלַי, and in that case the example would belong to No. 1) ; after a participle,

---

[1] In יֵדַע מִנֶּגֶן 1 S 16¹⁶, which appears to be a case of this kind, two different readings are combined, יֵדַע לְנַגֵּן and the simple מִנֶּגֶן.

[2] This kind of subordination is frequent in Arabic and in Syriac (cf. e. g. the Peshiṭtâ, Luke 18¹³) ; as a rule, however, a conjunction (corresponding to our *that*) is inserted. Cf. moreover, the Latin *quid vis faciam?* Terence ; *volo hoc oratori contingat*, Cicero, Brut. 84 ; and our *I would it were* ; *I thought he would go*.

2 S 21⁴.—A perfect is possibly subordinated in La 1¹⁰; but the explanation of בָּאוּ as a relative clause is preferable.

d   2. Instead of subordination (as in the cases mentioned in *a–c*), the *co-ordination* of the complementary verbal idea in the finite verb (cf. above, *c*) frequently occurs, either—

(*a*) With the second verb co-ordinated in a form exactly corresponding to the first (but see below, *e*) by means of וְ (וַ, וָ).[1] As a rule, here also (see above, *a*) the principal idea is introduced only by the second verb, while the first (especially הוֹסִיף, יָסַף,[2] שׁוּב) contains the definition of the manner of the action, e.g. Gn 26¹⁸ וַיָּשָׁב וַיַּחְפֹּר *and he returned and digged*, i.e. he digged again; 2 K 1¹¹·¹³; in the perfect consecutive, Is 6¹³; with הוֹסִיף, e.g. Gn 25¹ *and Abraham added and took a wife*, i.e. again took a wife; Gn 38⁵ and frequently; with הוֹאִיל in the jussive, Jb 6⁹; in the imperative (cf. § 110 *h*), Ju 1⁹ הוֹאֶל־נָא וְלִין *be content, I pray thee, and tarry all night* (cf. the English *he was persuaded and remained*, for *to remain*); 2 S 7²⁹; with מָהַר Gn 24¹⁸·²⁰, &c.; with חָפַד Ct 2³.

e   **Rem. 1.** Instead of an exact agreement between co-ordinate verbal forms, other combinations sometimes occur, viz. imperfect and perfect consecutive (cf. § 112 *d*), e.g. Dt 31¹² *that they* יִלְמְדוּ וְיָרְאוּ אֶת־יְהֹוָה *may learn, and fear the Lord*, i.e. *to fear the Lord*; Is 1¹⁹, Ho 2¹¹, Est 8⁶, Dn 9²⁵ᵇ; perfect and imperfect, Jb 23³ (*O that I knew how I might find him*); perfect and imperfect consecutive, Jos 7⁷, Ec 4¹·⁷; jussive and imperative, Jb 17¹⁰; cf., finally, Gn 47⁶ וְאִם־יָדַעְתָּ וְיֶשׁ־בָּם *and if thou knowest and there are among them*, &c., i.e. that there are among them.

f   2. Special mention must be made of the instances in which the natural complement of the first verb is suppressed, or is added immediately after in the form of an historical statement, e.g. Gn 42²⁵ *then Joseph commanded and they filled*[3] (prop. that they should fill, and they filled . . . ; cf. the full form of expression in Gn 50²); a further command is then added by means of לְ and the infinitive; Ex 36⁶; another instance of the same kind is Gn 30²⁷ *I have divined and the Lord hath blessed me*, &c., i.e. that the Lord hath blessed me for thy sake.

g   (*b*) With the second verb (which, according to the above, represents the principal idea) attached *without the copula*[4] in the same mood, &c, In this construction (cf. § 110 *h*) the imperatives קוּמִי, קוּמָה (קוּם,

---

[1] Cf. the English colloquial expression *I will try and do it.*

[2] Of a different kind are the cases in which יָסַף with a negative is co-ordinated with a verb to emphasize the non-recurrence of the action; cf. Nu 11²⁵ *they prophesied and added not*, sc. to prophesy, i.e. *but they did so no more*; Dt 5¹⁹, Jb 27¹⁹ (reading וְלֹא יֹאסִיף).

[3] Cf. the analogous examples in Kautzsch's *Gramm. des Bibl. Aram.*, § 102.

[4] To be distinguished, of course, from the cases in which two equally important and independent verbs are used together without the copula in vigorous poetic imagery, e.g. Ex 15⁹, Jb 29⁸, &c.

&c.) and לְךָ (לְכָה, לְכִי, &c.) are exceedingly common with the sense of interjections, before verbs which express a movement or other action, e.g. קוּם הִתְהַלֵּךְ *arise, walk,* Gn 13¹⁷, 19¹⁵, 27⁴³; in the plural, Gn 19¹⁴; Ex 19²⁴ לֶךְ־רֵד *go, get thee down;* 1 S 3⁹; with a following cohortative, 1 S 9¹⁰ לְכָה נֵלֵכָה *come, let us go;* Gn 31⁴⁴ and frequently.—Also with שׁוּב (a periphrasis for *again*) in the perfect, Zc 8¹⁵; in the imperfect, Mi 7¹⁹, ψ 7¹³, 59⁷, 71²⁰; in the jussive, Jb 10¹⁶; in the cohortative, Gn 30³¹; in the imperative, Jos 5², 1 S 3⁵ *lie down again;* הוֹאִיל (sometimes to express the idea of *willingly* or *gladly*) in the perfect, Dt 1⁵, Ho 5¹¹; in the imperative, Jb 6²⁸; הִרְבָּה=*much,* 1 S 2³ אַל־תַּרְבּוּ תְדַבְּרוּ גְּבֹהָה *do not multiply* and *talk,* i.e. talk not so much *arrogancy;* in the imperative, ψ 51⁴; הָחֵל, Dt 2²⁴ הָחֵל רָשׁ *begin, possess;* La 4¹⁴ יָכֹל, בְּלֹא יוּכְלוּ יִגְּעוּ *without men's being able to touch,* &c.; מִהֵר=*quickly,* in the perfect, ψ 106¹³; in the imperative, Gn 19²², Ju 9⁴⁸, Est 6¹⁰.—Other examples are: Ho 9⁹ הֶעְמִיקוּ=*deeply, radically;* Zp 3⁷ הִשְׁכִּים=*early* (even in the participle, Ho 6⁴, 13³); Is 29⁴ שָׁפֵל=*low,* cf. Jer 13¹⁸; Jos 3¹⁶ תָּמַם=*wholly;* ψ 112⁹ פִּזַּר=*plentifully.*

Rem. This co-ordination without the copula belongs (as being more *h* vigorous and bolder) rather to poetic or otherwise elevated style (cf. e.g. Is 52¹, Ho 1⁶, 9⁹ with Gn 25¹, &c.). Asyndeton, however, is not wanting even in prose; besides the above examples (especially the imperatives of קוּם and הָלֵךְ Gn 30³¹, Dt 1⁵, 2²⁴, Jos 3¹⁶, 1 S 3⁵) cf. also Neh 3²⁰, 1 Ch 13². For special reasons the verb representing the principal idea may even come first; thus Is 53¹¹ יִרְאֶה יִשְׂבָּע *he shall see, he shall be satisfied* (sc. with the sight), for the satisfaction does not come until after the enjoyment of the sight; Jer 4⁵ קִרְאוּ מַלְאוּ *cry, fill,* i.e. cry with a full (loud) voice.

§ 121. *Construction of Passive Verbs.*

Blake, 'The internal passive in Semitic,' *JAOS.* xxii.

1. Verbs which in the active take *one* accusative (either of the *a* proper object, or of the *internal* object, or of some other nearer definition; cf. § 117 *a, p, u*) may in the passive, according to our mode of expression, be construed *personally,* the object of the active sentence now becoming the subject, e.g. Gn 35¹⁹ וַתָּמָת רָחֵל וַתִּקָּבֵר *and Rachel died, and was buried,* &c. The passive, however, is also used *impersonally* (in the 3rd sing. masc.), either absolutely, as Dt 21³·⁴, Is 16¹⁰, Ez 16³⁴ (with a dative added, 2 S 17¹⁶, Is 53⁵, La 5⁵), or, more frequently, with the object of the active construction still subordinated in the accusative,[1] e.g. Gn 27⁴² וַיֻּגַּד לְרִבְקָה אֶת־דִּבְרֵי עֵשָׂו *and there were told* (i.e. one told) *to Rebekah the words of Esau;* 2 S 21¹¹, 1 K 18¹³.

---

[1] When this is not recognizable either by the *nota accusativi,* or by its disagreement with the passive form in gender, number, and person, it

b   Other examples are: after Niph., Gn 4¹⁸ וַיִּוָּלֵד לַחֲנוֹךְ אֶת־עִירָד *and unto Enoch was born Irad* (cf. Nu 26⁶⁰, and after an infinitive, Gn 21⁵); Gn 17⁵, 21⁸ (after an infinitive); 29²⁷ (unless וְנִתְּנָה is 1st plur. cohortative); Ex 21²⁸, 25²⁸, Lv 6¹³, Nu 7¹⁰ (after an infinitive); 26⁵⁵ (cf. verse 53); Dt 20⁸ (where, however, for יִמַּס the Hiph. יָמֵס should be read, according to 1²⁸); Jos 7¹⁵, Is 16¹⁰; with the object preceding, Ex 13⁷, Lv 2⁸, 19²⁰, Nu 16²⁹, Dan 9²⁴.¹— Also after Pu'al, Jer 50²⁰; *before* Pu'al, Is 14³ אֲשֶׁר equivalent to the internal object עֲבֹדָה=*which they have caused to be served by thee*); Jb 22⁹; according to the Masoretic text also Gn 46²², where, however, the Samaritan and LXX read יֻלְּדָה for יֻלַּד; the Samaritan in Gn 35²⁶ and 46²⁷ also reads יֻלָּדוּ, and this (or יֻלַּד) should certainly be read instead of יֻלְּדוּ in 2 S 21²².—After Hoph., Ex 10⁸, 27⁷, Lv 10¹⁸, 16²⁷, Nu 32⁵, 1 K 2²¹, Pr 16³³, Jb 30¹⁵; after the infinitive Hoph., Gn 40²⁰, Ez 16⁴ᶠ, 27⁷; *before* Hoph., Is 17¹, 21², Ho 10⁶, Zc 13⁶; after the infinitive Hothpa'el, Lv 13⁵⁵ᶠ.

c   **2.** Verbs which in the active take two accusatives (§ 117 *cc*) retain in the passive construction at least *one* accusative, namely that of the second or remoter object, whilst the nearer object now becomes the subject. Thus, corresponding to אֲשֶׁר אַרְאֶךָּ *which I will show thee* (Gn 12¹) the passive is אֲשֶׁר אַתָּה מָרְאֶה (Ex 25⁴⁰) *which thou hast been shown*, i. e. which has been shown to thee; cf. Ex 26³⁰ (but in Lv 13⁴⁹ with an accusative of the person); Jb 7³. In ψ 22¹⁶ מֻדְבָּק מַלְקוֹחָי depends on an assumed transitive הִדְבִּיק governing two accusatives (= *my tongue is made to cleave to my jaws*); also in Is 1²⁰, חֶרֶב תְּאֻכְּלוּ *ye shall be devoured with the sword*, חֶרֶב is not an *accus. instrumenti*, but most probably an accusative of the object retained from the active construction.²

d   Rem. 1. Examples of the retention of the second accusative are—(*a*) with *verba induendi* and *exuendi* (§ 117 *cc*), ψ 80¹¹ כָּסּוּ הָרִים צִלָּהּ *the mountains were covered with the shadow of it* (the vine); Pr 19²³. So also some of the examples in § 116 *k* of passive participles of these verbs, Ju 18¹¹, 1 S 2¹⁸, 17⁵, 1 K 22¹⁰,

---

naturally cannot be determined whether the construction is really impersonal. The construction itself can only be explained by supposing that while using the passive form the speaker at the same time thinks of some author or authors of the action in question, just as on the theory of the Arab grammarians a *concealed agent* is included in every passive. This accounts for the possibility (cf. § 144 *g*) of using the active without a specified subject as a periphrasis for the passive.

¹ In 2 K 18³⁰ יִתֵּן is to be read or אֶת־ is to be omitted, as in the parallel passage Is 36¹⁵.

² In the active, the sentence would be *I will cause the sword to devour you*; by the rule stated above, under *c*, this would become in the passive, *the sword* (nom.) *shall be made to devour you* (acc.). Instead of this, the remoter object is here made the subject, and the nearer object is retained in the accusative. Otherwise, the only possible explanation would be, according to the Arabic idiom, *to cause one to devour the sword* (remoter object), i. e. to give him over to it. It would then be simplest to read תְּאֻכְּלוּ.

Ez 9[2.3] ;[1] with the accusative preceding, Neh 4[12].—(*b*) with *verba copiae* and *inopiae,* Ex 1[7], Is 38[10] (equivalent to *I must forego the residue of my years*) ; Is 40[20].—(*c*) an accusative of the result (§ 117 *ii*) with the passive, Is 6[11], Zc 14[4], Jb 28[2] ; with the accusative preceding, Is 24[12], Mi 3[12] (Jer 26[18]), Jb 15[7], 22[16].[2] Also in Ez 40[17] and 46[23], the accusative preceding עָשׂוּי (in 41[18] follow- ing it) can only be taken as the accusative of the result ; some general idea, such as that of *place,* is to be understood as the subject of עָשׂוּי.—(*d*) an accusative of the member or part specially affected by the action (§ 117 *ll*), Gn 17[11], 14[24], Ju 1[7] (accusative *before* part. pass.) ; 2 S 15[32] (accusative with suffix after the part. pass.).

2. Both accusatives are retained in an unusual manner after the passive of a *verbum implendi* in Nu 14[21] ; instead, however, of the *Niph.* וַיִּמָּלֵא the *Qal* (which is sometimes used transitively elsewhere) should simply be read with the LXX ; similarly in ψ 72[19], although there the LXX also translate the passive.

3. The efficient cause (or personal agent) is, as a rule, attached to the passive by לְ (thus corresponding to the Greek and Latin dative), e. g. Gn 25[21] וַיֵּעָתֶר לוֹ יְהֹוָה *the Lord let himself be intreated by him* ; cf. Lv 26[23], ψ 73[10] and the blessing בָּרוּךְ הוּא לַיהֹוָה *blessed be he of the Lord* Ru 2[20] ; cf. Gn 14[19], Ju 17[2b], 1 S 15[13] ; also in the plural, 1 S 23[21] (2 S 2[5], ψ 115[15]).—*Before* the verb, Pr 14[20] and frequently ; less com- monly by מִן (called מִן of origin=*coming from*), e. g. Gn 9[11] ; *before* the verb, ψ 37[23], Jb 24[1] ; by בְּ (*instrumenti*) [rarely, König § 106], Gn 9[6] (בָּאָדָם *by man*) ; Nu 36[2], Is 14[8 b] [but ?=*wherewith it was worked* (§ 52 *e*) *with thee* ; cf. Dt 21[3], König § 106 ; and see בְּ עָבַד in the Lexicon], Ho 14[4], always to introduce a personal agent.—On the con- nexion of the passive participle with a genitive of the agent, cf. § 116 *l.*

II. Syntax of the Noun.

§ 122. *Indication of the Gender of the Noun.*

Cf. F. Schwabe, *Die Genusbestimmung des Nomens im bibl. Hebr.,* Jena, 1894, and especially the thorough investigation by K. Albrecht, ' Das Geschlecht der hebr. Hauptwörter,' in *ZAW.* 1895, p. 313 ff., and 1896, p. 61 ff. H. Rosenberg, 'Zum Geschlecht der hebr. Hauptwörter,' in *ZAW.* 1905, p. 325 ff. (supple- menting Albrecht's work by a treatment of the gender of many nouns in the Mishna) ; and his 'Notizen aus der tannaitischen Literatur . . .' *ZAW.* 1908, p. 144 ff.

1. According to § 80 *a,* Hebrew, like the other Semitic languages, distinguishes only a *masculine* and *feminine* gender.   To indicate the

---

[1] Analogous to הַלָּבֻשׁ הַבַּדִּים *who was clothed in linen,* Ez 9[3], would be וְהַנּוֹתָר אֶת־הֶהָמוֹן הַזֶּה 2 Ch 31[10] ; but we must certainly read there וְנוֹתַר with the LXX.—Still less can ψ 87[3] be so explained, נִכְבָּדוֹת being not an accusative, but the subject of a noun-clause.   On the other hand, שָׁלוֹחַ 1 K 14[6] may be explained with Ewald in the sense of *being charged with* something, so that, like צֻוָּה, it may be construed with an accusative.

[2] In reality וַיָּרֻם Ex 16[20.26] (*it became putrid*) is equivalent to a passive (*it was changed*), to which תּוֹלָעִים is added as an accusative of the result.

latter a special feminine ending is generally used (§ 80 *b* and § 87 *i*) both in the singular and plural (see, however, § 87 *p*), its use being most consistent in adjectives and participles; cf. § 87 *r*. The employment of these special endings is most natural when by means of them the feminine names of persons or animals are distinguished from the masculine of the same stem and the same formation, e. g. אָח *brother*, אָחוֹת *sister*; עֶלֶם *a young man*, עַלְמָה *a young woman, maid*; פַּר *iuvencus*, פָּרָה *iuvenca*; עֵגֶל *vitulus*, עֶגְלָה *vitula*. On the other hand, the feminine plays an important part in denoting the gender of whole classes of ideas (see below, *p*, &c.), which the Hebrew regards as feminine. The language, however, is not obliged to use the feminine ending either for the purpose of distinguishing the *sex* of animate objects (see *b*), or as an indication of the (*figurative*) gender of inanimate things which are regarded as feminine (see *h*).

b   2. The distinction of *sex* may be effected even without the feminine ending, (*a*) by the employment of words of different stems for the masculine and feminine; (*b*) by the different construction (either as masculine or feminine) of the same word (*communia*). But the distinction may also, (*c*) in the case of names of animals, be entirely neglected, all examples of a species being included under one particular gender, either masculine or feminine (*epicoena*).

c   Examples of (*a*) are: אָב *father*, אֵם *mother*; אַיִל *ram*, רָחֵל *ewe*; תַּיִשׁ *he-goat*, עֵז *she-goat*; חֲמוֹר *he-ass*, אָתוֹן *she-ass*; אַרְיֵה *lion*, לָבִיא *lioness*. Sometimes with the feminine ending as well, e.g. עֶבֶד *male slave, man-servant*, אָמָה or שִׁפְחָה *female slave, maid*; חָתָן *bridegroom*, כַּלָּה *bride*.

d   Of (*b*): גָּמָל *camel*. Plur. גְּמַלִּים construed as masculine, Gn 24⁶³; as feminine, Gn 32¹⁶; בָּקָר collect. *oxen*, Ex 21³⁷, construed as masculine, but in Gn 33¹³, Jb 1¹⁴ as feminine. In Jer 2²⁴ the construction of פֶּרֶה *wild ass*, changes directly from the masculine (intended as epicene) to the feminine. Cf. the Greek ὁ, ἡ παῖς· ὁ, ἡ βοῦς.

e   Of (*c*): analogous to the epicene nouns of other languages, many species of animals which are strong and courageous, are regarded in Hebrew as always masculine, while the weak and timid are feminine; cf. ὁ λύκος, ἡ χελιδών, and the German *der Löwe, der Adler*, &c., but *die Katze, die Taube*, &c. Similarly in Hebrew, e.g. אַלּוּף *ox* (ψ 144¹⁴ even referring to cows when pregnant), דֹּב *bear*, Ho 13⁸ דּוֹב שַׁכּוּל (*a bear that is bereaved of her whelps*; cf., however, 2 K 2²⁴, Is 11⁷), זְאֵב *wolf*, כֶּלֶב *dog*, all masculine; but אַרְנֶבֶת *hare*, יוֹנָה *dove*, חֲסִידָה *stork*, דְּבוֹרָה *bee*, נְמָלָה *ant*, &c., feminine.

f   Rem. 1. Masculine nouns which either have a separate feminine form or might easily form one, are but seldom used as epicene; such are, חֲמוֹר *ass*, 2 S 19²⁷ for אָתוֹן; אַיָּל *hart*, ψ 42² for אַיָּלָה. In Gn 23³ ᶠᶠ· מֵת *a dead body*, refers more especially to the body of a woman; אָמוֹן *a master workman*, in Pr 8³⁰ refers to wisdom (חָכְמָה feminine, cf. Plin. 2, 1 *natura omnium artifex*); and our use of *friend, teacher, servant, neighbour,* either as masculine or feminine; in German, *Gemahl*[1] spouse, also for fem. *Gemahlin,* &c.).

2. Of words denoting persons נַעַר *παῖς,* according to the formerly common *g* opinion, was in early times used as epicene (see, however, above, § 2 *n*). The use of the plural נְעָרִים in Jb 1[19] and Ru 2[21] in the sense of *young people* (of both genders) does not, however, prove this. In this and in similar cases (cf. e. g. אֹתָם Gn 1[27] and אֶתְהֶם 32[1]) the masculine as *prior gender* includes the feminine.[2]

3. The following classes of ideas are usually regarded as feminine,[3] *h* although the substantives which express them are mostly without the feminine ending:[4]

(*a*) Names of *countries* and *towns,* since they are regarded as the mothers[5] and nurses of the inhabitants; e. g. אַשּׁוּר *Assyria,* אֱדֹם *Idumaea,* צֹר *Tyre;* cf. also such expressions as בַּת בָּבֶל, בַּת צִיּוֹן *daughter of Babylon, daughter of Zion,* &c. On the other hand appellatives which are originally masculine, remain so when used as place-names, e. g. Am 5[5] בֵּית־אֵל, הַגִּלְגָּל, &c.

Rem. The same proper nouns, which as names of countries are regarded *i* as feminine, are frequently used also as names of the people, and may then, like national names in other languages, be construed as masculine (the national name almost always being used also as the personal name of the supposed ancestor of the people); thus יְהוּדָה masc. Is 3[8], &c., *Judaei;* but

---

[1] So in early Arabic, *ba'l* (lord) and *žaug̀* (conjux) are used both for *maritus* and *uxor;* *'arūs* for *bridegroom* and *bride;* the later language, however, distinguishes the feminine from the masculine in all these cases generally by the ending *a* (*at*). In early Arabic also the feminine ending is commonly omitted in such participles as *ḥāmil, bāṭin* (gravida), and the like, which from the nature of the case can only be used of females. Thus also אֹמֵן, at least in Nu 11[12] (Is 49[23]?), probably means *nurse* (for אֹמֶנֶת 2 S 4[4], &c.), not *nursing-father.*

[2] The Arab grammarians call this use of the masculine plural and dual (e. g. *el-abawāni,* the two fathers, i. e. *parentes*) *taghlīb* or *the making* (the masculine) *prevail* (over the feminine).—Cf. M. Grünert, *Die Begriffs-Präpon-deranz und die Duale a potiori im Altarab.,* Vienna, 1886.

[3] The masculine gender is attributed 'by the Hebrews and the Semites generally to whatever is dangerous, savage, courageous, respected, great, strong, powerful . . . ; the feminine to whatever is motherly, productive, sustaining, nourishing, gentle, weak, . . . subject, &c.' (Albrecht, *ZAW.* 1896, p. 120 f.).

[4] When, on the other hand, words *with* a feminine-ending, such as קֶשֶׁת a *bow* (stem קוש), עֵת *time* (see the Lexicon), are sometimes construed as masculine, this is owing probably in some cases to a misunderstanding of the formation of the word, the ת of the feminine being regarded as a radical.

[5] Cf. *a city and a mother* (אֵם) *in Israel,* 2 S 20[19]. In the same way אֵם (like μήτηρ, *mater*) on Phoenician coins stands for *mother-city,* μητρόπολις. The same figure is used in such expressions as *sons of Zion,* ψ 149[2]; *sons of Babylon,* Ez 23[15], &c., as also in speaking of the suburbs of a city as its *daughters,* e. g. Jos 15[45 ff.], &c.—The comparison of Jerusalem to a woman is especially frequent in allegorical descriptions, e. g. Ez 16[23], La 1[1], &c.

Is 7⁶, fem., *Judaea*; אֱדֹם masc., *Idumaei*, Nu 20²⁰; fem., *Idumaea*, Jer 49¹⁷. Nevertheless, it sometimes happens that by a very common transference of thought (just as we say *Turkey concludes peace*) these names are construed as feminine, even when they denote not the country but the inhabitants; so יְהוּדָה La 1³; cf. Gn 41⁸, Ex 10⁷, 12³³, 1 S 17²¹, 2 S 8², 24⁹, Is 7², 21², 42¹¹, Jer 50¹⁰, Jb 1¹⁵. Hence the frequent personification of nations (as well as of countries and towns, see *h*, note 5) as female beings, e. g. Is 50¹, 54¹ᶠ·, and the use of the expressions בַּת בָּבֶל Is 47¹ ᶠ·, בַּת צִיּוֹן &c. (see above) as collective poetical personifications of the people.

k   (*b*) Appellative nouns, which denote a *circumscribed space*, such as אֶרֶץ earth, land, תֵּבֵל world, שְׁאֹל the abode of the dead, כִּכָּר circle (of the Jordan valley), עִיר a town, בְּאֵר a well, צָפוֹן the north, תֵּימָן the south.

l   In the majority of nouns denoting place the gender is variable, e. g. אֹרַח and דֶּרֶךְ a way (usually feminine; the masculine gender only begins to predominate with Ezekiel; cf. Albrecht, l. c., 1896, p. 55), גַּיְא (גַּי) valley, גַּן garden (fem. Gn 2¹⁵, unless לְעָבְדָה, &c., is to be read), הֵיכָל palace, temple, חָצֵר court, כֶּרֶם vineyard, שַׁעַר door,¹ &c.; also מָקוֹם place, at least in Gn 18²⁴ (referring to Sodom), Jb 20⁹, and 2 S 17¹² K°*thîbh*, is construed as feminine. The mountains and hills commanding the surrounding country are almost without exception masculine (see Albrecht, l. c., p. 60 f.).

m   (*c*) The names of *instruments, utensils,* and (on the same analogy) *members* and *parts of the body* in man or beast, since these are all regarded as subservient and subordinate (consequently as feminine).

n   Thus חֶרֶב sword, יָתֵד tent-peg, כַּד bucket, כּוֹס cup, נַעַל shoe, עֶרֶשׂ bed, &c.; in other cases, as אָרוֹן chest, ark (with the article הָאָרוֹן), תַּנּוּר oven, the gender is variable. ('Instruments for binding or holding, girdles and the like, as constraining and mastering, are masculine,' Albrecht, l. c., p. 89.)—Also אֹזֶן ear (and in general, members occurring in pairs, Albrecht, l. c., p. 73 f.), אֶצְבַּע finger (and so probably בֹּהֶן thumb, great toe), יָד and כַּף hand, יָמִין right hand, רֶגֶל foot, בֶּרֶךְ knee, יָרֵךְ thigh, כָּתֵף shoulder, לְחִי cheek, בֶּטֶן belly, כָּנָף wing, קֶרֶן horn, שֵׁן tooth; as a rule also זְרוֹעַ arm (masc. Is 17⁵, &c.), לָשׁוֹן tongue (masc. ψ 22¹⁶, Pr 26²⁸, &c.), עַיִן eye (masc. Zc 3⁹, &c.), שׁוֹק thigh (masc. Ex 29²⁷).²

o   (*d*) Certain names of natural forces or substances are feminine, being probably regarded as instruments, while in the names of the heavens, the heavenly bodies and natural phenomena, the masculine generally predominates (cf. Albrecht, l. c., p. 323 ff.); thus feminine are שֶׁמֶשׁ sun (but often also *masc.*, ψ 19⁶, 104¹⁹); אֵשׁ (Ethiopic '*ĕsât*)

---

¹ מַחֲנֶה camp is feminine only when it is a collective, denoting the persons in a camp.

² אַף nose, גִּיד sinew, זָנָב tail, חֵךְ palate, כָּבֵד liver, לֵב, לֵבָב heart, מֵעִים, רַחֲמִים bowels, מֵצַח forehead, עוֹר skin, עֹרֶף back of the neck, פֶּה mouth, צַוָּאר neck, רֹאשׁ head, שְׁכֶם shoulder, also רֶחֶם womb, except in Jer 20¹⁷, are invariably construed as masculine.—עֶצֶם bone is common.

fire (rarely *masc.*); נֹ֫גַהּ *brightness*, אֶ֫בֶן *a stone*, as a rule also רוּחַ *wind*, *spirit*; נֶ֫פֶשׁ *breath*, *soul*; also אוֹר *light* in Jer 13¹⁶, Jb 36³², and others.

4. The following classes of ideas, which are also regarded as *p* feminine in Hebrew (see above, *h*), are usually indicated by the feminine *form*, notwithstanding their occasional transference to masculine persons (see *r* and *s*):

(*a*) Abstracts¹ (sometimes along with masculine forms from the same *q* stem, as נְקָמָה *vengeance*, as well as נָקָם, עֶזְרָה *help*, as well as עֵ֫זֶר), e. g. אֱמוּנָה *firmness*, *faithfulness*, גְּבוּרָה *strength*, גְּדֻלָּה *greatness*, מְלֵאָה *fullness*, מֶמְשָׁלָה *dominion*, &c. Similarly, the feminine (sing. and plur.) of adjectives and participles is used substantivally in the sense of the Latin and Greek *neuter*, e. g. נְכוֹנָה *stedfastness*, ψ 5¹⁰, טוֹבָה *goodness*, רָעָה *evil*, Gn 50²⁰, נְקַלָּה *a light thing* (i. e. a trifling thing), Jer 6¹⁴; so especially in the plural, e. g. גְּדֹלוֹת *great things*, ψ 12⁴; הַנֶּהֱרָסוֹת *the ruined places*, Ez 36³⁶, along with הַנְּשַׁמָּה *that which was desolate*, טֹבוֹת *kindnesses*, 2 K 25²⁸, נְכֹחוֹת *uprightness*, *honesty*, Is 26¹⁰, נְעִימוֹת *amoena*, ψ 16¹¹ (but in verse 6 in the same sense נְעִימִים), נִפְלָאוֹת *wonderful things*, Ex 34¹⁰ and frequently, קָשׁוֹת *hard things*, *roughly*, Gn 42⁷·³⁰ (but cf. also רֵיקִים *vain things*, Pr 12¹¹, 28¹⁹). Cf. moreover, the very frequent use of זֹאת, הִיא (as well as זֶה and הוּא), Ju 14⁴, ψ 118²³, &c., in the sense of *hoc*, *illud* (also הֵ֫נָּה equivalent to *illa*, Is 51¹⁹): also the use of the feminine form of the verb in Is 7⁷ לֹא תָקוּם וְלֹא תִֽהְיֶה *it shall not stand, neither shall it come to pass*; cf. Jer 10⁷; so too the suffixes Gn 15⁶, Ex 10¹¹, Jb 38¹⁸, referring back to a whole statement.²

(*b*) Titles and designations of office, properly a subdivision of the abstract *r* ideas treated above, under *q*, and specially noticed here only on account of their peculiar transference to concrete male persons. Thus we have קֹהֶ֫לֶת Ec 1¹, &c. (as a title of Solomon), properly no doubt *that which takes part in* or *speaks in a religious assembly*, hence LXX ἐκκλησιαστής, i. e. *concionator, preacher*; the proper names סֹפֶ֫רֶת Ezr 2⁵⁵, Neh 7⁵⁷, and פֹּכֶ֫רֶת Ezr 2⁵⁷, Neh 7⁵⁹, and the foreign word פֶּחָה *viceroy*; in the plural כֵּנוֹת prop. *cognomina*, then *like-named, colleagues*; פַּרְעוֹת *princes* (if this be the true meaning).³ All these words, in accordance with their meaning, are construed as masculine (in Ec 7²⁷ instead of אָמְרָה ק׳ the words should rather be divided as אָמַר הַקּ׳; cf. 12⁸).

---

¹ Cf. the list of masculine and feminine abstracts in Albrecht, l. c., 1896, p. 111 ff.

² While in all these instances it is simplest to speak of the *feminine* in Hebrew as being used *for the neuter* (which in Latin, Greek, and German is commonly employed for similar purposes), it must yet not be forgotten that since the language is wholly wanting in *neuters*, the Semitic mind regarded the above-mentioned forms primarily as actual feminines. Hence the Arab commentators are accustomed to explain the feminines of adjectives and participles (which would be neuter in Latin, &c.) by supplying a feminine substantive.

³ This use of the feminine form is far more frequent in Arabic, Ethiopic, and Aramaic; cf. e. g. in Arabic *ḫalifa* (fem. from *ḫalif*, following after, taking the place of) in the sense of *the* successor or representative (of Muhammad), and *'allāma* (*great wisdom*) as a title of learned men. Analogous to this is the Latin *magistratus*, *magistracy*, for *magistrate*, and our *his Majesty, Excellency, Highness*, &c.

s   Abstract ideas include also—

(c) *Collectives* in the fem. form,[1] generally fem. participles used substantively, especially as the comprehensive designation of a number of *persons*, e. g. אֹרְחָה (fem. of *travelling*), prop. *the travelling* (company), i. e. travelling persons (a caravan) ; גּוֹלָה (fem. of גֹּלֶה *one going into exile*) *the company of exiles* (also frequently used of those who had returned home again) ; יוֹשֶׁבֶת (that which inhabits) i. e. *the population*, Is 12⁶, Mi 1¹¹ ᶠ· ; אֹיֶבֶת (prop. that which is hostile) *the enemy*, Mi 7⁸·¹⁰ (cf. Mi 4⁶ ᶠ· *the halting, cast off, driven away*, i. e. *those who halt*, &c.) ; דַּלָּה (the abject) *the poorest sort* ; of living beings which are not persons, cf. חַיָּה (that which lives) in the sense of *cattle, beasts* ; דָּגָה *a shoal of fish*, Gn 1²⁶ (but in Jon 2² as a *nomen unitatis*, cf. *t*, for דָּג *a fish*, which in verses 1 and 11 is used as the *nomen unitatis*).   Cf., moreover, נְבֵלָה *dead body*, Is 26¹⁹, &c. (construed as masculine), for ·*a heap of dead bodies*.—On the collective poetic personification of a nation, by means of בַּת *daughter*, in בַּת בָּבֶל, בַּת עַמִּי (equivalent to בְּנֵי עַמִּי) *my countrymen*, see above, *i*.

t   (d) Conversely the feminine form of substantives is sometimes used (as in Arabic) as a *nomen unitatis*, i. e. to indicate a *single* example of a class which is denoted by the masculine form ; cf. אֳנִי *a fleet* (1 K 9²⁶), אֳנִיָּה *a single ship* (Jon 1³ ff.) ; צַיִד *hunting, game*, צֵידָה Gn 27³ Kᵉth. (צֵידָ Qᵉrê) *a piece of venison* ; שֵׂעָר *hair* (coll.), שַׂעֲרָה *a single hair* (Ju 20¹⁶ ; in the plural, ψ 40¹³, 69⁵) ; שִׁיר *a poem*, frequently collective, שִׁירָה *a single song* ; so probably also תְּאֵנָה *a fig* (the corresponding masculine *tin* is collective in Arabic) ; שׁוֹשַׁנָּה *a lily* (also שׁוּשָׁן) ; לְבֵנָה *a brick* (Arab. *libina*, but *libin* collective), &c.

u   (e) The feminine is also used for things *without life* (as being weaker or less important), which are named from their resemblance to *organic* things expressed by the corresponding masculine form ; cf. יָרֵךְ *side* (of the body), *thigh*, יַרְכָה or יְרֵכָה *back part, border* (of a country, house, &c.) ; מֵצַח *forehead*, מִצְחָה *greaves*.   On a similar distinction between the masculine for natural, and the feminine for artificial objects, see § 87 *o*.

v   Rem. The juxtaposition of the masculine and feminine from the same stem serves sometimes to express entirety ; e. g. Is 3¹ מַשְׁעֵן וּמַשְׁעֵנָה *stay and staff*, i. e. every kind of support (unless we omit verse 1ᵇ as a gloss and take *staff* as =*staff-bearer, official* ; the list of officials begins in verse 2) ; cf. Is 16⁶, Pr 8¹³. For similar groupings in the case of persons, see Is 43⁶, 49²², 60⁴ (*sons and daughters*) ; 49²³, Ec 2⁸.

§ 123. *The Representation of Plural Ideas by Means of Collectives, and by the Repetition of Words.*

a   Besides the plural endings treated in § 87 *a–i*, the language employs other means to express a plurality of living beings or things :

(a) Certain words employed exclusively in a collective sense, while the individual members of the class are denoted by special words (*nomina unitatis*, but not in the same sense as in § 122 *t*).

---

[1] Cf. in Greek ἡ ἵππος, *the cavalry* (as well as τὸ ἱππικόν), ἡ κάμηλος, Hdt. 1, 80, &c., *the camel corps*.

Thus בָּקָר *cattle, oxen* [1] (even joined with numerals, e.g. Ex 21³⁷ חֲמִשָּׁה בָקָר *five head of cattle*), but שׁוֹר *an ox*; צֹאן *small cattle*, i.e. sheep and goats (μῆλα), cf. Jb 1³ שִׁבְעַת אַלְפֵי־צֹאן *seven thousand sheep*; but שֶׂה *a single head of small cattle* (a sheep or a goat). Other more or less common collectives are: זַיִן (prop. *that which prowls or roams*) *wild beasts*, טַף (perhaps prop. *tripping*) *a number of little children*; דֶּשֶׁא *fresh green herb*, i.e. *young plants*, יֶרֶק *green*, i.e. *vegetation in general*; עוֹף *birds, fowl*; רֶכֶב *chariots* or *cavalcade*, רִמָּה *worms*, רֶמֶשׂ *creeping things* (of small creatures), שֶׁרֶץ *swarming things*.

(*b*) The collective use of substantives which at the same time serve as *nomina unitatis*; thus, אָדָם (never in plur.) means both *man* (homo) and *men* (homines); אִישׁ *a man* (vir) and *men* (viri); אִשָּׁה *woman* and *women* (Ju 21¹⁶, 1 S 21⁶); אַרְבֶּה *a locust*, but usually *a swarm of locusts*; נֶפֶשׁ *soul* and *souls* (persons); מַקֵּל *staff* and *staves* (Gn 30³⁷); עַיִט *a bird of prey* and *birds of prey*; עָלֶה *a leaf* and *foliage*; עֵשֶׂב *a plant* and *plants, herbs*; עֵץ *a tree* and *trees* (as it were *foliage*); פְּרִי *fruit* and *fruits*; שִׂיחַ *a shrub* and *shrubs*; in isolated instances also nouns like עֶבֶד *man-servant*, שִׁפְחָה *maid-servant*, חֲמוֹר *ass*, שׁוֹר *ox* (cf. Gn 32⁶).—On the singular (especially of gentilic names) with the article (which may, however, be omitted in poetry, cf. e. g. ψ 12² חָסִיד, Pr 11¹⁴ יוֹעֵץ) to include all individuals of the same species, cf. § 126 *l*. On the special meaning of the plurals formed from certain collectives, see § 124 *l*.

(*c*) The feminine ending; see § 122 *s*.

(*d*) The repetition of single words, and even of whole groups of words, especially to express entirety, or in a distributive sense. The following cases are more particularly to be noticed:

1. The repetition of one or more words to express the idea of *every, all*, as יוֹם יוֹם Gn 39¹⁰, &c., *day by day, every day*; שָׁנָה שָׁנָה *year by year*, Dt 14²²; אִישׁ אִישׁ *every man*, Ex 36⁴; with בְּ before each, as בַּבֹּקֶר בַּבֹּקֶר Ex 16²¹ *every morning* (and similarly before a group of words, Lv 24⁸), for which the *distributive* לְ is also used, לַבֹּקֶר לַבֹּקֶר 1 Ch 9²⁷, and with *one plural* לַבְּקָרִים ψ 73¹⁴, לִבְקָרִים Jb 7¹⁸ parallel with לִרְגָעִים *every moment*. Somewhat different are the instances with בְּ before the second word only, e. g. יוֹם בְּיוֹם *day by day*, 1 Ch 12²²; שָׁנָה בְשָׁנָה *year by year*, Dt 15²⁰, 1 S 1⁷ (but in verse 3 מִיָּמִים יָמִימָה), כְּפַעַם בְּפַעַם Nu 24¹, Ju 16²⁰, 20³⁰ ᶠ·, 1 S 3¹⁰ *as at other times*. Also with the two words united by means of *wāw copulative*, אִישׁ וָאִישׁ ψ 87⁵, or אִישׁ וָאִישׁ Est 1⁸; דּוֹר וָדוֹר *all generations*, Dt 32⁷; יוֹם וָיוֹם Est 3⁴; cf. Est 8⁹,

---

[1] The plural form בְּקָרִים from בָּקָר is found only in very late Hebrew, Neh 10³⁷ (where according to the Mantua edition, Ginsburg, &c., even צֹאנֵינוּ *our sheep*, is also to be read; Baer, however, has צֹאנֵנוּ), and 2 Ch 4³. In Am 6¹² read, with Hitzig, בַּבָּקָר יָם.

Ezr 10¹⁴, 1 Ch 26¹³ and often (cf. Cheyne, *Bampton Lectures*, 1889, p. 479, according to whom the use of the ‎ו‎ copulative with the second word is especially common in Ch and Est, and therefore belongs to the later language; Driver, *Introd.*⁶, p. 538, No. 35); sometimes (but with the exception of ‎ψ‎ 45¹⁸ only in very late passages) with a pleonastic ‎כָּל־‎ preceding, ‎ψ‎ 145¹³, Est 2¹¹, 9²⁸, 2 Ch 11¹², &c.

d   2. Repetition of words in an expressly *distributive* sense[1] (which may to some extent be noticed in the examples under *c*) equivalent to *one each*, &c., e. g. Nu 14³⁴ *forty days* ‎יוֹם לַשָּׁנָה יוֹם לַשָּׁנָה‎ *counting for every day a year*; cf. Ez 24⁶, Ex 28³⁴ (three words repeated); also with the addition of ‎לְבַד‎ *apart*, ‎עֵדֶר עֵדֶר לְבַדּוֹ‎ *every drove by itself*, Gn 32¹⁷; cf. Zc 12¹². Most frequently with the addition of a numeral (for the simple repetition of numerals for the same purpose, cf. § 134 *q*), and with the words not only in groups of two (Lv 24⁸, Nu 13², 31⁴) or three (Nu 7¹¹, 17²¹), but even of six (Ex 26³) or seven (Ex 25³³, 26¹⁹·²¹·²⁵); in Ex 25³⁵ five words even three times repeated.[2]

e   3. Repetition to express an exceptional or at least superfine quality; e. g. 2 K 25¹⁵ *which were of gold, gold, of silver, silver*, i. e. made of pure gold and pure silver; Dt 2²⁷ ‎בַּדֶּרֶךְ בַּדֶּרֶךְ‎ *only along by the* high *way*; cf. Nu 3⁸, 8¹⁶ *they are given, given to him*, i. e. given exclusively for his service, for his very own. Also with a certain hyperbole in such examples as 2 K 3¹⁶ ‎גֵּבִים גֵּבִים‎ *nothing but trenches*; Gn 14¹⁰ ‎בֶּאֱרֹת חֵמָר‎ *all asphalt-pits.*—Repetition serves to intensify the expression to the highest degree in Ju 5²² *by reason of the violent pransings of his strong ones*, Ex 8¹⁰ (*countless heaps*), and Jo 4¹⁴ (*countless multitudes*); cf. also ‎מְעַט מְעַט‎ Ex 23³⁰ *by little and little, very gradually*; cf. § 133 *k*.

f   4. Repetition with the copula to express *of more than one kind*; thus Dt 25¹³ (Pr 20¹⁰) ‎אֶבֶן וָאָבֶן‎ *a weight and a weight*, i. e. two kinds of weight (hence the addition *great and small*); ‎ψ‎ 12³ ‎בְּלֵב וָלֵב‎ *with two kinds of heart*, i. e. *with a double-dealing heart*; cf. the opposite ‎בְּלֹא לֵב וָלֵב‎ 1 Ch 12³³.

§ 124. *The Various Uses of the Plural-form.*[3]

a   1. The plural is by no means used in Hebrew solely to express a number of individuals or separate objects, but may also denote them collectively. This use of the plural expresses either (*a*) a combination of various external constituent parts (plurals of *local extension*), or (*b*) a more or less intensive focusing of the characteristics inherent in the idea of the stem (*abstract plurals*, usually rendered in English by forms in *-hood, -ness, -ship*). A variety of the plurals described under (*b*), in which the secondary idea of *intensity* or of an *internal*

---

[1] Cf. in the New Testament St. Mark 6³⁹ ᶠ· συμπόσια συμπόσια, πρασιαὶ πρασιαί (Weizsäcker, *tischweise, beetweise*).

[2] These repetitions of larger groups of words belong entirely to the *Priestly Code* in the Pentateuch, and are unquestionably indications of a late period of the language. Of quite a different kind are such examples as Ez 16⁶, where the repetition of four words serves to give greater solemnity to the promise, unless here, as certainly in 1²⁰, it is a mere *dittography*; the LXX omit the repetition in both passages.

[3] Cf. Dietrich, 'Über Begriff und Form des hebr. Plurals,' in the *Abhandl. zur hebr. Grammatik*, Leipzig, 1846, p. 2 ff.

multiplication of the idea of the stem may be clearly seen, is (*c*) the *pluralis excellentiae* or *pluralis maiestatis*.

Examples of (*a*): Plurals of *local extension* to denote localities in general, but *b* especially level surfaces (the *surface-*plural), since in them the idea of a whole composed of innumerable separate parts or points is most evident, as שָׁמַיִם (§ 88 *d*) *heaven* (cf. also מְרוֹמִים *heights of heaven*, Is 33¹⁶, Jb 16¹⁹; elsewhere מָרוֹם); מַיִם *water*; יַמִּים (the broad surface of the sea) poetically for יָם *sea*; פָּנִים (prop. the side *turned towards* any one, then) *surface* in general, usually *face*; אֲחוֹרִים *the back*, Ex 26¹², 33²³, &c., צַוָּארִים *neck, nape of the neck* [1]; also מְרַאֲשׁוֹת *the place at the head*, מַרְגְּלוֹת *place at the feet*; עֲבָרִים *place on the other side* (of a river); מַעֲמַקִּים *depth*, מֶרְחַקִּים (also מֶרְחָק) *distance*, מִשְׁכָּבִים *bed*, Gn 49⁴ (unless, with Dillmann, it is to be explained in the sense of *double bed*, i.e. *torus*), מִשְׁכָּנִים ψ 46⁵, and מִשְׁכָּנוֹת 43³, 84², 132⁵, *dwelling* (perhaps also אֹהָלִים *encampment*, in passages like 1 S 4¹⁰). The last four belong, however, to poetic style, and are better reckoned amongst the *plurals of amplification* treated under *d–f*. So perhaps יְצֻעִים *bed* (ψ 63⁷, Jb 17¹³; but Gn 49⁴, ψ 132³, &c., in the singular); probably, however, יְצֻעִים (prop. *strata*) refers to a number of coverings or pillows.

The plural of extension is used to denote a lengthened period of *time* in עוֹלָמִים *eternity* (everlasting ages).

Rem. The plural of extension includes also a few examples which were *c* formerly explained as simply poetic plurals, e.g. Jb 17¹ קְבָרִים לִי *graves are (ready) for me*, i.e. the place where there are many of them (as it were the *graveyard*) is my portion, Jb 21³², 2 Ch 16¹⁴; cf. 2 K 22²⁰.

Of (*b*): the tolerably numerous abstract plurals, mostly of a particular *d* form (*qᵉṭûlim*, *qiṭṭûlim*, &c.), may be divided into two classes. They sum up either the *conditions* or *qualities* inherent in the idea of the stem, or else the various single *acts* of which an action is composed. Cf. for the first class, כְּלוּלוֹת and בַּחוּרוֹת בְּחֻרִים *youth*, זְקֻנִים *old age*, נְעוּרִים *youth*; בְּתוּלִים *maidenhood*, *bridal state*; מְגוּרִים *condition of a sojourner*; בְּשָׂרִים *fleshliness* (only in Pr 14³⁰), חַיִּים *life* (the abstract idea of the qualities of a living being); שַׁכּוּלִים *childlessness*, סַנְוֵרִים *blindness*, עַוְעִים *perverseness*.

There are also a number of plurals, found almost exclusively in poetry *e* (sometimes along with the stem), which are evidently intended to intensify [2] the idea of the stem (plural of amplification), as אוֹנִים *might*, Is 40²⁶; אֱמוּנִים (as well as אֱמוּנָה) and אֱמוּנוֹת *faithfulness*; אַשְׁרֵי (according to § 93 *l*, only in the construct state plural or with suffixes = *the happiness of*), *happy*; בְּכֹשָׁרוֹת (complete) *prosperity*, ψ 68⁷; בִּינוֹת Is 27¹¹ and תְּבוּנוֹת Is 40¹⁴, &c. (keen) *understanding*; עֵצוֹת (true) *counsel*, Dt 32²⁸; דֵּעִים Jb 37¹⁶ and דֵּעוֹת

---

[1] Cf. the same use of the plural in τὰ στέρνα, τὰ νῶτα, τὰ τράχηλα, *praecordia*, *cervices*, *fauces*; on plurals of extension in general, cf. the prepositions of place and time in the plur. form, § 103 *n*. סְפָרִים is not a case in point, in the sense of *letter* (properly a sheet folded into several pages; elsewhere also סֵפֶר) 1 K 21⁸ ff., 2 K 10¹, 19¹⁴ (Is 37¹⁴; referred to afterwards by the *singular* suffix); Is 39¹, Jer 29²⁵, 32¹⁴ (*after* being folded, previously סֵפֶר).

[2] Cf. A. Ember, 'The pluralis intensivus in Hebrew,' *AJSL*. 1905, p. 195 ff.

1 S 2³ (thorough) *knowledge*; בַּטֻּחוֹת Jb 12⁶ and מִבְטַחִים Is 32¹⁸ (full) *confidence*; בְּרָכוֹת (abundant) *blessing*, ψ 21⁷; גְּבוּרוֹת (exceptional) *strength*, Jb 41⁴; הַוּוֹת ψ 5¹⁰ (very) *wickedness*; חֲמוּדוֹת Dn 9²³ (greatly) *beloved*; חֵמוֹת ψ 76¹¹, &c. (fierce) *wrath*; חֲרָפוֹת Dn 12² (utter) *contempt*; יְשֻׁעוֹת (real) *help*, Is 26¹⁸, &c.; מַרְאֹת Gn 46² (an important) *vision*; מֵישָׁרִים *uprightness*; תַּהְפֻּכוֹת *perversity*; נְקָמוֹת (complete) *vengeance*, Ju 11³⁶, &c.; חֲשֵׁכִים and מַחֲשַׁכִּים (thick) *darkness*; מִסְתָּרִים a (close) *hiding-place*; נְגִידִים *nobility*; שְׁמָנִים Is 28¹ *fatness*; צַחְצָחוֹת (complete) *aridity*; מַמְתַּקִּים *sweetness*; מַחֲמַדִּים *preciousness*; שַׁעֲשֻׁעִים *delight*; עֲדָנִים and תַּעֲנוּגִים *pleasure*; רַחֲמִים *compassion*; מְנֻחֹת ψ 23² *rest, refreshment*; מְהוּמֹת Am 3⁹ *tumult*. Probably also יְדִידֹת (heartfelt) *love*, ψ 45¹; מְרֹרוֹת (extreme) *bitterness*, Jb 13²⁶; מִרְמוֹת (base) *deceit*, ψ 38¹³; צְדָקוֹת (true) *righteousness*, Is 33¹⁵, &c.; שְׂמָחוֹת (the highest) *joy*, ψ 16¹¹. On the other hand, חָכְמוֹת *wisdom* (Pr 1²⁰, &c.) can hardly be a *plural* (=the essence of wisdom, or wisdom personified), but is a singular (see § 86 *l*).

A further extension of this plural of amplification occurs according to P. Haupt's very probable suggestion (*SBOT*. Proverbs, p. 40, line 50, &c.) in יְאֹרִים *the great river* (of the Nile, generally יְאֹר) Is 7¹⁸, 19⁶ (though with the predicate in the plural), Ez 30¹², ψ 78⁴⁴, but in Is 37²⁵, Ez 29³ the usual explanation, *arms* or *channels of the Nile*, can hardly be avoided; also in נְהָרוֹת ψ 24² of the ocean, which encircles the earth, 137¹ of the *great river*, i. e. the Euphrates, but in Is 18¹ נַהֲרֵי כוּשׁ is evidently a numerical plural.—In Pr 16¹³ מְלָכִים (acc. to P. Haupt=the *great king*) is very doubtful. In נְשִׂיאֵי Ez 19¹ the second *yôdh* is evidently due to dittography, since יִשְׂרָאֵל follows.

f   The summing up of the several parts of an action is expressed in חֲנֻטִים *embalming*, כִּפֻּרִים *atonement*, מִלֻּאִים (prop. *filling*, sc. of the hand) *ordination to the priesthood*, שִׁלֻּחִים *dismissal*, שִׁלֻּמִים *retribution*, פִּתֻּחִים *engraving* (of a seal, &c.); אֲהָבִים *fornication*, זְנוּנִים *whoredom*; נִאֻפִים *adultery*; נִחֻמִים (prop. no doubt, warm compassion) *consolation*, תַּחֲנוּנִים *supplication*, נְדֻדִים Jb 7⁴ (restless) *tossing to and fro*, פְּלָאִים *wonder* La 1⁹, עֹלֵלוֹת *gleaning*; perhaps also נְגִינוֹת ψ 4¹, 6¹, &c., if it means *the playing on stringed instruments*, and שַׁלְמֹנִים Is 1²³ *bribery*, unless it be a plural of number.[1]

g   Of (c): the *pluralis excellentiae* or *maiestatis*, as has been remarked above, is properly a variety of the abstract plural, since it sums up the several characteristics[2] belonging to the idea, besides possessing the secondary sense of an *intensification* of the original idea. It is thus closely related to the plurals of amplification, treated under *e*, which are mostly found in poetry.

---

[1] Mayer Lambert in *REJ*. xxiv. 106 ff., enumerates no less than ninety-five words ending in *îm*, which in his opinion are to be regarded as *pluralia tantum*.

[2] The Jewish grammarians call such plurals רִבּוּי הַכֹּחוֹת *plur. virium* or *virtutum*; later grammarians call them *plur. excellentiae, magnitudinis*, or *plur. maiestaticus*. This last name may have been suggested by the *we* used by kings when speaking of themselves (cf. already 1 Macc. 10¹⁹, 11³¹); and the plural used by God in Gn 1²⁶, 11⁷, Is 6⁸ has been incorrectly explained in this way. It is, however, either *communicative* (including the attendant angels; so at all events in Is 6⁸, cf. also Gn 3²²), or according to others, an indication of *the fullness of power and might* implied in אֱלֹהִים (see Dillmann on Gn 1²⁶); but it is best explained as a plural of *self-deliberation*. The use of the plural as a form of respectful address is quite foreign to Hebrew.

So especially אֱלֹהִים *Godhead, God* (to be distinguished from the numerical plural *gods*, Ex 12¹², &c.). The supposition that אֱלֹהִים is to be regarded as merely a remnant of earlier polytheistic views (i. e. as originally only a numerical plural) is at least highly improbable, and, moreover, would not explain the analogous plurals (see below). That the language has entirely rejected the idea of numerical plurality in אֱלֹהִים (whenever it denotes *one* God), is proved especially by its being almost invariably joined with a singular attribute (cf. § 132 *h*), e.g. אֱלֹהִים צַדִּיק *ψ* 7¹⁰, &c. Hence אֱלֹהִים may have been used originally not only as a numerical but also as an abstract plural (corresponding to the Latin *numen*, and our *Godhead*), and, like other abstracts of the same kind, have been transferred to a concrete single god (even of the heathen).

To the same class (and probably formed on the analogy of אֱלֹהִים) belong *h* the plurals קְדֹשִׁים *the Most Holy* (only of Yahweh), Ho 12¹, Pr 9¹⁰, 30³ (cf. אֱלֹהִים קְדֹשִׁים Jos 24¹⁹, and the Aram. עֶלְיוֹנִין *the Most High*, Dn 7¹⁸·²²·²⁵); and probably תְּרָפִים (usually taken in the sense of *penates*) the image of a god, used especially for obtaining oracles. Certainly in 1 S 19¹³·¹⁶ only *one* image is intended; in most other places a single image *may* be intended[1]; in Zc 10² alone is it most naturally taken as a numerical plural. In Ec 5⁷ גְּבֹהִים *supremus* (of God) is doubtful; according to others it is a numerical plural, *superiores*.

Further, אֲדֹנִים, as well as the singular אָדוֹן, (lordship) *lord*, e.g. אֲדֹנִים קָשֶׁה *i* a *cruel lord*, Is 19⁴; אֲדֹנֵי הָאָרֶץ *the lord of the land*, Gn 42³⁰, cf. Gn 32¹⁹; so especially with the suffixes of the 2nd and 3rd persons אֲדֹנֶיךָ, אֲדֹנָיו *ψ* 45¹², אֲדֹנָיו, &c., also אֲדֹנֵינוּ (except 1 S 16¹⁶); but in 1st sing. always אֲדֹנִי.[2] So also בְּעָלִים (with suffixes) *lord, master* (of slaves, cattle, or inanimate things; but in the sense of *maritus*, always in the singular), e.g. בְּעָלָיו Ex 21²⁹, Is 1³, &c.[3]

On the other hand, we must regard as doubtful a number of participles in *k* the plural, which, being used as attributes of God, resemble *plurales excellentiae*; thus, עֹשַׂי *my Maker*, Jb 35¹⁰; עֹשֶׂיךָ Is 54⁵; עֹשֶׂיהָ *ψ* 149²; עֹשֶׂיךָ Is 22¹¹; נֹטֵיהֶם *stretching them out*, Is 42⁵; for all these forms may also be explained as singular, according to § 93 *ss*.[4]—לְגֹשָׂיו Is 3¹² might also be regarded as another instance, unless it be a numerical plural, *their oppressors*; moreover, מְרִימָיו *him who lifteth it up*, Is 10¹⁵ (but read probably מְרִימוֹ); שֹׁלְחָיו *him who sendeth him*, Pr 10²⁶, 22²¹ (so Baer, but Ginsburg שֹׁלְחֶךָ), 25¹³ (in parallelism with אֲדֹנָיו). These latter plurals, however (including מְרִימָיו), may probably be more simply explained as indicating an indefinite individual, cf. *o* below.—For שֹׁמְרֶיךָ *ψ* 121⁵ (textus receptus) and בּוֹרְאֶיךָ Ec 12¹ (textus receptus) the singular should be read, with Baer.

---

[1] Even in Gn 31³⁴, notwithstanding the plural suffix in וַתְּשִׂמֵם and עֲלֵיהֶם, since the construction of these abstracts as numerical plurals is one of the peculiarities of the E-document of the Hexateuch; cf. Gn 20¹³, 35⁷, and § 145 *i*.

[2] On אֲדֹנִי (for אֲדֹנַי) as a name of God, cf. § 135 *q*.

[3] Euting, *Reise in Arabien*, p. 61, mentions the interesting fact that the subjects of the Emir of Ḥâyel commonly speak of their ruler as *šiyûkh*, a plur. majestatis = *the great sheikh*.

[4] בְּעָלָיךָ, which in Is 54⁵ is in parallelism with עֹשַׂיִךְ, must then be explained as merely formed on analogy.

l   Rem. I. (*a*) Coherent substances, &c., are mostly regarded as *single*, and are, accordingly, almost always represented by nouns in the singular, cf. אָבָק *fine dust*, אֵפֶר *ashes*, בַּד *linen*, בְּדִיל *lead*, זָהָב *gold*, כֶּסֶף *silver*, נְחֹשֶׁת *brass*, חָלָב *milk*, יַיִן *wine*, עָפָר *dust, the ground*, עֵץ *wood*.   Plurals are, however, formed from some of these words expressing materials in order to denote separate portions taken from the whole in manufacture (*plurals of the result*) or parts otherwise detached from it; thus, בַּדִּים *linen garments*; כְּסָפִים *silver pieces*, Gn 42²⁵·³⁵; נְחֻשְׁתַּיִם (dual) *fetters of brass*; עֵצִים *ligna* (*timber* for building or *sticks* for burning); also in a wider sense, בְּדִילִים *particles of alloy* to be separated by smelting, Is 1²⁵; עֲפָרוֹת *fragments of earth*, Pr 8²⁶, cf. Jb 28⁶ עַפְרֹת זָהָב *dust of gold*.

m   (*b*) To the class of *plurals of the result* belong also a few names of natural products, when represented in an artificial condition; thus, חִטִּים *wheat* in grain (threshed wheat), as distinguished from חִטָּה *wheat* (used collectively) in the ear; cf. the same distinction between כֻּסְּמִים and כֻּסֶּמֶת *spelt*; עֲדָשִׁים and עֲדָשָׁה (the singular preserved only in the Mishna) *lentils*; שְׂעֹרִים and שְׂעֹרָה *barley*; also פִּשְׁתִּים *linen*, פֵּשֶׁת (to be inferred from פִּשְׁתִּי) *flax*.

n   (*c*) Finally, the distinction between דָּם *blood* and דָּמִים requires to be specially noticed. The singular is always used when the blood is regarded as an organic unity, hence also of menstrual blood, and the blood of sacrifices (collected in the basin and then sprinkled), and in Nu 23²⁴ of the blood gushing from wounds. On the other hand, דָּמִים as a sort of plural of the result and at the same time of local extension, denotes *blood which is shed*, when it appears as blood-stains (Is 1¹⁵) or as blood-marks (so evidently in Is 9⁴). But since blood-stains or blood-marks, as a rule, suggest blood shed in murder (although דָּמִים also denotes the blood which flows at childbirth or in circumcision), דָּמִים acquired (even in very early passages) simply the sense of a *bloody deed*, and especially of *bloodguiltiness*, Ex 22¹ᶠ·, &c.

o   In some few cases the plural is used to denote an indefinite singular; certainly so in Dt 17⁵ אֶל־שְׁעָרֶיךָ *unto* one of *thy gates*; Zc 9⁹ בֶּן־אֲתֹנוֹת (cf. Ct 2⁹); Ex 21²² יְלָדֶיהָ (where evidently only *one* child is thought of, though certainly in connexion with a contingency which may be repeated); cf. also Ec 4¹⁰ (*if one of them fall*).—So probably also Gn 8⁴, 1 S 17⁴³, Dn 2¹, Neh 3⁸, 6²; but *not* Gn 19²⁹, since the same document (Gn 13¹²) makes Lot dwell *in the cities* of the Jordan valley; in Gn 21⁷ בָּנִים denotes the class with which the action is concerned. In Ju 12⁷ instead of the unusual בְּעָרֵי גִלְעָד *in the cities of Gilead* (formerly explained here as *in one of the cities of Gilead*) we should most probably read, with Moore (*SBOT.* Judges, p. 52), בְּעִירוֹ בְּמִצְפֵּה גִלְעָד *in his city, in Mizpeh* (in) *Gilead*.

p   **2.** When a substantive is followed by a genitive, and the compound idea thus formed is to be expressed in the plural, this is done—

     (*a*) Most naturally by using the plural of the *nomen regens*, e.g. גִּבּוֹרֵי חַיִל *mighty men of valour* (prop. heroes of strength), 1 Ch 7²·⁹; so also in compounds, e.g. בְּנֵי יְמִינִי 1 S 22⁷, as the plur. of בֶּן־יְמִינִי *Benjamite*; but also

q   (*b*) By using the plural of *both* nouns,[1] e.g. גִּבּוֹרֵי חֲיָלִים 1 Ch 7⁵;

---

[1] Cf. König, *Lehrgebäude*, ii. 438 f., according to whom the plural of the principal word exercises an influence on the determining genitive.

שְׁנֵי־לֻחֹת אֲבָנִים and in prison houses, Is 42²²; cf. Ex 34¹, &c.,
two tables of stone (but Ex 31¹⁸ לֻחֹת אֶבֶן); Nu 13³², Dt 1²⁸, Jos 5², 6⁴,
2 K 14¹⁴, 25²³, Is 51⁹, Jer 41¹⁶, Ezr 3³, &c. עַמֵּי הָאֲרָצוֹת the people of the
country; 2 Ch 26¹⁴; so perhaps בְּנֵי אֵלִים sons of God, ψ 29¹, 89⁷
(according to others sons of gods); or finally even

(c) By using the plural of the *nomen rectum*; ¹ e. g. בֵּית אָבוֹת Ex 6¹⁴, *r*
Nu 1²·⁴ᶠᶠ·, &c., as plur. of בֵּית אָב *father's house, family*; בֵּית הַבָּמוֹת *the
houses of the high places*, 2 K 17²⁹ (also בָּתֵּי הַבָּמוֹת 23¹⁹); בֵּית עֲצַבֵּיהֶם
the houses of their idols, 1 S 31⁹, Ez 46²⁴; cf. also Ju 7²⁵ *the head of Oreb
and Zeeb*, i. e. the heads, &c.

Rem. When a substantive (in a distributive sense) with a suffix refers *S*
back to a plural, the singular form of the substantive suffices, since the idea
of plurality is already adequately expressed by the suffix, e. g. פִּימוֹ *os* (for *ora*)
eorum, ψ 17¹⁰; יְמִינָם *their right hand*, ψ 144⁸ [so in the English RV.], for
hands.

§ 125. *Determination of Nouns in general. Determination of Proper Names.*

Brockelmann, *Grundriss*, i. 466 ff.

1. A noun may either be determinate in itself, as a proper name *a*
or pronoun (see below, *d* and *i*), or be made so by its context. In
the latter case, the determination may be effected either by prefixing
the article (see § 126), or by the connexion of the noun (in the
construct state) with a following determinate genitive, and consequently also (according to § 33 *c*) by its union with a pronominal
suffix (§ 127 *a*). It is to be taken as a fundamental rule, that the
determination can only be effected in *one* of the ways here mentioned;
the article cannot be prefixed to a proper name, nor to a noun
followed by the genitive, nor can a proper name be used in the
construct state. Deviations from this rule are either only apparent
or have arisen from a corruption of the text.

Rem. Only in a few passages is a noun made expressly *indeterminate* by the *b*
addition of אֶחָד in the sense of our indefinite article; cf. Ex 16³³, Ju 9⁵³, 13²,
1 S 1¹, 7⁹·¹², 1 K 13¹¹, 19⁴, 20¹³, 22⁹, 2 K 4¹, 8⁶, 12¹⁰, Ez 8⁸, Dn 8³, 10⁵ (in 8¹³
אֶחָד קָדוֹשׁ i. e. *one*, viz. *a holy one*, is opposed to another).

It is further to be noticed, that in Hebrew the phenomenon sometimes *C*
occurs, which the Arab grammarians call *indeterminateness for the sake of
amplification*; e. g. Is 31⁸ *and he shall flee* מִפְּנֵי־חֶרֶב *from a sword*, i. e. *from an
irresistible sword* (God's sword); cf. Is 28² בְּיָד; 2 S 6² שֵׁם; Ho 3¹ אִשָּׁה *such
a woman*, without doubt to be referred to the Gomer mentioned in cap. 1;

---

¹ Cf. Brockelmann, *Grundriss*, i. 482.

Am 6¹⁴ גּוֹי ; ψ 77¹⁶ בְּזֹרֵעַ ; Pr 21¹² צַדִּיק, if with Delitzsch it is to be referred to God ; Jb 8¹⁰ מִלִּים meaning *important words*, but in 15¹³ מִלִּין *reproachful words*. Cf. on this point, § 117 *q*, note 3, and Delitzsch, *Psalmen*, ed. 4, p. 79.

d   2. Real *proper nouns*, as being the names of things (or persons) only *once* met with, are sufficiently determinate in themselves. Such names, therefore, as סְדֹם, כְּנַעַן, יַעֲקֹב, דָּוִד, יהוה do not admit of the article,[1] nor can they be in the construct state. On the other hand, not only *gentilic* names (as denoting the *various* individuals belonging to the same class), but also all those proper names, of which the appellative sense is still sufficiently evident to the mind, or at least has been handed down from an earlier period of the language, frequently (often even as a rule) take the article (according to § 126 *e*), and may even be followed by a genitive.

e   Examples. Like the above-mentioned proper names of individuals, countries, and cities, so also national names, which are identical in form with the name of the founder of the race (e.g. מוֹאָב, אֱדוֹם, יִשְׂרָאֵל), are always determinate in themselves. Of gentilic names (e.g. הָעִבְרִי *the Hebrew*, הָעִבְרִים *the Hebrews*, Gn 40¹⁵ ; הַכְּנַעֲנִי *the Canaanite*) the plural פְּלִשְׁתִּים, even when meaning *the Philistines*, is generally used without the article (but in 1 S 4⁷, &c., הַפְּ׳) ; so always כַּפְתֹּרִים.—Evident appellatives (like such modern names as *the Hague, le Havre*) are הַגִּבְעָה *the hill*, in the construct state גִּבְעַת שָׁאוּל, i.e. *the Gibeah named after Saul* to distinguish it from others ; הָרָמָה *the height* ; הָעַי *the heap* ; הַלְּבָנוֹן (prop. *the white mountain*) *the Lebanon* ; הַיְאֹר (prop. *the river*) *the Nile*, cf. Am 8⁸ כִּיאוֹר מִצְרַיִם *like the river of Egypt* ; הַיַּרְדֵּן *the Jordan* (according to Seybold, *Mittheil. und Nachr. des DPV.*, 1896, p. 11, probably *the drinking-place* [ירד, Arab. *warada*, meaning orig. *to go down to drink*]).

f   Rem. 1. In a few instances original appellatives have completely assumed the character of real proper names, and are therefore used without the article ; thus אֱלֹהִים *God*, to denote the one true God (as elsewhere יהוה) Gn 1¹ and so generally in this document of the Pentateuch up to Ex 6, elsewhere sometimes הָאֱלֹהִים ὁ θεός (cf. § 126 *e*) ; also the sing. אֱלוֹהַּ *God*, עֶלְיוֹן *the Most High*, and שַׁדַּי *the Almighty* never take the article.—Moreover, אָדָם *Adam* from Gn 5¹ onwards (previously in 2⁷, &c., הָאָדָם *the first man*) ; שָׂטָן *Satan*, 1 Ch 21¹ (but Zc 3¹, Jb 1⁶, &c., הַשָּׂטָן *the adversary*) ; cf. אֹהֶל מוֹעֵד *the tent of revelation* (i.e. the tabernacle), always without the article.

g   To the class of nouns originally appellative, which the language regards

---

[1] Consequently, הַמְנַשֶּׁה Dt 3¹³, Jos 1¹², &c. (in the Deuteronomist) in the combination שֵׁבֶט הַמְנַשֶּׁה (for which elsewhere שֵׁבֶט מְנַשֶּׁה) is to be regarded *not* as a proper name but as a gentilic name (= *the tribe of the Manassites*), for which in Dt 29⁷ הַמְנַשִּׁי is used, as in 10⁸ הַלֵּוִי שׁ׳ *the tribe of the Levites*, and in Ju 18¹ הַדָּנִי שׁ׳ *the tribe of the Danites*.—In Jos 13⁷ הַמְנַשֶּׁה (like gentilic names in ◌ִי) is even used adjectivally.

as proper names, and which consequently never take the article, belong also certain archaic words mostly used only by poets, such as שְׁאוֹל *Hades*, תֵּבֵל *world*, תְּהוֹם *ocean*, of the body of water which encircles the earth, Gn 1², &c. ; but Is 63¹³, ψ 106⁹ בַּתְּהֹמוֹת *through the depths*, viz. of the Red Sea.[1]

2. When nouns which the usage of the language always treats as proper *h* names occasionally appear to be connected with a following genitive, this is really owing to an ellipse whereby the noun which really governs the genitive, i. e. the appellative idea contained in the proper name, is suppressed. So evidently in the case of יְהֹוָה צְבָאוֹת *Yahweh* (the God) *of hosts* ; the fuller form יהוה אֱלֹהֵי צְבָאוֹת 2 S 5¹⁰, &c., or יהוה אֱלֹהֵי הַצְּבָאוֹת Am 3¹³, &c., is a secondary expansion of the original יְהֹוָה צְבָאוֹת ; אֱלֹהִים in ψ 59⁶, 80¹⁵·²⁰, 84⁹ is due to the mechanical substitution of אֱלֹהִים for יהוה affected in the 2nd and part of the 3rd book of the Psalms. So also in geographical names such as אוּר כַּשְׂדִּים *Ur* (the city) *of the Chaldees*, Gn 11²⁸; אֲרַם נַהֲרַיִם *Aram* (the region) *of the two rivers* ; בֵּית לֶחֶם יְהוּדָה *Bethlehem* (the city) *of Judah* ; אָבֵל בֵּית מַעֲכָה 2 S 20¹⁴, &c., to distinguish it from אָבֵל מַיִם *Abel by the water*, 2 Ch 16⁴; יָבֵישׁ גִּלְעָד 1 S 11¹, &c.; יַרְדֵּן יְרֵחוֹ Nu 22¹, 26³·⁶³, &c.; on Ju 8³² cf. § 128 c; צִיּוֹן קְדוֹשׁ יִשְׂרָאֵל *the Zion of the Holy One of Israel*, Is 60¹⁴; but in 1 S 1¹ for צוֹפִים read צֹפִי *a Zuphite*. Some of these examples (cf. also Am 6²) come very near to the actual construct state (cf. above, גִּבְעַת שָׁאוּל), since e.g. the addition of the genitive serves to distinguish the place from four others called Aram (see the Lexicon), or from another Bethlehem. Aram, Bethlehem, &c., are accordingly no longer names found only in one special sense, and therefore also are no longer proper names in the strictest sense.

3. Of the pronouns, the personal pronouns proper (the separate *i* pronouns, § 32) are always determinate in themselves, since they can denote only definite individuals (the 3rd person, also definite things). For the same reason the demonstrative pronouns (§ 34) are also determinate in themselves, when they stand *alone* (as equivalent to substantives), either as subject (Gn 5²⁹) or as predicate (e. g. זֶה הַיּוֹם *this is the day*, Ju 4¹⁴; אֵלֶּה הַדְּבָרִים *these are the words*, Dt 1¹), or as object (e. g. אֶת־זֹאת 2 S 13¹⁷), or as genitive (מְחִיר זֶה 1 K 21²), or finally when joined to a preposition (לְזֹאת Gn 2²³; בָּזֶה 1 S 16⁸, see § 102 *g*).

So also the personal pronouns הוּא, הִיא, הֵם, הֵמָּה, הֵנָּה when they *k* are used as demonstratives (=*is, ea, id, ille*, &c.) are always determinate in themselves, e. g. הוּא הַדָּבָר *that is the thing*, Gn 41²⁸. They

---

[1] That various other words, such as אֱנוֹשׁ *man*, צַלְמָוֶת *deep darkness*, רֹזֵן *prince*, שָׂדַי *field*, תּוּשִׁיָּה *effectual working*, are always found without the article is not to be attributed to any special archaism, but is to be explained from the fact that they belong solely to poetic language, which avoids the article ; in other cases, such as תַּרְדֵּמָה *deep sleep*, there is no occasion for the article in the passages we possess.

are made determinate by the article, when they are joined like adjectives (see § 126 *u*) with a determinate substantive, e. g. הָאִישׁ הַזֶּה *this man*; הָאֲנָשִׁים הָאֵלֶּה *these men*; בַּיָּמִים הָהֵמָּה וּבָעֵת הַהִיא *in those days, and in that time*, Jo 4¹. The demonstrative, however, even in this case, is frequently used *without* the article, as being sufficiently determinate in itself (cf. § 126 *y*).

§ 126. *Determination by Means of the Article.*

a 1. The article (הַ, הָ, הֶ, § 35) was originally, as in other languages (clearly in the Romance; cf. also ὁ, ἡ, τό in Homer), a demonstrative pronoun. The demonstrative force of the article, apart from its occasional use as a relative pronoun (see § 138 *i*), appears now, however, only (*a*) in a few standing phrases, and (*b*) in a certain class of statements or exclamations.

b   (*a*) Cf. הַיּוֹם *this day, hodie* (§ 100 *c*); הַלַּיְלָה *this night*, Gn 19³⁴; הַפַּעַם *this time*, Gn 2²³; הַשָּׁנָה *this year* (= in this year) Is 37³⁰, Jer 28¹⁶.

(*b*) includes those instances in which the article, mostly when prefixed to a participle, joins on a new statement concerning a preceding noun. Although such participles, &c., are no doubt primarily regarded always as in apposition to a preceding substantive, the article nevertheless has in some of these examples almost the force of הוּא (הִיא, הֵמָּה) as the subject of a noun-clause; e. g. ψ 19¹⁰ *the judgements of the Lord are true* . . . , verse 11 הַנֶּחֱמָדִים וגו׳ prop. *the more to be desired than gold*, i. e. *they are more to be desired, or even they, that are more to be desired*,[1] &c.; cf. Gn 49²¹, Is 40²² ᶠ·, 44²⁷ ᶠ·, 46⁶, Am 2⁷, 5⁷, ψ 33¹⁵, 49⁷ הַבֹּטְחִים in the parallel half of the verse continued by a finite verb); ψ 104³, Jb 6¹⁶, 28⁴, 30³, 41²⁵ and frequently. When such a participle has another co-ordinate with it, the latter is used *without* the article, since according to the above it strictly speaking represents a second predicate, and as such, according to *i*, remains indeterminate; e. g. Jb 5¹⁰ *who giveth* (הַנֹּתֵן) *rain, &c., and sendeth* (וְשֹׁלֵחַ), &c.

c   The article is sometimes used with similar emphasis before a substantive, which serves as the subject of a compound sentence (§ 140 *d*); e.g. Dt 32⁴ הַצּוּר תָּמִים פָּעֳלוֹ i.e. as a fresh statement (not in apposition to the preceding dative), really equivalent to *he is a rock, perfect in his work* (i. e. *whose work is perfect*); cf. ψ 18³¹.

d   2. The article is, generally speaking, employed to determine a substantive wherever it is required by Greek and English; thus:

(*a*) When a person or thing already spoken of is mentioned again, and is consequently more definite to the mind of the hearer or reader; e. g. Gn 1³ *and God said, Let there be light*: verse 4 *and God saw the light* (אֶת־הָאוֹר); 1 K 3²⁴ *fetch me a sword: and they brought the sword*; Ec 9¹⁵. (In 2 S 12² therefore לְעָשִׁיר must be read.)

---

[1] On the analogous use of the article before participles which have a verbal suffix, as in ψ 18³³, &c., cf. above, § 116 *f*.

(*b*) With a title understood and recognized by every one, e. g. הַמֶּלֶךְ שְׁלֹמֹה ὁ βασιλεὺς Σαλωμών: Gn 35⁸ *under the oak* (the well-known oak which was there).

(*c*) With appellatives to denote persons or natural objects which are unique, e. g. הַכֹּהֵן הַגָּדוֹל *the high priest*, הַשֶּׁמֶשׁ *the sun*, הָאָרֶץ *the earth*.

(*d*) When terms applying to whole classes are restricted (simply by *e* usage) to particular individuals (like ὁ ποιητής, meaning Homer) or things, e. g. שָׂטָן *adversary*, הַשָּׂטָן *the adversary*, Satan; בַּעַל *lord*, הַבַּעַל *Baal* as proper name of the god; הָאָדָם *the* (first) *man*, *Adam*; הָאֱלֹהִים[1] or הָאֵל ὁ θεός, *the one true God* (cf. also ὁ Χριστός in the New Testament); also הַנָּהָר *the river*, i. e. *Euphrates*; הַכִּכָּר *the circle*, sc. of the Jordan, *the Jordan plain* [Gn 19¹⁷, &c.].

(*e*) Very often with the vocative, e. g. 2 S 14⁴ הוֹשִׁעָה הַמֶּלֶךְ *help, O king*; Zc 3⁸ יְהוֹשֻׁעַ הַכֹּהֵן הַגָּדוֹל *O Joshua the high priest*; 1 S 17⁵⁸, 24⁹, 2 K 9⁵; in the plural, Is 42¹⁸, Jo 1²·¹³; but cf. also Jos 10¹², Is 1², 49¹³ (שָׁמַיִם and אֶרֶץ); 23¹⁶, Ho 13¹⁴, Jo 1⁵, ψ 34¹², Ec 10¹⁷, 11⁹, &c.[2] The vocative occurs *without* the article in Is 22², since it has been already defined by a preceding accusative.

Rem. Strictly speaking in all these cases the substantive with the article *f* is really in apposition to the personal pronoun of the 2nd person, which is either expressly mentioned or virtually present (in the imperative), e. g. 1 S 17⁵⁸ *thou, the young man*. But such passages as Is 42¹⁸, where the vocative precedes the imperative, prove that in such cases the substantive originally in apposition eventually acquired the value of a complete clause.

(*f*) With words denoting classes (see particulars under *l*). *g*

(*g*) In a peculiar way, to specify persons or things, which are so far definite as to be naturally thought of in connexion with a given case, and must be assumed accordingly to be there (see *q–s*).

(*h*) With adjectives (also ordinal numbers and demonstrative pronouns used adjectivally) which are joined to substantives determined in some way (see *u*).

Rem. The article may be omitted in *poetry* in all the above-mentioned *h* cases; in general it is used in poetry far less frequently than in prose. Its use or omission probably often rests on rhythmical grounds;[3] it is sometimes omitted also for rhetorical reasons. Cf. e. g. אֶרֶץ for הָאָרֶץ ψ 2²; מְלָכִים as vocative, verse 10; מֶלֶךְ for הַמֶּלֶךְ 21²; שְׁמֶךָ גָּדוֹל וְנוֹרָא (contrary to *u, v*) 99³. In the instances in which the ה of the article is omitted after a prefix (§ 35 *n*), the vowel of the article is often retained after the prefix even in poetry, e. g. בַּשָּׁמַיִם ψ 2⁴, &c.

---

[1] On the subsequent change of אֱלֹהִים, אָדָם, שָׂטָן into real proper names by the omission of the article, cf. above, § 125 *f*.

[2] For further exceptions see Nestle, *ZAW*. 1904, p. 323 ff.

[3] Cf. the useful statistics of J. Ley in the *Neue Jahrbücher für Philologie und Pädagogik*, 2te Abteilung, 1891, Heft 7–9, and M. Lambert, 'L'article dans la poésie hébr.,' *REJ*. 37, 263 ff.

i   (*i*) On the other hand, the article is always omitted when a person or thing is to be represented as indefinite (or indefinable) or as yet unknown; consequently also before the predicate, since this is from its nature always a general term, under which the subject is included, e.g. Gn 29⁷ עוֹד הַיּוֹם גָּדוֹל *as yet the day is great*, i.e. it is yet high day; 33¹³, 40¹⁸, 41²⁶, Is 66³.

k   Rem. 1. As exceptions to the above rule it is usual to regard those examples in which a determinate adjective or participle (equivalent to a relative clause) is used apparently as a predicate, e.g. Gn 2¹¹ הוּא הַסֹּבֵב *it is the compassing*, i.e. *that is it which compasseth*; 42⁶, 45¹², Ex 9²⁷, Dt 3²¹, 8¹⁸, 11⁷, 1 S 4¹⁶, Is 14²⁷, Mal 3² (cf. in Greek, e.g. St. Mat. 10²⁰, where Winer, *Gram. des neutest. Sprachidioms*, § 58, 2, Rem., explains οἱ λαλοῦντες as a predicate with the article). In reality, however, these supposed predicates are rather subjects (acc. to § 116 *q*), and the only peculiarity of these cases is that the subject is not included under a general idea, but is equated with the predicate.
      2. Sometimes the article is used with only one of two parallel words, as Na 1⁵ הֶהָרִים and הַגְּבָעוֹת, 2 Ch 3¹⁷ מִיָּמִין and מֵהַשְּׂמֹאול.

l   3. The use of the article to determine the *class* is more extensive in Hebrew than in most other languages. In this case the article indicates universally known, closely circumscribed, and therefore well defined classes of persons or things. The special cases to be considered are—

m   (*a*) The employment of general names as collectives in the singular, to denote the *sum total* of individuals belonging to the class (which may, however, be done just as well by the plural); e.g. *the righteous, the wicked man*, Ec 3¹⁷; *the woman*, i.e. *the female sex*, 7²⁶; הָאֹיֵב *th. enemy*, i.e. *the enemies* (?) ψ 9⁷; הָאֹרֵב *the lier in wait*, i.e. *the liers in wait*; הֶחָלוּץ *the armed man*, i.e. *soldiers*; הַמְאַסֵּף *the rearguard*; הַמַּשְׁחִית *the spoiler*, 1 S 13¹⁷;[1] so also (as in English) with names of animals, when something is asserted of them, which applies to the whole species, e.g. 2 S 17¹⁰ *as the courage of* הָאַרְיֵה *the lion*. Especially also with gentilic names, e.g. *the Canaanite*, Gn 13⁷ (cf. 15¹⁹ᶠ.); so in English *the Russian, the Turk*, &c., in Attic writers ὁ Ἀθηναῖος, ὁ Συρακόσιος, &c.

n   (*b*) Names of materials known everywhere, the elements and other words denoting classes, even though only a part and not the whole of them is considered, in which case in other languages, as e.g. in English, the article is usually omitted (cf., however, our *to fall into the water, into the fire*, &c.), e.g. Gn 13² *and Abram was very rich* בַּמִּקְנֶה בַּכֶּסֶף וּבַזָּהָב *in cattle, in silver and in gold*; Jos 11⁹ *and he burnt their chariots* בָּאֵשׁ *with fire*; cf. Gn 6¹⁴, 41⁴² (unless this means, *the chain* necessarily belonging to the official dress); Ex 2³, 31⁴ (35³²), Is 1²², &c, and בַּשֶּׁמֶן *with oil*[2] very commonly in the sacrificial laws, Ex 29²,

---

[1] But in Ex 12²³ הַמַּ׳ is either to be explained as *the destroyer* (now mentioned for the first time) according to *q*, or a particular angel is meant whose regular function it was to inflict punishments. Others again take הַמַּ׳ even in Ex 12²³ impersonally = *destruction*.

[2] In nearly all the above examples the presence of the article is only indicated by the vowel of the prefix (בַּ, כַּ, לַ) and might therefore be merely

&c., and also Dt 33²⁴, 2 S 1²¹, Is 1⁶, ψ 23⁵, &c. Similarly the article is used with terms of measurement, as הָאֵפָה Ex 16³⁶, &c. : הַחֹמֶר and הַבַּת Ez 45¹¹; הָעֹמֶר Ex 16²²; בַּחֵבֶל 2 S 8².

(c) The expression of abstract ideas of every kind, since they are likewise used to represent whole classes of attributes or states, physical or moral defects, &c.; e.g. Pr 25⁵ (בְּצָרֶק); Gn 19¹¹ *and they smote the men* . . . בַּסַּנְוֵרִים *with blindness*; Am 4⁹, &c.; but in הַחֹשֶׁךְ Is 60² the article is no doubt due to dittography of the ה, and the parallel וַעֲרָפֶל has no article.

(d) *Comparisons*, since the object compared is treated not (as usually in English) individually but as a general term, e. g. Is 1¹⁸ *white* בַּשֶּׁלֶג *as snow*, בַּצֶּמֶר *as wool*; *red* כַּתּוֹלָע *like crimson*; Is 34⁴ *and the heavens shall be rolled together* כַּסֵּפֶר *as a scroll*; cf. Nu 11¹², Ju 8¹⁸, 16⁹ *as* פְּתִיל־הַנְּעֹרֶת *a string of tow is broken*; 1 S 26²⁰, 1 K 14¹⁵, Is 10¹⁴, 24²⁰, 27¹⁰, 29⁸, 53⁶, Na 3¹⁵, ψ 33⁷, 49¹⁵; cf. also such examples as Gn 19²⁸, Ju 14⁶, where the object compared is determined by a determinate genitive which follows (according to § 127 a).

Examples of indeterminate comparisons are rare, and perhaps due only to the Masora,—so at least in the case of singulars, while in such plurals as those in Gn 42³⁰, 1 K 10²⁷, Jo 2⁴·⁷, the omission of the article may be explained by the ordinary rules. On the other hand, the article is regularly omitted when the object compared is already defined by means of an attribute (or relative clause, Jer 23⁹, ψ 17¹²), e.g. Is 16² כְּעוֹף נוֹדֵד קֵן מְשֻׁלָּח *as wandering birds*, (as) *a scattered nest* (but cf. 10¹⁴ (כַּקֵּן); 14¹⁹, 29⁵ כְּמֹץ עֹבֵר (but ψ 1⁴ (כַּמֹּץ); Jer 2³⁰, Pr 27⁸, Jb 29²⁵, 30¹⁴.—In comparisons with persons also the Masora seems to avoid the use of the article, as in כְּגִבּוֹר Jb 16¹⁴ and seven other places (כַּגִּבּוֹר only in Is 42¹³), כְּאָב Jb 31¹⁸, כְּגֶבֶר Jb 38³, 40⁷.

4. Peculiar to Hebrew [1] is the employment of the article to denote a single person or thing (primarily one which is as yet unknown, and therefore not capable of being defined) as being present to the mind under given circumstances. In such cases in English the indefinite article is mostly used.

Thus Am 5¹⁹ *as if a man did flee from a lion* (הָאֲרִי, i.e. the particular lion pursuing him at the time), *and a bear* (הַדֹּב) *met him*, &c., cf. 3¹², 1 K 20³⁶ (John 10¹²); also Gn 8⁷ᶠ·, 14¹³ הַפָּלִיט, i.e. *one that had escaped*, the particular one who came just then; so also Ez 24²⁶, 33²¹; cf. 2 S 15¹³); Gn 15¹·¹¹, 18⁷ *the servant*, who is regarded as being constantly at hand and awaiting his commands; cf. 2 S 17¹⁷ (but הַנַּעַר Nu 11²⁷ is used like הַפָּלִיט above); Gn 19³⁰, unless בַּמְּעָרָה means in *the* well-known *cave*; בַּמָּקוֹם Gn 28¹¹, according to Dillmann, upon *the* place suitable for passing the night, or the right place, but it may possibly also refer to *the* sanctuary of Bethel afterwards so sacred and celebrated; Gn 42²³, 46², 50²⁶, Ex 2¹⁵, 3², 4²⁰, 21²⁰ (2 S 23²¹), Lv 23⁴², 24¹⁰ (Samaritan יִשְׂרָאֵל without the article); Nu 17¹¹, 21⁶·⁹, 25⁶, Dt 19⁵, Jos 2¹⁵, Ju 4¹⁸, 8²⁵, 13¹⁹, 16¹⁹, 19²⁹, 20¹⁶, 1 S 17³⁴, 19¹³, 21¹⁰, 2 S 17¹⁷, 1 K 6⁸, 13¹⁴ (? most

---

due to the masoretic punctuation. There is, however, no reason to doubt the correctness of the tradition. The same is true of the examples under n and o.

[1] Cf., however, analogous examples in biblical Aramaic in Kautzsch's *Gramm. des Bibl. Aram.*, § 79 f, e. g. Dn 2¹⁴, 3², &c.

probably a particular tree is meant) ; 19⁹, Is 7¹⁴ (הָעַלְמָה‎, i.e. *the particular maiden*, through whom the prophet's announcement shall be fulfilled ; we should say *a maiden* [cf. Driver on 1 S 1⁴, 6⁸, 19¹³] ; Jb 9³¹.

s　So always *to write in the book* (or *on the scroll*, Nu 5²³, Jer 32¹⁰), i.e. not in *the* book already in use, but in the book which is to be devoted to that purpose, equivalent to *in a book, on a scroll*, Ex 17¹⁴, 1 S 10²⁵, Jb 19²⁸. Especially instructive for this use of the article is the phrase וַיְהִי הַיּוֹם‎, which does not simply refer back to the previous narrative in the sense of *the same day*, but is used exactly like our *one day* (properly meaning on the particular day when it happened, i.e. *on a certain day*), 1 S 1⁴, 14¹, 2 K 4⁸, 11¹⁸, Jb 1⁶·¹³. In Gn 39¹¹ even כְּהַיּוֹם הַזֶּה‎.

t　The article is sometimes used in this way before collectives in the singular, which are not meant to denote (like the examples given under *l*) a whole class, but only that part of it which applies to the given case ; thus הָעֹרֵב‎, הַיּוֹנָה‎ Gn 8⁷, הַצִּרְעָה‎ Ex 23²⁸.

u　5. When a substantive is defined by the article, or by a suffix, or by a following genitive determinate in any way (see the examples below), the attribute belonging to it (whether adjective, participle, ordinal, or demonstrative pronoun) necessarily takes the article (see, however, the Rem.), e.g. Gn 10¹² הָעִיר הַגְּדֹלָה‎ *the great city* ; Dt 3²⁴ יָדְךָ הַחֲזָקָה‎ *thy strong hand*. A genitive following the substantive may, according to § 127 *a*, be determined either by the article, e.g. 1 S 25²⁵ אִישׁ הַבְּלִיַּעַל הַזֶּה‎ *this worthless man* (prop. *man of worthlessness* ; cf. also such examples as 2 Ch 36¹⁸, where the article is prefixed only to a second genitive following the noun) ; or as a proper name, e.g. Dt 11⁷ מַעֲשֵׂה יְהוָֹה הַגָּדֹל‎ *the great work of the Lord* ; or by a suffix, e.g. Is 36⁹ עַבְדֵי אֲדֹנִי הַקְּטַנִּים‎ *the least of my master's servants*.

v　When several attributes (whether connected by *Wāw* or not) follow a determinate substantive, each of them takes the article, e.g. Dt 10¹⁷ הָאֵל הַגָּדֹל הַגִּבֹּר וְהַנּוֹרָא‎ *the great God, the mighty, and the terrible.* Cf. also Ex 3³, Dt 1¹⁹, in both of which places a demonstrative with the article also follows the adjective,[1]

Rem. 1. The article is, however, not infrequently used also—

w　(*a*) With the attribute alone, when it is added to an originally indefinite substantive as a subsequent limitation ; so always with ordinal numbers after יוֹם,[2] e.g. Gn 1³¹ (cf. 2³, Ex 20¹⁰, &c.) יוֹם הַשִּׁשִּׁי‎ *the sixth day* (prop. *a day* namely

---

[1] The demonstrative used adjectivally is generally placed *after* the adjective proper ; in such cases as עַמְּךָ הַזֶּה הַגָּדֹל‎ 2 Ch 1¹⁰ the adjective forms a further (fresh) addition to עַמְּךָ הַזֶּה‎.

[2] Cf. Driver, *Tenses*, 3rd ed., § 209 ; M. Lambert, *REJ.* 31, 279 f.—The omission of the article from the substantive is not to be regarded in *this* instance as an indication of late style, and consequently cannot be put forward as a proof of the late origin of the ' Priestly Code ' (cf. Dillmann on Gn 1³¹, Holzinger, *Einl. in d. Hexateuch*, p. 465, and especially Driver in the *Journal of Philology*, xi. 229 f., against Giesebrecht in *ZAW.* 1881, p. 265 f.). On the other hand, the common omission of the article from the substantive before a determinate adjective (e.g. כְּנֶסֶת הַגְּדוֹלָה‎ *the great synagogue*, in the Mishna ; cf. Segal, *Miśnaic Hebrew*, p. 19 ff.) is certainly a later idiom.

the sixth; but יוֹם שֵׁנִי *a second day*, Gn 1[8]); Ex 12[15] מִיּוֹם הָרִאשֹׁן *from the first day onward* (not before Dn 10[12] and Neh 8[18] is מִן־הַיּוֹם הָרִאשׁוֹן used instead of it). On the other hand, the article is *always* found after בְּ, hence בַּיּוֹם הַשִּׁשִּׁי, &c., although it is possible that the original reading in these cases was בְּיוֹם, and that the article is only due to the Masora. In Ju 6[25] the text is evidently corrupt (see verse 26).—Especially also in certain frequently recurring combinations as in particularizing the gates in Jer 38[14], Ez 9[2], &c., Zc 14[10], and courts in 1 K 7[8.12], &c., Ez 40[28]; and very often when the attribute consists of a participle, e.g. Dt 2[23], Ju 21[19], 1 S 25[10], Jer 27[3], 46[16] הַחֶרֶב הַיּוֹנָה *the sword which oppresses*(?); Ez 14[22], Zc 11[2] *Keth.* (*the impenetrable forest?*) Pr 26[18], ψ 119[21].

Of the other examples, Gn 21[29] (where, however, the Samaritan reads *x* (הכבשׂות), 41[26] (but cf. verse 4), Nu 11[25], Ju 16[27], 1 S 17[17] may at any rate be explained on the ground that the preceding cardinal number is equivalent to a determinant; in Gn 1[21], 28[9.10], &c., the substantive is already determined by כָּל־, and in 1 S 14[29] (וּדְבַשׁ) by מֵעַט.—In 1 S 12[23], 2 S 12[4], Is 7[20] (where, however, הַשְּׁבִירָה might also be understood as a subsequent explanation of בְּתַעַר) and Neh 9[35], the omission of the article after the preposition is certainly due merely to the Masora. In 1 S 16[23] (unless רוּחַ אֱלֹהִים is to be read twice), Zc 4[7] (where however אֶת הָהָר is probably meant), ψ 104[18] (where a ה precedes הָרִים, hence probably a case of haplography), the omission of the article before א, ר (?) and ה may be due to a regard for euphony (see *z* below). On the other hand, in 1 S 6[18] (read הָאֶבֶן הַגְּ), 17[12] הַזֶּה is a later addition), 19[22] (cf. the LXX), Jer 17[2], 32[14], 40[3] *Keth.*, Ez 2[8] (read גּוֹ or omit גּוֹיִם with Cornill), Mi 7[11], ψ 62[4], either the text is corrupt, or the expression incorrect. But in 2 K 20[13], Jer 6[20], Ct 7[10] acc. to D. H. Müller (*Anzeiger der Wiener Akad.,* phil.-hist. Kl. 1902, no. *x*) הַטּוֹב is the genitive of a substantive, *aromatic oil, sweet cane* (in Jer 6[20] read וְקָנֶה), *like spiced wine.* In Is 39[2] read שֶׁמֶן הַטּוֹב and in ψ 133[2] כַּשֶּׁמֶן הַטּ'.

(*b*) *No* article with the attribute, while the substantive is determined *y* either by the article, or a suffix, or a following genitive. Thus the article is sometimes omitted with demonstratives, since they are already to a certain extent determined by their meaning (cf. also the Mêša' inscription, l. 3, הבמת זאת *this high place*); as with הוּא Gn 19[33] (evidently for euphony, and so probably often); 30[16], 32[23], 1 S 19[10]; with הִיא Gn 38[21]; with זוּ ψ 12[8] (according to the Masora זוּ is a relative pronoun here, as always elsewhere); with אֵלֶּה 1 S 2[23], according to the present corrupt text (the original reading כָּלְעַם יהוה became כָּלְעַם אֱלֹהִים, and אֱלֹהִים was then corrupted to אֵלֶּה); so, almost without exception, when the substantive is determined only by a suffix, e.g. Jos 2[20], Ju 6[14], 1 K 10[8], 2 K 1[2] and 8[8 f.], where חֳלִי, as in Jer 10[19], has arisen by contraction from חָלְיִי, or we should simply read חָלְיִי (in all these passages with זֶה); Gn 24[8] (with זֹאת); Ex 10[1], 1 K 22[23], Jer 31[21] (with אֵלֶּה).

The article is sometimes omitted also with the attributes referring to proper names,[1] as צִידוֹן רַבָּה Jos 11[8], 19[28], חֲמָת רַבָּה Am 6[2]. Other examples are Jos 16[3.5], 18[13], 1 K 9[17] (but in 1 Ch 7[24], 2 Ch 8[5] with the article). In Gn 7[11], &c., תְּהוֹם רַבָּה is also a case of this kind, תְּהוֹם being used (almost always without the article) as a sort of proper name; cf. also אֵל עֶלְיוֹן *the most high*

---

[1] Cf. Nöldeke, *Beiträge zur semit. Sprachwiss.*, p. 48, n. 1.

God and אֱלֹהִים חַי *the living God*. In Ju 1¹⁵ גֻּלֹּת עִלִּית and גֻּ׳ תַּחְתִּית are strange ; Jos 15¹⁹ has עִלִּיוֹת גֻּ׳ and גֻּ׳ תַּחְתִּיוֹת.

z   Of the remaining examples Is 11⁹ explains itself ; the direct connexion of the attribute with its substantive is broken by the insertion of לַיָּם. In Ez 34¹², Hag. 1⁴ (as Wellhausen says, a good instance of a Hebrew adjective in the stative form = וְהֵם סְפוּנִים), ψ 143¹⁰, Ct 6¹²(?) the substantive is also (see above) determined by a suffix, and consequently the attribute is less closely attached ; the same applies to Gn 37², 42¹⁹, 43¹⁴, ψ 18¹⁸, except that in these passages the omission of the article before ר, א, ע may at the same time be due to considerations of euphony (as also in Jos 16¹ before ע, Nu 14³⁷ before ר, 28⁴, Ez 10⁹ before א, 21¹⁹ before ח).¹ In 1 S 13¹⁷ᶠ. (אֶחָד) and 2 K 25¹⁶ (שְׁנַיִם after a determinate substantive), the attribute again, being a numeral, is determinate in itself (see above, x) ; in Is 65² the לֹא prevents the use of the article ; finally, in 2 Ch 26¹⁵ בַּחֵצִים and בָּאֲבָנִים are to be read, as in Jer 2²¹ גֶּפֶן for הַגֶּפֶן, in 22²⁶ אֶרֶץ for הָאָ׳ ; in 2 S 6³ omit חֲדָשָׁה, and in Ez 39²⁷ omit רַבִּים. Without any apparent reason the article is omitted in Dn 8¹³ and 11³¹.

aa   2. When, as in Mi 7¹² (יוֹם הוּא *in that day ?*), the article is omitted from both substantive and demonstrative, and in Ezr 3¹², the demonstrative even precedes (הַבַּיִת הַזֶּה = זֶה הַבַּיִת), this is obviously due in both cases to a radical corruption of the text (not only in the words quoted). In Jos 9¹² לַחְמֵנוּ is either in apposition to the independent demonstrative זֶה (= *this our bread*, &c.), as in verse 13 נֹאדוֹת is to אֵלֶּה, or they are complete sentences, *this is our bread*, &c. So also in Ex 32¹ מֹשֶׁה (= *that [iste] Moses*, &c.), and in ψ 48¹⁵ אֱלֹהִים are to be taken in apposition to זֶה. On ψ 68⁸ and Is 23¹³ cf. § 136 d.

§ 127. *The Noun determined by a following Determinate Genitive.*

Brockelmann, *Grundriss,* i. 475.

a   When a genitive, determined in any way, follows a *nomen regens*, it also determines the *nomen regens*, which, according to § 89 a, is always in the construct state. Moreover, every pronominal suffix attached to a substantive is, according to § 33 c, to be considered as a genitive determinate by nature. An independent genitive may be determinate—

(*a*) By its character as a *proper name* (according to § 125 a), e. g. דְּבַר יְהוָֹה *the word of the Lord*.

(*b*) By having the article, e. g. אִישׁ הַמִּלְחָמָה (prop. the man of the war) *the soldier* (but אִישׁ מִלְחָמָה Jos 17¹, *a soldier*) ; אַנְשֵׁי הַמִּלְחָמָה

---

¹ The same reason no doubt also favoured the omission of the article before הוּא and אֵלֶּה, see above, under y. Also in Is 23⁷ (*is this your joyous* . . . ?) the article is omitted before עַלִּיזָה probably only for euphony.

Nu 31⁴⁹, *the soldiers*; דְּבַר הַנָּבִיא *the word of the prophet*, Jer 28⁹ (but e. g., on the other hand, מִצְוַת אֲנָשִׁים מְלֻמָּדָה *a commandment of men which hath been taught*, Is 29¹³; דְּבַר־שֶׁקֶר *word of falsehood*, Pr 29¹²).

(*c*) By the addition of a pronominal suffix (see above), e. g. בֵּית־אָבִי *my father's house.*

(*d*) By construction with another genitive determined in some way, e. g. Gn 3² מִפְּרִי עֵץ־הַגָּן *of the fruit of the trees of the garden.* Thus in Is 10¹² four, and in 21¹⁷ even five, members of a series are determined by a concluding determinate genitive.

Rem. 1. The above explains also the various meanings of כֹּל (prop. a *b* substantive in the sense of *aggregate, whole*), according as it is followed by a determinate or indeterminate genitive. In the former case כֹּל has the meaning of *the entirety*, i. e. *all, the whole* (like the French *tous les hommes, toute la ville*), e. g. כָּל־הָאָרֶץ *the whole* (prop. the entirety of the) *earth*, כָּל־הָאָדָם *all men*;[1] Ex 18²², Nu 15¹³, Jer 4²⁹, and cases like Nu 4²³·⁴⁷, 21⁸ where כָּל is followed by a singular participle with the article. On the other hand, before an indeterminate genitive כֹּל is used in the more indefinite (individualizing) sense of *of all kinds, any* (cf. *tout homme, à tout prix*), or distributively *each, every*, e. g. כָּל־עֵץ *every* (kind of) *tree*, Gn 2⁹; cf. 4²², 24¹⁰, 1 Ch 29²; כָּל־דָּבָר *any thing*, Ju 19¹⁹; בְּכָל־יוֹם *every day, every time*, ψ 7¹².

It is, however, to be observed— *c*
(*a*) That the article may in this case also (see § 126 *h*) be omitted in poetic style, although the substantive is to be regarded as determinate, e. g. כָּל־שֻׁלְחָנוֹת *all* (the) *tables*, Is 28⁸.

(*b*) That the meaning *every* is frequent even before singulars used collectively; afterwards the idea of *quisque* passes naturally into that of *totality*, e. g. כָּל־חַי *each living thing*, i. e. *every* (not *every kind of*) *living thing*; כָּל־בָּשָׂר *all flesh*, i. e. *all men* or *all living creatures* (with the article only in Gn 7¹⁵ before a relative clause, and in Is 40⁶); sometimes also כָּל־עֵץ *all trees*, כָּל־עוֹף *all birds*; finally—

(*c*) That before the names of members of the human body, כָּל־ frequently (as being determinate in itself) denotes the entirety, e. g. Is 1⁵ *the whole head, the whole heart* (the sense required by the context, not *every head, &c.*, which the expression *in itself* might also mean); 9¹¹, 2 K 23³, Ez 29⁷ all (i. e. *the whole of*) *their shoulders . . . all* (*the whole of*) *their loins*; 36⁵.—On כֹּל with a suffix when it follows a noun in apposition (e. g. Is 9⁸ הָעָם כֻּלּוֹ *the people, all of it*, i. e. *the whole nation*, more emphatic than כָּל־הָעָם, cf. Driver on 2 S 2⁹), as well as when it follows absolutely in the genitive (= *all men, every one*, e. g. Gn 16¹²),[2] see the Lexicon, pp. 481ᵇ, 482ᵇ.

2. Gentilic names (or patronymics), derived from compound proper names *d* (consisting of a nomen regens and genitive), are determined by inserting the article before the second part of the compound (since it contains the original

---

[1] הָאָדָם being a collective, cf. כָּל־הָאִישׁ 2 S 15², *all men*, כָּל־הַבֵּן Ex 1²² *all sons*, כָּל־הַבַּת *all daughters*; in itself כָּל־הָאָדָם could also mean *the whole man.*

[2] In Ezr 10¹⁷ instead of בַּכֹּל אֲנָשִׁים read simply בְּכָל־הָאֲנָשִׁים.

genitive), e.g. בֶּן־יְמִינִי (see § 86 h) *a Benjamite*; בֶּן־הַיְמִינִי Ju 3[15], &c., *the Benjamite*; בֵּית הַלַּחְמִי *the Bethlehemite*, 1 S 16[1], &c. (cf., however, 1 Ch 27[12] Qᵉrê בֵּית־הַשִּׁמְשִׁי *the Beth-shemite*, 1 S 6[14]; (לְבֶן יְמִינִי; אֲבִי הָעֶזְרִי *the Abiezrite*, Ju 6[11], &c., cf. 1 K 16[34].

e 3. In a few instances the nomen regens appears to be used indefinitely notwithstanding a following determinate genitive; it is not so, however, in Gn 16[7], where the reference is to a well-known fountain; 21[28], where in the original context there must have been some reason for *the seven ewe lambs of the flock*; 2 S 12[30] *the spoil found in the city*; but it often is so before a proper name, as in Ex 10[9] חַג יְהֹוָה *a feast of the Lord* (unless it is *the* spring festival), Dt 7[25], and frequently תּוֹעֲבַת יְהֹוָה *an abomination unto the Lord*; cf. also Gn 46[34], Dt 22[19] *a virgin of Israel*; 1 S 4[12] *a man of Benjamin*; Pr 25[1], Ct 2[1], 3[9]; similarly before appellatives with the article (or before a genitive determined by a suffix, as in Lv 14[34]), 1 S 20[20] *three arrows*; 2 S 23[11] חֶלְקַת הַשָּׂדֶה *a plot of the ground* (but see Gn 33[19], Jos 24[32]); Ju 13[6], Jer 13[4], 41[16], Ct 1[11.13 f.], 5[13], 7[3], 8[2]. On the other hand, שִׁיר הַמַּעֲלוֹת in the titles of Psalms 120 to 134 (except 121[1], שִׁיר לַמַּעֲלוֹת) was most probably originally the title of a collection, in the sense of '*the pilgrimage-songs*' (according to § 124 r), and was subsequently added to these Psalms severally.—In Ex 20[24] בְּכָל־הַמָּקוֹם *in all the place*, sc. of the sanctuary, is a dogmatic correction of בְּכָל־מָקוֹם, *in every place*, to avoid the difficulty that several holy-places are here authorized, instead of the one central sanctuary. In Gn 20[13] also כָּל־הַמָּקוֹם (unless it means *in the whole place*) is remarkable, since elsewhere *every place* is always (8 times) כָּל־מָקוֹם.

f 4. The deviations mentioned under *e*, from a fundamental rule of syntax, are in some cases open to suspicion on textual grounds, but much more doubtful are the instances in which the article is found before a noun already determined in some other way, as—

(*a*) Before a noun which appears to be determined by a following independent determinate genitive. The least questionable are the instances in which the genitive is a *proper name*, since these may be elliptical forms of expression like the apparent construction of proper names with a genitive, noticed in § 125 h, e.g. Nu 21[14] הַנְּחָלִים אַרְנוֹן *the valleys*, namely the valleys *of Arnon*; 2 K 23[17] הַמִּזְבֵּחַ בֵּית־אֵל *the altar*, namely the altar *of Bethel* (i.e. with the suppression of the real nomen regens, מִזְבַּח without the article; by the pointing הַמִּזְבֵּחַ the Masora evidently intends to allow the choice either of reading הַמִּזְבֵּחַ or correcting it to מִזְבַּח); הָאֵל בֵּית־אֵל *the God of Beth-el*[1] (equivalent to הָאֵל אֶל ב'), Gn 31[13] (the LXX read הָאֵל הַנִּרְאֶה אֵלֶיךָ בַּמָּקוֹם *the God who appeared to thee in the* holy *place*); הַמֶּלֶךְ אַשּׁוּר *the king of Assyria*, Is 36[16] (probably a scribal error due to verse 13; it does not occur in the parallel passage, 2 K 18[31]), cf. Jos 13[5], 2 K 25[11], Jer 38[6], Ez 47[15]; in the vocative, Jer 48[32], La 2[13]. On the other hand, שָׂרָה אִמּוֹ Gn 24[67] is no doubt

---

[1] According to Philippi (*St. Constr.*, p. 38) בֵּית־אֵל is rather a case of 'subposition' in the accusative, as also הַדֶּרֶךְ חֶתְלֹן Ez 47[15] (for which, however, in 48[1] there is the correct reading דֶּרֶךְ חֶתְלֹן *by the way to Hethlon*; and in fact, Ez 47[15] may without difficulty be explained in this way; so שֵׁשׁ Ex 39[27] as an accusative of the material.

only a subsequent insertion; so also יִשְׂרָאֵל Jos 8³³ᵇ (cf. LXX), 2 S 20²³, 2 K 7¹³, הַמֶּלֶךְ 1 S 26²² after הַחֲנִית (simplified by the Masora to חֲנִית Qᵉⁱʳᵉ̄); עֲלִיַּת אָחָז 2 K 23¹², אַשּׁוּר Is 36⁸ (cf. 2 K 18²³), הַקֹּדֶשׁ Ez 46¹⁹ (unless the article with לִשְׁכוֹת is to be omitted), also הַתָּמִיד Dn 8¹³, and עֹדֵד הַנָּבִיא 2 Ch 15⁸. In Ex 9¹⁸ read with the Samaritan לְמִיּוֹם; in 2 S 19²⁵ לֶכֶת might possibly be taken in apposition to לְמִן הַיּוֹם; in 2 K 10¹ restore אֶת־בְּנֵי, with the LXX and Lucian, before אַחְאָב; in 2 K 25¹⁹ omit the article, as in Jer 52²⁵, before סֹפֵר.

A similar ellipse must be assumed in 2 K 23¹⁷ *the sepulchre is the* g sepulchre *of the man of God* (but most probably קֶבֶר has dropped out after הַקֶּבֶר) and ψ 123⁴ (cf., however, the LXX, and observe that in the parallel member the genitive is paraphrased by לְ).—In Jos 3¹⁴ הַבְּרִית (verse 17 בְּרִית יהוה) has been added to the original הָאָרוֹן by a redactor; cf. similar syntactically impossible additions in verse 11 (also in 1 S 4³, &c., where the LXX still had simply אֲרוֹן יהוה); in הַיָתֵד Ju 16¹⁴ the Masora evidently combines two different readings הַיָתֵד and הָאָרֶג; and similarly in Jer 25²⁶ (where הָאָרֶץ was only subsequently introduced into the text), the two readings מַמְלְכוֹת and הָא׳ הַמַּמְלָכוֹת are combined.—In Jos 8¹¹, 1 K 14²⁴, Jer 31⁴⁰, Ez 45¹⁶ the article, being usual after כָּל־, has been mechanically added, and so also in 2 Ch 8¹⁶ after עַד־; in 2 K 9⁴ the second הַנַּעַר (instead of נַעַר) is occasioned by the first; in Ez 7⁷ מְהוּמָה belongs as a nominative to what follows; in Ez 8²⁹ the meaning perhaps is *in the chambers, in the house of the Lord,* or the article is to be omitted; in 1 Ch 15²⁷ the text is manifestly corrupt.

Of another kind are the instances in which a determinate noun is followed h by a definition of the material *in apposition* (hence, not in the genitive; cf. § 131), e.g. Zc 4¹⁰ הָאֶבֶן הַבְּדִיל *the weight, the lead,* i.e. *the leaden weight;* Ex 39¹⁷, 2 K 16¹⁴ הַנְּחֹשֶׁת, both here and in verse 17, is probably only a later addition, while הַמְּסְגְּרוֹת הַמְּכֹנוֹת in verse 17 has arisen from a confusion of two readings, מִסְגְּרוֹת מְהַמְּכֹנוֹת and מִסְגְּרוֹת הַמְּכֹנוֹת (הַמְּסְגְּרוֹת). In Jer 32¹² also הַמִּקְנֶה (unless the article is simply to be omitted) is in apposition to הַסֵּפֶר.

(*b*) Before a noun with a suffix (which likewise represents a determinate i genitive; see above, at the beginning of this section). This does not apply to cases in which a *verbal* (i.e. *accusative*) suffix is affixed to a participle which has the article, e.g. הַמַּכֵּהוּ Is 9¹², *the one smiting him;* in Dt 8¹⁵, 13⁶ also ךְ is a verbal suffix, but hardly the וֹ in הָעֹשֵׂהוּ for הָעֹשָׂהוּ Job 40¹⁹, nor the ־ֶה in הַיֹּלְדָה Dn 11⁶; § 116 *g*. For הָעֶרְכְּךָ Lev 27²³, read עֶרְכְּךָ as in verses 2, 3, 5, 7, 13, &c., twelve times (but cf. also the note on § 128 *d*).—Of the remaining examples כַּנֻּבְרַתָּה Is 24² (probably an intentional alliteration with the eleven other words beginning with כָּ), לַמַּעַנֵהוּ Pr 16⁴, and בְּעֹרֵינוּ (so Baer, following the best authorities) Ezr 10¹⁴, rest only on the authority of the Masoretes, not of the authors. So also in הָאֹהֱלִי Jos 7²¹, הַחֶצְיוֹ Jos 8³³ (previously חֶצְיוֹ), הֶהֲרוּתֶיהָ 2 K 15¹⁶ (dittography of the ה), the article is simply to be omitted as syntactically impossible; the וֹ of הַדִּבְּרוֹן Mi 2¹² is the copula belonging to the next word.

§ 128. *The Indication of the Genitive Relation by means of the Construct State.*

Cf. especially Philippi's work cited at the head of § 89.

a 1. The genitive relation is regularly expressed (see § 89) by the close connexion of the *nomen regens* (in the construct state) with the *nomen rectum* (in the genitive). Since only *one* nomen regens can be immediately connected with a nomen rectum, it follows that the same genitive cannot depend on two or more *co-ordinate* nouns, but a second (sometimes even a third, &c.) regens must be added with a suffix referring to the nomen rectum, e.g. בְּנֵי דָוִד וּבְנֹתָיו *the sons of David and his daughters* (not בְּנֵי וּבְנוֹת דָּוִד); cf. 1 K 8²⁸.[1] The language also prefers to avoid a series of several co-ordinate[2] genitives depending upon one and the same nomen regens (such as occur in Gn 14¹⁹, Nu 20⁵, 31⁵⁴ [1 Ch 13¹], 1 S 23⁷, 2 S 19⁶, Is 22⁵, ψ 5⁷, 8³),[3] and rather tends to repeat the nomen regens, e.g. Gn 24³ אֱלֹהֵי הַשָּׁמַיִם וֵאלֹהֵי הָאָרֶץ *the God of heaven and the God of the earth* (so in Jer 8¹ the regens is five times repeated). A lengthened series of genitives may, however, be formed by a nomen rectum serving at the same time as *regens* to a genitive depending on it (cf. § 127 *a* [*d*]); e.g. Gn 47⁹ יְמֵי שְׁנֵי חַיֵּי אֲבֹתַי *the days of the years of the life of my fathers*; cf. Jb 12²⁴, where there are three genitives, Is 10¹² four, and 21¹⁷ five (unless the last three are in apposition). As a rule, indeed, such an inconvenient accumulation of genitives is avoided by means of a circumlocution in the case of one of them (see § 129 *d*).

b Rem. As the fundamental rules stated above are the necessary consequence not merely of *logical* but more especially of *rhythmical* relations (see § 89 *a*), we must feel the more hesitation in admitting examples in which genitives are supposed to be loosely attached to forms other than the construct state. Some of these examples (the supposed genitives following a regens which is determined by the article) have been already discussed in § 127 *f–h*. Compare, moreover:

c (*a*) Genitives after the absolute state, e.g. Is 28¹ גֵּיא־שְׁמָנִים הֲלוּמֵי יָיִן *the fat valley of them that are overcome with wine.* The usual explanation that גֵּיא־שְׁמָנִים forms *one* single idea (in German *Fettigkeitstal*), on which the

---

[1] Very rare, and only possible in very rapid utterance, are such exceptions as Ez 31¹⁶ (מִבְחַר וְטוֹב־לְבָנוֹן); Pr 16¹¹.—In Is 11² *the spirit of knowledge and of the fear of the Lord,* דַּעַת may at any rate also be taken as an absolute genitive, so also סֵפֶר Dn 1⁴.

[2] In ψ 114¹ a second genitive is added even without the copula, but the parallelism of the members renders any misunderstanding impossible.

[3] In almost all these instances the two (or three) genitives form one closely connected whole, as *heaven* and *earth, sons* and *daughters.*

genitive הַלּוּחֵי יֵין then depends, in reality, explains nothing ; the text is almost certainly corrupt. In Dt 15¹⁸ מִשְׁנֶה would be expected ; in Jos 3¹¹ הַבְּרִית is a later addition ; in Is 32¹³ (מְשׂוֹשׂ), and ψ 68²² (שֵׂעָר), the absolute for the construct state probably rests only on the authority of the Masoretes. In Ju 6²⁵ ᶠᶠ· the text is obviously in confusion. In Ju 8³² (cf. 6²⁴) בְּעָפְרָה should come either after וַיִּקָּבֵר or at the end of the verse, unless, with Moore, we omit אֲבִי הָע׳ as a gloss (from 6²⁴) ; in Is 63¹¹ מֹשֶׁה is probably a gloss on יְמֵי־עוֹלָם which has crept into the text ; in 2 S 4² לְאִישׁ־בֹּשֶׁת, according to the LXX, has dropped out before בֵּן ; in Ez 6¹¹ רְעוֹת is to be omitted with the LXX ; if originally in the text, it could only be genitive (= *all abominations of evils*), not an adjective ; Pr 21⁶ the text is altogether uncertain (the LXX read מוֹקְשֵׁי for (מְבַקְשֵׁי) ; in 1 Ch 9¹³ the preposition לְ (after a לְ) has dropped out before מְלֶאכֶת (cf. 12²⁵).—Elsewhere (Dt 3⁵, 1 K 4¹³, 2 Ch 8⁵) the supposed genitives are to be taken rather as words of nearer definition standing in apposition, i. e. *with high walls, gates, and bars*. In Jer 8⁵ יְרוּשָׁלִַם is either in apposition to הָעָם הַזֶּה or is better (since not in the LXX) omitted as a gloss.

(*b*) Genitives after a noun with a suffix (where the suffix prevents the direct *d* government by the *nomen regens*). Thus in Lv 27³·⁵·⁶, where הַנֶּעֱרָךְ after עֶרְכְּךָ¹ might be taken, contrary to the accents, as subject of the following clause ; in Lv 5¹⁵·²⁵ the suffix may refer to Moses. In Lv 6³ מִדּוֹ בַד *his garment*, namely the garment *of linen*, unless simply in apposition, cf. § 131 *d* (or read מִדֵּי(?)) ; Lv 26⁴², where בְּרִיתִי יַעֲקוֹב וגו׳ could at most be explained as an ellipse for בְּרִיתִי בְּרִית יַעֲקֹב, cf. § 125 *h* (probably, however, it is a case of dittography of the י, which was repeated also before אַבְרָהָם ; so Valeton, *ZAW.* xii. 3) ; equally strange is בְּרִיתִי הַיּוֹם Jer 33²⁰, &c. On the other hand, אִם יִהְיֶה נְבִיאֲכֶם יְהוָה Nu 12⁶ could not possibly mean *if your prophet be a prophet of the Lord* ; the text is manifestly corrupt (probably נְבִיאֲךָ מִיַּהְוֶה is to be read, with Marti). In ψ 45⁷ כִּסְאֲךָ אֱלֹהִים (usually explained as *thy divine throne*), אֱלֹהִים is most probably a later addition [another suggestion is to read כֵּאלֹהִים *like God('s throne)*: cf. § 141 *d*, note]. In Jer 52²⁰ two readings are probably combined, לְנְחֹשֶׁת כָּל־הַכֵּלִים without any addition, and לִנְחֻשְׁתָּם. In Nu 25¹² שָׁלוֹם is in apposition to בְּרִיתִי. On דַּרְכֵּךְ זִמָּה Ez 16²⁷, cf. § 131 *r*.

(*c*) The interposition of a word is assumed between כָּל־ (*the whole*; cf. *e* § 127 *b*) and the genitive governed by it in 2 S 1⁹, Jb 27³ (עוֹד), and, if the text is correct, in Hos 14³ (תִּשָּׂא). In reality, however, in all three places the genitive relation is destroyed by the transposition of the words (instead of עוֹד כָּל־, &c.), and כָּל is rather to be taken adverbially (equivalent to *wholly*), e. g. 2 S 1⁹ because *my life is yet wholly in me*, i. e. my whole life ; cf. Philippi, *Stat. Constr.*, p. 10.—On the instances in which the original construct state אַיִן *non-existence* is used without a following genitive, see the negative sentences, § 152 *o*.

2. The dependence of the nomen rectum on the nomen regens by *f* no means represents merely what is, properly speaking, the genitive relation (see the examples under *g–i*). Very frequently the nomen

---

¹ Halévy, *J. A.* xiv. 548, removes the difficulty by pointing עֲרֻכְּךָ.

rectum only adds a nearer definition of the nomen regens, whether by giving the name, the genus or species, the measure, the material, or finally an attribute of it (*genit. epexegeticus* or *appositionis*,[1] see the examples under *k–q*).

Examples. The *nomen rectum* represents—

g   (*a*) A *subjective genitive*, specifying the possessor, author, &c., e. g. בֵּית־הַמֶּלֶךְ *the king's house*; דְּבַר יהוה *the word of the Lord*.

h   (*b*) An *objective genitive*, e. g. Ob[10] מֵחֲמַס אָחִיךָ *for the violence done to thy brother*[2] (but in Ez 12[19] מֵחֲמַס is followed by a subjective genitive); Pr 20[2] אֵימַת מֶלֶךְ *the terror of a king*; Gn 18[20] זַעֲקַת סְדֹם *the cry concerning Sodom*; Is 23[5] שֵׁמַע צֹר *the report of (about) Tyre*, cf. 2 S 4[4]; Am 8[10] אֵבֶל יָחִיד *the mourning for an only son*; Dt 20[14] שְׁלַל אֹיְבֶיךָ *praeda hostibus tuis erepta*; cf. Is 3[14]. In a wider sense this includes such examples as דֶּרֶךְ עֵץ הַחַיִּים *the way of* (i. e. *to*) *the tree of life*, Gn 3[24]; cf. Pr 7[27], Jb 38[20]; דֶּרֶךְ הַיָּם *the way of* (by) *the sea*, Is 8[23]; זִבְחֵי אֱלֹהִים *the sacrifices of* (i. e. *pleasing to*) *God*, ψ 51[19]; שְׁבֻעַת יהוה *the oath of* (i. e. *sworn before*) *the Lord*, 1 K 2[43]; דִּבְרֵי לְמוּאֵל *the words of* (i. e. *addressed to*) *L.*, Pr 31[1].

i   (*c*) A *partitive genitive*; this includes especially the cases in which an adjective in the construct state is followed by a general term, e. g. חַכְמוֹת שָׂרוֹתֶיהָ *the wisest of her ladies*, Ju 5[29]; cf. for this way of expressing the superlative, § 133 *h*, and also *r* below.

k   Merely formal genitives (*genit. explicativus* or *epexegeticus*, *genit. appositionis*) are those added to the construct state as nearer definitions—

  (*d*) Of the *name*, e. g. נְהַר פְּרָת *the river Euphrates*; אֶרֶץ כְּנַעַן *the land of Canaan*; בְּתוּלַת יִשְׂרָאֵל *the virgin Israel* (not *of Israel*), Am 5[2].

l   (*e*) Of the *genus*, e. g Pr 15[20] (21[20]) כְּסִיל אָדָם *a fool of a man* (= *a foolish man*); cf. Gn 16[12], Is 1[4], 29[19], Ho 13[2], Mi 5[4], &c.

m   (*f*) Of the *species*, e. g. אֲחֻזַּת קֶבֶר *a possession of a burying-place*, i. e. *hereditary sepulchre*, Gn 23[4], &c.; תְּאֵנֵי הַבַּכֻּרוֹת *the early figs*, Jer 24[2]; אֹהֶל בֵּיתִי *the tabernacle of my house*, i. e. *my dwelling-place*, ψ 132[3].

n   (*g*) Of the *measure, weight, extent, number*, e. g. מְתֵי מִסְפָּר *people of number*, i. e. *few in number*, Gn 34[30], Dt 26[5]; cf. also Ez 47[3–5] *waters of the ankles, waters of the loins, waters of swimming*, i. e. which reached up to the ankles, or loins, or necessitated swimming; but in verse 4 in apposition (?) מַיִם בִּרְכַּיִם.

o   (*h*) Of the *material*[3] of which something consists, e. g. כְּלִי חָרֶשׂ *a vessel of earthenware*, Nu 5[17]; כְּלֵי כֶסֶף *vessels of silver* (cf. the French *des vases d'or*); אֲרוֹן עֵץ *an ark of wood*, שֵׁבֶט בַּרְזֶל *a rod of iron*, ψ 2[9]; cf. Gn 3[21], 6[14], Ju 7[13], &c.

---

[1] The latter term is preferred especially by König, *Theol. Stud. und Krit.*, 1898, p. 528 ff.

[2] Cf. in Latin a similar use of the genitive after *iniuria* (Caes. *B. G.* 1, 30), *metus* (*hostium, Pompeii*, &c.), *spes*, and other words. In Greek, cf. εὔνοια τῶν φίλων, πίστις τοῦ θεοῦ, ὁ λόγος ὁ τοῦ σταυροῦ, 1 Cor. 1[18].

[3] In the almost entire absence of corresponding adjectives (אָרוּז *made of cedar*, a denominative from אֶרֶז, and נָחוּשׁ *brazen* are the only examples), the language regularly has recourse to the above periphrasis. On the form *qāṭūl*, as expressing an inherent property, cf. § 50 *f*; cf. also the proper name, בַּרְזִלַּי *ferreus*.

(*i*) Of the *attribute* of a person or thing, e. g. Gn 17⁸ אֲחֻזַּת עוֹלָם *an everlasting* **p** *possession*; Pr 17⁸ *a precious stone*; cf. Nu 28⁶, Is 13⁸, 28⁴, ψ 23², 31⁸, Pr 5¹⁹, 14⁵, Jb 41¹⁹, and the examples of the genitive with a suffix given in § 135 *n*. Such a periphrasis for the expression of attributes frequently occurs, even when the corresponding adjectives are in use. Thus especially קֹדֶשׁ *holiness* very frequently serves as a periphrasis for the adjective קָדוֹשׁ (e. g. בִּגְדֵי הַקֹּדֶשׁ *the holy garments*, Ex 29²⁹), since קָדוֹשׁ is used almost exclusively in reference to persons (hence also with עַם and גּוֹי *people*, and with שֵׁם the *name* of a person); the only exceptions are מָקוֹם קָדוֹשׁ *holy place*, Ex 29³¹, &c.; מַיִם קְדֹשִׁים *holy water*, Nu 5¹⁷; קָדוֹשׁ as the predicate of יוֹם *day*, Neh 8¹⁰ᶠ·, and of מַחֲנֶה *camp*, Dt 23¹⁵. So also the use of צַדִּיק *righteous* is always confined to persons, except in Dt 4⁸; elsewhere the periphrasis with צֶדֶק or צְדָקָה is always used, e. g. מֹאזְנֵי צֶדֶק *just balances*, Lv 19³⁶.

In a wider sense this use of the genitive also includes statements of the **q** purpose for which something is intended, e. g. צֹאן טִבְחָה *sheep for the slaughter*, ψ 44²³; מוּסַר שְׁלוֹמֵנוּ *the chastisement designed for our peace*, Is 53⁵; cf. 51¹⁷ (*the cup which causes staggering*), ψ 116¹³; finally, also, the description of the material, with which something is laden or filled, e. g. 1 S 16²⁰ חֲמוֹר לֶחֶם וְנֹאד יַיִן *an ass laden with bread and a bottle of wine* (but probably עֲשָׂרָה is to be read for חֲמוֹר); cf. Gn 21¹⁴, Pr 7²⁰, &c.

Rem. 1. Certain substantives are used to convey an attributive idea in the **r** construct state before a partitive genitive; thus מִבְחַר *choice, selection*, as in Gn 23⁶ מִבְחַר קְבָרֵינוּ *the choice of our sepulchres*, i. e. our choicest sepulchres; Ex 15⁴, Is 22⁷, 37²⁴; other examples are, Is 1¹⁶ *the evil of your doings*, emphatically, *for your evil doings*; Is 17⁴, 37²⁴ (= *the tall cedars thereof*), ψ 139²², Jb 15²⁶.— This is the more common construction with the substantive כֹּל *entirety*, for *all, the whole, every*, see § 127 *b*; it is also frequent with מְעַט *a little*, for *few*, 1 S 17²⁸, &c.

2. To the periphrases expressing attributive ideas (see *p* above) by means **s** of a genitive construction may be added the very numerous combinations of the construct states אִישׁ *a man*, בַּעַל *master, possessor*, בֶּן *son*, and their feminines and plurals (including מְתֵי *men*, used only in the plural), with some appellative noun, in order to represent a person (poetically even a thing) as possessing some object or quality, or being in some condition. In English, such combinations are sometimes rendered by single substantives, sometimes by circumlocution. Examples:—

(*a*) Of אִישׁ, &c. : אִישׁ דְּבָרִים *an eloquent man*, Ex 4¹⁰ (but אִישׁ שְׂפָתַיִם Jb 11² **t** *a man of lips*, i. e. *a boaster*); אִישׁ לָשׁוֹן = *a slanderer*, ψ 140¹²; אִישׁ דַּעַת *a man of knowledge*, Pr 24⁵; אִישׁ חֵמָה *a wrathful man*, Pr 15¹⁸; אִישׁ דָּמִים *a man of blood*, 2 S 16⁷, ψ 5⁷; cf. further, 1 S 16¹⁸, 1 K 2²⁶, Is 53³, Pr 19⁶, 26²¹, 29¹, Ezr 8¹⁸; also אֵשֶׁת מִדְיָנִים *a contentious woman*, Pr 27¹⁵; in the plural, e. g. Gn 6⁴ אַנְשֵׁי הַשֵּׁם *the men of renown, famous*; cf. Gn 47⁶, Is 41¹¹, Jb 34⁸·¹⁰ (אַנְשֵׁי לֵבָב *men of understanding*); with מְתֵי, e. g. Is 5¹³ מְתֵי רָעָב *famished men*; but read probably מְזֵי רָעָב *weak with hunger*); ψ 26⁴, Jb 11¹¹, 22¹⁵.

(*b*) Of בַּעַל, &c. : בַּעַל שֵׂעָר *hairy*, 2 K 1⁸; בַּעַל הַחֲלֹמוֹת *the dreamer*, Gn 37¹⁹; **u** cf. Na 1², Pr 1¹⁷, 18⁹ (*a destroyer*), 22²⁴, 23² (*disposed to eat, greedy*), 24⁸; feminine

בַּעֲלַת־אוֹב *a woman that hath a soothsaying spirit*, 1 S 28⁷; cf. Na 3⁴; in the plural, e.g. בַּעֲלֵי חִצִּים *archers*, Gn 49²³, בַּעֲלֵי בְרִית *confederates*, Gn 14¹³; בַּעֲלֵי שְׁבוּעָה *sworn supporters*, Neh 6¹⁸.

v　(c) Of בֶּן־, &c.: בֶּן־חַיִל *a hero, warrior*, 1 K 1⁵²; בֶּן־מֶשֶׁק *heir*, Gn 15²; בֶּן־שָׁנָה *yearling*, Ex 12⁵, &c.; בֶּן־מְאַת שָׁנָה *centum annos natus*, Gn 21⁵; בֶּן־מָוֶת *worthy to die*, 1 S 20³¹ (Luther, 2 S 12⁵ *ein Kind des Todes*); cf. Dt 25² בִּן־הַכּוֹת *worthy to be beaten*. Feminine, e.g. בַּת־בְּלִיַּעַל *a wicked woman*, 1 S 1¹⁶; frequently also אִישׁ בְּלִיַּעַל, בְּנֵי ב׳, אַנְשֵׁי ב׳, and even simply בְּלִיַּעַל, like the Latin *scelus* for *scelestissimus*, 2 S 23⁶, Jb 34¹⁸. Plural masculine, e.g. בְּנֵי מְרִי *children of rebellion*, Nu 17²⁵. בֶּן־ is used poetically of things without life, e.g. Is 5¹ בֶּן־שָׁמֶן *a fat*, i.e. a fruitful (hill); Jon 4¹⁰ בִּן־לָיְלָה i.e. *grown in a night*; Jb 41²⁰ *son of the bow* (i.e. an arrow); so also בְּנֵי רֶשֶׁף = *sparks*, Jb 5⁷; La 3¹³; בָּנוֹת Ec 12⁴ *the daughters of song*, probably meaning the individual notes.

There is another use of בֶּן־ or בְּנֵי to denote membership of a guild or society (or of a tribe, or any definite class). Thus בְּנֵי הָאֱלֹהִים or בְּנֵי אֱלֹהִים Gn 6²·⁴, Jb 1⁶, 2¹, 38⁷ (cf. also בְּנֵי אֵלִים ψ 29¹, 89⁷) properly means not *sons of god(s)*, but beings of the class of אֵלִים or אֱלֹהִים; בְּנֵי־הַנְּבִיאִים 1 K 20³⁵ (singular in Am 7¹⁴) persons *belonging to the guild of prophets*; בֶּן־הָרַקָּחִים Neh 3⁸ *one of the guild of apothecaries*, cf. 3³¹ where בְּנֵי־הַצֹּרְפִים is to be read. Similarly בְּנֵי שִׁלֵּשִׁים Gn 50²³ are most probably not *great-grandsons* but grandsons, i.e. those belonging to the third generation. Cf. also בְּנֵי הַגֵּרְשֻׁנִּי Nu 4²⁷ ᶠ· *Gershonites*, בְּנֵי הַקְּהָתִים 2 Ch 20¹⁹, &c., *Kohathites*; בְּנֵי קֶדֶם *dwellers in the East*.

w　3. Special mention must be made of the not infrequent idiom by which adjectives (sometimes also ordinals, see § 134 *o*) are added in the genitive, like substantives, rather than as attributes in the same state, gender, and number as the noun which they qualify; thus, Is 28⁴ צִיצַת נֹבֵל *the flower of that which fades*, for which verse 1 has צִיץ נֹבֵל *the fading flower*; cf. further, Is 22²⁴, Jer 22¹⁷ (?), 52¹³, ψ 73¹⁰, 74¹⁵ (but אֵיתָן may be a substantive), 78⁴⁹; also the use of רַע as a substantive, e.g. in Pr 2¹⁴ ᵇ, 6²⁴ (אֵשֶׁת רָע),&c.. analogous to the New Testament phrase ὁ οἰκονόμος τῆς ἀδικίας, Luke 16⁸, and the French *un homme de bien*.¹—Finally, an adverb (treated as a substantive) may likewise be used as an epexegetical genitive; cf. דְּמֵי חִנָּם *blood shed without cause*, 1 K 2³¹; Pr 24²⁸, 26²; Ez 30¹⁶ (יוֹמָם).

x　3. The epexegetical genitives include finally the numerous nearer definitions which follow the construct state of adjectives (and of active and passive participles, or verbal adjectives, cf. § 116 *f–l*). For, while the word of nearer definition is added to the verb in the accusative (e.g. חָלָה אֶת־רַגְלָיו *he was diseased in his feet*, 1 K 15²³), it may, with participles and verbal adjectives, be either in the accusative

---

¹ On the other hand, in such passages as Is 36² (2 K 18¹⁷), Zc 14⁴, Ec 8¹⁰, &c., there is no apparent reason why the Masora requires the construct state instead of the absolute; hence חֵיל Is 36² and גִּיא Zc 14⁴ must be intended as forms of the absolute state, shortened in consequence of their close connexion.

(§ 116 *f* and *k*) or in the genitive, the case of a word depending on a noun. Such a genitive relation is usually termed an *improper annexion*. The nearer definition contains a statement either of the *material*, e. g. Ex 3⁸, &c., אֶרֶץ זָבַת חָלָב וּדְבַשׁ *a land flowing with milk and honey*; or of the *means*, e. g. חַלְלֵי־חֶרֶב *slain with the sword*, Is 22²; or the *cause*, Ct 2⁵ *sick of love*; or of the *scope* of the attribute,[1] e. g. Gn 39⁶ יְפֵה־תֹאַר *fair of form*; cf. Gn 41²·⁴, Ex 34⁶, Is 1⁴, Jer 32¹⁹, Na 1³, ψ 119¹, Jb 37¹⁶; or of the *manner*, e. g. ψ 59⁶ בֹּגְדֵי אָוֶן *faithless ones of wickedness* (wickedly faithless).

Especially frequent is the use of this genitive to name the part of *y* the body described as being affected by some physical or mental condition, e. g. ψ 24⁴ נְקִי כַפַּיִם *clean as regards hands*, &c.; 2 S 9³, Is 6⁵, Jb 17⁹; Is 19¹⁰ אַגְמֵי־נָפֶשׁ *grieved in soul*; 1 S 1¹⁰, Jb 3²⁰. Also such examples as Am 2¹⁶, Pr 19¹, where a suffix is attached to the substantive, must be regarded as instances of the genitive construction, on the analogy of Pr 14², see § 116 *k*.

§ 129. *Expression of the Genitive by Circumlocution.*

Besides the construction of a nomen rectum dependent upon a nomen *a* regens in the construct state (§§ 89 and 128), the connexion of two nouns may also be effected otherwise, either by simply attaching the dependent noun by means of the preposition לְ, which, according to § 119 *r*, expresses, besides other ideas, like that of *belonging to*,[2] or by the addition of a relative clause (אֲשֶׁר לְ, see *h* below).

1. The introduction of a genitive by לְ sometimes occurs even when the *b* construction with the construct state would be equally possible, e. g. 1 S 14¹⁶ הַצֹּפִים לְשָׁאוּל *the watchmen of Saul*; ψ 37¹⁶, 2 Ch 28¹⁸ (where indeed the circumlocution makes the sense much plainer); as a rule, however, this use is restricted to the following cases :—

(*a*) To prevent a nomen regens being determined by a following determinate *c* genitive, e. g. 1 S 16¹⁸ בֵּן לְיִשַׁי *a son of Jesse* (בֶּן־יִשַׁי would be, according to § 127 *a*, *the son of Jesse*); cf Gn 14¹⁸, 36¹², 41¹², Nu 16²² (27¹⁶), 1 S 17⁸, 2 S 19²¹, ψ 122⁵. Hence, regularly מִזְמוֹר לְדָוִד (ψ 3¹, &c.) *a psalm of David* (properly belonging to David as the author), for which לְדָוִד *of David* is used alone elliptically in ψ 11¹, 14¹, &c. Such a case as לְדָוִד מִזְמוֹר (ψ 24¹, &c.) is not to

---

[1] Cf. the Latin *integer vitae scelerisque purus ; tristes animi*, &c.
[2] Cf. the σχῆμα Κολοφώνιον in Greek, e. g. ἡ κεφαλὴ τῷ ἀνθρώπῳ for τοῦ ἀνθρώπου (Bernhardy's *Syntax*, p. 88). The Arab grammarians distinguish a twofold genitive, one of which may be resolved by לְ, and the other by מִן [see Wright's *Arabic Grammar*, vol. ii, § 75 ff.]. The *de* of the Romance languages is a development of the latter idea ; the Gascon, however, says e. g. *la fille à Mr. N.*. laying stress upon the idea of *belonging to* and not that of *origin*, as in *la fille de ... of the literary language.

be regarded as a transposition, but מִזְמוֹר is used epexegetically for the general term omitted before לְדָוִד (as it were, a poem *of David, a psalm*). Moreover, the introduction of the author, poet, &c., by this *Lamed auctoris* is the customary idiom also in the other Semitic dialects, especially in Arabic.

d (*b*) When a genitive is to be made dependent on a nomen regens, which is itself composed of a nomen regens and rectum, and represents, as a compound, one united idea, e. g. Ru 2³ חֶלְקַת הַשָּׂדֶה לְבֹעַז *the portion of field belonging to Boaz* (חֶ׳ שְׂדֵה בֹעַז would be *the portion of the field of Boaz*); 2 K 5⁹ *at the house-door of Elisha*. This especially applies to the cases in which the compound regens represents a term in very common use, the fixed form of which cannot be altered, e. g. 1 K 14¹⁹ עַל־סֵפֶר דִּבְרֵי הַיָּמִים לְמַלְכֵי יִשְׂרָאֵל *in the book of the chronicles of the kings of Israel*; 15²³, &c.; cf. also Jos 19⁵¹.

e (*c*) When for any other reason the construction with the nomen regens in the construct state is inadmissible; cf. e. g. Lv 18²⁰, where שְׁכָבְתְּךָ, on account of the suffix, cannot be used in the construct state; but Lv 15¹⁶ ᶠᶠ·, &c., שִׁכְבַת־זֶרַע; Ju 3²⁸ *the Jordan fords of Moab* (יַרְדֵּן as a *proper name* cannot be used in the construct state); Ex 20⁵ *upon the third and upon the fourth generation of them that hate me*; וְעַל־רִבֵּעִים must be kept in the absolute state for the sake of conformity with עַל־שִׁלֵּשִׁים, and for the same reason also לַאֲלָפִים לְאֹהֲבַי.

f (*d*) After statements of number in such cases as Gn 8¹⁴ בְּשִׁבְעָה וְעֶשְׂרִים יוֹם לַחֹדֶשׁ *on the seven and twentieth day of the month*; cf. 7¹¹, 16³ and frequently, or as in Hag 1¹ בִּשְׁנַת שְׁתַּיִם לְדָרְיָוֶשׁ *in the second year of Darius*; the numeral here is always one compound idea with the substantive numbered, and consequently (as in the examples under *b*) does not admit of being in the constr. st. with a genitive. The same naturally applies also to such examples as 1 K 3¹⁸ בַּיּוֹם הַשְּׁלִישִׁי לְלִדְתִּי *on the third day of my giving birth* (i. e. after my giving birth). Cf also the standing phrase בְּאֶחָד לַחֹדֶשׁ *on the first* (day) *of the month*, Gn 8⁵ and frequently.

g Rem. In cases like 2 S 3² *and his firstborn was Amnon* לַאֲחִינֹעַם *of Ahinoam*, the genitive expressed by circumlocution with לְ is in reality dependent on a regens which is omitted (בֶּן לַאֲחִינֹעַם *a son of Ahinoam*); cf. 2 S 3³·⁵, 1 K 14¹³, Am 5³ (unless לְבֵית יִשְׂרָאֵל originally depended on *thus spake the Lord*), and the remarks on לְדָוִד מִזְמוֹר under *c* above.

h 2. The periphrastic expression of the genitive by means of אֲשֶׁר לְ is used principally to state the *possessor*, e. g. Gn 29⁹ הַצֹּאן אֲשֶׁר לְאָבִיהָ *her father's sheep* (prop. *the sheep which* belonged *to her father*); Gn 47⁴ and frequently. So also (according to § 128 *a*) when a genitive depends on more than one substantive, e. g. Gn 40⁵ *the butler and the baker who* (belonged) *to the king of Egypt* (וְאֹפֶה מֶלֶךְ מִצְרָיִם would indicate only the baker as belonging to the king); or when a genitive (as in the examples under *d* above) is added to a compound, which expresses one united idea (Ru 4³); or when, as a fixed term (e. g. a title), it appears always in the same form, e. g. Ct 1¹ שִׁיר הַשִּׁירִים אֲשֶׁר לִשְׁלֹמֹה *the Song of songs, of Solomon*; 1 S 21⁸, 2 S 2⁸, 1 Ch 11¹⁰; cf. also Gn 41⁴³.[1]

---

[1] In New Hebrew שֶׁל (derived from אֲשֶׁר לְ = שֶׁלְ, see § 36, and cf. Ct 1⁶, 3⁷ שֶׁלִּשְׁלֹמֹה, שֶׁלִּי) is used like the simple relative דִּי, דְּ in Aramaic, as an independent sign of the genitive.

§ 130. *Wider Use of the Construct State.*

The construct state, which, according to § 89 *a*, primarily represents *a* only the immediate government by one substantive of the following word (or combination of words), is frequently employed in rapid narrative as a connecting form, even apart from the genitive relation; so especially—

(1) Before prepositions,[1] particularly in elevated (prophetic or poetic) style, especially when the nomen regens is a participle. Thus before בְּ, שִׂמְחַת בַּקָּצִיר *the joy in the harvest*, Is 9², 2 S 1²¹, ψ 136⁸ᶠ·; in participles, Is 5¹¹, 9¹, 19⁸, ψ 84⁷, and especially often when בְּ with a suffix follows the participle, e. g. ψ 2¹² כָּל־חוֹסֵי בוֹ; cf. Na 1⁷, Jer 8¹⁶ (ψ 24¹); ψ 64⁹ (unless רֹאֶה should be read); 98⁷·²—Before לְ, Ho 9⁶ (but read probably מֵחֲמַדֵּי כַסְפָּם); ψ 58⁵ (before לָמוֹ); Pr 24⁹, Jb 18², La 2¹⁸ (before לָךְ); 1 Ch 6⁵⁵, 23²⁸; in participles, Ez 38¹¹, Jb 24⁵; before לְ with an infinitive, Is 56¹⁰, and again before לְ with a suffix, Gn 24²¹, Is 30¹⁸, 64³;[3]—before אֶל־, Is 14¹⁹, Ez 21¹⁷;—before אֶת־ (*with*), Is 8⁶;—before מִן, Gn 3²², Is 28⁹ (a participle); Jer 23²³, Ez 13², Ho 7⁵;—before עַל־, Ju 5¹⁰;—before בִּלְתִּי, Is 14⁶;—before the *nota accus.* אֵת, Jer 33²²;—before a locative (which in such cases also serves as a genitive), Ex 27¹³, Jer 1¹⁵.

(2) Before *wāw copulative*, e. g. Ez 26¹⁰; but חָכְמַת Is 33⁶, גִּילַת 35², *b* and שָׁבְרַת 51²¹ may be cases of an intentional reversion to the old feminine ending *ath*, in order to avoid the hiatus (וָ) וְ וָ הָ—.

(3) When it governs the (originally demonstrative) pronoun אֲשֶׁר; *c* so especially in the combination מָקוֹם אֲשֶׁר, Gn 39²⁰, 40³, *the place where* (prop. *of that in which*) *Joseph was bound*; cf. § 138 *g*; or בִּמְקוֹם אֲשֶׁר Lv 4²⁴·³³, 2 S 15²¹, 1 K 21¹⁹, Jer 22¹², Ez 21³⁵, Ho 2¹. We should expect בַּמָּקוֹם אֲשֶׁר הַמָּקוֹם אֲשֶׁר, as in Gn 35¹³, &c., *at the place which . . .*, cf. § 138; but אֲשֶׁר is treated as a nomen rectum instead of as an attribute.

---

[1] Cf. König, 'Die Ueberwucherung des St.-constr.-Gebrauchs im Semit.,' *ZDMG.* 53, 521 ff.

[2] In Ju 8¹¹ the article is even used before a construct state followed by בְּ, in order to determine the whole combination שְׁכוּנֵי בָאֳהָלִים *tent-dwellers*, taken as one word; cf., however, the remarks in § 127 *f–i* on similar grammatical solecisms.

[3] These are to be distinguished from the cases where לְ follows a construct state, which in conjunction with מִן (and the following לְ) has become a sort of preposition or adverb of place; thus, we have מִבֵּית־לְ Ex 26³³ (for which in Ez 1²⁷ merely בֵּית לְ) meaning simply *within*; מִימִין לְ (2 K 23¹³, Ez 10³) *on the right hand* (i. e. south) *of*; מִצָּפוֹן לְ (Jos 8¹¹·¹³, &c., Ju 2⁹) *on the north of*; cf. also Jos 15²¹ and מִן לִפְנֵי Neh 13⁴.

Cf. also א׳ מִיּוֹם followed by a *perfect* in 1 S 29⁸, and א׳ יְמֵי Lv 13⁴⁶, Nu 9¹⁸.¹

d   (4) When it governs independent sentences (cf. § 155), which virtually stand to the construct state (as nomen regens) in a sort of genitive relation, e. g. Ex 4¹³ בְּיַד־תִּשְׁלָח prop. *by the hand of* him whom *thou wilt send*; Nu 23³ דְּבַר מַה־יַּרְאֵנִי *the matter of* that *which he shall show me*, i. e. whatever he shall; Is 29¹ קִרְיַת חָנָה דָוִד *the city where David encamped*; Jer 48³⁶, ψ 16³ (if the text be right), 65⁵ (Pr 8³²), ψ 81⁶, Jb 18²¹ *the place of him that knoweth not God*; Jb 29¹⁶, La 1¹⁴ (if the text be right) *into the hands* of those against whom *I cannot stand*.² In Gn 39⁴ (כָּל־יֶשׁ־לוֹ) the כָּל־ takes after it a noun-clause, and in Ex 9⁴, still more boldly, a subst. with לְ.—Very often a *time-determination* governs the following sentence in this way; thus אַחֲרֵי followed by a perfect, Lv 25⁴⁸, 1 S 5⁹; בְּיוֹם ψ 102³ (before a noun-clause), Ex 6²⁸, Nu 3¹, Dt 4¹⁵, 2 S 22¹, ψ 18¹, 59¹⁷, 138³ (in every case before a following perfect), ψ 56¹⁰ (before an imperfect); מִיּוֹם followed by the perfect, Jer 36²; כָּל־יְמֵי Lv 14⁴⁶, 1 S 25¹⁵, Jb 29² (כִּימֵי *as in the days when* . . .³; cf. כִּימוֹת and שְׁנוֹת before a perfect, ψ 90¹⁵); בְּעֵת before a perfect, Jer 6¹⁵ (cf. 49⁸, 50³¹); before an imperfect, Jb 6¹⁷; תְּחִלַּת before a perfect, Ho 1².

e   (5) Connected with a following word in apposition; certainly so in such cases as בְּתוּלַת בַּת־צִיּוֹן *the virgin, the daughter of Zion*, Is 37²²; cf. 23¹², Jer 14¹⁷; also 1 S 28⁷ אֵשֶׁת בַּעֲלַת־אוֹב *a woman, possessor of a soothsaying spirit*; cf. Dt 21¹¹.—Gn 14¹⁰, Ju 19²² (but read probably אֲנָשִׁים with Moore, as in Dt 13¹⁴, Ju 20¹³, 1 K 21¹⁰); 2 K 10⁶, 17¹³ *Qᵉrê*; Jer 46⁹, ψ 35¹⁶ (?), 78⁹, Jb 20¹⁷ᵇ (unless נֶהֱרֵי or נַחֲלֵי be a gloss).

f   Rem. Some of the above passages may also be explained by supposing that there exists a real genitive relation towards the preceding construct state, which has been, as it were, provisionally left *in suspenso*, in consequence of the insertion of some interrupting word, e. g. Is 37²², &c.; Jb 20¹⁷ᵃ. Elsewhere (Dt 33¹⁹, ψ 68³⁴) the *nomen regens* probably governs the following construct state directly.⁴

---

¹ In Dt 23⁵ the construct state governs a sentence introduced by the *conjunction* אֲשֶׁר (עַל־דְּבַר אֲשֶׁר *by reason of the fact that*, i. e. *because*); so also in 1 S 3¹³.

² Probably Gn 22¹⁴ is also to be so explained (contrary to the accents), and certainly (contrary to the very unnatural division of the verses) 2 Ch 30¹⁸, which should read on thus: יְהֹוָה הַטּוֹב יְכַפֵּר בְּעַד כָּל־לְבָבוֹ הֵכִין *the good Lord pardon every one that setteth his heart to seek God.* [See Wickes' *Accentuation of the Twenty-one Prose Books of the Old Testament*, p. 140.]

³ Cf. Na 2⁹ מִימֵי הִיא, usually explained to mean *from the days* that *she* hath been, but the text is evidently very corrupt.

⁴ So also Is 28¹⁶ *a corner stone of the preciousness* (יְקָרַת is a *substantive* not an *adjective*) *of a fixed foundation*, i. e. *a precious corner stone of surest foundation.*—In 2 S 20¹⁹ the text is wholly corrupt; in ψ 119¹²⁸ read כָּל־פִּקּוּדֶיךָ.

(6) The numeral אַחַד *one* for אֶחָד in close connexion, and even with *g* small disjunctives, e. g. Gn 3²², 48²², 1 S 9³, 2 S 17²², Is 27¹², Zc 11⁷.

The character of these passages shows that the numeral here cannot be in the construct state, but is merely a rhythmical shortening of the usual (tone-lengthened) form.

§ 131. *Apposition.*

1. Apposition in the stricter sense is the collocation of two sub- *a* stantives in the same case in order to define more exactly (or to complete) the one by the other, and, as a rule (see, however, below, under *g*), the former by the latter. Apposition in Hebrew (as in the other Semitic languages[1]) is by no means confined to those cases in which it is used in English or in the classical languages. It is not infrequently found when either the *subordination* of one substantive to the other or some more circumstantial kind of epexegetical addition would be expected.

2. The principal kinds of apposition in Hebrew are :—

(*a*) The collocation of *genus* and *species*, e. g. אִשָּׁה אַלְמָנָה *a woman b* (who was) *a widow*, 1 K 7¹⁴; נַעֲרָה בְתוּלָה *a damsel* (that is) *a virgin*, Dt 22²³·²⁸, Ju 4⁴, 19¹, 21¹², 1 S 30¹⁷, 1 K 1²; cf. Gn 13⁸, 21²⁰ (where, however, קֶשֶׁת is probably an explanatory gloss); Ex 24⁵ (1 S 11¹⁵), 2 S 15¹⁶, 1 K 3¹⁶, 5²⁹ (but probably סֵבֶל should be read instead of סַבָּל); Is 3²⁴ (unless מַעֲשֶׂה is to be read), Jer 20¹. Perhaps also כֹּהֵן הָרֹאשׁ *the priest* (who is) *the chief man*, 2 K 25¹⁸, &c.; others take כֹּהֵן as constr. st.—In 2 S 10⁷ read כָּל־הַצָּבָא הַגִּבֹּ' with the LXX, as in the parallel passage 1 Ch 19⁹ for כָּל־צָבָא הַגִּבּ', which is evidently meant to refer to the reading in 2 S.

(*b*) Collocation of the *person* or *thing* and the *attribute*, e. g. Jb 20²⁹ *c* (27¹³) זֶה חֵלֶק־אָדָם רָשָׁע *this is the portion of a man*, (who is) *a wicked man* (but רָשָׁע might also be an adject.); cf. Pr 6¹².—Lv 6¹³, 16⁴ (where, however, קֹדֶשׁ is probably a gloss); Pr 22²¹ אֲמָרִים אֱמֶת *words* (which are) *truth*; (immediately after אִמְרֵי אֱמֶת) cf. 1 S 2¹³, Mi 1¹¹ (where, however, בֹּשֶׁת is most probably a gloss on עֶרְיָה); Zc 1¹³ (=*comfortable words*); ψ 45⁵ (?), 68¹⁷ (cf. verse 16). In a wider sense this includes also such cases as ψ 60⁵ יַיִן תַּרְעֵלָה *wine* which is *staggering* (intoxicating drink), which causes staggering[2]; 1 K 22²⁷, 2 Ch 18²⁶ מַיִם לַחַץ (in

---

[1] On certain uses of apposition peculiar to the Semitic languages, cf. the exhaustive discussion by Fleischer, ' Ueber einige Arten der Nominalapposition im Arab.' (*Kleine Schriften,* ii. 16); [and see also Driver, *Tenses,* Appendix IV.]

[2] Unless it is to be translated *thou gavest us intoxication to drink as wine* (and so in 1 K 22²⁷ *give him affliction to eat as bread*, &c.) ; cf. ψ 80⁶ and the analogous examples of apposition in the form of a second accusative in § 117 *kk*. More-

Is 30²⁰ parallel with לֶחֶם צָר) *water* which is *affliction*, drunk in trouble (imprisonment). Still more boldly, 1 K 5³ בָּקָר רְעִי *oxen* which were taken out of the *pastures*, and 1 K 6⁷ *undressed stones* which come from the *quarry*, probably a corruption of מִפִּסָּע. A person and a condition are in apposition in Ez 18⁶ (unless בְּנִדָּתָהּ is to be read).— In 1 S 4¹ read אֶבֶן הָעֵזֶר', as in 5¹, 7¹².

d (*c*) Collocation of the *person* (Dt 28³⁶) or *thing* (form) and *material*,[1] or of the *place* or *measure* and its *contents*, e.g. 1 Ch 15¹⁹ בִּמְצִלְתַּיִם נְחֹשֶׁת *with cymbals* which were *brass*, i.e. of brass; cf. Ex 26²⁵, Dn 11⁸, 1 Ch 28¹⁵·¹⁸ (?); Ex 28¹⁷ *four rows*, namely *stones* (for which 39¹⁰ has טוּרֵי אָבֶן); cf. 2 Ch 4¹³, Lv 6³ (see, however, § 128 *d*); 2 K 7¹ סְאָה סֹלֶת *a seah* of *fine flour*; cf. 2 K 7¹⁶·¹⁸, Gn 18⁶, Ex 16³³, Lv 5¹¹, Ru 2¹⁷, 1 K 16²⁴, 2 K 5²³ כִּכְּרַיִם כֶּסֶף *two talents* of *silver*;[2] cf. 5¹⁷, Ex 39¹⁷, Ez 22¹⁸ (if the text be right). With the *material* placed before the *measure*, Ex 30²³ᶠ·.—A *period of time* and its *contents* are placed in apposition חֹדֶשׁ יָמִים *a month* of *days*, i.e. a month's time=for a whole month, Gn 29¹⁴, Nu 11²⁰·²¹, cf. Dt 21¹³, 2 K 15¹³, and שְׁנָתַיִם יָמִים *two years' time*, i.e. two full years, Gn 41¹, 2 S 13²³, 14²⁸, Jer 28³·¹¹, Dn 10²ᶠ·.

Finally, under this head may be included all the cases in which a numeral (regarded as a substantive) is followed by the object numbered in apposition, e.g. שְׁלֹשָׁה בָנִים *trias* sc. *filii*, § 97 *a* and § 134 *b*.

e (*d*) Collocation of the *thing* and the *measure* or *extent*, *number*, &c., e.g. Nu 9²⁰ יָמִים מִסְפָּר *days*, (a small) *number*, i.e. only a few days; כֶּסֶף מִשְׁנֶה *money, repetition*, i.e. twice as much money, Gn 43¹² (unless כֶּסֶף be constr. st.); מֵי בִרְכַּיִם *water* which was of the measure of the *knees*, which reached to the knees, Ez 47⁴ (also מֵי מָתְנַיִם *water that was to the loins*, in the same verse). This likewise includes the cases in which a noun is followed in apposition by a numeral (see § 134 *c*) or an adverb, originally conceived as a substantive, e.g. Neh 2¹² אֲנָשִׁים מְעַט *men, a few*, i.e. some few men; 1 K 5⁹ תְּבוּנָה הַרְבֵּה *understanding, much-making*, i.e. much understanding, unless הַרְבֵּה is to be taken as an adverb with וַיִּתֵּן, as in 2 S 8⁸ with לָקַח.

---

over, having regard to יַיִן הָרֶקַח *spiced wine*, Ct 8², and עַיִר פֶּרֶא *a wild ass's colt*, Jb 11¹² (in which passages יַיִן and עַיִר must certainly be in the construct state) we cannot but ask whether the Masora does not intend the יַיִן in ψ 60⁵ to be taken as construct state (for which elsewhere יֵין).

[1] Cf. also the examples treated above in § 127 *h*.

[2] On the anomalous form כִּכְּרַיִם (instead of כִּכָּרַיִם; cf. כִּכְּרַיִם immediately before), see § 88 *b*.

(e) Collocation of the *thing* and its *name*, e.g. בְּהַרְרָם שֵׂעִיר *in their* **f** *mountainous district, Seir* (perhaps only a later gloss), Gn 14⁶; הָאָרֶץ כְּנַעַן *the land Canaan* (כנען probably only a later gloss), Nu 34²; cf. Ezr 9¹, 1 Ch 5⁹ (see under *g* below).—For examples of nouns in the construct state before a noun in apposition, see § 130 *e*.

Rem. 1. Only in certain combinations does the noun of nearer definition **g** come first, e.g. הַמֶּלֶךְ שְׁלֹמֹה, הַמֶּלֶךְ דָּוִד *king David, king Solomon* (less frequently דָּוִד הַמֶּלֶךְ as in 2 S 13³⁹, 1 K 2¹⁷, 12², 2 K 8²⁹, 9¹⁵, and in late Hebrew, Hag 1¹·¹⁵ [cf. the Aramaic order דריוש מלכא], and often in Chron.).—A chiasmus occurs in Is 45⁴, the name standing after the defining noun in the first part of the verse, and before it in the parallel clause.

2. When the *nota accusativi* (אֵת, אֶת־) or a preposition precedes the first **h** substantive, it *may* be repeated before the noun in apposition, e.g. Gn 4², 22², 24⁴, 47²⁹, Is 66²¹; this usually occurs when the nearer definition precedes a *proper name*. As a rule, however, the repetition does not take place (Dt 18¹, Jer 33¹⁸, 1 S 2¹⁴). A noun in apposition is made determinate, even after a noun with a prefix, in the ordinary way, e.g. 2 Ch 12¹³ בִּירוּשָׁלַיִם הָעִיר *in Jerusalem, the city which,* &c.[1]

3. Sometimes a second adjective is used in apposition to a preceding **i** adjective, in order to modify in some way the meaning of the first, e.g. Lv 13¹⁹ בַּהֶרֶת לְבָנָה אֲדַמְדָּמֶת *a white-reddish* (light red) *bright spot.*

4. *Permutation* is to be regarded as a variety of apposition. It is not com- **k** plementary like apposition proper (see *a* above), but rather *defines* the preceding substantive (or pronoun, see below), in order to prevent any possible misunderstanding. This includes cases like Gn 9⁴ *with the life thereof* (which is) *the blood thereof*; Ex 22³⁰, Dt 2²⁶, 1 S 7⁹, 2 K 3⁴ *an hundred thousand rams, the wool,* i.e. the wool of the rams ; Jer 25¹⁵ *this cup of the wine,* that is *of fury* (but הַחֵמָה is probably a gloss) ; Is 42²⁵ *he poured upon him fury,* namely *his anger* ;[2] but especially the examples in which such a permutative is added to a preceding pronoun, viz.—

(a) To a separate pronoun, e.g. Ex 7¹¹; with regard to the vocative, cf. **l** § 126 *f*.

(b) To an accusative suffix, e.g. Ex 2⁶ *she saw him, the child* (unless אֶת־הַיֶּ׳ **m** be a later gloss) ; Ex 35⁵, Lv 13⁵⁷ᵇ, 1 K 19²¹ (where, indeed, הַבָּשָׂר appears to be a late gloss) ; 21¹³, 2 K 16¹⁵ *K⁽ᵉth⁾.,* Jer 9¹⁴, 31², Ez 3²¹, Ec 2²¹ (according to Delitzsch rather a double accusative).[3]

(c) To a noun-suffix, e.g. Ez 10³ בְּבֹאוֹ הָאִישׁ *when he went in, the man*; 42¹⁴; **n** cf. Pr 13⁴ (?), Ez 3¹²; so also after a preposition with suffix, e.g. Ec 4¹⁰ אִי לוֹ הָאֶחָד *woe to him, the one alone*; with a repetition of the preposition, Nu 32³³, Jos 1² לָהֶם לִבְנֵי יִשְׂרָאֵל *to them, to the children of Israel*; Ju 21⁷, Jer 51⁵⁶,

---

[1] In 1 K 11⁸ participles after לְכָל־נָשָׁיו, as in 2 K 10⁶ after אֶת־גְּדֹלֵי הָעִיר, in 19² after a determinate accusative, and in Hag 1⁴ after בְּבָתֵּיכֶם, are used *without* the article ; these, however, are probably to be explained not as in apposition, but according to § 118 *p*.

[2] But מַיִם Gn 6¹⁷ (cf. 7⁶) is to be regarded as a later gloss upon the archaic מַבּוּל.

[3] For וַיִּשֵּׁנוּ 1 S 21¹⁴ either וְיִשְׁנֶה is to be read or the *K⁽ᵉthibh⁾* is to be explained according to § 75 *b*, note. Also יְלַכְדֻנוּ Pr 5²² has hardly preserved the correct form.

Ez 42⁵ (?), Dn 11¹¹, 1 Ch 4⁴², 2 Ch 26¹⁴.¹—Cf. finally, Ct 3⁷, where the suffix precedes the genitive periphrastically expressed by שֶׁלּ/, as in Ez 9¹, where the genitive is expressed by לְ.²

o   Of a different kind are the cases in which the permutative with its proper suffix follows as a kind of correction of the preceding suffix, e. g. Is 29²³ *when he* (or rather) *his children see*, &c. (but יְלָדָיו is clearly a gloss) ; cf. ψ 83¹² ; in Jb 29³ read בְּהִלּוֹ (infin. Hiph.) or at least its syncopated form בַּהִלּוֹ.

p   5. Cases of apposition in a *wider sense* are those in which the nearer definition added to the noun was originally regarded as an *adverbial accusative* ; on its use with the verb and on the relative correctness of speaking of such an accusative in Hebrew, cf. § 118 *a* and *m*. Owing to the lack of case-endings, indeed, it is in many instances only by analogies elsewhere (especially in Arabic) that we can decide whether the case is one of apposition in the narrower or in the wider sense ; in other instances this must remain quite uncertain. However, the following are probably cases of apposition in the wider sense :—

q   (*a*) Such phrases as מִשְׁנֶה כֶּסֶף *a double amount in money*, Gn 43¹⁵ ; cf. Jer 17¹⁸ ; 1 S 17⁵ *five thousand shekels in brass*, but this might also be taken (as in *d*) *shekels* which were *brass* ; certainly such cases as Jb 15¹⁰ *older than thy father in days*, and the expression of the superlative by means of מְאֹד (originally a substantive), e. g. טוֹב מְאֹד *very good*, Gn 1³¹ (cf. also Ec 7¹⁶ צַדִּיק הַרְבֵּה *righteous over much*), and the very frequent הַרְבֵּה מְאֹד prop. *a much-making exceedingly*, i. e. *exceedingly great*, Gn 15¹, 41⁴⁹, also Pr 23²⁹ פְּצָעִים חִנָּם *wounds without cause*,³ perhaps also Gn 34²⁵ (בֶּטַח).

r   (*b*) A few examples, in which an epexegetical substantive is added to a substantive with a suffix ; thus, Ez 16²⁷ מִדְרְכֵּךְ זִמָּה *of thy conduct in lewdness* (but it is also possible to explain it (as in *c*) *of thy conduct*, which is *lewdness*) ; cf. Ez 24¹³, 2 S 22³³ מָעוּזִּי חָיִל *my fortress in strength*, i. e. my strong fortress (cf., however, ψ 18³³) ; Hb 3⁸, ψ 71⁷. While even in these examples the deviation from the ordinary usage of the language (cf. § 135 *n*) is strange, it is much more so in חֲבֻלָתוֹ חוֹב Ez 18⁷, i. e. according to the context *his pledge* for *a debt* ; Ezr 2⁶² כְּתָבָם הַמִּתְיַחְשִׂים, i. e. *their register*, namely of *those that were reckoned by genealogy* (but perhaps הַמִּתְיַ׳ is in apposition to the suffix in כְּתָבָם), also the curious combinations (mentioned in § 128 *d*) of בְּרִיתִי with a proper name (Lv 26⁴²), and in Jer 33²⁰ with הַיּוֹם.⁴

---

¹ But in Is 17⁶ we should certainly divide the words differently and read אַחֲרִית הַשְּׂמָחָה ; בִּסְעִפֵי הַפֹּרִיָּה, in Jer 48⁴⁴ read אֵלֶּה for אֵלֶיהָ, and in Pr 14¹³ in Gn 2¹⁹ נֶפֶשׁ חַיָּה is a late gloss upon לוֹ, and in Ez 41²⁵ אֶל־דַּלְתוֹת הַהֵיכָל a gloss on אֲלֵיהֶן.

² Some of the examples given above are textually (or exegetically) doubtful, whilst in the case of others, especially those from the later Books, we cannot help asking whether such a prolepsis of the genitive by means of a suffix (as e. g. Ez 10³) is not due to the influence of Aramaic, in which it is the customary idiom ; cf. Kautzsch's *Gramm. des Biblisch-Aram.*, § 81 *e* and § 88.

³ In ψ 69⁵ חִנָּם (like שֶׁקֶר *in a false way, falsely*, ψ 35¹⁹ and 38²⁰) is used as an *adverbial accusative* with a participle ; cf. § 118 *q*.

⁴ But in Nu 25¹² שָׁלוֹם may also be explained, according to *c*, as really in apposition. Cf. on the whole question Delitzsch, *Psalmen*, 4th ed., p. 203, note 1.

6. In Dt 33⁴ מוֹרָשָׁה, perhaps מוֹר' לְקִהְלַת is to be read), 33²⁷ (מְעֹנָה), Ju 7⁸ *S* (צֵדָה), the absolute state appears to be used instead of the construct to govern a following logical genitive; this, however, cannot be explained either as a special kind of apposition, or (with Hitzig) as a peculiarity of the dialect of Northern Palestine, but is merely a textual corruption. On the other hand, in Jb 31¹¹ עָוֹן is evidently intended to combine the readings עֲוֹן פְּלִילִים and עָוֹן פְּלִילִי (as in verse 28).—The remarkable combination אֱלֹהִים צְבָאוֹת in ψ 80⁸·¹⁵ is due to the fact that in ψψ 42–83 אֱלֹהִים has almost throughout been subsequently substituted by some redactor for the divine name יהוה; on יהוה צְבָאוֹת cf. § 125 *h*. In ψ 59⁶, 80⁵·²⁰, and 84⁹ יהוה has been reinstated in the text before אֱלֹהִים צְבָאוֹת.¹

7. Lastly, the nearer definition (qualification) of a noun may be effected by *t* means of a preposition (either with a suffix or with an independent noun), but must then be distinguished from the cases in which the preposition is dependent on a verb or verbal idea, e. g. Gn 3⁶ *and she gave also* לְאִישָׁהּ עִמָּהּ *unto her husband with her* (= *her husband who was with her*); in Gn 9¹⁶ (*that I may remember the everlasting covenant between God and every living creature of all flesh*) and other places, the qualification of the noun is itself also qualified.

§ 132. *Connexion of the Substantive with the Adjective.*²

1. The adjective (like the participle used adjectivally), which serves *a* as an *attribute* of a substantive, stands *after* the substantive, and agrees with it in *gender* and *number*, e. g. אִישׁ גָּדוֹל *a great man*, אִשָּׁה יָפָה *a beautiful woman*. If the substantive is immediately connected with a genitive, the attribute follows the latter, since, according to § 89 and § 128 *a*, the construct state and the genitive belonging to it are inseparably united, e. g. Est 8¹⁵ עֲטֶרֶת זָהָב גְּדוֹלָה *a great crown of gold.*— On the attribute when attached to a *determinate* substantive, see above, § 126 *u*.

---

¹ Without this assumption it would be inconceivable that יהוה אֱלֹהֵי צְבָאוֹת should not have been written; that the author of these Psalms regarded צְבָאוֹת already as an independent name of God (so Gesenius and Olshausen) is out of the question.

² On the expression of attributive ideas by substantives, cf. above, § 127 *h*, and § 128 *o*, with the note; § 135 *n* and § 141 *c* (substantives for adjectives as predicates of noun-clauses) and § 152 *u* (periphrases for negative qualities). On the use of the feminine of adjectives (and participles) to express abstract ideas, see § 122 *q*. It remains to mention further the employment (mostly only in poetry) of certain epithets in place of the substantives to which the quality in question belongs; e. g. אָבִיר *the strong one*, i. e. *God*; אַבִּיר *the strong one*, i. e. *the bull* (in Jer 8¹⁶, &c., *the horse*); קַל *swift* = *the runner* (of the horse, Is 30¹⁶); לְבָנָה *alba*, i. e. *luna*; פֹּרִיָּה (*fructifera*) *a fruitful tree*, Is 17⁶ (so פֹּרָת Gn 49²²); רֹבֵץ *a croucher*, i. e. *a crouching beast of prey*, Gn 4⁷. Cf. also רוֹזֵן (*gravis, augustus*) and נָשִׂיא (*elatus?*), i. e. *a prince*. The use of adjectives and participles for substantives is much more extensive in Arabic. In Greek and Latin poetical language cf. such examples as ὑγρή = *the sea*; *merum* for *vinum*, &c.

b Rem. 1. Where an adjectival attribute appears to stand *before* its substantive (according to the usual explanation, for the sake of special emphasis) the relation is really appositional in character; thus, Is 10³⁰ עֲנִיָּה עֲנָתוֹת *O thou poor one, Anathoth!* (but probably עֲנִיָּה *answer her*, is to be read); cf. 23¹², 53¹¹ (*a righteous man, my servant*; but in 28²¹ זָר and נָכְרִי are *predicates* preceding the substantives); Jer 3⁶·¹⁰ f., ψ 18⁴ *him who is worthy to be praised will I call upon, the Lord*; 92¹² (apposition after participles).—But רַבִּים and רַבּוֹת *many*, are sometimes placed, like numerals, before the substantive, Jer 16¹⁶, Neh 9²⁸ (in ψ 145⁷ רַב is a *subst. regens*, in 89⁵¹ the text is corrupt); an appositional relation can scarcely be intended in these instances.

c 2. In a few expressions (mostly poetic) the adjective appears not as an attribute *after* the substantive, but in the construct state governing it; so in the singular, Ex 15¹⁶ (unless גָּדֵל should be read); 1 S 16⁷ (*the height of his stature*); in the plural, 1 S 17⁴⁰ חַלֻּקֵי אֲבָנִים *smooth ones of* (among) *stones*, i.e. *smooth stones*; Is 35⁹, Ez 7²⁴, ψ 46⁵, and with a following collective instead of a plural, e.g. Is 29¹⁹ אֶבְיוֹנֵי אָדָם *the poor among men*, i.e. *poor men*; Jer 49²⁰, Zc 11⁷; cf. in Latin *canum degeneres*. However, in almost all these cases the adjective which is made into a *regens* is strongly emphatic, and is frequently equivalent to a superlative (see below, § 133 *g*).

d 3. When *two* adjectives follow a feminine, sometimes only that standing next to the noun takes the feminine termination, e.g. 1 K 19¹¹ רוּחַ גְּדוֹלָה וְחָזָק וגו' (but read גְּדוֹל); 1 S 15⁹ (but cf. § 75 *y*); Jer 20⁹, ψ 63². A similar dislike of the feminine form may also be observed in the case of verbal predicates referring to feminine subjects, cf. § 145 *p* and *t*.

When an attribute qualifies several substantives of different genders, it agrees with the masculine, as being the *prior gender* (cf. § 146 *d*), e.g. Neh 9¹³ חֻקִּים וּמִצְוֹת טוֹבִים; Jer 34⁹, Zc 8⁵.

When *three* attributes follow a substantive, the first two may stand without a conjunction, and the last be attached by *wāw copulative*, cf. Zc 1⁸.

e 4. After feminines plural ending in ים— (§ 87 *p*) the adjectival attribute (in accordance with the fundamental rule stated above, under *a*) takes the ending וֹת, e.g. Is 10¹⁴ בֵּיצִים עֲזֻבוֹת *forsaken eggs*; Gn 32¹⁶. For a strange exception see Jer 29¹⁷ (differently in 24²).

f 5. With regard to *number* it is to be remarked that—

(*a*) Substantives in the *dual* are followed by adjectives (or participles) in the *plural*, e.g. ψ 18²⁸ (Pr 6¹⁷) עֵינַיִם רָמוֹת *haughty eyes*; Is 35³, Jb 4³ f., cf. § 88 *a*.

g (*b*) *Collective* ideas are not infrequently joined with the *plural* of the adjective or participle (*constructio ad sensum*); thus, e.g. צֹאן *sheep* [with *fem. plur.*], Gn 30⁴³, 1 S 25¹⁸; עַם = *men*, 1 S 13¹⁵, Is 9¹; כָּל־יִשְׂרָאֵל = *all the Israelites*, 1 S 2¹⁴; גָּלוּת = *the exiles*, Jer 28⁴; cf. also נֶפֶשׁ שְׁנָיִם *two souls*, Gn 46²⁷.[1] Cf. similar phenomena in the connexion of collectives with plural predicates in § 145 *c*.

h (*c*) The *pluralis excellentiae* or *pluralis maiestatis* is joined, as a rule, to the singular of the attribute, e.g. ψ 7¹⁰ אֱלֹהִים צַדִּיק; 2 K 19⁴·¹⁶ (= Is 37⁴·¹⁷); Is 19⁴; but cf. אֱלֹהִים חַיִּים[2] Dt 5²³, 1 S 17²⁶·³⁶, Jer 10¹⁰, 23³⁶, perhaps also

---

[1] But it is impossible to take תְּמִימִם in Ez 46⁶ as an attribute of בָּקָר; probably it is a correction intended to harmonize the passage with Nu 28¹¹, where *two* young bullocks are required.

[2] Cf. 1 S 28¹³, where אֱלֹהִים (in the sense of *a spirit*) is followed by עֹלִים as a second accusative; conversely in 1 S 19¹³·¹⁶, a singular suffix refers back

Ex 20³ אֱלֹהִים אֲחֵרִים = *another god*, and Jos 24¹⁹ אֱלֹהִים קְדֹשִׁים (but cf. above, § 124 *g–k*). On the other hand, 1 S 4⁸ is to be explained as having been said by the Philistines, who supposed that the Israelites had several gods. On the connexion of אֱלֹהִים with a plural predicate, see § 145 *i*.

2. On the adjective (in the construct state) governing a following genitive, see § 128 *x*; for the participle in the same construction, see § 116 *f–l*.

§ 133. *The Comparison of Adjectives. (Periphrastic Expression of the Comparative and Superlative.)*

A. Wünsche, ' Der Komparativ im Hebr. im Lichte der arab. Gramm.,' in *Vierteljahrsschrift für Bibelkunde*, 1904, p. 398 ff.

1. Hebrew possesses no special forms either for the comparative or *a* superlative of the adjective.[1] In order to express a comparative, the person or thing which is to be represented as excelled in some particular quality is attached to the attributive word by the preposition מִן (מִ׳), e. g. 1 S 9² גָּבֹהַּ מִכָּל־הָעָם *higher than any of the people*. The fundamental idea evidently is, *tall away from all the people* (beyond all the people); cf. Ju 14¹⁸ מַה־מָּתוֹק מִדְּבַשׁ וּמֶה עַז מֵאֲרִי *what is sweeter than honey ? and what is stronger than a lion ?* Ez 28³, Am 6². Frequently an infinitive appears as the object of the comparison, e. g. Gn 29¹⁹ *it is better that I give her to thee, than that I should give her*, &c.; Ex 14¹², ψ 118⁸ᶠ.[2]

Rem. 1. This use of מִן is also very common when the attributive idea is *b* represented by an intransitive verb, e. g. 1 S 10²³ וַיִּגְבַּהּ מִכָּל־הָעָם *and he was higher than any of the people*; Na 3⁸, Jb 7⁶. Elsewhere, especially after transitive verbs, מִן rather represents (on its different senses see § 119 *v–z*) the idea

---

to תְּרָפִים *household god* (but not so in Gn 31³⁴), as in ψ 46⁴ to the plural of amplification יַמִּים *sea*. On the other hand, it is very doubtful whether רַבָּה ψ 78¹⁵ is to be regarded as an attribute of תְּהֹמוֹת and not rather as the adverb, *abundantly*.

[1] There is in Arabic a special form of the adjective (the *elative*) for the comparative and superlative, which in Hebrew would have the form אַקְטַל. Instances of it, perhaps, are אַכְזָר *daring, cruel*, אַכְזָב *deceptive* (of a brook drying up), and its opposite אֵיתָן (contracted from *'aitan*) *constantly flowing*, *perennis*. These forms are, however, used without any perceptible emphasis, and cannot be regarded as more than isolated relics of an elative formation which has become obsolete, much as the Latin comparative disappears in Italian, and still more so in French, and is supplanted by the circumlocution with *più, plus*.

[2] In Ju 11²⁵ the adjective is specially intensified by repetition, *art thou so much better than Balak ?* It would also be possible, however, to translate *art thou really better . . . ?*

of a *separation, distinction* or *superiority* of one person or thing *from* or *over* others.[1] This is evident in such cases as בָּחַר מִן־ *to choose* something (to prefer it) *before* something else, e. g. Jb 7¹⁵, cf. Dt 14² (also מִן־ . . . יִתְרוֹן *the excellence of . . . over . . .*, Ec 2¹³); it is also seen in examples like Gn 37³ וְיִשְׂרָאֵל אָהַב אֶת־יוֹסֵף מִכָּל־בָּנָיו *now Israel loved Joseph more than all his* (other) *children*; 29³⁰, 1 S 2²⁹, Ho 6⁶.²

c　2. A somewhat different idea underlies the use of מִן־ after adjectives, or intransitive verbs possessing an attributive sense, when the thought to be expressed is that the quality is *too little* or *too much* in force for the attainment of a particular aim or object, e. g. Is 7¹³ הַמְעַט מִכֶּם *is it a small thing* (i. e. too little) *for you to . . . ?* Jb 15¹¹; after an intransitive verb, e. g. Gn 32¹¹ *I am too insignificant* (קָטֹנְתִּי) *for all the mercies* (I am not worthy of . . .), &c.; cf. also the expressions כָּבֵד מִן־ *to be too heavy for one*, Ex 18¹⁸, Nu 11¹⁴, ψ 38⁵; קָשָׁה מִן־ *to be too hard for one*, Dt 1¹⁷; מָעַט מִן־ *to be too few for something*, Ex 12⁴; גָּבַר מִן־ *to be too strong for one*, ψ 65⁴; עָצַם מִן־ *to be too mighty for one*, Gn 26¹⁶; רוּם מִן־ *to be too high for one*, ψ 61³; צַר מִן־ *to be too narrow for one*, Is 49¹⁹; קָצַר מִן־ *to be too short for something*, Is 50², and very frequently נִפְלָא מִן־ *to be too wonderful for one* (and, consequently, inconceivable or unattainable), Gn 18¹⁴, Dt 17⁸, 30¹¹, Jer 37¹⁷, Pr 30¹⁸; in ψ 139⁶ פְּלִיאָה in the same sense is followed by מִן.—This use is especially seen in the numerous instances in which the attribute is followed by מִן־ with an infinitive, e. g. 1 K 8⁶⁴ *the brazen altar . . . was* קָטֹן מֵהָכִיל *too little to receive* (to be able to receive) *the burnt offering*, cf. Gn 4¹³, 36⁷ *too great for them to dwell together*; after verbs, e. g. Ex 12⁴, Is 28²⁰, ψ 40⁶. Finally, cf. רַב לָכֶם מִן־, followed by the infinitive, *it is enough* (prop. *too much*) *for you to . . .*, meaning *ye have . . . long enough*, 1 K 12²⁸; cf. Ex 9²⁸ and Ez 44⁶ (מִן־ followed by a substantive).³

d　In all these instances מִן־ expresses either the *removal* of a thing *from* a person, or the *severance* of the person from some aim or object; cf. also the expression לֹא־יִבָּצֵר מֵהֶם כֹּל וְגוֹ *nothing will be unattainable for them* (prop. there shall not be cut off from them anything which, &c.), Gn 11⁶, Jb 42³.

e　3. The attributive idea, on which מִן־ logically depends, must sometimes, in consequence of a pregnant use of the מִן־ (see the analogous examples in § 119 *f*), be supplied from the context, e. g. Is 10¹⁰ וּפְסִלֵיהֶם מִירוּשָׁלִַם *whose graven images were more numerous than* those at *Jerusalem*, &c.;⁴ Mi 7⁴ *worse than a thorn hedge*; ψ 62¹⁰ *lighter than a breath*; Jb 11¹⁷ *clearer than the noonday*; Ec 4¹⁷ *better than*, &c.

---

[1] Cf. the Latin ablative with the comparative; also the etymology of such words as *eximius, egregius*, and the Homeric ἐκ πάντων μάλιστα, Il. 4, 96; ἐκ πασέων, 18, 431.

[2] On the other hand, the phrase צָדַק מִן־ expresses not a comparison, but only a relation existing between one person and another; thus, in Gn 38²⁶ צָדְקָה מִמֶּנִּי means, *she is in the right as against me*; cf. ψ 139¹², Jb 4¹⁷, 32².—In Pr 17¹² *rather* (to meet with so and so) *than . . .* is expressed by וְאַל־ before the second member.

[5] Cf. also 2 K 4³, where the idea of *doing something too little* is paraphrased by the Hiph. הַמְעִיט = *do not too little*, sc. לִשְׁאֹל *in borrowing empty vessels*.

[4] With this *comparatio decurtata*, cf. the still bolder pregnant construction in ψ 4⁸, מֵעֵת *greater gladness than at the time*, &c.

2. The correlative comparatives *greater—less* (*older—younger*) are *f* expressed by the simple adjective with the article (*the great,* equivalent to *the greater,* &c.); Gn 1[16], 19[31.34], 27[15], 29[16.18.26].

3. To express the *superlative* it is also sufficient (see above, *f*) to *g* make the adjective determinate, either by means of the article or a following partitive genitive (or suffix); in this case the article or genitive indicates that the attribute in question belongs especially to one or more definite individuals;[1] e.g. 1 S 9[21] הַצְּעִרָה *the least*; 16[11] הַקָּטָן *the little one,* i.e. the *youngest* of eight sons; 17[14] David was הַקָּטָן *the youngest, and the three great,* i.e. elder, &c.; Gn 42[13], 44[2], Ct 1[8].—So also with a qualifying adjective, e.g. Gn 9[24] בְּנוֹ הַקָּטָן *his youngest son*; cf. Jos 14[15]; also with a following genitive, 2 Ch 21[17] קְטֹן בָּנָיו *the youngest of his sons*: Pr 30[24] *the least upon the earth*; with suffix, Mi 7[4] טוֹבָם *their good one,* i.e. the best of them; Jon 3[5] מִגְּדוֹלָם וְעַד־קְטַנָּם *from the greatest of them even to the least of them*; cf. the inverse order in Jer 6[13], 31[34].

Rem. 1. The above examples apply only to the most common *relative h* attributes (*great, small, good*), and to expressions which by usage easily came to be recognized as periphrases for the superlative. Other adjectives, however, when followed by a partitive genitive, also acquire the sense of a superlative; this appears from the context, e.g. Dt 33[19] *the most hidden treasures of the sand*; Ju 5[29] *the wisest amongst her ladies*; Is 14[30], 19[11], 23[8 f.], 29[19], Jer 49[20], Ez 28[7], Zc 11[7], ψ 45[13], Jb 30[6] (*in the most horrible of valleys*), 41[22]; probably also ψ 35[16]. On this government by the adjective generally, cf. § 132 *c.*—Moreover, the combination of a substantive in the construct state with an adjective used substantivally (§ 128 *w*) sometimes serves as a periphrasis for the superlative, e.g. Is 22[24] כֹּל כְּלֵי הַקָּטָן *all the smallest vessels.* On Ct 7[10] see § 126 *x.*

2. Other periphrases for the superlative are the use of a substantive in the *i* construct state before the plural of the same word (which is naturally to be regarded as a partitive genitive ; cf. our *book of books*), e.g. Ex 26[33] קֹדֶשׁ הַקֳּדָשִׁים *the most holy place*; שִׁיר הַשִּׁירִים (Ct 1[1]) *the most excellent song*; cf. Gn 9[25] (= *servus servorum, the lowest servant*); Nu 3[32], Dt 10[17] (ψ 136[2.3])[2] ; 1 K 8[27], Is 34[10] (cf. Gal 1[5], Rev 22[5]); Jer 3[19], Ez 16[7], 26[7] (*king of kings,* of Nebuchadrezzar; cf. 1 Tim 6[15], Rev 17[14], 19[16], and another kind of periphrasis in ψ 95[3]); Ec 1[2]. Similarly in Jer 6[28] two participles are combined, and in Ho 10[15] two substantives in the singular. Finally, the same object is attained by connecting one substantive in the construct state with another of the same stem (שַׁבַּת שַׁבָּתוֹן *a sabbath of solemn rest,* i.e. an obligatory day of rest, Ex 31[15], &c.) or of the same meaning (e.g. חֹשֶׁךְ אֲפֵלָה *a thick darkness,* Ex 10[22]).

3. The intensification of attributes by means of repetition belongs rather *k* to rhetoric than to syntax, e.g. Ec 7[24] עָמֹק עָמֹק *exceeding deep*; 1 S 2[3], Pr 20[14] ; the adjective is even used three times in Is 6[3].—Cf. the repetition of adverbs for the same purpose in Gn 7[19], Nu 14[7] (מְאֹד מְאֹד *exceedingly,* also מְאֹד בִּמְאֹד Ex 1[7], &c.); Ez 42[15].—On the other hand, in Dt 28[43] the repetition expresses

---

[1] Cf. also עֶלְיוֹן *the one above,* i.e. *the Most High.*

[2] *God of gods, and Lord of lords,* just as the supreme god of the Babylonians is called *bēl bēlī* (Tiele, *Compend. der Rel.-Gesch.,* p. 87).

a continuous progress, *higher and higher* . . . *lower and lower*; in Dt 2²⁷ (see § 123 *e*) and 16²⁰ (*nothing but justice*) the constancy of the action. Cf. Ex 23³⁰ מְעַט מְעַט *little by little, very gradually.*[1]

l The repetition of substantives serves also as a periphrasis for the superlative in such cases as לְדֹר דֹּר (Ex 3¹⁵) = *to the remotest generations*; cf. 17¹⁶, Jer 6¹⁴, 8¹¹ (*perfect peace*); Ez 21³² (עַוָּה three times);[2] 35⁷, Na 1²; cf. also Ho 2²¹ᶠ· and the emphatic combination of synonymous verbs in Is 33¹⁰. Sometimes the completeness of an action or state is expressed by placing together two or even three substantives of the same stem and of similar sound, cf. Is 22⁵, Ez 6¹⁴ (33²⁸ ᶠ·, 35⁸); 32¹⁵, Na 2¹¹, Zp 1¹⁵ (Jb 30³, 38²⁷).

§ 134. *Syntax of the Numerals.*

Cf. the exhaustive statistics collected by Sven Herner, *Syntax der Zahlwörter im A. T.*, Lund, 1893. E. König, ' Zur Syntax der Zahlwörter im A. T.,' *AJSL.* xviii. 129 ff.

a 1. The numerals from 2 to 10, as being originally abstract substantives,[3] may be connected with their substantives in three different ways. They may stand either —

(*a*) In the construct state *before* the substantive (the object numbered being consequently in the genitive), e. g. שְׁלֹשֶׁת יָמִים *a triad of days,* i. e. three days; שְׁנֵי הָאֲנָשִׁים *the two men*; or

b (*b*) In the absolute state *before* it (the object numbered being in apposition, § 131 *d*), e. g. שְׁלֹשָׁה בָנִים *a triad,* viz. *sons*, i. e. three sons; שְׁנַיִם אֲנָשִׁים *two men*; or

c (*c*) In the absolute state (likewise in apposition) *after* the object numbered, e. g. בָּנוֹת שָׁלֹשׁ. So especially in long lists, since in these the substantives naturally come first, e. g. Gn 32¹⁵. Nu 7¹⁷, 28¹⁹. Apart from such cases, the frequency of this order in the later Books is due to the fact that the character of the numeral tended more and more to become adjectival rather than substantival.[4]

---

[1] Adverbs of the same stem are connected in this way in Nu 6⁹, Is 29⁵, 30¹³; of different stems in Is 5²⁶ and Jo 4⁴. In Nu 12² the particles רַק אַךְ appear to be placed together for a similar purpose, equivalent to *simply and solely.*

[2] Different in kind from the triple utterance of the same words in 2 S 18³³, Jer 7⁴ and 22²⁹, and the double exclamation in Jer 4¹⁹ and La 1¹⁶ (?).

[3] Cf. § 97 *a*, where it is shown that the masculine is the original form of the numerals (used for both genders), and that the feminine was afterwards differentiated and used with masc. nouns, primarily in the second decade and then in the first as well.

[4] From Herner's tables (op. cit., pp. 55–66) it appears, according to p. 68, that in the documents J, E, D of the Pentateuch, and in Jos 1–12, Judges, Samuel, Isaiah, Jeremiah, the Minor Prophets, Psalms, Megilloth, and Job, the numeral never, or very rarely, stands *after* its noun; in Kings and Ezekiel it stands several times *after*; in the Priestly Code nearly always *after*; in Chronicles, Ezra, Nehemiah, and Daniel, nearly as often *after* as *before* the noun. In Ex 28¹⁰ the Masora makes the numeral in the genitive follow the construct state of the substantive numbered; we should, however, read וְאֶת־שְׁמוֹת הַשִּׁשָּׁה; for the omission of the article before שֵׁ, cf. § 126 *w.*

Rem. In Lv 24²² אֶחָד follows the construct state מִשְׁפָּט, but here as in *d* Nu 15¹⁶ מִשְׁפָּט should be read. In Gn 42¹⁹ אֶחָד is in apposition to a substantive with a suffix (= *one of you brethren*; but verse 33 *the one of you brethren*). In Nu 31²⁸ אֶחָד precedes the substantive in the Aramaic manner (= *one each*). —For מְאָה־שָׁנָה (Gn 17¹⁷, &c.) we find regularly in the Priestly Code (except in Gn 17¹⁷, 23¹) מְאַת שָׁנָה (Gn 5³, &c.) *an hundred years*. On the connexion of abstract numerals with suffixes, as שְׁנֵיהֶם *their duality*, i. e. *they two*, Gn 2²⁵, &c.² (also with a strengthening separate pronoun, as שְׁנֵינוּ אֲנַחְנוּ 1 S 20⁴²), cf. § 97 *i*.

2. The numerals from 2 to 10 take the object numbered in the *e* plural,¹ with very few exceptions, such as Ex 16²² (where שְׁנֵי הָעֹמֶר = *the double of an omer*), 2 K 22¹, Ez 45¹, cf. 2 K 8¹⁷ and 25¹⁷ *Keth*. The numerals from 11 to 19 generally take the plural, but with certain substantives frequently used with numerals the singular is more common (see further, under *f*). The tens (from 20 to 90), when they precede, take the singular (in the accusative, cf. § 131 *p*) of certain nouns frequently used with numerals (אֶלֶף *a thousand*, אִישׁ, שֶׁקֶל, נֶפֶשׁ, כַּר, יוֹם—but only in Ezekiel and the Priestly Code), otherwise the plural, as עָרִים, בָּנוֹת, בָּנִים (but cf. also Ju 11⁵³), &c.; on the other hand, the plural is necessary when they follow the object numbered in apposition (e. g. אַמּוֹת עֶשְׂרִים *twenty cubits*, 2 Ch 3³ᶠ·; with the exception of 2 S 24²⁴, only in late Books). After מֵאָה and אֶלֶף the substantive numbered may be used either in the singular or plural, see further under *g*.

Rem. 1. After the numerals from 11 to 19 the singular is used, as a rule, *f* with יוֹם *day*, שָׁנָה *year*, אִישׁ *man*, נֶפֶשׁ *soul* (person), שֵׁבֶט *tribe*, מַצֵּבָה *pillar* (Ex 24⁴), sometimes with אַמָּה *cubit*, חֹדֶשׁ *month*, עִיר *city*, שֶׁקֶל *shekel* (compare our *four-year-old*, *ten pound*), e. g. Dt 1² אַחַד עָשָׂר יוֹם (cf., however, such exceptions as Dt 1²³, Jos 4², &c.).—Substantives other than these are used in the plural with the numerals from 11 to 19, and the numeral may even follow the substantive, especially in later passages, as Nu 7⁸⁷ᶠ·, 1 Ch 4²⁷, 25⁵.

2. After מֵאָה (מְאַת) [so almost exclusively in the Priestly Code, e. g. always *g* אֲלָפִים, אַלְפֵי, אֶלֶף (מָאתַיִם, מֵאוֹת) and אֶלֶף אֲלָפִים (אֲלָפַיִם, [מְאַת אֶלֶף] the substantives אִישׁ, אֶלֶף, אַמָּה, רַגְלִי, יוֹם, צֶמֶד (except in Ez 40²⁷), are regularly used in the singular, generally also שֶׁקֶל, כַּר, כִּכַּר, שָׁנָה (with the exception of Jos 7²¹, 2 S 14²⁶, &c.); cf., moreover, Gn 33¹⁹, 24⁶⁰ (אַלְפֵי רְבָבָה), Est 1¹, Ju 21¹², Dt 7⁹, 1 K 5¹², 2 Ch 9¹⁵.—Examples of the *plural* after מֵאָה are Gn 26¹², 1 S 18²⁵, 2 S 16¹, 1 K 18⁴; after מְאַת Ex 38²⁷; after מֵאוֹת Ju 15⁴, 2 S 8⁴, 1 K 10¹⁷,

---

¹ On examples such as Gn 46²⁷ (נֶפֶשׁ שְׁנַיִם *two souls*), cf. § 132 *g* (collectives joined with the plural of the adjective).

Ez 42¹⁷; after מֵאתַיִם 1 S 25¹⁸, 1 K 7²⁰; after אֶלֶף 1 S 25², 1 K 3⁴, 5⁶, 2 K 3⁴, ψ 90⁴; after אֲלָפִים 1 S 17⁵, Jb 42¹²; after אַלְפֵי Mi 6⁷; after אֲלָפִים Is 36⁸.— In Dn 12¹¹ the plural יָמִים precedes the numeral *twelve hundred*.

h 3. Numerals compounded of tens and units (like 21, 62) take the object numbered either *after* them in the singular (in the accusative), e. g. Gn 5²⁰ שְׁתַּיִם וְשִׁשִּׁים שָׁנָה *two and sixty years* (שָׁנָה in the singular, according to *e*, since it conforms to the ten immediately preceding; but also שְׁלֹשִׁים וּשְׁמֹנֶה שָׁנָה Dt 2¹⁴), or *before* them in the plural, especially in the later Books, Dn 9²⁶, &c.; or the object is repeated (but only in 1 K 6¹, and the Priestly Code; sometimes even several times, e. g. Gn 23¹, 25⁷·¹⁷ thrice) in the plural with the units, and in the singular with the tens and hundreds, e. g. Gn 12⁴ חָמֵשׁ שָׁנִים וְשִׁבְעִים שָׁנָה *seventy and five years*; Gn 23¹ מֵאָה שָׁנָה וְעֶשְׂרִים שָׁנָה וְשֶׁבַע שָׁנִים *an hundred and twenty and seven years.* Cf. Gn 5⁶ ᶠᶠ.

i Rem. 1. It may further be remarked with regard to the order, that the thousand or thousands always precede the hundreds, &c., and the hundreds almost always come before the smaller numbers (in Kings and Ezekiel sometimes, and in the Priestly Code usually, after the smaller numbers), the tens in the earlier Books (documents J and D of the Pentateuch, in Joshua 1–12, Judges, Samuel, Isaiah, and also in Ezra and Nehemiah) *before* the units, but in Jeremiah, Ezekiel, the Priestly Code, Joshua 13–24 *after* the units (see Herner, *op. cit.*, p. 73). After the hundreds the smaller number is very frequently added without וְ, especially in Ezra, Nehemiah, and Daniel.

On the syntax of the cardinals in general :—

k 2. The cardinals are determined by the article, when they refer back (without being connected with the object numbered; cf., however, Lv 25¹⁰ ᶠ·, Nu 16³⁵, Jos 4⁴, 2 S 23¹³) to a number or list already mentioned, e. g. Gn 2¹¹ שֵׁם הָאֶחָד פִּישׁוֹן *the name of the one* (the first) *is Pishon*; Gn 14⁹ *four kings against the five* (enumerated in verse 2); cf. 1 Ch 11²⁰ ᶠ·, and the determinate tens in Gn 18²⁹·³¹ ᶠ·. A demonstrative with the article may also be added to a numeral determined in this way, e. g. Dt 19⁹ (but cf. also Gn 9¹⁹, 22²³, where the numeral and demonstrative are practically determinate in themselves). In the case of the numerals from 11 to 19 the article may stand either before the unit (1 Ch 25¹⁹, 27¹⁵) or before עָשָׂר (Jos 4⁴); it is used before all three members of a compound number (273) in Nu 3⁴⁶.

l In apposition with any determinate substantive the cardinal number is used *without* the article, not only when it precedes the substantive, as in Jos 15¹⁴ אֶת־שְׁלֹשָׁה בְּנֵי הָעֲנָק, where שְׁלֹשָׁה is equivalent to a substantive determinate in itself; cf. Gn 18²⁸, Jos 6⁸·²², 1 S 17¹⁴, 1 K 11³¹, and the passages discussed above in § 126 *x*, Gn 21²⁹, &c.), but also when it follows the substantive, e. g. 1 K 7²⁷·⁴³ ᶠ· עֶשֶׂר and עֲשָׂרָה; the omission of the article may here, as in the cases noticed in § 126 *z*, be also due to the dislike of a hiatus, but cf. also שָׁנַיִם 2 K 25¹⁶ after a determinate substantive. The fact that it is by nature determinate would also be a very simple explanation of אֶחָד Nu 28⁴, 1 S 13¹⁷ ᶠ·, Jer 24², Ez 10⁹, instead of the more usual הָאֶחָד, and of אַחַת 1 S 1² for הָאַחַת.

Such cases as שִׁבְעַת הַיָּמִים Ju 14¹⁷ (which is determined by a following *m* determinate genitive) are explained from § 127 *b*; 1 Ch 9²⁵ perhaps from § 126 *q*; in Is 30²⁶ probably the light of all the seven days of the week is meant; on the other hand, in 1 S 9²⁰ and 25³⁸ the article is, with Wellhausen, to be omitted.

3. Certain specifications of *measure, weight,* or *time,* are commonly omitted *n* after numerals, e.g. Gn 20¹⁶ אֶלֶף כֶּסֶף *a thousand* (shekels) *of silver;* so also before זָהָב Gn 24²², 1 K 10¹⁶, Is 7²³, cf. ψ 119⁷². Moreover, Ru 3¹⁵ שֵׁשׁ שְׂעֹרִים *six* (ephahs) *of barley;* 1 S 10⁴ שְׁתֵּי־לֶחֶם *two* (sc. *loaves,* see verse 3) *of bread,* cf. 17¹⁷ עֲשָׂרָה לֶחֶם; 2 S 16¹, where before קַיִץ *a measure,* or perhaps some term like *cakes,* is to be supplied.—The number of cubits is stated in the Priestly Code (Ex 26², &c.) and in 1 K 6 and 7 (otherwise only in Ez 40⁵·²¹, 47³, Zc 5², 1 Ch 11²³, 2 Ch 4² ᶠ·) by the addition of בָּאַמָּה prop. *by the cubit.* Also in Ex 27¹¹ the Samaritan and LXX read בָּאַמָּה after אֹרֶךְ, and in 27¹⁵ אַמָּה after עֶשְׂרֵה.

4. The *ordinals* above 10 have no special forms, but are expressed *o* by the corresponding cardinals, which may then stand either before or after the object numbered, e.g. Gn 7¹¹ בְּשִׁבְעָה עָשָׂר יוֹם *on the seventeenth day;* Dt 1³ בְּאַרְבָּעִים שָׁנָה *in the fortieth year;* cf. Gn 14⁵, 2 K 25²⁷, and, with repetition of שָׁנָה in a compound number, 1 K 6¹; such a cardinal occurs without בְּ (and therefore in the *accus. temporis,* according to § 118 *k*) in Gn 14⁴ (the Samaritan, however, has וּבִשְׁלֹשׁ); with the article (but without a numbered object, see under *k*), 1 K 19¹⁹.[1]—On the position of the numeral as a genitive following its noun, cf. e.g. 1 K 16¹⁰ בִּשְׁנַת עֶשְׂרִים וָשֶׁבַע *in the twenty and seventh year,* and with a determinate numeral, Ex 12¹⁸, Nu 33³⁸, Dt 15⁹. In this case, however, שָׁנָה is very frequently repeated, e.g. Gn 7¹¹, 2 K 13¹⁰; after a determinate numeral, Lv 25¹⁰.[2]

Rem. In numbering days of the month and years, the cardinals are very *p* frequently used instead of the ordinals even for the numbers from 1 to 10, e.g. בִּשְׁנַת שְׁתַּיִם 1 K 15²⁵; בִּשְׁנַת שָׁלֹשׁ 2 K 18¹, &c., cf. Dt 15⁹. The months themselves are always numbered by the ordinals (בַּשֵּׁנִי, בָּרִאשׁוֹן, &c., up to בָּעֲשִׂירִי), but not the days of the month, e.g. בְּאֶחָד לַחֹדֶשׁ Gn 8⁵, &c., בְּאַרְבָּעָה בִּשְׁעָה לַחֹדֶשׁ 2 K 25⁸, בְּשִׁבְעָה לַחֹדֶשׁ Ez 1¹, &c., בַּחֲמִשָּׁה לַחֹדֶשׁ Zc 7¹; בְּתִשְׁעָה לַחֹדֶשׁ Lv 23³² (always, however, בֶּעָשׂר לַחֹדֶשׁ *on the tenth day of the month*). On the

---

[1] Somewhat different from this is Ex 19¹⁵ *be ready* לִשְׁלֹשֶׁת יָמִים prop. *after three days,* i.e. *on the third day* (in verses 11 and 16 and in Ezr 10⁸ the ordinal is used), also 1 S 30¹³ כִּי חָלִיתִי הַיּוֹם שְׁלֹשָׁה *because three days agone I fell sick,* prop. *to-day three* (days).

[2] All these expressions may indeed be explained by supposing that, e.g. in Lv 25¹⁰, the proper meaning is *the year of the fifty years* which it completed, i.e. *the fiftieth year;* but it is more correct to regard שְׁנַת or בִּשְׁנַת in such cases not as a real *nomen regens,* but simply as a connective form to be explained on the analogy of the cases mentioned in § 128 *k*.

omission of יוֹם in all these cases see under *n*; only in late passages is יוֹם added, e. g. 2 Ch 29¹⁷ בְּיוֹם שְׁמוֹנָה לַחֹרֶשׁ; Ezr 3⁶ מִיוֹם אֶחָד לַחֹרֶשׁ.—Finally, when the year is stated by בִּשְׁנַת governing a determinate ordinal, viz. 2 K 17⁶ בִּשְׁנַת הַתְּשִׁיעִית *in the ninth year*; 2 K 25¹ (in Jer 52⁴ בְּשָׁנָה), Jer 28¹ *Keth.*, 32¹ *Keth.*, 46², 51⁵⁹, Ezr 7⁸; בִּשְׁנַת in such cases is again (see note 2 on *o*) to be explained according to § 128 *k*. This is supported by the fact that the Masora on Jer 28¹, 32¹ requires in the *Qerê* בַּשָּׁנָה for בשנת.

q 5. *Distributives* are expressed either by repetition of the cardinal number, e. g. Gn 7⁹·¹⁵ שְׁנַיִם שְׁנַיִם *two and two*; 2 S 21²⁰ שֵׁשׁ וָשֵׁשׁ *six each*; with the numbered object also repeated, e. g. Jos 3¹² אִישׁ אֶחָד אִישׁ אֶחָד לַשֵּׁבֶט *for every tribe a man*; Nu 13², 34¹⁸ אֶחָד מִן, as in Neh 11¹, *one out of every ten*); cf. § 123 *d*; or a periphrasis with לְ אֶחָד is used, Nu 17¹⁸, Dt 1²³, cf. Is 6² לְאֶחָד after *six wings* twice repeated; the simple distributive לְ is, however, sufficient (as in לַבְּקָרִים, § 123 *c*), e. g. לְמֵאוֹת וְלַאֲלָפִים *by hundreds and by thousands*.

r 6. The *multiplicatives* are expressed either (like the ordinals above 10, see under *o*) by the cardinals (in the feminine, probably owing to the omission of פַּעַם, פְּעָמִים; so König, *Lehrgeb.*, ii. 228), as שְׁתַּיִם *twice*, Jb 40⁵; שֶׁבַע *seven times*, Lv 26²¹·²⁴, Pr 24¹⁶; cf. also אַחַת *once*, 2 K 6¹⁰, Jb 40⁵, for which in Jb 33¹⁴ בְּאַחַת¹ along with בִּשְׁתָּיִם (the latter also in 1 S 18²¹); or by the *dual* of the numeral, thus שִׁבְעָתַיִם Gn 4¹⁵ (in verse 24 along with the cardinal 77 for 77 times); Is 30²⁶, ψ 12⁷, 79¹²; אַרְבַּעְתַּיִם 2 S 12⁶;² or periphrastically by פַּעַם *a time* (prop. *a step*, with the article, הַפַּעַם *this time*; cf. also בַּפַּעַם הַזֹּאת, with בְּ, like בְּאַחַת above), as פַּעַם אַחַת *once* (Neh 13²⁰ פַּעַם וּשְׁתָּיִם *once and twice*), בְּעָמַיִם *twice*, שָׁלֹשׁ פְּעָמִים (for which in Ex 23¹⁴, Nu 22²⁸·³² שָׁלֹשׁ רְגָלִים) *three times*; cf. Ez 41⁶ *thirty-three times*; 2 S 24³ *an hundred times*; Dt 1¹¹ *a thousand times*; 1 K 22¹⁶ עַד־כַּמֶּה פְעָמִים *until how many times*, i. e. how often. Cf. also עֲשֶׂרֶת מֹנִים *ten times*, Gn 31⁷·¹⁴, and רַבּוֹת עִתִּים *many times*, Neh 9²⁸.—In Gn 43³⁴, *five times* is expressed by חָמֵשׁ יָדוֹת (prop. *five hands*),³ and in Ex 16⁵ the *double* is expressed by מִשְׁנֶה עַל־ (prop. *a repetition over and above that which*, &c.).—Of the ordinals שֵׁנִית is used as a numeral adverb, Gn 22¹⁵, &c., *a second time*, cf. the Latin *tertium consul*; בַּשְּׁלִישִׁת *the third time*, 1 S 3⁸; פַּעַם חֲמִישִׁת *a fifth time*, Neh 6⁵; בַּשְּׁבִעִית *at the seventh* (time), 1 K 18⁴⁴, and בַּפַּעַם הַשְּׁ׳ Jos 6¹⁶.

---

¹ But בְּאַחַת Nu 10⁴ is to be translated *on one* (trumpet).

² Probably also כִּפְלַיִם Jb 11⁶ (from כֶּפֶל *doubling*) does not mean *doubled* but *manifold*.

³ But אַרְבַּע הַיָּדוֹת Gn 47²⁴ means *the* (other) *four parts*; cf. 2 K 11⁷, Neh 11¹.

Rem. The collocation of a numeral with the next above it (either in the *S* same or in different sentences) is a rhetorical device employed in *numerical sayings* to express a number, which need not, or cannot, be more exactly specified. It must be gathered from the context whether such formulae are intended to denote only an insignificant number (e. g. Is 17⁶, *two* or at the most *three*), or a considerable number, e. g. Mi 5⁴. Sometimes, however, this juxtaposition serves to express merely an indefinite total, without the collateral idea of intensifying the lower by means of the higher number. Thus *one* and *two* are connected by וְ, Dt 32³⁰, Jer 3¹⁴, Jb 33¹⁴, 40⁵ (without וְ, ψ 62¹²) ; *two* and *three*, Is 17⁶ (Sirac 23¹⁶, 26²⁸, 50²⁵), and without וְ, 2 K 9³², Ho 6², Am 4⁸ ; *three* and *four*, Jer 36²³, Am 1³⁻¹¹, Pr 30¹⁸, 21²⁹ (Sirac 26⁵), and without וְ, Pr 30¹⁵; *four* and *five*, without וְ, Is 17⁶ ; *six* and *seven*, Jb 5¹⁹, Pr 6¹⁶ ; *seven* and *eight*, Mi 5⁴, Ec 11² ; (*nine* and *ten*, Sirac 25⁷).

III. Syntax of the Pronoun.

§ 135. *The Personal Pronoun.*

1. The *separate* pronouns,—apart from their employment as the *a* subject in noun-clauses (cf. § 141 *a*) and the idiom mentioned under *d–h,*—are used, according to § 32 *b*, as a rule, only to give express emphasis to the subject; e. g. Gn 16⁵, 2 S 24¹⁷ אָנֹכִי i. e. *I myself*, so also אֲנִי 2 S 12²⁸, 17¹⁵ (after the verb), Ez 34¹⁵, ψ 2⁶; ¹ but 1 S 10¹⁸, 2 S 12⁷, Is 45¹² אָנֹכִי *I* and none else; cf. also אֲנִי אֲנִי *I, I !* Ho 5¹⁴, &c.; אַתָּה Gn 15¹⁵, Ju 15¹⁸, 1 S 17⁵⁶ (as in 20⁸, 22¹⁸, Ex 18¹⁹, Dt 5²⁴, Ju 8²¹, after the imperative); 1 K 21⁷; אַתֶּם Gn 9⁷, Ex 20¹⁹ (after the verb, Ju 15¹²); fem. Gn 31⁶; הוּא 1 S 22¹⁸; הִיא Gn 3²⁰, Ju 14³; הֵמָּה Jer 5⁵.— Sometimes, however, the separate pronoun appears to be placed before the verb more on rhythmical grounds, i. e. in order to give the statement a fuller sound than that of the bare verbal form (cf. the similar use of the infinitive absolute, § 113 *o*). Thus Gn 14²³, ψ 139², and most clearly in such passages as Gn 21²⁴, 47³⁰, Ex 8²⁴, Ju 6¹⁸, 11⁹, 1 S 12²⁰, 2 S 3¹³, 21⁶, 1 K 2¹⁸ (in solemn promises). The same explanation applies to אֲנִי at the beginning of sentences, e. g. Gn 24⁴⁵, Ho 5³, 10¹¹, 12¹¹, ψ 39¹, 82⁶, Jb 5³. ²

Rem. 1. Different from this is the pleonastic addition of the separate *b* pronoun immediately *after* the verb (according to Delitzsch on Ct 5⁵ perhaps

---

¹ Also הוּא, הִיא *he himself, she herself* (of persons and things), e.g. Is 7¹⁴ אֲדֹנָי הוּא *the Lord himself*; Est 9¹ הֵמָּה הַיְּהוּדִים *the Jews themselves*. In the sense of *the same* (ὁ αὐτός) or (*one and*) *the same*, הוּא is used in Is 41⁴, 43¹⁰·¹³, 46⁴, 48¹² (always אֲנִי הוּא), ψ 102²⁸ (אַתָּה הוּא), and probably also Jb 3¹⁹.—The position of הֵמָּה, as an accusative of the object, before a perfect in 1 Ch 9²², can at most be explained on the analogy of Aramaic (Ezr 5¹²).

² As early as the Mêša‘ inscription (line 21 ff.) אנך frequently stands at the beginning of a new sentence after the dividing stroke.

a trace of popular language), e.g. 1 S 23²² (?), Ct 5⁵, and (like other indications of the very late origin of the book) very frequently in Ecclesiastes, e.g. 1¹⁶, 2¹·¹¹·¹⁵, 3¹⁷ᶠ· and thirteen other places; in Aramaic, Dn 5¹⁶.

c 2. Substantival subjects also are somewhat frequently resumed, and thus expressly emphasized, by the insertion of the corresponding separate pronoun of the 3rd person before the predicate is stated, e. g. Gn 3¹² *the woman whom thou gavest to be with me, she* (הִיא) *gave me*, &c.; 14²⁴ (הֵם); 15⁴, 24⁷, &c.; but הוּא in Is 7¹⁴ after the predicate and subject is equivalent to *he himself*.[1]

d 2. Not infrequently the separate pronoun serves to give strong emphasis to a suffix of the same person which precedes (or sometimes even to one which follows), whether the suffix be attached to a verb (as accusative) or to a noun or preposition (as genitive). In English such an emphasis on the pronoun can generally be rendered only by laying greater stress upon it, or sometimes by repeating it; cf., on the contrary, the French *mon livre à moi*. The separate pronoun in such instances is not to be regarded as a *casus obliquus* (accusative or genitive), but as the subject of an independent sentence, the predicate of which must in each case be supplied according to the context.

e Examples of emphasis :—

(*a*) On a *verbal* suffix by means of אֲנִי (אָֽנִי), Gn 27³⁴ בָּרֲכֵנִי גַם־אָנִי *bless me, even me also* (prop. *bless me, I also* would be blessed); Zc 7⁵; cf. also Ez 6³, 34¹¹·²⁰ הִנְנִי אָֽנִי; by אַתָּה (אָֽתָּה) Pr 22¹⁹ (but the text is most probably corrupt). —The separate pronoun *precedes* in Gn 24²⁷ (אָנֹכִי); 49⁸ (אַתָּה, not *Judah, thou art he whom*, but *Judah thee, thee thy brethren shall praise !*), and Ec 2¹⁵ גַּם אָנִי.

f (*b*) On a noun-suffix with a substantive, by means of אֲנִי 2 S 19¹, Pr 23¹⁵; by אַתָּה 1 K 21¹⁹ אֶת־דָּמֲךָ גַּם־אָתָּה *thy blood, even thine*; by הוּא 2 S 17⁵, Jer 27⁷, Mi 7³; by אֲנַחְנוּ 1 S 20⁴², after שְׁנֵינוּ, but without special stress; Neh 5² (?); by אַתֶּם Nu 14³²; by הֵם ψ 38¹¹ (without special stress), הֵמָּה ψ 9⁷.—The separate pronoun *precedes* in Jb 21⁴ (אָנֹכִי); Gn 40¹⁶, Is 45¹², 1 Ch 28² (אֲנִי); Zc 9¹¹ (אַתְּ); Jos 23⁹ (אַתֶּם); Ez 33¹⁷ (הֵמָּה).—In ψ 89⁴⁸, where אֲנִי might be taken as strengthening חֶלֶד (equivalent in sense to חֶלְדִּי), we should read אֲדֹנָי for אֲנִי, as in verse 51.

g (*c*) On a suffix united with a preposition, 1 S 25²⁴ בִּי אֲנִי *upon me, upon me*; 1 K 1²⁶ אֲנִי . . . לִי; 2 Ch 35²¹ לֹא־עָלֶיךָ אַתָּה *not against thee*; 1 S 19²³ עָלָיו גַּם הוּא *upon him also*; Dt 5³ כִּי אִתָּנוּ אֲנַחְנוּ *but with us, even us*; Hag 1⁴ לָכֶם אַתֶּם *for you yourselves*; Jer 25¹⁴ בָּם גַּם־הֵמָּה.—The separate pronoun *precedes* in 1 S 12²³ . . . לִי; אָנֹכִי; 1 K 1²⁰ עָלֶיךָ . . . אַתָּה; Mi 5¹ מִמְּךָ . . . אַתָּה, and 2 Ch 28¹⁰ אַתֶּם עִמָּכֶם.

h The same principle also explains Gn 4²⁶ לְשֵׁת גַּם־הוּא *to Seth, to him also* (not גַּם־לוֹ); cf. 10²¹, and Ex 35³⁴, Nu 4²².

---

[1] Analogous to this is the resumption of a noun dependent on a preposition, by means of a pronominal suffix united with the same preposition, e. g. Gn 2¹⁷, 2 S 6²², 2 K 22¹⁸, or of an object by means of the *nota accusativi* אֵת with suffix, e. g. 1 S 15⁹ (where וְנִמְאֶסֶת is certainly to be read), Is 8¹³.

3. The *oblique* cases of the personal pronouns expressed by means of *i* a preposition (or the *nota accus.* אֵת) with a suffix may be used either in a demonstrative or reflexive sense,[1] as לוֹ *to him*, but also *to himself*, e.g. Ju 3[16] *and Ehud made* לוֹ *for himself a sword*, cf. Gn 33[17]; so also לָהֶם *sibi*, Is 3[9]; אֵלָיו *unto him*, and Gn 8[9] *unto himself*; אִתּוֹ *with him*, and Gn 22[3] *with himself*; עִמָּהּ *with her*, and 1 S 1[24] *with herself*; also apparently as a pleonastic *dativus ethicus* (see § 119 *s*), Jb 12[11], 13[1].

Rarely, and only when marked emphasis is intended, is the *accusative* *k* of the reflexive pronoun represented by the *nota accusativi* אֵת with a suffix (this being ordinarily expressed by the reflexive conjugations *Niph'al* and *Hithpa'ēl* [2]); thus, אֹתָם *se ipsos*, Ex 5[19], Jer 7[19] in sharp antithesis to הָאֹתִי; Ez 34[2.8.10]. Cf. § 57 at the end, together with note 2.

Rem. There is a similar emphasis in Is 49[26] on בְּשָׂרָם and דָּמָם in the *l* sense of *their own flesh, their own blood*. On the sometimes demonstrative, sometimes reflexive meaning of noun-suffixes of the 3rd person singular and plural, cf. § 91, *p* and *q*. For other circumlocutions to express the idea of *self*, see § 139 *f*.

4. The *possessive pronouns* are, according to § 33 *c*, expressed by *m* the *suffixes of the noun* (in the genitive),[3] which may represent either a *subjective genitive*, or (like the genitives proper, § 128 *h*) an *objective genitive*, e.g. חֲמָסִי *the wrong done against me*, Gn 16[5], Jer 51[35]; cf. Gn 9[2], 18[21], 27[13] (2 S 16[12] *Keth.*); Gn 30[23], 39[21] (cf. Ex 3[21], &c.); 50[4], Ex 20[20], 21[35], Ju 4[9], 13[12] (מַעֲשֵׂהוּ *the treatment of him*); Is 56[7], Jer 9[7], Na 3[19], Pr 1[27], 24[22], Jb 20[29], 23[14], 34[6]. Cf. also such pregnant expressions as ψ 20[3] יִשְׁלַח עֶזְרְךָ *he will send thy help* (*help for thee*), i.e. he will send thee help; Gn 30[18], 39[21], Ex 2[9], Is 1[26] (*and I will restore judges for thee*); Ez 37[15].

When several substantives are co-ordinated, the pronominal suffix must be attached to each singly, e.g. Gn 36[6] *and Esau took* אֶת־נָשָׁיו וְאֶת־בָּנָיו וְאֶת־בְּנֹתָיו *his wives and his sons and his daughters*, &c.; 38[18], &c. In 2 S 23[5] the text is hardly correct.

---

[1] As in Luther's Bible *jm* (*ihm*), *jr* (*ihr*) for *sich*, and in our version *him, her* for *himself, herself*.

[2] *Niph'al* according to § 51 *e* (like *Hithpa'ēl* according to § 54 *f*) may also include the *dative* of the reflexive pronoun.

[3] Like the substantival genitive, according to § 129 *h*, the possessive pronoun may also be paraphrased by a relative clause, e.g. Ru 2[21] הַנְּעָרִים אֲשֶׁר לִי *the young men, which are to me*, i.e. *my young men*; so especially, when the substantive, which should take a genitive suffix, is already followed by a genitive, e.g. 1 S 17[40]. In this case, however, the suffix also is sometimes attached pleonastically, e.g. Ct 1[6] כַּרְמִי שֶׁלִּי *my vineyard, which* belongs *to me*. Cf. Ct 3[7], and the analogous pleonasms in 2 S 22[2] (but see ψ 18[2]) and ψ 27[2].

n **5.** When the genitive, following a construct state, is used periphrastically to express the idea of a material or attribute (§ 128 *o* and *p*), the pronominal suffix, which properly belongs to the compound idea (represented by the *nomen regens* and genitive), is, like the article (§ 127), attached to the second substantive (the genitive), e. g. הַר־קָדְשִׁי prop. *the hill of my holiness,* i. e. my holy hill, ψ 2⁶, &c.; עִיר קָדְשֶׁךָ *thy holy city,* Dn 9²⁴; אֱלִילֵי כַסְפּוֹ *his idols of silver,* Is 2²⁰, 30²², 31⁷; ¹ cf. Dt 1⁴¹, Is 9³, 28⁴, 41¹¹, Ez 9¹ᶠ., ψ 41¹⁰, 150¹, Jb 18⁷ צַעֲדֵי אוֹנוֹ *his steps of strength;* 38⁶; after an adjective as *nomen regens,* Is 13³ (Zp 3¹¹) עַלִּיזַי גַּאֲוָתִי *my proudly exulting ones.*—On the same analogy is the use of e. g. כְּלֵי מִלְחַמְתּוֹ Dt 1⁴¹ *his weapons of war* [cf. Is 41¹²]; Is 56⁷ בֵּית תְּפִלָּתִי *my house of prayer,* although the genitive here does not convey the idea of an attribute.

o Rem. 1. Through a weakening in the distinction of gender, which is noticeable elsewhere (cf. § 110 *k*, 144 *a*, 145 *p, t, u*) and which probably passed from the colloquial language² into that of literature, *masculine* suffixes (especially in the plural) are not infrequently used to refer to *feminine* substantives; thus a noun-suffix in the singular, Ex 11⁶, 25¹⁹, Ju 11³⁴;³ in the plural, Gn 31⁹, 32¹⁶, 41²³, Ex 1²¹, 2¹⁷, Nu 2⁷·⁷ (but the feminine suffix twice immediately after, and so the Samaritan also in verse 7); 36⁶ (Samaritan אֲבִיהֶן, but also בְּעֵינֵיהֶם); Ju 19²⁴, 21²², 1 S 6⁷·¹⁰ᵇ (בְּנֵיהֶם); 9²⁰, Is 3¹⁶, Ez 23⁴⁵ᶠᶠ. (alternating with הֵן); Am 4¹ᶠ. (but afterwards a feminine suffix); Jb 1¹⁴, 39³ חֶבְלֵיהֶם in parallelism with יַלְדֵיהֶן; 42¹⁵, Ct 4², 6⁶, Ru 1⁸ᶠᶠ. (along with feminine suffixes); Dn 1⁵, 8⁹. Verbal suffixes in the singular, Ex 22²⁵; in the plural, Ju 16³, Pr 6²¹, Jb 1¹⁵. But Gn 26¹⁵·¹⁸, 33¹³, Ex 2¹⁷, 1 S 6¹⁰ᵃ are to be explained according to § 60 *h.* On הֵמָּה as feminine, see § 32 *n.* On the use of the masculine in general as the *prior gender,* see § 122 *g.*

p 2. The suffix of the 3rd person singular feminine (as also the separate pronoun הִיא Nu 14⁴¹, Jos 1c¹³, Ju 1⁴) sometimes refers in a general sense to the verbal idea contained in a preceding sentence (corresponding to our *it*); thus the verbal suffix, Gn 15⁶, Nu 23¹⁹, 1 S 11², 1 K 11¹², Is 30⁸, Am 8¹⁰; cf. Gn 24¹⁴ (בָּהּ *thereby*), 42³⁶, 47²⁶, Ex 10¹¹ (אֹתָהּ *that*), Is 47⁷. Elsewhere the suffix of the 3rd singular feminine refers to the plurals of things, e. g. 2 K 3³

---

¹ On the other hand, more explicitly in prose, Gn 44² אֶת־גְּבִיעִי גְּבִיעַ הַכֶּסֶף *my cup, the silver cup.*

² According to Diehl (see the title at the head of § 91 *a*), who adduces numerous instances on pp. 44 ff., 54 ff., 67 f., many of these cases may be set down to corruption of the traditional text, while the sudden (and sometimes repeated) change of gender in suffixes is mainly due to the influence exercised on the copyists by the Mishnic and popular Aramaic dialects, neither of which recognizes such distinctions. Such influence, however, is insufficient to explain the large number of instances of this weakening, occurring even in the earlier documents.

³ The Masora reckons six instances of מִמֶּנּוּ, where מִמֶּנָּה would be expected (Ju 11³⁴, where, however, the text is most probably corrupt), Ex 25¹⁵ (?), Lv 6⁸, 7¹³, 27⁹, Jos 1⁷; almost all these passages can, however, be easily explained in other ways.

[but see Kittel; so 13[2.6.11]; 10[26], but LXX מַצֵּבַת], Jer 36[23], Jb 6[20] (if the text is correct), 39[15] (read תְּחָמֵם in v. 14), and to the plurals of names of animals, Is 35[7], Ezr 11[5]. Conversely, plural suffixes refer to collective singulars, e.g. in Gn 15[13], Nu 16[3], 1 S 2[8], Zp 2[7] [but read עַל הַיָּם]; and to a verbal idea contained in the preceding clause, in Ez 33[18], Jb 22[21] בָּהֶם *thereby*), Ez 18[26], 33[19] עֲלֵיהֶם *on that account, thereby*).[1] But the suffix in נְתַנוֹ Dt 21[10] refers to the collective idea contained in אֹיְבֶיךָ; in Jon 1[3] עִמָּהֶם refers to the sailors included in sense under the term אֳנִיָּה. In Jos 2[4] read וַתִּצְפְּנֵם; in Is 30[6] (מֵהֶם), 38[16], ψ 19[5] (בָּהֶם) the text is most probably corrupt.

3. In a few examples the force of the noun-suffix or possessive pronoun *q* has become so weak that the language appears to be almost entirely unconscious of it. Thus in אֲדֹנָי *my Lord*, usually explained as being from the *pluralis maiestatis* אֲדֹנִים (§ 124 *i*) with the suffix of the 1st singular (always with *Qameṣ* to distinguish it from אֲדֹנַי *my lords*, Gn 19[2]; but see note below), used exclusively of God, not only in addressing him (Gn 15[2], 18[3], ψ 35[23]), but ultimately (see, however, the note below), without any regard to the pronoun, as equivalent to *the Lord*.[2] On אֲדֹנָי as a *Qᵉrê perpetuum* of the Masoretes for יהוה see § 17 *c* and § 102 *m*.

A similar loss of vitality in the suffix is generally assumed in יַחְדָּו prop. *in r his unitedness*, i.e. *he &c. together*, e.g. כָּל־הָעָם יַחְדָּו Ex 19[8]; then, without regard to the suffix, even after the 1st person אֲנַחְנוּ יַחְדָּו 1 K 3[18] in reference to two women; Is 41[1], Jb 9[32], Neh 6[2.7]; after the 2nd person, Is 45[20], &c. But the supposed pronominal suffix is perhaps rather to be explained, with Brockelmann, *ZA*. xiv. 344 f., as an old adverbial ending, which survives in the Arabic adverbs in *u* and in Assyrian.—Cf. further כֻּלָּם prop. *their entirety*, but also after the 2nd person equivalent to *all together*, 1 K 22[28], Mi 1[2] (*hear, ye peoples, all of you*; cf. § 144 *p*), and even before the 2nd person, Jb 17[10] (in 1 S 6[4] read לָכֶם with the LXX).—On the redundant suffix in הֶעָרֵבֻךְ Lv 27[23], cf. § 127 *i*.

---

[1] In 2 K 7[10] for שֹׁעֵר (the LXX had שַׁעַר) read שֹׁעֲרִי.

[2] Cf. the same weakening of the force of the possessive pronoun in רַבִּי prop. *my master*, from the second century A.D. onwards *the master*; so also in Syriac מרי *my lord*, and ultimately as a title *the lord*; in Italian *Madonna*, French *Madame, Notre Dame, Monsieur, Monseigneur*, &c. It can, however, hardly be doubted that the regular distinction between אֲדֹנָי as a holy name, and אֲדֹנַי as an ordinary appellative is merely due to the practice of the later Rabbis. G. H. Dalman, *Der Gottesname Adonaj und seine Geschichte* (Berlin, 1889), in an exhaustive discussion, shows that apart from the book of Daniel and the eight critically doubtful passages, in which אדני is used by God himself, there is nowhere any necessity to regard the suffix as *entirely* meaningless, since אדני is always used either in an address *to* or (like אֲדֹנָי, which also is never a mere phrase or title) in reverent language *about* God— as the Lord of the speaker—like the Assyrian *bêli-ia, my lord*. Against any original distinction between אֲדֹנָי and אֲדֹנַי it may be urged especially that when unconnected with suffixes the singular אָדוֹן is always used of God, and not the *pluralis maiestatis* presupposed by אֲדֹנַי.

§ 136. *The Demonstrative Pronoun.*

a　　The *demonstrative pronouns* are זֶה, fem. זֹאת, plur. אֵלֶּה (§ 34), *hic, haec (hoc), hi,* &c., and the personal pronoun הוּא, likewise used as a demonstrative, fem. הִיא, plur. masc. הֵמָּה, fem. הֵנָּה (§ 32 *b*), *is, ea (id),* or *ille,* &c., *ii, eae* or *illi,* &c. The distinction between them in usage is that זֶה (like *hic,* ὅδε) almost always points out a (new) person or thing present, while הוּא (like *is, ille,* αὐτός, ἐκεῖνος) refers to a person or thing already mentioned or known (see the examples below).[1]

b　　Rem. 1. Compare the instructive examples in Gn 32³, Ju 7⁴ *of whom I say unto thee, this* (זֶה) *shall go with thee, he* (הוּא) *shall go with thee* (so afterwards with negatives). Moreover, הַיּוֹם הַזֶּה *this day,* i.e. the actual day on which one is speaking or writing (Gn 26³³, &c.), but הַיּוֹם הַהוּא the day or period of which the historian has just been speaking (Gn 15¹⁸, 26³²) or of which the prophet has just been foretelling (Is 5³⁰, 7¹⁸·²⁰ ᶠᶠ·) and of which he continues to speak or foretell. Nevertheless זֶה and אֵלֶּה are also found in certain common combinations where הוּא and הֵמָּה would be expected, and vice versa; thus almost always בַּיָּמִים הָהֵמָּה, הַדָּבָר הַזֶּה, plur. הַדְּבָרִים הָאֵלֶּה, but בַּיָּמִים הָהֵם or בַּיָּמִים הָהֵם.—With a secondary sense of contempt (like Latin *iste*) זֶה occurs, e.g. in 1 S 10²⁷, 21¹⁶, 1 K 22²⁷, Is 6¹⁰, &c. In the sense of the neuter, *this,* זֹאת is more common than זֶה, as Is 5²⁵, 43⁹, &c., but הוּא more common than הִיא.

c　　2. Both זֶה and הוּא are sometimes used almost as enclitics to emphasize interrogative words (like the Latin *nam* in *quisnam*; cf. also *quis tandem*); e.g. Jb 38² מִי זֶה *who now* (darkeneth, &c.) . . . ? 1 S 17⁵⁵ ᶠ·, Is 63¹, Jer 49¹⁹, ψ 24⁸, 25¹², &c; מַה־זֶּה *what now?* 1 S 10¹¹; *how now?* Gn 27²⁰; *why now?* Ju 18²⁴; but before the verb עָשָׂה it is usually מַה־זֹּאת Gn 3¹³, 12¹⁸, Ex 14⁵, Ju 15¹¹; לָמָּה־זֶּה *wherefore now?* Gn 18¹³, 25²², 1 S 17²⁸, 2 S 12²³, &c.—So also מִי־הוּא Is 50⁹, Jb 4⁷ ᶠᶠ·; and still more emphatically מִי הוּא־זֶה ψ 24¹⁰, Jer 30²¹.

d　　3. זֶה is likewise used as an enclitic (see *c* above): (*a*) *of place,* in such passages as Gn 27²¹ הַאַתָּה זֶה וגו׳ *whether thou* (that art here) *be my son Esau?* 2 S 2²⁰ *is it thou?* הִנֵּה־זֶה *behold, here,* 1 K 19⁵, Is 21⁹;[2] cf. also the strengthen-

---

[1] On זֶה and הוּא standing separately as determinate in themselves, see § 125 *i*. On the use of determinate demonstratives as adjectives, see § 126 *u*.

[2] On the other hand, it is very questionable whether זֶה in ψ 104²⁵ (זֶה הַיָּם), Is 23¹³ (זֶה הָעָם), Ju 5⁵, ψ 68⁹ (זֶה סִינַי) can be taken, according to the common explanation, simply as a prefixed demonstrative particle (*the sea yonder,* &c.). In ψ 104²⁵ הַיָּם may be in apposition to זֶה; cf. § 126 *aa,* on Ex 32¹, and Zc 5⁷, where אִשָּׁה אַחַת is in apposition to זֹאת depending on הִנֵּה, and also Ez 40⁴⁵, where הַלִּשְׁכָּה is in apposition to זֹה; otherwise it is most naturally taken as the subject, *this is the sea.* Is 23¹³, Ju 5⁵, 1 K 14¹⁴, and ψ 68⁹ might also be explained in the same way; but in these passages the text is almost certainly

ing of the separate pronoun by הוּא Is 43²⁵ (אָנֹכִי‎), 1 S 7²⁸, Is 37¹⁶, ψ 44⁵ (אַתָּה‎), and אֵלֶּה הֵם *these are*, Gn 25¹⁶, 1 S 4⁸; (*b*) *of time*: עַתָּה זֶה *now*, 1 K 17²⁴; *just now*, 2 K 5²²; and rather frequently before words denoting number, e. g. Gn 27³⁶ זֶה פַעֲמַיִם *twice, now*; cf. 31³⁸, 2 S 14², Jb 1¹², 7³, 19³; separated from the numeral in Gn 31⁴¹ זֶה־לִּי elliptically for *this*, i. e. this present period, *is to me*, i. e. makes altogether, *twenty years*, &c. The other examples are similarly elliptical.

§ 137. *The Interrogative Pronoun.*

The interrogative pronoun מִי *who* may refer either to a masculine *a* or feminine person (Ct 3⁶), or even to a plural, e. g. מִי אַתֶּם *who are ye?* Jos 9⁸; מִי־אֵלֶּה Gn 33⁵, Nu 22⁹ (more minutely, מִי וָמִי Ex 10⁸, i. e. *who exactly, who in particular?*). It is used of the neuter only when the idea of a person is implied, e. g. מִי־שְׁכֶם *who are the Shechemites?* Ju 9²⁸, 13¹⁷, Gn 33⁸, Mi 1⁵; even more boldly, with the repetition of a מִי used personally, in 1 S 18¹⁸, 2 S 7¹⁸.—Another interrogative is אֵי־זֶה *which, what?*; of persons only in Est 7⁵.

Moreover, מִי may also be used in the sense of a genitive, e. g. *b* בַּת־מִי אַתְּ *whose daughter art thou?* Gn 24²³, 1 S 17⁵⁵,⁵⁶,⁵⁸; דְּבַר מִי *whose word?* Jer 44²⁸, 1 S 12³; in the accusative, אֶת־מִי *quemnam?* 1 S 28¹¹, Is 6⁸; with prepositions, e. g. בְּמִי 1 K 20¹⁴ (in an abrupt question *by whom?*); לְמִי Gn 32¹⁸; אַחֲרֵי מִי 1 S 24¹⁵.—Similarly מָה, מַה־, מֶה־, *what?* is used for the nominative, or accusative, or genitive (Jer 8⁹), or with prepositions, e. g. עַל־מָה *whereupon?* Is 1⁵, Jb 38⁶; *why?* Nu 22³², &c.; עַד־מָה *quousque?* ψ 74⁹. [1]

Rem. Both מִי and מָה are used also in indirect questions (on the merely *c* relative distinction between direct and indirect questions in Hebrew, see the *Interrogative Sentences*), e. g. Gn 39⁸ (but read מֵאוּמָה with Samar. and LXX), 43²², Ex 32¹.—On the meaning of מִי and מָה as interrogatives is based also their use as *indefinite pronouns* (equivalent to *quisquis, quodcunque* or *quicquam*), e. g. Ex 32²⁶, Ju 7⁸, 1 S 20⁴, Is 50¹⁰ (read יִשְׁמַע in the apodosis), 54¹⁵, Pr 9⁴·¹⁶, 2 Ch 36²³; even שְׂמָרוּד־מִי *have a care, whosoever ye be*, 2 S 18¹² (unless לֹי is to be read, with the LXX, for מִי); so also מָה (*whatever it be*) Jb 13¹³, 1 S 19³, 2 S 18²²·²³; cf. Nu 23³ וּדְבַר מַה־יַּרְאֵנִי *and whatsoever he showeth me*. Cf. also מִי אֲשֶׁר *whosoever* Ex 32³³, 2 S 20¹¹, and מִי־הָאִישׁ אֲשֶׁר *any man who* Dt 2c⁵ᶠᶠ,

---

corrupt. In Ju 5⁵ in fact זֶה סִינַי is most probably to be regarded with Moore as a very early gloss, which subsequently found its way from this passage into ψ 68.

[1] A quite different use of מָה was pointed out (privately) by P. Haupt in Ct 5⁸ *will ye not tell him?* i. e. *I charge you that ye tell him*, and 7¹ = *look now at the Shulamite*, corresponding to the late Arabic *mā tarā*, *just see!* *mā taqûlu*, *say now!* It has long been recognized that מָה is used as a negative in Ct 8⁴.

Ju 10¹⁸. A still further weakening of the *indefinite* use of מָה is the combination מַה־שֶּׁ *that which*, Ec 1⁹, 3¹⁵ (just like the Syriac דְּ מָא); cf. Est 8¹, and מָה . . . בַּל Pr 9¹³, מָה . . . לֹא Neh 2¹², *nothing whatever.*—On מְאוּמָה *quicquam*, *anything at all* (usually with a negative), and as an adverb *in any way*, 1 S 21³, see the Lexicon.

§ 138. *The Relative Pronoun.*

Cf. Philippi, *Stat. constr.* (see heading of § 89), p. 71 f., and especially V. Baumann, *Hebräische Relativsätze*, Leipzig, 1894.

a　　Relative clauses are most frequently (but not necessarily; cf. § 155 *b*) introduced by the indeclinable אֲשֶׁר (see § 36).[1] This is not, however, a relative pronoun in the Greek, Latin, or English sense, nor is it a mere *nota relationis*,[2] but an original *demonstrative* pronoun [as though *iste, istius,* &c.].[3] Hence it is used—

(1) In immediate dependence on the substantival idea to be defined, and virtually in the same case as it (hence belonging syntactically to the main clause); e. g. Gn 24⁷ . . . הוּא יִשְׁלַח . . . יְהֹוָה אֲשֶׁר לְקָחַנִי *the Lord, iste, he took me . . . he shall send,* &c. (=*who took me*); Gn 2² *and God finished* מְלַאכְתּוֹ אֲשֶׁר עָשָׂה *his work, istud, he had made* (it). Such qualifying clauses may be called *dependent relative clauses.*

b　　Rem. 1. In the above examples אֲשֶׁר in Gn 24⁷ is virtually in the nominative, in Gn 2² in the accusative. A further distinction between the examples is that in Gn 24⁷ the main idea (יהוה), to which אֲשֶׁר is added in apposition, is only resumed in the qualifying clause by the subject (*he*) inherent in

---

[1] The etymology of the word is still a matter of dispute. Against the identification of אֲשֶׁר, as an original substantive, with the Arabic *'aṯar, trace*, Aram. אֲתַר *place, trace*, Nöldeke urges (*ZDMG.* xl. 738) that the expression *trace of . . .* could hardly have developed into the relative conjunction, while the meaning of *place* has been evolved only in Aramaic, where the word is never used as a relative. According to others, אֲשֶׁר is really a compound of several pronominal roots; cf. Sperling, *Die Nota relationis im Hebräischen*, Leipzig, 1876, and König, *Lehrgeb.*, ii. 323 ff., who follows Ewald and Böttcher in referring it to an original אֶשֶׁל. According to Hommel (*ZDMG.* xxxii. 708 ff.) אֲשֶׁר is an original substantive, to be distinguished from שְׁ and שַׁ (an original pronominal stem), but used in Hebrew as a *nota relationis*, or (as זֶה and זוּ are also sometimes used, see below, *g* and *h*) simply for the *relative pronoun*. Baumann (op. cit., p. 44) sees in the Assyrian *ša*, Phoenician, Punic, and Hebrew שְׁ, the ground-forms, of which the Phoenician and Punic אֲשׁ (see above, § 36 note) and the Hebrew אֲשֶׁר are developments.

[2] E. g. like Luther's use of *so*, in *die fremden Götter, so unter euch sind*, Gn 35².

[3] This is the necessary conclusion both from the analogy of the Arabic *'allaḏi*, which is clearly a demonstrative (like the Hebr. הַלָּז, הַלָּזֶה), and from the use of זֶה and זוּ as relatives.

לְקָחַנִי, while in Gn 2² it is not resumed at all. This suppression of the retrospective pronoun[1] takes place especially when it (as in Gn 2²) would represent an accusative of the object, or when it would be a separate pronoun representing a nominative of the subject in a noun-clause, e.g. Gn 1⁷ הַמַּיִם אֲשֶׁר מִתַּחַת לָרָקִיעַ *the waters, those, under the firmament,* &c. In negative sentences, however, the retrospective pronoun is not infrequently added, e.g. Gn 17¹² הוּא; 7² הִיא; 1 K 9²⁰ הֵמָּה; Dt 20¹⁵ הֵנָּה; but cf. also אֲשֶׁר הוּא חַי Gn 9³. The addition of הִיא in a verbal clause, 2 K 22¹³, is unusual.

The very frequent omission of the retrospective pronoun is noticeable in cases where the predicate of the qualifying clause is a *verbum dicendi,* e.g. Nu 10²⁹ *we are journeying unto the place,* אֲשֶׁר אָמַר יְהוָֹה אֹתוֹ אֶתֵּן לָכֶם *that* place, the Lord said (of it), *It will I give to you;* cf. Nu 14⁴⁰, Ju 8¹⁵, 1 S 9¹⁷·²³, 24⁵, 1 K 8²⁹, Jer 32⁴³.

2. When the substantive, followed by אֲשֶׁר and the qualifying clause, *c* expresses an idea of *place,* it may also be resumed by the adverbs of place שָׁם *there,* שָׁמָּה *thither,* מִשָּׁם *thence,* e.g. Gn 13³ עַד־הַמָּקוֹם אֲשֶׁר־הָיָה שָׁם אָהֳלֹה *unto the place, that one, his tent had been there,* i.e. *where his tent had been*; cf. Gn 3²³ מִשָּׁם, Ex 21¹³ שָׁמָּה. But even in this case the retrospective word may be omitted, cf. Gn 35¹⁴, Nu 20¹³, Is 64¹⁰, where שָׁם would be expected, and Gn 30³⁸, Nu 13²⁷, 1 K 12², where שָׁמָּה would be expected.—When the appositional clause is added to a word of time, the retrospective pronoun is always omitted, e.g. 1 S 20³¹ *for all the days,* אֲשֶׁר בֶּן־יִשַׁי חַי *those—the son of Jesse is living* (*in them*); cf. Gn 45⁶, Dt 1⁴⁶, 9⁷, 1 K 11⁴²; see Baumann, op. cit., p. 33.

3. If the governing substantive forms part of a statement made in the *d* first or second person, the retrospective pronoun (or the subject of the appositional clause) is in the same person, e.g. Gn 45⁴ *I am Joseph,* אֲשֶׁר־מְכַרְתֶּם אֹתִי *he—ye sold me,* i.e. *whom ye sold;* Nu 22³⁰, Is 49²³; 41⁸ *thou, Jacob,* אֲשֶׁר בְּחַרְתִּיךָ *he—I have chosen thee;* Jer 32¹⁹, Ec 10¹⁶ᶠ·; Gn 15⁷ *I am the Lord,* אֲשֶׁר הוֹצֵאתִיךָ *he—I brought thee out,* &c., Ex 20² (Dt 5⁶).

(2) Not depending (adjectivally) on a governing substantive, but *e* itself expressing a substantival idea. Clauses introduced in this way may be called *independent relative clauses.* This use of אֲשֶׁר is generally rendered in English by *he who, he whom,* &c. (according to the context), or *that which,* &c., or sometimes *of such a kind as* (*qualis*), cf. Ex 14¹³ᵇ, and in a dependent relative clause Is 7¹⁷. In reality, however, the אֲשֶׁר is still a demonstrative belonging to the construction of the main clause as subject or object, or as a genitive dependent on a noun or preposition, e.g. Nu 22⁶ אֲשֶׁר תָּאֹר יוּאָר *iste—thou cursest* (him)—*is cursed,* i.e. *he whom thou cursest,* &c.; Ex 22⁸; [2] אֲשֶׁר as object, Gn 44¹,

---

[1] The instances in which, instead of a retrospective pronoun, the main idea itself is repeated (Gn 49³⁰, 50¹³, Jer 31³²) are most probably all due to subsequent amplification of the original text by another hand.

[2] The absolute use of אֲשֶׁר is very peculiar in the formula אֲשֶׁר הָיָה דְבַר יי׳ אֶל־ *this* (is it)—*it came as the word of the Lord to* ..., Jer 14¹, 46¹, 47¹, 49³⁴.

49¹, 1 S 16³ᶠᶠ·, Mi 6¹ (אֶת אֲשֶׁר); and even preceding the verb, e. g. Is 52¹⁵, ψ 69⁵; אֲשֶׁר as genitive, Ez 23²⁸ *I will deliver thee* בְּיַד אֲשֶׁר שָׂנֵאת *into the hand of those—thou hatest* (them); depending on a pre-position, e. g. לַאֲשֶׁר Gn 44⁴, 2 K 10²²; בַּאֲשֶׁר Gn 21¹⁷, שָׁם הוּא בַּאֲשֶׁר *in that* (place)—*he is there,* i. e. *where he is*; cf. Ju 17⁸ and Ru 1¹⁶ אֶל־אֲשֶׁר *whither*; ¹ 1 K 18¹² עַל־אֲשֶׁר *whither*; מֵאֲשֶׁר Ex 5¹¹.

f　From these examples it follows that in independent relative clauses the retrospective suffix, or adverb of place, may be, and in fact generally is, omitted. As a rule, however (as in the dependent relative clause), this does not apply to cases in which the retrospective pronoun, by the construction of the sentence, depends on a preposition,² e. g. Gn 44⁹ᶠ· וָמֵת ... אִתּוֹ יִמָּצֵא אֲשֶׁר *he—it* (the cup) *is found with him,—shall die* (for the *Wāw* of the apodosis in וָמֵת cf. § 143 *d*). In such cases אֲשֶׁר preceded by the preposition is quite anomalous, as in Gn 31³² תִּמְצָא אֲשֶׁר עִם *with whomsoever thou findest*, where אֲשֶׁר is a relative pronoun in the English sense; on the other hand, in Is 47¹² (and probably also 56⁴) בַּאֲשֶׁר is to be explained (with Baumann, op. cit., p. 37) by reference to 47¹⁵, as a demonstrative pronoun, *stand now with thine enchantments . . . , with those—thou hast laboured* (with them).

[With regard to the preceding explanation of אֲשֶׁר, the student will of course understand that, in Hebrew as we know it, אֲשֶׁר never occurs as a mere demonstrative. A particle which, whatever its origin, is uniformly used with reference to something in another, contiguous clause, will naturally have acquired in practice that force which we denote by the term 'relative'.]

g　Like the original demonstrative pronoun אֲשֶׁר, the demonstratives proper זֶה, זוֹ, זוּ (the last commonly),³ and sometimes the article, are used somewhat frequently in poetic language to introduce both dependent and independent relative clauses. With regard to the construction of זֶה, &c., the remarks on אֲשֶׁר, under *a* and *e*, also hold good.

Examples:—

(*a*) זֶה in apposition to a governing substantive in the nominative, ψ 104²⁶ בּוֹ־לְשַׂחֶק יָצַרְתָּ זֶה לִוְיָתָן (there is) *leviathan, he—thou hast formed* (him), i. e. *whom thou hast formed*; Is 42²⁴ (זוּ); in the accusative, Is 25⁹, ψ 74² (in both cases with a retrospective pronoun; זוּ is used without it in ψ 132¹²); in apposition to a genitive dependent on a preposition, Pr 23²² יְלָדֶךָ זֶה לְאָבִיךָ שְׁמַע *hearken unto thy father, him—he begat thee,* i. e. *who begat thee*; ψ 17⁹ (זוּ).—In ψ 104⁸ לָהֶם יָסַדְתָּ זֶה אֶל־מְקוֹם *unto the place which thou hadst founded for them* (cf. § 130 *c*), זֶה is in the genitive after the construct state מְקוֹם *to the place of that, thou hadst*

---

¹ In Zc 12¹⁰ also, instead of the unintelligible אלי את אשר, we should probably read אֶל־אֲשֶׁר, and refer the passage to this class.

² Such a strong ellipse as in Is 31⁶, where מִמֶּנּוּ would be expected after העמיקו, is only possible in elevated poetic or prophetic language.

³ The etymological equivalent דִּי, דְּ in Aramaic is always a relative.

founded (it) *for them*; on the same analogy we may also take, with Baumann (op. cit., p. 48), ψ 78⁵⁴ (חַר זֶה) and Ex 15¹³ (עַם־זוּ גָאָלְתָּ), 15¹⁶, Is 43²¹, ψ 9¹⁶, 10², 31⁵, 32⁸, 62¹², 142⁴, 143⁸ (all examples of זוּ).

To introduce independent relative clauses זֶה is used as a nominative in *h* Jb 19¹⁹; as accusative, Jb 15¹⁷ and זוּ Hb 1¹¹, ψ 68²⁹ (after a preposition, זֶה Ex 13⁸; but the text is evidently corrupt).

(*b*) More certain examples of the use of the article as a relative pronoun *i* (more correctly, perhaps, of the demonstrative which is otherwise used as article) are 1 Ch 26²⁸ כֹּל הַהִקְדִּישׁ שְׁמוּאֵל *all that Samuel had dedicated*, &c.; 1 Ch 29⁸ (where נִמְצָא can only be *perfect Niph'al*); 2 Ch 29³⁶, Ezr 10¹⁴. In connexion with a plural, Jos 10²⁴ *the chiefs of the men of war* הַהֹלְכוּ אִתּוֹ *who went with him*; Ezr 8²⁵, 10¹⁷, 1 Ch 29¹⁷. Finally, in the sense of *id quod*, Jer 5¹³ (where, however, we should read with the LXX הַדָּבָר). Cf. moreover, 1 S 9²⁴ *the thigh* וְהֶעָלֶיהָ *and that which was upon it* (but see *k* below); 2 Ch 1⁴ בַּהֵכִין equivalent to בַּאֲשֶׁר הֵכִין *to the place, that he had prepared.*

In all the examples adduced except 1 S 9²⁴ (where וְהֶעָלֶיהָ should probably *k* be read for וְהֶעָלֶיהָ) the הַ is followed by undoubted perfects; almost all the examples, moreover, belong to the latest Books (Ezra and Chronicles). On the other hand, another series of instances (even in the older texts) is extremely doubtful, in which the Masora likewise requires perfects, either by placing the tone on the penultima, as in Gn 18²¹, 46²⁷, Jb 2¹¹ הַבָּאָה; Is 51¹⁰ הַשָּׂמָה; Ez 26¹⁷ הַהֻלָּלָה Ru 1²², 2⁶ and 4³ הַשָּׁבָה, or by the punctuation, Gn 21³ הַנּוֹלַד; 1 K 11⁹, Dn 8¹ הַנִּרְאָה; Is 56³ הַנִּלְוָה, while no doubt the authors in all these cases intended participles (and in fact perfect participles, cf. § 116 *d*) with the article, thus הַבָּאָה, &c., Ez 26¹⁷ הַהֻלָּלָה for הַמְהֻלָּלָה according to § 52 *s*, and in the other examples הַנִּלְוָה, הַנִּרְאָה, הַנּוֹלַד.

§ 139. *Expression of Pronominal Ideas by means of Substantives.*

Analogous to the periphrases for expressing materials and attributes *a* by means of substantives (§ 128 *o* and *p*), is the use of substantives to represent certain kinds of pronominal ideas, for which no special expressions exist. Thus—

1. אִישׁ, אִשָּׁה *man, woman*, are used to express— *b*
(*a*) The idea of *each, every* (in the sense of each severally) with reference to persons,[1] and even animals (Gn 15¹⁰), e.g. Gn 10⁵, feminine Ex 3²²; אִישׁ is the object, e.g. in Jer 12¹⁵. On אִישׁ–אִישׁ cf. § 123 *c*.

In a few passages אִישׁ in the above sense is placed for the sake of emphasis *c* before the governing noun (always a substantive with a suffix), thus מִיַּד אִישׁ אָחִיו Gn 9⁵, according to the usual explanation, stands for מִיַּד אֲחֵי אִישׁ *at the hand of the brother of every man*. But although the explanation seems to be

---

[1] As a rule אִישׁ is used in the particularizing sense of *each man*, with the plural of the verb, e.g. Gn 44¹¹; sometimes, however, as subject to a verb in the singular, e.g. Gn 44¹³.

supported by Gn 42²⁵ and Nu 17¹⁷, it is inconceivable that such an inversion of *nomen regens* and *rectum* should occur. It is more likely, either that the second substantive is in apposition to אִישׁ (thus Gn 9⁵ *at the hand of every man, his brother*, [unless it is a combination of the two readings מִיַּד אִישׁ and [מִיַּד הָאָדָם]; similarly 15¹⁰ *and he laid each* or, more exactly, *one piece of it*, &c., and so probably also Nu 17¹⁷ *every one*, sc. *his name*), or אִישׁ precedes as a kind of *casus pendens*, and only receives its nearer definition from the following substantive with suffix; thus Gn 41¹², 42²⁵ (according to the context = *to every one in his sack*); 42³⁵, where צְרוֹר־כַּסְפּוֹ בְּשַׂקּוֹ is virtually the predicate of אִישׁ; Ex 12⁴, 28²¹, Nu 5¹⁰, 26⁵⁴, 2 K 23³⁵, and especially Zc 7¹⁰.[1]

d (*b*) *Any one, some one*, e.g. Gn 13¹⁶, Ct 8⁷, with a negative *no one*;[2] so after אֶל־ Ex 16¹⁹·²⁹; before לֹא Gn 23⁶ and frequently.—Instead of אִישׁ we sometimes find in a similar sense אָדָם *man, homo*, e.g. Lv 1² (cf. כְּאַחַד הָאָדָם *as any one else*, Ju 16⁷·¹¹), נֶפֶשׁ (*soul*) *person*, Lv 2¹, 5¹, &c., and in a neuter sense דָּבָר (prop. *word, thing*) for *anything*, Gn 18¹⁴, or כָּל־דָּבָר Lv 5², Nu 31²³. With a negative דָּבָר means *nothing*; thus after אַל־ Gn 19⁸; after לֹא Ec 8⁵.— Cf. finally, מֵאַחַד *any one*, Dt 15⁷; *anything*, Ez 18¹⁰ (but in Lv 4², 5¹³ מֵאַחַת) and the expressions noticed in § 144 *e*. The latter include also instances like Ez 18³² *I have no pleasure* בְּמוֹת הַמֵּת *in the death of him that dieth*, i.e. *of any man*.

e (*c*) In connexion with אָחִיו *his brother* or רֵעֵהוּ *his neighbour*, אִישׁ *one*, masc. (as אִשָּׁה *one*, fem., in connexion with אֲחוֹתָהּ *her sister* or רְעוּתָהּ *her neighbour*) is used to represent the ideas of *alter—alter, the one—the other*[3] (in reference to persons, animals, or things without life; see the Lexicon) or the idea of *one another*, e.g. Gn 13¹¹ *and they separated themselves* אִישׁ מֵעַל אָחִיו *the one from the other*; Ex 26³ *five curtains* (יְרִיעֹת fem.) *shall be coupled together* אִשָּׁה אֶל־אֲחֹתָהּ *one to another.*

f 2. נֶפֶשׁ *soul, person* expresses the idea of *self*,[4] both in the singular, Pr 19⁸·¹⁶, 29²⁴, Jb 18⁴ (in all cases נַפְשׁוֹ equivalent to *himself*) and in the plural, Jer 37⁹, &c. Similar to this is the use of בְּקִרְבָּהּ Gn 18¹² (prop. *in her inward part*) in the sense of *within herself*.[5]

---

[1] Cf. on the whole question the thorough discussion by Budde, *Die bibl. Urgeschichte*, p. 283 ff.: according to him, the words in Gn 9⁵ are to be rendered *at the hand of one another* (from men mutually) *will I require it*. [In support of this view, Budde points to Zc 7¹⁰ וְרָעַת אִישׁ אָחִיו אַל־תַּחְשְׁבוּ בִּלְבַבְכֶם, which in the light of 8¹⁷, וְאִישׁ אֶת־רָעַת רֵעֵהוּ אַל־תַּחְשְׁבוּ בִּלְבַבְכֶם, can only, he observes, be rendered 'and devise not *the hurt of one another* in your heart'. So also König, *Syntax*, § 33.]

[2] Cf. also אֵין־אִישׁ Gn 39¹¹. On the expression of the idea of *no one* by means of אַיִן with a following participle, see the *Negative Sentences*, § 152 *l*.

[3] Elsewhere זֶה . . . זֶה are used in a similar sense, Ex 14²⁰, Is 6³; also הָאֶחָד . . . הָאֶחָד 2 S 14⁶, or the substantive is repeated, e.g. Gn 47²¹ (*from one end . . . to the other end*).

[4] On the representation of this idea by pronouns, separate and suffixed, see § 135 *a, i* and *k*.

[5] In a similar way the idea of *self* in Arabic, as in Sanskrit (*átman*), is paraphrased by *soul, spirit*; in Arabic also by *eye*; in Rabbinic by גּוּף *body*,

3. עֶצֶם *bone* (then metaphorically for *substance*) expresses the idea of *self*, **g** *selfsame, very same*, in reference to *things* (as נֶפֶשׁ to persons, e.g. בְּעֶצֶם הַיּוֹם הַזֶּה *in the selfsame day*, Gn 7¹³, cf. Jos 10²⁷, Ez 24²; כְּעֶצֶם הַשָּׁמַיִם לָטֹהַר *as it were the very heaven for clearness*, Ex 24¹⁰; בְּעֶצֶם תֻּמּוֹ *in the very fullness of his strength* (= *in the midst of his full strength*), Jb 21²³.

4. The simple plural of words denoting time sometimes includes also the **h** idea of *a few, some*;[1] thus יָמִים *a few days*, Gn 24⁵⁵, 40⁴ (here even of a longer period, = *for some time*); Is 65²⁰, Dn 8²⁷ (on the other hand, Gn 27⁴⁴, 29²⁰ יָמִים אֲחָדִים; see § 96 under אֶחָד); שָׁנִים *some years*, Dn 11⁶·⁸.

גֶּרֶם or עֶצֶם *bone*, in Ethiopic and Amharic by *head*, in Egyptian by *mouth, hand*, &c.; cf. also the Middle High German *min lip, din lip*, for *ich, du*. However, נֶפֶשׁ in such cases is never (not even in Is 46² נַפְשָׁם *they themselves*) a merely otiose periphrasis for the personal pronoun, but always involves a reference to the *mental* personality, as affected by the senses, desires, &c.

[1] *Some* in reference to persons in Ex 16²⁰ is expressed by אֲנָשִׁים, and in Neh 5²⁻⁴ by יֵשׁ אֲשֶׁר *sunt qui*, with a participle following.

CHAPTER II

THE SENTENCE

I. The Sentence in General.

§ 140. *Noun-clauses, Verbal-clauses, and the Compound Sentence.*

a   1. Every sentence, the subject and predicate of which are nouns
or their equivalents (esp. participles), is called a *noun-clause*, e. g.
יְהוָה מַלְכֵּנוּ *the Lord is our king*, Is 33²²; וְאַנְשֵׁי סְדֹם רָעִים וְחַטָּאִים *now the
men of Sodom were wicked and sinners*, Gn 13¹³; פֶּה לָהֶם *a mouth is
theirs*, ψ 115⁵; see further, § 141.

b   2. Every sentence, the subject of which is a noun (or pronoun
included in a verbal-form) and its predicate a finite verb, is called
a *verbal-clause*, e. g. וַיֹּאמֶר אֱלֹהִים *and God said*, Gn 1³; וַיַּבְדֵּל *and he
divided*, 1⁷; see further, § 142.

c   Rem. In the last example the pronominal subject is at least indicated by
the preformative (י), and in almost all forms of the perfect by afformatives.
The 3rd pers. sing. perf. however, which contains no indication of the
subject, must also be regarded as a full verbal-clause.

d   3. Every sentence, the subject or predicate of which is itself a full
clause, is called a *compound sentence*, e. g. ψ 18³¹ הָאֵל תָּמִים דַּרְכּוֹ *God—
his way is perfect*, equivalent to *God's way is perfect*; Gn 34⁸ שְׁכֶם בְּנִי
חָשְׁקָה נַפְשׁוֹ בְּבִתְּכֶם *my son Shechem—his soul longeth for your daughter*;
see further, § 143.

e   4. The above distinction between different kinds of sentences—
especially between noun- and verbal-clauses—is indispensable to the
more delicate appreciation of Hebrew syntax (and that of the Semitic
languages generally), since it is by no means merely external or
formal, but involves fundamental differences of meaning.   Noun-
clauses with a substantive as predicate, represent something *fixed*,
a state or in short, *a being* so and so; verbal-clauses on the other
hand, something *moveable* and *in progress*, an *event* or *action*.   The
latter description is indeed true in a certain sense also of noun-clauses

with a participial predicate, except that in their case the event or
action (as distinguished from that expressed by the verbal-clause) is
of a fixed and abiding character.

Rem. By the Arab grammarians every clause beginning with an inde- *f*
pendent subject is regarded as a noun-clause, and every clause beginning
with a finite verb as verbal. If a finite verb follows the noun-subject the
two together (since the verb comprises its own subject and is thus a complete
verbal-clause) form a compound noun-sentence, just as when the predicate
consists of an independent noun-clause. Though this definition of the
different kinds of sentence, which we formerly accepted (in § 144 *a* of the
22nd to the 24th German editions of this Grammar), is rejected above, *a–d*,
we must, nevertheless, mention here the point in which this more complicated view of the Arab grammarians may be regarded as at least relatively
correct, namely, in classifying verbal-clauses according as the subject precedes
or follows the verb, a distinction which is often of great importance in Hebrew
also; see further, in § 142 *a*.

§ 141. *The Noun-clause.*

1. The *subject* of a noun-clause (see § 140 *a*) may be— *a*

(*a*) A substantive, e. g. וְנָהָר יֹצֵא מֵעֵדֶן *and a river went out* (was
going out) *of Eden,* Gn 2¹⁰.

(*b*) A pronoun, e. g. Gn 7⁴ אָנֹכִי מַמְטִיר *I will cause it to rain;* 14¹⁸
וְהוּא כֹהֵן *and he was priest;* 2²³ (זֹאת) before a feminine predicate, as
אֵלֶּה before a plural in Ex 32⁴); מִי חָכָם *who is wise?* Ho 14¹⁰.—In
1 Ch 5² וּלְנָגִיד מִמֶּנּוּ *and of him* one became *a prince,* the subject is
contained in מִמֶּנּוּ.¹

2. The *predicate* of a noun-clause may be— *b*

(*a*) A substantive, e. g. Dt 14¹ בָּנִים אַתֶּם וגו׳ *ye are children of the
Lord your God;* Gn 42¹³. Specially characteristic of the Semitic mode
of expression are the cases in which both subject and predicate are
substantives, thus emphasizing their identity ('the thing is its
measure, material, or equivalent'), e. g. Ez 41²² הַמִּזְבֵּחַ עֵץ . . . וְקִירֹתָיו עֵץ
the altar (was) *wood . . . , and the walls thereof* (were) *wood,* i. e. of
wood. Cf. below, *c.*

(*b*) An adjective or participle, e. g. Gn 2¹² וּזְהַב הָאָרֶץ הַהִיא טוֹב *and
the gold of that land is good;* וְעֶפְרוֹן יֹשֵׁב *now Ephron was sitting,* &c.,
Gn 23¹⁰.² Very frequently such noun-clauses, attached by *Wāw* to
a verbal-clause, are used to represent a state *contemporaneous* with
the principal action; cf. *e* below.

(*c*) A numeral, e. g. Gn 42¹³ שְׁנֵים עָשָׂר עֲבָדֶיךָ *the twelve* (of us) *are
thy servants.*

---

¹ For other remarkable instances of ellipse in the Chronicler, see Driver,
Introduction, ed. 8, p. 537, no. 27.
² Cf. the numerous examples in § 116 *n–p.*

(*d*) A pronoun, e. g. Gn 10¹² (הִיא), Ex 9²⁷ (אֲנִי), Gn 24⁶⁵ (מִי), 1 K 9¹³ (מֶה).¹

(*e*) An adverb or (esp. if formed with a preposition) any specification of time, place, quality, possessor, &c., which may be regarded as the equivalent of a noun-idea, e. g. שָׁם הַבְּדֹלַח *there is the bdellium*, Gn 2¹²; אֵי הֶבֶל *where is Abel?* 4⁹; לְעוֹלָם חַסְדּוֹ *his mercy endureth for ever*, ψ 136¹ᶠ·; עֹשֶׁר בְּבֵיתוֹ *riches* are *in his house*, ψ 112³; לוֹ אֲנַחְנוּ *we are his*, ψ 100³ *Qᵉrê.*

C Rem. 1. The employment of a substantive as predicate of a noun-clause is especially frequent, either when no corresponding adjective exists (so mostly with words expressing the material; cf. § 128 *o*) or when the attribute is intended to receive a certain emphasis. For in all cases there is a much greater stress upon a substantival predicate,² since it represents something as *identical* with the subject (see above, *b* [*a*]), than upon an adjectival or verbal predicate; cf. Ct 1¹⁰; ψ 25¹⁰ *all the paths of the Lord are* חֶסֶד וֶאֱמֶת *lovingkindness and truth* (i. e. *wholly lovingkindness*, &c.; cf. Jer 10¹⁰); Ez 38⁵, ψ 10⁵, 19¹⁰, 23⁵, 88¹⁹, Pr 3¹⁷,³ Jb 22¹², 23², 26¹³, Ru 3². Sometimes the emphasis on the predicate is obtained by the use of the plural form (according to § 124 *e*), e. g. ψ 110³ *thy people are* נְדָבֹת *altogether willingness*; Ct 5¹⁶, Dn 9²³.

d Sometimes the boldness of such combinations is modified by the repetition of the subject, as *regens* of the predicate, e. g. Jb 6¹² אִם־כֹּחַ אֲבָנִים כֹּחִי *is my strength the strength of stones?* Pr 3¹⁷. That the language, however—especially in poetry—is not averse even to the boldest combinations in order to emphasize very strongly the unconditional relation between the subject and predicate, is shown by such examples as ψ 45⁹ *myrrh and aloes and cassia* are *all thy garments* (i. e. so perfumed with them that they seem to be composed of them); Ct 1¹⁵ *thine eyes* are *doves*, i. e. dove's eyes (but 5¹² כְיוֹנִים);⁴ ψ 23⁵, 109⁴, Jb 8⁹, 12¹², Ct 2¹³. In prose, e. g. Ex 9³¹, Ezr 10¹³ הָעֵת וּשְׁמִים *the season* is *rain showers*, i. e. *the rainy season*; with a bold enallage of the number, Gn 34³⁰ וַאֲנִי מְתֵי מִסְפָּר *and I* (with my family) *am persons few in number.* For similarly bold expressions with הָיָה cf. Gn 11¹, 12², Ex 17¹², Is 5¹², Jer 2²⁸, and again with a bold enallage of the number, Jb 29¹⁵ *I was eyes to the blind, and feet was I to the lame*, but in prose, Nu 10³¹ *and thou shalt be to us* לְעֵינָֽיִם.

---

¹ Why in these examples the pronouns, notwithstanding appearances to the contrary, are to be considered as predicates and not as subjects, may be seen from what has been remarked above, § 126 *k*.

² The same naturally applies to most of those cases which are not pure noun-clauses, but have the substantival predicate connected with the subject by הָיָה (e. g. Gn 1² *and the earth was a waste and emptiness*; cf. ψ 35⁶, Pr 8³⁰, Jb 3⁴) or where a preposition precedes the substantival predicate, as ψ 29⁴ *the voice of the Lord is with power*, i. e. *powerful.*

³ שָׁלוֹם here, as in Jb 21⁹, is evidently a substantive after a plural subject; on the other hand, it is doubtful whether שָׁלֵו in such passages as Gn 43²⁷, 2 S 20⁹, ψ 120⁷, &c., is not rather to be regarded as an adjective.

⁴ As a rule, in such comparisons כְ (which is then to be regarded as *nominative*) stands before the predicate, e. g. Is 63² *wherefore* are *thy garments* כְּדֹרֵךְ בְּגַת *like* those of *one that treadeth in the wine-press?* (prop. *the like of one that treadeth, instar calcantis*); Jer 50⁹. The comparison is then much less emphatic than in the noun-clauses cited above.

2. The noun-clause connected by *wāw copulative* to a verbal-clause, or its *e* equivalent, always describes a state *contemporaneous* with the principal action, or (when the predicate is a transitive participle) an action represented in constant duration (cf. § 107 *d*, as well as § 116 *n* and *o*), e.g. Gn 19¹ *and the two angels came to Sodom at even,* וְלוֹט יֹשֵׁב *while Lot sat,* &c. ; 18¹·⁸·¹⁶·²²⁰, 25²⁶, Ju 13⁹, 1 S 1⁶, 2 S 4⁷, 11⁴ (always with a participle) ; with an adjectival predicate, Gn 18¹² ; with a substantival predicate, 18²⁷ ; with an adverbial predicate, 9²³. Not infrequently such a *circumstantial* clause indicates at the same time some contradictory fact, so that וְ is equivalent to *whereas, whilst, although,* e.g. Gn 15², 18²⁷, 20³, 48¹⁴ (*although he was the younger*) ; Ju 16¹⁵ *how canst thou say, I love thee,* וְלִבְּךָ אֵין אִתִּי *whereas thine heart is not with me ?* 2 S 3³⁹, ψ 28³ *whilst mischief is in their hearts.* These clauses describing a state are, however, only a subdivision of the large class of circumstantial clauses, on which see § 156.

3. As the examples given under *a* and *b* show, the syntactical *f* relation existing between the subject and predicate of a noun-clause is as a rule expressed by simple juxtaposition, without a *copula* of any kind. To what period of time the statement applies must be inferred from the context ; e. g. 1 K 18²¹ יְהוָֹה הָאֱלֹהִים *the Lord* is *the true God ;* 1 S 9¹⁹ ; Is 31² גַּם־הוּא חָכָם *yet he also* is *wise ;* Gn 42¹¹ ; on the other hand, Gn 19¹ וְלוֹט יֹשֵׁב *and* (=while) *Lot was sitting ;* Ez 28¹⁵ ; Gn 7⁴ אָנֹכִי מַמְטִיר *I am raining,* i. e. *I will rain.* Sometimes even a jussive or optative is to be supplied as predicate, Gn 27¹³ *upon me be thy curse ;* Gn 11³, 20¹³, Ex 12². Cf. § 116 *r*, note.

Not infrequently, however, a connexion is established between subject *g* and predicate (*a*) by adding the separate pronoun of the 3rd person singular or plural, expressly resuming and therefore strengthening the subject, or (*b*) (especially for the sake of a more exact specification of time) by the help of the verb הָיָה. The first of these will be a *compound* sentence, since the predicate to the main subject consists of an independent clause.

Examples of (*a*): Gn 41²⁶ *the seven good kine* שֶׁבַע שָׁנִים הֵנָּה *they* are *seven h years ;* Dt 1¹⁷, 4²⁴ ; Ec 5¹⁸ זֶה מַתַּת אֱלֹהִים הִיא *this—it* is *a gift of God ;* Nu 3²⁷ אֵלֶּה הֵם ; in a question, Gn 27³⁸. Sometimes הוּא is used in this way to strengthen a pronominal subject of the first or second person, and at the same time to connect it with the predicate which follows,[1] e. g. אָנֹכִי אָנֹכִי הוּא Is 43²⁵ *I, even I,* am *he that blotteth out,* &c. ; 51¹² ; אַתָּה הוּא 2 S 7²⁸, Is 37¹⁶, ψ 44⁵, Neh 9⁶·⁷ ; in an interrogative sentence, Jer 14²² ;[2] in Jer 49¹² הוּא in a *verbal*-clause strengthens אַתָּה.

---

[1] On a similar use of the separate pronoun of the third person in Aramaic (Dn 2³⁸, Ezr 5¹¹, &c.) see Kautzsch, *Gramm. des Bibl. Aram.*, § 87. 3.

[2] This is of course to be distinguished from the use of הוּא (to be inferred from the context) as predicate in the sense of ὁ αὐτός ; see above, § 135 *a*, note 1 ; or such cases as Dt 32³⁹ *see now* אֲנִי הוּא *that I, even I,* am *he ;* 1 Ch 21¹⁷.

i   Of (*b*): naturally this does not apply to the examples, in which הָיָה, in the sense of *to become, to fare, to exist*, still retains its full force as a verb, and where accordingly the sentence is verbal, and not a noun-clause; especially when the predicate precedes the subject. On the other hand, such examples as Gn 1² *and the earth was* (הָיְתָה) *waste and emptiness*, can scarcely be regarded as properly verbal clauses; הָיְתָה is used here really only for the purpose of referring to past time a statement which, as the description of a state, might also appear in the form of a pure noun-clause; cf. Gn 3¹. This is especially true of the somewhat numerous instances in which הָיָה occurs as a connecting word between the subject and the participial predicate; e. g. Ju 1⁷, Jb 1¹⁴ (immediately afterwards a pure noun-clause). The imperfect of הָיָה announces what is future in Nu 14³³, &c.; cf. § 116 *r*. However, especially in the latter case, הָיָה is not wholly without verbal force, but comes very near to being a mere copula, and this use is more frequent in the later books[1] than in the earlier.

k   Rem. On the employment of יֵשׁ *existence*, and אַיִן *non-existence*, which were originally substantives (on their tendency to be used as verbs, equivalent to *est*, and *non est*, cf. § 100 *o*, and the *Negative Sentences*, § 152) as a connecting link between a pronominal subject and a participial predicate (especially in conditional and interrogative sentences, Gn 24⁴²·⁴⁹, 43⁴, &c.), see above, § 116 *q*, and the various kinds of subordinate clauses mentioned in §§ 150, 159.

l   **4.** The natural *arrangement* of words in the noun-clause, as describing a state, is *subject—predicate*; the principal stress falls on the former since it is the object of the description. Very frequently, however (and not merely in poetry, where greater freedom is naturally allowed in the arrangement of words), the reverse order is found, i. e. *predicate—subject*. The latter order *must* be used when special emphasis is laid on the predicate,[2] or when it consists of an interrogative word; thus with a substantival predicate, e. g. Gn 3¹⁹ עָפָר אַתָּה *dust thou art*; 4⁹, 12¹³ (*my sister*, not my wife); 20²·¹², 29¹⁴, Is 6³ᵇ, Jb 5²⁴, 6¹²; with an adjectival predicate, e. g. Is 6³ᵃ, 28²¹, Jer 10⁶; with a participle, Gn 30¹, 32¹²; with an interrogative pronoun, e. g. Gn 24⁶⁵;[3] with an adverbial interrogative, e. g. Gn 4⁹.

m   Rem. On the above cf. the exhaustive investigations of C. Albrecht, 'Die Wortstellung im hebr. Nominalsatze,' *ZAW*. vii. 218 ff. and viii. 249 ff.; with a complete list of the exceptions to the order *subject—predicate*, p. 254 ff. The predicate *must* precede for the reasons stated (an *adjectival predicate* is particularly emphatic when it has the force of a comparative, e. g. Gn 4¹³; the predicate expressed by means of a preposition precedes most frequently when it serves to convey the ideas of *having, possessing*, e. g. Gn 18¹⁴, 29¹⁶, &c.; cf. also 26²⁰, 31¹⁶·⁴³).

n   The predicate *may* precede: (*a*) when the subject is a pronoun, for 'the person assumed to be generally known, does not excite the same interest as

---

[1] According to Albrecht, *ZAW*. viii. 252, especially in Deuteronomy and in the Priestly Code.

[2] For the same reason specifications of place (e. g. Gn 4⁷) or other adverbial qualifications may stand at the beginning of the sentence.

[3] The only exceptions, according to Albrecht (see the Rem. above), are Ex 16⁷·⁸.

that which is stated about him ;' (b) 'in order not to be a mere appendage to a subject which consists of several words,' e.g. 2 K 20¹⁹ ; (c) in interrogative sentences (with a substantival or adjectival predicate or one compounded with a preposition), e.g. 1 S 16⁴ ; finally (d) in a relative clause, when the predicate is adverbial or compounded with a preposition, as a rule closely united (by Maqqeph) with אֲשֶׁר, e.g. Gn 2¹¹ אֲשֶׁר־שָׁם ; 1²⁹ᶠ· אֲשֶׁר־בּוֹ.

§ 142. *The Verbal-clause.*

1. By § 140 f there is an essential distinction between verbal- *a* clauses, according as the subject stands before or after the verb.   In the verbal-clause proper the principal emphasis rests upon the action which proceeds from (or is experienced by) the subject, and accordingly the verb naturally precedes (*necessarily* so when it is in the perf. consec. or imperf. consec.).   Nevertheless, the subject does sometimes precede even in the verbal-clause proper, in the continuation of the narrative, e.g. Gn 7¹⁹, 1 S 18¹, 2 S 19¹² ; especially so if there is special emphasis upon it, e.g. Gn 3¹³ (it is not I who am to blame, but) *the serpent beguiled me*, cf. Gn 2⁵, &c.[1]   In the great majority of instances, however, the position of the subject at the beginning of a verbal-clause is to be explained from the fact that the clause is not intended to introduce a new fact carrying on the narrative, but rather to describe a *state*.   Verbal-clauses of this kind approximate closely in character to noun-clauses, and not infrequently (viz. when the verbal form might just as well be read as a participle) it is doubtful whether the writer did not in fact intend a noun-clause.

The particular *state* represented in the verb may consist—   *b*

(a) Of an act completed long before, to which reference is made only because it is necessary for understanding the sequel of the principal action. If the predicate be a perfect (as it almost always is in these cases), it is generally to be rendered in English by a pluperfect ; cf. the examples discussed above in § 106 f (1 S 28³, &c.) ; also Gn 6⁸ (not *Noah found grace*) ; 16¹, 18¹⁷, 20⁴, 24¹, 39¹ (*and Joseph* in the meanwhile *had been brought down to Egypt*) ; 41¹⁰, Ju 1¹⁶, 1 S 9¹⁵, 14²⁷, 25²¹, 1 K 1¹, &c.—In a wider sense this applies also to such verbal-clauses as Gn 2⁶ (see further, § 112 e), since when they serve to represent an action continuing for a long period in the past, and thus to some extent a state.

(b) Of a fact, contemporaneous with the principal events or continuing as *C* the result of them.   To the former class belong all those instances in which the predicate is combined with הָיָה (provided that הָיָה has not, as in Gn 1², 3¹, &c., been weakened to a mere copula, in which case the precedence of the subject is fully explained from the character of the clause as a noun-clause ; cf. § 141 i, and the examples of הָיָה, &c., with a participle, § 116 r) ; as an example of the second class, cf. e.g. Gn 13¹² אַבְרָם יָשַׁב בְּאֶרֶץ־כְּנַעַן וגו' *Abraham* accordingly *continued to dwell in the land of Canaan*, but *Lot dwelt*, &c.

---

[1] This of course applies also to the cases, in which the subject consists of a strongly emphasized personal pronoun, e.g. Gn 32¹³ אַתָּה *thou thyself* ; 33³ הוּא *he himself.*

d   Rem. 1. The close relation between verbal-clauses beginning with the subject and actual noun-clauses, is seen finally from the fact that the former also are somewhat frequently added with ֥ (or subordinated) to a preceding sentence in order to lay stress upon some accompanying circumstance; on such noun-clauses describing a *state* or *circumstance*, cf. § 141 *e*. This is especially the case, again, when the circumstantial appendage involves an antithesis; cf. Gn 18¹⁸ *seeing that* nevertheless *Abraham shall surely become*, &c.; 24⁵⁶, 26²⁷, Is 29¹³, Jer 14¹³, ψ 50¹⁷, Jb 21²², and such examples as Gn 4²·⁴, 29¹⁷, where by means of ֥ a new subject is introduced in express antithesis to one just mentioned. Moreover, in the examples treated above, under *b* and *c* (1 S 28³, &c.), the subject is frequently introduced by ֥, which then corresponds to the Greek δέ, used to interpose an explanation, &c., see Winer, *Gramm. des neutest. Sprachidioms*, § 53. 7 *b*.

e   2. By a peculiar construction verbal-clauses may be joined by means of ֥ and a following subject to participial clauses, e.g. Gn 38²⁵ הִיא מוּצֵאת וְהִיא שָׁלְחָה *she was already brought forth, when she sent*, &c.; 44³·⁴, Ju 18³, 19¹¹, 2 S 20⁸; for other examples, see § 116 *u* (where it is pointed out, note 1, that the apodosis also frequently appears in the form of a *noun*-clause, a further proof of the close relation between verbal-clauses beginning with the subject and noun-clauses proper). Without doubt there is in all these cases a kind of inversion of the principal clause and the temporal subordinate clause; the latter for the sake of greater emphasis being raised to an independent noun-clause, while the real principal action is added as though it were an accompanying circumstance, and hence in the form of an ordinary circumstantial clause. [Cf. Driver, *Tenses*, § 166 ff.]

f   2. According to what has been remarked above, under *a*, the natural *order of words* within the verbal sentence is: *Verb—Subject*, or *Verb—Subject—Object*. But as in the noun-clause (§ 141 *l*) so also in the verbal-clause, a variation of the usual order of words frequently occurs when any member of the sentence is to be specially emphasized by priority of position.[1] Thus the order may be :—

(*a*) *Object—Verb—Subject*: Gn 30⁴⁰, 37⁴, 1 S 15¹, 2 K 23¹⁹ and frequently. Naturally the examples are far more numerous, in which the object precedes a verbal form which includes the subject in itself, e.g. Gn 3¹⁰·¹⁴·¹⁸, 6¹⁶, 8¹⁷, 9¹³, Ex 18²³, Ju 14³, 1 S 18¹⁷, 20⁹, 21¹⁰, 2 K 22⁸, Pr 13⁵, &c.

(*b*) *Verb—Object—Subject*: Gn 21⁷, Nu 5²³, 1 S 15³³, 2 S 24¹⁶ (but הַמַּלְאָךְ is probably only a subsequent addition); Is 19¹³, ψ 34²², Jb 11¹⁹, &c.

(*c*) *Subject—Object—Verb*: Is 3¹⁷, 11⁸, 13¹⁸, Ho 12¹¹, ψ 6¹⁰, 11⁵, Jb 29²⁵.[2]

---

[1] Not infrequently also the striving after *chiasmus* mentioned in § 114 *r*, note, occasions a departure from the usual arrangement of words.

[2] This sequence occurs even in prose (Gn 17⁹, 23⁶, &c.); it is, however, more doubtful here than in the above prophetical and poetical passages, whether the preceding subject should not be regarded rather as the subject of a compound sentence (§ 143), the predicate of which is an independent verbal-clause; this would explain why the verbal-clause is usually separated from the subject by one of the greater disjunctives.—On the other hand, the sequence *Subject—Object—Verb* is quite common in Aramaic (e.g. Dn 2⁷·¹⁰); cf.

(d) *Object—Subject—Verb* (very rarely): 2 K 5¹³, Is 5¹⁷, 28¹⁷, ψ 51⁵, Pr 13¹⁶ (read כֹּל).[1]

(e) A substantival complement of the verb היה is placed first in Is 18⁵ וּבֹסֶר גֹּמֵל יִהְיֶה נִצָּה *and a ripening grape the flower becometh.*

Rem. Of specifications compounded with a preposition those of *place* stand *g* regularly after the verb, unless they are specially emphatic as e. g. Gn 19², 30¹⁶, 32⁵, Mi 5¹, Est 9¹² ; in Gn 29²⁵ בְרָחֵל with בְ *pretii* precedes for the sake of emphasis. Cf., however, in Gn 35¹³ the order *verb*—specification of *place— subject.*—The remoter object precedes for the sake of emphasis, e. g. in Gn 13¹⁵ (26³), 15³ ; even before the interrogative, Gn 27³⁷ (cf. Jer 22¹⁵ where the subject precedes an interrogative, and 1 S 20⁸, Jb 34³¹ where a prepositional specifi- cation precedes). — Prepositional specifications of *time*, such as בְּרֵאשִׁית (Gn 1¹), בַּתְּחִלָּה, בַּיּוֹם הַהוּא, &c. (but not בְּרִאשֹׁנָה, רִאשֹׁנָה, nor the simple רִאשֹׁנָה, לְעוֹלָם), stand, as a rule, before the verb, provided it be not in the perf. consec. or imperf. consec. ; so also certain adverbs of time, such as אָז, עַתָּה, whilst others like תָּמִיד, עוֹד regularly follow the verb.

§ 143. *The Compound Sentence.*

A compound sentence (§ 140 d) is formed by the juxtaposition of *a* a subject[2] (which always precedes, see *c*) and

(a) An independent noun-clause, which (α) refers to the principal subject by means of a pronoun, e. g. Na 1³ יְהֹוָה בְּסוּפָה דַרְכּוֹ *the Lord— in the storm is his way;* 2 S 23⁶, ψ 18³¹, 104¹⁷, 125², Ec 2¹⁴; cf. also Gn 34²³, where the predicate is an interrogative clause.—A personal pronoun is somewhat frequently used as the principal subject, e. g. Is 59²¹ וַאֲנִי זֹאת בְּרִיתִי אֹתָם *and as for me, this is my covenant with them,* &c.; Gn 9⁹, 17⁴, Is 1⁷, 1 Ch 28²;[3] with an interrogative noun-clause, Gn 37³⁰, Jb 21⁴, 38¹⁹:—or (β) is without a retrospective suffix (in which case naturally the connexion between the subject and predicate is much looser), e. g. 1 S 20²³ *and as touching the matter which,* &c. . . . *behold the Lord is between thee and me for ever;* Pr 27².

Gesenius, *Comm.* on Is 42²⁴, and Kautzsch's *Gramm. des Bibl. Aram.*, § 84. 1 b. The pure Aramaic usage of placing the *object* before the *infinitive* occurs in Hebrew in Lv 19⁹, 21²¹, Dt 28⁵⁶, 2 S 11¹⁹, Is 49⁶, 2 Ch 28¹⁰, 31⁷, 36¹⁹ (?).

[1] This sequence occurs more frequently in noun-clauses with a participial predicate, e. g. Gn 37¹⁶, 41⁹, 2 S 13⁴, &c., in interrogative sentences, e. g. 2 K 6²², Jer 7¹⁹ ; in all which cases the emphasized object is placed before the natural sequence of *subject—predicate.* [Cf. Driver, *Tenses*, § 208.]

[2] In Gn 31⁴⁰ a verbal-clause (הָיִיתִי *I was*) occurs instead of the subject, and is then explained by another verbal-clause.

[3] In 1 Chr 28² (cf. also 22⁷ אֲנִי (אֲנִי הָיָה עִם־לְבָבִי might also be taken as strengthening the pronominal suffix which follows (equivalent to *I myself had it in my mind*), as e. g. Ez 33¹⁷ *whereas their own way is not equal* ; cf. § 135 f.

b (*b*) An independent verbal-clause: (*a*) with a retrospective suffix,[1] e. g. Gn 9⁶ (cf. § 116 *w*); 17¹⁵ *as for Sarai thy wife, thou shalt not call her name Sarai*; 26¹⁵, 28¹³, 34³, Ex 30³⁷, 32⁵, 1 S 2¹⁰, 2 K 10²⁹, Is 9¹, 11¹⁰, Ez 33², Ho 9¹¹, ψ 11⁴, 46⁵, 65⁴, 74¹⁷, Dn 1¹⁷; with a pronoun as the principal subject, Gn 24²⁷; (*β*) without a retrospective suffix, Is 19¹⁷ *every one* that *mentions it* (Judah) *to it* (Egypt), *it* (Egypt) *is afraid.*

c Rem. 1. In all the above examples prominence is given to the principal subject (by its mere separation from the context by means of a greater disjunctive, as a *casus pendens*[2]) in a manner which would be quite impossible in a simple noun or verbal-clause (e. g. Na 1³ if it were דַּרְכּוֹ יְהֹוָה בְּסוּפָה); cf. the French *c'est moi qu'on a accusé.* But the statement or question contained in the clause which forms the predicate also receives greater weight. For the same purpose other members of the sentence also are sometimes placed at the beginning and resumed again by a following suffix; thus the object, Gn 13¹⁵, 21¹³, 35¹², 47²¹ (with the Samaritan and LXX read perhaps הֶעֱבִיר); 1 S 25²⁹; a specification of place, Gn 2¹⁷, 2 K 22¹⁸, &c.; a substantive with לְ, 1 S 9²⁰, 2 S 6²³; cf. the examples in § 135 *a*.—In Nu 15²⁹ a dative is co-ordinated with the *casus pendens*, i. e. there is a transition to a different construction.

d 2. To compound sentences belong also the numerous examples already treated in the account of the tenses, where the predicate of a *casus pendens* is introduced by the *wāw apodosis.* The isolation and prominence of the principal subject is in this case still more marked than in the instances treated above; on the *casus pendens* with a following imperfect consecutive (e. g. Jer 6¹⁹, 33²⁴), cf. § 111 *h*; with a following perfect consecutive (e. g. Ex 4²¹, 12⁴⁴, Nu 23³, 1 S 25²⁷, 2 S 14¹⁰, Is 9⁴, 56⁶ᶠ·), § 112 *t* and *mm*; on the participle as *casus pendens*, § 112 *oo* and § 116 *w*.—In Jb 15¹⁷ *wāw apodosis* follows with the cohortative; in Jb 23¹², ψ 115⁷, the imperfect is separated by לֹא from the *wāw apodosis*; in Jb 4⁶ as for *thy* hope, it is *the integrity of thy ways*, 36²⁶, Ec 5⁶, an incomplete noun-clause is appended by *wāw apodosis.* On *wāw apodosis* after disconnected specifications of time, cf. § 112 *oo* at the end, and Gn 40⁹, 2 S 15³⁴ וְעַתָּה וַאֲנִי עַבְדֶּךָ *and now* (so far as the present is concerned) *I will be thy servant*, Nu 12¹², Jer 4¹ (*me thou needest not fear*).

e 3. Sometimes a substantive introduced by לְ (*in respect to*; cf. § 119 *u*) serves the same purpose as the *casus pendens* beginning the sentence, as Nu 18⁸ (unless the לְ here serves to introduce the object, according to § 117 *n*); Is 32¹ (where, however, וְשָׂרִים should most probably be read); Ec 9⁴, 1 Ch 7¹, 24²⁰ᶠᶠ·, 2 Ch 7²¹. On the other hand, ψ 16³, 17⁴, 32⁶, 89¹⁹, 119⁹¹, are very doubtful. The suggestion of P. Haupt (*Johns Hopkins University Circulars*, xiii. no. 114; Baltimore, 1894) also deserves attention, that in passages like Ec 9⁴, and in לְכֹל Gn 9¹⁰, 23¹⁰, Ex 27³·¹⁹, Ez 44⁹, &c., לְ is not the preposition, but an emphasizing particle, answering to the Arab. *lă, surely*; Assyrian *lû*; with כֹּל it is equivalent to *in short*. Cf. also לְ--לְ *sive—sive, et—et*, Jos 17¹⁶, Ezr 1¹¹, Assyrian *lû—lû*.

---

[1] Cf. the Mêša' inscription, l. 31, *and Horonain, therein dwelt*, &c.

[2] But this term must not (any more than that formerly used 'the subject preceding *absolutely*') be misunderstood to mean that the principal subject is, as it were, floating in the air, and that the whole sentence results in an anacoluthon. On the contrary, to the Semitic mind, such sentences appear quite as correctly formed as ordinary noun- and verbal-clauses.

§ 144. *Peculiarities in the Representation of the Subject (especially in the Verbal-clause).*

1. According to § 40 ff. most forms of the finite verb include a *a* specification of the subject in the form of *personal afformatives* (in the imperfect also in the form of preformatives). Not infrequently, however, masculine forms are used in referring to feminines, e.g. וַיְדַעְתֶּם Ez 23⁴⁹; עֲשִׂיתָם Ru 1⁸; in the imperfect, Jo 2²², Ct 2⁷; in the imperative, Am 4¹, Zc 13⁷ (for other examples, see § 110 *k*). On emphasizing the pronominal subject by the addition of the separate pronoun, see § 135 *a* and *b*.

On the masculine as *prior gender*, cf. § 122 *g*; on similar anomalies in the use of the personal pronoun, § 135 *o*, in the connexion between substantive and adjective, § 132 *d*, between subject and predicate, § 145 *p, t, u*.

2. The third person singular is often used impersonally, especially *b* in the masculine, e.g. וַיְהִי *and it came to pass*, וְהָיָה *and it shall come to pass*; חָרָה followed by לוֹ, &c., *it became hot to him*, i.e. *he became angry*, Gn 4⁶, &c.; וַיֵּצֶר לוֹ lit. *and it became strait to him, he was distressed*, Gn 32⁸;¹ also in the feminine, e.g. 1 S 30⁶ (Ju 10⁹) וַתֵּצֶר לְדָוִד; Ju 11³⁹, Jer 7³¹, Ez 12²⁵, Jb 15³² (unless תְּמוּרָתוֹ in verse 31 be the subject); cf. also the impersonal passives, Is 1⁶ (רֻכְּכָה), 29⁶ (תִּפָּקֵד). Somewhat different are the instances in which the 3rd singular feminine occurs as the predicate of a feminine subject which is not mentioned, but is before the mind of the speaker, e.g. Is 7⁷, 14²⁴, Jer 10⁷, Jb 4⁵, 18¹⁵ (in 2 K 24⁷ כָּל־אֲשֶׁר is used in this way with a feminine predicate, and in Jer 19⁵ אֲשֶׁר alone); different, too, are the instances in which the 3rd singular masculine refers to an act just mentioned, e.g. Gn 17¹¹ וְהָיָה *and this* (the circumcision) *shall be a token of a covenant*, &c.

Rem. The expressions for natural phenomena may be either in the 3rd *c* sing. masculine or feminine, e.g. אוֹר *it becomes light*, 1 S 29¹⁰ (but with an explicit subject, Gn 44³); וַיָּאוֹר *and it became light*; so also יַחְשַׁךְ *it grows dark*, Jer 13¹⁶; but וְחָשְׁכָה Mi 3⁶; תָּעֻפָּה *though there be darkness*, Jb 11¹⁷; תַּמְטִיר *it rains*, Am 4⁷ (where, however, the context requires the reading אַמְטִיר); ψ 50³ נִשְׂעֲרָה *it is tempestuous*.

---

¹ In Arabic and Ethiopic the masculine is commonly used in this case, in Syriac the feminine.—The forms חַם *hot*, טוֹב *good, well*, מַר *bitter*, צַר *narrow*, רַע *evil* (frequently joined by לִי, לוֹ, &c.), which many regard as impersonal, are no doubt to be regarded in most cases not as forms of the 3rd pers. sing. perf., but, with Hupfeld on ψ 18⁷, as adjectives.

d　**3.** The indefinite personal subject (our *they, one,* the French *on,* and the German *man*[1]) is expressed—

(*a*) By the 3rd person singular masculine, e. g. קָרָא *one* (sc. any *one who named* it, see the Rem.) *called* (or *calls*) it, Gn 11⁹, 16¹⁴, 19²², Ex 15²³; וַיִּקְרָא Gn 35⁸·¹⁰, 2 S 2¹⁶, Is 9⁵; וַיֹּאמֶר *one said,* Gn 48¹, 1 S 16⁴;[2] other examples are Gn 38²⁸ *one put out a hand*; Nu 23²¹, 1 K 22³⁸, Is 6¹⁰ וְרָפָא לוֹ *and one heals them*; 8⁴ (יִשָּׂא); 46⁷ (יִצְעַק); Am 6¹², Mi 2⁴, Jb 27²³; by the 3rd singular feminine (יְלָדָה) Nu 26⁵⁹.

e　Rem. The Jewish commentators, following the Arab grammarians, usually explain these singulars by the addition of the participle (generally determinate) of the same stem, e. g. קָרָא הַקֹּרֵא. This view is supported by the fact that such a complement sometimes occurs, e. g. Is 16¹⁰ יִדְרֹךְ הַדֹּרֵךְ *the treader treads out,* for *one treads out*; 28⁴·²⁴ (*doth one plow continually?*); Dt 17⁶ (Ez 18³²), Dt 22⁸, 2 S 17⁹ (Ez 33⁴), Jer 9²³; with an indeterminate participle (as in Arabic, e.g. *qāla qāʾilun,* a *sayer says,* i. e. *some one says*), e. g. Nu 6⁹, Am 9¹; cf. above, § 116 *t,* and, on the whole question, Driver on 1 S 16⁴.

f　(*b*) Very frequently by the 3rd plural masculine, e. g. Gn 29² *for out of that well* יַשְׁקוּ *they* (i. e. people generally) *watered the flocks*; 26¹⁸, 35⁵, 41¹⁴, 49³¹, 1 K 1², Is 38¹⁶, Ho 12⁹, Jb 18¹⁸, 34²⁰, Est 2², Neh 2⁷.

g　Rem. The 3rd plur. also is sometimes used to express an indefinite subject, where the context does not admit of a human agent or at least not of several, e.g. Gn 34²⁷. In such a case the 3rd plur. comes to be equivalent to a passive, as very commonly in Aramaic (see Kautzsch's *Gramm. des Bibl. Aram.,* § 96. 1 *c*); e.g. Jb 7³ *wearisome nights* מִנּוּ־לִי *have they allotted to me* (equivalent to *were allotted to me*; to make 'invisible powers' the subject is a merely artificial device); Jb 4¹⁹, 6², 18¹⁸, 19²⁶, 34²⁰, Ez 32²⁵, ψ 63¹¹, Pr 2²² (in parallelism with a passive); 9¹¹.

h　(*c*) By the 2nd singular masculine, e. g. Is 7²⁵ לֹא־תָבוֹא שָׁמָּה *one will* (or *can*) *not come thither* (prop. *thou wilt* . . .); Jer 23³⁷, Pr 19²⁵, 30²⁸ (unless the reading should be תִּתְפֹּשׂ). Cf. also עַד־בֹּאֲךָ or simply בֹּאֲךָ (Gn 10¹⁹·³⁰, 13¹⁰ בֹּאֲכָה) prop. *until thy coming,* i. e. *until one comes.*

i　(*d*) By the plural of the participle, e. g. Jer 38²³ *and all thy wives and thy children* מוֹצִאִים (prop. *are they bringing out*=) *they will bring out,* &c.; cf. Is 32¹², Ez 13⁷, Neh 6¹⁰ (*for some are coming to slay thee*)

---

[1] In 1 S 9⁹ הָאִישׁ (prop. *the man*) is used in exactly the same sense as our *one.*

[2] Elsewhere in such cases וַיֹּאמְרוּ usually occurs (but not in the perfect, e. g. 1 S 23²²), so that it is doubtful whether the present reading of Gn 48¹, &c., would not be better explained according to § 7 *d,* note. In Gn 48² for the extraordinary וַיַּגֵּד the common form וַיֻּגַּד is to be read; so in 50²⁶ for וַיִּישֶׂם (after a plural) either וַיִּישַׂם or the 3rd plur.; in 2 K 21²³ וַיִּקְבְּרוּ.

and the passages discussed above, § 116 t.[1] In 1 K 5¹ the text is corrupt.

(e) By the passive, e. g. Gn 4²⁶ אָז הוּחַל לִקְרֹא *then* (*was it begun=*) *k* *began men to call upon*, &c. (but read זֶה הֵחֵל *he began*).

4. A peculiar idiom, and one always confined to poetic language, *l* is the not infrequent occurrence of two subjects in a verbal sentence,[2] one of the person and the other of the thing. The latter then serves —whether it precedes or follows—to state the instrument, organ, or member by which the action in question is performed, and may be most often rendered in English by an adverb, as a nearer definition of the manner of the action. All the examples of this kind have this in common, that the subject denoting the thing takes a suffix in the same person as the personal subject.[3] They are thus distinguished from the *accusatives* treated in § 117 s, with which they are often confused.

(a) Examples where the subject denoting the *thing* precedes, קוֹלִי אֶל־יְהֹוָה *m* אֶקְרָא *my voice—I cry unto the Lord*, i. e. *I cry aloud unto the Lord*, ψ 3⁵, 27⁷, 142² ; פִּי־קָרָאתִי *my mouth—I cried*, i. e. *I cried aloud*, ψ 66¹⁷ (cf. 17¹⁰) ; Is 26⁹ נַפְשִׁי *with my soul*, i. e. *fervently*, and parallel with it אַף־רוּחִי ; but נַפְשִׁי ψ 57⁵ is rather a periphrasis for the 1st pers. *I*.

(b) Where the subject denoting the *thing* follows, צַהֲלִי קוֹלֵךְ *cry—thy voice* (i. e. aloud), Is 10³⁰ ; so also after an imperative, ψ 17¹³ (חַרְבֶּךָ) and verse 14 (יָדְךָ) ; 60⁷, 108⁷ (יְמִינְךָ) ; after a perfect, Hb 3¹⁵ (סוּסֶיךָ) ; after a cohortative, ψ 108² (אַף־כְּבוֹדִי). The subject denoting the *thing* stands between the personal subject and the predicate in ψ 44³ אַתָּה יָדְךָ.[4]

Rem. 1. Sometimes (as in other languages) an action is ascribed to a *n* subject which can only have been performed at his direction by another

---

[1] That this form of expression also (see *g*) comes to be equivalent to a passive is seen from the analogy of such Aramaic passages as Dn 4²², which exclude any idea of human agency. Cf. Kautzsch, *Gramm. des Bibl. Aram.*, § 76. 2 *e* at the end, and in post.-bibl. Hebrew, e. g. *Pirqê Aboth* 2, 16 ; 3, 5, &c.

[2] Two subjects occur in a noun-clause in ψ 83¹⁹.

[3] In Ex 6³ שְׁמִי is subordinated to the following passive נוֹדַעְתִּי (§ 121 *b*) ; in 1 S 25²⁶·³³ יָדִי, יָדְךָ are subjects to the infinitive absolute הוֹשֵׁעַ, according to § 113 *gg*. In ψ 69¹¹ read וָאֶעֱנֶה for וָאֶבְכֶּה.

[4] In several of the above examples it might naturally be supposed that the subject denoting the thing (especially when it follows the verb) is to be explained rather as a *casus instrumentalis*, i. e. as an accusative, analogous to the adverbial accusatives in § 118 *q*. But although it is true that the subject denoting the thing often defines more closely the manner in which the action is performed, and although in similar (but still different) examples, ψ 89², 109³⁰, Jb 19¹⁶, פִּי occurs with בְּ *instrumentale*, the explanation given above must nevertheless be accepted.

person ; cf. e. g. Gn 40²² (41¹³), 41¹⁴, 43³⁴ (*and he commanded to set before them,* &c.) ; 46²⁹, 2 S 12⁹.

O   2. Supposed ellipses of a definite subject are due either to a misunderstanding of the passage, or to a corruption of the text.   Thus in 1 S 24¹¹ after וְתָּחָם either עֵינַי has dropped out (through confusion with עָלֶיךָ) or we should read with the LXX וָאָחֹם. In 2 S 13³⁹ (וַתְּכַל דָּוִד) the text is obviously corrupt.

p   3. In poetic (or prophetic) language [1] there sometimes occurs (supposing the text to be correct) a more or less abrupt transition from one person to another.   Thus from the 2nd to the 3rd (i. e. from an address to a statement), Gn 49⁴ (?), Is 31⁶ (?), 42²⁰, 52¹⁴, 61⁷, Mal 2¹⁵ (where, however, for יָבֹד we should undoubtedly read תִּבְגֹּד) ; ψ 22⁹ [and regularly after a vocative, Is 22¹⁶, 47⁸, 48¹, 54¹·¹¹, Jer 22¹⁶, 49⁴·¹⁶, Am 5⁶ᶠ·, Mic 1² (= 1 K 22²⁸), Mal 3⁹, 2 K 9³¹ ; and after הוֹי Is 5⁸, 29¹⁵, Jer 22¹³].   From the 3rd to the 2nd pers., Dt 32¹⁵, Is 1²⁹ (but read probably חֲמַדְתֶּם for חֲמַדְתָּם, which has caused the insertion of אֲשֶׁר), 5⁸, Jer 29¹⁹, Jb 16⁷, cf. also Dt 32¹⁷.   From the 1st to the 3rd pers., La 3¹ (in a relative clause).   In Jb 13²⁸ the 3rd pers. וְהוּא is probably employed δεικτικῶς for the 1st.

§ 145. *Agreement between the Members of a Sentence, especially between Subject and Predicate, in respect of Gender and Number.*

a   1. As in other languages, so also in Hebrew, the predicate in general conforms to the subject in gender and number (even when it is a pronoun, e. g. זֹאת בְּרִיתִי *this is my covenant,* Gn 17¹⁰).   There are, however, numerous exceptions to this fundamental rule.   These are due partly to the *constructio ad sensum* (where attention is paid to the meaning rather than to the grammatical form ; see *b–l* below), partly to the position of the predicate (regarded as being without gender) *before* the subject.

b   2. Singular nouns which include in themselves a collective idea (§ 123 *a*), or which occasionally have a collective sense (§ 123 *b*), may readily, in accordance with their meaning, be construed with the plural of the predicate, whether it precedes or follows.   This is also the case, when the collective is itself feminine but represents, exclusively or at least generally, masculine persons.

Examples:—

c   (*a*) Of collectives proper (cf. § 132 *g*) : (α) with the predicate preceding, Gn 30³⁸ תֵּלַאןָ הַצֹּאן (cf. 30³⁹, 31⁸ and 33¹³) ; Ju 1²²ᶠ· בַּיִת representing persons belonging to the tribe ; Mi 4³ גּוֹי ; 2 K 25⁵ חַיִל *army* ; Pr 11²⁶ לְאֹם

---

[1] In prose, Lv 2⁸ ; but וְהִקְרִיבָהּ here is hardly the original reading.   Different from this is Gn 26⁷, where there is a transition to direct narration.

the people; Nu 10³ כָּל־הָעֵדָה *all the congregation* (cf. 1 K 8⁵); 1 K 1⁴⁰, Is 9⁸, 25³, Am 1⁵ עָם; 1 S 17⁴⁷, Ezr 10¹² קָהָל *assembly.* Cf. also the construction of national names, as אֲרָם (§ 122 *i*), e. g. 1 K 20²⁰ וַיָּנֻסוּ אֲרָם *and the Syrians fled*; 1 S 4⁵.—(β) with the predicate following, 1 K 8⁵ צֹאן וּבָקָר *sheep and oxen*, construed with the plural in the following relative clause; Jb 1¹⁴ הַבָּקָר הָיוּ חֹֽרְשׁוֹת *the cattle* (cows) *were ploughing*; 2 S 3¹ and 1 Ch 10⁶ בַּיִת=*family* (in 1 S 6¹³ בֵּית שֶׁמֶשׁ on the analogy of names of countries, is used for *the inhabitants of Bethshemesh*); Ho 11⁷, Ezr 4⁴ עָם; ψ 68¹¹ חַיָּה *herd* [if correct, figuratively for *people*]; Is 26¹⁹ נְבֵלָה *dead bodies*; Is 27¹¹ קָצִיר *boughs*; 1 S 4¹ יִשְׂרָאֵל, preceded by a predicate in the singular.

(*b*) Of substantives occasionally used as collectives: (*a*) with the predicate *d* preceding, Gn 34²⁴ זָכָר; Ju 9⁵⁵, 15¹⁰ אִישׁ; Is 16⁴ רֹמֵס *the treader down.*—(β) with the predicate following, Jb 8¹⁹ אַחֵר=*others*; Ez 28³ סָתוּם *a secret*; [ψ 9⁷, and even after זֶה Jb 19¹⁹.]

(*c*) Of feminines as collective terms denoting masculine persons: (*a*) with *e* the predicate preceding, 1 S 17⁴⁶ וְיֵדְעוּ כָּל־הָאָרֶץ *that all the earth may know*, i. e. all the inhabitants of the earth; cf. Dt 9²⁸, ψ 66¹, 96¹·⁹, &c.; Am 1⁸ שְׁאֵרִית *remnant*; (ψ 33⁸ כָּל־הָאָרֶץ).—(β) with the predicate following, Gn 41⁵⁷, 2 S 15²³, 1 K 10²⁴, Gn 48⁶ מוֹלֶדֶת *issue*; 1 S 2³³ כָּל־מַרְבִּית *all the increase*; Jb 30¹² פִּרְחָח *rabble.* In Hag 2⁷ read חֶמְדַת with the LXX.

Examples of predicates in the singular, notwithstanding the collective *f* meaning of the subject, occur in Gn 35¹¹, Ex 10²⁴, 14¹⁰, Dt 1³⁰, &c.—For examples of bold enallage of the number in noun-clauses with a substantival predicate, see above, § 141 *c*.

Rem. Not infrequently the construction begins in the singular (especially *g* when the predicate precedes; see *o* below), but is carried on, after the collective subject has been mentioned, in the plural; e. g. Ex 1²⁰ וַיִּרֶב הָעָם וַיַּֽעַצְמוּ מְאֹד *and the people multiplied, and waxed very mighty*; 33⁴.

3. On the other hand, plurals which have a singular meaning *h* (§ 124 *a*) are frequently construed with the singular, especially the *pluralis excellentiae* or *maiestatis* (§ 124 *g–i*; on the union of these plurals with attributes, cf. § 132 *h*), as אֱלֹהִים Gn 1¹·³, &c. (but see the Rem.), אֲדֹנִים *master*, Ex 21⁴ בְּעָלִים *master, owner*, Ex 21²⁹; cf., moreover, פָּנִים with the singular, Jb 16¹⁶ *K*ᵉ*th.*, Pr 12¹⁰.—So feminine forms with a masculine meaning are construed with a masculine predicate, e. g. Ec 12⁹ הָיָה קֹהֶלֶת חָכָם *the preacher was wise.*

Rem. The construction of אֱלֹהִים *God* with the plural of the predicate may *i* be explained (apart of course from such passages as 1 K 19², 20¹⁰, where the speakers are heathen, and אֱלֹהִים may, therefore, be a numerical plural) partly as an acquiescence in a polytheistic form of expression, partly from the peculiar usage of one of the early documents of the Hexateuch, called *E* by Wellhausen, &c., *B* by Dillmann; cf. his commentary on Numbers—Joshua, p. 618, and above, § 124 *g*, note 2. So Gn 20¹³ (but in conversation with a heathen); 31⁵³, 35⁷, cf. also Jos 24¹⁹. That this construction was afterwards studiously avoided from fear of misconception, is shown by such passages as Neh 9¹⁸ compared with Ex 32⁴·⁸, and 1 Ch 17²¹ compared with 2 S 7²³. Cf. Strack's excursus on Gen 20¹³ in *Die Genesis*, Munich, 1905, p. 77.

k **4.** Plurals of names of animals or things, and of abstracts, whether they be masculine or feminine, are frequently construed with the feminine singular of the verbal predicate [1] (on the collective sense of the feminine form, cf. § 122 *s*); thus Jo 1²⁰ בְּהֲמוֹת שָׂדֶה תַּעֲרֹג *the beasts of the field long*; Jer 12⁴ (where the predicate precedes), cf. also Jb 12⁷; names of things with the predicate preceding occur in 2 S 24¹³, Is 34¹³, Jer 4¹⁴, 51²⁹, ψ 18³⁵, 37³¹, 73² *K*ᵉ*th.*, 103⁵ (unless הַמְחֻדָּשׁ is to be read for תִּתְחַדֵּשׁ), Jb 14¹⁹, 27²⁰; with the predicate following, Gn 49²² (בָּנוֹת=*branches*); Dt 21⁷, 1 S 4¹⁵ (וְעֵינָיו קָמָה),[2] 2 S 10⁹, Is 59¹², Jer 2¹⁵ *K*ᵉ*th.*, 48⁴¹, 49²⁴, Pr 15²², 20¹⁸, Jb 41¹⁰.[3]

l **5.** Moreover, the plural of persons (especially in the participle) is sometimes construed with the singular of the predicate, when instead of the whole class of individuals, each severally is to be represented as affected by the statement. Undoubted examples of this *distributive* singular are Gn 27²⁹ (Nu 24⁹) אֹרְרֶיךָ אָרוּר וּמְבָרֲכֶיךָ בָּרוּךְ *those that curse thee, cursed be* every one of them, *and those that bless thee, blessed be* every one of them; Ex 31¹⁴, Lv 17¹⁴ and 19⁸ (in both places the Samaritan has אֹכְלוֹ); Is 3¹² unless נֹשָׁיו is to be regarded as a *pluralis maiestatis* according to § 124 *k*; Pr 3¹⁸.³⁵ (?), 18²¹ (?), 21²⁷ᵇ, 27¹⁶, 28¹ᵇ, 28¹⁶ *K*ᵉ*th.*

m Rem. Analogous to the examples above mentioned is the somewhat frequent[4] use of suffixes in the singular (distributively) referring to plurals; cf. the *verbal*-suffixes in Dt 21¹⁰, 28⁴⁸, Am 6¹⁰; and the *noun*-suffixes in Is 2⁸, 30²², Jer 31¹⁴, Ho 4⁸ (but since וֹ follows, נַפְשׁוֹ is undoubtedly a dittography for נֶפֶשׁ), Zc 14¹², ψ 5¹⁰ (where, however, פִּימוֹ is clearly to be read with all the early versions); 62⁵, 141¹⁰ (?), Jb 38³², Ec 10¹⁵ [but LXX הַכְּסִיל]; finally, the suffixes with prepositions in Is 2²⁰ אֲשֶׁר עָשׂוּ־לוֹ *which they made* each one *for himself* (according to others, *which they (the makers) made for him*); 5²⁶, 8²⁰, Jb 24⁵, in each case לוֹ; in Gn 2¹⁹ לוֹ refers to the collectives חַיָּה and עוֹף; cf. further, Jos 24⁷, Is 5²³ מִמֶּנּוּ after צַדִּיקִים (but read probably צַדִּיק with the LXX, &c.). Conversely in Mi 1¹¹ עָבְרִי לָכֶם [cf. Jer 13²⁰ *K*ᵉ*th.*], but the text is undoubtedly corrupt.

---

[1] Cf. in Greek the construction of the neuter plural with the singular of the predicate τὰ πρόβατα βαίνει; in Attic Greek the plural of the predicate is allowed only when the neuter denotes actual persons, as τὰ ἀνδράποδα ἔλαβον. In Arabic also the *pluralis inhumanus* (i. e. not denoting persons) is regularly construed with the feminine singular of the attribute or predicate, as are all the *plurales fracti* (properly collective forms).

[2] On the possibility of explaining forms like קָמָה as 3rd plural feminine, cf. above, § 44 *m*; but this explanation would not apply to all the cases under this head, cf. Jo 1²⁰, ψ 37³¹, 103⁵.

[3] In Pr 14¹ an abstract plural חָכְמוֹת (to be read thus with 9¹, &c., instead of חַכְמוֹת) is construed with the singular; but cf. § 86 *l*, § 124 *e*, end.

[4] In several of the above examples the text is doubtful, and hence Mayer Lambert (*REJ.* xxiv. 110) rejects the theory of distributive singulars generally. [Cf. Driver, *Jeremiah*, p. 362, on 16⁷.]

6. Subjects in the dual are construed with the plural of the predicate, *n* since verbs, adjectives, and pronouns, according to § 88 *a*, have no dual forms; thus עֵינַיִם, Gn 29¹⁷ וְעֵינֵי לֵאָה רַכּוֹת *and Leah's eyes were dull*; 2 S 24³, Is 30²⁰, Jer 14⁶, Mi 7¹⁰, ψ 18²⁸, 38¹¹ (on the other hand, in 1 S 4¹⁵ the predicate is in the feminine singular *after* the subject, and in Mi 4¹¹ *before* it; on both constructions cf. *k* above); so also אָזְנַיִם *ears*, 2 Ch 6⁴⁰; יָדַיִם *hands*, Is 1¹⁵, Jb 10⁸, 20¹⁰ (in Ex 17¹² even with the plural masculine כְּבֵדִים; cf. *p*); שְׂפָתַיִם *lips*, 1 S 1¹³, Jb 27⁴; שָׁדַיִם *breasts*, Ho 9¹⁴.

7. Variations from the fundamental rule (see above, *a*) very fre- *o* quently occur *when the predicate precedes the subject* (denoting animals or things ¹). The speaker or writer begins with the most simple form of the predicate, the uninflected 3rd singular masculine, and leaves us without indication as to which of the following subjects (and so which gender or number) is to define the predicate thus left temporarily indefinite.² Thus inflexions are omitted in—

(*a*) The verb, with a following singular feminine, Is 2¹⁷ וְשַׁח גַּבְהוּת הָאָדָם *and bowed down shall be the loftiness of man*; 9¹⁸, 14¹¹, 28¹⁸, 47¹¹; 1 S 25²⁷ (see note 1 below); 1 K 8³¹ᵇ, 22³⁶, 2 K 3²⁶, Jer 51⁴⁶, Ec 7⁷; with a following plural masc., Is 13²² וְעָנָה אִיִּים *and there shall cry wolves*, &c.; Ju 13¹⁷ *Kᵉth.*, 20⁴⁶, 1 S 1², 4¹⁰, 2 S 24¹⁵, 1 K 13³³, Jer 51⁴⁸, ψ 124⁵, Est 9²³ (see note 1 below); Gn 1¹⁴ יְהִי מְאֹרֹת *let there be lights*; with a following plural feminine, Dt 32³⁵, 1 K 11³ᵃ, Is 8⁸, Jer 13¹⁸, Mi 2⁶, ψ 57²; before collectives and mixed subjects, e. g. Gn 12¹⁶, 13⁵, 30⁴³, 32⁶, &c.; before a following dual, Is 44¹⁸, ψ 73⁷ (where, however, with the LXX עֵינָמוֹ should be read).

Rem. 1. The instances in which a preceding predicate appears in the *p* plural masculine before a plural (or collective singular) feminine of persons (Ju 21²¹, 1 K 11³ ᵇ), of animals (Gn 30³⁹ where however יֵצְאוּ may refer specially to male animals) or of things (Lv 26³³, Jer 13¹⁶, Ho 14⁷, ψ 16⁴, Jb 3²⁴, Ct 6⁹), or before a dual (2 S 4¹, Zp 3¹⁶, 2 Ch 15⁷) are to be explained not on the analogy of the examples under *o*, but from a dislike of using the 3rd plur. fem. imperf., for this is the only form concerned in the above examples (cf., however, Na 3¹¹ תְּהִי instead of תְּהְיֶי); cf. the examples of a following predicate in the 3rd plur. masc., instead of the fem., under *t* and *u*, and on an analogous phenomenon in the imperative, see § 110 *k*.

2. As in the case of verbs proper so also the verb הָיָה, when used as a *q* copula, frequently remains uninflected before the subject; cf. Gn 5²³ ᶠᶠ, 39⁵,

_____

¹ Only rarely does an uninflected predicate precede a personal subject, as 1 S 25²⁷ (but הֱבִיאָה should probably be read, as in verse 35); Est 9²³ (before a plur. masc.). Such examples as Jb 42¹⁵ are to be explained according to § 121 *a*.

² In a certain sense this is analogous to the German *es kommt ein Mann, eine Frau*, &c.

Dt 21³ (according to the accents) ; 22²³, Is 18⁵ וּבֹסֶר גֹּמֵל יִהְיֶה נִצָּה *and a ripening grape the flower becometh.*

r   (*b*) The adjective in a noun-clause, e.g. ψ 119¹³⁷ יָשָׁר מִשְׁפָּטֶיךָ *upright* are *thy judgements*; cf. verse 155.[1]—On the other hand, רֹעֵה in רֹעֵה צֹאן עֲבָדֶיךָ *thy servants are shepherds*, Gn 47³, is either an unusual orthography or simply a misspelling for רֹעֵי.

s   Rem. 1. As soon as a sentence which begins with an uninflected predicate is carried on after the mention of the subject, the gender and number of the subsequent (co-ordinate) predicates must coincide with those of the subject, e.g. Gn 1¹⁴ יְהִי מְאֹרֹת . . . וְהָיוּ (see *o* above) ; Nu 9⁶, Ez 14¹ ; cf. also Gn 30³⁹ (see *p* above).

t   2. The dislike mentioned in *p* above, of using the feminine form (cf., further, § 144 *a*, with the sections of the Grammar referred to there, and below, under *u*), is exemplified sometimes by the fact that of several predicates only that which stands next to the feminine substantive is inflected as feminine (cf. the treatment of several attributes following a feminine substantive, § 132 *d*); thus in Is 14⁹ רָגְזָה, and afterwards עוֹרֵר (but עֹרֵר is better taken as an infin. abs. = *excitando*, reading הֵקִם for הֵקִים) ; 33⁹ אָבַל אֻמְלְלָה אָרֶץ *mourneth, languisheth the land.* Cf. Jer 4³⁰, Jb 1¹⁹, and the examples (§ 47 *k*) where only the first of several consecutive forms of the 2nd sing. fem. imperf. has the afformative *î*, Is 57⁸, Jer 3⁵, Ez 22⁴, 23³² (תִּהְיֶה after תִּשְׁתִּי) ; on the converse sequence of genders in imperatives, Na 3¹⁵, cf. § 110 *k*.—Of a different kind are instances like Lv 2¹, 5¹, 20⁶, where נֶפֶשׁ *person* (fem.) as the narrative continues, assumes (in agreement with the context) the sense of a masculine person.

u   3. The instances in which the gender or number of the *following* predicate appears to differ from that of the subject are due partly to manifest errors in the text, e.g. Gn 32⁹ read with the Samaritan הָאֶחָד instead of הָאַחַת ; וְהָיָה then follows correctly ; 1 S 2²⁰ read with Wellhausen שָׁאַל, according to 1²⁸, instead of שָׁאֵל ; 1 S 16⁴ read וַיֹּאמְרוּ ; Ez 18²⁹ instead of יִתָּכֵן read the plural as in verse 25 ; so also Ez 20³⁸ for יָבוֹא,[2] and in Jb 6²⁰ for בָּטַח ; in La 5¹⁰ read נִכְמָר, and cf. in general, § 7 *d*, note ; 1 Ch 2⁴⁸ read יָלְדָה ; in Jer 48¹⁵ also the text is certainly corrupt. Other instances are due to special reasons. The anomalies in Is 49¹¹, Ho 14¹, Pr 1¹⁶ (after רַגְלָיו), ψ 11⁴ (after עֵינָיו), 63⁴, Pr 5², 10²¹·³² 18⁶, 26²³, Jb 15⁶ (all after שְׂפָתַיִם), Pr 3² (after מִצְוֹתַי), ψ 102²⁸, Jb 16²² (after שָׁנוֹת), Dn 11⁴¹ (read וְרַבּוֹת), and perhaps Gn 20¹⁷ are also to be explained (see *p*) from the dislike of the 3rd plur. fem. imperf. ; moreover, in Jer 44¹⁹, Pr 26²³ the plur. masc. even of a participle occurs instead of the plur. fem.—In Gn 31⁸ ͟ᶠ· יִהְיֶה, after a plural subject, is explained as a case of attraction to the following singular predicate.[3]—In Gn 4⁷ רֹבֵץ

---

[1] This does not include such cases as Jb 24⁷·¹⁰, where עָרוֹם is rather to be explained as an accusative denoting a state, § 118 *n*.

[2] יבוא probably an error for יבאו. The Masora on Lv 11³⁴ reckons fourteen instances of יָבֹא, where we should expect the plural.

[3] So also the pronoun הוּא emphatically resuming the subject (see § 141 *h*) is attracted to the predicate in number in Jos 13¹⁴ אִשֵּׁי יְהוָֹה . . . הוּא נַחֲלָתוֹ *the offerings of the Lord . . . that is his inheritance* ; in number and gender, Lv 25³³ *Qᵉrê* ; Jer 10³.

is a substantival participle (*a lurker, a coucher*). In Gn 47²⁴ יִהְיֶה remains undefined in gender (masc.), although the noun precedes for the sake of emphasis; so also in Gn 28²², Ex 12⁴⁹, 28⁷·³², Nu 9¹⁴, 15²⁹, Jer 50⁴⁶, Ec 2⁷ (הָיָה לִי as if the sentence began afresh, *and servants born in my house . . . there fell to my lot* this possession also). In Jb 20²⁶ לֹא־נֻפַּח may (unless אֵשׁ is regarded as masculine, § 122 o) be taken impersonally, *fire, without its being blown upon.*—In Is 16⁸ and Hb 3¹⁷ the predicate in the singular is explained from the collective character of שְׁדֵמוֹת (see *h* above); on the other hand, the masculine form of the predicate is abnormal in ψ 87³, Pr 2¹⁰, 12²⁵, 29²⁵, Jb 8⁷, 36¹⁸.

§ 146. *Construction of Compound Subjects.*

1. When the subject is composed of a nomen regens (in the construct *a* state) with a following genitive, the predicate sometimes agrees in gender and number not with the nomen regens, but with the genitive, when this represents the principal idea of the compound subject.[1] Thus 1 S 2⁴ קֶשֶׁת גִּבֹּרִים חַתִּים *the bow of the mighty men is broken*, as if it were *the mighty men with their bow are broken*; Ex 26¹², Lv 13⁹, 1 K 1⁴¹ (but the text is clearly very corrupt), 17¹⁶, Is 2¹¹, 21¹⁷, Zc 8¹⁰, Jb 15²⁰, 21²¹, 29¹⁰, 32⁷ (רֹב שָׁנִים equivalent to *many years*); 38²¹; with the predicate preceding, 2 S 10⁹, unless it is to be explained according to § 145 *k*.

Rem. 1. The cases in which קוֹל (*voice, sound*) with a following genitive *b* stands at the beginning of a sentence, apparently in this construction, are really of a different kind. The קוֹל is there to be taken as an exclamation, and the supposed predicate as in apposition to the genitive, e.g. Gn 4¹⁰ *the voice of thy brother's blood, which crieth* (prop. *as one crying*) . . . ! = *hark! thy brother's blood is crying,* &c.; Is 13⁴, 66⁶. In Is 52⁸ an independent verbal-clause follows the exclamation *the voice of thy watchmen !*; in Jer 10²² and Ct 2⁸ an independent noun-clause; in Is 40³ קוֹל קֹרֵא *the voice of one that crieth !* i.e. *hark ! there is one crying* is followed immediately by direct speech; in Mi 6⁹ קוֹל *hark !* may be used disconnectedly (cf. the almost adverbial use of קוֹל in § 144 *m*) and יְהוָה be taken as the subject to יִקְרָא.

2. When the substantive כֹּל (כָּל־) *entirety* is used in connexion with a *c* genitive as subject of the sentence, the predicate usually agrees in gender and number with the genitive, since כֹּל is equivalent in sense to an attribute (*whole, all*) of the genitive; hence, e.g. with the predicate preceding, Gn 5⁵ וַיִּהְיוּ כָּל־יְמֵי אָדָם *and all the days of Adam were*, &c. (in 5²³, 9²⁹ וַיְהִי; but the Samaritan reads ויהיו here also); Ex 15²⁰; with the predicate following, ψ 150⁶, &c. Exceptions are, e.g. Lv 17¹⁴ (but cf. § 145 *l*), Jos 8²⁵, Is 64¹⁰, Pr 16², Na 3⁷. On the other hand, in such cases as Ex 12¹⁶ the agreement of the

---

[1] Sometimes, however, the attraction of the predicate to the genitive may be merely due to juxtaposition.

H h 2

predicate with ־כָּל is explained from the stress laid upon the latter, כָּל־מְלָאכָה
לֹא being equivalent to *the whole of work* (is forbidden).

d **2.** When the subject of the sentence consists of several nouns
connected by *wāw copulative*, usually

(*a*) The predicate *following* is put in the plural, e. g. Gn 8²² *seed
time and harvest, and cold and heat . . . shall not cease* (לֹא יִשְׁבֹּתוּ);
after subjects of different genders it is in the masculine (as the *prior
gender*, cf. § 132 *d*), e. g. Gn 18¹¹ אַבְרָהָם וְשָׂרָה זְקֵנִים *Abraham and Sarah
were old*; Dt 28³², 1 K 1²¹.

e Rem. Rare exceptions are Pr 27⁹ שֶׁמֶן וּקְטֹרֶת יְשַׂמַּח־לֵב *ointment and perfume
rejoice the heart*, where the predicate agrees in gender with the masculine
שֶׁמֶן (as in Is 51³ with שָׂשׂוֹן); on the other hand, in Ex 21⁴ (where הָאִשָּׁה
וִילָדֶיהָ are the subjects) it agrees with הָאִשָּׁה as being the principal person ;
in the compound sentence, Is 9⁴, it agrees with the feminine subject immediately preceding.[1]

f (*b*) The predicate *preceding* two or more subjects may likewise be
used in the plural (Gn 40¹, Jb 3⁵, &c.); not infrequently, however,
it agrees in gender and number with the first, as being the subject
nearest to it. Thus the predicate is put in the singular masculine
before several masculines singular in Gn 9²³, 11²⁹, 21³², 24⁵⁰, 34²⁰,
Ju 14⁵; before a masculine and a feminine singular, e. g. Gn 3⁸, 24⁵⁵
then said (וַיֹּאמֶר) *her brother and her mother* ; 33⁷; before a masculine
singular and a plural, e. g. Gn 7⁷ וַיָּבֹא נֹחַ וּבָנָיו *and Noah went in, and
his sons*, &c.; Gn 8¹⁸ (where feminines plural also follow); 44¹⁴, Ex 15¹,
2 S 5²¹; before collectives feminine and masculine, 2 S 12².

g Similarly, the feminine singular occurs before several feminines
singular, e. g. Gn 31¹⁴ וַתַּעַן רָחֵל וְלֵאָה *then answered Rachel and Leah* ;
before a feminine singular and a feminine plural, e.g. Gn 24⁶¹; before
a feminine singular and a masculine singular, Nu 12¹ וַתְּדַבֵּר מִרְיָם
וְאַהֲרֹן *then spake Miriam and Aaron*; Ju 5¹; before a feminine
singular and a masculine plural, e. g. Gn 33⁷ (cf., on the other hand,
ψ 75⁴ נְמֹגִים אֶרֶץ וְכָל־יֹשְׁבֶיהָ *dissolved are the earth and all the inhabitants
thereof*). The plural feminine occurs before a plural feminine and
a plural masculine in Am 8¹³.—In Jer 44²⁵ for אַתֶּם וּנְשֵׁיכֶם read אַתֶּם
הַנָּשִׁים with the LXX, and cf. verse 19.

h (*c*) When other predicates follow after the subjects have been
mentioned, they are necessarily put in the plural ; cf. Gn 21³², 24⁶¹,
31¹⁴, 33⁷, &c., and § 145 *s*.

---

[1] Similarly with a mixed object, Gn 33² *he put . . . Leah and her children
after*; אַחֲרֹנִים agrees with the masculine immediately preceding.

§ 147. *Incomplete Sentences.*

1. Sentences are called *incomplete*, in which either the subject or *a* the predicate or both must in some way be supplied from the context.[1] Besides the instances enumerated in § 116 *s* (omission of the personal pronoun when subject of a participial clause) and the periphrases for negative attributes § 152 *u*, this description includes certain (noun-) clauses introduced by הִנֵּה (see *b* below), and also a number of exclamations of the most varied kinds (see *c* below).

Rem. Incomplete sentences are very common in Chronicles, but are mostly due to the bad condition of the text; cf. Driver, *Introd.*[6], p. 537, no. 27. Thus in 2 Ch 11[22 *b*] restore חָשַׁב, with the LXX, before לְהַמְלִיכוֹ; in 35[21] add בָּאתִי, with the LXX, after הַיּוֹם and read פְּרָת for בֵּית; in 2 Ch 19[6] and 28[21] the pronoun הוּא is wanted as subject, and in 30[9] the predicate יִהְיוּ; cf. also the unusual expressions in 1 Ch 9[33] (Ezr 3[3]), 1 Ch 15[13] (*ye were not present?*), 2 Ch 15[3], 16[10.12 (bis)], 18[3].

2. The demonstrative particle הֵן, הִנֵּה *en, ecce* may be used either *b* absolutely (as a kind of interjection, cf. § 105 *b*) before complete noun- or verbal-clauses, e. g. Gn 28[15] וְהִנֵּה אָנֹכִי עִמָּךְ *and, behold! I am with thee*; 37[7], 48[21], Ex 3[13], 34[10], or may take the pronoun, which would be the natural subject of a noun-clause, in the form of a suffix, see § 100 *o*. Whether these suffixes are to be regarded as in the accusative has been shown to be doubtful in § 100 *p*. However, in the case of הִנֵּה the analogy of the corresponding Arabic demonstrative particle ʼ*inna* (followed by an accusative of the noun) is significant.[2] If הִנֵּה with a suffix and a following adjective or participle (see the examples in § 116 *p* and *q*) forms a noun-clause, the subject proper, to which הִנֵּה with the suffix refers, must, strictly speaking, be supplied again before the predicate.[3] Sometimes, however, the pronoun referring to the subject is wanting, and the simple הִנֵּה takes the place of the

---

[1] This does not apply to such cases as Gn 33[8], where an infinitive with לְ appears alone in answer to a question, the substance of the question being presupposed as a main clause; cf. also Gn 26[7], where הִיא must again be supplied after אִשְׁתִּי.

[2] On the same analogy any substantive following הִנֵּה would have to be regarded as originally a virtual accusative. Since, however, Hebrew does not possess case-terminations (as the Arabic does, and uses the accusative necessarily after ʼ*inna*), it is very doubtful whether, and how far, substantives following הִנֵּה were felt to be accusatives.

[3] That these are real noun-clauses and that the participle (e. g. מֵת in הִנְּךָ מֵת Gn 20[8]) cannot be taken as a second accusative (as it were *ecce te moriturum*), is also shown by the analogy of Arabic, where after ʼ*inna* with an accusative the predicate is expressly in the *nominative*.

subject and copula (as Gn 18⁹ הִנֵּה בָאֹהֶל *behold* she is *in the tent*; 42²⁸), or there is no indication whatever of the predicate, so that the sentence is limited to הִנֵּה with the suffix, as in the frequent use of הִנְנִי, הִנֵּנִי *here am I*, in answer to an address. Elsewhere a substantive follows הִנֵּה (or הֵן Gn 11⁶, Jb 31³⁵), and הִנֵּה then includes the meaning of a demonstrative pronoun and the copula, e. g. Gn 22⁷ הִנֵּה הָאֵשׁ וְהָעֵצִים *here is the fire and the wood*, &c.; 12¹⁹ *behold* thou hast *thy wife!* Ex 24⁸; with reference to the past, e. g. Am 7¹ וְהִנֵּה לֶקֶשׁ וגׄ *and lo*, it was *the latter growth*, &c. By a very pregnant construction the simple הִנֵּה is used as the equivalent of a sentence in Jb 9¹⁹, *lo, here am I!*

C 3. Examples of exclamations (threatening, complaining, triumphing, especially warlike or seditious) in which, owing to the excitement of the speaker, some indispensable member of the sentence is suppressed, are—(*a*) with suppression of the predicate (which has frequently to be supplied in the form of a jussive), e. g. Ju 7²⁰ *a sword for the Lord and for Gideon!* (verse 18 without חֶרֶב); 2 S 20¹ and 2 Ch 10¹⁶ (cf. also 1 K 22³⁶) *every man to his tents, O Israel!* (i. e. *let every man go to or remain in his tent*); without אִישׁ 1 K 12¹⁶; moreover, Is 1²⁸, 13⁴ (on the exclamatory קוֹל equivalent to *hark!* cf. § 146 *b*); 28¹⁰, 29¹⁶ (הַפְכְּכֶם *O your perversity!* i. e. how great it is!); Jer 49¹⁶ (if תִּפְלַצְתְּךָ be equivalent to *terror be upon thee!*); Jo 4¹⁴, Mal 1¹³ הִנֵּה מַתְּלָאָה *behold what a weariness!*); Jb 22²⁹; perhaps also Gn 49⁴ פַּחַז כַּמַּיִם *a bubbling over as water* (sc. happened), unless it is better to supply a subject אַתָּה (*thou wast*).—(*b*) With suppression of the subject, Ju 4²⁰, cf. § 152 *k*; Jb 15²³ אַיֵּה *where* sc. is bread?—(*c*) With suppression of both subject and predicate, Ju 7¹⁸ (see above); 1 K 12¹⁶ (see above); 2 K 9²⁷ גַּם אֹתוֹ *him also!* explained immediately afterwards by הַכֻּהוּ *smite him!* Ho 5⁸ *after thee, Benjamin!* sc. is the enemy (differently in Ju 5¹⁴); ψ 6⁴, 90¹³, Hb 2⁶ עַד־מָתַי; ψ 74⁹ עַד־מָה.—On וְלֹא *and if not* (unless וְלוֹ is to be read), 2 S 13²⁶, 2 K 5¹⁷, see § 159 *dd*.

d Rem. 1. To the class of incomplete sentences naturally belong exclamations introduced by interjections אֲהָהּ, אוֹי, הוֹי, הַס;¹ cf. § 105. After the first two the object of the *threat* or *imprecation* follows regularly with לְ (cf. vae tibi) or אֶל־ or עַל־, e. g. אוֹי לָנוּ *woe unto us!* 1 S 4⁸, Is 6⁵; cf. also אֲהָהּ לַיּוֹם *alas for the day!* Jo 1¹⁵; on the other hand, the object of *commiseration* (after הוֹי) follows mostly in the vocative, or rather in the accusative of exclamation (cf. vae te in Plautus); so in lamentation for the dead, הוֹי אָחִי *alas, my brother!* 1 K 13³⁰,

---

¹ We do not consider here the cases in which these interjections (e. g. הַס Ju 3¹⁹, Am 6⁰) stand quite disconnectedly (so always אָח and הֶאָח).

Jer 22¹⁸ ; הוֹי גּוֹי חֹטֵא *ah, sinful nation!* Is 1⁴, 5⁸·¹¹·¹⁸·²⁰·²² (*ah! they that . . .*).—
For הַם cf. Hb 2²⁰, Zp 1⁷, Zc 2¹⁷.

2. Finally, instances of noun-clauses shortened in an unusual manner *e*
may perhaps occur in יְדֵיהֶם and רַגְלֵיהֶם ψ 115⁷, for יָדַיִם לָהֶם *they have hands,*
&c.; cf. verses 5 and 6 פֶּה־לָהֶם, &c. Perhaps also וּפִילַגְשׁוֹ Gn 22²⁴, and
וְחֶלְיוֹ Ec 5¹⁶ are to be regarded in the same way, but hardly נְבִיאֲכֶם Nu 12⁶ ;
cf. § 128 *d* above.

II. Special Kinds of Sentences.

§ 148. *Exclamations.*

The originally interrogative מָה is used to introduce exclamations *a*
of wonder or indignation=*O how!* or ridicule, *why! how!* sometimes
strengthened by זֶה or זֹאת according to § 136 *c*.—Astonishment or
indignation at something which has happened is introduced by אֵיךְ
how (likewise originally interrogative) with the perfect; the indignant
refusal of a demand by אֵיךְ (but also by מָה Jb 31¹) with the imperfect;
an exclamation of lamentation by אֵיכָה, less frequently אֵיךְ *how!*; in
Jo 1¹⁸ by מָה.

Examples :—

מָה (or מַה־ with a following *Dageš*, see § 37) expressing admiration (or *b*
astonishment) before verbal-clauses, e.g. Gn 27²⁰ (מַה־זֶּה) ; 38²⁹, Nu 24⁵ (*how
goodly are . . .!*); ψ 21², Ct 7² ; before the predicate of noun-clauses, e.g.
Gn 28¹⁷, ψ 8² ; mockingly before the verb, 2 S 6²⁰ (*how glorious was . . .!*);
Jer 22²³, Jb 26²·ᶠ· ; indignantly, Gn 3¹³ (מַה־זֹּאת ; 4¹⁰, 20⁹, 31²⁶ *what hast thou
done!*

אֵיךְ with the perfect, e.g. Gn 26⁹, ψ 73¹⁹ ; in scornful exclamation, Is 14⁴·¹² ;
in a lament (usually אֵיכָה), 2 S 1²⁵·²⁷ ; with the imperfect, in a reproachful
question, Gn 39⁹, 44⁸, ψ 11¹, 137⁴ ; in a mocking imitation of lament, Mi 2⁴.

אֵיכָה with the perfect, Is 1²¹, La 1¹ ; with the imperfect, La 2¹, 4¹.

Rem. 1. The close relation between a question and an exclamation appears *c*
also in the interrogative personal pronoun מִי in such cases as Mi 7¹⁸ מִי־אֵל כָּמוֹךָ
who is a God like unto thee? and so in general in *rhetorical* questions as the
expression of a forcible denial ; similarly in the use of an interrogative
sentence to express a wish, see §§ 150 *d*, 151 *a*.
2. A weaker form of exclamation is sometimes produced by the insertion *d*
of a corroborative כִּי *verily, surely,* before the predicate, Gn 18²⁰ ; cf. 33¹¹,
Is 7⁹, and the analogous cases in the apodoses of conditional sentences,
§ 159 *ee*.

§ 149. *Sentences which express an Oath or Asseveration.*

The particle אִם, in the sense of *certainly not,* and אִם־לֹא (rarely כִּי *a*
Gn 22¹⁶) in the sense of *certainly,* are used to introduce promises or
threats confirmed by an oath (especially after such formulae as חַי־יְהֹוָה,

כִּי נִשְׁבַּעְתִּי ¹,חֵי אָנִי, חַי אָנִי, &c., as well as after imprecations, see below), and also simple asseverations, e.g. 1 S 2³⁰, 2 S 20²⁰, Jb 27⁵ after חָלִילָה לִי *far be it from me*, but mostly without any introductory formula.

b Rem. No certain explanation of these particles has yet been given. According to the usual view, phrases expressing an oath depend on the suppression of an imprecation upon oneself, e.g. *the Lord do so unto me, if I do it* equivalent to *I certainly will not do it*; then naturally אִם־לֹא properly *if I do it not* equivalent to *I certainly will do it*. It is indeed difficult to understand such self-imprecations, put into the mouth of God, as in Dt 1³⁴ᶠ·, Is 14²⁴, 22¹⁴, Jer 22⁶, Ez 3⁶, 35⁶, ψ 95¹¹. Possibly, however, the consciousness of the real meaning of the formula was lost at an early period, and אִם־לֹא simply came to express *verily*, אִם *verily not*.—In 1 S 25²², where, instead of a self-imprecation, a curse is pronounced upon others, read לְדָוִד with the LXX for לְאֹיְבֵי דָוִד.

Examples :—

c (*a*) The particles אִם and אִם־לֹא used after the utterance of an oath and after formulae of swearing, e.g. 2 S 11¹¹ (see note on *a*) חַי־יְהֹוָה וְחֵי נַפְשֶׁךָ אִם־אֶעֱשֶׂה אֶת־הַדָּבָר הַזֶּה *as the Lord liveth, and as thy soul liveth, I will not do this thing*; 1 S 14⁴⁵, 2 K 5¹⁶ (after חַי יְהֹוָה; in 1 S 14³⁹ and 29⁶ חַי־יְ is followed by a simple כִּי); Ct 2⁷, 3⁵ (after הִשְׁבַּעְתִּי *I adjure you*); cf. also Gn 14²³, 21²³, 26²⁹; spoken by God, Dt 1³⁴ᶠ·, 1 S 3¹⁴, ψ 95¹¹; similarly אִם־לֹא Gn 24³⁷ᶠ·; spoken by God, Is 14²⁴, where אִם־לֹא occurs first with the perfect in the sense of a prophetic perfect, § 106 *n*, but in the parallel clause with the imperfect; Jer 22⁶; in Gn 31⁵² the negative oath introduced by אִם־אָנִי, אִם־אַתָּה is immediately afterwards continued by לֹא with the imperfect.— In Ez 34¹⁰ the threat introduced in verse 8 by אִם־לֹא is, after a long parenthesis, resumed with הִנְנִי.

d (*b*) אִם and אִם־לֹא after formulae of cursing, e.g. 1 S 3¹⁷ כֹּה יַעֲשֶׂה־לְּךָ אֱלֹהִים וְכֹה יוֹסִיף אִם־תְּכַחֵד מִמֶּנִּי דָבָר וג' *God do so to thee, and more also!* thou shalt not hide anything from me, &c.; cf. 1 S 25²². On the other hand, כִּי follows the curse, in 1 S 14⁴⁴, 1 K 2²³ (here with a perfect), and in 2 S 3³⁵ כִּי אִם; in 1 S 25³⁴ the preceding כִּי is repeated before אִם; in 1 S 20¹³ the purport of the asseveration is repeated (after the insertion of a conditional sentence) in the perfect consecutive.

e (*c*) אִם and אִם־לֹא as simple particles of asseveration, e.g. Ju 5⁸ מָגֵן אִם־יֵרָאֶה וָרֹמַח וג' *truly, there was not a shield and spear seen*, &c.; Is 22¹⁴, Jb 6²⁸ (in the middle of the sentence); after חָלִילָה חָלִילָה *absit*, 2 S 20²⁰; אִם־לֹא with the imperf. Is 5⁹, with the perfect, Jb 22²⁰.

---

¹ Also combined חַי־יְהֹוָה וְחֵי נַפְשֶׁךָ 1 S 20³, 25²⁶ *as the Lord liveth, and as thy soul* (i.e. *thou*) *liveth!* (Also in 2 S 11¹¹ read חַי־יהוה instead of the impossible חֵיֶךָ). On חַי and חֵי in these noun-clauses (prop. *living is the Lord*, &c.), cf. § 93 *aa*, note.

§ 150. *Interrogative Sentences.*

H. G. Mitchell, 'The omission of the interrogative particle,' in *Old Test. and Sem. Studies in memory of W. R. Harper*, Chicago, 1907, i, 113 ff.

1. A question need not necessarily be introduced by a special *a* interrogative pronoun or adverb. Frequently[1] the natural emphasis upon the words is of itself sufficient to indicate an interrogative sentence as such; cf. Gn 27²⁴ אַתָּה זֶה בְּנִי עֵשָׂו *thou art my son Esau?* (but cf. note 1 below) Gn 18¹², Ex 33¹⁴ (פָּנַי יֵ); 1 S 11¹² שָׁאוּל יִמְלֹךְ עָלֵינוּ *Saul shall reign over us?* 1 S 22⁷, 2 S 16¹⁷, 18²⁹ שָׁלוֹם לַנַּעַר *is it well with the young man?* (but cf. note 1); 1 S 16⁴, 1 K 1²⁴, Is 28²⁸, Ho 4¹⁶, Zc 8⁶ (*should it also be marvellous in mine eyes?*); Pr 5¹⁶. So especially, when the interrogative clause is connected with a preceding sentence by וְ, e.g. Jn 4¹¹ וַאֲנִי לֹא אָחוּס *and I should not have pity?* Ex 8²² *will they not stone us?* Ju 11²³, 14¹⁶, 1 S 20⁹, 24²⁰, 25¹¹, 2 S 11¹¹, 15²⁰, Is 37¹¹, 44¹⁹ᵇ, Jer 25²⁹, 45⁵, 49¹², Ez 20³¹, Jb 2¹⁰, 10⁹; or when (as in some of the examples just given) it is negative (with לֹא for הֲלֹא *nonne?*), 2 K 5²⁶ (but cf. note 1), La 3³³.[2]

Rem. The statement formerly made here that the interrogative particle is *b* omitted especially before gutturals, cannot be maintained in view of Mitchell's statistics (op. cit. p. 123 f.). The supposed considerations of euphony are quite disproved by the 118 cases in which הַ or הֶ occurs before a guttural.

2. As a rule, however, the simple question is introduced by *He c interrogative* הֲ (הַ; as to its form, cf. § 100 *k–n*), *ne? num?* the disjunctive question by הֲ (*num? utrum?*) in the first clause, and אִם[3] (also וְאִם, less frequently אוֹ) *an?* in the second, e.g. 1 K 22¹⁵ ... הֲ…ֵלֵךְ

---

[1] Mitchell (op. cit.) restricts the number of instances to 39, of which he attributes 12 (or 17) to corruption of the text. Thus in Gn 27²⁴ he would read, with the Samaritan, הַאַתָּה as in verse 21, in 1 S 16⁴ הֲשָׁלֹם, in 2 S 18²⁹ הֲשָׁלוֹם as in verse 32; similarly he would read the interrogative particle in 2 K 5²⁶, Ez 11³, Jb 40²⁵, 41¹; 1 S 30⁸, 2 K 9¹⁹, Ez 11¹³, 17⁹.

[2] But in 1 S 27¹⁰ instead of אַל־ (which according to the usual explanation would expect a negative answer) read either אֶל־מִי (עַל־מִי) with the LXX, or better, אָן (אָנָה) *whither?* with the Targum. In 2 S 23⁵ read הֲלֹא חֶפְצִי with Wellhausen.

[3] Quite exceptional is the use of the particle אִין *num?* (common in Aramaic) in 1 S 21⁹ וְאִין יֶשׁ־פֹּה *num est hic?* The text is, however, undoubtedly corrupt; according to Wellhausen, *Text der Bücher Sam.*, the LXX express the reading רְאֵה הֲיֵשׁ; but cf. the full discussion of the passage by König, *ZAW.* xviii. 239 ff.—The above does not apply to interrogative sentences introduced by interrogative pronouns (§ 37) or by the interrogatives compounded with מָה *what?* such as בַּמָּה *how many?* לָמָּה *why?* (see § 102 *k*), מַדּוּעַ *why?* (§ 99 *e*), or by אַיֵּה *where?* אֵיךְ, אֵיכָה *how?* (§ 148), &c. On the transformation of

אִם נֶחְדָּל ¹ *shall we go . . . or shall we forbear?* Cf. also אָן *where?*
whither? אָנָה *whither,* and J. Barth, *Sprachwiss. Untersuchungen,*
i. 13 ff.

d   The particular uses are as follows :—

(*a*) The particle הֲ stands primarily before the simple question, when the
questioner is wholly uncertain as to the answer to be expected, and may be
used either before noun-clauses, e. g. Gn 43⁷ הַעוֹד אֲבִיכֶם חַי הֲיֵשׁ לָכֶם אָח
is your father yet alive? have ye another brother? for הֲיֵשׁ cf. Gn 24¹³, 1 S 9¹¹;
for הֲכִי *is it that?* Jb 6²²; for הֲכִי יֵשׁ *is there yet?* 2 S 9¹ (but in 2 S 23¹⁹ for
הֲכִי read הִנּוּ with 1 Ch 11²⁵); for הַאֵין *is there not?* 1 K 22⁷, &c.; or before
verbal-clauses, e. g. Jb 2³ *hast thou considered* (הֲשַׂמְתָּ לִבְּךָ) *my servant Job?*
In other cases הֲ (=*num?*) is used before questions, to which, from their tone
and contents, a negative answer is expected, e. g. Jb 14¹⁴ *if a man die,* הֲיִחְיֶה
shall he indeed live again? Sometimes a question is so used only as a rhetorical
form instead of a negative assertion, or of a surprised or indignant refusal,²
e. g. 2 S 7⁵ הַאַתָּה תִבְנֶה־לִּי בַיִת *shalt thou build me an house?* (in the parallel
passage 1 Ch 17⁴ לֹא אַתָּה וג׳ *thou shalt not,* &c.); Gn 4⁹ הֲשֹׁמֵר אָחִי אָנֹכִי *am I my
brother's keeper?* cf. 2 K 5⁷, and the two passages where הֲ is used before the
infinitive (*constr.* Jb 34¹⁸, *absol.* Jb 40²; on both, see § 113 *ee*, with the note).
—On the other hand, in 1 K 16⁸¹ for הֲנָקֵל (after וַיְהִי) read הֲנָקֵל.

e   Rem. 1. A few passages deserve special mention, in which the use of the
interrogative is altogether different from our idiom, since it serves merely to
express the conviction that the contents of the statement are well known
to the hearer, and are unconditionally admitted by him. Thus, Gn 3¹¹ *surely
thou hast eaten;* Gn 27³⁶ הֲכִי קָרָא *prop. is it so that one names?* &c., i. e. *of a truth
he is rightly named Jacob;* Gn 29¹⁵ *verily thou art my brother;* Dt 11³⁰, Ju 4⁶,
1 S 2²⁷ *I did indeed,* &c.; 20³⁷, 1 K 22³ *ye know surely . . .;* Mi 3¹, Jb 20⁴.—
In 1 S 23¹⁹ (cf. ψ 54²) a surprising communication is introduced in this way
(by הֲלֹא) in order to show it to be absolutely true, and in Am 9⁷ a concession
is expressed by הֲלוֹא *I have, it is true,* &c. Finally, we may include the
formula of quotation הֲלֹא הִיא כְתוּבָה Jos 10¹³ or הֲלֹא־הֵם כְּתוּבִים equivalent
to *surely it is, they are* written (the latter in 1 K 11⁴¹, 14²⁹, and very often
elsewhere in the books of Kings and Chronicles), synonymous with the
simple formula of assertion הִנֵּה כְתוּבָה 2 S 1¹⁸, and הִנָּם כְּתוּבִים 1 K 14¹⁹,
2 K 15¹¹, 2 Ch 27⁷, 32³².

Of very frequent occurrence also are questions introduced by לָמָה, which
really contain an affirmation and are used to state the reason for a request or
warning, e. g. 2 S 2²² *turn thee aside . . . wherefore should I smite thee to the ground?*
i. e. *otherwise I will* (or *must*) *smite,* &c.; cf. 1 S 19¹⁷, and Driver on the passage;
2 Ch 25¹⁶; also Gn 27⁴⁵, Ex 32¹² (Jo 2¹⁷, ψ 79¹⁰, 115²); Ct 1⁷, Ec 5⁵, 7¹⁷, Dn 1¹⁰.

---

pronouns and adverbs into interrogative words by means of a prefixed אֵי, see
the Lexicon.

¹ On the use of the *imperfect* in deliberative questions, see § 107 *t*; on the
perfectum confidentiae in interrogative sentences, see § 106 *n*.

² Analogous to this is the use of the interrogative מָה in the sense of a
reproachful remonstrance instead of a prohibition, as Ct 8⁴ מַה־תָּעִירוּ *why
should ye stir up?* i. e. *pray, stir not up;* cf. also Jb 31¹; see above, § 148.

2. The rare cases in which a *simple* question is introduced by אִם (as some- *f* times in Latin by *an? is it?*) are really due to the suppression of the first member of a double question; thus 1 K 1²⁷, Is 29¹⁶, Jb 6¹², 39¹³.

(*b*) Disjunctive questions are, as a rule, introduced by הַ–אִם (*utrum—an?*) *g* or sometimes by וְאִם¹–הַ, e. g. Jo 1², Jb 21⁴ (even with הַ repeated after וְאִם in a question which implies disbelief, Gn 17¹⁷). In Jb 34¹⁷, 40⁸ᶠ· special emphasis is given to the first member by הַאַף prop. *is it even?* The second member is introduced by אוֹ *or* in 2 K 6²⁷, Jb 16³, 38²⁸, 31³⁶ (Mal 1⁸ הֲ אוֹ), in each case before מ, and hence no doubt for euphonic reasons, to avoid the combination אִם מ/; cf. also Ju 18¹⁹, Ec 2¹⁹.

Double questions with (וְאִם)אִם–הֲ need not always be mutually exclusive; *h* frequently the disjunctive form serves (especially in poetic parallelism; but cf. also e. g. Gn 37⁸) merely to repeat the same question in different words, and thus to express it more emphatically.   So Jb 4¹⁷ *shall mortal man be just before God? or* (אִם) *shall a man be pure before his Maker?* Jb 6⁵ᶠ·, 8³, 10⁴ᶠ·, 11²·⁷, 22³, Is 10¹⁵, Jer 5²⁹. The second member may, therefore, just as well be connected by a simple וְ, e. g. Jb 13⁷, 15⁷ᶠ·, 38¹⁶ᶠ·²²·³²·³⁹; cf. also ψ 8⁵ after מָה; Jb 21¹⁷ᶠ· after כַּמָּה; or even without a conjunction, Jb 8¹¹, 22⁴; after מָה ψ 144³.

(*c*) With regard to *indirect* questions[2] after verbs of inquiring, doubting, *i* examining,[3] &c., simple questions of this kind take either הֲ *whether*, Gn 8⁸,⁴ or אִם Gn 15⁵, 2 K 1², Ct 7¹³; even before a noun-clause, Jer 5¹; in 1 S 20¹⁰ the indirect question is introduced by אוּ, i. e. probably *if perchance*. In disjunctives (*whether—or*) אִם–הַ Nu 13¹⁸ at the end (or אִם־לֹא הַ Gn 24²¹, 27²¹, 37³², Ex 16⁴), and הַ–הֲ Nu 13¹⁸, which is followed by אִם–הַ; also הַ–אוֹ Ec 2¹⁹. The formula אִם יוֹדֵעַ מִי has an affirmative force, *who knows whether ... not*, like the Latin *nescio an*, Est 4¹⁴.

In Jon 1⁷·⁸ the relative pronouns שֶׁ and אֲשֶׁר owing to the following *k* לְמִי have become also interrogative, *for whose cause?*

(*d*) זֶה and הוּא (cf. § 136 *c*) immediately after the interrogative serve to *l* give vividness to the question; so also אֵפוֹא (for which אֵפוֹ five times in Job) *then, now,* Gn 27³³ הוּא מִי־אֵפוֹא *who then is he?* Ju 9³⁸, Is 19¹², Jb 17¹⁵; אַיֵּה אֵפוֹ

---

[1] וְאִם occurs in Pr 27²⁴ after a negative statement; we should, however, with Dyserinck read וְאֵין. Not less irregular is הֲלֹא instead of אִם לֹא in the second clause of Ju 14¹⁵, but the text can hardly be correct (cf. Moore, *Judges*, New York, 1895, p. 337); in 1 S 23¹¹ the second הֲ introduces a fresh question which is only loosely connected with the first.—In Nu 17²⁸ and in the third clause of Jb 6¹³, הַאִם is best taken with Ewald in the sense of הֲלֹא, since אִם from its use in oaths (see above, § 149 *b*) may simply mean *verily not*.

[2] It should here be remarked that the distinction between direct and indirect questions cannot have been recognized by the Hebrew mind to the same extent as it is in Latin or English. In Hebrew there is no difference between the two kinds of sentence, either as regards mood (as in Latin) or in tense and position of the words (as in English). Cf. also § 137 *c*.

[3] In Gn 43⁶ the הֲ after לְהַגִּיד is explained from the fact that the latter, according to the context, implies *to give information upon a question*.

[4] Also in Ec 3²¹ we should read הָעֹלָה and הַיֹּרֶדֶת (*whether—whether*) instead of the article which is assumed by the Masora.

where then is . . . ? However, אֵפוֹא may also be placed at the end of the entire question (Ex 33¹⁶, Is 22¹; also Ho 13¹⁰, since either אֱהִי is a dialectical form of אַיֵּה, or אַיֵּה should be read instead of it) or at the beginning of the question proper, after a strongly emphasized word, as in Gn 27³⁷. [1]

m   (e) Sometimes one interrogative governs two co-ordinate clauses, the first of which should rather be subordinated to the second, so that the interrogative word strictly speaking affects only the second; thus Is 5⁴ after מַדּוּעַ *wherefore looked I . . . and it brought forth?* i.e. wherefore brought it forth, while I looked, &c.; Is 50²; after הַ Nu 32⁶, Jer 8⁴, also Nu 16²² (read הָאִישׁ); after הֲלֹא Jos 22²⁰; after לָמָּה Is 58³, 2 Ch 32⁴; after אֶל־מִי Is 40²⁵. [2] But הֲ Jb 4² and הֲלֹא 4²¹ are separated from the verb to which they belong by the insertion of a conditional clause.

n   3. The affirmative answer is generally expressed, as in Latin, by repeating the emphatic word in the question (or with the second person changed to the first, Gn 24⁵⁸, 27²⁴, 29⁵, Ju 13¹¹), Gn 29⁶, 37³²ᶠ·, 1 S 23¹¹, 26¹⁷, 1 K 21¹⁰, Jer 37¹⁷. (On וָיֵשׁ *if it be so* in the corrected text of 2 K 10¹⁵, see § 159 *dd*.) As a negative answer the simple לֹא is sometimes sufficient, as in Gn 19², 1 K 3²², &c.; cf. § 152 *c*; and in Ju 4²⁰ the simple אָיִן equivalent to *no* or *no one*.

§ 151. *Desiderative Sentences.*

a   A wish may be expressed not only by the simple imperfect (§ 107 *n*), cohortative (§ 108, especially with נָא § 108 *c*), jussive (§ 109; with נָא § 109 *b*), imperative (§ 110 *a*), perfect consecutive (§ 112 *aa*) or by a simple noun-clause (§ 116 *r*, note, and § 141 *g*) but also in the following ways :—

1. By exclamations in the form of *interrogative* clauses : [3] especially sentences with מִי followed by the imperfect as being the mood of that which is still unfulfilled but possible, and hence also of that which is desired, e. g. 2 S 15⁴ מִי־יְשִׂמֵנִי שֹׁפֵט *who maketh me judge ?* i. e. *O that I were made judge!* 1 S 20¹⁰, 2 S 23¹⁵. On the other hand, מִי with the perfect (Gn 21⁷, Nu 23¹⁰, 1 S 26⁹, Is 53¹, &c.) or participle (ψ 59⁸, Pr 24²², &c.), rather expresses a rhetorical question, i. e. a denial, cf. § 150 *d*. Especially frequent is the use of מִי־יִתֵּן (prop. *who gives ?*) to introduce all kinds of desiderative clauses (see under *b*).—In Mal 1¹⁰ the desiderative clause proper is co-ordinated with an interrogative clause,

---

[1] On the other hand, in Jb 9²⁴ and 24²⁵ אֵפוֹ is not prefixed to the מִי, but appended to the conditional sentence.

[2] Cf. the analogous sentences after יַעַן *because*, Is 65¹², Jer 35¹⁷; after causal אֲשֶׁר 1 S 26²³; after כִּי Is 12¹; likewise after גַּם § 153 at the end; after פֶּן־ Dt 8¹²⁻¹⁴, 25³, Jos 6¹⁸, 2 S 12²⁸.

[3] The transition from a question to a wish may be seen, e. g. in Nu 11⁴ *who shall give us flesh to eat?* i. e. *O that we had flesh to eat!*

מִי נִם־בָּכֶם וְיִסְגֹּר דְּלָתַיִם *would that one were among you and would shut the doors*, i. e. O that one would shut the doors!

Rem. Sometimes the original sense of מִי־יִתֵּן is still plainly discernible, *b*
e. g. Ju 9²⁹ מִי־יִתֵּן אֶת־הָעָם הַזֶּה בְּיָדִי *who gives this people into my hand?* equivalent to, O that this people were given into my hand! cf. ψ 55⁷. In these examples, however, מִי־יִתֵּן is still equivalent to *O had I!* and in numerous other instances the idea of *giving* has entirely disappeared, מִי־יִתֵּן having become stereotyped as a mere desiderative particle (*utinam*). Its construction is either—

(*a*) With the *accusative* (in accordance with its original meaning) of a substantive, Dt 28⁶⁷ *would that it were even! ... morning!* Ju 9²⁹, ψ 14⁷ (53⁷), 55⁷; with an accusative and a following infinitive, Jb 11⁵; with two accusatives, Nu 11²⁹, Jer 8²³; with the accusative of an infinitive, Ex 16³, 2 S 19¹ מִי־יִתֵּן מוּתִי אֲנִי תַחְתֶּיךָ *would that I had died for thee* (for אֲנִי cf. § 135 *f*); of a participle, Jb 31³⁵; of a personal pronoun (as a suffix), Jb 29² (with a following בְּ; but מִי־יִתְּנֵנִי Is 27⁴ and Jer 9¹ with a following accusative is not simply equivalent to מִי־יִתֵּן לִי, but is properly *who endows me with*, &c.; cf. § 117 *ff*).—With a still greater weakening of the original meaning מִי־יִתֵּן is used with an adjective in Jb 14⁴ *could a clean thing but come out of an unclean!* i.e. *how can a clean thing come*, &c.; similarly in Jb 31³¹ *who can find one that hath not been satisfied!*

(*b*) With a following perfect, Jb 23³ (cf. § 120 *e*); with a perfect consecutive, *c*
Dt 5²⁶ *O that they had such an heart!*

(*c*) With a following imperfect, Jb 6⁸, 13⁵, 14¹³; in Jb 19²³ the imperfect is *d* twice added with *Wāw* (cf. *a* above, on Mal. 1¹⁰).
On the cohortative in the apodosis to such desiderative clauses, cf. § 108 *f*.

2. The wish may also be expressed by the particles אִם (ψ 81⁹, 95⁷, *e* 139¹⁹, Pr 24¹¹, 1 Ch 4¹⁰; always with a following imperfect) and לוּ (for which in ψ 119⁵ we have אַחֲלַי, 2 K 5³ אַחֲלֵי, from אָח *ah!* and לוּ=לֻא; both with a following imperfect) *si, o si! utinam.*[1] לוּ is followed by the imperfect, Gn 17¹⁸, Jb 6²; by the jussive, Gn 30³⁴ (rather concessive, equivalent to *let it be so*); by the perfect, as the expression of a wish that something might have happened in past time (cf. § 106 *p*), Nu 14² לוּ מַתְנוּ *would that we had died*; 20³ and Jos 7⁷ (both times וְלוּ); on the other hand, Is 48¹⁸ and 63¹⁹ (both times לוּא) to express a wish that something expected in the future may already have happened.—On לוּ with the imperative (by an anacoluthon) Gn 23¹³ cf. § 110 *e*. On the perfect after כִּי אִם Gn 40¹⁴, 2 K 5²⁰, cf. § 106 *n*, note 2.

---

[1] Cf. a similar transition from a conditional to a desiderative particle, in consequence of the suppression of the apodosis, in the English, *O if I had!* and the like; e.g. Nu 22²⁹ *if there were* (לוּ יֵשׁ) *a sword in my hand now had I surely killed thee!*

§ 152. *Negative Sentences.*

a **1.** Besides the use of rhetorical questions (§§ 150 *d*, 151 *a*), independent sentences are made negative by the adverbs לֹא (Jb 6²¹, where instead of the *K*ᵉ*th.* לֹו we must evidently read לֹא; perhaps preserved as a substantive)=the Greek οὐ, *not*, אַל־=μή (Jb 24²⁵ as a substantive), אֵין (*it is*) *not*; טֶרֶם *not yet*, אֶפֶס *not*, אַפְסִי (cf. § 90 *m*) *not*. The forms בַּל, בְּלִי, בִּלְתִּי *not* belong almost entirely to poetry.—With regard to לֹא and אֵין the main distinction is that verbal-clauses (rarely noun-clauses, see *e*) are regularly negatived by לֹא (besides its use as negativing *single* words[1]), while אֵין is used exclusively with noun-clauses (see the examples below).

b The conjunctions פֶּן־ and לְבִלְתִּי *that not*, serve to negative dependent clauses. The particular uses of these particles are as follows:—

(*a*) לֹא (less frequently לוֹא), like οὐ, οὐκ, is used regularly for the *objective*, *unconditional* negation, and hence is usually connected with the perfect or imperfect (as indicative); on לֹא with the imperfect to express an unconditional prohibition, see § 107 *o*; on its use with the jussive, see § 109 *d*.—On הֲלֹא for לֹא *nonne*, in interrogative sentences, cf. § 150 *a*. In connexion with בָּל, כָּל־ (=*any*), לֹא is used to express an *absolute* negation, *nullus, none whatever* (cf. the French *ne ... personne, ne ... rien*), usually in the order לֹא ... כֹּל, e.g. Gn 3¹ לֹא תֹאכְלוּ מִכֹּל עֵץ הַגָּן *ye shall not eat of any tree of the garden*; 9¹¹, Ex 10¹⁵, 20¹⁰, Lv 7²³, Dt 8⁹, Jer 13⁷, 32¹⁷ לֹא ... כָּל־דָּבָר *nothing at all*; cf. the same statement in the form of a rhetorical question, Jer 32²⁷); Pr 12²¹, 30³⁰

---

[1] Especially in compounds, e.g. לֹא־אֵל lit. *a no-God* (Germ. *Ungott*) who is indeed called a god, but is not really a god, Dt 32²¹; לֹא אֱלֹהַּ verse 17, cf. Jer 5⁷, 2 Ch 13⁹; לֹא־עָם lit. *a not-people* (Germ. *Unvolk*), Dt 32²¹; לֹא דָבָר *a nothing*, Am 6¹³; לֹא עֵץ lit. *not-wood*, Is 10¹⁵; לֹא־אָדָם, לֹא־אִישׁ lit. *not-man*, superhuman (of God), Is 31⁸; לֹא־צֶדֶק *unrighteousness*, Jer 22¹³, cf. Ez 22²⁹; לֹא־סְדָרִים *disorder*, Jb 10²²; לֹא־חָמָס *not-violence*, 16¹⁷; after לְ Jb 26²⁶·⁻ (לֹא־בֹחַ, לֹא־עֹז *helplessness*, לֹא חָכְמָה *insipientia*); cf. also Is 55² בְּלוֹא לְשָׂבְעָה *for what is unsatisfying*; ψ 44¹³, Jb 8¹¹, 15³², 1 Ch 12³³.—In Nu 20⁵ a construct state with several genitives is negatived by לֹא.—Also לֹא is used with an infinitive, Nu 35²³; with an adjective, לֹא חָכָם *unwise*, Dt 32⁶, Ho 13¹³; לֹא־חָסִיד *impius*, ψ 43¹; לֹא־עָז and לֹא־עָצוּם *not strong*, Pr 30²⁵·; לֹא־כֵן *unsuitably*, 2 K 7⁹; לֹא־טוֹב *not-good*, Is 65², Ez 20²⁵, &c.; לֹא טָהוֹר *not-clean*, 2 Ch 30¹⁷; with a participle, e.g. Jer 2² (*unsown*); 6⁸, Ez 4¹⁴, 22²⁴, Zp 2¹, 3⁵; the Masora, however, requires נֻחָמָה in Is 54¹¹, נֶעֱזָבָה in 62¹², נוֹשָׁבָה in Jer 6⁸, רֻחָמָה in Ho 1⁶, i.e. always 3rd sing. fem. perf. in pause=*she was not comforted*, &c., and consequently not compounds, but either relative clauses or (Is 54¹¹, Ho 1⁶, and especially 2²⁵) main clauses instead of proper names.—On the above compounds generally, cf. the dissertation mentioned in § 81 *d*, note 2; on their use in sentences expressing a state, to convey attributive ideas, see *u* below.

מִפְּנֵי־כֹל . . . לֹא and turneth *not away for any*; 2 Ch 32¹⁵; but cf. also the inverted order, Ex 12¹⁶ כָּל־מְלָאכָה לֹא־יֵעָשֶׂה *no manner of work shall be done*; 12⁴³, 15²⁶, 22²¹, Lv 16¹⁷, Jb 33¹³, Dn 11³⁷. The meaning is different when כֹל by being determinate is used in the sense of *whole*, e. g. Nu 23¹³ כֻּלּוֹ לֹא תִרְאֶה *thou shalt not see them all*, but only a part.

Analogous to כֹּל . . . , לֹא is the use of לֹא . . . אִישׁ Gn 23⁶, &c., in verbal-clauses in the sense of *no one at all, not a single one*. On אֵין־כֹּל *nothing at all*, see under *p*.

Rem. 1. The examples in which לֹא is used absolutely as a negative answer, *c* equivalent to *certainly not! no!* must be regarded as extremely short verbal-clauses, e. g. Gn 19² (לֹא according to the context for לֹא נָסוּר &c.); 23¹¹, 42¹⁰, Hag 2¹², Jb 23⁶, sometimes with a following כִּי *but*, Gn 19² (see above); Jos 5¹⁴, 1 K 3²².

2. The negation of *noun*-clauses by לֹא (as opposed to the regular negation *d* by אֵין) always includes a certain emphasis, since the force of the negation falls rather upon a particular word (cf. e. g. Ez 36³²), than upon the whole clause. In 2 S 3³⁴ יָדֶיךָ לֹא־אֲסֻרוֹת *thy hands were not bound*, a participle is thus specially negatived by לֹא; cf. ψ 74⁹, where, however, לֹא is separated from the participle by אֲנַחְנוּ, and Jb 12³. As a rule, noun-clauses with a pronominal subject are thus negatived by לֹא, Gn 20¹², Nu 35²³ (Dt 4⁴², 19⁴); 1 S 15²⁹, 2 S 21², Jer 4²², ψ 22⁷, Jb 28¹⁴, parallel with אֵין; generally with לֹא before a substantival predicate, e. g. Ex 4¹⁰ לֹא אִישׁ דְּבָרִים אָנֹכִי *I am not a man of words*; Am 5¹⁸.—Noun-clauses with a substantival subject, Gn 29⁷, Nu 23¹⁹, Is 22², 44¹⁹, Hag 1², ψ 22³, Jb 9³², 18¹⁷, 21⁹, 22¹⁶, 36²⁶ (with ו of the apodosis); 41²; in Jb 9³³ even לֹא יֵשׁ *non est* is used instead of אֵין.—In Pr 18⁵ לֹא is used before an adjectival predicate; in 1 S 20²⁶ (where a preceding noun-clause is negatived by בִּלְתִּי) read לֹא טֹהַר with the LXX, for לֹא טָהוֹר. On לֹא for אֵין in circumstantial clauses to express attributive ideas, see *u* below.

3. As a rule לֹא stands immediately before the verb, but sometimes is *e* separated from it (frequently to bring into special prominence another word which follows it); thus Jb 22⁷, Ec 10¹⁰ before the object and verb; Nu 16²⁹ before the subject and verb; Dt 8⁹, 2 S 3³⁴, ψ 49¹⁸, 103¹⁰, Jb 13¹⁶, 34²³ before a complementary adjunct. In Dt 32⁵ לֹא according to the accentuation even stands at the end of the clause (*they offend him not*); but undoubtedly לֹא בָנָיו are to be taken together.—On the position of לֹא with the infinitive absolute, see § 113 *v*.

(*b*) אַל־ is used like μή and *ne* to express a *subjective* and *conditional* negation, *f* and hence especially in connexion with the jussive (§ 109 *c* and *e*) to introduce prohibitions, warnings, negative desires, and requests. On אַל־ with the imperfect, see § 107 *p*; with the cohortative, see § 108 *c*; on 2 K 6²⁷, see § 109 *h*.

Rem. 1. אַל־ (like לֹא, see note on *a* above) may be used to form a compound *g* word, as in Pr 12²⁸ אַל־מָוֶת *not-death* (immortality); though all the early versions read אֶל־מָוֶת. The instances in which אַל appears to stand absolutely, equivalent to *no, certainly not* (like μή for μὴ γένηται), e. g. Ru 1¹³ אַל בְּנֹתַי *nay, my daughters*, and Gn 19¹⁸, 33¹⁰ (אַל־נָא), are also due (see under *c*) to extreme shortening of a full clause (in 2 S 13²⁵ such a clause is repeated immediately afterwards); thus in 2 S 1²¹, Is 6²², ψ 83² יְהִי is evidently to be supplied, and in Jo 2¹³, Am 5¹⁴, Pr 8¹⁰ the corresponding jussive from the preceding imperatives, in Pr 17¹² from the preceding infinitive absolute.

h 2. אַל־, like לֹא, regularly stands immediately before the verb, but in Is 64⁸, Jer 10²⁴, 15¹⁵, ψ 6², 38² before another strongly emphasized member of the sentence.[1]

i (c) אֵין construct state (unless it be sometimes merely a contracted connective form, cf. שְׁנֵים for שְׁנַיִם § 97 *d*) of אַיִן *non-existence* (as also the absolute state, see below) is the negative of יֵשׁ *existence*; cf. e.g. Gn 31²⁹ with Neh 5⁵. As יֵשׁ (*he, she, it is, was,* &c.) includes the idea of *being* in all tenses, so אַיִן, אֵין includes the idea of *not being* in all tenses. Hence—

k (1) The absolute state אַיִן, with an evident transition to the meaning of a verbal predicate, *there does not exist,* always *follows* the word negatived, e.g. Is 37³ (2 K 19³) וְכֹחַ אַיִן לְלֵדָה *and strength does not exist to bring forth*; Gn 2⁵ אַיִן *was not present*; Ex 17⁷ אִם־אָיִן *or is he not?* after הֲיֵשׁ *is he ...?* (cf. Nu 13²⁰); Lv 26³⁷, Nu 20⁵, Ju 4²⁰ (אָיִן *no*). In 1 S 9⁴ and 10¹⁴ אַיִן is used in reference to a plural; 1 K 18¹⁰, Is 41¹⁷, 45²¹, 59¹¹, Mi 7², Pr 13⁴, 25¹⁴, Jb 3⁹ וָאָיִן *and let there be none, let none come!* Ec 3¹⁹.—Cf. finally אִם־אַיִן *if it be not so,* Gn 30¹, Ex 32³², Ju 9¹⁵, 2 K 2¹⁰.—Quite anomalous is אָיִן Jb 35¹⁵ before a perfect as an emphatic negation; the text, however, can hardly be correct.

l (2) The construct state אֵין stands in its natural position immediately before the substantive whose non-existence it predicates, or before the subject of the sentence which is to be negatived. To the former class belong also the very numerous instances in which אֵין is joined to a participle, e.g. 1 S 26¹² וְאֵין רֹאֶה וְאֵין יוֹדֵעַ וְאֵין מֵקִיץ *and there was not one seeing,* &c., i.e. *and no man saw it, nor knew it, neither did any awake*; so especially וְאֵין with a participle in subordinate *circumstantial* or *descriptive* clauses, such as Is 5²⁹ וְאֵין מַצִּיל רֵפְלִיט *and he shall carry it away,* while there is none delivering, i.e. *without any one's delivering* it; ψ 7³, &c.; Lv 26⁶ &c., וְאֵין מַחֲרִיד *without any one's making you afraid*; cf. § 141 *e.* אֵין is used as the negation of an entire noun-clause, e.g. in Gn 39²³, Nu 14⁴² אֵין יְהוָֹה בְּקִרְבְּכֶם *the Lord is not among you*; Gn 37²⁹ אֵין־יוֹסֵף בַּבּוֹר *Joseph was not in the pit.*

m (3) When the subject which is to be negatived is a personal pronoun, it is joined as a suffix to אֵין, according to § 100 *o*, e.g. אֵינֶנִּי *I am not, was not, shall not be*; אֵינְךָ, fem. אֵינֵךְ, *thou art not,* &c.; אֵינֶנּוּ, fem. אֵינֶנָּה *he, she is not,* &c.; also absolutely, Gn 42¹³ *he is* (5²⁴ *he was*) no longer *alive*; אֵינָם *they are not,* &c. When the accompanying predicate is a verb, it follows again (see *l*) in the form of a participle, since אֵין always introduces a noun-clause, e.g. Ex 5¹⁰ אֵינֶנִּי נֹתֵן *I will not give*; 8¹⁷, Dt 1³².

n Rem. In Neh 4¹⁷ אֵין אֲנַחְנוּ for אֵינֶנּוּ is due to its being co-ordinate with three other (substantival) subjects; these are again expressly summed up in אֵין־אֲנַחְנוּ.—In Hag 2¹⁷ אֵין אֶתְכֶם the pronominal complement of אֵין appears

---

[1] In Jer 51³ the pointing אֶל־ occurs twice instead of אַל־, and is thus, in the opinion of the Masoretes, equivalent to *against* him that *bendeth*; but undoubtedly we should read אַל־.

to follow with the sign of the accusative;[1] but most probably we should read with the LXX שְׁבְכֶם for אֶתְכֶם.

(4) The fact that אֵין (like אַיִן) always includes the idea of a verb (*is not, O was not*, &c.) led finally to such a predominance of the verbal element, that the original character of אֵין as a construct state (but cf. *i* above) was forgotten, and accordingly it is very frequently separated from its noun (substantive or participle); especially so by the insertion of shorter words (of the nature of enclitics), e. g. בּוֹ Is 1[6], לוֹ Lv 11[10.12], לָהּ Gn 11[30], גַּם ψ 14[3], שָׁם Ju 18[10], Ex 12[30]; but cf. also ψ 5[10], 6[6], 32[2], and אֵין used absolutely in Ex 22[2], 1 K 8[9], Ru 4[4].—Hence, finally, even the transposition of אֵין and its noun became possible, e. g. Gn 40[8] and 41[15] וּפֹתֵר אֵין אֹתוֹ *and an interpreter there is not of it*; Gn 47[13], Ju 14[6], 1 S 21[2], Is 1[30], Jer 30[13], Hb 2[19], Pr 5[17] (וְאֵין) = *neve sint*; cf. *k* above, on Jb 3[9]); 30[27].—In Gn 19[31], Ex 5[16] אֵין is placed between the subject and predicate.

Rem. 1. Like כֹּל . . . לֹא or לֹא . . . כֹּל (see *b* above) so also אֵין כֹּל *p* expresses an *absolute* negation, e. g. Ec 1[9] אֵין כָּל־חָדָשׁ *there is no new thing*, &c. ; 2 S 12[3], Dn 1[4] (cf. also אֵין מְאוּמָה *there is nothing*, 1 K 18[43], Ec 5[13]); as also כָּל־ . . . אֵין Hb 2[19]; cf. מְאוּמָה אֵין Ju 14[6].

2. Undoubtedly akin to אֵין in origin is the negative syllable אִי occurring *q* in the two compounds אִי כָבוֹד (as a proper name, 1 S 4[21]; Baer אִי־כָבוֹד) and אִי־נָקִי *not innocent*, Jb 22[30]; but the proper name אִיתָמָר is doubtful, and the fem. אִיזֶבֶל very doubtful. In Ethiopic this אִי is the most common form of negation, prefixed even to verbs.

(*d*) טֶרֶם *not yet*, when referring to past time is used, as a rule (§ 107 *c*), *r* with the imperfect, Gn 2[5] טֶרֶם . . . כֹּל *none* . . . *yet*; see *b* and *p* above; Gn 19[4], 24[45], Jos 2[8], 1 S 3[3]; with the imperfect in the sense of a present, Ex 10[7] הֲטֶרֶם תֵּדַע *knowest thou not yet?* Ex 9[30]; but cf. Gn 24[15], and בְּטֶרֶם with the perfect in ψ 90[2] (but see § 107 *c*), Pr 8[25].

(*e*) אֶפֶס (prop. a substantive, *cessation*) *no longer*, including the verbal idea *S* of *existing*, cf. Dt 32[36], Is 45[6.14], 46[9]; used absolutely, Am 6[10] in the question הַאֶפֶס עוֹד אִישׁ *is there none left?* &c., 2 S 9[3]; frequently also in the sense of *non nisi*; with ִי paragogic (§ 90 *m*) אַפְסִי Is 47[8.10], Zp 2[15] אֲנִי וְאַפְסִי עוֹד *I am, and there is none else.*

(*f*) בַּל,[2] in poetic and prophetic style, and with a certain emphasis, = לֹא, *t* is used with the imperfect, e. g. Is 26[14], 33[20.23] (immediately afterwards with a perfect); Ho 7[2], ψ 49[13], Pr 10[30] (but Is 14[21] before the jussive, = אַל־); before an adjective, Pr 24[23]; before a preposition, ψ 16[2], Pr 23[7].

(*g*) בְּלִי with a perfect, Gn 31[20], Is 14[6]; with an imperfect, Jb 41[18]; to negative a participle, Ho 7[8], ψ 19[4]; to negative an adjective, 2 S 1[21].

(*h*) בִּלְתִּי to negative an adjective, 1 S 20[26]; on בִּלְתִּי Ez 13[3], see *x*; on

---

[1] According to De Lagarde, *Novae psalterii graeci editionis specimen*, p. 26, ψ 3[3] יְשׁוּעָתָה is also an accusative after אֵין.

[2] Evidently from בָּלָה *to waste away*, from which stem also בְּלִי and בָּלַת (whence בִּלְתִּי § 90 *m*), originally substantives, are formed.

לְבִלְתִּי as the regular negative with the infinitive construct, see § 114 *s*; on לְבִלְתִּי as a conjunction, see *x* below.

On אִם as a negative particle in oaths (*verily not*), see § 149 *c* above.

u Rem. on בְּלִי, אֵין, לֹא. To the category of negative sentences belongs also the expression of negative attributes by means of בְּלִי, לֹא *not* (both so used almost exclusively in poetic language) or אֵין with a following substantive, mostly in the simplest form of circumstantial clause; e.g. 2 S 23⁴ בֹּקֶר לֹא עָבוֹת *a morning* when there are *not clouds*, i.e. *a cloudless morning*; cf. Jb 12²⁴, 26²ᵇ, 38²⁶ (לֹא־אִישׁ *where no man is*, i.e. *uninhabited*); 1 Ch 2³⁰·³² לֹא בָנִים *childless*; so also בְּלִי e.g. Jb 24¹⁰ and אֵין e.g. ψ 88⁵ *I am as a man* אֵין־אֱיָל *there is not help*, i.e. *like a helpless man*; Is 9⁶ אֵין־קֵץ *endless*; 47¹, Ho 7¹¹; אֵין־מִסְפָּר *countless*, Ct 6⁸, &c., but usually (ψ 104²⁵, &c.) like a proper circumstantial clause (cf. § 141 *e*) connected by *Wāw*, וְאֵין־מִסְפָּר.—Less frequently such periphrases take the form of relative clauses (cf. § 155 *e*), e.g. Jb 30¹³ לֹא עֹזֵר לָמוֹ they *for whom there is no helper*, i.e. *the helpless* (but probably עֹזֵר is only an intrusion from 29¹², and we should read עֹצֵר *without any one's restraining them*; in 29¹² translate *the fatherless and him that had none to help him*; in ψ 72¹² וְאֵין־עֹ' is used in the same sense); Hb 1¹⁴; with אֵין Is 45⁹ *thy work* is that of a man *who hath no hands*; Zc 9¹¹ *out of the waterless pit*.[1]

v How far such compounds finally came to be regarded by the language simply as negative adjectives, may be seen partly from the fact that they (as also relative clauses analogous to the above) are frequently co-ordinated with real adjectives, Jo 1⁶, ψ 72¹², Jb 29¹²; cf. also Is 59¹⁰, where כְּאֵין־עֵינַיִם is parallel with בְּעִוְרִים; partly from their being introduced by the sign of the dative לְ, e.g. Is 40²⁹ (= *and to the powerless*); Jb 26²ᵃ·³, Neh 8¹⁰.

w (*i*) פֶּן־ *lest, that not*, at the beginning of a clause expressing a fear or precaution, hence especially after such ideas as *fearing*, Gn 32¹², &c. (cf. δείδω μή, *vereor ne*), *taking heed*, frequently after הִשָּׁמֶר, הִשָּׁמְרוּ Gn 24⁶, 31²⁴, &c., *taking care*, 2 K 10²³, &c. Not infrequently the idea on which פֶּן־ depends, is only virtually contained in the main clause, e.g. Gn 19¹⁹ *I cannot escape to the mountain* (because I am afraid), פֶּן־תִּדְבָּקַנִי הָרָעָה *lest some evil overtake me*; Gn 26⁹, 38¹¹; also in Gn 44³⁴ from the rhetorical question *how shall I . . . ?* we must understand *I cannot*, governing פֶּן. This is especially the case after an appeal to do or not to do an action by which something may be prevented (in which case פֶּן־ is simply equivalent to the final *ne*); cf. e.g. Gn 11⁴, 19¹⁵, Nu 20¹⁸ (where פֶּן־ *lest* is separated from the verb by a strongly emphasized substantive); Ju 15¹² after *swear unto me*; Pr 24¹⁸.—In Gn 3²² *and now, lest he put forth his hand*, &c., פֶּן is to be regarded as virtually dependent on a cohortative, which immediately afterwards (verse 23) is changed into an historic tense; cf. also Gn 26⁷, 31³¹, 42⁴ Ex 13¹⁷, 1 S 13¹⁹, 27¹¹, ψ 38¹⁷, in every case after כִּי אָמַרְתִּי, כִּי אָמַר, &c. = *I thought*, &c., *I must beware lest*, &c.

Rem. According to § 107 *q*, פֶּן is naturally followed by the imperfect; for the exceptions, 2 S 20⁶, 2 K 2¹⁶, see § 107 *q*, note 3; cf. moreover, 2 K 10²³ רְאוּ פֶּן־יֵשׁ־פֹּה *look lest there be here*, &c.

---

[1] In Pr 9¹³ (perhaps also 14⁷; but see Delitzsch on the passage) a verbal clause is used co-ordinately in this way as a periphrasis for an adjective.

(k) לְבִלְתִּי *that . . . not*, with the imperfect, Ex 20²⁰, 2 S 14¹⁴ (in Jer 23¹⁴ *x*
read the infinitive שׁוּב for שָׁבוּ, in 27⁸ יָבֹא for בֹּאוּ). In Ez 13³ בִּלְתִּי רָאוּ
is a relative clause governed by לְ = *according to* things which *they have not seen*.

2. Two negatives in the same sentence do not neutralize each other *y*
(as in *nonnulli, non nemo*), but make the negation the more emphatic
(like οὐκ οὐδείς, οὐκ οὐδαμῶς, *nulli—non, nemo non*); e. g. Zp 2² (if the
text is correct) בְּטֶרֶם לֹא־יָבוֹא *before there shall* (not) *come.*[1] This
especially applies to the compounds formed by the union of אֵין or בְּלִי
with מִן־ *without* (§ 119 *y*), e. g. Is 5⁹ (6¹¹) מֵאֵין יוֹשֵׁב (for which in
Jer 2¹⁵ מִבְּלִי יֹשֵׁב), prop. *without no inhabitant*, i. e. *so that no inhabitant
is left there.* On the other hand, in Is 50² מֵאֵין מַיִם the מִן־ is causative,
because there is no water; as also in Ex 14¹¹ הֲמִבְּלִי אֵין־ *is it because
there were no . . . ?* 2 K 1³·⁶·¹⁶. In Ec 3¹¹ מִבְּלִי אֲשֶׁר לֹא *except that (yet
so that man cannot, &c.).*

3. The negative sometimes extends its influence from the first to *z*
a second negative sentence parallel with it (which may or may not
have *Wāw*); e. g. 1 S 2³ *talk not so much arrogancy; let* (not) *boasting
come out of your mouth*; Ex 28⁴³, Lv 19¹², 22⁹·¹⁵ *f.*, Nu 16¹⁴, 23¹⁹, Dt 7²⁵,
Is 23⁴, 28²⁷, 38¹⁸, 47¹⁴, Ez 16⁴⁷, ψ 9¹⁹, 13⁵, 35¹⁹, 38², 44¹⁹, 75⁶, Jb 28¹⁷ (so
לָמָּה לֹא *why . . . not ?* in Jb 3¹¹ also affects the parallel clause).

§ 153. *Restrictive and Intensive Clauses.*

The particles אַךְ, רַק *only*, serve to introduce restrictive clauses, and
גַּם, אַף *also, besides, even*, intensive clauses. It is to be observed that
the force of these particles does not necessarily affect the word which
immediately follows (as is the case with אַךְ Gn 7²³, 34¹⁵; רַק Gn 6⁵,
Am 3²; even הֲרַק אַךְ *hath he indeed only ?* Nu 12²; גַּם Gn 27³⁴, Jb 7¹¹;
אַף Dt 15¹⁷), but very frequently extends to the whole of the following
sentence. Thus with אַךְ, e. g. Nu 14⁹, 1 K 17¹³, Pr 17¹¹, Jb 13¹⁵, 14²²,
16⁷, 23⁶; רַק Gn 20¹¹, 24⁸, ψ 32⁶, Pr 13¹⁰; גַּם Gn 27³³, 32²¹ (גַּם הִנֵּה), 44¹⁰;
1 S 22⁷, 28²⁰, Zc 9¹¹, Pr 17²⁶, 20¹¹; אַף Jb 14³, 15⁴.—In Mal 1¹⁰ and
Jb 2¹⁰ גַּם is placed before two co-ordinate sentences, although, strictly
speaking, it applies only to the second. Cf. the analogous examples
in § 150 *m*.

---

[1] In 1 K 10²¹ אֵין־כֶּסֶף goes with what precedes and must be emended,
with the LXX and Lucian, to כִּי הַכֶּסֶף.

§ 154. *Sentences connected by Wāw.*

a　*Wāw copulativum*[1] (וְ) serves to connect two or more sentences, or single words (on its various vocalization, cf. § 104 *d–g*). Its use, however, is by no means restricted merely to joining sentences which

---

[1] For further particulars of the use of *wāw copulativum*, see Gesenius' *Thesaurus*, i. 393 ff. On its use in the co-ordination of similar tenses and moods (e. g. five imperfects consecutive in Gn 25³⁴, five perfects with וְנָם) as well as of dissimilar tenses and moods, the remarks made in the treatment of the tenses will suffice. With regard to the connexion of single *nouns* by וְ (which strictly speaking is always really a contraction of so many clauses into a single sentence) the following observations may be made :—

(*a*) Contrary to English usage, which in lengthy enumerations uses the *and* to connect only the last member of the series, in Hebrew *polysyndeton* is customary, as in Gn 12¹⁶ wāw copulativum six times, 24³⁵ seven times, 15¹⁹ ᶠᶠ· nine times, and in Jos 7²⁴ ten times. Sometimes, however, only the last two words are joined (so in a series of three members, Gn 5³², 10¹, 11²⁶, 13², 14¹, 30³⁹, &c.; the last three out of a series of four, Jer 2²⁶) ; less frequently only the first two, ψ 45⁹ ; cf. § 132 *d*. The formula תְּמוֹל שִׁלְשׁוֹם *yesterday* (and) *the day before yesterday*, Ex 5⁸, &c., is always without the copula. On the other hand, the *constructio asyndetos* in a series of verbs is used as a rhetorical expedient to produce a hurried and so an impassioned description ; e. g. Ju 5²⁷ *at her feet he bowed, he fell, he lay* ; Ex 15⁹, Dt 32¹⁵, 1 S 15⁶, Jer 4⁷, Am 5²¹, ψ 10¹⁰, 14¹, 45⁵, Jb 20¹⁹, 28⁴, 29⁸, Ct 2¹¹, 5⁶, &c.

(*b*) Frequently *wāw copulativum* is also *explanatory* (like *isque, et—quidem*, and the German *und zwar*, English *to wit*), and is then called *wāw explicativum*, e. g. Gn 4⁴ *and* (i. e. namely) *of the fat thereof* (unless it is simply copulative) ; Ex 24¹², 25¹² (*to wit two*) ; 27¹⁴, 28²³, Ju 17³ (in וּמַסֵּכָה ; here as often elsewhere, to introduce an explanatory gloss, cf. Is 17⁸, Ez 3¹⁵, and especially P. Haupt, *SBOT.* Isaiah, p. 90, l. 21 ff.), 1 S 17³⁴ *and that too with the bear* ; 2 S 13²⁰, Is 57¹¹, Jer 17¹⁰, Am 3¹¹, 4¹⁰, Ze 9⁹, Pr 3¹², Neh 8¹³, 2 Ch 23¹⁰ (but in 1 S 28³ the וּ before בְּעִירוֹ is to be omitted with the LXX) ; cf. also such combinations as מִן—וְעַד *from . . . and even to . . .*, Gn 13³, 14²³, 19⁴·¹¹, &c.—In 1 S 6¹¹ (see Driver on the passage), 2 S 1²³, &c., וּ is equivalent to *yea, and* ; in Is 32⁷ *even.*

וּ is used to express emphasis (=*and especially*), e. g. in Gn 3¹⁶ וְהֵרֹנֵךְ ; Is 2¹, ψ 18¹, perhaps also in Jb 10¹⁷ *yea, a whole host* ; 2 Ch 16¹⁴.—An undoubted example of what is called *wāw concomitantiae* occurs in Jb 41¹² *a seething pot* וְאַגְמֹן *with burning rushes* ; cf. Ex 10¹⁰ (*with your little ones*), 12⁸, Lv 1¹², Is 42⁵. In Arabic this *wāw concom.* is followed by the accusative.

וּ—וּ is used in the sense of *both—and* in ψ 76⁷, Dn 1³, 8¹³. On וּ—וּ as meaning *sive—sive*, cf. § 162 *b*.

(*c*) See the Lexicon on adverbs used in a copulative sense, such as גַּם *also, moreover*, summing up a number, e. g. גַּם־שְׁנֵיהֶם *both together*, Gn 27⁴⁵, Pr 17¹⁵ ; גַּם־כֹּל *all together* ; as an intensive *and*, e. g. Gn 30⁸, 37⁷, 1 S 30⁸ ; cf. also such examples as 1 S 24¹² *see, yea see!* גַּם—גַּם or וְגַם—גַּם Gn 24⁴⁴ = *both—and* ; גַּם occurs three times in Gn 24²⁵ and 32²⁰ ; also אַף, which is generally still more intensive, in the sense of *also, in addition to this, even*, and belongs rather to poetry, and to the later language ; frequently also equivalent to a mere *and*, but sometimes adversative *but now*, ψ 44¹⁰, &c. ; and אַף—אַף (also three times), equivalent to *both—and* ; cf. גַּם וְאַף *and even*, Lv 26⁴⁴ ; אַף־כִּי prop. *add to this also that*, equivalent to *not to mention*, according to the context either *quanto magis* or *quanto minus*.

are actually co-ordinate. Frequently the language employs merely the simple connexion by *Wāw*, even to introduce an antithesis (Gn 17²¹, 19¹⁹, Lv 2¹², Jb 6²⁵, and very frequently in circumstantial noun-clauses), or when one of the two clauses is not co-ordinated, but subordinated to the other. On the use of וְ to introduce circumstantial clauses, cf. especially § 141 *e* and § 142 *d*; introducing causal clauses, § 158 *a*; comparative clauses, § 161 *a*; final clauses, § 165 *a*; consecutive clauses, § 166 *a*. On *wāw apodosis*, cf. § 143 *d*, and the sections there cited; on the use of *Wāw* in numerical sayings, cf. § 134 *s*.

Rem. Sometimes wāw copulativum joins a sentence apparently to what *b* immediately precedes, but in reality to a sentence which is suppressed and which must, therefore, be supplied from the context. So especially וְ with imperatives to express inferences, e.g. 1 K 2²² וְשַׁאֲלִי *ask now rather*; Ez 18³² *for I have no pleasure in the death of him that dieth* . . ., וְהָשִׁיבוּ *wherefore turn yourselves*. Also at the beginning of a speech in loose connexion with an act or speech of another person, e.g. Ex 2²⁰, 2 S 18¹¹, 24³, 2 K 4¹⁴·⁴¹, 7¹³, 2 Ch 25⁹; cf. also Jos 7⁷ (וְלוּ), ψ 2¹⁰, 4⁴, Is 8⁷. Sometimes the suppression of the protasis is due to passionate excitement or haste, which does not allow time for full expression; this is especially illustrated by Nu 12¹⁴, 20³ (וְלוּ), 1 S 10¹², 15¹⁴, 22¹⁴, 28¹⁶, 2 S 18¹², 24³, 1 K 2²² (וְלָמָּה), 2 K 1¹⁰, 7¹⁹ (cf. verse 2); Is 3¹⁴, Zc 2¹⁰, ψ 2⁶ (at the same time a circumstantial clause *whereas I = and yet I have*, &c.); cf. also a new clause beginning with the formula of wishing וּמִי Nu 11²⁹, Ju 9²⁹; on the disconnected use of וְלֹא and וַיֵּשׁ cf. § 159 *dd*.

§ 155. *Relative Clauses.*

See V. Baumann, *Hebräische Relativsätze*, Leipzig, 1894 (cf. the heading of § 138 above); G. Bergsträsser, ʻDas hebr. Präfix שׁ,ʼ *ZATW.* 1909, p. 40 ff.[1]

1. By § 138 *a, e*, relative clauses are divided into two classes: those *a* which are used for the nearer definition of a noun (substantive or pronoun), and those which are not dependent on a noun. The former may be called *incomplete*, the latter *complete* relative clauses.

Complete relative clauses, as a rule (see the exceptions under *n*), *b* are introduced by the originally demonstrative pronoun אֲשֶׁר; see further in § 138 *e*. Similarly, incomplete relative clauses may also be introduced by אֲשֶׁר, or by some other demonstrative pronoun; see further in § 138 *a* and *g-k*. Very frequently, however, especially

---

[1] In this exhaustive article the author shows that between שׁ (on the pronunciation see § 36) and אֲשֶׁר there is syntactically no primary difference, but only a secondary distinction which arose in the course of the development of the language, namely that אֲשֶׁר is preferred in combinations which are customary in the old literary language, and שׁ in those which are derived from the popular language or from Aramaic.

in poetic style, the attributive relation is expressed by simple co-ordination.[1]

c The governing substantive or pronoun is frequently (in certain cases *always*) resumed by a pronominal suffix or an adverb. The resumption may, however, be omitted, just as in relative clauses introduced by אֲשֶׁר, &c.; see § 138 *f*.

d In Arabic a distinction is made between relative clauses used for the nearer definition of a *determinate* substantive (*ṣila*), and those which are attached to an *indeterminate* substantive (*ṣifa*). The former must be introduced by the demonstrative pronoun *allaḏī*, the latter are always simply co-ordinated. The same distinction was no doubt originally observed in Hebrew, since simply co-ordinated relative clauses are most commonly found after *indeterminate* substantives (see the examples below), and in cases like Dt 28⁴⁹ (גּוֹי אֲשֶׁר לֹא־תִשְׁמַע לְשֹׁנוֹ) *a nation whose tongue thou shalt not understand*; cf. Is 66¹³, and especially 1 S 3¹¹), the addition of אֲשֶׁר is explained from the special stress laid on the indeterminate substantive,[2] *a nation of such a kind, thou understandest not their tongue*. On the other hand, in poetic style at least, אֲשֶׁר is somewhat frequently omitted even after a determinate noun, but only rarely in prose (except by the Chronicler; cf. 1 Ch 9²², 12²³, 29¹ (read prob. אֲשֶׁר for אֶחָד), 2 Ch 15¹¹; after־כָּל 1 Ch 29³, 2 Ch 18²³, 30¹⁷, 31¹⁹, Ezr 1⁵, but also Gn 39⁴; for further instances, see Driver, *Introd.*⁸, p. 537, no. 30); so Ex 18²⁰, Ju 8¹, 20¹⁵, 1 K 13¹² (=which way), so 2 K 3⁸, 2 Ch 18²³; Neh 13²³; after a pronominal subject, 1 S 6⁹. In Jer 52¹² for עֹמֵד read עָמַד with the LXX.

e 2. If the nearer definition of a substantive or pronoun is effected by simple co-ordination of the relative clause, it may take the form—

(*a*) Of a noun-clause, e. g. 2 S 20²¹ *a man of the hill country of Ephraim* שֶׁבַע שְׁמוֹ *whose name was Sheba*; Zc 6¹², Jb 1¹, 3¹⁵ *with princes* זָהָב לָהֶם *that had gold*; ψ 11⁴, Pr 22¹¹; when referring to a noun-suffix, e. g. ψ 49¹⁴ זֶה דַרְכָּם כֵּסֶל לָמוֹ *this is the way of them who have* (self-)*confidence*.—On periphrases of this kind to express negative attributes, as in Jb 38²⁶ עַל־אֶרֶץ לֹא־אִישׁ *on a land* where *no man is*, see § 152 *u*, and cf. for this very short form of the relative clause, Gn 15¹³ בְּאֶרֶץ לֹא לָהֶם *in a land* that belongs *not to them*; Dt 32¹⁷ (לְשֵׁדִים לֹא אֱלֹהַּ2); Hb 1⁶, Pr 26¹⁷ (לֹא־לוֹ).

f (*b*) Of a verbal clause.

Here we must distinguish the cases in which the retrospective pronoun—

(1) Is the subject of the relative clause, and is contained in the

---

[1] The old view that all these cases arise from the *omission* of אֲשֶׁר is incorrect. These co-ordinated attributive clauses are rather a mere subdivision of the various kinds of circumstantial clauses (see § 156) which may be attached to a *nomen regens*. Cf. in English *this is the letter* (which) *he wrote to me*.

[2] So Baumann, *op. cit.*, p. 14 f., following Böttcher, *Lehrbuch*, ii. 80.

verb; so after a determinate substantive, ψ 34⁹ *happy is the man*
יֶחֱסֶה־בּוֹ *that trusteth in him*; Jb 3³ᵇ הַלַּיְלָה אָמַר *the night which said*;
after כָּל־ ψ 71¹⁸; referring to a vocative, which is determinate in
itself even without the article, Is 54¹, or to a noun-suffix (see under *e*),
ψ 16⁴; after an indeterminate substantive, e. g. Jb 31¹² *it is a fire*
(that) *devoureth unto Abaddon*; Dt 32¹⁷ᵇ, 1 S 6⁹, Is 55¹³, 56², ψ 68³¹, 78⁶,
Pr 30¹⁷, La 1¹⁰, 2 Ch 28⁹; referring to the suffix in הִנְנִי Is 28¹⁶, prop.
behold me, who have laid, &c., but perhaps the participle יֹסֵד is to be
read; 29¹⁴, 38⁵ (but probably again the participle יֹסֵף should be read
instead of the imperfect); Ez 25⁷. The relative clause is used in this
way especially to supply the place of an adjective, e. g. Gn 49²⁷ זְאֵב
יִטְרָף *a wolf that ravineth*, i. e. *a ravining wolf*; Is 51¹²; to express a
negative quality, e. g. Is 40²⁰, Ho 4¹⁴ עָם לֹא־יָבִין *an undiscerning people*.

Rem. Very frequently such relative sentences are attached to substantives *g*
which have the particle of comparison כְּ, e. g. Jb 7² כְּעֶבֶד יִשְׁאַף־צֵל *as a servant
that earnestly desireth the shadow*, &c.; Dt 32¹¹, Is 62¹, Jer 23²⁹, Ho 6³, ψ 42², 83¹⁵,
Jb 9²⁶, 11¹⁶; so also after כְּמוֹ ψ 58⁵; after a determinate substantive, e. g.
Is 53⁷ (but the better reading is כַּשֶּׂה without the article), 61¹⁰ᶠ·, Hb 2¹⁴,
ψ 49¹³·²¹, 125¹; see also the examples under *h*. Sometimes it seems simpler
in such cases, to take the verb directly as predicate to the preceding
substantive, and to explain כְּ (for כַּאֲשֶׁר; see *Comparative Clauses*, § 161 *b*) as
a conjunction—a view which even Hupfeld was ready to accept, at least as
regards ψ 90⁵, 125¹, Is 53⁷, 61¹¹, but it can hardly be right.

(2) The cases in which the retrospective pronoun represents an *h*
accusative of the object, or would do so if not suppressed, as it usually
is in such cases in relative clauses with אֲשֶׁר, cf. § 138 *b*. Examples
with the retrospective pronoun are, Dt 32¹⁷ אֱלֹהִים לֹא יְדָעוּם *gods whom
they knew not* (see also the end of the verse); after a substantive with כְּ
(see above, *g*), Jer 23⁹, Jb 13²⁸. Without a retrospective pronoun,
after a determinate substantive, Ju 8¹, ψ 33¹² (preceded by a relative
clause with אֲשֶׁר); Jb 28¹. Other examples of this kind, though the
article is omitted according to poetic usage, are Is 15⁷ (יִתְרָה עָשָׂה, for
which Jer 48³⁶ יִתְרַת עָשָׂה with the substantive in the construct state
governing the relative clause, see § 130 *d*), ψ 7¹⁶, 51¹⁰, La 1²¹.—Without the retrospective pronoun, after an indeterminate substantive, e. g.
Is 6⁶ רִצְפָּה בְּמֶלְקָחַיִם לָקַח מֵעַל הַמִּזְבֵּחַ *a live coal which he had taken with
the tongs from off the altar*; Ex 15¹⁷, Is 42¹⁶ (48¹⁷, ψ 25¹², all after
בְּדֶרֶךְ; but ψ 32⁸ (בְּדֶרֶךְ־זוּ תֵלֵךְ); Is 64²; Ec 10⁵ (in 6¹ the same clause
with אֲשֶׁר); moreover, in Jer 14¹⁸ read with the LXX אֶל־אֶרֶץ לֹא יָדְעוּ
into a land (that) *they know not*.

(3) The cases in which the retrospective pronoun is dependent on *i*
a preposition, or its place is taken by the adverb שָׁם, as in Jer 2⁶ end.

Thus after a determinate substantive, צוּרִי אֶחֱסֶה־בּוֹ *my rock in which I take refuge*; Ex 18²⁰, Is 42¹; in Jb 3³ᵃ also, the omission of the article with יוֹם is only a poetic licence. After an indeterminate substantive, Jer 2⁶, last clause but one; ψ 32².

k In this case also the retrospective word is not infrequently suppressed, giving rise to extremely short, bold expressions, such as Is 51¹ *look unto the rock* חֻצַּבְתֶּם (whence) *ye were hewn, and to the hole of the pit* נֻקַּרְתֶּם (whence) *ye were digged*; Jb 21²⁷ *the devices* (wherewith) *ye act violently against me.*—A retrospective adverb is suppressed in Jb 38¹⁹ *where is the way* (to the place where) *the light dwelleth?* cf. 38²⁴.

l Rem. 1. The omission of the retrospective word occurs most frequently in relative clauses which are governed by the construct state of a preceding substantive (especially an expression of time) and hence are virtually in the genitive. In addition to the instances already given in § 130 *d*, cf. the following: after בְּיוֹם Lv 7³⁵, ψ 56¹⁰; after מִיּוֹם Jer 36²; after simple יוֹם ψ 56⁴ (יוֹם אִירָא *on the day* when *I am afraid*); after בְּעֵת 2 Ch 29²⁷ (בְּעֵת הֵחֵל הָעוֹלָה *at the time* when *the burnt offering began*); 20²², 24¹¹, Jb 6¹⁷; after לְעֵת Dt 32³⁵; after עַד־עֵת Mi 5²; after מֵעֵת ψ 4⁸ *thou hast put gladness in my heart more than* (their gladness) *at the time* (when) *their corn and their wine are increased.*

m 2. The agreement (§ 138 *d*) of the retrospective pronoun with a pronominal regens in the 1st or 2nd person also takes place in a simple co-ordinated relative clause in 1 S 26¹⁴ *who art thou* (that) *criest?* Cf., however, Is 63¹⁹ *we are become* as they *over whom* (בָּם not בָּנוּ) *thou no longer bearest rule.*

n 3. Occasionally—chiefly in poetic or otherwise elevated style—even *independent* relative clauses are simply co-ordinated with a regens, whereas we should expect them always to be preceded by a demonstrative pronoun, on the analogy of the examples in § 138 *e*. The suppressed pronoun would stand—

(*a*) As subject, Is 41²⁴ *an abomination* (is he) *that chooseth you* (but read perhaps לִבְחֹר); Jb 30¹³, cf. § 152 *u*.

(*b*) As object, Is 41², with a retrospective pronoun; Mal 2¹⁶ וְכִסָּה *and him that covereth* (or read וְכִסָּה?); Jb 29¹² *I delivered . . . the fatherless also, and him that had none to help him.*

(*c*) In the genitive governed by a substantive (cf. § 130 *d*), Ex 4¹³ שְׁלַח־נָא בְּיַד־תִּשְׁלָח *send, I pray thee, by the hand of* him *whom thou wilt send*, i.e. by the hand of some one else; ψ 65⁵ and Pr 8³², verbal-clauses after אַשְׁרֵי *O the happiness of* the man, &c.; ψ 81⁶, 141⁹, Jb 29¹⁶, La 1¹⁴; after כָּל־ Gn 39⁴, but we must certainly read here, with the Samaritan and LXX, כָּל־אֲשֶׁר יֶשׁ־לוֹ as in verses 5 and 8; Ex 9⁴; verbal-clauses after כָּל־ 1 Ch 29³, 2 Ch 30¹⁹, 31¹⁹, Ezr 1⁵.

(*d*) Governed by a preposition; so verbal-clauses after אַחֲרֵי Jer 2⁸; after אֶל־ (= *to the place where*), 1 Ch 15¹², but Ex 23²⁰ before the same verb אֲשֶׁר אֶל־הַמָּקוֹם; after בְּ Jer 2¹¹, 2 Ch 1⁴ (בְּהַכִין=בְּהֵ'=*to the place where*); after לְ Is 65¹ לְלוֹא שָׁאֵלוּ by them *that asked not* for me . . . לְלֹא בִקְשֻׁנִי them *that sought me not*; Ez 13³ that which *they have not seen*, but the text is hardly correct; after עַל ψ 119¹³⁶, cf. § 158 *b*; after עַם 2 Ch 16⁹.—A noun-clause follows לְ in Neh 8¹⁰. An analogous instance in Aramaic is Ezr 5¹⁴ *to one whose name was Sheshbazzar* [so in the papyri, see the Lexicon, p. 1116ᵃ].

§ 156. *Circumstantial Clauses.*

1. The statement of the particular circumstances under which *a* a subject appears as performing some action, or under which an action (or an occurrence) is accomplished, is made especially (apart from relative clauses, see § 155) by means of noun-clauses connected by *Wāw* with a following subject (see further on this kind of *circumstantial clause* in § 141 *e*), and by verbal-clauses (see § 142 *d*). Very frequently, however, such statements of the particular circumstances are subordinated to the main clause by being simply attached, without *Wāw*, either as noun-clauses, sometimes extremely short (see *c*), or as verbal-clauses (see *d–g*).

Rem. Among relative clauses of this kind the commonest are the various *b* noun-clauses, which are most closely subordinated to a preceding substantive without אֲשֶׁר, e. g. Gn 16¹²; also statements of weight, Gn 24²²; of name, Jb 1¹ (also introduced by וּשְׁמוֹ Gn 24²⁹, 1 S 1¹, &c., or וּשְׁמָהּ Gn 16¹, 22²⁴, &c.); of a condition of body, Ju 1⁷, and others.—Noun-clauses which begin with *wāw* and the *predicate* have a somewhat more independent character than those introduced by *wāw* and the *subject*[1] (Gn 19¹, &c.). The former, however, are also to be regarded as circumstantial clauses, in so far as they describe a *state* which is simultaneous with the principal action ; thus Is 3⁷ *I will not be an healer*, וּבְבֵיתִי אֵין לֶחֶם *while in my house is neither bread nor clothing* ; Is 6⁶ (Am 7⁷) ; 2 S 13¹⁸, 16¹. Cf. also the instances in § 152 *l* of וְאֵין followed by a participle, as וְאֵין מַצִּיל, &c.

2. Characteristic examples of circumstantial *noun*-clauses are Gn 12⁸ *c* and *pitched his tent* בֵּית־אֵל מִיָּם וְהָעַי מִקֶּדֶם *with Bethel on the west and Ai on the east*; Nu 22²⁴, 2 S 18¹⁴ *through the heart of Absalom,* עוֹדֶנּוּ חַי *while he was yet alive*; Jer 30⁶, Ez 9² (cf. Ct 3⁸), Na 3⁸, Zc 14⁵, 2 Ch 23¹⁰; with the predicate preceding, e. g. 1 S 26¹³, ψ 32⁸.—In Gn 41²⁹ a noun-clause serves to announce a state in the future.—We may also include here certain set phrases, as פָּנִים אֶל־פָּנִים *face to face* (prop. *while face was turned towards face*), Gn 32³¹, Ex 33¹¹, Dt 34¹⁰,

---

[1] In Dt 32³¹ this form of sequence appears to be selected for another purpose, *and indeed our enemies are judges* thereof, with *wāw* emphatic ; to take it as a circumstantial clause is too artificial.

&c.; [1] so also *to cast oneself down*, אַפַּ֫יִם אַ֫רְצָה *the face* being turned *to the earth*, Gn 19¹, &c. (for אַ֫רְצָה we find אֶ֫רֶץ in 1 K 1³¹, Is 49²³).[2]—Cf. finally the formula אֵם עַל־בָּנִים *mother with children*, Gn 32¹²; cf. Ho 10¹⁴ and § 119 *aa* note 2.

Rem. On circumlocutions of this kind to express negative attributes by means of short noun-clauses (complete or incomplete), cf. § 152 *u*.

d　3. As circumstantial *verbal*-clauses,[3] we find (1) sometimes affirmative clauses (see below), but far more frequently (2) negative clauses (see *f*), and among these (3) a certain number of expressions which may be regarded simply as equivalent to negative adverbial ideas (see *g*).

Examples of (1) Is 5¹¹ᵇ woe unto them, that tarry late in the evening, יַ֫יִן יַדְלִיקֵם *while wine inflames them*; Is 1⁵, 10²⁴, 30³¹, Jer 7²⁶, 20¹⁵, ψ 4³, 5¹², 21¹³, 62⁵. The circumstantial verbal-clause is used to particularize an action which has before been expressed generally, in Gn 44¹², 48¹⁴ = *crossing his hands*; Dt 2²⁷, Ju 6¹⁹; antithetically, 1 K 13¹⁸ כִּחֵשׁ לוֹ *wherewith however he lied unto him*. The verbal-clause seems to assign a reason in ψ 7⁷ מִשְׁפָּט צִוִּ֫יתָ *since thou hast commanded judgement*; a consequence in ψ 103⁵.[4]

e　Rem. On the cases in which an imperfect in the sense of a final clause is subordinated to a verb of motion (generally קוּם), see § 120 *c*.

f　Of (2), subordinate verbal-clauses with לֹא (in English usually rendered by *without* and the gerund, if the subject be the same as in the principal clause), e.g. Lv 1¹⁷ לֹא יַבְדִּיל *without dividing it asunder*; Jb 31³⁴; לֹא with the perfect is so used in Gn 44⁴, Ex 34²⁸, 1 S 30², Jb 20²⁶ (*without its being blown upon it*). With a different subject, equivalent to a consecutive clause in English, Is 27⁹ לֹא־יָקֻ֫מוּ *so that they shall rise up no more*.—Moreover, verbal-clauses in the same sense (*without doing*, &c.) are frequently connected by וְלֹא; cf. 1 S 20², Jb 24²², 42³; in a concessive sense, Is 33¹, ψ 44¹⁸.

g　Of (3), cf. לֹא יָדַע (prop. *he knows it not*) *unawares*, ψ 35⁸, Pr 5⁶ לֹא יַחְמֹל *unsparingly*, Is 30¹⁴ (after an infinitive absolute); Hb 1¹⁷, Jb 6¹⁰ (but וְלֹא יַחְמֹל Jb 16¹³, 27²²; see *f* at the end); לֹא כִחֵ֫דוּ (prop. *they hide not*) *openly*, Is 3⁹ (but

---

[1] The expression הִתְרָאָה פָנִים *to look one another in the face* (i. e. to contend in combat) 2 K 14⁸·¹¹, 2 Ch 25¹⁷·²¹, is probably only a shortened form for הִתְרָאָה פָנִים אֶל־פָּנִים.

[2] That אַ֫רְצָה (אֶ֫רֶץ) is really to be regarded as a virtual predicate to אַפַּ֫יִם, and not אַפַּ֫יִם as a *casus instrumenti*, is seen from Is 49²³, where אַפַּ֫יִם אֶ֫רֶץ precedes the verb.

[3] Some examples of these have been already discussed in another connexion above, § 120 *a–c*.

[4] In Gn 21¹⁴ the circumstantial verbal-clause שָׂם עַל־שִׁכְמָהּ is only due to a harmonizing transposition; read וְאֶת־הַיֶּ֫לֶד שׂ׳ ע׳ שׁ׳. According to the source used in cap. 21 Ishmael was still a young child; according to 17²⁵ he was about 16 or 17 years old.

Jb 15¹⁸ (וְלֹא כָתֲדוּ) ; בְּלִי חָשַׂךְ (prop. *he restrains not*) *unceasingly*, Is 14⁶ ; בַּל־יִמּוֹט

Jb 41¹⁵ (ψ 93¹) (בַּל־תִּמּוֹט) and לֹא יִמּוֹט Is 40²⁰ (*without tottering*) *immovably* ; cf.

also לֹא אֶמְעָד *without wavering*, ψ 26¹.

§ 157. *Object-Clauses (Oratio Obliqua).*

Clauses which depend on a transitive verb, especially on what are *a* called *verba cordis*, i. e. verbs denoting any mental act, such as *to see*, *to hear*, *to know*, *to perceive*, *to believe*, *to remember*, *to forget*, *to say*, *to think*, &c., may be subordinated to the governing verb without the help of a conjunction by simple juxtaposition (§ 120 *a*), or they may be co-ordinated with it either with or without *wāw copulative* (§ 120 *d–h*). As a rule, however, the objective clause is introduced by the conjunction כִּי *that*, less frequently by אֲשֶׁר *that.*[1]

Examples:—

(*a*) Object-clauses without a conjunction. Besides the passages mentioned in § 120 (especially under *e*) there are a number of examples, in which a clause depending on a *verbum dicendi* or *sentiendi* (the *oratio obliqua* of the Latin and English Grammar) is added in the form of an independent noun-clause or verbal-clause ; e. g. Gn 12¹³ אִמְרִי־נָא אֲחֹתִי אָתְּ *say, I pray thee, thou art my sister* ; ψ 10¹³, Jb 25⁸ᵃ·¹⁴, Neh 6⁶ ; Zc 8²³ (after שָׁמַע) ; ψ 9²¹ (after יָדַע) ; verbal-clauses, e. g. ψ 50²¹ *thou thoughtest* הֱיוֹת־אֶהְיֶה כָמוֹךָ *I was surely like thyself* [but read הָיֹו for הֱיוֹת] ; Gn 41¹⁵, Ju 9⁴⁸ *what ye have seen me do* ; Is 48⁸, Ho 7².

(*b*) Object-clauses introduced by כִּי, e. g. Gn 6⁵ וַיַּרְא יְהוָֹה כִּי רַבָּה רָעַת הָאָדָם *b* *and the Lord saw that the wickedness of man was great*, &c.—Direct narration also is very frequently introduced by כִּי (analogous to the ὅτι *recitativum* ; frequently, indeed, with the secondary idea of a particle of asseveration, as in Gn 26⁹, 27²⁰), e. g. Gn 21³⁰, 22¹⁶ ᶠ·, 26²², 29³², 37³⁵, Jos 2²⁴, &c., even when the direct narration is not expressly indicated, Gn 4²⁵, 3²³¹, 41⁵¹ ᶠ·, Ex 18⁴.—On the expression of a second object by means of a clause introduced by כִּי, see § 117 *h*.[2]

(*c*) Object-clauses introduced by אֲשֶׁר, e. g. Est 3⁴ כִּי־הִגִּיד לָהֶם אֲשֶׁר־הוּא *c* יְהוּדִי *for he had told them that he was a Jew* ; 1 S 18¹⁵, Ez 20²⁶, Ec 8¹²,[3] even before direct narration, 1 S 15²⁰, 2 S 1⁴. Somewhat frequently אֲשֶׁר is preceded by

---

[1] On these clauses with כִּי and אֲשֶׁר and generally on clauses which we should render as subordinate, cf. P. Dörwald 'Zur hebr. Syntax' in *Neue Jahrbb. für Philol. und Pädag.* 1890, p. 115 ff.

[2] Instead of a complete objective clause we sometimes find a kind of accusative and infinitive construction, especially after נָתַן (prop. *to give up*) in the sense of *to allow*, e. g. Nu 21²³ וְלֹא־נָתַן סִיחֹן אֶת־יִשְׂרָאֵל עֲבֹר בִּגְבֻלוֹ *and Sihon did not suffer Israel to pass through his border* ; 20²¹ ; followed by an infinitive with לְ, e. g. Gn 20⁶, 31⁷, Ex 3¹⁹.—Cf. also the analogous examples in Dt 28⁵⁶ (after נָסָּה *to venture* ; see § 113 *d*) ; Ju 11²⁰ (after הֶאֱמִין *to trust*) ; 1 K 19⁴ (after שָׁאַל *to request*).

[3] In Jer 28⁹ a *subject*-clause is thus introduced by אֲשֶׁר instead of the usual כִּי.

the *nota accusativi* אֵת־ (equivalent to *the circumstance, the fact, that*), e. g. Jos 2¹⁰, 1 S 24¹¹·¹⁹, 2 S 11²⁰, Is 38³, but in Gn 30²⁹, Dt 29¹⁵ equivalent to *the way in which*.

§ 158. *Causal Clauses.*

a A complete clause, assigning the reason for statements, demands, threats, &c., sometimes follows with the simple *wāw copulative*, e. g. ψ 60¹³ *give us help against the adversary, and* (for) *vain is the help of man*; Gn 6¹⁷ (וַאֲנִי), 22¹², Ex 23⁹, Jb 22¹², perhaps also ψ 7¹⁰; or even without *Wāw*, e. g. Gn 17¹⁴. As a rule, however, special conjunctions in various combinations are used to introduce causal clauses.

b The most common causal conjunctions are יַעַן כִּי Is 3¹⁶, &c., and יַעַן אֲשֶׁר *because, prop. on account of the fact that*; both, however, may also be shortened to the simple יַעַן Nu 20¹², &c., or to כִּי *because*, Gn 3¹⁴·¹⁷, &c., or to אֲשֶׁר Gn 30¹⁸, 31⁴⁹, 34¹³·²⁷, 1 S 15¹⁵, 20⁴², 26¹⁶·²³, 1 K 3¹⁹, 8³³, Ho 14⁴, Zc 1¹⁵; also בַּאֲשֶׁר Gn 39⁹·²³. On the other hand, the simple יַעַן is sometimes repeated for emphasis, יַעַן וּבְיַעַן (something like the German *sintemal und alldieweil*) Lv 26⁴³, Ez 13¹⁰ (without וּ 36³); also עַל־אֲשֶׁר 2 S 3³⁰, and עַל־כִּי 1 Dt 31¹⁷, Ju 3¹², Mal 2¹⁴ *on the ground that*; עַל־דְּבַר אֲשֶׁר *because of the circumstance that*, Dt 23⁵; עַל־כָּל־אֹדוֹת אֲשֶׁר *for this very cause that*, Jer 3⁸. But just as the simple יַעַן is used for יַעַן אֲשֶׁר, so also the simple עַל with the perfect stands for עַל־אֲשֶׁר ψ 119¹³⁶, Ezr 3¹¹; cf. עַל־בְּלִי Gn 31²⁰ and מִבְּלִי Dt 28⁵⁵ both with the perfect, equivalent to *because . . . not*.—Cf. further עֵקֶב אֲשֶׁר Gn 22¹⁸, 26⁵, 2 S 12⁶, all with the perfect, and עֵקֶב כִּי (2 S 12¹⁰ with the perfect; Am 4¹² with the imperfect) prop. *in return for the fact that*; similarly again the simple עֵקֶב Nu 14²⁴ with the perfect, and Dt 7¹², 8²⁰ with the imperfect; finally, מֵאֲשֶׁר Is 43⁴ *arising from the fact that*, = *because*; תַּחַת אֲשֶׁר 1 S 26²¹, &c., and תַּחַת כִּי Dt 4³⁷, Pr 1²⁹ *for the reason that*.

c Rem. 1. The preposition עַל־ (*because of, on account of*) with the infinitive (§ 114 *e*) is frequently used as the equivalent of a full causal clause; cf. e. g. Am 1³·⁶·¹³, 2¹·⁶. Such a construction with the infinitive may, however, according to § 114 *r*, be continued by means of a finite verb, in which case עַל־ governs the verb as a conjunction; e. g. Am 1⁹ . . . וְלֹא זָכְרוּ עַל־הַסְגִּירָם *because they delivered up . . . and remembered not*, &c.; 1¹¹, 2⁴; without *Wāw*, Is 30¹⁴.

d 2. The choice of tense is regulated by the general principles stated in § 106 ff., viz. the perfect (cf. especially § 106 *f*) refers to causes already brought fully into effect, the imperfect to those which may contingently arise; cf. e. g. Dt 7¹², 8²⁰, 1 K 8³³, where the imperfect leaves the possibility still open that the persons addressed will perhaps escape the threatened punishments by avoiding disobedience.—Cf. further, § 111 *h* on the imperfect consecutive, and § 112 *nn* on the perfect consecutive in the apodosis to causal clauses.

---

¹ Also כִּי־עַל־כֵּן prop. *for therefore*, Gn 18⁵, 19⁸, 33¹⁰, 38²⁶, Nu 10³¹, 14⁴³, 2 S 18²⁰ Q°rê, and אֲשֶׁר עַל־כֵּן Jb 34²⁷, always mean *forasmuch as*.

§ 159. *Conditional Sentences.*

Cf. H. Ferguson, 'The Use of the Tenses in Conditional Sentences in Hebrew' (*Journal of the Society of Bibl. Lit. and Exeg.*, Middletown, Conn., June and September, 1882).—P. Friedrich, *Die hebr. Conditionalsätze*, Königsberg, 1884 (Inaug.-Diss.).—Driver, *Use of the Tenses*, 3rd ed., p. 174 ff.

1. The great variety of construction in conditional sentences is *a* owing to the fact that it frequently depends on the subjective judgement of the speaker, whether he wishes a condition to be regarded as *capable of fulfilment* (absolutely, or at least possibly), thus including those already fulfilled, or as *incapable of fulfilment*. On this distinction depends the choice both of the conditional particle to be used (see below), and especially (as also in Greek and Latin) of the tense. The use of the latter is naturally determined according to the general principles laid down in § 106 ff.[1] In the following sketch, for the sake of clearness, conditional sentences *without* conditional particles will be first discussed (under *b*), and afterwards sentences *with* these particles (under *l*).

2. The relation between condition and consequence may be expressed, *b* as in English, by the simple juxtaposition of two clauses. At the same time, it is to be observed in general as a fundamental rule (in accordance with the original character of the two tenses), that the *imperfect*, with its equivalents (the jussive, cohortative, imperative, perfect consecutive, and participle), is used to express a condition and consequence which are regarded as being *capable of fulfilment* in present or future time, while the *perfect* represents a condition already fulfilled in the past, and its consequence as an accomplished fact. The other use of the perfect—to represent conditions regarded as *impossible*—occurs only in connexion with particles.

Examples :—

(*a*) *Imperfect* (cf. § 107 *x*) in protasis and apodosis, Jos 22¹⁸, ψ 104²⁸ ᶠᶠ. *C* תִּתֵּן לָהֶם ² יִלְקֹטוּן (if) *thou givest unto them, they gather*, &c. ; ψ 139¹⁸, Pr 12¹⁷, Jb 20²⁴, Ec 1¹⁸, Neh 1⁸ ; with an interrogative imperfect in the apodosis, Ju 13¹² ; with the jussive, Jb 10¹⁶ ; with the cohortative, Pr. 1²³ ; with the perfect, Is 26¹⁰ (*yet will he not learn righteousness* ; the apodosis forcibly denies

---

[1] It may, moreover, happen that a different idea is introduced in the apodosis, from that with which the protasis started—a source of many further variations.

[2] On the termination וּן- cf. § 47 *m*. In verse 28 *b* also יִשְׂבְּעוּן is probably to be explained from its immediately preceding the greater *pause*. These terminations in verses 28–30 and ψ 139¹⁸ can scarcely have any connexion with the conditional sentence, although it is strange that וּן- in Nu 32²³ appears after אִם־לֹא in the protasis. In Nu 16²⁹, 32²⁰ וּן- as before אֹ (as in Jb 31¹⁰ in the apodosis) is to be explained from the dislike of hiatus.

what the imperfect in the protasis had represented as still conceivable; cf. Ho 8[12]); with the perfect consecutive, Gn 47[25], Ex 33[5]; with the protasis suppressed, Jb 5[8] (see § 107 *x*).

d (*b*) *Jussive* in protasis (cf. § 109 *h*, *i*) and apodosis, ψ 104[10] תְּשֶׁת־חֹשֶׁךְ וִיהִי לָיְלָה (if) *thou makest darkness, it is night*; imperfect in the apodosis, ψ 104[29 *b*]; cohortative Pr 1[23]. Also in Ex 7[9] יְהִי לְתַנִּין *it shall become a serpent*, is the apodosis to a suppressed protasis *if thou cast it down*; so in 2 K 5[10] וְיָשֹׁב is the apodosis to a protasis *if thou wash*, contained in what precedes.

e (*c*) *Cohortative* (see § 108 *e*) in the protasis; perfect in the apodosis, ψ 40[6]; imperfect consecutive, Jb 19[18] אָקוּמָה וַיְדַבְּרוּ־בִי (if) *I arise, they speak against me*; on the cohortative in the apodosis, cf. § 108 *f*.

f (*d*) *Imperfect consecutive* in the protasis (§ 111 *x*), ψ 139[11] וָאֹמַר *if I say*, &c. (with a noun-clause as the apodosis); with a frequentative perfect consecutive in the apodosis, 1 S 2[16].

g (*e*) *Perfect consecutive* in the protasis and apodosis (see the examples, § 112 *kk* and *ll*), Gn 44[22] עָזַב אָבִיו וָמֵת *and should he leave his father, his father would die*; 9[15], 44[29], Ex 4[14], 12[13], 1 S 16[2], 19[3], 2 S 13[28], 1 K 8[30]; with frequentative perfects, Ex 16[21] (referring to the past, Jer 20[9]); with imperfect in the apodosis (being separated from the *Wāw* by לֹא), Nu 23[20], Jb 5[24]; introduced by an infinitive absolute, 1 K 2[37]; an interrogative clause in the apodosis, Lv 10[19]; a noun-clause, ψ 37[10], Jb 7[21].

h (*f*) *A simple perfect* (to represent actions which are to be regarded as completed) in the protasis and apodosis, Pr 18[22] מָצָא אִשָּׁה מָצָא טוֹב *has one found a wife, he has found a good thing*; an imperfect in the apodosis, Jb 19[4], 23[10]; an imperfect consecutive, Ex 20[25], Pr 11[2], Jb 3[25], 23[13 *b*], 29[11]; an interrogative clause, Nu 12[14], Jb 7[20] *if I have sinned* (prop., well, now I have sinned!) *what can I do unto thee?* 21[31], 35[6], Am 3[8]; a noun-clause, Jb 27[19].

i (*g*) *A participle* as *casus pendens* (cf. § 143 *d*, and the sections of the Grammar there cited, esp. § 116 *w*) or a complete noun-clause in the protasis; the apodosis mostly introduced by *wāw apodosis*, e.g. Pr 23[24] *Keth.* יוֹלֵד חָכָם וְיִשְׂמַח בּוֹ *if one begetteth a wise child, he shall have joy of him*; with perfect frequentative in the apodosis, 1 S 2[13], &c.; but also with a simple imperfect, e.g. Ex 21[12] (cf. § 112 *n*); with an interrogative imperfect, 2 K 7[2.19]; with an interrogative perfect, Ju 6[13].

k (*h*) *Infinitive with preposition* (also as the equivalent of a conditional clause) in the protasis, and a perfect consecutive in the apodosis (cf. § 112 *mm*), e.g. 2 S 7[14 ff.] בְּהַעֲוֹתוֹ וְהֹכַחְתִּיו וְגֹ׳ *if he commit iniquity, I will correct him*; Ex 34[34 f.] (with imperfect, followed by perfects frequentative in the apodosis).

Rem. On the expression of condition and consequence by means of two co-ordinate *imperatives*, see § 110 *f*.

l 3. Particles used to introduce conditional sentences are אִם (for which in the later and latest Books sometimes הֵן, see below, under *w*) and לוּ[1] (1 S 14[30], Is 63[19]; לוּא; Ec 6[6], Est 7[4] אִלּוּ, from אִם לוּ) *if*, negative אִם לֹא and לוּלֵא (לוּלֵי) *unless*; כִּי *supposing that* (Lat. *ut*), *in case that*, sometimes used almost in the same sense as אִם. With regard to the difference between אִם (אִם לֹא) and לוּ (לוּלֵא), the fundamental rule is that אִם is used if the condition be regarded either as already fulfilled, or if it, together with its consequence, be thought of as possibly (or

---

[1] On לוּ cf. Kohler in Geiger's *Zeitschr. für Wiss. und Leben*, vi (1868), p. 21 ff.

probably) occurring in the present or future. In the former case, אִם
is followed by the perfect, in the latter (corresponding to the Greek
ἐάν with the present subjunctive) by the imperfect or its equivalent
(frequently in the apodosis also). On the other hand, לוּ (לֻלֵא) is used
when the condition is to be represented as *not fulfilled* in the past,
or as *not capable of fulfilment* in the present or future, and the consequence accordingly as not having occurred or never occurring. In the
former case, לוּ and לוּלֵא are necessarily followed by the perfect (mostly
also in the apodosis) corresponding to the Greek εἰ with the indicative
of an historic tense, and the Latin imperfect or pluperfect subjunctive.
In the latter case (which is extremely rare) the perfect, or the participle, or even the imperfect, may be used.

Rem. Since it again frequently depends on the subjective judgement of the *m*
speaker (see under *a*), whether a condition is to be regarded as possible or
impossible, we cannot wonder that the distinction between אִם and לוּ is not
always consistently observed. Although naturally לוּ and לוּלֵא cannot take
the place of אִם and אִם לֹא (on the strange use of לוּ in Gn 50¹⁵ see below),
yet conversely אִם is sometimes used where לוּ would certainly be expected ;
cf. e.g. ψ 50¹², 137⁵, 139⁸, Ho 9¹² (cf. verse 11). These examples, indeed (אִם
with the imperfect), may without difficulty be explained from the fact that
the connexion of לוּ with the imperfect was evidently avoided, because the
imperfect by its nature indicates a still unfinished action, and consequently
(as opposed to לוּ) a still open possibility. But אִם is also used for לוּ in connexion with the perfect, especially when an imprecation is attached by the
apodosis to the condition introduced by אִם, e.g. ψ 7⁴ ff. . . . . אִם־עָשִׂיתִי זֹאת
יְרַדֹּף וג׳ *if I have done this . . ., let the enemy pursue my soul*, &c., cf. Jb 31⁹ ff.
The speaker assumes for a moment as possible and even actual, that which
he really rejects as inconceivable, in order to invoke the most severe punish-
ment on himself, if it should prove to be the case.
On the frequent addition of an infinitive absolute to the verb in clauses
with אִם see § 113 *o* above.

Examples :—
A. אִם 1. with *perfect* in the protasis to express conditions, &c., which have *n*
been completely fulfilled in the past or which will be completely fulfilled in
the future (the perfect is here equivalent to the *futurum exactum*, § 106 *o*).
The apodosis [1] takes—

    (*a*) A *perfect* also, e. g. Pr 9¹² אִם־חָכַמְתָּ חָכַמְתָּ לָּךְ *if thou art wise, thou art wise
for thyself*; ψ 73¹⁵ (see below on לוּ).

    (*b*) *Imperfect*, e. g. Dt 32⁴¹ אִם־שַׁנּוֹתִי *if I whet my glittering sword* . . . אָשִׁיב
I will render vengeance, &c. ; Jb 9¹⁵ f. ³⁰ (in both cases we should expect
לוּ rather than אִם ; so also in ψ 44²¹ f., with an interrogative imperfect in
the apodosis) ; Jb 11¹³ (the apodosis is in verse 15).

    (*c*) *Jussive* (or *optative*), e. g. Jb 31⁹ ff. (see *m* above) ; Gn 18³.

---

[1] We are not here concerned with the fact that the logical apodosis (the
consequence of the condition) is sometimes mentioned before the condition ;
as in Gn 18²⁸·³⁰, Ju 11¹⁰, ψ 63⁶ f., 137⁶, and according to Dillmann Is 4⁴.

o   (d) *Perfect consecutive* (see the examples in § 112 *gg*), e. g. Gn 43⁹ אִם־לֹא
הֲבִיאֹתִיו וג' *if I bring him not . . . then I shall have sinned*, &c. ; Ju 16¹⁷, 2 S 15³³,
2 K 7⁴. On the other hand, e. g. Gn 47⁶, Mi 5⁷, Jb 7⁴ refer to actions already
completed ; in Gn 38⁹ and Nu 21⁹ the perfect with ו is a perfect frequentative
and refers to past time.

   (e) *Imperfect consecutive* (see § 111 *q*), e.g. Jb 8⁴ *if thy children have sinned*
(חָטָאוּ) . . . , וַיְשַׁלְּחֵם *he has delivered them*, &c.

   (f) *Imperative*, e. g. Gn 50⁴ אִם־נָא מָצָאתִי חֵן בְּעֵינֵיכֶם דַּבְּרוּ־נָא וג' *if now
I have found grace in your eyes, speak, I pray you*, &c.; the imperative precedes
in Gn 47¹⁶ and Jb 38⁴·¹⁸.

p   (g) A (complete or incomplete) noun-clause, e.g. Jer 14¹⁸ (a vivid realization
of the future) *if I have gone forth into the field* (= *if I go*, &c.), *then, behold, the
slain with the sword!* &c. ; Pr 24¹⁴ (apodosis with *wāw apodosis*).

q   2. אִם with *imperfect* in the protasis, to express what is possible in the
present or future, as well as (according to § 107 *b*) what has continued or
been repeated in the past. The apodosis takes—

   (a) The *perfect*, e.g. Nu 32²³ וְאִם־לֹא תַעֲשׂוּן כֵּן הִנֵּה חֲטָאתֶם *but if ye will not do
so, behold, ye have sinned*; here the apodosis represents the time when the
consequence has already taken place; so also Jb 20¹²⁻¹⁴. On the other
hand, Nu 16²⁹ (as also 1 S 6⁹ and 1 K 22²⁸) is a case of a pregnant construction,
if these men die as all men die, then (it will follow from this) *the Lord hath not
sent me*.

r   (b) The *imperfect*, e.g. 2 K 7⁴ אִם־יְחַיֻּנוּ נִחְיֶה *if they save us alive, we shall live*, &c.;
Gn 13¹⁶, 18²⁸·³⁰, 28²⁰ ᶠᶠ·, Ex 20²⁵ (the second imperfect is equivalent to a jussive) ;
Is 1¹⁸, 10²², Am 9²⁻⁴, ψ 50¹² (where אִם ironically represents an impossibility
as possible) ; Jb 8⁵ ᶠ· (with the insertion of a second condition in the form of
a noun-clause) ; 9³·²⁰, 14⁷ ; a frequentative imperfect referring to the past,
Gn 31⁸ אִם־כֹּה יֹאמַר *if* (ever) *he said thus . . .* , וְיָלְדוּ *then they bare . . .* ; Ex 40³⁷.
In Gn 42³⁷ the consequence (on תָּמִית cf. § 107 *s*) precedes the condition.

   (c) The *jussive* (or *optative*), e.g. ψ 137⁵ ; cf. § 109 *h*.

   (d) The *cohortative*, e.g. Gn 13⁹, Jb 31⁷ ; cf. § 108 *f*.

s   (e) The *perfect consecutive* (see the examples in § 112 *ff* and *gg*), e.g. 1 S 20⁶
אִם־פָּקֹד יִפְקְדֵנִי אָבִיךָ וְאָמַרְתָּ *if thy father miss me at all, then shalt thou say*, &c. ;
Gn 24⁴¹, Ju 4²⁰ ; with a frequentative perfect consecutive, Gn 31⁸ *if he said
(as often happened) . . . , then*, &c.

   (f) The *imperfect consecutive* ; so perhaps ψ 59¹⁶, if וַיָּלִינוּ is to be explained
according to § 111 *t*.

   (g) The *imperative*, e.g. Gn 31⁵⁰, 1 S 20²¹ (with *wāw apodosis*, but in verse 22
simply לֵךְ), 21¹⁰, Jb 33⁵.

t   (h) A noun-clause, e.g. Gn 4⁷, ψ 139⁸, Jb 8⁶, 31²⁶ ᶠ·

   3. אִם with *cohortative*, e.g. Gn 30³¹ ; cf. the passages in § 108 *e*.

u   4. אִם with *infinitive*, Jb 9²⁷ אִם־אָמְרִי prop. *if my saying is* (but probably we
should read אָמַרְתִּי).

v   5. אִם with a noun-clause, e.g. Dt 5²² (in the apodosis a perfect with
wāw apodosis), Gn 27⁴⁶, Ju 9¹⁵ (imperative in the apodosis) ; 11⁹ (imperfect in
the apodosis) ; 2 S 12⁸ (cohortative in the apodosis) ; Ho 12¹² ; especially
if the subject of the conditional clause be a personal pronoun. In an
affirmative sentence this pronoun is often joined to יֵשׁ, in a negative sentence
to אֵין (cf. on both, § 100 *o*), while the predicate (cf. § 116 *q*) is represented
by a participle, usually expressing the future, e. g. Ju 6³⁶ ᶠ· אִם־יֶשְׁךָ מוֹשִׁיעַ

if thou wilt save, &c. ; Gn 24⁴⁹ אִם־יֶשְׁכֶם עֹשִׂים *if ye will deal*, &c. ; 1 S 23²³. In Gn 24⁴² ᶠ· the condition is expressed in a more humble form by the addition of נָא. With אֵין אִם־ Gn 43⁵ וְאִם־אֵינְךָ מְשַׁלֵּחַ *but if thou wilt not send*, &c. ; 20⁷ (with imperative in the apodosis) ; Ex 8¹⁷, 9² ᶠ·, 1 S 19¹¹ (all with a participle also in the apodosis). But יֵשׁ and אַיִן may also be used after אִם without a suffix ; thus יֵשׁ Gn 23⁸, 1 S 20⁸, 2 K 9¹⁵, &c., אִם־אַיִן (*if it be not the case*) Gn 30¹, Ex 32³², Ju 9¹⁵, 2 K 2¹⁰ ; cf. also אִם־כֵּן *if it be so*, Gn 25²².

B. הֵן *if*, generally supposed to be originally identical with הֵן *behold!*[1] *w* Probably, however, הֵן *if*, is a pure Aramaism, and since the Aramaic word never has the meaning *behold*, it is at least improbable that it had originally any connexion with הֵן or הִנֵּה. Cf. Ex 8²², Lv 25²⁰, Is 54¹⁵, Jer 3¹, Hag 2¹², 2 Ch 7¹³, and frequently in Job, as 9¹¹·¹², 12¹⁴·¹⁵, 19⁷, 23⁸, 40²³, always with wāw apodosis following, except in 13¹⁵, where consequently the meaning *see* is no doubt preferable.

C. לוּ (לוּלֵי) לֻלֵא, לוּ *if*, *if not*.   *x*

1. With *perfect* in the protasis and apodosis (cf. § 106 *p*), e. g. Ju 8¹⁹) אִלּוּ is used in the same sense as לוּ in Est 7⁴, cf. Ec 6⁶ (with a question in the apodosis).—With the perfect in protasis and apodosis after לוּלֵא Gn 31⁴², 43¹⁰, Ju 14¹⁸, 1 S 25³⁴, 2 S 2²⁷, Is 1⁹. On the other hand, in Dt 32²⁹ לוּ with a perfect is followed by an imperfect in the apodosis, *if they were wise, they would understand this* ; in Mi 2¹¹ by a perfect consecutive.

2. With *imperfect* after לוּלֵא Dt 32²⁷, אָגוּר probably as the *modus rei repetitae*, *y* *were it not that I ever and again feared*, &c. ; so also the imperfect after לוּ with the apodosis suppressed, Gn 50¹⁵ *supposing that Joseph should hate us* ; since, according to the context, the danger was real, the use of לוּ here is strange ; conversely in other cases, e. g. ψ 73¹⁵, Jb 9¹⁵ ᶠ·³⁰, לוּ would be more natural than אִם.

3. A noun-clause occurs after לוּ 2 S 18¹², 2 K 3¹⁴, ψ 81¹⁴, all with imperfect *z* in the apodosis ; Jb 16⁴ יֵשׁ לוּ, with cohortative in the apodosis.

D. כִּי *supposing that, if* :—

1. כִּי with *perfect* in the protasis, e. g. Nu 5²⁰ וְאַתְּ כִּי שָׂטִית *but thou, if thou* *aa* *hast gone astray*, &c. ; with a frequentative perfect consecutive in the apodosis, Jb 7¹³ ᶠ· ; with an imperfect consecutive, Jb 22²⁹.

2. כִּי with *imperfect* in the protasis, e. g. ψ 23⁴ גַּם כִּי־אֵלֵךְ *yea, though I walk* *bb* (*have to walk*) . . . , *I will fear no* (לֹא־אִירָא) *evil* ; 37²⁴ ; Ex 21² כִּי־תִקְנֶה עֶבֶד עִבְרִי וג׳ *if thou buy an Hebrew servant, six years shall he serve* (but in verses 3–5 a series of definite conditions with definite consequences is introduced by אִם ; so also the כִּי in verse 7 is followed in verses 8–11 by the special cases with אִם ; cf. also verse 17 ff.) ; cf. Gn 4²⁴, 24⁴¹, Jb 38⁵ ; with a perfect consecutive in the apodosis, Gn 32¹⁸ ᶠ·, Ex 18¹⁶ ; with a noun-clause, Is 1¹⁵.

3. כִּי with a *noun-clause* (and imperfect in the apodosis), 2 S 19⁸.

Remarks.

1. In 2 K 5¹³ the particle אֲבִי (Masora אָבִי, probably in the sense of *my* *cc* *father*) appears exceptionally for לוּ ; its meaning here is unquestionable, but

---

[1] There could be no doubt of their identity if וְהִנֵּה in 1 S 9⁷, 2 S 18¹¹, simply meant *if*. We must, however, keep to the meaning *but behold*.

its origin is obscure. Cf. the exhaustive discussion of Delitzsch and Wetzstein on Jb 34³⁶, where this אבִי appears to be used as a desiderative particle.—Sometimes when one case has been already discussed, another of the same character is added by means of אוֹ *or*, e. g. Ex 21²⁶ אוֹ נוֹדַע וג' *or* (another possible case) *it is known that*, &c., i. e. *but if it be known*, &c., LXX ἐὰν δέ, Vulg. *sin autem*; cf. Lv 4²³·²⁸, 5¹, 25⁴⁹, 2 S 18¹³; with a following imperfect, Ez 14¹⁷ᶠ·—On the hypothetical use of אֲשֶׁר (which is interchangeable with כִּי in other senses also) Lv 4²² (in verses 3 and 27 אִם), Dt 11²⁷ (verse 28 אִם), Jos 4²¹, see the Lexicon.

dd   2. The conditional sentence is frequently found in an abridged form, where the suppressed clauses can be easily supplied from the context; cf. Gn 13⁹, 24⁴⁹, 1 S 2¹⁶ וְאִם־לֹא *and if not*, i. e. *and if thou wilt not give it to me, then I take* it (perfect according to § 106 *n*) *by force*; cf. 1 S 6⁹. The use of וְיֵשׁ alone in Ju 6¹³ is peculiar, as also וְיֵשׁ in 2 K 10¹⁵ (where read with the LXX וַיֹּאמֶר יְהוּא וְיֵשׁ) in the sense of *if it be so*.—In 2 S 13²⁶, 2 K 5¹⁷ וְלֹא alone appears to be used in the sense of *if really . . . not*, in each case with a following jussive equivalent to *may there at least*, &c. (cf. § 143 *d*); but perhaps with Matthes, *ZAW*. 1903, p. 122 ff., following Kuipers, we should read וְלוּ *would that!*—In 1 S 13¹³, Jb 3¹³ the condition must be supplied from the preceding clause to complete the sentence introduced by כִּי עַתָּה, in Jb 31²⁸ by כִּי, in 2 K 13¹⁹ by אָז.—The apodosis also appears sometimes in an abridged form (e. g. Gn 4²⁴, Is 43²) or is entirely suppressed, e. g. Gn 30²⁷, 38¹⁷, 50¹⁵ (see *y* above), Ex 32³², ψ 27¹³, Jb 38⁵, where properly הַגֵּד must be supplied with כִּי תֵדַע as in verses 4 and 18; cf. § 167 *a*.—In ψ 84, instead of the apodosis *I exclaim* which we should expect, the exclamation itself follows.

ee   3. The absolute certainty with which a result is to be expected is frequently emphasized by the insertion of כִּי Is 7⁹; כִּי אָז 2 S 2²⁷, 19⁷, Jb 11¹⁵; or כִּי עַתָּה *now verily*, Nu 22²⁹, 1 S 14³⁰ after לוּ, Gn 31⁴², 43¹⁰ after לוּלֵי, Jb 8⁶ after אִם. On this *corroborative* כִּי cf. such passages as Gn 18²⁰, &c., and § 148 *d*. On כִּי אִם after an oath cf. 163 *d*.

ff   4. Sometimes the force of a hypothetical particle extends beyond the apodosis to a second conditional clause, as in the case of אִם Pr 9¹², Jb 10¹⁵, 16⁶, 22²³, and כִּי Is 43².

gg   5. In Ex 33²⁰ a negative statement takes the place of a condition with a negative consequence, *for a man doth not see me and live*, instead of *for if a man sees me, he does not live*; cf. the similar passages, Dt 22¹·⁴ *thou shalt not see . . . and hide thyself*, instead of *if thou seest . . . thou shalt not hide thyself*.

§ 160.   *Concessive Clauses.*

a   Besides the use of the imperative in the sense of a concession, meant either seriously (§ 110 *a*) or mockingly (§ 110 *f*), and of concessive circumstantial clauses (§ 141 *e*, § 142 *d*, and § 156 *f*), concessive clauses may be introduced—

(*a*) By a simple אִם *if*: thus Jb 9¹⁵ with perfect, *if* (= *though*) *I had been in the right*; Is 1¹⁸ and 10²² with imperfect in reference to a contingent event.

b   (*b*) By גַּם כִּי *yea though*, Is 1¹⁵ with imperfect; for which we find simply גַּם in Is 49¹⁵ with imperfect, *yea, though these may forget, yet* . . .; on the other hand, with perfect, Jer 36²⁵, ψ 95⁹, Neh 6¹; finally כִּי גַם *even if, though*, Ec 4¹⁴.

(c) By the preposition עַל־ governing a complete noun-clause, as Jb 16¹⁷ C עַל לֹא־חָמָס בְּכַפָּי *notwithstanding* that *no violence is in mine hands*, or a verbal-clause, Is 53⁹. On עַל־ with the infinitive in a similar sense (equivalent to *in addition to the fact* that = *notwithstanding* that), cf. § 119 aa, note 2.

§ 161. *Comparative Clauses.*

1. A comparison between two facts is sometimes established by *a* simply uniting them with *wāw copulative*, especially in gnomic poetry, when facts of a moral nature are compared with those of the physical world, e. g. Jb 5⁷ *man is born unto trouble, and the sons of flame fly upward*, i. e. as the sparks by nature fly upward, so man, &c.; Jb 12¹¹ (in an interrogative form; in 34³ the same comparison as a statement); 14¹¹ᶠ·, Pr 17³, 25³, 26³·⁹·¹⁴, 27²¹, &c.[1] Even without the connecting וְ Jb 24¹⁹ *drought and heat consume the snow waters*, שְׁאוֹל חָטָאוּ *so doth Sheol those who have sinned* (cf. § 155 n); cf. Jer 17¹¹.

2. The conjunction כַּאֲשֶׁר (cf. § 155 g; the simple אֲשֶׁר occurs in the *b* same sense in Ex 10⁶, 14¹³, 34¹⁸) *as, quemadmodum*, is used as a comparative conjunction (Ob ¹⁵), frequently with כֵּן *so*, corresponding to it in the apodosis, Is 31⁴, 52¹⁴ᶠ·. Sometimes, however, כֵּן (*so also*) occurs even after independent statements, Is 55⁹, Jer 3²⁰.—Exact coincidence of two facts is expressed in Ec 5¹⁵ by כָּל־עֻמַּת שֶׁ־ [2] *in all points as*.

Rem. On the use of כְּ *as*, with single nouns or pronouns to introduce C comparisons, cf. 118 s; on the alleged use of כְּ as a conjunction (equivalent to כַּאֲשֶׁר), cf. § 155 g.—It is to be further remarked that כְּ—כְּ when used in correspondence with one another, *as—so* (e. g. Lv 7⁷, Ju 8¹⁸, Is 24², Ho 4⁹; also *so—as*, Gn 18²⁵, 44¹⁸, Dt 1¹⁷, 1 K 22⁴; in Jos 14¹¹, 1 S 30²⁴ כְּ—וּכְ; ψ 127⁴ and often, כֵּן—כְּ, cf. Jo 2⁴), are not to be regarded as conjunctions, but as virtual substantives with a following genitive; כָּכֶם כַּגֵּר יִהְיֶה Nu 15¹⁵ properly means *the like of you shall be the like of the stranger*, i. e. *your duty shall be* (also) *the stranger's duty*; cf. Lv 24²².

---

[1] On this *wāw adaequationis*, and in general on these proverbial comparisons, see Delitzsch, *Das Salomonische Spruchbuch*, p. 9 f. Moreover, instead of entire clauses, the nouns alone (without predicates) are frequently grouped together, e. g. Pr 25²⁵, 26²¹, 27²¹ (called by Delitzsch, the 'emblematic Mashal'). The expressions נֶחְשַׁב עִם prop. *to be counted with some one*, ψ 88⁵, and נִמְשַׁל עִם *to be likened with some one*, ψ 28¹, 143⁷, also arise from the idea of comparison implied in grouping things together. On this use of עִם cf. Jb 9²⁶, where *with* is equivalent to *like*.

[2] In spite of its form this particle has originally nothing to do with כָּל־, כֹּל *all*. The expression is compounded of כְּ and לְעֻמַּת, like the Aramaic כָּל־קֳבֵל for כְּלָקֳבֵל; cf. M. Lambert, *REJ.* xxx. 47.

§ 162. *Disjunctive Sentences.*

a   The introduction of another possible case, excluding that which preceded, is effected by אֹו *or*, e.g. Ex 21³⁶, equivalent to the Latin *vel*; but also equivalent to *aut* with an exclusive antithesis, 2 K 2¹⁶; so Is 27⁵ אֹו =*it would then happen that*, for which elsewhere אֹו כִּי.

b   In the sense of *sive—sive* we find אֹו—אֹו, or אִם—אִם, or וְאִם—אִם (see the examples in the Lexicon), also }—} Lv 5³, Nu 9¹⁴, Dt 24⁷, Is 2¹³ᶠᶠ·, Jer 32²⁰, ψ 76⁷, Jb 34²⁹, perhaps also Ex 21¹⁶ (but not Pr 29⁹; cf. Delitzsch on the passage), and לְ—לְ (see § 143 *e*); cf. also גַּם—גַּם (in Gn 24⁴⁴ גַּם—וְגַם) *both—and*; but גַּם לֹא—גַּם לֹא (in Gn 21²⁶ וְגַם לֹא—גַּם לֹא; Zp 1¹⁸ גַּם—גַּם..., לֹא) *neither—nor*. On disjunctive questions, see § 150 *g*.

§ 163. *Adversative and Exceptive Clauses.*

a   **1.** After negative sentences (especially after prohibitions) the antithesis (*but*) is introduced by כִּי אִם, e.g. 1 S 8¹⁹ *and they said, Nay, but we will have a king over us*; ψ 1², &c.; frequently also by כִּי alone, e.g. Gn 18¹⁵, 19², or even simply connected with }, Gn 17⁵, וְהָיָה as perfect consecutive; 42¹⁰; cf. Ex 5¹⁸.

b   Rem. Sometimes the negation is only virtually contained in the preceding sentence, e.g. in the form of a rhetorical question (Mi 6³ᶠ·) or of conditions which are to be regarded as not having been fulfilled (Jb 31¹⁸); כִּי or כִּי אִם in such cases becomes equivalent to *nay, rather*.

c   **2.** *Exceptive* clauses, depending on another sentence, are introduced by אֶפֶס כִּי *except that*, and (again after negative sentences, see *a* above) כִּי אִם [1] *unless*; especially כִּי אִם with the perfect (equivalent to *unless previously*) after imperfects which contain a declaration, e.g. Gn 32²⁷ *I will not let thee go, except thou hast* previously *blessed me*; Lv 22⁶, Is 55¹⁰, 65⁶, Am 3⁷, Ru 3¹⁸. Finally, בִּלְתִּי אִם *unless*, Am 3⁴ (with perfect after a rhetorical question), or simply בִּלְתִּי Gn 43³ with a noun-clause, *except your brother be with you*; Is 10⁴ after a rhetorical question, with a verbal-clause.

---

[1] Very probably this use of כִּי אִם arises from the original meaning *for if, surely if* (כִּי in an affirmative sense); so evidently in Ex 22²² as a forcible resumption of the preceding אִם. Thus, e.g. Ju 15⁷ is simply *surely when I have been avenged of you, after that I will cease*, equivalent to, I will not cease, until I have, &c. When the exception follows, an ellipse must be assumed, e.g. Ru 3¹⁸ *surely* (or *for*) *when he has finished it* (then the man will rest). It is far less natural to assume such an ellipse with כִּי אִם *but* (before entire clauses as before single nouns); see *a* above.

Rem. The principal statement, to which כִּי אִם appends an exception, *d* must sometimes be supplied from the context; thus, Gn 40[14] (I desire nothing else) *except that thou remember me*, equivalent to *only do thou remember*, &c. (cf. § 106 *n*, note 2; but it is probably better to read אַךְ for כִּי). Cf. Mi 6[8], where כִּי אִם, equivalent to *nothing but*, is used before an infinitive, and Jb 42[8], equivalent to *only*, before a noun. Similarly when כִּי אִם after an oath introduces an emphatic assurance, e. g. in 2 K 5[20] *as the Lord liveth* (I can do nothing else) *except I run after him*, &c.; cf. 2 S 15[21] K[e]*th.*, Jer 51[14], Ru 3[12] K[e]*th.*, and even without the oath, Ju 15[7]; cf. the Rem. on *c*.

§ 164. *Temporal Clauses.*

1. The relations of time existing between two different actions or *a* events are frequently expressed without the aid of a conjunction simply by juxtaposition:—

(*a*) Actions or events are represented as wholly or in part *simultaneous* by connecting a noun-clause with another noun-clause or verbal-clause introduced by וְ (or וְהִנֵּה), e. g. Gn 7[6] *and Noah* was *six hundred years old* (prop. *a son of six hundred years*), וְהַמַּבּוּל הָיָה *and* (i. e. *when*) *the flood was*. This is especially the case when the predicate of the noun-clause (frequently introduced by עוֹד *still*) is expressed by an active participle, e. g. Jb 1[16 f.] עוֹד זֶה מְדַבֵּר וְזֶה בָּא וג׳ *he* was *yet speaking, and there came another*, &c.; see the numerous examples in § 111 *g* and § 116 *u*. Instead of a complete noun-clause there often occurs a simple *casus pendens* after כָּל־ with a participial attribute in the sense of *whenever any one* . . ., e. g. 1 S 2[13] כָּל־אִישׁ זֹבֵחַ זֶבַח וּבָא וג׳ *whenever any man offered sacrifice, then came*, &c.; 2 S 2[23], &c.; see the examples (in which the second member is generally introduced by *wāw apodosis*) in § 116 *w*.

(*b*) Sequence is expressed by the juxtaposition *b*

(1) of two imperfects consecutive, e. g. Gn 24[19] וַתְּכַל לְהַשְׁקֹתוֹ וַתֹּאמֶר *and when she had done giving him drink, she said*, &c.; 28[8 f.], 29[31], 30[8], 32[26], &c.; cf. § 111 *d*;

(2) of a noun-clause with a passive participle as predicate, and a verbal-clause attached by וְ, e. g. Gn 38[25]; cf. § 116 *v*; in Gn 49[29] an imperative follows without וְ;

(3) of two perfects (frequently with the secondary idea of rapid succession [1] of the two actions or events in past time), e. g. Gn 19[23] הַשֶּׁמֶשׁ יָצָא . . . וְלוֹט בָּא וג׳ *the sun was just risen* . . ., *and* (=*when*) *Lot came*, &c., cf. 1 S 9[5], 2 S 2[24]; Gn 44[3 f.], Ju 3[24], 15[14], 20[39 f.]—In all these examples the subject follows immediately after the connective *Wāw*, and then the (simple) perfect. On the other hand,

(4) a perfect consecutive follows another perfect consecutive to express the contingent succession of future actions, e. g. Gn 44[4] וְהִשַּׂגְתָּם וְאָמַרְתָּ אֲלֵהֶם

---

[1] This secondary idea is implied here by the mere co-ordination of two independent *verbal*-clauses, just as the idea of simultaneous occurrence (according to § 116 *u*, note 1) is implied in the co-ordination of a noun-clause with another clause. In Gn 27[30] the immediate succession is especially emphasized by אַךְ and the infinitive absolute, *Jacob was yet scarce gone out* . . . *then Esau his brother came*; in 1 K 9[24] by אַךְ only· in ψ 48[6] by כֵּן and the addition of two more perfects without וְ.

and when thou dost overtake them (as soon as thou shalt have overtaken), *thou shalt say unto them.* Naturally, examples of this kind are very closely related to conditional sentences; see, therefore, the examples in § 112 *kk* and § 159 *g*. On the connexion of an imperfect consecutive or a perfect with detached expressions of time (as equivalent to complete clauses), cf. § 111 *b*; on the imperfect consecutive after וַיְהִי and a statement of time, cf. § 111 *g*; on the perfect consecutive following a detached statement of time, as in Ex 16⁶, cf. § 112 *oo*.—In 1 S 29¹⁰ an imperative with וְ follows the perfect consecutive.

C (5) The fact that one action or event has not yet taken place on the occurrence of another, is expressed by טֶרֶם (an adverb, not a conjunction) with the imperfect (according to § 107 *e*). The apodosis, which may consist of a subject and perfect or even of a noun-clause (Gn 24¹⁵),[1] is then connected by וְ (or וְהִנֵּה) as in the examples above, under no. 3, e.g. Gn 19⁴ (cf. Jos 2⁸) טֶרֶם יִשְׁכָּבוּ וְאַנְשֵׁי הָעִיר . . . נָסַבּוּ וג׳ *they had not yet lain down, and* (= *when*) *the men of the city . . . compassed*, &c.; Gn 24²⁵.

d **2.** Conjunctions used to introduce temporal clauses are כִּי (with perfect, e.g. Gn 6¹, Ju 1²⁸, 16¹⁶, 1 S 1¹²; with imperfect, Gn 4¹², 12¹², 24⁴¹, Ex 3²¹, Lv 21⁹, Dt 31²¹, Is 1¹², 8¹⁹) and אֲשֶׁר [2] *when* (כִּי with the imperfect also = *as often as*, ψ 8⁴; with perfect Jb 1⁵); less frequently אִם [3] (joined with a perfect), e.g. Gn 38⁹, Nu 21⁹, Ju 6³, ψ 41⁷, 94¹⁸, cf. also Is 24¹³ = *quotiescunque*; also in the same sense with an imperfect, Nu 36⁴; with a perfect, equivalent to the *futurum exactum*, Is 4⁴. Other conjunctions of time are the compounds כְּמוֹ *when*, Gn 19¹⁵; כַּאֲשֶׁר *when, after that*; עַד־כִּי, עַד־אֲשֶׁר *until* (also the simple עַד, e.g. Gn 38¹¹, Jos 2²², 1 S 1²² [with the imperfect = *only when*, as in 2 S 10⁵]); 2⁵, &c.; especially in the formula עַד־בִּלְתִּי הִשְׁאִיר לוֹ *until there was none left remaining to him* (where indeed it would be very natural to read הַשְׁאִיר the infin. constr., as elsewhere after בִּלְתִּי, § 114 *s*) Nu 21³⁵, Dt 3³, Jos 8²², 11⁸ (but 1 S 14¹⁹ *while, as long as*); עַד אֲשֶׁר לֹא *before that*, Ec 12¹·²·⁶ with an imperfect, as in Pr 8²⁶ עַד with a perfect; עַד־אִם, עַד־אֲשֶׁר אִם *until the time when*; אַחֲרֵי־אֲשֶׁר (for which in Ez 40¹ אַחַר־אֲשֶׁר; Lv 25⁴⁸, 1 S 5⁹ simply אַחֲרֵי; Lv 14⁴³, Jer 41¹⁶, Jb 42⁷ simply אַחַר) *after that*; מֵאָז (prop. *since that time*; the dependent clause is attached to it in the same way as the attributive clause to the demonstrative אֲשֶׁר § 138 *e*) *since*, Gn 39⁵; בְּטֶרֶם (and simply טֶרֶם § 107 *c*) *before*; קַרְמַת (for קַרְמַת אֲשֶׁר) *before*, ψ 129⁶.

e Rem. 1. With regard to the tenses used with the above conjunctions, the rules are practically the same as those given in § 158 *d* for causal clauses. The perfect indicates actions completed in the past or future (in the former case corresponding to the Latin pluperfect, § 106 *f*, and in the latter to the

---

[1] On the perfect in the protasis, which is critically doubtful, cf. § 107 *c*.
[2] On אֲשֶׁר as an original demonstrative, cf. § 138 *a*; hence עַד־אֲשֶׁר נָשׁוּב is properly *up to that* (moment)—*we shall return*.
[3] Cf. the frequent use of *wenn* [prop. *if*] for *wann* [= *when*] in German.

Latin *futurum exactum*, § 106 *o*), the imperfect denotes actions occurring contingently in the future. On בְּטֶרֶם, טֶרֶם, and עַד with the imperfect as a *tempus historicum*, cf. 107 *c*.

2. Clauses introduced by עַד, עַד־כִּי, or עַד־אֲשֶׁר, sometimes express a limit *f* which is not absolute (terminating the preceding action), but only relative, beyond which the action or state described in the principal clause still continues; thus, עַד with the imperfect, ψ 110¹; עַד־כִּי with the perfect, Gn 26¹³, with impf. 49¹⁰; עַד־אֲשֶׁר with the perfect, Gn 28¹⁵; with the imperfect, ψ 112⁸.—Like the Arab. حَتّٰى, עַד may even introduce a main clause; e.g. Ex 15¹⁶ עַד־יַעֲבֹר prop. no doubt = thus it came to this—*they passed through*, i.e. *so they passed through*.

3. The infinitive construct governed by a preposition (§ 114 *d, e*) is very *g* frequently used as the equivalent of a temporal clause; the infinitive with בְּ may usually be rendered by *when, as,* or *whilst*; the infinitive with כְּ by *when, as soon as* (in Pr 10²⁵ followed by a noun-clause introduced by *wāw apodosis*), or, when referring to the future, by *if*; the infinitive after מִן by *since*. According to § 111 *g* such statements of time are generally preceded by וַיְהִי and the apodosis follows in the imperfect consecutive; hence in 1 S 17⁵⁵ (cf. Driver on the passage) וְכִרְאוֹת with a simple perfect following, is unusual. On the continuation of these two infinitival constructions by means of the perfect consecutive, cf. § 112 *v*, and in general, § 114 *r*.—With the participle, בְּ appears to be used as the equivalent of a conjunction in כְּמֵשִׁיב *as he drew back*, Gn 38²⁹ (unless we should read כְּהָשִׁיב [or כְּמוֹ הָשִׁיב, cf. Gn 19¹⁵]), and in כְּפֹרַחַת *when it budded*, 40¹⁰.

§ 165. *Final Clauses.*[1]

1. Like most of the dependent clauses hitherto treated, the final *a* clause may also be joined by a simple *wāw copulative* to the main clause, unless the final clause is directly subordinated to the governing verb.

Examples of the connexion: (*a*) of a final imperfect (or jussive?) with a perfect by means of וְ, La 1¹⁹, see § 107 *q*; with an interrogative sentence, 2 S 9¹·³, Jb 38²⁴; with an optative, ψ 51⁹; with an imperative, 1 K 11²¹; (*β*) of a cohortative with an imperative by וְ, Gn 29²¹, 1 S 15¹⁶, or a jussive, Neh 2⁵ (§ 108 *d*); (*γ*) of a jussive with an imperative by וְ, Ex 9¹, 2 S 16¹¹, 1 K 5²⁰, ψ 59¹⁴, 86¹⁷; with a jussive, Jb 21¹⁹, or cohortative, § 109 *f, g* (cf. also 2 S 24²¹ the infinitive with לְ, Jon 1¹¹ מָה with the 1st plur. imperf., and 2 Ch 29¹⁰ עִם־לְבָבִי, which are equivalent to cohortatives); (*δ*) of an imperative with a jussive, cohortative, or interrogative sentence by וְ, § 110 *i*; (*ε*) of a perfect consecutive after another perfect consecutive, Lv 14³⁶; after an imperfect, § 112 *m* and *p*; similarly after a jussive, § 112 *q*; after an imperative, § 112 *r*.—On negative final clauses joined by וְלֹא to the imperfect (so Ex 28⁴³, 30²⁰; and 2 S 13²⁵ after אַל־נָא with a jussive in the main clause) see the Rem. on § 109 *g*. In Ex 28³², 39²³ the negative final clause is simply connected by לֹא.—On the use of an historical statement after verbs of command-

---

[1] Cf. H. G. T. Mitchell, *Final Constructions of Biblical Hebrew*, Leipzig, 1879.

ing, where we should expect a final clause (e.g. Neh 13⁹ *then I commanded, and they cleansed*, equivalent to *that they should cleanse, and they cleansed* ; in Jb 9⁷ a negative final clause is connected in this way by וְלֹא), cf. § 120 *f*.

For examples of the direct subordination of the final imperfect (without וְ) see § 120 *c*.

b **2.** Final conjunctions are לְמַעַן אֲשֶׁר *to the end that* ; also simply לְמַעַן Gn 12¹³, 27²⁵, Ex 4⁵, ψ 51⁶, &c.; בַּעֲבוּר אֲשֶׁר prop. *for the purpose that*, Gn 27¹⁰, and simply בַּעֲבוּר Gn 27⁴, Ex 9¹⁴, 20²⁰; also the simple אֲשֶׁר[1] Dt 4¹⁰·⁴⁰, 6³, 32⁴⁶, Jos 3⁷, Neh 8¹⁴ᶠ·; negatively, אֲשֶׁר לֹא Gn 11⁷, 24³, 1 K 22¹⁶; or שֶׁ· Ec 3¹⁴; also negatively, עַל־דִּבְרַת שֶׁלֹּא *for the matter (purpose) that . . . not*, Ec 7¹⁴; לְבִלְתִּי with imperfect, Ex 20²⁰, 2 S 14¹⁴ *that . . . not.*—Quite exceptional is the use of מִן־ (if the text be right) in Dt 33¹¹ מִן־יְקוּמוּן, with the imperfect, equivalent to *that . . . not* [in prose, מִקּוּם].

c Rem. All the conjunctions here mentioned are naturally always used with the imperfect, see § 107 *q* (on the apparent exception in Jos 4²⁴, see § 74 *g*).— On the negative conjunctions אַל and פֶּן *that not, lest*, see § 152 *f* and *w*. On the infinitive with לְ[2] (also לְמַעַן Gn 18¹⁹, 37²², &c.) as the equivalent of a final clause (Gn 11⁵, 28⁴, &c.), see § 114 *f, h, p*. On the continuation of such infinitival constructions by means of the finite verb, see § 114 *r*. On the negation of the final infinitive by לְבִלְתִּי, § 114 *s*. On the preposition מִן with a substantive or infinitive as the equivalent of a negative final clause (Gn 31²⁹, 1 S 15²³, &c.), see § 119 *x* and *y*.

§ 166. *Consecutive Clauses.*

a **1.** Consecutive clauses are added by means of simple *wāw copulative* with the jussive,[3] especially after negative and interrogative sentences, e.g. Nu 23¹⁹ לֹא אִישׁ אֵל וִיכַזֵּב וּבֶן־אָדָם וְיִתְנֶחָם *God is not a man, that he should lie, and* (i. e. neither) *the son of man, that he should repent* ; Is 53² וְנֶחְמְדֵהוּ; Ho 14¹⁰ מִי חָכָם וְיָבֵן אֵלֶּה נָבוֹן וְיֵדָעֵם *who is wise, that he may understand these things? prudent, that he may know them?* Jb 5¹² וְלֹא=*so that . . . not*; in Pr 30³ וְ is separated from the predicate by the object. In Gn 16¹⁰ a negative consecutive clause comes after a cohortative, and in Ex 10⁵ after a perfect consecutive.—On the other hand, in Jb 9³²·³³ the jussive in the sense of a consecutive clause is attached without *Wāw* to the preceding negative sentence (in

---

[1] In Ez 36²⁷ a final clause is introduced by אֵת אֲשֶׁר, thus at the same time taking the form of an object-clause.

[2] On לְ as a supposed conjunction (equivalent to the Arabic *li*) 1 K 6¹⁹, see § 66 *i*.

[3] That such examples as וִיכַזֵּב are to be regarded as jussive is probable from the analogy of Ho 14¹⁰ and Jb 9³³.

verse 32 a second jussive follows, likewise without *Wāw, for he is not a man, as I am, that I should answer him,* that *we should come together in judgement*).   On the imperfect consecutive as expressing a logical consequence, see § 111 *l*; on the perfect consecutive as a consecutive clause after a participle, see § 112 *n*.

2. Conjunctions introducing consecutive clauses are again (see *b* § 157 *c*, note 3) כִּי and אֲשֶׁר=*so that*; especially again after interrogative sentences, according to § 107 *u*; cf. Nu 16¹¹, כִּי with the imperfect, *that ye murmur*; but in Gn 20¹⁰ with the perfect, in reference to an action already completed. On אֲשֶׁר with the imperfect (or jussive) equivalent to *so that*, cf. further Gn 13¹⁶, 22¹⁴; with perfect and imperfect, 1 K 3¹²ᶠ·, with the demonstrative force clearly discernible, depending on לֵב; on אֲשֶׁר לֹא=*ut non*, cf. Dt 28³⁵, 1 K 3⁸, 2 K 9³⁷.

On מִן with a substantive or infinitive as the equivalent of a consecutive clause, see § 119 *y*.

§ 167. *Aposiopesis, Anacoluthon, Involved Series of Sentences.*

1. *Aposiopesis* is the concealment or suppression of entire sentences *a* or clauses, which are of themselves necessary to complete the sense,[1] and therefore must be supplied from the context.   This is especially frequent after conditional clauses; besides the examples already given in § 159 *dd*, cf. also Ex 32³² (the LXX and Samaritan supply שָׂא); Nu 5²⁰, Ju 9¹⁶ (in verse 19, after a long parenthesis, an imperative follows as the apodosis to this conditional clause); 1 S 12¹⁴ᶠ·, 2 S 5⁸ (where indeed the text is probably very corrupt; cf. the addition in 1 Ch 11⁶); 2 S 23¹⁷, ψ 27¹³, 1 Ch 4¹⁰.   For other examples of various kinds, see § 117 *l*, and especially § 147; in Aramaic, Dn 3¹⁵.—On Gn 3²², cf. § 152 *w* at the end.

2. *Anacoluthon* is the change from a construction which has been *b* already begun to one of a different kind.   It is found especially after long parentheses, because the speaker has either lost sight of the beginning of his sentence, or for the sake of clearness purposely makes a new beginning; thus Gn 20¹³, 31⁵² and Ez 34¹⁰ (cf. § 149 at the end); Nu 14²¹ᶠᶠ·, 32²⁰ᶠᶠ·, Dt 17²ᶠᶠ·, 24¹ᶠᶠ·, 29²¹ᶠᶠ·, Ju 10¹¹ (where, after a series of intermediate sentences, the predicate *I saved you* is sup-

---

[1] But those cases are not to be regarded as examples of aposiopesis, in which the answer, being closely connected with the question, is given simply in the infinitive with לְ; cf. § 147 *a*, note 1.

pressed; but the text can hardly be correct); perhaps also Is 66[18] (cf., however, Delitzsch on the passage, which is certainly corrupt).[1] On Gn 23[13] (אֹל with the imperative), see § 110 *e*.

c **3.** We may mention as instructive examples of *involved series* of sentences Gn 24[14] and [42 ff.], and Gn 28[6 ff.].

---

[1] On the other hand, from the Semitic point of view the various kinds of compound sentences are *not* to be regarded as instances of anacoluthon, e.g. Gn 17[14.17], nor even Gn 31[40] (cf. § 143).

THE PARADIGMS.

In the paradigms of the verbs, those forms which are to be especially noticed by the beginner are marked throughout by an asterisk as model forms. Thus e.g. in the strong verb the 3rd *sing. fem.* קָטְלָה is the model for קָטְלוּ, which likewise has only a vocalic afformative, and קָטַלְתְּ is the model for קָטַלְתְּ, קָטַלְתִּי and קָטַלְנוּ, which in the same way have a toneless afformative beginning with a consonant. On the other hand, the forms קְטַלְתֶּם and קְטַלְתֶּן, where the affix beginning with a consonant has the tone, stand by themselves.— In the table of the pronouns the asterisk has a different meaning; see the footnote there.—The bracketed forms (from Paradigm G onwards) are merely analogous formations not occurring in the Old Testament.

The newly added paradigm (Q) consists of forms actually found, belonging to various verbs.

A. The Personal

Nominative of the Pronoun, or *Pronomen separatum.*	Accusative of the Pronoun,
	A.
	Simple form.
Sing. 1. *comm.* אָנֹכִי, in pause אָנֹ֫כִי ; אֲנִי, in pause אָ֫נִי *I.*	נִי ; ־ֵ֫נִי ; ־ַ֫נִי *me.*
2. { *m.* אַתָּה (אַתְּ), in pause אָ֫תָּה ; *f.* אַתְּ (אַתִּי) } *thou.*	ךָ ; ־ְךָ, in pause ־ָ֫ךְ, ־ֶ֫ךָ } *thee.* ךְ ; ־ֵךְ ; ־ָ֫ךְ, ־ֶ֫ךָ
3. { *m.* הוּא *he.*	הוּ ; וֹ, (ה)־ֹ ; ־ֵ֫הוּ ; ־ָ֫הוּ *him.*
f. הִיא *she.*	הָ ; ־ֶ֫הָ ; ־ָ֫הּ *her (eam).*
Plur. 1. *comm.* אֲנַ֫חְנוּ (נַ֫חְנוּ), in pause אֲנָ֫חְנוּ (נָ֫חְנוּ) *we.*	נוּ ; ־ֵ֫נוּ ; ־ָ֫נוּ *us.*
2. { *m.* אַתֶּם *f.* אַתֵּן, אַתֵּ֫נָה } *you.*	כֶם ; ־ְכֶם } *you.* [כֶן ; ־ְכֶן]
3. { *m.* הֵם, הֵ֫מָּה *f.* הֵ֫נָּה } *they.*	(הֶם), ם ; ־ָ֫ם, ־ֵ֫ם, ־ָ֫מוֹ * ; ־ָ֫ם, (־ָ֫ם), ־ֵ֫מוֹ * *them (eos).* [הֶן], ן ; ־ָ֫ן, (־ָ֫ן) ; [־ֵ֫ן] *them (eas).*

Pronoun.[1]

or *Suffixum Verbi.*	Genitive of the Pronoun, or *Suffixum Nominis* (*Pron. possessivum*).	
B. With *Nûn energicum.*	**A.** Attached to a sing. noun.	**B.** Attached to a noun plur. or dual.
‑֫נִּי ; ‑֫נִי	‑ִי *my* (prop. gen. *mei*).	‑ִי *my.*
‑֫ךָ, (‑ְךָ) not found.	ךָ, ‑ְךָ, in pause ‑֫ךָ } *thy* (prop. ךְ, ‑ֵ־, (‑ְךִ)) } *tui*).	‑ֶ֫יךָ } ‑ַ֫יִךְ } *thy.*
(‑ְ‑נְהוּ), ‑֫נּוּ ; (נוֹ)	הוּ, וֹ ; ‑ֵ֫הוּ, וֹ (הֹ) *his* (*eius* and *suus*).	יו‑ָ, ‑ָיו, (‑ֵ֫יהוּ *) *his.*
‑֫נָּה	הָ ; ‑ֶ֫הָ ; ‑ָ֫הּ *her.*	‑ֶ֫יהָ *her.*
‑֫נּוּ ? (see § 58 *k*)	נוּ ; ‑ֵ֫נוּ ; (נָ֫וּ) *our.*	‑ֵ֫ינוּ *our.*
these forms are not found.	כֶם ; ‑ְכֶם } *your.* כֶן ; ‑ְכֶן }	‑ֵיכֶם } *your.* ‑ֵיכֶן }
	הֶם ; ‑ָם, ‑֫מוֹ * } *their.* הֵן, הֶן, ‑ָן }	‑ֵיהֶם, ‑ֵ֫ימוֹ * } *their.* ‑ֵיהֶן }

[1] Forms with an asterisk are exclusively poetic, those in parentheses ( ) are rare, those in brackets [ ] do not occur (cf. § 58 *a*, note).

B. Strong

		Qal.			Niph'al.	Pi'ēl.
Perf. Sing.	3. m.	*קָטַל	*כָּבֵד	*קָטֹן	*נִקְטַל	*קִטֵּל, קִטַּל
	3. f.	*קָטְלָה	*כָּבְדָה	קָטְנָה	*נִקְטְלָה	*קִטְּלָה
	2. m.	*קָטַ֫לְתָּ	*כָּבַ֫דְתָּ	קָטֹ֫נְתָּ	*נִקְטַ֫לְתָּ	*קִטַּ֫לְתָּ
	2. f.	קָטַלְתְּ	כָּבַדְתְּ	קָטֹנְתְּ	נִקְטַלְתְּ	קִטַּלְתְּ
	1. c.	קָטַ֫לְתִּי	כָּבַ֫דְתִּי	קָטֹ֫נְתִּי	נִקְטַ֫לְתִּי	קִטַּ֫לְתִּי
Plur.	3. c.	קָטְלוּ	כָּבְדוּ	קָטְנוּ	נִקְטְלוּ	קִטְּלוּ
	2. m.	*קְטַלְתֶּם	*כְּבַדְתֶּם	*קְטָנְתֶּם	נִקְטַלְתֶּם	קִטַּלְתֶּם
	2. f.	קְטַלְתֶּן	כְּבַדְתֶּן	קְטָנְתֶּן	נִקְטַלְתֶּן	קִטַּלְתֶּן
	1. c.	קָטַ֫לְנוּ	כָּבַ֫דְנוּ	קָטֹ֫נּוּ	נִקְטַ֫לְנוּ	קִטַּ֫לְנוּ
Inf.		*שָׁכֵב, קְטֹל			*הִקָּטֵל	*קַטֵּל
Inf. absol.		*קָטוֹל			*הִקָּטֹל, נִקְטֹל	*קַטֹּל, קַטֵּל
Imp. Sing.	2. m.	*קְטֹל	*כְּבַד		*הִקָּטֵל	*קַטֵּל
	2. f.	קִטְלִי	*כִּבְדִי		הִקָּטְלִי	קַטְּלִי
Plur.	2. m.	קִטְלוּ	כִּבְדוּ		הִקָּטְלוּ	קַטְּלוּ
	2. f.	*קְטֹ֫לְנָה	*כְּבַ֫דְנָה		*הִקָּטַ֫לְנָה	*קַטֵּ֫לְנָה
Impf. Sing.	3. m.	*יִקְטֹל	*יִכְבַּד	יִקְטַן	*יִקָּטֵל	*יְקַטֵּל
	3. f.	תִּקְטֹל	תִּכְבַּד	תִּקְטַן	תִּקָּטֵל	תְּקַטֵּל
	2. m.	תִּקְטֹל	תִּכְבַּד	תִּקְטַן	תִּקָּטֵל	תְּקַטֵּל
	2. f.	*תִּקְטְלִי	*תִּכְבְּדִי		*תִּקָּטְלִי	*תְּקַטְּלִי
	1. c.	אֶקְטֹל	אֶכְבַּד	אֶקְטַן	אֶקָּטֵל	אֲקַטֵּל
Plur.	3. m.	יִקְטְלוּ	יִכְבְּדוּ		יִקָּטְלוּ	יְקַטְּלוּ
	3. f.	*תִּקְטֹ֫לְנָה	*תִּכְבַּ֫דְנָה		*תִּקָּטַ֫לְנָה	*תְּקַטֵּ֫לְנָה
	2. m.	תִּקְטְלוּ	תִּכְבְּדוּ		תִּקָּטְלוּ	תְּקַטְּלוּ
	2. f.	תִּקְטֹ֫לְנָה	*תִּכְבַּ֫דְנָה		תִּקָּטַ֫לְנָה	תְּקַטֵּ֫לְנָה
	1. c.	נִקְטֹל	נִכְבַּד		נִקָּטֵל	נְקַטֵּל

Shortened Impf. (Jussive).

		Qal.			Niph'al.	Pi'ēl.
Part. act.		*קֹטֵל	כָּבֵד	קָטֹן	*נִקְטָל	*מְקַטֵּל
pass.		*קָטוּל				

Verb.

Pu'al.	Hiph'il.	Hoph'al.	Hithpa'ēl.
*קֻטַּל	*הִקְטִיל	*הָקְטַל	*הִתְקַטֵּל
*קֻטְּלָה	*הִקְטִילָה	*הָקְטְלָה	*הִתְקַטְּלָה
*קֻטַּלְתָּ	*הִקְטַלְתָּ	*הָקְטַלְתָּ	*הִתְקַטַּלְתָּ
קֻטַּלְתְּ	הִקְטַלְתְּ	הָקְטַלְתְּ	הִתְקַטַּלְתְּ
קֻטַּלְתִּי	הִקְטַלְתִּי	הָקְטַלְתִּי	הִתְקַטַּלְתִּי
קֻטְּלוּ	הִקְטִילוּ	הָקְטְלוּ	הִתְקַטְּלוּ
קֻטַּלְתֶּם	הִקְטַלְתֶּם	הָקְטַלְתֶּם	הִתְקַטַּלְתֶּם
קֻטַּלְתֶּן	הִקְטַלְתֶּן	הָקְטַלְתֶּן	הִתְקַטַּלְתֶּן
קֻטַּלְנוּ	הִקְטַלְנוּ	הָקְטַלְנוּ	הִתְקַטַּלְנוּ
wanting.	*הַקְטִיל	wanting.	*הִתְקַטֵּל
*קֻטֹּל	*הַקְטֵל	*הָקְטֵל	*הִתְקַטֵּל
	*הַקְטֵל		*הִתְקַטֵּל
wanting.	*הַקְטִילִי	wanting.	*הִתְקַטְּלִי
	הַקְטִילוּ		הִתְקַטְּלוּ
	*הַקְטֵלְנָה		*הִתְקַטֵּלְנָה
*יְקֻטַּל	*יַקְטִיל	*יָקְטַל	*יִתְקַטֵּל
תְּקֻטַּל	תַּקְטִיל	תָּקְטַל	תִּתְקַטֵּל
תְּקֻטַּל	תַּקְטִיל	תָּקְטַל	תִּתְקַטֵּל
*תְּקֻטְּלִי	*תַּקְטִילִי	*תָּקְטְלִי	*תִּתְקַטְּלִי
אֲקֻטַּל	אַקְטִיל	אָקְטַל	אֶתְקַטֵּל
יְקֻטְּלוּ	יַקְטִילוּ	יָקְטְלוּ	יִתְקַטְּלוּ
*תְּקֻטַּלְנָה	*תַּקְטֵלְנָה	*תָּקְטַלְנָה	*תִּתְקַטֵּלְנָה
תְּקֻטְּלוּ	תַּקְטִילוּ	תָּקְטְלוּ	תִּתְקַטְּלוּ
תְּקֻטַּלְנָה	תַּקְטֵלְנָה	תָּקְטַלְנָה	תִּתְקַטֵּלְנָה
נְקֻטַּל	נַקְטִיל	נָקְטַל	נִתְקַטֵּל
	*יַקְטֵל		
	*מַקְטִיל		*מִתְקַטֵּל
*מְקֻטָּל		*מָקְטָל	

C. Strong Verb

Suffixes		1 Sing.	2 Sing. m.	2 Sing. f.	3 Sing. m.
Perf. Qal	3. m.	קְטָלַ֫נִי שְׁכֵחַ֫נִי	קְטָֽלְךָ	קְטָלֵ֫ךְ	קְטָלָ֫הוּ קְטָלוֹ
	3. f.	קְטָלַ֫תְנִי	קְטָלַ֫תְךָ	קְטָלָ֫תֶךְ	קְטָלַ֫תְהוּ קְטָלַ֫תּוּ
	2. m.	קְטַלְתַּ֫נִי	—	—	קְטַלְתָּ֫הוּ קְטַלְתּוֹ
	2. f.	קְטַלְתִּ֫ינִי	—	—	קְטַלְתִּיהוּ
	1. c.	—	קְטַלְתִּ֫יךָ	קְטַלְתִּיךְ	קְטַלְתִּ֫יו קְטַלְתִּ֫יהוּ
Plur.	3. c.	קְטָל֫וּנִי	קְטָל֫וּךָ אֲהֵב֫וּךָ	קְטָל֫וּךְ	קְטָל֫וּהוּ
	2. m.	קְטַלְתּ֫וּנִי	—	—	קְטַלְתּ֫וּהוּ
	1. c.	—	קְטַלְנ֫וּךָ	קְטַלְנ֫וּךְ	קְטַלְנ֫וּהוּ
Inf. Qal		קָטְלִי קָטְלֵ֫נִי	כָּתְבְּךָ קָטְלְךָ	קָטְלֵ֫ךְ	קָטְלוֹ
Imp. Qal 2. (from an *Imperf.* in *a* שְׁמָעֵ֫נִי, שְׁלָחֵ֫נִי)		קָטְלֵ֫נִי	—	—	קָטְלֵ֫הוּ
Impf. Qal	3. m.	יִקְטְלֵ֫נִי יִלְבָּשֵׁ֫נִי	יִקְטָלְךָ יִלְבָּשְׁךָ	יִקְטְלֵךְ יִלְבָּשֵׁךְ	יִקְטְלֵ֫הוּ יִלְבָּשֵׁ֫הוּ
3. m. with *Nûn energ.*		יִקְטְלַ֫נִּי	יִקְטָלְךָ	—	יִקְטְלֶ֫נּוּ
Plur.	3. m.	יִקְטְל֫וּנִי	יִקְטְל֫וּךָ	יִקְטְל֫וּךְ	יִקְטְל֫וּהוּ יִנְאָל֫וּהוּ
Perf. Pi̇ʿēl	3. m.	קִטְּלַ֫נִי	קִטֶּלְךָ	קִטְּלֵ֫ךְ	קִטְּלוֹ

with Suffixes.

3 Sing. f.	1 Plur.	2 Plur. m.	2 Plur. f.	3 Plur. m.	3 Plur. f.
קְטָלָהּ	קְטָלָנוּ	wanting.	wanting.	{ קְטָלָם / לְבֶשָׁם }	קְטָלָן
קְטָלַתָּה	קְטָלַתְנוּ	—	—	קְטָלָתַם	wanting.
קְטַלְתָּהּ	קְטַלְתָּנוּ	—	—	קְטַלְתָּם	wanting.
קְטַלְתִּיהָ	קְטַלְתִּינוּ	—	—	קְטַלְתִּים	wanting.
קְטַלְתִּיהָ	—	קְטַלְתִּיכֶם	wanting.	קְטַלְתִּים	קְטַלְתִּין
קְטָלוּהָ	קְטָלוּנוּ	wanting.	wanting.	קְטָלוּם	קְטָלוּן
wanting.	קְטַלְתֻּנוּ	—	—	wanting.	wanting.
קְטַלְנוּהָ	—	קְטַלְנוּכֶם	wanting.	קְטַלְנוּם	wanting.
קְטָלָהּ	קְטָלֵנוּ	{ כָּתְבְּכֶם / קְטָלְכֶם }	wanting.	קְטָלָם	קְטָלָן
{ קְטָלָהָ / קְטָלָהּ }	קְטָלֵנוּ	—	—	קְטָלֵם	—
{ יִקְטְלֶהָ / יִלְבָּשֶׁהָ / יִקְטְלָהָ }	{ יִקְטְלֵנוּ / יִלְבָּשֶׁנּוּ }	יִקְטָלְכֶם	wanting.	יִקְטְלֵם	wanting.
יִקְטְלֶנָּה	יִקְטָלְנוּ	—	—	—	—
יִקְטְלוּהָ	יִקְטְלוּנוּ	יִקְטְלוּכֶם	wanting.	יִקְטְלוּם	wanting.
קִטְּלָהּ	קִטְּלָנוּ	wanting.	wanting.	קִטְּלָם	קִטְּלָן

D. Verbs primae gutturalis

	Qal.	Niph'al.	Hiph'îl.	Hoph'al.
Perf. Sing. 3. m.	עָמַד	‎*נֶעֱמַד	*הֶעֱמִיד	*הָעֳמַד
3. f.	עָמְדָה	*נֶעֶמְדָה	הֶעֱמִידָה	*הָעֳמְדָה
2. m.	עָמַ֫דְתָּ	נֶעֱמַ֫דְתָּ	הֶעֱמַ֫דְתָּ	הָעֳמַ֫דְתָּ
2. f.	עָמַדְתְּ	נֶעֱמַדְתְּ	*הֶעֱמַדְתְּ	הָעֳמַדְתְּ
1. c.	עָמַ֫דְתִּי	נֶעֱמַ֫דְתִּי	הֶעֱמַ֫דְתִּי	הָעֳמַ֫דְתִּי
Plur. 3. c.	עָמְדוּ	נֶעֶמְדוּ	הֶעֱמִידוּ	הָעֳמְדוּ
2. m.	*עֲמַדְתֶּם	נֶעֱמַדְתֶּם	הֶעֱמַדְתֶּם	הָעֳמַדְתֶּם
2. f.	*עֲמַדְתֶּן	נֶעֱמַדְתֶּן	הֶעֱמַדְתֶּן	הָעֳמַדְתֶּן
1. c.	עָמַ֫דְנוּ	נֶעֱמַ֫דְנוּ	הֶעֱמַ֫דְנוּ	הָעֳמַ֫דְנוּ
Inf.	*עֲמֹד	*הֵעָמֵד	הֶעֱמִיד	
Inf. absol.	עָמוֹד	*נַעֲמוֹד, הֵאָסֹף	*הַעֲמֵד	*הָעֳמֵד
Imp. Sing. m.	*עֲמֹד, *חֲזַק	*הֵעָמֵד	הַעֲמֵד	
f.	עִמְדִי, חִזְקִי	הֵעָמְדִי	הַעֲמִ֫ידִי	
Plur. m.	עִמְדוּ, חִזְקוּ	הֵעָמְדוּ	הַעֲמִ֫ידוּ	wanting.
f.	*עֲמֹ֫דְנָה, *חֲזַ֫קְנָה	הֵעָמַ֫דְנָה	הַעֲמֵ֫דְנָה	
Impf. Sing. 3. m.	*יַעֲמֹד, *יֶחֱזַק	*יֵעָמֵד	*יַעֲמִיד	*יָעֳמַד
3. f.	תַּעֲמֹד, תֶּחֱזַק	תֵּעָמֵד	תַּעֲמִיד	תָּעֳמַד
2. m.	תַּעֲמֹד, תֶּחֱזַק	תֵּעָמֵד	תַּעֲמִיד	תָּעֳמַד
2. f.	*תַּעַמְדִי, *תֶּחֶזְקִי	תֵּעָמְדִי	תַּעֲמִ֫ידִי	*תָּעֳמְדִי
1. c.	*אֶעֱמֹד, אֶחֱזַק	אֵעָמֵד	אַעֲמִיד	אָעֳמַד
Plur. 3. m.	*יַעַמְדוּ, *יֶחֶזְקוּ	יֵעָמְדוּ	יַעֲמִ֫ידוּ	יָעֳמְדוּ
3. f.	תַּעֲמֹ֫דְנָה, תֶּחֱזַ֫קְנָה	תֵּעָמַ֫דְנָה	תַּעֲמֵ֫דְנָה	תָּעֳמַ֫דְנָה
2. m.	תַּעַמְדוּ, תֶּחֶזְקוּ	תֵּעָמְדוּ	תַּעֲמִ֫ידוּ	תָּעֳמְדוּ
2. f.	תַּעֲמֹ֫דְנָה, תֶּחֱזַ֫קְנָה	תֵּעָמַ֫דְנָה	תַּעֲמֵ֫דְנָה	תָּעֳמַ֫דְנָה
1. c.	נַעֲמֹד, נֶחֱזַק	נֵעָמֵד	נַעֲמִיד	נָעֳמַד
Shortened Impf. (Jussive).			יַעֲמֵד	
Part. act.	עֹמֵד	*נֶעֱמָד	*מַעֲמִיד	
pass.	עָמוּד			מָעֳמָד

E. Verbs mediae gutturalis.

	Qal.	Niph'al.	Pi'ēl.	Pu'al.	Hithpa'ēl.
Perf. Sing. 3. m.	שָׁחַט	נִשְׁחַט	*בֵּרַךְ	*בֹּרַךְ	*הִתְבָּרֵךְ
3. f.	*שָׁחֲטָה	*נִשְׁחֲטָה	בֵּרְכָה	[בֹּרְכָה]	הִתְבָּרְכָה
2. m.	שָׁחַטְתָּ	נִשְׁחַטְתָּ	בֵּרַכְתָּ	בֹּרַכְתָּ	הִתְבָּרַכְתָּ
2. f.	שָׁחַטְתְּ	נִשְׁחַטְתְּ	בֵּרַכְתְּ	בֹּרַכְתְּ	הִתְבָּרַכְתְּ
I. c.	שָׁחַטְתִּי	נִשְׁחַטְתִּי	בֵּרַכְתִּי	בֹּרַכְתִּי	הִתְבָּרַכְתִּי
Plur. 3. c.	*שָׁחֲטוּ	*נִשְׁחֲטוּ	בֵּרְכוּ	בֹּרְכוּ	הִתְבָּרְכוּ
2. m.	שְׁחַטְתֶּם	נִשְׁחַטְתֶּם	בֵּרַכְתֶּם	בֹּרַכְתֶּם	הִתְבָּרַכְתֶּם
2. f.	שְׁחַטְתֶּן	נִשְׁחַטְתֶּן	[בֵּרַכְתֶּן]	בֹּרַכְתֶּן	הִתְבָּרַכְתֶּן
I. c.	שָׁחַטְנוּ	נִשְׁחַטְנוּ	בֵּרַכְנוּ	בֹּרַכְנוּ	הִתְבָּרַכְנוּ
Inf.	שְׁחֹט	הִשָּׁחֵט	*בָּרֵךְ	wanting.	*הִתְבָּרֵךְ
Inf. absol.	שָׁחוֹט	נִשְׁחוֹט	*בָּרֵךְ		
Imp. Sing. m.	*שְׁחַט	הִשָּׁחֵט	*בָּרֵךְ		*הִתְבָּרֵךְ
f.	*שַׁחֲטִי	*הִשָּׁחֲטִי	*בָּרְכִי	wanting.	[הִתְבָּרְכִי]
Plur. m.	שַׁחֲטוּ	הִשָּׁחֲטוּ	בָּרְכוּ		[הִתְבָּרְכוּ]
f.	שְׁחַטְנָה	הִשָּׁחַטְנָה	*בָּרֵכְנָה		הִתְבָּרֵכְנָה
Impf. Sing. 3. m.	*יִשְׁחַט	יִשָּׁחֵט	*יְבָרֵךְ	*יְבֹרַךְ	*יִתְבָּרֵךְ
3. f.	תִּשְׁחַט	תִּשָּׁחֵט	תְּבָרֵךְ	תְּבֹרַךְ	תִּתְבָּרֵךְ
2. m.	תִּשְׁחַט	תִּשָּׁחֵט	תְּבָרֵךְ	תְּבֹרַךְ	תִּתְבָּרֵךְ
2. f.	*תִּשְׁחֲטִי	*תִּשָּׁחֲטִי	תְּבָרְכִי	[תְּבֹרְכִי]	[תִּתְבָּרְכִי]
I. c.	אֶשְׁחַט	אֶשָּׁחֵט	אֲבָרֵךְ	אֲבֹרַךְ	אֶתְבָּרֵךְ
Plur. 3. m.	יִשְׁחֲטוּ	יִשָּׁחֲטוּ	יְבָרְכוּ	יְבֹרְכוּ	יִתְבָּרְכוּ
3. f.	תִּשְׁחַטְנָה	תִּשָּׁחַטְנָה	תְּבָרֵכְנָה	תְּבֹרַכְנָה	תִּתְבָּרֵכְנָה
2. m.	תִּשְׁחֲטוּ	תִּשָּׁחֲטוּ	תְּבָרְכוּ	תְּבֹרְכוּ	תִּתְבָּרְכוּ
2. f.	תִּשְׁחַטְנָה	תִּשָּׁחַטְנָה	תְּבָרֵכְנָה	תְּבֹרַכְנָה	תִּתְבָּרֵכְנָה
I. c.	נִשְׁחַט	נִשָּׁחֵט	נְבָרֵךְ	נְבֹרַךְ	נִתְבָּרֵךְ
Impf. with Suff.	יִשְׁחָטֵהוּ				
Part. act.	שֹׁחֵט	נִשְׁחָט	*מְבָרֵךְ		*מִתְבָּרֵךְ
pass.	שָׁחוּט			*מְבֹרָךְ	

L l 2

		Qal.	Niph'al.	Pi'ēl.
Perf. Sing.	3. m.	שָׁלַח	נִשְׁלַח	*שִׁלַּח
	3. f.	שָׁלְחָה	נִשְׁלְחָה	שִׁלְּחָה
	2. m.	שָׁלַחְתָּ	נִשְׁלַחְתָּ	שִׁלַּחְתָּ
	2. f.	*שָׁלַחַתְּ	*נִשְׁלַחַתְּ	*שִׁלַּחַתְּ
	1. c.	שָׁלַחְתִּי	נִשְׁלַחְתִּי	שִׁלַּחְתִּי
Plur.	3. c.	שָׁלְחוּ	נִשְׁלְחוּ	שִׁלְּחוּ
	2. m.	שְׁלַחְתֶּם	נִשְׁלַחְתֶּם	שִׁלַּחְתֶּם
	2. f.	שְׁלַחְתֶּן	נִשְׁלַחְתֶּן	שִׁלַּחְתֶּן
	1. c.	שָׁלַחְנוּ	נִשְׁלַחְנוּ	שִׁלַּחְנוּ
Inf.		*שְׁלֹחַ	*הִשָּׁלֵחַ	*שַׁלֵּחַ
Inf. absol.		שָׁלוֹחַ	נִשְׁלוֹחַ	שַׁלֵּחַ
Imp. Sing.	m.	*שְׁלַח	*הִשָּׁלַח	*שַׁלַּח
	f.	שִׁלְחִי	הִשָּׁלְחִי	*שַׁלְּחִי
Plur.	m.	שִׁלְחוּ	הִשָּׁלְחוּ	שַׁלְּחוּ
	f.	*שְׁלַחְנָה	הִשָּׁלַחְנָה	*שַׁלַּחְנָה
Impf. Sing.	3. m.	*יִשְׁלַח	*יִשָּׁלַח	*יְשַׁלַּח
	3. f.	תִּשְׁלַח	תִּשָּׁלַח	*תְּשַׁלַּח
	2. m.	תִּשְׁלַח	תִּשָּׁלַח	תְּשַׁלַּח
	2. f.	תִּשְׁלְחִי	תִּשָּׁלְחִי	תְּשַׁלְּחִי
	1. c.	אֶשְׁלַח	אֶשָּׁלַח	אֲשַׁלַּח
Plur.	3. m.	יִשְׁלְחוּ	יִשָּׁלְחוּ	יְשַׁלְּחוּ
	3. f.	*תִּשְׁלַחְנָה	*תִּשָּׁלַחְנָה	*תְּשַׁלַּחְנָה
	2. m.	תִּשְׁלְחוּ	תִּשָּׁלְחוּ	תְּשַׁלְּחוּ
	2. f.	תִּשְׁלַחְנָה	תִּשָּׁלַחְנָה	תְּשַׁלַּחְנָה
	1. c.	נִשְׁלַח	נִשָּׁלַח	נְשַׁלַּח
Shortened Impf. (Jussive).				
Impf. with Suff.		יִשְׁלָחֵנִי		
Part. act.		*שֹׁלֵחַ	נִשְׁלָח	*מְשַׁלֵּחַ
pass.		*שָׁלוּחַ		

tertiae gutturalis.

Pu'al.	Hiph'îl.	Hoph'al.	Hithpa'ēl.
שֻׁלַּח	*הִשְׁלִיחַ	הָשְׁלַח	*הִשְׁתַּלַּח
שֻׁלְּחָה	הִשְׁלִיחָה	הָשְׁלְחָה	הִשְׁתַּלְּחָה
שֻׁלַּחְתָּ	הִשְׁלַחְתָּ	הָשְׁלַחְתָּ	הִשְׁתַּלַּחְתָּ
*שֻׁלַּחַתְּ	*הִשְׁלַחַתְּ	*הָשְׁלַחַתְּ	*הִשְׁתַּלַּחַתְּ
שֻׁלַּחְתִּי	הִשְׁלַחְתִּי	הָשְׁלַחְתִּי	הִשְׁתַּלַּחְתִּי
שֻׁלְּחוּ	הִשְׁלִיחוּ	הָשְׁלְחוּ	הִשְׁתַּלְּחוּ
שֻׁלַּחְתֶּם	הִשְׁלַחְתֶּם	הָשְׁלַחְתֶּם	הִשְׁתַּלַּחְתֶּם
שֻׁלַּחְתֶּן	הִשְׁלַחְתֶּן	הָשְׁלַחְתֶּן	הִשְׁתַּלַּחְתֶּן
שֻׁלַּחְנוּ	הִשְׁלַחְנוּ	הָשְׁלַחְנוּ	הִשְׁתַּלַּחְנוּ
	*הַשְׁלִיחַ		*הִשְׁתַּלַּח
	*הַשְׁלֵחַ	*הָשְׁלֵחַ	
	הַשְׁלַח		*הִשְׁתַּלַּח
	הַשְׁלִיחִי		הִשְׁתַּלְּחִי
wanting.	הַשְׁלִיחוּ	wanting.	הִשְׁתַּלְּחוּ
	הַשְׁלַחְנָה		*הִשְׁתַּלַּחְנָה
יְשֻׁלַּח	*יַשְׁלִיחַ	יָשְׁלַח	יִשְׁתַּלַּח
תְּשֻׁלַּח	תַּשְׁלִיחַ	תָּשְׁלַח	תִּשְׁתַּלַּח
תְּשֻׁלַּח	תַּשְׁלִיחַ	תָּשְׁלַח	תִּשְׁתַּלַּח
תְּשֻׁלְּחִי	תַּשְׁלִיחִי	תָּשְׁלְחִי	תִּשְׁתַּלְּחִי
אֲשֻׁלַּח	אַשְׁלִיחַ	אָשְׁלַח	אֶשְׁתַּלַּח
יְשֻׁלְּחוּ	יַשְׁלִיחוּ	יָשְׁלְחוּ	יִשְׁתַּלְּחוּ
תְּשֻׁלַּחְנָה	תַּשְׁלַחְנָה	תָּשְׁלַחְנָה	*תִּשְׁתַּלַּחְנָה
תְּשֻׁלְּחוּ	תַּשְׁלִיחוּ	תָּשְׁלְחוּ	תִּשְׁתַּלְּחוּ
תְּשֻׁלַּחְנָה	תַּשְׁלַחְנָה	תָּשְׁלַחְנָה	תִּשְׁתַּלַּחְנָה
נְשֻׁלַּח	נַשְׁלִיחַ	נָשְׁלַח	נִשְׁתַּלַּח
	יַשְׁלַח		
	*מַשְׁלִיחַ		*מִשְׁתַּלֵּחַ
מְשֻׁלָּח		מָשְׁלָח	

CC²

G.   *Verbs mediae geminatae*

		Qal.	Niph'al.
Perf. Sing.	3. m.	*סָבַב, תַּם	*נָסַב, נָמֵס
	3. f.	סָבְבָה, תַּמָּה	*נָסַבָּה
	2. m.	*סַבּוֹתָ	*נְסַבּוֹתָ
	2. f.	סַבּוֹת	נְסַבּוֹת
	1. c.	סַבּוֹתִי	נְסַבּוֹתִי
Plur. 3.	c.	סָבְבוּ, תַּמּוּ	נָסַבּוּ
	2. m.	סַבּוֹתֶם	נְסַבּוֹתֶם
	2. f.	סַבּוֹתֶן	נְסַבּוֹתֶן
	1. c.	סַבּוֹנוּ	נְסַבּוֹנוּ

	Qal.	Niph'al.
Inf.	*סֹב	*הַסֵּב
Inf. absol.	סָבוֹב	הִמֵּס, הִסּוֹב

Imp. Sing. m.	*סֹב	הִסַּב
f.	*סֹבִּי	*הִסַּבִּי
Plur. m.	סֹבּוּ	הִסַּבּוּ
f.	[סֻבֶּינָה]	[הִסַּבֶּינָה]

Impf. Sing.	3. m.	*יָסֹב (יֵסַל § 67 p) *יִסֹּב	*יִסַּב
	3. f.	תָּסֹב	תִּסֹּב	תִּסַּב
	2. m.	תָּסֹב	תִּסֹּב	תִּסַּב
	2. f.	*תָּסֹבִּי	תִּסְּבִי	*תִּסַּבִּי
	1. c.	אָסֹב	אֶסֹּב	אֶסַּב
Plur. 3. m.	יָסֹבּוּ	יִסֹּבוּ	יִסַּבּוּ
	3. f.	*תְּסֻבֶּינָה	[תִּסֹּבְנָה]	[תִּסַּבֶּינָה]
	2. m.	תָּסֹבּוּ	תִּסֹּבוּ	תִּסַּבּוּ
	2. f.	[תִּסֻבֶּינָה]	[תִּסֹּבְנָה]	[תִּסַּבֶּינָה]
	1. c.	נָסֹב	נִסֹּב	נִסַּב

Impf. with Wāw consec.	*וַיָּסָב (pause וַיִּסֹּב)
Impf. with Suff.	*יְסֻבֶּנִי

| Part. act. | סֹבֵב | נָסָב |
| pass. | *סָבוּב | (fem. נְסַבָּה) |

Hiph'îl.	Hoph'al.	Po'ēl.	Po'al.
*הֵסֵב, הֵסַב	*הוּסַב	*סוֹבֵב	*סוֹבַב
*הֵסֵבָּה	הוּסַבָּה	סוֹבְבָה	[סוֹבְבָה]
*הֲסִבּוֹתָ	[הוּסַבּוֹתָ]	סוֹבַבְתָּ	סוֹבַבְתָּ
הֲסִבּוֹת	הוּסַבּוֹת	סוֹבַבְתְּ	סוֹבַבְתְּ
הֲסִבּוֹתִי	[הוּסַבּוֹתִי]	סוֹבַבְתִּי	סוֹבַבְתִּי
הֵסַבּוּ, הֵחֵלּוּ	הוּסַבּוּ	סוֹבְבוּ	סוֹבְבוּ
הֲסִבּוֹתֶם	[הוּסַבּוֹתֶם]	סוֹבַבְתֶּם	סוֹבַבְתֶּם
הֲסִבּוֹתֶן	הוּסַבּוֹתֶן	סוֹבַבְתֶּן	סוֹבַבְתֶּן
הֲסִבּוֹנוּ	[הוּסַבּוֹנוּ]	סוֹבַבְנוּ	[סוֹבַבְנוּ]
*הָסֵב		סוֹבֵב	
הָסֵב	הָשֵּׁמָּה	סוֹבֵב	[סוֹבַב]
*הָסֵב		סוֹבֵב	
הָסֵבִּי	wanting.	[סוֹבְבִי]	wanting.
הָסֵבּוּ		סוֹבְבוּ	
[הֲסִבֶּינָה]		סוֹבֵבְנָה]	
*יָסֵב, יָסֵב	*יוּסַב, יֵסַב	יְסוֹבֵב	[יְסוֹבַב]
תָּסֵב	[תּוּסַב]	תְּסוֹבֵב	תְּסוֹבַב
תָּסֵב	תּוּסַב	תְּסוֹבֵב	תְּסוֹבַב
[תָּסֵבִּי]	*תּוּסַבִּי	[תְּסוֹבְבִי]	תְּסוֹבְבִי
אָסֵב	אוּסַב]	[אֲסוֹבֵב]	אֲסוֹבַב
יָסֵבּוּ, יָסֵבּוּ	יוּסַבּוּ	יְסוֹבְבוּ	יְסוֹבְבוּ
*תְּסִבֶּינָה	*[תּוּסַבֶּינָה]	[תְּסוֹבֵבְנָה]	תְּסוֹבַבְנָה
תָּסֵבּוּ	תּוּסַבּוּ	תְּסוֹבְבוּ	תְּסוֹבְבוּ
תְּסִבֶּינָה	תּוּסַבֶּינָה	[תְּסוֹבֵבְנָה]	תְּסוֹבַבְנָה
נָסֵב	נוּסַב]	נְסוֹבֵב]	נְסוֹבַב]
וַיָּסֵב			
*יְסִבֵּנִי (יִסָבְּכֶם)		יְסוֹבְבֵנִי	
*מֵסֵב		מְסוֹבֵב	
	מוּסָב		מְסוֹבָב

H. Verbs פ״נ.

NCC

	Qal.		Niph'al.	Hiph'il.	Hoph'al.
Perf. Sing. 3. m.	[נָגַשׁ]	נָפַל	*נִגַּשׁ	*הִגִּישׁ	*הֻגַּשׁ
3. f.			נִגְּשָׁה	הִגִּישָׁה	הֻגְּשָׁה
2. m.			נִגַּשְׁתָּ	הִגַּשְׁתָּ	הֻגַּשְׁתָּ
2. f.			נִגַּשְׁתְּ	הִגַּשְׁתְּ	הֻגַּשְׁתְּ
1. c.	*regular.*		נִגַּשְׁתִּי	הִגַּשְׁתִּי	הֻגַּשְׁתִּי
Plur. 3. c.			נִגְּשׁוּ	הִגִּישׁוּ	הֻגְּשׁוּ
2. m.			נִגַּשְׁתֶּם	הִגַּשְׁתֶּם	הֻגַּשְׁתֶּם
2. f.			נִגַּשְׁתֶּן	הִגַּשְׁתֶּן	הֻגַּשְׁתֶּן
1. c.			נִגַּשְׁנוּ	הִגַּשְׁנוּ	הֻגַּשְׁנוּ
Inf.	*גֶּשֶׁת	*נְפֹל	הִנָּגֵשׁ	*הַגִּישׁ	*הֻגַּשׁ
Inf. absol.	נָגוֹשׁ		נִגּוֹף, הִנָּגֵשׁ	*הַגֵּשׁ	*הֻגֵּשׁ
Imp. Sing. m.	*גַּשׁ	*נְפֹל	הִנָּגֵשׁ	*הַגֵּשׁ	
f.	גְּשִׁי	נִפְלִי	הִנָּגְשִׁי	הַגִּישִׁי	
Plur. m.	גְּשׁוּ	נִפְלוּ	הִנָּגְשׁוּ	הַגִּישׁוּ	*wanting.*
f.	גֶּשְׁנָה	נְפֹלְנָה	הִנָּגַשְׁנָה	הַגֵּשְׁנָה	
Impf. Sing. 3. m.	*יִגַּשׁ	*יִפֹּל	[יִנָּגֵשׁ]	*יַגִּישׁ	*יֻגַּשׁ
3. f.	תִּגַּשׁ	תִּפֹּל		תַּגִּישׁ	תֻּגַּשׁ
2. m.	תִּגַּשׁ	תִּפֹּל		תַּגִּישׁ	תֻּגַּשׁ
2. f.	תִּגְּשִׁי	תִּפְּלִי		תַּגִּישִׁי	תֻּגְּשִׁי
1. c.	אֶגַּשׁ	אֶפֹּל		אַגִּישׁ	אֻגַּשׁ
Plur. 3. m.	יִגְּשׁוּ	יִפְּלוּ	*regular.*	יַגִּישׁוּ	יֻגְּשׁוּ
3. f.	תִּגַּשְׁנָה	תִּפֹּלְנָה		תַּגֵּשְׁנָה	תֻּגַּשְׁנָה
2. m.	תִּגְּשׁוּ	תִּפְּלוּ		תַּגִּישׁוּ	תֻּגְּשׁוּ
2. f.	[תִּגַּשְׁנָה]	[תִּפֹּלְנָה]		[תַּגֵּשְׁנָה]	[תֻּגַּשְׁנָה]
1. c.	נִגַּשׁ	נִפֹּל		נַגִּישׁ	נֻגַּשׁ
Shortened Impf. (Jussive).				*יַגֵּשׁ	
Part. act.	נֹגֵשׁ		*נִגָּשׁ	*מַגִּישׁ	
pass.	נָגוּשׁ				מֻגָּשׁ

I. *Weak Verbs,* פ״א.

	Qal.	Niph'al.	Hiph'il.	Hoph'al.
Perf.	אָכַל	*נֶאֱכַל	*הֶאֱכִיל	*הָאֳכַל

Like Verbs *primae gutturalis.*

		Qal.	Niph'al.	Hiph'il.	Hoph'al.
Inf.		*אֱכֹל, אֲכָל	הֵאָכֵל	הַאֲכִיל	הָאֳכַל
Inf. absol.		אָכוֹל	הֵאָכֹל	wanting.	wanting.
Imp. Sing. m.		*אֱכֹל	הֵאָכֵל	הַאֲכֵל	
f.		אִכְלִי	&c,	&c.	wanting.
Plur. m.		אִכְלוּ			
f.		[אֱכֹלְנָה]			
Impf. Sing.	3. m.	*יֹאכַל *(in pause	*יֵאָכֵל	*יַאֲכִיל	*יָאֳכַל
	3. f.	(יֹאכַל) תֹּאכַל	&c.	&c.	&c.
	2. m.	תֹּאכַל			
	2. f.	תֹּאכְלִי			
	1. c.	*אֹכַל			
Plur.	3. m.	יֹאכְלוּ			
	3. f.	תֹּאכַלְנָה			
	2. m.	תֹּאכְלוּ			
	2. f.	[תֹּאכַלְנָה]			
	1. c.	נֹאכַל			
Impf. with Wāw consec.		*וַיֹּאמֶר *וַיֹּאכַל			
Part. act.		אֹכֵל	נֶאֱכָל	מַאֲכִיל	
pass.		אָכוּל			מָאֳכָל

WCC

		Qal.		Niph'al.
Perf. Sing	3. m.	יָשַׁב		נוֹשַׁב* 1ֹ = 10's
	3. f.			נוֹשְׁבָה*
	2. m.			נוֹשַׁבְתָּ
	2. f.			נוֹשַׁבְתְּ
	1. c.	regular.		נוֹשַׁבְתִּי
Plur.	3. c.			נוֹשְׁבוּ
	2. m.			נוֹשַׁבְתֶּם
	2. f.			נוֹשַׁבְתֶּן
	1. c.			נוֹשַׁבְנוּ
Inf.		יְסֹד, רֶשֶׁת, שֶׁבֶת*		הִוָּשֵׁב*
Inf. absol.		יָשׁוֹב*		wanting.
Imp. Sing.	m.	שֵׁב, דַּע*		הִוָּשֵׁב*
	f.	שְׁבִי		הִוָּשְׁבִי
Plur.	m.	שְׁבוּ		הִוָּשְׁבוּ
	f.	שֵׁבְנָה		[הִוָּשַׁבְנָה]
Impf. Sing.	3. m.	יֵשֵׁב*	יִירַשׁ*	יִוָּשֵׁב*
	3. f.	תֵּשֵׁב	תִּירַשׁ	תִּוָּשֵׁב
	2. m.	תֵּשֵׁב	תִּירַשׁ	תִּוָּשֵׁב
	2. f.	תֵּשְׁבִי	תִּירְשִׁי	תִּוָּשְׁבִי
	1. c.	אֵשֵׁב	אִירַשׁ	אִוָּשֵׁב*
Plur.	3. m.	יֵשְׁבוּ	יִירְשׁוּ	יִוָּשְׁבוּ
	3. f.	תֵּשַׁבְנָה	[תִּירַשְׁנָה]	[תִּוָּשַׁבְנָה]
	2. m.	תֵּשְׁבוּ	תִּירְשׁוּ	תִּוָּשְׁבוּ
	2. f.	[תֵּשַׁבְנָה]	[תִּירַשְׁנָה]	[תִּוָּשַׁבְנָה]
	1. c.	נֵשֵׁב	נִירַשׁ	נִוָּשֵׁב

Shortened Impf. (Jussive).
Impf. with Wāw consec.   וַיֵּשֶׁב*

Part. act.		יֹשֵׁב		נוֹשָׁב*
pass.		יָשׁוּב		

פ״ו (*for* פ״י).   L. *Verbs properly* פ״י.

Hiph'il.	Hoph'al.	Qal.	Hiph'il.
*הוֹשִׁיב	*הוּשַׁב	יָטַב	*הֵיטִיב
הוֹשִׁיבָה	הוּשְׁבָה		הֵיטִיבָה
הוֹשַׁבְתָּ	הוּשַׁבְתָּ		הֵיטַבְתָּ
הוֹשַׁבְתְּ	הוּשַׁבְתְּ		הֵיטַבְתְּ
הוֹשַׁבְתִּי	הוּשַׁבְתִּי	regular.	הֵיטַבְתִּי
הוֹשִׁיבוּ	הוּשְׁבוּ		הֵיטִיבוּ
הוֹשַׁבְתֶּם	הוּשַׁבְתֶּם		הֵיטַבְתֶּם
הוֹשַׁבְתֶּן	הוּשַׁבְתֶּן		הֵיטַבְתֶּן
הוֹשַׁבְנוּ	הוּשַׁבְנוּ		הֵיטַבְנוּ
*הוֹשִׁיב	*הוּשַׁב	יָטֵב	*הֵיטִיב
*הוֹשֵׁב		יָטוֹב	*הֵיטֵב
*הוֹשֵׁב			*הֵיטֵב
הוֹשִׁיבִי			הֵיטִיבִי
הוֹשִׁיבוּ	wanting.		הֵיטִיבוּ
[הוֹשֵׁבְנָה]			[הֵיטֵבְנָה]
יוֹשִׁיב	*יוּשַׁב	*יִיטַב	*יֵיטִיב
תּוֹשִׁיב	תּוּשַׁב	תִּיטַב	תֵּיטִיב
תּוֹשִׁיב	תּוּשַׁב	תִּיטַב	תֵּיטִיב
תּוֹשִׁיבִי	תּוּשְׁבִי	תִּיטְבִי	תֵּיטִיבִי
אוֹשִׁיב	אוּשַׁב	אִיטַב	אֵיטִיב
יוֹשִׁיבוּ	יוּשְׁבוּ	יִיטְבוּ	יֵיטִיבוּ
[תּוֹשֵׁבְנָה]	תּוּשַׁבְנָה	תִּיטַבְנָה	[תֵּיטֵבְנָה]
תּוֹשִׁיבוּ	תּוּשְׁבוּ	תִּיטְבוּ	תֵּיטִיבוּ
[תּוֹשֵׁבְנָה]	[תּוּשַׁבְנָה]	[תִּיטַבְנָה]	תֵּיטֵבְנָה
נוֹשִׁיב	נוּשַׁב	נִיטַב	[נֵיטִיב]
*יוֹשֵׁב			יֵיטֵב
וַיּוֹשֶׁב		וַיִּיטַב	וַיִּיטֶב
*מוֹשִׁיב		יָטֵב	מֵיטִיב
	*מוּשָׁב	יָטוֹב	

M.   Weak

			Qal.		Niph'al.	Hiph'il.
Perf. Sing.	3. m.		*קָם	*מֵת	*נָקוֹם	*הֵקִים
	3. f.		*קָ֫מָה	*מֵ֫תָה	*נָק֫וֹמָה	*הֵקִ֫ימָה
	2. m.		*קַ֫מְתָּ	*מַ֫תָּה	[נְקוּמֹ֫ותָ]	*הֲקִימֹ֫ותָ
	2. f.		קַמְתְּ	[מַתְּ]	נְקוּמֹות	הֲקִימֹות
	1. c.		קַ֫מְתִּי	מַ֫תִּי	נְקוּמֹ֫ותִי	הֲקִימֹ֫ותִי
Plur.	3. c.		קָ֫מוּ	מֵ֫תוּ	נָק֫וֹמוּ	הֵקִ֫ימוּ
	2. m.		קַמְתֶּם	[מַתֶּם]	נְקוּמֹותֶם	הֲקִימֹותֶם
	2. f.		[קַמְתֶּן]	[מַתֶּן]	[נְקוּמֹותֶן]	[הֲקִימֹותֶן]
	1. c.		קַ֫מְנוּ	כַּ֫תְנוּ	נְקוּמֹ֫ונוּ	הֲקִימֹ֫ונוּ
65 Inf.			*קוּם		*הִקּוֹם	*הָקִים
60 Inf. absol.			*קוֹם		*הִקּוֹם, נָסוֹג	*הָקֵם
Imp. Sing. m.			*קוּם		*הִקּוֹם	*הָקֵם
	f.		*ק֫וּמִי		[הִקּ֫וֹמִי]	*הָקִ֫ימִי
Plur. m.			ק֫וּמוּ		הִקּ֫וֹמוּ	הָקִ֫ימוּ
	f.		*קֹ֫מְנָה			[הָקֵ֫מְנָה]
Impf. Sing. 3. m.			*יָקוּם, יָבֹוא		*יִקּוֹם	*יָקִים
	3. f.		תָּקוּם		תִּקּוֹם	תָּקִים
	2. m.		תָּקוּם		תִּקּוֹם	תָּקִים
	2. f.		*תָּק֫וּמִי		[תִּקּ֫וֹמִי]	*תָּקִ֫ימִי
	1. c.		אָקוּם		אֶקּוֹם	אָקִים
Plur. 3. m.			יָק֫וּמוּ		יִקּ֫וֹמוּ	יָקִ֫ימוּ
	3. f.		*תְּקוּמֶ֫ינָה, תְּשֹׁבְ֫נָה			*תָּקֵ֫מְנָה, תְּקִימֶ֫ינָה
	2. m.		תָּק֫וּמוּ		תִּקּ֫וֹמוּ	תָּקִ֫ימוּ
	2. f.		תְּקוּמֶ֫ינָה			[תָּקֵ֫מְנָה]
	1. c.		נָקוּם		נִקּוֹם	נָקִים
Shortened Impf.			*יָקֹם			*יָקֵם
Impf. with Wāw consec.			וַיָּ֫קָם (pause *וַיָּקֹם)			וַיָּ֫קֶם
Impf. with Suff.			*יְשׁוּפֶ֫נִי			*יְקִימֶ֫נִי
50 Part. act.			*קָם		*נָקוֹם	*מֵקִים
Gp 50 pass.			*קוּם			

Verbs, ע״י.   N.   Weak Verbs, ע״י.

Hoph'al.	Pôlēl.	Pôlal.	Qal.	Niph'al.
*הוּקַם	*קוֹמֵם	*קוֹמַם	*קָם	*נָבוֹן
[הוּקְמָה]	קוֹמֲמָה	[קוֹמֲמָה]	*קָֽמָה	[נְבוֹנָה]
הוּקַמְתָּ	קוֹמַמְתָּ	קוֹמַמְתָּ	*קַֽמְתָּ	נְבוּנוֹת
הוּקַמְתְּ	[קוֹמַמְתְּ]	[קוֹמַמְתְּ]	קַמְתְּ	[נְבוּנוֹת]
[הוּקַמְתִּי]	קוֹמַמְתִּי	קוֹמַמְתִּי	[קַֽמְתִּי]	נְבוּנוֹתִי
הוּקְמוּ	קוֹמֲמוּ	קוֹמֲמוּ	קָֽמוּ	
[הוּקַמְתֶּם]	[קוֹמַמְתֶּם]	[קוֹמַמְתֶּם]	[קַמְתֶּם]	See
הוּקַמְתֶּן	קוֹמַמְתֶּן	קוֹמַמְתֶּן	[קַמְתֶּן]	Verbs ע״י.
[הוּקַמְנוּ]	[קוֹמַמְנוּ]	[קוֹמַמְנוּ]	קַֽמְנוּ	
*הוּקַם	קוֹמֵם		*קֻם	
			*קָם	
	קוֹמֵם		*קֻם	
	[קוֹמֲמִי]	wanting.	קֻֽמִי	
	קוֹמֲמוּ		קֻֽמוּ	
	[קוֹמֵמְנָה]		—	
*יוּקַם	יְקוֹמֵם	יְקוֹמַם	יָקִים	
תּוּקַם	תְּקוֹמֵם	[תְּקוֹמַם]	תָּקִים	
[תּוּקַם]	תְּקוֹמֵם	תְּקוֹמַם	תָּקִים	
תּוּקְמִי	[תְּקוֹמֲמִי]	תְּקוֹמֲמִי	תָּקִֽימִי	
[אוּקַם]	אֲקוֹמֵם	[אֲקוֹמַם]	אָקִים	
יוּקְמוּ	יְקוֹמֲמוּ	יְקוֹמֲמוּ	יָקִֽימוּ	
[תּוּקַמְנָה]	תְּקוֹמֵמְנָה	תְּקוֹמַמְנָה	תְּקִימֶֽינָה	
תּוּקְמוּ	תְּקוֹמֲמוּ	[תְּקוֹמֲמוּ]	תָּקִֽימוּ	
[תּוּקַמְנָה]	תְּקוֹמֵמְנָה	תְּקוֹמַמְנָה	תְּקִימֶֽינָה	
נוּקַם	[נְקוֹמֵם]	[נְקוֹמַם]	נָקִים	
			יָקֵם	
			וַיָּֽקֶם	
			יְרִיבֵֽנִי	
	מְקוֹמֵם		לָקִים, שָׁב	נָבוֹן
*מוּקָם		מְקוֹמָם	שִׂים, שׂוֹם	

O.   Weak

		Qal.		Niph'al.	Pi'ēl.
Perf. Sing.	3. m.	*מָצָא	מָלֵא	*נִמְצָא	דִּכָּא, מִצָּא
	3. f.	מָצְאָה	מָלְאָה	נִמְצְאָה	[מִצְּאָה]
	2. m.	*מָצָ֫אתָ	מָלֵ֫אתָ	*נִמְצֵ֫אתָ	*מִצֵּ֫אתָ
	2. f.	מָצָאת	מָלֵאת	נִמְצֵאת	[מִצֵּאת]
	1. c.	מָצָ֫אתִי	מָלֵ֫אתִי	נִמְצֵ֫אתִי	מִצֵּ֫אתִי
Plur.	3. c.	מָצְאוּ	מָלְאוּ	נִמְצְאוּ	מִצְּאוּ
	2. m.	מְצָאתֶם	מְלֵאתֶם	נִמְצֵאתֶם	מִצֵּאתֶם
	2. f.	[מְצָאתֶן]	[מְלֵאתֶן]	[נִמְצֵאתֶן]	[מִצֵּאתֶן]
	1. c.	מָצָ֫אנוּ	מָלֵ֫אנוּ	[נִמְצֵ֫אנוּ]	מִצֵּ֫אנוּ
Inf.		מְצֹא		הִמָּצֵא	מַצֵּא
Inf. absol.		מָצוֹא		נִמְצֹא	מַצֹּא
Imp. Sing. m.		*מְצָא		הִמָּצֵא	מַצֵּא
	f.	מִצְאִי		[הִמָּצְאִי]	[מַצְּאִי]
Plur. m.		מִצְאוּ		הִמָּצְאוּ	מַצְּאוּ
	f.	*מְצֶ֫אנָה		[הִמָּצֶ֫אנָה]	[מַצֶּ֫אנָה]
Impf. Sing.	3. m.	*יִמְצָא		*יִמָּצֵא	יְמַצֵּא
	3. f.	תִּמְצָא		תִּמָּצֵא	תְּמַצֵּא
	2. m.	תִּמְצָא		תִּמָּצֵא	תְּמַצֵּא
	2. f.	תִּמְצְאִי		תִּמָּצְאִי	[תְּמַצְּאִי]
	1. c.	אֶמְצָא		אֶמָּצֵא	אֲמַצֵּא
Plur.	3. m.	יִמְצְאוּ		יִמָּצְאוּ	יְמַצְּאוּ
	3. f.	*תִּמְצֶ֫אנָה		*תִּמָּצֶ֫אנָה	*תְּמַצֶּ֫אנָה
	2. m.	תִּמְצְאוּ		תִּמָּצְאוּ	[תְּמַצְּאוּ]
	2. f.	תִּמְצֶ֫אנָה		תִּמָּצֶ֫אנָה	תְּמַצֶּ֫אנָה
	1. c.	נִמְצָא		[נִמָּצֵא]	נְמַצֵּא
Shortened Impf. (Jussive).					
Impf. with Suff.		יִמְצָאֵ֫נִי, יִמְצָאֲךָ			יְמַצְּאֵ֫נִי
Part. act.		מֹצֵא		נִמְצָא	מְמַצֵּא
pass.		מָצוּא			

Verbs, ל"א.

Pu'al.	Hiph'îl.	Hoph'al.	Hithpa'ēl.
קְרָא [מֻצָּא	הִמְצִיא	[הֻמְצָא]	[הִתְמַצָּא
מֻצְּאָה	הִמְצִיאָה	הֻמְצְאָה	הִתְמַצְּאָה
מֻצֵּאתָ	*הִמְצֵּאתָ	*[הֻמְצֵּאתָ]	*הִתְמַצֵּאתָ
מֻצֵּאת	הִמְצֵאת	הֻמְצֵאת	[הִתְמַצֵּאת]
מֻצֵּאתִי	הִמְצֵּאתִי	הֻמְצֵּאתִי	הִתְמַצֵּאתִי
מֻצְּאוּ	הִמְצִיאוּ	הֻמְצְאוּ	הִתְמַצְּאוּ
מֻצֵּאתֶם	הִמְצֵאתֶם	הֻמְצֵאתֶם	[הִתְמַצֵּאתֶם]
מֻצֵּאתֶן	[הִמְצֵאתֶן]	הֻמְצֵאתֶן	הִתְמַצֵּאתֶן
[מֻצֵּאנוּ]	[הִמְצֵּאנוּ]	[הֻמְצֵּאנוּ]	הִתְמַצֵּאנוּ
wanting.	הַמְצִיא הַמְצֵא	wanting.	הִתְמַצֵּא wanting.
wanting.	הַמְצֵא הַמְצִיאִי הַמְצִיאוּ [הַמְצֶּאנָה]	wanting.	[הִתְמַצֵּא] הִתְמַצְּאִי הִתְמַצְּאוּ [הִתְמַצֶּאנָה]
יְמֻצָּא	יַמְצִיא	[יֻמְצָא]	יִתְמַצָּא
[תֻּמְצָא]	תַּמְצִיא	תֻּמְצָא	תִּתְמַצָּא
תֻּמְצָא	תַּמְצִיא	תֻּמְצָא	תִּתְמַצָּא
תֻּמְצְאִי	תַּמְצִיאִי	תֻּמְצְאִי	[תִּתְמַצְּאִי]
אֲמֻצָּא	אַמְצִיא	אֻמְצָא	[אֶתְמַצָּא]
יְמֻצְּאוּ	יַמְצִיאוּ	יֻמְצְאוּ	יִתְמַצְּאוּ
*תֻּמְצֶּאנָה	*תַּמְצֶּאנָה	*תֻּמְצֶּאנָה	[תִּתְמַצֶּאנָה]
תֻּמְצְאוּ	תַּמְצִיאוּ	תֻּמְצְאוּ	תִּתְמַצְּאוּ
תֻּמְצֶּאנָה	תַּמְצֶּאנָה	תֻּמְצֶּאנָה	[תִּתְמַצֶּאנָה]
[נְמֻצָּא]	נַמְצִיא	נֻמְצָא	[נִתְמַצָּא]
	יַמְצֵא		
	יַמְצִיאֵנִי		
	מַמְצִיא		מִתְמַצֵּא
מְמֻצָּא		מֻמְצָא	

P. Weak

	Qal.	Niph'al.	Pi'ēl.
Perf. Sing. 3. m.	‏*גָּלָה‏	‏*נִגְלָה‏	‏*גִּלָּה‏
3. f.	‏*גָּלְתָה‏	‏*נִגְלְתָה‏	‏*גִּלְּתָה‏
2. m.	‏*גָּלִיתָ‏	‏*נִגְלֵיתָ , ‎ ‎‏‎‏‎‏—‏יתָ‏	‏*גִּלִּיתָ‏
2. f.	‏גָּלִית‏	‏נִגְלֵית‏	‏גִּלִּית‏
1. c.	‏גָּלִיתִי‏	‏נִגְלֵיתִי‏	‏גִּלִּיתִי , גִּלֵּיתִי‏
Plur. 3. c.	‏*גָּלוּ‏	‏נִגְלוּ‏	‏גִּלּוּ‏
2. m.	‏גְּלִיתֶם‏	‏[נִגְלֵיתֶם]‏	‏גִּלִּיתֶם‏
2. f.	‏גְּלִיתֶן‏	‏[נִגְלֵיתֶן]‏	‏[גִּלִּיתֶן]‏
1. c.	‏גָּלִינוּ‏	‏נִגְלֵינוּ‏	‏גִּלִּינוּ‏
Inf.	‏*גְּלוֹת‏	‏*הִגָּלוֹת‏	‏*גַּלּוֹת‏
Inf. absol.	‏גָּלֹה‏	‏נִגְלֹה , הִגָּלֵה‏	‏גַּלֵּה , גַּלֹּה‏
Imp. Sing. m.	‏*גְּלֵה‏	‏*הִגָּלֵה‏	‏*גַּלֵּה , גַּל‏
f.	‏*גְּלִי‏	‏*הִגָּלִי‏	‏*גַּלִּ'‏
Plur. m.	‏גְּלוּ‏	‏הִגָּלוּ‏	‏גַּלּוּ‏
f.	‏*גְּלֶינָה‏	‏[הִגָּלֶינָה]‏	‏[גַּלֶּינָה]‏
Impf. Sing. 3. m.	‏*יִגְלֶה‏	‏*יִגָּלֶה‏	‏*יְגַלֶּה‏
3. f.	‏תִּגְלֶה‏	‏תִּגָּלֶה‏	‏תְּגַלֶּה‏
2. m.	‏תִּגְלֶה‏	‏תִּגָּלֶה‏	‏תְּגַלֶּה‏
2. f.	‏*תִּגְלִי‏	‏[תִּגָּלִי]‏	‏*תְּגַלִּי‏
1. c.	‏אֶגְלֶה‏	‏אֶגָּלֶה , אֶגָּ'‏	‏אֲגַלֶּה‏
Plur. 3. m.	‏יִגְלוּ‏	‏יִגָּלוּ‏	‏יְגַלּוּ‏
3. f.	‏*תִּגְלֶינָה‏	‏*תִּגָּלֶינָה‏	‏*תְּגַלֶּינָה‏
2. m.	‏תִּגְלוּ‏	‏תִּגָּלוּ‏	‏תְּגַלּוּ‏
2. f.	‏תִּגְלֶינָה‏	‏תִּגָּלֶינָה‏	‏תְּגַלֶּינָה‏
1. c.	‏נִגְלֶה‏	‏[נִגָּלֶה]‏	‏נְגַלֶּה‏
Shortened Impf.	‏*יִגֶל‏	‏*יִגָּל‏	‏*יְגַל‏
Impf. with Suff.	‏יִגְלְךָ , *יִגְלֵנִי‏		‏יְגַלְךָ , *יְגַלֵּנִי‏
Part. act.	‏*גֹּלֶה‏	‏*נִגְלֶה‏	‏*מְגַלֶּה‏
pass.	‏*גָּלוּי‏		

Verbs, ל״ה.

Pu'al.	Hiph'il.	Hoph'al.	Hithpa'ēl.
*גֻּלָּה	*הֻגְלָה	*הָגְלָה	*הִתְגַּלָּה
*גֻּלְּתָה	*הֻגְלְתָה	*הָגְלְתָה	[הִתְגַּלְּתָה]
*גֻּלֵּיתָ	*הֻגְלֵיתָ ,־ֵ־יתָ	*הָגְלֵיתָ	*הִתְגַּלֵּיתָ
[גֻּלֵּית]	הֻגְלֵית ,־ֵ־ית	[הָגְלֵית]	[הִתְגַּלֵּית]
גֻּלֵּיתִי	הֻגְלֵיתִי ,־ֵ־יתִי	הָגְלֵיתִי	הִתְגַּלֵּיתִי
גֻּלּוּ	הֻגְלוּ	הָגְלוּ	הִתְגַּלּוּ
[גֻּלֵּיתֶם]	הֻגְלֵיתֶם ,־ֵ־יתֶם	[הָגְלֵיתֶם]	הִתְגַּלֵּיתֶם
גֻּלֵּיתֶן	[הֻגְלֵיתֶן]	הָגְלֵיתֶן	[הִתְגַּלֵּיתֶן]
גֻּלֵּינוּ	הֻגְלֵינוּ	[הָגְלֵינוּ]	הִתְגַּלֵּינוּ
*גֻּלּוֹת	*הַגְלוֹת		*הִתְגַּלּוֹת
	הַגְלֵה	*הָגְלֵה	
	*הַגְלֵה		[הִתְגַּלֶּה] הִתְגַּל
wanting.	*הַגְלִי	wanting.	הִתְגַּלִּי
	הַגְלוּ		הִתְגַּלּוּ
	[הַגְלֶינָה]		[הִתְגַּלֶּינָה]
*יְגֻלֶּה	*יַגְלֶה	*[יָגְלֶה]	*יִתְגַּלֶּה
תְּגֻלֶּה	תַּגְלֶה	תָּגְלֶה	[תִּתְגַּלֶּה]
תְּגֻלֶּה	תַּגְלֶה	תָּגְלֶה	תִּתְגַּלֶּה
[תְּגֻלִּי]	*תַּגְלִי	*תָּגְלִי	*תִּתְגַּלִּי
[אֲגֻלֶּה]	אַגְלֶה	*אָגְלֶה	אֶתְגַּלֶּה
יְגֻלּוּ	יַגְלוּ	יָגְלוּ	יִתְגַּלּוּ
*[תְּגֻלֶּינָה]	*תַּגְלֶינָה	*תָּגְלֶינָה	[תִּתְגַּלֶּינָה]
תְּגֻלּוּ	תַּגְלוּ	תָּגְלוּ	תִּתְגַּלּוּ
תְּגֻלֶּינָה	תַּגְלֶינָה	תָּגְלֶינָה	[תִּתְגַּלֶּינָה]
[נְגֻלֶּה]	נַגְלֶה	[נָגְלֶה]	נִתְגַּלֶּה
	*יֶגֶל		*יִתְגַּל
	יַגְלֶךְ ,*יַגְלֵנִי		
	*מַגְלֶה		*מִתְגַּלֶּה
*מְגֻלֶּה		*מֻגְלֶה	

	1. *Sing.*	2. *Sing. m.*	2. *Sing. f.*
Perf. Qal. 3. *m.*	נָחַנִי	רְאֲךָ, עָשְׂךָ	
	P. עָשָׂנִי	*P.* קָנָךָ, עָנָךְ	
3. *f.*	עָשָׂתְנִי		
2. *m.*	רְאִיתַנִי		
	P. עֲנִיתָנִי		
2. *f.*	*Pi.* רִמִּיתִנִי		
1. *c.*		רְאִיתִיךָ	עֲנִּתִךְ
Plur. 3. *c.*	עָשׂוּנִי	רָאוּךָ	*Pi.* כִּסּוּךְ
1. *c.*		*Pi.* קִוִּינוּךָ	
Imper. 2. *m.*	(נְחֵנִי עֲנֵנִי(		
2. *f.*	*Hiph.* הַרְאִינִי		
Plur. 2. *m.*	*Pi.* כַּסּוּנִי		
Impf. 3. *m.*	יִרְאֵנִי	(יִפְדְּךָ יַחְתְּךָ(	
3. *f.*		תִּשְׁבֶּךָ	
2. *m.*	תִּרְאֵנִי		
2. *f.*			
1. *c.*		אֶרְאֶךָ אֶעֱנָךְ	אֶעֱרׇךְ
Plur. 3. *m.*	יַעֲשׂוּנִי	*Pi.* יְפַתּוּךָ	
2. *m.*	תִּצֹּנִּי		
1. *c.*			

with Suffixes.

3. Sing. m.	3. Sing. f.	1. Plur.	3. Plur. m.
עָשָׂהֹוּ	רָאָהּ	עָשָׂנוּ	עָשָׂם
כִּלַּתוּ *Pi.*	צִוְּתָה *Pi.*		הֶעֱלָתַם *Hiph.*
כִּפִּתוֹ *Pi.*	עֲשִׂיתָה	דִּבִּיתָנוּ *Pi.*	עֲנִיתָם
(עֲשִׂיתִיהוּ / רְאִיתִיו	רְאִיתִיהָ		רְעִיתִים
עֲשׂוּהוּ / קִנִּינֻהוּ *Pi.*	רָאֹוּהָ		שָׁבוּם
		הִרְאָנוּ *Hiph.*	רְעֵם
תְּלוּהוּ			הִכּוּם *Hiph.*
(יִרְאָהוּ / יִלְוֻנּ)	(יִרְאָהָ / יִרְאָנָּה)	יְצֻוֵּנוּ *Pi.*	(יְחִיֶּם / יַעֲשֵׂם)
תַּשְׁקֵחוּ *Hiph.*			
תַּעֲשֵׂנּוּ	תַּעֲשֶׂהָ	תַּתְעֵנוּ *Hiph.*	תּוֹרֵם / תְּכַסֵּים *Pi.*
אֶרְאֶנּוּ / אֶעֱנֶהוּ	אֶעֱשֶׂנָּה		אֶפְדֵּם
יְפַתּוּהָ *Pi.*	יַעֲשׂוּהָ	יְעַנּוּנוּ *Pi.*	
נַשְׁקֵנּוּ	נַעֲשֶׂנָּה		תִּצֻּם

I
INDEX OF SUBJECTS

The numbers refer to the sections, except where otherwise indicated.
N. = note.

II

INDEX OF HEBREW WORDS AND FORMS

The numbers refer to the sections : the 'superior' figures after the letters refer to the notes. Doubtful forms are marked ? Corrupt forms with †.

ה with Mappiq 14, as a weak consonant 23 k, l, in verbs ל״ה 75, as a mere vowel-letter 6 d, 7 b, c, 24 g

ה locale, origin 90 b, use 90 c–i, with constr. st. before a genitive 90 c, sometimes otiose 90 e, mere poetic ornament 90 f, g, in place-names 90 g¹, added in segholate nouns to the developed form 90 i, 93 i

הַ (Article) punc-

כְּשִׂית 20 g

כְּשֶׁל forms of 78 c

כְּתָב 25 c², a qiṭâl form 84ᵃ n, the â unchangeable 93 ww

כְּתְבוּנָם 91 e

כְּתָב־הַדָּת 9 u

כַּתֹּנֶת 95 r

כַּתַּר 65 e

לְ preposition 45 f, g; pointed לְ 102 f–i, 103 e, f; uses of 119 r–u; reflexive use 119 s; introducing the object 117 n; denoting the genitive 129; with a passive and with passive ideas 121 f; לְ inscriptionis 119 u; distributive 123 d; with the infinitive 114 f–s, ול with infin. 114 p; = in respect to 143 e; perhaps = Arab. lă, surely 143 e.

לֹא origin 100 a; in prohibitions 107 o; with the Jussive 109 d; as negative answer 150 n, uses of 152 a–d, u; negativing a single idea 152 a¹; exceptional positions of for emphasis 152 e; וְלֹא = in order that ... not 165 a; וְלֹא forming hypothetical sentence 159 dd

לֹא written for לוֹ 103 g

לַאֲדִיב 53 q

לָאוֹר 51 l, 72 v

לָאט 72 p

לֵאמֹר 23 d

לֶאְסֹר 28 b

לְבַד 119 c

לָבוּז 67 n

לְבוּר 67 r

לְבִיא 53 q, 72 z

לְבִיא ? 80 h

לְבִלְתִּי with infin. 114 s; with impf. 152 x

לְבֶן־ 93 dd

לְבָעֵר קֵץ 29 f

לְבָרָם 67 p

לֵדָה 69 c

לְדַרְיוֹשׁ 45 g

לָהּ 23 k, 103 g

לְהוֹשִׁיבִי 90 n

לִהְיוֹת 28 b

לְהָכִיל 68 i

לְהַנָּפָה 72 z

לְהַנְתִּיךָ 66 f

לְהָפִיר 67 w

לְהַפְרְכֶם 67 dd

לְהֵרָאוֹת 75 c

לְהֹשׁוּת 75 qq

לְהַשְׁמָעוּת 53 l

לוֹ written for לֹא 103 g

לוּ in wishes, its construction 151 e; in conditional clauses 159 l, m, x–z

לוּא 23 i

לוֹט 72 p

לְוִינוּ 91 k

לְוִיתָן 86 f

לֻגְלִי, לַהְלָא formation

27 w, in conditional clauses 159 l, m, x–z

לֹחַ 91 e

לַחְטִיא 53 q

לְחָיִם 88 b

לַחֲלֹק 53 q

לֶחֶם 22 h

לַחְמָם 28 b, 67 cc

לַחֲנָנָה 67 cc

לַחְפֹּר פֵּרוֹת ? 84ᵇ n

לָטַעַת 66 b

לַיהוָה 102 m

לַיְלָה 90 f

לִיסֹר 69 n, 71

לִירֹא 75 rr

לִירָשֵׁנוּ 69 m

לֵךְ imperative, for לְכָה 48 i; as an interjection 105 b

לְכָה pronoun, for לָךְ 103 g

לְכוּ 105 b

לֶלְאוֹת 93 x

לַלְבֵּן 53 q

ללה (Moab.) for לַיְלָה 7 f

לֶלֶת 19 d, 69 m

לָמָה, לְמָה, לְמָּה, לָמֶה its punctuation 49 f, g, 102 l in requests or warnings often nearly = lest 150 e

לָמוֹ 103 f³

לָמוֹ 103 k

לַמְחוֹת 53 q

לְמִינֵהֶם 91 k

לְמָן 119 c²

עָשׂוּי ptcp. passive 24 *b*, 75 *v*
עֲשׂוֹות 75 *v*
עֲשָׂרָה 80 *l*
עֲשָׂרָה אֲלָפִים 97 *g*
עֶשְׂרִים 93 *l*, 97 *f*
עָשׂוּ 93 *dd*
עֲשֻׂשָׂה 67 *cc*
עֲשֻׂשׂוּ 67 *cc*
עֲשִׂתִּי 97 *e*¹
עֲשְׂתֹּרֶת 95 *q*¹
עַתָּה 90 *h*
עַתִּיק 84ᵇ *f*
עֵת נִשְׁבֶּרֶת ? 116 *g*¹

פָּארָה 23 *c*
פַּרְהֶצּוּר 23 *k*¹
פִּדְיוֹם 85 *t*
פֶּה 96
פּוּגַת 80 *f*
פֶּחָם (Ne 5¹⁴) ? 91 *e*
פִּיּוֹת 96
פִּימוֹ 91 *f*
פֶּלֶא 93 *k*
פֶּלֶא 22 *e*
פֶּלֶג 52 *n*
פֶּן with imperf. (twice perf.) 107 *q* and note³, 152 *w* (end), after ideas of fearing 152 *w*
פִּנָּה 91 *e*
פְּנוּאֵל 90 *k*
פָּנִים 145 *h*
פָּנֵימוֹ 103 *f*³
פָּעַל 39 *e*, 41 *d*
פָּעֳלוֹ 93 *q*
פִּפִיּוֹת 96
פְּקַחְקוֹחַ† 84ᵇ *n*
פֶּרֶא 22 *e*

פְּרָאוֹת† 75 *rr*
פְּרֻדֶם 1 *i*
פְּרִי 93 *x*
פֶּרִי 9 *f*
פְּרִיץ 84ᵇ *f*
פָּרָשׁ 84ᵇ *b*
פַּרְשֵׁז 56
פָּרָשִׁים 93 *dd*
פֹּרַת 80 *g*
פְּתָאִים 93 *x*

צֹאן with 3rd fem. pl. 132 *g*, 145 *c*
צֹאנֵינוּ ? 123 *a*¹
צֵאת 69 *m*
צֵאת 95 *e*
צְבָאוֹת 125 *h*
צְבָאִים 93 *x*
צְבִיָּה 75 *qq*
צֶדֶק מִן 133 *b*²
צַדְקָתֶךָ 52 *p*
צָהֳרַיִם 88 *c*
צוֹר (verb) 67 *n*
צוּרִי 72 *s*
צוּרְנִים 86 *g*
צָחֶה 84ᵇ *c*
צִים, צִי† 93 *y*
צָלְלוּ 67 *cc*
צְלָלִי 10 *g*
צַלְמָוֶת 30 *r*, 81 *d*²
צֵלַע 93 *gg*
צֶלַע 93 *gg*
צְמִתְּתוּנִי† 55 *d*
צֶעֱקִי 46 *d*
צָפוּ passive ptcp. 75 *v*
צְפַרְדֵּעַ 81 *d*², 85 *w*
צִקּוֹן ? 44 *l*, 72 *o*

קָאם for קָם 9 *b*, 23 *g*, analogous cases 72 *p*
קָאת 80 *g*
קֶבָה-לִי 9 *v*, 67 *o*
קָבְנוּ the נ not compensatory 20 *o*, for קִבֵּנּוּ 67 *o*, doubtful form 100 *o*²
קֻבְּצָה 52 *l*
קָדְרַנִּית 85 *u*
קְדָשִׁים 9 *v*, 93 *r*
קָדְשִׁים 124 *h*
קֹהֶלֶת 145 *h*
קוֹל = *hark !* 146 *b*
קוֹלִי† constr. st. 90 *n*
קוּמָה 72 *s*
קוּמוּ צֵאוּ 20 *g*
קוֹמִים 72 *p*
קוֹף 1 *i*
קַרְחֹהוּ 21 *c*
קַח ? for לָקַח 19 *i*, 66 *g*
קְחָם ? for לְקָחָם 19 *i*, 66 *g*
קְחָם-נָא 58 *g*, 61 *g*, 66 *g*
קַחַת 66 *g*, 93 *h*
קָטְבְךָ 93 *q*
קְטָלַנִי 26 *g*
קְטָלַתּוּ 19 *f*
קָטְמֵנִי ? 93 *q*
קִטֵּר 52 *o*
קִיא 76 *h*
קִיו 76 *h*
קִימוֹר 84ᵃ *u*
קִים 72 *m*
קִימֵנוּ† 91 *f*
קַלּוּ 67 *ee*
קָם 72 *g*

INDEX OF PASSAGES

The references are to the sections and their marginal letters, except where otherwise indicated. N. = note.

Deuteronomy		
1 24	. . . .	120 *h*
27	. .	115 *c*, 115 *f*
28	. . .	124 *q*
33	. . . .	53 *q*
34	. .	65 *e*, 149 *b*
40	. . . .	119 *s*
41	. . . .	135 *n*
44	. 67 *g*, 67 *y*, 107 *g*	
46	. . . .	138 *c*
2 9	. .	75 *bb*, 119 *s*
13	. . . .	119 *s*
14	. . . .	134 *h*
23	. . .	126 *w*
24	20 *g*, 69 *f*, 75 *cc*, 110 *h*, 120 *g*, *h*	
27	108 *c*, 123 *e*, 133 *k*, 156 *d*	
28	. . . .	49 *m*
31	. .	67 *w*, 69 *f*
3 3	. . .	164 *d*
5	. . .	128 *c*
11	. . .	100 *i*
13	. . .	125 *d* N.
21	. . .	126 *k*
26	. . . .	69 *v*
4 1	. .	44 *d*, 69 *s*
8	. . .	128 *p*
10	. .	115 *d*, 165 *b*
15	. .	52 *o*, 130 *d*
20	. . . .	74 *l*
21	. . . .	54 *k*
26	. . . .	51 *k*
36	. . . .	61 *d*
39	. .	2 *i*, 72 *w*
41	. . . .	90 *c*
5 3	. . . .	135 *g*
6	. .	15 *p*, 138 *d*
9	. . . .	60 *b*
12	. . .	113 *bb*
19	. . .	120 *d* N.
23	. . . .	132 *h*
24	. . . .	32 *h*
26	. .	115 *d*, 151 *c*
6 3	. .	118 *g*, 165 *b*
7	. . . .	119 *l*
11	. . .	49 *m*, 96
17	. . . .	58 *g*
7 5	. . . .	52 *n*
15	. . . .	60 *d*
16	. .	72 *r*, 109 *d*
24	. . . .	53 *l*
25	. . . .	127 *e*
8 3	. .	44 *l*, 72 *o*
5	. . . .	61 *h*
9	. . . .	93 *aa*
13	. . . .	75 *u*
14	. . . .	116 *f*
15	. . . .	127 *i*
16	. .	44 *l*, 72 *o*
19	. . . .	106 *i*

Deuteronomy		
9 7	. . . .	138 *c*
8	. . . .	54 *k*
18	. . . .	54 *k*
10 5	. . . .	29 *g*
17	102 *m*, 126 *v*, 133 *i*	
19	. . .	112 *aa*
22	. . . .	119 *i*
11 2	. . . .	117 *l*
15	. . . .	49 *m*
30	. . . .	150 *e*
12 3	. . . .	52 *n*
14	. . . .	61 *h*
13 1	. . . .	109 *d*
3	. . . .	60 *b*
6	. . . .	116 *f*
9	. . . .	109 *d*
14 17	. . . .	80 *k*
15 2	. . . .	113 *gg*
7	. 119 *w* N., 139 *d*	
14	. . . .	93 *k*
18	. . 128 *c*, 133 *k*	
16 6	. . . .	119 *g*
13	. . . .	93 *k*
20	. . . .	133 *k*
17 2	. . . .	167 *b*
5	. . . .	124 *o*
6	. . . .	144 *e*
8	. . . .	102 *h*
14	. . 44 *d*, 49 *m*	
17	. . . .	109 *g*
18 1	. . 68 *c*, 131 *h*	
16	. . . .	109 *d*
19 5	. . . .	126 *r*
20 2	. . . .	61 *d*
5	. . . .	137 *c*
8	. . . .	121 *b*
14	. . . .	128 *h*
21 3	. . 121 *a*, 145 *q*	
4	. . . .	121 *a*
7	. . 44 *m*, 145 *k*	
8	. . . .	55 *k*
10	. . 135 *p*, 145 *m*	
11	49 *m*, 96, 130 *e*	
13	. . . .	101 *a*
22 1	. . . .	159 *gg*
19	. . 17 *c*, 127 *e*	
23	. . . .	131 *b*
23 5	. 61 *d*, 130 *c* N¹	
11	. . . .	20 *h*
15	. . 93 *ss*, 128 *p*	
25	. . . .	96
24 1	. . . .	167 *b*
4	. . . .	54 *h*
5	. . . .	51 *n*
10	. . . .	23 *d*
13	. . . .	58 *i*
25 2	. . 96, 128 *v*	
12	. . . .	67 *ee*
13	. . . .	123 *f*
26 5	. . . .	119 *i*
12	. . . .	53 *k*

Deuteronomy		
27 2	. . . .	72 *w*
6	. . . .	117 *hh*
9	. . . .	16 *b*
28 24	. . . .	58 *g*
36	. . . .	131 *d*
43	. . . .	133 *k*
48	. . 53 *l*, 145 *m*	
49	. . . .	155 *d*
52	. . . .	67 *v*
56	. 113 *d*, 142 *f* N.	
57	. . . .	74 *i*
59	. . . .	91 *n*
62	. . . .	119 *i*
66	. . . .	75 *rr*
67	. . . .	151 *b*
29 14	. . . .	100 *o* N.
15	. . . .	157 *c*
18	. . . .	69 *h* N.
21	. . . .	167 *b*
28	. . . .	5 *n*
30 4	. . . .	92 *b* N.
31 12	. . . .	120 *e*
16	. . . .	93 *gg*
21	. . . .	164 *d*
29	. . . .	74 *g*
32 1	. 2 *r*, 91 *l*, 117 *b*	
3	. . . .	69 *o*
4	. . . .	126 *c*
5	. . 13 *c*, 152 *a*	
● 6	20 *g*, 75 *ll*, 100 *i*, 152 *a* N.	
7	. 60 *f*, 87 *n*, 123 *c*	
8	. . 53 *k*, 109 *k*	
10	. . 58 *i*, 58 *k*	
11	. . 52 *n*, 155 *g*	
15	20 *g*, 144 *p*, 154 N (*a*)	
17	144 *p*, 152 *a* N., 155 *e*, 155 *f*, 155 *h*	
18	. . 75 *s*, 109 *k*	
20	. . . .	108 *a*
21	. . .	152 *a* N.
22	. . . .	69 *f*
24	. . 110 *h*, 116 *l*	
26	. 58 *a* N., 75 *mm*	
27	. . . .	139 *y*
28	50 *e*, 93 *qq*, 124 *e*	
29	. . . .	159 *x*
30	. . . .	134 *s*
31	. . . .	156 *b* N.
32	. . . .	20 *h*
35	52 *o*, 145 *o*, 155 *l*	
36	. 29 *v*, 44 *f*, 152 *s*	
37	. . 29 *t*, 75 *u*	
39	. . . .	141 *h* N²
40	. . . .	93 *aa* N.
41	. . . .	159 *n*
46	. . 117 *gg*, 165 *b*	
50	. . . .	110 *c*
33 2	. . . .	112 *pp*

Ecclesiastes

5	11	. . . . . 69 n
	14	. . . . 109 i
	15	. . . . 161 b
	16	. . . . 147 e
	18	. 112 pp N., 141 h
7	7	. . . . . 117 c
	16	. 54 c, 54 k, 131 q
	24	. . . . 133 k
	26	. . . . 75 oo
	27	. . . . 122 r
8	1	. . . 35 n, 75 rr
	10	54g, 119 ii, 128w N.
9	1	. . . . 93 ww
	4	. . . . 143 e
	12	. . . . . 52 s
	14	. . . 112 pp N.
10	5	. . 75 qq. 155 h
	15	. . . . 145 m
	17	. . . . . 91 l
	18	. . . . . 88 b
	20	. . . . . 53 n
11	2	. . . . 134 s
	3	. . . 23 i, 75 s
12	1	. . . . 124 k
	4	. . . 72 t, 128 v
	5	. . . . . 73 g
	6	. . . 67 q, 67 t
	7	. . . . 109 k
	9	. . . . 145 h

Esther

1	4	. . . . 93 ww
	5	. . . . . 74 h
	8	. . . . 123 c
	17	. . . . 93 m
2	9	. . . . . 75 v
	11	. . . . 123 c
3	4	. . . . 157 c
	8	. . . 100 o N.
4	2	. . . . 114 l
	8	. . . . 93 ww
6	13	. . . . 20 g
7	2	. . . . 109 f
	5	. . 74 g, 137 a
	8	. . . . 114 i
8	1	. . . . 137 c
	8	. . . . . 63 c
9	1	. . . 135 a N.
	6	. . . . 113 z
	7	. . . . . 2 s
	23	. 124 c, 145 o N.

Daniel

1	4	. . 23 c, 128 a N.
	5	. . . . 135 o
	10	. . . . 93 ss
	12	. . . . 75 cc
	13	. . . . 75 hh

Daniel

1	15	. . . . 93 ss
2	1	. . . . 124 o
	4	. . . . . 1 c
3	15	. . . . 167 a
8	3	. . . . 93 n
	9	. . . . 135 o
	11	. . . . 72 ee
	13	125 b, 126 z, 127 f
	22	47 k, 87 i, 95 u, 116 w
9	5	. . . . . 91 n
	13	. . . . 117 m
	19	. . . . . 48 i
11	6	116f, 127 i, 139 h
	11	. . . . 131 n
	20	. . . . 93 dd
	23	. . 53 l, 54 k
	35	. . . . 53 q
12	2	. . 102 b, 124 e
	7	. . 93 aa N.
	11	. . . . 134 g
	13	. . . . . 87 e

Ezra

2	62	. . . . 131 r
	69	. . . . . 97 g
3	3	. . 124 q, 147 a
	6	. . . . 134 p
	12	. . . . 126 aa
4	7	. . . . . 55 h
	8	. . . . . 1 c
6	21	. . . . . 8 k
7	12	. . . . . 1 c
	28	. . . . . 49 e
8	1	. . . . 64 i
	18	. . . . . 14 d
	23	. . . . . 51 n
	25	. . 93 oo, 138 i
	29	. . . . 127 g
	30	. . . . . 92 g
	36	. . . . 112 rr
9	6	. . . . . 22 s
10	13	. . . . 141 d
	14	. . 127 i, 138 i
	16	. . . . . 45 g
	17	. . . 127 c N.

Nehemiah

2	3	. . . . 67 dd
	7	. . . . . 68 g
	12	. . 131 e, 137 c
	13	. . . . . 5 n
3	8	. . 124 o, 128 v
	13	. . . . . 35 d
	31	. . . . 128 v
4	3	. . 49 e N., 53 n
	4	. . . . 119 m
	7	. . . . . 20 h

Nehemiah

4	9	. . 49 e N., 67 x
	12	. . 116 k N.
	17	. . . . 152 n
5	14	. . . . . 91 e
6	6	. . . . . 90 k
	8	. . 23 c, 74 i
	10	. . . . 144 i
	11	. . . . 100 m
7	2	. . . . 118 x
	64	. . . . . 64 i
	66	. . . . . 23 i
8	2	. . . . . 74 l
	8	. . . . . 2 t
	10	. 85 g N., 128 p, 152 v, 155 n
	11	. . . . 105 a
9	13	. . . . 132 d
	35	. . . . 126 x
10	37	. . . 123 r N.
	39	. . . . . 53 k
11	17	. . . . 53 q
12	44	. . . . . 95 k
	47	. . . . . 95 n
13	9	. . . . 165 a
	13	. . 53 g, 53 n
	16	. . . . . 9 b
	21	. . . . . 73 f
	24	. . . 2 a, 2 w

1 Chronicles

2	13	. . . . . 47 b
	30	. . . . 152 u
	48	. . . . 145 u
3	5	. . . . . 69 t
4	10	. . 61 a, 167 a
	42	. . . . 131 n
5	1	. . . . 114 k
	2	. . . . 141 a
	20	. . . . . 63 c
6	63	. . . . . 90 f
7	5	. . . . 124 q
8	8	. . . . . 52 o
	38	. . . . . 29 q
9	13	. . . . 128 o
	22	135 a N1, 155 d
	25	. . . . 134 m
	27	. . . . 123 c
	33	. . . . 147 a
10	2	. . . . . 53 r
	13	. . . . 114 k
11	6	. . . . 116 w
	39	. . . . . 23 f
12	2	. . 24 f N., 70 b
	8	. . . . 114 b
	17	. . . . . 61 c
	23	. . . . 155 d
	33	. . . . 123 f
	38	. . . . . 23 f